The Victoria History of the Counties of England

EDITED BY WILLIAM PAGE, F.S.A.

A HISTORY OF

GLOUCESTERSHIRE

VOLUME II

THE
VICTORIA HISTORY

OF THE COUNTIES
OF ENGLAND

GLOUCESTERSHIRE

PUBLISHED FOR

THE UNIVERSITY OF LONDON

INSTITUTE OF HISTORICAL RESEARCH

REPRINTED FROM THE ORIGINAL EDITION OF 1907

BY

DAWSONS OF PALL MALL

FOLKESTONE & LONDON

1972

Issued by
Archibald Constable and Company Limited
in 1907

Reprinted for the University of London
Institute of Historical Research
by
Dawsons of Pall Mall
Cannon House
Folkestone, Kent, England
1972

ISBN: 0 7129 0555 3

Originally printed in Great Britain by
Eyre & Spottiswoode, London
Reprinted in Belgium by Jos Adam, Brussels

INSCRIBED
TO THE MEMORY OF
HER LATE MAJESTY
QUEEN VICTORIA
WHO GRACIOUSLY GAVE
THE TITLE TO AND
ACCEPTED THE
DEDICATION OF
THIS HISTORY

Gloucester from the Severn

THE
VICTORIA HISTORY
OF THE COUNTY OF
GLOUCESTER

EDITED BY

WILLIAM PAGE, F.S.A.

VOLUME TWO

PUBLISHED FOR
THE UNIVERSITY OF LONDON
INSTITUTE OF HISTORICAL RESEARCH
REPRINTED BY
DAWSONS OF PALL MALL
FOLKESTONE & LONDON

CONTENTS OF VOLUME TWO

	PAGE
Dedication	v
Contents	ix
List of Illustrations	xiii
Editorial Note	xv
Ecclesiastical History . . . By Miss Rose Graham, F.R. Hist. S.	1
Religious Houses :— ,, ,, ,, ,,	
Introduction	52
Abbey of St. Peter at Gloucester	53
Abbey of Tewkesbury	61
Abbey of Winchcombe	66
Priory of Stanley St. Leonard	72
Priory of St. James, Bristol	74
Abbey of St. Augustine, at Bristol	75
Abbey of Cirencester	79
Priory of St. Oswald, Gloucester	84
Priory of Lanthony by Gloucester	87
Priory of Horsley	91
Priory of St. Mary Magdalen, Bristol	93
Abbey of Flaxley	93
Abbey of Hayles	96
Abbey of Kingswood	99
Priory of Beckford	102
Priory of Brimpsfield	102
Priory of Deerhurst	103
Priory of Newent	105
College of Westbury-on-Trym	106
Black Friars, Bristol	109
Grey Friars, Bristol	110
Augustinian Friars, Bristol	110
Carmelite Friars, Bristol	110
Friars of the Penance of Jesus Christ, or Friars of the Sack, Bristol	111
Black Friars, Gloucester	111
Grey Friars, Gloucester	111
Carmelite or White Friars, Gloucester	112
Crutched Friars of Wotton-under-Edge	112
Preceptory of Guiting	113

CONTENTS OF VOLUME TWO

PAGE

Religious Houses (*continued*)—

Preceptory of Quenington 113

Hospital of St. Mark, Billeswick, called Gaunt's Hospital 114

Hospital of St. Bartholomew, Bristol 118

Hospital of St. Lawrence, Bristol 119

Hospital of St. Mary Magdalen, Bristol 119

Hospital of St. Bartholomew, Gloucester 119

Hospital of St. Margaret, Gloucester 121

Hospital of St. Mary Magdalen, Gloucester 122

Hospital of St. John, Cirencester 122

Hospital of St. Lawrence, Cirencester 123

Hospital of St. Thomas, Cirencester 123

Hospital of Longbridge, by Berkeley 123

Hospital of Lorwing 124

Hospital of St. John the Baptist, Lechlade 125

Hospital of Winchcombe 126

Hospital of Tewkesbury 126

Hospital of Holy Trinity, Stow-on-the-Wold 126

Social and Economic History . .   By Miss Ruth F. Butler, Oxford Honour School of Modern History 127

Table of Population, 1801–1901   By George S. Minchin 173

Industries :—

Introduction . . . .   By Miss R. F. Butler and Miss C. Violet Butler, Oxford Honour School of Modern History . 189

Wool . . . . .   By Miss R. F. Butler 193

Waterproofs, Ropes, and other Textiles . . .   ,, ... 199

Timber, etc. . . .   By Miss C. V. Butler 199

Engineering and Metal Industries   By Miss R. F. Butler 202

Bell-Founding . . .   ,, ... 204

Pins . . . .   By Miss C. V. Butler 206

Printing and Paper . .   By Miss R. F. Butlfr 208

Leather . . . .   ,, ... 209

Soap and Chemicals . .   ,, ... 210

Milling, Malting and Brewing .   ,, ... 211

Sugar and Chocolate . .   ,, ... 212

Glass, Pottery, Bricks and Building Materials . . .   ,, ... 213

Handicrafts . . .   ,, ... 215

Mining . . . .   By George R. Lewis, Ph.D. and C. H. Vellacott, B.A. 215

Agriculture . . . .   By Robert Anderson, F.S.I. . . . 239

Forestry . . . .   By J. Nisbet, D.Oec. and C. H. Vellacott, B.A. 263

CONTENTS OF VOLUME TWO

PAGE

Sport, Ancient and Modern . . Edited by E. D. Cuming

    Stag-Hunting . . . . By H. S. Kennedy Skipton 287

    Fox-hunting . . . .

        The Berkeley Hunt . . By H. O. Lloyd Baker 288

        The Cotteswold . . By H. S. Kennedy Skipton . . . 290

        The North Cotteswold .   ,, ... 292

        The Vale of White Horse

          (Cirencester) . . .   ,, ... 293

    Harriers . . . .   ,, ... 295

    Coursing . . . By J. W. Bourne 295

    Racing . . . . By T. J. Longworth 296

    Falconry . . . . By Charles A. Witchell 299

    Shooting . . . . By the Rev. A. R. Winnington Ingram, M.A. . 299

    Wild-fowling . . . By W. Lock Mellersh . . . 301

    Angling . . . . By J. W. Willis-Bund, M.A., LL.B, F.S.A. . 303

    Golf . . . . By A. Hoare 304

    Athletics . . . . By J. E. Fowler Dixon 306

        The Cotteswold Games . By E. D. Cuming 306

    Cricket . . . . By Sir Home Gordon, Bart. . . . 306

Schools . . . . . . By A. F. Leach, M.A., F.S.A. . . . 313

LIST OF ILLUSTRATIONS

PAGE

Gloucester from the Severn . . By William Hyde . . . . . *frontispiece*

Ecclesiastical Map of Gloucestershire . . . . *facing* 48

Gloucestershire Monastic Seals :—

      Plate I . . . . *full-page plate facing* 66

      Plate II . . . . ,, ,, ,, 98

A Balk or Dividing Strip, showing the Meerstone, Upton
St. Leonards . . . .

View of Lynches at Upton St. Leonards, looking North-
east . . . . ,, ,, ,, 164

Plan of Common Field at Upton St. Leonards, showing
Method of holding by Strips . . . . ,, ,, ,, 166

Stocking-loom Needle 198

Bell-founder's Seal from River Thames 205

Gloucester Stop used by Hendley 205

Rudhall's Bell Mark 205

Bell Ornamentation by the Rudhalls 206

Running Grape Ornamentation by Purdue 206

Purdue's Initial Cross 206

Bell Mark of Robert Purdue 206

EDITORIAL NOTE

THE Editor desires to express his thanks to the **Rt. Hon. Sir Charles Dilke, bart., LL.M., F.S.A.,** and Mr. W. R. Champness for kindly revising the section of the article on Industries dealing with Mining in the county and making some valuable additions, and also to Sir Charles Dilke and Mr. Philip Baylis, deputy surveyor of the Forest of Dean, for doing the same with regard to the article on Forestry. He has also to acknowledge his indebtedness to Mr. H. B. Walters, M.A., F.S.A., for information supplied with regard to the article on bell-founding, to Messrs. William Pollard and Co. for permission to reproduce drawings from the late Canon Ellacombe's *Church Bells of Gloucestershire*, and to Canon Scobell and the Cotteswold Naturalists' Field Club for permission to reproduce illustrations from the *Proceedings* of that Society.

A HISTORY OF
GLOUCESTERSHIRE

ECCLESIASTICAL HISTORY

THE early evidence of Christianity in Gloucestershire is very slight, and of British Christianity there is scarcely a trace.[1] 'Four stones marked with the Christian monogram found in the Roman villa at Chedworth, a few tiles marked IHS, and a tombstone which is probably Christian, discovered at Sea Mills in 1873, complete the tale.'[2] Excavations on the sites of the great Roman cities of Gloucester and Cirencester have as yet shed no light on Christian worship among the provincials. The name of Bishop Eldad, who held the see of Gloucester when Hengist invaded Britain, has been handed down by tradition.[3] Thomas, who was translated to London about 542, is said to have witnessed the destruction of Gloucester and to have fled with his clergy into Wales in 586.[4]

In 577 the West Saxons conquered the lower Severn Valley.[5] Three Roman cities, Cirencester, Gloucester and Bath, lay within the district, and were connected by splendid roads. The British kings, Commagil, Condidan, Farinmagil, joined forces and met the invaders under their leader Ceawlin at Deorham. They were utterly defeated, the cities were captured and burnt, the Britons fled and the country was occupied by a tribe of the West Saxons, called the Hwiccas. After another victory over the Britons at Feathanlea[6] in 584, the kingdom of the Hwiccas probably embraced a third part of Warwickshire, all Worcestershire, and Gloucestershire east of the Severn and Leadon.[7] The Britons held the land beyond the Severn for some time longer, and it was at Aust,[8] a ford of the river, that about 603 the British bishops came reluctantly to hold a conference with St. Augustine, which proved fruitless, and the British church continued in isolation. It is probable that for nearly eighty years the Hwiccas remained heathen. Though they were a West Saxon people, before the middle of the seventh century their land became a dependent province of the kingdom of Mercia,[9] which was under the rule of the heathen Penda. After his death at the battle of the Winwaed in 655, Christianity spread rapidly in Mercia.[10] There is no evidence to connect the work of the first Mercian bishops of Lichfield with the most

---

[1] According to Geoffrey of Monmouth, Christianity was introduced into Gloucestershire during the rule of King Lucius (Geoffrey of Monm. *Hist. Brit.* ed. 1844, p. 74). The legend of the burial of the king in 156 may perhaps testify to the truth that Christianity spread into the district soon after it was brought into Britain (Ibid. 76 ; *Brist. and Glouc. Arch. Soc. Trans.* xv, 120).

[2] *Brist. and Glouc. Arch. Soc. Trans.* xv, 121.

[3] Ibid. 122 ; Geoffrey of Monm. op. cit. 137.

[4] Ibid.

[5] *Arch. Journ.* xix, 194–5.

[6] *Brist. and Glouc. Arch. Soc. Trans.* xx, 269–72.

[7] Ibid. xv, 127.

[8] Ibid. xx, 290–2 ; *Clifton Antiq. Club Proc.* iv, 43–7.

[9] Ibid. xv, 125.

[10] Hunt, *Hist. of the Engl. Church*, i, 104.

remote portion of the kingdom, the province of the Hwiccas,[1] but within a few years they became Christians, and in 680 Bede records that Ebba, queen of the South Saxons, had been baptized among her own people the Hwiccas :[2] 'She was the daughter of Eanfrid, the brother of Eanher, who were both Christians with all their people.' The first religious settlement in Gloucestershire of which any record exists was at Tetbury, and in 680 it was already well known as a monastery.[3] The organization of the church among the Hwiccas was promoted by two ealdormen, Osric and his brother Oshere. In 676 Osric founded a monastery at Bath, and in the charter of endowment proclaimed his purpose of founding a bishop's seat, and monasteries for men and women.[4] In or about 680 the Mercian diocese was divided into five sees, and the bishop's seat for the province of the Hwiccas was set at Worcester.[5] The bounds of the diocese were those of the province, and thus it came about that Gloucestershire west of the Severn and the Leadon was not included in the diocese of Worcester, but became a part of the diocese of Hereford, which was founded about the same time. In or about 681 Osric founded a monastery at Gloucester,[6] choosing, as at Bath, a Roman city which was again occupied, on account of its position on the great roads of the district. Cirencester probably still lay waste.[7] It is impossible to trace the gradual growth of the church in Gloucestershire, but at the beginning of the ninth century there were monasteries which were virtually mission stations at Beckford,[8] Berkeley,[9] Cheltenham,[10] Cleeve,[11] Deerhurst,[12] Twyning,[13] Westbury,[14] Winchcombe,[15] Withington[16] and Yate.[17] Several of these, like Whitby, were no doubt double houses in which an abbess bore rule over both men and women. Some were family monasteries, and grave abuses crept into them.[18] As the work of the mission stations extended, the parochial system gradually developed, but its history is very obscure. The monasteries seem to have supplied a sufficient number of clergy for the diocese, and in 824 two hundred and ten priests gathered at Westbury-on-Trym to witness the final settlement of the dispute between the churches of Worcester and Berkeley.[19] Churches were built on the estates of the great minsters, and enjoyed the same privileges.[20] A record has by chance preserved the name of Wulfhun, the villagers' priest of Woodchester in 896,[21] and it is probable that at that time priests were already settled in other villages,[22] but no evidence has as yet come to light to show when or how the bounds of the parishes were determined in Gloucestershire.[23]

In the middle of the tenth century monasticism scarcely existed in England :[24] King Alfred's attempts to revive the regular life had failed; some of the minsters were homes of married priests, and others were ruinous and

---

[1] *Brist. and Glouc. Arch. Soc. Trans.* xv, 126. [2] Bede, *Hist. Eccl.* (ed. Plummer), i, 230.
[3] Birch, *Cart. Sax.* i, 93. [4] *Two chartularies of the Priory of St. Peter at Bath* (Somerset Rec. Soc.), i, 7.
[5] Stubbs, *Reg. Sacr. Angl.* 232, 233. [6] Birch, *Cart. Sax.* i, 95.
[7] *Brist. and Glouc. Arch. Soc. Trans.* xv, 135. [8] Birch, *Cart. Sax.* i, 429.
[9] Ibid. i, 438, 519. [10] Ibid. i, 429. [11] Ibid. i, 340.
[12] Ibid. i, 438. [13] Ibid. i, 489. [14] Ibid. i, 379.
[15] Ibid. i, 470. [16] Ibid. i, 225, 305.
[17] Ibid. i, 322. Beckford, Cheltenham, Cleeve, Tetbury, Westbury-on-Trym, Withington and Yate were afterwards absorbed by the cathedral monastery of Worcester ; cf. *Brist. and Glouc. Arch. Soc. Trans.* xx, 294.
[18] Ibid. xx, 296–8. [19] Haddan and Stubbs, *Councils and Eccl. Doc.* iii, 594.
[20] Ibid. iii, 653. [21] Birch, *Cart. Sax.* ii, 217.
[22] *Brist. and Glouc. Arch. Soc. Trans.* xv, 137. [23] Ibid. xx, 298.
[24] *Chron. Mon. de Abingdon* (Rolls Ser.), ii, 259.

deserted. Under the influence of Dunstan, archbishop of Canterbury, Ethelwold, bishop of Winchester, and Oswald, bishop of Worcester, and with the help of King Edgar, there was a brief but brilliant revival. When Oswald determined to introduce into his diocese the strict observance of the Benedictine rule, which he had himself learnt at Fleury, he differed from Ethelwold in at first avoiding the violent measure of expelling secular priests. The lands and church of Westbury belonged to Oswald's see, and soon after his consecration in 961 he sent to Fleury for an English monk named Germanus, who had gone thither from Winchester to study the observance of the rule of St. Benedict.[1] Germanus was appointed prior of a new foundation at Westbury, with twelve clerks and a number of boys under his rule, and Westbury thus became the centre of the Benedictine revival in Mercia ; the new monasticism flourished, and the number of monks increased. In 968 a monastery was founded at Ramsey in Huntingdonshire, and filled with monks from Westbury. In 969 King Edgar commanded the bishop to drive out the secular clerks.[2] It is probable that, as in the cathedral of Worcester,[3] some of the priests in the other monasteries of the province of the Hwiccas consented to become monks. It was from Westbury and Ramsey that Oswald chose rulers and monks for other Gloucestershire houses. Winchcombe became Benedictine in 969,[4] Deerhurst in 970.[5] Owing, possibly, to the hostility of Elfhere, ealdorman of Mercia, the houses of St. Peter and St. Oswald at Gloucester and the minsters of Berkeley and Cirencester escaped the influence of the Benedictine revival.[6] On the death of Edgar in 975 there was a revulsion of feeling in favour of the secular priests who had been ousted from the monasteries. In Mercia Elfhere incited the people to expel the monks,[7] and Abbot Germanus and his brethren were driven from Winchcombe, but after the death of Elfhere in 983 the persecution ceased.[8] The frequent and terrible ravages of the Danes from 980 to 1016 checked the progress of the monastic revival throughout England. When peace was restored, under Canute, the older generation of reformers in the church had passed away, and their successors were lesser men. In 1022 Wulfstan II, who held the sees of Worcester and York, introduced the Benedictine rule into the monastery of St. Peter at Gloucester, and the secular priests became monks, under the government of one of their number, Abbot Edric,[9] but the monastery did not prosper.[10] Writing in the reign of Henry I, William of Malmesbury said that 'Zeal and religion had grown cold many years before the coming of the Normans,'[11] and the condition of the Church in Gloucestershire, during the reign of Edward the Confessor, bears out the truth of his statement. The minster at Berkeley, with its great possessions, passed away from the Church into the hands of Earl Godwin.[12] Regenbald, dean of Cirencester, was a great pluralist, holding sixteen churches and lands in five different counties,[13] but the college itself was slenderly endowed ;[14] and

[1] *Chron. Abbatiae Rameseiensis* (Rolls Ser.), 42 ; *Historians of York* (Rolls Ser.), i, 424.

[2] *Flor. Wigorn.* (Engl. Hist. Soc.), i, 141.   [3] *Brist. and Glouc. Arch. Soc. Trans.* xviii, 118, 119.

[4] *Historians of York* (Rolls Ser.), i, 435.   [5] *Brist. and Glouc. Arch. Soc. Trans.* xviii, 128.

[6] Ibid. xviii, 130.   [7] *Historians of York* (Rolls Ser.), i, 445.

[8] *Brist. and Glouc. Arch. Soc. Trans.* xviii, 122.   [9] *Hist. et Cart. Glouc.* (Rolls Ser.), i, 8.

[10] Ibid. Dugdale, *Mon.* i, 564.   [11] Will. of Malmes. *De Gest. Reg. Angl.* (Rolls Ser.), ii, 304.

[12] *Brist. and Glouc. Arch. Soc. Trans.* xix, 80, 81.   [13] Round, *Feud. Engl.* 426 ; Dugdale, *Mon.* vi, 177.

[14] *V. C. H. Glouc. Relig. Houses, Cirencester*, 80.

the greater part of the lands belonging to the canons of St. Oswald at Gloucester were in the possession of another great pluralist, Stigand, archbishop of Canterbury.[1] It was perhaps because the monastery at Deerhurst was in decay that about 1059 Edward the Confessor granted much of the property to the Benedictine monastery at St. Denis, reserving the remainder for the new foundation of St. Peter at Westminster.[2] Tewkesbury was only a small cell of the Benedictine house of Cranbourne in Dorset.[3] In 1058, after the monastery of St. Peter at Gloucester had been destroyed by fire, it was rebuilt by Aldred, bishop of Worcester; but in 1061, on account of the expense, he took possession of some of the lands of the monks and annexed them to the see of York.[4] Monastic life at St. Peter's languished under the rule of Abbot Wilstan; and when he died in 1072, while on a pilgrimage to Jerusalem, the convent consisted only of two monks and eight novices.[5] It is probable, however, that zeal and energy were conspicuous in the monastery of Winchcombe ; Abbot Godric, who began to rule there in 1054, was one of Edward the Confessor's own chaplains.[6]

William of Malmesbury has given a striking account of the condition of the diocese of Worcester under Bishop Wulfstan (1062–95), from the biography by his chaplain, Coleman.[7] Wulfstan was of English birth, and was educated in the monasteries of Evesham and Peterborough, and at Worcester he filled the offices of schoolmaster and prior before he became bishop. He had not the learning of the Normans ; indeed, he neither knew nor cared to know 'the fables of the poets and the tortuous syllogisms of dialecticians.'[8] In 1078 Lanfranc contemplated deposing him on account of his ignorance, but wisely stayed his hand.[9] It is scarcely an exaggeration to say that no other bishop in England was in such close personal relations with his people.[10] Not only in his vigorous youth, but even when his hair was white with age, he travelled constantly throughout his diocese, holding large confirmations,[11] and never passing a church without going in to celebrate mass or to preach to the people in their own Saxon tongue.[12] He was a homely preacher, adapting his sermons to the understanding of his congregation, and everywhere the people flocked in great numbers to hear him.[13] He made a regular visitation of his see once a year, clergy and people being summoned to meet him by the two archdeacons of Worcester and Gloucester.[14] He was not only beloved by the poor, but high-born youths came under his influence, and put off their pride to serve the weak and lowly at his bidding.[15] He exerted all his power to stop the slave trade of Bristol, sometimes making a stay of two or three months to preach against it, until his efforts were successful.[16] It was perhaps in order that the bishops of the diocese might have a place of residence near the rapidly-growing port of Bristol that he restored the monastery at Westbury-on-Trym, rebuilding the church and

---

[1] Taylor, 'Domesday Surv. of Glouc.' (*Brist. and Glouc. Arch. Soc.*), 14, 95.
[2] *V. C. H. Glouc. Relig. Houses, Deerhurst*, 103.
[3] Ibid. *Tewkesbury*, 61.
[4] *Hist. et Cart. Glouc.* (Rolls Ser.), i, 9.
[5] Ibid. i, 10.
[6] cf. *V. C. H Glouc. Relig. Houses, Winchcombe*, 66.
[7] Wharton, *Vita S. Wulstani, Angl. Sacr.* ii, 241–70.
[8] Will. of Malmes. *Gesta Pontif.* (Rolls Ser.), 279.
[9] Ibid.
[10] Wharton, *Angl. Sacr.* ii, 261, &c.
[11] Ibid. 257. The numbers illustrate the usual exaggeration with regard to figures of the mediaeval writer.
[12] Ibid. 257.
[13] Ibid. 252.
[14] Ibid. 262.
[15] Ibid. 261.
[16] Ibid. 258.

making it dependent on the cathedral monastery of Worcester.[1] Before then there was but a single priest, and he seldom said mass.[2] Wulfstan built many churches on his own lands,[3] of which 231 hides lay in Gloucestershire,[4] and dedicated a great number of stone altars in place of the old wooden ones.[5] He also urged on the lords of manors the duty of building churches,[6] and the Domesday Survey is to some extent a measure of his success. Out of a total of about sixty parish churches, thirteen were on land belonging to religious houses,[7] the remainder on the property of the crown and of laymen.[8] It is probable that a number of other churches were already built,[9] for in Gloucestershire, as in many counties, there is evidence of some which are not entered in the survey, among them Deerhurst and Westbury-on-Trym, Pucklechurch and Churchdown.[10]

In 1100 there were churches at Standish, Hartpury, Brookthorpe, Churcham, and Taynton, and chapels at Nympsfield, Matson, Eycote, and Bulley,[11] and it may be that they were already built at the time of the survey. Of the churches of Berkeley and Berkleherness, which were granted to the monastery of St. Augustine, Bristol, about 1148,[12] only Berkeley is mentioned in the survey, and yet it was a prebendal church before the Norman Conquest.[13] Some of these parish churches were well endowed, the priests at Bibury and Cheltenham having three hides and a hide and a half, while those of Marshfield and Stow-on-the-Wold had each a hide.[14] The Church already owned a third of the profitable land of the county.[15]

The growth in wealth and importance of the religious houses in the first fifty years after the Conquest is remarkable. In 1072, when Serlo, a Norman monk of Mont St. Michel, became abbot of Gloucester, he found only two monks and eight novices; in 1100 there were more than sixty monks, a vast new church had been built and dedicated, and the possessions of the house had greatly increased.[16] Tewkesbury was but a small priory dependent on the monastery of Cranbourne in Dorset, until Robert Fitzhamon added largely to the endowment, and built a great church for the monks, who chose Tewkesbury for the mother-house and made Cranbourne a cell.[17] From Winchcombe

---

[1] Wharton, *Angl. Sacr.* ii, 262 ; cf. *V. C. H. Glouc. Relig. Houses, Westbury,* 107.

[2] Thorpe, *Diplomatarium Anglicum aevi Saxonici,* 447.

[3] Wharton, op. cit. ii, 253, 262.

[4] Taylor, *Analysis of the Domesday Survey of Gloucestershire,* 93.

[5] Wharton, op. cit. ii, 264 ; cf. Wilkins, *Concilia,* i, 365.   [6] Wharton, op. cit. ii, 262.

[7] Bibury, Withington, Cleeve, Prestbury, Olveston, Littleton-on-Severn, Stow-on-the-Wold, Bourton-on-the-Water, Broadwell, Upper Swell, Willersey, Weston-sub-Edge, Minchinhampton. Taylor, *Domesday Survey,* 101.

[8] Cheltenham, Awre, Berkeley, Marshfield, Bristol, Coln Rogers ?, Stanway, Clifford Chambers, Fairford, Dymock, Tidenham, Beckford and Ashton-under-Hill, two at Ampney, Bisley, Driffield, Rodmarton, Lasborough, Lower Guiting, Shipton Oliffe, Temple Guiting, Painswick, Quenington, Stratton, Siddington, Oakley, Hampnett, Tetbury, Tormarton, Stoke Gifford, Brimpsfield, Southrop ?, Barrington, South Cerney, Frampton Cotterell, Badminton, Brockworth, Salperton, Siddington, Greenhampstead, Side, Haselton, Bitton, Whitminster. Taylor, *Domesday Survey,* 100–102.

[9] Ibid. 102–104.   [10] Ibid. 102.

[11] *Hist. et Cart. Mon. Glouc.* (Rolls Ser.), i, 250 ; ii, 40.

[12] Wotton-under-Edge, Beverstone, Ashleworth and Almondsbury with dependent chapels. Red Book of St. Augustine's, Bristol, fol. 33 ; MSS. at Berkeley Castle.

[13] cf. charter of Adela, wife of Henry I, to Reading Abbey, Dugdale, *Mon.* iv, 42. 'Sciatis me concessisse et dedisse ecclesie de Redyng . . . ecclesias de Berkelei hernesse scilicet ecclesiam de Berkeley cum prebendis eidem ecclesie pertinentibus et prebendis duarum monialium et ecclesiam de Chamma. . . .' Earl Godwin seized the possessions of the nuns ; cf. supra, p. 3.

[14] Taylor, *Domesday Survey,* 104.   [15] Ibid. 98.

[16] *V. C. H. Glouc. Relig. Houses, Gloucester,* 53.   [17] Ibid. *Relig. Houses, Tewkesbury,* 62.

Prior Aldwyn set out with two deacons of Evesham to revive monastic life in Northumbria, and with the help of Walcher, bishop of Durham, they rebuilt the monasteries of Jarrow and Wearmouth.[1] Norman lords granted lands to Benedictine monasteries in Normandy, and alien priories were established at Newent,[2] Horsley,[3] and Brimpsfield.[4]

A number of new houses were founded before the middle of the twelfth century. Henry I was the great patron of the Augustinian canons who first came into England in 1108, and soon had several houses in Gloucestershire. In 1117 the king began to build a church and monastery for them at Cirencester, and fourteen years later they entered into possession, taking the place of the secular canons of the collegiate church.[5] Beckford was established as a cell to the Augustinian house of St. Barbe-en-Auge about 1135.[6] Lanthony-by-Gloucester was founded in 1136,[7] St. Augustine, Bristol, in 1148.[8] About 1150 they were installed in the collegiate church of St. Oswald at Gloucester by Henry Murdac, archbishop of York.[9] Although the Cistercians had fifty houses in England in 1152, and the general chapter of the order decreed that no more should be founded,[10] they had then only just gained a footing in Gloucestershire by a grant of lands in the Forest of Dean.[11] The Benedictine houses were steadily increasing their possessions, and two more priories were founded, Stanley St. Leonard,[12] and St. James, Bristol.[13]

There is evidence that in Gloucestershire, as elsewhere,[14] the troubles of Stephen's reign were favourable to the erection of parish churches. Moved by the tears and prayers of his tenants, William de Solers built the chapel of St. James in Postlip, that they might have a refuge from the attack of robbers.[15] He gave his tithes to Winchcombe, and the abbot and convent undertook to provide a chaplain to perform service daily in the presence of William de Solers and his heirs, and three times a week in their absence; half a virgate of land and a house were granted for the priest's residence.[16] Ralph of Worcester built a castle and a church at Hayles, and summoned Simon, bishop of Worcester, to dedicate the church,[17] but as the manor lay within the parish of Winchcombe the abbot and convent protested. However, Ralph cut off their supplies of food, and starved them into submission; Hayles was dedicated and became a mother-church with full rights of baptism and burial, charged only with the payment of 7s. a year to the sacrist of Winchcombe.[18] The whole question of church extension turned on the maintenance of the rights of the mother-church, which were safeguarded at the synod of Westminster in 1102,[19] when it was provided that no more chapels should be erected without the leave of the bishop of the diocese, and it was usual for the monasteries to petition the pope to confirm their rights.[20] A composition was generally made. In 1185 the abbot and convent of

[1] Simeon of Durham, Opera Omnia (Rolls Ser.), i, 108 ; ii, 201.
[2] V. C. H. Glouc. Relig. Houses, Newent, 105.   [3] Ibid. Horsley, 91.   [4] Ibid. Brimpsfield, 102.
[5] Ibid. Cirencester, 80.   [6] Ibid. Beckford, 102.   [7] Ibid. Lanthony-by-Gloucester, 87.
[8] Ibid. St. Augustine, Bristol, 75.   [9] Ibid. St. Oswald, Gloucester, 84.
[10] Guignard, Monuments primitifs de la règle Cistercienne, 273, cap. 86.
[11] V. C. H. Glouc. Relig. Houses, Flaxley, 93.   Kingswood was founded in 1139, but until recently it lay in Wiltshire.
[12] V. C. H. Glouc. Relig. Houses, Stanley St. Leonard, 73.   [13] Ibid. St. James, Bristol, 74.
[14] Cutts, Parish Priests and their People in the Middle Ages in England, 115.
[15] Royce, Landboc sive registrum monasterii de Winchelcumba, i, 81.
[16] Ibid.   [17] Ibid. 65.   [18] Ibid. 67.
[19] Cutts, op. cit. 113.   [20] Hist. et Cart. Mon. Glouc. (Rolls Ser.), iii, 3 ; i, 245.

Gloucester agreed with Nicholas FitzRobert that he and his successors might have a resident chaplain to serve the chapel of Nympsfield, provided that he paid £1 a year to the rector of Frocester, to whom the right of nominating a clerk as perpetual vicar of Nympsfield was reserved.[1] The vicar had the right of baptizing the children of his parish, and of burying persons who held less than half a virgate of land; but if through the inclemency of the weather it was not possible for the funeral of richer persons to take place at Frocester, the offerings were reserved to the mother-church. Architectural evidence shows that many of the Cotswold churches were built within a hundred years of the Norman Conquest.[2]

Advowsons of churches, as in France,[3] were lavishly granted to religious houses, with the laudable intention of putting patronage into the possession of those who might use it better than laymen. The churches of Dymock and Beckford were given to Newent;[4] the parish church of Brimpsfield to the monastery of St. Wandrille;[5] Thornbury, Old Sodbury, St. Peter at Bristol, Stanway, and others to Tewkesbury.[6] However, with the consent of the bishops, the new patrons charged the churches with the payment of a pension, or secured the greater part of the revenues by appropriating them to their own use. In 1100 Samson, bishop of Worcester, granted to the abbot and convent of Gloucester pensions of 2 marks each from Quenington and Nympsfield, £1 from St. John's, Gloucester, and 10s. each from Matson and Eycote.[7] Bishop Roger (1164–79) confirmed a pension of 5 marks from St. Mary de Lode, besides the tithes paid to the dependent churches of Maisemore, Barnwood, and Upton St. Leonard, which they might convert to their own use.[8] About 1194 Henry de Soilli, bishop of Worcester, allowed the abbot and convent of Winchcombe to draw a pension of 5 marks from Sherborne for the building and maintenance of the monastic church.[9] As early as 1100 the churches of Northleach, Standish, Hartpury, Brookthorpe, Churcham and Taynton, with dependent chapels, were appropriated by the bishops of Worcester and Hereford to the needs of the abbot and convent of Gloucester.[10] In 1184 Driffield and Preston were appropriated to the sacristy of Cirencester.[11]

The use by monasteries of the revenues of parish churches was not perhaps at that time the greatest evil of the system. The spiritual needs of the parishioners were neglected. The churches were served either by monks who from their training and life could have but little sympathy with the parishioners, or by a poorly paid chaplain who was removable at the will of the patrons. At the synod of Westminster in 1102 it was decreed that monks should not possess themselves of parish churches without the leave of the bishop, nor take so much of the profits as to impoverish the priests who served them.[12] It was, however, not until towards the end of the century that a decree of the Lateran Council of 1179 empowered the bishops to

---

[1] *Hist. et Cart. Mon. Glouc.* (Rolls Ser.), ii, 42–43.

[2] Taylor, *Domesday Survey of Gloucestershire*, 105.

[3] Cutts, op. cit. 95–96.

[4] *V. C. H. Glouc. Relig. Houses, Newent*, 105.

[5] Ibid. *Brimpsfield*, 102.

[6] *Journ. Arch. Assoc.* 1875, p. 289.

[7] *Hist. et Cart. Glouc.* (Rolls Ser.), ii, 41.

[8] Ibid. i, 328. The church of St. Mary and its dependencies were assigned to the office of the 'sacrist by Abbot Gilbert Foliot' (1139–48), cf. Reg. Frocester B. fol. 28 *d*., MSS. of Dean and Chapter of Gloucester.

[9] Royce, op. cit. ii, 275.

[10] *Hist. et Cart. Glouc.* (Rolls Ser.), i, 251; ii, 40.

[11] Fuller, *Cirencester Parish Church*, 72.

[12] Wilkins, *Concilia*, i, 383, cap. xxii.

create perpetual vicarages in appropriated churches.[1] In accordance with this decree the convent was bound to nominate a competent priest, who should be instituted by the bishop, and solely responsible to him for the fulfilment of his spiritual office, and to set aside a sufficient portion of the revenues to provide him with a house and maintenance as a perpetual endowment.[2] The bishops of Worcester acted promptly. A perpetual vicarage had been ordained for Nympsfield in 1185,[3] Cerney in 1190,[4] Kempsford in 1198,[5] and Coln St. Aldwyn in 1217.[6] A number were created by William of Blois (1218–36) and Walter Cantilupe (1237–66), among them Frocester,[7] Hardwick,[8] Sherborne,[9] Painswick,[10] Winchcombe,[11] Beckford,[12] Hatherop,[13] and Berkeley.[14] In 1240, at a synod in his cathedral church, Bishop Cantilupe insisted that vicarages should be created in all churches appropriated to monasteries, and that where the provision for vicars was insufficient it should be augmented within two months.[15] If the religious failed to act, the bishop's official and the archdeacon should compel them by sequestrating the fruits of their churches. He also ordered that before a stated time the houses should produce their title-deeds to prove their various claims to tithes. Peter Aquablanca, bishop of Hereford, ordained vicarages of the value of 14 marks in the churches of Newent[16] and Dymock.[17] In 1291 there were at least forty vicarages out of a total of about 200 benefices, and there were substantial charges on a number of other churches.[18] The number of vicarages, however, does not fully represent the appropriated churches, for some of the convents had papal bulls enabling them, in spite of ecclesiastical legislation, to serve the churches by one of their own number or by a paid chaplain. In this way, in 1242, Bishop Cantilupe was prevented from creating vicarages at Tewkesbury[19] and at St. James, Bristol.[20] From 1260 until 1380 the Augustinian canons from Bruton, who dwelt in the cell at Horsley, served the parish churches of Horsley and Wheatenhurst.[21] Until the dissolution the canons of Cirencester served the parish church[22] and the church of Cheltenham.[23] Papal indulgences worked infinite harm in the matter of appropriation. In 1191 Celestine III granted a bull to the abbot and convent of Gloucester, enabling them to appropriate a number of churches of which they had the advowsons when they fell vacant, notwithstanding the prohibition of the recent Lateran Council or of the bishop of the diocese.[24] In the same year he granted a similar bull to the abbot and convent of Cirencester for the churches of Ampney and Oxenton, and four years later for Cheltenham,[25] and in 1222 Honorius III confirmed the appropriation of

[1] Labbe, *Sacrorum Conciliorum Collectio* (ed. Cossart), xxii, 398, cap. i.
[2] Cutts, op. cit. 98. [3] *Hist. et Cart. Glouc.* (Rolls Ser.), ii, 42.
[4] Ibid. i, 230, 247. [5] Ibid. 229. [6] Ibid. 231.
[7] In 1225, ibid. iii, 31. [8] 1223–8, ibid. i, 336.
[9] (1218–24) Royce, op. cit. ii, 275. [10] MS. top. Glouc. C 5 fol. 644. (Bodl. Lib.).
[11] Royce, op. cit. i, 266. Giffard made a new ordination in 1288, annulling former ordinations.
[12] Before 1247 ; MS. Add. 18461, fol. 19 (B.M.).
[13] *Hist. et Cart. Glouc.* (Rolls Ser.), i, 328.
[14] Before 1255 ; Jeayes, *Catal. of Mun. of Lord Fitzhardinge*, 66. [15] Wilkins, *Concilia*, i, 674.
[16] MS. Add. 18461, fol. 13 (B.M.). [17] Ibid. fol. 14.
[18] *Pope Nich. Tax.* (Rec. Com.), 220–4.
[19] *Ann. Mon.* i, 126. [20] Ibid.
[21] *V. C. H. Glouc. Relig. Houses, Horsley*, 92.
[23] *V. C. H. Glouc. Relig. Houses, Cirencester*, 82, 83. [22] Fuller, *Cirencester Parish Church*, 81.
[25] Fuller, *Cirencester Parish Church*, 72. [24] *Hist. et Cart. Glouc.* (Rolls Ser.), iii, 11.

the parish church of Cirencester. Maurice of Arundel, archdeacon of Gloucester, complained to Gregory IX that the churches of Cheltenham and Cirencester had been appropriated to his damage and without his consent.[1] The papal delegates heard the cause at Hereford in 1230, and decided against the archdeacon. The case of the chapel of Wigwold, which was dependent on Cirencester, shows a scandalous disregard of the spiritual needs of the parishioners.[2] In 1236 the abbot and convent of Cirencester persuaded John Bisset, then lord of Wigwold, to release them from the duty of serving the chapel on condition that when he resided at Wigwold he could provide a priest at his own cost to perform the services, and that all fees should be paid over to the abbey. Bisset agreed to share expenses if the men of Wigwold indicted the abbot, and the chapel of the hamlet was thus converted into a private oratory. Bishop William of Blois prevented the abbot and convent of Tewkesbury from appropriating Fairford in virtue of a privilege granted by Honorius III in 1221.[3] On the death of the rector ten years afterwards several of the monks went to Fairford and occupied the church, but with the bishop's full knowledge they were expelled and so maltreated that they scarcely escaped alive, and the whole convent was excommunicated.[4] Bishop Cantilupe foiled a similar attempt at Thornbury.[5]

The endowment of the vicarages varied very much. Five marks was fixed as a minimum at the synod of Oxford in 1222,[6] the sum which had been assigned to the vicar of Coln St. Aldwyn in 1217,[7] all burdens being charged on the abbot and convent of Gloucester. In 1247 Peter Aquablanca, bishop of Hereford, ordered the abbot and convent of Cormeilles to find fourteen marks for the vicar of Dymock,[8] but in 1291 his portion was not worth six marks, while the rectorial dues amounted to thirty-nine.[9] William of Blois assigned two-thirds of the whole tithe of Sherborne to the abbot and convent of Winchcombe, and the remainder to the vicar,[10] and he seems to have made the same arrangement for the parish church of Winchcombe.[11] In both parishes there were serious quarrels between the collectors, which were probably reported to Bishop Giffard by the archdeacon of Gloucester, for in 1276 he charged his archdeacons to inquire whether the portions of the vicars were sufficient.[12] In 1298 he assigned the great tithes of Winchcombe to the abbot and convent, the small tithes, the tithe of wool, and all oblations and obventions to the vicar, but should his portion fall below £10 the convent was bound to pay him the difference.[13] In 1271 he gave the whole tithe of Sherborne to the convent, reserving for the vicar the offerings at the altar, his arable land, the right to put six beasts on the abbot's pasture, and the moiety of the tithe of hay of the parishioners; all sources of his revenue being valued at fifteen marks.[14] The vicar of Churcham had a bare maintenance: he and the deacon who helped him, for there were dependent chapels at Bulley and Highnam, lived at the expense of the abbot and convent of Gloucester on their manor of Churcham, and his horse was stabled and fed.[15]

---

[1] Fuller, *Cirencester Parish Church*, 75.
[2] Ibid. 74.
[3] *Cal. Papal L.* i, 81.
[4] *Ann. Mon.* (Rolls Ser.), i, 82.
[5] Ibid. i, 97.
[6] Wilkins, *Concilia*, i, 587, cap. xvi.
[7] *Hist. et Cart. Glouc.* (Rolls Ser.), i, 231.
[8] MS. Add. 18461, fol. 14.
[9] *Pope Nich. Tax.* (Rec. Com.), 161.
[10] Royce, op. cit. ii, 276.
[11] Ibid. i, 269.
[12] *Worc. Epis. Reg. Giffard* (Worc. Hist. Soc.), 90.
[13] Royce, op. cit. i, 270, 271.
[14] Ibid. ii, 277, 278.
[15] *Hist. et Cart. Glouc.* (Rolls Ser.), i, 267.

He was entitled to receive legacies and offerings at the altar in silver and in candles, but those of bread or food were handed over to the bailiff of the abbot and convent, who also took the whole of the tithe. The vicar was bound to find candles for the church and for the bailiff, and if he failed his horse's forage was stopped. He was obliged to entertain the archdeacon or any guests at his own expense, and to pay synodal dues. Thomas Cantilupe, bishop of Hereford, made a better provision for the vicar, granting tithes and offerings which were valued at £11 6s. 10d., and half an acre of land on which to build a manse.[1] In 1279 he bade the rural dean of the Forest admonish the abbot and convent of Gloucester to find a chalice for the church and to provide the timber and a site near the church for the vicar's house, and the vicar was ordered to build it before a certain day.[2] In spite of the bishop's ordinance, in 1291 the vicar's portion was only assessed at £5 6s. 8d., while the rectorial dues were £20.[3] The Taxation of Pope Nicholas (1291) shows that it was not unusual for the vicar only to get a fifth of the revenues; this was his portion at Hawkesbury,[4] and at Bisley he had less.[5] The rectorial dues of Berkeley, which fell to the convent of St. Augustine, Bristol, amounted to £24 6s. 8d.; the convent of Reading drew £13 6s. 8d.; the bishop of Worcester, £3 6s. 8d.; the convent of Stanley St. Leonard, £1; and the vicar had £12 13s. 4d.[6]

It was not only by appropriating the revenues of churches that the religious houses diminished the income of the parish priests. They obtained papal bulls exempting them from the payment of tithes from any land which they cultivated at their own expense, and from the tithe of the young of animals. Although an attempt was made at the Lateran Council of 1215 to prevent a further diminution of the income of the parochial clergy when monasteries acquired fresh lands, the Cistercians, Templars, and Hospitallers always maintained their immunities, and papal bulls were granted notwithstanding the prohibition of the Council.

Besides the ordination of vicarages there is other evidence that in the thirteenth century the bishops of Worcester were able and energetic prelates who ruled their diocese with watchful care, making visitations and issuing constitutions which show at least a high ideal of church life. In 1219 William of Blois decreed that no clerk should be admitted to any benefice not above the value of five marks unless he was already in priest's orders, and that he should be bound to reside, the reason being that so small a living could not support more than one man.[7] No priest might become a rural dean unless he held a benefice, and no rural deanery might be farmed. The bishop engaged in a serious dispute with the abbot and convent of Tewkesbury when they attempted to defy his authority in virtue of a papal bull, and although his measures were violent, he prevented them from appropriating Fairford.[8] In 1234 he deposed the abbot of St. Augustine's, Bristol, on account of his quarrels with the convent.[9]

In the years immediately after his consecration Bishop Walter Cantilupe (1237–1266) made a thorough visitation of his diocese. In accordance

---

[1] *Hist. et Cart. Glouc.* (Rolls Ser.), i, 249.
[2] Heref. Epis. Reg. Cantilupe, fol. 63 d.
[3] *Pope Nich. Tax.* (Rec. Com.), 161.
[4] Ibid. 220b. [5] Ibid. 221a.
[6] Ibid. 220b.
[7] Wilkins, *Concilia*, i, 571.
[8] *V. C. H. Glouc. Relig. Houses, Tewkesbury*, 62.
[9] *Ann. Mon.* (Rolls Ser.), i, 93.

with the decree of the legate Otho at the council of London in 1237,[1] he dedicated a great number of parish churches, bidding the priests write the year and day over the altar,[2] and keep the festival.[3] Among these was perhaps St. John's Church, Gloucester, for in 1234 the parson and parishioners undertook to build a new aisle.[4] In 1239 the bishop dedicated the churches of Tewkesbury Abbey,[5] St. James's Priory at Bristol,[6] Winchcombe Abbey[7] and of the abbey of St. Peter at Gloucester,[8] and in 1251 of Hayles Abbey.[9]

In 1240, at a synod in his cathedral church on the morrow of St. James's Day, he promulgated fifty-nine constitutions for the clergy.[10] Some of these embodied the decrees of Lateran Councils and synods of the English Church, others were adapted to the special needs of his diocese. He ordered that the churches should be cleansed of everything which defiled them, the roofs should be kept in good repair, and ornaments, including vestments, altar-cloths, chalices, pyxes, lenten veils, banners, and processional crosses, should be provided according to the resources of each church, but all must possess the necessary service-books.[11] The canon of the mass must be correct, and the feasts of the Church should be observed according to the Use of Sarum. The bishop had found that burial-grounds were put to uses which dishonoured the dead, and he ordered that they should be enclosed with a hedge or wall ; no unseemly games might be played within them, nor might they serve as a market-place,[12] and no markets might be held anywhere on Sundays.[13] Every baptismal church must possess a font of sufficient size and depth and decently covered. He told the parish priests that it was their duty to instruct their people every Sunday about having their children baptized and confirmed, especially as owing to the spread of error they no longer brought them on the vigils of Easter and Pentecost, the two days which had been solemnly set apart by the Church for baptism.[14] They should instruct them in the ten commandments, the seven sacraments of the Church, and about the seven deadly sins. Heathen beliefs still influenced the lives of the people, who resorted to soothsayers and fortune tellers and worshipped springs, and the bishop told the priests to forbid their parishioners to gather at Cerney, and at Rolla's Spring, near Gloucester, and other places. They should teach their parishioners how to make their confession once a year before they came to their Easter communion, and they should take no offerings from the poor. They should be diligent in visiting the sick. They were forbidden to ask fees for marriages or funerals, or for any of the sacraments, but if offered by the faithful, they might be accepted. If the parishioners kept back their tithes and had been solemnly admonished on three Sundays, the rectors might excommunicate them. The bishop bade the priests live as true scholars and

---

[1] Wilkins, *Concilia*, i, 650. [2] Ibid. 666. [3] Ibid. 678.
[4] *Cal. of Close*, 18 Hen. III, m. 31. [5] *Ann. Mon.* (Rolls Ser.), i, 112.
[6] Ibid. [7] Ibid. [8] *Hist. et Cart. Glouc.* (Rolls Ser.), i, 28.
[9] Dugdale, *Mon.* v, 686. [10] Wilkins, *Concilia*, i, 665–78.
[11] Ibid. 666, 'Missale, breviarium, antiphonarium, gradale, troparium, manuale, psalterium, ordinale in qualibet ecclesia propria volumus contineri' ; cf. Wordsworth and Littlehales, *Old Service Books of the English Church.*
[12] Cardinal Ottoboni forbade the use of churches as market places in 1267 ; Wilkins, *Concilia*, ii, 14. The holding of markets in cemeteries was forbidden by Edward I, 13 Edw. I, Winton, cap. 6.
[13] The Cirencester market was held on Sundays in 1131 ; Dugdale, *Mon.* vi, 177.
[14] Swete, *Services and Service Books before the Reformation*, 138.

disciples of Jesus Christ, having the ornament of a quiet spirit, keeping the tonsure, wearing a sober dress, not of silk or green or red in colour. They might not play at dice nor be present at public wrestlings nor take part in scotales or drinking bouts, and they should restrain their people also from scotales. Like the religious they were bidden to show hospitality so far as their means allowed of it. The archdeacons were ordered to make diligent inquiry about the celibacy of the clergy, and they were also to denounce rectors and vicars who had not sufficient learning, but they were to be chary in their use of excommunication, and were not to deprive the people of services by laying the church under an interdict when they could punish the priest by sequestrating his fruits. The archdeacons were to observe the statutes of the Lateran Council, and the councils of Oxford and London, and were not to travel with more than seven horses, or to demand money wrongfully for chrism and oil. The rural deans were to have no right to demand fees for inducting the clergy. In the larger churches with dependent chapels the bishop ordered the rectors to provide additional clergy, and if they failed to do so it should be done by the archdeacons. In churches near the schools of a city or castle the office of bearer of holy water should be given to scholars for their maintenance.[1] At the beginning of September every year, priests who had been ordained in another diocese and received benefices or served for a salary in the diocese of Worcester, were to be presented to the archdeacons or the bishop's official, that they might be approved or rejected according to their merits. If rectors and vicars had not taken priest's orders, the archdeacons should admonish them to be ordained as soon as possible. Vicars were bound to reside, and rectors might only absent themselves with the bishop's leave. Like his predecessor,[2] Cantilupe insisted that the decrees of successive Lateran Councils touching the relations between Jews and Christians should be observed; no Christian might be a servant in a Jewish household, nor give his money to a Jew to lend for usury, nor receive a Jew's money that it might be in safe custody in the parish church.[3] It is probable that, owing to the constitution of William of Blois, the scandal of pledging the books, vestments or ornaments of churches to the Jews had ceased.[4] In conclusion the bishop ordered that the constitutions should be observed in all the churches of his diocese, and he exhorted rectors and priests to strive with all their might to understand them and to fulfil them.[5] The clergy who were ignorant of them and failed to possess a copy would be fined 6s. 8d. for negligence.

The bishop also drew up statutes to be observed in the monasteries of his diocese, but he announced at the synod in 1240 that he would cause these to be published in the chapter-houses of the religious.[6] He made regular visitations of the monasteries, compelling the abbot and convent of Gloucester to admit him against their will in 1239,[7] and in 1242 removing the prior and other obedientiars from office.[8] In 1251, when the monastery was in debt to the amount of 3,000 marks, he forbade the reception and entertain-

---

[1] It was a usual provision for poor scholars, Cutts; *Parish Priests and their People*, 302, 303. Samson, abbot of Bury, was thus supported as a student at the university of Paris; *Mem. of St. Edmund's Abbey* (Rolls Ser.), i, 247.

[2] Wilkins, *Concilia*, i, 571.   [3] Ibid. 675.   [4] Ibid. 591.   [5] Ibid. 676.

[6] Ibid.   [7] *Ann. Mon.* (Rolls Ser.), iv, 430.   [8] Ibid. 433.

ment of guests.[1] In 1242 he visited St. Augustine's, Bristol, and compelled the abbot to resign.[2] He strove to enforce the constitutions for the reform of the Benedictine order, which were issued by Gregory IX in 1238 and by Innocent IV in 1253,[3] and accordingly in 1251,[4] and again in 1253,[5] he subjected Tewkesbury to a very strict visitation, when he himself examined the monks one by one, but found nothing of which he could complain.

In providing for the spiritual needs of the poor and the outcast, Bishops William de Blois and Cantilupe were helped by the coming of the friars into their diocese.[6] The Dominicans were established at Bristol in 1228, at Gloucester in 1239. The Franciscans went to Gloucester in 1231 and to Bristol in 1234. It is probable that as elsewhere the older orders were hostile to them, but only the Benedictines of St. James's Priory at Bristol are known to have manifested their resentment at the popularity of the friars. When in 1230, at the request of the Dominicans, Bishop William of Blois came to dedicate their altar and burial-ground, the monks protested, urging that the friars should be forbidden to receive oblation or to have a cemetery.[7] The chronicler of Tewkesbury records that the building of the friars' oratory was to the great prejudice and loss of the church of St. James.[8] It is significant, perhaps, of the power and influence of the friars in the diocese that at the synod in 1240 Bishop Cantilupe decreed that the anniversaries of St. Dominic and St. Francis should be kept as high festivals.[9] It is probable that like Grosseteste, bishop of Lincoln,[10] Cantilupe had difficulties with the alien priories, which claimed exemption from episcopal visitation, and had the right of presentation to several parish churches. In 1264 he made an agreement with the abbot and convent of St. Denis by which the abbot appointed one of his monks as prior of Deerhurst and presented him to the bishop by reason of his cure of souls in that church,[11] for the nave was parochial. The prior was bound to obey the bishop in all things saving the privileges of the monastery of St. Denis. In 1260 Cantilupe gave his consent to the grant of the priory of Horsley, which was a cell of the Benedictine monastery of Trouarn, to the Augustinian canons of Bruton,[12] and the priory thus became subject to the regular visitation of the bishop.[13] The establishment of the collegiate church of Westbury-on-Trym may most probably be ascribed to him, though its subsequent importance was due to his successor.[14]

Like Grosseteste he was opposed to the spoliation of the church to fill the treasuries of the crown and papacy.[15] In the barons' war he espoused the cause of Simon de Montfort, and was excommunicated by the papal legate, Cardinal Ottoboni, in 1265. Afterwards, when he was dying, he was reconciled and absolved by the legate.

---

[1] *Ann. Mon.* (Rolls Ser.), i, 146.
[2] Ibid. iv, 433. *V. C. H. Glouc. Religious Houses, Bristol,* 76.
[3] Matt. Paris, *Chron. Maj.* (Rolls Ser.), iii, 499–516 ; vi, 234.
[4] *Ann. Mon.* (Rolls Ser.), i, 146.
[5] Ibid. 152.
[6] *V. C. H. Glouc. Religious Houses, Friaries,* 109, 111.
[7] *Ann. Mon.* (Rolls Ser.), i, 94.
[8] Ibid.
[9] Wilkins, *Concilia,* i, 675.
[10] *Roberti Grosseteste Epistolae* (Rolls Ser.), 168, 319.
[11] *Worc. Epis. Reg. Giffard* (Worc. Hist. Soc.), 10.
[12] *Cartul. of Bruton and Montacute* (Somerset Rec. Soc.), 76.
[13] *V. C. H. Glouc. Religious Houses, Horsley,* 91.
[14] Ibid. *Religious Houses, Westbury,* 107.
[15] *V. C. H. Worcester,* ii, 20, 'Eccles. Hist.' ; *Ann. Mon.* (Rolls Ser.), iv, 180.

The episcopal registers of Worcester, Hereford, and York give a clear view of the ecclesiastical organization of Gloucestershire in the latter half of the thirteenth century. The county east of the Severn constituted the archdeaconry of Gloucester,[1] and was divided into the rural deaneries of Campden, Stow, Cirencester, Fairford, Winchcombe, Stonehouse, Hawkesbury, Bristol,[2] Dursley, and Gloucester. The jurisdiction of Bibury was exempt from the visitation of the archdeacon,[3] but not from that of the bishop.[4] In virtue of a papal privilege granted by Urban II (1088–1099) and confirmed by Eugenius III (1145–53), the abbot and convent of the Augustinian monastery of Oseney sent one of their brethren to serve the parish church of Bibury and the dependent chapels of Aldsworth, Barnsley, and Winson.[5]

The jurisdiction of St. Oswald's, by a grant from William Rufus in 1094, was a peculiar of the see of York.[6] It included the priory of St. Oswald, Gloucester, and the chapels of Churchdown, Norton, Sandhurst, and Compton Abdale,[7] and was administered by a dean or keeper,[8] who installed the priors of St. Oswald's[9] and received and transmitted procurations to the archbishop of York,[10] unless he came on a personal visitation. The prior and convent of St. Oswald's were in the habit of obtaining chrism and oil from the bishops of Worcester, but as they had attempted to exercise ecclesiastical jurisdiction over the monastery, Archbishop Corbridge (1300–1304) bade the canons send to Southwell for the chrism and oil, and pay pentecostals and Peter's pence to the dean of his jurisdiction.[11]

The county west of the Severn and the Leadon was in the diocese and archdeaconry of Hereford. The rural deanery of the Forest contained all the Gloucestershire parishes save those of Newland and English Bicknor and Preston, which were in the deanery of Ross,[12] and Staunton in the deanery of Irchinfield.

The zealous administration of Bishop Cantilupe bore fruit, and the carefully kept register of his successor Godfrey Giffard (1268–1302) shows that the evils of non-residence and pluralism were not very prevalent in Gloucestershire. In accordance with Bishop Cantilupe's constitution, a number of licences were granted to rectors to farm their churches and study canon law and theology at a university.[13] When rectors under age were presented

---

[1] *Worc. Epis. Reg. Giffard* (Worc. Hist. Soc.), the first extant register of the see.

[2] Including the city of Bristol with the exception of the small part beyond the Avon which lay in the diocese of Bath and Wells. It was a privilege of the burgesses of Bristol, which was confirmed to them by Robert Kilwardby, archbishop of Canterbury (1273–79), that they could not be cited to appear before the ordinary of the bishop of Worcester outside the rural deanery of Bristol. Bickley, *Little Red Book of Bristol*, i, 93 ; Worc. Epis. Reg. Reynolds, 42, 'as his predecessors had granted.'

[3] *Valor Eccl.* (Rec. Com.), ii, 220 ; Thomas, *Survey of Worcester*, App. 14.

[4] *Worc. Epis. Reg. Giffard* (Worc. Hist. Soc.), 272. In 1285 the abbot and convent of Oseney agreed to pay an annual procuration of four marks to the bishop in lieu of giving him food and lodging at their monastery.

[5] Ibid. 14. Entries of presentations of canons of Oseney to the cure of souls of Bibury occur frequently in the registers. In 1535 the rectory was farmed. *Valor Eccles.* (Rec. Com.), ii, 220. The jurisdiction of Bibury remained a peculiar after the Reformation, and in 1813 the archdeacon was still excluded. Ibid. 512.

[6] Archbishop Peckham and Bishop Giffard in vain attempted to exercise jurisdiction over it. *V. C. H. Glouc. Relig. Houses, St. Oswald, Gloucester*, 85.

[7] *Worc. Epis. Reg. Giffard* (Worc. Hist. Soc.), 138 ; *Valor Eccl.* (Rec. Com.), ii, 487.

[8] York Archiepis. Reg. Wickwane, 570. [9] Ibid. 574. [10] Ibid 571, *Valor Eccl.* (Rec. Com.), ii, 487.

[11] *Historians of York* (Rolls Ser.), ii, 225. [12] *Pope Nich. Tax.* (Rec. Com.), 161.

[13] *Worc. Epis. Reg. Giffard*, 13, Licence in 1268 to the rectors of Coates and St. Lawrence, Bristol, to let their church to farm and reside at the schools ; also 47, 50.

to the bishop, he himself committed the custody of the church to a priest that there might be no neglect of the cure of souls.[1]

In 1284, on the presentation of the prior and convent of Lanthony, he instituted Geoffrey of Ludlow to the rectory of St. Mary de Crypt, Gloucester ; but although a priest he had insufficient learning, and the bishop committed the custody of the parish to John de Butterley.[2] In 1269 John Everard, a poor clerk, petitioned the bishop to grant him the vicarage of Berkeley then vacant, according to a mandate from Alexander IV to the abbot and convent of St. Augustine, Bristol, to collate him to their next vacant benefice.[3] Giffard, however, told the dean of Dursley not to admit John Everard, because he was only in minor orders,[4] and on account of the neglect of the cure of souls he gave the custody of Berkeley to Simon de Otindon, a priest, without prejudice to the patrons.[5] The religious houses presented clerks in minor orders[6] as often as lay patrons did, and in 1290 the bishop instituted Walter Froucester, a deacon, to the vicarage of Berkeley ;[7] and two years later, in virtue of a papal dispensation because he was a vicar, he went away to study theology for five years.[8] However, although the greater part of the revenues was alienated,[9] there is evidence of vigorous church life in Berkeley, for in 1278 the parishioners undertook to find five marks a year for the maintenance of a priest in their chantry of the Virgin.[10] The rebuilding of much of the church took place in the reign of Edward I.[11] In parishes where the rector could no longer fulfil his duties, owing to old age or illness, the bishop committed the custody of the church to a neighbouring incumbent that he might make due provision for the maintenance of the services. In 1288 the custody of Coates was given to the rector of Ampney St. Mary,[12] and in 1291 that of Wotton to a canon of Westbury.[13] In 1276 Richard of Studley, rector of both Twyning and Bledington, was indebted to many creditors whom he could not pay, and submitted his case to the bishop.[14] He seems also to have served the Lady chapel of Winchcombe, and he had a lodging in the monastery. The bishop decided that as ' his mature age merited a rest from labour,' the abbot of Winchcombe should receive his rents, maintain him in food, wine, raiment, shoes, and bedclothes, and let him have his lodging in the monastery. The abbot should also provide a clerk to say the hours with the rector, and a groom and a boy to wait on him. He was to satisfy the rector's creditors, cause the churches to be properly served, and bear all charges.

In accordance with Bishop Cantilupe's constitution vicars were bound to reside, and it was decided at the council of Hartlebury in 1300 that if they absented themselves for a year they were legally deprived.[15] A curious case occurred at Sherborne in 1284. The vicar stated that he could not reside for fear of death and dread of his enemies, and Giffard decided that he should have his maintenance from the abbot of Winchcombe, who should provide a fit priest to undertake the cure of souls.[16]

---

[1] *Worc. Epis. Reg. Giffard*, 442. In 1294 he committed to John de Winterbournestoke the administration of the fruits and goods of the church of Cromhall and of Roger de Kingston, clerk, aged ten, presented but not instituted because he was a minor.

[2] Ibid. 248.   [3] Ibid. 27.   [4] Ibid. 34.   [5] Ibid. 33.   [6] Ibid. 434, &c.   [7] Ibid. 338.
[8] Ibid. 420.   [9] *Pope Nich. Tax.* (Rec. Com.), 220b.   [10] *Worc. Epis. Reg. Giffard* (Worc. Hist. Soc.), 99.
[11] Cook, *Handbook to Berkeley*, 26.   [12] *Worc. Epis. Reg. Giffard* (Worc. Hist. Soc.), 319.
[13] Ibid. 351 ; cf. 336, 428.   [14] Ibid. 86.   [15] Ibid. 517.   [16] Ibid. 242.

Supported by the authority of Archbishop Peckham's constitutions of 1279,[1] Giffard enforced the decree of the Council of Lyons in 1274, by which clerks who were not already priests when presented to livings, were compelled to take orders within a year. The case of Campden illustrates the difficulties with which the bishop had to contend owing to the claims of patrons and appeals to the papacy. In 1282 Edmund de Mortimer, rector of Campden, was deprived by Giffard because, although he had held the living for three years, he had neglected to take priest's orders.[2] Adam of Avebury was collated as rector by the bishop, but Edmund de Mortimer refused to give up corporal possession, and the church was laid under an interdict.[3] It was of no avail; and as the parishioners suffered, Giffard bade the dean of Campden remove the interdict and admonish Edmund de Mortimer to retire from the church and houses belonging to it.[4] Edmund de Mortimer appealed to the Court of Arches,[5] and thence to the Papal Curia, and in 1283 the judges delegated to act by Martin IV decided that he was the true rector, that the sentence of excommunication on him and his adherents was not binding, that he should have quiet possession of his church, and they condemned the bishop to pay 100 marks for expenses.[6] The bishop and Adam of Avebury appealed, and in consequence the judgement was reversed and Edmund de Mortimer was deprived and ordered to pay them £100.[7] They could not get it from him, and in 1284 the rectors of Blockley and Longborough were directed to induce him to find the money under sentence of the greater excommunication.[8] However, Adam of Avebury was not left in peaceful possession of the rectory, and in January, 1284, the dean of Campden received a mandate to go with four or five parish priests and warn those who had ejected Adam to deliver the church and houses to him under pain of excommunication.[9] The church was again laid under an interdict.[10] The cause of the fresh disturbance was the claim of the abbot and convent of Chester to present to the rectory,[11] and early in 1284 they recovered their right in the king's courts.[12] Giffard received a writ to admit a fit person on their presentation;[13] their nominee was a deacon named Henry of Upavon, and as Giffard refused, a suit in the Court of Arches followed,[14] and the dean of Arches ordered the sequestration of the fruits of Campden.[15] Giffard appealed to the Papal Curia against the sequestration,[16] and judges were delegated to hear the case.[17] The bishop was unsuccessful, and in August, 1284, he instituted Henry of Upavon.[18]

The bishop paid particular care to the fabrics of churches, insisting in September, 1270, that the chancel of Henbury-in-Salt-Marsh should be fitly rebuilt by the vicar and portioners before 1 August, 1271.[19] In 1282 the parishioners of Frocester were summoned to appear before the consistory court in the church of St. Nicholas at Gloucester to show cause why they had not repaired and roofed their chapel.[20] Their reply was that they had made an agreement with the vicar by the terms of which he was bound to undertake the repairs on condition of receiving a third of the mortuaries.[21]

---

[1] Wilkins, *Concilia*, ii, 36.   [2] *Worc. Epis. Reg. Giffard* (Worc. Hist. Soc.), 144.   [3] Ibid. 140.
[4] Ibid. 140.   [5] Ibid. 144.   [6] Ibid. 187.   [7] Ibid. 226.
[8] Ibid. 226.   [9] Ibid. 188.   [10] Ibid. 224.   [11] Ibid. 223.
[12] Ibid. 188.   [13] Ibid.   [14] Ibid. 193.   [15] Ibid. 209.   [16] Ibid. 223.
[17] Ibid. 211.   [18] Ibid. 246.   [19] Ibid. 43.   [20] *Hist. et Cart. Glouc.* (Rolls Ser.), i, 310.
[21] A mortuary was a due paid to the church upon the decease of a parishioner. A man might not dispose of his goods by will without first assigning therein a sufficient mortuary to the church; Phillimore, *Eccl. Law*, i, 873.

The vicar admitted it, and was ordered to act upon it. The archdeacon of Gloucester resented Giffard's activity in the matter of defects of chancels, and made a formal complaint in 1301, to which the bishop replied that he only intermeddled at the time of his visitation.[1]

In dealing with pluralism, of which scarcely any instances occur, he was strongly supported by Archbishop Peckham, who wrote to the precentor of Wells in 1283, insisting that he should resign the church of Welford-on-Avon.[2] Some livings were so poor that licences to hold more than one were occasionally granted; in 1298 Giffard allowed Walter of Cheltenham to hold the rectory of Sapperton with those of Ampney St. Mary and Withington on account of their poverty.[3] A bad case of pluralism came to the notice of Archbishop Winchelsey in the course of his metropolitical visitation in 1301.[4] Thomas of Stoke, incumbent of Kempsey in Worcestershire, had the care of the church of Duntisbourne Abbots, was vicar of Standish, and rector of Cam; but as during the voidance of the see the archbishop proceeded against him, he resigned Kempsey in 1302.

Some relaxation of discipline and extravagance of living in the religious houses, especially among the Augustinian canons, were reformed by Giffard,[5] and at the close of his episcopate the condition of the monasteries of Gloucestershire satisfied him and also Archbishop Winchelsey[6] when he came on his metropolitical visitation in 1301. The bishop was a warm supporter of the friars, and in his will remembered all their houses in his diocese.[7] The Carmelites established themselves at Gloucester and Bristol about 1267,[8] and in 1275 Giffard sent a mandate to all the clergy to admit the Franciscans to preach the crusade in their churches and grant indulgences.[9] After a bitter controversy with the chapter of his cathedral church, he increased the endowment and importance of the collegiate church of Westbury-on-Trym, which had probably been refounded by Bishop Cantilupe, but he did not succeed in reserving a prebendal stall for his successors.[10]

In 1290 the steadily increasing national hostility to the Jews led to their banishment from England. Through the influence of his mother, Eleanor of Provence, Edward I had ordered the Jews of Gloucester to be deported to Bristol with their chirograph chests and all their goods in 1275,[11] and in the same year an incident at Bristol showed how they drew upon themselves the hatred of their Christian neighbours. Bishop Giffard issued a mandate to the deans of Westbury and Bristol to excommunicate certain Jews of Bristol and to forbid all traffic with them because they were guilty of iniquitous insults, blasphemies, and injuries, and of an assault on the chaplain of St. Peter's, when he administered the Holy Eucharist to a sick person in the Jewry.[12]

---

[1] *Worc. Epis. Reg. Giffard* (Worc. Hist. Soc.), 551.   [2] Ibid. 191.   [3] Ibid. 494.

[4] *Reg. Sede Vac.* (Worc. Hist. Soc.), 28. Kempsey was in the bishop's gift; the abbot and convent of Gloucester were patrons of the three other livings.

[5] *V. C. H. Gloucester, post, Relig. Houses, Cirencester, Lanthony, Bristol, Horsley, Tewkesbury, Gaunt's Hospital, Lechlade, Longbridge-by-Berkeley.*

[6] Winchelsey's injunctions to Gloucester were in great part a confirmation of ordinances drawn up by the abbot and convent. Ibid. *Relig. Houses, Gloucester, Gaunt's Hospital.*

[7] *Brist. and Glouc. Arch. Soc.* xx, 152.   [8] *V. C. H. Glouc. Relig. Houses, Carmelites,* 110, 112.

[9] *Worc. Epis. Reg. Giffard* (Worc. Hist. Soc.), 83.

[10] *V. C. H. Glouc. Relig. Houses, Westbury,* 107.

[11] *Select Pleas, Starrs and Records of the Jewish Exchequer* (Selden Soc.), 85.

[12] *Worc. Epis. Reg. Giffard* (Worc. Hist. Soc.), 71.

A HISTORY OF GLOUCESTERSHIRE

In accordance with the terms of an agreement between the prior of Worcester and the archbishop of Canterbury in 1268, the prior of Worcester administered the spiritualities of the diocese during voidances of the see, paying two-thirds of the fees which were received to the archbishop.[1] In exercising his rights of visitation the prior came into conflict with several of the religious houses of Gloucestershire in the first years of the thirteenth century,[2] but as he was supported by the archbishop his claims were afterwards recognized. The agreement was confirmed at each voidance, but after 1435 the archbishops sent commissioners to act for them.[3]

The registers of the bishops of Worcester testify to careful administration of the diocese during the fourteenth century. Visitations usually occurred at regular intervals, and were undertaken by the bishop's official or by a vicar-general if the bishop was absent on affairs of state. During his metropolitical visitation in 1301 Archbishop Winchelsey discovered that in the deanery of Bristol an evil custom had arisen of charging a christening fee of twopence, and he bade the rural dean proclaim that such exactions would bring on the offender the penalty of the greater excommunication.[4] The parish clergy bore a high character, and cases of moral delinquency were very rare. Simon de Preus of Great Tew, who held the rectory of Tetbury of the gift of the abbot and convent of Eynsham, incurred considerable debts, presumably when he was at Oxford, for among his creditors were a mercer and a grocer of that town.[5] He was summoned to appear in the king's court in 1302[6], in 1304,[7] and again in 1307.[8] In 1306 Bishop Gainsborough allowed him to farm his church for five years to the rector of Swalcliffe, near Banbury, who undertook to pay debts to the amount of £100.[9] The agreement was that the rector should receive all the tithes and give Simon 4 marks, besides the offerings at the altar, and that Simon should find two chaplains and a deacon to serve the church, and provide lights, incense, bread and wine, and bell-ropes.

There was considerable activity in the rebuilding of churches in the earlier years of the century. The parish church of Cam was dedicated in 1308,[10] Badgeworth, Harescombe, Elmore, Fretherne, Frampton, Tetbury, Dry Marston, Tredington, and Shipton in 1315.[11] Much new work was undertaken in the abbey churches of Winchcombe, Gloucester, Tewkesbury, Bristol, and Lanthony,[12] and the religious succeeded in appropriating a number of churches in aid of their building funds, for, in accordance with Cardinal Ottoboni's constitution of 1268, no bishop might assign a parish church to the uses of a monastery unless it was overwhelmingly burdened by poverty.[13] It was therefore usual for the religious to frame a petition to the bishop, setting forth a most distressful tale of murrains, fires, floods, pestilences, the great cost of hospitality, the burden of taxation, and often urging that the fabric of their church threatened ruin and must be repaired at great expense.

[1] *Reg. Epistolarum Peckham* (Rolls Ser.), ii, 632 ; *Reg. Sede Vac.* (Worc. Hist. Soc.) ; *V. C. H. Worcester*, ii, 21, *Eccles. Hist.*
[2] *V. C. H. Glouc. Relig. Houses, Tewkesbury, Winchcombe, Cirencester, Horsley, Gloucester.*
[3] Cant. Archiepis. Reg. Morton, fol. 170, 171 ; *Reg. Sede Vac.* (Worc. Hist. Soc.), ii, 408-46, 227.
[4] Worc. Epis. Reg. Gainsborough, fol. 3.   [5] Ibid. fol. 41.
[6] *Reg. Sede Vac.* (Worc. Hist. Soc.), 26.   [7] Worc. Epis. Reg. Gainsborough, fol. 53.
[8] *Reg. Sede Vac.* (Worc. Hist. Soc.), 129.   [9] Worc. Epis. Reg. Gainsborough, fol. 41.
[10] Ibid. Reynolds, fol. 12.   [11] *Glouc. N. and Q.* ii, 13.
[12] *V. C. H. Glouc. Relig. Houses.*   [13] Wilkins, *Concilia*, ii, 10.

The bishop directed that an inquisition should be held, and if he was satisfied with the report he granted the petition. Thus Childs Wickham was appropriated to Bordesley in 1302,[1] Wotton to St. Augustine's, Bristol, in 1312,[2] South Cerney to Gloucester in 1317,[3] Longborough to Hayles in 1325,[4] Duntisbourne to Dore in 1229,[5] Tytherington to Lanthony in 1330,[6] Tetbury to Eynsham in 1331,[7] Campden to Chester in 1340,[8] while Tewkesbury secured Thornbury in 1315[9] and Fairford in 1333.[10] In the deanery of the Forest the bishops of Hereford appropriated Newland to the bishop of Llandaff in 1303[11] and Newnham to St. Bartholomew's Hospital at Gloucester in 1333.[12] The religious usually got possession on the death of a rector, but sometimes they persuaded him to resign in their favour, as in the case of Thornbury, when the rector secured a pension of 100 marks a year during his lifetime.[13] When the monasteries were in great need of money some of the clergy had sufficient means to purchase corrodies, which provided them for life with lodgings, food, lights and firing for themselves and one or two servants.[14] There was great extravagance in several of the larger monasteries,[15] and the bishops attempted to bring their finances into a sounder condition by insisting on the rendering of accounts and controlling the granting of corrodies. Relaxation of discipline occasionally called for a comment, and a disputed election at Lanthony in 1324 resulted in fierce internal dissensions;[16] but except at Bristol in 1320,[17] when one canon was charged with evil living, nothing more serious than an accusation of worldliness could be brought against the religious.

The Black Death reached England in the autumn of 1348, but Gloucestershire was not affected until the early spring of 1349.[18] The plague was at its worst in the summer months, and Bishop Wulstan de Bransford instituted to many vacant livings, himself falling a victim on 6 August. Bristol suffered severely,[19] but it seems that in the rest of the county the mortality was not nearly so great as in East Anglia.[20] Between March and September about eighty livings had to be filled on account of the deaths of the incumbents.[21] It is probable that there were many more deaths among the unbeneficed clergy, for in February, 1350, soon after his accession to the see, Bishop Thoresby wrote to his vicar-general, the prior of Lanthony, lamenting that on account of the scarcity of priests many churches were ill served.[22] Between January and September, 1350, he held eight large ordinations.[23] The economic results of the pestilence seriously affected the position of the clergy and of the monasteries. The scarcity of labourers produced a great and permanent rise in wages, and in Gloucestershire as elsewhere the

---

[1] *Reg. Sede Vac.* (Worc. Hist. Soc.), i, 79.   [2] Worc. Epis. Reg. Reynolds, fol. 76.
[3] Ibid. Cobham, fol. 56.   [4] Ibid. fol. 113.   [5] Ibid. Orlton, fol. 16, i.e. Duntisbourne Rous.
[6] Ibid. fol. 21.   [7] Ibid. fol. 23 *d.*   [8] Ibid. Bransford, fol. 41.
[9] Ibid. Maidstone, fol. 22.   [10] Ibid. Orlton, fol. 54 *d.*
[11] Heref. Epis. Reg. Swinfield, fol. 140.   [12] Ibid. T. Charlton, fol. 34.
[13] Worc. Epis. Reg. Maidstone, fol. 22.
[14] Royce, *Landboc monasterii de Winchelcumba,* i, 262, 300, 320, 333.
[15] *V. C. H. Glouc. Relig. Houses, Gloucester, Winchcombe,* 57, 69.
[16] Ibid. *Lanthony,* 89.   [17] Ibid. *Bristol,* 77.
[18] Worc. Epis. Reg. Bransford, pt. 2, fol. 10.   [19] Seyer, *Memoirs of Bristol,* ii, 143.
[20] Jessopp, *Diocesan History of Norwich,* 118–21.
[21] Worc. Epis. Reg. Bransford, pt. 2, 10–12 *d.* ; *Reg. Sede Vac.* (Worc. Hist. Soc.), 231–5 ; Heref. Epis. Reg. Trelleck, 21–24.
[22] Worc. Epis. Reg. Thoresby, fol. 6 ; cf. 20 *d.*   [23] *V. C. H. Worc.* ii, 32, 'Eccl. Hist.'

unbeneficed clergy were discontented with their salaries,[1] which were fixed by Islip, archbishop of Canterbury, at 7 marks a year in 1354.[2] They tried to supplement them by wandering out of the parishes to which they were attached, and charging higher fees for masses for the dead, but Bishop Thoresby inhibited them from doing so.[3] Although supported by parliamentary legislation in 1362,[4] the ecclesiastical authorities found great difficulty in limiting the stipends of curates and chantry priests.[5] The problem of making adequate provision for the spiritual needs of the people was more acute on account of the non-residence of rectors and vicars, and on 26 February, 1350, Bishop Thoresby sent a mandate to his sequestrator general to deprive the absent priests of their benefices and take the fruits.[6] In 1362 Bishop Barnet attempted to enforce residence on penalty of excommunication, as many rectors had farmed their churches and were away without licence.[7] The very numerous exchanges of benefices also illustrate the restlessness of the clergy, and in 1391 Archbishop Courtenay issued a mandate to his suffragans to deal severely with 'choppe-churches,' who trafficked in benefices and were guilty of simony.[8] Though many of the parish priests lacked learning, John Trevisa, the vicar of Berkeley, has won a great reputation for his translation of the *Polychronicon* of Ralph Higden, which he completed in 1387.[9]

Many of the monasteries in the county were seriously embarrassed by the falling off of their revenues.[10] In 1353 a royal commission was appointed to have the custody of Winchcombe until the debts had been discharged,[11] and in 1366 St. Augustine's, Bristol, was also in the hands of the king's commissioners.[12] The bishops attempted to restore order by issuing injunctions for the better administration of the finances,[13] but the religious were bent on adding to their income by further appropriations of parish churches. Awre was assigned to St. Oswald's, Gloucester, in 1351,[14] Cam to St. Peter's, Gloucester,[15] in 1361, Twyning to Winchcombe in 1379,[16] Toddington to Hayles in 1386.[17] By means of papal bulls the religious baffled the bishops' opposition, and in spite of the decrees of councils and synods they appropriated the vicarages of churches which they already held to their own use, thus securing the whole of the revenues and serving the church by one of their own number or by a salaried chaplain. The vicarages of St. Nicholas, Bristol, and Berkeley were given to St. Augustine's, Bristol, in 1399,[18] the vicarage of Winchcombe to the monastery in 1398.[19] In 1402 Boniface IX allowed the abbot and convent of Winchcombe to appropriate Bledington without making any provision for a vicar,[20] but the bishop compelled them to do so.[21] In 1411 the rich benefice of Westbury-on-Severn was appropriated to the college of vicars choral of Hereford by Bishop Mascall.[22] After the Black Death it became customary

---

[1] Worc. Epis. Reg. Thoresby, fol. 6.
[2] Wilkins, *Concilia*, iii, 30.
[3] Worc. Epis. Reg. Thoresby, fol. 49.
[4] 36 Edw. iii, cap. 8.
[5] Worc. Epis. Reg. Barnet, 11 *d.* 17 *d.* ; Wakefield, 130 ; Morgan, 5.
[6] Ibid. Thoresby, fol. 26.
[7] Ibid. Barnet, fol. 2 *d.*
[8] Worc. Epis. Reg. Wakefield, fol. 97 ; Wilkins, *Concilia*, iii, 215.
[9] *Polychronicon Ranulphi Higdeni* (Rolls Ser.), i, lix.
[10] *V. C. H. Glouc. Relig. Houses, Winchcombe*, 70.
[11] Ibid.
[12] Ibid. *Bristol*, 77.
[13] Ibid. *Gloucester, Bristol, Tewkesbury, Cirencester*, 58, 63, 77, 82.
[14] Heref. Epis. Reg. Trelleck, fol. 102.
[15] Worc. Epis. Reg. Brian, i, fol. 35.
[16] Royce, op. cit. ii, 95–101.
[17] Worc. Epis. Reg. Wakefield, fol. 116.
[18] *Cal. Pap. Letters*, vi, 191.
[19] Royce, op. cit. ii, 139–45.
[20] Ibid. ii, 42.
[21] Worc. Epis. Reg. Clifford, fol. 76.
[22] Heref. Epis. Reg. Mascall, fol. 43.

to assign a fixed sum to vicars instead of a portion of the tithes, and the amount tended to increase. The portion of the vicar of Cam was fixed at 20 marks in 1361,[1] and the vicars of Horsley and Wheatenhurst each received 12 marks in 1380.[2] If the rectory, with the exception of the tithe barns, was not allotted to the vicar, the religious were bound to build him a suitable manse near the church, but the cost of keeping it in repair fell upon his successors. The question of the responsibility of repairing or rebuilding the chancel depended entirely on the arrangement in the ordination of the vicarage ; at Thornbury[3] and Fairford[4] the burden was laid upon the vicar, at Tytherington[5] and Longborough[6] it rested with the religious, while at Standish,[7] with its three dependent chapels, the cost was divided. During the rule of Prior William de Cheriton (1377–1401) the convent of Lanthony rebuilt the chancels of Henlow, Painswick, Haresfield, and Awre.[8] The absence of any clear stipulation in the case of churches which had been appropriated at an early date led to several lawsuits. John Brighampton, the vicar of Winchcombe, disputed the responsibility of repairing the chancel and the glass in the windows with the convent, and Bishop Brian gave it as his decision that the vicar was liable.[9] Between thirty and forty years afterwards, another vicar, Thomas Power, denied his liability and was excommunicated by Bishop Wakefield. Power appealed to the Court of Arches, and thence to the papal curia, appealing again after judgement had been given against him in 1389. He lost his case and was condemned to pay the cost of the two suits at the curia, amounting to 135 gold florins. The vicars of Sherborne also went to law with the convent of Winchcombe about the rebuilding and repairing of the chancel, but a final judgement was given against them in 1387.[10] In a dispute between the abbot of Pershore and the vicar of Hawkesbury in 1420, the vicar alleged that since time immemorial his predecessors had been free from the burden of repairing the chancel, but the arbitrators decided that it ought to be done by him and his successors.[11] In the ordinations of vicarages by Bishop Clifford (1401–7) the duty of maintaining the chancel was assigned to the religious.[12] Acting upon the statute of 15 Richard II,[13] which was confirmed by Henry IV in 1403,[14] he decided that the convent of Gloucester should pay 24 marks instead of 12 to the vicar of Holy Trinity, Gloucester, and that the vicar of Bledington should have 20 marks instead of 10.[15]

The teaching of Wycliffe and of his chief followers among the early Lollards had a strong influence in the county. John Aston, one of the most zealous of the poor priests, preached at Gloucester on St. Matthew's Day, 1383, against the indulgences which were being sold in aid of the bishop of Norwich's crusade.[16] John Purvey, who lived for some years at Lutterworth with Wycliffe, taught and preached in Bristol, and there about 1388 he probably completed his revision of the Wycliffe Bible.[17] In 1387 Bishop

[1] Worc. Epis. Reg. Brian, i, fol. 35.
[2] Ibid. Wakefield, fol. 133 *d.* 134.
[3] Ibid. Maidstone, fol. 36.
[4] Ibid. Orlton, fol. 54.
[5] Ibid. fol. 48 *d.*
[6] Ibid. Cobham, fol. 118.
[7] Ibid. Bransford, fol. 139,
[8] MS. Top. Glouc. C. 5, 650–2, Bodl. Lib.
[9] Royce, op. cit. ii, 45–76.
[10] Ibid. 281–4.
[11] *Reg. Sede Vac.* (Worc. Hist. Soc.), 428.
[12] Worc. Epis. Reg. Clifford, fol. 72 *d.* 73 *d.* 76.
[13] Stat. of Realm, 15 Ric. II, cap. 6.
[14] Ibid. 4 Hen. IV, cap. 12.
[15] Worc. Epis. Reg. Clifford, fol. 72 *d.* 76.
[16] *Chronicon Henrici Knighton* (Rolls Ser.), ii, 178.
[17] Ibid. 179.

Wakefield issued a mandate to the archdeacon of Gloucester and all the clergy, forbidding them to allow Aston, Purvey, Nicholas of Hereford, John Parker, Robert Swinderby, or any of their following to preach again in their churches or cemeteries or anywhere in their parishes.[1] Nevertheless the teaching bore fruit, and throughout the fifteenth century Lollard beliefs held ground among the artisans of Bristol, for they were not stamped out as in the diocese of Norwich.[2] In 1420 William Taylor, a well-known Lollard who was burnt at Smithfield three years afterwards, preached at Holy Trinity, Bristol, by the invitation of the vicar, Thomas Drayton.[3] On the information of a Carmelite friar, the mayor and sheriff arrested Taylor and Drayton. In the trial at the Worcester consistory court it was alleged that they had drawn many away from the Catholic faith. Drayton was charged with preaching that the prayers of a priest living in mortal sin availed no more than the lowing of cattle or the grunting of pigs, and with making use of the parable of the pharisee and the publican in an attack on the religious orders. He denied these charges, but submitted himself to correction for committing the cure of souls in his church to Taylor, who had so inflamed the people that they were 'almost in insurrection.' When the monks of Worcester elected Bishop Bourchier in 1433, they urged that he was 'very necessary for the expulsion of heresies which were daily exercised in divers parts of the diocese.'[4] Yet in the ten years of his episcopate Bourchier is only recorded to have petitioned Henry VI to order the arrest of a heretic named John Brent of Bristol in 1436.[5] When William Fuere, a weaver of Gloucester, was tried before Bishop Carpenter in 1447, he said that he had learnt his opinions from a number of weavers dwelling in Bristol whom he mentioned by name.[6] William Smyth, a smith by trade, had given him the English book which had been taken from him, bidding him study it that he might know the reason of his beliefs. Fuere admitted that he had held and taught that the Church ought not to have possessions, that friars should not beg but labour with their hands, that although pilgrimages might be laudable no offerings should be made at shrines, that relics should not be venerated, and that Sunday should be kept like the Sabbath of the Old Testament. He consented to abjure his heresies, and was condemned as a penance to visit all the churches of Gloucester on Good Friday to adore the cross, and to be publicly whipped in the market-place on Easter eve. When James Willis, a 'lettered' weaver, aged fifty-nine, was tried for heresy before Chedworth, bishop of Lincoln, in 1462, he said that he had served his apprenticeship as a weaver in Bristol.[7] He knew the Epistles of St. Paul and the Apocalypse in English, and had bought the books from William Smyth of Bristol, who taught him his doctrines, and was himself afterwards convicted of heresy in the diocese of Winchester and burnt. Only one case of heresy in a country parish is entered in the bishops' registers of the fifteenth century. In 1425 the abbot of Winchcombe arrested John Walcote, the curate of Hazleton, and sent him to Bishop Morgan for trial; he admitted his errors and was reconciled to the Church.[8] As a portion of a manuscript of three treatises by Wycliffe, now in

[1] Wilkins, *Concilia*, iii, 202.
[3] Worc. Epis. Reg. Morgan, fol. 16–18.
[5] Worc. Epis. Reg. Bourchier, fol. 26.
[7] Linc. Epis. Reg. Chedworth, fol. 57 *d*.

[2] Jessopp, *Diocesan Hist. of Norw.* 137, 147.
[4] *Reg. Sede Vac.* (Worc. Hist. Soc.), 431.
[6] Ibid. Carpenter, i, fol. 58.
[8] Worc. Epis. Reg. Morgan, fol. 46 *d*.

the Imperial Library at Vienna, was transcribed by two Bohemians at Kemerton about 1407, it is possible that the rector sympathized with the Lollards.[1]

It was perhaps with the object of checking the spread of heresy through the circulation of Wycliffite books that Bishop Carpenter rebuilt the library of the Calendars of Bristol.[2] This gild ' of the commonalty, clergy, and people' of Bristol was reputed in 1318 to have been founded before the end of the tenth century.[3] In 1340 Bishop Wulstan de Bransford ordained that the college should consist of one priest-prior and eight chaplains to celebrate daily for the souls of the brethren and benefactors. All members of the gild were bound to be present at mass in the church of All Saints on the first Monday of each month.[4] In 1464 Carpenter decreed that the prior should be a bachelor of theology or a master of arts, with a good knowledge of the Old and New Testaments, and sufficiently instructed to preach the Word of God. He gave him the custody of the library, providing that it should be open on feast days for two hours both before and after nine to any who cared to enter, and that the prior should expound any difficult passages to the readers to the best of his ability.[5] The prior was also bound to preach four sermons a year, one in the church of the canons of St. Augustine, one in St. Mary Redcliffe, and two at Keynsham, in memory of a benefactor.[6] Carpenter may also have desired to give opportunities of study to the numerous parish and chantry priests of Bristol and the neighbourhood, for lack of learning among the clergy was notorious. An attempt to find a remedy was made at the meeting of convocation of the province of Canterbury in 1438, when it was provided that no priest should be presented to a benefice unless he had the degree of doctor of theology or law, or master of arts, or bachelor in some faculty.[7] Carpenter showed his anxiety to promote education by stipulating when he appropriated the parish church of Clifton to the dean and chapter of Westbury-on-Trym that they should maintain a grammar-school-master to teach all who came to him without charging any fees.[8] He rebuilt the college of Westbury, and revised the statutes and ordinances with the object of extending its sphere of usefulness.[9] Throughout his long episcopate of thirty-two years (1444–76) Bishop Carpenter ruled his diocese with great vigour, and even during the Wars of the Roses there was much rebuilding of churches by prosperous wool merchants and other traders. The chancel of the great parish church at Winchcombe was built by Abbot William Winchcombe, the parishioners found £200 for the nave, and Ralph Boteler, lord of Sudeley, helped them to finish the work.[10] In 1470 Conrad Nye, vicar of Lechlade, appeared before the bishop at Cirencester, and stated that he and his parishioners, with the aid of other good Christians, had rebuilt the nave.[11] The obligation of rebuilding the chancel rested on the vicar and on the prior of the hospital of St. John the Baptist, but with the help of some friends he intended to bear the whole cost of the work, provided that his successors were not thereby made liable for the whole of the repairs. As the fortunes of the

[1] *Brist. and Glouc. Arch. Soc. Trans.* xix, 34.
[2] Worc. Epis. Reg. Carpenter, i, fol. 197.
[3] Toulmin Smith, *English Gilds* (Camd. Soc.), 287.
[4] Barrett, *Hist. of Bristol*, 449–58.
[5] Worc. Epis. Reg. Carpenter, i, fol. 197.
[6] Ibid. 206 d.
[7] Worc. Epis. Reg. Bourchier, fol. 37.
[8] Ibid. Carpenter, i, fol. 183 d.
[9] *V. C. H. Glouc. Relig. Houses, Westbury-on-Trym,* 108.
[10] Dugdale, *Mon.* ii, 298–9.
[11] Worc. Epis. Reg. Carpenter, ii, 9.

hospital were at a very low ebb, Cecily, duchess of York, took its possessions for the endowment of a chantry of the Virgin for three chaplains in the parish church in 1473,[1] and three years later John Twyning of Cirencester founded the chantry of St. Blaise.[2] In 1475, by agreement with the abbot and convent of St. Peter's, the archdeacon of Gloucester gave up his official residence in Gloucester in exchange for the rectory of Dursley,[3] a benefice which was held by his successors for more than 400 years.[4]

For the space of sixty years after the death of Carpenter, the see of Worcester was filled by bishops who were occupied with affairs of state and left the administration of their diocese to suffragan bishops and vicars-general.[5] Visitations took place at regular intervals, and fees were collected. The condition of the monasteries called forth no comment, the larger houses were prosperous, the religious were occupied with the suitable maintenance of their services, with much new building, and with the management of their property. A case of heresy here and there is noted in the registers; in 1514 Avice Dedwood of Bisley abjured her opinions about the Eucharist when brought to trial before the vicar-general at Gloucester.[6] In 1509 Thomas Higons, a labourer of Mitcheldean, who was suspected of heresy and of favouring heretics, was condemned to do penance in Hereford Cathedral and in his parish church.[7] It is probable that opinions hostile to the teaching of the Church were disseminated from Bristol, for in 1498 it is said that many arrests were made, some persons were burnt, others abjured their errors and bore faggots on their backs in open penance.[8] Yet as the vicars-general were mainly occupied in the formal discharge of their duties, the reformers usually preached without molestation. About 1520 William Tyndale was a tutor in the house of Sir John Welsh at Little Sodbury, and on Sundays he preached there or in neighbouring parishes, and often at Bristol.[9] In 1531 the will of a Gloucestershire knight, William Tracy of Dodington, was brought before the notice of convocation on account of the manifest heresies which it contained.[10] Tracy had been one of Tyndale's friends, and convocation ordered that his body should be dug up and burned. The prolocutor gave notice at the same time of heresies in the will of Thomas Brown of Bristol.[11] In 1533 Bristol was much stirred by the Lenten sermons of Latimer in the churches of St. Nicholas, St. Thomas, and at the Black Friars.[12] A priest complained to convocation that by decrying the worship of the Virgin and the saints, and mocking at pilgrimages, Latimer had 'very sore infect' the town.[13] The mayor had invited him to Bristol again at Easter, but he was forbidden to preach anywhere within the diocese of Worcester without the bishop's licence.[14] His opponents—Edgeworth, Hubbardin, and others—delivered sermons against his opinions, but they attacked the divorce of Henry and Katherine, and commissioners were appointed by Cromwell to investigate the cause of the disturbances. The upshot of the matter was that some of Latimer's opponents were imprisoned, others fled, and Cranmer licensed him to preach anywhere

---

[1] Ibid. 30 d.; Dugdale, *Mon.* vii, 683.
[2] Dugdale, *Mon.* vii, 683.
[3] Worc. Epis. Reg. Carpenter, 77.
[4] Blunt, *Chapters of Parochial Hist.* 33.
[5] Creighton, *Historical Essays and Reviews*, 227–32.
[6] Worc. Epis. Reg. Silvester de Giglis, fol. 107 d.
[7] Heref. Epis. Reg. Mayhew, fol. 52 d.
[8] Seyer, *Memoirs of Bristol*, ii, 215.
[9] Ibid. *Dict. Nat. Biog.* lvii, 424.
[10] Wilkins, *Concilia*, iii, 746.
[11] Ibid.
[12] Demaus, *Hugh Latimer*, 162.
[13] Strype, *Eccl. Memorials*, i, 248.
[14] Demaus, op. cit. 163–74; *L. and P. Hen. VIII*, vi, No. 247.

in the province of Canterbury. Some attempt was made to check the spread of Lutheran opinions by licensing preachers who were proved free of heresy. In 1527 Bishop Booth allowed John Reynolds, a Dominican friar of Gloucester, to preach and explain the Word of God through the deanery of the Forest.[1] In 1533 the vicar-general of Worcester licensed five friars to preach in Latin or in English in parish churches or other suitable places throughout the diocese.[2] In 1535 the curate of Winchcombe complained to Cromwell that the abbot of Hayles had hired ' a great Golyas, a subtle Dun's man, yea a great clerk, as he sayeth, a bachelor of divinity of Oxford, to catch me in my sermons.'[3] This preacher had studied the works of Sir Thomas More, and was a staunch upholder of the teaching and traditions of the church.[4]

In 1535 Latimer was appointed to the vacant see of Worcester, and during the four years of his episcopate he was a ' diligent and vigilant pastor,' exhibiting such ' study, readiness, and continual carefulness in teaching, preaching, exhorting, visiting, correcting, and reforming, either as his ability could serve, or else the time would bear.'[5] In the autumn of 1537 he made a thorough personal visitation of the diocese, and found much ignorance and negligence among the clergy, to whom he gave a number of injunctions.[6] He insisted that every one of them should provide for their own use before Christmas a whole Bible, or at least a New Testament, both in Latin and English, and read and study not less than one chapter every day. They must also possess *The Institution of a Christian Man*, which had been drawn up by the bishops, and published by the king's authority in May. He forbade them to set aside preaching ' for any manner of observance in the church, as procession and other ceremonies.' He desired the chantry priests especially to teach such of the children of the parish as would come to them, at the least to read English, and forbade the clergy to discourage any lay person from the reading of any good books either in Latin or in English. So great was the ignorance of some of the laity for lack of instruction, that the bishop declared that no young man or woman should be admitted to receive the sacrament of the altar until he or she should openly say the Pater Noster in English in the church after mass or evensong.

The inclination of the people of Bristol to Lutheran opinions probably led the Scotch reformer, George Wishart, to take refuge there. In 1539 the rural dean of Bristol reported that he was persuading many of the commons of the town to heresy, and after a trial before Archbishop Cranmer and several of the bishops he was condemned to bear a faggot in the church of St. Nicholas, and in Christchurch, and about those parishes.[7]

The dissolution of the monasteries began during Latimer's episcopate, and he suggested to Cromwell that two or three houses in every county should be spared to 'maintain teaching, preaching, studying with prayer, and good housekeeping.'[8] In Gloucestershire only three houses came under the Act of 1536 for the dissolution of the lesser monasteries, St. Oswald's at Gloucester, Flaxley, and St. Mary Magdalen's at Bristol.[9] Kingswood and all the houses of friars in Bristol and Gloucester were surrendered in 1538. Lanthony was

[1] Heref. Epis. Reg. Booth, fol. 140 d.
[2] Worc. Epis. Reg. de Ghinucci, fol. 60.
[3] L. and P. Hen. VIII, ix, No. 747.
[4] Latimer's Remains (Parker Soc.), ii, 374.
[5] Foxe, Acts and Monuments (ed. 1847), vii, 461.
[6] Abingdon, Antiq. of Worc. Cath. 157, 162.
[7] Ricart's Calendar (Camd. Soc.), 55.
[8] Latimer's Remains (Parker Soc.), ii, 411.
[9] V. C. H. Glouc. Relig. Houses.

surrendered in March, 1539, and in December the commissioners arrived to take the surrenders of the remaining houses, completing their work at Tewkesbury on 9 January, 1540. The endowment of the new sees at Gloucester and Bristol was contemplated by Henry VIII, and accordingly the commissioners arranged for the maintenance of the services at Gloucester until the king's pleasure was made known. Fourteen monks were at once dismissed with pensions, twenty-two others were left in the monastery under the charge of the late prior of the cell of St. Guthlac at Hereford, stipends were provided for singing men and choristers, and wages for bellringers and a number of servants.[1] The canons were all dismissed from St. Augustine's, Bristol, and the custody of the monastery was committed to Mannyng, the king's farmer.[2] At the wish of Latimer, Holbeche, prior of Worcester, had been nominated as suffragan bishop of Bristol in 1538.[3]

The dissolution of the religious houses caused but little discontent in the county, because the middle class, which gained most by the spoliation of the Church, was so large and prosperous.[4] A large number of church livings were transferred from ecclesiastical to lay patronage, but the change was not so sudden as it appeared to be, for there is evidence that in the sixteenth century some of the religious houses sold the right of presentation to benefices,[5] and that they farmed the rectorial tithes.[6] Thus at South Cerney in 1510 the lessee of the rectorial tithes undertook to keep the chancel in repair, and though timber and stone were provided from the land of the abbot and convent of Gloucester, he had to bear the cost of carriage and of quarrying.[7] The inhabitants of Tewkesbury had always used the nave of the abbey as their parish church, and they purchased the transepts, choir, and chapels, except the Lady chapel, from Henry VIII for £453.[8]

In 1541 Henry VIII founded the bishopric of Gloucester, erecting the late Benedictine monastery into a cathedral church, dedicated to the Holy Trinity, and fixing the county bounds as those of the diocese.[9] The jurisdiction of St. Oswald was taken from the see of York; the deanery of the Forest from the see of Hereford;[10] and the town of Bristol, with the exception of a few parishes in the diocese of Bath and Wells, was included in the new diocese of Gloucester. The new chapter consisted of a dean and six canons, and the right of presenting them was reserved to the crown. The bishopric was endowed with part of the possessions of the monastery, and the remainder fell to the dean and chapter. The abbot's lodging was assigned as the bishop's palace. In 1542 the king founded the bishopric of Bristol,[11] including in the new diocese the city and county of Bristol, the manor of Leigh in Somerset, and the county of Dorset, which was taken from the diocese of Salisbury. The church of St. Augustine's Abbey became the

---

[1] Aug. Off. Bk. 494, fol. 93.   [2] Ibid. fol. 48.   [3] Demaus, *Hugh Latimer*, 290.

[4] Creighton, *The Story of some English Shires*, 267.

[5] Reg. Braunche, fol. 90, MSS. Dean and Chapter of Gloucester; MS. Rawlinson, B. 326, fol. 106, 123 (Bodl. Lib.).

[6] *Valor Eccl.* (Rec. Com.), ii, *passim*.

[7] Reg. Braunche, fol. 95 *d.*; cf. Reg. Newton, fol. 66; Reg. Parker, i, 172 *d.*; MSS. Dean and Chapter of Gloucester.

[8] Dugdale, *Mon.* ii, 58.   [9] Rymer, *Foedera*, xiv, 724.

[10] No mention was made of exemption from the jurisdiction of the archdeacon of Hereford, and he continued to exercise it in the deanery of the Forest until 1836, *Lond. Gaz.* 1836, p. 1735.

[11] Rymer, *Foedera*, xiv, 748.

cathedral, which like Gloucester was dedicated to the Holy Trinity, and was served by a dean and six canons. The bishopric of Gloucester was united to Worcester in 1552, when Bishop Hooper was transferred to Worcester,[1] but after his deprivation in 1555 they were again separated.

Having endowed two sees in the county with a scanty portion of monastic lands, Henry VIII diminished the pension list by making choice of the late religious in his appointments. John Wakeman, abbot of Tewkesbury, became bishop of Gloucester ; William Jennings, prior of St. Oswald's, Gloucester, was the first dean, and two or three of the monks of St. Peter's became prebendaries.[2] Paul Bush, prior of Edington, became bishop of Bristol ; the dean was William Snowe, prior of Bradenstock.[3] Neither Wakeman nor Bush exercised any strong influence on the progress of the reformation in the county.

Early in the fifteenth century the poverty of the parochial clergy was recognized as a serious question, and at convocation in 1439 it was decided that all vicarages should be augmented to ten marks.[4] There were at that time sixty-two beneficed cures in Gloucestershire which did not exceed that sum.[5] The *Valor Ecclesiasticus* illustrates the small provision for the clergy in a considerable number of parishes. In the deanery of Stowe out of thirty livings ten were vicarages, in three other cases the rectories were appropriated to religious houses, and there was no separate endowment of a vicarage ; thirteen livings were of the value of £10 and under, three only reached between £20 and £30.[6] Out of twenty-five livings in the deanery of Winchcombe, nine were under £10, and four churches were served by paid chaplains who usually received a stipend of £5 6s. 8d.[7] There were a considerable number of chantries which had been founded in many town and country parishes of the county from the thirteenth century onwards.[8] The chantry priests often helped the parish clergy, and sometimes they acted as schoolmasters. The chantry of 'Our Ladie Service' in St. Nicholas, Bristol, was founded to maintain a priest ' to be at all divine service and assistance to the curate and other in ministration of the sacraments to the great multitude of people in the parish,' and in 1548 there were 800 houseling people.[9] The chapel of the Assumption in the same parish was endowed to find certain priests and clerks, who amongst other duties distributed money to the poor and to prisoners. In seventeen parishes in Bristol there were in all thirty chantries. At Henbury-in-the-Salt-Marsh the parishioners had purchased lands and tenements for the maintenance of a priest to help the curate in a scattered parish with 600 houseling people.[10] At Tewkesbury the parishioners formerly maintained three priests out of certain rents, making up the residue of their own devotion.[11] The priest of Grendor's chantry in the church of Newland was bound to keep a grammar school ' half free,' charging scholars learning grammar 8d. a quarter, and those learning to read only 4d.[12] At Campden the priest

---

[1] *Cal. of S.P. Dom.* 1547–80, p. 39.
[2] Fosbrooke, *Hist. of Glouc.* (ed. 1819), 219–28.
[3] Nicholls and Taylor, *Bristol, Past and Present*, 67–68.
[4] Worc. Epis. Reg. Bourchier, fol. 63.
[5] Ibid. fol. 87 ; Heref. Epis. Reg. Spofford, i, fol. 197 *d*.
[6] *Valor Eccl.* (Rec. Com.), ii, 436–40.
[7] Ibid. 440–4.
[8] Worc. Epis. Reg. *passim ;* Glouc. Chant. Cert. Nos. 21 and 22, P.R.O. ; 22 has been printed in *Brist. and Glouc. Arch. Soc. Trans.* viii, 232–308.
[9] *Brist. and Glouc. Arch. Soc. Trans.* viii, 237–9.
[10] Ibid. 252.
[11] Ibid.
[12] Ibid. 292.

of Barnard's service had a free grammar school which was attended by from sixty to eighty scholars.[1] The sum total of the yearly revenues of the chantries in Gloucestershire amounted to £1,300 6s. 3¼d.[2]

By the Chantries Act of 1548 almost all these endowments were confiscated.[3] Cirencester was thus deprived of the provision for the service of half a dozen priests, an organ player, choirmaster, and choir boys.[4] In 1552 the parishes suffered a further wrong when the plate was seized by the crown. In some places the parishioners, probably anticipating the spoliation, had already sold some of their plate ; the churchwardens of All Saints', Gloucester, disposed of pyxes, candlesticks, copes, and one bell, thus realizing £31 15s. 3d., with the proceeds of which they executed certain repairs, purchased a Bible, two psalters, and the Paraphrases of Erasmus, and seated the church at a cost of £22.[5] The accounts of the churchwardens of St. Ewen's, Bristol, show that the plate was of great value;[6] they had sold but a little when the commissioners seized the whole of the remainder, returning them but one chalice.[7] At St. Nicholas in 1519 the plate weighed 694 oz. of silver, there were seven chalices, and the commissioners returned one weighing 15 oz.[8]

In 1551 John Hooper was consecrated bishop of Gloucester. He had spent the last few years of the reign of Henry VIII abroad, first at Strasburg and then at Zurich, and had many friends there among the reformers.[9] He accepted the views of Zwingli, disbelieving in the Real Presence.[10] For some months before his consecration on 8 March he was engaged in a controversy with Archbishop Cranmer about the use of vestments, but he at length consented to wear them at the consecration, in the king's presence, and in his cathedral church.[11] Immediately afterwards he went to his diocese and sent a letter to his clergy, announcing his impending visitation.[12] He threw himself into his work with such energy that on 3 April his wife wrote to Bullinger entreating him to counsel prudence, because the bishop was preaching four, or at least three, times every day.[13] He drew up fifty-two articles of religion [14] to which he required the clergy to subscribe.[15] Insisting on his own views of the sacrament of the Eucharist, he ordered that the altars should be taken down, and instead an ' honest table, decently covered,' should be erected ' in such place as shall be thought most meet.' He forbade the use of lights ' on the Lord's board,' the elevation of the host, and the ringing of the sacring bell. While desiring the clergy to move their people ' to the often and worthy receiving,' in no wise permitting one neighbour to receive for another, as was common in the diocese, he taught that as many as were present at the time of administration ought to communicate. He also forbade prayers for the dead, the worship of the saints, and all such ceremonies as the distribution of palms, creeping to the cross, and the Easter sepulchre. He told the clergy that it was not sufficient to speak in the mother tongue, but

---

[1] *Brist. and Glouc. Arch. Soc. Trans.* viii, 280.   [2] Ibid. 307.   [3] *Stat. of Realm*, 1 Edw. VI, cap. 14.
[4] Fuller, *Cirencester Parish Church*, 10–14.   [5] *Brist. and Glouc. Arch. Soc. Trans.* xii, 80.
[6] Ibid. xv, 139–82, 254–96.   [7] Ibid. xii, 91.   [8] Ibid. 89.
[9] Hooper, *Later Writings* (Parker Soc.), ix ; *Zurich Letters* (Parker Soc.), *passim*.
[10] Wakeman, *Hist. of the Church of Engl.* 291.
[11] Strype, *Memorials of Cranmer* (ed. 1840), i, 302.   [12] Ibid. ii, 869.
[13] *Zurich Letters* (Parker Soc.), i, 108.   [14] Hooper, op. cit. 120–9.
[15] Strype, op. cit. ii, 871.

that there must be clear and distinct pronunciation, and ordered them to preach every Sunday and festival day, and catechize the children in the afternoon. He bade them bestow their time on reading and study instead of mis-spending it in hunting and hawking, and told them plainly that the marriage of the clergy was holy and agreeable with God's Word. In the course of his visitation during the year, he issued thirty-one injunctions.[1] He ordered that all roodlofts, screens, tabernacles, and sepulchres should be removed ; that all images painted on the walls should be defaced ; that when any glass windows were repaired or new made, no saints should be portrayed, but if they wanted anything painted, it should be either branches, flowers, or posies taken out of Holy Scripture. After a separate examination of 311 of the clergy, he discovered that 168 were unable to repeat the ten commandments, thirty-one of them being further unable to state in what part of the scriptures they were to be found.[2] Forty-one could not tell where the Lord's Prayer was written, and of these thirty-one did not know who the Author was. Some of the clergy were men of learning, and found favour with him, among them the incumbents of St. Michael and Holy Trinity, Gloucester, Cleeve, Tewkesbury, Alderton, Kemerton and Cold Aston.[3] The bishop ordered that in the course of the next year all the clergy should learn by heart and recite to him or his assigns the books of Genesis and Deuteronomy, the Gospel of St. Matthew, and the Epistle to the Romans in Latin and in English. He told them to fix the hours for morning and evening prayer on Sundays, and other holy days, with the advice and consent of the whole parish, that no one might have an excuse for absence, and on Mondays, Wednesdays, and Fridays at least one member of every household should be present at the services. He found it necessary to forbid the holding of markets on Sundays during the hours of service 'within the church, churchyard, or parish.' He also insisted that there should be ' no noise, bruit, walking, talking or jangling, or any other unquiet behaviour in the church in the time of service.' William Phelps, the curate of Cirencester, in contempt of previous royal injunctions was teaching the doctrine of Transubstantiation to his people, but on 27 April, 1551, he accepted the articles administered to him by Hooper, renouncing his errors and false opinions.[4] John Wynter, the parson of Staunton, made a formal profession of his belief in the articles in the cathedral on 8 November.[5] Early in 1552 Hooper was translated to Worcester on the understanding that he should hold the see of Gloucester *in commendam*, but within a few months it was united to Worcester. On 6 July, after a brief visit to Worcester, he informed secretary Cecil that the negligence and ungodly behaviour of the ministers in Gloucestershire compelled him to return.[6] ' I have spoken with the greatest part,' he wrote, ' and I trust within these six days to end for the time with them all.' He urged that the forty-two articles which had been recently drawn up should be issued with the king's authority; he would force the ministers to confess them openly before their parishioners, as their private subscription to them on paper proved useless. ' I have a great hope of the people,' he added.

---

[1] Hooper, op. cit. 130–40. [2] Ibid. 151.
[3] Transcript of Hooper's Visitation Book, MS. Misc. 1, iii, 17–77, *passim*, Dr. Williams's Lib.
[4] Hooper, op. cit. 152 [5] Ibid. 154.
[6] Strype, op. cit. ii, 871.

After the accession of Mary, Hooper remained in his diocese, 'to live and die with his sheep.'[1] On 20 March, 1554, he was deprived of the see of Gloucester on the ground of his marriage, evil deserts, and a bad title.[2] After almost a year's imprisonment he was condemned as an obstinate heretic, and sent to Gloucester to be burnt on 9 February, 1555, 'for the example and terror of others such as he hath there seduced and mistaught.'[3] Bishop Bush was deprived of the see of Bristol on 13 March, 1554, on account of his marriage,[4] but as his wife died, he become rector of Winterbourne.[5]

Between 16 May, 1554, and 19 April, 1555, fifty-four of the clergy in the diocese of Gloucester were deprived of their livings, all of them probably because they had married.[6] Some of them forsook their wives and were reconciled to the Church.[7] Not one of them suffered death in the Marian persecutions. When Williams, the chancellor, was reminded by Thomas Drowry, a blind boy of Gloucester on trial for heresy, of his own sermon in the cathedral against Transubstantiation, he replied 'Do as I have done, and you shall live as I do and escape burning.'[8] Jennings, the dean, changed his opinions with the circumstances, and held his preferment until his death in 1565.[9] Neither Brooks, bishop of Gloucester, nor Holyman, bishop of Bristol, showed any great zeal in administering the statutes against heretics. The victims were few. A bricklayer of Gloucester was burnt with the blind boy in 1555;[10] John Piggott suffered at Little Sodbury in 1556;[11] Thomas Benion was burnt at Bristol in 1556; a weaver and a shoemaker in 1557.[12] Edward Horne suffered at Newent in 1558.[13]

During a visitation of the diocese of Gloucester in 1556, Bishop Brooks issued a number of injunctions to the clergy and laity, which curiously resemble and yet contrast with those of Hooper.[14] He bade all the clergy who had the gift and talent of preaching occupy themselves frequently in the same, not forgetting to declare the right use of the ceremonies of the Church ; such as could not preach should earnestly study the scriptures that they might account to the ordinary each year how they profited therein. On St. Andrew's Day, in annual remembrance of the reconciliation to the Catholic Church, all the parishioners should be present at a solemn procession and hear a sermon or homily setting forth the great benefit of the same. The names of such persons as did not make their confession in Lent should be certified to the ordinary. All parishioners should resort to their churches, especially at mass, and at the time of the elevation kneel reverently where they could see and worship the sacrament, 'not lurking behind pillars or holding down their heads.' The beneficed clergy should repair their chancels and manses with all convenient speed, and the churchwardens should see their churches and churchyards repaired before the following midsummer, and buy at the parish charge a decent tabernacle set in the midst of the high altar with a taper or lamp burning before it, a rood five feet long at least, with the Virgin, St. John, and the patron saint, not painted on cloth or boards, but cut out

---

[1] Hooper, *Later Writings* (Parker Soc.), xxii.
[2] *V. C. H. Worcester*, ii, 46, *n* 1, 'Eccl. Hist.'
[3] Hooper, *Later Writings* (Parker Soc.), xxv.
[4] Frere, *The Marian Reaction*, 20.
[5] *Dict. Nat. Biog.* viii, 33.
[6] Frere, op. cit. 49, 57. The returns for the diocese of Bristol are missing.
[7] Wilkins, *Concilia*, iv, 146.
[8] *Narratives of the Reformation* (Camd. Soc.), 19–20.
[9] Ibid. 21, *n. a.*
[10] Stratford, *Great and Good Men of Gloucestershire*, 91.
[11] Ibid. 93.
[12] Nicholls and Taylor, *Bristol Past and Present*, ii, 20.
[13] *Narratives of the Reformation* (Camd. Soc.), 69.
[14] Wilkins, *Concilia*, iv, 145–8.

in timber or stone. The churchwardens' accounts for Minchinhampton and several of the parishes of Bristol illustrate the changes in the reigns of Edward VI, Mary, and Elizabeth.[1]

On the accession of Elizabeth the see of Gloucester was vacant, and the bishop of Bristol died within a month. Both sees remained unfilled until 19 April, 1562, when Richard Cheyney was consecrated bishop of Gloucester, and on account of the slender endowment he was allowed to hold the bishopric of Bristol *in commendam*. There were very few changes among the clergy ; between 1558 and 1564 the dean of Bristol and one prebendary, two prebendaries of Gloucester, and nine incumbents were deprived.[2] Unlike the other Elizabethan bishops, Cheyney held the Lutheran view of the sacrament, and objected to signing the articles in 1563, on account of the second ' only ' in No. 28, though Guest, bishop of Rochester, explained that the word was intended to safeguard, not to deny, the Real Presence.[3] In 1568 he preached three sermons in the cathedral of Bristol which gave great offence to some of the Puritan citizens. The sheriffs, two aldermen, and thirty-five other persons made a formal complaint to the queen of his ' strange, perilous, and corrupt doctrine.'[4] They objected to his teaching that they should follow the fathers and doctors of the Church, although Calvin was opposed to some of them. He also said that Luther wrote a very evil book against free will, and that he himself was of the mind of Erasmus. Pointing to the strife among the reformers of Germany and Switzerland, he bade them follow neither this city nor that, but ' the catholic and universal consent.' Cheyney wrote to Cecil in his own defence, telling him that many liked his sermons well, for he merely upheld the authority of the Catholic Church, the fathers, and general councils.[5] Complaining of one Norbrooke, a preacher in Bristol against free will, he said, ' If young and hot heads shall be suffered to say and preach what they list in matters of great weight, there must needs ensue a Babylonical confusion.' He also notified that there were two in his diocese who administered the communion, christened, married, &c., but were not in orders.

In reply to the queen's mandate of 15 October, 1577, for a return of such persons as refused to come to church, Cheyney said that some supposed to savour of papistry alleged sickness, others alleged debt and a fear of a process, and a third sort commonly called Puritans wilfully refused, not liking the surplice, ceremonies, and other services.[6] These had been arraigned and indicted in several sessions, and were in prison. A week later he sent a full return of such absentees in the diocese of Gloucester as were presented by sworn men in every parish, making in all seventy-five persons.[7] It is probable that many of these were Puritans,[8] for when a separate return of Popish recusants was made in 1592, after the teaching of the seminary priests had influenced many waverers in other dioceses, only twenty names were notified in Gloucestershire.[9] Among these were six gentlemen, seven yeomen, one husbandman, two labourers, and three spinsters. In 1602 twenty-two recusants, of whom ten were women, paid fines.[10]

[1] *Arch.* xxxv. 415–8. Nicholls and Taylor, op. cit. ii, 152, 163, 175, 210, 221, 254.
[2] Gee, *The Elizabethan Clergy*, 272, 278.
[3] Frere, *Hist. of the Engl. Church*, 1558–1625, p. 163. *Brist. and Glouc. Arch. Soc. Trans.* v, 226.
[4] *Brist. and Glouc. Arch. Soc. Trans.* 229–32.   [5] Ibid. 227–9.   [6] Ibid. 232.   [7] Ibid. 234–6.
[8] Harl. MS. 594, 225–55 (B.M.).   [9] *Exch. L.T.R. Recusant R.* (Pipe Off. Ser.), i.   [10] Ibid. xi.

Cheyney's successor in 1581 was Bullingham, who had been deprived of his two livings in Gloucestershire on the accession of Elizabeth, but soon afterwards accepted the doctrines of the Reformation.[1] He also held the see of Bristol *in commendam* until 1589, when Fletcher, dean of Peterborough, was appointed.

The early years of the sixteenth century are marked by the spread of Puritan views in the county. None of the five bishops of Gloucester during that time was in any way conspicuous except Miles Smith (1612–25), a man of considerable learning, and one of the translators of the Bible, yet a stiff Calvinist. Thornborough was the most influential of the four contemporaneous bishops of Bristol, and his visitation articles show a determination to enforce ecclesiastical discipline and to remedy such abuses as pluralism and unlicensed preaching.[2] An arbitrary use of power brought him into conflict with the mayor and corporation.[3] With the leave of the dean and chapter they erected a gallery near the pulpit in the cathedral for their own use, but in 1608 the bishop ordered that it should be immediately removed, because it made the cathedral look like a playhouse. The citizens complained to the king, who appointed commissioners to investigate the case, and the bishop was ordered to reconstruct the gallery at his own expense. Accordingly he placed it three feet above the ground, and removed the pulpit to such a distance that the preacher could not be heard in the gallery. In consequence of this and other disputes the corporation attended service for some years at St. Mary Redcliffe. Yeaman, who was vicar of St. Philip's, Bristol, for over twenty years, had strong Puritan leanings and influenced a large congregation by his zealous preaching.[4] In 1619 the corporation of Gloucester provided that a yearly sum of money should be assigned for the maintenance of a lecturer to preach twice a week in the city on the ground that insufficient care had been taken 'for the settling and establishing of the public preaching of God's Word.'[5] Lectureships were founded and endowed in other places, and the Puritans thus had the opportunity of hearing 'preaching' ministers of their own persuasion on Sunday afternoons. At Deerhurst, Hayles, and Winchcombe seats for communicants were set up round three sides of the chancel, and the communion table stood in the middle.[6] At Dursley in 1618 a new 'table board' of Puritan fashion took the place of the Elizabethan communion table.[7] John Sprint, the Puritan vicar of Thornbury, was persuaded to conform by Samuel Burton, archdeacon of Gloucester, to whom, in 1618, he dedicated his book, *Cassander Anglicanus, shewing the Necessitie of Conformity to the prescribed ceremonies of the Church*.[8] William Woodwall, the curate of Stroud, was a social reformer rather than a Puritan. In a notable sermon preached in 1609 he attacked the pursuit of wealth on account of the suffering which it entailed on the poor, and lashed the increasing love of luxury and amusement among the rich.[9]

James I was informed that there was 'scarce ever a church in England so ill governed and so much out of order' as Gloucester, and in 1616 on the

---

[1] *Dict. Nat. Biog.* vii, 250–1. [2] *Second Rep. of Ritual Com.* 1867–8, App. E. 440.
[3] Britton, *Bristol Cathedral*, 29. [4] *Broadmead Records* (Hanserd Knollys Soc.), 8.
[5] Lloyd, *The State of Religion in Gloucester*, 1640–50.
[6] *Brist. and Glouc. Arch. Soc. Trans.* xxv, 285–7 ; Hayles about 1600, Deerhurst before 1606, Winchcombe probably a little later. The arrangement continued until recently.
[7] Blunt, *Chapters of Parochial History*, 59. [8] *Glouc. N. and Q.* ii, 327. [9] Ibid. i, 201.

death of Dean Field he appointed William Laud, bidding him reform and set in order what he found amiss.[1] In January, 1617, the dean and chapter decreed 'that the communion table should be placed altarwise at the upper end of the quire close to the east wall . . . as was the custom in the royal chapel and in most of the cathedral churches.' They subsequently assigned £60 a year for the repair of the fabric, and appealed to the gentry of the county for their assistance towards the erection of a new organ. The moving of the communion table gave great offence to Bishop Smith and to the Puritan party in Gloucester.[2] The bishop protested that if any such innovations were brought into that cathedral, he would never more come within the walls, and is said to have adhered to his resolution. A libellous letter about popish superstitions was cast into the pulpit of St. Michael's where the sub-dean preached, but Jones, one of the aldermen, committed some of the dispersers of the libel to prison.

Goodman filled the see of Gloucester during the important years preceding the Great Rebellion. His sermons attracted the attention of Bishop Andrewes and others of that school, who befriended him ; in 1617 he was made a canon of Windsor, and in 1625 he became bishop of Gloucester with licence to hold his canonry and other benefices *in commendam*.[3] A sermon which he preached before the king in 1626 on the Real Presence made a great stir both at the court and in the country, because he was supposed 'to trench too near the borders of popery.'[4] The king referred the consideration of it to Abbot, Andrewes, and Laud, who reported that though the words were incautious they contained no innovation on the doctrine of the Church of England. However, unlike Laud and other bishops of the same views, Goodman was not a vigorous opponent of the teaching of the Roman Church, and in 1635 his intercourse with certain Roman Catholics gave rise to a suspicion that he was a secret member of their communion. It is certain that as a bishop he was not loyal to his metropolitan. Yet in some directions he exercised a strong influence over his diocese. In 1629 he wrote to inform his clergy that he had lately erected a library at Gloucester for the use of his brethren throughout the diocese, and for gentlemen and strangers who were students. He urged them to give a book or the price of it, unless they were hindered by their poverty.[5] In his visitation articles in 1634 and 1640 he endeavoured to enforce obedience to the Canons of 1604, and inquired whether the fabrics of churches were in good repair within and without, and if there was 'a convenient seat for the minister to read service in,' 'a comely pulpit with a decent cloth or cushion and a cover for the same,' 'a comely large surplice,' 'a decent communion table with a seemly carpet and a cloth of fine linen to cover the same at the time of communion,' 'a fair communion cup of silver with a cover agreeable for the same' and all other necessary ornaments.[6] He asked if any of the parishioners omitted to kneel in the prayers and stand in the creed, and if they wilfully refused to do 'some humble and lowly reverence of body when the Lord Jesus is mentioned,' and whether any resorted 'unto barns, fields, woods, or private houses to any extraordinary exposition of Scripture or conferences together.' He inquired

[1] *Laud's Works*, iv, 233 ; vi, pt. i, 239 ; Heylin, *Cyprianus Anglicus*, 69.
[2] Heylin, op. cit. 69, 70.   [3] *Dict. Nat. Biog.* xxii, 131.   [4] Heylin, op. cit. 153.
[5] MS. Sloane, 1199, fol. 92b (B.M.).   [6] *Second Rep. of the Ritual Com.* App. E, 542–7.

if there were any who wrongfully took advantage of the king's Declaration of Sports, indulging in recreation without having attended church. He bade every incumbent or curate endeavour, if possible, especially in market towns, to read short morning prayers at six o'clock 'before men go to their work,' and advised preachers to set store not so much on 'long preaching or often preaching' as on 'painful and profitable preaching,' and to labour not 'to nourish and increase controversies in religion but rather to reconcile them' . . . and to instruct their people 'in points of devotion, piety, charity, mortification, and such like necessary principles and articles of our faith wherein all Christians agree.' In the report of the diocese which he sent to Laud in 1634, he certified that he had put down some lecturers and set up others, but he neither knew nor could conjecture that there was any one 'unconformable man in all his diocese.'[1] 'If it be true,' commented Laud, 'it is a great clearing of those parts which have been so much suspected.'

Goodman also stated that he had been obliged to ordain 'some very mean ministers to supply cures as mean,' and in 1635 he informed Laud that the county was very full of impropriations, which made the ministers poor, and their poverty made them 'fall upon popular and factious courses.'[2] Referring to the appropriations of Berkeley, Wotton, Almondsbury, and Ashleworth, Smyth, the steward of the Berkeleys, wrote: 'Three of the cures in those great and populous parishes are now served by poor hirelings with beggarly stipends.'[3] 'Appropriations are yet suffered to live in this daylight of the Gospel to the great hindrance of learning, the impoverishment of the ministry, the decay of hospitality and infamy of our religion and profession.'[4] Among the Puritan preachers who had been deprived for nonconformity was Humphrey Fox, who lost the cure of Forthampton about 1630, and lived at Tewkesbury until 1640.[5] John Geering, the minister of Tewkesbury, was summoned before the High Commission Court in 1631, and was suspended and deprived by Goodman.[6] John Workman, who had held the corporation lectureship in St. Michael's, Gloucester, for thirteen years, was tried by the High Commission Court for sermons in which he had not only preached rabidly against pictures and images in churches and the crime of dancing, but had attacked the clergy with great violence, and prayed from the pulpit for the States of Holland and the king of Sweden before the king's majesty.[7] He was suspended, excommunicated, ordered to recant his 'erroneous and scandalous doctrine,' condemned in costs and imprisoned. The corporation, in defiance of the court's decision, granted him an annuity of £20, and accordingly the mayor and aldermen were summoned as delinquents, their deed was cancelled, and two of the defendants were fined £10 each. There is some evidence of opposition to the king's Declaration of Sports. In 1633 Richard Capel, who had held the rich living of Eastington for twenty years and was a noted preacher, resigned on the plea that he could not first read God's command to keep holy the Sabbath day, and then King Charles's command to break it.[8] The preacher of the afternoon sermon at Ashton-under-hill in 1635 inveighed against the profanation of the Sabbath by sports.[9]

[1] *Laud's Works*, v, pt. ii, 330. [2] Ibid. 336. [3] Smyth, *Lives of the Berkeleys* (ed. Maclean), i, 68.
[4] Ibid. iii, 88. [5] *Glouc. N. and Q.* i, 412.
[6] Ibid. 431 ; *Rep. of Cases in Courts of Star Chamber and High Com.* (Camd. Soc.), 244.
[7] *Laud's Works*, iv, 236 ; Lloyd, *State of Religion in Glouc.* 32.
[8] *Glouc. N. and Q.* ii, 522. [9] Ibid. 449.

ECCLESIASTICAL HISTORY

After his metropolitical visitation of Gloucester in 1635, Laud issued several injunctions to the dean and chapter.[1] He ordered that the muniments should be set in order and kept in the former muniment room under the charge of the chapter clerk. The petty canons and singing-men should have their houses according to the Chapter Act when he was dean, and the choristers, whose bad behaviour was most unseemly, should be kept under strict discipline. All preachers in the cathedral should say the whole of the bidding prayer as enjoined in the 55th Canon of 1604. He required the chapter also to substitute movable seats for all fixed seats in the nave, as ' contrary to the course of cathedrals,' with the exception of those used by the mayor and his brethren, and by the dean and prebendaries during sermon time.

The condition of Bristol Cathedral and the order of the services there were far less satisfactory to Laud than they were at Gloucester. Most of the clergy were guilty of non-residence, and had recently framed a statute fixing twenty-eight days as sufficient.[2] The places allotted by the foundation were not filled, an usher was needed and two more petty canons, while the other four officiated elsewhere; some of the singing-men were clerks of parishes in the city, or organists, which hindered their attendance at the cathedral. In 1537 Robert Skinner became bishop of Bristol, and Laud reported to the king that he had taken great care in his first visitation, and if he continued would quickly settle the diocese into better order.[3] However, Skinner complained that ' they of the preciser faction ' endeavoured to disquiet the people daily, by strange inventions, giving out that the liturgy for Scotland had sundry notorious points of popery in it. In 1639 the diocese was reported to be in good order.[4] Yet for some years previously there had been a conventicle of Puritans at a house in the High Street.[5] Some who refused to kneel at the communion took houses in parishes outside the diocese of Bristol, and went thither with their families to spend Sunday.[6] Among them was Dorothy Kelly, who sat sewing in her open shop on Christmas Day in contempt of ' invented times and feasts.'[7] In 1639 she married a Puritan clergyman named Hazzard, who was chosen by the parishioners of St. Ewens as their minister. In 1640 Mrs. Hazzard and four other persons, including Bacon, a young minister, seceded and met by themselves, and shortly afterwards, under the teaching of Cann, a Baptist minister, the Baptist community of Bristol was established. In the space of three years it increased to 160 persons from the city and neighbourhood.

The Puritan party in Gloucestershire was also gaining in strength, and in 1640 John Allibond, curate of St. Nicholas, Gloucester, noted the names of their leaders in the county election, in a satirical letter to Heylin, ' principally men of our own coat, a pack of deprived, silenced, or puritanically affected men.'[8] Besides Geering, Fox and his sons Help-on-High and Sion-Build, he mentioned Marshall of Elmore, who ' practises conformity more out of awe than love, as does also Stansfield, a lecturer of Rodborough'; Guilliam of Hatherley, Prior of Sandhurst, Baxter of Forthampton, Whynnell,

---

[1] *Laud's Works*, v, pt. ii, 479.
[2] *Hist. MSS. Com. Rep.* v, App. pp. 141–4.
[3] *Laud's Works*, v, pt. ii, 353.
[4] Ibid. 368.
[5] *Broadmead Rec.* (Hanserd Knollys Soc.), 11.
[6] Ibid. 13.
[7] Ibid. 15–28.
[8] *Glouc. N. and Q.* i, 413.

'our learned lecturer of Gloucester, who last summer made an expedition into Scotland for bachelor in divinity, but was fain to return as wise as Waltham's calf and so still continues,' Jones of Tytherington, Workman the younger, and Stubbes, Sir Robert Cooke's chaplain. Nelmes, Edwardes, and Alderman Pury were the mainstay of the party in Gloucester; Pury is described by Allibond as 'sometimes a weaver, now an attorney, whom I think nothing has so much endeared as his irreverence in God's house, sitting covered when all the rest sit bare.'

In 1641 Gloucestershire was one of eleven counties which sent a petition to parliament for the abolition of episcopacy.[1] Speaking on the Root-and-Branch Bill in the Commons on 15 June, 1641, Alderman Pury proposed a scheme for the employment of the revenues of the dean and chapter of Gloucester :—

> If the dean and three prebends, being but seven in all to be now taken away, will be preaching ministers, there is sufficient maintenance for so many of them as have not too much besides, and yet to reserve so large a salary as now is allowed for so many singing-men then in holy orders as cannot preach. . . . . Out of the manors and lands the said cathedral living to be made a parochial church, £200 or more may be allowed for a learned preaching minister there, and £100 per annum each for two such others to assist him ; and then the rest of the said manors and lands may be employed to other godly, pious, and charitable uses as the wisdom of the king and parliament shall think fit.[2]

These moderate opinions ultimately prevailed among the corporation, for although the cathedral was in danger of destruction, as certain persons agreed among themselves to divide the plunder, they had only pulled down part of the little cloisters and removed the battlements from the Lady chapel when their work was arrested.[3] About 1653 John Dorney, the town clerk, exhorted the officers of the city to take charge of this its greatest ornament,[4] and three years later the cathedral, cloisters, library, and free school with the residences of the schoolmaster and usher were granted by Act of Parliament to the mayor and burgesses 'for the public worship of God, the education of children in learning, and for such other public and charitable uses as they may deem fit.'[5]

In 1640 Bishop Goodman was tried with Laud and the other bishops who had signed the Canons. In 1642 he was released and ordered to return to his diocese, but in the next year his palace at Gloucester was sacked and he fled.[6] When the war broke out Archdeacon Robinson was seized at Dursley, set on horseback with his face towards the tail, and hurried away to prison at Gloucester.[7] He subsequently took the covenant and accepted the sequestered living of Hinton near Winchester. In 1641 the vicar of Painswick and the rector of Downham were sequestered,[8] and at least twenty-four other country clergy were afterwards deprived of their livings[9] or severely mal-treated by the soldiers of the Parliament.[10] Although the new incumbents were bound to pay them a fifth of the revenues for their maintenance, they often had difficulty in getting it.[11] Churchwardens' accounts illustrate the

---

[1] Shaw, *Hist. of the Eng. Church*, 1640–60, i, 26, 38.
[2] Ibid. 90.
[3] Britton, *Glouc. Cathedral* (Essay on the Abbey), 18.
[4] Ibid.
[5] Stevenson, *Cal. of Rec. Cor. of Glouc.* 45.
[6] *Dict. Nat. Biog.* xxii, 250–1.
[7] Walker, *Sufferings of the Clergy*, 33.
[8] Shaw, op. cit. ii, 297.
[9] Walker, op. cit. *passim*.
[10] Ibid. 242, 282.
[11] Ibid. 200, 397, 398.

changes under the Commonwealth. At Dursley[1] the communion rails which had been set up in 1636 were destroyed, there was again a 'table board,' in the nave; instead of the surplice, Book of Common Prayer, and double gilt communion cup, there were, in 1643, the Presbyterian directory for public worship, two pewter platters, a salver and bowl. In 1648 a bason was bought and the font was screwed up. No less a sum than £11 5s. 8d. was spent on replacing old glass with plain glass. The windows at Fairford were taken out and hidden to save them from destruction,[2] but those at Rendcombe, which are said to have resembled the Fairford ones, were broken.[3] When Sudeley Castle was captured by the parliamentarians in 1643 they smashed the tombs of the Chandos family in the chapel, turned the tower into a stable, made the chancel their slaughter-house, and used the communion table as a chopping board.[4] The mayor of Bristol in 1655 caused the lead to be stripped from the cathedral and cloisters, but other members of the corporation intervened, and orders were issued that the lead should be sold for the repair of the building.[5] When the city was occupied by the soldiers of the parliament in 1642, Christchurch was used as barracks, and the organs and windows were broken.[6] At St. Mary Redcliffe images and ornaments were defaced, brasses were torn up, the organ was broken, and a bonfire was made of prayerbooks, homilies, cushions, and cassocks, and even Bibles were burnt.[7]

When Episcopacy was abolished and the use of the Book of Common Prayer was forbidden, dissensions broke out among the Puritans. In 1643, during the occupation of Bristol by the royalist army, the Baptist community dispersed.[8] On their return in 1645 'the heads and minds of many of the members were filled with controversies, insomuch that every meeting almost was filled with disputes and debates.' A number of them chose Mr. Ingello for their teacher, and sat under his ministry for four or five years. However, his 'flaunting apparel' and love of music offended some of them, and they secured the services of Mr. Ewins of Llanvaches in his stead. An Act for the consolidation of parishes in Bristol, for the better maintenance of the ministers and more frequent preaching, was passed in 1650, and the mayor made Mr. Ewins lecturer for the city. The chief representative of the Presbyterian party was Ralph Farmer, who became the lecturer at St. Nicholas and minister of St. James.[9] In 1659 his friend, a tanner named William Grigge, published a little book for sale at three farthings, in which he inveighed against Cromwell's 'wicked toleration' and 'liberty of conscience,' whereby Bristol was become 'the receptacle of blasphemers.' The Quakers who first appeared in Bristol in 1653 were treated with the utmost severity, but they gave some provocation. On 10 December, Elizabeth Marshall went to 'Nicholas steeple-house' to deliver a message to Ralph Farmer, and when he was about to administer the holy communion, she cried out, 'Woe, woe, woe from the Lord to them who take the Word of the Lord in their mouths and the Lord never sent them.'[10] They also caused disturbances at services in other churches, and roused much animosity against themselves. Hope Well Fox, who had become minister of Lydney, personally assaulted the Quakers

[1] Blunt, *Chap. of Par. Hist.* 59, 60.   [2] Joyce, *The Fairford Windows*, 43.
[3] *Glouc. N. and Q.* vi, 49.   [4] Dent, *Annals of Winchcombe and Sudeley Castle*, 260.
[5] Britton, *Bristol Cathedral*, 52.   [6] Nicolls and Taylor, *Bristol Past and Present*, ii, 177.
[7] Ibid. 210.   [8] *Broadmead Rec.* (Hanserd Knollys Soc.), 31–39.
[9] Nicholls and Taylor, op. cit. iii, 35.   [10] Ibid. ii, 285.

in his parish with extreme violence.[1] Many people flocked to hear the preaching of John Camm, John Audland, Edward Burrough, and Francis Howgill.[2] A strange belief gained ground in Bristol that the 'Society of Friends' were really Franciscan Friars, and in 1654 the magistrates issued a warrant for their arrest as emissaries from Rome.[3]

In 1644 Richard Baxter noted that he had seen the first contentions between ministers and Anabaptists at Gloucester ; Hart and Vaughan drew many to separation on another side, and during the war, Bacon, a preacher in the army, drew some to Antinomianism.[4] A great disputation took place between Corbet, the minister of St. Mary de Crypt, and Bacon, who was subsequently ordered to depart from the city. In 1645 the Common Council petitioned the Parliament to unite some of the churches and settle a maintenance for them out of the revenues of the see, and to settle £200 a year on an orthodox divine to preach twice a week in the cathedral. The consent of Parliament was not obtained until 1648, but the Council at once appointed Jackson, and in 1654 he was succeeded by James Forbes. Between 1654 and 1660, at the request of some of his hearers, who desired ' to have a church erected for Christ,' Forbes formed a church on the congregational plan ; ' there was only the parochial worship, save that a few Arminians and Socinians kept themselves distinct.' The Socinians were perhaps the converts of John Biddle, who became master of the Crypt Grammar School in 1641, and has been called the father of English Unitarianism.[5] The spread of Socinianism and other doctrines alarmed the Presbyterian party in Parliament, and in 1648 they proposed an ordinance making death the penalty for such opinions. Some of the London ministers supported it and sixty-five ministers in Gloucestershire testified that they were in agreement with them.[6]

The clergy, though harassed and persecuted, looked forward to the restoration of the Church of England to its rightful position.[7] In spite of the severe legislation of the Parliament there is evidence that the liturgy was not altogether disused. Bishop Juxon was living on his estate at Little Compton, and every Sunday at Chastellon House he celebrated divine service according to the rites of the Church of England, which was attended by many of the inhabitants of Little Compton and Chastellon.[8] Among those who were ordained by Robert Skinner, the ejected bishop of Oxford, was George Bull,[9] who shortly afterwards settled in the small living of St. George, near Bristol. His parish was full of Quakers and other sectaries, but he gained a wonderful influence over them by his life and preaching. He used prayers from the liturgy which he knew by heart, and pursued the same course at Suddington St. Mary, to which he was presented in 1658, the living of Suddington St. Peter being united to it in 1662.

At the Restoration the sees of Gloucester and Bristol were vacant. William Nicolson who was appointed to Gloucester had been a fearless champion of the Church during the Commonwealth, when he had supported himself by keeping a private school at Llanvihangel in partnership with Jeremy Taylor and William Wyatt, afterwards precentor of

[1] Besse, *Sufferings of the Quakers*, 210.   [2] Ibid. 39.   [3] Ibid. 40.
[4] Lloyd, *State of Religion in Glouc.* ' Barton Street Chapel.'   [5] Lloyd, Ibid. ' John Biddle.'
[6] *Glouc. N. and Q.* i, 329.   [7] Overton, *Life in the Engl. Ch.* 1660–1714, p. 3.
[8] Hook, *Lives of the Archbps. of Cant.* xi, 419.   [9] Nelson, *Life of George Bull* (ed. 1846), 22–25, 41.

Lincoln.[1] There were many nonconformists in his diocese, and he treated them with some consideration. Out of 2,000 ministers who were ejected from their livings in England on St. Bartholomew's Day 1662, because they could not sign the Act of Uniformity, there were only twenty-six in the diocese of Gloucester.[2] Several of the best and most able of the Puritans were among them. Alexander Gregory had held the living of Cirencester since the reign of James I, and was much beloved by his parishioners; before the Restoration Bull often preached for him, and he married Gregory's daughter Bridget. After his deprivation he was respectfully visited by both churchmen and nonconformists. William Tray of Oddington was an Oxford man of considerable learning, and Nicolson offered him as good a living as any in the diocese if he would conform. James Forbes and Increase Mather gave up their ministry at Gloucester. During Nicolson's episcopate order was gradually restored. His visitation articles in 1664 mark not only his effort to enforce uniformity by requiring returns of papists and sectaries, but an earnest attempt to reform abuses.[3] He insisted strictly on the residence of the clergy, and made careful inquiries about the repair of fabrics of churches, steeples and bells, and about the provision of a font of stone with a convenient cover, a communion table, paten, chalice and flagons. His consecration of the font in the cathedral in 1664 gave occasion for the publication of a violent pamphlet by Ralph Wallis, the well-known Gloucester Puritan who had taken refuge in London.[4] At Suddington the teaching of Bull brought about a strong revival of church life;[5] he catechized the youth of his parish with great care, taught the observance of holy days and fasts, above all of Good Friday; he refused to baptize in private houses except as the rubric directs, and administered the sacrament seven times a year, which, though not as often as he desired, was oftener than usual in small villages. His ministry at Avening, to which he was presented in 1685, was no less successful.[6] Many of the parishioners were very 'loose and dissolute,' and yet many more disliked the liturgy; but their attendance at public worship became regular, they brought their children to be baptized, and became 'very decent' in behaviour. The persecution of the Quakers who met at Cirencester, Aylburton, Nailsworth, Broad Campden, and Tewkesbury, was mainly the work of the magistrates, who administered the penal laws with much severity.[7] Until the Act of Toleration was passed in 1689, the sufferings of the Quakers in Bristol were still greater,[8] and the Baptist community, which met at the Friars in Lewin's Mead, was likewise persecuted.[9] In 1682 over 1,500 dissenters were under prosecution in the city, and in a news letter it was reported that at the next sessions 'about 500 families must desert their heresies, which many have done already, and meet together to hear preaching in the king's forest adjoining.'[10] The bishops of Bristol actively enforced the penal laws. However, these probably had little effect in checking nonconformity. In 1672, when Charles II issued an indulgence, licences were granted to Congregational and Presbyterian ministers at Ashchurch, Beckford, Berkeley, Bitton, Bourton-on-the-

---

[1] Dict. Nat. Biog. xli, 27.
[3] Articles of Visitation within the Archdeaconry of Glouc. 1664.
[5] Nelson, Life of Bull, 52, &c.
[7] Besse, Sufferings of the Quakers, i, 208–28.
[9] Broadmead Records (Hansard Knollys Soc.), 71, &c.

[2] Calamy, Ejected Ministers, iii, 493–506.
[4] Silawl, More News from Rome.
[6] Ibid. 298.
[8] Ibid. 45–70.
[10] Hist. MSS. Com. Rep. vii, 406.

Water, Bristol,[1] Campden, Chipping Sodbury, Cirencester, Cleeve, Clonwell, Deerhurst, Dursley, Dymock, Elington, Farmcote, Glastry, Hope, Horsley, Horton, Huntley, King's Stanley, Little Dean, Longford, Longhope, Marshfield, Nailsworth, Oddington, Painswick, Ruardean, Shipton, Stinchcombe, Stretton, Tetbury, Tewkesbury, Uley, Westerley, Wickham, Wickwar, Winchcombe, Woodland, and Wotton-under-Edge.[2]

Bishops Ironside, Carleton, and Gulston were zealous in restoring order in the Church and its services.[3] In 1670 £1,300 was spent on the cathedral and prebendal houses, and over £300 between 1681 and 1685 in repairing the pavement, painting the east end of the choir, and otherwise ornamenting the interior of the cathedral.[4] In 1684 John Lake, who held the see only for a year, established a weekly communion service in the cathedral in spite of the dean's opposition.[5] In 1687 a colony of Huguenot refugees was established in Bristol and, with the consent of the mayor and corporation, Bishop Trelawney granted them the use of the former chapel of Gaunt's Hospital.[6]

Robert Frampton, who had been dean of Gloucester since 1673, became bishop in 1681. Like Bull, he had received holy orders during the Commonwealth from the deprived bishop of Oxford, and was a zealous Churchman.[7] He made regular visitations of his diocese, preached frequently in all parts of it, and often catechized the children.[8] Although the most honourable and steadfast of the Puritans had quietly given up their livings in 1662, a number of their weaker brethren became conformists though not Churchmen.[9] Twenty years afterwards there were still some of them in the diocese of Gloucester,[10] and Frampton exerted himself to remedy their disaffection. He visited their churches, preaching the sermon himself and constraining them to read the whole of the prayers, 'which some congregations would not fail to exact of them afterwards.' One clergyman urged in defence of his neglect that the length of the service hindered him from praying so long in the pulpit as he would. The bishop remonstrated with him, and said in conclusion, 'I am apt to believe that if some of your prayer were repeated to you, you would not be so fond of it.' However, ' he was obliged to confine him to the Canon for the pulpit and the Act of Uniformity for the desk,' and he charged the churchwardens to see that he did his duty. In another parish in which he had read the litany, the churchwardens begged him on his next visit to use the same prayer ' with which they were mightily edified,' not knowing it to be part of the liturgy on account of the neglect of the incumbent. On his death Frampton appointed a worthy successor. In another parish in which the church was neglected for meeting-houses in neighbouring villages, the bishop went to preach himself, and procured other able men to do the same. The parishioners excused themselves for their neglect by pleading that the income was only £8 a year, which discouraged any minister from coming to reside there, and drove to a near conventicle many of those who did not care to walk

---

[1] There were six dissenting chapels in Bristol in 1674. Fuller, *Dissent in Bristol.*
[2] *Cal. S. P. Dom.* May–Sept. 1672, p. 743 ; 1672–3, p. 687.
[3] Articles at first episcopal visitation of Gilbert, bishop of Bristol, 1662 ; Articles of William, bishop of Bristol, 1681.
[4] Britton, *Bristol Cathedral*, 52.
[5] Overton, *Life in the Engl. Ch.* 1660–1714, p. 10.
[6] *Brist. and Glouc. Arch. Soc. Trans.* xv, 183.
[7] Simpson Evans, *Life of Robert Frampton*, 11.
[8] Ibid. 132, 138, 140, 144.
[9] Overton, op. cit. 1660–1714, p. 10.
[10] Simpson Evans, op. cit. 133–40.

two or three miles to church. They were willing to subscribe to the maintenance of a clergyman, and accordingly the bishop contributed himself and induced some of the gentry of the county to bear their share. He chose a man who soon filled the neglected church, preaching twice every Sunday and catechizing often. He held the vicarage of Standish near Gloucester with its three dependent chapels *in commendam*, and on one occasion he addressed the people in the conventicle on the borders of the parish, preventing the servant of the justice of the peace and other persons from defacing the windows and seats. A great number of nonconformists were cited before the consistorial court, and over 900 of them were persuaded by Frampton and other divines to conform.[1] He exercised great care in collating to benefices and in examining candidates for holy orders, and if he was obliged to reject any for lack of knowledge, he encouraged them to continue their studies.[2] He steadily opposed the arbitrary measures of James II. When the fellows of Magdalen College were ejected, he presented one of them to the church of Sandhurst, and refused to institute the nominee of the Roman Catholic fellows to the living of Slimbridge.[3] When the second Declaration of Indulgence was issued in 1688, Frampton forbade any of his clergy to read it in their churches; very few did, and one was deserted by his whole congregation, who left the church.[4] He was absent from London when the petition was signed by the seven bishops, arriving half an hour too late to append his signature. He visited his brethren in the Tower, and was dissuaded by Sancroft from presenting a petition of his own on the next day. On the accession of William III he scrupled to take the oath of allegiance, and in 1689 was deprived of his bishopric with the other nonjurors. With the connivance of the government he retained the living of Standish, of which the net income was only £40 a year.[5] There he lived in retirement for sixteen years, dying at the age of eighty-six. He undertook the afternoon service himself, omitting the names of the royal family in the prayers, and expounded the catechism to the children with such weighty plain truths as might be instructive to the parents. Only six of his clergy followed his example in refusing to take the oaths.[6] Though Trelawney, bishop of Bristol, was imprisoned in the Tower for signing the petition, he did not afterwards become a non-juror.

Frampton's successor was Edward Fowler, one of the most distinguished Whig prelates of his age.[7] He held the see for twenty-four years and made regular visitations. In his charge to the clergy in 1707 he discoursed on the animosities of professed Church of England men to one another, deprecating the blackening distinctions of High Church and Low Church, and assuring them that there was no ground for the popular cry of the Church in danger.[8]

In 1715 the nonconformists were established in thirty-four places in Gloucestershire, and possessed forty-eight chapels, of which twenty-five

---

[1] Simpson Evans, op. cit. 142.   [2] Ibid. 177.   [3] Ibid. 154.
[4] Ibid. 151.   [5] Ibid. 190, 208.
[6] Overton, *The Nonjurors*, Appendix, *passim*. Their names were James Kirkham, rector of Wickwar, Richard Saffyn, vicar of Berkeley, William Robinson, Humphrey Jervis Robson, vicar of Stonehouse, and Joseph Perkins. Thomas Bayley, rector of Slimbridge, and John Talbot, rector of Fretherne, refused at first, but took the oath afterwards.
[7] Abbey, *The Engl. Ch. and its Bishops*, 1700–1800, p. 118.
[8] Charge to the clergy of the diocese of Gloucester, 1707.

belonged to the Baptists.[1] Twenty years later there were over 8,000 non-conformists in the county.[2]

In 1735 Martin Benson became bishop of Gloucester. Unlike many of his brethren, he was no seeker after preferment, and though Gloucester was one of the poorest bishoprics, he declared his intention of refusing any offer of translation.[3] He spent large sums of money on the cathedral and the palace. 'His purity,' wrote Porteus, bishop of London, 'though awfully strict, was inexpressibly amiable. It diffused such a sweetness through his temper and such a benevolence over his countenance, as none who were acquainted with him, can forget.'[4] In a letter of commission which he issued shortly before his primary visitation, he expressed his determination ' to continue the ancient authority and use of rural deans,'[5] and his contemporary, Archbishop Secker, stated that he completely revived it.[6] Clerical poverty was a serious problem: in 1736 there were 168 livings in the county of which the revenues did not exceed £50 a year.[7]

Of the later bishops of the eighteenth century, Warburton (1760–79) alone, on account of his learning and great industry as a writer, has any special claim to distinction. Dr. Newton, afterwards bishop of Bristol, preached the sermon at his consecration, and said :

> When divines eminent for literature, conspicuous as preachers, illustrious as authors, are advanced to the first stations in the Church, it is not only a security to religion but an encouragement to learning, and a strong incitement to others to prosecute the same studies and to excel in the same useful arts.[8]

Warburton's influence over his clergy was exerted chiefly in that direction. In his charge in 1761 he exhorted them not ' to mistake the completion of their academic courses for the completion of their theologic studies,' and to extend their knowledge that they might be able to oppose and discourage ' fanaticism, whether spiritual or literary, bigotry, whether religious or civil, and infidelity, whether philosophical or immoral.'[9] However, he determined to see that no candidates should be presented for confirmation except such as were duly prepared.[10] Tucker, then dean of Gloucester, was exemplary ' in keeping his residence and performing his duties, in managing the chapter estates, in living hospitably, in repairing and improving his house, and in adorning the church and churchyard.' He was a man of ' strong and lively parts,' but like the bishop also ' of strong passions,' and Bishop Newton regretted that they were not in friendship and harmony.[11]

It was owing to the poverty of the see of Bristol, which in 1761 brought in little more than £300 a year, that in the eighteenth century most of the sixteen bishops were ' birds of passage,'[12] and held some other emolument *in commendam*. Two of them made their influence felt in the diocese. Joseph Butler, author of the *Analogy*, was appointed in 1738 and held the see until 1750, when he was translated to Durham. In 1740 he also became dean of St. Paul's, then resigning the benefice of Stanhope and a prebend at Rochester. Out of the revenues of the deanery he repaired and rebuilt the palace at

---

[1] Records of Nonconformity, MS. i, fol. 13 ; Dr. Williams's Lib.   [2] Ibid. MS. ii, 42.
[3] *Dict. Nat. Biog.* iv. 258.   [4] Spooner, *Bishop Butler*, 11.
[5] Dansey, *Horae Decanicae Rurales*, 421.   [6] *Secker's Charges*, 186.
[7] Return made by the Governors of Queen Anne's Bounty in 1736, pp. 70, 88.
[8] Watson, *Life of William Warburton*, 495.   [9] Ibid. 593.
[10] Ibid. 510.   [11] *Works of Thomas Newton*, i, 79.   [12] Ibid. 148.

Bristol.[1] He provided new fittings for the chapel and put a cross of white marble, let into a black background, under the east window. So strong was the feeling of the times that he was accused of popish leanings on account of his use of such an ornament and his taste for reading lives of the saints. He exercised great care in accepting candidates for ordination, and in his choice of the clergy for preferment and promotion. Thomas Newton (1760–81), who was also dean of St. Paul's from 1768 until his death, set his face against certain abuses. He spent several months every summer at Bristol, except when prevented by illness, hoping that by his example the cathedral clergy might be induced to reside. ' Alas ! ' he wrote, in 1781, ' never was church more shamefully neglected. The bishop has several times been there for months together without seeing the face of dean or prebendary, or anything better than a minor canon.'[2] He remonstrated with the chapter for their neglect, pointing out that

> their want of residence was the general complaint not only of the city, but likewise of all the country, that great numbers resorted every year to the wells and generally came at least on a Sunday to see the cathedral, that they were astonished at finding only one minor canon both to read and to preach, and perhaps administer the sacrament.

Reminding them that ' there were those who contended for the worthlessness and uselessness of deans and chapters,' he said that no more flagrant instance of good pay received and little duty done could be found than in the church of Bristol. He grieved over the neglect of the cathedral, for while the dean of Gloucester was improving and beautifying his church, ' poor Bristol lay utterly neglected, like a disconsolate widow.' He rejoiced over the appointment of Dean Hallam in 1781, hoping that he would rectify all irregularities and restore the good old order and discipline of the church. Between 1763 and 1777 he delivered five charges to the clergy of his diocese.[3] Like Warburton he desired to raise the standard of learning, and on admonishing them how to study the scriptures he said : ' I must suppose that you are able to read the scriptures in the original languages. If you have not already attained, it should be your endeavour to attain this knowledge.'[4] In speaking on the supposed increase of popery in 1766 he lamented that eagerness after pleasure and indifference to religion had taken possession of too many of the clergy.[5] They not only neglected their studies, but the necessary duties of their calling. Incumbents did not reside in their parishes, and there was a lack of resident curates. He advised the clergy to get Bishop Gibson's collection of the principal tracts and discourses written against popery, which, though consisting of three large volumes in folio, could be purchased at a moderate price. He congratulated himself on having had the aid of Grenville in suppressing a ' masshouse' which was to be opened at Bristol.[6] In 1790, eight years after his death, the Jesuits opened St. Joseph's Chapel in Trenchard Street.[7] During the next forty years the number of Roman Catholics increased so rapidly that the pro-cathedral of Clifton was begun in 1834. It was opened in 1848, and two years later Pius IX established a see at Clifton.

The full force of the Methodist movement was felt in Gloucestershire. George Whitefield was the son of the proprietor of the Bell Inn at Gloucester.[8]

[1] Spooner, op. cit. 23. [2] Thomas Newton, op. cit. i, 126–8. [3] Ibid. iii, 433–515.
[4] Ibid. 443. [5] Ibid. 461. [6] Ibid. 459.
[7] Nicholls and Taylor, *Bristol Past and Present*, ii, 274. [8] *Dict. Nat. Biog*, lxi, 85.

He went to Pembroke College, Oxford, as a servitor, and there came under the influence of the Wesleys, joining their religious society in 1733. On his return to Gloucester he formed a little society on the Methodist model. In 1736 he was ordained deacon by Bishop Benson. His remarkable gift for preaching was at once made manifest; the earnestness of his first sermon in the church of St. Mary de Crypt at Gloucester is said to have driven fifteen persons mad. In 1737 he was curate of Stonehouse for two months, and his popularity was extraordinary. In 1739, after his return from a missionary journey to North America, he came to Bristol, and being unable to get permission to preach in any of the city churches, he delivered his first field sermon to the neglected colliers of Kingswood on Saturday, 17 February. On Sunday he preached to an immense congregation in St. Mary Redcliffe, and on Monday in the church of St. Philip. The chancellor summoned him to appear before him on Tuesday, and threatened that if he preached or expounded anywhere without a licence, he would first suspend and then excommunicate him.[1] Nevertheless Whitefield preached the next day to nearly 2,000 colliers at Kingswood, and two days later to between 4,000 and 5,000. He summoned the Wesleys to join him, and on 31 March John Wesley arrived. 'I could scarce reconcile myself at first,' he wrote in his journal, 'to the strange way of preaching in the fields, of which he set me an example on Sunday, having been all my life (till very lately) so tenacious of every point relating to decency and order, that I should have thought the saving of souls almost a sin if it had not been done in a church.'[2] On 2 April he himself began his work as a field preacher, and in the course of the next few days he addressed large gatherings at Baptist Mills, Hanham Mount, Rose Green, Two-Mile-Hill, Fishponds, and the Bowling Green.[3] On 12 May the foundation-stone was laid of a building in the Horse Fair near St. James's church, which was intended to contain the societies of St. Nicholas and Baldwin Street and their acquaintance.[4] Thenceforth Bristol was one of the chief centres of the itinerant ministry of John and Charles Wesley. In 1742 the class meeting with its weekly contributions originated there.[5] On his frequent journeys between Bristol and London during the next few years [6] Wesley preached in many places in Gloucestershire; for instance, in 1739 at Thornbury and Gloucester,[7] at Runwick, Stanley St. Leonard, and on Hampton Common to between five and six thousand persons;[8] in 1742 at Painswick, Stroud, and Henbury;[9] in 1743 at Gutherton near Tewkesbury;[10] in 1745 to the miners at Colesford.[11] As elsewhere, the preaching of Wesley and Whitefield chiefly influenced the lower middle class and the poor. Their work at once attracted the attention of Bishop Butler, and in 1740 he sent for Wesley and raised an objection to the form of the doctrine of justification by faith which Wesley taught, on the ground that it was not in accordance with the teaching of the Church of England.[12] He censured the encouragement given by both Wesley and Whitefield to violent physical manifestations of the sense of conversion among their hearers. According to Wesley's account of the conversation, the bishop

[1] Nicholls and Taylor, op. cit. ii, 292.
[2] *Works of John Wesley* (ed. 1829), i, 185.
[3] Ibid. 185–192 ; Pawlyn, *Bristol Methodism*, 21.
[4] *Works of John Wesley*, i, 192.
[5] Pawlyn, op. cit. 29.
[6] *Works of John Wesley*, i, ii, *passim*.
[7] Ibid. i, 211.
[8] Ibid. 229.
[9] Ibid. 381–3.
[10] Ibid. 436.
[11] Ibid. 482.
[12] Spooner, *Bishop Butler*, 25.

said ' You are not commissioned to preach in this diocese, therefore I advise you to go hence.'[1]   He replied that having been ordained as a Fellow, he was not limited to any particular cure, and therefore held that he had an indeterminate commission to preach in any part of the Church of England. However, Butler determined to provide for the spiritual needs of Kingswood; a church was built and endowed, and a new parish was created by Act of Parliament.[2]   He intervened between Whitefield and the chancellor of the diocese, and secured him the opportunity of preaching for any of the clergy who wished for his aid.[3]   The strength of the methodist movement excited the displeasure of Bishop Newton.   In his charge to the clergy in 1766 he said: ' We should be sedulous to guard our people against methodism as we would guard them against popery.'[4]   He was convinced that from methodism to popery was a natural and easy transition, and saw a remarkably striking parallel between the saints of methodism and the saints of Rome, commending Bishop Lavington's book on the subject to his clergy.[5]   In very forcible language he deplored the lack of religion among high and low, rich and poor,[6] and in 1777 he delivered a charge entitled ' A Dissuasive from Schism.'[7]   He expressed his strong disapproval of men professing themselves members of the Church of England, who pretended to hold her doctrines and articles in greater reverence and purity than others, ' and yet contrary to all order and decency, in open violation of the laws of the Church as well as of the State, divine as well as human, set up separate congregations, erect tabernacles, preach in the fields and corners of the streets.' ' Many of them, ordained and licensed only by themselves, invade the priest's offices, revile the clergy of the Established Church, rob them as much as they can of the affections of their parishioners, and even of their parochial dues.' ' For shame,' he concluded, ' let them no longer pretend to be of the Church of England.'   Bishop Warburton looked upon Wesley and Whitefield as tiresome fanatics, and wrote *The Doctrine of Grace* in ridicule of them.[8] ' Were we to make our estimate of the present state of the religious world from the journals of modern fanatics, we should be tempted still to think ourselves in a land of pagans, with all their prejudices full blown upon them.' ' What, for instance, more strongly tends to tumult and disorder, than for one, who professes to propagate only the plain old religion of the Church of England, to set at nought its established discipline by invading the province of the parochial minister ; by assembling in undue places and at unfit times ?' He concluded his book by counselling the clergy to avoid bigotry, to favour toleration, to discountenance fanaticism, and to prevent schism, as far as possible, by judicious conciliation and correct example.   John Andrews, curate of Stinchcombe, was openly attached to methodism, and had even preached in Lady Huntingdon's chapel at Bath.[9]   In 1763 Warburton wrote threatening to revoke his licence unless he held morning and afternoon services in his parish on Sundays, and resided there continuously, ' not so much from the good you are likely to do there, as to prevent the mischief you may do by rambling about in other places.'   Whether owing to the influence of their

[1] *Works of John Wesley* (ed. 1856), xiii, 470–2.
[2] Spooner, *Bishop Butler*, 26.   [3] Ibid.   [4] Newton, op. cit. iii, 456.
[5] Ibid. 455.   [6] Ibid. 470.   [7] Ibid. 501.
[8] Watson, *Life of Warburton*, 525–39.   [9] Ibid. 543.

bishops or no, the clergy of Gloucestershire showed little sympathy with the Methodists. The Baptists of Bristol were also hostile to them.[1]

The fabrics of many churches were much neglected after the Reformation until the nineteenth century. However, churchwardens' accounts and other sources furnish some illustrations of repairs and rebuilding. A certain amount of money was expended at Cirencester in the early years of the seventeenth century,[2] but in 1639 the condition of the church is described in a quaint petition to Archbishop Laud :—

> I am in comeliness not much inferior to the cathedral church of Bath, but for want of whiteliming of marl look rustily. My windows are particoloured, white in one place and red in another, but I was founded with rich coloured glass, such as is in Fairford church near me in this diocese, which is kept decently to this day. The chancel where is received the sacrament is unceiled like a barn, my pavement is worn out and very unhandsome.

Laud threatened the churchwardens with proceedings in the Court of High Commission, and some repairs were executed. In 1704 there was a heavy rate for repairs. In 1734 Bishop Benson cited the parishioners to show cause why they should not rebuild the battlements, and they replied that battlements were useless and expensive, and the fabric was stronger and better without them. Dursley steeple fell in 1699, and the parishioners at once decided to petition for a brief in aid of the rebuilding, spending £17 1s. 9d. on beer at the meetings for the same.[3] The work was begun in 1708, and as the brief brought in £567 13s. 9d. and the cost of the work only amounted to £569 8s., the parishioners did not contribute a penny. The repairs of Tewkesbury in 1720 were estimated at £3,929; a brief only brought in £1,470, but nevertheless the work was completed in 1726.[4] The rebuilding of Tetbury was a memorial of the generosity and business capacity of the vicar and some of his parishioners in the face of much opposition ; the scheme was first mooted in 1729, but the work was not begun until 1777.[5] The rebuilding of several churches in Bristol is a mark of the prosperity of the city in the eighteenth century.[6]

The history of the Church in the nineteenth century is a record of steady progress which can be but faintly outlined here. One of the first symptoms of the renewal of activity was the foundation in 1780 of a Sunday school in Gloucester, which was the joint work of Thomas Stock, rector of St. John the Baptist, and Robert Raikes.[7] In a charge to the clergy of the diocese of Gloucester in 1807, Bishop Huntingford bade them beware of giving encouragement either to critics who attacked the church on the plea that the clergy did not preach the Gospel, or to others who called them Methodists.[8] Three years later he urged them to be circumspect and zealous in their duties.[9] In 1813, out of 274 benefices in the diocese, 165 were without resident incumbents ; of these, however, 51 were served by resident curates, 20 by clergy who held a second benefice, and in 46 of them the bishop had granted licence of absence because there was no parsonage house.[10] In 1815 Henry Ryder succeeded to the see. Four years earlier he had

[1] Nicholls and Taylor, *Bristol Past and Present*, ii, 292.   [2] Fuller, *Cirencester Parish Church*, 17–19.
[3] Blunt, *Chapters of Parochial History*, 65–68.   [4] Bennet, *History of Tewkesbury*, 144.
[5] Lee, *History of Tetbury*, 102–7.   [6] Barrett, *History of Bristol*, 466, 480, 495.
[7] *Lond. Quart. Review*, April, 1878, pp. 11–17.
[8] Charge to the clergy of the diocese of Gloucester, 1807.   [9] Ibid. 1810.   [10] *Parl. Papers*, 1817.

openly identified himself with the evangelical party.[1] He was an indefatigable bishop and attempted to animate the clergy with his own spirit, bidding them preach sermons of an evangelical nature, insisting that by their reading and earnestness they should do justice to the liturgy and rightly administer the sacraments.[2] Regretting the number of non-resident clergy, he pointed out that it was due to the great neglect of parsonage houses in former times and to the narrow incomes of some livings which made licensed pluralities almost a necessity. Although the population of the diocese had increased in eighty years by about one-third, the decrease in full services in parish churches was a little less than a third, again owing to the poverty of livings. During Ryder's episcopate John Keble, 'the true primary author'[3] of the Oxford movement, became curate of Southrop in 1823.[4] In the two years of his stay there his Oxford pupils, Robert Wilberforce, Isaac Williams, and Hurrell Froude, were much with him. From 1826 to 1835 he lived at Fairford as curate to his father, the vicar of Coln St. Aldwyn, publishing *The Christian Year* in 1827.[5] In 1833 he preached the summer assize sermon at Oxford on National Apostasy, and wrote No. 4 of the *Tracts for the Times*.[6]

Bishop Kaye, who succeeded to Bristol in 1821 and held the see for eight years before he was translated to Lincoln, stimulated a revival of teaching and discipline, admonishing his clergy to preach sermons which should reach the hearts of the people and to conform to ritual.[7] As in other dioceses, the record of the Church in 1833 was very different from that of 1800.[8] In his charge to the clergy of Gloucester in 1828, Bishop Bethell said : 'I have reason to flatter myself that the spiritual duties of this diocese are performed for the most part in a satisfactory and efficient manner.'[9] In 1832 Bishop Monk declared that non-residence ought to be called the misfortune rather than the opprobrium of the church in that diocese, for in nearly every case the cause was the want of a parsonage house ; over 100 parishes were destitute of anything which could be converted into a residence, and in these, almost without exception, there were sectarian congregations.[10] Although there were many cases of two benefices held by the same person on account of extreme poverty, there was not a single pluralist enjoying excessive revenues. The question of augmenting small livings was a difficult one, for in 1836 out of 279 benefices 123 were in the gift of private individuals;[11] however, the bishop set aside a tenth of his income for that purpose. After a visit to Cheltenham in 1836, Charles Simeon wrote : 'I have almost had a heaven upon earth. The churches so capacious, and so filled ; the schools so large, so numerous, so beneficial ; the people so full of love ; the ministers such laborious and energetic men.'[12]

As a result of the Ecclesiastical Commission in 1836 the see of Bristol was united to Gloucester, the new diocese of Gloucester and Bristol consisting of the county of Gloucester and the northern part of Wiltshire.[13] The

---

[1] *Dict. Nat. Biog.* l, 46. [2] Three charges to the clergy of the diocese of Gloucester.
[3] J. H. Newman, *Apologia*, ch. i, p. 17 ; Overton, *The Anglican Revival*, 34.
[4] Coleridge, *Memoir of Keble*, 108–10. [5] Ibid. 146, 154.
[6] Ibid. 218 ; Overton, op. cit. 54. [7] Charge to the clergy of the diocese of Bristol, 1821.
[8] Overton, *The English Church of the Nineteenth Century*, 8.
[9] Charge to the clergy of the diocese of Gloucester, 1828. [10] Ibid. 1832. [11] *Parl. Papers*, 1836.
[12] Carus, *Life of Charles Simeon*, 783. [13] *Lond. Gaz.* 1836, p. 1734 ; 1837, p. 2174.

new archdeaconry of Bristol contained in Gloucestershire the rural deaneries of Bristol, Cirencester, Fairford, and Hawkesbury. Monk exercised great influence during the twenty-six years of his episcopate. He extended and revived the functions of the rural deans.[1] In 1848, when the number of benefices was 424, there were 301 resident incumbents, and the number of curates had greatly increased.[2] A hundred parsonages were built or enlarged, and fifty-four new churches were consecrated by him.[3] He himself spent upwards of £8,000 on the augmentation of small livings, and the clergy and laity also gave generous help to the same object. In 1864, when Bishop Ellicott delivered his charge at his primary visitation, there were only twenty parishes without a resident clergyman, though 114 benefices were still without parsonages.[4] In thirty-one churches there were three full services on Sundays, and twenty with only one. In 124 churches, however, the Holy Communion was administered six times a year or less, and only fourteen churches had weekly celebrations. During his long episcopate, which lasted until 1905, the work of the Church extended and prospered greatly.[5] The cathedrals of Bristol and Gloucester were restored, many new churches were built, and a great number of others were restored or enlarged. In 1882 the archdeaconry of Cirencester was constituted.[6] In 1884 the Bristol Bishopric Act was passed, by which provision was made for a new see of Bristol when the necessary endowment was secured, and the division took place in 1897.[7]

APPENDIX

ECCLESIASTICAL DIVISIONS OF THE COUNTY

When the sees of Worcester and Hereford were created about 680,[8] Gloucestershire was divided between them, the western portion beyond the Severn and the Leadon being in the diocese of Hereford.

Shortly after the Norman Conquest the archdeaconry of Gloucester was constituted to contain all that part of the county which lay in the diocese of Worcester.[9] The remainder was assigned to the archdeaconry of Hereford.

In 1094 the jurisdiction of St. Oswald's, which included the priory of St. Oswald, Gloucester, and several adjacent chapels, was constituted a peculiar of the archbishopric of York.[10]

In 1291 the archdeaconry of Gloucester was divided into the eleven rural deaneries of Campden, Stow, Cirencester, Fairford, Winchcombe, Stonehouse, Hawkesbury, Bitton, Bristol, Dursley, and Gloucester.[11] Five parishes in the north-east of the county lay in the deanery of Blockley, in the archdeaconry of Worcester.[12] The rural deanery of the Forest in the archdeaconry of Hereford contained all the remaining parishes save those of Newland, English Bicknor, and Preston, which were in the deanery of Ross, and Staunton in the deanery of Irchinfield.[13]

[1] Dansey, *Horae Decanicae Rurales*, 421. [2] *Parl. Papers*, 1850.
[3] Charge of Bishop Baring to the clergy of the diocese of Gloucester and Bristol, 1857.
[4] Charge to the clergy, 1864.
[5] Ibid. 1873, *Records of Diocesan Progress, passim*.
[6] *Lond. Gaz.* 1882, p. 6242. [7] Ibid. 1897, p. 3787.
[8] *V. C. H. Glouc. Eccl. Hist.* 2.
[9] Phillimore, *Eccl. Law* (ed. 1873), i, 240; Wharton, *Angl. Sac.* ii, 262.
[10] Wharton, *Angl. Sac.* i, 295; *Historians of York* (Rolls Ser.), iii, 21.
[11] *Pope Nich. Tax.* (Rec. Com.), 220-4.
[12] Ibid. 217*b*. [13] Ibid. 161.

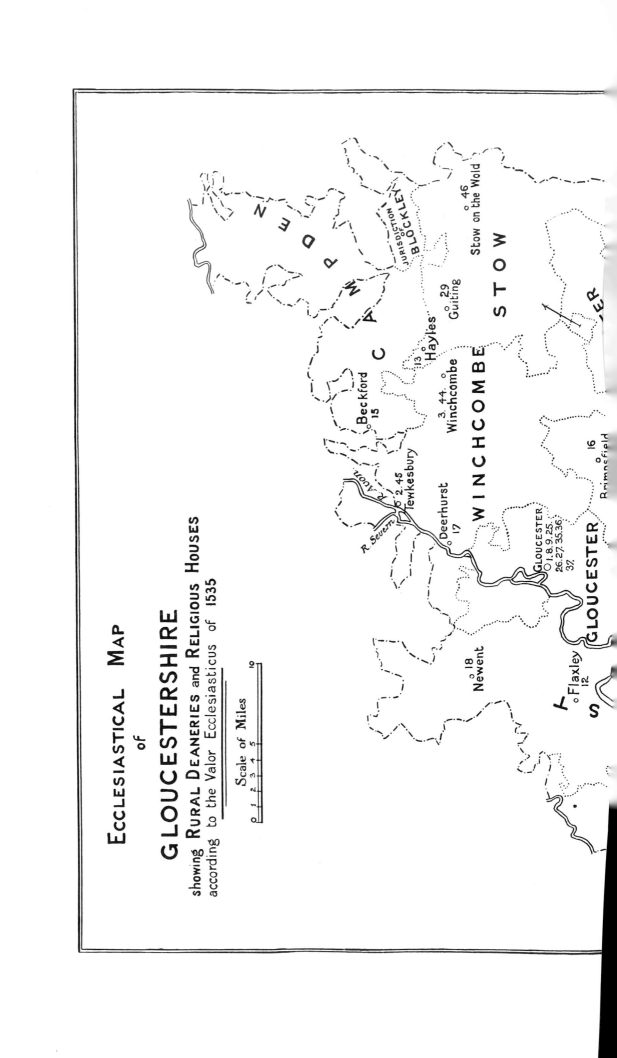

ECCLESIASTICAL MAP
of
GLOUCESTERSHIRE

showing RURAL DEANERIES and RELIGIOUS HOUSES
according to the Valor Ecclesiasticus of 1535

Scale of Miles

0 1 2 3 4 5   10

C A M P D E N

JURISDICTION OF BLOCKLEY

Stow on the Wold
°46

°29 Guiting

Haytes
13°

Beckford
°15

3. 44. ° Winchcombe

WINCHCOMBE   STOW

R. Avon
5 2.45 °Tewkesbury

Deerhurst
17°

R. Severn

GLOUCESTER
° 1.8.9.25.
26.27 35.36.
37.

16
°Brimpsfield

°18 Newent

L °Flaxley
12

GLOUCESTER

S

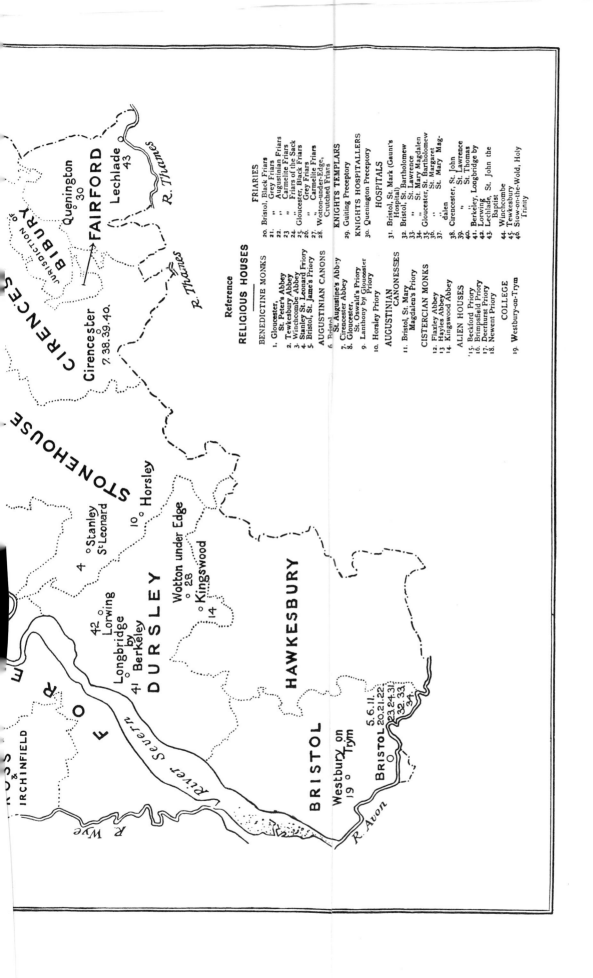

Reference

RELIGIOUS HOUSES

BENEDICTINE MONKS
1. Gloucester, St. Peter's Abbey
2. Tewkesbury Abbey
3. Winchcombe Abbey
4. Stanley St. Leonard Priory
5. Bristol, St. James's Priory

AUGUSTINIAN CANONS
6. Bristol
7. St. Augustine's Abbey
8. Cirencester Abbey
9. Gloucester, St. Oswald's Priory, Lanthony by Gloucester Priory
10. Horsley Priory

AUGUSTINIAN CANONESSES
11. Bristol, St. Mary Magdalen's Priory

CISTERCIAN MONKS
12. Flaxley Abbey
13. Hayles Abbey
14. Kingswood Abbey

ALIEN HOUSES
15. Beckford Priory
16. Brimpsfield Priory
17. Deerhurst Priory
18. Newent Priory

COLLEGE
19. Westbury-on-Trym

FRIARIES
20. Bristol, Black Friars
21. " Grey Friars
22. " Augustinian Friars
23. " Carmelite Friars
24. " Friars of the Sack
25. Gloucester, Black Friars
26. " Grey Friars
27. " Carmelite Friars
28. Wotton-under-Edge, Crutched Friars

KNIGHTS TEMPLARS
29. Guiting Preceptory

KNIGHTS HOSPITALLERS
30. Quenington Preceptory

HOSPITALS
31. Bristol, St. Mark (Gaunt's Hospital)
32. Bristol, St. Bartholomew
33. " St. Lawrence
34. " St. Mary Magdalen
35. Gloucester, St. Bartholomew
36. " St. Margaret
37. " St. Mary Magdalen
38. Cirencester, St. John
39. " St. Lawrence
40. " St. Thomas
41. Berkeley, Longbridge by
42. Lorwing
43. Lechlade, St. John the Baptist
44. Winchcombe
45. Tewkesbury
46. Stow-on-the-Wold, Holy Trinity

ECCLESIASTICAL HISTORY

In 1535 the rural deanery of Bitton had been absorbed into that of Hawkesbury,[1] but there were no other changes.[2]

In 1541 the bishopric of Gloucester was created, and the bounds of the diocese became those of the county. Thus the jurisdiction of the archbishop of York over the peculiar of St. Oswald was abrogated, the rural deanery of the Forest and the parishes in the deaneries of Ross and Irchinfield were taken from the diocese of Hereford, but remained in the archdeaconry of Hereford.[3] In 1542 the bishopric of Bristol was created, and the city and rural deanery of Bristol were taken out of the diocese of Gloucester.[4]

In 1836 the sees of Gloucester and Bristol were united as the bishopric of Gloucester and Bristol, and the archdeaconry of Bristol was constituted, the rural deaneries of Bristol, Cirencester, Fairford, and Hawkesbury being taken out of the archdeaconry of Gloucester.[5] The deanery of the Forest was transferred from the archdeaconry of Hereford to the archdeaconry of Gloucester.[6]

In 1882 the archdeaconry of Cirencester was constituted to include the six rural deaneries of Campden, Stow, Northleach north and south, Fairford, and Cirencester.[7]

In 1897 the diocese of Bristol was created, and the rural deaneries of Bristol, Stapleton, and Bitton were taken out of the diocese of Gloucester.[8]

At the present time (1906) the list of parishes under the deaneries is as follows :—

THE DEANERY OF GLOUCESTER : containing the forty-four parishes of Arlingham, Ashleworth, Barnwood, Brockworth, Brookthorpe with Whaddon, Churchdown, Edge, Elmore, Framilode, Fretherne, All Saints Gloucester, St. Aldate Gloucester, St. Catherine Gloucester, Christchurch Gloucester, St. Mark Gloucester, St. John the Baptist Gloucester, St. James Gloucester, St. Mary de Crypt with All Saints and St. Owen Gloucester, St. Mary de Lode with Trinity Gloucester, St. Michael with St. Mary de Grace Gloucester, St. Paul Gloucester, St. Luke Gloucester, St. Nicholas Gloucester, Mariners' Church Gloucester, Harescombe with Pitchcombe, Haresfield, Hartpury, Hempstead, Hucclecote, Lassington, Longney, Maisemore, Matson, Moreton Valence, Norton, Quedgeley, Randwick, Sandhurst, Saul, Standish with Hardwicke, Twigworth, Upton St. Leonard, Wheatenhurst (or Whitminster), Great Witcomb.

THE DEANERY OF DURSLEY : containing the twenty-two parishes of Berkeley with Purton Wick, Breadstone, Sharpness and Newport Church, Beverstone, Cam, St. Bartholomew, Lower Cam, Coaley, Dursley with St Mark's Chapel, Falfield, Frampton-on-Severn, Hill, Kingswood, Lasborough with Weston Birt, Newington Bagpath with Kingscote, North Nibley with Ridge Chapel, Oldbury-on-Severn, Ozleworth, Rockhampton, Slimbridge, Stinchcombe, Stone, Thornbury, Uley with Owlpen, Wotton-under-Edge.

THE DEANERY OF THE FOREST, NORTH : containing the twenty-four parishes of Awre, Blaisdon, Blakeney, Bromsberrow, Churcham with Bulley Chapel, Dymock, Flaxley, Gorsley with Clifford's Mesne, Highnam, Huntley, Kempley, Lea, Longhope, Minsterworth, Newent, Newnham, Oxenhall, Pauntley, Preston, Rudford, Taynton, Tibberton, Upleadon, Westbury-on-Severn.

THE DEANERY OF THE FOREST, SOUTH : containing the twenty-four parishes of Abenhall, Beachley, English Bicknor, Bream, St. Briavels, Clearwell, Coleford, All Saints Viney Hill Forest of Dean, Christchurch Forest of Dean, Holy Trinity Forest of Dean, St. John (Cinderford) Forest of Dean, St. Stephen (Cinderford) Forest of Dean, Woodside Forest of Dean, Hewelsfield, Littledean, Lydbrook, Lydney with Aylburton, Mitcheldean, Newland with Redbrook, Parkend, Ruardean, Staunton, Tidenham with St. Luke's Chapel at Tutshill, Woolastone with Alvington Chapel and Lancaut Chapel.

THE DEANERY OF BISLEY : containing the seventeen parishes of Bisley, Brimpsfield, Bussage, Chalford, Cranham, Edgeworth, Elkstone, France-Lynch, Miserden, Oakridge, Painswick, Sapperton with Frampton Mansel, Shepscombe, Slad with Uplands, Stroud, Holy Trinity Stroud, Syde, Whiteshill, Winstone.

THE DEANERY OF STONEHOUSE : containing the twenty parishes of Amberley, Avening, Brimscombe, Cainscross, Cherrington, Eastington, Frocester, Horsley with Chavenage, Leonard

---

[1] *Valor Eccl.* (Rec. Com.), ii, 491, 492.

[2] The peculiar jurisdiction of Bibury (Ibid. ii, 452), had long been exempt from the visitation of the archdeacon. Thomas, *Survey of Worcester*, App. 14. The peculiar jurisdiction of Blockley contained those parishes which were in the deanery of Blockley.

[3] Rymer, *Foedera*, xiv, 724.

[4] Ibid. 748.

[5] *Lond. Gaz.* 1836, pp. 1734-5.

[6] Ibid. p. 1737.

[7] Ibid. 1882, p. 6242.

[8] Ibid. 1897, p. 3787.

Stanley, Minchinhampton, Nailsworth, Nympsfield, Rodborough, Rodmarton, Selsley, Shipton Moyne, King's Stanley, Stonehouse, Tetbury, Woodchester.

THE DEANERY OF WINCHCOMBE: containing the twenty-one parishes of Ashchurch, Bishop's Cleeve with Stoke Orchard, Corse, Deerhurst with Apperley, Down Hatherley, Elmstone with Hardwick and Uckington, Forthampton, Hasfield, Kemerton, Leigh, Oxenton, Staverton with Boddington, Sudeley, Tewkesbury, Holy Trinity Tewkesbury, Tirley, Tredington, Twyning, Walton Cardiff, Winchcombe with Gretton, Woolstone.

THE DEANERY OF CHELTENHAM: containing the twenty-eight parishes of Badgeworth with Bentham, Charlton Abbots, Charlton Kings Holy Apostles, Charlton Kings St. Mary with St. Matthew Cheltenham, Holy Trinity Cheltenham, Christ Church Cheltenham, All Saints Cheltenham, St. James Cheltenham, St. John Cheltenham, St. Luke Cheltenham, St. Mark Cheltenham, St. Paul Cheltenham, St. Peter Cheltenham, St. Stephen Cheltenham, Coberley *alias* Cubberley, Colesbourne, Cowley, Dowdeswell, Leckhampton, St. Philip and St. James Leckhampton, Prestbury, Sevenhampton, Shurdington, Swindon, Upper Hatherley, Whittington, Withington.

THE DEANERY OF HAWKESBURY: containing the eighteen parishes of Acton Turville, Alderley, Great and Little Badminton, Boxwell with Leighterton, Charfield, Cromhall, Didmarton with Oldbury, Hawkesbury with Tresham, Hillsley, Horton, Rangeworthy, Old Sodbury, Little Sodbury, Chipping Sodbury, Tortworth, Tytherington, Wickwar, Yate.

THE DEANERY OF CIRENCESTER: containing the nineteen parishes of Ampney Crucis, Ampney, Bagendon, North Cerney, South Cerney with Cerney Wick, Cirencester with Watermoor, Coates, Daglingworth, Driffield, Duntisbourne Abbots, Duntisbourne Rous, Harnhill, Kemble, Poole-Keynes, All Saints Preston, Rendcombe, Siddington, Somerford Keynes with Sharncote, Stratton with Baunton.

THE DEANERY OF FAIRFORD: containing the fourteen parishes of Barnsley, Bibury with Winson, Coln St. Aldwyn, Down Ampney, Eastleach Turville with Eastleach Martin, Fairford, Hatherop, Kempsford with Whelford, Lechlade, Marston Meysey, Meysey Hampton, Poulton, Quenington, Southrop.

THE DEANERY OF NORTHLEACH: containing the sixteen parishes of Aldsworth, Aston Blank, Little Barrington, Cold Salperton, Chedworth, Coln St. Dennis, Coln Rogers, Compton Abdale, Farmington, Hampnett with Stowell, Hezleton with Yanworth, Northleach, Notgrove, Sherborne with Windrush, Shipton Oliffe with Shipton Sollars, Turkdean.

THE DEANERY OF STOWE: containing the twenty-two parishes of Great Barrington, Bledington, Bourton-on-the-Water with Clapton and Lower Slaughter, Broadwell with Adlestrop, Little Compton, Condicote, Lower Guiting with Farmcote, Temple Guiting, Hawling, Icomb, Longborough with Seizincote, Naunton, Oddington, Great Rissington, Little Rissington, Rissington Wick, Upper Slaughter, Stow-on-the-Wold, Sutton-under-Brails, Lower Swell, Upper Swell, Westcote.

THE DEANERY OF CAMPDEN: containing the thirty-two parishes of Alderton, Aston Somerville, Aston-sub-Edge, Batsford with Moreton-in-the-Marsh, Beckford with Ashton-under-Hill, Bourton-on-the-Hill, Buckland, Chipping Campden, Childswickham, Clifford Chambers, Didbrook with Pinnock, Hayles, and Hyde, Dorsington, Dumbleton, Ebrington, Hinton-on-the-Green, Lemington, Marston Sicca, Mickleton, Pebworth, Preston-on-Stour, Quinton, Saintbury, Stanton with Snowhill, Stanway, Todenham, Toddington with Stanley Pontlarge, Great Washbourn, Welford, Weston-upon-Avon, Weston-sub-Edge, Willersley, Wormington.[1]

THE DEANERIES OF BRISTOL, STAPLETON, AND BITTON

(Before the creation of the diocese of Bristol in 1897)

DEANERY OF BRISTOL: containing the parishes of Abbots Leigh, All Saints with All Hallows Easton, St. Augustine, St. Agnes, St. Barnabas, St. Bartholomew, Christchurch with St. Ewen, St. Clement, Emmanuel, St. Gabriel, St. George Brandon Hill, Holy Trinity, St. Philip and St. Jacob, St. James, St. John the Baptist, St. Jude, St. Lawrence, St. Luke Barton Hill, Christ Church Barton Hill, St. Mark Easton, St. Mary Redcliffe, St. Mary-le-Port, St. Matthew Kingsdown, St. Matthew Moorfields, St. Andrew Montpelier, St. Matthias (the Weir), St. Michael, St. Nathaniel, St. Nicholas with St. Leonard, St. Paul, St. Mary Tyndalls Park, St. Saviour's Woolcot Park, Redland, St. George (Gloucestershire), St. Peter, St. Silas, St. Simon, St. Stephen, Temple or Holy Cross, St. Thomas, St. Werburgh (Bristol), St. John with St. Michael and

---

[1] *Clergy List* for the diocese of Gloucester, 1906.

All Angels, St. Francis Ashton Gate, Holy Trinity Knowle, St. Luke, St. Paul, St. Peter Bishopworth, St. Raphael (Bedminster), St. Andrew with St. James, St. Andrew the Less, Christchurch, All Saints, St. John the Evangelist, St. Paul, St. Peter Clifton Wood, Holy Trinity, Emmanuel (Clifton).

The Deanery of Stapleton : Almondsbury, Alveston, Bishopston (St. Michael and All Angels), Compton Greenfield, Downend, Elberton, Filton Fish Ponds, Frenchay, Henbury with Aust, Northwick and Redwick Churches, Horfield, Littleton-on-Severn, Mangotsfield, Olveston, Pilning (St. Peter), Shirehampton, Stapleton, Stokebishop (St. Mary Magdalene), Stoke Giffard, St. Michael Two Mile Hill, Westbury-on-Trym with Redland Chapel, Winterbourne St. Michael, Winterbourne Downe (All Saints).

The Deanery of Bitton : Cold Ashton, Bitton, Coal Pit Heath, Dodington, Doynton, Dyrham, Frampton Cotterell, Hanham-Abbots, Christ Church, Iron Acton, Kingswood (Holy Trinity), Marshfield, Oldland, Pucklechurch with Abson Church, Siston, Tormarton with West Lytleton, Wapley with Codrington, Warmley, Westerleigh, Wick.[1]

---

[1] The deaneries of Bristol, Stapleton, and Bitton are taken from the *Clergy List* of 1896, before these parishes were transferred to the diocese of Bristol ; since that date the new deaneries of Bedminster, Clifton, and East Bristol have been formed from parishes in Bristol and Stapleton.

THE RELIGIOUS HOUSES OF GLOUCESTERSHIRE

INTRODUCTION

Monasticism had a very strong influence on the history of Gloucestershire on account of the great possessions of the religious houses.

The chief Benedictine monasteries had their origin before the beginning of the ninth century. Gloucester was founded about 681, Tewkesbury about 715, Winchcombe in 798. Of the smaller houses of the order, Deerhurst was founded about 804, and became a cell of the monastery of St. Denis about 1059. The priories of Newent, Horsley, and Brimpsfield were established as cells of Benedictine monasteries in Normandy in the reign of William the Conqueror. The priory of St. James, Bristol, was founded about 1137, Stanley St. Leonard in 1146.

Before the middle of the twelfth century the Augustinian canons had four important houses. In 1131 they took the place of the secular canons of Cirencester. The monastery of Lanthony by Gloucester had its origin in 1136; St. Augustine's, Bristol, in 1148. The secular canons of St. Oswald's Minster at Gloucester gave place to Augustinians about 1150. Beckford was founded as a cell to St. Barbe-en-Auge, about 1135. The priory of St. Mary Magdalen, Bristol, which after the Norman conquest was the only monastery for women in Gloucestershire, was founded for Augustinian canonesses before 1173. In 1260 Horsley became a cell of Bruton, in Somerset.

Although the Cistercians came to England in 1128, and spread rapidly in the north and in the marches of Wales, the small monastery of Flaxley, in the Forest of Dean, was not founded until about 1151. The more noted house of Hayles had its origin in 1246.

The preceptories of the Templars and Hospitallers were established at Guiting and Quenington before the end of the twelfth century. In 1222 the Carthusians settled for a few years at Hatherop, but afterwards moved to Hinton in Somerset.

In the thirteenth century the Friars came to Bristol and Gloucester.

Westbury-on-Trym, which was a Benedictine monastery in the tenth century, and again after the Norman Conquest, probably became a collegiate church of secular canons in the middle of the thirteenth century.

Hospitals at Bristol, Gloucester, Cirencester, Berkeley, Lechlade, and elsewhere were founded, some for lepers, others for the sick and needy.

HOUSES OF BENEDICTINE MONKS

I. THE ABBEY OF ST. PETER AT GLOUCESTER

In or about 681, with the consent of Ethelred, king of Mercia, Osric, under-king of the Hwiccas, founded a monastery at Gloucester in honour of St. Peter and St. Paul.[1] It is possible that a monastery for men was attached to it as to many other monasteries for women which were founded before the eighth century.[2] Osric's sister, Cyneburh, was consecrated as the first abbess by Bosel, bishop of Worcester.[3] She died in 710, and was succeeded by her sister, Eadburh.[4] On her death in 735, Eva was consecrated abbess by Wilfrid, bishop of Worcester.[5] During the rule of the three abbesses monastic life flourished,[6] and the possessions of the house increased.[7] But on the death of Eva in 767 no successor was appointed,[8] and it seems probable that the nuns dispersed during the confusion of civil strife in England. According to the writer of the *Memoriale* the monastery was deserted for the space of fifty years.[9] It has been suggested that King Offa took the lands of the monastery into his own hands as he did those of the abbey of Bath.[10] Bernulph, king of the Mercians (ob. 823), is said to have rebuilt the church, and to have endowed a body of secular priests with the former possessions of the nuns, and in addition five hides in Standish.[11]

Gloucester was untouched by the monastic revival in the reign of King Edgar. However, in 1022 Wulfstan II, who held the sees of both Worcester and York, changed the community of secular priests into a convent of Benedictine monks and put them under the rule of Abbot Edric.[12] According to one tradition, the men of Gloucester resented the reform, and killed seven of the monks,[13] and in atonement for that deed, Wulfin le Rue gave Churcham and Highnam to the convent. There is no evidence of a violent expulsion of the secular priests,[14] and Abbot Edric

is said to have been one of them.[15] The house did not flourish, lands at Badgeworth and Hatherley were sold,[16] and the monastic buildings were destroyed by fire.[17] In 1058 Edric was succeeded by Wilstan, a monk of Worcester.[18] Aldred, then bishop of Worcester, rebuilt the church from the foundations; to recoup the expense he took possession of the lands of the monks at Leach, Oddington, Standish, and Barton, and annexed them to the see of York, to which he succeeded in 1061.[19] At the time of the Norman Conquest monastic life languished at Gloucester, as in many other houses. In 1072 the convent consisted only of two monks and eight novices, and Abbot Wilstan had gone on a pilgrimage to Jerusalem.[20] After his death in that year, Serlo, a Norman monk of Mont St. Michel, was appointed by William the Conqueror. The monastery prospered exceedingly under his vigorous rule, and before 1087 he recovered the manors of Frocester and Coln St. Aldwyn, which had been alienated by his predecessor.[21] In the *Domesday Survey* the possessions of the convent in Gloucestershire[22] also included the manors of Boxwell, Buckland, Aldsworth, Hinton, Highnam, and Preston, of the old endowment, Ledene of the gift of Walter de Lacy,[23] Duntisbourne, of the gift of his wife;[24] in Hampshire,[25] Linkenholt, the gift of Ernulf de Hesding in 1082;[26] in Worcestershire[27] half a hide in Wick; in Herefordshire[28] the manors of Westwood, Brompton, and Lea, making in all 89½ hides. In 1093 Abbot Serlo regained the manor of Nympsfield.[29] In 1095, with the aid of the king, he compelled Thomas, archbishop of York, to restore all the lands at Leach, Oddington, Standish, and Barton,[30] which had remained in the possession of the see of York since 1058, when Aldred seized them. William the Conqueror gave the convent the manor of Barnwood[31] and the church of St. Peter Mancroft at Norwich.[32] When William II lay sick at Gloucester in 1093, he gave the church of St. Gundelay at Newport and fifteen

[1] *Hist. et Cart. Mon. Glouc.* (Rolls Ser.), i, 3, 4.
[2] Hunt, *Hist. of the Engl. Ch.* i, 182; R. *Hist. Soc. Trans.* xiii, 168–83.
[3] *Hist. et Cart. Glouc.* (Rolls Ser.), i, 4.
[4] Ibid. 6. She is here described as the widow of Wulphere, king of the Mercians, but this is impossible; cf. *Brist. and Glouc. Arch. Soc. Trans.* xv, 130.
[5] *Hist. et Cart. Glouc.* i, 7. She was however neither the sister of Cyneburh, nor the widow of Wulphere; cf. *Brist. and Glouc. Arch. Soc. Trans.* xv, 130.
[6] *Hist. et Cart. Glouc.* i, 6, 7.   [7] Ibid. 4.
[8] Leland, *Itin.* (ed. 1711), iv, fol. 171b.
[9] Dugdale, *Mon.* i, 563.
[10] *Brist. and Glouc. Arch. Soc. Trans.* xvi, 215.
[11] Dugdale, op. cit. i, 563.
[12] Ibid.; *Hist. et Cart. Glouc.* i, 8.
[13] Dugdale, op. cit. i, 563.
[14] *Hist. et Cart. Glouc.* i, 8.

[15] Dugdale, op. cit. i, 563.
[16] *Hist. et Cart. Glouc.* i, 8.
[17] Dugdale, op. cit. i, 564.
[18] *Hist. et Cart. Glouc.* i, 9.
[19] Ibid.   [20] Ibid. 10.
[21] Ibid.
[22] *Dom. Bk.* (Rec. Com.), 165b.
[23] *Hist. et Cart. Glouc.* (Rolls Ser.), i, 92.
[24] Ibid. 73.
[25] *Dom. Bk.* (Rec. Com.), 43.
[26] *Hist. et Cart. Glouc.* (Rolls Ser.), i, 93.
[27] *Dom. Bk.* (Rec. Com.), 174.
[28] Ibid. 181.
[29] *Hist. et Cart. Glouc.* i, 101.
[30] Ibid. 11.   [31] Ibid. 65.
[32] Ibid. 102.

hides.[1] Henry I granted the manor of Maisemore in 1101.[2] Lands and churches in the marches in Wales were lavishly presented by Norman lords; in 1088 Bernard of Newmarch gave the manor of Glasbury and the church of Cowarne;[3] Robert Fitzhamon granted the church of Lancarvan and fifteen hides at Penhow.[4] In 1100 Harold, lord of Ewyas, founded and endowed the cell of Ewyas in Herefordshire.[5] In the following year Hugh de Lacy gave the collegiate church of St. Peter at Hereford.[6] The church of St. Martin in the Vintry, London, was the gift of Ralph Peverel.[7] The number of monks increased rapidly, and in 1104 was said to have reached 100.[8] However, in a charter granted by Samson, bishop of Worcester, on 23 July, 1100, he expressly stated that Serlo had gathered around him more than sixty monks, and that the possessions of the house scarcely sufficed to provide for them.[9] In 1089[10] the foundation-stone was laid of a new church which was dedicated on 13 July, 1100, with great pomp by Samson, bishop of Worcester, Gundulf, bishop of Rochester, and Hervey, bishop of Bangor.[11] Two years later the building suffered some damage by fire.[12] On the death of Serlo in 1104, Prior Peter became abbot.[13] Building and the acquisition of property continued, and Henry I gave the manor of Abload and Paygrove Wood in exchange for some land in Gloucester on which the castle was built.[14] Learning flourished, Abbot Peter had long been an earnest student of the Scriptures, and he gave many books to the library.[15] In 1122, during the rule of his successor, William Godemon, the monastery suffered serious damage by fire.[16] The convent appears to have already enjoyed the privilege of freedom of election,[17] and in 1130, Walter de Lacy, who had entered the monastery under Abbot Peter at the age of seven, was unanimously chosen.[18] On his death in 1139 the monks elected Gilbert Folliot, a monk of Cluny,[19] and when he was promoted to the see of Hereford in 1148, their choice fell on the sub-prior Hamelin.[20] Under these three abbots the possessions of the house continued to increase very rapidly. In 1134 the cell of Kilpeck, in Herefordshire, was founded and endowed by Hugh Fitzwilliam.[21] In 1135,

Robert Curthose, a former benefactor,[22] received honourable burial within the church.[23] To find a light at the high altar for his brother's soul, Henry I gave the manor of Rodley, with a wood and fishery.[24] Robert, earl of Gloucester (ob. 1146), gave lands at Tregoff and Penhow in Glamorganshire.[25] The dependent priory of St. Guthlac at Hereford was founded between 1139 and 1148, with the aid of the bishop, Robert de Bethune.[26]

In 1141 Maurice of London founded and endowed the cell of Ewenny in Glamorganshire.[27] In 1144 the lands at Glasbury were exchanged for the manor of Eastleach.[28] In 1146 the college of secular canons at Stanley St. Leonard was given to the monastery by Roger of Berkeley III, with the consent of the prior and canons, and became another cell.[29]

In 1155 the secular canons of Bromfield in Shropshire surrendered their collegiate church to the monastery,[30] and themselves became Benedictines in the new cell. The old claim of the see of York to the manors which had been surrendered by Archbishop Thomas in 1095, was again put forward by Archbishop Roger. After a journey to the papal court, Abbot Hamelin made a final settlement by granting Oddington, Condicote, and Cherdington to the archbishop.[31]

In spite, or perhaps on account of the very rapid expansion, there are indications of that financial embarrassment which becomes so marked a feature in the history of the monastery in the thirteenth and fourteenth centuries. The revenues were very large, but they frequently proved insufficient. In 1146, for a loan of £80, the abbot and convent handed over the manor of Tregoff, their land at Penhow, and the church of Lancarvan to Robert Fitzharding for a term of five years.[32] If they were able to repay him before the time had expired, he undertook to restore the property at once. The intellectual condition of the monastery was flourishing. Of the monks who are known to have added their works to the library, Benedict[33] wrote a life of St. Dubricius about 1130, and Osbern was conspicuous among his contemporaries for his knowledge of philosophy and theology.[34] The letters

---

[1] *Hist. et Cart. Glouc.* i. 102.
[2] Ibid. 100.   [3] Ibid. 80.
[4] Ibid. 93.   [5] Ibid. 76, 285.
[6] Dugdale, op. cit. iii, 621 ; *Hist. et Cart. Glouc.* (Rolls Ser.), i, 84.
[7] *Hist. et Cart. Glouc.* (Rolls Ser.), i, 94.
[8] Ibid. 13.   [9] Ibid. ii, 40.   [10] Ibid. i, 11.
[11] Ibid. 12.   [12] Ibid.
[13] Ibid. 13, 14.   [14] Ibid. 59.
[15] Ibid. 13.   [16] Ibid. 14.
[17] Ibid. iii, 3. It was confirmed by Innocent III in 1200.
[18] Ibid. i, 15.   [19] Ibid. 18.
[20] Ibid. 19.   [21] Ibid. 91.

[22] Dugdale, op. cit. i, 551.
[23] *Hist. et Cart. Glouc.* (Rolls Ser.), i, 15.
[24] Ibid. 110, 111.   [25] Ibid. 115.
[26] Ibid. 85. The date 1163 is obviously incorrect. Robert de Bethune died in 1148. As the foundation took place while he was bishop of Hereford and Gilbert Folliot was abbot of Gloucester, it must fall between 1139 and 1148. Cf. Giles, *Letters of Gilbert Folliot*, i, 161.
[27] *Hist. et Cart. Glouc.* 75.
[28] Ibid. 80.   [29] Ibid. 113.
[30] Ibid. 19, 66.   [31] Ibid. 19.
[32] Glouc. Orig. Chart. Court of Chancery (P.R.O.).
[33] Hardy, *Catalogue of Materials* (Rolls Ser.), ii, 178.
[34] Ibid. ii, 238 ; Bibl. Reg. 6, D. xi (B.M.).

of Gilbert Folliot bear witness to his reputation for elegant scholarship and wisdom.[1]

He assigned the church of Glasbury, the tithes of Talgarth and those from the lordship of Brecon to the precentor to find parchment and ink to increase the library.

Between 1163 and 1179 one of the western towers fell while Roger, bishop of Worcester, was celebrating mass, and although the church was thronged with people they all escaped unhurt.[2] In 1168 the ritual murder of a boy named Harold was attributed to the Jews of Gloucester.[3] Abbot Hamelin and the monks gave the body honourable burial in their church.

The house suffered severely from the financial extortions of John. The chalices and silver vessels had been sold for Richard I's ransom in 1194,[4] and other chalices were sold to meet the king's demands in 1210.[5] On 28 October, 1216, Henry III, then a boy of nine years old, was crowned king of England by Guala, the papal legate, and other bishops, in the great church of the monastery.[6] A market in the manor of Northleach was granted by Henry III in 1222,[7] and in 1227 a fair on the vigil, feast, and morrow of St. Peter and St. Paul.[8] The church of Frocester was appropriated to the house by William of Blois, bishop of Worcester, in 1225;[9] in 1231 20 marks out of the revenues of the church of Newport were assigned to provide wine for the convent.[10] Some of the monastic offices were destroyed in a fire which did much damage in the town in 1222.[11] Building continued steadily. The central tower was erected under the supervision of Elias the sacrist about 1222;[12] he also made the monks' stalls and constructed an aqueduct.[13] In 1232 Henry III granted 100 oaks in the forest of Dean for the work of the church;[14] in the following year he gave ten,[15] and in 1234 he allowed the abbot to have a horse going to the forest to fetch dead wood to his mill at Rodley, to melt lead for the roof of the church of the monastery, every day from the Feast of the Purification until three weeks after Easter.[16] In 1227 the Lady chapel, which had been built and endowed by a benefactor named Ralph de Wilington, was completed.[17] The church was

dedicated in 1239 by Walter Cantilupe, bishop of Worcester.[18]

In 1242 the vaulting of the nave, which, possibly from poverty, had been undertaken by the monks themselves, was finished.[19] The south-west tower was begun immediately and completed within a few years.[20]

Yet there are indications of mismanagement and lack of order. In 1239 the convent vainly attempted to deny the right of visitation to the bishop of Worcester,[21] and when Walter Cantilupe exercised that right in 1242 he removed the prior and other obedientiars from office.[22] Under the rule of John de Felda (1243–63) the monastery became heavily in debt. The exactions of both crown and papacy were felt as a very serious burden by most of the religious houses during those years, but building and the acquisition of land were probably responsible for financial difficulties. In 1246 the old frater was pulled down and a new one was begun.[23] Five years later the house owed 3,000 marks, and the abbot and convent were in such straits that they appealed to Bishop Cantilupe for help,[24] and he forbade the reception and entertainment of guests. Nevertheless in 1260 the abbot purchased from Laurence de Chandos 55 acres of arable land in Brockworth, 40 acres of meadow, and Buckholt Wood, covering 300 acres.[25] John de Felda's successor, Reginald de Homme, found a debt of 1500 marks in 1263.[26] In 1271 John de Breton, bishop of Hereford, allowed the abbot and convent to appropriate the church of Great Cowarne,[27] but the abbot's difficulties were so great that in 1272 he appealed to the crown. On 24 January, 1273, until the king should arrive in England, Reginald de Akele was given the custody of the monastery, which was reported to be decayed.[28] As was usual in such commissions he doubtless received the whole of the revenues, made provision for the abbot and convent and such servants as were necessary, and used the remainder to pay off the debts. However, on the accession of John de Gamages in 1284 the house was again in debt to the amount of 1,000 marks.[29]

The most interesting event in the abbacy of Reginald de Homme was the foundation in 1283 of a college at Oxford for monks of Gloucester by John Giffard, lord of Brimpsfield.[30] It bore the name of Gloucester Hall, but within a few years other Benedictine monasteries began

---

[1] Giles, op. cit.; *Hist. et Cart. Glouc.* (Rolls Ser.), i, 18.

[2] Wharton, *Angl. Sacr.* ii, 428.

[3] *Hist. et Cart. Glouc.* (Rolls Ser.), i, 20, 21.

[4] Ibid. 23. [5] Ibid. 24.

[6] Ibid. [7] Ibid. 104.

[8] Chart. R. 11 Hen. III, pt. i, m. 11.

[9] *Hist. et Cart. Glouc.* (Rolls Ser.), i, 78.

[10] Ibid. 28. [11] Ibid. 26.

[12] Ibid. 25. [13] Ibid. 28.

[14] *Cal. of Close*, 16 Hen. III, m. 10.

[15] Ibid. 17 Hen. III, m. 15.

[16] Ibid. 18 Hen. III, m. 31.

[17] *Hist. et Cart. Glouc.* (Rolls Ser.), i, 27.

[18] Ibid. 28. [19] Ibid. 29.

[20] Ibid. 29, 30.

[21] *Ann. Mon.* (Rolls Ser.), iv, 430.

[22] Ibid. 433.

[23] *Hist. et Cart. Glouc.* (Rolls Ser.), i, 30.

[24] *Ann. Mon.* (Rolls Ser.), i, 146.

[25] *Hist. et Cart. Glouc.* (Rolls Ser.), i, 65.

[26] Ibid. 31. [27] Ibid.

[28] *Cal. of Pat.* 1 Edw. I, m. 18.

[29] *Hist. et Cart. Glouc.* (Rolls Ser.), i, 39.

[30] Ibid. 32.

to send students there and to have their own lodging within the college.[1] In 1298 William de Brok, a monk of Gloucester, was the first Benedictine to gain the degree of doctor in theology. The day of his inception, 11 June, was made the occason of a great gathering of Benedictines at the college.[2]

Fifty monks, including the priors of the cells, took part in the election of John de Gamages in 1284.[3] As prior, first of Ewenny,[4] and afterwards of St. Guthlac's, Hereford,[5] he had already gained some profitable experience of administration, and during the twenty-two years of his rule he effected many reforms. The life and management of the monastery satisfied even so stern a visitor as Giffard, bishop of Worcester, had shown himself to be elsewhere. The injunctions[6] sent in 1301 by Winchelsey, archbishop of Canterbury after his metropolitical visitation were in great part a confirmation, on the petition of the abbot and convent, of ordinances which they had made. In accordance with these, no one might henceforth become a monk, unless he were whole in body and mind, lettered and skilled in song, and of tried character. The abbot's household was strictly limited at home and when he went abroad, and he was not allowed to hold property of his own. The common seal could only be used in the presence of the greater or wiser part of the chapter. The duties of the chamberlain in providing clothes were carefully defined. No pensions or liveries might be granted except for the manifest use of the house and then only with the consent of the bishop of the diocese. No obedientiar might sell lands or grant corrodies, and thus burden his office, without the knowledge of the abbot and the consent of the chapter. Among the injunctions added by the archbishop was one for a strict yearly audit of the accounts of bailiffs of manors and of the obedientiars of the monastery. He limited the number of dogs kept for the chase, forbade the monks to play draughts, practise the use of the bow, or to enter alone any house in Gloucester or to wander about the countryside.

Owing to the abbot's watchful care, the manors were well stocked and profitable.[7] The number of sheep was increased to 10,000, and in one year 46 sacks of wool were sold, realizing probably over 550 marks.[8] More land was purchased in the manor of Upton, much building went on in the different manors, and included the abbot's chamber at Hartpury, the great granary at Frocester, and new houses at Upleadon.[9] Abbot John de Gamages' gifts to the church included plate and vestments, and an altar in honour of St. Paul was dedicated in 1306.[10] Among the books which de Gamages added to the library was a 'Legenda Sanctorum' and a cartulary.[11] It was during his rule that Robert of Gloucester compiled a chronicle in English verse of over 12,000 lines.[12] He wrote the praises of England as the best of all lands,[13] and desired that English should be spoken by great folk as well as by low-born men.[14] Abbot John de Gamages remembered the loss and damage when the escheators held the lands of the house in the vacancy before his accession,[15] and in 1306 he obtained from Edward I a concession to the prior and convent to retain the custody of the monastery lands during each successive voidance on condition that they rendered 200 marks for four months, and if it lasted longer, a further payment at the same rate.[16]

The first dispute with the prior of Worcester, who claimed the right of visitation of the diocese during a vacancy of the see, took place during the abbacy of John de Gamages. On 15 March, 1302, the prior appeared before the gates of the monastery and was refused admittance,[17] because the house had been visited twice within a year by Bishop Giffard and Archbishop Winchelsey. The prior excommunicated the abbot and convent.[18] They at once appealed to Winchelsey, archbishop of Canterbury, against the sentence, and the prior petitioned for the preservation of his lawful jurisdiction. The prior cited the abbot to appear before him on 21 March, 1302, in the parish church of Winchcombe, but as he did not come he was declared contumacious. However, the official of the archbishop intervened, inhibited the prior from taking any further proceedings, and summoned him to appear before the Court of Arches. In July he was compelled to absolve the abbot and convent from the sentence of excommunication.

The quarrel was renewed during the next vacancy of the see.[19] On 20 March, 1308, the prior of Worcester wrote to inform Abbot Thoky that he should visit Gloucester on the vigil of Palm Sunday. The abbot refused to admit the prior, and the controversy continued till 1309, when Winchelsey proposed to arbitrate, and both parties consented. His decision was that the priors of Worcester had had, and ought to have,

---

[1] *Brist. and Glouc. Arch. Soc. Trans.* xvi, 106.
[2] *Hist. et Cart. Glouc.* (Rolls Ser.), i, 34.
[3] Ibid. iii, 26.   [4] Ibid. i, 39.
[5] Ibid. iii, 22.   [6] Ibid. lxxxiv–xcii.
[7] Ibid. i, 39.
[8] cf. Cunningham, *Growth of English Industry and Commerce,* i, 640 (ed. 1905).

[9] *Hist. et Cart. Glouc.* i, 40 (Rolls Ser.).
[10] *Worc. Epis. Reg.* Gainsborough, fol. 11.
[11] *Hist. et Cart. Glouc.* i, 40 (Rolls Ser.).
[12] *Chronicle of Robert of Gloucester* (Rolls Ser.). It is probable, though not absolutely certain, that he was a monk of Gloucester, cf. i, v–vii, xii–xiv.
[13] Ibid. i, 1–3.   [14] Ibid. ii, 544.
[15] Ibid i, 36.
[16] *Cal. of Pat.* 34 Edw. I, m. 13.
[17] *Ann. Mon.* (Rolls Ser.), iv, 551.
[18] *Worc. Reg. Sede Vac.* (Worc. Hist. Soc.), 11, 62.
[19] Ibid. 122–5.

the right of visiting the monastery of St. Peter at Gloucester. In spite of this award, the abbot and convent offered resistance at the next vacancy, and in December, 1313, Thoky and eleven of the great officers were excommunicated.[1] However, in 1317 the prior of Worcester's claims were admitted,[2] and no further controversy was raised during later vacancies.

The most interesting feature of the history of the monastery throughout the fourteenth century is the continuance of the building, which only falls within the scope of this article in so far as it throws light on the financial position of the house. Abbot Thoky continued the policy of his predecessors, and of him, too, the chronicler wrote: 'He obtained many good things in building and other ornaments' for the church.[3] On the feast of the Epiphany, 1300, a fire which began in a timbered house in the great court spread to the small bell-tower, the great camera, and the cloister.[4] The dorter suffered some damage; in 1303 it was pulled down to build a new one, which was not finished till 1313.[5] About 1318 the south aisle was rebuilt at great cost.[6] It was most probably in aid of the expenses that, in 1318, the abbot and convent sought to obtain from Cobham, bishop of Worcester, the appropriation of the church of South Cerney, urging that they were oppressed by grievous burdens, and that ruin threatened the fabric of their church.[7] The bishop ordered an inquisition.[8] The administration of the house was known to be unsatisfactory, and after the visitation, during the vacancy of the see in 1317, the prior of Worcester issued letters of absolution to Abbot Thoky, who was found to have transgressed certain rules, and especially the injunctions of Robert Winchelsey, archbishop of Canterbury.[9] On 18 March, 1318, Bishop Cobham wrote to remind the abbot that he had already bidden him to desist from wasting the goods of the house, and to compel others to refrain also.[10] Nevertheless, the abbot retained Walter de la Hurst as cellarer, who had already entirely cut down the woods of Littleton and Linkenholt in Hampshire, and was now felling those of Hope Mansel and Birdwood in Herefordshire. There can be no doubt that the maintenance of lavish hospitality was a serious drain on the finances of the house, and it would be felt chiefly by the office of the cellarer. However, in 1323 the bishop was satisfied, and effected the appropriation of South Cerney.[11] A

new and important source of revenue was obtained in 1327. After the murder of Edward II at Berkeley Castle, the abbots of Bristol, Kingswood, and Malmesbury feared the vengeance of Roger Mortimer and Queen Isabella if they gave the king burial in any one of their churches.[12] Edward II was well known to Abbot Thoky, who had entertained him sumptuously at Gloucester, and he sent an escort to Berkeley to bring the body of the king to Gloucester, where it was buried with great honour near the high altar on the north side of the choir. It is somewhat strange, after the misgovernance of the king and the general unrest throughout the country during his reign, that his tomb became immediately an object of pilgrimage. According to the chronicler, the crowds which flocked thither were so great that the town of Gloucester could scarcely contain them.[13] Moreover, the offerings were so numerous and costly that the new work in the south transept was completed in 1335. The offerings at the tomb also paid for the vaulting of the choir in the time of Adam of Staunton.[14] In consideration of the great expenses incurred at the funeral of his father, Edward III granted many privileges to the monastery. In 1328 he diminished the payment to the crown during each voidance of the abbey, fixing it at the rate of £100 a year.[15] At the same time he also granted a licence to appropriate the churches of Chipping Norton, Cam, and Wyrardisbury.[16] These were not effected for some time, and in 1345, in exchange for the advowson of Wyrardisbury, Edward III granted the manor of King's Barton by Gloucester, the weir of Minsterworth, and half the weir of Duneye at a fee farm rent of £48 a year.[17] In 1336 he granted the hundred of Dodeston for a fee farm rent of £12 a year.[18]

The manor of Standish, which had been given to St. Peter's by Bernulph, king of the Mercians, when he founded a college of secular priests,[19] had from an early date been assigned to charity. In 1202 Mauger, bishop of Worcester, made an ordinance that it should be restored to the use of the poor, except in case of great necessity, and that the revenues should be administered for them by the almoner.[20] In 1301 Winchelsey, archbishop of Canterbury, issued an injunction that the poor should not be defrauded of the profits of the manor.[21] In 1346 Wulstan de Bransford was compelled to intervene again on their behalf.[22] In 1535, according to his ordinance, as much as £92 was distributed

[1] *Worc. Reg. Sede Vac.* (Worc. Hist. Soc.), 145.
[2] Ibid. 183.
[3] *Hist. et Cart. Glouc.* (Rolls Ser.), 41.
[4] Ibid. 35.   [5] Ibid. 41.   [6] Ibid. 44.
[7] Worc. Epis. Reg. Cobham, fol. 56.
[8] Ibid.
[9] *Worc. Reg. Sede Vac.* (Worc. Hist. Soc.), 188.
[10] Worc. Epis. Reg. Cobham, fol. 56.
[11] Reg. Froucester A. No. liii (MSS. of Dean and Chapter of Glouc.).

[12] *Hist. et Cart. Glouc.* (Rolls Ser.), i, 44, 45.
[13] Ibid. 46.   [14] Ibid. 47.
[15] *Cal. of Pat.* 2 Edw. III, pt. i, m. 25.
[16] Ibid.
[17] Ibid. 1 Ric. II, pt. ii, m. 23.
[18] Ibid.   [19] Dugdale, *Mon.* i, 563.
[20] Worc. Epis. Reg. Bransford, fol. 112 d.
[21] *Hist. et Cart. Glouc.* (Rolls Ser.), i, lxxxviii.
[22] Worc. Epis. Reg. Bransford, fol. 112 d.

to the poor from the issues of the manor of Standish,[1] over and above other regular alms.

It is not easy to discover the mortality from the Black Death. In 1339 the number of the monks was forty-six,[2] in 1351 it was only thirty-six,[3] but during the abbacy of John Boyfield (1377–81) there were fifty-four monks,[4] so the numbers suffered no permanent diminution. The register of Thoresby, bishop of Worcester, bears witness to serious internal discord in 1350. The custom, or, as the bishop termed it, corruption, had grown up of allowing the monks so much a year for their food and clothes.[5] In 1350 Abbot Staunton experienced some difficulty in carrying on the administration of the house, the revenues being seriously diminished. Accordingly he abolished this custom, and provided the food and clothing. Although his object was evidently to economize, for he had been obliged to borrow money, the monks complained to the bishop of his action as an infringement of their privileges. However, the abbot seems to have effected his purpose, for on his death in 1351 he left the house free of debt and with 1,000 marks in the treasury.[6]

During the abbacy of Thomas Horton between 1368 and 1374, the new work in the north transept was completed at a total cost of £581 0s. 2d., out of which the abbot contributed no less than £444 0s. 2d.[7] Further building was undertaken;[8] vestments, silver vessels, and candlesticks were among his gifts, and at his own cost he purchased the tenement of Le Wast near Lettrington, and defrayed the expenses of the appropriation of Cam, which, although sanctioned by Edward III in 1328, had not as yet been effected. It became more and more necessary to make out a good case to induce bishops to consent to the appropriation of churches by religious houses, and the petition of the abbot and convent to Brian, bishop of Worcester, was strongly worded.[9] They urged that their buildings within and without the monastery were ruinous and in need of costly repair; the property in Wales from which they derived the greater part of their food was in the hands of enemies; their lands were sterile and numbers of their sheep had died in the pestilence. These arguments found favour with the bishop and he allowed the appropriation of Cam. Abbot Horton proceeded to charge the revenues of Cam with a provision of cakes, wines, and a pittance of fruit for the keeping of his anniversary.[10]

In 1359 the abbot and convent were able to

withdraw their monks from the cell of Ewyas in Herefordshire, on the plea that its revenues no longer sufficed for the maintenance even of a prior.[11]

The revenues of the house, which under Abbot Boyfield (1377–81) were said to be greatly reduced through inundations, pestilences, and excessive hospitality, amounted to 1,700 marks a year.[12] There were at that time fifty-four monks besides the abbot and 200 servants. The most important event of his rule was the meeting of Parliament at Gloucester in 1378 from 22 October to 16 November.[13] Richard II and the court lodged in the abbeys of Gloucester and Tewkesbury. Parliament met in the great guest-hall of St. Peter's. The place was more like a fair than a house of religion, and games were played on the cloister garth. According to the chronicler Boyfield was a gentle, simple-minded man, and his enemies gave him little rest.[14] He engaged in a dispute with Wakefield, bishop of Worcester, who is said to have demanded a sum of money on the resignation of Abbot Horton, and to have defamed the convent at the papal curia. In spite of the grant by Edward III of a reduction in the sum due to the crown during a vacancy, in 1377 the escheator demanded 200 marks.[15] A lawsuit followed, but at length judgement was given in favour of the abbot and convent. It was probably in consequence of these troubles, that, when Abbot Walter Froucester succeeded in 1381, he found a debt of 8,000 florins,[16] but under his rule the monastery recovered its prosperity.[17] The cloisters which had been begun by Abbot Horton were completed, much rebuilding took place on the manors, and they were well stocked with cattle and sheep. He pursued a very deliberate policy of increasing the rental of the house by appropriating churches. Richard II and John of Gaunt supported the petition of the abbot and convent to Urban VI in which they asked to be allowed to appropriate the vicarage of St. Mary de Lode, and to serve the church by one of their own number or a secular clerk removable at will.[18] They urged that 1,700 marks a year was not sufficient to maintain forty-four monks and 200 servants, and to meet other charges. After an inquiry which Urban VI directed the abbot of Winchcombe to hold, the appropriation was effected. On 30 June, 1391 he also consented to the appropriation of the parish church of Chipping Norton, which was worth 70 marks a year.[19] It was urged that the convent was

---

[1] *Valor Eccles.* (Rec. Com.), ii, 411.
[2] *Worc. Reg. Sede Vac.* (Worc. Hist. Soc.), 281.
[3] Fosbrooke, *History of Gloucester* (ed. 1819), 175.
[4] Ibid.
[5] Worc. Epis. Reg. Thoresby, fol. 9, 24, 24 d.
[6] *Hist. et Cart. Glouc.* (Rolls Ser.), i, 48.
[7] Ibid. 50.   [8] Ibid. 49–51.
[9] Worc. Epis. Reg. Brian, fol. 36.
[10] *Hist. et Cart. Glouc.* (Rolls Ser.), i, 51.

[11] Reg. Froucester A, No. xc (MSS. of Dean and Chapter of Glouc.).
[12] Fosbrooke, *History of Gloucester*, 175.
[13] *Hist. et Cart. Glouc.* (Rolls Ser.), i, 52–4.
[14] Ibid. 52.   [15] Ibid. iii, xxv, xxvi.
[16] Ibid. i, 57.   [17] Ibid. 55–8.
[18] *Cal. Papal L.* v, 599.
[19] Ibid. v, 599–600; cf. Linc. Epis. Reg. Buckingham Mem. fol. 443 d.

obliged to maintain three or four monks at Gloucester Hall in Oxford, and furnish them each with 15 marks a year, which they then had difficulty in doing.[1] On 30 April, 1391, Richard II granted the advowson of the church of Holy Trinity, Gloucester, with the chapel of St. Mary, Grasslane, to the abbot and convent.[2] According to the petition to Boniface IX, the revenues of the convent had then reached 2,000 marks.[3] However, owing to representations which were made to him in 1402 he insisted that vicarages should be created.[4] Boniface IX also granted to Walter Froucester the privileges of a mitred abbot.[5] During his rule the muniments of the house, which were kept in the treasury,[6] appear to have been set in order. It was probably by his wish and influence that one of the monks compiled the chronicle which briefly relates the lives and good deeds of the abbots, concluding with Walter Froucester.[7] Several registers were compiled by him, and of these two have survived.[8] One of them contains a collection of royal charters and a series of documents referring to churches appropriated to the monastery.[9] The other, which was compiled in 1393, contains documents arranged in distinct sections, concerning the property of ten of the officers of the house, viz. : of the sacrist, almoner, hostiller, sub-almoner, master of the works, chamberlain, masters of the frater, the farmery, and Lady Chapel, and precentor.[10] The office of master of the works existed under Abbot Henry Foliot (1228–43),[11] it was perhaps created by him after the death of Elias, the sacrist, in 1237.[12] A register of the property of the common fund of the convent, which was administered by treasurers or receivers,[13] seems also to have been compiled at this time.[14] The other officers of the house, who are known to have held property[15] are the prior, kitchener, custos or master of the churches, and master or monk of the town. A document which may probably be assigned to the first half of the fourteenth century shows the relative value of the property held by each of these officers at a time when the total revenue

of the monastery amounted to £1,623 16s. 4d.[16] It is interesting to note that at Gloucester the common fund was large, its income being nearly £830. The abbot's personal income was only £10. In view of the great expenditure of Abbot Horton, it may perhaps be concluded that he appropriated the offerings at the tomb of Edward II to his office, or that he got a larger share of the common fund. The separate income of the abbot, though usual in Benedictine houses, was contrary to the injunction of Winchelsey, archbishop of Canterbury of 1301.

The fifteenth century is almost barren of interest save in the continuance of the building. The west front was the work of Abbot Morwent (1420–37)[17] the rebuilding of the central tower was begun by Abbot Sebroke (1450–7)[18] and finished after his death by a monk named Tully. The Lady chapel was built during the rule of Richard Hauley (1457–72) and William Farley (1472–98).[19] In 1428 the cell of Kilpeck was united to the mother house by Thomas Spofford, bishop of Hereford.[20] When Thomas Polton, bishop of Worcester, visited the monastery early in 1429 he was extremely dissatisfied with its condition ; pressure of other business apparently compelled him to depart in some haste, and he appointed a commissioner to conclude his work.[21] Abbot Boulers (1437–50) was a shrewd man of affairs and was sent on an embassy to Rome in 1449, when the convent allowed him £400 for his expenses.[22] In 1450 he was seized by Richard, duke of York, and imprisoned for a time in Ludlow Castle. In that year he was promoted to the bishopric of Hereford ; in 1453 he was transferred to Lichfield, and shortly before his death in 1459 he willed his books to the library at Gloucester. In 1484 Richard III granted in mortmain to Abbot Farley £20 a year, the reduced fee farm payable by the burgesses of Gloucester.[23]

At the elections of the Abbots Braunche and Newton, there were hot disputes in the monastery. Matters reached such a pass that in 1500, and again in 1510, the king issued a mandate to the prior to maintain order.[24] In 1510 there were forty-eight monks in the house, two who were scholars at Oxford, and fifteen who were at the four cells.[25] All these assembled to elect an abbot, and the choice of the majority fell on John Newton, a bachelor of divinity, then prior

[1] *Cal. Papal L.* v, 599–600.
[2] *Cal. of Pat.* 14 Rich. II, pt. 2, m. 17.
[3] *Cal. Papal L.* v, 600.
[4] Ibid. 601.
[5] *Hist. et Cart Glouc.* (Rolls Ser.) i, 56.
[6] Ibid. iii, 106. [7] Ibid. i, 1–58.
[8] Reg. Froucester A. and B. (MSS. of Dean and Chapter of Glouc.).
[9] Ibid. A. [10] Ibid. B.
[11] Ibid. Registrum Magistri Operis, fol. 3 *v*, 6.
[12] *Hist. et Cart. Glouc.* (Rolls Ser.), i, 28.
[13] Ibid. iii, 105.
[14] An index, as far as Brompton, of the manors belonging to the common fund of the monastery, is to be found on fol. 1 of Froucester A. Brompton occurred on fol. 16, and it may be concluded that the index ends abruptly, because the scribe discovered that he was entering it in the wrong volume.
[15] *Hist. et Cart. Glouc.* (Rolls Ser.), 232, 233.

[16] Ibid. iii, 233, 234.
[17] Fosbrooke, *History of Gloucester*, 177.
[18] Ibid. 178. [19] Ibid. 179.
[20] Heref. Epis. Reg. Spofford, i, fols. 113–4 *d.*
[21] Worc. Epis. Reg. Pulton, fol. 59 *d.*
[22] Fosbrooke, op. cit. 177–8.
[23] *Cal. of Pat.* 1 Ric. III, pt. iv. m. 24.
[24] Fosbrooke, op. cit. 178 ; *Hist. et Cart. Glouc.* (Rolls Ser.), iii, p. xxxv.
[25] *Hist. et Cart. Glouc.* (Rolls Ser.), iii, pp. xxxii–xxxiv.

of St. Guthlac's, Hereford, but sixteen voted for John Huntley, the cellarer, and appealed to the bishop of Worcester. However, Newton was declared elected. On his death four years later William Malvern or Parker, also an Oxford scholar, who had taken the degree of bachelor of divinity, was peacefully chosen.[1] The registers of the last three abbots have survived,[2] and relate chiefly to the granting of leases and presentations to livings. The manumission of bondmen occurs not infrequently, and corrodies were granted to faithful servants. In 1507 a doctor entered into a contract to live in the monastery and give his services ; he was allowed to go away and see his friends for a week in each quarter.[3] In 1515 an annuity was granted to John Tucke, a bachelor of arts, in exchange for his services as master of the grammar school and of the song school.[4] He was appointed to instruct in grammar the younger monks, thirteen boys of the almonry, and five or six boys who 'were apt in learning to sing.' A special building in the monastery was set apart and known as the schoolhouse in or before 1378.[5]

In 1516 Abbot Parker made a fresh provision for the distribution of a portion of the alms, which were charged on the manor of Standish. In accordance with the ordinance made by Bishop Wulstan de Bransford in 1346 it was usual every year to give away corn, gowns, and money within the monastery. These occasions were marked by much unseemly behaviour, ' brawling, swearing, blaspheming, and fighting,' ' sick and unthrifty persons' resorted thither to the great disquiet of the monastery.[6] As a remedy the abbot and chapter founded a fraternity of the Holy Cross of thirteen poor and honest men to be called Peter's men, who were to be supported chiefly out of the alms from Standish. They were to be chosen from among the fathers and brethren of the monks, servants who had spent their youth in true service to the house, or from impoverished and decayed tenants, preferably those of Standish.

The acknowledgement of the royal supremacy was signed by the abbot and thirty-five monks, 31 August, 1534.[7] In 1538 Henry VIII sent an imperative request to the abbot and convent to recall the prior and monks from the cell of Stanley St. Leonard and grant a lease thereof to Sir William Kingston. They had no choice

but to comply.[8] In 1539 Abbot Malvern died.[9] The monasteries were being surrendered everywhere. On 9 June, 1539, the prior, Gabriel Morton, wrote in the name of the convent to notify the abbot's death to Cromwell and to ask how to proceed in petitioning for a new election.[10] No reply seems to have been vouchsafed. On 2 January, 1540, the monastery with its cells was surrendered,[11] and the prior was discharged with a pension of £20. The receiver had the same amount, and twelve other monks had pensions varying from £10 to £5.[12] Other monks and some of the servants of the house who were left at the monastery under the charge of Thomas Bisley, late prior of St. Guthlac's until a scheme should be framed for a bishopric, also received pensions.[13]

The clear yearly value of the property of the monastery in 1535 amounted to £1,430 4s. 3d., and including the four cells of Stanley St. Leonard, Ewenny, St. Guthlac's, Hereford, and Bromfield, £1,846 5s. 9d.[14]

The possessions of the monastery included rents and tenements in Gloucester of the value of over £150 a year, the manors of Tuffley, Hartpury, Maisemore, Highnam, Droiscote, a third of Lassington, Abload, Barnwood, Brookthorpe, and Harescombe, Abbot's Barton, Matson, Wotton, Longford, Upton, Preston, King's Barton, the hundred of Dodeston, the manors of Boxwell and Leighterton, Frocester, Rudge and Farley, Upleadon and Highleadon, Cubberley, the borough and manor of Northleach and Eastington, the manors of Aldsworth, Coln Rogers, Coln St. Aldwyn, Eastleach, Ampney St. Peter, Duntisbourne, Buckland and Staverton, Hinton, Clifford, Standish, Churcham, Rudford, and Rodley in Gloucestershire ; in Hampshire the manors of Linkenholt and Littleton ; in Herefordshire of Hope Mansel, Brompton, Monkhide, Ullingswick, Dewchurch and Kilpeck ; in Glamorganshire of Tregoff ; and the rectories of St. Mary de Lode, Holy Trinity with the chapel of Grasslane in Gloucester, Hartpury, Maisemore, Barnwood, Frocester, Northleach, Coln St. Aldwyn, Kempsford, South Cerney, Standish, Churcham, Cowarne, Tregoff, Glasbury and Devennock, Newport

---

[1] *Hist. et Cart. Glouc.* (Rolls Ser.), iii, pp. xlviii, xlix.

[2] Registers of Braunche, Newton and Parker (2 vols.). (MSS. of Dean and Chapter of Glouc.)

[3] Reg. Braunche, fol. 145.

[4] Reg. Parker, i. fol. 24 ; *Hist. et Cart. Glouc.* (Rolls Ser.), iii, 290 ; cf. *Valor Eccles.* (Rec. Com.), ii, 411.

[5] *Hist. et Cart. Glouc.* i, 53 (Rolls Ser.).

[6] Ibid. iii, lxxvi–lxxxix.

[7] Ibid. l–liii.

[8] Reg. Parker, ii. fol. 163. (MSS. of Dean and Chapter of Glouc.)

[9] *L. and P. Hen. VIII*, xiv, pt. i, No. 1096. The belief that Abbot Parker refused to surrender his house and therefore lost his pension is first found in Brown Willis. Cf. Dugdale, *Mon.* i, 536. Cf. *Hist. et Cart. Glouc.* (Rolls Ser.), iii, l–liii. It has also given rise to the theory that Abbot Parker's body was not buried in his tomb in the choir.

[10] Ibid.

[11] Ibid. xv, No. 139 iv.

[12] *Hist. et Cart. Glouc.* (Rolls Ser.), iii, p. liv.

[13] *L. and P. Hen. VIII*, xv, No. 139, iv ; Aug. Off. Bk. 494, fol. 93.

[14] *Valor Eccles.* (Rec. Com.), ii, 422.

and Chipping Norton, besides pensions and charges.[1]

ABBOTS OF GLOUCESTER.[2]

Edric, 1022
Wilstan, 1058
Serlo, 1072
Peter, 1104
William Godemon, 1113
Walter de Lacy, 1130
Gilbert Folliot, 1139
Hamelin, 1148
Thomas, 1179
Henry Blunt, 1205
Thomas of Bredon, 1223
Henry Foliot, 1228
John de Felda, 1243
Reginald de Homme, 1263
John de Gamages, 1284
John Thoky, 1306
John Wygmore, 1328
Adam of Staunton, 1337
Thomas Horton, 1351
John Boyfeld, 1377
Walter Froucester, 1381
Hugh of Morton, 1412
John Morwent, 1420
Reginald Boulers, 1437
Thomas Sebroke, 1450
Richard Hauley, 1457
William Farley, 1472
John Malvern, 1498
Thomas Braunche, 1500
John Newton, 1510
William Parker or Malvern, 1514

DEANS OF GLOUCESTER [3]

William Jennings, prior of St. Oswald's, Gloucester, 1541
John Man, warden of Merton College, Oxford, 1566
Thomas Cowper, 1569
Lawrence Humphrey, 1571
Anthony Rudd, 1585
Griffith Lewis, 1594
Thomas Moreton, 1607
Richard Field, 1609
William Laud, 1616
Richard Senhouse, 1621
Thomas Winniffe, 1624
George Warburton, 1631
Accepted Frewen, 1631
William Brough, 1643
Thomas Vyner, 1671
Robert Frampton, 1673
Thomas Marshall, 1681

William Jane, 1685
Knightly Chetwood, 1707
John Waugh, 1720
John Frankland, 1723
Peter Allix, 1729
Daniel Newcombe, 1730
Josiah Tucker, 1758
John Luxmoore, 1800
John Plumbtree, 1808
Edward Rice, 1825
Henry Law, 1862
H. D. M. Spence, 1886

A seal of the fifteenth century represents St. Peter seated in a carved gothic niche with a crocketed canopy and tabernacle work at the sides ; on his head a triple crown, in his right hand a crozier, in the left two keys ; in base a shield of arms, two keys in saltire, wards upwards, over all a sword of St. Paul in pale, hilt downwards.[4] The legend is :—

SIGILLUM · COMMUNE · MON. . . . . SANCTI ·
PETRI · GLOUCESTRIE.

The private seal of Abbot Staunton represents the abbot standing on a carved corbel in a niche ; in his right hand a pastoral staff, in his left a book.[5]

2. THE ABBEY OF TEWKESBURY

According to the chronicle of Tewkesbury, Oddo and Dodo, two Saxon lords who lived during the reign of three Mercian kings, Ethelred, Kenred, and Ethelbald, founded the first monastery at Tewkesbury.[6] Modern research has shown that Oddo lived at least 300 years[7] after Dodo. It may be concluded that Dodo was the founder of Tewkesbury. In 715 he began to build a church in honour of the Virgin at a place which was said to have received its name from Theokus, a hermit, who was reputed to have dwelt there about 655. The endowment consisted of Stanway and other lands. In the course of the next 200 years the monastery was plundered and burnt on divers occasions. About the year 800 a Mercian lord named Hugh is said to have been a patron of the house ; he buried Brictric, king of Wessex, within the church and was himself laid to rest there in 812. About 980 Aylward Meaw founded and endowed a monastery at Cranbourne in Dorset for monks who should keep the strict rule of St. Benedict, and he made the priory of Tewkesbury a cell to that house.

At the Norman Conquest the lands of Aylward's grandson, Brictric, were confiscated, and

---

[1] *Valor Eccles.* (Rec. Com.), ii. 409–18.
[2] The list is taken from Dugdale, *Mon.* i, 531–6, which has been carefully checked.
[3] The deans of Gloucester up to 1825 are taken from Le Neve, *Fasti Ecclesiae Anglic.* corrected by T. Duffus Hardy.

[4] Birch, *Catalogue of Seals in British Museum*, i, 566.
[5] Ibid. 567.
[6] Dugdale, *Mon.* ii, 59.
[7] *Brist. and Glouc. Arch. Soc. Trans.* xxv, 78 ; Blunt, *Tewkesbury Abbey*, 15–17.

the patronage of Cranbourne and Tewkesbury passed to the crown.[1] About 1087, by the advice of Lanfranc, archbishop of Canterbury, and Osmund, bishop of Salisbury, William Rufus appointed Gerald, a Norman monk of Winchester, as abbot of Cranbourne. In the same year he gave the honour of Gloucester to Robert Fitzhamon, a Norman lord. The possessions of the priory of Tewkesbury consisted of lands at Stanway, Toddington, Lemington, Great Washbourn, Fiddington, Natton, and Stanley Pontlarge.[2] It has been conjectured that some of these possessions were the gift of Duke Oddo, who built the Saxon chapel at Deerhurst in 1056, and was a great benefactor of the church.[3] Under the influence of his wife Sibilla, Robert Fitzhamon began to build a new church and monastic offices at Tewkesbury, and he greatly increased the endowment.[4] In 1102, Gerald, abbot of Cranbourne, and his monks entered the new monastery at Tewkesbury, leaving only a prior and two monks at Cranbourne, which became a dependent cell.[5] In 1105, with the advice and consent of Robert Fitzhamon, Abbot Gerald divided the possessions of the house and endowed the offices of cellarer, chamberlain, sacrist, precentor, and almoner.[6] There were at that time fifty-seven monks,[7] these with the prior of Cranbourne and his two brethren making sixty, probably the full complement. The gift of the manor of Ampney Crucis was confirmed in 1101.[8] In 1106 Henry I granted a charter confirming the possessions of the monastery, which already included many churches of which a number were afterwards appropriated.[9] Tewkesbury profited by the conquests of Norman lords in Wales and received before 1103, amongst other benefices, the parish church of St. Mary of Cardiff with eight dependent chapels.[10]

In 1109 Abbot Gerald resigned and returned to Winchester.[11] In 1123 the church was dedicated by Theulf, bishop of Worcester.[12] About 1137, Robert, earl of Gloucester, founded the priory of St. James at Bristol as a dependent cell to Tewkesbury,[13] and he is also said to have been the founder of the cell at Cardiff.[14] Learning and literature probably flourished under Abbot Alan (1186–1202), who had been prior of Canterbury. He himself wrote one of the lives of St. Thomas of Canterbury and made a collection of his letters.[15] His successor, Walter, found the house in debt to the amount of 700 marks,[16] but was able to restore its finances to a flourishing condition.

Abbot Peter was engaged in a number of law-suits in defence of the rights of the house.[17] In 1221 owing to disturbances in Wales, he was obliged to recall the monks from the cell of Cardiff and let the priory on lease for some years.[18] The Irish lands at Dungarthan held of the gift of John, brought no profit and were sold for £80 to the bishop of Dublin in 1224.[19] There were several disputes with the bishops of Worcester.[20] In 1231, in virtue of a papal privilege of 1221,[21] several of the monks of Tewkesbury entered into possession of the vacant church of Fairford with the object of appropriating it for the monastery.[22] They were expelled by the nominee of Bishop William of Blois and the whole convent was excommunicated. Early in 1232 the abbot died and was buried within the church. The bishop ordered his body to be cast out as he was still under sentence of anathema,[23] and as the monks refused he again excommunicated them. He then attempted to hinder their right of freedom of election which they obtained from Hubert de Burgh as the guardian of Richard de Clare, the patron of the house.[24] On 1 May he absolved the convent,[25] and a week later the prior, Robert of Forthampton, was elected. He was an able and vigorous abbot, bent on maintaining the rights of the monastery against both episcopal and lay encroachments, and in developing its resources in all directions. There was no saint's shrine to which the report of miracles attracted pilgrims and their offerings, but Tewkesbury possessed a number of relics, and accordingly the feast of the Holy Relics was celebrated on 2 July, and a number of miracles are said to have occurred in 1232[26] and 1250.[27] At the second dedication of the church, 18 June, 1239, Walter Cantilupe, bishop of Worcester, granted an indulgence to those who visited it during the feast of the dedication and its octave and on the feast of the Relics.[28] He subjected the house to a very strict visitation in 1251[29] and again in 1253,[30] but on each occasion it was triumphantly recorded in the annals that he found nothing amiss.

[1] Dugdale, *Mon.* ii, 60.
[2] *Dom. Bk.* (Rec. Com.), 163*b*.
[3] *Brist. and Glouc. Arch. Soc. Trans.* xxv, 81.
[4] Dugdale, op. cit. ii, 60.
[5] *Ann. Mon.* (Rolls Ser.), i, 44 ; Dugdale, op. cit. ii, 60.
[6] Dugdale, op. cit. ii, 81.　　[7] Ibid.
[8] Ibid. 65.　　[9] Ibid. 66.　　[10] Ibid. 67.
[11] *Ann. Mon.* (Rolls Ser.), ii, 43.　　[12] Ibid. i, 45.
[13] Dugdale, op. cit. iv, 333 ; ii, 70.
[14] Ibid. iv, 632.

[15] Hardy, *Catalogue of Materials* (Rolls Ser.), ii, 322 ; *Materials for the Hist. of Thomas Becket* (Rolls Ser.), ii.
[16] *Ann. Mon.* (Rolls Ser.), i, 56.
[17] Ibid. 64, 65, 70.　　[18] Ibid. 65.　　[19] Ibid. 67.
[20] Dugdale, op. cit. ii, 79 ; *Cal. Papal L.* i, 95 ; *Ann. Mon.* i, 68.
[21] *Cal. Papal L.* i, 81.
[22] *Ann. Mon.* i, 82.
[23] Ibid. 83, 84.
[24] Dugdale, op. cit. ii, 81.　　[25] Ibid. 80.
[26] *Ann. Mon.* (Rolls Ser.), i, 84–6.
[27] Ibid. 141.　　[28] Ibid. 112.
[29] Ibid. 146.　　[30] Ibid. 152.

Between 1271 and 1276 the abbot and convent petitioned Gregory X for his support in effecting the appropriation of the church of Fairford. In addition to the usual plea of the heavy expense of hospitality, they urged that the nave was in so dangerous a condition that it could not be used for service, and that its repair would be very costly.[1] Gregory X granted the request.

The condition of the house was unsatisfactory when Godfrey Giffard visited it in 1279.[2] Extravagance and maladministration roused his indignation. He ordered that gluttony and drunkenness should cease; that the monks should eat to live and not live to eat; and that no drinking should take place except in the frater. The great obedientiars and other officers were bidden to fulfil their duties with more care.

Soon after the death of Giffard, which took place on 26 January, 1302, the prior of Worcester determined to exercise his rights of visitation in the diocese during a vacancy. On 13 March, 1302, he was refused admission at Tewkesbury,[3] because the monastery had been visited twice within a year.[4] The prior of Worcester at once excommunicated the abbot and nine chief officers of the house. They appealed to Robert Winchelsey, archbishop of Canterbury, against the sentence, and the prior wrote to the archbishop, asking him to preserve his lawful jurisdiction. The official of the archbishop inhibited the prior of Worcester from proceeding with the excommunication of the abbot and convent of Tewkesbury, and cited the prior to appear before the Court of Arches, and the sentence of excommunication was removed. No resistance was made to the visitation during the next vacancy in 1308.

In 1314 a licence was obtained from Edward II for the appropriation of the churches of Thornbury and Fairford.[5] Bishop Maidstone allowed the licence for Thornbury to take effect immediately, on the ground that, although the monastery was amply endowed by Gilbert de Clare, it was so much oppressed by misfortunes and the attacks of enemies, that speedy succour was needed.[6] There were outstanding debts, and a fire had wrought havoc among the monastic buildings. Indeed, the main interest of Tewkesbury in the fourteenth and fifteenth centuries is in the progress of the new building.

In 1332 the abbot and convent petitioned John XXII to urge the bishop of Worcester to act on the papal licence, which had been granted more than sixty years before, for the appropriation of Fairford,[7] and in 1333 Orlton consented.

In 1345 the abbot and convent were able, with the aid of Hugh Despenser, to appropriate the church of Llantrisant in the diocese of Llandaff.[8] Out of its revenues twenty marks were assigned for the keeping of his anniversary, and thirty marks for a pittance for the monks.[9] In 1347 the number of monks in the house was thirty-seven.[10]

When Henry Wakefield, bishop of Worcester, made a visitation in 1378, he found much to criticize.[11] No yearly statement showing the financial position of the house was made by the abbot to the chapter. Some of the obedientiars were respecters of persons, sparing some and unduly chastising others. The monks were ill-fed, the bread was poor and badly baked, the ale was weak and very new. Sick brethren in the farmery were neglected and had no doctor. The education of the younger monks was neglected. Relations and friends were badly served in the hostelry, neither vessels, napkins, nor towels were provided for their use; the office of hostiller was not filled, and the revenues of the church of Ampney Crucis, which had been appropriated for the purpose of hospitality, were diverted to other uses. The bell-tower was in a dangerous condition. The bishop ordered the abbot to produce the annual account without fail, to appoint a doctor immediately, and a competent teacher before Michaelmas; to remove indiscreet obedientiars and appoint others within a month, among them an honest and discreet hostiller, to see that everything was provided for the comfort of guests before 1 August. It was to be the abbot's duty to know that bread and ale of the quality and quantity formerly provided for the monks were baked and brewed by the servants, and as the monks used to get capons, chickens, or pigeons for supper, he was to see that their needs were supplied. The bishop bade the sacrist repair the bell-tower, so far as his means allowed, before the feast of St. Andrew. It had become customary for the monks once a year, on one of the occasions when they were bled, to withdraw to the Mythe for a change from Sunday to the following Friday. The bishop decided that the stay was too long, and said that the monks must content themselves with their wonted comforts at that time.

The Despensers and Beauchamps, who in turn succeeded to the honour of Gloucester, were, like the De Clares, generous patrons of the monastery, and some, at least, of the new building in the fourteenth and fifteenth centuries was at their expense. Henry VI granted the patronage of the alien priory of Goldcliff in Mon-

---

[1] Worc. Epis. Reg. Orlton, fol. 54 d.
[2] Worc. Epis. Reg. Giffard (Worc. Hist. Soc.), 104.
[3] Worc. Reg. Sede Vac. (Worc. Hist. Soc.), 62, 63.
[4] Ann. Mon. iv, 551.
[5] Cal. of Pat. 8 Edw. II, pt. i, m. 12.
[6] Worc. Epis. Reg. Maidstone, fol. 7 d.
[7] Ibid. Orlton, fol. 54 d.

[8] Cal. of Pat. 19 Edw. III, pt. ii, m. 1; cf. ibid. 17 Edw. III, pt. ii, m. 27.
[9] Dugdale, Mon. ii, 62.
[10] Worc. Epis. Reg. Bransford, fol. 137. Forty monks, including the priors of three cells, were present at the election of Thomas of Legh.
[11] Ibid. Wakefield, fol. 133.

mouthshire to Henry, earl of Warwick, with licence to appropriate it to Tewkesbury. In 1442, with the full approval of Eugenius IV, Goldcliff Priory was made a cell of Tewkesbury.[1] It was stated that the revenues of the monastery did not then exceed 2,000 marks, and the priory was worth £200 a year. The abbot and convent were bound to maintain a prior and two monks in priest's orders at Goldcliff. In 1445 the three monks of Tewkesbury were expelled from Goldcliff by the Welsh, but in 1447 they again took possession of it.[2] Their enjoyment of its revenues was short, for in 1450 the priory was granted by Henry VI to Eton College.[3] In 1462 Edward IV revoked the grant of Henry VI and restored Goldcliff Priory to Tewkesbury. However, in 1467, he again granted Goldcliff to Eton College, and compensated Tewkesbury by the gift of the alien priory of Deerhurst.[4] The condition of the grant was that the abbot and convent of Tewkesbury should maintain a prior and four monks at Deerhurst, and a secular priest to serve the parishioners as vicar. The union of Deerhurst with Tewkesbury was confirmed by Carpenter, bishop of Worcester, in 1469.[5]

In 1471 some of the fugitives from the battle of Tewkesbury fled to the church and were there slain by the pursuers. On 30 May the bishop of Down and Connor purified the sanctuary after its pollution by blood.[6] Among the dead who were buried by the monks was Prince Edward, the only son of Henry VI.

The appetite of the abbot and convent for the appropriation of churches was insatiable. Tarrant Monachorum in Dorsetshire had been appropriated before 1439,[7] Penmark in the diocese of Llandaff between 1420 and 1443, Sherston before 1471.[8] On the plea that the revenues of the Lady Chapel had declined in value, and that they desired to increase the splendour of the services therein, in 1470 the monks appropriated the church of Holy Trinity, Bristol, but two years later they consented to a revocation and received instead the church of Compton Parva.[9] However, there is evidence in 1494 that the convent was seriously embarrassed, for heavy legal expenses had been incurred in suits about both Goldcliff and Deerhurst.[10] The number of monks in the house in that year was thirty-three ;[11] a survey of their finances obliged them to seek an increase of their revenues, and a further appropriation of churches was the easiest

method. Fields, meadows, and rich pastures in their manors of Kingston and Wyke in Sussex had been swallowed up by the sea. Some of their lands in other parts of England were untilled and unoccupied, and they received £100 a year less on that account. In 1494 William Smith, bishop of Lincoln, allowed them to appropriate the church of Great Marlow, which they had attempted in 1242, when Robert Grosseteste rebuffed them. At the beginning of the sixteenth century they were confronted with further difficulties. The great bell-tower, the cloister, and other houses and buildings in the monastery were said to be in a ruinous condition ; some of their manor houses and barns were in the same plight. On account of insufficient revenues the number of monks and servants had been greatly diminished, and hospitality, a heavy burden, was not maintained as it should have been.[12] Accordingly, in 1500, the church of Taynton was appropriated, with the consent of William Smith, bishop of Lincoln,[13] and the church of Eastleach Turville, by the permission of the vicar-general of Silvester de Giglis, bishop of Worcester.[14] Five years later the church of Wotton-under-Edge in Gloucestershire was also appropriated.[15]

The clear value of the possessions of the monastery, including the cells of Deerhurst, St. James Bristol, and Cranbourne, amounted in 1535 to £1,598 10s. 3d.[16] The revenues of the great officers of the religious houses are but rarely indicated in the *Valor Ecclesiasticus*. At Tewkesbury they are set forth with admirable clearness. The lands and churches assigned in the ordinance of 1105 remained in the hands of the same officers. The abbot received £253 14s. 7¼d. He had acquired for his office several of the most profitable manors formerly belonging to the priory of Deerhurst, and all the five recently appropriated churches. It is clear that before the dissolution, as at Winchcombe, he also administered the revenues of the cellarer, which amounted to £842 18s. 11d., and thus had entire control over two-thirds of the income of the house.[17]

He seems to have acquired arbitrary power, for it is noted in the *Valor* that he had the right of appointing and removing all the officers of the house at his sole will and pleasure. The visitations of the vicars-general of the four Italian

[1] Dugdale, *Mon.* vii, 1021.
[2] Ibid. ii, 64.   [3] Ibid. vii, 1021.
[4] Ibid. iv, 664.
[5] Worc. Epis. Reg. Carpenter, ii, fols. 1–6.
[6] Massé, *Tewkesbury Abbey*, 14.
[7] Dugdale, op. cit. ii, 64 ; cf. *Cal. of Pat.* 7 Ric. II, pt. i, m. 44.
[8] Dugdale, op. cit. ii, 64.
[9] Worc. Epis. Reg. Carpenter, ii, fol. 7 d, 28.
[10] Linc. Epis. Reg. Wolsey and Atwater, fol. 61–65.
[11] Cant. Archiepis. Reg. Morton, fol. 169.

[12] Worc. Epis. Reg. Silvester de Giglis, fol. 128.
[13] Linc. Epis. Reg. Smith, fol. 37–52.
[14] Worc. Epis. Reg. Silvester de Giglis, fol. 128.
[15] Ibid. fol. 183.
[16] *Valor Eccles.* (Rec. Com.), ii, 471–86. The revenues of the cells of Deerhurst, St. James Bristol, and Cranbourne were valued respectively at £134 8s. 0¾d, £55 7s. 4d., £37 19s. 5d. The apparent decline in the value of the priory of Deerhurst is accounted for by the appropriation to the abbot of several of its manors.
[17] Ibid. 480–6.

bishops who held the see of Worcester from 1497 to 1535 appear to have been of a purely formal character, and the abbots therefore met with no interference. The household management was conducted on the generous if not extravagant scale of a great Benedictine monastery, and included maintenance and wages for 144 servants. The provision of spices, always an important item in monastic accounts, had been assigned to a special officer, the master of the spices, who had £47 13s. 11d. for that purpose. The kitchener received £32 13s. 1d., the master of the frater £1 4s. 4½d. The exercise of hospitality must have fallen to the abbot and cellarer, for the hostiller had only £3 5s. 2d., the clear proceeds from the church of Ampney Crucis. The almoner after setting aside £15 6s. 4d. in special alms, which included clothing for sixteen poor scholars, and provision for a number of boys who were clothed, fed, and educated at the expense of his office, had £35 13s. 4d. It would, however, be misleading to suppose that this sum represented the charity of the monastery, for fixed alms occur as a charge on the revenues of most of the other officers. The income of the chief prior was £9 9s. 8d. The chamberlain who furnished the clothes of the house and probably the liveries of many of the servants received £83 1s. 6d. The sacrist had £42 4s. 7d., the master of the Lady Chapel £12 3s. 1½d.

The monastery, including the three cells, was surrendered on 9 January, 1540.[1] It is probable that the number of monks then in the house was about thirty-seven; thirty-six were included in the pension list,[2] and of these a prior and two monks lived at each of the cells. John Wakeman, the abbot, received a pension of £266 13s. 4d., and drew it until September, 1541, when he was consecrated to the newly-founded see of Gloucester. The prior got £16 a year, the priors of the cells of Deerhurst and St. James, Bristol, £13 6s. 8d., the prior of Cranbourne and one other monk £10, two of them £8, another £7, and the remaining twenty-seven £6 13s. 4d. each. Wages were paid up to date to 144 servants.[3]

The possessions[4] of the monastery included the manor and borough of Tewkesbury, the manors of Coln St. Dennis, Compton Parva, Preston-upon-Stour, Alvescot, Welford, Washbourne, Prescot, Gotherington, Tredington, Fiddington, Oxenton, Walton Cardiff, Forthampton, Ampney Crucis, Hosebridge, Lemington, Church Stanway in Gloucestershire, the manor of Pull Court, a moiety of the manor of Queenhill, the manors of Bushley, Pirton, Ashton Keynes and Leigh, in Worcestershire, the manor of Burnet in Somerset, the manor of Taynton in Oxfordshire; in Dorsetshire the manors of Cranbourne, Chettle, Upwimborne, Boveridge with Estworth, Tarrant Monachorum; in Sussex the manors of Kingston and Wyke; in Devon the manors of Loosebeare and Midlande; rents in Gloucester, Cardiff and other places; and the rectories of Tewkesbury, Fiddington, Walton-Cardiff, Aston-upon-Carron, Southwick and Tredington, Compton Parva, Preston-upon-Stour, Washbourn, Forthampton, Thornbury, Ampney, Fairford, Eastleach, Wotton-under-Edge, Marshfield in Gloucestershire, Sherston and Aldington in Worcestershire, Taynton in Oxfordshire, Great Marlow and Chetelhampton in Buckinghamshire, St. Wenne and Crewenne in Cornwall, Tarrant Monachorum in Dorset, Kingston in Sussex, in Wales Llantwit, Llanblethian, Llantrisant, Penmark with the chapel of St. Donat and Cardiff, and tithes and pensions in a number of other churches in England and Wales, and the priories of Deerhurst, St. James Bristol, and Cranbourne.

ABBOTS[5] OF TEWKESBURY

Gerald, appointed by William Rufus
Robert, 1110, ob. 1123
Benedict, 1124
Roger, 1137
Fromund, 1162, ob. 1178
Robert, 1182
Alan,[6] 1187
Walter,[7] 1202
Hugh,[8] 1214, ob. 1215
Bernard elected but not consecrated
Peter, 1216
Robert III,[9] 1232
Thomas of Stoke, 1255
Richard of Norton, 1276
Thomas of Kempsey, 1282
John Coles, 1328
Thomas of Legh, 1347
Thomas of Chesterton, 1361
Thomas Parker, 1389
William of Bristol, 1420 or 1421
John of Abingdon,[10] 1444
John Galeys,[11] occurs 1453, ob. 1468
John Strensham, 1468
Richard Cheltenham, 1480
Henry Beeley, 1509, occurs 1529
John Walker, ob. 1531
John Wakeman, 1531

---

[1] L. and P. Hen. VIII, xv, No. 139, iv.
[2] Dugdale, op. cit. ii, 83.
[3] Ibid. 58.
[4] Valor Eccl. (Rec. Com.), ii, 471-86.

[5] The list is taken from Dugdale, Mon. ii, 53-6. It has been carefully checked, and additions are noted.
[6] Ann. Mon. Rolls Ser. i, 53.
[7] Ibid. i, 56, 57.
[8] Ibid. 61.   [9] Ibid. 83.
[10] Heref. Epis. Reg. Spofford, ii, fol. 4.
[11] B.M. MS. Cole, xxvii, p. 206. It has been suggested, with great probability, that John of Abingdon and John Galeys are identical.

A seal of the fifteenth century represents three heavily canopied niches; in the centre the Assumption of the Virgin, standing with hands uplifted in prayer, within an oval vesica of clouds, upheld by an angel above it; on the left St. Peter with nimbus, book and keys; on the right St. Paul with nimbus, sword and book, each saint slightly turned to the virgin; over the central canopy a smaller niche containing the Trinity; in base an angel holding in front a shield of arms, a cross engrailed supported by two lions couchant guardant addorsed.[1]

The legend is—

SIGILLVM . COMMVNE . EC . . . IE . . .
NCTE . MARIE . DE . TEVKESBVRY

3. THE ABBEY OF WINCHCOMBE

In 798 Cenwulf, king of the Mercians, began to build a great monastery at Winchcombe.[2] The church was dedicated in 811 with much splendour by Wulfred, archbishop of Canterbury, in the presence of Sired king of East Anglia, Cuthred king of Kent, thirteen bishops, ten ealdormen, and a great concourse of people.[3] When at the end of the fifteenth century, Abbot Richard Kidderminster began to write the history of the monastery, he could not gather any certain information as to the endowment provided by Cenwulf.[4] He believed that it consisted of lands at Sherborne, Bledington, Enstone, Honeybourne, Adelmington, Alne, Twyning, Charlton Abbots, Stanton, Snowshill, and Newton.[5]

In 821 Cenwulf died. Soon afterwards, according to the legend, his little son and successor, Kenelm, was murdered in a wood at Clent in Worcestershire, at the instigation of his ambitious sister, Cwenthryth.[6] In after ages it was said that a dove flew into St. Peter's at Rome and laid a letter written in English on the high altar. An Englishman took it, and read how the little king was slain, and his body lay hidden in the wood. The pope sent letters to the English kings to tell them of the deed. The body was found and taken to Winchcombe for burial. Thus St. Kenelm became the patron saint of the monastery.

During the next 150 years monasticism decayed greatly throughout England, and at Winchcombe, as in many other religious foundations, monks gave place to secular clerks.

In 969, during the Benedictine revival, Oswald, bishop of Worcester, compelled the secular clerks who were then dwelling at Winchcombe to withdraw.[7] In their place he put monks who should keep the strict rule of St. Benedict, as it was then observed at Fleury, and appointed Germanus, dean of Ramsey, as their abbot. On the death of King Edgar there was a revulsion of feeling in Mercia in favour of the secular priests who had been ousted, and in 975 the monks of Winchcombe were expelled, and returned to the monastery at Ramsey from which they had come.[8] It is probable that the monks were reinstated before many years had passed,[9] as in the reign of Edward the Confessor (1042–66) it had become one of the foremost Benedictine houses. On the death of Abbot Godwine in 1053, Aldred, bishop of Worcester, undertook to rule the monastery,[10] and it was in his hands until 17 July, 1054, when Edward the Confessor appointed one of his chaplains, by name Godric.[10] Winchcombe was within Harold's own earldom of Wessex, and William the Conqueror had reason to think that the monks were hostile to him. In or about 1068 he deposed Godric, and sent him as a prisoner to Gloucester, and afterwards put him under the charge of Athelwig, abbot of Evesham, a staunch supporter of the Norman rule.[11] William entrusted the monastery to the custody of Athelwig for the space of three years until he appointed Galandus, a Norman monk.[12]

The rule of Galandus was marked by a quickening of monastic life which everywhere attended the efforts of the vigorous Norman abbots, and at Winchcombe manifested itself more especially in a notable mission to Northumbria. Accompanied by two deacons from Evesham, Prior Aldwyn set out on foot, with an ass to carry his books, altar plate, and vestments.[13] With the aid of Walcher, bishop of Durham, they rebuilt the monasteries of Jarrow and Wearmouth, and gave a strong impulse to monastic revival in the north.

In 1087 the possessions of Winchcombe included, in addition to the endowment attributed to Cenwulf,[14] lands at Alderton, Frampton, Hidcote, and Windrush, making in all 109 hides, which were valued at £82.[15]

On 15 October, 1091, the church of Winchcombe was struck by lightning, and the tower rent in twain.[16] In 1151 the church and monastic buildings again suffered serious damage by fire,[17] books and charters being then destroyed.

---

[1] Birch, *Catalogue of Seals in the B.M.* i, 768.

[2] Dugdale, *Mon.* ii, 300.

[3] Ibid. 301.   [4] Ibid. 302.   [5] Ibid. 300.

[6] *Hist. of the Ch. of York* (Rolls Ser.), i, 435. *Chronicon abbatiae Rameseiensis* (Rolls Ser.), 42.

[7] Ibid. 72, 73. *Hist. of the Ch. of York* (Rolls Ser.), i, 443. *Flor. Wigorn* (Engl. Hist. Soc.), i, 144.

[8] Ealdorman Elfhere died in 983; under his son Elfric the persecution ceased. *Brist. and Glouc. Arch. Soc. Trans.* xviii, 222.

[9] *Flor. Wigorn.* (Engl. Hist. Soc.), i, 211.

[10] Ibid.

[11] Freeman, *Norman Conquest*, iv, 177.

[12] Ibid.; Dugdale, op. cit. ii, 302.

[13] Simeon of Durham, *Opera omnia* (Rolls Ser.), i, 108; ii, 201.

[14] Cf. supra.

[15] *Dom. Bk.* (Rec. Com.), 157, 165*b*, 239.

[16] MS. Cotton. Tiberius, E. 14, fol. 20*v*.

[17] Royce, *Landboc sive Registrum Monasterii de Winchelcumba*, i, 83.

ST. PETER'S ABBEY, GLOUCESTER

ST. PETER'S ABBEY, GLOUCESTER

TEWKESBURY ABBEY

LANTHONY PRIORY BY GLOUCESTER

GLOUCESTERSHIRE MONASTIC SEALS : PLATE I

In 1175 Abbot Henry obtained from Alexander III a bull confirming the lands and churches then held by the monastery, and at the same time restraining the abbots from alienating any of them without the consent of the chapter.[1] The pope also exempted the monks from payment of tithes on land newly brought into cultivation by them or at their expense, or on the young of their flocks and herds. In a general interdict he allowed them to hold services with closed doors and without ringing of bells. Prior Crispin, a man of pure and religious life, was elected by the monks in 1181.[2] His skill in worldly matters showed itself in the policy, continued by his successor, of buying up lands and rights.[3] He proposed to rebuild the cloisters, but died suddenly within a year.[4]

The name of Abbot Robert III (1194–1221) was gratefully remembered at Winchcombe. During his rule the new church was completed, and the building of the cloisters and monastic offices followed.[5]

In or about 1194 Henry de Soilli, bishop of Worcester, allowed the convent to draw a yearly pension of five marks from the church of Sherborne for the building and maintenance of their church.[6] In 1206, with the consent of the chapter, Abbot Robert set aside the tithes of Stanton and Snowshill for a fabric fund, decreeing that except at a time of famine and distress the endowment should not be diverted to any other purpose.[7] At a considerable cost he made an aqueduct by which water was carried in leaden pipes to the abbey from a spring at Hanwell.[8] He increased the revenues of the obedientiars,[9] and assigned certain rents in Gloucester to provide wine for the convent on St. Margaret's Day.[10] He instituted a solemn mass of the Virgin on the morrow of St. Kenelm, and 'because the labourer is worthy of his hire,' he decreed that all who took part in it should be present at a feast of geese and wine afterwards.[11] As a provision for charity he decreed that 100 poor should be feasted each year on the morrow of All Saints.[12] In or about 1200, at the heavy price of over £558, he obtained from William de Bethune the manors of Yanworth, Hazleton and Halling at a fee farm rent of £20 a year,[13] which was reduced in 1208 to £10.[14] In 1217 Daniel de Bethune remitted another £1, and gave the monastery the advowsons of the churches in

the three manors.[15] In or before 1251 the rent was remitted altogether.[16]

About 1224 the church of Sherborne was appropriated to the monastery for the use of hospitality.[17] It was probably in accordance with the constitution of the legate Otho,[18] that the abbey church was solemnly dedicated by Walter Cantilupe, bishop of Worcester, on 13 October, 1239.[19]

The abbacy of John Yanworth (1247–82) was marked by somewhat reckless expenditure. The acquisition of land was pursued at all costs. About 1250 the manor of Dry Marston was purchased from the prior and convent of Coventry for the large sum of 1,130 marks and a yearly rent of £1.[20] In 1251 rights of free warren were granted by Henry III in the demesne lands of nineteen manors belonging to the convent.[21] Another of the abbot's early acts was to petition Alexander IV to allow him to cancel long leases granted by his predecessors, which he urged were greatly to the detriment of his house.[22] On 4 January, 1254, Alexander IV sent a mandate to Robert, abbot of Tewkesbury, to recover any of the lands of Winchcombe which had been unlawfully alienated.[23] Abbot Kidderminster noted that Yanworth increased the property of the monastery in tithes, possessions, and spiritualities.[24] The building of the Lady Chapel in the cemetery continued.[25] During the last few years of his rule very lavish corrodies were granted in exchange for sums of ready money or as a reward for faithful service. In 1276 Henry Addie and Agnes his wife purchased a bountiful supply of daily food for life for fifty-five marks.[26] In 1278 a wise provision was made for Walter the mason of Hereford, who bound himself to serve the abbot and his successors all his life, to finish the new work as well as he knew how, and to undertake no other building except for the king.[27] He was allowed to build a chamber for himself next the granary, for which the abbot was to find the stone and timber. He boarded with the abbot's chief servants, but if he were ill and confined to his room he was to have an allowance of two monk's loaves, two noggins of beer, and two dishes from the abbot's kitchen. Food, clothes, and provender were provided for his two servants and two horses. Each year he was promised a robe for himself like that of the steward, and if incapacitated by continuous sickness or old age he was to have the same allow-

[1] Royce, op. cit. ii, 89 ; Dugdale, op. cit. ii, 303.
[2] Royce, op. cit. i, 69.   [3] Ibid. 197, 198.
[4] Ibid. 70.
[5] Ibid. 73 ; Dugdale, op. cit. ii, 312.
[6] Royce, op. cit. ii, 275.   [7] Ibid. i, 73.
[8] Dugdale, op. cit. ii, 312.
[9] Royce, op. cit. i, 150, 156.
[10] Ibid. i, 167.   [11] Ibid. 242, 243.
[12] Dugdale, op. cit. ii, 312.
[13] Ibid. ; Royce, op. cit. i, 109 ; ii, 309, 310.
[14] Royce, op. cit. ii, 312.

[15] Ibid. 313.   [16] Ibid. 111.   [17] Ibid. 275.
[18] Wilkins, Concilia, i, 650.
[19] Ann. Mon. (Rolls Ser.), i, 112.
[20] Dugdale, op. cit. ii, 312 ; Royce, op. cit. i, 11.
[21] Cal. Chart. R. 35, Hen. III, m. 7.
[22] Royce, op. cit, ii, 87.   [23] Ibid.
[24] Dugdale, op. cit. ii. 312.
[25] Royce, op. cit. ii, xliv; i, 245, 247.
[26] Ibid. i, 124 ; cf. 121, 125.
[27] Ibid. 138.

ances, but to content himself with one servant and one horse. Thirty years later he was still in the service of the house, and paid the costs of the appropriation of the church of Enstone.[1] In 1329 it was ordained that ten marks should be set aside each year for the keeping of his anniversary.[2]

On the resignation of John Yanworth in 1282, Walter of Wickwane, the cellarer, was elected. He found the monastery in debt to the sum of above 930 marks.[3] Being a shrewd and able man of business, he not only extricated the house from its difficulties, but added very largely to its possessions. About 1288[4] he obtained the appropriation of the parish church of St. Peter at Winchcombe from Godfrey Giffard, bishop of Worcester, and in 1309 the appropriation of Enstone from John Dalderby, bishop of Lincoln.[5] He also secured the great and small tithes of the demesne of Halling, Cutsdean, Sponley, Hazleton, and Yanworth.[6] Among his other acquisitions were the grange of Corndean; land in Thrupp and Coates to provide comforts for the monks when they were bled; and lands in Twyning, Gretton, Frampton, Honeybourne, Sherborne, and elsewhere, which added £15 to the rental of the monastery.[7] The property which he obtained in London in 1301, in the parish of St. Bride, Fleet Street, consisted of a messuage with a hall, chambers, and stables, and served as the abbot's lodging,[8] for he and his successors were regularly summoned to attend Parliament.[9] He bought timber for sixteen granaries and many sheepfolds and for buildings within the abbey.[10] In 1299 he obtained a confirmation from Edward I of the lease of Lindley Warren from John of Sudeley for sixty years.[11] In 1276 a licence was granted him to enclose 60 acres of waste lands at Enstone,[12] in 1307 to assart 115 acres of waste land in Whichwood Forest,[13] and in 1311 to enclose another 60 acres of waste land in the manor of Enstone.[14] He was generous in his dealings with the convent, and increased the revenues of the prior, sacrist, almoner, hostiller, master of the farmery, precentor, pittancer, kitchener, and chamberlain, and made provision for a larger daily allowance of bread to the monks.[15] Probably in aid of the building fund, he obtained from Nicholas IV in 1291 an indulgence of a year and forty days for penitents who visited the monastery on the feasts of the Virgin and St. Kenelm.[16] He caused the presbytery and the chapels on the north side of it to be vaulted.[17] It is difficult to realize how the money was obtained for the accomplishment of his objects. Over £1,050 was paid in taxes to the crown and the papacy between 1282 and 1311.[18] The grange of Corndean was given by Oliver, brother of Ralph of Sudeley, for the support of two monks,[19] but the lease of Lindley Warren cost £60.[20] The expenses of the sacrist who was the officer responsible for the building at Winchcombe were exceeding his receipts,[21] and in aid of the vaulting he was allowed 4s. from each shop owned by the convent within the north gate of Gloucester, the tithe of lambs at Winchcombe, and the whole tithe of Sudeley.[22] Before 1307 William of Cherington gave £40 for the fabric.[23] In that year, because, as they urged, the resources of the monastery did not suffice for the completion of the fabric and the maintenance of alms and hospitality, and the house was already in debt, the abbot and convent succeeded in appropriating the church of Enstone.[24] Though assessed only at 40 marks,[25] its revenues amounted to 80 marks,[26] but the convent did not enter into immediate enjoyment of them, for, probably in order to induce William de Haustede, the rector, to resign in their favour, they were obliged to guarantee him a pension of that amount.[27] In 1309 the convent owed £200 to Hugh of Normanton.[28] The assessment of the temporalities of Winchcombe in 1291 amounted to under £110,[29] but there were other sources of revenue. At the beginning of the fourteenth century, forty sacks of wool were sold on an average every year at the rate of 13 marks a sack.[30] Several corrodies were granted, but these do not seem to have brought in any considerable sum of money. However, the administration and discipline of the house satisfied so stern a visitor as Giffard, bishop of Worcester,[31] proved himself to be in other monasteries, and so vigorous a reformer as Winchelsey, archbishop of Canterbury, when he came thither on his metro-

---

[1] Worc. Epis. Reg. Orlton, fol. 31 d.; Royce, op. cit. ii, lxiii.

[2] Royce, op. cit, ii, lxiii.

[3] Dugdale, op. cit. ii, 304.

[4] Royce, op. cit. i, 268.   [5] Ibid. 313.

[6] Dugdale, op. cit. ii, 304.   [7] Ibid.

[8] Ibid.; Cal. of Pat. 29 Edw. I, m. 21.

[9] The abbot was summoned first in 1265; cf. Dugdale, op. cit. viii, app.

[10] Ibid. ii, 304.   [11] Cal. of Pat. 27 Edw. I, m. 12.

[12] Royce, op. cit. ii, 25.   [13] Ibid. 27; i, 301.

[14] Cal. of Pat. 4 Edw. II, pt. ii, m. 8.

[15] Dugdale, op. cit. ii, 305–9; Constitutiones Walteri de Wykewane.

[16] Cal. Papal L. (Rolls Ser.) i, 541.

[17] Dugdale, op. cit. ii. 304.   [18] Ibid.

[19] Royce, op. cit. i, 290.

[20] Cal. of Pat. 27 Edw. I, m. 12.

[21] Dugdale, op. cit. ii, 309.   [22] Ibid.

[23] Ibid. 308; Royce, op. cit. i, 299.

[24] Royce, op. cit. ii, 44.

[25] Ibid. Pope Nich. Tax. (Rec. Com.), 233 b.

[26] Royce, op. cit. ii. lxiii. Worc. Epis. Reg. Orlton, fol. 31 d.

[27] Royce, op. cit. i, 259, 260.

[28] Cal. of Close, 3 Edw. II, m. 16 d.

[29] Pope. Nich. Tax (Rec. Com.) 45, 228, 233.

[30] Cunningham, Growth of English Industry and Commerce, i, 640 (ed. 1905).

[31] No corrections at Winchcombe are entered in Giffard's Register (Worc. Hist. Soc.).

political visitation in 1301.[1] When Bishop Maidstone visited the monastery in 1315, the year after the death of Abbot Walter, he found nothing to correct.[2] The gates of the monastery were closed against the prior of Worcester in 1302, when he attempted a visitation during the vacancy of the see, because the house had been so recently visited both by Giffard and Winchelsey.[3] In 1314 Abbot Walter's last benefaction was to secure for the prior and convent the right of administering the possessions of the monastery during vacancies for a fine of £40 on each occasion, thus excluding the escheators.[4]

His successors emulated his policy of expansion, but lacked his ability and force of character. The next thirty years was a period of extravagance and maladministration. In 1318 the manor of Rowell was purchased from the abbey of St. Evroul at an initial cost of £550, and a yearly rent of £20.[5] A hundred marks were paid for an assart at Enstone.[6] Thirty-three acquisitions of messuages, lands, and rents in Winchcombe, Coates, and Greet were made without the licence of the crown to appropriate in mortmain, and in 1344 the convent was fortunate in obtaining, on the intercession of John Stratford, archbishop of Canterbury,[7] a pardon and a licence to retain this property. There was some reckless speculation in corrodies. As these included grants of perpetual sustenance and sometimes clothes and lodging as well, and were in fact annuities, their profitableness depended on the lives of the individuals who purchased them. In 1317 Margery, daughter of Bertram of Alderton, obtained one for 140 marks.[8] In 1320, when the convent was in urgent need of money, John de Somery, rector of Bishampton, who already held a corrody,[9] paid 140 marks for further privileges.[10] Many other corrodies are entered in the *Landboc*,[11] in which there are other indications of financial difficulties.

In 1321 a bond of £60, payable at the rate of £10 a year, was given to Robert Dastyn for corn already received from him.[12] In 1328 £76 0s. 8d. was due to Robert Pope, a burgess of Gloucester, for cloth.[13] The injunctions issued on 12 July by Orlton, bishop of Worcester, after his visitation in 1329, throw a strong light on the internal life of the monastery.[14] The finances were in great disorder. Orlton decreed that the abbot and obedientiars should render their accounts, before 8 September, to the convent, or those of the monks who were elected for that purpose, and that for the future the accounts should be regularly presented. Two treasurers were to be appointed to administer the common fund of the convent, and by the will of the chapter the obedientiars should be compelled to contribute to it if necessary. The abbot was bidden to restore to the obedientiars the rents and issues of the possessions assigned to their offices, which he was said to have taken from them. Neither woods, wool, nor corrodies were to be sold without the consent of the chapter. Trustworthy bailiffs were to be appointed to the custody of the manors. If the obedientiars served their office faithfully they were not to be removed at the abbot's whim, and he was to consult the chapter on matters of business. The common seal was to be in safe keeping. The extravagant household of both abbot and convent was to be cut down, superfluous servants dismissed, and the provision of horses and robes for unnecessary persons diminished. The lives of the monks called forth some strictures. They were bidden to attend the services regularly, to be silent in church, cloister, frater and dorter, instead of chattering and listening to vain tales. The evil custom of sitting drinking after dinner and after compline was to be abolished. The monks were to keep within the precincts instead of wandering in the town and countryside, unless they were sent abroad on the business of the house. At the request of the abbot and convent, Orlton made fresh appointments to some of the offices, but shortly afterwards, on 7 December, 1329, as the abbot pleaded that his privileges had been thus infringed, the bishop allowed him to remove those obedientiars and make his own choice.[15] In 1340 he resigned on account of old age and harassing cares, a liberal provision was made for him by the chapter, and he was given a chamber in the farmery.[16] There was some irregularity in the choice of his successor, William of Sherborne, and Wulstan de Bransford, bishop of Worcester, declared the election invalid, but to avoid any difficulties he himself appointed the monks' nominee.[17] William of Sherborne's rule was unfortunate. On 20 July, 1346, Thomas of Berkeley was appointed to arrest Hugh Becyn, a chaplain, John his brother, and their confederates, who, as soon as the king had gone abroad, came openly in arms to Winchcombe, broke into the abbey, carried away a large quantity of its goods, assaulted the monks and their servants and other men,

[1] Royce, op. cit. i, 271 ; cf. Cant. Archiepis. Reg. Winchelsey, in which there are no corrections.
[2] Worc. Epis. Reg. Maidstone, fol. 24.
[3] *Ann. Mon.* (Rolls. Ser.), iv, 551. However, the prior's right of visitation was subsequently admitted ; cf. *Worc. Reg. Sede Vac.* (Worc. Hist. Soc.), 61, 211.
[4] Dugdale, op. cit. ii, 309.
[5] Ibid. ii, 312. Royce, op. cit. ii, 121, 122.
[6] Dugdale, op. cit. ii, 312.
[7] *Cal. of Pat.* 18 Edw. III, pt. ii, m. 37.
[8] Royce, op. cit. i, 329. [9] Ibid. 320.
[10] Ibid. 323. [11] Ibid. i, 322–58 *passim*.
[12] Ibid. i, 336. [13] Ibid. 362.

[14] Worc. Epis. Reg. Orlton, fol. 31 d.
[15] Ibid. fol. 11.
[16] Ibid. Bransford, fol. 14, 34 d., 38.
[17] Ibid. fol. 35.

and still besieged the monastery.[1] In June, 1351, John Thoresby, bishop of Worcester, sent a mandate to the archdeacon of Worcester, to visit the house and make an inquiry into the alienation and dilapidation of its goods, and other excesses.[2] In 1352 certain of the monks came to the bishop in London and made grave complaints against the abbot.[3] In July the bishop commissioned the prior of Worcester and Henry de Neubold to put an end to the dissensions which had arisen.[4] On 26 August, he summoned Abbot Sherborne to London,[5] and on 18 September, arrived at Winchcombe to conduct his own investigation.[6] Nineteen monks besides the abbot appeared before him on chapter. The abbot proffered his resignation, and the bishop accepted it on the ground that the late dissensions threatened the dispersion of the monks, and the ruin of the monastery. The profits of the manor of Twyning were assured him for his life, and in his stead Richard of Ipwell was elected and confirmed.[7] He was confronted with a very difficult position, and in 1353 Edward III intervened. With the assent of Reginald Brian, bishop of Worcester, and at the request of the abbot and convent, he entrusted the custody of the house to four commissioners.[8] It was said that through lack of governance in the past the monastery was so heavily burdened with debt, and its fortunes were for other reasons so miserably depressed, that its possessions did not suffice for the maintenance of the convent nor the payment of creditors. Almsgiving had ceased, and it was feared that the monks would be constrained to disperse. Accordingly the commissioners were to administer the finances, provide for the sustenance of the convent and the necessary staff of servants for almsgiving and other good works, and with the advice of some of the more discreet monks, sell the residue to pay off the debts. The crisis was indeed the Nemesis of undue expansion, doubtless hastened by the loss of revenue after the visitation of the Black Death in 1349.[9] After order had thus been restored, disputes again arose between the abbot and monks, and on the resignation of Richard of Ipwell in 1359, the experiment was tried of electing a monk from another house. The choice fell on Walter of Winferton, then cellarer of Worcester,[10] and under his rule the monastery slowly regained its former position. In 1362 Edward III granted a licence to appropriate in mortmain the church of Twyning,[11] which was worth forty marks, but

the consent of Wakefield, bishop of Worcester, was not secured until 1379.[12] The abbot and convent urged on him that, owing to the loss of their tenants and servants in the pestilence, their rental had fallen by one half, and in fact their whole income did not exceed 500 marks. The buildings of the monastery and on the manors were in a ruinous condition, and in 1373 a licence to embattle and crenellate the abbey was granted by Edward III.[13] Hospitality was a heavy charge, and wrongful, costly, and vexatious lawsuits had been brought against the convent; among these the convent probably reckoned the suits with the vicars of Sherborne and Winchcombe.[14]

In 1391, for a payment of 50 marks, Richard II granted that, on the death of a knight, by name John atte Wode, the abbot and convent and their successors should have the jurisdiction over the hundreds of Kiftesgate, Holford and Greston, and the profits of the markets and fairs of Winchcombe, at the fee farm rent of £38 a year to the Exchequer.[15]

At the election of William Bradley in 1395 there were nineteen monks,[16] so the numbers had not increased since 1359. In 1398 he received for himself and his successors from Boniface IX the rights of a mitred abbot, which added to his dignity and importance.[17] In the same year, with the assent of the pope, Richard II, and Tidman of Winchcombe, bishop of Worcester, the vicarage of the parish church was appropriated to the monastery.[18] In 1402, when their revenues had reached 1,000 marks, they obtained a papal bull enabling them to appropriate the church of Bledington, which was worth 25 marks a year.[19] Boniface IX gave them leave to serve the church either by a monk or secular priest whom they could remove at will, but in 1406 they were obliged to acquiesce in the ordination of a perpetual vicarage of the value of 10 marks by Clifford, bishop of Worcester.[20]

When the monastery was visited by Bishop Polton in 1428, he found that it was out of debt and very prosperous and peaceful.[21] Under

[1] *Cal. of Pat.* 20 Edw. III, pt. iii, m. 10 *d.*
[2] Worc. Epis. Reg. Thoresby, fol. 28 *d.*
[3] Ibid. fol. 52.   [4] Ibid. fol. 51 *d.*
[5] Ibid. fol. 52.   [6] Ibid. fol. 52–4.
[7] Ibid. fol. 53.
[8] Pat. 27 Edw. III, pt. ii, m. 17.
[9] Royce, op. cit. ii, 97.
[10] Dugdale, op. cit. ii, 312.
[11] *Cal. of Pat.* 3 Ric. II, pt. ii, m. 38.

[12] Royce, op. cit. ii, 95–101.   [13] Ibid. 129.
[14] Ibid. ii, 45–66, 281, cf. *V.C.H. Glouc.* 'Eccles. Hist.' p. 21.
[15] Royce, op. cit. ii, 16. The grant had been made to the convent by Hen. III in 1223 for a ferm of £50, but only 'usque ad ætatem nostram,' *Cal. of Pat.* 8 Hen. III, m. 12. It was not afterwards renewed to them; cf. Royce, op. cit. ii, 19–22.
[16] *Worc. Reg. Sede Vac.* (Worc. Hist. Soc.), 367.
[17] *Cal. Papal L.* v, 162. Royce, op. cit. ii, 41, but there wrongly assigned by the editor to the year 1303. Had he lived to revise his work finally, he would doubtless have discovered the error.
[18] Ibid. ii, 139–45; cf. *V. C. H. Glouc.* 'Eccles. Hist.' p. 20.
[19] Royce, op. cit. ii, 42; *Cal. of Pat.* 6 Hen. IV, pt. 1, m. 8.
[20] Worc. Epis. Reg. Clifford, fol. 76.
[21] Royce, op. cit. ii, 499.

the rule of John Cheltenham (elected 1423) it had become an example to other monasteries, a comfort and relief to the bishop. The important register which bears John Cheltenham's name was compiled by him.[1] There were still some lay brothers in the monastery at the time of his installation,[2] but the number of monks did not increase by more than one or two.

The prosperity of both town and abbey manifested itself during the Wars of the Roses in the building of the great parish church. The chancel was erected by Abbot William Winchcombe (1454–74), the parishioners found £200 for the nave, and Ralph Boteler, lord of Sudeley, helped them to finish the work.[3] In 1480, in exchange for quarried stone to the value of £100 for the building of St. George's Chapel at Windsor, Edward IV granted a licence to the abbot and convent to appropriate lands in mortmain to the yearly value of £20.[4]

Abbot Richard Kidderminster (1488–1525) was a man of affairs, a trusted servant of Henry VIII and Wolsey, as well as a truly religious man, a scholar, and an able administrator. At the age of fifteen he was admitted as a novice, and four years later was sent to the Benedictine College of Gloucester Hall at Oxford.[5] Under his rule the number of monks reached twenty-seven.[6] In the words of Brown Willis: 'By his encouragement of virtue and good letters he made the monastery flourish so much that it was equal to a little university,'[7] but without further evidence it would be difficult to say whether there was any such revival of learning at Winchcombe as at Canterbury.[8] Abbot Kidderminster was a keen student of history, and in his searches among the charters and records of the house, many of which he found torn and almost illegible, he had cause to deplore the carelessness of his predecessors.[9] He conceived and carried out his scheme of compiling a great register, which was divided into five sections. In the first part he treated of the foundation of the monastery, and owing to the destruction of the earlier records in the fire of 1151, he had great difficulty in coming to any definite conclusion. With scrupulous regard for accuracy, he wrote: 'What truth there may be in these things I know not, for as I have never read them among our antiquities, I should not dare to write them'[10]; the second part contained papal and episcopal privileges and instruments relating to pensions and tithes; the

third, royal charters and privileges; the fourth, a collection of documents connected with the possession and acquisition of all the property of the house; and the last consisted of a series of brief lives of the abbots. But the register met the fate of the earlier charters, though not before it had been seen and used by Dugdale. In 1666 it was in the chambers of Sir William Morton in Serjeants' Inn, and perished in the Great Fire.[11] Among his other works was a book on the sanctity of the persons of the clergy, and a treatise against Luther.[12] In 1510 he preached before the king at Greenwich, and in 1514 he delivered a famous sermon at Paul's Cross in defence of the privileges of the clergy.[13] In 1510 he obtained from Henry VIII a grant of the manor of Sudeley, the advowson of the chapel, and the lands formerly held by Sir Ralph Boteler, at a rent of £60 a year.[14] In 1512 he accompanied Fisher, bishop of Rochester, and the prior of the Hospitallers on an embassy to Pope Julius II.[15] He favoured the divorce of Katherine of Aragon, and sought Cromwell's friendship at the beginning of the great minister's career. He resigned his office in 1525, and in 1531, shortly before his death, he attributed his neglect in writing to Cromwell, to his advanced age and sickness.[16]

The galling nature of the injunctions which were sent to the monasteries by Cromwell in 1535 was very apparent at Winchcombe. Abbot Mounslow and the convent petitioned Cromwell that some of these might be modified.[17] They were virtually prisoners within the precincts. Accordingly they asked that the abbot might have licence to take one or two of his brethren with him as chaplains when he went out of the monastery, and that he might send any of his brethren to preach the Word of God abroad. They desired that the abbot might receive women of nobility and others of sad and good conversation, being friends, mothers, or kinswomen to him or his brethren, to his hall at dinner or supper, and that women might come into the church for divine service. As the monks were limited to the use of one gate, they reminded Cromwell that of the two gates of the monastery, one opened on to the town where there was always a porter, and the other into the fields. If this were shut, corn and hay would have to be carried half a mile about. They also prayed that the church doors might stand open at mass and evensong. As the abbot was bound daily to expound part of the rule of St. Benedict in English, they asked that he might have licence to appoint a deputy. The injunctions were subversive of discipline. Any

---

[1] Royce, op. cit. ii.   [2] Ibid. ii, 5.

[3] Dugdale, op. cit. 298–9.

[4] *Cal. of Pat.* 20 Edw. IV, pt. ii, m. 24.

[5] Royce, op. cit. ii, xxxiii.

[6] Cant. Archiepis. Reg. Morton, fol. 171 *d*.

[7] Dugdale, op. cit. ii, 299.

[8] Gasquet, *The Eve of the Reformation*, 22–6 (ed. 1905).

[9] Dugdale, op. cit. ii, 301.

[10] Ibid. 302.

[11] Ibid. 299.

[12] Ibid. 299. Royce, op. cit. ii, xxxiv.

[13] Dugdale, op. cit. ii, 299. Royce, op. cit. ii, xxxiv.

[14] Royce, op. et loc. cit.   [15] Ibid.

[16] Ibid.   [17] *L. and P. Hen. VIII*, ix, No. 1170.

monk who wished to complain of his superior or of his brethren had a right to appeal to Cromwell and to be furnished with money and means. The abbot told his monks that he would shortly expound the rule in chapter, but as he delayed a day or two the sub-chamberlain demanded a licence from him to complain to Cromwell on that account, and because the abbot had invited the prior and chanter to dinner.[1] One of the brethren, John Horwood, wrote a treatise 'against the usurped power of the bishop of Rome,' which he sent to Cromwell. He could not endure 'the straitness of the religion,' the customary abstinence, the frater, and other observances, and was excused by Cromwell from getting up for matins.[2] He also desired a capacity to take a benefice without changing his habit. On 7 December the abbot complained to Cromwell of the disobedience of two of his brethren.[3] They had eaten meat on the first Thursday in Advent, refused to do penance, and said they would eat it on Friday if they could get it. The appointment by Cromwell of Anthony Saunders, the curate of Winchcombe, to preach to the monks, was an obvious source of friction. On 3 February, 1535, he complained of the hindrances put in his way by the abbot,[4] and on 2 November he asked Cromwell to appoint a convenient hour in the forenoon for him to read to the monks. 'They will not come in due time,' he wrote, 'they set so much by their popish service.'[5] There was no opposition to the royal supremacy, which was acknowledged on 25 August, 1534, by the abbot and twenty-four monks.[6]

The monastery was surrendered on 23 December, 1539. The abbot received a pension of £140 and forty loads of wood, the prior one of £8, nine monks had £6 13s. 4d. and seven others received £6 each.[7]

The clear yearly value of the property of the monastery in 1535 amounted to £759 11s. 9¼d.; [8] in the hands of the crown bailiff in 1540 it brought in £945 3s. 11¼d. The possessions of the convent in Gloucestershire included the manors of Winchcombe, Twyning, Sherborne, Staunton, Snowshill, Honeybourne, Dry Marston, Adelmington, Bledington, Yanworth, Hazleton, Rowell, Halling, Charlton Abbots, Naunton, Frampton, Coates, Sudeley, the hundreds of Kiftesgate, Holford, and Greston, rents in Winchcombe and Gloucester, the rectories of Winchcombe, Twyning, Staunton, and Bledington, in Oxfordshire the manor and rectory of Enstone, in Warwickshire the manor of Alne.

ABBOTS OF WINCHCOMBE [9]

Livingus (?), occurs 851 (?)
Germanus, *circa* 969–75
Godwine or Eadwine, 1044, died 1053
Godric or Eadric, 1054–72
Galandus, 1075
Ralph I, 1077
Girmind, 1095
Godfrey, 1122
Robert I, 1138
William, 1152
Gervase, 1157
Henry, 1171
Crispin, 1181
Robert II, 1182
Ralph II, 1184
Robert III, 1194
Thomas, 1221
Henry of Tudington, 1232
John Yanworth, 1247
Walter of Wickwane, 1282
Thomas of Sherborne, 1314
Richard of Idbury, 1315
William of Sherborne, 1340
Richard of Ipwell, 1352
Walter of Winferton, 1359
William Bradley, 1395
John Cheltenham, 1423
William Winchcombe, 1454
Thomas Twining, 1474 [10]
John Twining, 1477
Richard Kidderminster, 1488
Richard Mounslow, 1525

A seal of the fifteenth century represents the Virgin crowned, seated in a canopied niche, the Child standing on her right knee, in her left hand a sceptre (?); overhead, in a smaller niche, the Trinity; on each side, in a smaller canopied niche, a saint full-length; in base, under a round-headed arch, Oswald, bishop of Worcester, half-length, with mitre and pastoral staff, between two shields of arms, a saltire for Winchcombe Abbey; below the shields the initial letters W W for William of Winchcombe (1454–74).[11]

The legend is :—

s' : AB[BAT]IS : ET : CONVĒT : DE : WYNC

4. THE PRIORY OF STANLEY ST. LEONARD

In or about 1131 Roger of Berkeley II founded on his manor of Stanley a small house of canons which was dedicated to St. Leonard.[12]

[1] *L. and P. Hen. VIII*, ix, No. 314.
[2] Ibid. Nos. 321, 322.
[3] Ibid. No. 934.
[4] Ibid. viii, No. 171.
[5] Ibid. ix, No. 747.
[6] *Dep. Keeper's Rep.* vii, App. ii, 304.
[7] *L. and P. Hen. VIII*, xv, No. 139, iv.
[8] *Valor Eccles.* (Rec. Com.), ii, 461.

[9] The list, which is taken from Royce, *Landboc sive Registrum Monasterii Winchelcumba*, ii, xvi–xxxv (cf. also Dugdale, *Mon.* ii, 297-9), has been carefully verified.
[10] *Cal. of Pat.* 17 Edw. IV, pt. i, m. 11.
[11] Birch, *Catalogue of Seals in British Museum*, i, 809.
[12] *Brist. and Glouc. Arch. Soc. Trans.* viii, 197, *The Earlier House of Berkeley*.

Nothing is known of the foundation except that it was a college of secular canons. In 1146, with the consent of the prior and canons, Roger of Berkeley III gave the church of Stanley St. Leonard to the Benedictine abbey of St. Peter at Gloucester,[1] and it became a cell to that house. The endowment of the priory consisted of the churches of Ozleworth, Coaley, Arlingham, Slimbridge and Uley,[2] and in 1156 he added the church of Cam,[3] the church of Easton Grey,[4] a mill and messuage in Coaley,[5] and Fyfacre Wood.[6] In 1224 a dispute arose between Thomas of Berkeley, and Thomas, abbot of Gloucester, about the church of Slimbridge. The abbot renounced his rights in exchange for a grant of the hospital of Lorwing with its lands and appurtenances.[7]

There is no evidence as to the number of monks who were usually at the priory, but probably it did not exceed three or four. Monks usually disliked being sent to a cell. After his visitation of Gloucester in 1301, Winchelsey, archbishop of Canterbury, decreed that the brethren should be sent to dwell for a time at any of the cells, and also recalled, by a council consisting of the abbot, prior, sub-prior, third prior, precentor and five of the older monks who held no office.[8] Their stay should not exceed a year, and until they had spent a year in the monastery after their return, they could not again be sent to a cell unless they were contentious or out of health. The priors of the cells were bound to provide all things for the monks except clothes and boots. Like the other cells of Gloucester, Stanley St. Leonard was at no time wealthy, and in 1317, on account of a general complaint of poverty from the priors, Abbot Thoky decreed that they should receive a mark a year from the mother house for each of their brethren.[9] The prior was doubtless appointed by the abbot and convent. He was summoned to be present at the election of an abbot,[10] and in 1510[11] and 1514[12] the two monks who were with him at the cell, also recorded their votes. The house was subject to the visitation of the bishop of Worcester.[13]

In 1361, at the urgent petition of the abbot and convent of Gloucester, Reginald Brian, bishop of Worcester, appropriated the church of

Cam to their use.[14] According to an ordinance of Abbot Horton, the custody of the church was left to the prior of Stanley St. Leonard, but he was bound to pay over a fixed sum out of the issues to the obedientiars of Gloucester for the provision of cakes, wines and a pittance of fruit on the abbot's anniversary.[15]

In 1535 the clear yearly value of the cell was £106 17s.[16] Its possessions included rents in the vill of Stanley St. Leonard, in Slimbridge, Stinchcombe, Easton Grey and elsewhere, the manor of Lorwing, the rectories of Cam, Arlingham, Coaley, Stanley St. Leonard and other tithes and pensions.[17] At that time there were only three monks at the priory.[18] As the revenues were under £200 a year the priory was visited by the commissioners who were appointed under the Act of 1536 for the suppression of the lesser monasteries. The prior showed that his house was appropriated to St. Peter's, Gloucester. The commissioners gave him an injunction to appear before the chancellor and council of the Court of Augmentations on 16 June, 1536, upon pain of a fine of 500 marks.[19] On 11 June, 1538, Henry VIII sent an imperative request to the abbot and convent of Gloucester to recall the monks from Stanley St. Leonard and grant a lease of the priory to Sir William Kingston.[20] They had no choice, and on 18 July the lease was drawn up at a rent of £36 13s. 4d., and a payment of king's tenths of £8 2s. 4d.[21] On the surrender of the monastery of Gloucester on 2 January, 1540, the rent passed to the crown.[22]

PRIORS OF STANLEY ST. LEONARD

Tabrith, occurs 1146 [23]
Thomas of Tyringham, occurs 1284 [24]
John Crosse, occurs 1449 [25]
Peter, occurs circa 1494 [26]
William Monynton, occurs 1510 [27]
Richard Wolryge, occurs 1514 [28]
John Rodley, 1535 [29] and 1538 [30]

[1] Hist. et Cart. Mon. Glouc. (Rolls Ser.), i, 113.
[2] Ibid.
[3] Ibid. 114 ; Dugdale, Mon. iv, 470 ; Red Book of St. Augustine's, Bristol, fol. 80, Berkeley Castle MSS.
[4] Ibid.
[5] Hist. et Cart. Glouc. (Rolls Ser.), i, 113.
[6] Ibid. 114.
[7] Ibid.; Dugdale, op. cit. iv, 469.
[8] Hist. et. Cart. Glouc. i, lxxxvii (Rolls Ser.).
[9] Ibid. i, 42. [10] Ibid. iii, 22.
[11] Ibid. xxxiv. [12] Ibid. xlix.
[13] Worc. Epis. Reg. Giffard (Worc. Hist. Soc.),

[14] Worc. Epis. Reg. Brian, fol. 36.
[15] Hist. et Cart. Glouc. (Rolls Ser.), i, 51.
[16] Valor Eccles. (Rec. Com.), ii, 419.
[17] Ibid.
[18] Dugdale, op. cit. iv, 469.
[19] Dublin Rev. April, 1894, p. 276.
[20] Reg. Parker, ii, fol. 163 (MSS. of D. and C. of Glouc.).
[21] Ibid.
[22] Dugdale, op. cit. iv. 469.
[23] Hist. et Cart. Glouc. (Rolls Ser.), 113.
[24] Ibid. iii, 23.
[25] Dugdale, op. cit. iv, 469.
[26] MS. Furney, 3, Brist. and Glouc. Arch. Soc. Lib.
[27] Hist. et Cart. Glouc. (Rolls Ser.), iii, p. xxxiv.
[28] Ibid. iii, xlix.
[29] Valor Eccl. (Rec. Com.), ii, 419.
[30] Reg. Parker, ii, fol. 163 (MSS. of D. and C. of Glouc.).

434.

5. THE PRIORY OF ST. JAMES, BRISTOL

The priory of St. James, Bristol, was founded about 1137, by Robert, earl of Gloucester, as a cell to the Benedictine monastery of Tewkesbury.[1] He set aside a tenth of the stone which had been brought from Normandy for the keep of Bristol Castle for the building of a Lady chapel in his new foundation.[2] He died 31 October, 1147, and was buried in the choir.[3] His son William, earl of Gloucester, completed the endowment which was confirmed by Henry II about 1181.[4] It included the manor of Ashley, the profits of his fair at Bristol in the week of Pentecost, a tenth of the rent of the earl's mills at Newport, a tenth penny of the rent of that vill in Monmouthshire, of his forest, and of three other mills, a burgage in the new part of the town which was then growing up around the castle on the land which separated it from the monastery. For the sustenance of the monks he gave the church of Escremoville in the diocese of Bayeux, and all the churches of his fee in Cornwall, viz. Eglosbrech, Connarton, Egloshale, Eglossant, Egloscrawen, with the chapel of Bennarton, and Melidan, with the chapel of St. Germoch.

The priors were appointed absolutely at the will of the abbot and convent of Tewkesbury,[5] and in the absence of other evidence, it may be concluded that the monks were sent there for a time from the mother house. The priors were usually summoned to take part in the election of the abbot.[6] The house was subject to the visitation of the bishop of Worcester.[7]

In 1230 the prior and monks of St. James were in conflict with the Dominicans, who had built an oratory within their parish.[8] When, at the request of the friars, William of Blois, bishop of Worcester, came to dedicate their altar and burial-ground, the monks protested against the dedication; they petitioned that their privileges might remain intact, and that the friars should be forbidden to receive oblations or to have a burial-place. However it is recorded in the Annals of Tewkesbury that the bishop did not desist from the dedication nor the friars from building and taking offerings, to the great prejudice and loss of the church of St. James.

It was doubtless to attract offerings that in 1238 the prior and convent persuaded Walter de Cantilupe, bishop of Worcester, to institute the Feast of Relics which was celebrated on the Thursday of the week of Pentecost, when Bristol was thronged with visitors to the fair.[9] He granted an indulgence of fifteen days to all who came to the church and gave alms. Probably the offerings were needed for the fabric, as some building was then proceeding, and on St. Luke's Day 1239, Cantilupe dedicated the church.[10]

It is evident from the charter of Henry II that, as at Tewkesbury, the nave of the priory church had always been used by the parishioners.[11] In virtue of a papal bull the prior and convent had the right of sending a monk to serve the parishioners or of appointing a chaplain, and in 1242 they successfully resisted Walter de Cantilupe's attempt to create a perpetual vicarage.[12] In 1374 the parishioners undertook to build a bell-tower, but they resisted the obligation to rebuild the roof of the nave, and the prior and convent agreed to undertake it for an annual payment of 3s. 6d. in Redland.[13]

In 1310 the prior and convent proved their right to take 3d. for every hogshead of wine which came to the port of Bristol from twelve o'clock on the Saturday before the Feast of St. James for a full week.[14]

In 1394 a dispute with the steward of the honour of Gloucester was concluded.[15] When he came to hold a court at Bristol he claimed hospitality for a day and a night at the priory for himself, his bailiffs, servants and horses, but on inquiry he failed to prove the right.

The history of this priory, as of most other cells, was uneventful. It was reckoned as part of the possessions of the abbey of Tewkesbury, which was surrendered on 9 January, 1539.[16] There were probably at that time not more than three or four monks, and they would be included in the pension list of Tewkesbury. The prior received £13 6s. 8d. a year.[17]

In 1535 the clear yearly value of the property was £57 7s. 4d.[18]; of this sum over £31 was drawn from rents in Bristol and the immediate neighbourhood.

PRIORS OF ST. JAMES, BRISTOL

Jordan, ob. 1231 [19]
Henry of Washbourn, resigned 1234 [20]
Thomas of Keynsham, appointed 1234 [21]
Thomas de Stokes, occurs 1255 [22]
Richard of Devizes, appointed 1255 [23]

[1] Dugdale, *Mon.* iv, 333.
[2] Ibid. iv, 335.   [3] Ibid. 333.
[4] Ibid. 335. Bickley, *Little Red Book of Bristol,* i, 108. Dugdale, op. cit. ii, 69.
[5] *Ann. Mon.* (Rolls Ser.), i, 94, 157, 169.
[6] Worc. Epis. Reg. Bransford, fol. 132 d.
[7] *Worc. Epis. Reg. Giffard* (Worc. Hist. Soc.), 234 ; Montacute, fol. 48 d.
[8] *Ann. Mon.* (Rolls Ser.), i, 78.

[9] Ibid. 110.   [10] Ibid. 112.
[11] Dugdale, op. cit. iv, 335.
[12] *Ann. Mon.* i, 126.
[13] Nicholls and Taylor, *Bristol Past and Present,* ii, 30.
[14] Bickley, *Little Red Book of Bristol,* i, 241.
[15] Birch, *Orig. Doc. relating to Bristol,* p. 299, *n.* 49.
[16] Dugdale, op. cit. ii, 57.
[17] Ibid.
[18] *Valor Eccles.* (Rec. Com.), ii, 484, 485.
[19] *Ann. Mon.* (Rolls Ser.), i, 80.
[20] Ibid. 94.   [21] Ibid.   [22] Ibid. 155.
[23] Ibid. 157.

William Isaac, appointed 1262 [1]
Henry, occurs 1310 [2] and 1311 [3]
William of Campden, occurs 1347 [4]
Thomas Norton, occurs 1374 [5] and in 21 Ric. II.
Richard Worcester, occurs 1394 [6] and 1400 [7]
William Newport, occurs 1454 [8]
William, occurs 1465 [9]

John Aston, occurs 1486 [15]
Robert Cheltenham, occurs 1523 [16]
Robert Circeter, occurs 1535 [17] and 1539 [18]

The prior's seal attached to a deed dated 1486 [19] is a small signet, and represents an eagle displayed, within a cabled border. [20]

HOUSES OF AUGUSTINIAN CANONS

6. THE ABBEY OF ST. AUGUSTINE AT BRISTOL

The monastery of St. Augustine was founded as a house of Augustinian canons by Robert Fitzharding, [10] a rich citizen of Bristol. During the civil war he supported the cause of the Empress Matilda and her son, and in reward was granted the lordship of Berkeley. [11] In 1142 he resolved to found a religious house in his manor of Billeswick. [12] The church and monastic offices were six years in building. On 11 April, 1148, the church was dedicated by the bishops of Worcester, Exeter, Llandaff, and St. Asaph, and six canons from Wigmore entered into possession of the new monastery. [13] The endowment consisted of the manors of Billeswick, Almondsbury, Horfield, Ashleworth, Cromhall, Leigh near Bristol, Cerney, Fifhide, lands and tenements at St. Katherine's of the fee of Portbury, at Arlingham, at Blakenford, rents in Bristol, the churches of Tickenham, Were, Poulet, Portbury, Berkeley, Wotton, Cromhall, Beverstone, Ashleworth, Almondsbury, Cheshull, Portishead, Langstone, Rualach, and St. Nicholas, Bristol, the gift of Robert Fitzharding and his sons. [14] As some of the manors were held by Fitzharding of the crown in chief, and were confirmed to the canons 'in

perpetual alms' by Henry, duke of Normandy, he was reputed a founder of the house. [21] He granted the canons a rental of 10 marks, and promised another gift of equal value when he came into his kingdom. [22] The monastery prospered greatly; before 1189 the canons had received numerous other benefactions, including the churches of Clevedon, Finemere, Halberton, Grantendon, All Saints, Bristol, and in Wales lands at Penarth and the church of Romeney. [23] In or before the reign of Richard I they acquired lands and several churches in Ireland. [24] Thus it is clear that the monastery was liberally endowed, and successive lords of Berkeley [25] showed themselves generous patrons of the foundation of their ancestor, Robert Fitzharding, who died a canon of the house. [26] However, its history is marked by financial embarrassment and a lack of governance which led to internal dissensions.

The monastery was subject to the visitation of the bishops of Worcester. In 1234 William of Blois deposed Abbot David on account of his quarrels with the convent. [27] One of the first acts of his successor, William of Bradstone, was to conclude an important agreement in 1234 with the mayor and commonalty of Bristol, by which they acquired for nine marks sufficient land on St. Augustine's Marsh to make a new quay. [28] In the following year the abbot and convent began to build the church of St. Augustine the Less for persons dwelling on their side

[1] *Ann. Mon.* (Rolls Ser.), i, 160.
[2] *Cal. of Pat.* 4 Edw. II, pt. i, m. 22 d.
[3] Birch, *Orig. Doc. relating to Bristol,* n. 36.
[4] Worc. Epis. Reg. Bransford, fol. 132 d.
[5] Nicolls and Taylor, *Bristol Past and Present,* ii, 30.
[6] Ibid. ii, 36. Birch, op. cit. No. 77.
[7] Birch, op. cit. No. 132. *Cal. of Pat.* 2 Hen. IV, pt. 7, m. 11.
[8] Bickley, *Little Red Book of Bristol,* i, 236.
[9] Bickley, *Calendar of Bristol Deeds,* n. 262.
[10] Dugdale, *Mon.* vi, 363; Smyth, *Lives of the Berkeleys* (ed. Maclean), i, 36.
[11] Ibid. i, 42. [12] Ibid. 26.
[13] There is some confusion about the date; cf. *Ricart's Calendar* (Camd. Soc.), p. 22. *Brist. and Glouc. Arch. Soc. Trans.* xiv, 125; Smyth, op. cit. i, 35; Dugdale, op. cit. vi, 344.
[14] Dugdale, op. cit. vi, 366; Smyth, op. cit. i, 36, 45, 51, 66. Some of these possessions were granted at the dedication. The manor of Berkeley and Berkleherness was not made over to Robert Fitzharding by Henry, duke of Normandy, until 1152; *Brist. and Glouc. Arch. Soc. Trans.* viii, 205.

[15] Harl. Chart. 75, A. 29 (Brit. Mus.)
[16] Jeayes, *Catalogue of Muniments of Lord Fitzhardinge,* p. 107.
[17] *Valor Eccles.* (Rec. Com.), ii, 484, 485.
[18] Dugdale, op. cit. ii, 57.
[19] Harl. Chart. 75, A. 29 (Brit. Mus.)
[20] Birch, *Catalogue of Seals in Brit. Mus. MSS. Dep.* i, 461.
[21] Red Book of St. Augustine's, Berkeley Castle MSS. fols. 17, 18.
[22] Ibid. fol. 18. [23] Ibid. fol. 18–20.
[24] Ibid. fol. 21 v. The possessions in Ireland included the rectories of Casteldonagh, Dissert, and Kilferagh, the rectory of Inhorollyn, besides lands; *L. and P. Hen. VIII,* xii, pt. ii, No. 1310 (26) and (39).
[25] Smyth, op. cit. i, 86, 109, 127, 201.
[26] *Brist. and Glouc. Arch. Soc. Trans.* xiv, 125.
[27] *Ann. Mon.* (Rolls Ser.), i, 93.
[28] *Ricart's Calendar* (Camd. Soc.), 28, 29; cf. Bickley, *Little Red Book of Bristol,* i, 22.

of the new quay.[1] Abbot Bradstone was compelled to resign after a visitation of the convent by Walter Cantilupe, bishop of Worcester, in 1242.[2] His successor was William Longe, the chamberlain of Keynsham. During his rule there were lawsuits and disputes with the hospital of St. Mark's, Billeswick, about rights of pasture and of burial on the land between the two houses. The question was finally settled by Bishop Cantilupe in 1259.[3]

At his visitation in 1278 Bishop Giffard discovered that the monastery was in a most unsatisfactory state.[4] There was neglect in the services; the abbot had not enough learning to preach; the canons broke the rule of silence in cloister, frater, and elsewhere, and indulged in slanderous talk. They even feigned illness as an excuse for drinking together in the farmery. Discipline had broken down and the temporal affairs were in great disorder. The abbot had too large and extravagant a household, and by collusion with him the bailiffs evaded rendering accounts of their manors. The bishop made a vigorous effort to reform the house. He insisted that the canons should keep the rule of silence, and devote their time in the cloister to study and meditation. They were only to go beyond the precincts when urged by necessity, and then two together, with the leave of the abbot or prior. Corrections in chapter should be made without respect of persons. The abbot was ordered to have only a moderate household, consisting of one or two chaplains and two or three squires. Superfluous and useless persons were to be removed from the household of the convent, and the grainger, vendor of corn, and the porter who collected the rents were to be deprived of their offices. To ensure better financial management the bishop enjoined that the abbot should appoint two canons as treasurers with the consent of the greater part of the convent. The treasurers should receive all the money of the house, keep account of the same, and deliver by tally to the abbot and obedientiars as much as was needed for the use of the community.[5] All obedientiars and bailiffs were bound to present

their accounts to be audited at the beginning of the year. No corrodies might be sold without the consent of the bishop. Two years later as Abbot John de Marina was unable through illness to attend to the government of his house, Giffard sent his official, together with William le Rous, a canon of Westbury, to do what they deemed necessary for the honour of the convent.[6] The abbot resigned soon afterwards.[7] In 1284 Giffard visited the house again and found that under Abbot Hugh all was in good order, except that the late abbot was living on one of the convent manors, and that the house was burdened with a debt of £300 because Bogo de Clare had taken away a church worth £100 a year.[8] In 1285 the abbot complained to Edward I that, being at Cardiff, he was seized and imprisoned by Gilbert and Bogo de Clare, and the king issued a commission for his release.[9] A compromise was effected. The abbot and convent agreed to pay Bogo de Clare a hundred marks a year for his life, and they recovered possession of the churches of Romeney and St. Melan which had previously been appropriated to them.[10] In the same year the king intervened to restore the financial stability of the house. He sent a mandate to the constable of Bristol Castle, directing him with the advice of the abbot, prior, chamberlain, and older canons, to remove all unnecessary members of the household, to retrench the expenditure, to depute one or two canons to collect the revenues, and after providing for the reasonable maintenance of the house to apply the remainder to the payment of its great debts.[11]

The rule of Abbot Knowle (1306–32) was eventful. In 1307 the abbot and convent were involved in a struggle with the prior of Worcester over the right of visitation, which he claimed to exercise during a vacancy of the see.[12] On 20 December the prior wrote stating his intention of visiting the monastery on 16 January, and the abbot acknowledged his letter. Through pressure of business the prior could not come in person, but sent commissioners, who were not admitted, and as they could get no reply of any kind they excommunicated the abbot and convent. Appeals were made to the court of Canterbury and to the papal *curia*. The abbot successfully defended his conduct, for that occasion only, on the plea that the prior had not come in person.[13]

The new choir was built in great part during Knowle's abbacy.[14] Other works were also under-

[1] Britton, *History and Antiquities of Abbey and Cathedral of Bristol*, 9.

[2] *Ann. Mon.* (Rolls Ser.), iv, 433. Barrett (*History of Bristol*, p. 261) states that in 1237 Cantilupe removed the prior and other officers, and that William of Bradstone then resigned. It is clear that the abbot did not resign until 1242.

[3] Red Book of St. Augustine's, Berkeley Castle MSS. fol. 206 *v*–9 *v*.

[4] *Worc. Epis. Reg. Giffard* (Worc. Hist. Soc.), 100–2.

[5] The common treasury, out of which all expenses were met, was an essential feature of observances of Augustinian canons of St. Victor. Martène, *De Antiquis Ecclesie Ritibus*, iii, 70; cf. Clark, *Customs of Augustinian Canons*, p. 188, cap. xl. Giffard added that, although many times ordered, this was not observed.

[6] *Worc. Epis. Reg. Giffard* (Worc. Hist. Soc.), 123.

[7] *Cal. of Pat.* 8, Edw. I, m. 3; 9 Edw. I, m. 30.

[8] *Worc. Epis. Reg. Giffard* (Worc. Hist. Soc.), 233.

[9] *Cal. of Pat.* 13 Edw. I, m. 2 *d*.

[10] Ryley, *Pleadings in Parliament*, 165.

[11] *Cal. of Pat.* 13 Edw. I, m. 2.

[12] *Worc. Reg. Sede Vac.* (Worc. Hist. Soc.), 117–20.

[13] Ibid.

[14] *Brist. and Glouc. Arch. Soc. Trans.* xiv. 128.

taken and the cost was a heavy charge upon the revenues of the house. In 1311 the abbot and convent petitioned Bishop Reynolds to appropriate the church of Wotton to their needs.[1] They stated that the greater part of the church was destroyed from the foundations on account of its age and weakness, and that the rest threatened ruin. They had already spent large sums, and would be obliged to spend still more on the new work. Hospitality in a port like Bristol was a serious burden; owing to the persecution of powerful enemies their income had been diminished by one-third for the last eighteen years,[2] and they were heavily in debt. The bishop sent a commissioner to inquire into the matter, and he reported that the truth was well known in Bristol.[3] Some years ago the poverty of the house was so great that the canons, having nothing to eat or drink, went out into the town to borrow food or get it from charity. In 1313 the appropriation of Wotton was effected, and about £30 was added to the revenues.[4] After his visitation in 1320 Bishop Cobham expressed grave dissatisfaction.[5] He insisted that the convent should give up keeping hounds, and that the almoner should be removed from office because his administration gave cause for scandal. The bishop also ordered that an inquiry should be made about one canon who was charged with evil living, and another who was said to sow discord among the brethren. He enjoined that proper care should be taken of the sick in the farmery, that a sufficient allowance of food should be provided for the brethren, instead of money to buy what they needed for themselves, that the dorter should be roofed as quickly as possible, and that the mass of the Virgin should be celebrated with due solemnity. When Bishop Wulstan de Bransford visited the house in 1339 he found, 'God be praised,' that its condition was far more worthy of commendation than of correction, but nevertheless he was constrained to issue some injunctions.[6] It was unseemly that the church should be ruinous (*patere ruinis*) and he bade the sacrist see that a roof was put on to it. He forbade the canons, both young and old, to go out of the precincts without leave, and insisted on regular attendance at divine service. As reading without understanding profited nothing, he said that the canons must either speak Latin or French to each other. In 1341 the abbot secured exemption from attendance at Parliament.[7]

There is no exact evidence of the mortality at St. Augustine's, when the Black Death visited Bristol in 1349. When William Coke was

elected in 1353, the convent consisted of eighteen canons, of whom fifteen were priests and three subdeacons.[8] It is probable that several of them died during the second visitation of the plague in 1361, for in 1363 Abbot Coke obtained a bull from Urban V by which canons might be ordained priests at the age of twenty-two.[9] In 1365 he resigned and was succeeded by Henry Shellingford. On 1 April, 1366, Edward III took the monastery under his special protection, and entrusted the custody to Maurice of Berkeley IV and three other commissioners.[10] He intervened because it was likely that the poverty of the house would compel the canons to disperse. The abbots had resorted to disastrous financial shifts. They had sold corrodies to persons of evil life who were then living within the precincts; they had made bad bargains for the convent in the leases which they had granted, and the expenses of their households were excessive. The monastery was heavily in debt. The commissioners were ordered to collect and receive all the revenues, make sufficient allowance for the canons and a moderate number of servants, apply the residue to the payment of debts and remove all suspected persons from the house. Five years later, on 26 October, 1371, Edward III wrote to William of Lynn, bishop of Worcester, attributing the misfortunes of the monastery to the misrule of Abbot Henry Shellingford.[11] The king sent a mandate to the bishop to make a personal visitation with the object of reforming the house. At the same time the abbot, canons, and servants were bidden to obey the bishop[12] William of Lynn died in 1373, apparently without fulfilling the king's mandate. Walter Legh, prior of Worcester, acted during the voidance of the see, and in 1374 issued a series of injunctions for the better government of the monastery, by which the arbitrary power of the abbot was limited.[13] It was provided that five of the elder and more discreet canons should be elected to act as the abbot's council for the transaction of the important business of the house. The obedientiars were to be chosen from among the members of the council and bound to render an account of their administration at least once a year. The abbot was to appoint seven canons to have the custody of the common seal. Two or three canons should be chosen by the abbot and council to act as receivers and treasurers, and the revenues should be expended by order of the abbot and council. Two other receivers were to be appointed in like manner to keep the moneys due from the spiritualities. The abbot and council were to appoint the secular officers. Provision was also made for the supply of better

[1] Worc. Epis. Reg. Reynolds, fol. 27 d.
[2] *Ann. Mon.* iv, 542.
[3] Worc. Epis. Reg. Reynolds, fol. 76.
[4] *Pope Nich. Tax* (Rec. Com.) 220b.
[5] Worc. Epis. Reg. Cobham, fol. 68 d.
[6] Ibid. Bransford, fol. 14 d.
[7] *Cal. of Pat.* 15 Edw. III. pt. i, m. 13.

[8] *Worc. Reg. Sede Vac.* (Worc. Hist. Soc.), 197.
[9] Nicholls and Taylor, *Bristol Past and Present*, ii, 63, *n.* 1.
[10] Pat. 40, Edw. III, pt. i, m. 36.
[11] Worc. Epis. Reg. Lynn, fol. 51.   [12] Ibid.
[13] *Worc. Reg. Sede Vac.* (Worc. Hist. Soc.) 318–20

bread and ale, and of sufficient meat and fish, also for the care of the sick in the farmery. The secular clerks, who sang in the Lady chapel, were to have their maintenance, 'as was accustomed of old time.' Order was thus restored, and the monastery prospered under the rule of Abbots Cernay and Daubeney (1388–1428). In 1398 Boniface IX granted the right of wearing a mitre to Abbot Daubeney and his successors.[1] In 1399 the revenues did not exceed 800 marks,[2] and the abbot and convent obtained papal bulls enabling them to appropriate the perpetual vicarages of St. Nicholas,[3] Bristol, and of the parish church of Berkeley,[4] valued together at 45 marks, with leave to serve the churches by a canon or a fit priest of their appointment. Much rebuilding on the manors of the convent went on during the abbacy of Walter Newbery,[5] but dissensions again broke out,[6] and in 1451 he was deposed and one of the canons named Thomas Sutton usurped his office. For five years Sutton wasted the goods of the house and sold quit rents for money to defend his position. He was expelled, and Walter Newbery restored to office by Thomas Bourchier, archbishop of Canterbury, in 1456; Sutton appealed to the pope in vain.[7] During the next eighty years the history of the convent was untroubled and the abbot and canons concentrated their attention on the care of the fabric of their church, on new monastic offices and the rebuilding of houses and granges on their manors.[8] In 1491 the convent consisted of seventeen canons, of whom eight were novices.[9] The vicar of St. Augustine the Less was paid to teach the younger canons and other boys in the grammar school within the abbey.[10] The clear income of the monastery amounted to £667 5s. 5d., the expenditure to £488 10s. 4½d. In 1498 the number of canons had increased to twenty-four.[11] Abbot Newland was keenly interested in the history of the monastery. In or about 1489 he compiled and translated into English a chronicle of the abbots of Bristol and of the lords of Berkeley, which is known as 'Abbot Newland's Roll.'[12]

'Full much convenient it thinketh me,' he wrote, 'that all religious men know by name their foundators and special benefactors for whom they ought most devoutly to pray for, which for the love of God and in perpetual alms have given and procured to be given

unto them great possessions and liberties. And for this cause moved I the foresaid John Newland Abbot for my more larger knowledge and information of my brethren canons present.'[13]

Dissensions, which lasted for some years, broke out between the monastery and town in 1515. The cause of the first dispute is obscure. Fox, bishop of Winchester, who intervened, suggested to Wolsey that as it was a perilous matter he should send for some of the canons and order them 'after his wisdom,' or appoint a commission; 'and that three young fools which sue for voices in the choir, though they be not in sacris, shall be expelled.'[14] During the rule of Abbot Somerset (1526–33), two choristers refused to pay the 'King's silver,' and their goods were distrained by the collectors.[15] The abbot arrested the officers, the mayor and commonalty imprisoned the servants of the convent. The abbot, 'with a riotous company,' attempted to force the prison but failed. The matter was finally referred to arbitration, and the award was that the choristers should pay their taxes; that the prisoners of both parties should be released; that the mayor and council should attend service in the college as usual; and that the abbot and his successors, 'in token of submission for their contempt,' should thenceforth, upon Easter Day, in the afternoon, and on the Monday in the forenoon, meet or wait for them at the door of the grammar school at Froom Gate, and bear them company to the college.

In 1534 the abbot and eighteen canons subscribed to the royal supremacy.[16] In the following year the house was visited, under the royal commission to Cromwell, by Richard Layton, who gave the abbot the irritating injunctions framed by his master.[17] Shortly afterwards the abbot wrote to Cromwell, pleading for some relaxation.[18] He desired licence for himself, for his health's sake, to walk to his manor places near Bristol, and also within the green and canons' marsh adjacent to the precincts. He prayed for himself and his brethren that, if they kept away from the town, they might walk three or four together, juniors with seniors, about the hills and fields, to refresh their minds and to 'laxe their veynes,' whereby they might be more apt for the service of God night and day. 'Further,' he added, 'we desire to have some poor honest woman to keep us if any pestyfer plague or distress of sickness do fall amongst us.'

In 1536 the Irish possessions of the monastery were confiscated under a statute of 3 Ric. II concerning the lands of absentees, although the abbot and convent had hitherto been licensed to hold them.[19] On 9 December, 1539, the royal

---

[1] *Cal. Papal L.* vi, 161.   [2] Ibid. 191.
[3] Ibid.   [4] Ibid.
[5] Britton, *Bristol Abbey and Cathedral*, 48–51; *Brist. and Glouc. Arch. Soc. Trans.* xiv, 130; Worc. Epis. Reg. Alcock, fol. 77 d.
[6] *Brist. and Glouc. Arch. Soc. Trans.* xiv, 129; Britton, *Bristol Abbey and Cathedral*, 16.
[7] Britton, op. cit. and loc. cit.
[8] *Brist. and Glouc. Arch. Soc. Trans.* xiv, 130; xv, 71–5.
[9] Britton, op. cit. 17–20.   [10] Ibid.
[11] Cant. Archiepis. Reg. Morton, fol. 170 d.
[12] *Brist. and Glouc. Arch. Soc. Trans.* xiv, 117–30.

[13] Ibid. 119.   [14] *L. and P. Hen. VIII,* ii, 194.
[15] Britton, op. cit. 21, 22.
[16] *Dep. Keeper's Rep.* vii, App. ii, 17.
[17] *L. and P. Hen. VIII,* viii, No. 215.
[18] Ibid.   [19] Ibid. xii, No. 1310 (26, 39).

commissioners arrived to receive the surrender.[1] The abbot secured a pension of £80 a year, and eleven canons received sums varying from £8 to £6. Wages were paid to forty-six officers and servants. The custody of the church, houses, and buildings was entrusted to Mannyng, the king's farmer, until His Majesty's pleasure was further known.

The clear yearly value of the property in 1539 was £692 2s. 7d.[2]

ABBOTS OF ST. AUGUSTINE, BRISTOL[3]

Richard, 1148
John, 1186
David, 1216
William of Bradstone, 1234
William Longe, 1242
Richard of Malmesbury, 1264
John de Marina, 1275
Hugh of Dadington, 1280[4]
James Barry, 1294
Edmund Knowle, 1306
John Snowe, 1332
Ralph Asch, 1341
William Coke, 1353
Henry Shellingford, 1365
John Cernay, 1388
John Daubeney, 1393
Walter Newbery, 1428, deposed 1451
Thomas Sutton, 1451
Walter Newbery, restored 1456
William Hunt, 1472
John Newland, 1481
Robert Elyot, 1515
John Somerset, 1526
William Burton, 1533
Morgan ap Gwilliam, 1537

DEANS OF BRISTOL

William Snow, last prior of Bradenstoke, 1542
John Whiteheare, or Whythere, 1551
George Carew, 1552, deprived 1553
Henry Joliffe, 1554, deprived 1558
George Carew, restored 1559, resigned in 1570, on being made dean of Exeter
John Sprint, archdeacon of Wilts 1571
Anthony Watson, 1590. In 1596 he was made bishop of Chichester, but held the deanery *in commendam* until 1597
Simon Robson, 1598
Edward Chetwynd, 1617

Mathew Nicholas, 1639. Dean of St. Paul's, Lond., 1660
Henry Glemham, 1660. Bishop of St. Asaph, 1667
Richard Towgood, 1667
Samuel Crossman, 1683
Richard Thompson, 1684
William Levett, 1685
George Royse, 1694
Robert Boothe, 1708
Samuel Creswick, 1730. Dean of Wells, 1739
Thomas Chamberlayne, 1739
William Warburton, 1757. Bishop of Gloucester, 1759
Samuel Squire, 1760
Francis Ayscough, 1761
Cutts Barton, 1763
John Hallam, 1781. Appointed Canon of Windsor, 1775
Charles Peter Layard, 1800
Bowyer Edward Sparke, 1803
John Parsons, 1810
Henry Beeke, 1813
Thomas Musgrave, nominated 1837. Promoted to see of Hereford, 1837
John Lamb, 1837, *ob.* 1850
Gilbert Elliott, 1850
Francis Pigou, 1891

A seal of the fourteenth century represents the priory church with two saints, an archbishop on the left and a bishop on the right, in doorways; in base, under a niche on the left, a bishop with pastoral staff; under a similar niche on the right, a destroyed subject; in the field over the roof, two estoiles and as many sprigs of foliage.[5]

The legend is—

SIGILLV̄ . CO . . . A . . . STOLIA (?)

An abbot's seal of the twelfth century represents the abbot, full-length, with vestments, partly embroidered: in the left hand a pastoral staff, in the right hand a book.

The legend is—

SIGILL' . IOH'IS . ABBATIS : S̄C̄I . AUG : DE . B . . ISC (?)

7. THE ABBEY OF CIRENCESTER

In the reign of Edward the Confessor there was a collegiate church of secular canons at Cirencester,[6] but it is impossible to write of its origin with any certainty. When Christianity was introduced into the province of the Hwiccas in the middle of the seventh century, the Roman city of Corinium still lay waste.[7] On the authority of a manuscript, which cannot now be

---

[1] Aug. Off. Bk. 494, fol. 47.   [2] Ibid.
[3] The list of Abbots has been taken from *Abbot Newland's Roll, Brist. and Glouc. Arch. Soc. Trans.* xiii, 126–30. It differs slightly from the list in Dugdale, *Mon.* vi. 364 ; there, Philip, who became abbot of Byland, is said to have been the second abbot of Bristol. The statement occurs in the first edition of the *Monasticon*. It is unlikely that if Philip were the second abbot, he would be omitted from Abbot Newland's Roll.
[4] *Cal. of Pat.* 8 Edw. I, m. 3 ; 9 Edw. I, m. 30. Not 1286 as in Newland's Roll.

[5] Birch, *Catalogue of Seals in British Museum*, i, 460.
[6] *Dom. Bk.* (Rec. Com.) 166b.
[7] *Brist. and Glouc. Arch. Soc. Trans.* xv, 135.

traced, Collinson declared that the minster was founded by Alwyn, a Saxon thane, in the reign of King Egbert.[1] In the middle of the thirteenth century the tradition of the monastery was that it had been founded for three hundred years.[2] The college was but slenderly endowed, possessing in the reign of Edmund the Confessor, and again in 1086, only two hides of land in the hundred of Cirencester, six acres of meadow, and a vill in Wick, besides a portion of wood given by King William.[3] The dean of Cirencester[4] was Regenbald, the chancellor of Edward the Confessor, who has been called the first great pluralist;[5] in 1086 he held sixteen churches, and lands in five different counties.

Henry I was a great benefactor of the Order of Augustinian canons, which was first established in England in 1108.[6] At Cirencester, as in a number of other minsters, they were introduced in place of the secular canons. In 1117 Henry I began to build a new church and monastery at Cirencester.[7] Though the church was not dedicated until 1176,[8] the buildings were so far advanced in 1131 that Serlo was consecrated as the first abbot, and the Augustinian canons entered into possession of them.[9] In 1133 Henry I gave a charter to the abbot and convent, granting them all the possessions of Regenbald.[10] The endowment included two hides in Cirencester, a third part of the toll from the Sunday market, two-thirds of the tithe of the royal demesne of Cirencester, and the whole tithe of the parish; the churches of Preston, Driffield, Ampney St. Mary, and Cheltenham, besides lands in those places, and at Norcote, Driffield, Wadle, Aldsworth, Elmstone, and Wick in Gloucestershire; the churches of Latton, Eisy, Penesey, and Avebury, with lands in those places, and two houses in Cricklade in Wiltshire; the churches of Milborne, Frome, and Wellow, and lands in Somerset; the church of Pulham with ten hides, wood and meadow in Dorsetshire; the churches of Cookham, Bray, Hagbourne, Shrivenham, besides ten hides at Eston in Berkshire; Boicote, with one hide and a mill in Oxfordshire; the churches of Rowell and Brigstock in Northamptonshire; and three messuages in Winchester. The king added from his own demesne 'the sheriff's hide,' in Cirencester, for gardens and a mill; a stream and the wood of Oakley, reserving to himself the right of hunting and of making assarts. He also reserved among Regenbald's possessions the life interests of Roger, bishop of

Salisbury, William FitzWarin, and Nicholas, nephew of the bishop of Winchester; and he safeguarded the life interest of the secular canons in their prebends.

During the greater part of the reign of Henry II the abbot and convent held the manor of Cirencester of the crown at a fee farm rent.[11] In 1190 they purchased from Richard I the town and manor of Cirencester with Minety, the seven hundreds, for £100, and a fee farm rent of £30 a year.[12] In 1203 the abbot bought the right of excluding the sheriff from his liberties except for pleas of the crown.[13] In 1222 Henry III allowed the abbot to build a gaol.[14] The trade of the town, which increased rapidly in the twelfth and thirteenth centuries,[15] was entirely under the abbot's control. He took the profits of the weekly market in virtue of Richard I's grants of the manor. In 1215 Abbot Alexander Neckham obtained the right of holding a fair for eight days at the feast of All Saints,[16] in 1253 Abbot Roger secured the privilege of holding another fair on the vigil, feast, and morrow of St. Thomas the Martyr, and the five following days.[17] These successive grants of privileges put the town entirely into the abbot's power.[18]

Alexander Neckham, one of the most learned men of his age in England, was abbot from 1213 to 1217. He was a Master of Arts of the University of Paris, and had taught in the grammar school at Dunstable and St. Albans before he entered the monastery at Cirencester.[19] He was interested in science rather than in history, and in his chief work, 'De Naturis Rerum,'[20] he aimed at compiling a manual of scientific knowledge. There is no evidence to gauge his influence at Cirencester, no writings of the canons are known to have survived, and it nowhere appears that they kept a chronicle.

Cirencester was subject to the visitation of the bishops of Worcester. The letter written by Bishop Giffard, after his visitation of the monastery in 1276, reveals maladministration and weak government.[21] Under the rule of Abbot Henry de Munden, the prior, William de Haswell, had exercised, or perhaps usurped, great power,

[11] *Brist. and Glouc. Arch. Soc. Trans.* ix, 298. For the history of the relations between the monastery and town of Cirencester cf. Fuller, *The Manor and Town (Brist. and Glouc. Arch. Soc. Trans.* 298–344), drawn from the chartularies of the monastery, now at Thirlstane House, Cheltenham, as well as from public records.

[12] Cart. Antiq. Ric. I, S 12.
[13] Cart. R. 5 John, 2.
[14] Close R. 6 Hen. III, m. 13.
[15] *Brist. and Glouc. Arch. Soc. Trans.* ix, 319.
[16] Cart. R. 17 John, 4.
[17] Ibid. 37 Hen. III, 10.
[18] *Brist. and Glouc. Arch. Soc. Trans.* ix, 300–21.
[19] Hardy, *Catalogue of Materials* (Rolls Ser.), iii, 58.
[20] *De Naturis Rerum* (Rolls Ser.).
[21] *Worc. Epis. Reg. Giffard* (Worc. Hist. Soc.), 86, 87.

[1] Collinson, Hist. of Somerset, ii, 191.
[2] *Brist. and Glouc. Arch. Soc. Trans.* xvi, 221.
[3] *Dom. Bk.* (Rec. Com.), 166b.
[4] *Brist. and Glouc. Arch. Soc. Trans.* xiv, 227.
[5] Round, *Feudal England*, 426.
[6] Gasquet, *English Monastic Life*, 225.
[7] *Flor. Wigorn.* (Eng. Hist. Soc.), ii, 70.
[8] *Roger of Hoveden* (Rolls Ser.), ii, 101.
[9] *Brist. and Glouc. Arch. Soc. Trans.* xvii, 47.
[10] Dugdale, *Mon.* vi, 177.

and it is likely that he held the office of treasurer. At the visitation he was accused of being a drunkard, to the damage of the house and the scandal of many. He was negligent and remiss in spiritual and temporal matters, being himself a man of evil life. Discipline was relaxed, and he was charged with having spent a great part of the substance of the house on his kinsfolk ; with alienating the silver vessels and ornaments of the church ; with pledging the credit of the house for debts of other persons. The bishop was told that owing to his conduct the monastery was so seriously embarrassed that the most discreet abbot would find difficulty in redeeming its fortunes. In 1298 Giffard restored the church of Ampney St. Mary to the monastery on the ground that it had been appropriated since the foundation of the house, and had been lost through the nepotism of a former abbot.[1] When the prior of Worcester attempted to visit the abbey in 1302, during the voidance of the see after the death of Giffard, he was refused admittance because the house had already been visited twice within two years.[2] During the rule of Abbot Henry de Hamptonet there was a crisis in the relations of the convent with the town.[3] In 1301 Edward I issued a commission of oyer and terminer to William de Bereford and Henry Spigurnel on the complaint of the poor men of Cirencester that the abbot, two canons, and others, had extorted from them, for the first time, great sums of money by undue distraints ; had entered their houses, assaulted and imprisoned some of them ; consumed the goods of some, and carried away the goods of others ; taken some of their beasts and impounded others, detaining them until a great part died of hunger, and driving some to places unknown.[4] A number of tenants attempted to avoid the obligation of taking their corn to be ground at the abbot's mills by using handmills in their houses. At different times between 1300 and 1305, the abbot's bailiff and others broke into the houses of several men of Cirencester and seized their mill-stones ; some they broke, others they carried off to the monastery.[5] When the jurors presented their complaint before the justices of Traylbaston at Gloucester in 1305, they replied that it was a question of tenure. The town was at the abbot's mercy, and it was agreed that twenty men of Cirencester should execute a deed on behalf of themselves and the whole community, stating that they had made a false complaint, and binding themselves to pay 100 marks to the abbot.[6]

In 1306 the convent secured the important privilege of retaining the custody of the property of the house during the voidance on the death of an abbot. For the right of excluding the escheators they covenanted to pay the king £100 for a voidance of three months or less.[7] In the following year the abbot died. Forty canons were present at the election of Hamptonet's successor, Adam de Brokenborough.[8] It took place during a voidance of the see of Worcester, and probably owing to some informality in the proceedings the prior of Worcester declared the election invalid, but understanding that Adam de Brokenborough was 'a discreet man, esteemed for his learning and virtuous habits and actions . . . and circumspect in spiritual and temporal matters,' he collated him to the office of abbot.[9] The penalty for disregard of the statute of mortmain was heavy, and in 1313 the abbot and convent were compelled to pay a fine of £200 for the royal pardon because they had received a number of parcels of lands, tenements, and shops in Cirencester without the late king's leave to acquire them in mortmain.[10] In 1314 they paid another fine of £20 for obtaining the appropriation of Ampney St. Mary from Bishop Giffard without licence,[11] and £5 for acquiring lands in Minety in mortmain in the reign of Edward I.[12] Heavy law costs were incurred in defending the abbot's rights to take tallage from his tenants. In 1312 Master Nicholas de Stratton impleaded the abbot for an illegal tallage, and although according to the townsmen of Cirencester he was afterwards beaten and slain by the abbot's servants, the suit dragged on until 1321, when Edward II granted a charter confirming the abbot's right.[13]

In 1325 during the rule of Richard of Charlton (1320–35), disquieting rumours of evil-living among the canons reached Cobham, bishop of Worcester.[14] Although he had visited the monastery nothing sinister had come to his knowledge. Nevertheless, on account of popular reports, which may, indeed, have been spread by the resentful townsmen, the bishop bade the abbot discover the truth of the matter ; if any of the canons were found guilty and remained contumacious their names were to be sent to him. The bishop's aid was not invoked.

About 1342 the strife with the town broke out again.[15] Owing to the development of the wool-trade many of the men of Cirencester were very prosperous, and keenly resented their position as the abbot's tenants. They preferred a bill of complaint into chancery charging the abbot, William Hereward, and his predecessors with encroachments on the king's rights and

---

[1] *Worc. Epis. Reg. Giffard* (Worc. Hist. Soc.), 508.
[2] *Ann. Mon.* (Rolls Ser.), iv, 551 ; *Worc. Reg. Sede. Vac.* (Worc. Hist. Soc.), 68.
[3] *Brist. and Glouc. Arch. Soc. Trans.* ix, 311–15.
[4] *Cal. of Pat.* 24 Edw. I, m. 28 *d.*
[5] *Brist. and Glouc. Arch. Soc. Trans.* ix, 314, 315.
[6] Ibid.

[7] *Cal. of Pat.* 35 Edw. I, m. 43.
[8] *Worc. Reg. Sede Vac.* (Worc. Hist. Soc.), 101.
[9] Ibid. 102.
[10] *Cal. of Pat.* 7 Edw. II, pt. i, m. 17.
[11] Ibid. pt. ii, m. 15.   [12] Ibid. m. 4.
[13] *Brist. and Glouc. Arch. Soc. Trans.* ix, 317, cf. xx, 116.
[14] Worc. Epis. Reg. Cobham, fol. 112.
[15] *Brist. and Glouc. Arch. Soc. Trans.* ix, 321–8.

their own. In 1342 the abbot and his followers imprisoned several of the townsmen by pretext of their suit 'until they made very grievous fines for their ransoms.' In 1343 twenty men of Cirencester were summoned to Westminster and swore to the truth of the bill of complaint. They declared that the king was the patron of the parish church, but that since the reign of John the abbot and convent had taken possession of it. They also administered the hospitals of St. John and St. Laurence to their own advantage. Other encroachments on the rights of the crown were enumerated ; but the townsmen put forward a monstrous claim on their own behalf. They swore that Henry I gave a charter to the burgesses of Cirencester granting them the same liberties as the burgesses of Winchester. They had only a copy of that charter to produce, because they alleged that in 1292 the abbot bribed the burgess who had the custody of it, got possession of it and burnt it. The charter was a forgery, though it is possible that it was first produced when the abbot purchased the manor from Richard I and the burgesses of Cirencester were fined for false presentment. The case was several times adjourned. Finally the abbot compounded with the king for £300 and obtained a charter in 1343 confirming and defining his franchises.[1] Abbot Hereward had other claims on the gratitude of the canons besides the victory over the townsmen.[2] He freed the convent from the heavy load of debt with which it was burdened at the time of his election in 1336. In the first ten years of his rule a new nave was built, and houses within the precincts and on the manors were erected at great cost. In 1346 he made provision for the maintenance of a chaplain to sing mass daily in the Lady Chapel, and for the keeping of his anniversary. Thus shortly before the Black Death the monastery was very prosperous. There is no record of the mortality among the canons or in the town of Cirencester. Bishop Wulstan de Bransford died on 8 August,[3] and only a week afterwards the prior of Worcester began to exercise his right of visiting the diocese during the voidance of the see.[4] In October he proposed to visit Cirencester, but the abbot and convent declined to receive him on the plea that they were only subject to visitation by a papal legate, the metropolitan, and the bishop of the diocese.[5] They were supported by the official of the court of Canterbury. However, an agreement was made shortly afterwards strictly defining and limiting the prior's rights. He might only inquire whether the mass of the Virgin was celebrated daily with devotion, and whether a chapter was held each day. He might only

enter the house with one monk and one secular clerk. His procuration was fixed at 4 marks, he had no right to any hospitality, and he could not lodge in the monastery with his household and carriages. It is probable that the discipline of the house was lax, Abbot Hereward was an old man, and in 1350 Edward III exempted him from attendance at Parliament on account of his age and infirmity.[6] In 1351 Thoresby, bishop of Worcester, wrote to him grieving that there were evil reports of the canons, and that he did not do his duty as abbot.[7] Thoresby told him to reform the convent by his own power without appealing to the bishop for help. He ought to forbid the canons to leave the kingdom on any business without permission, and to see that, unless they were fulfilling the duties of their office, they remained within the cloister. He should compel the officers to render a yearly account of their receipts and expenditure. Abbot Hereward died soon afterwards, and his successor, Ralph of Estcote, was elected in May, 1352.[8] Owing to the scarcity of labour the abbot and convent had, perhaps, unusual difficulty in exacting the services of the townsmen of Cirencester. In 1370 they obtained an exemplification under the great seal of the record of 1225, in which the services of tenants of the manor were defined.[9]

Lack of governance and discipline characterized the rule of Nicholas of Ampney when Bishop Wakefield visited the monastery in 1378.[10] William Tresham held the office of sub-prior, treasurer, and keeper of the parish church. The bishop ordered that another keeper should be appointed because in the discharge of that office he was often outside the monastery. Within six days the abbot was bidden to choose another canon to act as treasurer with William Tresham. The whole of the revenues from manors, churches, and other sources were to be paid to the treasurers instead of to any other officers. The almoner was to be removed from office on account of the scandal caused by his maladministration. The precentor was also to be removed. Within six days the abbot was to make new appointments to the offices of almoner, precentor, and keeper of the parish church, with the advice and consent of the older and wiser canons. The bishop found that the bread was badly baked, and that the beer was weak. He enjoined the abbot to see that the cellarer provided good bread, fish, and beer. The conduct of some of the canons had given rise to grave scandal, among them the keeper of the parish church of Cheltenham, who was to be deprived of his office. The abbot was ordered to see that these disobedient brethren did not go beyond the

[1] Cart. R. 17 Ed. III, No. 13.
[2] Worc. Epis. Reg. Bransford, fol. 110 d.
[3] Ibid.
[4] Worc. Reg. Sede Vac. (Worc. Hist. Soc.), 250.
[5] Ibid. 253–5.
[6] Cal. of Pat. 24 Edw. III, pt. i, m. 29.
[7] Worc. Epis. Reg. Thoresby, fol. 49.
[8] Ibid. fol. 46.
[9] Brist. and Glouc. Arch. Soc. Trans. ix, 330–1.
[10] Worc. Epis Reg. Wakefield, fol. 132.

precincts and that they underwent canonical penance. He must have succeeded in restoring order for some years, as when Courtenay, archbishop of Canterbury, came to Cirencester on metropolitical visitation in 1384 he apparently found no cause for censure.[1] Yet in 1389 the abbots of Lanthony Secunda and Oseney received a special commission from the general chapter of Augustinian canons to visit the monastery of Cirencester on account of disorders therein.[2]

In 1385 some of the townsfolk attacked the abbey. Richard II issued a commission to the keepers of the peace in Gloucestershire upon information that divers of the king's lieges of Cirencester had assembled and gone to the abbey and done unheard-of things to the abbot and convent and threatened to do all the damage they could.[3] The townsfolk were kept in check for a few years, but in 1400, when they rendered Henry IV a signal service by crushing the rebellion of the earls of Salisbury and Kent, whom they beheaded in the market-place,[4] they seized the opportunity to put forward their complaints against the abbot and his predecessors.[5] At the king's command an inquisition was held by the sheriff. Five juries from the town and the neighbourhood testified against the abbot, and it was claimed that the town of Cirencester had not been parcel of the manor until 1208, when the abbot compelled the townsmen to perform villein service. The king's decision was postponed, and there is no record of it. In 1403 the townsmen petitioned Henry IV to allow them to have a gild merchant.[6] The sheriff held an inquisition at Gloucester in 1403, and twelve knights of the county set forth the abbot's franchises. Nevertheless, the king gave a charter to the men of Cirencester granting their petition, so that the abbot and convent were obliged to submit. The townsmen established their gild merchant, and entirely controlled the trade of the town ; but they had no justification for withholding their services and absenting themselves from the manorial courts. In 1409 Abbot John Leckhampton obtained a further confirmation of Richard II's confirmation of the charters concerning the lands, manors, and liberties of the abbey.[7] In 1410 Henry IV ratified the charters of John and Henry III, granting the right of holding the two yearly fairs to the abbot. In 1413 the abbot attempted to distrain for services due to him ; a riot followed, and his officers were beaten and wounded. Henry IV died on 20 March, and on 5 June the abbot secured another exemplification of the record of 1225, defining the services of the tenants of the manor.[8] The townsmen saw that further

resistance was useless. The abbot impleaded a number of them for withdrawing their services for thirteen years, and heavy damages were awarded. In 1414, with the abbot's consent, Henry V granted them a general pardon. In 1418 the abbot petitioned that the charter granting the gild merchant might be made void. The Court of Chancery found that Henry IV's charter was contrary to the previous rights of the abbot, and annulled it. The strife thus ended in the complete triumph of the monastery over the town.

The history of the monastery during the last hundred years of its existence is quite obscure. At a visitation during the voidance of the see of Worcester in 1428, there were twenty-four canons, of whom one was a scholar at Oxford.[9]

In 1534 the abbot and twenty canons subscribed to the royal supremacy.[10] Five years later, 19 December, 1539, they surrendered their house to the royal commissioners.[11] The abbot received a pension of £200 a year, the prior £13 6s. 8d., the cellarer £8, twelve canons £6 13s. 4d. each, and another £5 6s. 8d., while William Phelps became vicar of the parish church.[12] Wages were paid to 110 officers and servants of the household.[13]

In 1535 the clear yearly value of the property of the monastery was £1,051 7s. 1¼d.[14] The abbot also held the office of cellarer, and had control over £859 17s. 6d. of the revenues. These were drawn from the bailiwicks of the town and seven hundreds of Cirencester, the manors of Cirencester, Minety, Driffield, Preston, Ampney St. Mary, Nutbeme, Walle, Salperton, Througham, and lands at Cheltenham, Daglingworth, Shipton Moyne, and Weston Birt, in Gloucestershire ; the manors of Frome and Milborne Port, in Somerset ; Pulham, in Dorsetshire ; Latton, in Wiltshire ; Shrivenham, Hagbourne, and Eston, in Berkshire ; Bradwell and Abberbury in Oxfordshire ; Brigstock and Rowell in Northamptonshire ; rents in London, Bristol, Cirencester ; and the rectories of Cirencester, Cheltenham, Frome, Milborne Port, Latton, Wellow, Milton, Avebury, Eton in Wiltshire, Cookham, Bray, Hagbourne, Stanyarn, Brigstock, Rowell, besides tithes in other places.

ABBOTS OF CIRENCESTER [15]

Serlo, 1131 [16]
Andrew, 1147
Adam, 1176

[1] Cant. Archiepis. Reg. Courtenay, fol. 127.
[2] M. S. Top. Glouc. C. 5, fol. 651 (Bodl. Lib.).
[3] Cal. of Pat. 8 Ric. II, p. ii, m. 26 d.
[4] Brist. and Glouc. Arch. Soc. Trans. ix, 330.
[5] Ibid. 330-4. [6] Ibid. 334-6.
[7] Ibid. 336. [8] Ibid. 337-8.
[9] Cant. Archiepis. Reg. Morton, fol. 171.
[10] Dep. Keeper's Rep. vii, App. ii, 283.
[11] Dugdale, Mon. vi, 178. [12] Ibid.
[13] Aug. Off. Bk. 494, fol. 59-60.
[14] Valor Eccles. (Rec. Com.), ii, 463-71.
[15] Dugdale, op. cit, vi, 176. The list has been carefully checked. Only corrections are marked in the footnotes.
[16] Brist. and Glouc. Arch. Soc. Trans. xvii, 47.

Robert, 1183 (died same year)
Robert, 1183
Richard, 1187
Alexander Neckham, 1213
Walter, 1217
Hugh of Bampton, 1230
Roger of Rodmarton, 1238
Henry de Munden, 1266
Henry de Hamptonet, 1281
Adam Brokenborough, 1307
Richard of Charlton, 1320, resigned 1335 [1]
William Hereward, 1335
Ralph of Estcote, 1352
William de Marteley, 1358
William de Lynham, 1361 [2]
Nicholas of Ampney, 1363
John Leckhampton, 1393 [3]
William Best, 1416
William Wotton, 1429
John Taunton, 1440
William George, 1445
John Sobbury, 1461
Thomas Compton, 1478
Richard Clive, 1481
Thomas Aston, 1488, resigned 1504
John Hakton, 1504
John Blake, *circa* 1522

A seal of the fourteenth century represents the Coronation of the Virgin, in a canopied niche on a carved corbel.[4]

8. THE PRIORY OF ST. OSWALD, GLOUCESTER

The minster of St. Oswald at Gloucester was founded and richly endowed by Ethelfleda, the Lady of the Mercians, and her husband Ethelred.[5] In 909 they brought thither from the ruined monastery of Bardney the body of Oswald, king of Northumbria.[6] Their church was served by a body of secular canons.[7]

In the reign of Edward the Confessor, Stigand, archbishop of Canterbury, a great pluralist, obtained possession of the lands of the canons.[8] After his disgrace in 1070, the property passed into the hands of Thomas, archbishop of York,[9] and was entered under the estates of the church of York in the Domesday Survey of Gloucestershire, together with the lands of the monastery of

St. Peter, which had been appropriated by Archbishop Aldred.[10] For a long period before the Norman Conquest, the sees of Worcester and York were held jointly ; the house of St. Oswald, Gloucester remained under the jurisdiction of the see of York until 1536. In 1094 Thomas, archbishop of York, claimed jurisdiction in the diocese of Lincoln, and to end the controversy William Rufus gave the new monastery of Selby and the minster of St. Oswald, Gloucester to the see of York.[11] The minster was accounted a free chapel royal,[12] and by the act of the king was created a peculiar of the see of York. In 1095, Archbishop Thomas was compelled to restore the manors of the monastery of St. Peter at Gloucester,[13] and William of Malmesbury said that the canons of St. Oswald's raged because the archbishop parted with lands which ought to have been theirs.[14] It is certain that they had a real grievance because the archbishop retained for his see a considerable portion of the lands of the canons, which was afterwards known as the barony of Churchdown.[15]

The jurisdiction of St. Oswald was confirmed to the archbishop of York by Pope Paschal II in 1106, by Calixtus II in 1120, and again by Alexander III in 1177.[16] The archbishops of Canterbury and the bishops of Worcester were unwilling to surrender their claims,[17] and did not finally abandon them before the beginning of the fourteenth century.

Until the accession of Henry Murdac to the see of York in 1147, the minster of St. Oswald was served by secular canons who were supported out of their own prebends.[18] The

---

[1] *Cal. of Pat.* 9 Edw. III, pt. i, m. 5.
[2] *Worc. Epis. Reg. Barnet*, fol. 25 d.
[3] *Cal. of Pat.* 17 Ric. II, pt. ii, m. 34.
[4] Birch, *Catalogue of Seals in British Museum*, i, 511.
[5] William of Malmesbury, *Gesta Pontif. Angl.* (Rolls Ser.), 293.
[6] Ibid. *Angl. Sax. Chron.* (Rolls Ser.) ii, 77.
[7] Hunt, *History of the English Church*, 291. There is no evidence to support William of Malmesbury's statement that Ethelred and Ethelfleda put monks at St. Oswald's.
[8] Taylor, *Domesday Survey of Gloucestershire*, 95.
[9] Ibid. 95.

[10] Ibid. 94.
[11] *Historians of the Church of York* (Rolls Ser.), iii, 21 ; Wharton, *Anglia Sacra*, i, 295.
[12] *Suppression of the Monasteries* (Camden Soc.), 124.
[13] *Hist. of Cartul. S. Petri Glouc.* (Rolls. Ser.), i, 11.
[14] William of Malmesbury, *Gest. Pontif. Angl.* (Rolls Ser.), 263 *n*.
[15] Taylor, *Domesday Survey of Gloucestershire*, 95. In 1536, the archbishop's barony of Churchdown was valued at £186 18s. 0¼d., while the temporalities and spiritualities of St. Oswald's were only worth £90 10s. 2½d., cf *L. and P. Hen. VIII*, x, No. 86. *Valor Eccles.* (Rec. Com.), ii, 487.
[16] *Historians of the Church of York* (Rolls Ser.), iii, 28, 43, 85.
[17] In 1174, Richard, archbishop of Canterbury, coming to Gloucester, suspended the clerks and officials of the archbishop of York because they refused him the canonical obedience of other clerks of his province. Strife between the archbishops followed, the canons successfully appealed to the pope cf. Twysden. *Decem. Scriptores*, 1100, 1101, 1102, 1167. In 1242 Walter Cantilupe, bishop of Worcester, held an ordination at the priory, cf. Wharton, *Angl. Sac.* i, 491.
[18] *Historians of the Church of York* (Rolls Ser.) ii, 386. The prebend then held by Nicholas consisted of a mill, a hide and a virgate at Norton, and the tithe of a hide at Pirton ; York Archiepis. Reg. Melton, 425.

church was in great part rebuilt by Archbishop Thurstan (1119–40).[1] Archbishop Henry Murdac (1147–53), who had been abbot of Fountains and was full of zeal for the new religious orders, changed the minster of St. Oswald into a priory of regular canons of the Order of St. Augustine with the full approval of Pope Eugenius III.[2] He chose Humphrey, a canon of the Augustinian house of Lanthony by Gloucester, as prior with the consent of two of the secular canons, Nicholas and Aelward.[3] Nicholas became a regular canon of the new foundation, Aelward received a prebend at Beverley, two others resigned their prebends into the archbishop's hands, and he dispossessed the two remaining canons of their prebends on the ground that they had received them from a lay hand.[4] He endowed the convent with these six prebends and two fisheries on the Severn near the church of his own gift, and property at Cerney. As however the endowment was insufficient, he lent them his possessions at Compton for four years or until he came to Gloucester, promising either to grant them Compton in perpetuity or to give them an equivalent. The dependence on the see of York was strictly emphasized ; unlike other Augustinian houses, the canons of St. Oswald never acquired the right of free election to the office of prior.[5]

The monastery was at no time prosperous. It was frequently visited by Archbishop Walter Gray (1214–55) ; in 1231 he sent the prior and several of the canons into exile because, through their maladministration, the house was heavily in debt to the Jews.[6] In 1230 they had sold their lands at Culkerton to the Cistercian house of Kingswood for £100.[7] However in 1232 the archbishop allowed the canons to return.[8] After a visitation in 1250 he sent a number of injunctions for the government and administration of the house.[9] He insisted that the prior should only transact important business with his consent, or that of a deputy whom he might appoint, and with the advice of the wiser members of the convent. No canon or lay

brother might be admitted without the bishop's consent. The common seal was to be in the custody of three or four canons. Accounts were to be rendered at least twice a year. It appears that there was some friction between the canons and the lay brothers, for the archbishop declared that the canons should always and everywhere have dominion over the others. At the same time he forbade the canons to make hay or take any share in agricultural labour. He ordered the prior to be with the canons in the dorter and frater, and to be diligent in correcting his brethren in chapter, but in all charity, not reproaching them before seculars, or punishing them severely without the consent of the convent. It is probable that the prior neglected the admonition, for in 1251 the archbishop deposed him, and appointed the sub-prior in his stead.[10] At the same time he restored certain benefices to the convent. In 1280 Archbishop Wickwane appointed Richard of Bathampton as prior, hoping that so good and skilful a ruler would be able to restore the fortunes of the priory.[11] The rule of Richard of Bathampton and his successors was marked by an acute conflict with the archbishop of Canterbury and the bishop of Worcester. In 1280 Bishop Giffard promulgated a sentence of excommunication against the prior for contempt in not appearing at the citation of Archbishop Peckham.[12] The prior relied on papal support. By apostolic authority he forbade the bishop under grave penalties to execute the mandate of the archbishop of Canterbury, his official, or the dean of Arches, or the mandate of the precentor or the sub-prior of St. Bartholomew, Smithfield, against himself, the abbot of Winchcombe or others adhering to them.[13] On 23 March 1283 Archbishop Peckham charged Bishop Giffard to promulgate his sentence of excommunication against the prior and six canons.[14] Edward I intervened and bade the archbishop revoke his sentence.[15] The archbishop replied that the king had been deceived ; although royal free chapels were exempt from episcopal visitation, when they were alienated from the king's hands and given to others they returned to their first nature of subjection to the prelates and lost their exemption. He had excommunicated the prior and senior canons, because they did not receive him at his visitation. 'We do not wish,' he wrote, 'saving your reverence, to revoke the aforesaid sentence except by form of law.'[16] In 1287 Peckham sent another mandate to Giffard to promulgate the

[1] William of Malmesbury, *Gesta Pontif. Angl.* (Rolls Ser.) 293.

[2] Simeon of Durham, *Opera* (Rolls Ser.), ii, 328.

[3] York Archiepis. Reg. Melton, fol. 425.   [4] Ibid.

[5] Ibid. Wickwane, fol. 574, provision of Richard of Bathampton to the office of prior, 'nostro prioratui S. Oswaldi Glouc. iam vacanti et ad provisionem seu collacionem nostram ordinariam libere et plene pertinenti.' Cf. *Suppression of the Monasteries* (Camden Soc.), 124.

[6] *Ann. Mon.* (Rolls Ser.), i, 78.

[7] *Hist. MSS. Com. Rep.* App. i, 335. Cf. *Brist. and Glouc. Arch. Soc. Trans.* xxii, 182.

[8] *Ann. Mon.* (Rolls Ser.), i, 87.

[9] The injunctions are entered in *York Archiepis. Reg. Giffard* (Surtees Soc.), 203 ; 'ea quae in aliis nostris visitationibus ipsis iniunximus renovantes, superaddentes quaedam nova.'

[10] *Ann. Mon.* (Rolls Ser.), i, 146.

[11] York Archiepis. Reg. Wickwane, fol. 574.

[12] *Worc. Epis. Reg. Giffard* (Worc. Hist. Soc.), 122.

[13] Ibid. 154. In consequence, in 1282 Giffard forbade the dean of Pershore to execute his mandate.

[14] *Reg. Epis. Peckham* (Rolls Ser.), ii, 527 ; *Worc. Epis. Reg. Giffard* (Worc. Hist. Soc.), 192.

[15] *Reg. Epis. Peckham* (Rolls Ser.), ii, 547.

[16] Ibid.

sentence of excommunication in his diocese, to cause the prior and canons to be denounced as excommunicate, and to forbid all the faithful in Christ to eat, drink, buy, sell or communicate with them in any way until they should receive absolution.[1] He bade the bishop inquire in the town of Gloucester and the neighbourhood, and cite all who should have communicated with them.[2] Apparently the sentence was revoked by the keeper of the spiritualities of Canterbury after Peckham's death.[3] Bishop Giffard was not deterred from attempting to exercise rights of jurisdiction over the prior and canons. In 1300 he appointed two commissioners to visit the priory.[4] He excommunicated the prior, sub-prior, sacrist, precentor, cellarer, and elder canons, because they refused to admit John, bishop of Llandaff, to hold an ordination in their church, by his authority. They claimed an exemption but it was well-known that Walter de Cantilupe, bishop of Worcester, had held an ordination there in 1242.[5] The convent suffered from the effect of the excommunication. In 1301, one of the canons appeared before the justices at Worcester, and declared that the bishop had done them much evil that year, causing them to be so straitened that the greater part of the convent had suffered from illness.[6] At the instance of the prior and convent, Edward I summoned Giffard to appear before him and his justices, but he died very shortly afterwards.[7] To avoid further trouble with the bishops of Worcester, Corbridge, archbishop of York, bade the prior and canons get the chrism and oil from Southwell, and pay pentecostals and Peter's pence to the dean of the archbishop's jurisdiction of St. Oswald.[8] Accordingly they did so. Gainsborough, bishop of Worcester, complained of their action to the king at the Parliament of Carlisle in 1307,[9] but he was inhibited from exercising any ecclesiastical jurisdiction over the priory,[10] and in 1318 Edward II issued a general prohibition against any encroachment on the liberties and privileges of St. Oswald's Priory.[11] In 1374 when the see of York was vacant, and the prior of Worcester was visiting the diocese of Worcester during a voidance of that see, Edward III forbade him to act to the prejudice of the archbishopric of York.[12]

The rapid appointments and removals of priors in the first few years of the fourteenth century testify to misfortune and lack of governance.[13] After a personal visitation of the monastery in 1309, Archbishop Greenfield ordered that the injunctions of Archbishop Gray should be strictly observed, and he made further provision to insure financial stability.[14] He insisted that a full statement of the rents, revenues, and stock should be presented to him every year, and that no corrodies should be sold, no manors or granges let, no lands alienated without his special permission. Two bursars should be appointed by the convent as receivers of all moneys, and the muniments like the common seal should be under the charge of three or four of the canons.

There are only glimpses of poverty in the later history of the priory. In 1335 Archbishop William of Melton granted a licence to the prior and convent to borrow £100 for the foundation of a chantry.[15] In 1417 the prior and convent petitioned Edmund Lacy, bishop of Hereford, to appropriate the church of Minsterworth to them.[16] They pleaded dire distress, their house was ruinous, their rents and profits were so diminished that the canons had but a bare living. Their losses were very heavy from pestilences and murrains, and they had also suffered from the misgovernment of former priors, and they were oppressed by an insupportable load of debt. The bishop ordered an inquisition to be made into the state of affairs at the priory. He was satisfied of the truth,[17] and consented to the appropriation of the church.[18] In 1462 the canons of St. Oswald were reduced to such penury that they were exempted from payment of tenths.[19]

The priory came under the Act of 1536 for the suppression of the lesser monasteries. On 23 April, 1536, Edward Lee, archbishop of York, besought Cromwell to spare the house.

It is not of foundation a monastery of religious men, he wrote, but is *libera capella archiepiscopi.* No man hath title in it but the archbishop : the prior thereof is removable at my pleasure and accountable to me, and the archbishop may put there if he will, secular priests, and so would I have done at my entry, if I had not there found one of mine acquaintance whom I judged meet to be there under me.[20]

His appeal was of no avail. On 4 September a commission was issued for a survey of those monasteries in Gloucestershire of which the revenues fell below £200 a year, with a view of taking them over on the king's behalf.[21] The

[1] *Worc. Epis. Reg. Giffard* (Worc. Hist. Soc.), 309.
[2] Ibid. 310.
[3] *Brist. and Glouc. Arch. Soc. Trans.* xiii, 126.
[4] *Worc. Epis. Reg. Giffard,* (Worc. Hist. Soc.), 531.
[5] Ibid. 532.
[6] Ibid. 543.
[7] *Historians of the Church of York* (Rolls Ser.), ii, 224.
[8] Ibid. 225. [9] Ibid. 224.
[10] *Brist. and Glouc. Arch. Soc. Trans.* xiii, 126, York Archiepis. Reg. Greenfield bet. fols 34, 35.
[11] *Brist. and Glouc. Arch. Soc. Trans.* xiii, 126.
[12] *Worc. Reg. Sede Vac.* (Worc. Hist. Soc.), 306.

[13] Cf. list of priors, and York Archiepis. Reg. Greenfield, i, fol. 45 *d* ; ii, fol. 44.
[14] York Archiepis. Reg. Greenfield, i, fol. 45.
[15] Ibid. Melton, fol. 546.
[16] Heref. Epis. Reg. Lacy, fol. 4.
[17] Ibid. fol. 16. [18] Ibid. fol. 17.
[19] Worc. Epis. Reg. Carpenter, i, fol. 178 ; 'per casus fortuitos . . . quasi destruct. seu nimium deminut. et depauperat '
[20] *Suppression of Monasteries* (Camden Soc.), 124.
[21] *Dublin Review,* April, 1894, p. 250.

commissioners reported that at St. Oswald's there were seven canons, all priests, 'by report of honest conversation.'[1] Five of them wished to continue in religion, only two desired to have 'capacities' that they might get benefices. Their household consisted only of eight servants. The church was ruinous, though the house had been lately repaired, and the priory was in debt to the amount of £124 9s. It was dissolved not long afterwards. The prior received a pension of £15,[2] but the other canons had nothing.[3]

In 1535 the clear yearly value of the possessions amounted to £90 10s. 2½d.[4] The property included the manors of Pirton, Norton, and Tulwell, rents in Gloucester and elsewhere, the rectory of Minsterworth, and the chapels of Churchdown, Norton, Sandhurst, and Compton Abdale.[5]

PRIORS OF ST. OSWALD, GLOUCESTER

Humphrey, canon of Lanthony by Gloucester, 1153[6]
Anketil, occurs circa 1155–9[7]
William, occurs 1230[8]
William, occurs 1260[9]
Richard, ob. 1281[10]
Richard of Bathampton, 1281[11]
Guido, ob. 1289[12]
Peter de Malburn, 1289, removed 1301
Walter of Bingham, 1301, removed 1310[13]
Humphrey of Lavington, 1310
Walter of Bingham, removed 1312[14]
John of Ayschwell, 1312[15]
Richard of Kidderminster, 1312, removed 1314[16]
John of Ayschwell, 1314[17]
William Heved, 1352
Thomas Dick, 1398
John Players, 1404
John de Shipston, 1408
John Suckley, 1433
John Higins, 1434
John Inglis, canon of Cirencester, 1447

[1] Dublin Review, April 1894, p. 276.
[2] L. and P. Hen. VIII, xiii, pt. i, p. 575.
[3] Gasquet, Henry VIII and the English Monasteries, ed. 1899, 181.
[4] Valor Eccles. (Rec. Com.), ii, 487.   [5] Ibid.
[6] Simeon of Durham Opera (Rolls Ser.), ii, 328.
[7] Round, Cal. of Doc. in France illustrative of the History of Great Britain and Ireland, i, 377.
[8] Hist. MSS. Com. Rep. v, App. i, 335.
[9] Brist. and Glouc. Arch. Soc. Trans. xiii, 128. He is not the same as William occurring in 1230, for a prior was deposed in 1251; cf. Ann. Mon. (Rolls Ser.), i, 146.
[10] York Archiepis. Reg. Wickwane, fol. 574.
[11] Ibid. fol. 574.
[12] Brist. and Glouc. Arch. Soc. Trans. xiii, 128.
[13] York Archiepis. Reg. Greenfield, i, fol. 45 d.
[14] Ibid. ii, fol. 44.   [15] Ibid.
[16] Ibid. fol. 50 d.   [17] Ibid.

Nicholas Falkner, canon of Lanthony by Gloucester, 1491
William Jennings, 1530

A seal of the twelfth century is in shape a pointed oval, and represents a saint full length, in vestments partly embroidered, lifting up his right hand in benediction, in his left hand a book; before him a church with porch or transept, masoned walls, ornamental tiles or shingles on the roof, and a cross at each gable end; in the field, on the left a crescent, on the right an estoile.[18]

9. THE PRIORY OF LANTHONY BY GLOUCESTER

In or about 1108 Hugh de Lacy founded a monastery dedicated to St. John the Baptist for Augustinian canons in the valley of the Hodenay, beneath the Hatteril Hills in Monmouthshire.[19] During the reign of Henry I this monastery of Lanthony prospered greatly, and the number of canons increased to forty.[20] Owing to the disturbances which broke out immediately after the death of Henry I the canons were reduced to desperate straits; a Welsh lord took refuge in the monastery with his women-folk, and enemies cut off the canons' supplies of food.[21] In dire distress they sent a messenger to Robert de Bethune, bishop of Hereford, their former prior. He invited the convent to take refuge with him, and provided for their use a chapel, storehouse, barns, and other offices. Some of the canons chose to remain at Lanthony;[22] the greater number, under the prior, Robert de Braci, took refuge with the bishop, and stayed with him for two years at his expense. In 1136 at his request Milo, earl of Hereford and constable of Gloucester, offered the canons a hide of land close to the town of Gloucester.[23] With the money which they had brought from Wales, and with the bishop's help, the canons at once began to build a new church, and on 10 September, 1137,[24] it was dedicated to the Virgin by Robert, bishop of Hereford, and Simon, bishop of Worcester. Buildings were ready for the habitation of the canons, and the convent from Hereford entered into possession of them. The new foundation was called Lanthony Secunda to distinguish it from the Welsh house, which was thenceforth called Lanthony Prima. On the occasion of the dedication Milo, earl of Hereford, confirmed the gifts of his ancestors, Roger of Gloucester and Walter the constable of the castle, and added churches and lands for the support of the canons.[25]

[18] Birch, Catalogue of Seals in the British Museum, i, 568.
[19] Dugdale, Mon. vi. 130.
[20] Ibid. 131.   [21] Ibid. 132, 133.
[22] Ibid. 132.   [23] Ibid. 136.
[24] Ibid. 137.   [25] Ibid. 136, 137.

Thus this endowment included, besides the site, the meadow called Castle Mead, a tithe of the fishery by the castle and of Quedgeley, the chapel within the castle, the chapels of St. Kinburga and Elmore, besides other tithes in the earl of Hereford's demesnes. Afterwards he granted the church of Barton in Hampshire and in 1141 the manor of Heyhampstead.[1] In 1137 Robert de Braci died, and was succeeded as prior by William de Wycombe, the familiar friend of Robert de Bethune. The chronicler implies that Robert de Bethune stipulated for the return of the canons to the mother church if peace were concluded, leaving only thirteen of their number at Gloucester.[2] In 1146, at the bishop's request, Pope Eugenius III confirmed the possessions of the two priories, and decreed that the house at Gloucester should continue as a cell to the mother church of St. John the Baptist.[3] The canons of Gloucester were soon afterwards joined by a band of twenty brethren, who were constrained to leave the mother house because their property lay barren.[4] Robert de Bethune granted lands and churches in the diocese of Hereford that the newcomers might not be a burden on the younger foundation. The thought of returning to the mother house was hateful ; they appreciated the contrast between the town of Gloucester and the desolate Hatteril mountains.[5] The chronicler told how he had heard some of the canons say that they wished each stone of the mother church was a hare, and others that they longed for the earth to open and swallow it up. They devoted their revenues to the fabric of the new church to the neglect of the elder. As it could not be deserted, all the old, weak, and more humble brethren were sent thither and left in want of clothing and food, while the canons at Gloucester enjoyed plenty. Everything of value was gradually removed to Gloucester, the books of the library, silken cloths, charters, and muniments, even the bells.[6] William de Wycombe, himself a man of austere life, strove, though in vain, to maintain discipline at Gloucester.[7] The canons hated him, and used his work on the life of Robert de Bethune to get rid of him. In the course of a serious quarrel, the bishop excommunicated Milo, earl of Hereford, and in 1143, while under the ban, he was killed when hunting in the Forest of Dean. William de Wycombe, the bishop's familiar friend, wrote vehemently against the tyrant, as he styled the earl. The canons informed his son Roger, earl of Hereford

of this, and he swore vengeance on the house. William de Wycombe resigned, and left Gloucester to dwell for the rest of his life at Canon Frome in Herefordshire. His successor, Clement, compelled the brethren to dwell with him for a year at the mother house leaving but thirteen at Gloucester, but they would not stay ;[8] on account of St. John, he said, 'we shall all descend into hell.' The Welsh house pleased him as a place for study[9] and prayer[10] but the chronicler deemed that the wisdom of the serpent would have profited him more than the innocence of the dove.[11]

It is difficult to discover the relations between the two houses during the latter half of the twelfth century. In 1157 Adrian IV confirmed a composition which had been made by Prior Clement, but the details are not forthcoming.[12] The Bohuns were generous patrons of the monastery at Gloucester. In the reign of Henry II Margery de Bohun, the daughter of Milo, earl of Hereford, gave the manor of South Cerney,[13] his son Henry gave the churches of Haresfield and Caldicote, in 1161.[14] In 1198, Richard I confirmed the possessions and liberties of the priories of St. Mary and St. John the Baptist in one charter.[15] The Irish Conquest brought a great increase of property ; Hugh de Lacy II gave lands to Lanthony Prima,[16] other benefactors favoured Lanthony Secunda.[17] Shortly before 1205 Hubert Walter, archbishop of Canterbury, required Mauger, bishop of Worcester, and Giles, bishop of Hereford, to consider the question of a repartition of the possessions of the two priories as a former division had been made void.[18] In 1205 it was agreed that each monastery should have its own prior and convent and that neither should be subject to the other.[19] The possessions were to be divided, but no record of the settlement is known to have survived. Later evidence suggests that the mother house had the lands and churches in the counties of Monmouth, Hereford, and Wales, while the monastery at Gloucester kept the lands and other possessions in that county.[20] In 1211 an amicable composition was made about the Irish property.[21]

The Irish possessions were an important but fluctuating source of revenue. One or two of the canons acted as the prior's proctors in Ireland,[22]

---

[1] Dugdale, *Mon.* vi, 137.

[2] Ibid. 132.

[3] *MS.* Top. Glouc. C. 5, Bodl. Lib. fol. 607. This manuscript of Richard Furney, archdeacon of Surrey (*ob.* 1752), contains a valuable collection of notes extracted from a series of registers of Lanthony by Gloucester which were then in the possession of the Scudamores of Holme Lacy.

[4] Dugdale, op. cit. vi. 132.   [5] Ibid. 133.

[6] Ibid. 133.   [7] Ibid. 133.

[8] Ibid. 134.

[9] Cf. *MS.* Top. Glouc. C. 5, fol. 644.

[10] *Giraldus Cambrensis, Opera* (Roll Ser.), vi, 30.

[11] *Mon.* vii, 134.

[12] MS. Top. Glouc. C. 5, fol. 607.

[13] *Brist. and Glouc. Arch. Soc. Trans.* xviii, 43.

[14] Ibid. xix, 283.

[15] MS. Top. Glouc. C. 5, fol. 609.

[16] Dugdale, *Mon.* vi, 138.

[17] MS. Top. Glouc. C. 5, fol. 613.

[18] Ibid. 611.   [19] Ibid. 612.

[20] Fosbrooke, *Hist. of Glouc.* 293 note *b*.

[21] MS. Top. Glouc. C. 5, fol. 613.

[22] *Cal. of Pat.* Edw. I, Edw. II, Edw. III, *passim*.

living at the grange of Dulek in East Meath.[1] They transmitted the proceeds to England, and in one year, during the rule of Prior Walter (1283–1300), the sum amounted to £81 5s. 7d.[2] In 1291 the English temporalities were assessed at less than £80.[3] The profits of the wool-trade were a valuable asset: in 1318 or 1319 a burgess of Cirencester covenanted to purchase the wool of the convent for that year for 100 marks.[4] It is impossible to ascertain the exact income of the monastery, but until late in the fourteenth century there is evidence of financial embarrassment. Laxity of discipline and maladministration were revealed at the visitation of Giffard, bishop of Worcester, in 1276.[5] Divine service was neglected, the prior and obedientiars absented themselves too frequently, the sacred vessels and other ornaments of the church were pledged to creditors. The canons went out into the town without licence, and the finances were in confusion. The bishop enjoined more regular attendance in church and forbade the canons to go beyond the precincts without leave. He insisted that the almoner should be removed from his office, and suggested that a more cautious cellarer should be chosen, while better appointments might be made to the offices of sub-cellarer and kitchener. To insure more prudent management, he ordered that two of the wiser and more careful canons should be chosen by the prior and convent to receive all the money of the house and act as treasurers; they were to be bound to render an account four times a year in the presence of the prior, obedientiars, and the wiser members of the convent. Two or three canons should be chosen to act as the prior's council in spiritual and temporal matters. Without their consent he might not transact any business touching the churches, manors, or granges, nor appoint either secular bailiffs or lay brothers to hold the custody of them. The bailiffs were to render their accounts at least once a year. As the house was heavily burdened with liveries and corrodies, the bishop forbade that these should be granted without his special licence. He also attempted to check sales and alienations in perpetuity. He threatened those who were guilty of disobedience to their superiors with condign punishment.

On 1 April, 1301, the vigil of Easter, the monastery suffered a great disaster, the church with its four bell towers was burnt, and only the bare walls were left standing.[6] The rebuilding was a heavy charge. In 1308, Henry Woodlock, bishop of Winchester, appropriated the rectory of Barton Lacy to the prior and convent; they pleaded their losses from hostile

invasions of their Irish possessions, and the burden of hospitality.[7] Edward II remitted the payment of a fine of sixty marks for the licence.[8] Serious quarrels followed the resignation of Prior William de Pendebury in 1324.[9] Acting on a mandate from Edward II, on 5 April Bishop Cobham ordered him to go to the Augustinian monastery of Studley until after the election [10] of a new prior. Some of the canons chose Robert of Gloucester, others Walter de Longeneye,[11] and both parties presented their candidates to the king for confirmation. On 24 May, 1324, in consequence of these discords, Edward II gave the custody of the monastery to his servant, Adam de Helnak, and bade him dispose of the revenues of the house with the counsel of the sub-prior.[12] For two years the convent was without a head, some of the canons set the sub-prior at defiance, and it was reported to Bishop Cobham that they wandered at will to the dwellings of the great, robbed the manors on the plea that they had come thither as proctors, impoverished the monastery, and withheld hospitality. On two occasions the bishop wrote in remonstrance to the sub-prior.[13] In 1326 the rival candidates agreed to submit their claims to John Stratford, bishop of Winchester.[14] The late prior, William de Pendebury, declared that the election was invalid, stating that he was taken by the secular power, and kept in prison until he resigned, but he revoked his resignation.[15] The bishop of Winchester weighed the evidence, and decided that William de Pendebury was the lawful prior, and bade the convent render obedience to him.[16] Walter de Longeneye was to remain at the monastery with the same privileges as were granted to Prior William de Ashwell when he resigned his office. At the request of Robert of Gloucester he was permitted to enter the abbey of St. Thomas at Dublin with an allowance of forty marks a year for his life, and had leave to take his books with him.[17] After his reinstatement William de Pendebury ruled the monastery for thirty-six years. He found that the house was not only seriously impoverished but heavily in debt.[18] In a lamentable petition to Bishop Orlton, in which the misfortunes of the great fire, frequent ravages of Irish lands, floods, and murrains were set forth, the prior and convent pleaded for the appropriation of the church of Tytherington. In 1330, after due investigation, Orlton granted their request, and four years

[1] MS. Top. Glouc. C. 5, fol. 635.
[2] MS. Corpus Christi Coll. Oxon. No. 154, fol. 387.
[3] Pope Nich. Tax. (Rec. Com.), 233.
[4] Brist. and Glouc. Arch. Soc. Trans. xviii, 44.
[5] Worc. Epis. Reg. Giffard (Worc. Hist. Soc), 87.
[6] Hist. et Cart. Mon. Glouc. (Rolls Ser.), i, 35.

[7] MS. Top. Glouc. C. 5, fol. 647.
[8] Cal. of Pat. 2 Edw. II, pt. i, m. 2.
[9] Ibid. 17 Edw. II, pt. ii, m. 27.
[10] Worc. Epis. Reg. Cobham, fol. 102.
[11] Cal. of Pat. 17 Edw. II, pt. ii, m. 27.   [12] Ibid.
[13] Worc. Epis. Reg. Cobham, fols. 111, 112 d.
[14] Ibid. 124 d.   [15] Ibid. 125.
[16] Ibid. 125, 126.   [17] Ibid. 126.
[18] Worc. Epis. Reg. Orlton, fol. 21.

later Thomas Charlton, bishop of Hereford, appropriated the church of Kington with its three dependent chapels to their needs.[1] In 1342 the priory was still in serious straits, and on that account Edward III took the house under his special protection, with all its lands and rents in Ireland.[2] As the financial condition of the monastery was unstable, the economic effects of the Black Death were very severe. The mortality in the house was great, out of thirty canons nineteen died.[3] On 20 September, 1351, Thomas of Berkeley gave the advowson of the church of Aure to Lanthony in exchange for the manor of Coaley.[4] The prior and convent at once took steps to secure the appropriation of the church, pleading amongst other reasons that owing to the pestilence the rents and services of their tenants were irrecoverably withdrawn. On 3 October John Trelleck, bishop of Hereford, granted the appropriation.[5]

On the installation of Prior William de Cheriton in 1377 the debts of the house amounted to £128 8s. 4d.,[6] but during the twenty-four years of his rule the monastery regained some measure of prosperity. The prior engaged in several lawsuits, and recovered some houses and £50 in money from the commonalty of Gloucester. In spite of the statute of 3 Ric. II concerning the lands of absentees from Ireland he secured the possession of the Irish estates for his house. The chapel of the Trinity, the cloister, and granary of the priory were rebuilt, and new halls, granges, and mills were built on several of the manors. In the fifteenth century the monastery was uniformly prosperous, the priors were able administrators, and discipline was well maintained. Under John Garland (1436–57) several registers were compiled, and the muniments were set in order.[7] There were not as many canons as before the Black Death : in 1409 there were seventeen canons besides two in minor orders,[8] in 1436 the numbers had risen to twenty-six, and there were again two in minor orders,[9] in 1457 twenty-two canons were present at the election of John Heyward.[10] Henry Deane was then a scholar at Oxford, ten years later he succeeded to the office of prior. He was in high favour with Edward IV, and in 1477 was one of his chaplains.[11] The priory of Lanthony Prima had fallen on evil days ; it was said that the

services were neglected, and that hospitality and almsgiving had ceased.[12] The convent consisted only of four canons besides the prior, who was charged with waste and destruction, and accordingly on 10 May, 1481, Edward IV granted it and all its possessions to Henry Deane and the convent of Lanthony by Gloucester for a fine of three hundred marks.[13] Thus Lanthony Prima became a cell to Lanthony Secunda, and was served by a prior and four canons from that house. In 1496 Henry Deane became bishop of Bangor ; in 1500 he was transferred to Salisbury, but he retained the office of prior of Lanthony[14] by Gloucester until his promotion to the see of Canterbury in 1501. In spite of considerable revenues, the monastery was again embarrassed in 1518, and the vicar-general of Bishop Silvester de Giglis pleaded to the treasurer and barons of the Exchequer that it might be exonerated from payment of the tenth.[15] As a reason he urged the ruin of the conventual church and the great expense of rebuilding.

In 1534 the acknowledgement of the royal supremacy was signed by the prior and twenty-two canons of Lanthony Secunda and the prior and four canons of Lanthony Prima.[16] In 1536 when, under the Act of 3 Ric. II, Henry VIII seized the possessions of English monasteries in Ireland, Lanthony was deprived of about a third of its revenues.[17] On 4 March, 1537, the prior wrote to Cromwell asking, on account of his great loss in Ireland, for leave to recall the prior and canons from Lanthony Prima, that the profits of the cell might be used for the maintenance of his house.[18] It is not clear if Cromwell consented. On 10 March, 1539, the royal commissioners arrived to receive the surrender of Lanthony Secunda, and the deed was signed by the prior and twenty-four canons, including the prior of Lanthony Prima.[19] Richard Hempstead secured a pension of £100 a year, the rest of the canons were awarded pensions varying from £8 to £4.[20]

In 1535 the clear yearly revenues of the monastery amounted to £648 19s. 10¾d.[21] The possessions included the manors of Barrington Magna, Quedgeley, and Elmore, Hempstead, Brockworth, Painswick, Haresfield, Prestbury, Colesborne, Aylberton, Ocle, Westbury, Frome Canonicorum, Monkton and Lanwarne, Falley, Alvington, Boroughhill, Tytherington, Turkdean and Northleach, Eyleworth, Caldicote, South

---

[1] MS. Top. Glouc. C. 5, fol. 648.
[2] *Cal. of Pat.* 16 Edw. III, pt. ii, m. 2.
[3] MS. Top. Glouc. C. 5, fol. 648.
[4] Ibid. 648 ; Smyth, *Lives of the Berkeleys* (ed. Maclean), i, 146.
[5] Heref. Epis. Reg. Trelleck, fol. 102.
[6] MS. Top. Glouc. C. 5, fols. 650–2.
[7] Ibid. 656.   [8] Ibid. 653.
[9] Worc. Epis. Reg. Bourchier, fols. 17–21.
[10] MS. Top. Glouc. C. 5, fol. 657.
[11] *Cal. of Pat.* 17 Edw. IV, pt. i, m. 5.

[12] Dugdale, op. cit. vi, 139.   [13] Ibid. 139.
[14] MS. Top. Glouc. C. 5, fol. 658.
[15] Ibid. 661.
[16] *Dep. Keeper's Rep.* vii, App. ii, 290 (74, 75).
[17] *L. and P. Hen. VIII*, xii, pt. ii, No. 1310 (i), 21 (ii). The clear revenues of the Irish possessions for a year and a half amounted to £514 9s. 6d.
[18] Ibid. i, No. 569.
[19] *Dep. Keeper's Rep.* viii, App. ii, p. 22.
[20] MS. Top. Glouc. C. 5, fol. 662.
[21] *Valor Eccles.* (Rec. Com.), ii, 430.

Cerney, Widmarshmore, Cherington, Henlow, rents in Gloucester and Cirencester, and the rectories of Barrington Magna, Barrington Parva, Windrush, Hempstead, Brockworth, Painswick, Haresfield, Prestbury, Frome Episcopi, Boroughhill, Tytherington, Caldicote, Barton Lacy, Cherington, Kington, Staunton Lacy, Llantrisant, Weobley and Awre, and the chapel of St. Kinburga at Gloucester.[1] The property of Lanthony Prima yielded £99 19s. 0½d.[2]

PRIORS OF LANTHONY BY GLOUCESTER [3]

Robert de Braci, 1137[4]
William de Wycombe, 1137[5]
Clement, 1150,[6] occurs *circa* 1170[7]
Roger of Norwich occurs 1178[8]
Geoffrey de Henlow occurs 1191[9] and 1203[10]
Martin occurs 1203[11]
Gilbert occurs *circa* 1203[12]
Walter of Monmouth occurs 1207[13]
John de Heyhampstead occurs 1217,[14] ob. 1240[15]
Geoffrey de Banbury resigned 1251[16]
Edward or Everard, 1251[17]
William de Ashwell occurs 1267[18] and 1276[19]
Walter de Martley elected 1283,[20] occurs 1300[21]

John Chaundos occurs 1300[22] and 1320[23]
William de Pendebury resigned 1324,[24] reinstated 1326,[25] ob. 1362[26]
Simon de Brockworth, 1362,[27] ob. 1376 or 1377[28]
William de Cheriton, 1377–1401[29]
John Lymnor, 1401[30]
John Wyche, 1409–36[31]
John Garland, 1436–57[32]
John Heyward, 1457[33]
Henry Deane, 1467[34]
Edmund Forrest, 1501,[35] occurs 1525[36]
Richard Hempstead or Hart occurs 1534–39[37]

A seal of the fifteenth century represents the Virgin crowned, seated in a heavily canopied niche, with tabernacle work at the sides, the Child with nimbus on her right knee, at her feet a lion passant.

The legend is :—

SIGILLVM COMVNE PRIORIS ET CONVENTVS ECCL'IE BEATE MARIE LANTHONI IVX. GLOUCESTRM [38]

10. THE PRIORY OF HORSLEY

In the reign of William the Conqueror, Roger Montgomery, earl of Shrewsbury, endowed the Benedictine abbey of St. Martin at Trouarn in Normandy with the manors of Horsley in Gloucestershire and Runckton in Sussex.[39] Another Norman lord, Robert de Romeliolo, gave the church of St. Andrew at Wheatenhurst near Horsley.[40] A prior and monks from Trouarn lived in the cell at Horsley until 1260.[41] In that year the abbot and convent of Trouarn gave all their property in England to the abbot and convent of Bruton in exchange for their possessions in the dioceses of Coutance and Bayeux.[42] Thus Horsley ceased to be an alien priory, and became a dependent cell of Bruton, which had been founded as a house of Augustinian canons in 1142 by William de Mohun.[43]

[1] *Valor Eccles.* (Rec. Com.), ii, 423–30.
[2] Ibid. 431.
[3] In the list given by Dugdale, *Mon.* vi, 127, the priors of Lanthony Prima and Lanthony Secunda are confused. The list in MS. Cotton, Julius D. x, was evidently compiled by a canon of Lanthony Prima, and the five priors after the partition belong to that house. In *Anglia Sacra*, ii, 322, Wharton introduced another source of error by confusing the Cluniac Priory of Lenton with Lanthony. Thus Matthew (or Peter) prior of Lenton, who became abbot of Bardney in 1214, disappears from our list. Cf. *Ann. Mon.* (Rolls Ser.), iii, 40. Thomas of Elmham, a monk of St. Augustine's, Canterbury, is also wrongly included by Wharton and Dugdale.
[4] Dugdale, op. cit. vi. 133.   [5] Ibid. 133.
[6] MS. Top. Glouc. C. 5, 643.
[7] Jeayes, *Catalogue of Muniments of Lord Fitzhardinge at Berkeley Castle*, p. 11.
[8] MS. Top. Glouc. C. 5, 643.
[9] Ibid. 644.
[10] In 1203 he became bishop of St. David's ; *Ann. Mon.* (Rolls Ser.), i, 57 ; *Giraldus Cambrensis* (Rolls Ser.), i, 108, 112, 306; iii, 82, 259–62.
[11] MS. Cotton, Julius D. x, fol. 32 ; MS. Top. Glouc. C. 5, 644.
[12] *Brist. and Glouc. Arch. Soc. Trans.* xxv. p. 224.
[13] MS. Top. Glouc. C. 5, 644.   [14] Ibid.
[15] *Ann. Mon.* (Rolls Ser.), i, 116.
[16] Ibid. 146 ; MS. Top. Glouc. C. 5, 645.
[17] *Ann. Mon.* (Rolls Ser.), i, 146 ; MS. Top. Glouc. C. 5, 645.
[18] Ibid. 646.   [19] Ibid.
[20] *Worc. Epis. Reg. Giffard* (Worc. Hist. Soc.), 174.
[21] MS. Top. Glouc. C. 5, 646.

[22] *Cal. of Pat.* 28 Edw. I, m. 15.
[23] Ibid. 13 Edw. II, m. 17.
[24] Ibid. 17 Edw. II, pt. ii, m. 27.
[25] Worc. Epis. Reg. Cobham, fol. 125, 126.
[26] MS. Top. Glouc. C. 5, 648.
[27] Ibid. 649.   [28] Ibid.   [29] Ibid.
[30] Ibid. 653.   [31] Ibid. 654, 655.
[32] Ibid. 656 ; Worc. Epis. Reg. Bourchier, fol. 17.
[33] MS. Top. Glouc. C. 5, 657.
[34] Ibid. 657.
[35] Ibid. 660 ; Worc. Epis. Reg. Silvester de Giglis, fol. 182 d.
[36] MS. Top. Glouc. C. 5, 661.
[37] *Dep. Keeper's Rep.* vii, App. ii, 290.
[38] Birch, *Catalogue of Seals in the British Museum*, i, 614.
[39] Dugdale, *Mon.* vii, 1030, 1031.
[40] Ibid. 1031.   [41] Ibid.
[42] *Cartul. of Bruton and Montacute* (Somerset Rec. Soc.), 76.
[43] Ibid. xviii.

In 1262 Walter Cantilupe, bishop of Worcester, admitted Stephen, a canon of Bruton, on the presentation of the prior of that house, to the care, rule and custody of the priory of Horsley.[1] The cell was managed entirely for the interests of the mother house, and in 1271, on the request of his brother, Walter Giffard, archbishop of York, Godfrey Giffard, bishop of Worcester, granted that the prior of Horsley should dwell at Bruton or elsewhere for four years, and that the prior of Bruton should administer the fruits of Horsley as should seem expedient to him, for the payment of the debts of his house, which was then greatly impoverished.[2] In 1276 Giffard ordered that on the presentation of the prior of Bruton, the prior of Horsley should have the cure of souls of Horsley and Wheatenhurst, with all offerings and oblations, and should have with him one canon regular, chosen by the prior of Bruton.[3] Difficulties again arose in 1283. The bishop wrote to the prior of Bruton, stating that having been lately at Horsley he found that hospitality was withdrawn and charity banished, and that the profits of the priory were converted to alien and strange uses. The bishop therefore admonished the prior not to take more from the priory of Horsley than was anciently 'accustomed and due.'[4]

In 1307 the prior of Horsley resisted the commissaries of the prior of Worcester when they attempted to visit his house during the vacancy of the see. He was excommunicated, and made an appeal to the archbishop of Canterbury, but afterwards withdrew it, and acknowledged the right of the prior of Worcester to visit the priory.[5]

In 1349 Prior Henry de Lisle determined to go on a pilgrimage to Rome, and on 31 December, when the bishopric was vacant, the prior of Worcester granted him a licence to set out, on the understanding that the prior of Bruton had given his consent.[6] He showed himself strangely neglectful of his duties, and in 1355 Edward III ordered an inquisition to be made into the devastations and dilapidations of Henry de Lisle at Horsley.[7] The jurors declared that he had cut down trees and sold wood to the value of £100, and also sold eighty oxen and cows which fell in as heriots at the time of the plague. He had spent £60 in going to Rome and Venice without the licence of the prior of Bruton.[8] In 1357 he resigned,[9] but the conduct of William Cary, who became prior in 1363,[10] gave rise to still greater dissatisfaction. At an inquisition[11] made by command of the king in 1369 it was stated that the prior had withdrawn all hospitality for seven years, although he was bound to provide dinner every day for six poor people in his hall.[12] He had leased the manor of Horsley for the term of his own life to the prior of Bruton without the king's consent;[13] and, although two voidances had occurred, the profits had gone to the prior of Bruton instead of to the crown. Probably on account of diminished revenues the prior and convent of Bruton were anxious to withdraw the canons from Horsley. For a payment of twenty marks, Edward III restored the manor of Horsley, which had been seized by the escheators; and agreed that henceforward no prior of Horsley should be nominated, and that vicarages should be created in the churches of Horsley and Wheatenhurst,[14] but some years passed before the king's grant took effect. During the vacancy of the see on 30 July, 1375, the prior of Worcester sent a mandate to the rural dean of Stonehouse to sequester the fruits of the priory and of the two churches on account of the absence of the prior, the peril of souls therefrom, and the withdrawal of hospitality, adding that the buildings of the priory had in great part collapsed and the profits of the house had been wasted.[15] The sequestrator was negligent, and on 16 August another commissioner was appointed in his stead,[16] but William Cary succeeded in preventing the seizure of the profits of the churches.[17] In the following year Henry Wakefield, bishop of Worcester, determined to put an end to the scandal. The bishop of Bath and Wells had excommunicated William Cary for leaving his house without permission from Bruton, and on 26 March, 1376, Bishop Wakefield sent a mandate to the deans of Gloucester and Stonehouse to denounce the prior of Horsley as excommunicate,[18] and the dean of Stonehouse was bidden to sequester the fruits of the priory.[19] On 5 July the bishop made a new ordinance by which the prior of Bruton was able not only to present the prior of Horsley but to recall him.[20] Nothing further is known of William Cary; but the prior of Bruton did not appoint a successor. Acting on the charter of Edward III he retained the manor. In 1380 Bishop Wakefield created vicarages in the churches of Horsley and Wheatenhurst.[21] Possibly a part of the priory buildings served as a manse for the vicar of Horsley. The history of the cell thus came to an end in 1380.

[1] *Cartul. of Bruton and Montacute* (Somerset Rec. Soc.), 77.
[2] *Worc. Epis. Reg. Giffard* (Worc. Hist. Soc.), 46.
[3] *Cartul. of Bruton and Montacute,* 79.
[4] *Worc. Epis. Reg. Giffard* (Worc. Hist. Soc.), 216.
[5] *Worc. Reg. Sede Vac.* (Worc. Hist. Soc.), 120, 121.
[6] Ibid. 245.
[7] *Cartul. of Bruton and Montacute,* 90.
[8] Ibid. 93.
[9] *Worc. Epis. Reg. Brian,* fol. 22 *d.*
[10] Ibid. Barnet, fol. 4 *d.*

[11] *Cartul. of Bruton and Montacute,* 95.
[12] Ibid.
[13] Ibid. ; Dugdale, op. cit. vii, 1031.
[14] Ibid.   [15] *Reg. Sede Vac.* 347.
[16] *Worc. Reg. Sede Vac.* (Worc. Hist. Soc.), 347.
[17] Ibid. 348.
[18] Worc. Epis. Reg. Wakefield, fol. 7 *d.*
[19] Ibid. fol. 8.   [20] Ibid.
[21] Ibid. fols. 14, 133 *d.,* 134.

PRIORS OF HORSLEY[1]
Stephen, 1262,[2] occurs 1269[3]
Walter de Horwood, occurs 1271[4]
Richard de la Grave, 1292[5]
William, 1298[6]

William de Milverton, *ob.* 1329[16]
Laurence de Haustede, 1329[17]
Henry de Lisle, 1335,[18] resigned 1357[19]
Richard de Holt, 1357,[20] resigned 1363[21]
William Cary, 1363[22]

HOUSE OF AUGUSTINIAN CANONESSES

11. THE PRIORY OF ST. MARY MAGDALEN, BRISTOL

The priory of St. Mary Magdalen at Bristol was founded in or about 1173, and endowed with 'competent' possessions, by Eva, widow of Robert Fitzharding, who is said to have been the first prioress.[7] It was a house of canonesses of the order of St. Augustine,[8] and as such was subject to the visitation of the bishop of Worcester, which was regularly exercised.[9] The canonesses had the right of free election after obtaining a *congé d'élire* from the lords of Berkeley,[10] but on more than one occasion either they did not avail themselves of the right[11] or they neglected some formality, which gave the bishop the power to appoint. In 1421 he set aside their election as invalid,[12] but nominated the prioress of their choice. From the thirteenth century onwards the community was very poor, and on that account was exempt from payment of procurations to the bishop at his visitation,[13] and from taxation.[14] The priory came under the Act of 1536 for the suppression of the lesser monasteries. On 3 August a commission was issued for a survey of those monasteries in Bristol

of which the revenues fell below £200 a year, with a view of taking them over on the king's behalf.[23] The commissioners reported that at the priory of St. Mary Magdalen there were two religious, 'by report of honest conversation whereof one professed being governor impotent and aged; the other a young novice desiring continuance in religion.'[24] They had two servants, a man and a laundress. The church and house were in good repair. The yearly value of the property was set down at £21 13s. 2d. The house was probably dissolved immediately afterwards.[25]

PRIORESSES OF ST. MARY MAGDALEN, BRISTOL

Eva,[26] *ob.* 1173
Agnes of Gloucester,[27] 1347
Matilda de Luttelton, 1349,[28] resigned 1356[29]
Margery Long, 1363[30]
Elizabeth Wodecroft, 1369,[31] occurs 1386[32]
Alice Clayville, *ob.* 1421[33]
Joan Waleys, 1421[34]
Elizabeth Went, occurs 1499[35]
Katherine Brown, occurs 1507,[36] *ob.* 1520[37]
Eleanor Graunte, 1520[38]

HOUSES OF CISTERCIAN MONKS

12. THE ABBEY OF FLAXLEY

The Cistercian monastery of Flaxley, sometimes called Dean, was founded between 1151 and 1154 by Roger, son of Milo Fitzwalter, earl of Hereford.[15] According to tradition he chose

as a site the spot on which his father had been killed while hunting in 1143.[39] Between 1151 and 1154 Henry, duke of Normandy and count of Anjou, confirmed to the monks of the Cistercian Order the grants which Roger, earl of

---

[1] It has not been possible to trace the names of the priors of the first foundation who were appointed by the abbot and convent of Trouarn.
[2] *Cartul. of Bruton and Montacute,* 77.
[3] *Worc. Epis. Reg. Giffard* (Worc. Hist. Soc.), 21.
[4] Ibid. 46.   [5] Ibid. 425.   [6] Ibid. 507.
[7] Smyth, *Lives of the Berkeleys;* (ed. Maclean), i, 44; Dugdale, *Mon.* iv, 589.
[8] Worc. Epis. Reg. Morgan, fol. 6 d.; *Dublin Review,* 1894, p. 275.
[9] *Worc. Epis. Reg. Giffard* (Worc. Hist. Soc.), 234.
[10] Smyth, *Lives of the Berkeleys* (ed. Maclean), ii. 79. *Worc. Epis. Reg. Giffard* (Worc. Hist. Soc.), 263.
[11] Worc. Epis. Reg. Bransford, fol. 145.
[12] Ibid. Morgan, fol. 6 d.
[13] Ibid. *Giffard* (Worc. Hist. Soc.) 234; *Sede Vac. Reg.* (Worc. Hist. Soc.), 120.
[14] Ibid. Clifford, fol. 70 d.
[15] Dugdale, *Mon.* v, 589; Crawley-Boevey, *Cartul. of Flaxley,* 1; *Engl. Hist. Rev.* 1893, p. 648.

[16] Worc. Epis. Reg. Orlton, fol. 33. He may be the prior who was appointed in 1298.
[17] Ibid. fol. 33.
[18] Ibid. Montacute, fol. 20.
[19] Ibid. Brian, i, fol. 22 d.   [20] Ibid.
[21] Ibid. Barnet, fol. 4 d.   [22] Ibid.
[23] *Dublin Review,* April, 1894, p. 250.
[24] Ibid. 275.
[25] *L. and P. Hen. VIII.* xi, 307.
[26] Dugdale, *Mon.* iv, 589.   [27] Ibid.
[28] Worc. Epis. Reg. Bransford, fol. 145.
[29] Ibid. Brian, fol. 17.   [30] Ibid. Barnet, fol. 27.
[31] Ibid. Lynn, fol. 20 d.
[32] *Cal. of Pat.* 10 Ric. II, pt. i, m. 33.
[33] Worc. Epis. Reg. Morgan, fol. 6 d.
[34] Ibid. fol. 6 d.
[35] Birch, *Orig. Doc. relating to Bristol,* No. 143.
[36] Ibid. No. 106.
[37] Worc. Epis. Reg. Jerome Ghinucci, fol. 2.
[38] Ibid. fol. 2.
[39] *Cartul. of Flaxley,* 4.

Hereford, had made to them according to the tenor of their charter, viz. a place in the valley of Castiard, the land called Westdean, a forge at Edland, all the land under the old castle of Dean which remained to be assarted, and the assarts, a fishery at Rodley called Newerre, a meadow in Pulmede, all easements in the Forest of Dean, all the demesne of Dymock, and the lands belonging to Walfric, half the wood at Dymock, all the tithes of chestnuts in Dean, the lands of Geoffrey son of Walfric and of Leofric de Staura, which the earl of Hereford released.[1] It is clear from this charter that the site had been given but the buildings, even if they had been begun, were not sufficiently advanced for habitation. There was as yet no convent of monks at Flaxley, and Henry therefore confirmed the grant to the Cistercian Order. There can be little doubt that the first monks of Flaxley came from Bordesley in Worcestershire, which had been founded in 1138.[2] In 1158 Henry II gave the monks of Flaxley a charter confirming his former grant.[3] In aid of the building which was in progress Henry II granted the right of taking wood and other materials without committing waste in the forest.[4] The monks had already built for the lay brothers granges at Westdean and Wallmore, where the king had given them 200 acres of his assarts, with meadows and pastures. They had the right of common of pasture for their cattle, swine, and all other beasts within the forest.

When the visitors of the order came to England in 1187 Abbot Waleran resigned, and Alan, a monk of Bordesley, was elected in his stead.[5] Towards the end of the twelfth century the abbot and convent were rapidly increasing their possessions. Many of these lay in the parish of Westbury-on-Severn, which was only two miles from Flaxley.[6] Like other houses of the Cistercian Order, Flaxley was exempted by papal bulls from the payment of tithes from land which they brought into cultivation or cultivated at their own expense, and of all tithes of the young of their animals.[7] It was a privilege which pressed hard on the parish priests. Diminishing tithes probably kindled the bitter animosity of Walter Mapes, archdeacon of Oxford (ob. circa 1210), who, amongst other preferments, held the rectory of Westbury-on-Severn.[8] The abbot and convent of Flaxley were willing to pay sums of ready money and take lands for a term of years in pledge. In 1195 Walter Mapes witnessed an agreement by which Philip de Dunie pledged lands in Westbury for terms of eight and twelve

years for 4 marks down.[9] As the monks of Flaxley were sheep farmers, it was obviously to their advantage to secure fresh pastures ; the wool trade was a great source of profit, and money in hand allowed them to make bargains profitable to themselves. A notable case occurs in the acquisition of land at Ragel, afterwards called Rochelbury. In 1193 Philip de Burci gave all his land at Ragel to William de St. Leger in perpetuity at a fee farm rent of 2s.[10] As his part of the bargain William de St. Leger paid a debt of 87½ marks which Philip de Burci owed to Manasser, a Jew of Bristol, gave him 15 marks down, and paid the rent for three years in advance. William de St. Leger granted the land to the abbot and convent of Flaxley to be held at ⅔ of a knight's fee, and for a yearly rent of 2s., which after thirty-one years had elapsed was to be paid, with an additional 2s., to Philip de Burci and his heirs. At the time of this grant the abbot and convent gave 20 marks to William de St. Leger, and he expressly stated that he paid the debts of Philip de Burci to Manasser the Jew, out of the money of the monks of Flaxley.

In 1193 Abbot Alan obtained a bull from Pope Celestine III confirming the liberties and immunities which his predecessors had granted to Flaxley.[11] As a Cistercian house, Flaxley was exempt from the visitation of the bishops of Hereford.

In the exercise of their privileges in the Forest of Dean, the abbot and convent came into conflict with the keeper, the constable of St. Briavel's Castle. Mandates were sent to him by Henry III in 1226, in 1231, and again in 1232 and 1234, to allow the abbot and convent of Flaxley to have all their rights of common of pasture.[12] In 1217 the constable of St. Briavel's was ordered to allow them to take timber according to their charters.[13] In lieu of the right to take fuel for their use throughout the forest, in 1227 Henry III granted the woods around the abbey, strictly defining their bounds.[14] Henry II, by the charter of 1158, had allowed the monks to set up their forge where they willed,[15] and they had secured the right of taking two dry oaks for fuel for the forge every week.[16] It was represented to Henry III that this was greatly to the detriment of the forest, and in 1258, after an inquisition, he withdrew the privilege and gave them instead the ' abbot's ' woods.[17]

In 1234, on the occasion of the movement against Henry III's foreign favourites, the monastery was embarrassed by the presence of the followers of Richard Earl Marshal who had

---

[1] Dugdale, op. cit. v, 590.
[2] *Engl. Hist. Rev.* 1893, p. 648 ; cf. *Cartul. of Flaxley*, 20.
[3] Dugdale, op. cit. v, 590 ; *Cartul. of Flaxley*, 19.
[4] Ibid. v, 590, No. ii.
[5] *Ann. Mon.* (Rolls Ser.), ii, 245.
[6] *Cartul. of Flaxley*, 230.   [7] Ibid. 178–82.
[8] *Dict. Nat. Biog.*; cf. *Giraldus Cambrensis* (Rolls Ser.), iv, 219.

[9] *Cartul. of Flaxley*, 163 ; cf. 161.
[10] Ibid. 185–90.   [11] Ibid. 178–80.
[12] Ibid. 23.   [13] Ibid. 24.   [14] Ibid. 108.
[15] Dugdale, op. cit. v, 590.
[16] *Cartul. of Flaxley*, 30. ' By the sufferance of Hen. II.'
[17] Ibid. 109.

taken refuge there.[1] On 6 March Henry III commanded the sheriff of Gloucester to take with him the constable of St. Briavel's and the king's coroners of the county, and go to the abbey of Flaxley to offer to persons there who were against the king that they should come out to stand their trial or else abjure the kingdom. The sheriff's men, armed with bows and hatchets, kept watch around the abbey and took fuel in the abbot's woods. The constable of St. Briavel's seized the abbot's horses, and was in consequence excommunicated by Hugh Foliot, bishop of Hereford. On 20 March Henry III sent a mandate to the constable to deliver up the horses, and to the bishop to remove the excommunication. On 28 March he ordered the constable to recompense the abbot for his burnt hedges, and commanded that the keepers of Richard Marshal's servants should remain outside, not inside, the gates of the monastery.

The revenues of Flaxley were never large, and in 1276 it was one of the poorer houses of the southern province, assessed only to pay £8 towards the 'courtesy' of £1,000 to Edward I, when Kingswood paid £13 16s. and Hayles £14 13s. 4d.[2] Like a number of other Cistercian monasteries,[3] it was heavily in debt. Building was going on in the reign of Henry III, for on several occasions the king granted oaks for the church and buildings of the abbey.[4] In 1277 Edward I appointed his steward, Ralph of Sandwich, to the custody during pleasure, of the abbey of Flaxley, because it was in debt to the king for a considerable sum, and would so continue for a long time, also on account of a loan contracted in the Jewry and elsewhere, and of various immense debts to merchants alien and denizen, and others.[5] In 1281 the king issued a mandate to Grimbold Pauncefort, the keeper of the Forest of Dean, to take the abbey of Flaxley under his special protection for three years, because it was burdened with debt and impoverished both by murrain among the sheep, upon which the monks mainly depended for their subsistence, as well as by sheriffs, bedels, foresters, and others consuming their goods by faculties, so that the abbey could no longer perform its customary distribution of alms or other works of mercy, and the monks were in danger of dispersion. He was bidden to apply the revenues thereof to the use of the said abbey, except such as were necessary for the maintenance of the abbot and convent and their households, and for the distribution of alms to the poor.[6] The situation appears to have been one of special difficulty, and two years later Edward I gave the

custody of Flaxley to Thomas de Basing, a citizen of London, bidding him apply the issues to the satisfaction of the multifarious and immense debts of the house.[7] A great murrain among sheep began in 1276 and lasted for several years.[8] The debts of Flaxley probably prevented the convent from restocking their pastures, and perhaps explain the fact that about the beginning of the fourteenth century the annual average sales of wool amounted only to six sacks a year, the prices varying from 15 to 8½ marks a sack, when Kingswood was selling forty sacks and Hayles twenty sacks.[9]

In 1335 misrule as well as misfortune brought the monastery once more into grievous pecuniary difficulties. Edward III gave the custody of Flaxley during his pleasure to the abbots of Bordesley and Dore, and the prior of the house.[10]

In 1353, in consideration of the great losses which the abbot and convent had sustained from the deer and other wild beasts of the forest, and from the expense incurred by many visits from the king, Edward III granted a yearly payment of £36 9s. 1d. out of the rents of newly assarted crown lands in the Forest of Dean.[11]

As one of the lesser monasteries Flaxley came under the Act of 1536. On 4 September a commission was issued for a survey of all those monasteries in Gloucestershire of which the revenues fell below £200 a year, with a view of taking them over on the king's behalf.[12] The commissioners reported that at Flaxley there were seven monks, all priests, 'by report of convenient conversation.'[13] Three of them desired to have 'capacities' that they might hold benefices, the other four wished to continue in religion. There was one lay brother, and the household consisted of eighteen servants. The house itself was in ruin and decay, and the church had been destroyed by fire; the bells had been melted and the metal sold for the restoration of the building. There is no evidence to show how soon afterwards the house was dissolved; on 21 March, 1537, the site and possessions of the late monastery were granted to Sir William Kingston.[14] The abbot, Thomas Were, retired to Aston Rowant in Oxfordshire.[15] Under the Act pensions were only provided for heads of houses; in the case of the Cistercian monasteries the monks who wished to continue in religion were usually received into the larger houses of the order, when possible into the

---

[1] *Cartul. of Flaxley*, 55–7.

[2] Harl. MS. (B.M.), 6603, fol. 384.

[3] *Roy. Hist. Soc. Trans.* xviii, 142.

[4] *Cal. of Close*, 15 Hen. III, m. 15. *Cartul. of Flaxley*, 25.

[5] *Cal. of Pat.* 5 Edw. I, m. 20.

[6] Ibid. 10 Edw. I, m. 22.

[7] Ibid. 11 Edw. I, m. 9.

[8] *Flor. Wigorn.* (Engl. Hist. Soc.), ii, 217.

[9] Cunningham, *Growth of English Industry and Commerce*, i, 633 (ed. 1905).

[10] *Cal. of Pat.* 9 Edw. III, pt. ii, m. 16. *Cartul. of Flaxley*, 117.

[11] Ibid. 116.

[12] *Dublin Review*, April, 1894, p. 250.

[13] Ibid, 275, 276.

[14] *L. and P. Hen. VIII*, xii, pt. i, No. 795 (42).

[15] *Cartul. of Flaxley*, p. 88.

mother house.[1] Nothing is known of the fate of the four monks of Flaxley who did not seek 'capacities.' Possibly they were received at Bordesley.

In 1535 the clear yearly value of the property was £112 3s. 1d.[2] The possessions of the monastery in Gloucestershire included the manors of Blaisdon, Wallmore, and divers lands and rents in Newnham, Polton, Howle, Goodrich, Climperwell, Arlingham, Dymock, Newland, Coleford, Staunton, and Little Dean, and the manor of Rochelbury, in Somerset.[3]

ABBOTS OF FLAXLEY[4]

Waleran, resigned 1187
Alan, el. 1187
Richard, el. *circa* 1200
William, el. Feb. 1277 (?)
Nicholas, 1288
William de Rya, 1314
Richard Peyto, 1372
William, 1426
— Berkeley, occurs 1476
John, el. 1509
William Beawdley, 1528
Thomas Were, 1532

The abbot's seal,[5] attached to a deed dated 1316, is in shape a pointed oval, and represents an abbot standing erect under a canopy, slightly ornamented, with a pastoral staff in his right hand, and holding with his left a book on his breast.

The legend is :—

S. ABBATIS DE FLAXLE.

The counterseal represents a hand with a pastoral staff and other ornaments, and the legend is—

CONTA SIGILL' ABBATIS DE FLAXLE.

13. THE ABBEY OF HAYLES

The Cistercian monastery of Hayles was founded in 1246 by Richard, earl of Cornwall.[6] When in great peril in a storm at sea on his way home from Gascony to Cornwall, he vowed that if he came safely to port he would found a monastery.[7] He fixed upon a site in his manor of Hayles. On 17 June, 1246, he was present with his brother, Henry III, at the dedication by William de Raleigh, bishop of Winchester, of the Cistercian church at Beaulieu.[8] The abbot of Beaulieu consented to send twenty monks and ten lay brothers to found a new monastery.[9] Thus Hayles became the daughter house of

Beaulieu, and in virtue of that tie was subject to the regular visitation of the abbot. In 1251 the church, cloister, dorter, and frater were finished at the sole cost of the founder, amounting to from 8,000 to 10,000 marks.[10] The church was dedicated on 5 November by Walter Cantilupe, bishop of Worcester, assisted by thirteen other bishops, who each dedicated an altar.[11] For the endowment of the monastery Richard gave the manor and church of Hayles,[12] and 1,000 marks to be expended either on the purchase of land or on buildings,[13] and Henry III granted a yearly rental of 20 marks.[14]

As a house of the Cistercian Order Hayles was exempt from the bishop's visitation. It has been recently stated that Giffard, bishop of Worcester, disregarded the immunity of the Cistercians, and visited their houses.[15] It is clear, however, from his register that he received procuration in food and drink at their houses solely in virtue of his visitation of the parish churches which they held,[16] and on other occasions he received a fee instead.[17] It was on account of a dispute concerning the parish church of Didbrook that in 1275 he laid an interdict upon the abbot of Hayles.[18] Probably the abbot yielded, for the bishop shortly afterwards removed it.[19]

The revenues did not suffice to meet expenses, and the building of granges for the lay brothers and servants, an essential step in the development of a Cistercian house, was doubtless a heavy charge. When James, abbot of Beaulieu, visited the monastery in 1261, he decreed that no further increase should be made in the number of monks or lay brothers until the debts were diminished.[20] He bade the cellarer and his colleague pay greater heed to the administration of property. Nine years later, when John, abbot of Beaulieu, came to Hayles he insisted that the alms which used to be given away at the great gate should not be withdrawn.[21] His other injunctions were directed towards keeping the rule of silence that quarrels among

---

[1] Gasquet, *Hen. VIII and the English Monasteries* (ed. 1899), pp. 181, 437 *n.* 2.

[2] *Valor Eccles.* (Rec. Com.), ii, 486.   [3] Ibid.

[4] *Cartul. of Flaxley,* 85, 86.

[5] Ibid. 97, 98.

[6] Dugdale, *Mon.* v, 686 ; *Ann. Mon.* (Rolls Ser.), ii, 337.

[7] Dugdale, op. cit. v, 688.

[8] *Ann. Mon.* (Rolls Ser.), ii, 337.   [9] Ibid.

[10] Dugdale, op. cit. v, 688.

[11] *Ann. Mon.* (Rolls Ser.), ii, 343.

[12] Dugdale, op. cit. v, 688.

[13] *Ann. Mon.* (Rolls Ser.), ii, 343.

[14] Ibid. Probably the manor of Pinnockshire was then granted by Henry III to the abbot and convent. Cf. Pipe R. 44 Hen. III, m. 2.

[15] *V.C.H. Worcestershire*, ii, 26, 'Ecclesiastical History' ; and 153, 'Religious Houses.' *Worc. Epis. Reg. Giffard* (Worc. Hist. Soc.), xcii, xciii, xcvi, 66–7, 81. There is absolutely no evidence that, as stated in the introduction to Giffard's register, the bishop attempted to enforce internal reforms at Hayles. On no occasion is it stated that the bishop 'visited' any Cistercian house, though in the printed text, p. 77, 'hospitare' is loosely rendered as 'visit.'

[16] *Worc. Epis. Reg. Giffard* (Worc. Hist. Soc.), 22, 235, 239.

[17] Ibid. 141.   [18] Ibid. 66–7.   [19] Ibid. 81.

[20] M.S. Reg. xii, E. xiv. 73–4 (B.M.).

[21] Ibid. fol. 75.

the brethren and vain chatter might be avoided, and the better care of the sick in the farmery. In 1276 Hayles was reckoned among the more prosperous houses of the Cistercian Order in the south of England, and paid £14 13s. 4d. out of the 'courtesy' granted to Edward I, which was the same amount as that given by the house of Bordesley in Worcestershire, and more than either Kingswood or Flaxley contributed.[1]

A gift from Edmund, earl of Cornwall, proved to be a constant source of revenue on account of the attraction which it offered to pilgrims. In 1267 he purchased from Florey V, count of Holland, a relic which was authenticated under the seal of the Patriarch of Jerusalem, afterwards Pope Urban IV, as some of the blood of Christ.[2] On 14 September, 1270, he gave a portion of this relic to Hayles. A polygonal apse of five chapels was added to the church to contain the shrine of the relic,[3] and the new work was dedicated by Giffard, bishop of Worcester, in 1277.[4] In 1277 Earl Edmund petitioned the bishop of Lincoln to appropriate to Hayles the churches of Hemel Hempstead and Northley, of which he had given the advowsons,[5] and Northley was appropriated in 1304.[6] It is probable that the well endowed churches of St. Paul and St. Breage in Cornwall were also his gift. In 1300 he granted his manor of Lechlade to Hayles at a fee farm rent of 100 marks.[7] When the manor reverted to the crown after his death in 1301, Edward I increased the rent to £100.[8] Hayles derived the greater part of its income from the profits of the wool-trade, and about the beginning of the fourteenth century twenty sacks a year were sold on an average, at prices varying from 10 to 7 marks a sack, according to the quality.[9] However, until the middle of the fifteenth century, the financial condition of the monastery was very unstable, and its history is a record of difficulties and of efforts to overcome them. The expenses of Lechlade were so heavy that it was useless to the monks, and they were obliged to give it up.[10] They had licence to exchange it in 1318 with Hugh Despenser the elder for the manor of Siddington by Cirencester and a rental of 10 marks in Chelworth, Wiltshire.[11] In 1317 they received a licence from Edward II to acquire in mortmain lands and rents not held in chief, to the value of £10 a year,[12] and before 1318 they had possession of the manor of Great Wormington in Gloucester-

shire.[13] In 1324 Hugh Despenser granted the advowsons of the churches of Longborough and Rodborne,[14] and the abbot and convent saw an opportunity to add to their revenues. In 1325 they set forth their distress in a long petition to Thomas Cobham, bishop of Worcester, urging him to appropriate Longborough to them.[15] The burden of it was that unless they could increase their income they must diminish the number of their brethren, and withdraw some of that hospitality which they had hitherto maintained 'according to the laudable custom of the kingdom of England.' Their buildings had been left unfinished by the founder and his son, they had not the promised rental of £200 a year, Lechlade had proved unprofitable, other endowments were in distant dioceses, and they had great difficulties in collecting their revenues. In the years of the great famine,[16] from 1314 to 1321, they had suffered heavily from sterile lands and murrain among cattle, and in 1325 Bishop Cobham consented to the appropriation of Longborough. In 1345 Abbot Thomas complained that Sir Walter Dastyn and others broke into his close and houses at Wormington, drove away horses, oxen, sheep, and swine which were worth 100 marks, and assaulted his men and servants.[17]

In 1347, at the request of Edward prince of Wales, Edward III granted a licence for the acquisition of lands and rents to the value of £20 a year,[18] and in 1392 the abbot and convent had secured them.[19] There is no indication of the effects of the Black Death in 1349, but when the pestilence recurred in 1361–2 many of the monks and lay brothers died.[20] The abbots of Hayles had often found some difficulty in collecting the revenues which accrued to the convent as rectors of the churches of St. Breage and St. Paul in Cornwall. It was usual for the abbot to send two of his monks to serve the churches and to receive the profits for his use.[21] In 1337 the king's aid was invoked against persons who threatened and assaulted their men and servants and carried away their goods.[22] Later in the fourteenth century the abbot leased the churches at a rent of 120 marks a year.[23] In 1395 there were arrears of 140 marks, and the tenants of the abbot were outlawed for non-payment.[24] When in 1386 Hayles was in sore

[1] Harl. MS. 6603, fol. 384 (B.M.).
[2] *Brist. and Glouc. Arch. Soc. Trans.* xxiii, 277 ; Harl. MS. 3725, fol. 13 *v*. (B.M.).
[3] Ibid. 278.
[4] Dugdale, *Mon.* v, 687 ; Harl. MS. 3725, fol. 15.
[5] Linc. Epis. Reg. Dalderby, Institutions, fol. 145.
[6] Ibid.
[7] Cart. R. 12 Edw. II, No. 17.   [8] Ibid.
[9] Cunningham, *Growth of English Industry and Commerce,* i, 634 (ed. 1905).
[10] Worc. Epis. Reg. Cobham, fol. 106.
[11] *Cal. of Pat.* 12 Edw. II, pt. i, m. 23.
[12] Ibid. 10 Edw. II, pt. ii, m. 30.

[13] Ibid. 12 Edw. II, pt. i, m. 17 *d*.
[14] Ibid. 17 Edw. II, pt. ii, m. 6.
[15] Worc. Epis. Reg. Cobham, fol. 106.
[16] Harl. MS. 3725, fol. 21.
[17] *Cal. of Pat.* 19 Edw. III, pt. iii, m. 9 *d*.
[18] Ibid. 21 Edw. III, pt. i, m. 17.
[19] Ibid. 16 Ric. II, pt. i, m. 17.
[20] *Brist. and Glouc. Arch. Soc. Trans.* xxii, 259.
[21] *Cal. of Pat.* 6 Edw. III, pt. ii, m. 2 ; cf. other references in *Cal. of Pat.*
[22] Ibid. 11 Edw. III, pt. i, m. 21.
[23] Ibid. 19 Ric. II, pt. ii, m. 36.
[24] Ibid.

need of a further source of revenue the abbot and convent commented on the difficulty of collecting their Cornish[1] rents. They petitioned Wakefield, bishop of Worcester, to appropriate the church of Toddington, with the chapel of Stanley Pontlarge, to their uses, putting forward the usual pleas of religious houses in the years after the Black Death. Their lands were sterile, their tenants and villeins had died in great numbers, they had lost their cattle by murrains. They even lacked necessary food and clothing; they were bound with a load of debt, while taxation was ever increasing. It is probable that as at Meaux and other Cistercian houses the lay brothers died out before the end of the fourteenth century. After inquiring into the truth of these statements, Bishop Wakefield granted the petition of the abbot and convent of Hayles. In 1394, when Herman, abbot of Stratford, came to Hayles as the visitor-general of the Cistercian order, he found but little to criticize.[2] In 1398 John, abbot of Beaulieu,[3] desired that better care should be taken of the sick, and that one of the monks should be chosen to provide the clothes of the brethren out of the proceeds of the parish churches of Rodbourne and Northley. Misfortune dogged the footsteps of the convent. In 1397 Henry of Alcester was elected abbot,[4] but six years later another abbot, Robert of Alcester, appealed to Henry IV to seize a vagrant monk, by name Henry of Alcester.[5] In 1413 Pope John XXIII granted for ten years a relaxation of ten years and ten quarantines of penance to penitents who on Whitsun Day and Corpus Christi and during those octaves visited the church of Hayles and gave alms for the maintenance of the fabric.[6] It was alleged that on account of the dilapidations left by the late Abbot Henry the monastery was in debt to the sum of 1,000 marks. The buildings were ruinous, the revenues scarcely amounted to £100 a year, and were insufficient for the sustenance of twenty-two monks, for hospitality, and other burdens. About 1431 Abbot William set out for the papal curia with the object of obtaining further aid.[7] He deputed Prior John of Alcester to govern during his absence, with two monks as his council, and power to summon others to advise him. All jewels and other valuables were to be kept in the treasury, and the convent seal was put in safe custody. A revival in the attraction of the relic of the Holy Blood was the result of the abbot's journey. Eugenius IV granted lavish indulgences to all who gave alms to the worship of God and the Precious Blood of

Hayles.[8] Further indulgences were granted in 1458 by Calixtus III, who exhorted all the faithful to help the monks of Hayles in repairing their ruined abbey,[9] and again by Paul II in 1468.[10]

The administration of the house caused grave dissatisfaction to the abbots of Waverley and Beaulieu, when they visited it in 1442.[11] The strict provisions of the Cistercian rule about finance were disregarded, so they bade the abbot render his accounts by Michaelmas, and immediately afterwards to appoint two bursars to receive all the moneys and supervise the expenditure of the house. They ordered that repairs, internal and external, of the monastery, should be carried out as quickly as possible, and they censured the general relaxation of discipline. It may be surmised that a period of prosperity began about the middle of the fifteenth century; much rebuilding took place, and at the dissolution the commissioners were loud in their praises of the administration of the property of the monastery.[12]

In 1535 Cromwell appointed Anthony Saunders, the curate of Winchcombe, to read to the monks of Winchcombe and preach in the parish.[13] On 2 November he complained to Cromwell of the abbot of Hayles—

I have small favour and assistance amongst Pharasaical papists. The Abbot of Hayles has hired a great Golyas, a subtle Dun's man, yea a great clerk, as he sayeth, a bachelor of divinity of Oxford to catch me in my sermons.

He added that this preacher rather maintained than spoke against the usurped power of the bishop of Rome. However, Abbot Stephen was not openly hostile to Cromwell. On 28 January, 1536, he wrote asking him to dispense with some of the new injunctions which were most galling to the religious.[14] Since Cromwell had visited the house, he wrote—

The number of my brethren is sore decayed. I have buried three, two are sore sick, one had licence to depart, and I have three in Oxford at divinity. I beg that I may take in more to help the choir.

On 18 June he told Cromwell that in accordance with his wish he had granted the farm of Longborough to Robert Hopper.[15]

In 1538 commissioners were appointed in every county to destroy the shrines. Latimer, bishop of Worcester, reported to Cromwell that the relic of the Holy Blood of Hayles seemed, after examination, to be 'an unctuous gum and

[1] Worc. Epis. Reg. Wakefield, fol. 116.
[2] MS. Reg. xii, E. xiv, fol. 84 v. (B.M.).
[3] Ibid. fol. 89 v.
[4] Worc. Epis. Reg. Winchcombe, fol. 16 d.
[5] Cal. of Pat. 5 Hen. IV, pt. i, m. 27 d.
[6] Cal. Papal L. (Rolls Ser.), vi, 376.
[7] MS. Reg. xii, E. xiv, fol. 75 v. (B.M.).

[8] Brist. and Glouc. Arch. Soc. Trans. xxiii, 279.
[9] Ibid. 279, xxii, 260.   [10] Ibid. 280.
[11] MS. Reg. xii, E. xiv, fol. 81 v. (B.M.).
[12] Wright, Suppression of the Mon. (Camden Soc.), 236-7.
[13] L. and P. Hen. VIII, ix, No. 747.
[14] Ibid. No. 192.
[15] Ibid. x, No. 1163.

ADAM OF STAUNTON,
ABBOT OF ST. PETER'S, GLOUCESTER,
1337

JOHN, ABBOT OF ST. AUGUSTINE'S,
BRISTOL

HAYLES ABBEY

ST. AUGUSTINE'S ABBEY, BRISTOL

ST. BARTHOLOMEW'S HOSPITAL,
GLOUCESTER

BLACK FRIARS, GLOUCESTER

GILBERT, PRIOR OF LANTHONY BY GLOUCESTER,
circa 1203

GLOUCESTERSHIRE MONASTIC SEALS : PLATE II

a compound of many things.'[1] It was dispatched to London, and on 24 November Hilsey, bishop of Rochester, preached at Paul's Cross, and there showed the Blood of Hayles, affirming it to be 'honey clarified and coloured with saffron, as had been evidently proved before the king and his council.'[2] Abbot Stephen wrote to Cromwell praying that he might destroy the empty shrine, 'lest it should minister occasion for stumbling to the weak.'[3]

On 24 December, 1539, the abbot and twenty-one monks surrendered the monastery.[4] Dr. London and his fellow-commissioners reported to Cromwell that they found—

the father and all his brethren very honest and conformable persons, and the house clearly out of debt. . . . The father had his house and grounds so well furnished with jewels, plate, stuff, corn, cattle, and the woods also so well saved, as though he had looked for no alteration of his house.[5]

A pension of £100 a year, with the manor-house of Coscomb, was assigned to the abbot ; the prior and one monk got £8 ; the rest received pensions varying from £7 to £1 6s. 8d. a year, and two monks were given vicarages.[6] Wages were paid to seventy servants of the household.[7]

In 1535 the clear yearly value of the property of Hayles amounted to £357 7s. 8½d.[8] The possessions of the monastery included the manors of Hayles, Pinnockshire, Nether Swell, Wormington, Coscomb, Longborough ; rents in the towns of Gloucester and Winchcombe ; lands and rents in Didbrook, Challingworth, and Farmcote, in Gloucestershire ; the manor of Rodbourne in Wiltshire ; pastures at Heathend in Worcestershire ; and the rectories of Hagley in Suffolk, Northley in Oxfordshire, St. Breage and St. Paul in Cornwall, Rodbourne in Wiltshire, Hayles, Didbrook, Longborough, and Toddington in Gloucestershire.

ABBOTS OF HAYLES [9]

Jordan, 1246 [10]
Hugh, occurs 1280 [11] and 1305 [12]

John of Gloucester, 1305,[13] occurs 1333 [14]
Thomas, occurs 1345 [15]
Nicholas of Hayles, 1351 [16]
Thomas, 1354 [17]
John of Gloucester, 1368 [18]
Robert, occurs 1380 [19]
Henry of Alcester, 1397 [20]
Robert of Alcester, occurs 1403,[21] ob. 1420 [22]
William Henley, 1420,[23] occurs 1435 [24]
Robert Laurak, 1451 [25]
William Whitchurch, 1464 [26]
Richard Wotton, 1479 [27]
John Combeck, occurs 1483 [28]
Thomas Stafford, 1483,[29] occurs 1503 [30]
Anthony Melton, occurs 1515,[31] ob. circa 1527 [32]
Stephen Sagar, 1527 [33]–39

A seal of the fifteenth century represents a monk standing on a flight of three steps, in his right hand a globular bottle with cylindrical neck or ampulla, with cross issuing from the mouth in allusion to the Holy Blood ; in the left hand a sprinkler ; the field resplendent with wavy branches of foliage with pierced cinquefoil flowers.[34]

The legend is :—

SIGILLV · FRATERNITAT' . MONASTERII · BEATE · MARIE · DE · HEYLES.ι

14. THE ABBEY OF KINGSWOOD

The monastery of Tintern was founded in 1131 as a daughter house of the Cistercian monastery of L'Aumone in the diocese of Chartres.[35] The monks rapidly increased in numbers, and in a few years' time, in accordance with the Cistercian usage, the abbot and convent were anxious to send out a colony of their brethren to found a daughter house.[36] Roger of Berkeley II purposed to give them the manor of

---

[1] Glouc. N. and Q. iv, 576.
[2] Wright, op. cit. 237 n.
[3] Glouc. N. and Q. iv, 575.
[4] L. and P. Hen. VIII, xv, No. 139, iv.
[5] Wright, op. cit, 236–7.
[6] Dugdale, Mon. v, 689.
[7] Aug. Off. Bk. 494, fol. 70.
[8] Valor Eccles. (Rec. Com.), ii, 456.
[9] The abbots of Hayles have been confused with the abbots of Hales Owen in Shropshire. A list of the abbots of Hales Owen is included in Gasquet, Coll. Angl. Premonstratensia (R. Hist. Soc.), ii, 237. Of these Walter de Hagge and Bartholomew are wrongly set down as abbots of Hayles by Dugdale, Mon. v, 687.
[10] Harl. MS. 3725, fol. 33 v. (B. M.).
[11] Brist. and Glouc. Arch. Soc. Trans. xxii, 258.
[12] Worc. Epis. Reg. Gainsborough, fol. 7.

[13] Ibid. fol. 30.
[14] Cal. of Pat. 6 Edw. III, pt. iii, m. 1.
[15] Ibid. 19 Edw. III, pt. iii, m. 9 d.
[16] Worc. Epis. Reg. Thoresby, fol. 35.
[17] Ibid. Brian, fol. 10.
[18] Heref. Epis. Reg. Charlton, fol. 32.
[19] Dugdale, Mon. v, 687.
[20] Worc. Epis. Reg. Winchcombe, fol. 16 d.
[21] Cal. of Pat. 5 Hen. IV, pt. i, m. 27 d.
[22] Worc. Epis. Reg. Morgan, fol. 15 d.
[23] Ibid.   [24] Ibid. Bourchier, fol. 10.
[25] Ibid. Carpenter, i, fol. 95.
[26] Ibid. fol. 185.
[27] Ibid. Alcock, fol. 52 ; on death of W. Whitchurch.
[28] Ibid. fol. 120 d.
[29] Ibid.
[30] Ibid. Silvester de Giglis, fol. 33.
[31] Ibid. fol. 142 d.
[32] Ibid. de Ghinucci, fol. 75 d.
[33] Ibid. fol. 75 d.
[34] Birch, Catalogue of Seals in British Museum, i, 580.
[35] Dugdale, Mon. v, 265 ; Ann. Mon. (Rolls Ser.), ii, 228.
[36] Dugdale, op. cit. v, 425.

Acholt at Kingswood, and obtained the consent of Henry I.[1] In 1139, in fulfilment of his uncle's wish, William of Berkeley made a grant of the manor,[2] which was confirmed by the Empress Matilda.[3] During the civil war the monks probably wished for a more retired site.[4] They purchased from John de St. John some lands at Hazleton, which had belonged to Reginald de St. Waleric, and had been confiscated by King Stephen.[5] There they settled for a short time. Probably about 1147 Reginald de St. Waleric recovered his lands and drove out the monks, who then returned to Kingswood.[6] In 1148 Roger of Berkeley III confirmed the lands at Kingswood to the abbot and convent.[7] They were not content to forego their lands at Hazleton and disputed the possession of them with Reginald de St. Waleric.[8] According to the story of the abbot of Tintern, Reginald de St. Waleric was bound, as an act of penance imposed upon him by the pope, to found a Cistercian monastery, and accordingly he agreed to restore Hazleton to the monks if they would remove thither from Kingswood. They consented. A few of the monks were left at Kingswood, but the greater number removed to Hazleton. There they were troubled by a lack of water, and Reginald removed them to Tetbury. Roger of Berkeley III then complained that Kingswood, which had been founded as an abbey by his predecessor, was practically only a grange to Tetbury. He insisted that he should either recover his lands at Kingswood, or that the convent should return thither from Tetbury. However, at the request of Stephen, and the petition of the general chapter of Citeaux he recognized Kingswood as a grange of Tetbury.[9]

But the embers of controversy were not yet extinguished. A chapter was held at Kirkstead, probably in 1149, to settle a dispute between Philip abbot of L'Aumone, and the abbot of Waverley, who both attended.[10] L'Aumone was the mother house of Waverley and Tintern.[11] It was then decided that the abbot of Waverley might build a monastery at Kingswood.[12] Pagan, abbot of Tetbury, who was present, acquiesced, although his monastery was but slenderly endowed, but he is said to have been a simple-minded man without guile. The king and Roger of Berkeley gave their consent, although the chapter at Kirkstead had ignored the rights of the convent of

Tetbury, and of the mother house of Tintern. The abbot of Waverley sent four monks to Kingswood to occupy the grange, but disputes followed, and a conference was held at Kingswood which was attended by many Cistercian abbots, monks, and lay brothers, besides Roger of Berkeley III, and a number of other persons. It was then decided that the abbot of Waverley should recall his monks from Kingswood, and that it should again become a grange to Tetbury. The site at Tetbury was very unsuitable in many ways, and the monks were constrained to fetch all their fuel from Kingswood. Bernard de St. Waleric obtained from Roger of Berkeley III a grant of forty acres of land at a place called Mireford, close to the water at Kingswood,[13] and in 1149 or early in 1150,[14] removed the monks thither from Tetbury. He made over this land to the brethren that they might build their abbey upon it.[15] At the same time he confirmed to them all the land that they had when they dwelt at Tetbury and at Hazleton. The Berkeleys of Berkeley Castle and of Dursley were also among the benefactors of Kingswood.

In 1180 Abbot Hugh was deposed[16] by the visitors of the order, and his successor, William, was deposed in the following year,[17] both probably for some lack of business capacity.

It was most likely owing to the profits from wool that in 1230 the abbot and convent were able to spend £100 in purchasing lands at Culkerton from the prior and convent of St. Oswald's, Gloucester.[18] In 1242 the revenues from all sources amounted to £288 17s. 1d., the expenses to £269 4s. 11½d., and at the end of the financial year the balance in hand was £174 17s. 1d.[19] In 1276 the monastery was one of the more prosperous houses of the southern province of the order, and contributed £13 16s. towards a 'courtesy,' which the Cistercians gave to the king.[20] About the beginning of the fourteenth century the annual sales of wool averaged forty sacks, at prices varying from 26 to 12 marks, according to the quality.[21] In 1291 the abbot and convent had eight granges on their lands at which their lay brothers and servants lived and worked.[22] The proceeds of

[1] Dugdale, op. cit. v, 427.
[2] Ibid. 425. Cf. *Brist. and Glouc. Arch. Soc. Trans.* viii, *The Earlier House of Berkeley*, 199, 200.
[3] Dugdale, op. cit. v, 426.
[4] Ibid. 425.   [5] Ibid.
[6] Ibid. 425.
[7] Ibid. v, 427, No. x.   [8] Ibid. 425.
[9] Ibid. 426, No. vi.   [10] Ibid. 426.
[11] *Engl. Hist. Rev.* 1893, p. 675.
[12] Dugdale, op. cit. v, 426.

[13] Ibid. v, 426, No. iv.
[14] *Hist. MSS. Com. Rep.* v, App. i, 337. Simon, bishop of Worcester (ob. 20 March, 1150) was one of the witnesses. The date of the final settlement at Kingswood, has, without sufficient evidence, been given as about 1170, e.g. Dugdale, *Mon.* v, 424, *Clifton Antiq. Club Proc.* iii, 223.
[15] *Hist. MSS. Com. Rep.* v, app. i, 337.
[16] *Ann. Mon.* (Rolls Ser.), ii, 242.
[17] Ibid.
[18] *Hist. MSS. Com. Rep.* v, App. i, p. 335.
[19] Ibid.
[20] MS. Harl. 6603, fol. 384 (B.M.).
[21] Cunningham, *Growth of Engl. Industry and Commerce* (ed. 1905), i, 632.
[22] *Pope Nich. Tax.* (Rec. Com.), 235.

spiritualities were very small, amounting only to £6 4s. 4d.,[1] and the monastery had but the one rectory of Kingswood.[2] In virtue of that possession the bishop of Worcester took procurations from the monastery, and in 1283[3] and 1293[4] Giffard lodged at the monastery instead of taking a fee.

The resources of Kingswood were much straitened after the Black Death, and although the generosity of the Berkeleys again stood the convent in good stead,[5] there were financial difficulties at the end of the fourteenth century. In 1398 Boniface IX granted a very lavish indulgence to penitents who visited the church of Kingswood on Whit Sunday and the four following days, and gave alms for the repair of the church.[6] It was stated in 1402 that on account of the lack of lay brothers the lands of the monastery were more than usually uncultivated, and that the revenues then scarcely amounted to £100.[7]

During the course of the fifteenth century the house regained some measure of prosperity. Manors and granges were let on lease, and shortly before the dissolution the convent only cultivated at their own expense a small portion of their land around the monastery.[8]

The abbot and convent showed a painful anxiety to stand well with Cromwell. On 21 January, 1535, the prior, Thomas Reading, sent Cromwell a little book which he had written in support of the royal supremacy, begging him ' to close up the eye of justice and open the eye of pity to me and the religious men of this house who have no succour except in your evangelical charity.'[9] On 9 September the abbot sent a friar as prisoner to Cromwell because he had preached in his church in support of the ecclesiastical headship of St. Peter.[10] The monastery was surrendered on 1 February, 1538, by the abbot, twelve monks, and one lay brother.[11] Probably on account of their extreme complaisance they all received a small sum of money ' for their reward and finding,' in addition to the promise of a pension. The abbot received £6 13s. 4d., and a pension of £50, the prior £3 6s. 8d. and a pension of £6 13s. 4d. the rest of the monks the sum of £2 13s. 4d. each and pensions of £4 13s. 4d., or £4.[12] The

novice had only £2, and the lay brother at his own request was sent to another religious house.

The clear yearly revenues of the monastery in 1538 amounted to £232 0s. 4d,[13] and were drawn from the demesne lands, the manors of Kingswood, Ozleworth, and Bagpath, Culkerton, the granges of Ilbery, Bagston, Redge, Hyll, Hazleton, Calcot, and land and rents in Acton, Wotton, Nibley, Dursley, Berkeley, Stone, Newport, Tetbury, Bley, Bristol, and Gloucester, and the rectory of Kingswood.

ABBOTS OF KINGSWOOD [14]

Pagan occurs *circa* 1149 [15]
Hugh deposed 1180 [16]
William succeeded 1180, deposed 1181 [17]
Eudo succeeded 1181 [18]
William succeeded 1188,[19] occurs *circa* 1212 [20]
John occurs 1241 [21]
Samson occurs 1263 [22]
Robert of Tetbury occurs 1303 [23]
Richard elected 1319 [24]
John Wodeland occurs 1441 [25]
Walter Deryngs occurs 1435 [26]
Thomas Neude occurs 1470 [27]
Thomas Pyrton elected 1482 [28]
John Sodbury occurs 1503 [29]
Robert Wolaston occurs 1515 [30]
William Bewdley occurs 1535 [31] and 1538 [32]

An abbot's seal of the thirteenth century represents the Virgin crowned standing under a crocketed canopy with trefoiled arch supported on slender shafts, the Child on her left arm ; in the field outside a hatched pattern ; in base a carved roundheaded arch, under it a destroyed figure of the abbot.[33]

---

[1] Dugdale, *Mon.* v, 424.
[2] Ibid. 428.
[3] *Worc. Epis. Reg. Giffard* (Worc. Hist. Soc.), 210.
[4] Ibid. 434.
[5] Smyth, *Lives of the Berkeleys*, i, 338, 347.
[6] *Cal. Papal L.* v, 263.
[7] Ibid. v, 514.
[8] Dugdale, *Mon.* v, 428.
[9] *L. and P. Hen. VIII*, viii, No. 79.
[10] Ibid. No. 315. [11] Ibid. xiii, pt. i, No. 199.
[12] Dugdale op. cit. v. 429. One monk was absent. *L. and P. Hen. VIII.* xiii, pt. i, 1051.

[13] Dugdale op. cit. v, p. 428.
[14] The abbots of Kingswood did not usually receive benediction from the bishops of Worcester. No list at all is given in the *Monasticon*.
[15] Dugdale op. cit. v, 426.
[16] *Ann. Mon.* (Rolls Ser.), ii, 242 ; Dugdale, op. cit. v, 426.
[17] *Ann. Mon.* (Rolls Ser.), ii, 242.
[18] Ibid.   [19] Ibid. 245.
[20] Jeayes, *Catalogue of Mun. of Lord Fitzhardinge*, p. 36.
[21] Ibid. No. 273.   [22] Ibid. No. 433.
[23] Ibid. No. 468.
[24] Worc. Epis. Reg. Cobham, fol. 13.
[25] *Hist. MSS. Com. Rep.* v, App. i, 337.
[26] Worc. Epis. Reg. Bourchier, fol. 10.
[27] Ibid. Carpenter ii, fol. 12.
[28] Ibid. Alcock, fol. 97.
[29] Ibid. Silvester de Giglis, fol. 33.
[30] Ibid. fol. 142 d.
[31] *L. and P. Hen. VIII*, viii, No. 315.
[32] Dugdale op. cit. v, 429.
[33] Birch, *Catalogue of Seals in British Museum*, i, 601.

ALIEN HOUSES

15. THE PRIORY OF BECKFORD

In the reign of Henry I Rabellus, the chamberlain of Normandy, gave the manor of Beckford-with-Ashton to the monastery of St. Barbe-en-Auge in Normandy,[1] which had been founded as a house of Augustinian canons in 1128.[2] A prior and one or two canons were sent over to occupy the cell.[3] In 1247 the abbot and convent of Cormeilles let the parish church of Beckford with the chapel of Aston at a rent of 60 marks to the prior and convent of St. Barbe-en-Auge.[4] The arrangement was recognized by Walter Cantilupe, bishop of Worcester, in 1248.[5] Another agreement to the same effect was concluded in 1267.[6] How long it lasted is uncertain;[7] in 1339 the prior of Beckford still paid procuration to the bishop for the parish church.[8]

The prior and convent of St. Barbe-en-Auge presented the prior of their choice to the bishop of Worcester, and the custody of the priory was committed to him as their proctor.[9] When the alien priories were seized by Edward I, Edward II, and Edward III, the prior seems to have retained his possessions on payment of a ferm to the exchequer.[10] In the reign of Richard II, however, the custody was granted first to one of the king's clerks in 1379 for a rent of 100 marks a year,[11] and in 1383 for life to a knight named Sir John Cheyne,[12] who was to hold it without rendering anything as long as the war lasted, and after peace was restored for 100 marks to the exchequer. It was a high demand, for in 1374 the value of the priory was only assessed at £40 a year.[13] At that time a prior and one canon dwelt there. In 1389 the prior and convent of St. Barbe-en-Auge confirmed the grant of the possessions of Beckford Priory to Sir John Cheyne.[14] In 1399, when Henry IV restored many of the alien priories which

were conventual, Sir John Cheyne urged that the manor of Beckford was not a conventual priory and had no spiritualities attached to it, and thus succeeded in obtaining a confirmation of the grant by Richard II in 1383.[15] Beckford came under the Act of 1414 for the suppression of the alien priories, and the manor was in the possession of the crown until 1443, when Henry VI granted it to his new foundation of Eton College.[16] In 1462 Edward IV revoked that grant, and added Beckford to the endowment of the collegiate church of Fotheringhay.[17]

PRIORS OF BECKFORD [18]

Peter de Hayn, ob. 1298 [19]
William de Bony, 1298 [20]
Lawrence Gerard occurs 1345 [21]
Robert occurs 1374 [22]

16. THE PRIORY OF BRIMPSFIELD

The alien priory of Brimpsfield was a cell of the Benedictine monastery of St. Wandrille in Normandy.[23] Although no exact information exists about the founder and the date of the endowment, there can be little doubt that one of the Giffards, after 1086 and probably before 1100, gave the church of Brimpsfield and a small grant of land to the abbot and convent of St. Wandrille.[24] The abbot and convent of St. Wandrille sent one of their monks to act as their bailiff or proctor, they presented him as prior to the bishop of Worcester, and the custody of the manor of Brimpsfield was committed to him; the bishop instituted him, and issued a mandate that he should be inducted into the priory.[25] Brimpsfield was not a conventual house, and accordingly, when the alien priories were seized in time of war against France, the custody was not restored to the prior for payment of a ferm to the exchequer, but remained in the king's

---

[1] Dugdale, *Mon.* vii, 1048.
[2] Ibid. 1112.   [3] Ibid. 1048.
[4] MS. Add. 18461, fol. 19 (B.M.).
[5] Ibid. fol. 22 *v.*   [6] Ibid. fol. 17 *v.*
[7] Cf. Newent, p. 106.
[8] Worc. Epis. Reg. Bransford, fol. 15 *d.* No instance occurs in any of the bishops' registers of a visitation of the priory.
[9] *Worc. Epis. Reg. Giffard* (Worc. Hist. Soc.), 505.
[10] Lawrence Gerard occurs prior of Beckford in 1345 (*Cal. of Close*, 19 Edw. III, pt. ii, m. 22 *d.*) when the alien priories were in the king's hands.
[11] *Cal. of Pat.* 2 Ric. II, pt. ii, m. 16.
[12] Ibid. 7 Ric. II, pt. i, m. 26.
[13] *Worc. Reg. Sede. Vac.* (Worc. Hist. Soc.), 308. In 1293 the manor with its goods and chattels was valued at £126 6s. 10d. per annum. MS. Donat. 6164, fol. 46 (B.M.).
[14] *Cal. of Pat.* 13 Ric. II, pt. i, m. 9.

[15] Ibid. 1 Hen. IV, pt. iii, m. 12.
[16] Dugdale, op. cit. vii, 1048.
[17] Ibid.
[18] Entries of the priors of Beckford, with one exception, are not to be found in the registers of the bishops of Worcester. This may be due to the fact that the prior had no spiritualities.
[19] *Worc. Epis. Reg. Giffard* (Worc. Hist. Soc.), 505.
[20] Ibid.
[21] *Cal. of Close*, 19 Edw. III, pt. iii, m. 22 *d.*
[22] *Worc. Reg. Sede. Vac.* (Worc. Hist. Soc.), 308.
[23] Dugdale, *Mon.* vii, 1048. St. Stephanus de Fontanello, i.e. St. Wandrille.
[24] Osbern Giffard held Brimpsfield in 1087; cf. Taylor, *Domesday Surv. of Glouc.* 272.
[25] *Worc. Epis. Reg. Giffard* (Worc. Hist. Soc.), 357, 365, 368 ; cf. notes to list of priors.

hands.[1] The manor was very small, and in an extent of 1293 its goods and chattels and yearly produce were only valued at £6 19s.[2] In 1374 the church was worth 12 marks a year.[3]

The priory was finally seized in 1414 under the Act for the confiscation of the alien priories. In 1441 Henry VI gave it to Eton College,[4] and Edward IV confirmed the grant in 1467.[5] However, in 1474 he bestowed the property on the dean and chapter of Windsor.[6]

PRIORS OF BRIMPSFIELD[7]

Gilbert, 1289[8]
Robert le Masiner, 1290[9]
Thomas le Brykebek, 1311[10]
Roger de Argenciis, 1327[11]
Richard de Hente, 1328[12]
Roger de Hegneto, 1329[13]
John Fabrun, 1361[14]
Peter le Cerbonour resigned 1363[15]
Simon Halley, 1363[16]

17. THE PRIORY OF DEERHURST

The origin and early history of Deerhurst are very obscure. According to Leland, a monastery at Deerhurst was known to Bede, but of this fact there is now no proof.[17] On the evidence of a document in the chartulary which was compiled by Heming, sub-prior of Worcester while Wulfstan was bishop (1062–95), there was a monastery at Deerhurst soon after 804.[18] Leland also stated that the Danes burnt Deerhurst.[19] The monastery was rebuilt in or before 970. St. Alphege in his youth was a monk of the house, and was even then conspicuous for his holy life.[20] It is probable that he became abbot in 970,[21] and that under him the strict observance of the

rule of St. Benedict was introduced into the monastery. Fervour and zeal probably languished at Deerhurst as in many other Benedictine houses in the first half of the eleventh century. It was perhaps as a measure of reform that about 1059[22] Edward the Confessor granted the greater part of the lands of Deerhurst to the Benedictine monastery of St. Denis, reserving the remainder for his new foundation of St. Peter, at Westminster.[23] Thus Deerhurst became an alien priory, and the first monk from St. Denis who came as prior was Baldwin, afterwards, in 1065, abbot of Bury St. Edmunds.[24] In 1069 William the Conqueror confirmed the possessions of Deerhurst Priory.[25] According to the Domesday Survey, the possessions of St. Denis in Gloucestershire amounted to 64 hides, and included the vills of Uckington, Staverton, Coln St. Dennis and Caldicot, Little Compton, Preston-on-Stour, and Welford, besides 30 burgess-tenements in Gloucester.[26]

Deerhurst was served by a prior and monks from St. Denis, who paid a yearly sum from the revenues of the priory to the mother house. In 1250 Matthew Paris records an extraordinary episode.[27] According to his statement, Richard, earl of Cornwall, when staying at St. Denis, purchased the priory of Deerhurst from the abbot, and caused the transaction to be ratified in the papal *curia*. The priory with the eight vills belonging to it was then worth £300 a year. On his return to England in 1250 Richard dispersed the monks of Deerhurst, took possession of the property, and proposed to build a castle on the banks of the Severn. His occupation of Deerhurst was only temporary, though why the transaction became void remains a mystery. In 1264 a composition was made between Walter Cantilupe, bishop of Worcester, and the abbot of St. Denis, by which it was agreed that the abbot should appoint one of his monks as prior of Deerhurst, and should present him to the bishop by reason of his parochial cure in that church, and not by reason of the priory.[28] The abbot might recall the prior by signifying his intention to the bishop. The prior was bound to obey the bishop in all things, saving the privileges of the monastery of St. Denis. In accordance with this composition, which was confirmed by Godfrey Giffard, bishop of Worcester, in 1270, the priors of Deerhurst were subsequently presented, instituted, and recalled. The bishops exercised the right of visitation in the church of Deerhurst on

---

[1] There is no record of any institution of a prior between 1327 and 1361, when the alien priories were restored.

[2] MS. Add. 6164 (B.M.), fol. 46.

[3] *Reg. Sede Vac.* (Worc. Hist. Soc.), 308.

[4] Dugdale, op. cit. vii, 1048.

[5] Ibid.   [6] Ibid.

[7] The list is necessarily very incomplete, as the sole source is the registers of Worcester.

[8] *Worc. Epis. Reg. Giffard* (Worc. Hist. Soc.), 357.

[9] Ibid. 368 ; ob. 1311, ibid. Reynolds, fol. 34 *d*.

[10] Ibid.

[11] Ibid. Cobham, fol. 131.

[12] Ibid. Orlton, fol. 16 *d*.

[13] Ibid. fol. 23.   [14] Ibid. Brian, fol. 31 *d*.

[15] Ibid. Barnet, fol. 26.   [16] Ibid.

[17] Leland, *Itin.* vi, 79. It has been suggested (*Brist. and Glouc. Arch. Soc. Trans.* xvi, 221) that Leland's statement is due to a misunderstanding. Cf. *Bede Hist. Eccles.* (Ed. Plummer), ii, 104.

[18] Dugdale, *Mon.* i, 591, No. xxiii.

[19] Ibid. iii, 664.

[20] Wharton, *Angl. Sacr.* ii, 123.

[21] *Brist. and Glouc. Arch. Soc. Trans.* xviii, 128.

[22] Dugdale, op. cit. iii, 664 ; Félibien, *Histoire de l'Abbaye de Saint Denis*, 126.

[23] *Brist. and Glouc. Arch. Soc. Trans.* xxv, 230–50.

[24] *Memorials of St. Edmund's Abbey* (Rolls Ser.), ii, 3.

[25] Doublet, *Histoire de l'Abbaye de Saint Denis*, 839.

[26] *Dom. Bk.* (Rec. Com.), 166.

[27] Matt. Paris, *Chronica Majora* (Rolls Ser.) v, 112.

[28] *Worc. Epis. Reg. Giffard* (Worc. Hist. Soc.), 10, 37.

account of the parochial cure, but had no jurisdiction over the monks of the priory.[1]

In 1319 Edward II granted the right of holding two fairs of three days in the manor of Deerhurst, at the feasts of the Invention and Exaltation of the Cross.[2] Like other alien priories, Deerhurst was seized on account of the revenues which were sent to the mother house during the wars with France. The effect of the king's action was that the prior and convent held their lands of him on payment of a ferm to the exchequer, which may have represented the amount sent yearly to the mother house.[3] The crown also presented to churches of which the advowsons belonged to the priory, as they fell vacant.[4] In time of war the abbots of St. Denis presented the priors to the king,[5] who notified to the bishop of Worcester his will that they should be instituted. In the reign of Edward III the alien priories were in the king's hands from 1337 to 1361.[6] In 1345 he leased the priory to Thomas de Bradeston for £110 a year.[7] Under such an arrangement as this the administration of property and receipt of revenues was, of course, taken from the prior, and there can be no doubt that Thomas de Bradeston was bound to pay the convent a fixed sum for their maintenance and the provision of a chaplain to serve the parishioners. However, the priory was then vacant, and when John Godelli was appointed in 1346 the king restored the custody to him on payment of £110 a year to the exchequer so long as the war lasted.[8] In 1389 the custody of the priory was granted to John Russell, a knight, and William Hitchcock, a chaplain, at a rent of £200.[9] The prior was entitled to receive 46 marks a year from certain tithes and oblations, and bound to find chaplains for the parish church. In a previous grant all the spiritualities of the priory were reserved to his use, and it is not clear if he was supposed to provide for himself and his monks and find the chaplains for 46 marks.[10] In 1394 John Russell complained that the prior had received the money and had not paid the salaries of the

chaplains.[11] On Christmas Eve, 1394, the prior was killed, but no presentation was made by the abbot of St. Denis, and after a vacancy of nearly three years the king presented John Todenham, a monk of St. Mary's, Thetford, to the priory.[12] The temporalities were still let for a ferm, and under that system it was inevitable that the property should suffer. In 1374 the value of its spiritualities and temporalities was estimated at only 200 marks, and at that time a prior and two monks were living at Deerhurst.[13] In 1400, immediately after the restitution of the priory to St. Denis by Henry IV,[14] the new prior, William Forestar, prevailed on the king to issue a commission to several persons, including the sheriff of Gloucester, to inquire about divers wastes, sales, and destructions committed on divers lands and possessions pertaining to the alien priory of Deerhurst, and the removal of divers charters, writings, rent rolls, and muniments by the late farmers of the priory and others of those parts.[15] The payment due from the prior to St. Denis was 120 marks a year,[16] which was probably made until 1415, when war broke out with France. Deerhurst was one of the alien priories which were not confiscated under the Act of Parliament of 1415.[17] It was not made denizen until 1443,[18] and in that grant Henry VI declared that he acted on the petition of Hugh de Mantyazon, who had been presented as prior by the abbot of St. Denis in 1411.[19] Deerhurst was placed on the same footing as other priories in England, and the right of freedom of election was assured to the convent. Four years later Henry VI cancelled the grant, and gave the priory and possessions of Deerhurst to Eton College.[20] In 1461 Edward IV granted Deerhurst to William Buckland, a monk of St. Peter's, Westminster, that it might be fully restored to the abbot and convent of St. Denis, provided that they supported monks, a secular chaplain, and servants, all of whom should be English, and that no pension or impost was paid to the mother house.[21] On 18 January, 1466, Carpenter, bishop of Worcester, collated William Buckland to the priory on the ground that there were not a sufficient number of monks to proceed to an election, and that the abbot of St. Denis had made no presentation.[22] In 1467 Edward IV took the priory from William Buck-

---

[1] *Worc. Epis. Reg. Giffard* (Worc. Hist. Soc.), 22, 382. The monks denied the right of the bishop to visit the priory, and although it is stated (ibid. p. lxxxix) that Giffard did so, there is no evidence of it. On the contrary he received procurations from the prior of Deerhurst on account of the parish churches which he held ; *Reg. Sede Vac.* (Worc. Hist. Soc.), 63, 121.

[2] Cart. R. 12 Edw. II, No. 19.

[3] *Cal. of Close*, 1 Edw. III, pt. i, m. 22 ; Pat. 39 Edw. III, pt. ii, m. 12.

[4] *Cal. of Pat.* 10 Edw. III, 11, 12, &c. *passim*.

[5] Ibid. 20 Edw. III, pt. i, m. 31 ; 1 Hen. IV, pt. v, m. 25.

[6] Dugdale, *Mon.* vii, 985.

[7] *Cal. of Pat.* 19 Edw. III, pt. ii, m. 31.

[8] *Cal. of Close*, 20 Edw. III, pt. i, m. 13.

[9] *Cal. of Pat.* 13 Ric. II, pt. i, m. 38.

[10] Ibid. 11 Ric. II, pt. i, m. 23.

[11] Ibid. 17 Ric. II, pt. ii, m. 39.

[12] Worc. Epis. Reg. Winchcombe, fol. 18 d. It was stated that the king had presented the last prior also.

[13] *Worc. Reg. Sede Vac.* (Worc. Hist. Soc.), 308.

[14] *Cal. of Pat.* 1 Hen. IV, pt. v, m. 25.

[15] Ibid. 1 Hen. IV, pt. v, m. 7 d.

[16] Félibien, *Histoire de Saint Denis*, 128.

[17] Dugdale, op. cit. iii, 664.

[18] Ibid. iii, 666.

[19] Worc. Epis. Reg. Peverell, fol. 37 d.

[20] Dugdale, op. cit. iii, 665.

[21] *Cal. of Pat.* 2 Edw. IV, pt. i, m. 5.

[22] Worc. Epis. Reg. Carpenter, i, fol. 192 d.

land, on the plea that he had only maintained one secular chaplain and no other monk besides himself, that he had wasted the revenues and withdrawn hospitality.[1] The king granted Deerhurst to Tewkesbury on condition that the abbot and convent should maintain a prior and four monks there, the prior to be appointed and removed at the will of the abbot.[2] At the same time Edward took the alien priory of Goldcliff from Tewkesbury and gave it to Eton College.[3] The possessions of Deerhurst in 1467 included the manors of Deerhurst, Hawe, Wolston, Uckington, Coln St. Dennis, Welford, Preston-on-Stour, and Compton in Gloucestershire, Taynton with La More in Oxfordshire, and the rectories of Deerhurst and Uckington.[4] The union of Deerhurst with Tewkesbury was confirmed by Carpenter, bishop of Worcester, in 1469.[5] The cell was surrendered as part of the possessions of the abbey of Tewkesbury on 9 January, 1540.[6]

PRIORS OF DEERHURST

Baldwin, occurs 1065 [7]
Stephen of Paris, instituted 1270 [8]
Robert of Elleboef, instituted 1272 [9]
Stephen de Moysiaco, instituted 1278 [10]
Peter de Thoriniaco, instituted 1302 [11]
Philip de Serinaco, instituted 1315,[12] deposed 1329 [13]
John de Vetolio, 1329,[14] recalled 1339 [15]
Ralph de Ermenovilla, 1339,[16] removed 1344 [17]
Thomas Graculi, 1344,[18] resigned or deprived 1345 [19]
John Godelli, 1346 [20]

John Coci, 1349 [21]
Peter Cudoe, ob. 1361 [22]
John de Medunta, admitted 1361 [23]
Peter Pounchefichet, occurs 1374,[24] ob. 1375 [25]
Droco Garnarii, admitted 1375,[26] ob. 1394 [27]
Vacant until 19 July, 1397 [28]
John Todenham, admitted 1397 [29]
William Forestar, admitted 1399 [30]
Hugh de Mantyazon, admitted 1411,[31] occurs 1443 [32]
William Buckland, 1461 [33]

After the union with Tewkesbury the priors were appointed solely at the will of the abbot and convent, and no record exists of their succession.

Robert Cheltenham, occurs 1535 [34]
James Bromsgrove, occurs 1539 and 1540 [35]

18. THE PRIORY OF NEWENT

About 1060 William FitzOsborn founded the Benedictine monastery of Cormeilles in Normandy,[36] and before the compilation of Domesday Book he added largely to the endowment out of his possessions in England. These included the manor of Newent of five hides, the church and all tithes and offerings, with the woods of Yarcledon, Tedeswood, Compton, Lind, Oakley, Melswick, Ongley, and all the assarts that belonged to Newent, Stanling, and Boulsdon with the chapel, the church of Taynton with the chapel of Pauntley, the church of Dymock, the tithe of his demesne, and one virgate; the vill of Kingston with appurtenances in West Kingston, the tithe of his demesne and a virgate, the churches of Maurdine, Kingsland, Martley, Suckley, Beckford, Lidiart, with tithes of his demesne, and a virgate in each place, and rents in Monmouth.[37] A cell to Cormeilles was established at Newent. The prior acted merely as the bailiff of the abbot and convent of Cormeilles, and transmitted the revenues and profits of the lands and churches to the mother house.[38] There is no evidence in the registers

---

[1] *Cal. of Pat.* 7 Edw. IV, pt. iii, m. 5 ; Worc. Epis. Reg. Carpenter, ii, fol. 1. It appears that William Buckland had already resigned, and that the abbot and convent of Tewkesbury hoped to acquire Deerhurst. Buckland's resignation was accepted by Bishop Carpenter, and with the consent of the proctor of Tewkesbury an annual pension of £10 was assigned to him on 28 September, 1466. Worc. Epis. Reg. Carpenter, i, fol. 213 *d.*
[2] Ibid. ii, 1–3.
[3] Ibid. ii, 3 ; Dugdale, op. cit. iv, 664.
[4] Worc. Epis. Reg. Carpenter, ii, 1–6.
[5] Ibid.
[6] *L. and P. Hen. VIII*, xv, No. 139, iv.
[7] *Memorials of St. Edmund's Abbey* (Rolls Ser.), ii, 3.
[8] *Worc. Epis. Reg. Giffard* (Worc. Hist. Soc.), 37.
[9] Ibid. 49.   [10] Ibid. 98.
[11] *Cal. of Pat.* 30 Edw. I, m. 33. Recalled before 1315, *pro meritis,* cf. Worc. Epis. Reg. Maidstone, fol. 33 *d.*
[12] Ibid.
[13] Ibid. 3 Edw. III, pt. i, m. 2.   [14] Ibid.
[15] Ibid. 12–14 Edw III, m. 17, 'for bodily weakness.'
[16] Worc. Epis. Reg. Bransford, fol. 32 *d.*
[17] *Cal. Papal L.* (Rolls Ser.), iii, 11, 16.
[18] *Cal. of Pat.* 18 Edw. III, pt. ii, m. 27.
[19] Worc. Epis. Reg. Bransford, fol. 94.
[20] Ibid. ; *Cal. of Pat.* 20 Edw. III, pt. i, m. 31.

[21] *Worc. Reg. Sede Vac.* (Worc. Hist. Soc.), 237.
[22] Worc. Epis. Reg. Brian, fol. 41 *d.*
[23] Ibid.
[24] *Worc. Reg. Sede Vac.* (Worc. Hist. Soc.), 308.
[25] Worc. Epis. Reg. Wakefield, fol. 2 *d.*   [26] Ibid.
[27] Ibid. Winchcombe, fol. 18 *d.*
[28] Ibid.   [29] Ibid.
[30] *Cal. of Pat.* 1 Hen. IV, pt. v, m. 25.
[31] Worc. Epis. Reg. Peverell, fol. 37 *d.*
[32] Dugdale, *Mon.* iv, 666.
[33] *Cal. of Pat.* 2 Edw. IV, pt. i, m. 5.
[34] *Valor Eccles.* (Rec. Com.), ii, 484.
[35] Dugdale, op. cit. ii, 57.
[36] Dugdale, *Mon.* vii, 1048.
[37] MS. Add. 18461 (B.M.) fol. 1 *v.*; cf. Dugdale, op. cit. vii, 1076.
[38] MS. Add. 18461, *passim.*

of the bishops of Hereford to show that they exercised any control over the bailiff,[1] or that they committed the custody of Newent to him by any formal act. On account of the possession of the churches of Kingsland, Dymock, and Newent with the chapel of Pauntley, in 1195 the bishop and chapter of Hereford made the abbot of Cormeilles a canon, assigned him a prebendal stall, and gave him a place in the chapter. He was bound to appoint a suitable vicar to make perpetual residence in his absence.[2]

In 1247 the abbot and convent of Cormeilles let the church of Beckford with the chapel of Aston at a rent of sixty marks to the prior and convent of St. Barbe-en-Auge, who possessed a cell at Beckford.[3] The arrangement was recognized by Walter Cantilupe, bishop of Worcester, in 1248.[4] Another agreement to the same effect was concluded in 1267.[5] How long it lasted is uncertain; in 1339 the prior of Beckford still paid procuration to the bishop for the parish church.[6] In 1373 it was declared that the crown had recently recovered the presentation to the church of Beckford which the abbot and convent of Cormeilles had held as appropriated to the cell of Newent.[7] However, in consideration of the cause of the recovery, which is not stated, Edward III granted it back to the abbot and convent.[8] It was not again leased to the prior of Beckford.[9]

In 1226 Henry III granted the right of holding a yearly fair in the manor of Newent;[10] in 1253 he confirmed the fair and added a weekly market.[11] On more than one occasion disputes arose with the escheators, who attempted to enter upon the possessions of the priory on the death either of the abbot of Cormeilles or of his bailiff the prior of Newent.[12] In 1320 a search was made among the records of the exchequer as far back as Richard I, and it was discovered that the crown had never had the custody of Newent Priory during such voidances. At the same time it was expressly stated that

the bailiff was appointed by the abbot and removable at his pleasure.

During the wars with France Newent was seized like other alien priories. In 1305 Edward I allowed the prior to have the custody by paying £120 a year into the exchequer.[14] It is not clear whether Edward III pursued the same course. In 1345 he granted the custody to Thomas de Bradeston for £130 a year,[15] but it is possible that it was a temporary measure, perhaps taken immediately on the death of a bailiff. In 1382, when the alien priories were again in the hands of the crown, the abbot and convent of Cormeilles granted their manor of Newent called 'priorie' to Sir John Devereux for his life, with remainder to his son, wife, and daughter.[16] Richard II allowed the grant on condition that during war with France the rent of £126 13s. 4d. should be paid to the exchequer, and that due provision should be made for divine service and other charges.[17] In 1399 Henry IV committed the custody of the manors of Newent and Kingston and the temporalities of the priory in Gloucestershire and Herefordshire to Sir John Cheyne for a ferm of £54, and £20 to be paid for the support of the prior and other charges, while the war with France lasted.[18] In 1400 Henry IV restored some of the alien priories, but Newent was not among them. On 11 February, 1401, he granted to Sir John Cheyne and a clerk, by name Thomas Horeton, the issues, rents, and profits pertaining to the rectories of Newent, Beckford, and Dymock for 150 marks a year.[19] In 1411 he granted all the possessions of the priory of Newent to his new foundation of the collegiate church of Fotheringhay.[20]

PRIORS OF NEWENT

William de Hakeville, occurs 1243[21]
Simon de Goupillariis, occurs 1290[22] and 1298[23]
John Fabri, occurs 1374[24]

COLLEGE

19. THE COLLEGE OF WESTBURY-ON-TRYM

It has been surmised that a monastery was founded at Westbury-on-Trym about 716.[13] It was

most probably a place of residence for a number of priests who lived their life in common, but were not under monastic vows. In 824 the cathedral church of Worcester obtained possession of the

---

[1] In 1289 the prior supplied Bishop Swinfield with hay, litter, and brushwood when he came to Newent on 20 December, but his act was gratuitous; cf. *Household Roll of Bishop Swinfield* (Camd. Soc.), ii, cxvi.
[2] Ibid. fol. 8 v., 9. [3] Ibid. fol. 19.
[4] Ibid. fol. 22 v. [5] Ibid. 17 v.
[6] Worc. Epis. Reg. Bransford, fol. 15 d.
[7] Pat. 47 Edw. III, pt. i, m. 29. [8] Ibid.
[9] *Worc. Reg. Sede Vac.* (Worc. Hist. Soc.), 308.
[10] Close R. 10 Hen. III, m. 8.
[11] Cart R. 37 Hen. III, m. 10.
[12] *Cal. of Pat.* 14 Edw. II, pt. i, m. 8.
[13] *Clifton Antiquarian Club Proceedings*, iv, 22–42.

[14] MS. Add. 18461, fol. 92.
[15] *Cal. of Pat.* 19 Edw. III, pt. ii, m. 31. In 1344 he was recognized as the abbot's proctor; *Cal. of Pat.* 18 Edw. III, pt. i, m. 3.
[16] Ibid. 5 Ric. II, pt. ii, m. 9.
[17] Ibid. [18] Ibid. 1 Hen. IV, pt. v, m. 4.
[19] Ibid. 2 Hen. IV, pt. ii, m. 31.
[20] Tanner, *Notitia Monastica*, ed. 1744, p. 379.
[21] MS. Add. 18461, fol. 29 v.
[22] *Household Roll of Bishop Swinfield* (Camd. Soc.), II, p. cxxxvii.
[23] Add. MS. 18461, fol. 33.
[24] *Worc. Reg. Sede Vac.* (Worc. Hist. Soc.), 308.

church and lands of Westbury.[1] Nothing is known of the fate of the minster during the Danish invasions, but it is unlikely that it escaped being plundered and burnt.[2]

Soon after his consecration Oswald, bishop of Worcester (961–992), determined to introduce the strict observance of the Benedictine rule into his diocese. He sent to Fleury for an English monk named Germanus, and appointed him prior of a new foundation at Westbury, which became the centre of the Benedictine revival in Mercia.[3] On the death of King Edgar there was a revulsion of feeling in favour of the secular priests who had been ousted during the monastic revival ;[4] the monks were expelled from several of the Mercian monasteries, and there is no evidence that they were afterwards reinstated at Westbury. The minster is not even mentioned in the Domesday Survey.

Some years later when Wulfstan, bishop of Worcester, restored the foundation, he said that Oswald's church had afterwards suffered great damage from pirates, and that it was ruinous through the neglect of its rulers.[5] There was but a single priest, and he seldom said mass.[6] Wulfstan recovered the church from William the Conqueror, rebuilt it, and making it dependent on the cathedral monastery of Worcester, he placed monks there under the rule of Colman.[7] He recovered by law some of the former possessions of Westbury, others by purchase, and on 8 September, 1093, he granted a charter confirming the endowment of 2½ hides and a virgate in Westbury, part of a wood called Aescgraf and 12 acres of meadow, 2½ hides and 28 acres of land in Henbury and in Charlton and Wick, the churches of Henbury and Stoke with all tithes, free from all service to king or bishop ; 1½ hides in Berwick, 1 virgate in Hazleton only owing service to the king. His successor, Samson (1096–1112) was a canon of Bayeux, and he took Westbury from the monks.[8] Bishop Simon (1123–51) restored the church of Westbury with its dependent chapels to the prior and convent of Worcester.[9] It has usually been assumed that afterwards Westbury was merely a parish church until 1288, when Bishop Giffard founded a college of canons against the will of

the prior and convent.[10] However, Giffard's register proves conclusively that from the earliest years of his episcopate a dean and canons were in possession of Westbury,[11] and, indeed, that his predecessor, Walter de Cantilupe, collated his clerks to the prebends of Westbury.[12] Giffard's correspondence with his agent at the papal *curia* in 1286 revealed his object.[13] He was anxious to be bishop of Westbury as well as of Worcester, that he might have his episcopal throne in a church of secular canons as well as in a Benedictine monastery. He petitioned Honorius IV that there might be granted to him and his successors for ever a prebend in the church of Westbury of the value of ten marks or pounds, and that he might make all churches of his patronage prebendal to Westbury.[14] The canons of Westbury were anxious that the bishop should be present in choir and chapter, and therefore possess a prebend in their church.[15] The reply to his request that he might make the churches of his patronage prebendal to Westbury was apparently favourable, for he collated his clerks to new prebends.[16] The prior and convent of Worcester complained to Nicholas IV, stating that the bishop had constituted the churches of Kempsey, Bredon, Wychendon, Bishop's Cleeve, and Weston-upon-Avon prebendal to Westbury against their wishes, and assigned them to certain clerks and members of his household whom he instituted as new canons of Westbury.[17] The prior and convent of Worcester had always possessed the right of instituting rectors to those churches during a vacancy of the see, and the bishop's action deprived them of their privilege. Nicholas IV directed that an inquiry should be made, but the judges whom he appointed were unwilling to act.[18] Although the prior and convent obtained a hearing of the king they gained nothing,[19] and in 1297 the Court of Arches decided in the bishop's favour.[20] Thus the result of Giffard's work was an increase in the number of prebendaries at Westbury, and a corresponding provision for them.[21] As the bishops collated to the deanery and the prebends their patronage was extended, though papal provisions were frequent.[22] The collegiate church was subject to the regular visitation of

[1] Haddan and Stubbs, *Church Councils*, iii, 394 ; cf. Dugdale *Mon.* i, 591, No. xxiii.

[2] *Clifton Antiq. Club Proc.* iv, 28.

[3] *Chronicon Abbatiae Rameseiensis* (Rolls Ser.), 42 ; *Historians of the Church of York* (Rolls Ser.), i, 424.

[4] *Chronicon Abbatiae Rameseiensis* (Rolls Ser.), 72–73.

[5] Dugdale, *Mon.* i, 591, No. xxii.

[6] Thorpe, *Diplomatarium Anglicum aevi Saxonici*, 447.

[7] Dugdale, *Mon.* i, 591 ; Wharton, *Angl. Sac.* ii, 242, 262.

[8] William of Malmesbury, *Gesta Pontif.* (Rolls Ser.), 290.

[9] Thomas, *Survey of Cathedral Church of Worcester*, 109, App. No. 9.

[10] e.g. Tanner, *Notitia Monastica* (ed. 1744), p. 142. *Clifton Antiq. Club Proc.* iv, 33.

[11] *Worc. Epis. Reg. Giffard* (Worc. Hist. Soc.), 20, 49, 54, 71, 123, &c.

[12] Ibid. 4.   [13] Ibid. 301–3.

[14] Ibid. 303.   [15] Ibid. 302.

[16] Ibid. 328, 336–7, &c.

[17] Ibid. 362.

[18] Ibid. 362–4. *Ann. Mon.* (Rolls Ser.), iv, 498.

[19] *Ann. Mon.* (Rolls Ser.), iv, 501–2, 504, 518

[20] *Worc. Epis. Reg. Giffard* (Worc. Hist. Soc.), 492.

[21] The prebends were Goodringhill, Laurensweston, Henbury, Aust and Halley.

[22] *Cal. Papal L.* (Rolls Ser.), *passim*.

the bishops of Worcester [1] and of the prior of the cathedral monastery during voidances.[2]

Bishop Carpenter (1444–76) was regarded as a second founder of the college of Westbury, which he dedicated to the Holy Trinity.[3] He realized the importance of an episcopal seat near the town of Bristol, as strongly as his predecessor Giffard had done, and alone of all the bishops of the see he is said to have adopted the style of bishop of Worcester and Westbury.[4] In 1447 he began to rebuild the college on a much larger scale, and revised its statutes and ordinances with the object of increasing its sphere of usefulness.[5] He founded and endowed a chapel in the church to be served by six priests,[6] built almshouses for six poor men[7] and six widows,[8] vesting the right of nomination in the dean and chapter. In 1463 he appropriated the parish church of Clifton to the college, with the proviso that the dean and chapter should find a master to teach grammar to those ministering in the church and any other persons whomsoever who came to him, without any charge, and should give him a residence in the college.[9] In 1473 he appropriated the parish church of Kempsey and its dependent chapels to Westbury, on the petition of the dean and chapter, showing that their revenues were insufficient.[10] Edward IV was a generous benefactor. In 1464 he gave the manor of Elmstree in Tetbury,[11] and in 1465 he granted the custody of the hospital of St. Lawrence, Bristol, in frankalmoigne.[12] In 1468 he gave the manor and church of Astley in Worcestershire.[13] From 1469 to 1474 William Canynges, the rich merchant who five times held the office of mayor of Bristol, was dean of Westbury.[14] In 1476 Bishop Carpenter was buried in the chancel.[15]

In 1534 the dean, one of the prebendaries, and the fellows of the college subscribed to the royal supremacy.[16] On 10 February, 1544, the college was surrendered into the king's hands.[17] In 1535[18] the college consisted of a dean, five prebendaries, a sub-dean, Bishop Carpenter's chaplain, a schoolmaster, eight fellows, four clerks, six aged priests, and twelve choristers. After the disbursements of alms according to the ordinances, the clear yearly value of the property amounted to £232 14s. 0¼d. The possessions of the college included the manors of Westbury, Clifton, Goodringhill, Wormington, Turkdean, Foxcote, Dowdeswell, and Elmstree in Gloucestershire; Astley, Shelve, Monehills, Greveley and Longborough in Worcestershire; Bereford in Warwickshire; Aston Tirrold and North Morton in Berkshire; rents in Bristol, Worcester, and elsewhere, the hospital of St. Lawrence, Bristol, and the rectories of Westbury and Kempsey.

DEANS OF WESTBURY-ON-TRIM[19]

Stephen, occurs 1285,[20] ob. 1291[21]
Hugh de Carnaria, 1291
Nicholas de Gore, occurs 1321 and 1323[22]
Ralph de Lacu, 1323
William Edington, occurs 1335
Adam de Aylincton, 1335
David Bracewell, 1395
Stephen Basset, occurs 1413
William Oxton, 1413
John Arundel, 1414
John Powle, occurs 1425
John Lowsby, 1425
Richard Ellis, 1425
John Kemmes, ob. 1451
William Okeborn, 1451
John Blakman, resigned 1458
Henry Sampson, 1458
William Caninges, 1469
Robert Slimbridge, 1474
William Vaus, occurs 1479
John Lyndsey, 1479, ob. 1488
Adam Redshelf, 1488
William Cretyng, occurs 1497
John Barlow, 1530–44[23]

A seal of the fifteenth century represents the Trinity in a canopied niche with elegantly carved side towers, each containing four small niches; on the carving on each side, a shield of arms; left, indistinct; right, paly of six, a chevron for John Carpenter, bishop of Worcester; in base under a depressed round-headed arch, between walls of masonry, the bishop, with mitre and pastoral staff, kneeling in prayer. The legend is :—

SIGILLVM . COMMUNE . COLLEGII . DE . WESTBURI .
WIGORNIĒSIS DE . . . . . .[24]

---

[1] Worc. Epis. Reg. passim.
[2] Worc. Reg. Sede Vac. (Worc. Hist. Soc.), passim.
[3] Valor Eccles. (Rec. Com.), ii, 432.
[4] Tanner, Notitia Monastica (ed. 1744), p. 142.
[5] Worc. Epis. Reg. Carpenter, i, fol. 183 d.
[6] Ibid. ii, fol. 25. Clifton Antiq. Club Proc. iv, 36.
[7] Worc. Epis. Reg. Carpenter, i, fol. 231, in 1466.
[8] Clifton Antiq. Club Proc. iv, 36. Valor Eccles. (Rec. Com.), ii, 434.
[9] Worc. Epis. Reg. Carpenter, i, fol. 183 d.
[10] Ibid. ii, fol. 25.
[11] Cal. of Pat. 4 Edw. IV, pt. i, m. 20.
[12] Ibid. 5 Edw. IV, pt. i, m. 6.
[13] Chart. R. 8 Edw. IV, No. 4.
[14] Clifton Antiq. Club Proc. iv, 36.
[15] Ibid. iv, 35.
[16] Dep. Keeper's Rep. vii, App. ii, 304.
[17] Ibid. viii, App. ii, 48.
[18] Valor Eccles. (Rec. Com.), ii, 434–5; cf. Clifton Antiq. Club Proc. iv, 36. Cant. Archiepis. Reg. Morton, fol. 170.

[19] The list is probably incomplete. With one or two exceptions it is taken from Tanner, Notitia Monastica (Ed. Nasmyth, 1744), App.
[20] Worc. Epis. Reg. Giffard (Worc. Hist. Soc), 263.
[21] Ibid. 349.   [22] Ibid. Cobham, fol. 25.
[23] Ibid. De Ghinucci, fol. 43.
[24] Birch, Catalogue of Seals in British Museum, i, 799.

FRIARIES

20. THE BLACK FRIARS, BRISTOL

The house of the Black Friars of Bristol was founded in the parish of the priory of St. James in 1227 or 1228, by Maurice de Gaunt, great-grandson of Robert Fitzharding, and Matthew de Gurnay.[1] In 1230, at the request of the friars, William of Blois, bishop of Worcester, came to dedicate their altar and burial-ground.[2] In 1232 Henry III granted a licence to the friars to enlarge their burial-ground,[3] and many of the Bristol citizens in the thirteenth, fourteenth, and fifteenth centuries willed their bodies to be buried in the cemetery of the Black Friars.[4] Henry III was a most generous benefactor of the friars. The church and priory were over forty years in building, and the timber came from the Forest of Dean, as the gift of the king,[5] and John de Plessetis earl of Warwick.[6] In 1232 Henry III allowed the friars to make a conduit to their house.[7] On several occasions he granted oaks for fuel.[8] In 1251, to enable them to pay their debts, he granted them 21 marks out of the exchequer.[9] He also granted them in perpetuity a moiety of the prisage of fresh fish which came into the port of Bristol. Gifts to friars are a regular feature of the bounty of later kings; in 1293 Edward I gave six oaks for fuel,[10] and when the provincial chapter met at Bristol on the Feast of the Assumption in 1302 he gave ten oaks for fuel.[11] On the next occasion, in 1323, Edward II gave £15 for the food of the fathers,[12] and in 1343 Edward III also gave £15 for the same object.[13] The evidence of the wills which are now extant shows that it was usual to re-

member the friars.[14] As late as 1532 Thomas V of Berkeley left £10 towards repairing the cloister of the Black Friars in Bristol.[15]

In 1532 or 1533 Hugh Latimer preached against purgatory and other hitherto accepted doctrines in the church of the Black Friars,[16] and the prior, John Hilsey, preached in reply. In 1534 Hilsey became provincial of the order in England, and was appointed by Henry VIII together with George Brown, prior of a house of Augustinians, to visit the houses of the orders of friars throughout England.[17] The object was to force the acceptance of the royal supremacy upon them, and to compel them to preach it to the people. On 9 June Hilsey secured the submission of the Black Friars at Bristol.[18] The greater part of them abandoned the convent and fled from England, leaving only the prior, William Oliver, and four brethren.[19] William Oliver's preaching got him into trouble in 1537,[20] and though he escaped condemnation he lost his office and probably fled[21] to the continent.

The houses of the friars were not included under the Act of 1536 for the suppression of the lesser monasteries. However, in 1537 the dissolution of the friaries was clearly contemplated.[22] On 9 December Richard Ingworth, formerly prior of the Dominican house of King's Langley, was consecrated suffragan bishop of Dover, and soon afterwards he received two commissions to visit the friars.[23] He was ordered to depose or suspend heads of houses against whom any charge was brought and to appoint others, and also to visit the convents, take possession of the keys, sequestrate goods, and make indentures and inventories. The friars were very largely dependent on private charity, which diminished as the result of the suppression of the lesser monasteries.[24] Accordingly they were reduced to great poverty which forced them to surrender their houses.[25] On 28 August, 1538, Richard Ingworth wrote to Cromwell that the Black Friars of Bristol were ready to give up their

---

[1] *Reliquary*, 1888, p. 71 (Palmer, *The Black Friars of Bristol*), from which most of the references are taken.

[2] *Ann. Mon.* (Rolls Ser.), i. 78 ; cf. St. James's Priory, Bristol, p. 74.

[3] Pat. 17 Hen. III, m. 8.

[4] Bickley, *Cal. of Bristol Deeds*, No. 114, &c.; *Reliquary*, 77.

[5] *Reliquary*, 72–73:—Four oaks for shingles, 1233; ten oaks out of Furches wood, 1240; ten oaks for timber, 1241; ten oaks, 1242; seven oaks, 1242; six oaks for the fabric of the church, 1245 ; six oaks for the work of the church, 1249 ; four oaks for timber, 1250; thirty oaks for timber, 1252 ; six oaks for timber, 1255 ; five oaks for timber, 1256 ; four oaks for timber, 1259 ; four oaks for timber, 1269 ; six oaks for timber, 1263. These were felled and delivered at the king's expense.

[6] Ibid. 72, 73.

[7] Ibid. 74.

[8] Ibid. 75.

[9] Ibid. 75.

[10] Ibid.

[11] Ibid.

[12] Ibid. 76.

[13] Ibid.

[14] *Notes on Bristol Wills* (1382–1595) ; *Reliquary*, 75.

[15] Smyth, *Lives of the Berkeleys* (ed. Maclean), ii, 669.

[16] *Reliquary*, 79.

[17] Gasquet, *Hen. VIII and the Engl. Mon.* (ed. 1899), 51, 52.

[18] *Reliquary*, 1888, p. 79.

[19] Ibid.

[20] *L. and P. Hen. VIII*, xii, pt. i, Nos. 508, 1147.

[21] *Reliquary*, 1888, p. 79.

[22] Gasquet, op. cit. 313.

[23] Ibid. ; Wilkins, *Concilia*, iii, 829, 835.

[24] Gasquet, op. cit. 317.

[25] Wright, *Supp. of the Mon.* (Camd. Soc.), 196 ; *L. and P. Hen. VIII*, xiii, pt. i, No. 1456.

house.[1] He took the surrender, which was signed by the prior and four others on 10 September.[2]

The seal represents St. Paul, a tall, bearded figure with nimbus, and loosely robed, in his right hand a sword, in his left a scroll.[3] The legend is :—

SIGILL · CONVENTVS · FRAT · PREDICATM̄ · BRISTOLL.

21. THE GREY FRIARS, BRISTOL

The house of the Grey Friars of Bristol in Lewensmead was founded before 1234.[4] In 1538 the mayor stated that the house was of the foundation and purchasing of the town, and was built by ancient burgesses at their own cost.[5] In 1236 Henry III gave fifteen oaks from the wood of Furches,[6] and afterwards he granted in perpetuity a moiety of the prisage of fresh fish which came into the port of Bristol.[7] The Franciscans were popular with the citizens of Bristol, and were often remembered in their wills.[8]

After a visit to Bristol in 1538 Richard Ingworth wrote, on 27 August, to tell Cromwell that the warden of the Grey Friars was 'stiff'; he was also warden of Richmond, 'yet for all his great port,' added Ingworth, 'I think him twenty marks in debt, and not able to pay it.'[9] There were clamorous creditors, but as the warden was absent they could not get payment.[10] On 10 September six friars surrendered the house to Ingworth.[11]

22. THE AUGUSTINIAN FRIARS, BRISTOL

The house of the Augustinian Friars of Bristol was founded in 1313 by Simon de Montacute, who gave them a piece of land 100 ft. square hard by the Temple Gate of the town.[12] In 1317 William de Montacute gave them an

adjacent plot for the enlargement of their dwelling-place.[13] The church was being built in 1329 when Ralph of Shrewsbury, bishop of Bath and Wells, granted an indulgence of forty days to all who should contribute to the fabric.[14] In 1344 Thomas of Berkeley gave four acres for the enlargement of the site.[15]

In 1538, when Richard Ingworth visited Bristol, he reported that the Austin Friars were 'stiff,' and would not give up their house.[16] On 27 August he told Cromwell that the prior had sold the plate and the timber that grew about the house for over 100 marks within the last three years, and that almost all was gone.[17] On 10 September the prior and seven friars surrendered the house to Ingworth.

23. THE CARMELITE FRIARS, BRISTOL

The house of the Carmelite Friars of Bristol, on the right bank of the Frome near the quay, is said to have been founded by Edward, prince of Wales, about 1267.[18] In 1358 the friars received a grant of land for the enlargement of their dwelling-place,[19] and until shortly before the dissolution the White Friars prospered; indeed, Leland wrote that the priory of the Carmelites was the fairest of all the houses of the friars in Bristol.[20] On 25 July, 1538, Richard Ingworth reported to Cromwell that the house was ready at the king's pleasure; the prior and sexton had fled since his last visit, but he had made sure of all the substance that was left.[21] Three days later he went with the four friars before the mayor, and they stated that divers priors had sold and plundered all the jewels and substance of the house, they were in debt, the charity of the people was very small, and they could not continue.[22] Accordingly they gave their house into the hands of the visitor,[23] and the sale of the goods satisfied the creditors.[24] Ingworth begged Cromwell that the four friars might have their capacities, for they had no money wherewith to purchase them. They had

[1] Wright, op. cit. 211.
[2] *L. and P. Hen. VIII*, xiii, pt. ii, No. 320. The inventory of the property (*Reliquary*, 1888, p. 80-2) shows that the Black Friars of Bristol were not reduced to such extreme poverty as many other houses.
[3] *Clifton Antiq. Club Proc.* iii, 159.
[4] In 1234 Henry III granted wood for fuel to the Friars Minor of Bristol; Close, 19 Hen. III, m. 36.
[5] *L. and P. Hen. VIII*, xiii, pt. ii, No. 322.
[6] Close, 20 Hen. III, m. 9.
[7] Bickley, *Little Red Book of Bristol*, i, 89.
[8] Weare, *Collectanea relating to the Friars Minor of Bristol*, 58–66.
[9] Wright, *Suppression of the Monasteries* (Camd. Soc.), 211.
[10] *L. and P. Hen. VIII*, xiii, pt. ii, No. 321.
[11] Ibid. For the inventory of goods, cf. Weare, *Collectanea*, 88–90.
[12] *Cal. of Pat.* 6 Edw. II, pt. ii, m. 2.

[13] Ibid. 11 Edw. II, pt. i, m. 10.
[14] Tanner, *Notitia Monastica* (ed. 1744), p. 483.
[15] *Cal. of Pat.* 18 Edw. III, pt. ii, m. 47.
[16] Wright, *Suppression of Monasteries* (Camd. Soc.), 211 ; *L. and P. Hen. VIII*, xiii, pt. i, No. 1456.
[17] Wright, op. cit. 211. For the inventory of goods cf. Weare, *Collectanea relating to the Friars Minor of Bristol*, 81, 82.
[18] Tanner, *Notitia Monastica* (ed. 1744), p. 483.
[19] Pat. 32 Edw. III, pt. ii, m. 15.
[20] Leland, *Itin.* v, 53 ; vii, 74.
[21] *L. and P. Hen. VIII*, xiii, pt. i, No. 1456.
[22] Weare, *Collectanea relating to the Friars Minor of Bristol*, 75.
[23] Ibid.
[24] Wright, *Suppression of the Monasteries* (Camd. Soc.), 198. For the inventory of goods cf. Weare, *Collectanea*, 76–78.

'a goodly house, meet for a great man,' but their only source of income was the garden.[1]

A seal of the fifteenth century represents an angel kneeling before the Virgin standing at a lectern, on which is an open book, a star of six points over her head.[2] Above the whole is a trefoiled canopy, with traceried tabernacle work, and at the sides panelled buttresses. In base, under a trefoiled canopy, is the demifigure of a friar holding up his hands in supplication with his hood thrown back.

24. FRIARS OF THE PENANCE OF JESUS CHRIST OR FRIARS OF THE SACK, BRISTOL

The Friars of the Sack were established in Bristol in or before 1266, when Henry III granted them six oaks from Selwood Forest for building.[3] The order was suppressed by the Council of Lyons in 1274, but some of the English settlements continued until the Dissolution.[4] The church of the Friars of the Sack in Bristol is mentioned in 1322,[5] but as yet no later reference has come to light. It is certain that they had no house in Bristol in 1538.[6]

25. THE BLACK FRIARS, GLOUCESTER

The house of the Black Friars of Gloucester was founded about 1239.[7] It is probable that Stephen, lord of Harnhill, gave the site, and that Henry III was also accounted a founder in virtue of his munificent gifts.[8] The house was over twenty-five years in building.[9] In 1246 the king gave 41 marks to buy a plot of land for the church, enlarging the churchyard, and making a road to the great thoroughfare of the town.[10] About 1265 the house was probably finished.[11] In the first half of the fourteenth century the number of friars varied from thirty to forty.[12] In 1365 a plot of

land was granted for the enlargement of the site.[13]

It is probable that, as at Bristol and elsewhere, many of the Black Friars of Gloucester fled from England in 1534 and 1535.[14] The few who remained were miserably poor. On 25 July, 1538, Richard Ingworth, the royal visitor, reported to Cromwell that the Black and White Friars were ready to surrender.[15] They were in great penury, and had sold the greater part of their goods. Their chalices were changed to tin and copper, and they had nothing left to purchase their capacities. The Black Friars had 'a proper little house,' but no rents, only their garden which they had let on lease to Master Bell, the alderman.[16] Three or four days later the prior and six friars declared before the mayor and aldermen that they could not keep the visitor's injunctions and continue in their house, and therefore they delivered it into Ingworth's hands for the king's use.[17]

A seal of the thirteenth century represents two figures : one bald-headed and bearded, in flowing garments, holding a book and a reversed sword by the point, probably St. Paul ; the other tonsured, in the habit of the Friars Preachers, holding a long cross and a book ; in base the demifigure of a prior at prayer.[18] The legend is :—

s' COMMUNE · FRM · PREDICATOR' · GLOUCESTRIE

26. THE GREY FRIARS, GLOUCESTER

The house of the Grey Friars of Gloucester, near the south gate of the town, was founded about 1231.[19] Thomas I of Berkeley gave the site,[20] and Henry III granted timber for building. Under the guidance of Agnellus of Pisa, provincial minister, the friars at first accepted only a small plot of land,[21] but about 1239 they needed more ground, and, by the persuasion of his wife, Thomas of Berkeley gave them all that he had at first offered them.[22] The enlargement of the site was sanctioned by Haymo of Faversham, the provincial minister ; he held that it was better for the friars to have land to cultivate that they might provide their sustenance instead of begging from others.[23] In 1239 Ralph of

[1] Wright, op. cit. 198.

[2] *Clifton Antiq. Club Proc.* iii, 200.

[3] Close R. 51 Hen. III, m. 10. For extracts from the constitutions of the order cf. *Eng. Hist. Rev.* ix, 121.

[4] Gasquet, *English Monastic Life*, 242.

[5] Bickley, *Calendar of Bristol Deeds*, No. 63.

[6] Wright, *Suppression of the Monasteries* (Camd. Soc.), 196, 211.

[7] *Arch. Journ.* vol. xxxix, 296–306.

[8] Ibid. 296; cf. *Monumenta Franciscana*, i, 36.

[9] Ibid.   [10] Ibid. 297.

[11] Ibid. 298. The church was not consecrated until 1284 ; *Worc. Epis. Reg. Giffard* (Worc. Hist. Soc.), 235.

[12] Ibid. 299. In 1321, 33 friars ; in 1324, 29 ; in 1326, 40 ; in 1328, 33 ; in 1337, 31.

[13] Ibid. 299.   [14] *Reliquary*, xviii, 21.

[15] *L. and P. Hen. VIII*, xiii, pt. i, No. 1456.

[16] Wright, *Suppression of the Monasteries* (Camd. Soc.), 199.

[17] Ibid. 200–2. For the inventory made in May, 1538, cf. *L. and P. Hen. VIII*, xiii, pt. i, No. 1109.

[18] *Arch. Journ.* xxxix, 306.

[19] In 1231 Henry III granted five trees from the Forest of Dean to the Friars Minor of Gloucester ' ad se hospitandos.' *Cal. of Close*, 15 Hen. III, m. 17.

[20] *Monumenta Franciscana* (Rolls Ser.), i, 35. Tanner, *Notitia Monastica* (ed. 1744), 151.

[21] *Monumenta Franciscana* (Rolls Ser.), i, 35, 59, *n.* 2.

[22] Ibid. 35.   [23] Ibid. 34.

Maidstone resigned the bishopric of Hereford, and entered the house of the Grey Friars of Gloucester.[1] In 1246 Henry III allowed them to hold schools of theology in a turret of the town wall.[2] In 1285 the friars again desired to enlarge their site, and sought permission to acquire a plot of land near their church.[3] They came into conflict with the Benedictines of St. Peter's, and appealed to Peckham, archbishop of Canterbury, himself a Minorite. In 1285 he wrote to the abbot and convent of Gloucester, bidding them satisfy the Grey Friars; it appeared that a man had desired to be buried in their churchyard, but that the monks had seized his body.[4] In the middle of the fourteenth century another dispute arose when the friars claimed the right to the water coming from a spring at Breresclyft, and it was settled in their favour through the intervention of the Black Prince in 1357.[5] In 1365 the friars acquired another half acre for the enlargement of their site.[6] There is no evidence of the mortality in the house during the Black Death; in 1337 the number of friars was thirty-one,[7] and the activity of the brethren a few years afterwards suggests that they suffered no permanent diminution in numbers. Towards the end of the fifteenth century a great part of the church was rebuilt. William, marquis of Berkeley, left £20 to the fabric by his will of 1491;[8] Maurice VI of Berkeley gave 10 marks for several years, and in 1520 he made a provision that if he died before the rebuilding of the church was complete, his executors should finish the work.[9] In 1538 Richard Ingworth, the royal visitor, reported to Cromwell that the Grey Friars was 'a goodly house, much of it new builded.'[10] It is probable that many of the Grey Friars fled abroad in 1534–5,[11] for only five remained at Gloucester in 1538.[12] They were not reduced to such straits of poverty as the Black and White Friars; nevertheless, on 28 July, they too stated in the presence of the mayor and aldermen that they could not keep the visitor's injunctions and continue in their house, and accordingly they delivered it into Ingworth's hands for the use of the king.[13]

27. THE CARMELITE OR WHITE FRIARS, GLOUCESTER

The house of the Carmelite Friars of Gloucester outside the north gate had its origin about 1268,[14] and was probably founded with the help of Queen Eleanor, Sir Thomas Giffard, and Thomas II of Berkeley.[15] In 1321 Henry de Ok gave a curtilage with stews, hays, dikes, walls and trees.[16] In 1337 the number of friars was thirty-one,[17] and in 1343 Edward III allowed them to acquire 3½ acres of land from Thomas of Berkeley, and a messuage from Richard of Hatherley for the enlargement of their manse.[18] In 1347, by an agreement with the prior and brethren of the hospital of St. Bartholomew, they obtained an aqueduct running through a leaden pipe from the spring called 'Gosewhyte-well' to their enclosure.[19]

On 25 July, 1538, Richard Ingworth, the royal visitor, reported to Cromwell that the Black and White Friars were ready to surrender.[20] The White Friars had but a small house, 'and in decay, and some houses taken down and sold.'[21] Their rents were only 20s. a year, and some ten years before they had received the money down for twenty years. Three or four days after Ingworth's report had been made the three remaining friars declared before the mayor and aldermen that they could not keep the visitor's strict injunctions and tarry in their house, and they therefore gave it into Ingworth's hands for the use of the king.[22]

28. THE CRUTCHED FRIARS OF WOTTON-UNDER-EDGE

In 1349 Edward III granted a licence for the foundation of a house of Crutched Friars at Wotton-under-Edge which should be endowed with lands of the yearly value of £10.[23]

[1] *Monumenta Franciscana* (Rolls Ser.), i, 59.
[2] Close, 30 Hen. III, m. 6.
[3] Inq. a.q.d. 13 Edw. I, No. 62.
[4] *Reg. Epis. Peckham* (Rolls Ser.), iii, 905.
[5] Stevenson, *Calendar of Records of the Corporation of Gloucester*, 352.
[6] Inq. a.q.d. 38 Edw. III, No. 3.
[7] *Brist. and Glouc. Arch. Soc. Trans.* xiii, 179.
[8] Smyth, *Lives of the Berkeleys* (ed. Maclean), ii, 134.
[9] Ibid. 201.
[10] Wright, *Suppression of the Monasteries* (Camd. Soc.), 199.
[11] Gasquet, *Hen. VIII and the English Monasteries* (ed. 1899), p. 313.
[12] Wright, op. cit. 201.
[13] Ibid. 202.

[14] On the morrow of the Epiphany, 1269, William de Beauchamp left a mark to the Carmelites of Gloucester; *Worc. Epis. Reg. Giffard* (Worc. Hist. Soc.), 8. On 18 January, 1270, Walter Giffard, archbishop of York, granted a licence to the friars of Mount Carmel who were dwelling at Gloucester to build an oratory by Brook Street outside Gloucester, as the site was within his jurisdiction; *York Archiepis. Reg. Giffard* (Surtees Soc.), 92.
[15] Ibid. 151.
[16] *Cal. of Pat.* 14 Edw. II, pt. ii, m. 17.
[17] *Arch. Journ.* xxxix, 299. Edward III gave a groat each to thirty-one Carmelites when he came to Gloucester in 1337.
[18] *Cal. of Pat.* 17 Edw. III, pt. ii, m. 15.
[19] Stevenson, *Calendar of the Records of the Corporation of Gloucester*, 343.
[20] *L. and P. Hen. VIII.* xiii, pt. i, No. 1456.
[21] Wright, *Suppression of the Monasteries* (Camd. Soc.), 199.
[22] Ibid. 201–2. For the inventory made in May, 1538, cf. *L. and P. Hen. VIII*, xiii, pt. i, No. 1109.
[23] *Cal. of Pat.* 23 Edw. III, pt. i, m. 23.

RELIGIOUS HOUSES

HOUSE OF KNIGHTS TEMPLARS

29. THE PRECEPTORY OF GUITING

The preceptory of the Templars at Guiting was founded about the middle of the twelfth century.[1] Gilbert de Lacy and Roger de Waterville gave lands at Guiting; Roger, earl of Hereford, and Roger d'Oilly were among the benefactors of the Templars in Gloucestershire.[2] At the survey of the lands of the order in 1185, the possessions of the preceptory of Guiting were valued at £11 10s. 6½d.[3] The preceptories were virtually cells of the head house of the Templars in London, which were established principally for the sake of managing the property of the order.[4] The community consisted of some serving brethren, a chaplain, and one or more knights under the rule of the preceptor, who was always a knight. After due provision was made for their maintenance and for hospitality, the surplus of the revenues was sent to the Master of the Temple, and transmitted by him to Palestine.

The destruction of the order in England has been carefully chronicled.[5] In obedience to the bull of Clement V, under writs from Edward II,

the Templars were suddenly arrested on 8 January, 1308, in all parts of England, and their property was seized for the king.[10] When they were transferred as prisoners to the Tower of London and to York and Lincoln Castles, in September, 1309, John de Coningston, the preceptor of Guiting, was sent to London.[11] Of all the Templars who were examined and tortured in England, only two serving brethren and one chaplain were constrained to admit the truth of the charges which were brought against them.[12] A compromise was at last effected. The Templars agreed to confess that they had erred in believing that the Master of their order, who was a layman, had the power of granting absolution, and that they were therefore guilty of heresy.[13]

They made a public abjuration of their error, and in June, 1311, were absolved and reconciled to the church.[14] Their property was confiscated, and a pension of 4d. a day was assigned to them. John de Coningston and six other Templars were sent to different monasteries in the diocese of Worcester to do penance, and their maintenance was a charge on the lands of Temple Guiting.[15]

HOUSE OF KNIGHTS HOSPITALLERS

30. THE PRECEPTORY OF QUENINGTON

The manor of Quenington was given to the Hospitallers by Agnes de Lucy and her daughter Sibilla,[6] and a preceptory was established there in or about 1193.[7] The manor of Wishanger was the gift of Asculf Musard.[8]

In 1338, when a survey was made of the possessions of the Hospitallers, the gross value of the preceptory was £179 8s. 4d.[9] The income was derived mainly from the manor of Quenington, lands at Wishanger, and the churches of Lower Guiting, Southrop, Down Ampney, and Siddington. The community consisted of the preceptor, two other knights, a chaplain, three clerks, and several servants. The cost of their maintenance, of hospitality, and other charges amounted only to £57 6s. 9d., and the residue of the income of the preceptory was paid to the treasurer of the Hospitallers in London. The Hospitallers experienced great difficulty in get-

ting possession of the lands of the Templars, which were granted to them by a bull of Clement V in 1312.[16] In 1338 the manors of Guiting and Bradwell and the church of Temple Guiting, worth in all 210 marks a year, were in the possession of Master Pancius, the king's doctor.[17] The church of Temple Guiting and the manor of Bradwell were probably annexed soon afterwards to the preceptory of Quenington,[18] but the Hospitallers never recovered possession of the manor of Guiting.

In 1535 the clear yearly value of the property amounted to £137 7s. 1½d.[19] The possessions of the preceptory included the manors of Quenington, Wishanger, Baunton, Calmsden and Hampenne in Gloucestershire; of Bradwell, Gosford, Sutton, and Clanfield in Oxfordshire; and the rectories of Temple Guiting, Lower Guiting, Southrop, Down Ampney, Siddington, Bradwell, and Kelmscott.[20]

The preceptory was surrendered as part and parcel of the possessions of the hospital of St. John at Clerkenwell in 1540.

---

[1] Dugdale, *Mon.* vii, 823.   [2] Ibid.
[3] Ibid.   [4] Addison, *The Knights Templars*, 93.
[5] Ibid. 459–559.   [6] Dugdale, *Mon.* vii, 836.
[7] Tanner, *Notitia Monastica* (ed. 1744), p. 148, before 1 John. An agreement with the prior and convent of Worcester was signed at the chapter at Quenington in 1193; cf. MSS. Dean and Chapter of Worcester, *Liber Pensionum*, fol. 1.
[8] Dugdale, op. cit. vii, 836.
[9] *The Hospitallers in England* (Camd. Soc.), 28, 29.

[10] Addison, *The Knights Templars*, 464.
[11] Ibid. 467, 468.   [12] Ibid. 530–7.   [13] Ibid. 540.
[14] Ibid. 541.   [15] Worc. Epis. Reg. Reynolds, fol. 64.
[16] Addison, *The Knights Templars*, 466, 553–7.
[17] *The Hospitallers in England* (Camd. Soc.), 193, 213.
[18] *Valor Eccles.* (Rec. Com.), ii, 463.   [19] Ibid. 463.
[20] Ibid. 462, 463. cf. *The Hospitallers in England* (Camd. Soc.), 26. The possessions of the preceptory of Clanfield had been united with it.

HOSPITALS

31. THE HOSPITAL OF ST. MARK, BILLESWICK, CALLED GAUNT'S HOSPITAL[1]

Maurice de Gaunt, great-grandson of Robert Fitzharding,[2] built an almonry in Billeswick and entrusted the administration of his charity to the monastery of St. Augustine's, Bristol.[3] On condition of a yearly gift of 60 loads of corn, of beans, and of peas, and a rental of £10, the abbot and convent undertook to feed one hundred poor people in the almonry each day and to maintain a chaplain.[4] In his will[5] Maurice de Gaunt provided a permanent endowment for the almonry, consisting of the manor of Poulet in Somersetshire, several mills, and rents in Bristol.[6] After his death on 30 April, 1230,[7] 'his nephew and heir,' Robert de Gurnay, confirmed the endowment,[8] and in 1232 Henry III confirmed the possessions of the master of the almonry of Billeswick, which also included the manor of Stokeland, the gift of Andrew Lutterel.[9] Robert de Gurnay made the hospital a separate foundation, independent of the monastery of St. Augustine, with a master and three chaplains as a governing body.[10] He granted that on the death of the master the administration of the property should be in the hands of the three chaplains; they might elect one of themselves or some other

person as master, and present him to Robert de Gurnay or his heirs, by whom he would be presented to the bishop of Worcester.[11] He decided that the daily allowance of each poor person should be bread of the weight of 45s. and oatmeal pottage.[12] He provided for twelve poor scholars to be admitted and removed at the will of the master, who would be bound to be present in choir at the services in black copes and surplices, under the control of one of their number who should know how to discipline and teach the others.[13] The abbot and convent of St. Augustine's resented the modification of the founder's will, which deprived them of the control of the hospital, and carried their claims before civil and ecclesiastical courts.[14] A settlement was effected in 1251.[15] The abbot and convent of St. Augustine's recognized the independence of the master and brethren of St. Mark's and their right to free burial within their walls. They renounced their claims in the manor of Poulet, and the master and brethren of St. Mark's agreed to pay tithes within the bounds of the parish of Poulet and Were. Both parties agreed to refer any subsequent disputes to the bishop of Worcester. In 1259 they called upon him to settle the question of rights of pasture on the land between their houses,[16] and Bishop Cantilupe judged it to be the burial ground of St. Augustine's, but decided that neither of them should pasture their cattle upon it. The possessions of the hospital, both by gift and purchase, steadily increased. In 1247 Henry III granted rights of free warren in Poulet and Stokeland,[17] and in 1257 the privilege of holding a yearly fair in the manor of Poulet on the vigil, feast, and morrow of St. John the Baptist.[18] In 1259 the hospital had acquired the manors of Herdicote and La Lee, lands in Bruham, a mill at Langford, rents in Bristol, and the advowsons of Stokeland and Quantoxhead.[19] In that year a new constitution, framed on that of the hospital of St. John the Baptist at Lechlade, was drawn up by Walter Cantilupe, bishop of Worcester, with the consent of Robert de Gurnay and his uncle Henry de Gaunt, the master of the hospital.[20] It provided, besides the

[1] The chief hospitals in Bristol are given below. Besides these Trinity Hospital was (Dugdale, *Mon.* vii, 774) founded about 1417 by John Barstaple, a merchant and burgess, for six poor men and six poor women and a priest to officiate for them. It was granted by Queen Elizabeth to the mayor and corporation and has had a continuous existence. St. Margaret's Hospital is mentioned by Leland. Lyon's Hospital is said to have been founded under Canning's will; almshouses of the old endowment are maintained in St. James's parish. The almshouses on St. Michael's Hill were founded in 1504 by John Foster for a priest, eight poor men, and five poor women. The hospital of St. John the Baptist by Bristol for lepers, and the hospital of St. Katherine in the manor of Bedminster, were in the county of Somerset and the diocese of Bath and Wells.

[2] Smyth, *Lives of the Berkeleys* (Maclean), i, 20.

[3] Jeayes, *Catalogue of Muniments of Lord Fitzhardinge at Berkeley Castle*, 78.

[4] Ibid.

[5] *Red Book of St. Augustine's, Bristol,* Berkeley Castle MSS. fol. 206 v.

[6] Tanner, *Notitia Monastica* (ed. 1744), 482.

[7] Smyth, *Lives of the Berkeleys,* i, 26.

[8] *Cal. Chart. R.* 17 Hen. III, m. 15; *Mon.* vii, 687.

[9] *Cal. Chart. R.* 17 Hen. III, m. 15.

[10] *Worc. Epis. Reg. Giffard* (Worc. Hist. Soc.), 18. One of the witnesses, William of Blois, bishop of Worcester, died 1236. The charter was probably granted before 1232; cf. notes 8 and 9.

[11] Dugdale, *Mon.* vii, 688.　　　[12] Ibid.

[13] *Worc. Epis. Reg. Giffard* (Worc. Hist. Soc.), 15.

[14] *Red Book of St. Augustine's,* Berkeley Castle MSS. fol. 206 v.

[15] Ibid. fol. 206 v. 207.　　[16] Ibid. fol. 209 v.

[17] *Cal. Chart. R.* 31 Hen. III, m. 4.

[18] Ibid. 41 Hen. III, m. 4.

[19] *Worc. Epis. Reg. Giffard* (Worc. Hist. Soc.), 15.

[20] Ibid. 15–18. It occurs also Cant. Archiepis. Reg. Winchelsey, fol. 81–82; for the brief following summary, and where differences occur, the Lambeth MS. has been followed.

three chaplains of the old foundation, for six clerks in minor orders and five lay brothers. The clerks were to serve the priests at mass, and if with the master's consent they took priest's orders they were still to serve each other, for unless the possessions of the hospital increased, the number of chaplains and clerks might under no circumstance exceed thirteen. The Use of Sarum was ordered. The master, chaplains, clerks, and brethren had one common dorter and frater. No secular might eat in the frater ; the master was bidden to entertain guests in a room set apart for him. Those who sought admission to the brotherhood underwent a year of probation. If they were found fitting they were then professed and took vows of chastity and obedience, promising to renounce private property, and to keep all the observances of the house. All the brethren bore on their habits the sign of the hospital, a white cross, and beneath it a red shield with three white geese. The master and chaplain wore black cloaks and amices, and when they went into the town black copes. Two chaplains, six clerks, and two lay brothers managed the daily distribution of food to the poor, which took place before the midday meal in the frater. The chaplains might write anything or set down music for the use of the house with the master's leave ; under the same condition lay brothers who were skilled in medicine might use their knowledge for the profit of the hospital. The house was subject to the visitation of the bishop of Worcester,[1] but Cantilupe granted for himself and his successors that it should be exempt from the payment of procurations and from the visitation of the archdeacon or his official.

In 1268 Prince Edward granted the manor of Winterbourne Gunner in Wiltshire,[2] and in 1272 the executors of William de Rumere, formerly treasurer of Wells, and of a canon named John of Hereford, delivered £80 to the master and brethren, who undertook to pay a yearly pension of £4 3s. 4d. to the dean and chapter of Wells for the stipend of a chantry priest and the maintenance of services for their souls.[3]

The daily provision of food for a hundred poor people was a heavy charge upon the income of the hospital, which in 1282 was returned by the master at only £20 4s. 8d.[4] When Bishop Giffard visited the house in 1279 he found that for four years past the feeding of the poor had been 'damnably omitted.'[5] He ordered that the alms should be duly made according to the ordinance of the foundation, and added an injunction that two brethren should be chosen to receive all moneys due to the house, and that

they should render a yearly account to the master and three or four of the wiser brethren. In 1281 the master disregarded the summons of Peckham, archbishop of Canterbury, to attend a provincial council at Lambeth, and in accordance with a mandate from the archbishop, Giffard suspended him from office for a time.[6] At his visitation in 1284 the bishop again discovered that the alms had been wholly withdrawn.[7] On the resignation of the master, Robert of Reading, in 1298, the hospital was involved in a lawsuit with the patron, John Ap Adam, who had married Elizabeth daughter and heiress of John de Gurnay, and now claimed the sole right of presentation.[8] The brethren showed Robert de Gurnay's charter, stating that they had elected one of themselves, William de Beaumier, and were willing to present him to the patron. They enforced their right. Edward I also instituted an inquiry to discover whether the custody of the hospital during the vacancy ought not to fall to the crown, but the jurors made a return in favour of the brethren.[9] During the vacancy John Ap Adam and others entered the manors of the house, carried off the corn and drove away the cattle, so that the brethren could not make their accustomed alms.[10] John Ap Adam charged them with neglecting the terms of their foundation.[11] He appears to have appealed to Giffard against the brethren, but the brief entry in the register is rather obscure ; as at the bishop's council at Hartlebury on 26 December, 1300, the answer to John Ap Adam's petition for changing the habit of the canons of St. Mark's was that they could not be changed without scandal.[12] The disputes were referred to Archbishop Winchelsey when he came on his metropolitical visitation in 1301.[13] On 24 July he decreed that the master and brethren should begin to feed 100 poor folk on Michaelmas Day and the three days following, but that in consideration of their losses for the rest of the year

[1] Cant. Archiepis. Reg. Winchelsey, fol. 82.
[2] *Brist. and Glouc. Arch. Soc. Trans.* iii, 246 ; Cart. R. 18 Edw. I, pt. i, No. 69.
[3] *Glouc. N. and Q.* i, 453.
[4] *Worc. Epis. Reg. Giffard* (Worc. Hist. Soc.), 143.
[5] Ibid. 104.

[6] Ibid. 138. For the archbishop's mandate, cf. *Registrum epistolarum Peckham Arch. Cant.* (Rolls Ser.), ii, 237-8. The cause of the suspension is omitted in the English summary in Giffard, p. 138, but it is clear from the mandate that the master's name was not on the first schedule of exempt monasteries, but on the second schedule sent by the archbishop, viz. the names of the heads of houses, not exempt from visitation, who had absented themselves from the council. Owing to a misunderstanding of the entry in Giffard's register, it has been recently stated that, although the hospital was exempt from visitation, Giffard regularly visited it ; *Reg. Giffard* (Worc. Hist. Soc.), lxxxviii, xcii, xcv.
[7] Ibid. 233.
[8] *Brist. and Glouc. Arch. Soc. Trans.* iii, 247.
[9] Ibid.
[10] In 1300 a commission of oyer and terminer was appointed, *Cal. of Pat.* 29 Edw. I, m. 35 d.
[11] Cant. Archiepis. Reg. Winchelsey, fol. 81.
[12] *Worc. Epis. Reg. Giffard* (Worc. Hist. Soc.), 516.
[13] Cant. Archiepis. Reg. Winchelsey, fol. 82 v.

they should only provide for thirty each day. In the next year they should feed sixty persons daily, and in the third year the full number of 100. He insisted that the master and obedientiars should render an account of expenses once a year, or oftener if needful, in the presence of the brethren. He utterly forbade seculars, and especially women, to enter the cloister or other private places of the house, and he prohibited the brethren from going outside the precincts except with a companion, when necessary, and with the master's leave. Although Winchelsey does not explicitly state that the brethren were to live according to the rule of St. Augustine, the petition of John Ap Adam, in 1300, about the 'canons' of St. Mark's suggests that, as is apparent before the middle of the fourteenth century, the community had already adopted the rule of St. Augustine and the customs of Augustinian canons, probably modifying the observances according to the needs of the house.[1] In 1312 the condition of the hospital caused grave dissatisfaction. Bishop Reynolds commissioned his official to hold an inquiry, because he had heard from four of the brethren that the master, William de Beaumier, was alienating the goods of the house.[2] Information also reached the bishop that the aforesaid brethren had committed grave offences against the observance of the rule.[3] Pending the inquiry the bishop forbade the master to take any steps against the brethren.[4] Nevertheless the master imprisoned William of Kent and imposed penance on him.[5] On inquiry his guilt was proved and, as he expressed great contrition, the bishop bade the master punish him according to the rule of the house, but with gentleness.[6] However, news of the master's violent conduct afterwards reached the bishop, and in October, 1313, he ordered William de Beaumier, under pain of the greater excommunication, to restore the erring brother to his former condition and bade the abbot of St. Augustine's see that it was done.[7]

The church of Stokeland was appropriated to the hospital in 1316.[8] In 1326 Edward II allowed the master and brethren to exchange their lands at Compton, Cheddar, and Netherwere with the bishop of Bath and Wells for the advowson of the church of Overstowey that they might appropriate it.[9] In 1336 Bishop Montacute visited the hospital, and it is briefly recorded in his register that he 'corrected' there.[10] A few years later the house was seriously in debt, in 1343 owing £20 to William de Langeford of Bristol,[11] and in 1344 £100 to Adam Brabazon, a fishmonger of London, and William de Stoures, a grocer of London.[12] In 1339 Bishop Wulstan de Bransford gave leave of a year's absence to the master, Ralph of Tetbury, to go on a pilgrimage to St. James of Compostella, and he committed the custody of the house to John of Stokeland.[13] In 1346 Ralph was still absent, and the nine brethren elected John of Stokeland[14] in his place.

The Black Death wrought great havoc in Bristol, and it is clear that the brothers of St. Mark's were fewer in number during the latter half of the century. After holding the office of master for ten years, Walter Browning resigned in 1370,[15] but two years later, owing to urgent necessity, he again consented to hold office[16] till 1391, when being very old and weak he finally resigned.[17] In consideration of his long and careful service he was assigned two rooms in the house and a daily allowance of food and drink for himself and his servant. There were then only three priests besides himself, and they constituted the whole community.[18] One of them, Thomas Over, had resigned the office of master in 1372.[19] Another, Philip Russell, attempted to secure it for himself by papal provision, but the letters in his favour arrived too late,[20] as William Lane, a canon of the monastery of St. Augustine, Bristol, had already been elected and confirmed.[21] However, he was not left in undisturbed possession. On 30 April, 1400, Henry IV granted the office of master to his clerk, John Trowbridge.[22] Lane remonstrated, and the appointment was revoked on 13 July.[23] In 1406 complaint was made to the king that works of piety, including the feeding of the poor, had been wholly omitted by William Lane, and that there were only three chaplains besides himself.[24] It was stated that the clear yearly

[1] In 1445, in return to the king's writ to scrutinize the registers, Bishop Carpenter stated that the house was dedicated for a master and convent of the order of St. Augustine, thus making the hospital a convent of Augustinian canons from its first foundation, which the evidence does not support. Worc. Epis. Reg. Carpenter, fol. 25 d. In 1346 nine of the brothers, who were competent to elect, stated that they lived according to the rules of St. Augustine and the regular observances of that house. Ibid. Bransford, fol. 97 d.

[2] Ibid. Reynolds, fol. 64 d.

[3] Ibid. fol. 77.   [4] Ibid. fol. 96.
[5] Ibid.   [6] Ibid. fol. 81 d.
[7] Ibid. fol. 96.
[8] Wells Epis. Reg. Drokensford (Som. Rec. Soc.), 109.

[9] Cal. of Pat. 20 Edw. II, m. 17. It was appropriated in or before 1327. Wells Epis. Reg. Drokensford (Som. Rec. Soc.), 270.
[10] Worc. Epis. Reg. Montacute, fol. 48 d.
[11] Cal. of Close, 17 Edw. III, pt. ii, m. 18 d.
[12] Ibid. 18 Edw. III, pt. i, m. 24 d.
[13] Worc. Epis. Reg. Bransford, fol. 8 d.
[14] Ibid. fol. 97 d.–98 d.
[15] Ibid. Brian, i, fol. 30 d.; Lynn, fol. 21.
[16] Ibid. Brian, &c. ii (numbered xi, 2), fol. 5.
[17] Ibid. Wakefield, fol. 82 d.
[18] Ibid. fol. 90.   [19] Ibid. Brian, &c. ii, fol. 5.
[20] Cal. of Pat. 17 Ric. II, pt. i, m. 18.
[21] Worc. Epis. Reg. Wakefield, fol. 90.
[22] Cal. of Pat. 1 Hen. IV, pt. vi, m. 3.
[23] Ibid. 1 Hen. IV, pt. vii, m. 2.
[24] Brist. and Glouc. Arch. Soc. Trans. iii, 249; Close R. 7 Hen. IV, m. 11.

value of the manor of Stokeland Gaunts and the lands of Gauntesham and Colle was £40. The manor and lands were seized into the king's hands in consequence, but after investigation they were restored to the master and brethren. The numbers did not again exceed four or five.[1] It is not clear how the charity of the hospital was exercised, and indeed its history in the fifteenth century is quite obscure; but apparently the administration satisfied so vigorous a ruler and reformer as Bishop Carpenter. In 1487 the tower of the church was finished.[2] Sir Robert Poyntz of Iron Acton (ob. 1520) built the Jesus Chapel, and founded a chantry therein.[3] In the sixteenth century the hospital, like a number of other religious houses, took gentlefolks as boarders. Among these, in 1535, was Lady Jane Guildford,[4] who had an annuity of £60. After the visitation by Cromwell's commissioners in 1535, women were excluded by the injunctions, and she wrote to Cromwell begging his favour. 'I have a lodging there chosen as meet for a poor widow to serve God in her old days. And I trust both for myself and my women like as we have been hitherto, to be of such governance with your licence to the same, that no inconvenience shall ensue thereof. And where hereto before I have been used from my house to go the next way to the church, for my ease, through the cloister of the same house to a chapel that I have within the quire of the same, I shall be content from henceforth, if it shall so seem convenient unto you, to forbear that, and to resort to the common place, like as others do, of the same church.' John Coleman, the master, urged Cromwell to dispense with the injunction forbidding any of the brethren to leave the precincts, because he was bound to ride from place to place about the profits of the house.[5]

In 1534 the master and four brethren acknowledged the royal supremacy,[6] and five years later, on 9 December, 1539, they surrendered the house to Cromwell's commissioners.[7] The master received a pension of £40; Richard Fletcher, the steward, got £6 13s. 4d., Thomas Pynchyn £6, and John Ellis was appointed curate of the parish of St. Mark at a salary of £8, but if he refused, a pension of £6 was to be awarded him.

Sixteen men and children, servants, and choristers of the house were paid £10 9s. 4d. in all for their wages and liveries. The clear yearly value of the property of the hospital amounted to £165 2s. 4½d., the manors of Erdcote Gaunts and Lee in Gloucestershire, Stokeland Gaunts, Overstowey, and Poulet Gaunts in

Somerset, and Winterbourne Gunner in Wiltshire, besides the rectories of Stokeland Gaunts and Overstowey.[8] The site and the greater part of the possessions were sold to the mayor and corporation of Bristol in 1541.[9]

MASTERS OF THE HOSPITAL OF ST. MARK

Henry de Gaunt (brother of the founder), occurs 1251,[10] resigned 1268[11]
Gilbert de Watham, 1268[12]
John of Trowbridge, resigned 1273[13]
Thomas, occurs 1282[14]
Robert of Reading, 1287,[15] resigned 1298[16]
William de Beaumier, 1298,[17] occurs 1313[18]
William, occurs 1330[19]
Ralph of Tetbury, occurs 1336,[20] resigned or deposed 1346[21]
John of Stokeland, 1346[22]
Richard of Yate, resigned 1360[23]
Walter Browning, 1360,[24] resigned 1370[25]
Thomas of Over, 1370,[26] resigned 1372[27]
Walter Browning, 1372,[28] resigned 1391[29]
William Lane, 1391,[30] occurs 1406[31]
John Molton, occurs 1424,[32] resigned 1442[33]
William Wyne, 1442,[34] resigned 1486[35]
Thomas Tyler, 1486[36]
Thomas, occurs 1501[37]
John Coleman, occurs 1534[38] to 1539[39]

The seal attached to the acknowledgement of the king's supremacy represents two crocketed canopied niches supported by crocketed buttresses.[40] In the sinister niche is a seated figure of St. Mark, writing his gospel on a desk or stand before him, holding in his right hand a stilus. On the dexter side before him is a lion sejant rampant. In the space above between the

---

[1] Worc. Epis. Reg. Bourchier, fol. 82.
[2] 'The Mayor's Chapel,' 26. (Clifton Antiq. Club).
[3] Ibid. 27.
[4] L. and P. Hen. VIII, ix, No. 289.
[5] Ibid. ix, No. 296.
[6] Dep. Keeper's Rep. vii, App. ii, 281.
[7] L. and P. Hen. VIII, xv, No. 139.

[8] Dugdale, op. cit. vii, 688.   [9] Ibid.
[10] Red Book of St. Augustine's, Bristol, fol. 20. MSS. of Berkeley Castle.
[11] Worc. Epis. Reg. Giffard (Worc. Hist. Soc.), 19.
[12] Ibid.   [13] Ibid. 59.
[14] Ibid. 153.   [15] Ibid. 304.
[16] Brist. and Glouc. Arch. Soc. Trans. iii, 247.
[17] Ibid.
[18] Worc. Epis. Reg. Reynolds, fol. 96.
[19] Cal. of Pat. 4 Edw III, pt. ii, m. 39.
[20] Ibid. 15 Edw. III, pt. i, m. 14.
[21] Worc. Epis. Reg. Bransford, fol. 97 d.
[22] Ibid. 97 d.–98 d.
[23] Ibid. Brian, i, fol. 30 d.
[24] Ibid.   [25] Ibid. Lynn, fol. 21.
[26] Ibid.   [27] Ibid. Brian, &c. ii, fol. 5.
[28] Ibid.   [29] Ibid. Wakefield, fol. 82 d
[30] Ibid. fol. 90.
[31] Brist. and Glouc. Arch. Soc. Trans. iii, 249.
[32] Cal. of Pat. 3 Hen. VI, pt. i, m. 22.
[33] Worc. Epis. Reg. Bourchier, fol. 82.
[34] Ibid.   [35] Ibid. Alcock, fol. 154 d.
[36] Ibid.
[37] MS. Harl. 6966, fol. 160 (B.M.).
[38] Dep. Keeper's Rep. vii, App. ii, 281.
[39] L. and P. Hen. VIII, xv, No. 139.
[40] Clifton Antiq. Club Proc. iii, 11, 12.

canopies is a heater-shaped shield, which was probably charged with the arms of the house, gules, three geese argent. In a compartment below the figures are two similar shields, probably containing the arms of the two founders; the sinister is shown to be paly or, three pales azure for Robert de Gurnay. Between these shields is another niche in which is a kneeling figure looking to the right. The legend is :—

S · CŌE · DOM' · MARCI · DE · SCI · BILLES VVYK · IVXTA · BRISTOLL

32. THE HOSPITAL OF ST. BAR-THOLOMEW, BRISTOL

Nothing is known of the foundation of the hospital of St. Bartholomew at Bristol. In 1275 the community consisted of brethren and sisters who had the right of free election of their master.[1] There is no evidence that any of the brethren beside the master were priests, and it is probable that both they and the sisters had been appointed at the original foundation to minister to the needs of the sick and poor, and were under vows. The endowment was very small.[2] The master was a secular chaplain;[3] in 1329 Robert de Merston was presented to Orlton, bishop of Worcester, as master or warden by John de la Warre, who claimed to be the patron, with the unanimous assent of the brothers and sisters.[4] In 1331 Orlton commended brother John de Merston to the community, to be admitted to the care and guidance of the hospital until he should order otherwise.[5] However, in the latter half of the fourteenth century and onwards, the de la Warres of Wickwar in Gloucester were recognized as the patrons,[6] and declared the house to be of their foundation.

In or before 1336 the brethren seem to have disappeared from the community,[7] and in 1340 a prioress ruled over it. In that year Wulstan de Bransford, bishop of Worcester, allowed the prioress and sisters to let on rent for a term of sixty years a piece of land and the old dorter in which they used to sleep when both brothers and sisters were dwelling in the hospital.[8] The prioresses maintained their position for over forty years, but when the hospital lacked a ruler in 1386, John de la Warre presented William Badesford to Henry Wakefield bishop of Worcester,[9] who ordered the archdeacon of Gloucester and the prior of St. James, Bristol, to inquire into the vacancy, and report

whether the hospital ought to be ruled by seculars or by regulars, by men or by women, who was the true patron, and what was the yearly value of the endowment.[10] The claim of John de la Warre to present a secular priest as supreme ruler was then established.[11] The question of the government was again raised in 1412, when the women again attempted to assert their claim to the supreme rule. By order of Bishop Peverell an inquisition was held to discover whether according to the ordination of the hospital it ought to be ruled by men or by women.[12] The jurors declared that the hospital ought to be ruled by men who were secular priests, and not by women, and added that it had always been ruled by men.[13] They were unable to ascertain the value of the endowment *propter grauissimam dilapidacionem*. Successive masters bore undisputed sway over both brothers and sisters.

In 1445, with the approval of the mayor and commonalty of Bristol, a fraternity of mariners was established in the hospital of St. Bartholomew.[14] A priest and twelve poor mariners were bound to remember in their daily prayers all 'merchants and mariners passing and labouring on the sea . . . to the port aforesaid.'

In 1531 Lord de la Warre conveyed the hospital and all its property to Robert Thorn to enable him to found a free grammar school at Westbury on Trym.[15]

MASTERS OF THE HOSPITAL OF ST. BARTHOLOMEW, BRISTOL

Walter,[16] 1319
John de Hulle, 1322,[17] resigned 1329[18]
Robert de Merston, 1329[19]
John de Merston, 1331[20]

PRIORESSES

Eleanor, occurs 1340[21]
Elizabeth Batte, became prioress 1363[22]
Joanna Joye, 1368[23]
Matilda Coveley, 1369[24]

MASTERS

William Badesford, 1386,[25] resigned 1389[26]
John Dauntre, 1389,[27] exchanged 1403[28]

[1] *Worc. Epis. Reg. Giffard* (Worc. Hist. Soc.), 76.
[2] *Worc. Reg. Sede Vac.* 120.
[3] Walter, vicar of St. Nicholas, Bristol, was appointed in 1319. Worc. Epis. Reg. Cobham, fol. 46 d.
[4] Ibid. Orlton, fol. 16 d.   [5] Ibid. fol. 45.
[6] Ibid. Wakefield, fol. 58.
[7] Ibid. Montacute, fol. 41 d.
[8] Ibid. Bransford, fol. 41.
[9] Ibid. Wakefield, fol. 45 d.

[10] Ibid.   [11] Ibid. fol. 58.
[12] Ibid. Peverell, fol. 41 d.   [13] Ibid.
[14] Bickley, *Little Red Book of Bristol*, ii, 186–92.
[15] Dugdale, *Mon.* vii, 774 ; Nicholls and Taylor, *Bristol Past and Present*, ii, 120.
[16] Worc. Epis. Reg. Cobham, fol. 46 d.
[17] Ibid. fol. 30.   [18] Ibid. Orlton, fol. 16 d.
[19] Ibid.   [20] Ibid. fol. 45 d.
[21] Ibid. Bransford, fol. 41.
[22] Ibid. Barnet, fol. 27.   [23] Ibid.
[24] Ibid. Whittlesey, fol. 27.
[25] Ibid. Wakefield, fol. 45 d.
[26] Ibid. fol. 58.   [27] Ibid.
[28] Ibid. Clifford, fol. 65 d.

John Prentys, resigned 1412 [1]
John Arundel, 1412 [2]
John White, 1457,[3] resigned 1463 [4]
William Attingham, 1463 [5]
Thomas Mark, resigned 1480 [6]
John Langrissh, 1480 [7]
James Butler, 1488 [8]
Humphrey Saville, 1511 [9]
George Croft, *circa* 1524–31 [10]

33. THE HOSPITAL OF ST. LAWRENCE, BRISTOL

The leper hospital of St. Lawrence, Bristol, was founded by King John when earl of Mortain, and in 1208 he gave a charter confirming the foundation.[11] The right of appointing the master was vested in the crown [12] until Henry V granted it to Humphrey, duke of Gloucester.[13] It is probable that the hospital was always very poor. In 1390 Richard II issued a commission to six persons to visit the hospital and correct abuses therein.[14] In the middle of the fifteenth century it had fallen into decay, and in 1465 Edward IV granted the custody to the dean and chapter of Westbury to increase their endowment.[15] In 1535 the clear yearly value of the possessions of the hospital was £12 8s. 2d.[16] The dean and chapter paid a salary of £2 to a priest to celebrate mass in the chapel, and gave 16s. to four poor almsfolk.[17] The hospital was surrendered as part of the possessions of Westbury in 1544.[18]

MASTERS OR WARDENS OF THE HOSPITAL OF ST. LAWRENCE [19]

Robert de Halwell, occurs 1321 [20]
Simon, occurs 1337 [21]
William Coterell, appointed 4 Feb. 1390 [22]

John Bell, appointed 16 Sept. 1390 [23]
Robert Bailly, appointed 28 Nov. 1390 [24]
Richard des Armes, 1393 [25]
William Ruddock, 1400 [26]
Walter Chivington, occurs 1438 [27]

34. THE HOSPITAL OF ST. MARY MAGDALEN, BRISTOL

The leper hospital of St. Mary Magdalen, Brightbow, is described by William of Worcester (1415–90) as an ancient foundation.[28]
A seal [29] of the fifteenth century represents St. Mary Magdalen standing in a canopied niche ; in her right hand an ointment box to which she is pointing with the left hand. The background is a diapered lozengy with a reticulated pattern, having a small spot in each space ; the edge engrailed ; in base an arcade. The legend is :—

s' HOSPETAL . MARIE . MAGDALENE . BRISTOLL
$\overline{IX}$. BRITBOW

35. THE HOSPITAL OF ST. BARTHOLOMEW, GLOUCESTER

According to a statement made by a jury of Gloucester in 1357,[30] a chaplain, by name Nicholas Walred, began, in the reign of Henry II, to build the west bridge over the Severn, and employed many workmen. William Myparty, a burgess of Gloucester, associated himself with the work and built a dwelling on a piece of ground which he held of the king in chief. Sick men and women found shelter there, besides the priest, the burgess, and the workmen. The community which there grew up had a continuous existence, and under the rule of a priest who wore the dress of a hermit, served the double purpose of maintaining the bridge and caring for the sick.[31] From the beginning of the thirteenth century there are records of grants of lands and rents by the burgesses of Gloucester.[32] The right of having a chantry chapel in the hospital was not secured until 1232, when William of Blois, bishop of Worcester, persuaded the abbot and convent of Gloucester, in whose parish the hospital lay, to give their consent, provided that the rights of the mother church were maintained.[33]

---

[1] Worc. Epis. Reg. Peverell, fol. 41 *d.*
[2] Ibid.
[3] Ibid. Carpenter, fol. 144 *d.*
[4] Ibid. fol. 180. [5] Ibid.
[6] Ibid. Alcock, fol. 77 *d.* [7] Ibid.
[8] Ibid. Moreton, fol. 27, collated by bishop *hac vice.*
[9] Ibid. Silvester de Giglis, fol. 71, on death of James Butler.
[10] Ibid. de Ghinucci, fol. 23.
[11] Dugdale, *Mon.* vii, 670.
[12] Tanner, *Not. Mon.* (ed. 1744), 481.
[13] Ibid.
[14] *Cal. of Pat.* 14 Ric. II, pt. i, m. 26 *d.*
[15] Ibid. 5 Edw. IV, pt. i, m. 6.
[16] *Valor Eccles.* (Rec. Com.), ii, 434.
[17] Ibid.
[18] *L. and P. Hen. VIII,* xix, pt. i, No. 120.
[19] The names of the masters do not occur in the registers of Worcester. Only a few have been found in the public records.
[20] *Cal. of Pat.* 14 Edw. II, pt. ii, m. 3.
[21] Ibid. 11 Edw. III, pt. i, m. 34.
[22] Ibid. 13 Ric. II, pt. ii, m. 7.

[23] Ibid. 14 Ric. II, pt. i, m. 23.
[24] Ibid. pt. i, m. 7.
[25] Ibid. 16 Ric. II, pt. iii, m. 9.
[26] Ibid. 1 Hen. IV, pt. vi, m. 32.
[27] *Clifton Antiq. Club Proc.* iii, 27.
[28] Nasmith, *Itin. Symonis Simeonis et Willelmi de Worcestre,* 205, 206 ; cf. *Pope Nich. Tax.* (Rec. Com.), 235.
[29] Birch, *Catalogue of Seals in British Museum,* i, 461.
[30] Dugdale, *Mon.* vii, 689. [31] Ibid.
[32] Stevenson, *Calendar of Records of Corporation of Gloucester, passim.*
[33] *Hist. et Cart. Glouc.* (Rolls Ser.), i, 245.

In 1229 Henry III gave the church of St. Nicholas to the prior, brethren, and sisters of the hospital of St. Bartholomew of Gloucester for the support of the poor,[1] and it was appropriated to their needs.[2] In virtue of that gift, the hospital was afterwards said to be of royal foundation. Soon afterwards the brethren and sisters obtained a licence to elect their prior.[3] The community seems to have consisted of several priests of the order of St. Augustine,[4] and a number of lay brothers and sisters to minister to the sick and poor.[5] It was subject to the visitation of the bishop of Worcester.[6]

Little is known of the history of the hospital except that it suffered greatly from poverty and maladministration under the rule of Nicholas de Hardwick and Walter Gibbes (1329–85). In 1333 Thomas Charlton, bishop of Hereford, appropriated the church of Newnham, of which the advowson was given by William de Bohun, earl of Northampton,[7] to the use of the prior and brethren.[8] There were then ninety sick in the hospital, among them the lame, the halt, and the blind, both men and women.[9] In 1344 Edward III appointed a commission to make a visitation of the hospital, which was reported to be greatly decayed.[10] Similar commissions were appointed in 1345[11] and in 1347,[12] and the report of the jurors summoned by the sheriff in 1357[13] has furnished the history of the first foundation of the hospital. Nicholas de Hardwick resigned in 1356;[14] he had granted several corrodies for life, and had thus so burdened the hospital that its resources no longer sufficed for the maintenance of the services, almsgiving, and other good works, and for the provision of food and clothing for the brothers and sisters.[15] Sums of money, jewels, corn, silver and brass vessels, beds, and household utensils given by men of Gloucester and elsewhere to the value of £100, which were under the charge of the prior and two of his brethren, had been dissipated and destroyed. After receiving this report, on 8 May, 1359, Edward III appointed five commissioners to effect a thorough reform, and directed all the inmates of the hospital to obey them.[16] An almost exactly similar account of the misdeeds of the prior and

his predecessor reached Richard II in 1381.[17] It was again stated that the brethren and sisters lacked food and clothing, and a commission appointed on 20 July[18] sent in a more detailed report before 26 October. Contrary to the ordinance of the foundation, the poor had been charged for admittance, and five cases were mentioned in which bed-money had been received.[19] Lands given for the benefit of the poor had been diverted to other uses, and a great building in the hospital set apart for the benefit of the poor had been unroofed, and the timbers and tiles taken for other purposes. There were further charges of dissolute living. Another commission was appointed on 26 October, 1381,[20] and a third on 12 March, 1382,[21] and in 1384 a fourth commission was bidden to make ordinance for the reformation of the hospital.[22] It is possible that there was some exaggeration in the charges, for the prior, Walter Gibbes, was not deposed, and on his death in 1385 one of the priests of the hospital, John Bulmyll, mentioned by name as an evildoer in one of the reports, was admitted by Bishop Wakefield as his successor, with the king's consent.[23]

On account of its poverty the hospital was exempted from taxation in 1401. In 1407 Henry IV confirmed the possessions of the hospital, and took the collectors of alms together with the hospital and its goods under his protection.[24] He granted that upon each vacancy the chaplains might elect a prior without obtaining a royal licence, the electors being only constrained to certify their choice to the bishop for his confirmation.[25]

In or before 1413 the prior and brethren sent a petition to John XXIII.[26] Although the chapel of Little Dean was dependent on the parish church of Newnham, which had been appropriated to the hospital for over sixty years, the inhabitants had had the chapel consecrated apparently as an independent church, without the licence of the ordinary or of the prior and brethren, and now withdrew the tithes which were due to the mother church of Newnham for the maintenance of their chaplain. The pope sent a mandate that the hospital should recover its rights.

In 1423 the hospital was so seriously embarrassed that Henry VI committed the custody to a commission consisting of the bishop of Worcester and five other persons.[27]

[1] Cart. R. 13 Hen. III, pt. i, m. 5.
[2] *Cal. Papal Letters*, vi, 395. *Valor Eccles.* (Rec. Com.), ii, 488.
[3] Dugdale, op. cit. vii, 689.
[4] *Cal. Papal Letters*, vi, 395.
[5] Cart. R. 13 Hen. III, m. 5.
[6] Worc. Epis. Reg. *passim*.
[7] *Cal. of Pat.* 17 Edw. III, pt. i, m. 7.
[8] Heref. Epis. Reg. Thomas Charlton, fol. 34.
[9] Ibid.
[10] *Cal. of Pat.* 18 Edw. III, pt. i, m. 6 *d.*
[11] Ibid. 19 Edw. III, pt. i, m. 9 *d.*
[12] Ibid. 21 Edw. III, pt. i, m. 8 *d.*
[13] Dugdale, *Mon.* vii, 689.
[14] Worc. Epis. Reg. Brian, fol. 15.
[15] Pat. 33 Edw. III, pt. i, m. 2 *d.*   [16] Ibid.

[17] *Cal. of Pat.* 4 Ric. II, pt. i, m. 26 *d.*
[18] Ibid.   [19] Ibid. m. 8 *d.*
[20] Ibid.
[21] Ibid. 5 Ric. II, pt. ii, m. 23 *d.*
[22] Ibid. 7 Ric. II, pt. ii, m. 17 *d.*
[23] Ibid. 8 Ric. II, pt. ii, m. 19.
[24] Stevenson, *Calendar of Records of Corporation of Gloucester*, 57.
[25] Ibid.; Worc. Epis. Reg. Clifford, fol. 70 *d.*
[26] *Cal. Papal Letters*, vi, 395.
[27] *Cal. of Pat.* 1 Hen. VI, pt. iv, m. 23

In 1451 an indulgence of forty days for the benefit of the poor was granted by Boulers, bishop of Hereford.[1] A similar indulgence was granted by Carpenter, bishop of Worcester, in 1450,[2] and in 1455[3] and 1462[4] he issued indulgences in aid of the repair of the bridge, which was doubtless at times a heavy charge on the revenues of the hospital.

In 1534 the prior and three chaplains acknowledged the royal supremacy.[5] In 1535 the gross revenues amounted to £85 7s. 1d.; of this sum £20 was derived from the rectories of St. Nicholas, Gloucester, and of Newnham, the remainder from tenements and lands in or near the city.[6] Only £30 0s. 3d. was expended on the maintenance of thirty-two almsfolk; the master and five chaplains drew nearly £50 in salaries.[7] Another survey of the hospital was made under the Chantries Act of 1547,[8] and it was not confiscated by the crown. In 1564 Queen Elizabeth granted the hospital to the mayor and corporation of Gloucester for the support of a priest, a physician or surgeon, and forty poor persons.[9] It has had a continuous existence to the present day.[10]

PRIORS OF ST. BARTHOLOMEW, GLOUCESTER

Adam, occurs *circa* 1230 and in 1245[11]
Walter, occurs 1248[12]
John, occurs 1253[13]
Walter, *circa* 1260[14]
John, *circa* 1270[15]
Adam of Garne, *circa* 1280[16]
John le Pessover, 1286[17]
John[18] or William[19] de Abbenhall, 1295
John de Okes, 1301[20]
John de Bicknor, 1326[21]
Nicholas de Hardwick, 1329,[22] resigned 1356[23]
Walter Gibbes, 1356[24]
John Bullmyll, 1385[25]

John Gloucester, 1404[26]
Thomas Carpenter, occurs 1413 and 1418[27]
William Wrecester, resigned 1425[28]
Stephen Myle, 1425[29]
William Sobbury *alias* Holway, 1460[30]
Richard Heyward, *ob.* 1476[31]
John Hasfield, elected 1476,[32] *ob.* 1487[33]
Richard Baker, 1487[34]
Thom Apowell, resigned 1510[35]
Andrew Whitmay, 1510,[36] occurs 1534[37]

A seal of the thirteenth century represents the martyrdom of St. Bartholomew, the saint standing between two executioners, one on the right with a large knife, the one on the left flaying him; in base under a trefoiled arch the prior kneeling in prayer to the right.[38]

36. THE HOSPITAL OF ST. MARGARET, GLOUCESTER

The hospital of St. Margaret and St. Sepulchre at Gloucester was probably founded about 1150,[39] and at the beginning of the thirteenth century the master, brethren, and sisters found kindly benefactors among the citizens of Gloucester.[40] The brethren and sisters were lepers, and until after the beginning of the fourteenth century the master was probably the chaplain who served the chantry. It lay within the parish of St. Peter's Abbey,[41] and the abbot presented to the chantry.[42]

In 1309, on the appeal of the brothers, Benedict of Paston, the official of Bishop Reynolds, came on a visitation on 27 April.[43] The master, who had been deputed to fill the office by a former official, was then broken down by age and ill-health. He resigned, and a chaplain named William Pouke was appointed by Benedict of Paston, and entrusted with the custody of the

---

[1] Heref. Epis. Reg. Boulers, fol. 3.
[2] Worc. Epis. Reg. Carpenter, i, fol. 81.
[3] Ibid. fol. 130 d. [4] Ibid. fol. 171.
[5] Dep. Keeper's Rep. vii, App. ii, 287.
[6] Valor Eccles. (Rec. Com.), ii, 488–9.
[7] Ibid. 488; cf. Leland, Collectanea, i, 79.
[8] Ibid. 490. [9] Cal. S. P. Dom. i, 333.
[10] Kelly, Direct. of Glouc. (ed. 1906).
[11] Stevenson, op. cit. 134. [12] Ibid. 189.
[13] Ibid. 209. [14] Ibid. 217.
[15] Ibid. 243. [16] Ibid. 269.
[17] Worc. Epis. Reg. Giffard (Worc. Hist. Soc.), 292.
[18] Ibid. 462.
[19] On Pat. 23 Edw. I, m. 12, the successor is entered as William de Abbenhale. William de Abbenhale was deposed, Cal. of Pat. 29 Edw. I, m. 16.
[20] Ibid. He died in 1326. Cal. of Pat. 20 Edw. II, m. 16.
[21] Ibid. 20 Edw. II, m. 14.
[22] Ibid. 3 Edw. III, pt. ii, m. 9.
[23] Worc. Epis. Reg. Brian, fol. 15. [24] Ibid.
[25] Cal. of Pat. 8 Ric. II, pt. ii, m. 19. On death of Walter Gibbes.

[26] Ibid. 6 Hen. IV, pt. i, m. 17. On death of John Bullmyll.
[27] Stevenson, op. cit. 381, 383.
[28] Worc. Epis. Reg. Morgan, fol. 42 d.
[29] Ibid. fol. 43.
[30] Ibid. Carpenter, i, fol. 154. On death of Stephen Myle.
[31] Ibid. Carpenter, ii, fol. 79 d. [32] Ibid.
[33] Ibid. Moreton, fol. 18 d. [34] Ibid.
[35] Ibid. Silvester de Giglis, fol. 66 d.
[36] Ibid. He was bishop of Chrysopolis, and acted as suffragan. V.C.H. Worcester, ii, 43, 'Ecclesiastical History.'
[37] Dep. Keeper's Rep. vii, App. ii, 287.
[38] Birch, Catalogue of Seals in British Museum, i, 568.
[39] Alured, bishop of Worcester (1158–63), granted the lepers the right of burial in their churchyard. Hist. et Cart. Glouc. (Rolls Ser.), ii, 7.
[40] Stevenson, Cal. of Records of Corporation of Glouc. passim.
[41] Hist. et Cart. Glouc. (Rolls Ser.), ii, 7.
[42] Ibid. iii, 31; cf. Worc. Epis. Reg. Gainsborough, fol. 37.
[43] Worc. Epis. Reg. Cobham, fol. 10.

spiritualities and temporalities of the house. The brethren and sisters were bidden to observe the injunctions of the bishop, especially that no brother or sister should be admitted by command or request of any lay knight or burgess, except with the assent of the bishop or his official.

In the middle of the fourteenth century the burgesses of Gloucester had secured control over the hospital. The commonalty elected one of the burgesses to act as master or supervisor,[1] and the management of the property of the hospital was under his charge. He was appointed perhaps for a year or a term of years, and his consent was necessary for the granting of leases.[2] A prior, who was perhaps the chaplain, bore rule over the brethren and sisters. Probably he too was appointed by the commonalty of Gloucester, for no collations are recorded in the registers of the bishops of Worcester. In 1518 the mayor, master of the hospital, and burgesses accepted William Ergan and Emmota his wife as a brother and sister, and granted the office of prior and governor to William Ergan, so at that date the prior was no longer of necessity the chaplain.[3] The inmates were then apparently almsfolk, for leprosy had greatly declined. In or about 1545 Henry VIII confirmed the custody of the hospital to the mayor and corporation.[4] The hospital has had a continuous existence until the present day.[5]

37. THE HOSPITAL OF ST. MARY MAGDALEN, GLOUCESTER

The leper hospital of St. Mary Magdalen, Gloucester, was founded for women, probably soon after the middle of the twelfth century.[6]

It has had a continuous existence as a home for the sick poor. In 1599 Queen Elizabeth granted it to the mayor and corporation of Gloucester.[7] In 1617, on information that for want of good governance the revenues had been much wasted, James I ordained that the government should be in the masters and governors, that they should be a body corporate with a common seal, and should have and enjoy the possessions of the hospital for the benefit of the inmates, and in addition a pension of £13 from the king, to be called 'King James's Pension,' as was formerly paid by the kings of England.[8] He

willed that the hospital should thenceforth be called the hospital of King James. However, it still bears the former name of St. Mary Magdalen.[9]

38. THE HOSPITAL OF ST. JOHN, CIRENCESTER

According to a statement of the townsmen of Cirencester in 1343, the hospital of St. John was founded by Henry I and endowed with a third of the tithe of the royal demesne of Cirencester, and three cartloads of underwood from his forest of Oakley every week.[10] They declared that by the king's provision a chaplain should sing mass daily in the oratory of the hospital, and should have a daily allowance of food from the monastery of Cirencester. The abbot and his predecessors since 1155 had appropriated the tithe, had made laymen wardens, and taken money for appointments for life. 'And so,' the townsmen continued, 'they have abated the said chantry of the king a long time; but that a widow from Cirencester, Aleyze de Weston, gave £60 to the abbot for having a chantry to chant for herself, as appears by a charter which they could show.'

It is probable that the hospital was founded by Henry I.[11] In 1222 Honorius III confirmed the appropriation of it to the abbot and convent.[12] There is no evidence to show that the hospital had a chapel which was served by its own chaplain from the time of the foundation. In 1319 Cobham, bishop of Worcester, notified to the master and the poor of the hospital that, whereas there were many old and feeble persons among them who were unable to attend mass at the parish church, he had granted a licence to them to build an oratory within the hospital and to have a priest to celebrate mass, saving the rights of the mother church.[13] An undated document in the chartulary of the monastery gives the abbot's consent, and provides that the mass in the chapel of the hospital should be celebrated after the mass in the parish church, and that the warden should pay to the convent all offerings made in the chapel.[14] The abbot and convent stated that the hospital was founded and built by their predecessors, and that they had always been in possession of the hospital free from the visitation of the ordinary, with full power over its affairs, and the right of appointment to the custody of it. The inmates were supported by the alms of the faithful, and the daily distribution of food by the almoner of the monastery, according to ancient custom.

The complaints of the townsmen were fruitless. On 20 September, 1348, for £300,

[1] Stevenson, op. cit. 351, 355, &c. The names of a number of other burgesses who held the office of master occur *passim*.

[2] Ibid. *passim*.   [3] Ibid. 426.

[4] Fosbrooke, *Abstracts of Records and MSS. relating to Gloucestershire*, i, 190.

[5] Kelly, *Direct. of Glouc.* (ed. 1906).

[6] *Brist. and Glouc. Arch. Soc. Trans.* xx, 131 ; *Worc. Epis. Reg. Giffard* (Worc. Hist. Soc.), 381.

[7] Fosbrooke, *Abstracts and Records relating to Glouc.* i, 192.

[8] Stevenson, *Cal. of Records of the Corporation of Glouc.* 68.

[9] Kelly, *Direct. of Glouc.* (ed. 1906).

[10] *Brist. and Glouc. Arch. Soc. Trans.* viii, 225.

[11] Ibid. 226.   [12] Ibid.

[13] Worc. Epis. Reg. Cobham, fol. 61 d.

[14] *Brist. and Glouc. Arch. Soc. Trans.* viii, 226.

Edward III gave a charter to the abbot and convent confirming their rights and privileges, including the appropriation of the hospital and the power of appointing and removing the custos.[1]

In 1535 the office of keeper of the hospital was held by one of the canons, and its income was reckoned as a part of the revenues of the monastery.[2] The gross yearly value was £6 5s. 4d.; there was a rent charge of 5s. 6d., and 13s. 4d. was paid for salt and flour to make pottage for the poor folk therein.[3] In the almoner's account a special alms of 6s. 8d. to the sisters of St. John is noted.[4] It is probable that they had their maintenance from the almoner. At the dissolution of the monastery the hospital was treated as a separate endowment, and continued. In 1546, as the result of the commission to inquire into hospitals and chantries, it was returned that the hospital was founded to find a master or keeper for ever with a salary of £2 15s. 4d., to find six poor folks for ever to have yearly 14s. 5d.; the gross income was £4 14s. 7d., the expenses were 10s. 6d., and the poor therefore got an additional sum of 14s. 4d.[5] The hospital was their parish church. It has had a continuous existence to the present day as an almshouse.[6]

39. THE HOSPITAL OF ST. LAWRENCE, CIRENCESTER

According to the statement of the townsmen of Cirencester in 1343, Edith Biset of Wiggold founded the leper hospital of St. Lawrence on land which she held of the king in chief.[7] The lepers used to be maintained partly by the alms of the townsfolk and partly from the lands and rents. They alleged that the charters of the hospital had been taken away by Adam abbot of Cirencester (1307–19); that brother John of Baudington, who had been appointed master by Adam de Orlton, bishop of Worcester (1327–32), was ousted in 1336 by the abbot and his council, and a sister appointed in his stead. The lands were worth 40s. a year. The truth seems to be that Abbot William Hereward converted the leper hospital into an almshouse for women, but the complaints of the townsmen were of no avail. In 1343 Edward III confirmed the hospital to the abbot and convent.[8] In 1546, at the inquisition into hospitals and chantries, a return was made that the hospital of St. Lawrence was

founded for two poor women, and that they had for their stipend the value of the land, which was worth £3 6s. 7d. a year.[9] There was no chapel in the hospital.[10] It has had a continuous existence as an almshouse.[11]

40. THE HOSPITAL OF ST. THOMAS, CIRENCESTER.

The hospital of St. Thomas at Cirencester was founded for four decayed weavers by Sir William Nottingham, who died in 1427.[12]

It has had a continuous existence.

41. THE HOSPITAL OF LONGBRIDGE BY BERKELEY [13]

The hospital of the Holy Trinity of Longbridge at the north end of Berkeley was founded by Maurice of Berkeley I, between 1170 and 1189.[14] The community consisted of a prior or master and a number of brethren to provide for the spiritual and temporal welfare of the sick poor who were received into the hospital.[15]

At the foundation of the hospital Maurice of Berkeley I guaranteed the rights of the abbot and convent of St. Augustine's, Bristol, to whom all the churches of the honour of Berkeley had been granted. It was agreed that all tithes and offerings should belong to the mother church of Berkeley, but that such offerings as were made by the parishioners on the feasts of St. John the Baptist and of St. Mary Magdalen should be assigned to the prior and brethren of the hospital.[16]

In 1269 Godfrey Giffard, bishop of Worcester, disputed the right of presentation to the hospital with Maurice of Berkeley.[17] It was then decided that the lords of Berkeley and the bishops of Worcester should present alternately, and this agreement was carefully observed.

The right of visitation was granted at the foundation, not to the bishop of Worcester, but to the abbot and convent of St. Augustine's, Bristol.[18] It was probably in virtue of their right of collation that the bishops of Worcester held inquisitions on two occasions. In 1275

---

[1] Cart. R. 17 Edw. III, No. 13.
[2] *Valor Eccles.* (Rec. Com.), ii, 471.
[3] Ibid.   [4] Ibid. 469.
[5] *Brist. and Glouc. Arch. Soc. Trans.* viii, 228; Certificate of Chantries, Glouc. 21.
[6] *Brist. and Glouc. Arch. Soc. Trans.* xvii, 53; Kelly, *Direct. of Glouc.* (ed. 1906). The chapel is only a ruin.
[7] *Brist. and Glouc. Arch. Soc. Trans.* xvii, 54.
[8] Cart. R. 7 Edw. III, No. 13.

[9] *Brist. and Glouc. Arch. Soc. Trans.* xvii, 56.
[10] Ibid.
[11] Kelly, *Direct. of Glouc.* (ed. 1906).
[12] Tanner, *Notitia Monastica* (ed. 1744), p. 152.
[13] The hospital of St. James and St. John, which was assigned by Tanner to Berkeley, was at Brackley in Northamptonshire; cf. *Cal. Charter Rolls* (Rolls Ser.), 12 Hen. III. m. 4.
[14] Dugdale, *Mon.* vii, 761; Smyth, *Lives of the Berkeleys* (ed. Maclean), 69.
[15] Ibid. 70, 71; cf. Jeayes, *Catalogue of Charters at Berkeley Castle*, 165.
[16] Smyth, op. cit. 69.
[17] *Worc. Epis. Reg. Giffard* (Worc. Hist. Soc.), 31.
[18] Smyth, op. cit. 69.

Godfrey Giffard sent a mandate to the prior of the hospital of Lechlade to visit the hospital of Longbridge and inquire concerning the condition of the brethren and other persons dwelling there,[1] as he hoped to bring it to a more prosperous state. In 1321 Thomas Cobham commissioned Nicholas de Gore to inquire into the condition of the property of the hospital, and to discover what had become of the books and ornaments of the chapel, and the muniments and seal. The sick poor had apparently been ousted.[2] On 30 March, 1322, after receiving the report of the commissioner, the bishop wrote to the rural deans, rectors, and vicars in the archdeaconry of Gloucester bidding them fulminate the sentence of excommunication in their churches against certain persons, both clerks and laymen, in that archdeaconry who were said to have taken away the property of the hospital, unless they should at once restore it to Stephen de Brampton, to whom the bishop gave the office of master.[3]

The hospital benefited greatly under the will of William, marquis of Berkeley, in 1492. He directed that his executors should purchase a rental of 22 marks to find two priests for the chapel of Longbridge, and should spend 100 marks in building a house for them, 40 marks more in buying vestments and ornaments for the chapel, and in addition should buy a papal indulgence, 'as large as may be had,' to worshippers therein on the feast of the Trinity, who offered prayers for the souls of himself, his father and son.[4] The hospital of Longbridge was suppressed under the Act for the dissolution of chantries of 1547.[5]

PRIORS OR MASTERS OF THE HOSPITAL OF LONGBRIDGE

Henry, occurs 1270,[6] ob. 1275 [7]
Robert de Werwich, 1275 [8]
Henry Hass, 1278 [9]
William de Cokebury, 1285 [10]
John of Newington, 1286 [11]
Stephen of Brampton, 1322 [12]
John de Barneby, 1331 [13]
Robert, 1349 [14]
Roger le Frend, 1355,[15] exchanged 1356 [16]

William le White, 1356,[17] exchanged 1357 [18]
Walter Launce, 1358 [19]
Nicholas Geoffrey, 1364,[20] exchanged 1370 [21]
Thomas Munday, 1370 [22]
Thomas Bristow, resigned 1401 [23]
Thomas Thame, 1401,[24] exchanged 1404 [25]
Reginald Powy, resigned 1406 [26]
Thomas Calle, 1406,[27] resigned 1409 [28]
William Rande, 1409,[29] resigned 1414 [30]
John Talbot, 1414 [31]
Richard Wude or Ward, 1422 [32]
Richard Vele, 1451 [33]
Richard Roos, 1455,[34] resigned 1465 [35]
Thomas Campden, 1465 [36]
John Campden, ob. 1486 [37]
John Wiche, 1486 [38]
William Wall, ob. 1511 [39]
Robert Davell, 1511,[40] resigned 1512 [41]
John Mogryche, 1512 [42]

A seal of the thirteenth century represents our Lord with nimbus, seated on a throne, lifting up the right hand in benediction, in the left hand a book.[43]

42. THE HOSPITAL OF LORWING

The hospital of Lorwing, between Berkeley and Dursley, was founded for a master and brethren by Maurice of Berkeley I between 1170 and 1189.[44] It had but a brief existence, for in 1225 Thomas of Berkeley I, the son of the founder, gave the endowment to the prior of Stanley St. Leonard, a cell of Gloucester, on condition that the abbot of Gloucester renounced all claims to the church of Slimbridge.[45]

[1] Worc. Epis. Reg. Giffard (Worc. Hist. Soc.), 72, 76.
[2] Worc. Epis. Reg. Cobham, fol. 74 d.
[3] Ibid. fol. 86.
[4] Smyth, Lives of the Berkeleys, 71.
[5] Ibid. 71.
[6] Jeayes, Catalogue of Mun. of Lord Fitzhardinge, 137.
[7] Worc. Epis. Reg. Giffard, 82.
[8] Ibid. 82.   [9] Ibid. 96.
[10] Ibid. 266.   [11] Ibid. 299.
[12] Worc. Epis. Reg. Cobham, fol. 86.
[13] Ibid. Orlton, fol. 46.
[14] Ibid. Bransford, ii, fol. 17.
[15] Ibid. Brian, i, fol. 11.
[16] Ibid. fol. 21.

[17] Ibid.
[18] Ibid. fol. 23.
[19] Ibid.
[20] Ibid. Whittlesey, fol. 4.
[21] Pat. 44 Edw. III, pt. ii, m. 8.
[22] Ibid.
[23] Worc. Epis. Reg. Clifford, fol. 10 d.
[24] Ibid. fol. 10 d.   [25] Ibid. fol. 22 d.
[26] Ibid. fol. 88.   [27] Ibid. fol. 88.
[28] Ibid. Peverell, fol. 16.
[29] Ibid. fol. 16.   [30] Ibid. fol. 64 d.
[31] Ibid. fol. 64 d.
[32] Ibid. Morgan, fol. 8.
[33] Ibid. Carpenter, i, fol. 94.
[34] Ibid. fol. 131.
[35] Ibid. fol. 191.
[36] Ibid.   [37] Ibid. Alcock, fol. 162.
[38] Ibid. fol. 162.
[39] Ibid. Silvester de Giglis, fol. 71 d.
[40] Ibid. fol. 71 d.   [41] Ibid. fol. 84.
[42] Ibid. fol. 84.
[43] Birch, Catalogue of Seals in British Museum, i, 645.
[44] Tanner, Notitia Monastica (ed. 1744), 148; Smyth, Lives of the Berkeleys (ed. Maclean), i, 69.
[45] Smyth, op. cit. 69.

43. THE HOSPITAL OF ST. JOHN THE BAPTIST, LECHLADE

The hospital of St. John the Baptist at Lechlade was founded in or before 1246 by Isabella de Mortimer.[1] She endowed it with land at the head of Lechlade Bridge, the bridge, chapel, and a mill. In 1246 the property of the hospital was confirmed by Henry III to be held in free alms.[2] The community seems to have consisted, according to the ordinance of the foundation, of seven priests of the order of St. Augustine, of whom one was prior or master, and a number of lay brothers and sisters to minister to the poor and sick, both men and women, who came to the hospital.

In 1252 the manor of Lechlade was granted to Richard earl of Cornwall, who thus became the patron of the hospital.[3] Before 1255 he and his wife Sanchia granted to the priests who served it the right of electing their prior or master, and endowed the hospital with the advowson of the parish church, retaining however the right of presenting to the vicarage.[4]

In the visitation of the diocese of Worcester which took place in 1290 and 1291, Bishop Giffard deputed one of his clerks, by name Nigel le Waleys, to visit the hospital. He fulfilled his office on 11 January, 1291,[5] and reported a most unsatisfactory state of affairs to the bishop. The services were neglected, regular discipline was not observed, and the administration was wasteful. On 17 February Giffard sent a mandate for the reform of the hospital.[6] He decreed that according to the will of the founders seven priests should perform the daily services, and that the prior and all the brethren should be present at the hours unless prevented by some honest cause. Silence was to be observed in church, dorter, frater, and cloister. Among the brethren there should be uniformity in dress; the sisters should have a suitable dress and take their food in the places assigned to them. As the vice of gluttony prevailed among them, neither brothers nor sisters should presume to eat or drink except at stated hours and places, unless they were ill or engaged in the service of the house; nor should they go beyond the precincts without leave. As hospitality ought to be observed with charity and cheerfulness, one kind and courteous brother was to be chosen to entertain guests, and another to receive the sick. The prior was bidden to render an exact account of the financial position of the house. Under pain of eternal damnation the bishop forbade that any possessions or rents given for the special use

of the poor and sick should be diverted to any other object. In 1300 matters were no better, and in January an inquisition into the state and condition of the hospital was held in the parish church.[7] The jurors declared that the prior had withdrawn several of the priests and expelled them and a number of lay brothers and sisters, also that he had alienated various lands and goods belonging to the hospital, including the books and ornaments of the church, but there is no evidence of the steps taken to restore order.

The maintenance of the bridge was a charge upon the hospital, and in 1338[8] and again in 1341[9] Edward III granted the right of taking tolls for a term of three years in aid of the repairs.

On 21 October, 1351, Bishop Thoresby sent a commission to Henry de Neubold, his vicar-general, and William Poty, the vicar of Lechlade, to punish Brother Ralph of Tetbury for laying violent hands on the brothers summoned before the bishop at his visitation of the hospital.[10] On 26 February, 1352, he appointed two commissioners to inquire into the excesses and defects of the hospital, to make corrections, and if necessary to remove the prior from office.[11] He had heard that the prior and brethren had put aside their habit and were going about as chaplains, celebrating masses and getting salaries, and they may perhaps have so acted under pressure of poverty. Later in that year the prior desired to be released from his office, because he wished to live a life of contemplation.[12] In or about 1374 Bishop William de Lynn attempted to reform the hospital. He found at his visitation that Prior Stephen of Newbury had diminished the services, wasted and defiled the goods of the house, and had led a dissolute life.[13] However, Stephen ignored the bishop's injunctions, and on 22 March, 1375, during the vacancy of the see, the prior of Worcester sent a mandate to the dean of Fairford and all rectors and vicars of that deanery to denounce him as excommunicate, and to summon him to appear before the prior or his commissary in the cathedral church of Worcester to receive condign punishment.[14] On 31 October he resigned.[15] On 10 November, 1384, when in the course of his metropolitical visitation Courtenay, archbishop of Canterbury, came to Lechlade, he found that the title of the prior, Richard Smyth, was defective. The right of presentation therefore fell to the archbishop, and on account of the upright character of the

---

[1] *Cal. of Chart. R.* 30 Hen. III, m. 6.
[2] Ibid.
[3] Ibid. 36 Hen. III, m. 10.
[4] Ibid. 39 Hen. III, m. 8 ; Dugdale, *Mon.* viii, 684.
[5] *Worc. Epis. Reg. Giffard* (Worc. Hist. Soc.), 381.
[6] Ibid. 391.
[7] Ibid. 537.
[8] *Cal. of Pat.* 12 Edw. III, pt. i, m. 6.
[9] Ibid. 15 Edw. III, pt. ii, m. 7.
[10] Worc. Epis. Reg. Thoresby, fol. 35.
[11] Ibid. fol. 49.   [12] Ibid. fol. 51 *d.*
[13] *Worc. Reg. Sede Vac.* (Worc. Hist. Soc.), 330.
[14] Ibid. 330.
[15] Worc. Epis. Reg. Wakefield, fol. 1 *d.*

man, he collated him to the office.[1] In 1388 the repair of the bridge was a further expense; it had been broken down by order of Thomas, duke of Gloucester, and Richard II therefore granted to the prior the right of taking tolls for the next three years.[2]

When John Wyham resigned in 1454 there were not enough brethren to elect a prior, and on the commendation of Richard, duke of York, then the patron, Bishop Carpenter collated William Littleton.[3] In 1462 the hospital was so much impoverished by misfortune that it was exempted from payment of the tenth.[4] About two years later Edward IV granted the advowson of the hospital to his mother Cecily, duchess of York, and on her presentation Bishop Carpenter collated William Lovel, who filled the office of prior for eight years.[5] The poverty of the house was very great, and the revenues were utterly inadequate to maintain the objects of its foundation.[6] In 1472 the duchess of York obtained a licence from Edward IV to found a chantry for three chaplains to celebrate divine service daily in the chapel of the Virgin in the parish church of Lechlade,[7] and William Lovel was empowered to transfer the whole of the possessions of the hospital to the chaplains of the chantry.[8] Out of the revenues the sum of ten marks a year was assigned by the duchess of York to be paid to the chaplain of the chantry of St. Blaise at Lechlade, which was founded at the same time by John Twynho.[9] Accordingly on 20 September, 1475, Bishop Carpenter effected the appropriation of the hospital to the chantry of St. Mary,[10] stipulating that the chaplains should keep the chapel of the hospital in repair, and hold services there on the vigil and feast of St. John the Baptist.[11]

PRIORS OF THE HOSPITAL OF ST. JOHN THE BAPTIST, LECHLADE

Peter of Pevensey, *ob.* 1283 [12]
William of Estham, 1283 [13]

Walter of Lambourne, occurs 1305 [14]
John of Lechlade, elected 1312 [15]
William of Tewkesbury, elected 3 April, 1330 [16]
Adam of Alcester, elected 15 April, 1330 [17]
Walter, resigned 1355 [18]
Stephen of Newbury, 1356,[19] resigned 1375 [20]
Richard, occurs 1384 [21] and 1388 [22]
John Wyham, 1442,[23] resigned 1454 [24]
William Littleton, 1454 [25]
Thomas Hedley, occurs 1464 [26]
William Lovel, 1464–72 [27]

44. THE HOSPITAL OF WINCHCOMBE

Leland stated that there was once a hospital in the town, but when he visited it only the name of 'Spittle remained in testimony thereof.'[28]

45. THE HOSPITAL OF TEWKESBURY

There was a leper hospital at Tewkesbury in 1200.[29]

46. THE HOSPITAL OF HOLY TRINITY, STOW ON THE WOLD

The hospital of Holy Trinity, Stow on the Wold, is said to have been founded before the Norman Conquest.[30] It was intended for the maintenance of poor women and a chaplain to serve them.[31]

In 1535 the yearly revenues amounted to £25 4s. 4d.[32]

[1] Cant. Archiepis. Reg. Courtenay, fol. 127 d.
[2] *Cal. of Pat.* 11 Ric. II, pt. ii, m. 32.
[3] Worc. Epis. Reg. Carpenter, i, fol. 118 d.
[4] Ibid. fol. 178.   [5] Ibid. fol. 186.
[6] Dugdale, *Mon.* vii, 683; Pat. 12 Edw. IV, pt. ii, m. 28.
[7] Ibid.   [8] Ibid.
[9] Ibid.
[10] Worc. Epis. Reg. Carpenter, ii, fol. 20 d. 30.
[11] Ibid. fol. 31 d.
[12] *Worc. Epis. Reg. Giffard* (Worc. Hist. Soc.), 283.
[13] Ibid.
[14] Worc. Epis. Reg. Gainsborough, fol. 7.
[15] Ibid. Reynolds, fol. 58 d.
[16] *Cal. of Pat.* 4 Edw. III, pt. i, m. 36.
[17] Ibid. m. 32.
[18] Worc. Epis. Reg. Brian, fol. 12 d.
[19] Ibid. fol. 15.
[20] Ibid. Wakefield, fol. 1 d.
[21] Cant. Archiepis. Reg. Courtenay, fol. 127 d.
[22] *Cal. of Pat.* 11 Ric. II, pt. ii, m. 32.
[23] Worc. Epis. Reg. Bourchier, fol. 89 d.
[24] Ibid. Carpenter, i, fol. 118 d.
[25] Ibid.   [26] Ibid. fol. 186.
[27] Ibid.
[28] Tanner, *Notitia Monastica* (ed. 1744), 152.
[29] Ibid. 148.   [30] Ibid. 145.
[31] Ibid. *Cal. of Pat.* 21 Edw. III, pt. iii, m. 9.
[32] *Valor Eccles.* (Rec. Com.), ii, 486.

SOCIAL AND ECONOMIC HISTORY

TO its triple division into vale, wold, and forest—a physical feature of which the effects are still discernible in the character and prejudices of the inhabitants—the county of Gloucester owes the prominent place which it has occupied in the past. Each has had its special industry ; each, by its special facilities, has aided the other. ·The Severn—the pride of the vale—was the earliest gate to the outer world possessed by a county almost enclosed by forest ; and the natural harbours, which it provided, made early Gloucestershire one of the foremost in the race for commercial prosperity. Thus Bristol and Gloucester set an industrial example to the inland parts of the shire ; the wolds helped on the towns by the fine growth of wool which was fostered on their pastures ; and the merchants of the towns were, in their turn, able to help the wolds when their main industry migrated thither. For, though the Forest was famous for its ironworks and its timber for ship-building, in early days it stood somewhat apart from the rest of the county, and the more important part of Gloucestershire's industrial history lies mainly in the upland district. The Cotswolds, in addition to their pastures, were rich in water-power, and thus drew to themselves in the sixteenth century the greater part of the woollen manufacture, while the two big ports devoted themselves more entirely to commerce across the seas. With its infinite variety, Gloucestershire could never lack a direction for its industrial energies ; and, when the woollen trade was languishing, a sudden fresh development of the iron industry in the Forest of Dean, about the middle of the nineteenth century, offered them a new outlet in what had hitherto been the most backward part of the county.

While—at any rate till recent times—Gloucestershire's prosperity has thus been chiefly due to commercial causes, its agricultural history must not be neglected. In Domesday we only find one town of any size, Gloucester, though Bristol, Winchcombe, and Tewkesbury possessed privileged tenants, known as burgesses ; and the county, as a whole, was inhabited by a thinly scattered agricultural population—rather poor, probably, for the value of the land was low.[1] Before, therefore, it is possible to treat of the industrial side of the history of the county, it will be well to describe the long period between the eleventh and the fifteenth century, when the bulk of the people were given over to rural pursuits.

In the main physical features that arise from the proportion of wild to cultivated land, the county did not differ very widely at the time of the Domesday Survey from its present condition. There were 469,035 acres of

---

[1] F. W. Maitland, *Domesday Book and Beyond*, 412–13.

ploughland and 1,769 acres of meadow in 1086, as compared with 111,101 acres of arable (besides 20,676 acres of orchard), and 203,902 acres of pasture (permanent, and hay in rotation) in 1895–9. As compared with 58,407 acres of woodland in 1895[1] Domesday mentions 80,760 acres, but this estimate must have been far below the real area covered with woods, as royal forests were omitted from the survey. Dean, beyond the Severn, was only one of the royal forests which bounded Gloucestershire on the west, south, and south-east. With Malvern Chase on the Worcestershire margin, Bedminster and Kingswood on the Somerset side, Braden Forest in North Wiltshire and Wychwood in Oxfordshire, it is hardly probable that the boundaries of the county were very closely respected. Probably there were debatable areas, adjoining these forests, which remained wooded and unenclosed. Buckholt, as its name implies, was already famous for its beechwoods, which, together with a wood at Frocester, provided Gloucester Abbey with the whole of its yearly stock of firewood in the thirteenth century.[2] Between Berkeley and Bristol there was another large tract of forest, called Horwood, which has now vanished, though traces of it long remained about Hawkesbury and Horton.[3] It was not disafforested till 1227–8, when the men of the neighbourhood paid Henry III the large sum of 700 marks (£466 13s. 4d.) in order to be quit of the interference of the royal foresters and the royal deer.[4]

While its principal characteristics have thus not materially altered since the days of Domesday, a Gloucestershire landscape between the eleventh and the fifteenth century lacked one very marked feature of the present day. Instead of lying amid fields enclosed by hedges, or by the stone-walls of the Cotswolds, each village was surrounded by two or three vast open fields, divided into strip-holdings with 'balks' of turf as their only boundary. The only enclosures to be seen were a few pieces of meadow-land, which, before the days of winter-roots, were doubly precious to the stock-owner. And this outward difference in the village was significant of a difference in the condition of its inhabitants. The average mediaeval villager was superior to his modern descendant in the fact that he was a landholder, and inferior in his personal subjection to dues and services of a more or less galling character. He was, in fact, unfree in the eye of the law. This is, at least, true of the average man in Gloucestershire, which was pre-eminently a county of villeins. In Domesday Book nineteen-twentieths of the population are recorded as unfree,[5] and an analysis of the extents of twenty-five manors belonging to Gloucester Abbey in the thirteenth century [6] shows very little advance in the number of freemen by that date (1266). At least three-quarters of these tenants were still unfree, and in some cases their descent from the villeins of the Domesday period can be traced with some certainty. The 'villanus' of the great survey was primarily a shareholder in the plough-team necessary to work a hide of land; his normal holding was a 'virgate,' or quarter of a hide,[7] and rendered him liable to contribute two oxen, or a quarter of a team,

---

[1] *Agric. Returns for* 1899 (Bd. of Agric.), *C.d.* 166.

[2] *Hist. et Cart. Mon. S. Petri Glouc.* (Rolls Ser.), iii, 107. This work will be referred to as *Glouc. Cart.* throughout this article.

[3] For notes from Domesday see C. S. Taylor, 'Analysis of Domesday Book for Gloucestershire,' *Brist. and Glouc. Arch. Soc. Trans.* 1889.   [4] J. Smyth, *Berkeley MSS.* iii, 237.

[5] i.e. serfs or villeins.   [6] *Glouc. Cart.* (Rolls Ser.), iii, 44–213.

[7] Both hide and virgate were rather vague measurements. In the *Glouc. Cart.* the latter varied from 28 to 80 acres, but the term is used especially to denote a peasant's holding.

to the plough which he shared with three other tenants of similar status. Coupled with the 'bordars,' a class of small holders also bound to contribute, though in a lesser degree, to a common team, the villani formed more than half the population of Gloucestershire in 1086.[1] Similarly, in the thirteenth-century extents, more than half[2] of the customary, or villein, land was held in virgates, or clear fractions of virgates. The temptation to see in the thirteenth-century virgatarius or 'yerdling' (i.e. holder of a virgate, or 'yardland') the direct descendant of the eleventh century 'villanus' is almost irresistible, and in some instances the coincidence works out very neatly. For instance, in Ledene (Upleadon) there were in 1086 eight yerdlings and one bordar; in 1266 there were eight and a quarter yard-lands, which gives one yardland to each villein and one quarter to the bordar. If we accept a difference in the size of the yardland[3] at the two periods, the majority of cases show very little change in the status of the population.

Upon the lands of Cirencester Abbey during the same period, for which we have one or two records in the Abbey Register,[4] only a slight advance towards freedom is evident. In an extent taken, probably, about the middle of Stephen's reign,[5] the thirteen serfs of Domesday re-appear in twelve men who 'were wont to labour' and one who 'used to hold his land by labour, but now by keeping a plough '—' tenet quadrantem terrae, quae fuit operaria, tenendo carucam.' In Domesday there were thirty-one villeins and ten bordars; in the extent there appear twenty-seven villeins, who perform services of ploughing, carrying, and haymaking; the remaining four must either be accounted for by an accumulation of several holdings into the hands of one tenant, or they may be found among eighteen tenants of the twelfth century, who 'pay a penny.' Possibly the descendants of the bordars, whose services can never have been very heavy, may also be found among these last. Two freemen are mentioned in both documents. In a still later inquisition of the same lands[6] which gives the tenures of 1187, these re-appear as two tenants by grand sergeanty.[7] At the same time, the number of customary tenants had fallen from fifty-two to thirty-six; but this change, again, probably indicates a tendency to consolidate holdings rather than any diminution of the proportion of villeins to freemen.

Villeinage being thus the typical condition of the Gloucestershire peasant in the thirteenth century, as well as in the eleventh, it may be well to define that condition as closely as possible. By strict legal theory a villein was without rights, or, at any rate, his rights were not such as could be asserted at common law. His land, his person, and his property were all,

---

[1] C. S. Taylor. op. cit.   [2] i.e. 486 out of 903 tenancies.

[3] The difference in size was sometimes 100 per cent. as may be seen from the following table :—

	Clifford	Frocester	Churcham	Northleach
Domesday villani	14	8	7	23
Domesday bordarii	—	7	2	16
Thirteenth-century virgates . .	28	$17\frac{3}{4}$	$14\frac{1}{2}$	46
Acres of thirteenth-century virgate .	36	48	48	68
Consequent acres of Domesday virgate	72	96	96	136

F. Baring, *Eng. Hist. Review*, xii, 285–290.

[4] Quoted, E. A. Fuller, 'Tenures of land in Cirencester,' *Brist. and Glouc. Arch. Soc. Trans.* ii.

[5] Cir. Abb. Reg. A 13*a*.   [6] Ibid. A 88*b*.

[7] i.e. personal service of some honourable kind; in this case it was acting as huntsman.

nominally, at his lord's disposal. Hence he could neither bequeath nor transfer his holding, which, strictly speaking, escheated to the lord on the death of the tenant. Ordinarily, however, his son would be allowed to succeed him on payment of a fine, and on going through the same formula of admittance as a new tenant. Here is a typical example from a Court Roll of Hawkesbury Manor :—

> A cottage and adjacent curtilage (i.e. small plot or garden) is remaining in the lord's hands. Thereupon comes Thomas Rooke and takes them, to hold according to the custom of the manor for life, paying all the same customary rents and services as did his father, William Rooke. He pays a fine of one shilling, and does fealty.[1]

Or a tenant might, by a fine paid during his lifetime, secure his son's succession to his tenement; e.g. at Bisley, 1354 :—

> Walter Tymbercombe, tenant of a messuage and half a yardland for his own and his wife's lifetime, gives to the lord a fine of 13s. 4d. in order that John, his younger son, may, after their deaths, hold the same for the same services.[2]

Or, again, the fine might be paid in the son's own name, as in an amusing instance at Hawkesbury (1448–9), where a child of six presented the lord with a salmon in order to obtain the reversion of his father's holding.[3] Fines for reversions are, indeed, of common occurrence in Manor Court Rolls, a fact which seems to indicate a great thirst for the holding of land. A fine would also often procure a licence to alienate land. Without such permission alienation by one villein tenant to another was void,[4] and ordinarily the form of surrender by the existing tenant and regrant to his would-be lessee was insisted upon.[5] Freeholders were, of course, exempt from these restrictions, as were burgage tenants,[6] who, at Cheltenham, for instance, in the fourteenth century could bequeath and alienate freely.[7] Wives, too, had rights of inheritance, varying from 'villein dower,' which allowed them the whole, to 'free-bench,'[8] which gave the wife of a copyholder a half of the husband's estate.[9] Still the legal theory that the tenant's rights were derived from the lord was kept up by the enforcement of fines and of the payment of heriots, and by the occasional deprivation of the tenant for misconduct, such as quitting the manor without leave, or persistent neglect to repair.[10]

The heriot itself was a sign of the lord's claim over his villeins' property; and 'merchet,' the fine exacted for marriage of a villein's daughter, was the result of the same theory. The death or the marriage of a villein were both equivalent in the lord's eyes to 'a transfer of property out of the range of his power.'[11] Merchet probably varied according to the steward's estimate of the value of the bride; 2s. only was paid by a base tenant of Cheltenham (1333) for leave to give his daughter in marriage, while 40s. was exacted

---

[1] Ct. R. (P.R.O.), portf. 175, No. 9, m. 1. Fitzherbert, a writer of the sixteenth century, gives the following form of fealty for a villein :—'Here you, my lord, that I, fro this day forth, to you shal be faithful and lowly, and to you shal do al the customes and services that I ought to do to you, for the landes that I hold of you in Vyllenage.'   [2] Ct. R. portf. 175, No. 7, m. 15.

[3] Ct. R. portf. 175, No. 53, m. 2.   [4] Cf. Hawkesbury Ct. R. 7 Hen. V, portf. 175, No. 50, m. 6.

[5] Cf. Hawkesbury Ct. R. 17 Ric. II, portf. 175, No. 46, m. 1.

[6] Burgage was a privileged tenure, usual in towns, and nearly resembling freehold.

[7] Ct. R. portf. 175, Nos. 25 and 26.

[8] Bisley Ct. R. Eliz. portf. 175, No. 13, m. 2. Also *Cal. of Rec. of Corp. of Glouc.* ed. W. H. Stevenson, No. 456.

[9] Murray, *New Eng. Dict.* 'Free-bench.' Also Pollock and Maitland, *Hist. of Eng. Law,* ii, 416–25.

[10] Cf. Bisley Ct. R. portf. 175, Nos. 7, 10, and 13.   [11] Vinogradoff, *Growth of the Manor,* 347.

(1407–8) from a tenant of the same manor before he could marry a widow with a messuage and two acres of land.[1]

Another way in which the lord's property might suffer loss was by the flight of a villein from the manor ; hence the reiterated, though usually fruitless, attempts of the manor courts to recover such fugitives by distraining their relatives.

Besides these restraints upon his personal liberty, the villein's time was greatly occupied by labour services to his lord, which, together with dues in kind at certain seasons and ' pannage ' (the money paid for pasturing his pigs in the woods), were all acknowledgements of the lord's superior rights over his land. Some description of these services (which were nicely adjusted to the value of the holding) may prove not uninteresting. At Cirencester, in the extent of Stephen's reign already quoted, besides the thirteen tenants who merely ' laboured,' we read that ' there is no man so free but he is bound to plough and carry with a waggon, if he has one, or with a cart.' Some tenants are described as bound to ' work among the swine,' or to do a day's haymaking. By 1187 the services are somewhat more defined. Some hold by ' keeping the lord's oxen,' others 'by fork and flail ' ; others work on three days every week for their lord, besides three days at harvest and three at haytime ; they pay toll, and cannot give their daughters in marriage without the lord's licence.[2]

Cirencester, however, was in ' Ancient Demesne,'[3] and its tenants had special privileges. The chartulary of St. Peter's Abbey, which contains an unrivalled series of manorial extents, provides more typical examples of the labour services of a villein.[4] On the manor of Clifford Chambers the tenant of a yardland (here 36 acres) was bound to pay the following services, or their equivalent in money.

To plough ½ acre in winter and again in Lent, and harrow the same at seedtime. Value 4d.

To work four days a week with one man from Michaelmas to 1 August, at ½d. a day.

To do summage or carry loads by cart to Gloucester twice a year. Value 8d.

To wash and shear sheep for two days. Value 1d.

To carry hay for one day (value 2d.) and three other days at ½d., besides manual labour, (value ½d.)

To carry brushwood (counted as a day's work).

To do two bederipes[5] with two men before 1 August. Value 3d.

From 1 August to Michaelmas he had to reap five days a week with one man at 1½d. a day.

To do eight bederipes with two men. Value 2s.

To carry the lord's corn twice a week for four weeks, at 1½d. a day.

To carry mows of corn to the lord's grange for one day. Value ½d.

To give an aid according to the quantity of his land and of his beasts.

If he brewed beer for sale, he must give to the lord 12 gallons, or the price thereof.

He paid pannage—1d. for a full-grown pig, ½d. for a young one.

He could not sell his ox or horse without the lord's licence.

He must ' redeem ' his son and daughter.[6]

His best beast must go to the lord as heriot on his death.

---

[1] Ct. R. portf. 175, No. 25, m. 9, and No. 26, m. 4.   [2] E. A. Fuller, op. cit.

[3] i.e. land which belonged to the crown at the time of the Domesday Survey.

[4] There were about a hundred and five manors in Gloucestershire (Hund. R. pp. 166–83). The twenty-five manors for which these extents exist are scattered all over the county. The services do not appear to have differed much in different parts. Representative examples have been chosen for quotation.

[5] i.e. reaping performed at lord's bidding.

[6] i.e. pay a fine for their marriage or admission into holy orders.

The total value of such a yerdling's services was £1 2s. 7d., besides which every customary tenant on the manor had to give a fixed aid of 20s. a year, and carry mill-stones for the lord's mill.[1] The services of a half-yerdling (or holder of half a yardland) were of a similar kind. At Churcham he performed a long tale of services, amounting in money value to £1 1s. 1½d., but his yearly aid was only 1s. 11½d.[2]

In the fourteenth century we still find long lists of services and dues in kind, supposed to be rendered by villein tenants. The following is an example from Minchinhampton, in the reign of Richard II :—' Ralph Deulee holds one yardland and pays 4s. 1d. rent. He must work every other week from Michaelmas to Gulaust (1 August) ; that is, from Michaelmas to the Feast of the Purification he will have a task of some sort, except that, when there is ploughing of the lady's (of the manor), he will work at the garden, until her oxen come home from ploughing. From the Feast of the Purification (2 February) to Hockday (second Tuesday after Easter), he will work the whole day, and while the lady is sowing he will come with his own horse and harrow her land. From Hockday to Michaelmas he will labour all the day. He will also perform dederip, wynerip, benrip, alerthe and alerip, and will plough twice a year and plough at denerthe, and weed and carry hay from Burnmore ; give pannage and toll, gather nuts (with an allowance from the lady of meat, cheese and bacon, while so engaged), and watch on the vigil of St. John the Baptist. He must also mow with two servants on Monday, and give a cock and eggs. His children must do dederips.'[3]

Rightless, unable to plead in the royal courts—the cultivation of his own land continually interrupted by labour on the demesne—this typical Gloucestershire villager may perhaps be thought to have led a hard life. Yet the very elaboration with which his duties were defined, the fact that manorial custom was the only standard to which he could appeal, constituted his strength. Customary law was, in some ways, a better defence against his lord than the law of the land could have been ; for, being unwritten, it could only be declared by the suitors of the manor court, who were, at the same time, fellow-tenants of the manor. The villein's time might be portioned out with irksome exactitude ; but, when once he had performed his allotted tasks, he was free to do what he chose, and his holding was attached to him almost as closely as he was to it. ' The very root of villeinage lay in the impossibility for owners and lords to work their dependants at their will and pleasure.' ' At no time was the tradition and authority of customary arrangements greater, nor directed to so close a regulation of all the details of rural life and work, than in the epoch of the theoretical sway of the lord's will. No period has produced such records of customary possession and customary services as the period when the extents and custumals of manorial administration were compiled.'[4] Moreover, commutation of service for money, which, as will appear later, was common by the fourteenth century, relieved the villein of most of the personal inconveniences of his position. Curiously enough, it was not the yerdlings, the

---

[1] *Glouc. Cart.* iii, 52–3. [2] Ibid. 137–8.
[3] Probably these terms have been confused by the clerk. They imply boon-work where drink is given. Rentals and Surv. R. 238. [4] Vinogradoff, *Growth of the Manor*, pp. 348, 349.

descendants of the Domesday 'villani,' who were thus emancipated the soonest. They were part of a primitive system for the provision of plough-teams, and their services accordingly were more easily computed and exacted. Thus it is among the small holders, either the descendants of the Domesday bordars and cotters, or new settlers, or the sons of villeins for whom the family holding provided no support, that money rents first appeared. In the thirteenth-century extent of Clifford Chambers,[1] there are two tenants, of a messuage and curtilage each, Adam the weaver, and William Marshall, who gave pannage and aid, and were subject to heriot, merchet, and toll for selling a horse, an ox, or beer; but had only to perform three days' service at haytime and three at harvest, the rest having been commuted for a rent of 1s. Next to them appears a Nicholas Hentelove, who held a messuage and curtilage and two acres of arable. He was subject to the same dues, but was free of the six days' labour, in return for the larger rent of 3s. Again, at Littleton,[2] there is a holding, consisting of a house and curtilage, which paid 2s. rent, owing only one bederipe, worth a penny, and services of sheep washing, shearing, and nut-gathering, each worth a halfpenny; while another holding of six acres is let 'at farm' for twenty pence, but owed, besides, labour worth 5s. 3½d., and a cock and hen for 'chirshec.' Some of these lesser holders were craftsmen or officials whose regular duties left them no time to work on the demesne, but who took up small plots of land to supply their own home needs. Such were the village miller (who, despite his small holding was one of the chief members of a mediaeval village), reaper, smith, or keeper of a bridge.[3] And, yet again, there were curious tenements, known as Honilond, Penilond, and Lundinar (i.e. Honeyland, Pennyland, and Mondayland), the status of the holders of which is somewhat mysterious. At Churcham[4] a croft containing four acres of Honeyland paid eight gallons of honey as rent; half a virgate of Pennyland paid a rent of 10s., an aid of 1s. 11½d., provided two men for 'metebedripes,'[5] and was subject to toll, pannage, merchet, and heriot. A Monday-man (who often held 'by copy'), for a messuage, curtilage, and four acres of arable, had to do manual labour one day a week[6] and other services amounting to 6s. 8d.; while a 'coterellus,' or cottager, held a messuage and curtilage by finding a man to work with him for eight bederipes (worth 1s.).

On the whole, therefore, these small holdings, 'clustered round' the regular settlement of the village shareholders, were bound less closely into the manorial economy; they 'sent out their hands to work for hire, managed the accessory industries of the village, and carried on cultivation by individualistic processes less dependent on the agrarian customs of the open field, and less burdened with service in regard to the manors.'[7] This freedom, however, brought with it some disadvantages. The regular villein could use the common wood for grazing and for repairs; he could put cattle, in numbers proportioned to the size of his holding, upon the waste, and, after the crops were gathered, upon the hay and corn fields of the village; he was also

---

[1] *Glouc. Cart.* iii, 49–55. [2] Ibid. 40–1.
[3] e.g. at Clifford Chambers, Adam Bruggemon, or Bridgeman, held a messuage, curtilage, and piece of pasture, in return for 2s. and keeping the bridge in repair. (*Glouc. Cart.*)
[4] *Glouc. Cart.* [5] Harvest-work when the lord provided food.
[6] Presumably on Mondays.
[7] Vinogradoff, op. cit. 353.

entitled to a share in the meadows, or closes. But the last two privileges, at any rate, were not accorded to the mere cottager.[1]

It is also probable that the main share in the open-field organization was accorded to those tenants (the whole or half-yerdlings) whose holdings properly belonged to it. Nor was this a trivial distinction; for in the management of the village fields the villagers preserved the main vestiges of primitive independence. Beneath the manorial framework, imposed from above for governmental and fiscal purposes, was always preserved the older communal organization which had grown up to meet economic needs. The government of the manor was, after all, controlled not by the lord, or the steward, alone, but by the lord sitting in his manorial court. Reading, in the records of these courts, the multitudinous details as to the cultivation of the common fields, one feels that it is to the voice of a village community that one is really listening. As long as he gets the fines of the court in acknowledgement of his superior rights, the lord is willing enough to allow the village to manage its agriculture in its own way; to present offenders against the open-field system, and even to pass by-laws for its regulation. Innumerable instances of such by-laws can be quoted. At Hawkesbury (1394–5) various tenants were fined for putting their beasts into the lord's stubble in August, 'contrary to the order of the lord and tenants.'[2] Rights of pasture were continually demanding legislation. The Hawkesbury court had again (1435) to issue an order 'by the assent of all the tenants there,' 'that henceforth no one shall pasture his cattle or pigs in the cornfields from after Martinmas till the last sheaf has been cleared, unless he guard them in his own pasture.'[3] At the same court[4] an order was issued for the tenants to 'pleach' a hedge which had 'bracks' (or gaps) in it, and make a gate. And yet again (1460) 'it is ordered by the assent of all the tenants' that a yerdling may have only two beasts feeding in Upton-combe during the summer; that a new 'hanging-gate' be erected by the Gloucester Weye; that the whole homage of Upton shall put 'meerstones' (stones marking boundaries of strips) in West-mede field; and that the tenants of one tithing shall not put their beasts into the 'several' field of another.[5] By-laws of this kind continued to be made as long as open fields existed. At Cheltenham, in the reign of Henry VIII, frequent orders were passed for the regulation of the common pasture;[6] and continual agreements had to be made as to the dates of enclosing hay and corn, and of taking down the same enclosures after the crops had been gathered. The Hawkesbury tenants (1451–2) forbid the men of Badmynton Tithing to enter the common stubble to pasture their sheep before the day appointed 'by their unanimous assent.'[7] At Bisley (1445) the 'free customary tenants present that John Benet has not enclosed his hedges at the times due by the ancient customs of the manor. He is fined the customary penalty, a sheep and a lamb, worth 1s. 6d.'[8] 'It is agreed (1598) that Litteridge (one of the Bisley fields) shall be opened on Trinity Day, and the corn carried within thirteen days; no one is to put beasts in the field till the last stack is carried.'[9] Unconsciously perhaps the lord himself fostered this corporate feeling by imposing

---

[1] Vinogradoff, op. cit. 353. [2] Ct. R. portf. 175, No. 46, m. 2. [3] Ibid. No. 52, m. 4.
[4] Ibid. [5] Ibid. No. 54, m. 6. [6] Ibid. No. 27.
[7] Ibid. No. 53, m. 5. [8] Ibid. No. 10, m. 8. [9] Ibid. No. 13, m. 11.

duties on the village as a community. The homage,[1] or the tithing, were frequently called upon to inspect and report upon doubtful cases of ownership, to declare customs or to amend nuisances. At Hawkesbury the head tithing-man of Upton is ordered to see that a hedge is mended before the next court, on pain of 1*s.* fine from everyone involved. 'The headman of Kylcote Tithing says that, by ancient custom, Thomas Blyke is bound to make and close a certain " lanewey." And the village say that Thomas Haynes has to assist him in shutting the " Blyndelane." The homage present that certain tenants are bound to make the " Lupeyate " (stile) of Upton, and it is ordered that the " Lupeyate " shall always stand where it now stands, towards the Falowfelde.'[2] Sometimes the lord commanded, or a tenant paid a fine to obtain a 'view' and report by the homage on some disputed boundary.[3] At Bisley (1401–2) the homage declared that the house and barn of William Tymberhulle were burnt down by his own negligence, and the court therefore ordered him to rebuild, on pain of forfeiting all his oxen.[4] And as late as the reign of Elizabeth we find the homage at the lord's command inspecting a piece of land on which three new cottages had been built, and examining the oldest tenants whether the land was waste of the queen's (as lady of the manor);[5] or the suitors at the woodcourt made a 'view' of a wood, and reported on the number of trees felled there in the year.[5] Again, the tenants who had common pasture at Waterlane were to assist the lord to maintain those rights by pulling down a cottage newly built upon the common, and removing the old woman who lived there to another house.[5] On one occasion in the same reign the various townships of the manor were made mutually responsible for each other's repairs.[6]

These illustrations are sufficient to show that, in its ecomonic aspect, the manorial system offered considerable scope for the villein to experience the pains and pleasures of self-government. Even the manorial woods, which, in any law court would probably have been adjudged private property of the lord, in the language of the court rolls are often known as the 'customary wood,' and he might encounter resistance from his tenants if he tried arbitrarily to regulate their use of it. At Hawkesbury (1318) a John Sinot refused to drive his pigs into the lord's wood at Martinmas, unless he 'might have them out again at Midsummer.'[7] The amount of wood, turf, and stones which each tenant might take was probably known by custom, for later on, when land was let by lease, these points were always specified with especial care. Some tenements were considered to possess 'wodecustome,' while others had none.[8] As late as the reign of Elizabeth tradition still preserved the ancient manorial customs of the Bisley Wood ;[9] nor was the voice of manorial custom less positive with regard to free tenants, who at the same court were declared to have no right to dig stones or clay in the customary wood.

---

[1] i.e. the whole body of tenants. [2] Ct. R. (Hen. V.), portf. 175, No. 50, m. 3–6.
[3] e.g. at Hawkesbury (1511–12). Ct. R. portf. 175, No. 59, m. 2, and at Cheltenham (1529). Ibid. No. 27; m. 13. [4] Ct. R. portf. 175, No. 9, m. 2. [5] Ibid. No. 13, m. 3.
[6] Ibid. m. 7. [7] Ibid. No. 42, m. 16. [8] Ibid. Nos. 7 and 12.
[9] 'No tenant having common in the customary wood can make easement there, or in the common fields, except for sheep.' Ibid. No. 13, m. 5.

These self-governing powers of the villeinage must not, however, be exaggerated. Over all matters from which he could derive profit the lord kept a tight hand by means of the various manorial officials. Some of these, such as the reeve or the woodward,[1] were, it is true, elective, but the privilege seems to have been little appreciated. This was due probably to the expenditure of time which the duties involved, to the odium incurred by carrying out the lord's commands upon a man's own fellows in the village, and to the fact that, by accumulation of precedent, the tenure of such offices was held equivalent to a confession of villein status. A villein was generally chosen as reeve : therefore, it was argued, a reeve must be a villein. Thus at Bisley in 1400 the steward ordered the homage to choose a reeve to serve the lord, and the freemen of the manor alleged that by ancient custom the reeve must be of villein blood. The steward made no objection, but the dubious character of the theory is shown by the fact that both free and bond shared in the election.[2] The mock officers still elected by some villages, such as the 'Mayor of Randwick,' may point to some ancient rights of election among the tenants of such manors. Ale-tasters, whose duty it was to inspect the measure and quality of the manorial ale, were also usually elected.[3] Above these elective officials, however, were the actual servants of the lord, such as the bailiff, who superintended the work on the manor ; the reaper, who performed most of the attachments necessary to bring up offenders ; the grainger, who was answerable for the corn ; and the head steward, who probably supervised all manors of the lord, passing from one to another, and checking the accounts of the local officers. At Bisley (1548) there were also overseers called 'ryders,' to whom, apparently, the tenants had to present accounts of 'theyr wood that they did fell, accordyng to the custom.'[4] (These may have resembled the tenants of Gloucester Abbey, who held their land by a riding service, see *infra*, p. 138.) Sometimes, too, there was a reeve appointed by the lord, besides the one chosen by the tenants, as on the very occasion quoted above at Bisley.[5] The authority of these seignorial representatives was strictly upheld. Thus Thomas Rolf of Cheltenham was distrained (1333) for falsely defaming the bailiff and ministers of the lord, when exacting an amercement from him,[6] and at Hawkesbury, in an amusing instance, all the officials seemed to need the support of the lord. The tithing-man (1292), Robert Greiway, and his neighbours said that, 'John de la Purye, on such a day, drove his horse through the corn ; that Walter, Sir John de Meise's servant, came and demanded of him whether he intended to trespass in the lord's meadow. John replied, "You shall soon see," and pushed down part of the wall of the meadow. Whereon the tithing-man and the reaper were sworn to attach John's beasts, but John came and removed them from the lord's park, without the bailiff's leave.'[7] That the office of grainger or bailiff was no sinecure is shown by the elaborate accounts, which are still preserved among the 'ministers' accounts' of Gloucestershire. Not a horse could be sold, a sheep be worried by dogs, or a bushel of seed be bought without a corresponding entry on the account

---

[1] e.g. Woodwards of Bisrugge, Tymbercombe and Okerugge, woods on Bisley manor (Edw. III and Ric. II.). Ct. R. portf. 175, Nos. 7 and 8.   [2] Ct. R. portf. 175, No. 9, m. 1.
[3] e.g. at Cheltenham, 1416. Ct. R. portf. 175, No. 26, m. 5.
[4] Ct. R. portf. 175, No. 12, m. 2.   [5] Ibid. No. 9, m. 1.
[6] Ibid. No. 25, m. 9.   [7] Ibid. No. 41, m. 5–6.

roll. The tenants might muddle along, amid endless difficulties and disputes, with their antique open-field system ; the lord's demesne, where it was enclosed, was managed on more economic lines. The following rules for the management of the manors of St. Peter's Abbey, in the thirteenth century, seem to show that the religious orders, at any rate, made businesslike landowners. Once a month the reeve was to cause these articles to be recited openly before himself and his companion, the reaper.

(1) A month before Michaelmas the bondmen were to be summoned each to the manor where he was born, and there, before the sergeant of the place, it was to be ascertained who were fit to be kept in the lord's service, and at what work, where, and at what wages, it being understood that whenever the bailiff of the place chose, they could be removed to another place, at the lord's convenience, saving to them their former wages.

(2) The servants were to take care of the horses, and perform such services as should be assigned to them on feast days ; and not to absent themselves without special licence.

(3) Servants in any way related to sergeant, reeve, bedel, or other superior, were not to serve under them, but elsewhere.

(4) The servants were to be at their ploughs at the proper hours, and to plough without injuring or distressing their beasts.

(5) No iron or nails were to be delivered to carters and ploughmen, without due inquiry by the reeve.

(6) Within each oxstall were to be mangers of equal length, containing a night's food for one team.

(7) No useless or unprofitable beasts were to be kept throughout the winter, to the waste of hay and fodder. No bullock was to be used for riding without good cause.

(8) No corn was to be sold, horse hired, servant engaged, or building begun without permission.

(9) Salt and flour were to be distributed to servants in proper quantities, and also to the 'deye' (dairy-maid), who was to swear to keep and distribute it properly.

(10) The deye was to account to the reeve every fortnight for the fowls, eggs, chickens, geese and ducks, in her charge.

(11) All calves, colts, lambs, and young pigs were to be marked.

(12) All labourers were to come early to work with proper tools, to perform their work faithfully, and go away at the appointed hours. None were to be allowed to work who were under age, or not of sufficient strength.

(13) No money was to be delivered to any but the reeve, who was to have entire charge of receipts and expenses. He was to have due regard for economy. His accounts were to be kept on a roll of parchment, with the proper title.

(Other rules follow as to boundaries, manure, reclaiming waste places, and collecting stubble for thatch.)

The reeve was to be elected by the 'community of the halimote,' which was to be answerable for his conduct to the bailiff.[1] The cellarer, who apparently acted as general steward to the monastery, was to audit the accounts of the lesser officers, and inquire as to their diligence, and as to the reverence and respect paid them by the workmen.[2]

Manorial officials must thus have formed a distinct class of the rural population of mediaeval Gloucestershire. Of another class, the freeholders, we have hitherto said little. In the twenty-five manorial extents of the Gloucester Chartulary, from which so many calculations have already been drawn, not more than a quarter of the tenants can possibly be considered free, and of these a large number seem to lie upon the border line. Of the clearly free tenant a Ralph Brun of Churcham may be taken as a type. For two yardlands of 48 acres each he paid £1 as rent, owed suit to the Churcham halimote and the courts of Gloucester, the hundred and the shire ;

---

[1] *Glouc. Cart.* iii, 213–21.   [2] Ibid. 108.

his land was subject to heriot, relief, and the lord's rights of wardship and marriage. He is said to hold by hereditary charter[1] and was clearly a socage tenant. Then there are a few tenants by sergeanty upon the manor of King's Barton, such as Thomas of the Smithy, who rendered 200 barbed arrowheads, worth 8s. 4d., for a yardland ; Robert Savage, who paid 10s. rent for a yardland and had to carry writs for the county ; Geoffrey of the Grove, who held a yardland by archery ;[2] others, when a monk rode on church business, had to find a squire with a proper horse, to follow him through England and serve him ; this squire had to carry on his own horse the furniture of the monk's bed, also a book, cresset, candles, two loaves, and half a sextary of wine or beer ; when he tarried within the monastery on account of such service, he was to receive every day two squires' loaves, with beer and one dish from the kitchen. If his horse died in the service, he was to be allowed 10s. This service was commuted by a William of Ocholte, in Upton, for attendance with towels when the abbot washed his hands on the feast of St. Peter and St. Paul.[3] Yet another curious service was that of Walter Freman of Hartpury, tenant of a messuage and six acres, for which he paid a sheep with twelve pence tied round its neck.[4]

Besides these obvious freeholders are others of very doubtful status. Directly following the freeholder of Churcham, in the extent just quoted, comes a Walter Wood, tenant by hereditary charter. For half a yardland he paid 10s. 3d., did suit to the courts of Gloucester and Churcham, owed pannage, and must do one ploughing called ' peniherthe.' So far he appears a tenant by socage, but the further information that he could not sell his ox, give his daughter in marriage or alienate his son, leaves us doubtful. On most of the extents, before the heading ' consuetudinarii ' there appear a number of tenants, holding by a few services, and subject to heriot and merchet, whose difference from the regular villein is hard to understand. At Eastleach for instance a yerdling held for the term of his life, for 5s.[5] He did three bederipes and two ploughings, owed suit to the halimote, paid pannage and hyndergeld and aid, at the same time as the customary tenants ; gave toll for ox and beer, and the lord had a heriot on his death. Small holdings, e.g. a messuage and curtilage, appear in numbers as liable to work at only hay time and harvest ; these were probably pieces of the demesne, let out to freeholders, who often held by villein tenure without losing their own freedom of status.[6] It is impossible definitely to place such men either among the free or the unfree ; they were really in a state of transition, attained in varying degrees and at varying moments in different parts of the county.

In the foregoing sketch of the manor and the various classes who inhabited it, most stress has been laid upon its economic aspect, and on the opportunities which it offered to the development of its communal, as opposed to its seignorial, elements. When we pass on to matters of law and justice, we find the two in conflict ; before the lord's court the people appear as tenants of a manor ; before the king's as members of a township. Both kinds of justice, however, were brought very close to the life of the ordinary man, and must have influenced his character and

---

[1] *Glouc. Cart.* iii, 133. [2] Ibid. iii, 69. [3] Ibid. iii, Introd. p. civ. [4] Ibid. iii, 77.
[5] Ibid. iii, 188. [6] cf. *Landboc Mon. B.M.V. et S. Cenhelmi de Winchelcumba*, ed. D. Royce, i, 219–25.

ways of thinking ; some description of the methods and constitution of the various courts may not therefore be out of place.

In the manor-court, where, in spite of legal theory, the distinctions into court baron, court leet, and court customary do not seem to have been very closely preserved, the lord tried cases arising from breaches of manorial custom, and offences of his tenants against himself. If, as was usual, he also possessed the right to hold 'view of frankpledge' and the 'assize of bread and beer,' he exercised no mean control over police matters, and, when holding a 'view,' he would probably take cognizance of such minor breaches of the peace as were left him by the ever-lengthening arm of royal justice.

Offences against the lord's own rights were promptly punished. Trespassers in the lord's wood, or cornfield, or pasture, occur innumerable times in every court-roll. The lord's ultimate interest in the land and property of his villeins was preserved by the infliction of fines for any injury to their holdings. 'William Smith of Badminton, in the manor of Hawkesbury (1324–5), has been ordered to repair his tenement; an inquest of neighbours report that he has only mended one corner, and his tenement is therefore forfeited to the lord.'[1] 'John Norton of Bisley is fined for breaking up the lord's land by digging and carrying away tiles and stones (1391) '; 'Nicholas Gale has cut the branches of an ash on the lord's demesne (1393) ';[2] 'William Upington has lessened the value of his holding by felling the greater part of his grove (1435).'[3] Woods in fact were so fruitful a source of trouble that in many manors there was a special 'Woodcourt and Woodward.' At Bisley (Hen. VI) the latter functionary was himself fined 1s. 11d. for felling a beech in the lord's private wood, and for taking charcoal thence ; while the homage of the woodcourt presented that various tenants had sold customable wood by loads.[4] As late as Elizabeth tenants were fined for taking 'Crabstockes,' and for 'shrouding ash-trees' in the lord's wood.[5] A small amount of poaching appears also on the records. Possibly most lords were not very particular on the subject, but at intervals fines are inflicted for the unlawful catching of rabbits, 'troughtes,' and partridges ;[6] and at Minchinhampton the lord obliged some of his customary tenants to aid him in guarding the hare-warren.[7] Even the clergy were not guiltless of sporting tastes, for in 1400 a writ was required against 'John Burgeys, chaplain of Stroud parish, and two others, who have hunted without leave in the lord's warren, and taken rabbits and hares.'[8] Bees' nests were the lord's perquisite, and at Hawkesbury (1294) a man was fined for not bringing him some bees found in a field.[9] The rights of tenants had to be similarly

---

[1] Ct. R. portf. 175, No. 43, m. 5.   [2] Ibid. No. 8.
[3] Ibid. No. 10, m. 5.   [4] Ibid.
[5] Ibid. Nos. 12 and 13. Fitzherbert tells us the special uses of these two trees. 'Sell the smalle asshes to cowpers for garches (hoops) and the gret asshes to whelewrightes, and the meane asshes to plowe-wrightes, and crabbe-trees to myllers to make cogges and ronges.' *Book of Husbandry* (ed. W. Skeat, 1882), pp. 85–6.
[6] Ct. R. portf. 175, Nos. 7, 10, 25.   [7] Rentals and Surv. R. 238.   [8] Ct. R. portf. 175, No. 9, m. 1.
[9] Ct. R. portf. 175, No. 41, m. 7. Tusser writing about 1580 gives an amusing description of the poacher of his day :

> 'At noone if it bloweth, at night if it shine,
>   Out trudgeth Hew Make-shift with hooke and with line.
> Such walke with a black or a red little cur,
>   That open wil quickly, if anything stur ;
> Then squatteth the master, or trudgeth away,
>   And after dog runneth as fast as he may.'
> —*Five Hundred Points of Good Husbandry* (ed. Eng. Dialect Soc.), 43.

guarded against each other. The lack of enclosures led to endless disputes. Beasts were continually trespassing and devouring corn ; one man would seize the opportunity of the yearly ploughing to break up a bit of his neighbour's land,[1] or to remove a boundary.[2] Small cases of debt came up to be tried,[3] and slanderous accusations were contested.[4]

Proceedings were, however, more interesting when the lord could hold a 'view of Frankpledge,' and small criminal offences were presented by the various tithings.[5] In these reports it is that we learn how common were brawls and robberies in the mediaeval world, and with what evident relish the 'hue and cry' was raised by anyone who thought himself or herself aggrieved. Gloucestershire women seem to have availed themselves of this privilege with almost excessive readiness; for fines were not infrequently imposed for 'hue and cry raised unjustly' by Alice So-and-so upon some William or John.[6] Assaults were perpetrated with every sort of implement—with stones and sticks, 'with an iron chain,'[7] 'with a Glayfe' (or sword),[8] 'with a Schefepyke.'[9] Walter Bodele of Hawkesbury complains that his wife and son beat and ill-used him because he drank the beer which his wife was keeping for mid-Lent.[10] 'A certain Eva of the same place was keeping her sheep in Upton field, and John Leverich came and dispersed them with his dog. On her demanding why he did so he replied nothing, but seized a stick and struck her repeatedly. John is therefore at mercy, and he and Eva give bail to appear at the next court (1290).'[11] Accusations are frequently met by a 'tu quoque.' William Palfreyman of Hawkesbury says a sow and a hogget of John Jones have trespassed in his close. Jones complains that Palfreyman has maliciously slain the aforesaid sow and hogget. Palfreyman denies the charge, and says the beasts were never killed, or even hurt by him or servant of his, but that they were 'found dead' (!) in his close. He is ordered to acquit himself by twelve hands (i.e. by the oath of twelve neighbours). In this he evidently succeeds, for at the next court (1406) John Jones is fined 3d. for unjust complaint against William Palfreyman.[12]

But perhaps the most frequent cases dealt with in the view were breaches of the rules as to the prices of victuals, tolls of millers, and of the assize of bread and beer. The latter was so common an offence that it must have been considered a regular source of revenue. For the lord's justiciary rights were mainly valued for their pecuniary value. All amercements,

---

[1] e.g. Hawkesbury, Ct. R. portf. 175, No. 50, m. 9. [2] Ibid. No. 48, m. 3.
[3] Ibid. m. 1. [4] Ibid. No. 41, m. 2.
[5] Articles for View of Frankpledge (*Glouc. Cart.* iii, 221–2). Inquiry to be made : of bloodshed, treasure trove, hue and cry raised and not followed, clipping of coin, assaults on women, pleas of replevin ; of bridges made and obstruction of streams, obstructions and encroachments of roads and footpaths, encroachments on king or lord, fugitives from justice who have since returned without warrant, receivers of robbers ; of those who are well clothed, and have nothing, neither labour, nor are merchants, nor keep inns ; of tanners ; of 'comelinges' not shown after three days ; of those who are twelve years old and not in tithing ; of those who were in a tithing and have left it without leave ; of those who have kept strangers without leave ; of Christian usurers, bakers or brewers selling contrary to the assize, false weights, and measures and tolls at the mill ; of those who have withdrawn from following the tithing ; whether those of twelve years are present as summoned ; whether the halmote be full ; of everything touching the crown or liberties of the lord ; whether the head servants and others are fit men, whether the ploughing beasts, meadows, and fields and woods are well looked after, and the land well tilled ; of those who put their sons in clerk's orders without leave ; of those who cut 'free wood' without leave, who overburden the common pasture, who marry their daughters without leave, who permit their houses to fall out of repair.
[6] e.g. Cheltenham Ct. R. portf. 175, No. 26. [7] Ibid. No. 27, m. 1.
[8] Ibid. No. 54, m. 1. [9] Ibid. No. 27, m. 2.
[10] Ibid. No. 41, m. 7. [11] Ibid. m. 4. [12] Ibid. No. 48, m. 1.

though 'affeered' (or apportioned) by the whole body of suitors, came into the lord's pockets, as did the money's worth of any instrument which had been used to 'draw blood' unlawfully. (A glayfe was worth 4*d.*; a stick was 'of no value.') Thus it is easy to understand the strictness with which the lord tried to enforce the duty of 'suit of court' upon his tenants—no easy task when big men like the priors of Gloucester and Llanthony were included among the suitors.[1] Distraints for default of suit were almost as common as distraints to do homage.[2] Fines, it is true, were more often to be counted by pence than by shillings, but altogether they amounted to a respectable sum, and were by far the most frequent punishment. 'Infangtheof,' or the right to hang offenders, was a special franchise,[3] and even then could only be exercised if the thief were caught 'hand-having' or the murderer 'red-handed'; lesser crimes were occasionally dealt with by the pillory or the tumbrel (ducking-stool). According to the returns of the Hundred Rolls and Placita Quo Warranto (1273 and 1275), a gallows was possessed by some forty-five manors, a pillory by thirteen, and a tumbrel by sixteen.[4]

Of these instruments of punishment the gallows, at any rate, became more and more an article not for use but for adornment, as royal justice gradually extended its scope. For seignorial franchises of this extended kind by no means tended towards the maintenance of law. The Hundred Rolls teem with complaints of the oppressive way in which they were exercised.[5] 'The bailiff of Slaughter has held a court, and, when contradicted by the suitors, shut the gates, and killed three of them.'[6] 'The liberties of Cheltenham, Slaughter, and Salmonsbury,' say the jurors of Holford and Gretestan, 'hinder common justice and subvert the royal power, because they obey neither the itinerant justices nor the King's servants.'[7] 'The bishop of Worcester holds the Hundred Court of Henbury, where he amerces men, rich or poor, strong or weak, free or serf, not, as is fitting, according to the amount of his crime, the assessment of his neighbours, nor by the form of the Great Charter, but at the will of his bailiff.'[8]

Forest privileges were abused by the earls of Sudleye[9] and Gloucester,[10] and the retainers of the latter magnate were uncontrolled in their misdeeds, to judge by an exciting story in the Hundred Rolls. The earl of Gloucester's men were stopping in Camden, and sent two grooms to get hay for their horses. On their way they met with lads and lasses jumping for doves, and one of the grooms said one of the lasses was a good jumper, and should have doves from him. Two jealous swains, resenting the interference, seized on the doves, called him a liar, and knocked him down. Thereon arose a fray between the earl's retainers and the young men of Camden and Weston, who, infuriated at the death of one of their party by an arrow, drove back the earl's men, and imprisoned two of them till the slayer should be delivered. In the end, however, the villagers got the worst of it, for the

---

[1] Ct. R. portf. 175, Nos. 25 and 44.   [2] Ibid. No. 7.

[3] Objections raised against the claim of Tewkesbury Abbey to exercise this franchise led to an interminable dispute between the abbot and the earl of Gloucester over the hanging of a certain 'John Milksop' in 1249; *Ann. Monast.* (Rolls Ser.), i, Introd. p. xxii–iii.

[4] These statistics are worked out Mr. J. Latimer, *Brist. and Glouc. Arch. Soc. Trans.* vol. xii.

[5] The period of which the Hundred Rolls treat was of course exceptional, but they show the extent to which the barons, when uncontrolled, abused their franchises.   [6] Hund. R. Glouc. 1, m. 1.

[7] Ibid. 4, m. 1.   [8] Ibid. 2, m. 1.

[9] Ibid. 5.   [10] Ibid. extr. Glouc. 3, m. 19.

earl's men returned, rescued the prisoners, and kept four of the Camdenites till a heavy ransom had been paid.[1]

The offending retainers in this case should have been brought to justice by the earl, in whose mainpast (or household) they were—servants being exempt from the general liability to be in frankpledge or tithing.[2] In spite of such exceptions, and of the fact that many lords could hold the view of frankpledge, the latter institution must have served as a check upon seignorial power, not so much directly, as by promoting a non-manorial form of organization among the villeins, and by bringing them into connexion with the network of royal justice. Whatever its exact origin, it was connected with the old Saxon principle that every man was responsible for police duties. For this purpose he was placed at twelve years old in a small group whose members were mutually responsible for each other's production, if criminal, before the representative of the king's justice. The tithing was thus part of a directly national system, and distinct from the older responsible unit, the family, of which manorial justice continued to avail itself as late as the fourteenth century.[3] The responsibility for its enforcement lay, not with the lord of the manor (though he might receive its fines), but with the township.[4]

If a criminal were not forthcoming, the amercement would naturally fall upon his tithing, unless the township had failed to place him in one, when the fine would fall upon the larger body. The township thus occupied a step higher in the scheme of local police, and had various other duties to perform.[5] It had to follow the hue and cry, to watch criminals who took sanctuary, and to keep watch and ward by a stipulated number of men from sunset to sunrise.[6] (Statute of Winchester, 1285.) In a thinly populated county like Gloucestershire there were, it is true, many cases in which a township was so small as to 'discharge its duty of having all its members in frankpledge and tithing by being itself a tithing and a frankpledge.'[7] In 1221 the township of Swell consisted of one tithing,[8] and in the fourteenth century, in the manors of Cheltenham and Hawkesbury,[9] which consisted of several townships, the two terms seem to have been quite interchangeable ; but this confusion between two grades does not interfere with the fact that in criminal as in economic matters the villein (for frankpledge soon became a preeminently villein institution) was allowed to act as a 'townsman' rather than as a mere tenant. And while the long arm of the law thus stretched forth a finger to maintain national institutions even amidst the manorial preserves, the full strength of its clutch was felt by the lords in the courts of the royal Justices. Here, before the whole community of the shire, criminals of every rank were accused by the representative juries of the hundreds, and received their due at the hands of the judge and the same juries. Even sheriffs were called to account at the eyre—answering for their own misdeeds and for the

---

[1] Hund. R. Glouc. 5. [2] cf. Chelt. Ct. R. 175, No. 27, m. 6.

[3] e.g. distraint of kinsmen of fugitive villeins at Hawkesbury ; Ct. R. portf. 175, No. 46.

[4] For neglect of and performance of this duty see Hawkesbury Ct. R. portf. 175, Nos. 41 and 53.

[5] See Pollock and Maitland, *Hist. of Engl. Law*, i, 550.

[6] For neglect to obey this rule the watchmen and constables of Cheltenham and eight neighbouring townships were distrained in 1333. Ct. R. portf. 175, No. 25, m. 9.

[7] Pollock and Maitland, op. cit. i, 556.

[8] *Glouc. Pleas of the Crown* (ed. F. W. Maitland), No. 1.

[9] Ct. R. portf. 175, Nos. 25 and 50.

profits of the hundred courts.[1] Here, too, no great man could override local tradition. It was the whole county which 'declared' to the king's judges 'its own special customs,' as to the methods of presenting Englishry,[2] the privileges of special districts such as the Forest of Dean, &c.,[3] while elected juries of various kinds played a prominent part in the decision of cases. All difficult civil cases required to be settled through an assize of twelve sworn men ; and in criminal cases, by the thirteenth century, the ordeal was also being superseded by trial by a jury of neighbours, usually the same as the jury of presentment, but sometimes assisted by four neighbouring townships. This method, known as 'putting oneself upon one's country,' was not however absolutely obligatory,[4] and in a few flagrant cases a criminal was hanged without either trial or ordeal, as when a murderer confessed his guilt by breaking prison and taking sanctuary at Newnham in 1221,[5] or was taken red-handed ;[6] but generally one or other method was employed. The form of procedure would run thus :

> Philip of Egham acknowledges himself a thief, and accuses William, son of Robert of Dimescherche, as his accomplice in stealing two horses, two cows and a mare in the fields of Littleton ; he offers to prove it by his body. William comes and denies the whole by his body, but offers no proof, and is not in pledge, nor does any man speak for him ; they go to the duellum, and Philip is defeated, and therefore hung.[7]

Hanging does not appear to have been a penalty at all commonly inflicted. At the eyre of 1221, the records of which we have been quoting, some two or three hundred cases of homicide were presented (probably an unusual number, as at least seven years had elapsed since the last eyre), but only fourteen persons were hanged and one mutilated, while about a hundred 'abjured the country' and were outlawed.[8] Thus Thomas Moraunt of Kiftsgate hundred who has killed Henry Baldewyn's son and fled to the church, acknowledges his guilt and abjures the country.[9] There are innumerable entries to the effect that robbery and murder have been committed 'by persons unknown ; no one is suspected by the jury.' (Some jurors had evidently a very loose memory for crimes ; in 1221 those of Blidsloe hundred could remember nothing to present ; their verdict was then 'committed to them to provide for it,' and after a brief interval, fourteen crimes were recalled to their minds.)[10] With regard to the murder fine, Gloucestershire had a few special rules. Proof of Englishry had to be given by two males on the father's side, and one on the mother's ;[11] a woman's evidence was rejected ;[12] the town of Gloucester was exempt, as was the forest region beyond the Severn ('Non jacet murdrum, ultra Sabrinam').[13] Accidental death did not, of course, give rise to the 'murdrum,' though the Sheriff Engelard did exact it on one occasion, when a boy was found drowned in Coln Rogers mill-dam.[14] Usually the judgement given was 'death by

---

[1] See *Glouc. Pleas of the Crown, passim.*

[2] Presentment of Englishry. By a statute of William I every township was fined for a murder committed within its boundaries, unless the victim was proved to be an Englishman.

[3] *Glouc. Pleas of the Crown,* Nos. 119, 128, 183. [4] Ibid. No. 213.

[5] Ibid. No. 316. [6] Ibid. No. 174.

[7] Ibid. No. 73. [8] In Gloucestershire anyone might kill an outlaw ; ibid. Introd. xxix.

[9] Ibid. No. 8. [10] Ibid. Nos. 388–401.

[11] Ibid. No. 1. [12] Ibid. No. 119.

[13] Ibid. Nos. 105 and 450. [14] Ibid. No. 92.

misadventure,' and the offending instrument of the death was 'deodand.'[1] But cases of obvious murder were not allowed to slip, and the judges firmly suppressed the lurking belief that they could still, like other offences of old, be commuted for a fine. At the eyre which we have quoted so often came up an interesting though complicated case, in which the kinsmen of a murdered man had agreed with his murderer to patch up the affair. Geoffrey of Sutton (under Brailes) had been slain by the powerful family of the Bassets. He had come into court to appeal them of his wounds, but died directly after, and Christina his wife had carried on the appeal at two county courts. Then 'finding it was no good,' she had given up the suit, and her daughter had been married to the murderer's son. The Basset brothers had all fled, except Robert, who had adroitly got himself placed upon the jury. For this concealment of crime the jurors were amerced by the judges, and with the aid of their own and four neighbouring townships promptly condemned Robert to be hanged. Christina was also fined, still protesting that the alliance was none of her doing,—in spite of the recorded fact that she had received a yardland from Robert, as her daughter's dower, and had paid the sheriff half a mark for his sanction of the whole settlement.[2] Only one worse crime than homicide is mentioned—arson—when the criminal was punished by his own weapon.[3]

In conclusion it may be noticed how large a proportion of deaths were due to affrays among men returning from ale-feasts.[4] One fatal quarrel took place over a game of dice.[5] One case of suicide occurs at Campden, when the dead man's chattels are forfeited to the crown.[6]

Such was the general fabric of life and interests in rural Gloucestershire between the eleventh and fifteenth centuries,—a period which can, more easily than any other, be treated as a whole, because of the extraordinary fixity and uniformity produced by the manorial system. With all its rigidity, however, the system could not be wholly proof against the economic and political changes which, from within and without, were at work to undermine it. Of these the economic development that was most sure to come, and most powerful in its effects, was the substitution of money-rents for labour services. The villein, we may be sure, was always ready to demand the removal of this, the most galling as it was the most essential characteristic of his position; and the lord, on his side, when the growth of population had provided a surplus of labourers for hire, profited by an arrangement which enabled him to engage them continuously. Even in the twelfth century, as we have seen, commutation of labour for money had begun at Cirencester;[7] and the process must have been at least in contemplation in 1266 on the manors of the Gloucester Chartulary, which invariably quotes the customary liabilities of the tenants both in their labour and their money value. By the reign of Edward I, *venditiones operum*, or sale of labour services, had become a regular item in the receipts of some manors. At Tidenham (1279), where there was a highly elaborate

---

[1] *Glouc. Pleas of the Crown*, No. 113. E.g. Walter of Andebirie has been crushed by his cart, loaded with corn. Judgement: misadventure. Worth of horse and cart 6s. 8d. Let it be given as to God, to Walter's poor sister, who is reported to be ill. [2] Ibid. No. 101.
[3] Ibid. No. 216. See the case of William the Miller, who burnt the abbot of Malmesbury's barn in Langtree hundred, 'et per preceptum Regis Johannis combustus,' was burnt by King John's order.
[4] Ibid. *passim*. [5] Ibid. No. 189. [6] Ibid. No. 22. [7] E. A. Fuller, op. cit.

scheme of demesne work for the year, we come across entries like the following : [1]

		£	s.	d.	
205 winter works sold for	. . . . .		8	0	(i.e. less than ½d. each)
176 autumn „	. . . . .	1	2	0	(i.e. 1½d. „)
258 boon-days in harvest, without food .	.	1	12	3	(i.e. less than 1d. „)
32 „ „ with food	. .		8	3	(3d. „)
9 ploughings	.	1	10½		(2½d. „)
67 „	.	11	2		(2d. „)
56 „	.	9	4		(2d. „)
Total 803 works sold for	.	£4	12	10½	(average about 1½d. „)

Or again, taking the services in a lump, 3,675 winter-works (Michaelmas to Midsummer) were sold at a halfpenny each, and 2,500 summer-works at a penny.[2]

By 1345 a few of the tenants of Cheltenham were being allowed to commute ploughing and harrowing services at a penny, and weeding at a halfpenny a work ;[3] and in 1380 Brimpsfield was following the same course, at very similar rates.[4] Land was, in fact, gradually coming to be considered a thing that could be held as well for money as for labour, though, even when commutation had taken place, older fashions were preserved in the expression, 'tenure by the service of so much money.'[5] At Minchinhampton, about the same date, tenements were held by a mixed rent, chiefly money, but with a few services included. For a messuage and yardland, for instance, the rent was 12s. to 20s. in money, besides one or two shillings-worth of labour.[6] (This, by the way, was a large sum, for at the Templars' property of Newington, not very far from Minchinhampton, the usual rent of such a holding in 1328 was 4s.)[7] By the next reign, however, these proportions were reversed,[8] and the rental contains long lists of labour service due from the tenants. This was probably part of the general effort of landlords over all the country to re-enforce their villein services, which had become once more the cheapest means of working their demesnes since the rise of prices and wages consequent upon the Black Death.

It is not easy to gather much information as to the ravages of this terrible pestilence in the rural parts of Gloucestershire. At Bristol we know that it raged with such fury in 1348 that 'the living were scarce able to bury the dead,' and the Gloucester folk refused all intercourse with the stricken city.[9] It is improbable, however, that the country people kept up such a boycott, and on the estates of the religious houses, at least, we have direct evidence of the effects of the plague. At Ham, near Berkeley, in 1349, as much land had escheated to the lord by deaths from pestilence as

---

[1] Mins. Accts. bdle. 859, No. 19. [2] Ibid. No. 21.
[3] Ibid. bdle. 851, No. 22. [4] Ibid. bdle. 850, No. 22.
[5] Cf. Bisley Ct. R. 24 Edw. III, portf. 175, No. 7, m. 2. 'A messuage and two acres let for the service of 2s. a year.' [6] Rentals and Surv. R. 237.
[7] C.C.C. Bursary Books, 21, p. 4. This reference is to one of two volumes, kept in the Bursary of Corpus Christi College, Oxford, which I was allowed to consult by the courtesy of the President and Fellows of the College. They contain deeds relating to the lands of the college in Gloucestershire from Edw. III to Jas. I, and are marked, Glouc. F. 1, 21, and Glouc. F. 2, 22.
[8] Cf. rent of Ralph Deulee, the tenant quoted above (p. 6), whose labour services amounted to the value of 10s., while his money-rent was only 4s. 1d. Rentals and Surv. R. 238.
[9] Gasquet, The Great Pestilence, 86, 92.

would have required 1,144 days' labour to clear at harvest. By 1353 Winchcombe Abbey was overwhelmed with debt, and Llanthony Priory was in difficulties owing to its almost entire loss of rents and services from the same cause. At Horsleigh Priory, too, some eighty tenants were reported to have died.[1] From this time onward, too, the disturbance of the rural population is testified by the frequent notices in court rolls as to ruined houses,[2] and the 'cert-money,' a contribution paid by each tithing to a lord holding view of frankpledge, diminished at Hawkesbury, as if from inability or recalcitrance on the part of the tenants.[3]

In the face of such changes, lords of manors struggled vainly to preserve the old order of things. The shortage of labour enabled the villein to do far better as a hired labourer at high wages than as a tenant subject to the old laborious services. If his lord insisted on a return to these, a villein not infrequently took to his heels. From 1352, right through the reigns of Richard II, the two Henrys, and Edward IV, manor-courts continued to issue orders for the return of runaway bondmen, who never re-appeared, though in one case a Bisley tenant, William Coptegue, sent word that he wished to come and claim his freedom. Four years later however he was still at Cirencester.[4] Thus the process of commutation went merrily on,[5] and the villein obtained by economic pressure what would never have been granted otherwise. From time to time, it is true, there occurred a few scattered instances of direct manumission, probably as an act of piety, by religious houses ;[6] but the rise of the villein took place mainly in two ways : by his hiring himself out as a free labourer, or by his conversion into what was practically a free rent-paying tenant.[7] In a large number of cases the taint of villeinage had been attached only to the holding, not to the tenant ; at Cirencester, in the twelfth century, for instance, it was ' the land ' of so and so that was said to ' owe bederipes,' toll or services.[8] Thus, when these services were commuted, there was little to distinguish the holders of customary land from others, and such holdings were let for the same sort of rents as free land.[9] In 1435–6 occurs the first mention at Hawkesbury of copyhold,[10] though the privileged tenants of Cirencester had attained it much earlier.[11] In Bisley and Culkerton it was not till the reign of Henry VIII that the term became common.[12] At Cheltenham, in 1450, services and their money values were still both quoted in a survey of the holdings ' by base tenure ' ;[13] by Henry VII only money-rents were given (the average for a messuage and half-yardland being 4s. 6d.) ;[14] by Henry VIII

---

[1] Gasquet, *The Great Pestilence*, 189 et seq. [2] e.g. Bisley Ct. R. portf. 175, Nos. 8–13.

[3] Ct. R. portf. 175, No. 52.

[4] Bisley Ct. R. portf. 175, No. 7–9 ; Hawkesbury Ct. R. portf. 175, No. 46–8, 56 ; Cheltenham Mins. Accts. bdle. 852, No. 23. [5] See also Bisley Mins. Accts. (1447–61), bdle. 850, Nos. 26, 27, 29.

[6] e.g. in 1326 by the abbot of Winchcombe (*Landboc.* i, 6), and in 1428, 1460, 1461, 1470, by the abbot of Cirencester (Cir. Cart. fol. 18, 41, 45, and 56. Rawlinson MSS. 326).

[7] In some cases the tenants simply demanded, and obtained easier rents, as at Cheltenham in 1452–3, when Sir Ralph Butler of Sudeley, called in to arbitrate between the tenants and their lady, the abbess of Sion, decided in favour of a reduction of the rents originally paid in lieu of service. Mins. Accts. bdle. 852, No. 25. [8] Cirencester Abbey Register, A 88*b*, as quoted by E. A. Fuller, op. cit.

[9] e.g. at Hawkesbury, 1418–19, 4 acres of customary land paid one capon every Hockday as rent, and a gallon of wine as tenant's fine on entry, and a messuage and two customary yardlands were let for a rent of 33s. 4d. and a fine of £2 6s. 8d. Ct. R. portf. 175, No. 50, m. 3 and 9.

[10] Ct. R. portf. 175, No. 52, m. 6. [11] E. A. Fuller, op. cit.

[12] Ct. R. portf. 175, No. 11 ; Rentals and Surv. portf. 7, No. 70.

[13] Rentals and Surv. R. 217. [14] Ibid. R. 223.

twenty-five customary holdings had become free.[1] At Minchinhampton the effort, noticed above, to revise labour-rents was abandoned by 1417, and the sale of labour amounted to £4 16s. 8d. in the yearly receipts.[2]

Leaving those villeins who after the catastrophe of the Black Death remained on the land and grew to be copyholders, we turn to the lot of those who, convinced that employers would be compelled to offer what wages they chose to demand, joined the ranks of the landless labourer. In spite of the Statutes of Labourers, prescribing a minimum rate, wages did rise as a whole in the latter half of the fourteenth century. [See App. I.] Between 1344 and 1389 at Cheltenham the wages of a thatcher and his boy rose from 2d. and 1d. to 4d. and 2d. respectively.[3] Prices paid for grinding corn rose in the following proportions :

1344			1379		
Wheat, per quarter	. .	2d.	Wheat, per quarter	. .	3d.
Barley ,, ,,	. .	1½d.	Barley ,, ,,	. .	2d.
Oats ,, ,,	. .	.1d.	Oats ,, ,,	. .	1½d.[4]

A carpenter's wages at Cheltenham rose from 4d. to 5d. a day between 1394 and 1448 ;[5] and a tiler's from 3d. to 4d. between 1389 and 1396, and to 5d. by 1448.[6] In 1422 a special session of the peace had to be held at Cheltenham to check the demands of the wage-earners. John Russell, a labourer, was fined for taking 1½d. a day for winter hoeing.[7] The shoe-makers, too, were pulled up for the high prices which they had charged for shoes ; some of them had taken as much as 7d. per pair, whereas at Bristol in 1403 the cobblers were only charging—[8]

For sewing yarking and finishing shoes called Quarterschone .	. 1s.	a dozen
,, ,, ,, ,, ,, Courseware .	. 7d.	,,
For making a pair of boots entirely	. 3d.	a pair
,, ,, Galoges (i.e. clogs)	. 2d.	,,

Weavers were fined for charging 2d. per ell for weaving cloth ; while butchers and bakers were also at fault for their excessive prices.[9]

While wages thus rose, the cost of most articles of food altered little. Corn, according to Thorold Rogers, varied hardly at all between the years 1201 and 1540, the average price being about 6s. per quarter.[10] Poultry remained extraordinarily steady, varying only from 1d. to 1½d. a cock, and from 1½d. to 2d. a hen, between the thirteenth and fifteenth centuries. Eggs were usually about forty a penny.[11] Nor did the cost of farm animals differ much during the same period. Sheep rose from 1s. to 1s. 6d. apiece between the reigns of Henry III and Edward III, and for the subsequent century remained steady. Pigs were 1s. 9d. each in 1280 at Tidenham, and at Cheltenham 90 years later were still from 1s. 4d. to 2s. The cost of 'affers,' or plough horses (of which a certain number were used in Gloucestershire instead of the ox),[12] sank slightly, being 7s. 6d. in 1289 and 6s. 8d. in 1369,

---

[1] Rentals and Surv. R. 226, 227.   [2] Ibid. R. 240.
[3] Mins. Accts. bdle. 851, Nos. 22, 24.   [4] Ibid. No. 22 ; bdle. 850, No. 22.
[5] Ibid. bdle. 852, Nos. 2, 23.   [6] Ibid. bdle. 851, No. 24 ; bdle. 852, Nos. 1, 23.
[7] Ct. R. portf. 175, No. 26, m. 7.
[8] *Little Red Book of Bristol*, ed. F. B. Bickley, ii, 101, et seq.
[9] Ct. R. portf. 175, No. 26, m. 7.
[10] *Six Centuries of Work and Wages*, 215.   [11] Mins. Accts. Glouc. *passim*.
[12] See *Glouc. Cart.* where six horses were considered able to pull an eight-ox plough.

while in 1389 a stray was sold for 2s. 6d. But horses vary so in quality that it is difficult to estimate their relative values ; in 1388 an ordinary horse was sold at Cheltenham for £3, and in 1460 a pair at Bisley were valued at £20 ; while a 'lord's horse' in 1438 cost £7 6s. 8d. And the price of oxen is also uncertain, averaging 7s. 6d. in the thirteenth century and rising to 20s. between 1360 and 1370, after which it gradually fell. By 1460 an ox was 13s. 4d., a heifer 6s. 8d., and a cow about 10s.[1] While raw products were little affected by the rise of wages, manufactured articles, the value of which was dependent on the cost of labour, immediately felt its effect ; for in the fourteenth century there were no middlemen, whose profits could be clipped when wages rose, but contracts were made directly between the consumer, who bought the material, and the producer, who worked it up under his orders. Neither the small holder nor the labourer were, however, greatly affected by such a rise. Their clothing could be largely manufactured at home ; their stock of farm implements, or of tools, was not extensive.

It would be interesting to calculate the yearly income and cost of living of a peasant in the fourteenth century. Rogers draws a picture of a small holder, with a wife and two children, whose yearly cost of living he puts at £8 (i.e., four quarters of wheat, £1 3s. 6d. ; malt, to supply four gallons of beer a week, 7s. 7d. ; 800 lb. of meat, at ¼d. per lb., 16s. 8d ; boots, 3s. 6d. ; clothing, &c., 13s. 6d.).[2] The rent of such a small holder, say for a house and yardland, would be from 5s. to 10s. ; but then it is hard to calculate the exact yield of such a holding, or to say what amount of their yearly expenses our small holder and his family would nullify by their own labour.

And the living of the hired labourer is even more difficult to picture, for, when wages were paid by the day, we are not usually told for how many days a week they were given. In Bristol, in the fourteenth century, labourers received no wage for holidays on which they did no work ;[3] but we have no general rule, and saints' days were so many that the question is important. Rogers calculates that the average labourer could earn the quarter of wheat necessary for his own annual consumption by about eighteen days' labour, and the artisan by fourteen days'.

But the most trustworthy idea of the style of living of the labourer may be derived from the agreements as to board and lodging made by those workmen who were hired by the year. In the thirteenth century a mason binds himself to serve the abbey of Winchcombe for life in return for the 'livelihood of a chief servant.' When well, he feeds at the abbey table ; when sick, he is entitled to have two monks' loaves of 3 lb. each, two noggins of ale, and two dishes from the abbot's kitchen. He is to have a robe like the steward's ; two wax candles every night, and four tallow candles a week.[4] This mason was evidently a skilled artisan. The living of a farm servant of the higher grade may be imagined from a 'corrody'[5] purchased from the same abbey by a bailiff in 1317. He bargains for three bushels of wheat every eight weeks, and three bushels of such corn as the abbey servants have ; two carcases of wethers on 1 November ; pottage, and a place at table.[6]

[1] Mins. Accts. Tidenham and Cheltenham.   [2] *Hist. of Agric. and Prices*, vol. i, ch. 29.
[3] *Little Red Book*, ii, 224 et seq.   [4] *Landboc*, i, 137–8.
[5] Purchasing a corrody from some great house was the mediaeval equivalent to purchasing an annuity.
[6] *Landboc*, i, 279–80.

SOCIAL AND ECONOMIC HISTORY

Even allowing for a lower scale of living for the ordinary labourer, his standard in the fourteenth century must thus have been fairly comfortable. Bread and ale were probably the staple articles of subsistence, to judge from these allowances of food and from the prominence given to the growth of wheat and barley in the manorial accounts. The price of these necessities was carefully regulated by the assize of bread and beer. According to a fourteenth-century ordinance at Bristol[1] beer was to be sold at ½d. a gallon when the prices of grain were, 3s. to 3s. 4d. a quarter for wheat, 1s. 8d. to 2s. for barley, 1s. 4d. for oats. Prices outside the city were slightly lower. A rather later ordinance[2] fixed ale at 1¼d. the gallon, and loaves at ½d. each.[3]

Besides bread, however, the peasant—and even the landless labourer, who probably was allowed some rights of common on the waste and the 'balks'—must have enjoyed abundance of eggs and poultry; butter, milk, and meat were all cheap, and fish were abundant in Gloucestershire. The finer sorts were chiefly preserved in the lord's fish ponds; but in the towns sea fish were imported in numbers, and at rates suitable for all classes.[4] The Severn, the 'speciall glory' among 'all good gifts,' as Malmesbury says, 'than which there is not any in all the land for Channell broader, for streame swifter, or for fish better stored,' had been famous as far back as Domesday, where Tidenham already appears as the great fishing manor. At that date it contained upon the Severn eleven fisheries in demesne, and forty-two held by villeins,[5] besides a few in the Wye, and the rent paid by its lord to Bath Abbey consisted of six porpoises and 30,000 herrings.[6] The existence of herrings in even a tidal river like the Severn certainly appears improbable; yet at Sodbury there is still a place called Herringbridge, and Smyth (seventeenth century) in the course of his 'cookish observations' expressly mentioned herrings as one of the fish caught at Berkeley.[7] But the great delicacy of the Severn was the lamprey, that 'fish of note and eminency, Gloucester's Royal Fish.' King John had a special liking for it, and quarrelled mightily with the men of Gloucester when 'they did not pay him sufficient respect in the matter of his lampreys.'[8] Henry III was regularly supplied with Severn lampreys and herrings, and Edward III was propitiated by the earl of Berkeley with a gift of six lampreys, costing the fabulous sum of £6 7s. 2d. The same prudent earl, evidently distrusting the provender of the north, took nine lamprey pies with him on the Scottish expedition of 1308. The bailiff of Cheltenham, early in the fifteenth century, was continually receiving orders to send lampreys to his mistress, the countess of Huntingdon, with minute instructions as to their baking, salting, and packing. Prices varied from 9d. to 5s. apiece.[9] The annual presentation of a lamprey

---

[1] *Little Red Book*, ii, 217.
[2] Ibid. p. 224–5.
[3] The weights of loaves were also very carefully fixed, through a long scale of different qualities of bread, which includes 'Simnel,' 'wastel,' 'cokel,' and 'bread of Our Lord,' and ends with 'horse bread'—a mixture of beans and other horse's food. Ibid. p. 237.
[4] See *Landboc*, Introd. p. xxxi.
[5] The same entry also mentions weirs called 'cytweras' and 'haecweras.' Seebohm considers the former to have resembled the 'puttchers,' 'putt-weirs,' or basket-weirs of the present day, and the latter to have been like the 'hackles' by which an eddy is formed to guide the fish into the stop-net. See *Engl. Village Community*, pp. 151–3, where an illustration of 'puttchers' is given.
[6] C. S. Taylor, op. cit.
[7] *Berkeley MSS.* iii, 319–20.
[8] *Glouc. Right Royal Fish*, 1902.
[9] Mins. Accts. bdle. 852.

pie to the king by the city of Gloucester is a custom of immemorial antiquity, revived, after sixty years' lapse, in 1893.[1] The other product for which Gloucestershire was famous was its wines, which, says William of Malmesbury, 'carry no unpleasant tartnesse, as being little inferiour in sweet verdure to the French wines.' 'Gloster,' sings Drayton,

> Herselfe did highly prize,
> When in her pride of strength she nourisht goodly vines,
> And oft her cares represt with her delicious Wines.[2]

Nor is this reputation mythical, for Domesday mentions a plot of vines at Stonehouse (where, by the way, there is still a farm called Vinegar Hill),[3] and later on a vineyard is mentioned both at Bisley (1324)[4] and Prinknash. Houses called 'the Vineyard' still exist in several places in the shire, while a vague local tradition tells of vine-roots dug up on the hillside beneath Birdlip.[5] 'There is not any county in England so thicke set with Vineyards' as Gloucestershire, said Malmesbury, who also described 'the Highwayes and Common Lanes clad with Apple trees and Peare trees; the ground of itselfe is so inclined to beare fruits, and these both in taste and beautie farre exceedinge others.'[6] This statement can be readily believed by anyone who has seen the orchards of modern Gloucestershire, though contemporary accounts say little on the subject. Apples were sold at 8d. per quarter at Tidenham in 1293-4,[7] but were apparently only a garden fruit; the almoner of Winchcombe Abbey (1270) distributed apples to the tenants, together with seed of leek and colewort.[8] Salt, another article of prime necessity in days when no fresh meat could be got all winter, was rather easily attained in Gloucestershire, owing to the proximity of the Worcestershire salt mines. At Wyche (Droitwich) salt works were owned by eight manors in the time of Domesday.[9] In the twelfth century Winchcombe Abbey had salt springs there,[10] as had Gloucester Abbey in the thirteenth century. At Hartpury several tenants owed the service of carrying loads from Wyche once a year.[11] The Saltway from Droitwich to Lechlade, where packs of salt were shipped to London, passed through Gloucestershire, by Hinton-on-the-Green, Toddington, Hayles, and Chedworth. At the latter place tolls on salt were a regular item in the lord's revenue.[12]

This discussion of the income and subsistence of the Gloucestershire peasant has led us rather far afield. Taking it as a whole, the lot of the labourer and small holder seems to have improved after the Black Death, but there were no changes of a rapid or startling nature. There was not a sudden rise of a system of bailiff-farming, or of leaseholding, as in some parts of England. Gloucestershire landlords were in no hurry to abandon the old leases for one life, even in the case of mills and quarries, which had always lain outside the regular manorial economy.[13] The rent in such cases in the middle of the fifteenth century at Hawkesbury varied from 13s. 4d. to 16s.

[1] *Right Royal Fish.*
[2] *Polyolbion*, 1889 reprint, p. 231.
[3] C. S. Taylor, op. cit.
[4] Atkyns, *Hist. of Glouc.* 2nd ed. p. 146.
[5] Add. MS. 24,783, fol. 209.
[6] Quoted in Gough, Glouc. 23.
[7] Mins. Accts. bdle. 859, No. 23.
[8] *Landboc*, i, 219-25.
[9] C. S. Taylor, op. cit.
[10] *Landboc*, i, 27.
[11] *Glouc. Cart.* iii, 68, 83.
[12] C. S. Taylor, op. cit.
[13] e.g. Cheltenham Ct. R. portf. 174, No. 50, m. 4. John Roche takes a quarry, according to the custom of the manor, for 4s. rent and ten feet of 'Sharpe crestys' (roof-tiles), 1419-20.

for a messuage and yardland,[1] and from 2s. to 9s. for a cottage and garden. At Cheltenham[2] a messuage and half-yardland were rented for about 4s. 8d. At Longney a messuage and yardland were 11s., with relief, heriot and suit of court.[3] But leases, of course, were sometimes given. As far back as 1270 two holdings were let 'at farm' for a term of ten years at Duntisbourne,[4] and in 1359 one brother leased to another at Temple Guiting two yardlands for a term of seven years.[5] Another case could be quoted of about the same date at Cheltenham.[6] Tithes were also occasionally let out at farm in the fifteenth century,[7] and so were whole manors.[8] But it was not till about 1512 that twelve-years leases between tenants became common at Cheltenham. The lessee generally undertook all services to the lord, and was allowed to lop and shroud, but not to top the trees.[9]

Towards the end of Henry VI's reign, however, a new and very significant form of short lease did begin to appear at Stroud and Bisley. This was the grant, for three or four lives, of mill-streams[10]—a sign that the industrial value of the water-power of that valley was beginning to be realized. It is, indeed, at this period that the greater frequency with which fulling-mills are mentioned reminds us that we are approaching the greatest period of Gloucestershire's prosperity—that of her upland woollen trade. But before discussing this, some retrospect of the preceding history of the great towns, where the industry was born and nursed, is necessary.

Among these, Gloucester and Bristol naturally take the first place, the first owing its existence mainly to political, the second to commercial, causes. In constitutional ways the capital town led the way. It was the first to obtain a charter of trading privileges in 1155;[11] in 1192 it had a guildhall,[12] and in 1200, when a more extended charter was granted to it by John, it already possessed a merchant guild.[13] But Bristol, though it obtained no charter till the reign of John, and had no merchant guild till 1242 (Inq. of 46 Edw. III, quoted by Mr. Bickley, Introd. to *Little Red Book*), soon outstripped Gloucester in wealth and commercial activity. Foreign trade went hand in hand with home industry, and by the fourteenth century there had sprung up a number of craft-guilds, ousting the guild-merchant, of which we hear little beyond its name. In Bristol, accordingly, we get the fullest accounts of the woollen industry in its first stage, when it was urban and guild-controlled.

Wool had played an important part in English history from the twelfth century, mainly as an item in the royal revenue; and when in 1297 Edward I raised his famous custom of half a mark on every sack of wool, Bristol's share in the export trade had been attested by a 'customer' of her own.[14] Despite various spasmodic efforts of the government to promote the consumption of English wool at home, Bristol[15] and other English seaports continued to be thronged by foreign merchants exporting the precious

[1] Ct. R. portf. 175, Nos. 52 and 53.
[2] Rentals and Surv. R. 216.
[3] *C. C. C. Bursary Books,* 22, p. 497.
[4] Ibid. p. 151.
[5] Ibid. 21, p. 151.
[6] Ct. R. portf. 175, No. 25, m. 3.
[7] Ibid. No. 52.
[8] See Hawkesbury Ct. R. portf. 175, No. 50, m. 7; also Cheltenham Mins. Accts. bdle. 853, No. 11.
[9] Ct. R. portf. 175, No. 27.
[10] Mins. Accts. bdle. 850, Nos. 26, 29.
[11] *Glouc. Cal.* No. 1.
[12] Pipe R. 4 Ric. I, m. 10.
[13] *Glouc. Cal.* No. 5.
[14] Smith, *Mem. of Wool,* 14.
[15] See Hund. R. 4 Edw. I, Rot. Extr. com. Glouc. No. 3, m. 18.

commodity, until Queen Philippa's introduction of Flemish weavers. In the development of the manufacture of cloth in England Bristol again played a representative part. Within two years of the law (passed 1337) protecting foreigners, some of them were being employed by Thomas Blanket at Bristol. Whether Blanket was himself a foreigner is not clear, though he certainly was not, as is asserted, the originator of the material called by his name, for that existed in England long before his arrival. Either by his nationality or by his neglect of guild rules,[1] he excited the jealousy of the townsmen, for in 1339 a writ had to be issued for the protection of 'Thomas Blanket and other citizens, who had caused instruments for the making of cloth to be set up in their own houses, and had caused weavers and other craftsmen to be hired,'[2] and had therefore been heavily fined by the mayor and bailiffs. Two years later, however, Blanket had acquired sufficient popularity to be elected bailiff himself, and from the time of his coming Bristol certainly throve. In 1353 a staple of wool was settled there[3] and evidently helped on the cloth manufacture, for from this time we find abundant ordinances for its regulation among the records of the Fullers', Dyers', and Weavers' Guilds. True, there is an anxiety about the reiteration of guild rules at this time, which indicates that the guilds were somewhat strained in the effort to receive, firstly, the workers from abroad, and secondly, the villein element which flooded in after the Black Death, to fill the gaps in the city population. Weavers had to be reminded (1346) that they must become burgesses of the city before they could ply their craft there. The width and quality of the cloth were again minutely prescribed, and a foreign instrument called a 'webanlam' was only permitted to be set up on payment of a fee to the mayor and aldermen. Another called 'Osetes' was forbidden, except to five men, because fraudulent cloth was made thereby.[4] The practice of new and unlawful methods was guarded against by the order that weavers' instruments must stand neither in solars nor in cellars, but only in halls and shops next the road, in sight of the people. No weaver was to work by night. Fullers, dyers, and weavers were warned not to deal with persons outside the craft. The town weaver must spin his thread at home, and not buy from any stranger. Cloth must not be sent outside the town to be fulled, nor wool to be woven, spun, or combed, without special permission from the aldermen.[5] Roving dyers who do not attend properly to their work are warned.[6] Prices were controlled too by ordinances limiting the sale of cloth to certain times and places (1370 and Ric. II). But the masters were in their turn assisted by the municipality in controlling the rate of wages, guild law having evidently proved an ineffective barrier to the general tendency of the times. Rates of wages were prescribed under severe penalties. In 1346 a woman called a 'Wedestere' had to be content with a penny a day, and a man engaged in fulling with fourpence a day. (This last, however, had, as is shown by an erasure, to be raised to 6d.)[7] In 1389 the master weavers were forbidden to pay their covenant servants more than a third part of the cloth made.[8] In 1406 the master fullers were again authorized to pay their labourers 4d. in the summer and 3d. in the winter, and four good men

---

[1] He appears to have collected his workmen in one building like a small factory; Ashley, *Econ. Hist.* pt. i, 202.   [2] Rhymer, *Foedera*, ii, 1098; Ashley, ibid.
[3] S. Seyer, *Memoirs of Bristol*, 139   [4] *Little Red Book*, ii, 40.   [5] Ibid. 2–9.
[6] Ibid. 39.   [7] Ibid. 12.   [8] Ibid. 59.

were ordered to be elected yearly to inquire into the observance of this rule and of others for the good of the craft, which was suffering great shame and disadvantage 'by the frauds and deceits of divers men ignorant of the said craft.'[1] The dyers, too, were ordered to close up their ranks, to put down the untrained workmen who were bringing discredit on their craft; and in 1425 their position was confirmed by royal charter. There is something familiar too in the cry of the masters in the next century.[2]

'Divers persons,' they complain, 'dailly taken upon theym to receyve into theire houses wollen yarn made of flokkes and thrummes (waste, or inferior wool), and the same yarn deceytefully weve in theire lomes into the liknesse of Brodemedes, that afterwards be sent into divers parties beyond see, and there solde to marchauntes straungiers as true drapery called Brodemedes, to the grete infamie and disclaundre of this worshipfull Towne.'

And while the manufacturer denounces shoddy, the voice of the unemployed is uplifted against alien immigration. In 1419 we read complaints of Irish weavers who eluded the rules for apprenticeship;[3] in 1461 even wives and daughters of weavers were forbidden any employment in weaving, 'by which many men gothe vagaraunt and unoccupied, and may not have ther labour to ther livyng,'[4] and in the next year fresh protests were made against those weavers who 'receyven Allions,' and 'for ther singular profit provokyn marchaunts . . . to bring into this Towne people of divers Countrees, not born under the King's obeisaunce but rebellious, which bene sold to them as hit were hethen people.'[5] The other crafts[6] were in equal difficulties over the uncraftlike spirit of the age. Men would get themselves shaved at home, or by their neighbours, to the grief of barber journeymen who had served their seven years' apprenticeship.[7] The cordwainers would not attend their own guild-meetings; and the hoopers were rebellious over the wages allotted them (covenant servants 40s. a year; journeymen 1s. a week and their 'table').[8] The tailors too (1401) had to issue regulations against bad work, and against tailors who were not members of the guild.[9]

Complex indeed was the web of interests through which the paternal municipality of the middle ages strove unflinchingly to find its way. In this case its efforts tended on the whole to the depression of the craftsmen, already weakened, as we have seen, by the crowding of the labour market. Their complaints that they were being deprived of their right to walk in the guild processions testified to their own sense of their declining position. Wealth could still be amassed in the cloth trade at the close of the fifteenth century (as is shown by the accounts of the Merchant Taylors, and by the frequency with which bequests of cloth and 'cloth-houses' occurred in the wills of Bristol burgesses of the period),[10] but not by the actual manufacturer. The age of the great merchants was approaching, and Bristol enjoyed as fine a succession of merchant princes as any town in the realm. Chief among

---

[1] *Little Red Book*, ii, 76.   [2] Ibid. 123.   [3] Ibid.
[4] Ibid. 127.   [5] Ibid. 128.
[6] *The Little Red Book* mentions seventeen craft-guilds, besides two religious fraternities, the Kalenders and Mariners.
[7] *Little Red Book*, ii, 135–41.   [8] Ibid. 159–66.
[9] The Merchant Taylors' Guild was founded by royal charter 1392, and continued to issue ordinances till 1640. It became finally extinct early in the nineteenth century. See F. F. Fox, *The Ancient Fraternity of Merchant Taylors of Bristol*.
[10] T. P. Wadley, 'Great Orphan Book, and Book of Wills,' *Brist. and Glouc. Arch. Soc. Trans.* 1886.

these were the Canynges, cloth merchants, whose wealth and pious munificence have a permanent memorial in Redcliffe church.[1]

The other towns of Gloucestershire also owed their prosperity largely to wool. Gloucester must have early had a weavers' guild, though I can find no authentic mention of such a body before 1545;[2] and the only answer to an inquiry as to the age of the fraternity in 1635 was that it had existed 'during the tyme whereof the memory of man is not to the contrary.'[3] But at the end of the twelfth and the beginning of the thirteenth century, when the rest of England was still clothed mainly in foreign cloth, 'Fuller,' 'Dyer,' and 'Weaver,' were already common names in Gloucester, and the tolls on wool and woad imported into the city show them to have been articles necessary to her craftsmen in the fourteenth century. Cloth was, however, still imported from Ireland and from Worthstede (probably the new 'worsted' manufacture of the Flemings).[4] In the fifteenth century 'Gloucester reds' were famous.[5] At Tewkesbury there was a 'Fullers' Street' as early as 1257.[6] In Cirencester, which is said to have been a clothing town in the first century A.D., the cloth trade had been encouraged by foreign merchants as early as 1315,[7] and even in the twelfth century we hear of merchants established there, and of Ralph the Weaver, Henry the Dobber (or Dyer), and Norman the Fell-monger.[8] Henry II is said to have granted a charter to weavers at Cirencester.[9] By the reign of Henry IV the weavers' fraternity was sufficiently important to be endowed with a hospital for poor members, though the guild did not actually secure a charter till the reign of Philip and Mary.[10] The town as a whole continued to flourish, though not a chartered borough, and though its only royal privilege was a guild-merchant, illegally granted by Henry IV in 1403, declared null by Henry V,[11] and not confirmed till Elizabeth.[12] But it could hold two fairs a year[13] and two markets a week,[14] when its merchants could buy up the produce of the upland districts.[15] In 1318 a Cirencester townsman, Geoffrey Merston, was purchasing of the prior of Llanthony his 'Coteswolde wool' at the rate of $11\frac{1}{2}$ marks (£7 13s. 4d.) the sack, the wool to be only 'good wool, dry and well cleaned.'[16] In 1341 there were ten wool merchants in the town, and Cirencester wool was known as far away as Florence.[17] That the county as a whole had a recognized position in the clothing trade by the end of the fourteenth century is shown by an Act of Parliament in 1389, regulating its sale in the counties of Somerset, Devon, Bristol, and Gloucester. Winchcombe too was an emporium for raw wool and other necessities of the cloth trade. Among the tolls on imports to the town[18] in

---

[1] H. R. Fox Bourne, *Engl. Merchants*, ch. iv. Sir Richard Whittington, the most famous of the fourteenth-century merchants, was a Gloucestershire man.   [2] *Glouc. Cal.* No. 1237.
[3] Exch. Dep. Mich. 11 Chas. I, No. 45.   [4] *Glouc. Cal.* No. 46.
[5] Rogers, *Hist. of Agric. and Prices*, iv, 567.   [6] *Ann. Monast.* i, 160.
[7] Madox, *Firma Burgi*, Lond. 1726, p. 273.
[8] Cir. Abb. Reg. A. 65 a. Cotton MSS. Vitellius, A. xi, 131–4. Quoted, E. A. Fuller, *Brist. and Glouc. Arch. Soc. Trans.* ix.   [9] Rudder, *Hist. of Gloucestershire*.
[10] *Hist. of Cir. and Tewkesbury*, Ciren. 1800.   [11] Chancery County Placita, Glouc. 47b.
[12] Confirm. R. 31–7 Eliz.   [13] Granted by John and Hen. III, Inq. a.q.d. 4 Hen. IV, No. 13.
[14] Ibid.   [15] For these references see E. A. Fuller, *Brist. and Glouc. Arch. Soc. Trans.* xviii.
[16] Reg. Ant. Llanthony Priory, A. ix, 2, No. 87. Transcript at Thirlestone House, Cheltenham. E. A. Fuller, *Brist. and Glouc. Arch. Soc. Trans.* xviii.   [17] E. A. Fuller, *Brist. and Glouc. Arch. Soc. Trans.* ix.
[18] The list is interesting as showing the articles in use even in a small fourteenth-century town. They include herrings, sea-fish, salmon, cattle, skins and hides, corn, salt, butter, tallow, wax and cheese, pepper, onions, almonds, figs and raisins, cinnamon, wire, coal, lead, pitch, oil, and tar. *Landboc*, Introd. p. xxxi.

1327 were included alum (used for dyeing), wool at $\frac{1}{2}d.$ per wey, woad 1*d.* per assize, cloth 1*d.* per bound trussel and $\frac{1}{2}d.$ per whole drap, teazles at 2*d.* per 1,000.[1] St. Kenelm's Fair (July 28) was the great occasion for the purchase of cloth and other articles at Winchcombe. In 1254 the abbot of Abingdon provided himself with cloth there,[2] and weavers and fullers are mentioned.[3] Winchcombe merchants, however, probably dealt more in the raw article. In 1276 they got into trouble by exporting wool, which a protective law of 1258 forbade, and some of them bribed the bailiff of the town to the extent of 1*s.* a sack, to wink at the rule.[4]

But wool-stapling had not yet reached its height. It was Edward IV's protection that did most to develop the English cloth trade, and so to provide a lucrative home market, and it is in the fifteenth century accordingly that men began to 'discover' the Cotswolds, to whose pastures, as Drayton wrote two centuries later, even

> Sarum's vale gives place ; tho' famous for her flocks,
> Yet hardly doth she tythe our Cotswold's wealthy locks.[5]

Cotswold, that ' great king of shepherds,' had, as we have seen, always been famous for its sheep. Domesday Book notes ' the sheep's wool ' at Cirencester as being the queen's due. In the thirteenth century it is said that 6,000 sheep were kept at Beverstone, and that the city of Gloucester owed 30,000 sacks of Cotswold wool every year to the crown.[6] In the fourteenth century we get a detailed account of sheep-farming in the ministers' accounts of Brimpsfield and Winstone. Here we learn the prices of sheep and fleeces, and the wages of shepherds and shearers, together with the cost of all their manifold requisites. Some 400 sheep seem to have been kept—a number betokening that the growth of wool was made a regular matter of business, for on most manors sheep were only kept in small numbers on the waste or the stubble. Here they were carefully enclosed in a fold, the steward paying 2*s.* for twenty-four hurdles made of the lord's wood. Sheep were shorn at five a penny, the men receiving free food and drink while at work. One permanent shearer was engaged, besides the shepherd, whose joint wages amounted to 18*s.* per annum. At lambing time the shepherd was allowed a boy to help him (at a wage of 1*s.* 6*d.*) and received a pound of candles (worth 2*d.*). The loss of lambs seems, however, to have been considerable. Out of a hundred and twenty, thirty-one died one year before weaning, and only seventy-seven finally survived. Once too we get a glimpse of the darkest of all the evils that beset the shepherd's charge. ' Twelve sheep, injured by night by dogs unknown, sold for £1 1*s.* 2*d.*' As a matter of fact, such a sale involved no very great pecuniary loss, as 1*s.* 8*d.* was quite an ordinary price for a sheep. Fleeces were sold at $6\frac{1}{2}d.$ each, lambskins at $7\frac{1}{2}d.$ Fresh wool fetched £9 13*s.* 4*d.* the sack ; refuse or broken wool about 3*d.* per lb. ' Red stuff for marking the sheep ' cost 8*d.* ; lard was bought at 10*d.* per gallon for mixing with tar to grease the sheep.[7]

---

[1] From the high price of teazles, which are used in the finishing process of cloth-making, they were probably still imported from abroad at this date. Later in the reign Gloucestershire is said to have led the way in the cultivation of teazles, and was long famous for the fineness of its growth. See Anne Pratt's *Flowering Plants, Grasses, and Ferns of Gt. Britain*, ii, 119. [2] *Chron. Monast. de Abingdone*, ii, 300–26.
[3] *Landboc.* Introd. pp. xxvii-xxx, 43, 195. [4] Hund. R. i, 74, 167, 174, 178.
[5] *Polyolbion*, 1889 reprint, p. 232. [6] Prize Essay on ' Cotswold Sheep' in *The Cotswold Flock Book*, vol. i.
[7] Mins. Accts. Ric. II. bdle. 850, No. 22.

But it was in the fifteenth century that sheep-farming became general on the wolds, and that Cotswold wool-dealers raised such splendid memorials of their wealth and piety as may be seen at Northleach and Chipping Camden.[1] The correspondence of the Cely family,[2] who were merchants of the staple at London in the time of Edward IV, gives interesting details as to their dealings with the woolmen of Northleach, Camden, and Chipping Norton. 'Good Cottyswolde woll' was in great request, and no less a person than the merchant Richard Cely, or his son, had to ride constantly into Gloucestershire to select the fleeces, and also personally to supervise their packing at London for shipment to 'Jorge Cely' at Calais. Pleasant expeditions they must have been to a gay young merchant like the younger Cely, whose hawk, we hear, provided him with sport by the way, and with a 'heronshaw' which proved useful in his courtship of an heiress at Northleach. Trade was anxious work, however, for prices were rising in consequence of foreign competition. 'I have not bogwyt thys yere a loke of woll,' complains the elder Cely in 1480, 'for the woll of Cottyswolde is bogwyt be the Lombardys.' And again, in the following year, he writes to his son at Calais: 'Ye avyse me for to by woll in Cottyswolde, bot it is at grete pryse, 13s. 4d. a tode, and gret ryding for woll in Cottyswolde as was onny yere this vii yere.' The average price of wool in the years 1471–80 was 5s. 4d. the todd, according to Thorold Rogers,[3] so that Cotswold wool must have been very highly rated at this time, though apparently a fictitious price was set upon it by the Northleach wool-dealer, Mydwynter, of whom Cely piously remarks, 'God ryd us of hym.' Even kings did not disdain to treat for it. In the middle of this century we meet with a special request from the Portuguese to the English king, for leave to export sixty sacks of Cotswold wool for making cloth of gold. In 1464 Edward sent to Henry of Castile a present of Cotswold rams, which are believed to have been crossed with the merino sheep, and greatly improved it.[4]

The consequent rise in the value of sheep-pastures becomes increasingly evident in the court rolls of the fifteenth and sixteenth centuries. The tenants of Hawkesbury Court, for instance, issued orders in 1466 'stinting' the number of sheep which might be kept on a common called 'Les Mores.'[5] Again in 1509 four tenants were accused of keeping flocks of sheep in the common fields of Hawkesbury, and in 1528 it was noted that the abbot of Gloucester had pasture there for 300 sheep.[6] At Temple Guiting, we hear of many transactions relating to sheep pastures in the reign of Henry VIII.[7] The dissolution of the monasteries, and consequent distribution of great estates, probably stimulated enclosures for sheep-farming in Gloucestershire, while the general break-up of old systems of life which followed that momentous event encouraged the woollen manufacture to proceed on freer lines. At Cirencester, says Leland, 'a right goodly clothing mill' was set up in the ruins of the abbey.[8] But the especial characteristic of the period is the development of the industry not in the towns but in

---

[1] Camden's great woolman, Grevel, was known as 'the flower of English wool merchants.'
[2] *The Cely Papers*, Camd. Soc. (3rd ser.), vol. i.
[3] *Hist. of Agric. and Prices*, iv, 328. See also App. ii, infra.   [4] *Cotswold Flock Book*, vol. i.
[5] Ct. R. portf. 175, No. 55, m. 5.   [6] Ibid. No. 59.
[7] e.g. Richard Wenman, merchant of the staple at Witney, sells a pasture for 800 sheep at Guiting for £66 12s. *C.C.C. Bursary Books*, 21, p. 289.   [8] Quoted, Ashley, pt. i.

the country districts. A certain amount of weaving had indeed always gone on in the villages. In the twelfth century the abbot of Winchcombe had a fulling-mill at Clively.[1] As far back as Edward I the tenants of Hawkesbury used to pay fines for leave to full their cloth elsewhere than at the lord's mill.[2] Several weavers, one dyer, and one fulling-mill are mentioned in the Gloucester Chartulary.[3] In 1353 there was a 'Hugh the Walker,' or Fuller, at Cheltenham,[4] and by the reign of Henry V, as we have seen, there were weavers there. Whether the Flemings, who did so much for the cloth industry in the towns, also settled in the country we do not know ; but the name 'Fleming' occurs more than once at and near Temple Guiting.[5] Possibly foreign workmen were introduced there by the Templars, who had built two fulling-mills in the neighbouring hamlet of Barton by 1185.[6] Probably most villages did some amount of weaving, for pieces of cloth seem to have been articles to be found in many houses. In 1418 the theft of a yard of cloth worth 3s. 4d. led to a highly entertaining quarrel at Hawkesbury.[7] In 1399 'cloth of blanket' was sold at about 2s. 6d. a yard at Cheltenham.[8] In the reign of Edward IV the fulling-mill at Hawkesbury was a valuable part of the lord's estate.[9] At Bisley a fulling-mill and messuage were let for 12s. per annum in 1439,[10] while Chalford Mill and tenements paid 16s. rent in the reign of Richard III. By 1485 the owner of this fulling-mill was unpopular, because of his prosperity, his new methods, or some other reason unknown, for he was attacked by a crowd of malefactors, 'vi et armis, viz. with swords, sticks, bows and arrows, scythes, jakkes, armour, &c., with intent to murder him, so that he was many times affrighted and disturbed, and was robbed of three Sherman Sherys, worth 30s.'[11] In 1515 the same mill and lands were let for £3 6s. 8d. a year.

Under Henry VIII fulling-mills also existed in considerable numbers at Kingswood, one being let for the high rent of £8 1s.[12] In 1532 a gig-mill and a fulling-mill at Cam were leased for twenty-one years to Alice, wife of John Tyndale. It was beginning, in fact, to be realized that the valleys about Stroud possessed superior facilities for the weaving and dyeing of cloth. In 1557 this development of the west received remarkable recognition in 'an Act touching the making of woollen cloth,' whereby an effort was made to confine the manufacture to the towns, the only favourable exceptions being a few specified districts, which included 'any towns or villages near the river Stroud in the county of Gloucester, where cloths have been made for twenty years past.' In an Act of 1565–6 this grace was again extended to 'the parts of Gloucestershire about Frome Water, Kingswood Water and Stroud Water.'[13]

Though its progress is marked by the grumblings common to English manufacturers of every age, the Cotswold woollen industry was evidently

---

[1] *Landboc*, i, 195. [2] Ct. R. portf. 175, No. 41.
[3] Vol. iii. [4] Ct. R. portf. 175, No. 25, m. 7.
[5] First at Little Utryngton, in Guiting, in 1328. *C.C.C. Bursary Books*, 21, pp. 3–5 ; 22, p. 139.
[6] Dugdale, *Mon.* (ed. 1661), ii, 529.
[7] The thief, declaring he 'would sooner mortify than stand to answer in court,' fled, leaving his cloak behind him. Ct. R. portf. 175, No. 50, m. 3. [8] Mins. Accts. bdle. 852, No. 2.
[9] Ct. R. portf. 175, No. 55. [10] Ibid. No. 10, m. 6.
[11] *C.C.C. Bursary Books*, 22, pp. 401–23. These shears were probably used for shearing off the nap, which was part of the process of finishing cloth.
[12] Rentals and Surv. portf. 7, No. 70. [13] John Smith, *Mem. of Wool*, pp. 70–9.

becoming a prosperous affair.[1] In 1585 Acts were passed regulating the breadth of Gloucestershire 'Whites and Reddes,' and protecting the Gloucestershire industries of woollen card-making and card-wire drawing.[2] About this date occurred an event which made the reign of Elizabeth rank equal with that of Edward III in the history of the cloth-manufacture—the immigration of Flemish weavers, refugees from Alva's persecutions. Two great clothing families, the Playnes and the Clutterbucks, who are still well known in the Stroud district, trace their descent to Huguenot ancestors. The name of Clutterbuck is found at King's Stanley as early as 1574, and early in the seventeenth century had spread to the surrounding villages of Eastington, Slimbridge, and Wotton-under-Edge.[3] The Playnes, who first settled in Kent, did not move till about the middle of the seventeenth century to Woodchester, where portions of their original mill may still be seen.[4] It may be noted that to Flemish influence is generally attributed the peculiar excellence of the farms and manor-houses of this portion of the Cotswolds.

Under this new stimulus numerous fresh mills were erected. Near Bubblewell, at Bisley, in 1586, we read of one with two 'rack-places' and a dyehouse. Ten years later William Esler, a Bisley tenant, was fined for cutting down an oak upon his tenement, and making thereof 'a boame for a loome.'[5]

All this growth and change naturally strained the old system under which the woollen industry had grown up. With the departure of the manufacture from the towns the guilds ceased to play an important part in its history. Weaving was now carried on under the domestic system, by which the master clothier gave out his wool to be spun and woven in the cottages of the workmen, or occasionally by a number collected under his own roof. The fulling and finishing of the cloth was then completed at a large mill, often the clothier's own property. The old merchants of the staple began to disappear, and we catch echoes of their dying plaints in the state papers of Elizabeth and James I. All their difficulties were ascribed to the covetousness of the merchant adventurers, who were said to monopolize the trade in the export of wool. Licences to export wool were being granted also to foreigners, whereby, says a petition of 1560, 'the merchants of the staple and their families are utterly decayed.' The merchant adventurers were evidently a pushing set of men, whose methods accorded ill with old ideas of a hard-and-fast delimitation of functions in commerce. They were also accused by the Gloucestershire clothiers (in 1577) of raising the price of wool,[6] so that some had been obliged to give over their businesses, and whole villages were decayed.[7] Foreigners, it was felt, should not be allowed to export wool, though there was objection to the establishment of a cloth staple to provide them with employment (1582).[8]

---

[1] The proverb, 'He'll prove a man of Dursley' (i.e. promise much and perform nothing), is due to the unenviable notoriety of a Gloucestershire clothier, in the time of Queen Mary. This was a certain Webb, of Dursley, who used 'to buy very great quantities of wooll out of most counties of England. At the weighinge whereof, he would ever promise out of that parcell a gown-cloth, peticote-cloth, apron, or the like to the good wife or her daughters, but never paid any thinge.' J. Smyth, *Berkeley MSS.* iii, 26–7.

[2] John Smith, *Mem. of Wool*, pp. 81–2.

[3] *Parish Registers of Glouc.* (ed. W. Phillimore), vol. i. See also Exch. Dep. Mich. 5 Jas. I, No. 35.

[4] For this information I am indebted to the courtesy of Mr. Arthur J. Playne, of Longfords, Minchinhampton. [5] Ct. R. portf. 175, No. 13, m. 10. [6] S.P. Dom. Eliz. cxiv, 32 and 34.

[7] Ibid. Add. ix, 56. [8] Ibid. clv, 80.

SOCIAL AND ECONOMIC HISTORY

Considerable confusion appears in descriptions of the industry at this period. Probably it was increasing in bulk, but was rather irregular in its profits, owing to the sudden influx of labour and capital, and owing also to the disturbance of the currency by the earlier Tudors. But questions of money value are notoriously hard to grasp, and in the sixteenth century high prices were always attributed to the covetousness of some class, and believed to be removable by government. The merchant of the staple died a natural death, and we hear no more of him. By fair means or foul, the cloth trade was evidently developing, for it now needed not only the home supply of wool, but imports from Spain. In 1567 125½ hundred lb. of Spanish wool were imported.[1] The development of the Spanish sheep was indeed encouraging other continental countries to make cloth,[2]—another cause probably of the anxiety of the English clothiers, who had hitherto had no rivals of importance outside Flanders.

In 1599 complaints were raised that the cloth dressers of England were suffering by the export of undressed cloth by the merchant adventurers, to be finished abroad.[3] Complaints were also raised that the alnager and sealer interfered with the manufacture (1576).[4] Nevertheless, clothiers and dyers rapidly assumed a leading part in the life of the southern Cotswolds, and considerable fortunes were amassed by some of them. In 1615 Painswick Court-house was purchased by Seaman, a wealthy clothier, and tithes of woad, grown by the Painswick dyers, formed an important item in the tithes paid to Painswick church.[5] In the second quarter of the century, however, a period of real depression began. In 1621 the Justices of the clothing counties received piteous petitions from the weavers, spinners, and fullers as to lack of work ' and, consequentlie, of means of reliefe for themselves and their families.' The clothiers were ordered to provide employment for the discharged workmen, but in their turn complained of the high price of wool, and of the monopoly in the export of cloth enjoyed by the merchant adventurers, who were not sufficient to 'take off' the bulk of the cloth. ' One Will Bennett, a very ancient and good clothier, doth offer to live by brown bread and water, rather than his great number of poore people should want work, if he had means to keep them in work.' Many of them declared they were forced to pawn their clothes to keep their people at work.[6] There were at this time, we learn, 1,500 looms in the county, and some 2,400 persons engaged in the clothing industry. To aid their distress, government could devise no better remedy than sumptuary laws, enjoining the wearing of English cloth (22 June, 1622) ; and later on, it appeared that it was the government regulations which were one cause of the distress. In 1633 petitions were presented to the Justices of Assize from 800 persons at Leonard Stanley and King's Stanley, 'hitherto employed in clothing, and now likely never to be employed again.' Proclamations forbidding gig-mills and the old-fashioned sort of rack [7] had entirely disturbed the makers of red and white broad cloth. So anxious were the ' red clothiers ' that they journeyed to London to further their petition, explaining that they did not now use the ' gig mills, prohibited

---

[1] Exch. Q.R. bdle. 457, No. 35.   [2] S.P. Dom. Add. iv, 29.
[3] S.P. Dom. Eliz. cclxx, 128.   [4] Lansd. 22 (36).
[5] *Hist. of Painswick Church*, S. Clair Baddeley. This may account for the prevalence of the common ' Dyer's Weed,' on the unenclosed ground above Painswick.
[6] S.P. Dom. Jas. I, cxxviii, 49.   [7] S.P. Dom. Chas. I, cclii, 21, and ccxxxvii, App. 16.

by statute, which are used with card wires, theirs being used only with small teazles, for the gentle raising of the cloth at the first work.' If they were not to have the moseing-mills, but to finish the cloth by hand, they would have to use king teazles, which could not be grown in less than two years.[1] In 1640 more successful complaints were made against the restrictions on the manufacture of says, or 'say dyed cloth' (cloth dyed before it was fulled).[2] But neither the gig-mills and moseing-mills nor the desired kind of rack were allowed, though the old restrictions (passed from 1328 to 1606) as to length, breadth, and weight of cloth were removed, and cloth was only to be rejected by the searcher for being falsely made, 'wasted in the hull, squaly, rowy, baudy, holes and the like.'[3] Thrum gatherers, or petty chapmen of cloth, were forbidden, and home-spinning for the market restricted, evidently in order to help the clothiers.

But the woes of the clothiers were not yet cured, when the Civil War was upon them. Some took an active part in the struggle, as Paine, a clothier, who fell with the colours in his hand ;[4] others obtained letters of protection, which availed little against the marauding hands of the soldiers, by whom the clothiers about Stroudwater 'were utterly undone.'[5] It is recorded that the garrison of Beverley Castle was reinforced during the rebellion to 'overawe the wealthy clothiers of Gloucestershire.' Towards the end of the seventeenth century the trade recovered, whether from natural causes or the action of government.[6] In 1677 Gloucestershire weavers were famous enough to be lured to Ireland by a London company.[7] From 1690 to 1760 appears to have been the period of greatest prosperity among the Gloucestershire clothiers, to judge by the numerous houses and tombstones which they have left as witnesses.[8] The dyers were gradually assuming a position of inferiority to the clothiers, who dictated prices to them, and exacted the last farthing for defects in the still difficult art of dyeing.[9]

The wages paid by the clothiers to their employees may be made out from a pamphlet of 1737, computing the amount of work provided in a week by one pack of wool, made into broad cloth :[10]

	£	s.	d.
One man to sort and dry it		8	o
Dyeing and cleaning, etc.	1	10	o
Four men and two boys to scrible it	2	8	o
Thirty women and girls to card and spin	6	o	o
Four boys to spoole and wind quills		10	o
Four women to burle it		12	o
Five „ to scour, full, row, shear, rack, and press it . .	3	4	o
Eight men to weave it	4	16	o
Total. 58 persons employed for a week at	19	8	o

[1] S.P. Dom. Chas. I, ccxliv, 1 and 45. [2] Ibid. cccliv, 29 and 84.
[3] Ibid. dxxxiv, No. 152. [4] *Bibliotheca Gloucestriana*, iii, p. cxliv.
[5] P. H. Fisher, *Notes and Recollections of Stroud.* See S.P. Dom. 1653, xxxvii, 36 ; also Hist. MSS. Com. Rep. iv, 63.
[6] The Acts for burying in woollens, passed by Charles II to encourage the cloth industry, are borne witness to in the parish register of Henbury. *Brist. and Glouc. Arch. Soc. Trans.* xii.
[7] See 'Dialogue between clothier, woolen draper, and yeoman.' Smith, *Mem. of Wool*, 227.
[8] See Bigland, *Gloucestershire*, vol. ii.
[9] In 1718 the prices received by dyers were : 'For colouring one cloth green, 40s. ; for colouring one cloth blue, 28s.–36s.; for woading (a sort of blue put on preparatory to black), 5s. to 24s., though (as was naively admitted), if a cloth was unusually long, and the dyers were forced to take the same price, they used to make the woad so much the worse in proporc'on as might make them amends.' *Cal. of Exch. Spec. Com.* June, 1718, 'at Strowde.' [10] *The Golden Fleece*, 1737.

In 1728, the Justices in quarter sessions, who had already turned their attention to the woollen industry, so far as to appoint 'Inspectors of Cloths, Racks, and Tentors' in Dursley, Uley, Bisley, and Wotton-under-Edge,[1] undertook also to regulate their wages, which were fixed according to the number of hundreds in the chain—i.e. for a chain of 600, 4d. per yard, and so on to 24,000, which would be 2s. the yard.[2] Indentures of apprenticeship were drawn up before the same body, which in 1714 recorded the following terms between Edward Wyat, weaver, of Horsley, and Francis Heskins, apprentice. Heskins is bound for 4¼ years, during which time he is to find himself in food, drink, washing, lodging, and apparel, and may go home every Saturday to Monday. His wages are to be : out of every shilling made by his master, 2½d. in the first year, 3d. the second and third years, 4d. the fourth year.[3]

At a second assessment in 1756 the rate of wages was, however, lowered 50 per cent.[4] by the Justices. A petition from the weavers of ' Hampton, Bisley, Stroud, Painswick, Wotton-under-Edge, Dursley, Horsley, King Stanley, and Rodborough,' presented 5 October, 1756, expressly complained that the masters neglected these regulations, by lengthening the chain upon the bar (from 600 threads to 900), so that a weaver could earn only 4d. by sixteen hours' labour. Many were thus being driven to seek relief from the parish.[5] The clothiers also appeared before the Justices, contesting the weavers' claims with a series of rather contradictory arguments. Weaving, they declared at first, was the work of old men, women, and children, who could not expect full wages. Further inquiry, however, brought out the fact that each loom required one master weaver, who might employ a journey-man, with whom profits were divided in the proportion 7 : 5, and a boy who acted as quill-driver for a very small wage. Often, however, a man and his family would work the loom together, and 13s. to 21s. a week could be earned thus by an industrious family. Instances were quoted of men who worked two looms, with hardly any hired aid, and earned as much as £80 or £90 in the year. It was a weaver's own fault, declared the masters, if he could not earn a good living. They struck, however, a more genuine note when they came to their own difficulties, declaring that the ' wise regulations ' as to measures and methods only hampered trade, and had already ruined the wool industry in other parts of the country, and that to force them to give higher wages would be to destroy their last chance of coping with French competition.[6] Here we probably touch the real trouble, which had already been discussed in 1739, in the letter of a manufacturer, entitled : ' A short account of the State of our Woollen Manufacture, from the Peace of Ryswick,

---

[1] *County Record Books.* There are two sets of books recording quarter sessions, kept in the custody of the clerk of the peace at the Shire Hall, Gloucester.

(a) *The Record Books,* 21 vols., for years 1660 to 1868, though not in an unbroken series.

(b) *The Minute Books,* 15 vols., 1791–1896, containing fuller reports.

[2] See *Record Books ;* also Timothy Exell, *A Brief Hist. of the Weavers of the County of Gloucester,* Stroud, 1838. [3] *Record Books.*

[4] *Record Books,* Mich. Session, 1756. 'White scoured work' was to be woven at 4¾d. ; 'medley work' at 4½d. for every yard, 1,000 threads wide ; 'Clayed work' at 6½d. for every yard and a half, 1,000 threads wide. Every 'hundred' was to contain 190 threads. If Irish warp or abb were used, the payment was to be slightly higher. N.B.—The number of hundred threads to the warp (or chain) determines the width or thickness of the cloth.

[5] *State of the Case and Narrative of the facts Relating to the late Commotions and Risings of the Weavers in the County of Gloucester :* London, 1757. [6] *State of the Case,* op. cit.

shewing their former Flourishing, and their Present Ruinous Condition, and that they always flourished when France could not get our Wool, but declined in Proportion to the quantities of Wool exported to them.' The same writer also speaks of the Irish export of wool as affecting English trade, while Defoe about the same time mentions the influence of French competition. Probably the masters were cutting down wages as low as they could; but a more potent cause of the weavers' special distress was the relaxation of the apprenticeship laws. Apprentices could now be taken very young, and the consequence was an undue increase in the number of weavers, as compared with workmen in other branches of the manufacture. Prices, too, were high at this time.[1] The weavers certainly conceived themselves to have just cause for complaint, for they refused to accept the Justices' decision against them, and raised a riot at Stroud, where several clothiers barely escaped with their lives. On 15 October, 1756, however, an agreement was arrived at, and from this time till 1802, though there may have been discontent, it took no open form. There were, we are told, no combinations of weavers or masters; no weavers needed parish relief; and some of their number made fortunes.[2] Possibly the masters did not fare so well as the men, for the complaints of decaying trade, first mentioned by Defoe,[3] still continued. Yet another writer in 1757 says that some clothiers were making a thousand cloths a year, and that the trade of Stroud was worth £50,000 a year.[4] Rudder, writing in 1779, laments the decay of the trade, yet gives a most attractive description of Chalford-Bottom, with its 'eight fulling-mills' and 'its great number of well-built houses, intermixed with rows of tenters, along the side of the hill, on which the Cloth is stretched.'[5] And though Defoe talks of declining trade, yet all the towns he describes as flourishing were connected with clothing—Cirencester, Tetbury, Marshfield, Minchinhampton, Stroud, Fairford, and Tewkesbury. Stroud is described by Defoe as mainly notorious for its dyeing 'of the beautifullest scarlets and other grand colours that are anywhere in England, perhaps in any part of the world.'[6] 'Cirencester is still a very good town, populous and rich, full of clothiers, and doing a great trade in wool.'[7] By this he means wool-stapling; that is buying up the wool, combing it, and getting it spun in the cottages, for in weaving Cirencester could not hope to vie with the superior water power of the Stroud valley. 'There are,' says a writer of 1800, 'numerous vestiges of the combers' wool-lofts still to be seen in some of their old houses, distinguished by doors in the garret walls, for the conveniency of taking in wool-packs';[8] and one firm of weavers was actually using the same stock-mill that Leland mentions as built by John Blake, the last abbot. The French war, he adds, had put an end to the wool-combing, but corn trade was flourishing, and prosperity generally augmented by a canal joining the Severn and Thames by means of the Churn.

Stow-on-the-Wold was another town still famous in Defoe's time, its ancient fairs being still the centre of commerce to all the Cotswold district. The main articles exchanged there were hops, cheese, and above all sheep, 'of which,' it is said, 'that above 20,000 are generally sold at one fair.'[9]

[1] *State of the Case*, op. cit.
[2] *Brief Hist. of Weavers*, &c.
[3] *Tour through Great Britain* (5th ed. 1753), ii, 37.
[4] *County Curiosities*, 1757; Gough, Glouc. 25.
[5] S. Rudder, *Hist. of Gloucestershire*, 289.
[6] Defoe, op. cit. ii, 316.   [7] Ibid. 268.
[8] *Hist. of Ciren. and Tewkesbury* (1800), 175.
[9] Defoe, op. cit. ii, 261.

SOCIAL AND ECONOMIC HISTORY

For still, as for so many centuries past, it was the Cotswold sheep which formed the main wealth of the hill district, ' so eminent for the best of sheep and the finest wool in the kingdom,' as Defoe says. Larger flocks could be kept, since the introduction of turnips in 1740 enabled the farmers to keep their sheep all winter, instead of sending them to the vale for winter grazing, as used to be the custom. Early in the eighteenth century there were said to be 400,000 sheep in the county,[1] but even so, the local supply could not equal the demands for the clothiers. Stroud alone needed two or three million fleeces in the year, and wool was bought up in all directions. ' The quantities sold here are incredible,' says Defoe.[2] From Berks, Bucks, Northants, and Oxon, waggons poured into Cirencester, while more enterprising dealers went to Kent, Ireland, and, as we have seen (*ante*, p. 159) to Spain. The merino sheep now far surpassed those of England in fineness of wool,[3] thanks to an early infusion of the Cotswold breed, the fleece of which was growing coarser in England, where it was enlarged by crossing with the Leicestershire. When Rudder wrote (1779) the price of Cotswold wool was low as compared even with some other English breeds, and it was used only for worsteds and coarse cloths.

But among towns Bristol towered above its contemporaries. Defoe in 1753 describes it as ' the greatest, the richest and the best Port of Trade in Great Britain, London alone excepted.'[4] The Craft Guilds had long been eclipsed by the Fellowship of Merchants, founded by William Canynges the younger in 1474,[5] and under their guidance the city had flung itself eagerly into foreign trade.[6] Bristol mariners had been among the first to catch the exploring spirit of the age. ' For the last seven years,' reported the Spanish ambassador in 1498, ' the people of Bristol have sent out every year two, three, or four light ships in search of the Island of Brazil.' In 1497 one of its merchants, the Portuguese John Cabot, started on the expedition which discovered Labrador, and a few years later three Bristol men, Warde, Ashehurst, and Thomas, discovered ' New-found-land,' for which feat they received from the royal purse the sumptuous reward of £20 ![7] With the discovery of the West began a new era in the city's prosperity. The clothing industry, which lingered in the city through the seventeenth century[8] and was so flourishing in the country, provided its merchants with abundant material for export ; and in the early sixteenth century one of its cloth merchants, Robert Thorne,[9] also developed the soap manufacture for which Bristol had been notorious since 1242.[10] In 1556 a society of merchant adventurers to Russia was founded under the headship of Cabot, a descendant of the discoverer.[11] In 1578 Frobisher returned to Bristol. Trade sprang up with the Guinea coast also, and in the seventeenth century Bristol merchants played a large share in supplying slaves to America and the West Indies, whence they brought back sugar and tobacco. It is curious to see how the old taint of slave-trading clung to the town ; not content with the supply of black slaves and of English criminals condemned to transportation, the ship-masters of Bristol

---

[1] *County Curiosities, or A New Description of Glouc.* 1757; Gough, op. cit. 25.
[2] Defoe, ii, 268.   [3] Ibid.
[4] Ibid. 292.   [5] H. R. Fox Bourne, *Engl. Merchants*, ch. iv.
[6] *Little Red Book*, ii, 206–10.   [7] H. R. Fox Bourne, op. cit.
[8] A petition of 1590 speaks of ' makyng and ventinge of collored clothes for the sea ' at Bristol.
[9] H. R. Fox Bourne, op. cit.   [10] Seyer, op. cit. ii, 14.   [11] Ibid. 238.

took to kidnapping children for the same purpose, until stopped, in 1685, by that angel of mercy, the Lord Chief Justice Jeffreys ![1] The West Indian trade, however, continued to be enormously profitable, and sugar-refining became almost the chief industry of the town. Pepys (in 1668) describes its glories and those of the ship-yards.[2]

At one time, indeed, the rivalry of Gloucester had threatened to be dangerous. In 1580 that city had received a royal charter, extending the jurisdiction of its port from Tewkesbury down to Berkeley, whereas hitherto the whole river as far as Gloucester had belonged to Bristol. 'Bystowe is maynteyned only by the trade of merchandizes,' pleads a petition of Bristol merchants :

> Gloucester is no place for trade or merchandize, because they have no lawfull wares meete to be transported in shippes, but yf they adventure anything at sea, the same is in small barkes with corn and prohibited wares, wherewith they make more profitable retournes than Brystall wythe their great shippinge and lawfull wares can doe.[3]

In 1626–7 the burgesses of Gloucester received a grant from the crown of the right to levy customs on all ships and merchandise passing through their port (except in the case of towns which, like Tewkesbury, had made special arrangements with them).[4] But the competition of the elder city was not really to be feared. As far back as 1487 the mayor of Gloucester had been complaining of ' the great ruin and decay of the said town, decayed within a few years to the number of three hundred or more dwelling places.'[5] The cloth industry continued, it is true, during the fifteenth or sixteenth century, but in 1646 it was at a low ebb ; nor did the introduction of various small industries, such as pin-making and silk-weaving, in the seventeenth and eighteenth centuries, do much to raise the position of the city.

Before entering on the last period of our county's industrial history, we must turn back to see how agriculture and commerce had been faring in the last three centuries. We have noticed already the tendency to enclose in the sixteenth century, an age in which men suddenly awoke to the advantages of abandoning the open-field system, either for agriculture or sheep farming. Fitzherbert was eloquent on the subject of enclosures, which he discovered to benefit rich and poor alike, for the landlord 'will be saved expence in labour,' and the 'ryche man shall not overeate the poore man with his catell.'[6] The court rolls of the period teem with notices of enclosures, which some manors favoured and others opposed. The queen objects to having her Bisley woods raided for material for hedges ;[7] the tenants of Cheltenham strive to enforce the old rules as to open-field upon each other ;[8] at Bisley tenants are fined for building a 'Piggis cot' on the common, and for keeping 'several' (or enclosed) a field which ought to lie in common.[9]

But the lords went on with their own enclosures, which by 1517 amounted to 3,650 acres on the estates of only twenty-two landlords.[10] In 1548 there were risings against enclosures in Gloucestershire and the west generally,[11] and complaints were raised in the clothing districts that farmers

---

[1] W. Hunt, *Bristol.*　　　　[2] Ibid.
[3] Harl. MSS. 368, quoted by F. D. Fosbrooke, *Hist. of City of Glouc.* p. 25.　　[4] *Glouc. Cal.* No. 31.
[5] Ibid. No. 59.　　[6] Fitzherbert, *Book of Husbandry,* 1534 (ed. W. Skeat, 1882), p. 77.
[7] Ct. R. portf. 175, No. 13.　　[8] Ibid. No. 27.　　[9] Ibid. No. 13.
[10] Inquest of Enclosures in Gloucestershire, Lansd. i, No. 58 (Plut. lxxiii, D, fol. 182.)
[11] See Evidence of Hales, Commissioner of Enclosures, in App. I, iii, to *Discourse of the Common Weal of this Realm of Engl.* 1581 (ed. Eliz. Lamond).

A Balk or Dividing Strip, showing the Meerstone,
Upton St. Leonard's

View of Lynches at Upton St. Leonard's, looking North-east

were becoming clothiers, and clothiers weavers.[1] This shows that the new woollen industry was carried on in conjunction with farming, the same man often growing the wool and hiring weavers to work it in one large room in his farmhouse.

This influx of trade into agriculture completed the destruction of the manorial system. Gloucestershire was one of the last counties where villeinage lingered. In a survey of the duke of Buckingham's lands at Thornbury in 1521, besides complaints of his enclosures of freeholds and copyholds to make his park and 'conyngry' (rabbit-warren), it was reported that there were 'of bondmen a good number.'[2] In 1567 almost the last case relating to villeinage was tried in the law courts, between the lord of Badminton and a certain Crouch, whom he claimed as his villein. In 1574, however, commissions were issued by the queen for enfranchisement of the remaining bondmen in Gloucestershire.[3] Henceforth copyholders, freeholders, and small farmers were all classed together among the famous 'yeoman' class of which we hear so much in the Civil War of the next century. Manor courts might continue, as at Guiting, into the eighteenth century,[4] but now that the judiciary rights of the lords were absorbed by the judges of the crown and justices of the peace they were of little importance. Where they survived they assumed more and more the character of a village meeting for the discussion of economic needs. At Weston-sub-Edge, till its enclosure in 1852, a special vestry meeting, the descendant of the old manor court, had the management of the common-fields, and elected the hayward and fieldsmen, or meresmen, receiving their yearly accounts, levying rates, and deciding in concert as to the course of crops, and the number of beasts which every occupier of a yardland might graze on the common pastures and fallows.[5] At Upton Saint Leonards, where the common-fields were not enclosed till 1897, where the 'meerstones' that divided the strips are still visible, and the newly-planted hedges are only a few feet high (1906), the governing assembly was a real manor court, with a jury of fifteen good and lawful men and a regular form of presentment. The holdings, which were partly freehold and partly copyhold, were still in scattered strips,[6] and very clear evidence of the effect of strip-ploughing upon a sloping ground may be seen in a field called 'the lynches.'[7] The holdings have been re-arranged and enclosed, with the result that the value of the land has risen enormously. Thirteen acres of allotments and two recreation grounds have been provided to atone to the labourer for the loss of common rights; and the old terms of the open-field—'balk,' 'meerstone,' and 'lammas-road'—are already

---

[1] Lamond, op. cit.
[2] I. S. Leadam, 'The Inquisition of 1517,' *Trans. of Engl. Roy. Hist. Soc.* (new ser.), vi, 167–344.
[3] I. S. Leadam, *Law Quarterly Rev.* ix, 348–65.
[4] See loose sheet in *C. C. C. Bursary Books*, 22, containing an account of a court-baron attended by two suitors.
[5] See C. R. Ashbee, *Last Records of a Cotswold Community*, which gives interesting extracts from the Fieldsmen's Books.
[6] See plan.
[7] See Seebohm, *Engl. Village Community*, pp. 5–6. On a slope 'the process of ploughing would result in the soil of the field travelling gradually from the top to the bottom of the field. But the balks between the strips would prevent this.' Thus 'every year's ploughing took a sod from the higher edge of the strip and put it on the lower edge; and the result was that the strips became in time long level terraces, one above the other, and the balks between them grew into steep rough banks of long grass, covered often with natural self-sown brambles and bushes.'

dying out.[1] At Westcot, however, a case of open-field still survives (1905).[2]

But we are advancing too rapidly on the subject of enclosures. In so far as they promoted the use for which the Cotswolds were best fitted, they added to the wealth of that district,—which, indeed, in the seventeenth century is always spoken of as highly prosperous. Even Camden had spoken of the ' golden fleeces ' of the Cotswolds, while Drayton writes enthusiastically of the shepherd's life there. Incidentally, too, he gives an interesting description of the Cotswold sheep of his day—

> No browne nor fulleyed black the face or legs doth streak,
> . . . but Cotswold wisely fills
> Hers with the whitest kind ; whose browes so wooly be
> As men in her faire sheepe no emptiness should see ;
> The Staple deep and thick, thro' to the very graine,
> Most strongly keepeth out the violentest rain ;
> And of the fleecie face, the flanke doth nothing lack,
> But everywhere is stored, the belly as the back,
> As white as winter's snowe. . . .
> The shepherd king,
> Whose flock hath chanced that yeere the earliest lambe to bring,
> In his gay Bauldric sits at his lowe grassie Bord,
> With flawns, curds, clowted-creame & country dainties stor'd ;
> And whilst the bag-pipe plays, each lustie jocund swaine
> Quaffs sillabubs in kans, to all upon the Plaine,
> And to their country-girles whose nosegayes they doe weare ;
> Some Roundelayes doe sing ; the rest the burthen bear.[3]

These were the jolly days of Cotswold when the rustic games for which it had once been famous,[4] but which had vanished under the Puritan *régime*, were revived by Drayton's friend, Mr. Robert Dover, in the reign of James I,[5] at Weston-sub-Edge. Here every Whitsuntide the Gloucester-shire youth contended in coursing, horse-racing, dancing, wrestling, throwing the 'sledge' (hammer ?), and the bar, while chess and kindred games went on in tents for their elders. Dover, a true sportsman,[6] and wise old country gentleman ; Dover the ' joviall,' the attorney who ' never tried but two causes, having always made up the difference,'[7] thus explains his motives, in reply to the ' Poeticall and Learned noble friends ' who had presented him with a volume of poems celebrating his games.

After speaking in praise of these old country sports he says that when men—

> Once those pastimes did forsake,
> And unto drinking did themselves betake,
> So base they grew, that at this present day
> They are not men, but moving lumps of clay.

---

[1] See 'The Common Fields at Upton Saint Leonards,' by Canon E. C. Scobell. *Cotteswold Naturalists' Field Club Proc.* xiii, pt. 3.   [2] H. A. Evans, *Highways and Byways of the Cotswolds*, p. 169.

[3] Drayton, *Polyolbion*, 1889 reprint (Spenser Soc.), p. 233.

[4] See Carving of a Whitsun Ale on north wall of Cirencester parish church.

[5] Cf. also Shakespeare, *Merry Wives*, Act I, scene 1. ' How does your fallow grey-hound, sir ? I heard say he was outrun on Cotsall.' Weston-sub-Edge Fieldsmen's Books mention the letting of the hill every year for the games. C. R. Ashbee, op. cit.

[6] The sporting spirit of the games is thus described, *Annalia Dubrensia* (ed. A. B. Grosart, 1877), p. 41 :

> ' Where horse not for his price doth ride,
> More than his truth (a match as faire),
> And greyhound is for Coller tried,
> More than for death of harmless Hare.'

[7] C. R. Ashbee, op. cit.

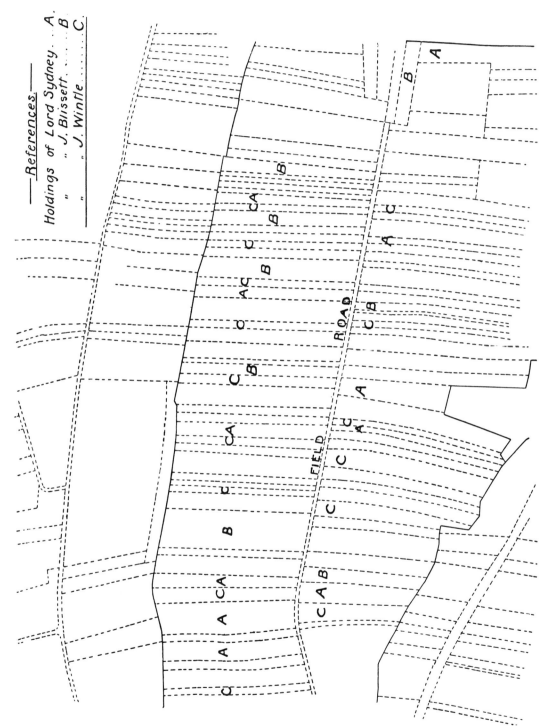

PLAN OF COMMON FIELD AT UPTON ST. LEONARD's, SHOWING METHOD OF HOLDING BY STRIPS

> I've heard our fine refined clergy teach,
> Of the commandment it is a breach
> To play at any Game, for gayne or coyne ;
> One silly beast another to pursue
> 'Gainst nature is, and fearefull to the view ;
> Mix'd dancing is a horrid wicked sin,
> And by the same much naughtinesse hath bin.

In consequence of these clerical teachings, he complains—

> The pipe and pot are now the onely Prise
> Which all our sprightfull youth doe exercise.
>
> .   .   .   .
>
> Yet I was bold, for better recreation,
> 'T' invent these sports to countercheck that fashion.
> I never thought that anyone of you
> In written poems would the same allow.

One cannot but applaud the honest old gentleman's simple lines and cry
'Amen' when he concludes—

> And let Content and Mirth all those attend
> That doe all harmlesse honest sports defend,

and wish with his friend, John Trussell, that—

> While that sheepe have woole or sheepheards sheepe
> Fame shall his actions in remembrance keepe.[1]

But there was a darker side to the agrarian revolution. Hastened as it
was by commercial needs, it brought a new commercial spirit into the dealings
of the legislature with the land. It was probably West Indian traders who
killed the tobacco-planting industry which had arisen in the time of the
Commonwealth about Cheltenham and Winchcombe. Successive Acts (from
1652 onwards) at last brought about its suppression, though in 1667 the
military had to be called in to support the sheriff, who found the local
magistrates far too sympathetic with the unfortunate tobacco-growers.[2]

Enclosures, too, could not be made without evictions, or at any rate
without a loss to the labourer of rights of common and pasture which he
had continued to enjoy long after he had ceased to be a landholder. In 1733
a bill for enclosing the commons and wastes of Bisley was thrown out in
response to a vehement petition from some of the inhabitants, the copyholders, labourers, and small freeholders. This document is interesting, as
giving information as to the woollen industry, and as expressing what was
probably a not uncommon view of enclosures. The common lands and
wastes amount now, it recites, to only 1,000 acres, which have always been
used for pasture by the people of Bisley, and have been freely built over
by the 'Carders, Spinners, Weavers, and numberless Artificers' employed in
the woollen manufacture.

> 'At present there are at least 800 such dwellings.' 'The small Pieces of Land that
> will be allotted them' (by the Bill of Enclosure) 'will bear no Proportion to the Benefit
> of the Commons, in which they were used to keep their cattle till their first grass is cut,
> and their latter grass fit to receive them. 'This Bill,' they declared, 'will entirely destroy
> several hundred industrious families, which are now settled upon these Commons . . . .
> and consequently must prejudice the Woollen Manufacture by removing the hands absolutely
> necessary for their business.'[3]

[1] *Annalia Dubrensia.*

[2] *Hist. MSS. Com. Rep.* xii, App. vii and ix. See also *Bib. Glouc. III,* cxxiv–vii. and S.P. Dom.
1654, lxxii, 27–29 and 65. In 1661 tobacco was 1*s.* a bundle in Gloucester (*Record Books*).

[3] 'Petition against Inclosing divers Parcels of Common and Waste Ground within the manor of Bisleigh,'
bound up in a miscellaneous volume in Bodleian ; Gough Glouc. 32.

The time at which enclosures began undoubtedly coincided with the rise of the vagrant trouble, a fact which confirms the general complaints by sixteenth-century writers, of the lack of subsistence for the small man after the enclosure of commons. In 1504 the Common Council of Gloucester, among various regulations for the improvement of the city's morals, for decency and good order, issued orders to all beggars and poor people to 'avoyde this towne, except such as hath been all dayez dwellyng' there, of whom a strict register was to be kept by the town clerk, and who were to wear the city livery.[1] These were the last efforts of the old order of things, when poverty could be limited and systematized. But the simultaneous breakdown of the guild system and of the manor were producing an irresistible tide of vagrancy, swelled by the general spirit of unrest and love of travel. In 1559 gipsies ('certain persons called Egyptians') were apprehended in Gloucestershire.[2] Successive poor laws, beginning in 1536 and culminating in Elizabeth's famous Poor Law of 1601, were the state's answer to the new problem of poverty and vagrancy which confronted it. From this time the parish was the unit for relief, and the parish accounts are full of items as to dealing with vagrants. Those who had a pass, or certificate, were helped on to their place of birth.[3] The impotent were to be provided for by a poor rate levied on the parish; the able-bodied were to be given work. In Gloucestershire poor-houses were not established till the eighteenth century (the earliest instance I can find is at Colesbourne in 1717[4]), but poor rates were levied for out-door relief, and the justices in quarter sessions were constantly called upon to settle disputes as to liability; 'Must Cubberly pay for the relief of the poor of Cowley?' and so on. With the quarter sessions, too, a statute of 1563 had placed the power of fixing rates of wages, and of apprenticing poor children. Punishments could be inflicted on those who refused either to be bound, or to receive, apprentices[5] to agricultural labour; rather more licence was allowed to the employers of artisan labour. In 1682 the Justices of the Seven Hundreds Division ordered 'all the younger people of the age to go to service, and live at their own hands, to appear before them, that care may be taken to apprentice them, and punish those that refuse.' The 'County Stock' could be drawn upon for the expenses of apprenticeship, and probably could well afford it.[6] In 1681 only five cases demanding poor relief came before the quarter sessions of Gloucester; in 1682, ten; in 1683, nineteen; in 1684, fourteen; in 1685, four; in 1686, seventeen.[7] But the fatal doctrine of Settlements (embodied in an Act of 1662) proved as much more expensive as it was more harmful than the old system. The cost of transporting vagrants (i.e. all who could not prove that they would never become chargeable) to their place of settlement now fell upon the county, which made constant attempts at economy. In 1712 the justices fixed the cost of conveying a vagrant at 4d. per mile, with 4d. a day for his maintenance, and ordered a stricter examination of travelling certificates, lest men should be 'encouraged to spend their lives in wandering from one part of the kingdom to another.' One would hardly think the poor law of the day offered much temptation to permanent tramping, but in

---

[1] *Hist. MSS. Com. Rep.* xii, App. pt. ix, 436–7.   [2] S. P. Dom. Eliz. vii, 20.
[3] e.g. Churchwardens' Accounts of Dursley, 1621–1734, frequent notices :—'To a poor man with a passe, 2s. To an Irish poor man with a certificate, 1s.'   [4] *Record Books.*
[5] See *Record Books,* 1682–3.   [6] Act of 1662.   [7] *Record Books.*

1716 the same order was repeated and a new house of correction built at Bristol for the detention of vagrants, and supposed saving of expense of their transport.[1] In 1801[2] the cost of transport was still the same, though 6d. was allowed for subsistence of the vagrant, and in 1803 the constables were warned that they were expected to travel fifteen miles a day with their victims, whether on foot or in a cart. But if the Act of 1672 was costly, the later poor laws of 1782 and 1796, which abandoned the workhouse test, and added allowances from the rates, to bring up wages to a supposed minimum standard of living, proved ruinous. The Settlement Act had caused endless disputes between parishes (one parish objecting to So-and-so being settled on it);[3] the allowance system led to a war of classes. Employers cut down wages, trusting to supplements from the rates; rate-payers struggled to keep down rates; labourers grew more and more idle and rebellious. An attempt was made to work upon the old spirit of local responsibility by the Settlement Act. Tithing-men of vills were still elected,[4] and the parish was organized as the unit of the poor law. But, in other respects, local self-government was practically extinct, and the county was managed chiefly by the justices of the peace. With the abandonment of the old systems of justice it was still only very slowly that the ancient cruel forms of punishment were dropped. In 1716 a man was put in the pillory at Newnham for shooting a deer in the Forest of Dean. In 1718 the ducking-stool was used for the last time at Bristol.[5] An accusation of witchcraft was brought as late as 1726 against a Winchcombe woman, who, however, was allowed to take out a warrant against her accusers; while about the same date occurred an appeal to a still more barbarous piece of legal usage—the *peine forte et dure*. The criminal, a house-breaker, was only induced to plead in court by the sheriff sending a carpenter 'to measure his body for an engine to press him.'[6] About 1770 whipping was revived by the justices,[7] and was a favourite form of punishment till 1789, when it was objected to at quarter sessions.[8] In 1779 occurred the last case of branding in Gloucestershire, at the Gloucester Booth Hall.

In 1795 the magistrates at Gloucester drew up a table, showing what they considered to be the minimum weekly income of the 'industrious poor.' Bread was then 1½d. per lb. (wheat 75s. 2d. per quarter), and 8 lbs. of bread per week were calculated as necessary for each member of a family. Another shilling a week was allowed for articles of necessity for the man, and 8d. for the wife. This brought the weekly income up to 7s. 8d. per week for a husband, wife and four children, with bread at the price then prevalent. A sliding scale was drawn up, allowing for the rise of bread to 3¼d. per lb., when the same family would receive 14s. 8d. The deficiency of a labourer's wage below this minimum was to be made good by the parish.[9] With this allowance we may compare that made in 1681, when wheat was only about 40s., to a poor woman with five children at Duntis-

---

[1] *Record Books.*   [2] *Minute Books*, vol. i.
[3] The Gloucestershire Justices had in 1725 to decide a difficult problem of settlement, when a man's bed was so placed that he lay in two parishes. It was determined that his settlement lay where his head lay, 'as being the more honourable part'; J. J. Powell, *Gloucestriana*, 'Journ. of a Glouc. Justice.'
[4] *Record Books.*   [5] W. Hunt, op. cit.   [6] J. J. Powell, op. cit.
[7] *Record Books.*   [8] Gough Glouc. 32.   [9] *Minute Books*, vol. i.

bourne Abbots, who received 25s. a week.[1] Eight pounds of bread was not a large allowance, for the Gloucester prisoners about 1790 were receiving 10½ lb. a week, besides a pint of strong soup, 'made from coarse but wholesome meat.'[2] After the rise of wheat in 1801 (to 119s. 6d. per quarter) the prisoner's weekly fare was, however, cut down to 7 lb.[3] In 1802 vain efforts were made by the magistrates at Gloucester to enforce the Ancient Assize of Bread, in order to keep down prices. This must have been the worst period in the history of the Gloucestershire labourer. In 1632, when wheat was 38s. 8d., an ordinary labourer's wage in Gloucestershire had been fixed by quarter sessions at 8d. a day, or 4s. a week, a carpenter's at 6s., and a tiler's at 7s. per week. In 1655 the same labourers received respectively 5s., 10s. and 7s. Wheat was then cheaper—20s. per quarter. In 1632 the labourer would thus have been very badly off, earning, according to Rogers' calculations, £10 8s. 4d., while the artisan earned £16 5s. Neither could have earned a proper living, which would have cost £16 8s. (allowing for a family of four persons). In 1655 provisions for a similar family would only have cost £9 7s. 4d., and wages had risen, so that an agricultural labourer could earn his store of food for the year by thirty-five weeks' labour, a chief carpenter or mason in nineteen weeks, and a tiler in thirty weeks.[4] We get no further statistics as to the wages of the agricultural labourer till 1769 (only two quarter sessions assessments having been preserved for Gloucestershire). Arthur Young reports that the average price of day labour in Gloucestershire was from 8d. to 10d. a day (4s. to 5s. a week) in winter and spring, 1s. in summer, and 1s. 8d. in harvest time. Wheat was threshed at from 10d. to 2s. per quarter, which he considers an unusually low rate.[5] Wheat was then about 35s. per quarter, so that the labourer's condition was nearly as bad in 1769 as it had been in 1632. Since the fourteenth century it had declined enormously, prices having risen by a multiple of 8 to 12, wages only by a multiple of 4.[6] Except in the richer parts of the Vale, Young seems to have been struck with the backward state of the county and lack of enclosures, of which only sixteen had been made in Gloucestershire in 1769. By 1801, however, some forty more enclosures had taken place, mainly in the Vale, or on the edges of the Wolds, and from this time onwards the process went on in an ever-increasing stream.[7] By 1821 when Cobbett's 'rural rides' first brought him to Gloucestershire, he was able to admire the Vale country as seen from 'Burlip Hill.' 'All here is fine; fine farms; fine pastures; all inclosed fields; all divided by hedges; orchards a plenty.' 'The girls at work in the fields are not in rags,' as in Wiltshire.[8] But for the hill country he does not find much good to say, except that the turnips were good, and that the ox-teams used for ploughing were 'some of the finest I ever saw.'[9] He notes the falling-off of the population about Withington, owing to the

---

[1] *Record Books.* [2] *Gough Glouc.* 32. [3] *Minute Books,* i.
[4] Rawlinson MSS. C. 358, quoted by Rogers, *Hist. of Agric. and Prices,* v, 622–3.
[5] *Tour through the Southern Counties,* 2nd ed. [6] Rogers, *Hist. of Agric. and Prices,* i, ch. 29.
[7] See Return of Commons (Inclosure Awards), Feb. 1894. The confusion of manors and townships, which has been noticed above (p. 142), was a considerable source of trouble when enclosures had to be made. Parishes were found to be much intermixed, and detached portions were common. In some cases several parishes held intermixed strips in one large common field. One enclosure near Gloucester included pieces of ten parishes. See Minutes of Evidence before Com. on Boundaries of Parishes, *Parl. Pap.* 1873, vol. viii (308). [8] *Rural Rides* (ed. W. P. Cobbett), i, 23–4. [9] Ibid. ii, 178.

change that had come over the woollen industry with the introduction of machinery.[1] The year 1821 was, indeed, noted in Gloucestershire for the heaviness of its poor rates, the total cost of apprehending and conveying vagrants being £2,074, as compared with £1,053 in 1817, and £1,055 in 1822.[2] This may have been due to the disturbance in the woollen industry, for it was about this period that the factory system was started. It was immensely unpopular with the weavers, who were already furious at the abolition of the apprenticeship laws, which they considered their protection (1802), and who now complained that they were driven from their houses to work as prisoners at the shop-looms.[3] In 1821 a reduction of wages by the masters was resisted by the weavers, more than a hundred of whom were imprisoned. In 1825 a printed agreement as to wages restored peace between the masters and men at Dursley, but was not accepted by the Stroud clothiers. In 1828 the latter reduced wages to a truckster's standard, in order to meet foreign competition,[4] and in 1830, finding it difficult to carry on the factory system by forcing the weavers to bring their looms to a central building, they introduced power looms. The weavers promptly struck, and a further reduction of wages in 1838 did not lessen the bitter feeling stirred up between them and the masters.[5]

It is difficult to get any clear account of the condition of the agricultural labourer in Gloucestershire in the first half of the nineteenth century. In 1836, when an inquiry was held as to causes of agricultural distress,[6] the three Gloucestershire farmers who gave evidence seemed agreed that, with low prices and wages of 8s. to 12s. a week, the labourer was better off than he had been for some time. It was the farmer who was hard hit by the low price of wheat, which had fallen in the Bristol market from 50s. per quarter in 1833 to 38s. 8d. in 1835.[7] Even so, however, the three witnesses did not think so very badly of the prospects of farming in Gloucestershire. The price of corn went on rising, till it reached 74s. in 1855, since when it has steadily fallen to 26s. in 1899.[8] From 1861, similarly, the census returns show a steady diminution in the agricultural population of the county. Yet, while land has been allowed to revert to pasture, and the amount of field labour has diminished, the wages of the labourer have increased. Between 1849 and 1853, when a bad harvest made prices high in spite of the repeal of the corn laws, his wage was about 7s. 6d. a week; in 1861 it was 10s. in the Vale, 9s. on the Hill; between 1865 and 1890 about 11s. In 1898 it ranged from 10s. to 15s., the average being about 13s. in summer and 12s. in winter. Cottages are sometimes allowed free, and in a few cases beer or cider is given, but, on the whole, allowances are less than in the fifties.[9]

On the whole, agriculture seems to have a brighter outlook in Gloucestershire at the present day. There is a considerable demand for small holdings (especially in the fruit districts along the Severn), which is a hopeful

---

[1] *Rural Rides* (ed. W. P. Cobbett), ii, 175.

[2] Accounts of Treasurers of the Counties of sums paid for Apprehension of Vagrants, *Parl. Pap.* 1823, vol. xv (No. 456).

[3] T. Exell, op. cit.   [4] Ibid.   [5] Ibid.

[6] 3rd Rep. of Select Com. on Agric. Distress, *Parl. Pap.* 1836, vol. viii (2), (No. 465).

[7] 2nd Rep. on Agric. Distress, *Parl. Pap.* 1836, vol. viii (1), (No. 189).

[8] Agric. Returns for 1899 (B. of Agric.), C. d. 166.

[9] Report of B. of Trade on Wages and Earnings of Agric. Labourers, *Parl. Pap.* 1900, vol. lxxxii. (C. d. 346).

sign, socially.[1] The towns, too, have begun to revive. Bristol, which lost its supereminent position in the West Indian trade owing to the rise of Liverpool, in the wool trade owing to London's rivalry, and in the sugar manufacture owing to Free Trade, has taken a new lease of life since 1888, when the city bought two new docks built at Avonmouth and Portishead, and took over the entire control of its own trade.[2] Gloucester has benefited enormously by the opening first, of the Berkeley Canal in 1827; secondly, by the formation of a canal joining the Stroudwater Canal, which completed the waterway between Gloucester and London (1836); and thirdly, by the improvement of her harbour at Sharpness (1874), which now permits the entrance of a ship of 4,000 tons. Cheltenham, which became a watering place in the latter half of the eighteenth century, is now one of the most thriving towns in the county. Even in the Stroud Valley, where the woollen industry has been passing through a terribly bad period, the manufacturers seem not unhopeful as to the future. Thus, though Gloucestershire has somewhat the air of a home of lost causes, though crumbling mills in half-forgotten valleys, and ruined cottages on her upland pastures, seem to testify to a greatness that has passed away, we cannot but hope that the county has a better future in store. The establishment of the Guild of Handicraft at Chipping Campden should set an example to all those who desire to see the return of industry to healthy and beautiful surroundings. In such a reformation Gloucestershire, with the variety of resources of which we have said so much, might play a leading part.

APPENDIX I[3]

TABLE OF WAGES[4] IN GLOUCESTERSHIRE, FOURTEENTH TO TWENTIETH CENTURY

Occupation	Date	Daily Wage	Occupation	Date	Daily Wage
		s. d.			s. d.
Carpenter . . .	1302	0 4	Tiler (cont.)	1673	1 0
	1371	0 4		1703	1 0
	1412	0 4		1870	4 0
	1449	0 5		1906	4s. to 6 8
	1570	0 10 to 1s.			
	1632	1 0		1266	0 0½
	1655	1 8		1345	0 1½
	1732	1 2		1371	0 1½
	1860	2 2 to 3s.		1412	0 2
	1906	3 9 to 8s.	Agricultural Labourer (i.e. weeding, ditching, or 'ordinary labour')	1551	0 6
	1302	0 4		1632	0 8
	1397	0 4		1655	0 10
Tiler	1449	0 5		1767	8d. to 1 2
	1493	0 6½		1836	1s. 6d. to 2 0
	1632	1 2		1850	1 2
	1655	1 2		1880	1 9
				1898	2 2

[1] H. Rider Haggard, *Rural Engl.* i. [2] W. Hunt, op. cit.
[3] Number in *italic* drawn from Rogers's average for whole country in that year.
[4] Drawn from Mins. Accts. Churchwardens Accts. two Quarter Sessions Assessments (Rawlinson MSS. C. 358), A. Young, 'Tour through Southern Counties,' Parl. Blue Bks., and Thorold Rogers, *Hist. of Agric. and Prices.*

APPENDIX II

TABLE OF PRICES OF COTSWOLD SHEEP AND WOOL, FOURTEENTH TO TWENTIETH CENTURY, COMPARED WITH AVERAGE COST OF THE SAME THROUGHOUT ENGLAND [1]

——	Date	Cotswold	Average (Ordinary Wool)	——	Date	Cotswold	Average
		s. *d.*				*s.* *d.*	
	1380	9 4	6*s.* 5*d.*		1371	1 6	1*s.* 7*d.* (1371–80)
	1421	13 1	7*s.* 5½*d.*		1426	1 2	1*s.* 6½*d.* (1421–30)
	1446	10 8	4*s.* 10½*d.* (1441–50)		1439	1 6	1*s.* 9*d.* (1431–40)
	1452	7 0	} 4*s.* 3½*d.* (1451–60)	Sheep . .	1592	10 0	9*s.* 0½*d.*
	1459	9 4			—	—	11*s.* 0½*d.* (1693–1702)
	1481	13 4 (unusually high)	4*s.* 8½*d.* (1481–90)		1836	33 0	—
Todd of Wool (28 lb.)					1906	40*s.* to 50*s.*	50*s.* to 60*s.*
	1550	under 19*s.*	} 15*s.* 8*d.* (1551–60)				Average 1260–1400 1 lb. 7¾ oz.
	1552	30 0			1411	1¾ lb.	
	1581	20 0	17*s.* (1571–82)		1449	1⅙ lb.	14 oz. (1450)
	1592	30 0	20*s.* (1583–1600)	Weight of fleece.	—	—	1 lb. 10 oz. (1570)
	1661	28 0	Spanish wool, 84*s.*; Herefords, 74*s.* 7½*d.*		—	—	3–4 lb. (1760) (A. Young)
	1779	24 10½	—		1836	6 lb.	—
	1836	45 0	—		1870	8–10 lb.	6–8 lb. (cross-bred)
	1840	70 0	—		1906	10–12 lb.	} 8–10 lb. (cross-bred); 10–14 lb.(Oxf.Down)
	1870	40*s.* to 45*s.*	40*s.* to 45*s.*				
	1906	28*s.* to 35*s.*	28*s.* to 36*s.*				

TABLE OF POPULATION, 1801 TO 1901
INTRODUCTORY NOTES

Area

The county taken in this table is that existing subsequently to 7 & 8 Vict., chap. 61 (1844). By this Act detached parts of counties, which had already for parliamentary purposes been amalgamated with the county by which they were surrounded or with which the detached part had the longest common boundary (2 & 3 Wm. IV, chap. 64—1832), were annexed to the same county for all purposes ; some exceptions were, however, permitted.

By the same Act (7 & 8 Vict., chap. 61) the detached parts of counties, transferred to other counties, were also annexed to the hundred, ward, wapentake, &c. by which they were wholly or mostly surrounded, or to which they next adjoin, in the counties to which they were transferred. The hundreds, &c. in this table are also given as existing subsequently to this Act.

As is well known, the famous statute of Queen Elizabeth for the relief of the poor took the then-existing ecclesiastical parish as the unit for Poor Law relief. This continued for some centuries with but few modifications ; notably by an Act passed in the thirteenth year of Charles II's reign which permitted townships and villages to maintain their own poor. This permission was necessary owing to the large size of some of the parishes, especially in the north of England.

In 1801 the parish for rating purposes (now known as the civil parish, i.e. 'an area for which a separate poor rate is or can be made, or for which a separate overseer is or can be appointed') was in most cases co-extensive with the ecclesiastical parish of the same name ; but already there were numerous townships and villages rated separately for the relief of the poor, and also there were many places scattered up and down the country, known as extra-parochial places, which paid no rates at all. Further, many parishes had detached parts entirely surrounded by another parish or parishes.

Parliament first turned its attention to extra-parochial places, and by an Act (20 Vict., chap. 19—1857) it was laid down (a) that all extra-parochial places entered separately in the 1851 census returns are to be deemed civil parishes, (b) that in any other place being, or being reputed to be, extra-parochial overseers of the poor may be appointed, and (c) that where, however, owners and occupiers of two-thirds in value of the land of any such place desire its annexation to an adjoining civil parish, it may be so added with the consent of the said parish. This Act was not found entirely to fulfil its object, so by a further Act (31 & 32 Vict., chap. 122—1868) it was enacted that every such place remaining on the 25 December, 1868, should be added to the parish with which it had the longest common boundary.

The next thing to be dealt with was the question of detached parts of civil parishes, which was done by the Divided Parishes Acts of 1876, 1879, and 1882. The last, which amended the one of 1876, provides that every detached part of an entirely extra metropolitan parish which is entirely

[1] Drawn from Mins. Accts., Parl. Papers, Cely Papers, A. Young, Thorold Rogers, Cotswold Flock Book, i, ii, and personal inquiry.

surrounded by another parish becomes transferred to this latter for civil purposes, or if the population exceeds 300 persons it may be made a separate parish. These Acts also gave power to add detached parts surrounded by more than one parish to one or more of the surrounding parishes, and also to amalgamate entire parishes with one or more parishes. Under the 1879 Act it was not necessary for the area dealt with to be entirely detached. These Acts also declared that every part added to a parish in another county becomes part of that county.

Then came the Local Government Act, 1888, which permits the alteration of civil parish boundaries and the amalgamation of civil parishes by Local Government Board orders. It also created the administrative counties. The Local Government Act of 1894 enacts that where a civil parish is partly in a rural district and partly in an urban district each part shall become a separate civil parish ; and also that where a civil parish is situated in more than one urban district each part shall become a separate civil parish, unless the county council otherwise direct. Meanwhile, the ecclesiastical parishes had been altered and new ones created under entirely different Acts, which cannot be entered into here, as the table treats of the ancient parishes in their civil aspect.

POPULATION

The first census of England was taken in 1801, and was very little more than a counting of the population in each parish (or place), excluding all persons, such as soldiers, sailors, &c., who formed no part of its ordinary population. It was the *de facto* population (i.e. the population actually resident at a particular time) and not the *de jure* (i.e. the population really belonging to any particular place at a particular time). This principle has been sustained throughout the censuses.

The Army at home (including militia), the men of the Royal Navy ashore, and the registered seamen ashore were not included in the population of the places where they happened to be, at the time of the census, until 1841. The men of the Royal Navy and other persons on board vessels (naval or mercantile) in home ports were first included in the population of those places in 1851. Others temporarily present, such as gipsies, persons in barges, &c. were included in 1841 and perhaps earlier.

GENERAL

Up to and including 1831 the returns were mainly made by the overseers of the poor, and more than one day was allowed for the enumeration, but the 1841–1901 returns were made under the superintendence of the registration officers and the enumeration was to be completed in one day. The Householder's Schedule was first used in 1841. The exact dates of the censuses are as follows :—

10 March, 1801	30 May, 1831	8 April, 1861	6 April, 1891
27 May, 1811	7 June, 1841	3 April, 1871	1 April, 1901
28 May, 1821	31 March, 1851	4 April, 1881	

NOTES EXPLANATORY OF THE TABLE

This table gives the population of the ancient county and arranges the parishes, &c. under the hundred or other sub-division to which they belong, but there is no doubt that the constitution of hundreds, &c. was in some cases doubtful.

In the main the table follows the arrangement in the 1841 census volume.

The table gives the population and area of each parish, &c. as it existed in 1801, as far as possible.

The areas are those supplied by the Ordnance Survey Department, except in the case of those marked ' e,' which are only estimates. The area includes inland water (if any), but not tidal water or foreshore.

† after the name of a civil parish indicates that the parish was affected by the operation of the Divided Parishes Acts, but the Registrar-General failed to obtain particulars of every such change. The changes which escaped notification were, however, probably small in area and with little, if any, population. Considerable difficulty was experienced both in 1891 and 1901 in tracing the results of changes effected in civil parishes under the provisions of these Acts ; by the Registrar-General's courtesy, however, reference has been permitted to certain records of formerly detached parts of parishes which has made it possible approximately to ascertain the population in 1901 of parishes as constituted prior to such alterations, though the figures in many instances must be regarded as partly estimates.

* after the name of a parish (or place) indicates that such parish (or place) contains a union workhouse which was in use in (or before) 1851 and was still in use in 1901.

‡ after the name of a parish (or place) indicates that the ecclesiastical parish of the same name at the 1901 census is coextensive with such parish (or place).

0 in the table indicates that there is no population on the area in question.

— in the table indicates that no population can be ascertained.

The word ' chapelry ' seems often to have been used as an equivalent for ' township ' in 1841, which census volume has been adopted as the standard for names and descriptions of areas.

The figures in italics in the table relate to the area and population of such sub-divisions of ancient parishes as chapelries, townships, and hamlets.

SOCIAL AND ECONOMIC HISTORY

TABLE OF POPULATION, 1801—1901

—	Acreage	1801	1811	1821	1831	1841	1851	1861	1871	1881	1891	1901
Ancient or Geographical County[1]	795,709	250,723	285,955	336,190	387,398	431,495	458,805	485,777	534,646	572,433	600,056	634,843

PARISH	Acreage	1801	1811	1821	1831	1841	1851	1861	1871	1881	1891	1901
Berkeley Hundred—Lower Division												
Almondsbury (part of)[2]:—												
Almondsbury Tything	7,009	350	402	477	517	603	599	686	600	2,188	2,047	2,160
Elberton ‡	1,531	179	191	203	199	190	204	180	163	158	144	132
Filton †‡	1,040	115	168	210	217	276	245	317	290	296	311	464
Henbury (part of)[3]	—	401	744	489	436	525	541	550	505	—	—	—
Hill ‡	2,053	220	228	259	257	227	216	216	218	206	214	200
Horfield †	1,299	119	146	198	328	620	1,221	1,746	2,985	5,739	8,202	13,975
Berkeley Hundred—Upper Division												
Arlingham	2,461	506	571	715	744	793	737	693	697	626	566	455
Ashleworth ‡	1,766	476	503	498	540	594	590	547	564	501	450	410
Berkeley:—	14,552	3,090	3,236	3,835	3,899	4,405	4,344	4,316	4,607	5,038	5,307	5,299
Berkeley †[4]	57	658	616	836	901	926	949	1,011	1,161	870	890	774
Alkington Tything †	4,099	816	893	1,101	1,167	1,175	1,134	1,010	921	854	818	771
Stone Chap.	4,410	835	269	963	903	296	276	277	260	818	830	766
Ham Tything			613			632	601	577	635			
Hamfallow Tything[5]	2,870	394		437	645	697	667	692	928	1,038	1,020	1,093
Hinton Tything	1,914	257	845	346	162	539	579	620	562	1,313	1,629	1,763
Breadstone Tything	1,202	130		152	121	140	138	129	140	145	120	132
Beverstone ‡	2,150	150	162	160	174	178	199	170	164	190	168	185
Cam †	2,946°	1,285	1,501	1,885	2,071	1,851	1,640	1,500	1,667	1,758	1,778	1,713
Coaley †‡	2,463°	800	909	1,117	1,124	979	788	777	780	735	654	618
Cromhall Abbots ‡	2,594	550	567	703	761	732	766	681	669	592	606	589
Dursley *†‡	1,059°	2,379	2,580	3,186	3,226	2,931	2,752	2,477	2,413	2,344	2,273	2,372
Kingscote †	1,810°	271	246	266	276	295	297	311	255	272	233	220
Kingswood ‡[6]	2,365	901	963	1,391	1,447	1,321	1,227	1,061	898	932	938	908
Newington Bagpath †	2,131°	217	205	247	258	278	239	242	223	207	185	146
North Nibley †‡	3,245°	1,211	1,290	1,553	1,562	1,305	1,133	1,020	944	820	801	722
Nympsfield †‡	1,472°	523	532	462	454	466	417	373	275	269	235	216
Owlpen †	720°	188	181	232	255	94	82	91	105	110	102	59
Ozleworth ‡	1,148	133	123	134	152	106	88	130	124	78	121	136

[1] *Ancient County.*—The county as defined by 7 & 8 Vic. c. 61, which altered Gloucestershire to the following extent:—(1) *Added to Gloucestershire*, Kingswood and Poulton parishes (from Wilts), parts of Iccomb ancient parish, viz. Church Iccomb township, and Overbury ancient parish, viz. the hamlets of Little Washbourne and Alstone (from Worcestershire); (2) *severed from Gloucestershire*, Widford and Shenington ancient parishes (to Oxfordshire), Little Compton and Sutton-under-Brailes ancient parishes (to Warwickshire), Minty ancient parish (to Wiltshire), and part of Lea ancient parish, viz. Lea Lower (to Herefordshire). In addition to these changes part of Broughton Poggs ancient parish, viz. Great Lemhill Farm, and part of Great Barrington ancient parish were also added to Gloucestershire by the same statute, from Oxfordshire and Berkshire respectively; these areas, however, had always been returned with Gloucestershire. The area is taken from the 1901 Census Volume. (See also notes to Welford and Bristol.)

[2] *Almondsbury Ancient Parish* is situated (1) partly in Berkeley hundred, Lower Division; (2) partly in Langley and Swinehead hundred, Lower Division; and (3) partly in Thornbury hundred, Lower Division. The limits of the Tythings were ill-defined, and the area and entire population (1881-1901) are entered in Berkeley hundred, Lower Division.

[3] *Henbury Ancient Parish* is situated (1) partly in Berkeley hundred, Lower Division, and (2) partly in Henbury hundred, Lower and Upper Divisions. The whole parish—area and population (1881-1901)—except the areas and populations of Aust, and Northwick with Redwick chapelries, is shown as Henbury Tything.

[4] *Berkeley Tything* included, in 1871, a number of workmen engaged in constructing Sharpness Docks.

[5] *Hamfallow.*—The increase in 1871 is ascribed to the presence of men engaged in constructing a new canal and some docks.

[6] *Kingswood* included, in 1841, eighty labourers employed on the Great Western Railway

TABLE OF POPULATION, 1801—1901 (*continued*)

Parish	Acreage	1801	1811	1821	1831	1841	1851	1861	1871	1881	1891	1901
Berkeley Hundred —Upper Division (cont.)												
Slimbridge † ‡ . .	3,747	770	794	807	923	866	859	789	854	854	872	804
Stinchcombe Par. Chap. † ‡	1,464°	419	371	432	352	393	354	340	334	336	315	278
Uley †	1,492°	1,724	1,912	2,655	2,641	1,743	1,327	1,230	1,156	1,043	930	954
Wotton-under-Edge † ‡	4,880°	3,393	3,800	5,004	5,482	4,702	4,224	3,673	3,651	3,349	3,254	2,979
Bisley Hundred												
Bisley †	7,927	4,227	4,757	5,421	5,896	5,339	4,801	4,692	4,985	5,169	5,202	4,811
Edgeworth ‡ . .	1,598	116	123	134	116	149	148	139	124	130	140	152
Miserden † ‡ . .	2,434°	469	502	514	441	509	489	503	452	430	369	337
Painswick † . . .	5,614	3,150	3,201	4,044	4,099	3,730	3,464	3,229	4,019	4,044	4,134	4,067
Sapperton † ‡ . .	3,908°	351	368	476	453	585	646	600	571	529	514	422
Stroud * † . . .	3,731	5,422	5,321	7,097	8,607	8,680	8,798	9,090	9,957	11,112	11,677	10,785
Winstone ‡ . . .	1,491	143	169	192	164	262	252	230	227	231	200	187
Bledisloe Hundred												
Alvington . . .	1,582	211	213	272	281	340	370	369	408	387	408	392
Awre	4,329	952	1,035	1,138	1,130	1,277	1,512	1,526	1,345	1,179	1,148	1,096
Lydney ‡ :—	7,075	1,032	1,160	1,393	1,534	1,885	2,577	2,889	3,353	3,194	3,632	4,290
Lydney . . .	5,185	783	820	1,040	1,746	1,417	1,989	2,285	2,692	2,545	2,944	3,559
Aylburton Chap.	1,890	249	340	353	388	468	588	604	661	649	688	731
Botloe Hundred												
Bromsberrow ‡ .	1,810	235	274	335	337	283	260	305	272	266	282	255
Dymock	7,009	1,223	1,342	1,558	1,656	1,776	1,771	1,870	1,778	1,529	1,401	1,316
Kempley ‡ . . .	1,593	218	286	301	302	342	305	311	306	281	272	210
Newent * . . .	8,091	2,354	2,538	2,660	2,859	3,099	3,306	3,182	3,168	2,889	2,605	2,485
Oxenhall † ‡ . .	1,887°	313	347	323	306	292	288	272	245	231	190	208
Pauntley † ‡. .	1,967°	215	230	280	263	249	256	233	205	216	183	188
Rudford (part of)† [1]	1,204°	87	94	97	103	125	136	105	141	124	125	113
Taynton ‡ . . .	2,521	378	416	516	555	634	631	689	635	568	487	463
Upleadon ‡ . . .	1,230	160	183	182	241	250	275	237	245	232	206	192
Bradley Hundred												
Aston Blank, or Cold Aston ‡	2,360	216	247	296	295	302	310	325	311	300	255	214
Bibury (part of) [2] :—												
Winson Chap. .	1,216	145	171	185	176	202	170	181	181	162	134	109
Coln Rogers ‡ . .	1,574	110	139	139	135	137	156	116	90	107	93	102
Compton Abdale †‡	2,215°	157	180	184	188	260	256	258	232	220	213	178
Dowdeswell ‡ . .	2,246°	196	185	181	232	249	304	350	331	483	283	255
Farmington ‡ . .	2,261	216	232	245	311	359	339	284	275	269	243	182
Hampnett [3] . . .	1,431	90	82	121	187	195	211	156	151	165	162	108
Hazleton ‡ :—	2,829	195	224	265	287	286	278	308	337	335	303	249
Hazleton . . .	1,566	98	111	146	164	193	189	185	208	196	172	145
Yanworth Chap.	1,263	97	113	119	123	93	89	123	129	139	131	104
Northleach ‡ :—	3,997	814	793	993	1,061	1,290	1,352	1,404	1,310	1,206	1,106	968
Northleach . .	43	664	647	773	795	939	931	962	901	831	787	661
Eastington Tything *	3,954	150	146	220	266	351	421	442	409	375	319	307
Notgrove ‡ . . .	1,724	214	211	198	166	181	195	162	165	132	133	134
Salperton ‡ . . .	1,401	186	162	173	216	206	145	189	141	145	131	139
Sevenhampton ‡ .	3,377	349	334	386	465	471	553	543	526	456	399	400
Shipton Oliffe † [4] }	2,210°	239	207	177	229	222	241	255	253	376	340	292
Shipton Sollars [4] }				62	98	126	96	80	118			
Stowell	851	13	34	33	43	42	28	41	46	50	83	67
Turkdean ‡ . . .	2,178	143	164	228	237	246	278	291	337	298	205	145
Whittington ‡ . .	1,479	194	198	215	247	231	233	217	183	225	179	187
Withington † . .	5,830°	572	650	759	743	818	823	783	768	626	589	630

[1] *Rudford Ancient Parish* is situated (1) partly in Botloe hundred, and (2) partly in Dudstone and King's Barton hundred, Lower Division. The entire area is entered in Botloe hundred.

[2] *Bibury Ancient Parish* is situated (1) partly in Bradley hundred, and (2) partly in Brightwells Barrow hundred.

[3] *Hampnett.*—The increase of population in 1831 is ascribed to the prisoners in the gaol being included.

[4] *Shipton Oliffe*, and *Shipton Sollars* were united for civil purposes, as Shipton, by the Act 34 & 35 Vic. c. 61.

TABLE OF POPULATION, 1801—1901 (*continued*)

Parish	Acre-age	1801	1811	1821	1831	1841	1851	1861	1871	1881	1891	1901
St. Briavels Hundred												
Abinghall † ‡ [1] . .	770	185	201	215	235	239	224	228	307	268	238	224
Bicknor, English [2].	3,209	465	500	534	598	576	584	592	601	665	623	544
Dean Forest [3] :—	12,530ᵉ	3,325	4,073	5,535	7,014	10,692	13,566	17,801	20,861	22,198	22,404	23,155
East Dean Township † [4]	2,495ᵉ	1,576	2,039	2,733	3,727	6,243	7,482	9,547	11,270	12,909	13,298	13,160
West Dean Township †	10,035ᵉ	1,749	2,034	2,802	3,287	4,449	6,084	8,254	9,591	9,289	9,106	9,995
Dean, Little † ‡ [5] .	495	541	754	807	617	828	947	887	884	823	816	769
Newland :—	8,797ᵉ	2,543	3,147	3,383	4,046	4,085	4,574	5,147	5,258	5,091	4,646	4,950
Bream Chap.			339	417	393	441	643	824	907			
Clearwell Tything and Chap.	8,743ᵉ	2,457	544	583	678	674	703	816	731	4,812	4,346	4,681
Coleford Chap.			1,551	1,804	2,193	2,208	2,310	2,600	2,718			
Newland Tything †			641	486	674	627	761	676	649			
Lea Bailey Tything †	54ᵉ	86	72	93	108	135	157	231	253	279	300	269
Flaxley †	1,749	135	158	196	186	229	242	272	1,090	1,278	1,229	1,340
Hewelsfield . .						319						
Brockwear Common Extra-Par.	1,592	298	349	434	535	212	497	417	395	402	409	353
Mitcheldean † ‡ .	627	563	535	556	601	665	662	689	742	711	730	631
Ruardean † ‡ . .	1,593	845	735	729	858	929	1,033	1,054	1,090	1,295	1,229	1,096
St. Briavels . .						585						
St. Briavels Common, including Lower Mean and Hudnells Extra Par.	4,796	670	867	1,112	1,124	661	1,194	1,261	1,315	1,143	1,112	1,065
The Fence, Extra Par.						41						
Staunton ‡ . . .	1,530	159	171	200	204	188	211	202	179	121	157	166
Brightwells— Barrow Hundred												
Aldsworth ‡ . . .	3,350	288	282	347	353	365	379	430	395	386	372	299
Barnsley ‡ . . .	2,163	271	279	318	318	305	322	327	292	276	227	222
Bibury (part of) [6] .	5,198	707	781	805	774	875	946	899	876	738	695	685
Coln St. Aldwyn ‡	2,666	385	380	393	441	428	492	516	523	443	406	340
Eastleach Martin, or Bouthrop †	1,966	210	215	231	159	186	197	216	165	146	147	146
Eastleach Turville †	2,630	370	370	333	370	421	446	506	503	435	374	295
Fairford ‡ [7] . . .	4,012	1,326	1,444	1,547	1,574	1,672	1,859	1,654	1,626	1,525	1,463	1,404
Hatherop ‡ . . .	2,123	247	269	290	326	358	375	323	283	347	307	295
Kempsford ‡. . .	4,963	656	657	838	885	998	1,003	1,007	950	828	790	711
Lechlade [8] . . .	3,870	917	993	1,154	1,244	1,300	1,373	1,354	1,294	1,198	1,266	1,179
Quenington ‡ . .	1,996	239	311	345	365	371	369	426	438	380	366	357
Southrop † ‡ . .	1,493	238	268	313	350	403	425	362	367	350	316	255
Cheltenham Hundred												
Charlton Kings. .	3,499	730	1,005	1,607	2,478	3,232	3,174	3,443	3,680	3,950	4,187	5,017
Cheltenham * . .	4,301	3,076	8,325	13,396	22,942	31,411	35,051	39,693	41,923	43,972	42,914	44,805
Leckhampton . .	1,614	225	242	318	929	1,770	2,149	2,523	3,265	3,501	3,363	3,781
Swindon ‡ . . .	730	116	162	201	225	204	221	227	239	201	243	233

[1] *Abinghall* included, in 1821, an extra-parochial district bordering on the Forest of Dean.

[2] *English Bicknor* includes the area and the population (1851–1901) of two formerly extra-parochial places, viz. Mailscot, and a place near New Weir, which were added to it under the Act 5 & 6 Vic. c. 48 (see also Forest of Dean).

[3] *Forest of Dean* was extra-parochial up till its division into two townships by the Act 5 & 6 Vic. c. 48.

[4] *East Dean Township* includes the area and the population (1861–1901) of Causeway, Little Dean Hill, Hinders Lane, Mousel Lane, and South Whites (or Whitehall), which were all reputed to be extra-parochial in 1861.

[5] *Little Dean* included, in 1821, an adjoining extra-parochial place containing 123 persons.

[6] See note (²), p. 176.

[7] *Fairford* —The removal of the pauper inmates of the asylum to the county asylum is given as the main cause of the decline in population in 1861.

[8] *Lechlade* includes Great Lemhill Farm, 1801–1901 (see note to Ancient County).

TABLE OF POPULATION, 1801—1901 (continued)

PARISH	Acre-age	1801	1811	1821	1831	1841	1851	1861	1871	1881	1891	1901
Cleeve, or Bishop's Cleeve, Hundred												
Bishop's Cleeve‡:—	8,669	1,355	1,416	1,548	1,642	1,944	2,117	1,970	2,066	1,825	1,794	1,790
Bishop's Cleeve Township †	—	431	394	458	550	682	745	703	704	650	657	686
Gotherington Hamlet	1,643	335	348	348	373	381	424	387	408	388	364	334
Stoke Orchard Hamlet	1,378	195	237	239	229	231	226	201	183	168	162	136
Southam and Brockhampton Hamlet †	—	202	207	248	223	278	290	248	264	238	310	291
Woodmancote Hamlet †	—	192	230	255	267	372	432	431	507	381	301	343
Crowthorne and Minty Hundred												
Ampney Crucis † ‡	2,660°	514	470	590	599	591	662	648	654	541	488	522
Ampney, Down ‡ .	2,541	279	324	365	463	425	443	429	381	345	304	260
Ampney St. Mary, or Ashbrook	1,371	167	168	130	115	121	125	125	99	129	113	94
Ampney St. Peter, or Easington †	533°	162	203	177	180	196	206	188	185	173	191	183
Badgington ‡ . .	1,146	133	125	137	167	172	183	175	178	181	182	150
Baunton	1,367	108	105	129	144	187	134	122	152	135	133	100
Cerney, South ‡ .	3,062	798	784	922	980	1,077	1,103	1,006	950	943	909	794
Coates †	2,514	226	259	309	343	373	400	417	452	464	434	311
Daglingworth ‡ .	1,923	215	230	253	239	302	320	355	351	333	301	297
Driffield	1,264	128	136	144	146	148	161	132	121	119	114	101
Duntisbourne Abbots (part of)[1]	2,332	245	175	171	171	215	207	237	196	289	285	230
Duntisbourne Rouse ‡	2,260	93	90	100	126	138	160	127	113	129	119	109
Harnhill . . .	708	71	65	75	71	97	77	88	65	71	56	59
Hampton, Meysey‡	2,022	315	333	362	364	410	376	352	383	332	324	291
Poulton ‡. . . .	1,600	306	305	309	368	371	408	454	499	457	406	376
Preston ‡. . . .	2,042	141	176	160	196	220	218	217	209	212	191	212
Siddington St. Mary and St. Peter ‡	2,137	325	321	349	409	469	502	474	520	481	571	501
Stratton	1,424	166	175	271	468	546	622	596	602	694	836	837
Deerhurst Hundred—Lower Division.												
Elmstone Hardwicke (part of):—[2] Uckington Chap.	884	153	154	179	175	200	173	195	172	145	148	124
Leigh ‡	1,504	303	300	340	355	489	470	428	386	337	337	315
Prestbury ‡ . . .	3,054	485	667	906	1,231	1,283	1,314	1,297	1,373	1,402	1,430	1,393
Staverton † . . .	720°	159	230	262	245	296	278	315	299	242	298	300
Tirley ‡	1,924	365	405	443	498	550	526	539	517	481	393	365
Woolstone ‡ . .	795	83	83	89	92	78	86	81	89	62	72	66
Deerhurst Hundred—Upper Division												
Coln St. Dennis ‡ .	1,789	163	162	179	176	200	229	206	211	192	200	149
Preston-on-Stour ‡	1,769	267	291	334	355	394	421	376	369	273	276	273
Welford (part of)[3]	1,853	516	477	641	604	608	605	627	634	585	461	467

[1] *Dunstisbourne Abbots Ancient Parish* is (1) partly in Crowthorne and Minty hundred, and (2) partly in Rapsgate hundred. The entire area and population (1801, and 1881–1901) are entered in Crowthorne and Minty hundred.

[2] *Elmstone Hardwicke Ancient Parish* is situated (1) partly in Deerhurst hundred, Lower Division, and (2) partly in Westminster hundred, Lower Division.

[3] *Welford Ancient Parish.*—The remainder is in Warwickshire (Barlichway hundred, Stratford Division). The entire population in 1801 is entered here.

TABLE OF POPULATION, 1801—1901 (*continued*)

PARISH	Acreage	1801	1811	1821	1831	1841	1851	1861	1871	1881	1891	1901
Dudstone and Kings Barton Hundred—Lower Division												
Churcham (part of) †[1]:—viz. Highnam, Linton and Over	2,004°	202	288	252	327	337	415	396	385	339	310	271
Hartpury ‡ . . .	3,670	567	682	811	880	877	884	843	830	803	781	775
Lassington ‡ . .	546	85	79	52	60	82	80	73	75	62	57	57
Maisemore † ‡ .	1,930°	343	408	404	423	421	471	516	484	491	433	456
Preston	897	87	90	87	79	75	80	78	82	61	76	76
Rudford (part of)[2] Highleadon Hamlet	—	78	78	92	100	105	96	97	103	96	91	105
Dudstone and Kings Barton Hundred—Middle Division												
Brookthorpe † . .	2,294	112	137	160	193	169	191	180	165	151	182	194
Elmore † ‡ . . .	1,486°	381	312	355	401	379	393	374	373	352	346	304
Harescombe † . .	478°	108	100	104	121	132	147	138	152	149	139	126
Hempsted † [3] . .	1,311°	159	128	157	165	224	251	424	475	714	761	867
Littleworth Extra Par.	12	150	268	237	615	427	479	501	586	557	506	459
Matson †	450°	51	55	35	55	61	53	32	62	73	59	162
Pitchcombe † . .	278	216	204	187	224	243	145	178	175	157	177	156
Prinknash Park Extra Par.	223	—	7	9	14	7	13	17	14	22	14	7
Quedgeley (part of) :—[4] Woolstrop Hamlet	—	35	38	36	39	46	57	55	64	—	—	—
South Hamlet extra Par. † [8]	—	60	52	391	834	1,055	1,739	2,248	2,802	3,521	4,202	6,122
St. Mary-de-Lode, (part of) :—[5]	1,470°	524	608	792	895	1,781	2,827	4,473	7,544	10,736	13,131	17,487
Barton St. Mary Hamlet †	—	412	497	670	786	1,674	2,696	4,335	7,348	10,480	12,810	16,972
Tuffley Hamlet †	—	112	111	122	109	107	131	138	196	256	321	515
St. Michael (part of) :—[6] Barton St. Michael Hamlet †	500°	285	287	337	676	1,116	1,744	2,315	3,005	3,338	3,772	4,474
Upton St. Leonard †	2,975°	621	713	895	898	893	1,124	1,035	1,309	1,430	1,539	1,454
Whaddon †	727°	88	114	139	152	132	120	125	127	111	138	141
Dudstone and Kings Barton Hundred—Upper Division												
Badgeworth † . .	3,927°	603	642	715	859	903	874	1,048	1,151	1,004	1,096	1,077
Barnwood † ‡ . .	1,471°	309	306	392	419	383	358	507	619	761	1,244	1,285
Brockworth ‡ . .	1,957	350	376	386	390	409	425	475	489	445	411	373
Churchdown :—	4,076°	644	783	954	982	999	1,043	1,119	1,050	1,139	1,209	1,660
Churchdown † .	—	410	438	515	517	544	585	659	621	686	750	989
Hucclecote Hamlet	—	234	345	439	465	455	458	460	429	453	459	671

[1] *Churcham Ancient Parish* is situated (1) partly in Dudstone and King's Barton hundred, Lower Division, and (2) partly in Westbury hundred.

[2] See note (1), p. 176.

[8] *South Hamlet.*—The area is included with that of *Hempsted.*

[4] *Quedgeley Ancient Parish* is situated (1) partly in Dudstone and King's Barton hundred, Middle Division, and (2) partly in Whitstone hundred, Upper Division. The entire area and population (1881-1901) is entered in Whitstone hundred, Upper Division.

[5] *St. Mary-de-Lode Ancient Parish* is situated (1) partly in Dudstone and King's Barton hundred, Middle Division; (2) partly in Dudstone and King's Barton hundred, Upper Division; and (3) partly in the city of Gloucester.

[6] *St. Michael Ancient Parish* is situated (1) partly in Dudstone and King's Barton hundred, Middle Division, and (2) partly in the city of Gloucester.

TABLE OF POPULATION, 1801—1901 (continued)

Parish	Acre-age	1801	1811	1821	1831	1841	1851	1861	1871	1881	1891	1901
Dudstone and Kings Barton Hundred—Upper Division (cont.)												
Hatherley, Down†‡	930°	119	122	170	150	212	240	192	194	193	172	184
Hatherley, Up‡ .	538	22	21	32	21	22	50	68	50	88	99	113
Norton † ‡ . . .	1,870°	303	356	349	423	427	467	458	430	429	354	377
St. Catherine (part of) :—[1]												
Longford St. Catherine Hamlet †	200°	84	192	113	160	170	205	213	255	335	274	243
St. Mary-de-Lode (part of) :—[3][4]	2,040°	297	353	589	1,069	1,332	1,674	2,158	2,525	3,592	3,901	4,712
Longford St. Mary Hamlet †[2]	—	82	—	102	178	239	315	418	401	441	520	736
Twigworth Hamlet †	59	59	59	90	87	136	185	178	188	182	204	177
Wotton Hamlet †[5]	—	156	294	397	804	957	1,174	1,562	1,936	2,969	3,177	3,799
North Hamlet Extra Par †[4]	—	—	—	—	—	362	368	490	473	509	629	581
Wotton Vill, Extra. Par. †[4]	—	—	—	—	—	44	56	91	512	541	559	565
Sandhurst † . . .	2,227°	365	399	473	434	540	494	549	602	462	447	417
Shurdington, Great †	383°	63	81	102	99	198	173	164	197	215	193	208
Witcombe Magna‡	942	119	135	155	174	179	167	165	181	159	123	126
Grumbalds Ash Hundred—Lower Division												
Acton Turville ‡ .	1,015	156	180	215	236	311	323	310	314	290	266	293
Dyrham and Hinton ‡	3,020	437	476	526	516	530	474	457	466	400	365	332
Dodington ‡ . .	1,496	95	113	106	113	143	135	126	136	140	131	132
Littleton, West .	1,013	100	88	109	128	158	161	120	116	101	100	69
Sodbury, Chipping ‡	107	1,090	1,235	1,059	1,306	1,273	1,195	1,112	1,157	1,067	1,028	1,177
Sodbury, Little † ‡	1,093	89	83	107	126	125	128	143	155	132	143	139
Sodbury, Old ‡[6] .	3,729	687	765	803	729	871	820	809	804	714	690	1,332
Tormarton . . .	2,656	225	252	320	402	462	463	454	418	424	347	340
Wapley and Codrington ‡	2,598	258	276	307	253	366	305	358	335	275	249	399
Grumbalds Ash Hundred—Upper Division												
Alderley † ‡ . . .	898°	212	197	235	200	174	145	98	100	93	78	91
Badminton, Great †	1,794	423	409	464	529	552	521	524	476	489	520	517
Boxwell and Leighterton ‡	2,313	217	254	297	297	334	285	255	255	253	266	254
Charfield ‡ . . .	1,383	247	250	344	487	471	515	629	634	553	540	556
Didmarton † . .	722	74	95	101	103	95	101	92	77	56	73	59
Hawkesbury † . .	9,770	1,396	1,482	1,834	2,182	2,231	2,185	2,173	2,145	1,948	1,795	1,656
Horton ‡	3,582	366	373	385	477	466	461	454	431	367	342	356
Oldbury-on-the-Hill †	1,346	239	317	371	414	483	485	440	415	386	328	276
Tortworth ‡ . .	1,577	269	303	277	266	240	237	235	231	199	216	222
Wickwar ‡[7] . .	2,328	764	805	919	972	1,125	966	949	902	917	933	905

[1] *St. Catherine Ancient Parish* is situated in (1) Dudstone and King's Barton hundred, Middle Division (where none is shown); (2) Dudstone and King's Barton hundred, Upper Division; and (3) the city of Gloucester.

[2] The population of *Longford St. Mary* is included with that of *Longford St. Catherine* in 1811.

[3] See note (5), p. 179.

[4] The areas of *North Hamlet* and *Wotton Vill* are included with that for the part of *St. Mary-de-Lode Ancient Parish* in Dudstone and King's Barton hundred, Upper Division.

[5] *Wotton Hamlet* includes (1861–1901) Wotton Hill, formerly extra-parochial, which was added to it under the Act 20 Vic. c. 19.

[6] *Old Sodbury.*—The increase of population in 1901 is mainly due to the presence of a large number of workmen engaged in constructing a railway tunnel.

[7] *Wickwar.*—The increase of population in 1841 is ascribed to the employment of labourers on the railway

TABLE OF POPULATION, 1801—1901 (*continued*)

Parish	Acreage	1801	1811	1821	1831	1841	1851	1861	1871	1881	1891	1901
Henbury Hundred—Lower Division												
Henbury (part of) :—[1]	8,862	897	1,030	1,155	1,243	1,250	1,219	1,207	1,344	2,605	2,356	2,266
Henbury Tything †	7,580	437	447	431	390	442	434	423	479	2,084	1,971	1,885
Northwick with Redwick Chap.†	1,282	137	180	257	285	256	259	267	341	521	385	381
Stowick Tything	—	323	403	467	568	552	526	517	524	—	—	—
Westbury-upon-Trym :—	5,456°	2,325	3,035	3,721	4,263	5,029	6,728	8,329	13,374	19,299	22,538	26,128
Westbury-upon-Trym †[2]	—	678	957	1,203	1,515	1,707	1,883	1,975	2,131	17,500	19,856	22,769
Shirehampton Chap. ‡[3]	—	354	490	635	420	671	632	731	1,056	1,799	2,682	3,359
Stoke, Bishop Tything[2]	—	1,293	1,588	1,883	2,328	2,651	4,213	5,623	10,187	—	—	—
Henbury Hundred—Upper Division												
Compton Greenfield † ‡	661	24	35	42	40	65	64	52	60	42	40	27
Henbury (part of) :—[1]	979	390	360	639	672	664	765	725	717	181	151	143
Aust Chap. †	979	140	174	192	203	191	213	187	175	181	151	143
Charlton Tything	—	99	186	296	310	329	411	425	401	—	—	—
Compton Tything	—	151	—	151	159	144	141	113	141	—	—	—
Stoke Gifford † ‡ .	2,323	281	315	376	441	480	488	445	430	342	359	390
Tytherington (part of) :—[4]												
Itchington Hamlet	—	73	124	144	126	149	120	—	—	—	—	—
Yate * ‡	4,081	654	717	827	824	1,057	1,080	1,138	1,194	1,255	1,190	1,279
Kiftsgate Hundred—Lower Division												
Aston Somerville ‡	1,004	87	88	110	103	89	89	105	151	110	107	99
Buckland ‡ . . .	2,275	328	324	382	403	377	368	355	354	283	259	283
Charlton Abbots †‡	2,190°	100	99	87	111	101	112	109	91	115	70	69
Childs Wickham ‡	1,898	351	352	428	415	469	466	440	463	450	400	396
Didbrook :—	2,578°	379	243	324	287	353	178	232	239	244	235	207
Didbrook † . .	1,528°	254	201	291	240	292	149	182	200	215	205	179
Pinnock and Hyde Township †	1,050°	125	42	33	47	61	29	50	39	29	30	28
Dumbleton ‡ . .	2,185	307	315	374	420	497	457	465	455	439	412	381
Guiting Power † ‡ .	3,380°	430	613	629	792	672	690	647	634	619	524	473
Guiting, Temple ‡ .	6,004	301	450	510	520	523	525	573	539	517	443	411
Hailes	1,447	111	122	136	123	120	90	102	91	57	63	82
Hawling † ‡ . . .	1,846°	192	209	195	202	217	212	171	206	154	132	130
Overbury (part of) :—[5]												
Little Washbourne Hamlet	—	59	68	55	51	37	29	28	28	22	16	21

[1] See note (3). p. 175.

[2] *Westbury-upon-Trym Tything* includes *Stoke Bishop Tything*, 1881–1901. Stoke Bishop Tything is said (1841) to be partly in the county of the city of Bristol ; it is, however, entirely entered in Henbury hundred, Lower Division. The 1811 population of Stoke Bishop is an estimate.

[3] *Shirehampton.*—The increase of population in 1871 is chiefly owing to the temporary presence of labourers employed in constructing new docks at the mouth of the Avon.

[4] *Tytherington Ancient Parish* is situated (1) partly in Henbury hundred, Upper Division, and (2) partly in Thornbury hundred, Lower Division. The entire area and population (1861-1901) are shown in Thornbury hundred, Lower Division. The increase of population in 1871 is attributed to the presence of labourers employed in constructing a railway.

[5] *Overbury Ancient Parish* is situated (1) partly in Kiftsgate hundred, Lower Division ; (2) partly in Kiftsgate hundred, Upper Division ; and (3) partly in Oswaldslow hundred, Middle Division (Worcestershire). The entire area (in Gloucestershire) is shown in Kiftsgate hundred, Upper Division.

TABLE OF POPULATION, 1801—1901 (*continued*)

Parish	Acre-age	1801	1811	1821	1831	1841	1851	1861	1871	1881	1891	1901
Kiftsgate Hundred—Lower Division (cont.)												
Roel Extra Par.	1,158	41	42	32	38	20	12	50	42	32	26	32
Snowshill . . .	2,325	263	272	301	292	298	303	235	260	255	240	214
Stanley Pontlarge	684	44	49	48	62	75	66	57	54	58	91	66
Stanton † . . .	1,650°	256	244	269	293	319	307	280	282	269	265	235
Sudeley Manor † ‡	2,622°	68	76	90	84	84	77	98	79	100	101	114
Toddington † . .	1,857°	268	261	355	290	229	189	153	221	212	236	202
Twyning † ‡ [1] . .	3,155°	752	813	849	942	970	1,011	992	1,004	857	889	855
Winchcombe * † ‡	5,700°	1,888	1,936	2,240	2,514	2,613	2,824	2,937	2,993	2,834	2,868	2,699
Wormington ‡ . .	532	91	81	83	96	73	62	79	86	94	87	79
Kiftsgate Hundred—Upper Division												
Aston-sub-Edge ‡ .	728	116	120	116	103	134	132	128	136	121	141	112
Batsford † . . .	932°	89	86	108	107	79	107	130	97	109	112	106
Chipping Campden ‡ [2]	4,699	1,700	1,684	1,798	2,038	2,087	2,351	1,975	2,013	1,861	1,736	1,542
Cow Honeybourne	1,377	274	286	333	329	327	343	360	379	367	428	432
Dorsington ‡ . .	989	100	103	121	122	141	115	118	94	94	114	59
Ebrington ‡ . .	2,974	464	359	535	573	583	594	570	548	543	538	491
Ilmington (part of):— [3]												
Lark-Stoke Hamlet	482	12	10	5	23	18	13	21	13	21	13	12
Longborough † . .	2,770°	473	502	526	619	625	656	655	616	572	552	462
Marston-Sicca, or Long Marston ‡	1,580	242	253	272	264	337	332	371	388	367	346	288
Mickleton :— ‡	3,813	489	565	574	679	698	829	743	760	752	720	660
Mickleton with Clopton [4]	*3,200*	*430*	*475*	*—*	*—*	*624*	*720*	*659*	*652*	*665*	*643*	*605*
Hidcote Bartrim Hamlet	*613*	*59*	*90*	*—*	*—*	*74*	*109*	*84*	*108*	*87*	*77*	*55*
Overbury (part of) :— [5]												
Alstone Hamlet †	1,060°	83	83	79	78	89	89	96	84	76	62	59
Pebworth ‡ . . .	3,056	579	591	620	578	829	737	736	803	691	641	539
Quinton :— ‡	3,457	485	554	598	609	666	587	557	627	647	565	502
Quinton . . .	*2,460*	*338*	*380*	*436*	*432*	*469*	*411*	*396*	*482*	*498*	*447*	*385*
Admington Hamlet	*997*	*147*	*174*	*162*	*177*	*197*	*176*	*161*	*145*	*149*	*118*	*117*
Saintbury ‡ . . .	1,379	152	147	156	123	133	138	121	135	127	122	117
Sezincote . . .	1,438	44	95	86	51	67	111	81	92	51	89	88
Swell, Upper ‡ . .	1,376	74	96	82	95	80	83	65	95	77	74	75
Weston-upon-Avon (part of) [6]	917	118	96	93	93	91	93	87	88	103	90	65
Weston-sub-Edge ‡	2,658	332	283	347	367	342	358	369	399	341	363	332
Willersey ‡ . . .	1,271	273	256	301	327	375	372	373	405	393	353	393
Duchy of Lancaster												
Bulley	963	176	203	237	216	229	241	226	199	152	166	134
Huntley ‡ . . .	1,439	313	357	405	464	511	555	533	516	416	422	445
Longhope ‡ . . .	3,153	636	646	790	873	929	1,070	1,104	1,088	971	972	863
Minsterworth † ‡ .	1,938°	354	420	462	496	498	494	463	459	418	429	384
Tibberton ‡	1,406	254	252	282	307	344	362	391	398	363	314	272

[1] *Twyning and Tewkesbury.*—There seems to have been some doubt as to the exact boundaries of these parishes with regard to each other, 1801–31.

[2] *Chipping Campden* includes 265 persons employed on railway works in 1851.

[3] *Ilmington Ancient Parish.*—The remainder is in Kington hundred (Warwickshire).

[4] *Mickleton with Clopton* includes sixty-seven labourers engaged in railway construction in 1851.

[5] See note (5), p. 181.

[6] *Weston-upon-Avon Ancient Parish.*—The remainder is in Alcester Division of Barlichway hundred (Warwickshire).

TABLE OF POPULATION, 1801—1901 (*continued*)

PARISH	Acreage	1801	1811	1821	1831	1841	1851	1861	1871	1881	1891	1901
Langley and Swinehead Hundred—Lower Division												
Almondsbury (part of) [1]	—	719	882	931	850	869	986	1,086	1,337	—	—	—
Alveston † ‡ [2] . .	2,554	412	524	657	800	841	847	841	857	811	759	720
Littleton-upon-Severn ‡	938	136	132	133	179	195	190	195	230	203	196	184
Olveston † ‡ . .	4,812	899	1,093	1,351	1,523	1,725	1,669	1,699	1,746	1,609	1,435	1,381
Rockhampton † ‡ [3]	1,224	160	152	159	220	208	235	248	219	220	195	183
Langley and Swinehead Hundred—Upper Division												
Bitton :—	7,191	4,992	6,061	7,171	8,703	9,338	9,452	9,630	10,320	11,662	13,785	16,539
Bitton Hamlet †	*3,379*	*1,094*	*1,186*	*1,788*	*2,258*	*2,413*	*2,395*	*2,537*	*2,577*	*2,788*	*2,895*	*3,032*
Hanham Chap.†	*1,210*	*795*	*934*	*1,086*	*1,212*	*1,217*	*1,180*	*1,224*	*1,328*	*1,633*	*1,993*	*2,158*
Oldland Chap. †	*2,602*	*3,103*	*3,641*	*4,297*	*5,233*	*5,708*	*5,877*	*5,869*	*6,415*	*7,241*	*8,897*	*11,349*
Doynton ‡ . . .	1,728	303	342	415	448	529	499	448	434	402	391	360
Frampton Cotterell †	2,125	1,208	1,419	1,610	1,816	1,991	1,837	1,931	2,075	1,983	1,960	2,118
Winterbourne † .	3,281	1,592	2,333	2,627	2,889	3,151	2,876	3,067	3,234	3,151	3,380	3,643
Longtree Hundred												
Avening [4] . . .	4,510	1,507	1,602	2,016	2,396	2,227	2,321	2,070	2,101	2,018	1,908	1,921
Cherington ‡ . .	2,267	173	167	215	251	220	220	232	237	210	199	181
Horsley [4] . . .	3,887	2,971	2,925	3,565	3,690	3,064	2,931	2,558	2,650	2,537	2,507	2,433
Minchinhampton [4]	4,791	3,419	3,246	4,907	5,114	4,890	4,469	4,147	4,361	4,561	4,544	4,372
Rodborough . .	1,317	1,658	1,628	2,038	2,141	2,147	2,208	2,165	2,359	2,759	2,955	3,378
Rodmarton . . .	4,145	305	286	357	369	431	416	401	392	382	412	420
Shipton Moyne ‡ .	2,360	273	298	390	389	353	403	407	367	420	380	340
Tetbury* ‡ . . .	4,627	2,500	2,533	2,734	2,939	2,982	3,325	3,325	3,274	3,349	3,237	3,057	2,894
Weston Birt with Lasborough ‡	1,904	157	122	198	138	166	234	190	282	194	258	186
Woodchester ‡ .	1,206	870	845	929	885	908	893	816	974	903	867	820
Pucklechurch Hundred												
Abson and Wick †	2,308	571	671	715	824	794	826	833	838	878	979	981
Cold Ashton ‡ . .	2,289	224	268	284	322	414	479	503	473	388	344	332
Pucklechurch † .	2,449	542	535	612	796	862	931	1,265	1,258	1,292	1,339	1,291
Siston	1,833	856	833	902	973	1,014	926	938	961	1,018	1,200	1,352
Westerleigh † . .	4,116	1,582	1,632	1,817	1,709	1,776	1,679	1,582	1,460	1,285	1,196	1,239
Rapsgate Hundred												
Brimpsfield ‡ . .	2,729	299	320	348	382	417	443	392	425	369	337	323
Cerney, North ‡ .	4,176	565	530	562	622	668	689	692	687	617	585	529
Chedworth ‡ . .	4,781	848	896	975	1,026	983	963	954	962	816	778	885
Coberley	3,639	161	164	237	181	231	243	343	343	326	346	323
Colesborne . . .	2,198	231	237	245	252	256	269	261	267	286	242	204
Cowley ‡	1,898	251	270	273	323	317	317	311	293	300	270	269
Cranham † ‡ . .	1,859	250	317	321	394	428	354	424	379	384	317	325
Duntisbourne Abbots (part of) :— [5]												
Duntisbourne Lear Tything	—	—	88	85	111	139	164	117	116	—	—	—
Elkstone ‡ . . .	2,116	299	285	296	299	335	336	320	302	237	199	222
Rendcomb ‡ . .	2,586	147	163	190	218	248	264	246	237	211	229	237
Side ‡	628	41	33	40	50	43	42	55	55	42	29	48

[1] See note ([2]), p. 175.

[2] *Alveston Ancient Parish* is partly in Langley and Swinehead hundred, Upper Division, but it is entirely entered in the Lower Division of the same hundred.

[3] *Rockhampton Ancient Parish* is partly in Berkeley hundred, Upper Division, but it is entirely shown in Langley and Swinehead hundred, Lower Division.

[4] *Avening, Horsley,* and *Minchinhampton* all contain part of Nailsworth chapelry. Nailsworth chapelry was however, entirely returned with Avening in 1821 and 1831. It appears to have been treated correctly at all the other censuses. [5] See note ([1]), p. 178.

TABLE OF POPULATION, 1801—1901 (*continued*)

PARISH	Acre-age	1801	1811	1821	1831	1841	1851	1861	1871	1881	1891	1901
Slaughter Hundred—Lower Division												
Barrington, Great † ‡	2,997	348	427	462	532	553	545	496	460	453	496	433
Barrington, Little † ‡	1,260	140	137	159	162	208	128	151	162	154	135	115
Bourton-on-the-Water	2,470	697	663	758	858	943	1,040	1,011	1,109	1,157	1,127	1,097
Clapton-on-the-Hill	819	103	104	118	109	117	112	123	138	133	115	103
Naunton ‡ [1] . . .	3,177	433	460	471	531	523	568	535	538	530	491	401
Rissington, Great ‡	2,493	349	361	446	468	483	493	499	481	413	419	347
Rissington, Little ‡	1,475	227	220	229	231	318	279	290	243	231	221	186
Rissington, Wyck	1,267	217	214	231	219	207	219	206	168	170	226	206
Sherborne [2] . .	4,567	526	506	525	767	637	674	584	564	573	516	484
Slaughter, Lower †	1,140°	198	232	242	258	222	230	212	202	212	250	260
Slaughter, Upper † ‡	1,390°	253	216	245	260	231	218	241	244	252	301	222
Windrush . . .	1,835	317	289	317	291	313	332	290	266	228	228	222
Slaughter Hundred—Upper Division												
Adlestrop . . .	1,306	225	228	229	193	200	196	184	192	165	164	190
Bledington ‡ . .	1,539	282	326	340	335	354	391	396	398	367	354	341
Broadwell, or Bradle	1,817	239	282	296	334	345	388	398	404	391	373	316
Condicote † ‡ [3] .	890°	115	124	165	142	165	174	182	191	169	113	118
Eyford	1,241	57	70	67	55	83	48	44	55	56	75	74
Iccomb :— ‡	1,184	112	143	164	148	162	140	164	188	153	135	149
Iccomb Hamlet	671	—	13	18	17	16	9	12	9	9	15	29
Church Iccomb Township	513	—	130	146	131	146	131	152	179	144	120	120
Oddington ‡ . .	1,813	421	412	458	539	525	545	588	552	502	470	402
Stow-on-the-Wold :— ‡	2,961	1,471	1,544	1,731	1,810	2,140	2,250	2,077	2,040	1,969	1,878	1,712
Stow-on-the-Wold	33	1,189	1,188	1,304	1,240	1,465	1,515	1,374	1,373	1,266	1,204	1,118
Donnington Hamlet	1,053	162	196	201	200	189	164	141	128	153	111	116
Maugersbury Hamlet *	1,875	120	160	226	370	486	571	562	539	550	563	478
Swell, Lower ‡ . .	2,347	239	235	263	298	352	431	449	456	407	405	341
Westcote ‡ . . .	1,548	127	131	185	188	240	242	245	236	185	206	202
Tewkesbury Hundred—Lower Division												
Ashchurch † ‡ . .	4,201°	558	571	643	649	743	786	771	747	670	703	749
Boddington † [4] . .	930°	273	338	413	421	414	443	392	455	412	370	402
Forthampton ‡ . .	2,540	449	477	474	459	460	468	442	430	413	402	351
Kemerton † ‡ . .	1,590°	427	496	520	599	561	528	559	534	484	469	483
Oxenton ‡ . . .	1,114	150	141	178	166	139	139	136	117	136	120	91
Tredington ‡ . .	1,021	121	167	138	132	163	143	117	155	110	104	102
Walton Cardiff ‡ .	649	62	55	51	57	69	60	70	68	60	60	55
Tewkesbury Hundred—Upper Division												
Alderton ‡ . . .	1,579	222	264	312	330	411	486	487	474	415	472	418
Bourton-on-the-Hill (part of) [5]	2,975	369	301	180	302	261	263	506	526	451	506	395

[1] *Naunton Ancient Parish* is partly in Bradley hundred, but it is entirely entered under Slaughter hundred, Lower Division.

[2] *Sherborne* in 1831 included a considerable number of men engaged in building Lord Sherborne's mansion. The decrease in population in 1861 is attributed to the establishment of a system which permits but one family in each cottage.

[3] *Condicote Ancient Parish* is partly in Kiftsgate hundred, Upper Division, but it is entirely entered under Slaughter hundred, Upper Division.

[4] *Boddington Ancient Parish* is partly in Westminster hundred, Lower Division, but it is entirely entered under Tewkesbury hundred, Lower Division.

[5] *Bourton-on-the-Hill Ancient Parish* is situated (1) partly in Tewkesbury hundred, Upper Division; and (2) partly in Westminster hundred, Upper Division. The entire area and population (1801, 1811, 1861–1901) are entered under Tewkesbury hundred, Upper Division.

TABLE OF POPULATION, 1801—1901 (*continued*)

Parish	Acreage	1801	1811	1821	1831	1841	1851	1861	1871	1881	1891	1901
Tewkesbury Hundred—Upper Division (cont.)												
Clifford Chambers‡	1,725	223	244	305	336	309	305	344	375	378	348	333
Lemington, Lower‡	859	61	63	67	56	53	58	57	63	54	75	67
Prescott Extra Par. †	430°	33	47	56	51	62	51	63	60	60	46	40
Stanway † ‡ . .	3,390°	342	403	415	401	384	359	378	335	307	310	305
Washbourne, Great ‡	638	89	99	80	87	100	117	83	115	82	83	85
Thornbury Hundred—Lower Division												
Almondsbury (part of)[1]	—	—	—	—	—	125	112	95	92	100	—	—	—
Iron Acton † ‡[2] .	2,952	860	897	1,122	1,372	1,342	1,265	1,234	1,189	1,156	1,034	1,059
Thornbury .—	11,570	2,692	3,321	3,760	4,375	4,706	4,614	4,494	4,670	4,164	4,106	3,974
Thornbury †[3]		*856*	*1,083*	*1,261*			*2,607*	*1,470*	*1,497*	*1,630*			
Kington Tything		*484*	*678*	*831*				*1,057*	*1,156*	*1,129*			
Morton and Falfield Tything	10,674	*670*	*814*	*844*		*4,044*	*1,001*	*1,041*	*884*	*937*	*3,917*	*3,872*	*3,735*
Oldbury-upon-Severn Chap.		*452*	*481*	*528*			*745*	*724*	*707*	*724*			
Rangeworthy Chap.‡	896	230	265	296	*331*	*353*	*322*	*250*	*250*	247	234	239
Tytherington (part of)[4]	2,236	295	317	330	350	347	345	447	523	445	464	441
Thornbury Hundred—Upper Division												
Marshfield ‡ . .	5,907	1,246	1,415	1,569	1,651	1,674	1,648	1,742	1,780	1,527	1,350	1,210
Tibaldstone Hundred												
Aston-under-Hill .	1,664	305	325	301	291	342	396	411	457	359	361	315
Beckford	2,778	459	460	442	433	461	450	473	545	461	433	450
Hinton-on-the-Green ‡	2,291	196	194	195	209	178	192	192	183	180	175	209
Westbury Hundred												
Blaisdon † ‡ . . .	927	152	207	243	255	264	299	282	241	203	203	222
Churcham (part of)[5]	2,275	327	465	481	581	533	610	606	536	510	411	369
Newnham ‡ . . .	1,937	821	952	1,012	1,074	1,105	1,288	1,325	1,483	1,455	1,401	1,184
Tidenham †[6] . .	6,285	696	918	1,102	1,180	1,443	1,753	1,661	1,519	1,515	1,733	1,701
Westbury-on-Severn * † ‡	8,206	1,651	1,765	1,889	2,032	2,225	2,498	2,501	2,495	2,262	2,005	1,868
Woolaston † . . .	3,303	613	646	884	880	1,022	1,110	971	998	866	859	848
Westminster Hundred—Lower Division												
Corse ‡	2,220	335	410	446	476	482	586	552	519	513	419	409
Deerhurst ‡[7] . .	3,138	646	741	742	869	937	892	930	910	832	712	701
Elmstone Hardwicke (part of)[8]	1,746	177	170	178	197	210	218	245	277	173	197	222
Hasfield ‡ . . .	1,446	187	265	237	245	304	300	299	300	246	225	206

[1] See note (2), p. 175.

[2] *Iron Acton Ancient Parish* is partly in Grumbalds Ash hundred, Lower Division, but it is entirely entered under Thornbury hundred, Lower Division.

[3] *Thornbury Tything.*—The increase in 1871 is attributed to the presence of labourers employed in railway construction. [4] See note (4), p. 181. [5] See note (1), p. 179.

[6] *Tidenham* includes in 1851 about fifty persons engaged in railway construction, and also some labourers employed on the tubular bridge across the Wye. It includes Lancaut.

[7] *Deerhurst Ancient Parish* is partly in Deerhurst hundred, Lower Division, but it is entirely entered in Westminster hundred, Lower Division.

[8] See note (2), p. 178.

TABLE OF POPULATION, 1801—1901 (*continued*)

Parish	Acre-age	1801	1811	1821	1831	1841	1851	1861	1871	1881	1891	1901
Westminster Hundred— Upper Division												
Bourton-on-the-Hill (part of)[1]	—	—	—	174	251	281	287	—	—	—	—	—
Moreton-in-the-Marsh	1,014	829	928	1,015	1,331	1,345	1,512	1,420	1,468	1,424	1,446	1,374
Todenham ‡ . .	2,481	339	363	440	481	474	462	408	396	321	349	292
Whitstone Hundred— Lower Division												
Eastington * † . .	2,042°	988	1,223	1,681	1,770	1,871	1,886	1,717	1,685	1,520	1,424	1,233
Frampton-upon-Severn † ‡	2,322	860	848	996	1,055	1,051	994	983	993	965	856	797
Frocester ‡ . . .	1,870	362	367	437	414	344	299	262	242	271	247	239
King's Stanley . .	1,719	1,434	1,722	2,269	2,438	2,200	2,095	2,038	2,212	2,117	1,982	1,845
Leonard Stanley † ‡	1,189	590	538	757	942	874	861	864	847	775	771	685
Stonehouse † [2] . .	1,786	1,412	1,711	2,126	2,469	2,711	2,598	2,614	2,797	3,251	3,729	4,091
Wheatenhurst, or Whitminster †	1,267	287	339	370	423	391	380	411	428	364	360	308
Whitstone Hundred— Upper Division												
Fretherne † . . .	558	117	160	210	224	242	267	237	211	239	230	346
Hardwicke † . . .	2,378°	341	423	446	459	540	564	625	628	645	657	599
Haresfield † . . .	2,155°	553	552	662	611	576	627	612	640	572	534	494
Longney † ‡ . . .	1,558	314	379	443	453	490	504	486	450	426	317	313
Moreton Valence †	672	265	312	348	324	344	307	337	376	339	340	241
Quedgeley (part of) † [3]	1,453°	165	195	227	258	230	344	353	400	474	464	457
Randwick † . . .	604	856	748	984	1,031	979	959	1,060	1,089	1,128	1,100	880
Saul †	572	349	365	467	443	477	550	607	614	597	580	400
Standish † . . .	3,022	504	474	525	536	540	534	525	528	489	436	386
City (and County) of Bristol [4]												
All Saints [5] . . .	2°	182	150	173	180	174	154	121	94	135	142	116
Castle Precincts Extra Par.	15	1,404	1,535	1,526	1,804	1,830	1,825	1,537	1,413	1,134	1,033	948
Christchurch, or Holy Trinity	5	690	894	1,029	1,193	1,092	1,079	1,073	1,241	830	570	98
St. Augustine-the-Less	160	5,377	6,495	7,321	8,358	9,242	9,891	10,476	10,380	9,167	8,490	7,020
St. Ewin	1	117	103	99	74	55	52	76	89	19	20	49
St. James (part of) [6]	70	7,307	8,241	8,804	10,488	10,555	10,658	10,325	9,802	8,420	7,831	6,588
St. John ‡ . . .	10	700	704	757	889	938	1,190	960	932	531	425	148
St. Leonard . . .	5	285	329	285	302	281	123	104	137	64	32	28
St. Mary-le-Port ‡ .	3	289	288	302	247	277	230	196	134	105	51	36
St. Mary Redcliff [4]	72	4,131	4,696	5,827	6,259	7,025	6,812	7,467	6,530	5,188	5,159	4,581
St. Michael . . .	103	2,786	3,103	3,445	3,836	4,254	4,431	4,922	4,918	4,899	5,305	4,718
St. Nicholas. . .	28	1,849	1,819	1,892	1,916	2,166	2,076	1,935	1,596	1,024	815	691
St. Paul (part of) [6]	127	4,958	6,056	7,320	9,146	10,762	10,758	11,397	12,612	15,083	16,282	14,207
St. Peter	12	1,566	1,546	1,623	1,776	1,545	1,470	1,472	1,168	912	793	679
St. Philip and St. Jacob (part of) [6]	31	2,355	2,834	3,673	3,886	4,110	4,522	4,378	4,078	3,560	2,754	1,906
St Stephen ‡ . .	32	1,761	1,671	2,078	1,278	2,269	2,778	2,680	2,302	1,994	1,714	1,239
Temple, or Holy Cross ‡ [4] .	85	3,716	4,690	5,343	5,981	6,189	6,060	5,592	4,450	3,764	3,556	2,448
St. Thomas ‡ [4] . .	20	1,195	1,294	1,276	1,361	1,403	1,508	1,276	768	650	577	336
St. Werburgh [5] .	3°	146	144	116	100	99	99	40	18	—	—	—

[1] See note (5), p. 184.

[2] *Stonehouse* includes Haywardsfield, which was formerly extra-parochial.   [3] See note (4), p. 179.

[4] Part of *Bristol*, viz. the *parishes of St. Mary Redcliff, St. Thomas*, and *The Temple*, was anciently in Somerset, but has always (1801–1901) been included in Gloucestershire.

[5] *All Saints Parish* includes *St. Werburgh Parish*, 1881–1901.

[6] *St. James, St. Paul*, and *St. Philip and St. Jacob Parishes* are partly in the county of the city of Bristol and partly in Barton Regis hundred.

TABLE OF POPULATION, 1801—1901 (continued)

PARISH	Acre-age	1801	1811	1821	1831	1841	1851	1861	1871	1881	1891	1901
Barton Regis Hundred												
Clifton . . .	834	4,457	6,981	8,811	12,032	14,177	17,634	21,375	26,364	28,695	29,345	27,761
St. George . . .	1,846	4,038	4,909	5,334	6,285	8,318	8,905	10,276	16,209	26,433	36,718	55,426
St. James (part of)—Out [1] St. Paul (part of)—Out [1]	440	1,897	2,427	3,605	4,495	6,139	7,935	9,944	13,841	19,114	24,042	26,505
Mangotsfield . .	2,606	2,492	2,901	3,179	3,508	3,862	3,967	4,222	4,533	5,707	7,247	10,015
St. Philip and St. Jacob (part of) [1]	736	8,406	10,702	11,824	15,777	21,590	24,961	31,753	42,287	50,108	51,624	49,402
Stapleton * . . .	2,573	1,541	1,921	2,137	2,715	3,944	4,840	5,355	6,960	10,833	14,589	21,236
Cirencester Borough												
Cirencester * ‡ . .	5,286	4,130	4,540	4,987	5,420	6,014	6,096	6,336	7,079	7,737	7,521	7,536
Tewkesbury Borough												
Tewkesbury * [2] .	2,532	4,199	4,820	4,962	5,780	5,862	5,878	5,876	5,409	5,100	5,269	5,419
City (and County) of Gloucester = 680° acres												
Holy Trinity. . .	5	501	627	586	685	591	612	539	540	493	416	316
College Precincts Extra Par. [3]	—	—	—	—	—	282	278	217	238	—	—	—
St. Aldate ‡ . . .	5	514	600	716	700	786	816	710	826	708	511	511
St. Catherine (part of) † [4]	—	707	806	1,047	1,106	1,445	1,717	2,265	2,593	2,600	3,265	4,610
St. John the Baptist †	—	925	1,119	1,277	2,465	3,380	4,081	3,682	3,883	3,694	3,786	3,297
St. Mary-de-Crypt	20	672	835	963	939	1,012	1,042	953	981	879	804	658
St. Mary-de-Grace	2	217	269	269	280	298	296	251	231	175	140	143
St. Mary-de-Lode (part of) † [5] [8]	—	983	756	1,265	1,917	1,840	2,055	2,047	2,160	2,416	2,240	1,830
St. Michael (part of) [6]	28	820	877	917	913	1,029	1,331	1,372	1,431	1,312	1,356	1,232
St. Nicholas † .	—	1,787	2,005	2,332	2,459	2,775	2,839	2,348	2,514	2,833	2,436	2,046
St. Owen. . . .	21	592	445	372	469	714	948	830	826	623	522	526

The following Municipal Boroughs and Urban Districts are co-extensive at the census of 1901 with one or more places mentioned in the table :—

Municipal Borough, or Urban District	Place
Awre U.D.	Awre parish (Bledisloe hundred)
Cirencester U.D.	Cirencester parish (Cirencester borough)
Newnham U.D.	Newnham parish (Westbury hundred)
Tewkesbury M.B.	Tewkesbury parish (Tewkesbury borough)

[1] See note (6), p. 186.   [2] See note (1), p. 182.

[3] *College Precincts* probably returned with the part of *St. Mary-de-Lode Ancient Parish in the City* 1801-31, and certainly so included 1881-1901.   The part of St. Mary-de-Lode in the City also includes Pool Meadow, 1851-1901, and probably 1801-41, which was formerly deemed extra-parochial.   Pool Meadow became a civil parish under the Act 20 Vic c. 19.   [4] See note (1), p. 180.

[5] See note (5), p. 179.   [6] See note (6), p. 179.

INDUSTRIES

THOUGH stress has already been laid upon the variety of the natural resources of Gloucestershire, only those acquainted with it would realize to what an extent these have tended to make it an industrial county. Over 60,000 of its inhabitants at the present day are pursuing industrial occupations, as compared with 25,000 engaged in agriculture.. Nor is this manufacturing class chiefly centred in Bristol and Gloucester. Probably few counties have so many rural industries, some of them contained in large factories in country towns, some of them conducted by one man in a mere village.

Gloucestershire industries fall chronologically and categorically into three divisions. The first comprises the period of industries based on natural resources, supplemented only by the simplest means of communication—roads. The second, from the 17th to the 19th century, includes the period of canals, when foreign products and influence made industries less local; the third, the period of railways, when a new and exotic set of industries was introduced.

Among natural resources, the influence of the pastures and water-power of the Cotswolds in giving rise to the woollen industry has been dealt with under the 'Social and Economic History' of the county, from which it is impossible to dissociate it. Almost equal in importance have been the mineral resources. The coal and iron mines of Bristol and the Forest of Dean will be fully spoken of further on. But the abundance of clay and building stone scattered over Gloucestershire has not been without effect upon its history. A considerable manufacture of bricks, tiles, and pottery is carried on from local resources, the clay being found in the Alluvium, or deposit of the Severn and Avon, and in the Lower and Middle Lias of the Vale and the Cotswolds respectively. The former beds are little worked owing to their comparative difficulty of access, except at Tewkesbury and in the neighbourhood of Gloucester, but the number of old pits in the Severn banks testifies to a common use of the alluvium in the past.

Stone, rather than brick, has however been the favourite building material of the past, and some 2,000 men are at this day engaged in quarrying. Red Millstone Grit and Pennant Sandstone are worked in the Bristol region, and Mountain Limestone and Conglomerate near Clifton, the latter having been used in the building of Clifton College. In the Cotswolds the abundance of building-stone found in the Inferior Oolite gave rise to considerable architectural skill at so early a date as the 15th century, and the local material employed harmonizes with the scenery to a striking degree. It has also occasioned the use of stone rather than hedgerows for enclosures—a very marked feature of the hill district at the present day. The limestone provides roofing material, and where these stone tiles, or 'slats,' have been used and have weathered in harmony with the walls of the building, the whole effect is singularly complete. That these building materials were early utilized and valued is shown by the frequent mention in Court Rolls of the letting of 'quarrs' (still the local pronunciation) and 'tylepitts.' Tiling and 'slatting' were certainly commoner than thatching, to judge from these records, a few extracts from which may give some idea of the materials and cost of building in mediaeval Gloucestershire.

In 1460 a new hall and 'crosschamber' were built for the abbess of Sion, on her manor of Cheltenham and Slaughter, for the sum of £55 odd[1]:

	£	s.	d.
Wages of carpenters	14	2	0½
,, sawyers	18	0	5
,, tiler	2	13	5
,, lathers	2	13	10
,, labourers	4	7	6½
,, dauber	2	18	10
Timber	1	19	10
Planks	0	11	4
Saw	0	0	9
Nails	0	12	5½
Moss	0	2	4
Lath-nails	0	15	0
Straw	0	1	6
Guestone	0	8	3
Crests	0	9	8
Splitting laths, &c.	0	18	8
Carriage of stuff	4	5	6½
Total	55	1	5

This house was presumably wattled, and the moss and straw were for the dauber. The laths were probably to bear the 'slats' for the roof. At this day the latter are laid on light wooden

[1] Mins. Accts. (P.R.O.), bdle. 853, No. 2.

cross laths, to which they are fixed by a wooden peg (lath-nail) through a hole in the upper end of the 'slat.' This peg is mentioned under the name of 'tyle-pynne' in a steward's account at Gloucester in 1493–4.[1] Crests are the stones on the ridge of the roof.

Again, in 1482, at Slaughter, a roof was repaired [2] :—

	£	s.	d.
5 loads of tiles	0	10	0
Crests	0	1	0
Mortar, lime and the laying it on .	0	5	2
Workman, carpenter, and timber .	0	4	10
To the man for 'ledding,' and workman's expenses	1	6	8
Total	2	7	8

In 1395 lath-nails were 1s. 6d. and laths 6s. 8d. per thousand.[3] Roofing was done in 1412 at 5s. for 1,000 tiles.[4] Walls were also made of stone as now. Stones for a wall round 'Haselangre' (Brimpsfield) were dug at 4d. a day, and the building done at 1s. 6d. per perch, including cost of carriage.[5] Walling is the only local craft still in common use. Very few men do 'slatting' properly, and the modern work seldom lasts so long as the old. Wattling, I believe, survives in the Campden district, where traditions lasted long unbroken, in consequence of the late date of the inclosure.

Rough Oolitic Limestone, suitable for walls and road-metal, is quarried in nearly every parish in the Cotswolds. In the south the chief building-stone is freestone, dug at Cleeve, Leckhampton, Painswick, Smith's Cross, and Brockhampton. In the northern Cotswolds 'yellow-bed' is chiefly worked for this purpose, quarries having been opened at Temple Guiting, Bourton on the Hill, Ebrington, and Chipping Campden. The Great, or Upper, Oolite is quarried at Minchinhampton, and is durable if properly seasoned. Good tilestones of Stonesfield slate are obtained at Sevenhampton, Eyford, Notgrove, and Througham, and rougher tiles of flaggy oolite have been got in many parts of the Cotswolds.

Gravel and sand, generally rather intermixed, occur near Cheltenham and in other localities. The gravel is chiefly composed of the rubble of the limestone, but can be used for paths and drives. On Cleeve Hill is a considerable deposit of finer sand, which was at one time exported to the Staffordshire Potteries. Down the Moreton Valley and the lower Severn stretch the gravel strata known as Northern Drift, which has been worked at Bredon, Shuthonger Common, Twyning Green, and Wainlode Hill.

The Keuper Marls contain various valuable deposits; ochre at Wick Rocks, near Mangotsfield; gypsum at Aust Cliff; and sulphate of strontium, which is worked at Yate and Wickwar and exported to Germany for use in beet-sugar refineries. There are also four groups of saline springs which, if they have not given rise to any large industries, have been the origin of Spas at Tewkesbury, Cheltenham, Gloucester, and Clifton.

To this list of natural sources of wealth must be added the abundance of forest-trees, which not only gave rise to the tanneries of Tewkesbury, Gloucester, and Bristol, and to innumerable modern timber industries, but made Bristol, till the 17th century, one of the chief shipbuilding ports of the kingdom. In the 16th century sieve-making, mainly a wooden industry, was carried on at Gloucester.[6]

The water-power, which has been mentioned as so valuable for fulling and dyeing cloth, was the occasion for the foundation of various other textile industries, such as silk, linen, and cottons. Silk must have been used at an early period for church embroidery (with a view to which an abbot of Cirencester in the 13th century wrote a book, 'De Natura Rerum,' explaining how to keep silk-worms); but the art of weaving it was probably introduced by French refugees of the 16th and 17th centuries. In 1637 silk-weaving was being practised at Gloucester.[7] At Chipping Campden and Blockley, about the year 1700, there were erected two silk-throwing mills, which made Campden famous for silk stockings in the 18th century, and which continued to work till some forty or fifty years ago.[8] Silk was also thrown at Tewkesbury between about 1840 and 1870, at which date the last firm, Iliffe's, migrated to Coventry. But the largest silk industry was in the Stroud Valley, where it was practised at one time in ten or a dozen mills. It has been killed off, however, by the hostile tariffs imposed about fourteen years ago by the French, who first drove the silk manufacturers out of French markets and have now undersold them in London. Such, at least, is the explanation of one who has been forced to close three silk mills, employing three or four hundred hands. At least eight other silk mills have followed suit, and an industry which forty years ago employed nearly a thousand persons is now almost extinct. The one exception is a new business at Langford Mill, Kingswood, where some two hundred persons are engaged in throwing silk for braid and fishing lines. Cotton and flax are also spun for the same purpose.

---

[1] *Hist. MSS. Com.* Rep. xii, App. ix, 423.
[2] Mins. Accts. bdle. 853, No. 7.
[3] Ibid. bdle. 852, No. 1.
[4] Ibid. bdle. 852, No. 5.
[5] Ibid. bdle. 850, No. 22.

[6] *Acts of P. C.* (New Ser.), xxi, 204.
[7] J. J. Powell, *Gloucestriana* : 'Early Trade Manuf. and Commerce of Glouc.'
[8] P. C. Rushen, *Hist. and Antiq. of Chipping Campden.*

With this exception, there has now been no flax industry in Gloucestershire for some years, though thirty-five years ago there were over a hundred hands employed in it. In 1838 a flax mill at Chipping Campden gave employment to forty-seven persons.[1] Linen used to be woven at Moreton-in-Marsh, and when the railway there was opened, the directors were each presented with fine linen table-cloths of local manufacture. This industry owed its rise to government protection, which had fostered the growing of flax at Moreton and Willersey as far back as 1787.[2]

A small cotton industry has existed for at least a century. A cotton-thread lace factory was founded at Tewkesbury at least as early as 1817, and in 1825 these works, the property of Messrs. Freeman in the Oldbury, were considered highly equipped for that date. The manufacture did not, however, survive later than 1850.[3] In 1803 there was a cotton-spinning mill at Bitton,[4] and by 1845 the Great Western Cotton Company had established its works at Barton Hill, Bristol. At the present day this firm employs some 1,500 workpeople, and exports largely to India and China.

Of other industries due to natural resources there only remain malting and brewing, which are hardly peculiar to the county, and cider-making, which has been the natural result of Gloucestershire's wealth in orchards. The earliest record of its manufacture that I have noticed is in about 1290 at Tidenham, a lay manor,[5] but it was probably practised first by religious houses, whose gardens were usually well stocked with fruit trees.

Methods of communication, even at the earliest period of the county's industrial history, were unusually good, in spite of the amount of hill and forest. This was mainly in consequence of the network of roads bequeathed by the Romans, and by the Britons before them. The central point of these is Cirencester, where the Foss Way, running north-east and south-west, cuts the lesser Ermine Street, which connects Cirencester with Gloucester, Ross, and ultimately Wales. Close to Cirencester this line of roads is crossed by the Akeman Street, which ran almost east and west, entering the county at Coln St. Aldwyn, and passing on by Cirencester to Rodmarton, Aust, and the Severn. The White Way from Winchcombe also ended at Cirencester. Besides these there was the Salt Way, from Droitwich to Lechlade, which entered the county near Hailes and ran down the eastern margin by Salperton and Coln St. Aldwyn ; a

track from Gloucester to Bristol, probably on the line of the existing road, and another trackway which nearly followed the present road through Birdlip, by the Seven Springs to Andoversford. The Portway, which started at Bath, ran by Gloucester past Kimsbury, Painswick, and Minchinhampton ; Buggilde's Way traversed the northern Cotswolds by Honeybourne, Broadway and Guiting, and passed out of the county at Bourton on the Water ; while the British Ryknield Road crossed the northern part of the county close to Tewkesbury. The Severn was crossed at Aust and Abone, probably, as well as Gloucester and Tewkesbury. At the present day, besides these two towns, there are bridges at Upton and Sharpness, and a passage at Newnham.

The canals made at the end of the 18th century and in the early years of the 19th gave means of industrial communication which supplemented and often superseded the less dependable road routes. First in date was the Stroudwater Canal, which, opened in about 1779, has had a useful and placid existence, and has connected the different manufactures of the Stroud Valley with the Severn estuary, and with the Gloucester and Berkeley Canal. Next, in 1798, the Hereford Canal was opened, although it did not for some years extend, as was intended, to Gloucester. It was bought about the middle of last century by the Great Western Railway, was neglected, and has been for some years derelict. In 1799, the Thames and Severn Canal, of which 26¼ out of a total length of 30 miles pass through Gloucestershire, began its troubled existence. It had been the ideal of various engineers of the early 18th and even the 17th centuries thus to join the upper waters of the Severn and Thames. Finally, at a cost of £245,000, the highest part of the intervening watershed was pierced by a tunnel of 1½ miles at Sapperton ; the rest of the incline was overcome by a double series of locks, and the canal, at last opened, had a steady success up to 1841, when its traffic amounted to 89,271 tons, with receipts of £11,330. Then adversity overtook it. The Great Western Railway opened its line from Cirencester to Swindon in that year, and in the sixty-five years that have since passed the canal first fell into partial disuse from obstructions in the Thames, was then bought by the Great Western Railway, and in 1893 formally closed. It was later purchased by a public trust, which, after the expenditure of £19,000, once earned a profit of £271 ; was again declared unworkable ; and in 1901 was finally taken over by the County Council, who have spent large sums on its repair, and hope eventually to make it successful, as supplying a means of communication to a large district at present ill-provided.

From these three comparatively unimportant canals we may turn to the great Gloucester and

---

[1] P C. Rushen, op. cit.
[2] Glouc. Record Books.
[3] J. Bennett, *Tewkesbury Yearly Reg.* i ; and *Hist. of Tewkesbury*, 202.
[4] Glouc. Quarter Sessions Minute Bks.
[5] Mins. Accts. bdle. 859, No. 21.

Berkeley Ship Canal, which by means of the Severn Navigation and the Worcester and Birmingham Canals opens up and connects the whole county with the Bristol Channel and the Midlands. It was begun in 1794, opened in 1827, and was until the completion of the Manchester Ship Canal the greatest of its kind in England. It gives a direct route of 16 miles to Gloucester, instead of the tortuous 28½ miles by river, which had always been dangerous to ships owing to the shifting sands of the Severn estuary, and to its exceptionally strong tides, which are the highest in Europe. So unwilling had foreign ships been to ascend the river, that we are told that 'in 1791 the arrival of one from Oporto was greeted with ringing of bells and firing of cannon.'[1] The success of the canal has been unbroken, and its cargo tonnage has risen steadily from 107,000 tons in 1827, with total receipts of £2,836, to 567,000 tons and £28,600 receipts in 1870, and to 1,053,000 tons of cargo in 1905, with a revenue of £35,374.[2] Thus since the opening of the New Entrance docks at Sharpness in 1875 the volume of cargo borne on the canal has doubled, and a further extension of the canal to supply another entrance at Shepherdine is contemplated. At present ships of 5,400 tons can be docked at Sharpness, while a 1,200-ton vessel can go up the canal, which is 18 ft. deep, to Gloucester.

There are various schemes afloat in the minds of business men of the county by which the inland navigation of the Severn district might be improved. Thus, it has been urged before the Canal Commission that, if the locks, etc. at Gloucester were improved, and if the Birmingham and Worcester Canal were enlarged, 100-ton vessels might pass direct from Sharpness to Gloucester up the Severn (which has been canalized by the commissioners to Worcester, and can carry boats of 160 to 200 tons), and thence to Birmingham and the Pottery district, thus saving the time and expense at present involved in transhipment into small barges. The journey by water from Sharpness to Birmingham, which is 76 miles, has been accomplished in 30 hours, and it has been calculated that the substantial lowering of freight thus possible[3] would at once secure a large share of carrying trade to the Canal Company, relieve the congestion in goods traffic, and definitely 'open the Midlands to the sea.' But that question does not concern Gloucestershire alone.

To the same period as that which saw the creation of the canal system, belong various small industries of more than local fame, such as the manufacture of hats at Frampton Cotterell and Bitton, and of carpets at Cirencester (first mentioned by Rudder in 1779).[4] Carpet-weaving died out at Cirencester in 1836, when many of the operatives migrated to Kidderminster, but it is still carried on at Stroud on a small scale. The hat industry, which consisted in felting wool, and covering it with rabbit-fur, began to decline between 1840 and 1850 with the introduction of silk hats; during this decade the population of Frampton Cotterell fell considerably. In 1871 the census reported only 15 persons in Gloucestershire as engaged in the felt industry (which presumably included hats). Edge-tools for curriers were made in the 18th century at Cirencester (where the manufacture still continues) and at Gloucester. Button-making, lace-making, and tobacco-dressing had been also carried on at Gloucester as far back as the 17th century;[5] wool-combing survived into the 19th century in places where the rest of the clothing industry had died out; and metal cards for clothiers were made at Dursley, Stroud, and Wotton under Edge at the close of the 18th century.[4] Till within living memory nails were manufactured at Tewkesbury, which had also long been so famous for its mustard as to give rise to the proverb, 'thick as Tewkesbury mustard,' quoted in Shakespeare's *Henry IV* (pt. ii, 4), à propos of Falstaff's wit. The secret of the peculiarly pungent flavour of this mustard is said to have been an admixture of horse-radish, added when the seed was being pounded.[6] The stocking-frame knitting of Tewkesbury and Cirencester, the pin-making and bell-foundry of Gloucester, are all industries of the old local type, which failed to survive the changed conditions of industry that followed the introduction of railways.

The main lines of Gloucestershire railway are the Great Western lines from Worcester to Oxford, viâ Evesham and Chipping Norton, and from Swindon to Gloucester and Bristol respectively; and the Midland line from Birmingham to Bristol, viâ Cheltenham, Gloucester, Coaley Junction, and Wickwar. From Wickwar a second branch passes westward to Lydney, by the Severn Bridge, built by the Midland Railway and opened in 1879. Eight years later the Great Western completed its scheme for the passage of the river by the Severn Tunnel, two miles below the junction of the Severn and Wye.[7]

With these improvements in communication, the industries of Gloucester and Bristol, which had passed through a period of stagnation, entered on one of rapid development. Docks were, and are still being, improved and the

[1] J. J. Powell, *Gloucestriana.*
[2] *Evidence before Royal Com. on Canals and Waterways,* May, 1906.
[3] To 4s. 3d. per ton as compared with the present railway rate of 6s. 8d. on similar goods.
[4] S. Rudder, *Hist. of Gloucestershire,* 63.
[5] Fosbrooke, *Hist. of Glouc.* 424.
[6] J. Bennett, *Hist. of Tewkesbury,* 201.
[7] In completing this vast undertaking as much water was pumped out as would form, it is computed, a lake 3,000 acres in extent and 10 feet deep. See T. A. Walker, *The Severn Tunnel.*

volume of trade has greatly increased. The rise of the engineering industry of the county has occurred mainly in the last thirty or forty years, and in Gloucester, at any rate, not more than five, out of the many flourishing firms at the present day, existed at the late Queen's accession.

This development of new manufactures is, perhaps, an even more interesting feature in the county's industrial history than the lengthy pedigree of some of the industries that have been described, for it gives good hope that Gloucestershire will be increasingly benefited by the new movement of industry from the Midlands to the coast, and from highly-rated cities to districts where production can be more cheaply and healthily carried on. At the same time such rural industries as fruit-growing and bee-keeping are developing. All along the Severn valley apples and pears are grown in large quantities for cider and perry, and orchard-planting is on the increase. In past years, however, many orchards have been suffered to become dilapidated, and much more might still be done in the way of fruit culture. Plums do

remarkably well near the Severn round Newnham and Westbury, and also in the Evesham district. At Frampton Cotterell and several places near Bristol, plums and strawberries are grown for the Bristol market. There and on the outskirts of the Forest of Dean, as well as on the Worcestershire border, a good deal of fruit is grown by small holders and owners, but on the whole Gloucestershire is an orchard county. A large percentage of the fruit is grown in farm orchards, but at Toddington, near Sudeley, where Beach's jam factory is situated, the Toddington Orchard Company have some 500 acres under fruit. The same place produces the largest amount of honey. The Bristol and Cheltenham districts are also active in bee-keeping, and in the more sheltered parts of the Cotswolds, especially near Stroud, Cirencester, and Andoversford, a large number of hives are kept. The industry suffers somewhat, however, from a lack of scientific knowledge, such as would be disseminated by a bee-keepers' association, though this is being to some extent remedied by the County Council's lectures and demonstrations in various parts of the county.

WOOL

A previous article [1] has already described the course of the clothing industry up to the introduction of power-machinery—a change which marks an impassable breach with the past. From that date its characteristics and the influences to which it is subject are sufficiently like those of the present day for it to be treated as a modern industry. For with the use of big and costly machinery came the concentration into large factories, which is the most familiar feature of modern manufactures, but was so distressing to observers of the 'forties' and 'fifties.' Long after the woollen industry had died out in Bristol and Gloucester it used to cover so large a district as is enclosed by Painswick and Bisley on the north, and Horsley and Wotton under Edge in the south. But in most of these villages deserted mills and houses of a size and style hardly in accord with their present surroundings now alone testify to their former greatness. If, as before said, we turn to the census reports, we should date the beginning of this decay at about 1830, from which time the population of the clothing district steadily decreased. The returns for 1851 expressly mention the decline of the woollen manufacture as the cause of the fall in population at Minchinhampton, Avening, Horsley, Randwick, Edge, Pitchcombe, Kingswood, Stinchcombe, Coaley, Uley, Cam, and Wotton under Edge. In 1861 the same tale of woe is told with regard to Nibley, Slimbridge, and

Eastington. Yet cloth manufacturers declare that the decline of their business did not set in till 1875, up to which time their prosperity had been steadily growing. The explanation, as already suggested, is to be found in the tendency of industry to concentrate when machinery is introduced into it. In Stroud only did the cloth manufacturers succeed in establishing power-looms, in the teeth of the weavers' opposition ; and in Stroud, alone among the Gloucestershire clothing towns, has the population grown unceasingly since 1831. About this date the first large power-loom shed was erected at Stafford's Mill. Elsewhere, with one exception, strikes have caused the gradual extinction of the industry.

The cause of this especial dislike of power-machinery in Gloucestershire is not hard to seek. The craft of the hand-loom weaver had a pedigree of almost unparalleled length. Both the art and the loom itself were often handed down from father to son, and their possession gave a sort of dignity and independence to the worker that were lost by factory work at daily wages. When the weaver bought his own yarn, and wove it at home, he was more or less his own master, doing long or short hours as suited the season or his own inclination. All the family could take their turns at the loom, the narrower kind being easily worked by a boy, a woman, or an old man. A narrow loom cost about £5, and lasted a long time without getting out of order. Broad looms were far less common in cottages, as they took up too much space for an

[1] See *ante*, 'Social and Economic History.'

ordinary room. The journeymen who sold the yarn were apt, it is true, to drive rather hard bargains with these home-workers, but on the whole the latter could earn a very fair living. An old weaver, who worked a hand-loom till about thirty years ago, computes the weekly earnings of himself and his wife together at about 30s. Each of them worked a loom, and could weave a piece (60 yds.) in a fortnight. For a piece they would be paid 30s. at the factories—where also they got their yarn, a chain and a half at a time. Most of the weavers were old men in his young days, says another of these survivors, who remembers the introduction of power-looms. The old men refused to be troubled with the new machinery, and it was chiefly women who took it up.

The hereditary prejudices of their operatives thus combined with the general fall in prices after 1815 to give the Gloucestershire clothiers a hard struggle in the first half of the nineteenth century. A Blue Book of 1800, called 'An account of the proceedings of the merchants, manufacturers, and others concerned in the wool and woollen trade of Great Britain,' contains the complaints of a west-country witness on the first score. 'The opposition that we generally meet with in the West of England to introducing machinery is so great,' he declared, 'that, until the Yorkshire manufacturers have stolen the article away from us, we are almost afraid to introduce it.'[1] Thus an improvement in the shearing process, called 'The Lewis cutting-machine,' though invented towards the end of the 18th century by a Stroud manufacturer, was rejected by the operatives. In 1820 the hand-mule was introduced—a species of machinery which, though not worked by steam, yet greatly reduced the amount of labour required for spinning. But up to 1851, when Gloucestershire broadcloth won high honours at the Great Exhibition, very little machinery was in use beyond the 'slubbing billy,' the hand-mule, and the power-loom. Between 1840 and 1850, however, the old system of milling, or hammering, the cloth by 'stocks' was superseded by a felting-machine, composed of a continuous series of rollers through which the cloth was passed, sometimes for so long a period as forty or fifty hours. In the course of the next decade an automatic spinning-mule, invented by Roberts, superseded both the hand-mule and the 'billy'; nor have later inventions been able to surpass the 'scroll' method of this mule for spinning woollen yarn. (Worsted, on the other hand, is now spun almost entirely upon a frame.) By about the year 1870 Mr. James Hollingworth had perfected his 'Dobcross' power-looms, which were rapidly taken up by woollen manufacturers and valued at what was then considered the high price of £50 apiece. Other improvements in machinery quickly

followed. The addition of a second warp-bar enabled 'backed' cloths to be made, while the multiplication of shuttles and healds permitted a far greater variety in weight and pattern than was ever dreamed of by workers of the old simple looms, on which threads were merely lifted alternately. Another advantage of the double warp-bar was that the same loom could be used for the production of either light or heavy cloths. Again, in 1882, Mr. Hollingworth produced a better and even more adaptable loom—an improved species of the 'Knowles' loom, all rights to which he had purchased from its American inventor. Thus to the same man we owe both the 'Knowles' and the 'Dobby,' the two great looms of the present day.

These improved methods of manufacture, together with the removal, in 1828, of the duties on the import of foreign wool, gave a great impetus to the Stroud clothing industry. Between 1851 and 1861 the number of persons in Gloucestershire engaged in all branches of the woollen industry rose from 4,459 to 7,050. The census figures for the next decade, however, show a decline in numbers by about a thousand; by 1881 the numbers had sunk to 4,958, and by 1901 to 3,321. More than one mill has failed since then, while others close occasionally, or are often worked at a loss.

The first decline in numbers between 1861 and 1871 must be accounted for by the displacement of labour due to the introduction of mechanical appliances—if manufacturers are right in admitting no diminution of prosperity until after 1875. While the same arguments may apply in some degree to the subsequent decline, there is no masking the general tendency of the trade during the last thirty years. In this period not a single new woollen mill has been built, and about twenty woollen businesses have come to an end. This may be ascribed to three main causes—foreign competition, slowness of manufacturers to follow changes of fashion, and, recently, high cost of raw material.

The high protective tariffs of America and the continent have undoubtedly had an effect on the Stroud woollen industry. New York alone now imports not much over a fortieth of what she took ten years ago. The cutting down of prices, consequent on the dumping of foreign woollen goods in England, falls with especial severity upon the broadcloth manufacture, which must always, and necessarily, be a costly one. This is due to the far more numerous and more elaborate processes required to produce smooth, highly finished cloth. Woven of woollen yarn, which is spun less tightly and strongly than worsted, broadcloth has to pass through the felting, fulling, and dressing processes in order to acquire proper strength and compactness. These are followed by finishing processes, which may be repeated an almost indefinite number of

[1] For this and other pieces of information see *Stroud Journal Supplement*, 13 May, 1904.

times, and demand both skill and judgement to regulate.[1]

This greater complexity of the woollen-cloth manufacture is probably one reason why Gloucestershire has lagged behind Yorkshire, which was the first to take up the worsted industry. The original disparity has been again accentuated by the rapid change of fashion that set in, when it was discovered how much greater variety of colour and design could be introduced into worsted cloth. Fancy tweeds were first brought in about 1830 and soon increased in popularity. Between 1842 and 1880 the improvement in worsted coatings was enormous, and at the present date they are almost exclusively worn in this country. Their neglect of this new fashion was due, it must be admitted, to short-sightedness on the part of Gloucestershire manufacturers ; and, while they could hardly have been expected to foresee the vast extent of the approaching change in the cloth trade, they have certainly stuck to their old methods of industry with somewhat unnecessary perseverance. Worsted cloth is now, however, being woven by a few of them with great success. The actual numbers employed in the worsted manufacture are hard to discover, as the last census did not quote them separately. In 1891 they amounted to sixty-seven as compared with four in 1851, but the numbers must now be considerably greater. Yet tradition and hereditary custom have both operated against such a development in the Stroud district, whereas Yorkshire had a larger population from which to draw its workers, and one that was quicker in appreciating new methods and inventions. The relative cost of coal in the two districts has been rather unfavourable to Gloucestershire manufacturers, who show also a lack of power to organize their trade that was noted as one of their defects as far back as 1779. And, lastly, the worsted fabrics adopted by the north lent themselves to the introduction of the shoddy manufacture to an extent impossible, even were it desired, in the broadcloth industry ; and thus Stroud clothiers fell behind yet a

[1] The most interesting processes of finishing are those performed by the teasing machine, which raises the nap of the cloth, and the shearer, which clips it off. The former consists of cylinders, closely studded with teazles, through which the cloth is passed ; the latter, of rollers, with spiral knives upon them, somewhat resembling a grass-lawn mower, but with the principle just reversed—the article to be shorn traversing, instead of being traversed by, the cutters. Before the invention of this machine the nap was clipped by hand. Teazles, it may be noticed, though some of them are now imported from France, have been largely grown in Gloucestershire, especially at Sandfield and Cromhall, where they find a congenial marly soil. With the change of fashion, and decline in the manufacture of highly finished cloth, teazles are, however, grown in ever smaller quantities, and there is said to have been only one lot to cut this year (1906) at Cromhall.

second stage in the general struggle for increased cheapness.

But by far the most immediate cause of difficulty to Gloucestershire industry has been the scarcity in the supply of the fine wool on which all makers of fine cloths rely. This is due to the eight-years' drought in Australia, which, since the introduction of the merino sheep by Macarthur, has produced the larger part of the fine wool imported by this country, the rest being supplied by New Zealand, South Africa, and the East Indies. The best of all still comes from Silesia, where the merino has been bred since 1765. Till within the last forty or fifty years, indeed, Stroud manufacturers used still to journey to Breslau personally to select their purchases of wool. Now, all their wool is bought at the London Wool Exchange. Spain, formerly their chief mart, had been given up after the Peninsular War, when the quality of the Spanish merino deteriorated. Though up to 1800 England was importing annually from Spain as much as 6,000,000 lb. of wool, by 1857 the yearly imports had fallen to 383,000 lb. Their place was taken by German wool, of which as much as 26,000,000 lb. was imported to England in 1830. After that date, however, Australia and South Africa drew up in the race. The imports from these two countries rose from 1,967,000 lb. and 33,000 lb., respectively, in 1830 to 49,209,000 lb. and 14,287,000 lb. in 1857, by which date German imports had fallen to 5,993,000. By 1869 Australia and the Cape were sending in some 200,000,000 lb. a year.

While discussing sources of raw material, it may be well to note the disuse of Cotswold fleeces, the fine quality of which originated the Gloucestershire woollen industry. This has been the result, partly of the deterioration of wool that accompanied the increase in the animal's bulk, partly of the great improvement of the merino breed elsewhere. Rudder, writing in 1779, mentions that the longer Cotswold wool was still combed for worsteds, and the shorter woven into army cloth [1]; now it is considered too coarse for anything but blankets or very rough materials. The only factories in which local, though not pure Cotswold, fleeces are used are those of a Stroud manufacturer, Mr. Apperly, who has of late begun to employ the wool from his own Hyde Farm, and from other celebrated flocks of the neighbourhood, such as those of Sir John Dorington and Sir Nigel Kingscote. After many experiments he has succeeded in softening the wool, so as to turn out an excellent material, known as ' Hydea ' cloth, for dresses, suitings, and overcoatings.

The main products of the Stroud Valley still, however, consist of smooth, highly finished cloths, such as hunting and military scarlets, white buckskins, doeskins, liveries, riding cords, beavers, meltons, vicunas, llamas and cheviots,

[1] S. Rudder, op. cit. 23.

and cloths for pianos, carriages, and billiard-tables. As the use of livery has greatly decreased of late, some enterprising firms have turned their attention with great success to motor caps and coatings.

There are now eleven surviving firms of cloth manufacturers, whose mills lie mainly in Stroud and its immediate neighbourhood. Dudbridge Mills are owned by Messrs. Apperly, Curtis & Co. whose business was established in 1794 by the grandfather of the present director, Mr. Alfred Apperly. They were rebuilt after the destruction of the old mills by fire in 1891, and are now some of the largest clothworks in the west of England. Their machinery is thoroughly up-to-date, and includes a self-acting feed for the carding machine, invented in 1851 by Mr. James Apperly and Mr. William Clissold. Of the 'Hydea' cloth manufactured by this firm mention has already been made; their other chief speciality is travelling-rugs, woven by a process of their own. They have their own dye-works on the premises, and do much of the dyeing required by other manufacturers. The only other large dye-works of the district are at Bowbridge, and are the property of Messrs. Strachan & Co. At their two cloth-mills, Lodgemore and Frome Hall, this latter firm manufacture dark and light cloth respectively, as it is all-important to the colour of light materials that they should be made in a different room from dark ones. Their products are mainly serges, liveries, box and billiard cloth, and riding cords. They are one of the few firms who still employ water-power in one department. At Lightpill Mills Messrs. Roberts, Jowlings & Co., established about 1850, carry on a smaller but fairly flourishing business, with thoroughly good machinery. Their cloths are mainly of the regular West of England type, and are still racked on the old plan, which turns out better results for heavy cloths than more modern rapid methods. The especial feature of these mills is the weaving of heavy beavers, to which a whole shed, with peculiarly heavy machinery, is devoted. Very similar styles of cloth, on a slightly smaller scale, are turned out by Messrs. Howard & Powell, at Wallbridge Mill, which has been working for at least eighty years.

The foregoing mills all stand conveniently close to the Stroud Canal and to the Midland and Great Western Railways. A little further out on the north, or Slade side of the town, stand Woodlands Mills, lately purchased by a Welshman, Mr. Humphreys. By adapting himself to the modern taste for tweeds and homespuns, and by importing a few workmen from his flannel factory in Wales to instruct the native workmen in new methods, he has established a thriving business, mainly with London and Manchester. A very large number of his looms are devoted to making material for motor-caps.

On the opposite side of the town stand Brimscombe Mills, the property of Messrs. P. C. Evans & Co. Established in 1855, they have been under the direction of five generations of the Evans family. Large improvements have been made recently, including the establishment of the first worsted-spinning plant of the district. At Minchinhampton, high up the valley of the Frome, is Longfords Mill, which has been for three centuries in the hands of the Playnes, originally a French Protestant family.

On a smaller stream, to the west of Stroud, are Ebley and Stanley Mills, the property of Messrs. Marling & Co., and Eastington Mill. Here Messrs. Hooper & Co. weave white cricketing flannels and white buckskins, besides the usual smooth cloth of the neighbourhood. Another Stonehouse firm (Messrs. R. S. Davies & Sons), owning two mills, has just closed a career begun in 1798.

The many cloth-mills formerly existing at Dursley and Wotton under Edge are now represented by two large firms. In the Nind Mills, Wotton under Edge, Messrs. Millman, Hunt & Co. possess a building that has been in use for three centuries. In 1893 they also took over the management of a neighbouring mill at Charfield. They are fortunate in their supply of water-power, which is sufficient to drive three large water-wheels. Their speciality is the manufacture of printers' blanketings. Cam Mills, Dursley, the property of Messrs. Hunt & Winterbotham, are some of the largest in the whole district, covering an area of eight acres, and employing over four hundred operatives. Within the last six or seven years they have been able to make extensive improvements, including special cottages for their work-people. Their works are self-contained, with carpenters' and fitters' shops attached to them. They weave almost every style of cloth produced in the Stroud Valley, including some made of pure English wool.

To turn to the condition of the operatives employed in the cloth manufacture, perhaps the first point to be noticed is the preponderance of female over male workers, in the proportion of about five to three. This feature dates probably from the introduction of the power-loom, when, as has been mentioned, women stepped in to fill the place of the more recalcitrant men. Wages are difficult to estimate, as every process of the manufacture is paid at a different rate and on a different scale. The elements taken into consideration in weaving, for instance, are the rate at which the loom runs, the number of picks per inch of woven cloth, and the number of shuttles or other complications of the process. Wages are paid sometimes by the week, but more often by the piece, and vary from 5s. to 17s. for female workers, and from 15s. to 35s. for males. The average weekly earnings, however, would be 12s. or 15s. in the case of a woman, and 18s. or 20s.

in the case of a man. Apprenticeship has now died out, but useful training in the theory of weaving is given to boys who care to learn upon the hand-looms of the Stroud School of Art. Elsewhere hand-looms have finally disappeared ; the last, probably, being those worked by a few old people at Uley and Dursley nearly twenty years ago. The census of 1901 recorded six 'persons engaged in woollen manufacture' in Gloucestershire as working in their own homes, but these were probably not weavers, but people engaged in some subordinate process of the manufacture.

Upon the whole, a general review of the Stroud cloth industry inclines one to be hopeful on its behalf. The number of hands that it employs is undoubtedly diminishing, having fallen from 6,589 in 1871 to 3,321 in 1901, but, according to a belief general among the manufacturers, the district has now a larger annual output of cloth than ever before, owing to the labour-saving appliances of modern machinery. It is a disappointing fact that such improvements have not led to any really corresponding growth in the volume of trade, but this, we have seen, has been largely due to the trend of English fashion in the direction of worsted cloths—a trend which is said, however, to have slightly diminished in the last three or four years. Gloucestershire woollen manufacturers have undoubtedly fallen behind in the race, but it is not too late for them to recover. The broadcloth manufacture, being one in which it is almost impossible to scamp work or conceal faults, has been so good an industrial education that its makers have never lost their high reputation for sound workmanship. And if the past twenty years have seen the collapse of many old clothing firms, they have also witnessed enormous improvements in mechanical plant, so that those mills that survive are now as well equipped as any in the country. The most hopeful sign of all, however, is the manufacture of tweeds and other rough coatings, taken up by the more progressive of the cloth firms. The extraordinary and growing success with which this has been attended affords, I think, strong ground for hope that, should other manufacturers follow this lead, the Gloucestershire woollen industry may yet enjoy its own again.

The manufacture of cloth is usually treated as the woollen industry *par excellence* of the west country, but there are two branches of Gloucestershire manufacture that must not be omitted from the same category. The first of these might seem akin to cloth-making, though, as a matter of fact, it has no special connexion with it. In the Brimscombe and Nailsworth valleys is carried on the manufacture of flock and shoddy—products both made out of old woollen rags. These are sorted, boiled (in the better factories), and dried in a temperature of 300° Fahrenheit, after which they are passed

through rollers studded with teeth, which tear the rags into shreds. The best resulting material, known as mattress wool, is not unlike freshly carded wool ; the lower grades, formed out of coloured rags, are less carefully shredded, and look much more lumpy. The lowest grade, known as flock, is prepared in a slightly different way. And yet a third process is required for shoddy, of which a small quantity is manufactured annually for Yorkshire spinners and weavers. The whole business in Gloucestershire is not large, the chief mills being those of Mr. Richard Grist at Brimscombe and Chalford, which turn out the more expensive kinds of mattress material, and Mr. Selwyn's Toadsmoor Mill, which produces the cheaper class of goods. A large amount of the raw material employed is carpet rags, imported from Holland for this purpose.

A more important sub-division of the woollen industry is hosiery, in the production of which some two hundred hands are now employed. The earliest form of this manufacture was stocking-frame knitting, which was invented in 1589, and introduced into Gloucestershire in the 18th century. In 1779 Rudder wrote of it as the chief occupation of Cirencester, Tewkesbury, Newent, and a few villages in that neighbourhood.[1] In Cirencester, as early as 1727, a charitable bequest had founded 'The Yellow School,' where twenty poor boys were to be taught stocking-frame knitting. By 1800 this was a thriving industry, though it did not survive much longer.[2] At Tewkesbury, thirty years later, some 800 frames (or looms) were at work, and 1,500 persons, or one quarter of the population, were employed in the stocking manufacture,[3] which consisted partly of silk and partly of wool. The Tewkesbury hosiers entered largely into the life of the old borough, and were evidently a luxurious class, for a clause in their apprenticeship indentures stipulated that they should not be given fish more than three times a week, as a consequence of the great number of salmon in the Severn.

The *Tewkesbury Yearly Register* of 1830 to 1848 gives interesting details as to the condition of the hosiery trade at that period. In November, 1831, says this publication—

in consequence of a disagreement between the hosiers and their workmen respecting wages, the latter, who compose a large body of the lower class of the town, assembled at the Cross in great numbers, and went round to their masters with certain demands, which were readily complied with.

On the ensuing day they increased their demands, and pressed them with such vehemence that the military had to be called out, and many special constables were sworn. Six years

---

[1] S. Rudder, op. cit. p. 63.
[2] *Hist. of Cirencester and Tewkesbury* (1800), 312–19.
[3] J. Bennett, *Hist. of Tewkesbury*, 202.

previously there had been a strike of frame-work knitters, and in 1814 a hosiery manufacturer had been threatened with death unless he raised the wages of his workmen. But the present moment, being that of the Bristol riots, was a specially alarming one. It was thought that

the turbulent behaviour of the stocking-makers was caused by some abandoned characters from Derby and Nottingham, who had made erroneous statements respecting the wages paid by the manufacturers in those towns.[1]

The influence of these agitators was counteracted by the wisdom of the magistrates, who induced the workmen 'to depute a committee to state their grievances in writing,' and thereby effected a peaceful compromise between them and the masters. In 1842 the hosiery trade suffered so great a depression that 220 frames were stopped for six weeks, and there was talk of providing employment for the knitters out of the poor-rates. Most fortunately this scheme was pronounced illegal by the Board of Guardians, and soon after trade improved sufficiently for work to be given at low wages, which the operatives thankfully accepted.[2] The decline in the hosiery hand-loom manufacture was, however, serious, as is shown by the census reports. By 1851 the number of persons employed in it had fallen to 276, and though the next decade showed a slight improvement in numbers, yet from 1861 they fell steadily, till in 1891 only fifty-seven persons were employed. Since then, however, the last census reports a rise in the number of hosiery employees to 216, thanks to the establishment of Messrs. Walker's hosiery factory at Dunkirk Mills, Nailsworth, in 1891. This firm, like many others, utilized a deserted cloth mill, the oldest part of which had been built in 1798, and has been described, under the title 'Enderley Mill,' in Mrs. Craik's *John Halifax, Gentleman.* Only stocking-wear is turned out, and this enjoys a fairly steady sale.

This revival, however, only replaces to a small degree the lack of employment created by the failure of the older Tewkesbury industry. Hand-looms of course, both singly and collectively, demanded far more employment of labour. Two thousand of them would not have turned out more goods than can six of the modern electric-power looms, which make 360 or 380 revolutions for five or six of the old sort; and two power-looms can be managed by one man. Each workman under the old system, however, earned about as much money as his modern successor. Moreover, in addition to the persons actually employed in weaving, the old industry gave employment to 500 or 600 persons in its accessory processes, such as seaming, scouring,

bleaching, sewing on calico bands and buttons to the hosiery garments, and embroidering or clocking the stockings. Framesmiths, who repaired the looms, and needle-makers, who made the special needles required for them, were also supported at Tewkesbury by the hosiery trade there. These needles were peculiarly formed with a hook or 'beard' at the knitting end, and with little lumps, or notches, at the other. The latter helped to fix the needle in the needle-mould, into which melted pewter was also

STOCKING-LOOM NEEDLE

poured. These 'heads' were then ready for insertion in the frame, which was made to carry a larger or smaller number, according to the width of work required. In the frame were also 'jacks' and 'sinkers,' which knitted the stitches all across the frame. About 1860 a time-saving invention was made in the 'carrier,' which enabled the yarn to be thrown more rapidly across the loom, but such small improvements could not save the hand-looms from going down before the flood of machine competition. Tewkesbury hosiers had not sufficient capital to set up the large power-looms, which cost some £700. Thus by 1875 the industry had sunk very low, and finally flickered out a few years ago. The last batch of hand-frames, which cost originally £400, were sold for 30s. as old iron by Mr. Wilkes, the last of the hand-loom manufacturers. His firm, established about 1829, worked for a Mr. Hooke of Exeter, and owned 40 looms. Up to the end he was constantly called on to supplement the work of the power-looms, which is undoubtedly inferior. The hand-loom stocking was far stronger, containing an average of nine or ten threads in thickness, and was looked over individually after weaving, in order that all dropped stitches might be picked up by hand. Hence hand-made hosiery is still in demand, and large quantities of hose used to be sent to Tewkesbury to be 'doctored' and sold as hand-manufactured. This is a curious instance of the harking-back of fashion.

In conclusion, it may be noticed that the woollen manufacture of Gloucestershire probably originated, though it does not now supply, the considerable clothing business in the county, especially at Stroud and Bristol. In the former town is a large production of ready-made clothing, mainly in the hands of Jews; in the latter is a corset manufacture that employs a very large number of hands, and is possibly descended from the 'whalebone boddes' made by the Merchant Taylors in the seventeenth century.[3]

[1] J. Bennett, *Tewkesbury Yearly Reg.* i, 70, 71.
[2] Ibid. ii, 81, 82.

[3] See F. F. Fox, *Anct. Frat. of Mer. Taylors,* 19–20.

WATERPROOFS, ROPES, AND OTHER TEXTILES

Besides her woollen fabrics Gloucestershire has a number of miscellaneous textile industries, due largely to the requirements of her shipping trade, or to her West Indian imports of hemp, rubber, oil-seed, &c. At Kingswood, Wotton under Edge, Messrs. Tubbs, Lewis & Co., whose silk-line manufacture has already been mentioned, carry on a considerable elastic industry, which employs some 700 hands. One of their three mills is entirely devoted to the spinning and weaving of elastic fabrics, for which purpose they have devised special looms. Here is made the 'Sandow Developer,' the production of which occupies 100 workpeople.

In Bristol are a considerable number of india-rubber factories connected with the motor and cycle trade, and also a large oilcloth manufacture. John Hare & Co., established in 1782, are the oldest firm of floorcloth makers. A guide-book of 1828 [1] describes a visit to their factory at Temple Gate and recites triumphantly that

the whole process is conducted on the premises, from spinning the flax, weaving, &c., with the manufacture of colours, to the completion in pieces 180 ft. long and 27 ft. wide, of the most rich and varied patterns, which are exported to all parts of the world.

The business is now carried on in conjunction with the grinding of oil and colours.

Sail-cloth was made at Bristol at the close of the 18th century,[2] but the only sail-makers now existing in the county are Messrs. Johns & Sons, one of the oldest firms in Gloucester. Canvas, sacking, and tarpaulin are made at Dursley by another long-established firm, Messrs. Champion & Sons, who manufacture mattings of flax, hemp, jute, and cocoanut fibre. Messrs. Yeo Brothers, of Bristol, are also engaged in the jute trade, and make up sacks and tarpaulins for sale. Waterproofs for hydraulic purposes are made at Arno's Vale, Bristol, by Messrs. Terrell & Sons, who have also acquired sole rights to manufacture several brands of 'Engine Packing.' For this fabric they employ linden bark, tape, hemp, cotton, asbestos yarns (both plain and metallic), and esparto grass, which last material passes through many intricate processes of boiling,

drying, crushing, twisting, and spinning. The engine-packing trade suffers, however, from the continual changes in the style of locomotives, which render it hard to be up to date.

Both Champion and Terrell are also rope-manufacturers. This old-established Gloucestershire industry, which flourished at Gloucester in 1720,[3] and at Tewkesbury as late as 1832, is now extinct in both these towns, while all over the county the number of rope-walks has diminished. Like other trades this manufacture has of late become increasingly centralized. Large rope-manufacturers now supply smaller firms, who retail from shops, whereas formerly the small rope-maker made and sold for himself in markets. Thus, while a few smaller firms, such as Champion's, do manufacture agricultural rope and twine, their principal business is in factoring, and Terrell's is by far the largest rope-making firm in the county. It was first established in Canon's Marsh about 1770, but moved a few years ago into larger premises, with a rope-walk 300 yards long. Here ropes of every size are turned out, from the largest hawser to the finest rat-line. The best large ropes, it is interesting to notice, are still made by hand, though machinery is perfectly satisfactory for smaller sizes. Binder-twine, for use on reaping machines, is made in enormous quantities, 100 tons being exported last July (1906) to Canada alone. The binder-twine and box-cord branch of the business is growing fast. Besides agricultural ropes, flexible steel wire ropes and rigging hawsers are supplied to the Admiralty, Lloyds, and other large shipping companies. But the railway connexion is perhaps the biggest, as, besides the 'engine-packing' manufacture, the company produce great quantities of carriage 'communication cord' for many of the principal railways.

The best material for ropes is Manilla hemp, of which an enormous amount is annually imported direct from the Philippine Islands. Owing to the superior length and toughness of its fibre it is mainly employed at Terrell's rope-walk, although Russian, Indian and New Zealand hemp, and coir yarn (a cocoanut fibre production) also enter largely into the manufacture.

TIMBER, ETC.

The woods of the Cotswolds and the Forest of Dean provided Gloucestershire in the past with an abundant supply of timber, and encouraged all the industries dependent on it to an extent

beyond the merely local hewing of wood and carpentering which every county must have practised. Now, although comparatively little local wood is used, and the native supplies are no longer a *raison d'être* of the trade, timber dealing, with its accessories, is one of the most important

[1] Mathew's *Bristol Guide*, 1828.
[2] *New History of Bristol*, published by W. Matthews, Bristol, 1794; p. 41.

[3] J. J. Powell, *Gloucestriana*.

industries in the county, employing, according to the census of 1901, nearly 7,000 persons. Besides these, large numbers are engaged in its transport.

The Forest of Dean will be dealt with elsewhere; but it may be observed that mention is made in the forest accounts as early as 1280, of the right to fell timber and burn charcoal within its limits.[1] In 1657 and 1668 Acts were passed for the preservation of the trees, the latter ordering the enclosure, and planting with oaks for the Royal Navy, of 11,000 acres of waste land in the forest; while during the Civil Wars, Sir J. Winter complained, in his narrative published in the reign of Charles II,[2] that from the time that his patent in the forest was interrupted by the civil troubles, until the Restoration, above 40,000 tons of timber were cut down by order of the House of Commons. Its importance for shipbuilding, &c., thus for long extended beyond the limits of the county. Now English timber, whatever be its intrinsic superiority, is both scarce and costly compared with similar foreign woods, and the trade in it is too unsystematic, or too purely local, for chronicling.

Foreign timber has far more than supplied its place, as regards quantity and importance. Bristol imported over £1,000,000 worth in 1905, and Gloucester, which is said to be the ninth town in order in the timber trade within the United Kingdom, imported to the value of nearly £600,000, out of a total of a little over £25,000,000 for the whole country.[3] As far back as the time of Elizabeth it is said that there were mills at Swinford for grinding logwood and other hard American woods for dyeing purposes. They were owned by the Tyndall family, and only closed in 1886.[4] The history of the origin of the Gloucester trade in foreign timber is curious. Up to 1736 the government had sold the oaks felled in the Forest of Dean to a local dealer, who squared them up roughly and sold them again at a great profit for the use of the royal docks. At length in 1736 the government realized the meaning of this ingenious transaction, and put a stop to it. The disappointed dealer then sold the three ships with which he had carried on the trade, and one of these, purchased by its previous captain, brought to Gloucester, as a speculation, the first

load of Norway deals. This, owing to the captain's fear of grounding with the falling tide, which has always been a difficulty in the port of Gloucester, was dumped at cost price in the yards of a riverside merchant, Mr. Morgan Price, who, however, profited so much by his venture when he came to resell, that he organized a regular service of vessels from abroad, which has continued in his family for 130 years.[5] His example was followed in a few years by one Cornelius Gardener, who brought wood up the river in trows and rafts; and the foreign timber trade, by means of the canals made in the early years of last century, was for a time probably the most important occupation of the lower Severn waterways. The volume of the imports has increased steadily throughout the century, and expanded at Gloucester in the ratio of 9 to 1 during the reign of Queen Victoria, with a temporary inflation in the years 1851–3, when the huts of the French army in the Crimea were supplied by the oldest firm, Price, Walker & Co.

This firm may be considered representative of the modern trade in the district. Its imports have, of course, extended beyond the Norway deals bought by its founder, to firwoods from Russia, Sweden, and Canada, pitch pine from the Gulf of Mexico, oaks from Prussia and Austria, &c. These are sawn on the premises by the most up-to-date machinery, and sent to different parts of England by rail and water. As many as 700 hands are often employed. Other firms in Gloucester are those of Messrs. Ashbee, Sons & Co., founded in 1872, who do a large business in foreign deals, &c., for building purposes; Messrs. Nicks & Co., founded in 1840, who, like those already mentioned, combine the import of timber with steam-sawing, &c., and whose speciality is creosoting wood; and some ten minor timber dealers; while in the Stroud Valley various firms have in the last seventy years carried on, by means of rail and canal, a fairly flourishing trade, largely in English wood.[6]

At Bristol the import of timber is carried on by about twenty-seven firms, among whom Messrs. Dentry, and Temple, Roger & Co. may be mentioned, while Messrs. Parsloe, and Harbour & Co. have important saw-mills.

Beside these large firms there are various small saw-mills which survive in different parts of the county, and represent the centralization of the scattered saw-pits that as late as twenty years ago were to be seen continually among the Cotswold woods. Of these that of Birdlip, founded more than one hundred years ago, and successfully employing twelve to twenty-one hands in the sawing, carpentering, and wheelwright's business of the district, may be taken as

---

[1] Mins. Accts. bdle. 850, No. 19.

[2] 'A true narrative concerning the woods and ironworks of the Forest of Deane,' *Bib. Glouc.* iii.

[3] The exact figures are £1,267,473: i.e. £374,477 sawn wood, £14,471 manufactured wood, £878,525 'other sorts' (part manufactured, &c.), for Bristol. Gloucester imported in 1905 hewn wood to the value of £5,029—a decrease of £4,445 on the preceding year, which had also seen a decrease; sawn wood, £537,774—a considerable increase. *Ann. Statement of Trade of United Kingdom with Foreign Countries and British Possessions*, 1906, ii. (C.d. 3022.)

[4] H. T. Ellacombe, *Hist. of Bitton* (1881), 227.

[5] Supp. to 56th *Ann. Rep. of Glouc. Chamber of Commerce*, 1897.

[6] There is a considerable trade in fir props for the north-western collieries from the Stroud larch-woods.

typical. Even in such mills, however, steam-power has of late largely superseded hand-labour, and the introduction of 'cheap and perishable' foreign doors, &c., which the large importers admit to be a notable recent feature of the trade, is a serious rival to their own production.

Allusion has been made to the county industries directly or indirectly connected with the timber trade. These are too numerous for detailed description, but a very brief account of them may be given. There is a large production of carriages, wagons, &c., both in Gloucester, where the well-known 'Railway Carriage and Wagon Co.' now employs from 1,100 to 1,400 hands, and has in the forty-six years since its establishment grown to be the largest manufacturing firm in the city, and one of the largest of its kind in the kingdom; and in Bristol, where a great trade is carried on by the Bristol Carriage and Wagon Works, the Stapleton Carriage and Wheel Works, &c. Joinery and cabinet-making are done on a large scale in both the large cities. There are the Whitehall Cabinet Works, among many in Bristol; while at or near Gloucester are the 'Gloucester Joinery Co.,' Mr. William Wibby, and Messrs. James Constance & Sons (founded in 1788) who do steam-turning and joining. A very large manufacture of furniture has since 1863 been carried on at Gloucester by J. Matthews & Co.; Mr. C. Jones, at Hatherley, has since 1885 managed what is said to be the largest step-works in existence; Messrs. Roberts, of Gloucester, employ about 150 operatives in the manufacture of different games and toys; the firm of Vowles & Sons, with ten other firms, &c., produces brushes at Bristol, and has recently started a branch in a disused cloth-mill at Stonehouse; while at Gloucester Messrs. Ireland & Co., brushmakers, have carried on their business since as far back as 1767, and Messrs. Morland have for more than fifty years made safety and other matches on a scale which is indicated by the fact that they can turn a ton of wood into matches in a day.

The manufacture of walking-sticks and umbrella handles, which is a speciality of the Stroud district, is carried on by so few firms in the country as to merit a rather more detailed account. With so much cheap local beech-wood as material, and with water-power and vacant cloth-mills available, the manufacture had a natural origin in the Golden Valley. It is not known, so far as I can ascertain, at what exact date it started; but sixty years ago it was prospering. For some time only common sorts were made—the black handles, carved according to traditional local patterns, representing the highest type. But the trade has progressed and enlarged, foreign woods are employed, and the five or six firms now producing umbrella-handles, while driving a keen competition among themselves, supply a large part of the demand of the country. Some of the materials are procured ready-made, i.e. the firms receive the celluloid, bone, or metal handles now so much in fashion, and fit them into specially prepared sticks, generally of beech-wood. Wooden handles of every grade are, however, manufactured on the spot, from olive, gorse, cherry, orange, American birch and maple, Congo-wood, and canes of different sorts, and pass through every stage of seasoning, stripping, bending, and varnishing within the factory. The present makers are Messrs. Hooper of Griffin Mill, Thrupp, whose firm claims to be the oldest, and employs about fifty hands; the Chalford Stick Co., with about one hundred hands; Messrs. A. J. Harrison & Co., founded in 1840 by Mr. Dangerfield, also at Chalford; Messrs. Nicks & Co. (now Walker) at Nailsworth; Messrs. Beard & Co., Horsley Mill, and Messrs. Workman at Woodchester.

It is principally for the very large English market that these firms produce. Complaints are raised of the 'excessive tariffs' which have nearly killed the former trade with France, Germany, Spain, and Italy, and of the dumping of foreign manufactured sticks by France, Austria-Hungary, and Germany. On the whole, however, this interesting special industry, like others in Gloucestershire long surviving the special advantages which caused its rise, may be said to be flourishing, and competition has at least led to 'economies in production' as regards utilization of 'waste' wood, and cane, to a degree which is really remarkable.[1]

There were, according to the census returns of 1901, 442 males and 264 females within the county engaged in the umbrella and stick manufacture.

The history of Gloucestershire shipbuilding is almost inevitably a part of the civic history of Bristol. It is true that the Severn towns have spasmodically attempted shipbuilding. At Gloucester a shipsmith is mentioned in 1230,[2] while Newnham in the 18th century produced a few ships 'of large burthen.'[3] But the Severn was too dangerous a river for shipbuilding to prosper on its banks, and it was Bristol, described as far back as 1141 by the *Gesta Stephani* as 'a port fit and safe for 1,000 vessels,' which up to the beginning of the 19th century was the chief source of vessels for the west of England. For the siege of Calais in 1347, Bristol supplied Edward III with 24 ships and 608 men,[4] and a little later in the reign gave him twenty-six vessels, while London gave but twenty-five, and only Fowey, Yarmouth, and Dartmouth supplied more. In the 15th century began its foreign shipping trade in organized form, when Canynges started a line of vessels for that purpose. In

---

[1] Thousands of 'pea-shooters,' for instance, are made out of odd ends of cane.
[2] W. H. Stevenson, *Glouc. Cal.*
[3] Rudder, op. cit. 572.
[4] Arrowsmith's *Dict. of Bristol*, 363.

1572 Bristol stands ninth with fifty-three vessels in a list of the merchant ships of sixteen principal ports of England,[1] and in 1594 Bristol had built seven ships in the previous thirteen or fourteen years,[2] while in 1653, when there was a great want of shipwrights at Woolwich, it was proposed to impress 100 from Bristol and the west country.[3] The profits of privateering gave an incentive to Bristol shipping during the 17th and 18th centuries. Sixty letters of marque were granted to local ships between 1626 and 1628,[4] and there were fifty-one Bristol ships engaged in attacking the French during the Seven Years' War, while in 1779 a ship ' pierced for sixteen six-pounders,' and chiefly manned by the Dean Foresters, was launched at Newquay, and letters of marque were requested from the government.[13] In 1781 the famous frigate *Arethusa* was built by the Royal Navy in the dockyards of Charles Hill & Sons, a firm of shipbuilders that still exists in Bristol.

From the end of the 18th century, however, shipbuilding at Bristol declined, until the invention of steamships revived it in another form.

ENGINEERING AND METAL INDUSTRIES[5]

If the local abundance of timber originated the shipbuilding of Bristol, it has been carried on by the industries that sprang from the mineral resources of the county. These were found mainly in the Forest of Dean, which had been already to some extent exploited by the Romans;[6] but mines were evidently worked as well in the Kingswood region, for Domesday mentions a rent of ninety pigs of iron, paid annually by six tenants at Pucklechurch. The Dean iron was exported down the Severn, and thus Gloucester naturally became a city of smiths. Giraldus Cambrensis, writing in the 12th century, describes it as famous for its ' ironworks, and smithery.'[7] In 1390 the city seal bore four horseshoes and horsenails, which suggests that the nail manufacture for the Royal Navy had not died out since the Domesday record.[8] Bolt Lane and Longsmith Street in Gloucester are names suggestive of the same industry, and large numbers of smiths' cinders are said to have been dug up in these streets. It is thought that Colstal, the old name of the Bareland, may indicate that coal and timber were supplied thence for the forges.[9] In 1240, at any rate, the Gloucester records mention a ' Jordan the nailer,' besides a needlemaker and innumerable smiths in both the 13th and 14th centuries.[10]

In the 17th century cutlery and wire-drawing were being carried on in Gloucester.[11] By the beginning of the 18th century an iron-rolling mill had been set up at Willsbridge, in the Bristol district,[12] and when Rudder wrote in 1779, iron and steel wire mills had been recently erected at Fromebridge, near Frampton on Severn. He also mentions brass-works at Warmley, in the parish of Bitton, and at Baptist Mills, on the Frome, near Bristol.[14] The former works, where wire and battery were made, were famous as the first place in England where brass and zinc were manufactured. The zinc industry was started about 1740 by William Champion, who employed Black Jack, or calamine from the Mendips, for his manufacture. The process is thus described :—

In a circular kind of oven are placed pots of about four feet in height, into the bottom of which is inserted an iron tube, which passes through the floor of the furnace into a vessel of water ; the pots are filled with a mixture of calamine and charcoal, and the mouths of each are then stopped with clay. The fire being properly applied, the metallic vapour of the calamine issues through the iron tube, and is condensed in small particles in the water, and being remelted is formed into ingots, and is sent out under the name of zinc or spelter.[15]

About 1758 the manufacture of brass was begun by William's brother, John Champion, who learnt the secret by going as a supposed beggar to Holland, and working in a brass factory. On his return he brought with him to Bitton five Dutch workmen, whose descendants still live in that parish. The Warmley works failed in 1770, and were sold to the Bristol Brass and Copper Co., founded in 1704 ; but an even higher fame was won by the brass-works at Hanham, two miles from Bristol, where a Mr. Emerson, formerly Champion's manager, made some of the purest brass in the world, ' free from knots,' and ' resembling gold.'[16] There were at the same date three large iron foundries in St. Philip's, Bristol, one of which had a steam-engine for boring cannon. Lead-works also existed, where melted lead, red and white lead, and small shot were manufactured. Bristol small shot, indeed, was at that date considered superior

[1] S.P. Dom. Add. Eliz. xxii, No. 1.
[2] S.P. Dom. Eliz. ccl, No. 33.
[3] *Cal. S.P. Dom.* (1653–4), p. 505.
[4] Arrowsmith, op. cit. 364.
[5] Number of persons employed, 1904 :—
Engineering, machinery and ship-building . 10,470
Brass and copper 461
Miscellaneous iron and steel 2,832
[6] See *infra*, ' Mining,' 216.
[7] ' Gloverniam ferream atque fabrilem,' *Gir. Camb.* (Rolls Ser.), vi, 171.   [8] See *infra*, p. 216b.
[9] J. J. Powell, *Gloucestriana*.   [10] *Glouc. Cal.*
[11] Fosbrooke, *Hist. of Glouc.* 424.
[12] H. T. Ellacombe, *Hist. of Bitton*, 231.
[13] Rudder, op. cit. 63.   [14] Ibid.
[15] H. T. Ellacombe, *Hist. of Bitton*, 229.
[16] *New Hist. of Bristol*, pub. by W. Matthews, 1794, pp. 39–40.

to all others. The lead must have been imported, as efforts to work native lead had proved useless. Yet, at some ancient date, lead-mines were probably worked near the Frome, for two Roman pigs of lead have been found in the river-bed, and at Penpark Hole, near by, is an old lead-mine, 200 ft. deep. It was examined in 1669 and in 1776, but no practical use could be made of it.[1]

The Bristol lead-works progressed, however, and by 1828, besides the shot manufacture, *Mathew's Guide* notices two sheet-lead and white-lead works. By 1863[2] there were eight sheet-lead makers. At the present day a large industry is carried on at the 'City Lead Works,' where 250 tons of sheets have been rolled in a single week. From 150 to 250 sheets (in sizes up to 50 ft. long and 8 ft. wide) are kept in stock, besides 1,500 coils of lead and compo pipe, and 1,500 lengths of large bore pipe. For making the latter, the company have a patent press, which will turn out ten tons a day.

Brass-founding also developed greatly at Bristol. By 1828 the Baptist Mills firm had become a company; the Hanham Works were turning out copper, spelter, zinc, brass battery, sheet-brass and wire; other brass and spelter works had sprung up at Crew's Hole, St. George's; and a zinc company had been established with a patent for malleable zinc for covering buildings. By 1863 there were eighteen brass-founders and braziers at Bristol, besides three bell-founders.[3] Tin-smelting was going on at Bedminster and Barton Hill, and there were already more than twenty iron-founders and engineers.

This brings us back to engineering as a whole, and to shipbuilding in particular. Gloucestershire may really claim to have produced the inventor of steamships, for, fifty years before Watt, a clock repairer of Chipping Campden, called Jonathan Hulls, discovered the first principle of steam locomotion. He never succeeded in combining his locomotive engine with an ordinary vessel, but placed it on a sort of steamtug. The first case in which the invention was tried was not however a success, and from lack of funds to experiment Hull gave up the attempt to improve it.[4]

Since this outburst in the early 18th century the county has shown no special inventive genius in the matter of ships, though it carries on a considerable modern business in building. The chief constructive dockyards are at Bristol, where *The Great Western*, the first steamship for regular Transatlantic trading, was built and launched in 1837. Owing to the obstructive policy of the Dock Company, how-

ever, Bristol did not pursue this advantage, and did not produce its second steamship *The Great Britain*, an iron screw vessel, till 1843, when Liverpool had already a service of four ships with New York. The same policy has continually retarded the shipping industry of Bristol. In 1871 a large steamship company was started, but suffered several misfortunes to its vessels. In 1881 the Great Western Steamship Company was formed, and built seven vessels for the Atlantic trade. It failed however to keep pace with Liverpool competition, and came to an end in 1896.[5]

In 1879 a fresh line of steamers between Bristol and New York was started by Messrs. Charles Hill & Sons, who have now in the Albion Dockyard one of the biggest shipbuilding industries in Bristol. Messrs. G. K. Stothert are another large shipbuilding company. In 1900 the former firm constructed the SS. *Bristol City*, of 2,511 tons gross—about the largest size of vessel that can be safely brought up to the centre of the city. Since that date, however, little shipbuilding has been done in Bristol beyond the construction of small tugs and lighters, which can be engined in the port. As there are no big marine engineering works in Bristol, engines for larger vessels, such as *The Bristol City*, have to be built elsewhere—a fact which, coupled with the absence of any large mills for rolling steel or iron plates, places Bristol shipyards at a disadvantage. Their total output, in fact, for 1905 was only ten vessels, with the small capacity of 1,471 tons.

At Gloucester Messrs. Summers & Scott have a small manufacture of steam launches, and ship machinery and equipment are made by Messrs. Newman, Hender & Co. of Woodchester, and Sisson & Co. of Gloucester. The latter firm supplied engines and boilers for all the fastest launches on Windermere. Boilers are manufactured separately by most of the steamship builders, and a special boiler composition is turned out by the Anti-Lithon Company at Bristol. 'Anti-Lithon' is a liquid formed of pure vegetable products, which forms a soft filmy covering on the metal of the boiler, besides precipitating all harmful ingredients in the water. It is designed to prevent the formation of 'scale,' which is apt to cause explosions in all classes of steam boilers.

The most interesting engineering industry of the county, after shipbuilding, is perhaps the manufacture of locomotives, of which Bristol is now the chief seat, though railway trucks were constructed in Gloucester in 1852 by Messrs. Butt & Co. (now general iron-founders). The Gloucester Wagon Co., too, has now a considerable manufacture of railway goods. At the Atlas Locomotive Works, Bristol, every sort of locomotive is built, except the heaviest engines

[1] J. Nicholls, 'Penpark Hole,' *Brist. and Glouc. Arch. Soc. Trans.* iv.
[2] See Mathew, *Brist. and Clifton Directory.*
[3] See *infra*, 'Bell-founding.'
[4] P. C. Rushen, *Hist. of Chipping Campden.*
[5] Arrowsmith, op. cit., 365–7.

for main-line traffic. The firm was founded about forty years ago, and has steadily developed, mainly since the purchase of the works by Mr. Thomas Peckett in 1880. In its early days the firm worked chiefly for the Midlands and South Wales, but it has now a considerable export trade. It built the engines for the first light railway in England, between Selsey and Chichester, and has supplied the government with locomotives for use in South Africa and the Soudan. Piecework, it is interesting to note, is not considered safe or satisfactory on such important works.

The other chief locomotive factory, carried on at Fishponds by the Avonside Engine Co., turns out railway steam motors and locomotives of the highest class. Founded in 1837 at St. Philip's, the business has grown so rapidly that, after being twice rebuilt on the original site, in 1905 a wholly new factory was erected with a yearly capacity of seventy-five complete locomotives. The firm numbers among its customers English, foreign, and South African railway companies, the state railways of Egypt and India, and the British War Office, but its principal output goes to South America, Australia, India, and Japan.

Gloucestershire also contains many general engineering firms, such as the High Orchard Works of Messrs. Summers & Scott (established in 1850) at Gloucester, who turn out heavy machinery for cake and flour mills and, in especial, for linoleum printing factories; and the milling machinery works of Messrs. Barron & Co. and Gardner & Co. Gloucester, with its large flour-milling business, has, in fact, closely followed or sometimes led the way in the vast improvements in milling machinery of the last forty years. Cheltenham and Tewkesbury contain small engineering works. Stroud has acquired a new lease of life from its modern foundries and engine-factories. Among other firms are the Stroud Metal Co., whose umbrella-fitting industry was called into existence by the local manufacture of umbrella-sticks; the Bowbridge Excelsior Engineering Co., who make all kinds of machinery and factory necessities, including mill-hoists, roofs, and girders, which they have supplied to many of the cloth-mills; the Ebley Iron Works, and the Dudbridge Iron Works, where flock machinery and gas engines are made respectively. Dursley is the seat of the only electric works in the county, those of Messrs. Lister & Co., who, besides electric motors and dynamos, have a large manufacture of agricultural and dairy machinery. Their Dursley-Pedersen cycle factory is, perhaps, the best known of the many Gloucestershire and Bristol cycle works, most of which are of no special note. Agricultural tools of the smaller sort are made at the Coaley Mills, by a firm established in 1744, and larger sorts by Messrs. Kell & Co. of Gloucester, who manufacture ploughs and drills of every description.

In the Bristol district, Messrs. Torrance & Sons of Bitton make paint and colour-grinding machinery, and Messrs. Gardiner & Co. of Bristol are large manufacturers of ornamental ironwork, such as wrought-iron gates and casements, besides lifts and safes. The largest galvanized-iron factory in Great Britain is also established at Bristol, under Messrs. Lysaght & Co. It was established in 1857, and now employs thousands of hands. The black sheet is produced at Newport, where is another branch of the same firm, but it is galvanized, corrugated, and packed at Bristol. Galvanized wire-netting is made in enormous quantities at Messrs. Lysaght's Netham spelter-works, as are also cisterns, tanks, and other agricultural requisites; while they also perform large contracts in general constructional engineering.

In concluding the subject, allusion may be made to an interesting institution, the Gloucester Machine Exchange, where machinery is bought, repaired, and kept ready for purchase or exchange, to the extent of 3,000 tons at one time.

BELL-FOUNDING[1]

For more than 600 years bell-founding has been a Gloucestershire industry. Originally an art practised only in monasteries, it was probably atttacted to Gloucestershire by the many religious houses settled there.[2] There are still extant a few bells bearing the arms of a see or abbey, such as those on bells in the cathedrals of Bristol and Gloucester, and on a bell now at Stoneleigh (Warw.), which bears the arms of Winchcombe Abbey. But ancient bells are hard to trace to their founders, owing to the pious reluctance of the latter to put their names upon the products of their art. Our knowledge of mediaeval bell-founders must therefore mainly be drawn

[1] See H. T. Ellacombe, *Church Bells of Glouc.*; article by H. B. Walters on 'Bells,' *Brist. and Glouc. Arch. Soc. Trans.* xviii; *Bells and Bell-founding*, by X.Y.Z. (Bristol, 1879).

[2] The religious light in which bells were regarded in the middle ages is illustrated by the rules of the Ringers' Gild at Bristol in the 14th or 15th century. There were stringent regulations as to the good character and reverence of the ringers, who were instructed to aim that 'our rich neighbours, hearing these loud cymbals with their ears, may by the sweet harmony thereof be enlarged in their hearts to pull one string to make it more sweet.'—L. T. Smith, *Eng. Gilds*, 288.

from written records. The earliest of these is of a John 'le Belyetare,' or bell-founder, who was

BELL-FOUNDER'S SEAL FROM RIVER THAMES

reeve of the city of Bristol in 1236. In 1270 the records of Gloucester tell of the death of 'Hugh the Bell-founder.' Hugh's business apparently descended to his daughter, Christiana, who is also described as a 'belyetare' in 1303,[1] and John of Gloucester, a famous founder of the next two reigns, was very probably of the same family. John made bells for Edward II,[2] and in 1346 cast four large bells for the West Tower of Ely Cathedral. A seal of about the year 1330, bearing a bell-founder's mark (a bell and laver) and also the inscription 'S' Sandre. de Gloucestre' has been fished out of the Thames, and given rise to various conjectures. All that can be safely asserted is that this seal was probably the property of one of the mediaeval bell-founders of Gloucester whose works have survived though their names have perished. But we believe that we can identify one 15th-century founder at Gloucester in Robert Hendley, whose name survives on the fourth bell of St. Nicholas, Gloucester. This bears the marks which Mr. Ellacombe, the great authority on Gloucestershire bells, has called, from their prevalence in the county, the 'Gloucester Cross and Stop.' Hendley was followed in the next century by William Henshawe and Richard Atkyns, the former of whom was in such repute at Gloucester that he was five times elected mayor between 1503 and 1520. It is his foundry which is believed to have given its name to 'Bell Lane.' Three other founders: I. B., who flourished 1580–1610, H. Farmer 1602–22, and J. Palmer 1621–62, were succeeded by the

GLOUCESTER STOP USED BY HENDLEY

Rudhalls, one of the most famous families of bell-founders that England has ever known. They came from Ross in Herefordshire. Abraham, the first of the Gloucester founders, died in 1735, 'famed for his great skill, beloved and esteemed for his singular good nature and integrity,' according to an inscription in the cloisters of his native cathedral. Between 1684, when he cast his first bell (now at Oddington), and 1715 Abraham Rudhall cast 1,291 bells, 'to the satisfaction,' says his catalogue, 'of them that understand music, ringing and good bells.' He was followed in succession

by his son Abraham and his descendants, Abel, Thomas, Charles, and John. The family cast altogether 4,521 bells, including four rings of 12, ten of 10, eighty-two of 8, two hundred and ninety-five of 6, and a hundred and thirty-one of 5 bells. Of these many found their way to the continent and even to America, but a very large number are still preserved in Gloucestershire. Their especial characteristic was the running ornament that decorates their inscriptions, which are excellent both in sense and workmanship. There is, too, a cheerful and patriotic tone about these legends. 'Peace and good neighbourhood' is a common one of Abraham Rudhall's. 'Let us ring for peace

RUDHALL'S BELL MARK

and plenty' is another of his at Alderton, bearing the date 1713. 'When you us ring we'll sweetly sing, A.R. 1739' is the legend on a bell at Withington. A Badgeworth bell relates the following piece of history :—

> Badgworth . Ringers . they . were . mad .
> Because . Rigbe . made . me . bad .
> But . Abel . Rudhall . as . you . see .
> Hath . made . me . bigger . than . Rigbe .

Perhaps one of the best surviving whole peals cast by the Rudhall foundry is the ring of eight in St. Stephen's Church, Bristol. The last of their bells in Gloucestershire were probably the third and tenor at Dymock, dated 1827 and 1829. On the extinction of the family in 1830 their business was sold to T. Mears, who shortly removed it to Whitechapel. Cainscross has a bell marked 'T. Mears, Gloucester & London, fecit. 1831,' and Tewkesbury Abbey has two bells 'cast at Gloucester by T. Mears, 1837.'

Bristol meanwhile had never wholly lost its early reputation for bell-founding. 'John le Belyetare' had been succeeded by two other mediaeval founders, John Gosselyn (c. 1450)[3] and William Warwick, the latter of whom has left bells at Yate and at Hereford Cathedral. Bells dating about 1400–50 are found in Gloucestershire with the stamp of a ship, indicating that they were cast in Bristol ; these may be the work of John Gosselyn. Subsequently we find many bells in Gloucestershire and Somersetshire bearing the initials R. T., H. I., and T. G. ; of these the last-named stand for Thomas Gefferies of Bristol, whose will is in existence, dated 1546. H. I. may have been

---

[1] W. H. Stevenson, *Glouc. Cal.*
[2] J. J. Powell, *Gloucestriana.*

[3] F. B. Bickley, *Little Red Book,* i, 88 ; ii, 161, 169.

his son, spelling his name Iefferies. We also hear of one John White of Bristol casting bells for Yatton in Somersetshire in 1485 and 1531; his will is dated 1540. In the 17th century the Purdues, who lived at Salisbury and Winchester, set up a bell-foundry at Bristol. Thirty-nine of their bells still survive in churches in this county. Their inscriptions were formed of large, flat letters, with a plain cross and a vine-leaf pattern. Early in last century a firm called Jefferies and Price cast a few bells at Bristol, of which two, dated 1840, survive at Iron Acton. But no worthy successors of the old bell-founders appeared in any part of the county till the comparatively recent revival of campanology, under the influence of Sir Edmund Beckett and the Rev. H. T. Ellacombe, author of *Church Bells of Gloucestershire*.

BELL ORNAMENTATION BY THE RUDHALLS

Under their guidance both bell-founders and bell-ringers have made enormous advances. There is now in Gloucestershire a 'Diocesan Association of Change-ringers,' founded in 1878, besides the old Society of St. Stephen's Ringers at Bristol, which still survives.

Bell-founding is now studied with such care that it has almost attained to the position of an exact science. Thanks to his knowledge of acoustics, the modern founder can cast his bells with an accuracy that was impossible to his mediaeval predecessors who, though some of their

bells will never be surpassed, turned out products of extremely varying quality.

One of the most scientific and successful of

RUNNING GRAPE ORNAMENTATION BY PURDUE

these modern firms is that of Messrs. Llewellins and James, who revived the art of bell-founding at Bristol in 1875. At their works at Castle Green they perform bell-founding of every class and scale, from musical hand-bells to complete rings. They also recast and tune old bells, and do their own bell-fitting and hanging, their frames being made either of seasoned oak, or of steel and cast-iron. By following out scientific principles Llewellins and James have arrived at a formula which gives almost exact results as to weight, dimensions, and tone. Slight differences between the actual and the calculated result in bell-founding are unavoidable, owing to the inequality of the moulding medium which, being formed of sand, is affected in varying degrees by the pressure of the fluid metal.

PURDUE'S INITIAL CROSS

At present most of the work of this firm is in the West of England and Wales, though some of it is found further afield. Bristol possesses numerous examples of their art, including a good light ring of six in St. Luke's Church, Bedminster. They have also done work in Gloucestershire at Painswick, Thornbury, and Chipping Sodbury. Including its general engineering department, this firm altogether employs about 180 workmen. The happy immunity from foreign competition which it enjoys in its bell department is due to the fact that bell- and

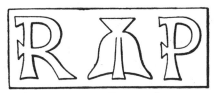

BELL MARK OF ROBERT PURDUE

peal-ringing is a peculiarly English practice, and not thoroughly understood in other countries.

PINS

Although the Gloucester pin manufacture was for two centuries the principal industry of the city, its history does not, like that of some local products, go back to any great antiquity. Various protective statutes from 1463 onward had prohibited the importation of pins into England and regulated their manufacture; and in 1605 there were in the country as many as 464 pin-makers, who were incorporated as a company. During the last thirty years of the 17th century, a commercial war on a small scale had raged between the Flemish and British pin-merchants, interesting in view of the present complaints of the Stroud pin manufacturers against Dutch competition. In 1571 (at which date, it may be mentioned, the English price of pins is rated at 4*d.* per 1,000), pins are included in a list of the principal products of the Low Countries; the latter were said to be raising their prices, and government retaliation was asked for.[1] Twenty years later, after some litigation, a suit against Flemish merchants for importing pins was dismissed; for a recent treaty made at Bristol had sanctioned their import, as the persistent stoppage of these products had been followed by the restraint of English cloth abroad.[2]

Despite the admission of foreign pins, which produced frequent complaints in the early years of the 17th century, it is at that period that the manufacture began in Gloucester. A general tradition ascribes its introduction in 1626 to one John Tilsley from Bristol. An unpretentious local ballad describes how 'Gentle Johnnie Tilsley came, And invented pins in Gloucester.' We need hardly, perhaps, believe the current statement that previously local wearers of pins had subsisted on 'prickles of thorns, curiously scraped and dried' by poor women in Wales.[3] There is an account of his original bargain with the mayor, which shows a desire, worthy of a modern municipality, to encourage the establishment of a fresh industry. He was to be provided with a house, to be lent £200, and to be supplied with thirty boys at least, who should learn the trade at wages of 12*d.* to 1*s.* 6*d.* per week for three years.[4] Tilsley's industry took root, fostered no doubt by the developing local brass and iron production in the 18th century. In 1712 the pin manufacture produced £80 a week, in 1744, £300,[5] while in 1781 it was said to return £20,000 per annum from London alone, besides an extensive country trade.[6] There were in 1802 nine factories employing at least 1,500 persons, and supplying a large market in Spain and America. In 1837 pin-making was still the most important industry of the city, though only three factories survived. 'The wire was drawn out and pointed in the

factory, the driving of which was by horse power. The heading, or "nobbing," was done in the homes of the workers.' Each pin is said to have passed through twenty-five hands, which process supplied Adam Smith with the illustration to his well-known chapter on the benefits of division of labour. 'Within living memory (1860) the sound of pin machines could be heard from nearly every door in the Island and in Leather Bottle Lane.'[7] The introduction of solid heads (invented almost accidentally in 1824) which required more elaborate machinery and necessitated the work being done entirely in the factory, probably caused the decline of the trade.[8]

Like many other early Victorian traders, the old pin manufacturers were unable to adjust themselves to changed conditions; heavy rating perhaps burdened them in the struggle, and although at Tewkesbury an enterprising pair of local tradesmen introduced a manufacture of 'superlative solid heads and improved points,' which enjoyed a boom for a short time, the firm of Kirby, Beard & Co., to whom the business was sold in 1849, were soon reduced to abandon it, while in 1855 the last Gloucester pin factory moved to Birmingham.

The manufacture of solid-headed pins is now only carried on in the county by Messrs. Critchley Bros., Wimberley Mills, Brimscombe, whose total output capacity in hairpins and solid-headed pins is 15 tons per week. Their firm, founded 60 years ago in the neighbourhood of Woodchester, employed in 1906 about 300 hands, and manufactured every kind of bone and solid-headed pin, from Kaffir pins $4\frac{1}{2}$ in. long to minnikin pins $\frac{5}{16}$ in. in length. The kindred production of wooden knitting-needles, crochet-hooks, &c., is carried on by them at Darkmills. Hairpins and safety-pins now seem to be taking the place once held by solid-headed pins as a local product. At Gloucester itself, the Gloucester Pin Co. (founded 1892) with seventy operatives, make hairpins (1 ton weekly) and hooks and eyes, while in the small town of Painswick three manufacturers[9] produce hairpins, hooks and eyes, and safety-pins in large quantities. At Woodchester and Wotton under Edge there are also pin factories; and there are at least two at Bristol. On the whole, the pin trade in its present form is, despite very strong foreign competition and protective duties, flourishing and expanding.

[1] S.P. Dom. Eliz. Add. xix, No. 63.

[2] S.P. Dom. Eliz. ccxxxix, No. 18.

[3] Fosbrooke, op. cit. 24.

[4] J. J. Powell, *Gloucestriana*.

[5] The *Gloucester Journal* of 1735 mentions 'a great trouble among the pin-makers, which is the chief manufacture of the city, and we hear that they have advanced the wages of their work-folks twopence in a shilling, from whence we infer that pins will soon be a *sharp* commodity, but it will be well if the masters do not *prick* their fingers by it.'

[6] Rudder, op. cit. 63.

[7] J. J. Powell, *Gloucestriana*.

[8] J. Platt, 'Progress of Manufactures in Glo'ster, 1837–97'; *Report of Glouc. Cham. of Com.* 1897.

[9] Watkins, Okey & Co, founded more than fifty years ago, specialize on hairpins; Cole & Co. make hairpins, hooks and eyes, and safety-pins; Savory & Sons produce hairpins, &c., and, unlike most makers, draw their own wire.

PRINTING[1] AND PAPER

If an entry in the Bristol Calendar for 1546 is correct,—and we have no information either to prove or disprove it,—Bristol was the seventh provincial town to possess a press. The Calendar of this date says that 'a press for printing was set up in the castle, which is used daily to the honour of God.' We hear no more, however, of printing in Bristol till 1643, when the king took the city, and brought there his printer, Robert Barker, the same man who had printed James I's Bible. His press sent out a number of royalist tracts, religious and political, of which twelve are still extant, but in 1645 Barker was driven away by the Parliamentarian capture of Bristol. Fifty years later the common council of Bristol decided that 'a printing-house would be useful in several respects,' and granted a licence to William Bonny, a London printer, to set up a press. He published the *Bristol Post-Boy*, a number of which for 5–12 August, 1704, is the earliest extant copy of an English provincial paper. The latest known copy is May, 1712, about which time Bonny's press probably came to an end. His most famous publication is an *Essay on the State of England in Relation to its Trade, its Poor, and its Taxes, by John Cary, Merchant of Bristol*, a work said by Locke to be the best discourse on the subject that he had ever read. It advocated the establishment of workhouses. The *Post-Boy* was printed on one small folio leaf of coarse, whitey-brown paper. Its successor, the *Bristol Postman, or Weekly Intelligence from Holland, France, Spain, etc., with General Occurrences, Foreign and Domestick*, was a much larger concern, containing twelve small quarto pages. At its head were woodcuts of a galloping postman and a ship in full sail. It was started in 1713 by Samuel Farley, printer, 'at the house in St. Nicholas St., near the church,' and sold at 'three-halfpence' 'delivered to any public or private house in this city,' and 'delivered for the country, twopence.' Farley also printed a tragedy of Hannah More's, called *The Inflexible Captive*, in 1774. Another paper, the *Bristol Weekly Mercury*, moderately described by its publisher, Henry Greep, as 'far excelling all other newspapers,' was started about the same time as the *Postman*, but was short-lived.

The 18th century also witnessed the establishment of various other local newspapers. Wotton under Edge is said in 1704 to have possessed a press, the property of John Exell. At Tewkesbury, between 1760 and 1780, Samuel Harward printed a number of rather famous penny chap-books, including the *Blind Beggar of Bethnal*

Green, and *Bite upon Bite; or, the Miser Outwitted by the Country Lass.* When he moved to Cheltenham in 1780, he was succeeded at Tewkesbury by Richard Dyde, as appears from a version of the Psalms issued by the latter and now in the Bodleian Library. Cirencester set up its press and produced a *Cirencester Post or Gloucestershire Mercury* about 1718. In 1722 the *Gloucester Journal* was founded by Robert Raikes and William Dicey. When the first Gloucester press was set up is, however, uncertain, as the imprint, 'T. Cobb, 1713, at Gloucester,' upon a political tract called *The Cobler of Gloucester, or Magna Carta discussed by a Poor Man and his Wife*, is probably fictitious. Raikes, father of the founder of Sunday schools, was a man of much public spirit, and was called before the House of Commons and imprisoned for publishing reports of their debates. His *Journal* has, however, continued in an unbroken series from 1722 to the present day, when it is the property of Messrs. Chance & Bland, who have also a general printing business of considerable size.

There are also various other printing houses in Gloucester, of which the most interesting is that established in 1858 by John Bellows, a Quaker of very high local reputation and author of a famous pocket-dictionary. This dictionary, though it contained nearly half a million words, weighed only $4\frac{1}{2}$ oz., owing to the lightness of the paper, which had been originally made for American greenbacks.

Bristol printing, meantime, pursued a steady course. The Farley family seem to have been enterprising, as they published between them seven papers in the 18th century. Felix Farley's *Bristol Journal*, begun in 1752, continued for 101 years, when it was incorporated with the *Bristol Times*. This again was incorporated in 1863 with the *Bristol Mirror*, and the paper is now published under the title of *Bristol Times and Mirror*. Many other papers have been published in Bristol, which contained nearly thirty printers by the end of the 18th century. Between 1815 and 1836 the stamp duty was 4*d*., besides a duty of 3*d*. per lb. on printing paper, and a tax of 3*s*. 6*d*. on each advertisement, so that the usual price for a copy of a newspaper was 7*d*.

A large number of papers are now published at Bristol, but there are no specially notable firms of printers. At Charfield, in an old cloth-mill, is the only large collotype-printing firm in the county, founded in 1894.

There is also a considerable paper manufacture in Gloucestershire. According to the census of 1901, only 233 men and 304 women in all were engaged in the occupation; but the

[1] See F. A. Hyett, *Brist. and Glouc. Arch. Soc. Trans.* xx ; also Arrowsmith's *Dict. of Bristol*.

production is very large in proportion to the number both of manufacturers and of operatives.

The Golden Valley Paper Mills, now in the possession of Mr. C. K. Smith, were founded about fifty years ago on the site of the brass-mills at Bitton.[1] The number of hands averages about 200, and the output was, in September, 1906, about fifty tons weekly—the machinery working by day and night. The qualities of paper made are tub-sized and engine-sized writing papers, envelope papers, drawing papers, and account-book papers.

Messrs. Evans, Adlard and Co., Postlip Mills, Winchcombe, are one of the largest and best-known of the British firms who manufacture blotting paper. Founded more than one hundred years ago[2] at a time when water-power was a necessity, the Postlip Mills were worked by the stream that is still used in the actual process of manufacture. The motive-power is now supplied by a 200 h.p. engine. Blotting-paper of every possible colour and quality, above the low grades, is made by the hundred hands employed in these mills and is exported in large quantities to Canada, the United States, and the Continent, in addition to its use in government offices, &c., at home. The firm also manufactures a pure filtration paper of its own for chemists; seidlitz paper, black needle paper, photographic paper, besides a special tub-sized, loft-dried paper used for exposing samples of different kinds.

There is a large paper-bag manufacture in the county, represented by Wellington & Co. in Gloucester, and by some four firms in Bristol, and wall-papers and cardboard boxes are also largely made; 178 males and 1,657 females were in 1901 engaged in these manufactures.

LEATHER

In 1904 over 13,000 persons in Gloucestershire were employed in leather manufactures, which included 460 tanners, 475 curriers, 547 saddlers, 94 glove-makers, and 11,540 bootmakers.[3] Tanning in particular has had a lengthy history in Gloucestershire, owing to the readiness with which hides could always be procured by river, and to the plentiful supply of oak-bark along the Severn and Wye. In Gloucester the records of tanning stretch back to very early times. From 1230 onwards tanners occur occasionally among lists of citizens. The building of Tanners' Hall in Hare Lane bears evidence to the importance of the trade, and in 1541 the Tanners' Gild drew up its ordinances. These, by the way, show that women, as well as men, were employed in the tanyards. No master was to keep 'a shopp or standinge bothe in the markett of Gloucester, to sell clowte leather,' nor was any member to buy 'clowte leather' to sell again.[4]

At Tewkesbury early details as to the abbey tannery are preserved in the kitchener's accounts. For instance, in 1385 the kitchener purchased 307 hides for £28 2s. 6d., and sold 373; 70s. worth of bark was bought, and 8s. 8d. worth of lime, while small sums were paid to the mender of vats and sieves, and 'to the cook at the time of larding.'[5] By the 16th century various dependent leather industries had grown up in Tewkesbury, which possessed a company of cordwainers and shoemakers, besides 'whittawyers, glovers, pouch-makers, and point—or shoelace—makers.'

Gloucester had not, apparently, a gild of cordwainers at an early date, though it had its single cobblers and glovers, who were fairly numerous from the 13th to the 15th century. Bristol, on the contrary, had a Cordwainers' or Coziers' Gild at least as soon as the 15th century. Its ordinances of 1407 have been already quoted.[6] At the same date provision was made for inspecting the trade and preventing the use of 'false leathers, dishonestly tanned or curried, called sole-leather or over-leather.' Before setting up as a craftsman, every apprentice must be certified as 'able and well-instructed in sewing, yarking (or preparing), and cutting, as pertaineth to the said craft.' No member was to tan leather for strangers.[7] In the 16th century 'points' were also being made at Bristol.[8] By the 18th century the tanyards there were important. At Tewkesbury the tanning trade is extinct, though it was still plied within living memory. Early in the 19th century Edmund Rudge, a Tewkesbury tanner, had a great character as a miser. Though reputed to be worth £100,000, he and his brother lived in the meanest way, feeding upon the 'rumps and bars' of their hides. He used to go weekly to Gloucester to purchase his own skins, which he wheeled to the quay himself by barrow-loads.[9]

There are still tanneries at Gloucester, and at Newnham, Winchcombe, and Leonard Stanley, but by far the largest business is now carried on

---

[1] H. T. Ellacombe, *Hist. of Bitton*, 232.

[2] Rudder says, in 1779, that fine writing-paper was then made at 'Postlip, in the parish of Winchcombe, Quenington, and Abbenhall,' and brown paper at a few other places.—*Hist. of Gloucestershire*, 63.

[3] *British and Foreign Trade and Industry* (2nd ser.), 1904 (c.d. 2337).

[4] *Hist. MSS. Com. Rep.* xii, App. ix, 527–9 (Records of Corp. of Glouc.).

[5] *Tewkesbury Yearly Reg.* ii, 274–80.

[6] See *ante*, 'Social and Economic History.'

[7] Bickley, *Little Red Book of Bristol*, ii, 101–14.

[8] *Acts of P.C.* (new ser.), viii (1571–75), 286.

[9] *Tewkesbury Yearly Reg.* ii, 147–8.

at Bristol, which tanned 250,000 hides in 1900, as compared with 187,000 in 1877. At one Bristol tanyard alone, that of Messrs. Parker in Whitehouse Street, 1,000 heavy hides can be turned out weekly. It is, in fact, for heavier leather that Bristol tanners are pre-eminent, and Bristol 'butts' have quite a name.[1] Oak-bark from Dean Forest is still used, though a foreign import called valonia (a sort of acorn) is also employed largely, as it enables skins to be tanned in four to eight months instead of in nine to eighteen. The Whitehouse Tannery is especially good in the finishing processes of the trade.

With all this leather trade an enormous boot manufacture has grown up in the county, employing, as we have seen, over 11,000 hands. In Bristol alone there are a hundred boot factories, with an annual capacity of 10,000,000 pairs of boots.

SOAP AND CHEMICALS

Soap is almost the oldest recorded manufacture of Bristol, which incurred great popular contempt in consequence among other English mediaeval towns. In 1242 Seyer's Memoirs record that 'this year grey soap was sold from this city to London by one John Lamb, who retailed it at a penny a pound, and black soap at a half-penny.'[2] In the 16th century white soap was one of the most important products of Bristol, and was exported by Thorne, one of Bristol's merchant-princes.[3] In the 17th century soap manufacturers suffered greatly from the effects of the special privileges granted in 1635 to a 'New Corporation of Soap-boilers at Westminster.' Government inspection, too, was a source of annoyance. New ingredients for soap were being discovered,[4] and in 1632 an assay-master of soap had been appointed.[5] In 1635 the amount of soap to be made yearly in Bristol was limited to 600 tons, the allotment for each manufacturer being made according to the annual proportion he was supposed to have made in the years 1630-2. This restriction led to many remonstrances from the Bristol soap-boilers. Richard Tovey petitioned the Council to the effect that he used to make at least 80 tons a year, but was now cut down to 24 tons.[6] Thomas Longman, describing himself as 'a young man governed by his company,' declared that he had 'conceived he did well therein, but perceiving they have run into contempt, he disavows their proceedings and submits to pay his Majesty what shall be ordered by the Board. He has undertaken the house and trading of his master, who made 200 tons of soap by the year;

20 tons a year is now allotted to him by his company, on which he is not able to subsist. He prays the Lords to settle his proportion, he giving caution to pay duty for all he shall make hereafter.'[7]

Disregarding this betrayal by one of their number, the other soap-boilers of the city presented a general remonstrance, declaring it impossible to obey the orders of the Council, which, besides restricting their output, limited their price to $3\frac{1}{2}d$. per lb. and their sale to Bristol and westward beyond the Severn, and imposed a tax of £4 on every ton of soap.[8] By 1637, however, they were only praying for the enforcement of these ordinances, in order to save them from worse at the hands of the London soap-boilers.[9] Not long after the unfortunate master, wardens, and others of the soap-makers of Bristol were in the Fleet prison for non-payment to the commissioners of arrears in making soap.[10]

It is perhaps not surprising that the interference of the Crown with their soap-trade was mentioned by Bristol citizens as one of their inducements to take the Parliamentary side in the Civil War. From this time we hear no special complaints from this industry, which has continued steadily through the 18th century to the present day. Messrs. Thomas and Bros., of the Broad Plain Soap Works, are now the last representatives of the Bristol soap-makers.

The soap industry now includes the manufacture of candles.

Chemical trades, which comprise, among other things, the manufacture of paint, ink, blacking, gunpowder and explosives, glue and varnish, employ about 1000 persons in the county. Of these, saltpetre and gunpowder used to be manufactured at Gloucester and Bristol during the Civil War.[11] In 1633 the Bristol powder-makers were purchasing saltpetre 'unlawfully made' at Sherston Magna in Wilts,[12] and when this had

---

[1] 'Butts' are the skin from an ox's back, and are used for boot-soles, machine-belting, and hard wear generally. They require much more tanning than the thinner parts of the hide.

[2] Sam. Seyer, *Mem. of Bristol,* ii, 14. About the same date there was a soap-maker at Gloucester, but this is a solitary instance of the trade occurring there. *Glouc. Cal.*

[3] H. R. Fox Bourne, *Engl. Merchants,* 105.

[4] Hitherto potash had been mainly used. See S.P. Dom. Jas. I, lxxxi, and clxxi, No. 69.

[5] S.P. Dom. Chas. I, ccix, No. 43.

[6] Ibid. cccviii, No. 15.

[7] S.P. Dom. Chas. I, cclxxxix, No. 94.

[8] Ibid. cclxxxviii, No. 49.

[9] Ibid. ccclxiii, No. 17.

[10] Ibid. ccclxxvii, No. 46.

[11] Ibid. cxliii, No. 67 ; and ccxi, No. 79.

[12] Ibid. ccl, No. 66.

been stopped, a petition was presented to the crown by John Corsley of Bristol, saying that although His Majesty had granted leave to the city to make 400 or 500 barrels of powder yearly, for their shipping, he could get no petre, and prayed that 200 lb. might be appointed him weekly from petremen near Bristol and Somerset. His petition was refused.[1]

How long the powder-trade survived the monopoly, after the immediate necessities of the war had been satisfied, I do not know. At the present date the chief representatives of the explosive trades are match factories at Bristol and Gloucester respectively. The former city had a saltpetre refiner and gunpowder and firework factories forty years ago, but these, I believe, are extinct. Early in the 19th century there were chemical works at Conham and Oldland Bottom, both near Bitton. At the former factory Prussian blue, hartshorn, and a compound called Gibbesium were turned out; the latter firm, that of Holbrow, Haynes, & Co., manufactured sal ammoniac, ivory black, &c., till 1840, when the works were closed, and were taken over ten years later by a chemical company at Netham.[2] Ink and vitriol were also made at Bristol in 1863. Chemicals for medicine, for dyes, and photography, besides essences for preserves and aerated waters are made by Messrs. Collett & Co, at

Gloucester. Annatto, a vegetable extract used for giving a light yellow colour to cheese and butter, has been manufactured since 1812 by Messrs. Baker & Co., St. Paul's, Bristol, but the business is a declining one, as the fashion in cheese colour has changed. The last survivor of the old charcoal works in the Forest of Dean, the Lydbrook Chemical Co., besides a large charcoal manufacture carried on both in the forest and in the factory, turns out the closely allied products of naphtha, tar, acetate of lime, blacking, &c.

Glue, varnish, and painters' colours are also manufactured at Bristol. The latter industry, in particular, is firmly rooted there, where it amounts perhaps to half a million pounds per annum. Probably, as already suggested, the oil and colour industry was originated by the lead manufacturers of the city in the 18th century. Artists' colours are not made, but only fire colours and earth colours, such as umbers, siennas, and red oxide. The latter are ground both dry and in oil, of which vast quantities are imported into Bristol—turpentine, petroleum, and, in particular, linseed and cotton oil. There are a few firms in Bristol which specialize in crushing linseed and cotton seed, though most of the oil and colour manufacturers do their crushing themselves.

MILLING, MALTING AND BREWING

The oil and cake mills carried on by Messrs. Foster Bros. at Gloucester Docks belong to the firm which first introduced the industry into Great Britain. Up to 1862 the works were at Evesham, but were then moved to Gloucester, where a new large plant was set up; 800 tons of seeds, mainly cotton seed from Egypt and linseed from India, Russia, and the Argentine, are manufactured weekly into various forms of cattle and sheep food, and some 120 workmen are employed, working by spells day and night. The mills, which have lately become a branch of the Bristol Oil and Cake Mills, Ltd., have a large export trade.

At Stroud there is a similar business carried on by Messrs. Townsend & Co. Another cattle food called 'dredge' is made at Gloucester by Messrs. Turner, Nott & Co., who are large corn merchants, both at Bristol and Gloucester; they once imported in one vessel 30,000 quarters of South American wheat, the largest single cargo of grain ever unloaded at Gloucester Docks. Large imports of corn are indeed needed in Gloucester, which is a great flour-milling centre. The Albert Flour Mills and the City Flour Mills, the two chief works of the kind in Glou-

cester, are large and well equipped, having both adopted the 'roller' system at an early date. They have between them a weekly capacity of 5,500 sacks. Both are situated in the Docks, and can thus deal with the grain direct on importation. In Gloucestershire, as in other counties, these large mills superseded to a considerable extent the small wind and water-mills, of which there used to be so many scattered over the country-side. A few still survive, as in the Painswick valley where an occasional old cloth mill is utilized for this purpose. Tewkesbury also has a considerable milling business.

Malting was long a staple industry at Tewkesbury, and indeed all over the county, as is testified by the old 'malt-houses.' In 1596 an order was issued by the Gloucester magistrates to limit the malt-houses, the excessive number of which caused a dearth of grain.[3] Corn and beer have of course been intimately connected since the days of the assize of bread and beer, which, as we have seen,[4] regulated their respective prices on a common scale. In 1500, when loaves at Gloucester were fixed at four a penny, one gallon of the best ale was to be sold for a penny, and thirteen gallons for twelve pence (an

---

[1] S.P. Dom. Chas. I, cclxv, No. 91.
[2] H. T. Ellacombe, *Hist. of Bitton*, 231.

[3] *Acts of P.C.* (new ser.), xxvi (1596-7), 174.
[4] See *ante*, 'Social and Economic History.'

early example of the baker's dozen), and of the second ale three for a penny 'well sodde and skommed.' The best grain was to be sold at three bushels a penny. 'No comon bruear' was to 'tappe non ale within ther owne houses.' 'No typler shall alter any ale which he or they shall receive and buy of any brewer, with barme, worte or any wyse' (1522).[1] A penny a gallon is the price often reiterated. In regulations for the 'bruars,' 1520, they are ordered to 'sylle xiii gallons of ale for the dozen, stonding mesure, with a cowle[2] sealed by the Meyre.' 'The typlar or sellar of ale shall lett sett at there howses a stone upright levelled, so that the bruar's men shall always sett there cowles sealed to trye truly there mesures.'[3] By 1620 the brewers of Gloucester had become a company.[4]

At the present day Gloucestershire enjoys a considerable industry in brewing and in the manufacture of ginger-beer and mineral waters. These industries are carried on at Gloucester, Stroud, Cheltenham, Tewkesbury, Wotton under Edge, Wickwar, Brimscombe, Nailsworth, Mitcheldean and Bristol (which had distilleries in 1794). Cider and perry are made by Daniel Phelps at Tibberton ; J. Harper & Sons at Ebley, Stroud ; by several Bristol manufacturers ; and for local consumption by half the farmers in the Vale.

There is also a manufacture of patent foods in Gloucestershire, especially by the Cheltine Food Co. in Cheltenham. At Stroud is a bacon-curing company that dates from 1819, and at Gloucester an ice-factory, very recently established, with a capacity of fifty tons of ice per week.

SUGAR AND CHOCOLATE

But the chief food products of Gloucestershire have been and are the sugar, sweets, and chocolate industries. Sugar refining, like the tobacco industry (which is still a large one),[5] grew up at Bristol in the 17th century in consequence of the West Indian Trade. Pepys describes the sugar refineries as one of the chief glories of Bristol (1698), and mentions that owing to the vaults beneath the streets for the storage of sugar, as well as wine, &c., only sleighs and small carts drawn by dogs were allowed. By 1795 Bristol sugar was the most esteemed in England, says Andrew Hooke in his 'Dissertations,' and there were twenty large sugar houses. The Bristol sugar refiners had bought up the sugar house at Gloucester, which had been flourishing about 1760.[6] Throughout the 19th century, however, the refining industry has declined. In 1828 there were only seven sugar houses ; in 1863, three.

The cause of this decline was, of course, the foreign sugar bounty system, which did enormous injury to the refineries of this kingdom. In Bristol only one held on till the Sugar Convention relieved the situation, and this is not always at work. But if refiners have suffered, the country as a whole has profited by the greater cheapness of sugar, which has practically founded two large British industries. In Bristol many more hands are now employed in the manufacture of sweets and chocolates than ever lost employ-

ment through the stopping of refineries. The output, too, has enormously developed both in bulk and in variety. Whereas under the old system of hand-manufacture, only 40 or 50 lb. of mint or rose lozenges would have been cut by hand in a day, an up-to-date modern firm, such as that of Champion, Davies & Co., turns out a ton or two per day from each of its machines. Almond comfits and other sweets covered with hard sugar were at first made in small quantities in hand-pans swung over an open fire, but are now made in batches of some cwt. in large revolving pans, steam-heated. Other articles of confectionery, now turned out in huge quantities, such as creams, gum goods, and gelatine work, were quite unknown to the trade in its early days. Many firms, such as that of Messrs. Richards & Co., are also employed in sugar importing and manufacturing, by which latter term is implied the making of icing and castor sugars from refined sugar, and the colouring of sugar known as 'yellow crystals,' made in imitation of yellow Demerara or cane crystals. While the Sugar Convention has assisted the refiners, it has injured the whole sugar manufacture, occasioning the close of many sweet factories at Bristol during the last three years.

Of the two great Bristol chocolate manufacturers, Packer and Fry, the latter is by far the more famous. The industry was founded about 180 years ago by Dr. Joseph Fry, a Quaker doctor of Bristol, great-grandfather of the chairman of the present company. His Quaker views probably increased his interest in this temperance drink, first introduced into England in 1656. He died in 1787, leaving the business to his wife, Anna Fry. In 1798 steam power was intro-

---

[1] *Hist. MSS. Com. Rep.* xii, App. ix, 442.
[2] Word connected with 'cooling-vat.'
[3] *Hist. MSS. Com. Rep.* xii, App. ix, 472.
[4] S.P. Dom. Jas. I, cxx, No. 140.
[5] One-eighth of the tobacco consumed in Great Britain is said to be manufactured at Bristol.
[6] J. J. Powell, *Gloucestriana.*

duced. To quote the *Bury and Norwich Post* of 6 June, 1798 :

Since the great improvement of the steam-engine, it is astonishing to what a variety of manufactures this useful machine has been applied ; yet it does not a little excite our surprise that one is used for the trifling object of grinding cocoa. It is, however, a fact that Mr. Fry of Bristol, the maker of the famous Churchman's Chocolate, has in his new manufactory one of these engines, for the sole purpose of manufacturing chocolate and cocoa. Either the consumption of this little article must far exceed our ideas, or, which we think much more likely, a very large proportion of what is drunk in this country must be made by him.

A few years later the *Times* was alluding to

the high repute of the preparation of Fry, which no less proves his superior skill and care, than the excellent solubility of the articles produced from his celebrated manufactory.

Since then the industry has grown steadily, and now, instead of the original building in Newgate Street, with a small number of employees, it occupies eight large buildings, in various streets, and employs fully 4,000 hands. The whole of these are not, it is true, employed in the actual cocoa manufacture, as all the chocolate boxes and cases are made on the premises by the company. Many tons of sugar, too, are melted down and used for flavouring and for paste. The preparation of the beans themselves requires elaborate machinery. After being roasted, they are shot down into galleries, cracked, winnowed by fans, and ground between granite rollers. The oil having then been extracted by heat, a fine paste appears, which is mixed with sugar, and finally made up into chocolate.

The firm has a large export trade, which has given rise to a whole new branch of their industry—the making of air-tight canisters. Their cocoa-beans are imported from Ceylon, the West Indies, Brazil and Central America.

GLASS, POTTERY, BRICKS AND BUILDING MATERIALS

Though there were a few glaziers and glass-wrights in Gloucester as far back as the 13th century,[1] it is to the brewing and mineral water trade of Gloucestershire that the glass industry of the county is mainly due. By the end of the 16th century it was reported that 'in Gloucestershire, one Hoe a Frenchman, hath built a glass house and furnace and doth make great quantities of glasses.' Hoe was condemned accordingly in the general order issued by the magistrates in 1598 to put down the manufacture of drinking-glasses, for which a patent had been granted to Sir Jerome Bowes.[2] By 1794, however, 'glass bottles were already a flourishing manufacture, occasioned by the demand for the export of Bristol waters, beer, cyder and perry.' Window-glass was also made. There were, altogether, says Matthews,[3] twelve glass-houses, which might ' be visited by presenting a small gratuity to the workmen, who, living in hot climates,' were ' very glad of some suction to moisten their clay.' By 1828 flint glass was being made at Bristol.[4] By 1863 a factory for glass bottles had been established by Messrs. Powell & Ricketts, still one of the chief representatives of what is now a flourishing Bristol manufacture.

Another Bristol industry due to similar causes is the manufacture of stoneware. A rough form of this was first introduced into England from Cologne in 1581, but no salt-glazed ware was made till 1670, when John Dwight of Fulham patented the invention. This was subsequently improved by the brothers Elers, and early in the 18th century was introduced into Bristol. The productions of these first stoneware manufacturers, of whom a number soon sprang up, consisted of demi-johns, sugar-pots, and jars and jugs grotesquely ornamented. They were all glazed with salt in the following way :

the ware was placed in the kilns on open shelves, built up tier on tier, so as to receive the full force of the fire direct. When the highest temperature was reached, common salt was thrown in through small holes in the crown of the kiln and volatilized in the great heat, the chlorine escaping in vapour, and the sodium combining with the silica of the clay to form a glass of silicate of soda, which covered the surface of the ware with a fine, thin film of hard glaze. In later days some most beautiful specimens of stoneware have been glazed thus, as, from its fineness and delicacy, this glaze is admirably adapted to set off artistically figured pieces of pottery.

In the year 1840 the stoneware industry was developed and improved by the substitution for salt of a liquid glaze, into which the ware was dipped, and which, when fired, gave the rich and highly vitrified enamel known as 'Bristol glaze.' Nearly the same ingredients are still used for the modern glazes which, being absolutely without lead or borax, are fluxed at an exceedingly high temperature. This, in conjunction with a dense, hard body, renders the ware specially adapted for resisting the action of

[1] *Glouc. Cal.*
[2] *Acts of P.C.* (new ser.) xxix (1598–9), 102.
[3] *New Hist. of Bristol* (1794), ch. 8.
[4] Mathews' *Brist. Guide* (1828).

spirits and acids of all kinds. Stoneware, it may be noted, unlike earthenware, is only fired once. The time spent in the kiln is about forty-eight hours, after which the ware undergoes cooling and testing processes that occupy about three weeks.

The chief modern representative of the industry is the firm of Messrs. Price, Powell & Co., at the 'Old Stoneware Potteries' in St. Thomas' Street. The firm of Messrs. Price, the oldest branch of the partnership, was established in 1740, since when it has gradually absorbed most of its smaller rivals. About 100 men and boys are employed in all sections of the manufacture, which includes the basket-making necessary for wickered jars. Every kind of stone jug, bottle, pan, filter, and barrel is produced, almost all being 'thrown' on the potter's wheel. The clays used are brought by vessel from Devonshire and Dorsetshire pits, where they are cut in square lumps. These are well dried and pounded up, then soaked and passed through pug mills which render the clay fit for use.

Ordinary clay pottery was made at Bristol from local clay in the reign of Edward I,[1] and the industry was in full swing in the 16th century. The 18th century produced two rather famous kinds of ware, Bristol porcelain and Bristol china. The former is described by a traveller in 1751 as made of 'calcined flint and the soapy rock at Lizard Point.' He also describes the 'beautiful white sauce-boats adorned with reliefs of festoons,' which are almost the only specimens of the porcelain with which we are now acquainted. This fabric was made in 'soft paste,' and differed wholly from 'Bristol china,' a far more famous product, much resembling Dresden china. In fact the cross, which is the mark of Bristol china, is often found in conjunction with the crossed swords of Dresden. The invention was due to Messrs. Champion and Cookworthy, who formed a company, under a patent, in 1770, but seven years later sold their factory to a Staffordshire firm, by whom it was finally closed in 1782. Champion's flower-groups were a triumph of 'hard-paste' modelling in biscuit. Specimens of his china are now rare, and highly valued by collectors.[2]

Elsewhere some of the oldest potteries in the county still survive at Cranham, where local tradition ascribes their foundation to the Romans. (Some connexion may possibly be traced between this theory and the Domesday record of five potters at Haresfield.) Two works exist at the present day, owned by Messrs. Ritchings and Stirling. The latter gentleman has in the last few years extended the industry, which formerly consisted only in the manufacture of flower-pots, pans, drain-pipes, and a few rough jars of brown ware, by introducing the art of green-glazing. Much ornamental pottery is now turned out.[3]

At a small factory at Coleford, which has been in existence nearly fifty years, brown ware, both glazed and unglazed, is also produced, besides chimney-pots, tiles, crests, fire-bricks, and building bricks. At Littleton upon Severn the 'Whale Brick and Tile Company,' founded about 1860, has works covering some sixteen acres and employing fifteen men, who make bricks, pipes, and ordinary red tiles. A brick-field is also worked at Dumbleton near Tewkesbury. Other clay-pits are opened in various parts of the Lias, notably at Robin's Wood Hill, Stroud, and Stonehouse. The 'Stonehouse Brick and Tile Company' possesses fine deposits of clay, which have already been worked to a depth of 100 ft. and show no signs of exhaustion. Starting on a small scale in 1890, the firm have been able to enlarge their works to the present yearly capacity of 10,000,000 bricks of every style, plain and ornamental, besides terra-cotta goods of various kinds. The factory is excellently equipped, having a chimney stack 200 ft. high, six steam-engines, and a hot-air drying plant.

There are also a number of brick-fields near Bristol, where, for a short time in the middle of the 17th century, 'potts of glass-house clay' were made by Dagney, an Italian, for use as smelting-forges in the Forest of Dean.[4]

While upon the subject of building, it may be well to notice two substitutes for brick and marble respectively, both manufactured in Gloucester. One is Calway's portable cement slabs, a composition of granite and cement, made in blocks ready for building, 2½ ft. long by 2 ft. wide, and 2 in. thick. The other invention is that of enamelled slate, which is manufactured by three Gloucester firms, Messrs. Gee & Sons, and Sessions & Sons, and the Phoenix Enamelled Slate Company. Here slate is given the veined appearance of marble by an interesting process called 'dipping.' The colours are placed on the surface of water, which is then shaken, so that a waving appearance is given to the colours. The slate is then dipped into the water, so that the colours adhere in the pattern produced by the ripples of the water. Gloucester is now so admittedly eminent in this particular trade that, when firms in other districts to which the manufacture has spread are in need of workmen, they advertise in Gloucester papers.

The total number of persons employed in the brick, cement, pottery, and glass industries in 1901 was 1,944.

---

[1] Bristol Mins. Accts. 28–29 Edw. I, bdle. 851, No. 7.
[2] See Arrowsmith's *Dict. of Bristol,* 328–9.

[3] These works have just closed (Sept. 1906).
[4] Dud Dudley, *Metallum Martis* (1665), p. 22.

INDUSTRIES

HANDICRAFTS[1]

Perhaps the most interesting of all the modern Gloucestershire industries are those pursued by the Gild of Handicraft at Chipping Campden, where it has been established since 1901. Founded in Whitechapel in 1888, the gild owed its inception to the desire of a Toynbee Hall Ruskin class to put into practice the principles which they had learnt. Three working craftsmen formed its original members, who were intended to receive recruits from a school of handicraft worked in connexion with the gild. This particular branch of the experiment failed from lack of support by educational authorities, but the productive work of the gild progressed rapidly, gradually including such handicrafts as cabinet-making, wrought-iron work, printing, book-binding, enamelling, jewellery, and silver and copper work. Partly from the necessity of finding more space for its growing activities, partly from a desire for purer air and healthier surroundings, the gild was moved five years ago from its quarters in Essex House to Chipping Campden, where its workshops were set up in a deserted silk-mill. 'On the ground floor of this building is the printing-room; on the central floor are the metal shops, where work the jewellers, the silversmiths, and the enamellers. On the upper floor the cabinet work and carving is done. In another building is the smithy, and away at a different part of the ground is the storage for timber and the power-house where the rough timber is sawn.' Over seventy men and boys are employed.

The artistic, social, and commercial success of the gild is a tribute at once to the truth of its principles—which are indeed those of Ruskin, Morris, and Carlyle—and to the skill with which these have been adapted to practical requirements. For though the industry is organized on a co-operative and profit-sharing basis, the need for flexibility and for skilled leadership has never been lost sight of. All designs are supervised by a chief designer, Mr. Ashbee, the lecturer to the original Ruskin class, while the business side of the enterprise is entrusted to a special director,

both of them being elected by the gild committee. In 1898 the gild was formed into a limited liability company.

Broadly speaking, the formation of the Gild of Handicraft 'implies a rebellion against inutilities, a conviction that machinery must be relegated to its proper place as the tool and not the master of the workman, that the life of the producer is to the community a more vital consideration than the cheap production which ignores it, and that thus the human and ethical considerations that insist on the individuality of the workman are of the first importance.' Its aim has been by reviving the system of apprenticeship and by training the craftsman in the whole of his work, not only in a section, to give him an understanding and joy in his work. With all the supervision that is given to the products of the gild's art, the greatest care is taken that each article should bear an individual stamp; and the stimulus thus given to the artistic sense and conscientiousness of the craftsmen is evidenced by the creative faculty which many of them display and by the beauty and thorough workmanship of all their productions. These are still of the class originally enumerated, furniture-making, printing, hammered metal-work, enamelling, and jewellery. The high reputation of the gild has brought to Campden a private artist in stained glass, and is further borne witness to by the many requests for lessons from its workmen, both in the Campden school of art and in technical schools all over the country.

This artistic character, if it is due to the principles on which the gild was founded, must also surely owe a great debt to the surroundings in which it is placed. Campden is a peculiarly beautiful village, untouched by architectural outrages, and still containing unspoilt several fourteenth and fifteenth century buildings. The workshops of the gild stand beside a stream, in the midst of a rose-garden; and altogether no better atmosphere, literal or metaphorical, could be found to inspire and contribute to the success of this attempt at the idealization of industry.[2]

MINING

The mining industry of Gloucestershire has been practically confined at all periods of its history to two districts—the valley between the Cotswolds and the Severn, and beyond that river the Forest of Dean. At the present time nearly three-quarters of the coal raised in the county, and its entire though meagre output of

iron, come from the second region, though at an earlier period the disparity of production between vale and forest may not have been so marked; it is therefore convenient to deal first with the

[1] See C. R. Ashbee, *An endeavour towards the teaching of John Ruskin and William Morris* (Essex House Press), from which the passages quoted are taken.

[2] For information in the whole of this article the writer is much indebted to *Industrial Gloucestershire*, published by Chance and Bland, Gloucester, and to the kindness of local persons interested in manufacture, especially to Mr. W. Stanton, of Stratford Lodge, Stroud.

mines to the west of the Severn, which may further claim a certain precedence from the peculiar interest attaching to the immemorial usages and customs which have governed their working.

No detailed description of the geology[1] of the Forest of Dean can be given here, but it may be stated briefly that the strata of the Carboniferous system form a basin which is more perfect than any other Coalfield in England,[2] the Coal Measures being encircled by belts of Millstone Grit and Carboniferous Limestone, while the last of these rests for the most part on the Devonians or Old Red Sandstone. On the south-eastern limits of the forest, however, near Blakeney and Lydney, the Carboniferous Limestone 'thins out' and ultimately disappears, owing to the overlapping of the Coal Measures which here apparently rest directly on the Old Red Sandstone. The coal field covers some 34 square miles, but of the fifteen fairly workable seams[3] of coal only eight or nine are two or more feet thick. Deposits of iron[4] have been found and worked, both in the lower part of the Millstone Grit and the upper portion of the thick Limestone formation.

Ample evidence[5] is forthcoming that the iron deposits in and about the Forest of Dean were known to the Romans and worked by them, and attention has been drawn by various observers to ancient excavations and surface-workings, some of which may be attributed to the period of the Roman occupation. What proportion of the 'cinders' found in the forest can claim an age equally great is rather difficult to determine; but in certain instances coins and other objects of the Roman period have been found in close connexion with heaps of slag. That the iron of Dean continued to be worked during at least the later Anglo-Saxon period is proved by the evidence of Domesday[6] that in the days of the Confessor Gloucester rendered to the king as part of its farm thirty-six dicres of iron, probably horse-shoes,[7] and 100 rods of iron suitable for making nails for the king's ships. This iron no doubt came from the Forest of Dean, for only about a hundred years after the entry of this render in the great survey, Gerald the archdeacon, in his *Itinerary*,[8] speaks of the 'noble forest of Dean (*Danubie*) which supplies Gloucester with venison and great store (*copiam*) of iron,' and many years before his book was written the Pipe Rolls of Henry II furnish abundant references to the iron industry of Gloucestershire. The implements of peace, and the missiles and engines of war, shoes for the king's horses, iron for the king's ships, were then largely procured from our county. As early as the Pipe Roll of the fourth year of this sovereign we hear of iron sent to Woodstock,[9] and later this brief entry is illustrated by a record[10] of the thirty-first year of '30 pickaxes, and 3 iron hammers and 4 iron levers sent to Woodstock for the king's work.' About 1166[11] £5 16s. was paid by the king's writ for '2 tuns (*tonellis*) full of arrows and engines sent over sea,' and four years[12] after, nails and rods were furnished for a ship, and under the account of Gloucester town we hear of £1 5s. 6d. paid for iron and nails for the horses of the king. A little later[13] the preparations for the Irish expedition left traces on the Gloucestershire Pipe Roll, '£1 2s. 11d. for 100 axes sent into Ireland,' while under the account of the town we have an entry of £6 15s. for 1,000 spades, and of £17 10s. for 60,000 nails sent to the same destination, while enormous quantities of nails were also dispatched for the repair of the royal palace at Winchester. But not the least interesting of these references to the great county industry is found at the end of Henry's reign,[14] '£8 16s. 3d. for iron for the king's works for his journey (*in itinere*) to Jerusalem,' that Crusade to which the broken warrior was vowed but which he was destined never to accomplish.

The Pipe Rolls of Richard carry on the story, and Gloucestershire is again to the fore in the preparations for the Eastern expedition,[15] £33 18s. being paid for 50,000 horse-shoes (*ferris equorum e duplici clavatura*), and £100 for iron for the furnishing of the royal ships. Four years[16] later a small payment of 11s. 9d. was made for the purchase of 12 quarters of iron for the repairs of the royal hunting-lodge at Brill (*Brehull*). Such notices of the requisition of iron from Gloucestershire when work was in progress at any of the royal houses are also found on the rolls of John,[17] and in his reign a considerable quantity of the metal was sent to Poitou.[18] These references illustrate clearly the importance of the industry, based largely on the output of the forest mines, which gave Gloucestershire a place of pre-eminence right into the fourteenth century, if

---

[1] See further *V.C.H. Glouc.* i, 'Geology,' and for a general description of the Forest of Dean, the 'Topography' and 'Forestry.'

[2] Hull, *Coal-Fields of Great Britain* (5 ed. 1905), p. 80.

[3] The actual number of existent seams, however, is stated by Mr. H. Bauermann, F.G.S., to be thirty-one. *Encycl. Brit.* vi, 50.

[4] J. D. Kendall, *Iron Ores of Great Britain*, 128.

[5] *V.C.H. Glouc.* i, 'Roman Remains.' Nicholls, *Iron Making in the Forest of Dean*, 7 et seq. *Trans. Bristol and Glouc. Arch. Soc.* ii, 216.

[6] *Dom. Bk.* i, 162a. C. S. Taylor, *Dom. Surv. of Glouc.* 126.

[7] Horse-shoes were a speciality of Gloucester manufacture. Note also the armorial bearings of the city. *Bristol and Glouc. Arch. Soc. Trans.* ii, 235–40.

[8] Giraldus Camb. *Opera* (Rolls Ser.), vi, 55.

[9] Hunter, *Pipe Rolls*, 168.

[10] Pipe Roll, 31 Hen. II.

[11] Ibid. 13 Hen. II.
[12] Ibid. 17 Hen. II.
[13] Ibid. 18 Hen. II.
[14] Ibid. 34 Hen. II.
[15] Ibid. 2 Ric. I.
[16] Ibid. 6 Ric. I.
[17] e.g. Pipe Rolls, 7 & 9 John.
[18] Ibid. 8 John.

not later, as the chief iron-producing district in the south of England.

Direct references to the ironworks of Dean Forest under the Angevin dynasty are, however, more scanty, but bear out the impression produced by the entries already cited. Henry Plantagenet[1] before his accession had confirmed the gifts of Roger, earl of Hereford, to Flaxley Abbey, as amongst which were included 'a certain ironwork at Edland,'[2] and after his coronation he again confirmed[3] the privileges of these Cistercians, using the significant words :

'Et de eadem foresta dedi eis . . . unam forgeam ferrariam ita liberam et quietam et operantem per omnia, sicut meae dominicae forgeae.'

As early, then, as the middle of the twelfth century, and probably before that time, the king's forges were at work in the forest, and the same remark may apply to itinerant forges in private hands. Among forges[4] known to have been authorized by Henry II may be mentioned those of Walter de Lascy and Richard de Eston. The second of these lay at Staunton. In this connexion may be cited an entry on the first Pipe Roll of King John that William the son of Hingan paid 10 marks for holding his 'fabrica'[5] in peace till the king's pleasure were ascertained.

Besides those already enumerated one of the best-known of these early itinerant forges was that of the Cantelupes, and the terms[6] of the grant to Mabel de Cantelupe in 1231 imply that the privilege was of long standing, 'as in the time of King John and his predecessors.' This forge lay at Etloe (Ettelawe), and was privileged to receive an oak every fifteen days from the forest as late as the middle of the reign of Henry III. The same family also

possessed three 'fossatas de bosco sicco,' doubtless charcoal pits for providing coals.[7]

Another forge of special interest, long worked by the Malemort family, lay in the demesne land near the castle of St. Briavel, and furnished for at least a century much of the war material, especially cross-bow quarrels required by the armies and garrisons[8] of successive kings. In the Pipe Roll of the eighth year of King John, after a notice of 1s. 6d. paid for the carriage of 2,000 quarrels to Montgomery, we read of William de Malemort, who has been forging quarrels, with two assistant journeymen (garcionibus), at 5d. a day, and of William the fletcher, who has 3d. a day, 7 marks 9s. and 4d. having been paid to them in wages for fifty-four days from the morrow of Michaelmas to the 3 March inclusive, while 30s. were expended in iron, charcoal (carbone), and other materials for the quarrels. And further details of the process of manufacture at this miniature arsenal are furnished by the account of Amaury de St. Amando, Constable of St. Briavel's, which is enrolled on the Pipe Roll[9] 20 Henry III. Another member of the family, possibly a son, John de Malemort, is still forging quarrels, and is paid the considerable sum of £14 5s. 4½d. for his expenses in iron, coals, wood (fusto), feathers for arrows, and bran and lard for preserving the quarrels (bren et lardio ad eos reservandos), also barrels for storing them, and a grindstone and a smithy for making them (domo fabrili ad eosdem fabricandos). This forge again was privileged to receive an oak a week, and other supplies from the forest, 'to the damage of the king and the detriment of the forest,' according to a 'Verdict[10] of the three foreign hundreds,' which is certainly earlier than 1258, and not improbably than 1250. And it may be noted that in this document John de Malemort is styled sheath-maker (gaynarius) of our lord the king,[11] but by 1282 he had apparently been succeeded by a son or other relative named Stephen. In the reign of Edward II, two members of this family, Richard and Osbert, were men of some local standing in the neighbourhood of Lydney.[12]

In the early 'Verdict' just cited, which seems to be an answer to the chapters of a regard, mention

---

[1] Dugdale, Mon. v, 590.

[2] Or Erdland, as in Forest Proc. K.R. bdle. 1, No. 25.

[3] He also granted them the two oaks a week which they received till about 1258. Cf. Forest Proc. K.R. bdle. 1, No. 25, and App. to Cart. of Flaxley.

[4] Close, 1 Hen. III, m. 11; and 4 Hen. III, m. 3.

[5] This entry occurs amongst the forest amercements, and thus we shall be tolerably safe in assuming that the 'fabrica' in question was an iron forge, that is, probably, a smelting-hearth or bloomery, with adjacent smithy. It is possible that the rare word 'blissahiis,' which occurs in connexion with ironworks in a mandate cited below, may be a local term for the smelting-hearths or small furnaces as distinguished from forges in the narrower sense. As Mr. H. S. Cowper, F.S.A., points out in discussing the 'Excavation at Springs Bloomery' (Arch. J. lv, 100), 'in all these smaller bloomeries [in the Furness district] there was a small smithy at hand for working up the metal on the spot.' In the Forest of Dean the same conjunction probably existed in most cases, and the word 'forge' may thus be understood. The Close Roll of 1 Hen. III, pt. ii, m. 15, supplies evidence that three classes of forges were then at work in the forest : those of the demesne, a few under licence, and the rest unauthorized.

[6] Pat. 16 Hen. III, m. 10.

[7] Forest Proc. K.R. bdle. 1, No. 25.

[8] Cf. in Pipe Roll Glouc. 13 Hen. III, a note of 15,000 quarrels to be delivered to the Constable of Winchester.

[9] m. 2.   [10] Forest Proc. K.R. bdle. 1, No. 25.

[11] Early in 1278 a mandate was sent to the Constable of St. Briavel's to allow John de Malemort to have two beech-trees from the forests for shafts ('flecchas') for quarrels, and two oak-trees to make two chests for the king's use, to place the said quarrels in.

[12] Harl. Chart. iii, C. 32. One of these is not improbably the 'Osbert le Gaynere' who accounts for wood sales in Dean in the early years of Edw. III. Exch. Accts. bdle. 140, No. 20.

is made of another forge [1] held by the Constable of the Castle of St. Briavel at that place 'which is supported by the wood felled for the forge of the said John [de Malemort] and from other perquisites.' Details are also available as to the forges then existing in the vills of the foresters. At Bicknor there were sometimes four and sometimes a lesser number. From each of these the Constable of St. Briavel's as warden of the forest received 7s. rent if they were at work all the year through (*si sunt arrantes continue per annum*), while the forester-in-fee or lord of the vill received 3d. a week from each forge. The charcoal for the support of the Bicknor forges was derived in part from Wales and in part from 'perquisita in foresta,' which may refer to the 'top and lop' and divers windfalls sold by the foresters. In Ruardean there were five forges and the conditions of tenure and working seem to have been similar to those prevailing in Bicknor. The eight forges of Great Dean paid similar dues, but it is distinctly stated that the charcoal with which they were fed was procured outside the forest. Little Dean returned four forges and the conditions under which they worked were similar to those in Bicknor and Ruardean. Besides these, Nigel of Lydney and Walter of Ewias had each a forge in Lydney, for which they each paid 7s. a year to the Constable of St. Briavel's Castle. By 1270 [2] the forges in the forest were at least forty-three in number, and by 1482 [3] had increased to more than sixty, and this in spite of strenuous protests made by the forest officials as to the damage done to the vert by their activity. The earlier account [4] of James Fressel for the Forest of Dean preserved on the Pipe Roll, 40 Hen. III, is interesting in this connexion as it shows that the 'great forge of the king' was then let on lease for £22 10s., while the issues of foreign forges amounted to £8 4s. 6d., and £4 9s. 3d. was returned from forges lately raised (*de novo levatas*) by 'the said James.'

The early smelting-hearths or bloomeries were no doubt of a very simple type, fed with charcoal, the fuel and mineral being placed in alternate layers. Yarranton in the seventeenth century contrasted the great bellows of his own time, driven by water-power, with the ancient foot blast. Improvements in detail were, however, doubtless made even in the mediaeval period as the 'cinders' of still earlier workers were already in request by the smelters of the day who were able to extract more metal.

During the reign of Henry III, and in fact right on into the fourteenth century Gloucestershire would seem in the south of England at least to have continued to hold its place of pride as the chief seat of the iron industry. Two instances may alone be cited here in illustration. In a letter [5] of Simon de Seinliz to Ralf Neville, bishop of Chichester, written sometime between 1224 and 1226, mention is made of ten marks' worth 'de minuto ferro' if it can be got, or if not five marks' worth of this kind and five 'de grosso ferro' to be obtained in Gloucestershire, and thence carried to Winchester to the bishop's house [6] there. One Henry de Kynard had suggested that the iron should be carted (*cartatum*) to Bristol in the first instance and not to Gloucester, but the writer preferred Gloucester since it could be conveyed thence to Winchester more easily and without greater expense. And farther afield even at Westminster Abbey Gloucester iron was appreciated and used, as the fabric rolls bear witness. [7]

Until the thirteenth century it is difficult to find direct and specific mention of Gloucestershire mines on private or public record, though indirect references are, as we have seen, very frequent indeed. One of the earliest detailed notices of both sea-coal and iron mines in Dean is found in the 'Verdict of the three foreign hundreds' already cited, which is, however, most unfortunately mutilated. From this it appears that about 1250 or earlier coal was worked in Blakeney, Staunton, and Abinghall. In Blakeney the Constable of St. Briavel's Castle and the forester-in-fee in charge of the bailiwick seem to have shared certain dues paid by the miners, and the same was the case at Staunton. In Abinghall on the other hand the Constable got nothing, but the forester-in-fee took a penny on each horse-load of coal. That mineral coal was ever used for the smelting-hearths at this time in Dean there is no evidence whatever, but there did exist some export trade [8] across the Severn. Mineral coal when first employed for burning seems to have been essentially the fuel of the less wealthy classes, and often restricted to special trades; the rich and noble [9] preferred the more aromatic fires of wood.

In 1282 [10] the regarders asserted that the king took any sea-coal found in Bearse, Ruardean, and Great and Little Dean. At the same time Ralf de Abbenhale held a coal-pit (*fossatum carbonis marini*) in the bailiwick of Abinghall and thence took coal, but the king got nothing. The same claims were set up by Cecily de Michegros in

---

[1] The word translated 'forge' throughout this document is in the original 'fabrica.' In the regard of 1282 however 'forgia' is employed.

[2] Forest Proc. Tr. of Rec. No. 29.

[3] Ibid. No. 30. They varied much from year to year. Rudder quotes the number as 72 from a record about this time. [4] m. 4.

[5] *Royal and Hist. Letters*, Hen. III. (Rolls Ser.), i, 278–9.

[6] The text reads 'hospitis' corruptly for 'hospitii.'

[7] Lethaby, *Westminster Abbey and the King's Craftsmen*, 141.

[8] Forest Proc. Exch. K.R. bdle. 1, No. 26.

[9] In 1257 Queen Eleanor left Nottingham for Tutbury 'quia . . . propter fumum carbonum maris nullo modo potuit demorari.' *Ann. Mon.* (Rolls Ser.), iii, 203.

[10] Forest Proc. Exch. Tr. of Rec. No. 31.

Bicknor, the warden of Staunton in that baili-wick, Walter de Astune in Blakeney, Nicholas de Lea in Lea, and the earl of Warwick in Lydney, but the regarders 'nesciunt quo war-ranto.' What was taken, as will be seen hereafter in the account of the free miners, was sometimes not so much the actual coal raised as certain dues levied thereon, and this is also borne out by the earlier 'Verdict.'

The account of the iron-mines given in the earlier finding is unfortunately mutilated, and as the facts stated do not seem to differ in essentials from those recorded by the regarders in 1282 it may be advisable to confine our attention to the later document. According to this, Ralf de Abbenhale had a mine in his bailiwick from which the king took nothing except six loads of ore (*minerie*) a week and paid therefor to the miners 6*d.* In Bicknor Cecily de Michegros and in Blakeney Walter de Astune claimed any mine (*mineriam*) if it were found. The king held the mine in the bailiwick of Great Dean and received from each workman raising three loads of ore (*minee*) per week one penny for that week. And when ore (*minea*) was first found the king must have one man working with the other miners in the mine (*mineria*), 'et conducet illum pro duobus denariis per diem et habebit partem lucri quantum eveniat uni operatori,' and just as in Abinghall the Crown claimed six loads of ore, 'que vocantur law-ore,' per week, for which 6*d.* was paid to the miner. In the bailiwick of Bearse there were more mines than in Dean, but under the same regulations, and the king received twenty-four loads per week as law-ore, for which he gave the miners 2*s.* In Staunton, again, the king had the mine, and the regulations were as in Dean except that he only took one halfpenny per week from each man who raised three loads. Again, if the king had an itinerant (*errantem*) forge the miners were bound to supply him with ore at a penny a load. He also had a right to a halfpenny on every load taken outside the forest, and the whole of these dues from the miners the king placed out at farm for £46.[1] Further, Sir Richard Talebot held the mine in Lea by unknown right, but the king had nothing from it. And again from the ore raised in the earl of Warwick's wood at Lydney the king took nothing except the customary due of a halfpenny a load on iron carried out of the forest.

The mediaeval mining in the Forest of Dean was naturally of a somewhat primitive character, open-cast workings being sufficient[2] in the case of the shallower deposits of limonite along the out-crop of the crystalline limestone known by the local name of 'crys' or 'crease.' Instances of old workings of this type are not uncommon in the Forest as at Dean Pool on the western side and elsewhere, and are often known by the local name of 'scowles.' Coal was, no doubt, often worked in the same way. The deeper deposits in the 'crease' are found in 'churns' or chambers, some quite small, others ranging to a capacity of 50,000 or 60,000 tons of ore. To reach these, bell or beehive-pits were probably sunk, a small pit being driven through the surface cover and widened below. When as much ore had been taken as could safely be removed, the working was left and a fresh pit opened up beside it.[3] Few of these pits were large enough to require the leaving of pillars or elaborate support. This method of working was especially useful in dealing with the irregular deposits of iron ore, connected by 'strings' or 'leads' which are characteristic of the Forest of Dean formations.

The equipment of a free miner is depicted in the heraldic crest on a mutilated brass of the fifteenth century within the Clearwell Chapel of Newland Church. He wears a cap and carries a candlestick between his teeth. In his right hand is a small mattock, while a mine-hod of wood hangs at his back from a shoulder-strap fastened to his belt ; his leathern breeches are tied with thongs below the knee. An interesting series of smiths' and miners' tools are also found represented on the font of Abinghall Church and the western face of its tower. Men of a sturdy race skilled in their own craft, the miners of Dean were fre-quently summoned to the Scottish wars[4] under the Edwards, and their pre-eminent services at the sieges of Berwick were traditionally associated with the customary laws and privileges to which we must next devote our attention. As, however, will be seen presently these customary rights dated from an earlier period, although it is not impossible that the hall-mark of a royal con-firmation may have followed faithful service at the wars ; but of such confirmation no absolute first-hand proof is at present known.

---

[1] This is confirmed by the account rendered for Dean by Ralf de Sandwich [Mins. Accts. bdle. 850, No. 19, 8–9 Edw. I (P.R.O.)] There the 'Issues of the Water of Severn (i.e. not of the weirs, which were in-cluded in the Rents of Assize, but the ½*d.* a load cus-toms duty) are £23,' and the 'issues of the Great and Small Mines of iron with coal £23 19*s.*' The rent of the forges, which was not included, of course, in the miners' payments, amounts to £12, which, as the rent for the full year was 7*s.* a forge, suggests that many of the sixty or more then existing were working short time. A comparison of the somewhat fragmen-tary accounts available shows that the amount received from the forges varied considerably at different periods.

[2] Kendall, *Iron Ores of Gt. Brit.*, 364.

[3] Galloway, *Annals of Coal Mining*, i, 32.

[4] And also for service across the Channel. From the Pipe R. 20 Edw. III, m. 8, we learn that Guy Brian 'vallettus Regis' had selected 60 miners in-cluding six master-miners to be sent to Portsmouth. For the five days' journey the master-miners were paid 4*d.* a day each, and the rest 3*d.* a day, and reasonable expenses were allowed for the six horses which bore the 'instrumenta eorundem mineratorum.' The whole sum spent was £4 5*s.*

Few subjects are so little known or appreciated as the special position and privileges of the mediaeval free miner and the relation in which he stood to the rest of the community. The origin of these privileges is obscure. Excluding England, two theories prevailed in the Middle Ages with regard to property in mines.[1] By the first the sovereign was looked upon as absolute proprietor, and the landowner had no rights, save to indemnification for property damaged. By the second, ownership of the surface carried with it a right to the mines beneath, but a third person was given power to acquire an interest when the owner was unable, or unwilling, to exploit them. In both cases the enjoyment of mines was subject to regulations from the Crown, which also commonly established a claim to one-tenth or other proportion of the produce, so that in practice the two theories might coincide.

In Germany,[2] the idea of a royalty in mines is supposed to have made its first appearance and to have obtained firmest footing; but even there no claims appear until the close of the eleventh century,[3] when the revival of Roman law cooperated with the assumed succession of the emperor to the rights of the Caesars, to give currency to the claims of sovereignty over mines. According to the Justinian Code,[4] one might work a gold mine upon condition of conforming to certain regulations and of giving preference in sales to the imperial fisc. By a constitution of Gratian,[5] also, a general permission had been given to take marble from the land of private persons upon payment of a tenth to the owner. The interpretation of these rules by the Lombard commentators[6] made them applicable to mines of all descriptions and in all countries, and the emperors in the twelfth century succeeded in enforcing their pretensions and in taking all mines under their peculiar care.[7]

It was found, however, that attempts to treat the miners as so many agricultural labourers would be disastrous. The technical difficulties connected with mining made it essential that the men be secured from interruption, and also

that skilled workmen be called in by special grants of privileges. The upshot was that the emperor, and his imitators, the lesser princes, gradually commuted their mining rights for a proportion of the produce, and threw open the mines to all comers under a series of charters,[8] the provisions of which we shall find exemplified in the main by the privileges of the Dean miners. Germany's policy was followed some centuries later by France, the edicts of Charles VI[9] and Louis XI[10] removing the miner from the power of the landlords and granting privileges to prospectors.

In England, in the same general period, we meet with similar codes, applied, however, not to all mines, but to several scattered communities— the lead miners of the MendipHills,[11] Derbyshire,[12] and Alston Moor,[13] the iron and coal miners of the Forest of Dean, and the tinners of Cornwall.[14] It would simplify matters, could we regard these codes as descended from Roman law, as was probably the case upon the continent. This explanation, however, is almost certainly inadmissible. The early references to the English miners' privileges give the impression of unwritten customary law, rather than of rights formally conferred by charter.[15] In Derbyshire the leadminers' customs rested upon immemorial usage,[16] which Edward I merely confirmed in 1288.[17] The Alston miners received a charter from Henry V,[18] but, again, nothing was granted which had not been previously enjoyed. The same may be said with regard to the Cornish and Devonshire tinners, whose liberties, first embodied in a royal charter of 1201,[19] and later added to in 1305,[20] seem for the most part to have rested upon tradition. What also seems strange is that, although these mining camps were operated under conditions of great liberality to the adventurer, all mines outside their limits should be the

---

[1] 'A Sketch of the Origin of Mining Laws in Europe,' by J. Hawkins, *Trans. Roy. Geol. Soc. Corn.* vi, 84–90.

[2] 'Observations on the Mining Law of Germany,' by C. Lemon, *Trans. Roy. Geol. Soc. Corn.* vi, 150–72.

[3] Hüllman, *Geschichte des Regalien*, 62; Eichorn, *Deutsche Staats und Rechtsgeschichte*, ed. 1834, ii, 424.

[4] Lib. xi, tit. 7b.

[5] Ibid. 3; *Theodosian Code*, lib. x, tit. 19; l. 1, 8, 10, 11, 14.

[6] See extracts from the gloss of Accursius and the Summa of Azo printed in Smirke, *Vice v. Thomas*, App. 104.

[7] See Charters of Mines, printed in the *Spicilegium Ecclesiasticum*; Luenig, *Reichs. Archiv.* and cited by Gmelin, *Geschichte des Teutschen Bergbau*, 220, 241.

[8] See von Cancrin, *Grundsäzze des Teutschen Bergrechts*, 149. A specimen charter is that of Iglau, Peithner, *Versuch, über die Natürliche und Politische Geschichte der Bohmischen und Märischen Bergwerke*, App.; Jare, *Voyages Métallurgiques*, iii, 461–511; Reyer, *Zinn*, 35, 53, 54, 56, 79.

[9] *Recueil des Anciennes Lois Francaises*, vii, 386–90.

[10] Ibid. x, 623; 'The Mining Laws of France,' by M. Migneron, *Trans. Roy. Geol. Soc. Corn.* vi, 239–58.

[11] Houghton, *The Compleat Miner*, pt. iii.

[12] Esch. Enr. Accts. 16 Edw. I, No. 34; Add. MS. 6682, fol. 65; *Compleat Mineral Laws of Derb.*

[13] Pat. 4 Hen. V, m. 8; 30 Edw. I, pt. iii, m. 23; Parl. R. i, 64.

[14] Pearce, *Laws and Customs of the Stannaries.*

[15] 'The Origins of Mining Law,' by J. Hawkins, *Trans. Roy. Geol. Soc. Cornw.* vi, 90.

[16] It is said that William I expressly refrained from disturbing them (Add. MS. 6682, fol. 197).

[17] Esch. Enr. Accts. 16 Edw. I, No. 34.

[18] Pat. 4 Hen. V, m. 8.

[19] Chart. R. 36 Hen. III, m. 18.

[20] Ibid. 33 Edw. I, m. 40, 41.

property of the king,[1] or of the owner [2] of the land. This is no place for a dissertation upon the general subject of the origins of English mining law, but it may be stated that while the king unquestionably tried to imitate the continental sovereigns in claiming all metallic mines,[3] this pretension was never permanently made good, except for the precious metals, other mines as a rule remaining the property of the ground lord.[4] Under these circumstances the existence, under peculiar mining codes, of several isolated tracts well known to be the seat of the oldest mines in England, seems due, not to any engrafting of Roman law from the continent, but, as the miners themselves declared, to usage time out of mind.[5]

Although certain of the rights of the fiee miners of Dean are alluded to in the verdicts and regards already quoted, we are obliged in order to obtain a connected view of these privileges to have resort to a seventeenth-century transcript [6] of the code of customary law which regulated the exercise of mining rights within the forest. This purports to be a memorandum

What the Customes and Franchises hath been that were granted tyme out of minde and after in tyme of the excellent and redoubted prince King Edward [7] unto the miners of the Forrest of Deane and the Castle of St. Bridvills ('Briavells' in *Editio Princeps*).

and is sometimes known as the 'Book of Dennis.'

There is unfortunately no evidence to show precisely when these customs were reduced to writing. Probably, however, this occurred before the Reformation, as the use of certain ecclesiastical terms would suggest, and at a time when the extended boundaries[8] of the forest reduced about 1301 had not been forgotten, for these are assumed in this *Book of Laws* as the area within which the privileges of the free miners operated, and there is no limitation as in later times to the hundred

of St. Briavel's. This summary record of their franchises, together with the regulations embodied in the later orders, seventeen in number, of their mine-court, formed the authoritative standard to which the free miners constantly appealed.

The first point alluded to in their code of customs is the trespass committed by anyone with 'boat, trowe, pinard, or any other vessel' who passes 'without gree made for the customes due to the king and also to the said miners for the myne (i.e. ore),' the penalty being forfeiture of vessel and cargo. This is worth notice as a possible explanation of the outrages perpetrated by the miners on Tewkesbury traders in the reign of Henry VI already mentioned in the 'Forestry' article of this volume.

The most characteristic and peculiar privilege to which the *Book of Laws* bears witness is that every free miner might with the approval of the king's gaveller [9] dig for iron ore [10] or coal where he pleased within the bounds of the forest whether on the royal demesne or on the lands of private persons.[11] In the latter case the lord of the soil as well as the king received a share in the newly-opened mine, as we might, even without this evidence, gather from the regards previously cited. In fact the lord was to be considered as the last man of the fellowship, and the gaveller in this case was also bound to mark out a 'convenient way next stretching to the king's highway.' In respect to the king's share it is laid down (in reference apparently to mines on the demesne) that

At all tymes the king's man shall come into the mine without any costes asking of him and shall bee the third better man of the fellowship in mayntenance and in helping of the myne and of the fellowship.

The gaveller should call at the works every Tuesday between 'Mattens and Masse' to receive the king's share one penny [12] from every miner. The miners again of the district beneath the wood [13]

---

[1] As in the case of mines royal (*Pipe R. of Cumb. Westmld. and Dur.* Introd. xxiv–xxvi ; Plowden, *Commentaries* (ed. 1761), p. 310.

[2] As in the coal mines in the north (Galloway, *Annals of Coal Mining and the Coal Trade*, i, 18, 21, 23, 24, 27, 37–39, 44, 59, 69, 73 ; Patrick, *Early Mining Records of Scotland*, Introd. xlv.).

[3] Dugdale, *Mon.* (ed. 1846), ii, 289 ; *Cal. Pat.* 1283, p. 73.

[4] Plowden, *Commentaries* (ed. 1761), p. 310.

[5] As Sir Charles Dilke, bart., reminds us, the usage of the oath taken 'touching a holly-wand' may suggest a possible pre-Roman or Celtic origin.

[6] First printed in 1687 from a transcript made in 1673, which is now at the Crown Office, Whitemead Park, but again, apparently from another copy, by Mr. Nicholls, *Ironmaking in the Forest of Dean*, 71 et seq.

[7] i.e., from internal evidence, probably Edw. I. But one fragmentary MS. copy discovered by Mr. Philip Baylis reads Edw. III.

[8] 'Betweene Chepstowe Bridge and Gloucester Bridge, the halfe deale of Newent, Ross Ash, Monmouth's Bridge and soe farr into the Seasoames as the Blast of a horne or the voice of a man may bee heard.'

[9] i.e. the king's receiver who took the gavel or rent on behalf of the Constable of St. Briavel's, and officially recognized or disallowed any new mine.

[10] Diggings for ochre were also included, at least in the seventeenth century, as appears from Exch. Dep. 27–28 Chas. II.

[11] At a later period, if not as early as the reign of Edw. I, gardens, orchards, and curtilages were excepted, according to the evidence of John Williams, deputy gaoler (gaveller) to Sir Baynham Throckmorton. Exch. Dep. Ord. Com. 27–28 Chas. II, Hilary, No. 21, Glouc. (P.R.O.).

[12] 'If so bee that the myner winns three seames of myne.'

[13] The division of the forest mining district into 'Above the Wood' and 'Beneath the Wood' seems of considerable antiquity. In the seventeenth century there was a deputy-gaoler for each district. St. Briavel's, Newland, Staunton, and Bicknor were then 'above the Wood,' and Mitcheldean, Little Dean, Abinghall, Flaxley, and part of the parishes of Awre and the Lea 'beneath the Wood.' Exch. Dep. ut supra.

'Mitcheldeane, Little Deane, and Riverdeane' (i.e. Ruardean), delivered to the king every week when at work 'twelve charges of mine by a certaine measure if they have soe much gotten by the week,' for which they were to be paid 12d. Mention is also made of the contribution to the king known as 'Lawe oare,' while on his side timber was to be allowed from the royal forest for the works of the miners. A consideration of this last proviso throws a welcome light on a presentment of the jurors at the regard[1] of 1282 that the 'foresters take the branches or rafters (*coporones lignorum*) delivered (*liberatorum*) to the miners, to the oppression of the miners, and make their profit of them' (*et faciunt inde commodum suum*). Indeed a comparison of the fragmentary notices relating to the mines in the 'Verdict' of 1244 (?) or the Regard of 1282 with the claims of the *Book of Laws* must inevitably lead to the conclusion that the main outlines at least of the mining customs of Dean were fixed as early as the reign of Edward I if not of Henry III, and that their origin possibly goes back to remote antiquity.

Besides the provisions already alluded to the *Book of Laws* laid down the well-known restriction that only persons born and abiding within the metes of the forest were to frequent the mines, while the rule as to the distances between the pits 'that noe man shall come within so much space that the miner may stand and cast ridding[2] and stones soe farr from him with a bale as the manner is' not only recalls the 'throw of the hache'[3] of the Mendip miners, but also suggests what we otherwise know to have existed, the open-cast and bell-pit systems of working. Again, the clause as to the miner's testamentary rights that he 'in his last days and at all tymes may bequeath and give his dole of the mine to whom he will as his own catele' is of interest from a legal standpoint when we consider the mediaeval testamentary practice, and may be compared with the rule existing in the Stannaries of Cornwall where the dormant liberty of mining was regarded as personal property.[4] Reference is also made in this compilation of the mining customs of Dean to the forest 'court of the wod' before the verderers at the 'Speech,' the procedure for the recovery of debts at St. Briavel's castle or gate where the creditor swore to the debt by his faith holding a stick of holly, and to the Court of Mine Law, consisting of the constable, gaveller,[5] the castle clerk, and the

miners themselves.[6] An attentive perusal of the account given of these legal formalities will induce a strong conviction in any reader acquainted with the legal phraseology of the Middle Ages that part at least of this *Book of Laws* was originally drawn up in Latin, though the English translation may be far older than the seventeenth century. And finally the prohibition of carts and wains, the allusions to a standard measure or 'bill^eyes,'[7] and to the miners' clothes and light, are all of interest and illustrate the extreme conservatism which has marked the usages and customs of the free-miners of the Forest of Dean.

The general purport of the laws of the Dean miners has now been given, but before closing this sketch of the mediaeval history of the mines it will be of interest to examine more carefully the constitution under which the work was carried on.

We have already seen in the case of the tinners of Cornwall[8] that the miners enjoyed peculiar forms of judiciary exemption from ordinary taxation, and miners' parliaments for legislative action, thus constituting, as it were, a state within a state, although subject, in the last resort, to the approval of the crown. All this, of course, was in addition to the basic privilege of free mining, with rights to wood and water. Now in the Forest of Dean the miners, both of coal and of iron, constituted a much less complex organization. Instead of, as in the

---

[1] Forest Proc. Tr. of Rec. No. 31.

[2] i.e. the surface material to be removed before the ore or coal was reached.

[3] Or 'hacke.' *The Ancient Laws of the Miners of Mendip* (1687), 4.

[4] Nicholls, *Iron-making in the Forest of Dean*, 79 n.

[5] In the seventeenth century there were two gavellers, or gaolers, acting as deputies for the chief gaveller. Exch. Dep. under Com. 27–28 Chas. II. Hilary, No. 21, Glouc. (P.R.O.).

[6] Two Chancery bills of the fifteenth century contain references to a court held at St. Briavel's Castle and may be noted here. In the first of these (Early Chanc. Proc. bdle. 12, No. 41), which may be dated about 11 Hen. VI, John Luke of Gloucester complained of the arrest of goods and merchandise to the value of £20 at Mitcheldean by Thomas and Harry White, who carried them to the 'Castell of St. Brevell,' where they were withheld from the owner until 'your said suppliant hadde found sufficient suerte to apere in his propere person in the courte holden there fro iij wokes to iij wokes,' while by 'favour of the court he was denied the right to make attornay in no wyse which is agayn the lawe.' He accordingly begs for writs of *subpoena*. About half a century after (Early Chanc. Proc. bdle. 60, No. 200) Richard Bassh and Thomas Bassh complained of one John Laurens who was alleged to have wrongfully 'affermyd a pleynt of detinue ayenst the seid Richard Bassh in the Court of Seynt Briavell . . . before the bailiffs theer which is the kinges court of record as it is and alwey hath byn pretended to be' concerning lands and tenements at Pyrton 'oute of the jurisdicion of the seid courte.' Further grievances were that within this court 'they dayly make new lawes at ther willes and call them from thensforth [cu]stomes,' and that no challenge of the jury was permitted.

[7] Nicholls, *Iron-making, ut supra*, 80. The official MS. copy reads 'belleye' (*ex inform.* Mr. Philip Baylis). Probably the measure contained in the miner's hod. Cf. term 'billy-boy' employed with regard to hod-carriers in the iron mines of Dean.

[8] *V.C.H. Cornw.* i, 'Tin Mining.'

INDUSTRIES

Stannaries, a hierarchy of mine officials, wardens, vice-wardens, stewards, receivers, controllers, and others, for the administration of the courts and the collection of taxes, we find the former duty carried on by the Constable of St. Briavel's Castle, while the king's gaveller, or his deputies, attended to such things as the collection of mining dues and the installation of new mines. Nor is there anything in the laws of the Dean miners to show that the forest miners were exempted from ordinary taxation, while it is a matter of record that they might be impressed by the king's officers for service in mines elsewhere.[1] The mine courts of the Forest of Dean were constituted of free miners, and were probably rudimentary in the extreme, such appeal as existed being to successive inquests of the miners from twelve to twenty-four, and then to forty-eight, when a final judgement was given.[2]

On the other hand, however, the constitution of the Dean miners went much farther than that of the Stannaries, the Mendip and Derbyshire lead miners, or those of Alston Moor. These latter bodies formed corporations quite distinct from the town gilds. In the latter the chief aim was the suppression of competition among members by means of regulations to check production and to restrict membership. On the other hand, the ordinary free miner was member of an organization which resembled rather the regulated trading company of the sixteenth and seventeenth centuries. No restrictions were laid upon output. Every miner might work in his own way and on whatsoever scale he might choose, and might sell his product for whatever price he pleased. The sole rules which bound him were those designed to facilitate the collection of the special royalties of the crown. Again, we find that the mining was free to all comers, foreigners[3] excepted, each man as he staked his claim becoming, *ipso facto*, a member of the community, and entitled to all the rights of a free miner. The elasticity of this simple constitution was undoubtedly the factor which preserved the early mine organizations throughout the centuries down to the present day, in spite of every change in industrial organization and tendencies.

To this state of affairs the Dean miners formed a strong exception. In the first place, the so-called free miners and their descendants residing in the forest constituted a close corporation. They and they alone, save for their apprentices, might work the coal and iron.[4] What the earlier regulations were concerning apprentices it is impossible to say, but by an order in 1668 no young man, although born in

the hundred, might work at coal or iron unless he had already worked a year and a day, or had been for five years an apprentice to a miner.[5] In 1737 the order was modified to the effect that no foreigner's son, even though born in the hundred, might become a miner unless he had undergone a seven years' apprenticeship.[6] It should be added that apprentices were rarely taken, the miners contenting themselves with the aid of their sons.[7]

This fact is the more readily understood when one recalls the petty size of the mines themselves. Strict custom required that the mines be worked by companies of four persons called 'verns' or partners,[8] the king being considered a fifth, by virtue of the fact that he was entitled in each mine to a seam of ore called the law acre,[9] besides another share if he chanced to be lord of the soil as well.[10] The verns must be free miners and must proceed in driving and working the level or sinking and working the water-pit by their own labour or that of their sons and apprentices;[11] and a further limitation, which applied only to coal carriers, was that they must rent land and keep their own houses.[12] Under these laws machinery could be erected only upon the express permission of the owner of the soil.[13] To these facts we must add the law applicable only to shallow mines, that the workings of a mine might be carried to an indefinite extent unless interrupted by another work.[14]

Another rule, equally restrictive of competition, was that passed in 1668 by the miners' parliament, giving to the free miners the sole privilege of carrying ore and coal;[15] and a supplementary regulation, designed to prevent the concentration of the business in the hands of a few, limited free miners to the use of four horses each,[16] and forbade wagons.[17] With these went another regulation which fixed the prices at which the ore and coal might be carried,[18] and in 1676, when the monopoly of cartage was abandoned, it was enacted that free miners were always to have a preference in loading at the pit. In the sale of ore and coal to out-

[5] Nicholls, *Forest of Dean*, 45-6.
[6] *Award of Dean Forest Commrs.* 13.
[7] *Fourth Rep. of Dean Forest Commrs.* 6.
[8] Cf. ibid. 8.
[9] Houghton, *Compleat Miner*, pt. ii, art. 16.
[10] Ibid. art. 14. As a matter of fact the king is referred to as owner of several iron-mines in Dean (*Cal. Close*, 1320, p. 278; 1328, p. 296; 1332, p. 443).
[11] *Fourth Rep.* 8.
[12] *Award*, 17; Nicholls, *Forest of Dean*, 46.
[13] *Award*, 24.   [14] Ibid. 13.
[15] Ibid. 1.
[16] Ibid. 14. Nicholls, *Forest of Dean*, 45.
[17] Galloway, *Annals of Coal Mining and the Coal Trade*, 209; Nicholls, *Forest of Dean*, 45.
[18] *Award of Dean Forest Commrs.* 13.

[1] Cf. *Cal. Close* (1319), p. 127.
[2] Nicholls, *Iron-making in the Forest of Dean*, 78.
[3] i.e. those not born in the forest.
[4] Cf. Houghton, *Compleat Miner*, pt. ii, art. 30, 36.

223

siders, moreover, the miners must not underbid one another. In all cases they were subject to bargains made by 'bargainers' appointed by the mine law court.[1] Lastly, the persistent antagonism of the miners to large enterprises, and their opposition of interests to the consumers of their products, is shown by the custom by which no miner might become the owner of a smithy without loss of his privileges.[2]

These restrictions, which cramped the productions of coal and iron, and deadened individual initiative, could not stand the test of time. Throughout the Middle Ages, indeed, they seem to have been maintained, but with the sixteenth and seventeenth centuries their maintenance became increasingly more difficult. Probably at an early date various irregularities had crept into the working of the rules. It had grown to be not unusual for outsiders, gentlemen of rank and influence, to be made free miners by a vote of the inhabitants of the forest,[3] while probably already the custom had been connived at[4] of the miners staking out claims and then leasing them to outsiders.[5] The great value of the iron deposits of Dean, as well as its timber, which the working of the mines and smelting houses endangered, at last led to a series of efforts on the part of the Crown and others to wrest the control from the miners.

From this somewhat lengthy digression as to the status and claims of the free miners, it is necessary to return to the general history of the mines which we have traced with some particularity to the reign of Edward I. From this point onward there is very little to add, in the mere outline that can be given here, to the valuable facts collected by Mr. Nicholls.[6] He points out that apparently there had been some diminution of the number of forges at work on the west side of the forest during the reign of Edward II, if a list of that date can be regarded as complete. But even if this is the case the amount of iron produced from the mines during the reign of Edward III must have been very considerable,[7] and it is necessary to bear in mind that they supplied not only the forges of the forest, but those of Caerleon, Newport, Berkeley, Monmouth, and Trelleck,[8] while iron implements

of all kinds long formed a particular speciality of the great fair at Gloucester.

It seems, however, that toward the end of the fourteenth century, if not before, a decline in the production of iron had taken place, possibly through the gradual exhaustion of the most accessible superficial deposits, although already recourse was being had to the re-smelting of the older 'cinders,' while the export trade to the south and east of England had diminished, partly through the increased import of iron from abroad, aided at a later period by the energetic exploitation of the ores of the Sussex Weald.

But while the amount of iron may have declined, there is some reason for supposing that the output of coal was gradually increasing, as was certainly the case in Kingswood, between the fourteenth and seventeenth centuries. As regards the methods of mining there is no reason to suppose that much advance occurred during this period, and about 1568 on the records[9] of one of the minor forest courts we meet with frequent presentments 'pro puteis non impletis,' which under the special circumstances of this forest may well refer to abandoned mine-pits.

With respect to the forges, however, the late sixteenth or early seventeenth century undoubtedly saw an advance: the old bloomeries were gradually passing and cast iron was being made in enlarged furnaces provided with a more powerful blast, advantage being taken of water-power when available. This introduction of a vastly more expensive and elaborate process necessitated the intervention of the capitalist and the syndicate. On 14 June we hear[10] of a 'bargayne' between the crown and Giles Brudges and others by which the adventurers were to have

libertye to erect all manner of workes, iron or other, by lande or by water, excepting wyer workes, and the same to pull downe, remove and alter att pleasure

and also 'libertye to take myne oare and synders, either to be used att the workes or otherwise.' The exception of wire-works is of great interest, and is doubtless due to the fact that a company[11] which included Sir Francis Bacon had already works of this description at Tintern and Whitebrook.

The important lease to William earl of Pembroke in 1611 of the castle of St. Briavel and of the Forest of Dean, and the lands, mines, and quarries belonging thereto, as well as a further grant of wood for his iron-works, has already been mentioned in the article on 'Forestry' in the present volume. This and some later leases resulted in serious trouble with the free miners, who saw their liberties threatened and who were possibly supported by iron-masters already settled in

---

[1] *Award of Dean Forest Commrs.* 14; Nicholls, *Forest of Dean*, 45.

[2] Houghton, *Compleat Miner*, pt. ii, art. 33.

[3] *Award of Dean Forest Commrs.* 13.

[4] Since this gave employment to many poor men.

[5] *Fourth Rep. Dean Forest Commrs.* 2; *Award of Dean Forest Commrs.* 21.

[6] *Iron-making in the Forest of Dean* (1866), and other works.

[7] A return of about the year 1341, printed by Nicholls, *Personalities of the Forest of Dean*, 21, gives the yearly profit of the mines and forges as £34, which certainly shows some decline since the days of Edw. I.

[8] Nicholls, *Iron-making in the Forest of Dean*, 72, 73.

[9] For. Proc. Exch. K.R. bdle. 1, No. 30.

[10] Lansd. MSS. 166, fol. 365 (B.M.)

[11] S.P. Dom. Jas. I, lxiii, 76.

the forest. The order of the Court of Exchequer on an information filed soon after the earl of Pembroke attempted to carry out the terms of his lease was practically a compromise between the parties, since it laid down, in spite of the enunciation of some strong doctrine as to crown rights, that no new diggers were to be allowed, ' but only such poor men as were inhabitants of the said forest.'

The iron-works in the forest were in this reign leased to Sir Basil Brook, who was succeeded by several other lessees or sub-lessees, the lease of the earl of Pembroke remaining in force. In the forest were cast the 610 guns ordered by the Crown in 1629 for the States General of Holland, which were possibly shipped at Bullo Pill on the Severn. Mr. Wyrrall, the indefatigable antiquary, transcribed a most valuable inventory dated 1635 of the iron-works in the forest used by the successive lessees. There were then furnaces at Cannop, Parkend, Soudley, and Lydbrook, and forges, including chafferies and fineries, at Parkend, Whitecroft, Soudley, and Lydbrook. From this survey it is quite clear that the stone body of the furnace was as a rule about 22 ft. square, while the water-wheel for the blast was not less than 22 ft. in diameter, and the two pairs of bellows measured 18 ft. by 4 ft. The inventory is astonishingly minute, and the list of tools extremely valuable to any investigators of the history of smelting, but we can only give a reference to them here.[1]

As this article is mainly concerned with mining we are unable to do more than allude to the attempts made to use mineral coal in the Dean iron-works, among which may be mentioned that by Captain Birch, Major Wildman, and others who erected in the Forest of Dean

large air furnaces, into which they introduced large clay pots, resembling those used at glass-houses, filled with various proportions of the necessary mixture of ores and charcoal. The furnaces were heated by the flame of pit-coal, and it was expected that, by tapping the pots below, the separated materials would flow out. This rude process was found entirely impracticable; the heat was inadequate to perfect separation, the pots cracked, and in a short time the process was abandoned altogether.[2]

The famous Dud Dudley maintained for some time a furnace in the forest, at which he partially solved the problem of fuel,[3] but he met with so many reverses, owing to the hostility of other

iron-masters and the dishonesty of his partners,[4] that he gave up the struggle.

After twenty-four years of leases,[5] during which frequent assaults upon the privileges of miners by royal patentees led to violent uprisings and riots among the former,[6] in 1637 a grant was made to Edward Terringham of

all mines of coal and quarries of grindstone within the Forest of Dean and in all places within the limits and perambulations thereof, as well those within his Majesty's demesne lands and the waste and soil there, as also all such as lay within the lands of any of his Majesty's subjects within the perambulation of the said Forest to His Majesty reserved or lawfully belonging, to hold for 31 years at the yearly rent of £30.[7]

Two years later, in 1640, the crown sold to Sir John Winter[8] all the mines, minerals, and stone quarries within the limits of the forest, to work and use the same together with all timber, trees, woods, and underwood growing in any part thereof, in consideration of £10,000 and the yearly sum of £16,000 for six years, and of a fee-farm rent of £1,950 12s. 6d. for ever. This bargain was equivalent to selling the forest altogether, and the inhabitants of the district, being greatly dissatisfied, took advantage of the approaching civil distractions to throw down the fences which Winter had already begun to make.[9] Winter's active part in the Civil War in behalf of the king led to the confiscation of his iron-works and the alienation of his claims to the forest.[10] What were the fortunes of the miners during this period it is difficult to say, other, perhaps, than that they were inclined towards the side of Parliament, and were plundered and pillaged by the troops of both armies.

Under the Commonwealth, owing to the difficulty experienced in meeting the demand for material consequent on the Dutch War, iron-works were erected in the forest for the service of the Navy. After the Restoration it was stated that the war-material thus procured from Dean was found ' inserviceable and layd by in the Tower as uselesse.'[11] This verdict is either much exaggerated or can only apply to

---

[1] Printed Nicholls, *Iron-making in the Forest of Dean*, 33–40. Cf. with this the Inventory of the Commonwealth Govt. Works, S. P. Dom. 1656, cxxx, 102. The seventeenth-century methods are vividly described by Parsons, whose account is cited by Nicholls, *Forest of Dean*, App. v.

[2] Galloway, *Annals of Coal Mining and the Coal Trade*, 253.

[3] For his experiments see Dud Dudley, *Metallum Martis*, 2–24; Percy, *Metallurgy of Iron and Steel*, 883; cf. Malynes, *Lex Mercatoria*, 269–70.

[4] *Metallum Martis*, 12–3, 16–20, 22–3. For subsequent efforts to smelt iron with pit-coal see Plot, *Hist. of Staff.* 128; Galloway, *Annals of Coal Mining and the Coal Trade*, i, 189; Percy, *Metallurgy of Iron and Steel*, 885.

[5] Cf. *Narrative of Forest of Dean*.

[6] Rudder, *Hist. of Glouc.* 30; *Hist. MSS. Com. Rep.* xii, App. pt. i, p. 430.

[7] Nicholls, *Forest of Dean*, 27; Galloway, *Annals of Coal Mining and the Coal Trade*, i, 207; cf. S.P. Dom. Chas. I, ccciii, 61; Chas. II, xvii, 61.

[8] For further details as to the history of the Forest of Dean during the seventeenth century see article ' Forestry ' in this volume.

[9] Nicholls, *Forest of Dean*, 28; *Narrative of Forest of Dean*, 34.

[10] Nicholls, *Forest of Dean*, 28–34.

[11] Add. MSS. (B.M.), 33058, fol. 85.

early samples, as the output was very considerable and sustained. In 1656 the stock[1] in hand at the iron-works was appraised at £9,446, 'which is profit above all charges,' while from September, 1654, to March, 1659, 701 tons of shot and 88 tons of iron fittings were made in the forest for the use of the Navy.[2]

At the Restoration, Winter's titles were returned to him, but under a new patent he confined his activities to the felling of timber in the forest, and the havoc he caused so aroused the king and Parliament as to lead to the important Act of 1668, which, besides its provisions relating to the timber of the forest, declared that all lawful rights and privileges relating to the Dean minerals were to continue, with permission to the crown to lease coal-mines and stone quarries for periods not exceeding thirty-one years.[3]

Some five years previous to the passing of this Act there took place in March, 1663, a session[4] of the Mine Law Court, whose date and proceedings have been preserved. It was held at Clearwell, before Sir Baynham Throckmorton, deputy constable of St. Briavel's Castle, and a jury of forty-eight free miners. The records of this court now at the Crown Office, Whitemead Park, printed by Mr. Nicholl,[5] show it to have been in some sense a parliament, similar to that of the tinners of Cornwall and Devon, and capable not merely of declaring the forest custom, but of framing new rules and regulations for the maintenance of the miners' privileges. These enactments had to do chiefly with the question of apprenticeship,[6] the miners' monopoly of coal cartage, and the fixing of prices by bargainers.

Yet even with this reassertion of the privileges of the free miners we find an ominous indication of the restriction of their ancient rights. In 1668 an Act was passed by Parliament with regard to the forest, providing, among other things, that all lawful rights and privileges relating to minerals in the forest were to continue, with permission to the crown to lease coal-mines and stone quarries for periods not exceeding thirty-one years.[7] The Dean Forest Commissioners, in their report of 1788, remark that

immediately after the Act of 1668 the colliers, who, it is said, now pretend to have a right to whatever timber they find necessary for carrying on their works in the Forest without paying anything for it, then purchased it from the crown.[8]

The second existing order of the Mine Law Court states that it met in 1674, on 9 March, at Clearwell, before Sir George Probert, deputy-constable at St. Briavel's Castle, chiefly with the design of raising a fund for defending in a legal way the right of the free miners and affording them support when injured at their work.[9]

To these ends a payment of 6d. per quarter was levied upon each miner digging for or carrying mineral, of fifteen years of age, as also upon every horse so used, payable within fourteen days, under a fine of 2s. Six collectors were to receive the above payments, to be remunerated at the rate of 1s. per quarter for each pound they gathered. Twice a year they handed in their accounts, under a penalty of £5 and perpetual exclusion from any office of trust if such were found defective. It appears, therefore, that the free miners valued their rights, and not only took thought for the morrow, but provided for it. They added the proviso that the servants of the deputy-constable should have the benefit of always being supplied first at the pit, showing that they knew something also of public diplomacy.

How strictly the enclosures were preserved at this time against all mining operations is shown by the refusal which Sir Charles Harbord gave to a petition presented to the Treasury by several gentlemen and freeholders of the parish of Newland for leave to make a coal level through an enclosure, although they were backed by Sir Baynham Throckmorton, deputy-governor of St. Briavel's Castle, who had also been one of the commissioners first appointed for carrying out the Act of 1668, and who gave it as his opinion that agreeing to the prayer of the petition would conduce to the preservation of the woods in the forest, and to the convenience and advantage of the country. The wording of the refusal was very peremptory, to the effect that 'the enclosures could only be preserved for timber by being kept discharged from all claims; that although miners and quarrymen had long been permitted to dig where they pleased, yet that they could not prove their right to do so; and, as to coal works, any such claims were unknown, much less any liberty of cutting his Majesty's woods for the support thereof.'[10]

The third of the Mine Law Courts was held in September, 1678, at Clearwell, before Sir Baynham Throckmorton, whose favour it shows the free miners were most anxious to preserve, since, upon the understanding that the former order of 1668, forbidding any foreigner to convey or deliver minerals, had proved prejudicial to him and his friends and tenants, they now revoked[11] the same, allowing any foreigner to carry fire or lime coal for his own use, besides which they constituted the marquis of Worcester, then constable of St. Briavel's Castle, as well

---

[1] S.P. Dom. 11 Nov. 1657, cxxx, 101–2.
[2] Ibid. 8 April, 1659, ccii, 70.
[3] 20 Chas. II, cap. 8.
[4] In 10 Chas. I, at a justice seat at Gloucester, the earl of Pembroke claimed the right to be the judge of the Mine Law Court (*Fourth Report Dean Forest Commrs.* 5). [5] *Forest of Dean,* 45–46.
[6] *Award of Dean Forest Commrs.* 13.
[7] Galloway, *Annals of Coal Mining and the Coal Trade,* i, 208 ; Nicholls, *Forest of Dean,* 42, 43, 231.
[8] Nicholls, *Forest of Dean,* 46.

[9] *Award of Dean Forest Commrs.* 17.
[10] Nicholls, *Forest of Dean,* 49.
[11] Ibid. 50.

as Sir Baynham Throckmorton, his deputy, 'free miners to all intents and purposes.'

One order of this court in 1678 is worth particular notice, because it shows that the miners of Dean were in the ' pit and adit ' stage of mining,[1] but the increasing length and cost of the adits, locally called ' surffes,' for draining the pits made it necessary to modify the old custom mentioned in the *Book of Laws* that the bounds of a mine were limited by the distance to which the miner could cast the rubbish from his pit. In consequence, when a ' surfe ' was driven by one party, other miners sank pits near to get a share of the free drainage, which was clearly inequitable. So it was laid down by this order that ' noe myner shall come to work within 100 yards of that surffe,' and we have already seen the distance was at a later time still further extended.

The fourth Mine Law Court was held in 1680 at the Speech House, a building then barely completed[2] for the purpose of carrying on the public business of the forest, which still stands. The order there passed implies that, although the last court had appointed six bargainers to deal with the difficult question of valuing the minerals offered for sale, inconvenience was yet experienced on this head. It was therefore decreed that a dozen Winchester bushels of iron ore should be delivered at St. Wonnarth's furnace for 10s., at Whitchurch for 7s., at Bishopswood for 9s., at Linton for 9s., at Longhope for 9s., at Flaxley for 8s., at Gainsmills (if rebuilt) for 7s., at Blakeney for 6s., at Lydney for 6s., at those in the forest lately demolished (if rebuilt) for the same as before, at Redbrook for 4s. 6d., at the Abbey (Tintern) for 9s., at Brockweir for 6s. 6d., at Redbrook Passage for 5s. 6d., at Gunspill for 7s. So also no house or smith's coal was to be delivered on the banks of the Wye below Huntsam Ferry for less than 8s. a dozen bushels, or for 4s. 6d. if only lime coal, and if above Huntsam 3s. 6d., on a forfeiture of one hundred dozen of good iron ore, the one half to His Majesty and the other to the miner that will sue for the same, together with loss of ' freedom ' and utter exclusion from the mine works—a very heavy penalty for such an offence, showing the arbitrary power assumed by the court, at one time conferring free minership upon strangers and foreigners, and at another deposing the free miner merely for an over or even an under charge.[3]

Mr. Nicholls points out that according to this order

the instructions given in 1674 to pull down the king's iron-works in the Forest had been so thoroughly executed that all furnaces were ere this demolished, leaving such only to be supplied with ore as were situated beyond the Forest limits. These furnaces

seem to have taken about six hundred dozen bushels of ore at one time, during the delivery of which no second party was allowed to come in. It is signed by fourteen out of the forty-eight free miners in their own hands, which is so far an improvement ; but if the iron trade was unpromising owing to the course which the government felt constrained to take lest the development should endanger the timber, it was not so with the coal, the getting of which the Crown would obviously regard with favour in the hope that it would relieve the woods from spoliation. Accordingly we shall find that from about this period, on through the next century, coal-works were constantly on the increase, so as eventually to throw the getting of iron ore into the shade. This last order cancelled an agreement passed by the Mine Law Court in 1675, to the effect that a legal defence fund be raised ; but it confirmed the decree of a former court forbidding any young man to set up for himself as a free miner, unless he was upward of twenty-one years of age, and had served, by indenture, an apprenticeship of five years, and had also given a bond of £10 to obey all the orders of the said court.[4]

The next or fifth session of the Mine Law Court was held at Clearwell in 1682. It confirmed for the most part the orders already issued, and further exacted the payment, within six days, of 6d. from every miner thirteen years of age and upwards, and an additional payment of 6d. for every horse used in carrying mineral, ' for raising a present sum of money for urgent occasions,'[5] and required all coal-pits which had been wrought out to be sufficiently secured.[6]

The sixth order of the Court of Mine Law records that it assembled in 1685 at Clearwell, before the deputy-constable of St. Briavel's. Its principal design seems to have been that of confirming the former 6d. rate, and authorizing the same to be raised to 10s. if necessary, toward keeping up a fund for supporting the miners' claims at law,[7] which of late they had been obliged to do in the Court of Exchequer against various interlopers. The order concludes with the following direction, ' that one-half of the jury should be of iron miners, and the other half colliers,' so rapidly had coal-mining advanced, and so important had its condition become. An examination of the original document shows this order to have been signed by one person writing down the names of the forty-eight free miners, since they all exhibit the same handwriting.[8]

The seventh of the orders still extant reports the court of the mine to have been held at Clearwell in 1687, and commences by stating that more money was wanted for legal purposes, and that every miner must pay 2s., with 2s. besides for every mine horse, toward meeting

[1] Galloway, op. cit. i, 209. [2] Ibid. 51.
[3] Nicholls, *Forest of Dean*, 52.
[4] Nicholls, *Forest of Dean*, 52, 53.
[5] *Award of Dean Forest Commrs.* 17.
[6] Nicholls, *Forest of Dean*, 53.
[7] *Award of Dean Forest Commrs.* 17.
[8] Nicholls, *Forest of Dean*, 54.

them. It likewise directed that each coal-pit and dangerous mine-pit, if left unworked for a whole month together, should be fenced with a stone wall or posts and rails, under penalty of 10s.

All previous orders fixing the prices at which the minerals of the forest were alone to be sold were now abolished, not having been found to answer ; and all miners were left at liberty to sell or carry and deliver their ore and coal to whom, where, or how they pleased ; and, whereas previously all colliers were entitled to be first served at the pits, now it was ordained that the inhabitants of the hundred should precede the trade, and that those miners only should keep horses who had land sufficient to feed them. The following provision speaks for itself :—

For the restrayning that pernicious and abominable sinne of perjury too much used in these licentious times, every myner convicted by a jury of 48 miners in the said court shall forever loose and entirely forfeit his freedome as touching the mines, and be utterly expelled out of the same, and all the working tooles and habitt be burned before his face, and he never afterwards to be a witness or to be believed in any matter whatsoever.[1]

A period of about five years from the time that the last was held brings us to the eighth record of the Mine Court in 1692. It was held, as usual, at Clearwell. The court levied a further contribution of 12d. upon every miner, with an additional 1s. on every mine horse, with which to clear off certain charges incurred in a recent suit in the Court of Exchequer at Westminster. It extended the protective distance of 100 yards, within which every pit was guarded from being encroached upon by any other work, to 300 yards. It also provided that no iron ore intended for Ireland should be shipped on the Severn or Wye for a less sum than 6s. 6d. for every dozen bushels. This order was signed by sixteen out of the forty-eight miners with their own hands, the rest making their marks only.[2]

Dr. Parsons, the antiquary, thus describes the industries of the forest at this time :—

It abounds, he says, with springs for the most part of a brownish or amber colour, occasioned by their passage through the veines of oker, of which there is a great plenty, or else through the rusty tincture of the mineralls of the ore. The ground of the Forest is more inclined to wood and cole than corn, yet they have enough of it too. The inhabitants are, some of them, a robustic wild people, that must be civilized by good discipline and government. The ore and cinder wherewith they make their iron (which is the great imployment of the poorer sort of inhabitants) is dug in the most parts of ye Forest, one in the bowells and the other towards the surface of the earth. But whether it be by virtue of the Forrest laws or other custome, the head Gaviler of the Forrest, or others deputed by him, provided they were born in the Hundred of St. Briavel's, may go into any man's grounds whatsoever within the limitation of the Forrest, and dig or delve for ore and cinders without any molestation. There are two sorts of ore ; the best ore is your brush ore, of a blewish colour very ponderous and full of slimy specks like grains of silver ; this affordeth the greatest quantity of iron, but being melted alone produceth a mettal very short and brittle. To remedy this inconvenience they make use of another material which they call cinder, it being nothing but the refuse of the ore after the melting hath been extracted, which being melted with the other in due quantity gives it that excellent temper of toughness for which this iron is preferred before any other that is brought from foreign parts. But it is to be noted that in former times when their works were few and their rents small, they made use of no other bellows but such as were moved by strength of men, by reason whereof their fires were much less intense than in the furnaces they now imploy ; so that having in them only melted downe the principal part of the ore, they rejected the rest as useless and not worth their charge ; this they called their cinder, and is found in an inexhaustible quantity throughout all parts of the country where any blomerys formerly stood, for so they were then called.[3]

The ninth Mine Law Court was held in 1694, and the tenth in 1701. The proceedings of the latter were as follows :—Certain temporary orders, dated 12 March, 1699, and 11 November, 1700, regulating the loading of horses and carts, forbidding any coal to be sent off by the River Wye below Welsh Bicknor, authorizing the raising of money for paying the costs of the miners' debts in law, securing the records of their court, and making the present deputy-constable of St. Briavel's Castle a free miner, were confirmed and made perpetual. Mention is also made for the first time of the 'utmost seventy,' being the greatest number ever comprised in the miners' jury. The order further directs that the records of mine law used at the hearings of the suit in the Exchequer be recorded and put into a chest to be left in the custody of Francis Wyndham, esq., whom the court had made a free miner, and that in paying any of the costs incurred in that cause a legal discharge be taken. Now the ton of twenty-one hundredweight was fixed as a weight of coal to be sold for 5s. to an inhabitant of the hundred, or for 6s. to foreigners ; and every pit was to be provided with scales. Upwards of twenty of the forty-eight miners who formed the jury at this court put their names to the above verdict, the rest being marksmen.[4]

In 1707,[5] and again in 1717,[6] two further sessions were held, the chief object of which seems to have been the raising of additional funds with which to defend the rights of the free miners against interlopers, as well as to enforce the prohibition of mineral lawsuits in

---

[1] Nicholls, *Forest of Dean*, 54.   [2] Ibid. 56.

[3] Nicholls, *Forest of Dean*, 56, 57.
[4] Ibid. 62 ; *Award of Forest of Dean Commrs.* 14.
[5] Nicholls, *Forest of Dean*, 63.   [6] Ibid. 65.

other than the Forest Mine Courts. The latter session we find also constituted the Honourable Matthew Morton, Thomas Gage, John Wyndham, Richard Machen, William James, and Christopher Bond, free miners, ' out of the due and great respect, honour, and esteem borne towards them.' We need not call in question the truthfulness of such protestations ; but, doubtless, had these miners perceived the inconsistency of such admission, they would not have so readily dispensed with the ancient regulations which restricted the fellowship of the mine to those who had worked therein. They were well intended at the time, but long afterwards weakened in a legal point of view the free miners' rights.

Only two years intervened between the holding of the court just mentioned, and the one which followed it at the Speech House. On this occasion certain previous orders were cancelled, and in their stead it was determined that no one living beyond the hundred of St. Briavel's should convey any coal out of the forest unless he belonged to the forest division of the county and carried for his own private use. A penalty of £5 was imposed upon any person under twenty-one years of age carrying ore or coal. All traffic in coal, either up or down the Wye, was to stop at Welsh Bicknor, between which and Monmouth Bridge no coal was to be pitched. At Monmouth fire coal was to be sold at 9s. the dozen bushels, smith's coal at 8s., and lime coal at 5s. 6d. Above Lydbrook on the Wye fire coal was to be sold at 8s. the ton or the dozen barrels, smith's coal at 6s., and lime coal at 3s. One free miner was not to sell any fire coal to another under 5s. per ton of 21 cwt.[1]

Nine years passed before another full Mine Court is recorded. On this occasion (1728) we find no less than nine gentlemen of the neighbourhood admitted to free mining privileges.[2] The distance of 300 yds., which by a former order in 1692 protected every pit from interruption, was now enlarged to 500 yds., and further the giving away of coals was prohibited under fine of £5.[2]

The fifteenth of the series of orders, enacted by that Mine Law Court, occurred in 1737. Owing to the injury which it was considered foreigners had done to the free miners by carrying coal out of the forest for merchandise, it was decided that for the future no such carrying should be allowed, except to certain persons named, under penalty of £5 or property to that amount. More outsiders were admitted to the fellowship, and a rule was made that a foreigner's son, born in the hundred and seeking to become a free miner, was to serve by indenture an apprenticeship of seven years.[3]

The sixteenth order of the same court was in 1741, when the following business was transacted. A £5 penalty was laid upon all miners who should send or carry any coals to Hereford or Monmouth by the Wye, except lime coal at the New Wears at 4s. the dozen bushels. A similar fine was imposed upon any inhabitant of the Forest division of the county who should presume to carry coal otherwise than for his own use ; so also no miner was to work more than two pits at one time, or to carry coal for any person not a free miner ; neither could he sell fire coal or stone coal charks under 7s. a dozen bushels, or 5s. if smith's coal, at Redbrook, which if refused there a ' forbid ' should be declared until the former coal was accepted. This order further enacted that if coal were found in any bargeman's boat and he refuse to say from whom he had it, a general ' forbid ' should be declared that no miner serve him with any more. A free miner was briefly defined to be 'such as have lawfully worked at coal a year and a day.' A foreigner selling coal at Hereford for less than 13s. per ton was to be summoned, or abide the consequence of a general forbid. Should there be at any time more than a sufficiency of coal for the trade on the Wye, the barge owners were to employ the service of the miners or be fined according their wages.[4]

We now arrive at the seventeenth or last order issued at the Mine Law Court. It dates 22 October, 1754, and records the election, as free miners, of no less than twenty-two gentry and notables.[5] As Mr. Nicholls remarks :—

So full a list of persons of influence and position as this order exhibits, lending their names to the free miners' society, indicates the existence of considerable importance in that body ; and yet this was the last court having forty-eight free miners on the jury, whose proceedings have been preserved, the fact being that they failed to agree in their verdicts, and then gentlemen refused to attend, owing, it is said, to the violent disputes and quarrels arising between foreigners possessed of capital, who now began to be admitted to the works, and the free miners. It is also reported that the decisions of the court were seldom observed, no Act of Parliament having passed to render them valid. The former protective distance between one mine and another was increased from 500 to 1,000 yards of any levels. The order concludes with directing that ' the water wheel engine at the Arling Green, near Broadmoor, be taken to be a level to all intents and purposes.' This machine was evidently the first of its kind erected in the Forest, as was also the steam engine which superseded it, each manifesting the improvements going on in the method of working the mines.

According to a paper examined by Mr. Mushet, and referring probably to the year 1720 or 1730, the iron-making district of the Forest of Dean contained ten blast furnaces, six in Gloucester-

---

[1] Nicholls, *Forest of Dean*, 66.   [2] Ibid. 66, 67.
[3] Ibid. 69 ; *Award of Dean Forest Commrs.* 13.   [4] Nicholls, *Forest of Dean*, 70.   [5] Ibid. 71.

shire, three in Herefordshire, and one at Tintern, making their total number just equal to that of the then iron-making district of Sussex.[1] In Mr. Taylor's map of Gloucestershire, published in 1777, iron furnaces, forges, or engines are indicated at Bishopswood, Lydbrook, The New Wear, Upper Redbrook, Parkend, Bradley, and Flaxley. Yet only a small portion of the mineral used at these works was obtained from the Dean Forest mines, if we may judge from the statement made in 1788 before the Parliamentary Commissioners to the effect that

there is no regular iron mine now carried on in the said Forest, but there are about twenty-two poor men who, at times when they have no other work to do, employ themselves in searching for and getting iron mine or ore in the old holes and pits in the said Forest, which have been worked out many years.[2]

From another source we learn that

at Tintern the furnace charge for forge pig iron was generally composed of a mixture of seven-eighths of Lancashire iron ore, and one-eighth part of a lean calcareous sparry iron ore from the Forest of Dean called flux, the average yield of which mixture was fifty per cent. of iron. When in full work Tintern Abbey charcoal furnace made weekly from twenty-eight to thirty tons of charcoal forge pig iron, and consumed forty dozen sacks of charcoal; so that sixteen sacks of charcoal were consumed in making one ton of pigs. This furnace was the first charcoal furnace which, in this country, was blown with air compressed in iron cylinders.[3]

In the same year, 1788, we are informed by the evidence of the gaveller that, according to an account made out in the previous August, there were then within the forest 121 coal-pits (thirty-one of which were not actually in work), which produced 1,816 tons of coal per week, and employed 662 free miners.[4]

Mr. Nicholls tells us that—

The existing remains of the coal-works of this period, combined with the traditions of the colliers, enable us to form an accurate idea of the way in which the workings were carried on. 'Levels,' or slightly ascending passages, driven into the hillsides till they struck the coal seam, appear to have been general. This was no doubt owing to the facility with which they effected the getting of the coal where it tended upwards into the higher lands forming the edge of the Forest Coal Basin, since they required no winding apparatus, and afforded a discharge for the water which drained from the coal beds. The usages observed at the works entitled the proprietors of their respective levels to so much of the corresponding seams of coal as they could drain, extending right and left to the limits awarded by the gaveller. So far this mode of procedure was satisfactory enough, and would no doubt have long continued to go on amicably, had not the principle, highly judicious in itself, that no workings were ever to intersect one another, but always to stop when the mattocks met, been

abused by driving 'narrow heading' up into different workings, whereby the rightful owner of the coal was stopped, and the other party enabled to come in and take it from him. Timber of considerable strength was required throughout the underground excavations to support the roof, hence proving a serious source of spoliation to the woods. Large slabs of it were also needed for the flooring, in order that the small coal-trams might be the more readily pushed forward over it, a space being left beneath for air to circulate, and for the water to run out.

If the vein of coal proposed to be worked did not admit of being reached by a level, then a pit was sunk to it, although rarely to a greater depth than 25 yards, the water being raised by buckets, or by a water-wheel engine, or else by a drain having its outlet in some distant but lower spot, such as is found to have led from the Broad Moor Collieries to Cinderford, a mile and upwards in length. The shaft of the pit was made of a square form, in order that its otherwise insecure sides might be the better supported by suitable woodwork, which being constructed in successive stages was occasionally used as a ladder, the chief difficulty being found in keeping the workings free from water, which in wet seasons not infrequently gained the mastery and drowned the men out.[5]

Reverting to the iron industry of Dean, we find in 1795 the beginning of the resumption of the manufacture of iron in the forest by means of pit-coal cokes at Cinderford. 'The conductors of the work succeeded,' according to Mr. Bishop,

in making pig iron of good quality; but from the rude and insufficient character of their arrangements, they failed commercially as a speculation, the quantity produced not reaching twenty tons per week. The cokes were brought from Broadmoor in boats, by a small canal, the embankment of which may be seen at the present day. The ore was carried down to the furnaces on mules' backs from Edge Hill and other mines. The rising tide of iron manufacture in Wales and Staffordshire could not fail to swamp such ineffectual arrangements, and as a natural consequence Cinderford sank.[6]

At Flaxley, during the eighteenth century, iron was still made in the old way with charcoal chiefly from Lancashire ore, water-power being used for the bellows and hammers. When the furnace was at work about twenty tons a week were reduced to pig iron; in this state it was carried to the forges where about eight tons a week were hammered out into bars and plough-shares ready for the smith.[7]

This practically ended the history of the Dean miners until the opening years of the nineteenth century. The social forces at work may be briefly summarized. The Dean miners, alone of all the mining population of England, had adopted a constitution which, in its exclusiveness and rigid protectionist features, can be compared only with those of the craft gilds of the sixteenth

---

[1] See Nicholls, *Forest of Dean*, 223.
[2] Ibid. 223–4. [3] Ibid. 224. [4] Ibid. 237.

[5] Ibid. 239–40.
[6] Ibid. 224–5.
[7] From a description by the Rev. T. Rudge in 1802.

century. The maintenance of these laws against outsiders, however, depended in the last resort, as was the case with the laws of other mining communities, upon the Crown itself; and, as time went on, this sanction became increasingly more difficult to obtain, the richness of the mineral deposits in the forest, as well as the importance of its timber for naval purposes, making it an object of cupidity on the part of even the Crown. In the seventeenth century we find the beginnings of an organized attack upon the forest privileges, which led at the outset to the miners fatally compromising their position by admitting that they held their place upon royal sufferance rather than by legal right. Thereafter, the history of the forest people is that of a continual and increasingly hopeless struggle against interlopers; the miners obstinately refusing to liberalize their laws, yet, on the other hand, often admitting outsiders to the privileges of their calling.

The year 1831 is chiefly remarkable for the riotous destruction committed on the fences and banks of the enclosures in the forest by the free miners, who by this time had become thoroughly exasperated at the usurpation of their old rights by 'foreigners' in whose hands, by this time, were the principal coal-works of the forest by purchase or lease from free miners.[1] Military force quelled these risings, but the feeling in the district was so strong that an Act was passed in the same year[2] authorizing the appointment of commissioners to investigate the complaints of the miners. The commissioners were instructed to ascertain the boundaries of the forest and the encroachments thereon; to inquire into the rights and privileges claimed by the free miners of the hundred of St. Briavel's; the constitution, powers, jurisdiction, and practice of the court held there, as well as respecting a court called the Mine Law Court; and to report on the expediency of parochializing the forest.

Under this Act a commission was appointed which held several sessions,[3] covering a period of as many years, during which the claims both of the free miners[4] and of outside parties having forest interests received an impartial hearing. The fourth report gives a summary of the rights and privileges claimed by the free miners derived chiefly from evidence taken in 1832. The commissioners however express the opinion that the persons by whom the mines were worked at an early period could not have been in the first instance free tenants of the crown. It is more likely that they were in a state of servitude,[5] and subject to the performance of labour required of them. The name 'free miners' by which they were, and

had been for centuries known, referred probably to some right or privilege distinct from their original condition, and it was not unreasonable to suppose that certain persons at some distant period, either by having worked for a year and a day, or by reason of some circumstance connected with the origin of the privilege were considered as emancipated, and thereupon became entitled, or were allowed to work the mines upon their own adventure, concurrently with, or subject to the right of the crown to a certain portion of the product.[6]

The report goes on to state that the franchise of the mine was unquestionably perpetuated by birth from a free father in the hundred of St. Briavel's, and afterwards working a year and a day in one of the mines and abiding within the hundred. The commissioners were, however, doubtful as to the necessity of birth from a free miner, inasmuch as the son of a 'foreigner' could obtain his freedom after an apprenticeship of seven years with a free miner.

Entering, in the next place, into a consideration of the actual claims of the free miners, the commissioners recognized the fact that while before the discontinuance in 1777 of the Mine Law Court the free miners rarely leased, mortgaged, or sold their works to outsiders, this practice had since then become so frequent that the greater part of the mining properties were in the hands of foreigners,[7] who, in absence of injunctions or 'forbids' from any mine court, worked them by the employment of hired labour.[8] They declared their opinion as to the settlement of these claims, suggesting at once the question 'whether they could now be maintained with advantage to the miners themselves or to the community,' connected, as they were, with a most defective system of working, productive of incessant disputes and expensive litigation, and occasioning never-ending jealousy.[9] 'Taking all the circumstances of the case into consideration,' they thus conclude, ' we are of the opinion that the monopoly and customary workings are practically at an end, and that, if individual claims were bought up, the whole coalfield might then be let by the crown as between landlord and tenant, defining the limits and regulating the workings.'

In the fifth and last report, the commissioners, among other things, notice the stone quarries which persons born within the hundred of St. Briavel's claimed the right of opening in the waste lands of the forest on payment of a fee of 3s. to the gaveller and a further yearly rent of 3s. 4d., according to the custom of at least the last century, a period too long to justify the withdrawal of any existing 'gale,' or mine share, unless with compensation. In view of this fact, in order to render the conditions for the working

[1] Nicholls, *Forest of Dean*, 110–12.
[2] 1 & 2 Will. IV, cap. 12.
[3] Cf. Nicholls, *Forest of Dean*, 113 et seq.
[4] Ibid. 120.   [5] Ibid. 4.

[6] *Fourth Rep. Dean Forest Commrs.* 4.
[7] Ibid. 8.   [8] Ibid. 9.   [9] Ibid. 10.

of the stone quarries more satisfactory, the commissioners could only advise the Crown to re-issue gales on liberal leases to applicants born within the hundred, a time-limit being assigned for putting in claims.

In 1838, the royal assent was given to 'an Act for regulating the opening and working of mines and quarries in the Forest of Dean and hundred of St. Briavel's by the agency of a board of commissioners.' Some idea may be formed of the necessity for such a mining commission, and of the difficulties which it had to overcome, from the following particulars, as Mr. Sopwith stated them in a paper read before the British Association at Newcastle in 1838 :—

Great distrust of any interference existed, and some of the mine-owners refused to allow of underground surveys being made. Numerous and conflicting parties were then working mines under customs which were totally inapplicable to the present state of mining ; destructive at once to the interests of the free miners of the forest, ruinous, as sad experience had shown, to the enterprizing capitalist ; and subversive to the rights of the crown. So great was the perplexity and so numerous and conflicting were the claims of contending parties, that the law advisers of the Board of Woods deemed it almost impossible to arrive at any satisfactory adjustment of them within the period of three years as named in the Dean Forest Mining Act. The ruinous and unsatisfactory state of the mines must appear obvious on a slight consideration. As no plans existed, it was impossible to tell to what extent or in what direction the underground works were being carried. The crossing of mattocks, that is to say, the actual meeting of workmen underground, was often the abrupt signal for contention ; the driving of narrow headings was a means by which one coal-owner might gain possession of coal which of right belonged to another ; and a pit, though sunk at a cost of several thousand pounds, had no secured possession of coal beyond 12 yards around it, that is, a tract of coal 24 yards in diameter. At 40 or 50 yards from such a work another adventurer might commence a pit, and have an equal right, if right it could be called, to the coal. If a long and expensive adit was driven, another one might be commenced only a few yards deeper ; and from such a state of things it is quite clear that great uncertainty and frequent losses inevitably ensued.[1]

The important Act[2] of 1838 provides that all male persons born and abiding within the hundred of St. Briavel's, being upwards of twenty-one years of age, and having worked a year and a day in a coal or iron-mine or stone quarry within the said hundred, should alone have the right to hold or dispose of such works, a register of all such persons being kept as 'free miners.' It suppressed all claims to pit timber with all 'customs,' and assigned to the commissioners under the Act the duty of fixing rents and royalties for twenty-one years, and to the

gaveller power to limit and regulate, as well as to enter and survey all works which might be re-awarded or galed. No engines were to be erected nearer than sixty yards to any enclosure, within which only air-shafts might be opened, and all unnecessary buildings were to be removed.

The duties of the Mining Commissioners were carried out with great ability and discretion, and in 1841 no less than 104 collieries and 20 iron-mines were defined and awarded, while certain regulations were drawn up for their working.

The later history of the iron-mines in the forest cannot be dealt with in any detail here. As has already been remarked, the greater proportion of the ore smelted at Tintern, Flaxley, and other places in the late eighteenth century had been brought from outside the forest. Much capital was lost in the first quarter of the nineteenth century in efforts to establish a stable iron-making trade in the forest, but after Mr. Mushet had given up the attempt as hopeless, Messrs. Teague, Montague, and James were more successful between 1825 and 1827. At Parkend especially a stable business was built up, and the Forest of Dean Iron Company, in the early 'sixties' of the last century, were producing upwards of 300 tons of pig iron per week, consuming weekly 350 tons of coke as well as 600 tons of iron ore obtained from the mines at Oakwood and China Eugene close by, and from the Perseverance and Findall Mine on the east side of the forest. At the same time there existed tin-plate works at Parkend, drawing two-thirds of the iron required from the local mines. They were carried on by Messrs. W. Allaway and Sons, who had similar works on a greater scale at Lydney.[3] Iron ore from Dean was also used to some extent at Soudley and Lydbrook, while the Vale Iron Works, near Cinderford, were at the same time supplied principally from the Shake-Mantle, Buckshraft, and St. Annal's mines. Indeed, in 1865, the yield of ore from the Buckshraft was no less than 46,127 tons.

The famous Westbury-Brook iron mine[4] on the eastern side of the forest was opened about 1837, immediately below the extensive 'old men's workings,' where many ancient mining implements were found. In 1864 and 1865 the average yearly output of iron ore from this mine was nearly 20,000 tons. The Old Sling Iron Mine

---

[1] Nicholls, *Forest of Dean*, 126–7.
[2] Stat. 1 & 2 Vict. cap. 43.

[3] In comparison it may be noted that for the year 1904 not a single blast-furnace for the making of pig-iron was returned for Gloucestershire ; *Coal and Iron Diary* (1906), 150. Even in 1878 there were 9 iron furnaces in the Forest, of which 2 were in blast, producing upwards of 40,000 tons of pig-iron. Hull, *Coalfields of Gt. Britain* (5th ed. 1905), 82, 83.
[4] A section of this mine, the deepest iron-mine in the Forest, will be found illustrated in Kendall, *Iron Ores of Gt. Britain*, 131.

on the west of the forest about 1860–6 yielded on an average 1,000 tons of haematite per month. This mine was opened in 1838 on the Clearwell Mean below ancient workings where picks and wooden shovels tipped with iron were discovered. Other important mines at this time were the Easter and the Dean's Meend.

The nineteenth century has seen considerable fluctuations in the output of the iron-mines of the forest. In 1828 only 9,800 tons of ore were produced, but in 1839 this had risen to 72,800 tons, and in 1871 there was a high water mark of 170,611. Since then we perceive a sorry falling off indeed, and in the present year (1906) the returns for Gloucestershire show only eleven iron mines[1] at work employing ninety-one persons, while the output for 1905 is estimated at 7,245 tons of iron ore, 2,662 tons of ochre, and a small quantity of red oxide of iron and umber. The various forms of iron ore are known locally as the 'brush,' the 'grey burler,' the 'brown burler,' the 'smith ore,' and the low grade 'grey ore,' and for the distinctions between them the reader must be referred to the technical handbooks.[2]

While the iron output of the forest has seriously diminished since the middle of the last century, the production of coal has increased nearly threefold. In 1856 the number of coal-works in the forest was estimated at 221, and the output 460,432 tons, of which the two largest and most highly organized, the Parkend Colliery and the Lightmoor Colliery, furnished 86,973 and 86,508 tons respectively. In 1898 the amount of coal raised in the Forest of Dean reached 1,176,712 tons, while the output for the whole of Gloucestershire in 1905 was 1,388,476 tons, a figure which probably indicates some decrease in the Forest of Dean on the figures of 1898, since at least one quarter of this must be deducted for the collieries in the Bristol and Kingswood coalfield across the Severn.

No attempt can be made here[3] to deal exhaustively with the Forest of Dean Coalfield from the technical standpoint, but a few remarks may be permitted on features of interest. Of the three series of seams the Woorgreens or uppermost are in the centre of the field, covering about 1,500 acres. Two seams, the Upper Woorgreens averaging 1 ft. 2 in. and the Lower Woorgreens 1 ft. 8 in. in thickness, have been worked, but only slightly. Between them and the Dogdelf lie two coal bands 6 in. thick. The Dogdelf, which may be regarded as the first of

the Middle Series, has only been mined to a small extent; its average thickness is 1 ft. 3 in. The Smith Coal, or Twenty-Inch seam, which lies from 5 to 12 yds. beneath the Dogdelf, is generally regarded as very unreliable, and probably a greater area of it has been left untouched than in any other of the upper seams, although it has been worked to some extent all over the forest. The Little Delf seam lies from half a foot to as much as 30 ft. below the last-mentioned seam, the average being about 18 ft. The specific gravity of its coal is said to be the highest of any seam in this field. The next seam, the Lowrey or Parkend High Delf, lies fairly regularly at a distance of from 15 to 18 yds. below the Smith Coal, with a general average thickness of from 1 ft. 4 in. to 2 ft. 6 in., the 'thick Lowrey' however showing an average section of 3 ft. 7 in. The coal procured here is of excellent quality, suited both for household use and the manufacture of gas. The next workable seam—the Starkey, like the Smith Coal—is of variable section, usually from about 1 ft. 5 in. to 2 ft. 6 in. The coal in the Rockey Delf, which lies about 15 yds. below the Starkey, has as fine an appearance as any in the forest. But to quote Mr. Joynes' account: 'as the name implies it is very hard itself and fairly hard to get.' Its average section may be taken as nearly 2 ft. Twenty-five yards below the Rockey is the Churchway High Delf, a good seam nearly worked out in the northern and north-eastern half of the coalfield; to this seam nearly all the pits working the Middle Series are sunk. In section it varies from 1 ft. 6 in. to 4 ft. In the northern part the Breadless, Upper Churchway, and Lower Churchway unite to form a fine working section, to the south they are separated by bands of 'dirt.' The No Coal seam, the last of the Middle Series, is from 15 to 19 yds. below the Churchway High Delf, but the coal is faulty and generally split up by bands of dirt. In consequence it has been mined little or not at all.

The next seam, the Brazilly, should more correctly have been classed in the Middle Series, as it is only 17 yds. beneath the No Coal, but between 80 and 90 yds. above the Yorkley. It is very variable in section. The Yorkley or Nag's Head, though to the north it runs thin, furnishes towards the south a hard house coal; in thickness it averages over 2 ft. The Whittington seam, 50 yds. and sometimes considerably more beneath the Yorkley, has been worked near the outcrop to the south and south-west of the coalfield; its average thickness may be accepted as about 1 ft. 9 in. The strata intervening between the Whittington and the famous Coleford High Delf are mainly grey sandstone. A fair average section of this seam, the finest in the district, may be reckoned at from 4 to 6 ft., though occasionally a thickness of 14 ft. has been found. The coal here is an excellent steam coal, but as a house coal is not so good as that

---

[1] But owing to the high price of iron now ruling others may soon be reopened.

[2] A good account is given in Kendall, op. cit. 134.

[3] For further details see an exhaustive paper by J. J. Joynes, 'Description of Seams, &c.,' in *Journ. Brit. Soc. Mining Students*, xi, 136 et seq. Also Hughes, *Textbook of Coal Mining*; Hull, *Coal Fields of Gt. Britain*, etc. We are also indebted to valuable notes furnished by Mr. W. R. Champness and other courteous informants.

found in the thin seams. Although worked to a great extent near the outcrop the deep portion of the Coleford High Delf awaits development on a large scale, and for this adequate capital is necessary. In this seam exists the peculiar disturbance known locally as 'the Horse,' which is not in a strict sense a geological fault, as there is no dislocation of the adjoining strata. According to Sir Henry De La Beche it resembles 'a channel cut amongst a mass of vegetable matter in a soft condition. It ranges south, 31 degrees east for a length of 2 miles and a breadth of from 170 to 340 yds., whilst a number of minor channels communicating with the main channel are called *lows*'. Mr. Buddle has suggested that 'the Horse' represents the channel of a river which formed the outlet of a lake where the vegetation producing the Coleford High Delf seam of coal was originally accumulated. The 'Horse' itself is formed of sandstone. About 43 yds. below the Coleford High Delf, and 504 yds. below the surface, lies the Upper Trenchard which has been worked to a slight extent on the western side and also near the southern outcrop, furnishing a good gas and steam coal. Its average thickness is said to be about 4 ft. The Lower Trenchard is separated from the Upper Trenchard by some 22 yds. of shale and sandstone, and is usually very thin. Beneath it lies a fire-clay 20 ft. thick, which has been worked along the western outcrop. This is the last seam of coal, and is succeeded by the Millstone Grit. The present resources of this coalfield are estimated in round figures at 250,000,000 tons.

Among the collieries of the Forest of Dean Coalfield may be mentioned the Addishill, Bridewell, Crown, Crump Meadow and Duck, Darkhill, East Slade, Forest Red Ash, Foxes Bridge, Gentlemen Colliers, Hopewell, Hulks, Lightmoor and Speech House Main, Little Brockhollands, Lydbrook Deep Level, New Fancy and Parkend Royal, New Mount Pleasant, Norchard, Princess Royal, Trafalgar, Wallsend, and Woorgreens. Of these the Lightmoor, Parkend, Trafalgar, Crump Meadow, and Foxes Bridge are the chief collieries now working the Middle Series [1] of seams at varying depths.[2] The Lightmoor Colliery, which is owned by Messrs. Henry Crawshay and Co. Ltd., and situate at Cinderford, is by far the largest of these, having an output of between 800 and 900 tons per day. Its depth is 300 yds. The Parkend and Fancy Collieries, owned by the Parkend Deep Navigation Collieries Ltd., and situate near Parkend, have an output of about 500 tons per day. The Fancy Colliery is 240 yards in depth. The Trafalgar Colliery, owned by the Trafalgar Colliery Co. Ltd., with a depth of 200 yds., is

situate near Drybrook, and has a daily output of about 500 tons. The Crump Meadow Colliery, 200 yds. in depth, is owned by the Lydney and Crump Meadow Colliery Co. Ltd., and is situate at Cinderford. Its output with that of the Duck Colliery is estimated at about 500 tons per day. The Foxes Bridge Colliery, which is the property of the Foxes Bridge Colliery Co. Ltd., is 300 ft. deep and situate at Cinderford. It also has a daily output of about 500 tons. These collieries working the thinner seams produce first-rate house coal.

Among the principal collieries working the lower series The Flour Mill Colliery near Bream, and the Park Gutter near Whitecroft, both owned by the Princess Royal Colliery Co. Ltd., have an output of 600 tons per day. The former works the Coleford High Delf Seam, and the latter the Yorkley. The Flour Mill Colliery is sunk to the depth of about 130 yds. The Old Norchard Colliery, owned by the Park Iron Ore Co., has an output of about 350 tons per day, produced from the Coleford High Delf Seam and the Trenchard Seam. It may be noted that the coal worked by the Park Iron Ore Co. Ltd. is won by means of a level driven from the surface to strike the seam. Another important colliery, the Lydbrook, owned by Messrs. Richard Thomas and Co. Ltd., and situate at Lydbrook, has an average output of about 350 tons per day, produced from the Coleford High Delf Seam. This colliery is said to be about 140 yds. in depth. Though fair house coal is got from the Yorkley Seam, the principal output of the collieries working the lower seams is in steam and gas coal.

'Longwall' working is adopted in the thin seams, and even in certain places in the Coleford High Delf, though here the 'pillar and stall' system has sometimes been preferred. Owing to the thinness of the seams it is necessary to be sparing in the driving of roads, and where the gradients of the seams are steep, hod-roads—or in rare cases inclines or jinney-roads—are 'driven to the rise at right angles to a main road, driven along the strike of the seam.'[3] The haulage system is sometimes of a primitive character and in the steep measures coal is brought down to the loading stage in hods mounted on two slides, a form of sledge drawn by boys.

The freedom of the pits from fire-damp, at least under present conditions, and the absence of faults of any great size in the formations, are attractive features in the coalfield of the Forest of Dean. But the varying thickness of seams, and the increasing quantity of water met with, present serious disadvantages. The latter circumstance is partly due to the fact that in the past the coal has been largely worked from the surface downwards along the outcrops of the seams, owing to the symmetrical regularity of

[1] Or Upper if only two series are recognized.
[2] The seams worked in all cases are the Churchway High Delf, Rockey, Starkey, Lowrey and Twenty Inch.

[3] Joynes, op. cit. 152 et seq.

the basin, with the result that water has accumulated in the hollows which have been left. Consequently extensive pumping installations are required in the deeper mines to deal with the water which pours in from the old shallow workings. In this connexion it may be mentioned to the credit of the Forest of Dean coalfield that the first application of electricity to pumping operations[1] in mines, at least in England, was made at the Trafalgar Colliery, where the new plant was installed by Mr. F. Brain, and commenced working as far back as December, 1882. Such success attended this innovation, that three more plants were erected in May, 1887, which still do a large part of the underground pumping work ; while in a still later installation the pump, at a maximum speed of 25 strokes, lifts 120 gallons per minute 300 ft. high.

The Gales of the Deep Series, amalgamated under recent legislation, can only be profitably worked by a syndicate of capitalists, but His Majesty's Inspector in his last *Report*[2] expressed the opinion that ' unless the matter is started under favourable auspices of management and capital (in cash, and not in shares), it would be likely to prove detrimental rather than advantageous,' and that in fact, ' it would be better for the responsible authorities to disallow any transfer of the Gales to fresh owners unless they were guaranteed efficient management and ample available capital to provide for the difficulties and eventualities to be expected.'[3]

For the sake of completeness, mention may be made here of what has been called the Newent coal-basin to the north of the present limits of the Forest, where the Coal Measures rest directly on the Old Red Sandstone. This tract lies about two miles west of Newent, and extends from May Hill northward towards the Malverns. Coal was formerly worked at Boulsdon to the south-west of Newent, where a seam from four to five feet thick was found at a depth of 123 ft., and also at Oxenhall on an estate then belonging to R. F. Onslow, esq., where a seam is said to have been discovered over 8 ft. in thickness. The easily accessible coal in this district, however, seems now for the most part to be exhausted. The iron furnace at Oxenhall, which Rudder[4] mentions as producing 20 tons of metal weekly in 1730, was perhaps supported with ore from outside the county, mixed with ' cinders ' from the Forest of Dean.

As in the case of the Forest of Dean, so on the eastern bank of the Severn, iron and coal have formed the staple product of the mines of the district which lies between Bristol and Tortworth. This area, if regarded apart from the great Somersetshire coalfield, of which it is a parcel, may be described as a pear-shaped basin,[5] bounded on the western, northern, and eastern sides by the Millstone Grit and the Carboniferous Limestone. The Coal Measures have been divided into an Upper Division (1,100 ft.) of sandstones, red clays, and shales, with six seams of coal at Parkfield and Coal Pit Heath, the Pennant Grit (2,000 ft.) with occasional seams of coal at Iron Acton, Winterbourne, Mangotsfield, and Kingswood, and the Lower Division (2,700 ft.) of sandstones and shales, with seams of coal varying from some thirty in the south to eight in the north, ironstones and fireclays at Kingswood, Bitton, Bristol, Yate, and Cromhall. To the south the faulted anticline[6] ranging east and west, which crosses the Frome two miles north of Bristol, is an important feature, as well as the overthrust fault first pointed out by Mr. Handel Cossham. There is considerable evidence of a third coalfield connecting that of the Forest of Dean with the Bristol area, and in a geological sense the entire mineral district of Gloucestershire may be regarded as a whole, since Coal Measures revealed by the railway cuttings at Almondsbury have also been proved in the Severn Tunnel and opened up beneath the adjacent alluvial low lands. But their working at a commercial profit seems at present unlikely.

Iron was probably worked to the east of the Severn at a much earlier period than coal, and it has even been suggested that the brown haematite of the Pennant Grit was mined near Iron Acton, Frampton Cotterell, and Rangeworthy during the period of Roman occupation.[7] The render of ninety blooms (*massas*) of iron mentioned in the Domesday[8] notice of Pucklechurch[9] suggests a considerable mining industry at that time within the manor, and there is some reason for supposing that it was from this source that the monks of Glastonbury obtained the ore for the forges which they had at work even before the Conquest. This documentary evidence is borne out by the traces of old workings which have been found within the hundred of Pucklechurch as at Cold Ashton and elsewhere,[10] while the heaps of ' cinders ' discovered at Iron Acton point to the early existence of iron forges in the district. It is impossible to state exactly when iron ceased

[1] Hughes' *Textbook of Coal Mining* (5th ed.), 414 et seq.) ; *Journ. Brit. Soc. Mining Students*, xi, 48.

[2] For 1905, published 1906.

[3] We are indebted to Sir Charles Dilke, bart. for information that two shafts are now being sunk to the Deep.

[4] Op. cit. 589.

[5] For a detailed account of the Geology, see *V.C.H. Glouc.* i ; Hull, *Coalfields of Gt. Britain* (5th ed.) ; and *Journ. Brit. Soc. of Mining Students*, xii, 161.

[6] As Mr. Hull has pointed out, op. cit. 69, ' The occurrence of the Pennant to the north of the fault has greatly retarded the development of the lower seams, which have been largely worked on the southern side of the anticlinal.'

[7] *Proc. Cotteswold Club*, iv, 28.

[8] *Dom. Bk.* 165a. [9] Which included Wick.

[10] Rudder, op. cit. 239.

to be raised about Pucklechurch, but it is possible that the deposits within easy reach had been worked out by the thirteenth century. It is at least fairly certain that the iron forges of Berkeley were towards the close of that century, if not before, supplied from the Forest of Dean. Iron ore has also been found elsewhere to the east of the Severn, as in the Marlstone of the Middle Lias at Upton Cheyney, North Nibley, and Stinchcombe, but does not repay the cost of working in the present conditions of trade. In the Bristol district no ironstone was returned as having been raised during 1905, according to the reports of His Majesty's Inspectors, under the Coal Mines Regulation Acts and the Metalliferous Mines Acts.

It is difficult to say exactly when coal was first worked to the east of the Severn, but probably at a later period than iron, as the early forges were fed with charcoal fuel, and coal when first dug was not welcomed by the wealthy for domestic use. From an entry on the patent roll,[1] 4 Edw. I, it is clear that coal had been dug in Kingswood in the reign of his predecessor, and probably even before that, as the constable of Bristol Castle is ordered to permit Petronilla de Vivonia, wife of David Le Blund, to dig sea-coal in her wood within the king's chase of Kingswood, inasmuch as it is proved by inquisition that she and her ancestors from time out of mind were wont to dig it in the said wood till Robert Waleraund, then constable, wilfully hindered her. By the year 1284, and perhaps much earlier, an entry of money received from sea-coal diggings within the limits of the forest of Bristol or Kingswood had become a regular item in the constable's accounts. This in the compotus[2] for the year 12–13 Edw. I amounted to 29s. 9d. In a similar account[3] for the years 24–28 Edw. I we are actually told the names of these early colliers—Richard Le Reve, Robert At Pyle, William Long, William Copep (junior), Robert Cory, John Chanflor, Alan North, Thomas Serle, David de Mogelane, and William Popok. During the last of the years accounted for a sum of 24s. was received from this source. It is probable, but not perhaps quite certain, that these moneys represented the sums paid for licences to dig, or the value of rent paid in kind. In a similar account[4] more than a hundred years later there is an entry of 26s. 8d. from the 'diggings *carbonum terrestrium* sold in this year.' If sea-coal is meant, the variant is very curious.[5]

By the early years of the seventeenth century the crown rights at Kingswood had in practice,

partly through careless leasing and partly through encroachment, shrunk within very narrow limits. Norden declared[6] in 1615 that the 'coale mines and all other profittes altogether are carryed from his Majestie by unknowne righte.' The production of coal had increased considerably, and although witnesses would confess to £200 worth only being taken, it was probably more than twice as much. A curious complaint made by Norden is worth notice, that the 'coale mines also devoure the principall hollies in all partes of the forest for the supportation of their pitts.' One Player was at this time the 'generall fermer of the coales,' no doubt under patent from the Crown. His monopoly[7] had been taken very ill by the citizens of Bristol, who had petitioned the Privy Council. They had been accustomed to buy coal at 3½d. a bushel, but Player would only allow a few pits to be worked, and thus by an artificial scarcity enhanced prices. Furthermore— for the most modern trust methods are no novelty beneath the sun—he had reduced the capacity of his sacks from 2 bushels to 1 bushel 3 pecks.[8]

In spite of the uncertainty of the crown rights still remaining in Kingswood, various leases were in the seventeenth century granted in reference to minerals, and the grantees often found themselves in consequent litigation with landowners and occupiers who alleged prescriptive rights. It may also be mentioned that under the Commonwealth (1657) iron-smelting with pit coal was tried near Bristol, but proved a failure, though Captain John Copley, the patentee, had the help of Dud Dudley.[9] By 1679 Kingswood had become such a typical colliery district that the coal-pits were recommended to visitors to the neighbourhood as a sight worth viewing,[10] and half a century afterwards a vivid picture of the condition of the miners will be found in the journals of Whitefield. Rudder,[11] writing of St. George's, Bristol, in 1779, declares that some of the coalpits were of prodigious depth, and particularly singles out the duke of Beaufort's mine at Two Mile Hill as being 107 fathoms deep. Already 'fire-engines' at this and other mines were in use for pumping out water, and local conditions had probably forced on a more extended use of machinery than at the same period in the Forest of Dean. At Westerleigh, also, and Abson and Wick, coal was being worked to a considerable extent at this time.

We are unable to trace in detail the later history of the Bristol coalfield, including under this name the whole mineral district between

---

[1] M. 4.　[2] Mins. Accts. bdle. 851, No. 1 (P.R.O.).
[3] Ibid. bdle. 851, No. 6.
[4] Mins. Accts. bdle. 840, No. 9 (13 Hen. IV– 1 Hen. V).
[5] Cf. however the 'carbonem terreum' of a Swansea charter of 1305 which apparently refers to mineral coal. Francis, *Charters Granted to Swansea,* 7.

[6] S.P. Dom. Jas. I, 1615, lxxxiv, 46.
[7] Harl. MS. 368, fol. 11.
[8] Cf. as to this last grievance an order (Egerton MSS. 2044, fol. 12), that in Bristol coal must either be sold in exact 1 or 2 bushel sacks or else 'by heape,' according to the statute bushel.
[9] Dud Dudley, *Mettallum Martis* (ed. 1665), 25.
[10] King, *Life of Locke* (ed. 1830), i, 250.
[11] Op. cit. 459.

Tortworth and the Avon, the coalpits at Yate, as well as the more extensive collieries of Kingswood and Pucklechurch. The seams worked vary much in thickness throughout the coalfield. The 'longwall' system of working is generally adopted now in the Bristol district and at Parkfield, but the 'pillar and stall' at the Yate and Coalpit Heath Collieries as well as at the Oldland Colliery near Golden Valley. Some of the seams in the Bristol district are fiery, but those worked at Parkfield appear fairly free from gas, though at Yate gas is said to be got in the Hard Seam.

At one of the deeper mines the temperature is said to vary from 65° F. at the surface to about 79° F. at a depth of 790 yds., the lowest point at which the coal is worked being about 820 yds. At present there are scarcely any artificial means of cooling the air except by the exhaust from compressed air engines, but it is not considered likely that the increase of temperature will make it impossible to work coal in the deeper levels of these mines, though the expense must of necessity become greater, and an advance will be made in the adoption of mechanical traction. No coal-cutting machinery is at present in use, and it is estimated that little difference exists in the amount of coal extracted per man between the deep mines and those more shallow.[1]

In the slightest mention of the Bristol mining district during the later nineteenth century, it is necessary to recall the name of Mr. Handel Cossham, who, from a clerk at Yate Colliery, rose to be the greatest colliery owner in the south-west of England. About 1875 he bought the freehold of the minerals of St. George's district and the lordship of the manor of Kingswood, as well as the duke of Beaufort's mining property at Stapleton.[2] In 1879 his firm was formed into a limited company, the Wethered family selling out the interest they had held, while Mr. Cossham acquired the predominant interest under the new arrangement. Till his death in 1889 he was the controlling power in the management of the Kingswood and Parkfield Collieries, and the property of the company comprised in 1891 about 3,000 acres of mineral freehold, with a daily output from the collieries of from 700 to 1,000 tons of steam and house coal, while employment was found above and below ground for an average of 1,500 persons.

Beside the Bedminster, Easton, Kingswood and Parkfield Collieries Co. other important firms

interested in the Bristol Coalfield are the Bristol United Collieries, A. Brand & Co., the Coal Pit Heath Co., Leonard Boult & Co. and the Oldland Colliery Co. The average yearly output from this field was from 1870–80, 524,156 tons, from 1880–90, 483,881 tons, from 1890–1900, 395,546 tons, and from 1900–3, 430,697 tons. In 1903, 411,077 tons were raised, and the district produces house coal, gas coal, bituminous, coking, and manufacturing coal as well as steam coal.

There can be little doubt that lead was worked at an early period within the borders of the present county of Gloucester, and probably by the Romans. Two dated pigs of lead[3] have been found in the bed of the Frome near Traitor's Bridge, and there is reason for supposing that they may have come from Penpark Hole, some 3½ miles to the north, which in the boundaries described in a Saxon charter of 882, is mentioned as the 'leadgedelf' or lead-diggings.[4] This extensive mine was further identified by two mining 'captains,' Sturming in 1669 and Collins in 1682, as having been worked for lead. Traces of old workings also exist, or existed, on Durdham Downs and at Clifton, especially at the junction of the Limestone and Lias, and as far north as Almondsbury. The mining of this metal in any quantity seems, however, to have ceased in Gloucestershire by the period of the Angevins, if not before, as in the reign of Henry II lead was more easily procured from Shropshire.[5]

Although lead in the form of argentiferous galena occurs rather widely, though in uncertain quantities, in the Bristol district, it has been worked to a very small extent to commercial advantage in modern times. About 1712 some attempt[6] was made to raise lead, calamine (the ore of zinc), and manganese at Durdham Downs, and an account or prospectus was issued which anticipated some of the characteristic features of the familiar financial literature of our own day, but the enterprise does not seem to have been of very long continuance. For many years zinc[7] was turned out in fair quantities by Mr. Champion and his successor from works established at Bristol about 1743, but the ore he employed came from beyond the Gloucestershire border, and probably from Somerset. In the late eighteenth century lead was occasionally worked, as by Mr. Freeman at Almondsbury in 1775, but apparently it was not found in payable quantities,[8] and the same remark applies to the workings at Abson and Wick, mentioned by Rudder.[9]

[1] For a technical account of the Somersetshire coalfield, which includes southern Gloucestershire, see a paper by Mr. G. E. J. McMurtrie, in *Journ. of the Brit. Soc. of Mining Students*, xii, 161 et seq. (1890); and Hull, *Coalfields of Gt. Britain* (5th ed.), 68 et seq. We are also under obligation for local information kindly furnished.

[2] Braine, *Hist. of Kingswood Forest*, 264.

[3] *Brist. and Glouc. Arch. Soc. Trans.* iv, 320 et seq.

[4] Birch, *Cart. Sax.* ii, 174 (No. 550); *Antiq. Mag.* iii, 279.

[5] Pipe Roll, 29 Hen. II, Glouc.

[6] R. Hunt, *Brit. Mining*, 831 et seq.

[7] Watson, *Chemical Essays* (ed. 1786), iv, 37, 38.

[8] *Brist. and Glouc. Arch. Soc. Trans.* iv, 324 et seq.

[9] *Gloucestershire*, 211.

Parsons, in his MSS. collections,[1] mentions argentiferous tin-ore at Siston, but the vein was probably quite inconsiderable, and the same may be said of the copper[2] lying in small perpendicular fissures, discovered in the eighteenth century by one Pope on a high hill towards the Severn, about half a mile from Henbury. The famous copper works at Bristol were certainly supplied with ore from Cornwall, and possibly from other places outside the county.

The last of the mineral products of the county which demands mention here is celestite, or strontium sulphate. The neighbourhood[3] of Bristol, even at the beginning of the last century, was known as one of the few localities in England where it was found, and about a generation ago large quantities were discovered in the course of excavations at Clifton, between Alma and Oak-field Roads and at Cotham. Much of this, however, was mixed with barium sulphate, the proportions varying from 99·1 of $Sr.SO_4$ to ·5 of $Ba.SO_4$ at Clifton Grove, to 89·1 of $Sr.SO_4$ to 10·9 of $Ba.SO_4$ at All Saints Road,[4] while in specimens found to the north of the mouth of the railway tunnel at Clifton, barium sulphate furnished a percentage of 74·1. Celestite has also been found in considerable quantities some miles to the north of Bristol, especially at Wickwar and Yate, and is worked commercially in shallow pits in the Keuper Red Marls. Indeed, in 1902 over 32,000 tons are said to have been raised in the Gloucestershire district (which, however, includes Somerset), but in 1905 the amount shipped from Bristol Docks had fallen to 14,294 tons with an estimated value of £13,936. This mineral is in demand amongst both the sugar refiners of Germany and the cotton manufacturers of northern England.

[1] Cited by Rudder, op. cit. 270.
[2] *Brist. and Glouc. Arch. Soc. Trans.* iv, 325.
[3] *Cotswold Nat. Field Club Proc.* x, 73.

[4] *Brist. Nat. Soc. Proc.* ii, 299 (new ser.).

AGRICULTURE

FOR many centuries the county of Gloucester has held a prominent place in the agriculture of the kingdom, originally by reason of the native breed of sheep which takes its name from the Cotswold Hills. The wool of this variety was once highly valued for the production of the fine fabrics that were formerly in great demand, not only in this country, but on the continent of Europe, and numerous large flocks were maintained in the county, which was for a long period the centre of the English wool trade.

Until the closing years of the eighteenth century the greater part of the arable land was cultivated on the unfenced, open-field system, it being the exception for agricultural holdings to be divided into fields by fences, or held, as it was then termed, 'in severalty.' There were generally two or three large arable fields in each parish divided into acre or half-acre strips among the tenants. Owing to the absence of fences the whole of each field was of necessity in the same crop, and in the Vale the usual course was to plant two successive corn crops followed by a fallow, while on the lighter land of the hills a fallow followed each crop of corn. Adjoining the village were crofts or pastures attached to each holding of arable land, which were mown for hay, or a meadow, of which every tenant might mow a portion, and in some cases a sheep or cow common, where the stock might graze at such times as there was no other pasturage available, which would be during the late summer and autumn. Turnips not having been introduced, the fallow field was sometimes sown with rye-grass to be fed, but even if left uncropped there was a quantity of couch-grass and weeds which was fed off until June or July, when the land was ploughed for wheat. After harvest the stubbles were thrown open, as well as the grazing common, and as the season advanced the live stock was brought home, and, when the lattermath of the pasture was gone, was as far as possible carried through the winter on hay. This system was terribly wasteful. The divisions, or baulks, in the arable fields occupied a considerable area of surface and bore no crop, while the absence of turnips, and consequent scarcity of winter food, made it impossible to carry the whole of the live stock through the winter. It was therefore necessary either to sell, or put out to agistment, every autumn, animals that should have been maintained on the holding. Beyond this the cultivation of the narrow detached strips entailed great waste of time, and these small holdings required a far larger strength in men, oxen, or horses, than would have been the case if they had formed part of a larger farm divided into fields and fenced. While each occupier's land lay in scattered strips all over the parish, any amelioration of the soil by drainage was impracticable, and it was hopeless to attempt any improvement in live stock so long as the sheep were sent out in a common flock, and the cattle in a common herd, to graze under the care of a common shepherd and herdsman respectively, the male animals being in some cases provided by the lord of the manor, and in others by the tenants. Under these conditions it was impossible to deal with the contagious diseases of live stock, and it will cause no surprise to find in the *Agricultural Survey of Gloucestershire*, drawn up by Rudge in 1805 for the Board of Agriculture, scab, or shab, described as ' a disease of the skin to which long-woolled sheep are more or less subject.'

The remedy for this state of affairs was to consolidate the various occupations, allotting to each the equivalent in value of the former holding, not in detached strips, but in compact blocks that might be enclosed within fences. Acts of Parliament were obtained to effect this change, the first Inclosure Act dealing with land in the county of Gloucester being that relating to the parish of Farmington, passed in 1714. Inclosures in the county did not, however, become general until the end of the eighteenth century, more than eighty Acts having been passed between 1760 and 1800.

An instructive comparison is appended by Rudge to his report concerning the state of the parish of Aldsworth before and after the inclosure. Previously the management of the arable land was in two shifts, that is, a corn crop and fallow alternately, one-half of the ploughed land being sown with wheat, barley, and oats, the other half being fallow, one-sixth of which was sown with peas, the remainder apparently being bare of crop, but full of weeds, until ploughed in July for the next year's corn. The acreage of pasture is not given. Before the inclosure the produce was as follows :—

Wheat, 200 acres, average 6 bushels per acre = 150 quarters.
Barley   ,,   ,,   ,, 10   ,,   ,,   ,, = 250   ,,
Oats   ,,   ,,   ,, 10   ,,   ,,   ,, = 250   ,,
Peas   100   ,,   ,, 6   ,,   ,,   ,, = 70   ,,

As regards live stock we are told that sheep bred were 200; full stock, 400; wool, at 8 fleeces per tod, 50 tods; 600 sheep were taken to agistment at 1*s.* per head; 10 beasts were bred and kept till four years old; 10 were sold yearly and 40 taken to agistment at 5*s.* per head.

After the inclosure the produce was increased to the following :—

Wheat   ...   390 acres at 12 bushels per acre = 585 quarters
Barley   ...   ,,   ,,   ,, 17   ,,   ,,   ,, = 825   ,,
Peas and Oats   ,,   ,,   ,, 19½   ,,   ,,   ,, = 950   ,,

Sheep bred annually, 1,800; beasts ditto, 12; sent to market, 20; wool at 5 fleeces per tod, 360 tods.

The net result of the inclosure of this parish would thus seem to be that 1,800 sheep were annually bred as compared with 200, 20 beasts against 10, and 360 tods of wool against 50, besides an additional 1,640 quarters of corn produced per annum. Aldsworth being a parish upon the Cotswold Hills, the following extract from Rudge's report referring to the Vale may be quoted :—

The claylands of the vale are thrown up in ridges much higher than would be necessary if proper drains were made for carrying off the stagnant water, which, however, is impracticable under the present management of the open common fields (a person six feet high may stand in some of the furrows and not be able to see the top of the second ridge from him). Where an inclosure has left the farmer at liberty to follow his own good sense and judgment, he reduces the higher ridges, fills the furrows, and brings the surface nearer to a level ; the superfluous water is collected from smaller drains and grips in large receiving sewers, and the deep furrows, which from redundancy of moisture carried little else but couch and aquatic plants, are brought back to an equal degree of fertility with the rest of the field. The farmer is aware of the evil, but his hands are tied up from improvement while the lands are entangled with each other, and subdivided among so many proprietors of different tempers and various degrees of industry.

Inclosure Acts, dealing with the open and common fields in the county, undoubtedly resulted in a greatly increased production of corn and meat, both on the hills and in the Vale, and enabled the cultivators of the soil to adopt a rational system or course of cropping, which is the foundation of the science and practice of agriculture. In the vale, drainage operations became possible, and were largely carried out, not only increasing the capacity of the soil for bearing crops, but having a most important effect on the health of the population, as well as of the live stock of every description. As underdrainage carried away the water, and made thorough cultivation of the heavy arable land possible, the high ridges were gradually got rid of, and the wide water trenches removed. In fact, it was now for the first time possible to get the water out of the land, instead of having to plough the land out of the water. Much of the earlier draining was, however, not so efficient as it would have been if the drains had been laid less deeply, and if pipes of larger size had been employed. In many cases, in heavy land, drains were cut 6 ft. deep if a fall could be got, and the subsidiary drains were often laid with pipes 1 in. in diameter. It is, however, scarcely possible at this date to appreciate the improvement of the heavy lands in the Vale brought about by drainage, as it is to realize their condition in the former state.

Under the old conditions agricultural operations must have been extremely tedious. Wheat was cut with the sickle, or fagging hook, and barley and oats mown with the scythe, and much of the corn must have been put together in bad condition. All the hay was also, of course, mown, turned, and raked into swaths by hand. Ploughs were heavy and cumbrous, and it is difficult to see how a tilth was obtained in the absence of the various drags and cultivators of the present day. Such drills as were in use were clumsy implements, covering little ground, and all the hoeing was done by manual labour. In winter the corn was threshed with the flail in the large barns, many of which still exist, and winnowing must have been very imperfectly performed with the means at command.

Now that the work of the farm is so largely carried on by machinery and horses, it is difficult to imagine how, under the old system, the various operations can have been completed in their season. Even with the help of string-binding reapers, grass-cutters, swath-turners, horse-rakes, American cultivators and pair-horse drills, and with the stimulating artificial fertilizers now available, it is not always possible to sow the seed and harvest the crop without suffering delay and loss from unseasonable weather.

The very comprehensive Report to the Board of Agriculture by Rudge, published in 1805, which has already been referred to, was followed by Bravender's Essay on *The Agriculture of Gloucestershire*, which gained the prize of the Royal Agricultural Society in 1850. These records afford an excellent opportunity of comparing the methods of the past with those of the present. In both attention is drawn to the practice of 'paring and burning' old sainfoin layers in preparation for turnips, as being essential to clean farming and the maintenance of fertility on the light soils of the Cotswold Hills. The operation consisted in cutting a thin slice from the surface with the breast-plough, an implement shaped like a spade, and fixed on a shaft with a crossbar at the end, which was held by the labourer in both hands and propelled from his thighs. The slice being cut was turned over by moving the cross-handle from right to left. When they were dry the turfs were gathered into heaps and stifle burned, not being allowed to burst into flame. The object of this operation was to destroy weeds, grubs of wireworm, and larvae of other harmful insects, as well as to provide a fertilizer for the turnip crop. The practice is immemorial on the Cotswold Hills, and Bravender remarks that he has known 'hundreds of farmers who have practised breast-ploughing and burning, but not one who has discontinued it.' In 1857 Voelcker described it as 'a practice, the advantages of which are fully confirmed and explained by modern chemical science.' Besides the old sainfoin layers, foul wheat stubbles were also breast-ploughed and burned with advantage. The great increase in the cost of manual labour, combined with the introduction of superphosphate of lime, dissolved bones, and other artificial manures, has led to a general discontinuance of this ancient and excellent practice, which had so much to recommend it. Another change that has taken place in the fifty years since the date of Bravender's essay is that oxen are no longer used as draught animals in the cultivation of the soil, which is now entirely effected by horses, with the occasional assistance of steam. In spite of the publication of the opinions of many practical men, based upon actual experience, and proving the superior economy of the ox-team as compared with horses, the former has now passed away—owing very greatly to the extreme difficulty of getting lads willing to work with the bullocks, such labour for some reason or other being considered derogatory—and is not likely to come back. Old and experienced cultivators of the light hill soils laid great stress on the benefit to the land caused by the treading of the ox-teams, and it was an undoubted preventive of wireworm, while upon the heavy soils where the land could only be cultivated for brief periods at certain seasons, and where it was consequently necessary to get a large area of land worked in a short time, an additional team or two of oxen, that were cheaply maintained, and when not required could be laid aside without detriment, enabled the work of the farm to be carried out with a less number of horses. The treading of cattle is also less inclined to poach the land when in a wet state, from the more gentle pressure of the hoof, and also from the fact that, unlike horses, the hind feet are, in walking, not placed in the exact spot that has just been trodden by the fore feet. In 1850 the practice of using the presser and roll to consolidate the soil before wheat-planting, and again in spring, was only just being substituted for the ancient custom of driving sheep and cattle over the land, and giving the flock a bare fold with the same object.

Gloucestershire shared in the agricultural prosperity of the kingdom from 1853 to 1874 due to the expansion of trade and manufactures, the gold

AGRICULTURE

discoveries in Australia and California, and the generally favourable seasons. In spite of deplorable losses from rinderpest, pleuro-pneumonia, and foot-and-mouth disease, the numbers of cattle and sheep increased and agriculture flourished. Wages, however, did not rise as quickly as the prices of commodities, and in the early seventies there were numerous strikes of farm labourers that were unprofitable both to employer and employed and created much ill-feeling on either side.

The general depression in the price of cereals, owing to imports from the United States, combined with the wet seasons, culminating in the disastrous year of 1879, occasioned great losses among arable farmers. In the Vale, in order to meet the altered circumstances, much of the heavier clay arable land was laid down to permanent pasture. In those cases where suitable mixtures of seeds were employed, and where the land was clean and in good heart, and so maintained by liberal manuring, useful pastures are now the result. On the hills, however, the soil does not adapt itself to pasture, the newly sown herbage being in a few years smothered by blackgrass (*Agrostis stolonifera*) and other natural and worthless weeds, and most of that which was laid down in the eighties, and intended to form permanent pasture, has either been broken up, or else, producing practically no crop, is now merely a run for stock. The general absence of springs on the hills also makes them unsuitable for grazing, necessitating constant hauling of water at a time when horses and men are urgently required on the arable land.

By the courtesy of Major Craigie, C.B., of the Board of Agriculture, the following statement showing the variations in area of the cultivated crops and the numbers of live stock of each kind in the county as returned to the Board is given. The period embraced is from 1875 to 1905 taken at intervals of five years, and it indicates, in a graphic manner, the way in which agriculturists have adapted themselves to the new conditions consequent on the depreciation in the value of cereal crops, and the variation in the numbers of live stock of the various descriptions kept under the altered circumstances of farming practice.

TABLES SHOWING THE ACREAGE UNDER EACH CROP AND THE NUMBER OF LIVE STOCK IN THE COUNTY OF GLOUCESTER IN EACH OF THE UNDERMENTIONED YEARS.

Total Acreage under Crops and Grass	1875	1880	1885	1890	1895	1900	1905
	642,463	653,828	659,011	659,336	656,488	661,441	657,549

		1875	1880	1885	1890	1895	1900	1905
Corn Crops	Wheat	89,924	79,086	67,827	62,125	37,509	47,379	45,738
	Barley, or Bere	44,954	41,807	33,997	31,801	32,904	28,237	23,092
	Oats	17,430	21,828	27,154	25,395	38,174	33,553	31,009
	Rye	252	222	312	229	383	449	317
	Beans	16,828	12,341	12,825	12,113	7,209	9,068	7,500
	Peas	8,549	5,568	4,544	4,286	4,424	2,809	2,177
	TOTAL	177,937	160,852	146,659	135,949	120,603	121,495	109,833

TABLES SHOWING THE ACREAGE UNDER EACH CROP AND THE NUMBER OF LIVE STOCK IN THE COUNTY OF GLOUCESTER IN EACH OF THE UNDERMENTIONED YEARS—*continued*.

	1875	1880	1885	1890	1895	1900	1905
Total Acreage under Crops and Grass	642,463	653,828	659,011	659,336	656,488	661,441	657,549
Green Crops — Potatoes	5,979	4,786	6,131	5,444	4,338	4,048	3,335
Turnips and Swedes	43,124	40,393	37,605	34,784	34,617	28,174	25,564
Mangold	3,744	3,259	3,920	3,815	3,733	5,470	5,087
Cabbage, K. Rabi and Rape	1,274	1,165	854	1,145	943	1,489	1,314
Vetches or Tares	} 13,925	10,549	12,100	9,247	5,222	6,189	4,253
Other Crops					1,440	1,665	1,623
TOTAL	68,046	60,152	60,610	54,435	50,293	47,035	41,176
Clover, Sainfoin and Grasses under Rotation — For Hay	49,927	*	55,530	54,247	56,026	53,432	52,585
Not for Hay	35,413	*	42,534	35,622	32,042	35,782	31,645
TOTAL	85,340	89,067	98,064	89,869	88,068	89,214	84,230
Permanent Pasture or Grass not broken up in Rotation — For Hay	130,990	*	131,635	151,715	151,772	148,198	152,116
Not for Hay	169,486	*	209,604	217,308	235,320	249,520	262,999
TOTAL	300,476	324,908	341,239	369,023	387,092	397,718	415,115
Flax	—	1	7	4	3	3	—
Hops	30	25	24	14	38	47	49
Small Fruits	*	*	*	926	1,780	1,498	1,650
Bare Fallow	10,634	18,823	12,408	9,116	8,611	4,431	5,496
Horses	23,955	25,779	26,455	27,268	27,737	27,530	29,726
Cattle	115,822	112,292	129,926	121,336	109,786	124,708	135,047
Sheep	453,881	354,621	393,149	375,712	347,011	364,785	348,808
Pigs	55,109	52,171	68,353	81,094	83,619	67,438	66,371

* Not separately distinguished.

The figures speak for themselves, and it is only necessary to make a few brief remarks on this instructive table. The decreases in the thirty years, as far as crops are concerned, are 68,104 acres of corn (of which 44,186 acres is wheat), 23,918 acres of turnips and green crops, and bare fallow is also 5,138 acres less. On the other hand we see that permanent pasture shows an increase of 114,639 acres.

As regards live stock there is an increase in cattle of 19,225, of horses 5,771, and pigs 11,262, and a decrease in sheep of 104,973.

Some further explanation of the live stock figures is necessary. The increase in the number of horses, in spite of the decreased acreage of cultivated land, is accounted for by the fact that in 1875 a large number of working oxen were kept upon the arable farms, which is no longer the case, and at

AGRICULTURE

the same time there has been an increased use of labour-saving implements in which horses take the place of manual labour. The impetus given to the breeding of Shire horses consequent upon the high prices that have been obtained is another element that must not be lost sight of.

The effect upon the agricultural population of the low prices of the produce of arable land and consequent increase of pasture is shown by the following table based upon the census and on the Agricultural Returns :

Year	Arable Land Acres	Number of Agricultural Labourers		
		Male	Female	Total
1871	352,613	18,579	2,007	20,586
1881	326,801	18,650	1,150	19,800
1891	286,194	15,386	530	15,916
1901	261,922	13,137	182	13,319

The practice of agriculture in the county of Gloucester is similar to that of other counties in that it is controlled and governed by conditions of soil, climate, and elevation.

The total area is about 806,000 acres, 2,500 acres being covered with water, 58,400 acres occupied by woods and plantations, and 8,300 acres being mountain and heath-land of nominal value used for sheep runs.

The number of agricultural holdings is 9,706 covering about 657,500 acres, of which 101,100 acres are occupied by owners of the land they cultivate. There are 2,807 holdings above 1 and not exceeding 5 acres, 3,834 above 5 and not exceeding 50 acres, 2,580 above 50 and not exceeding 300 acres, and 485 above 300 acres in extent.

For purposes of agricultural distinction the county may conveniently be divided into four portions as follows, although in each division many varieties of soil with consequent variation of agricultural management will be found :

1. The Cotswold Hills extending from Chipping Campden to Bath.
2. The portion of the Thames Valley lying to the south-east of the Cotswolds extending from Eastleach to Didmarton through Cirencester and Tetbury.
3. The part of the Vale of the Severn lying south-east of that river, extending from Tewkesbury to Bristol, and including part of the valley of the Warwickshire Avon.
4. The portion lying on the northern side of the Severn, including the Forest of Dean and Ryeland districts, extending from the River Wye on the west to the borders of Worcestershire and Herefordshire in other directions.

1.—The Cotswold Hills cover some 300,000 acres, and are situated geologically upon the Great and Inferior Oolitic Limestone rocks, interspersed with the Fuller's Earth and Stonesfield Slate. The soil on the Oolite is thin, being only from 3 to 6 inches deep, of a light description locally called Stonebrash. Although containing many stones, there is little or no sand, and it is of a hollow nature, requiring skill in giving it the necessary consolidation to enable the roots of plants to keep a firm hold in the ground. At the same time it is tenacious when wet, and great care must be exercised to avoid all treading and working unless the land is sufficiently dry. Strangers are often surprised to see three horses at length in a plough in this district, but the plough does not clean itself, and the work is not so easy as is imagined. As a general rule, however, a pair of horses is sufficient.

Owing to the prevalence of stone wall fences this district presents a bare appearance, though it is pleasantly broken up by the narrow valleys in which the villages are situated, where the soil is deeper, and which are generally well watered, being also beautified by ash and elm timber trees.

In order to prevent the fertilizing constituents from being washed into the rubbly underlying rock, and on account of its hollow character, it is important that this light, thin, brashy land should not be too deeply nor too often ploughed. On this soil more crops are probably in danger of being damaged by over-cultivation than by too little stirring, and the roll is an implement of greater importance than in many other districts.

The size of farms on the Cotswolds varies from about 200 to 1,000 acres, and upwards. A smaller holding than the former does not afford a living for the occupier and his family, unless the soil is more fertile and nearer to good markets than is, generally speaking, the case in this district. The usual course of husbandry is the five-course rotation, with certain variations necessitated by the seasons and the prices of the various descriptions of corn and live stock. About fifteen per cent. of the arable land is usually devoted to the growth of sainfoin, a most useful crop on the limestone, and an excellent sheep food. This crop usually stands from three to five years, when it is broken up and replaced by a similar acreage recently laid down. In this soil the deep-rooted lucerne should be cultivated more frequently. In the few instances where it has been tried the results have been most satisfactory, the crop yielding three good cuts a year. The remainder of the land is cropped as follows :—First year, wheat ; second year, turnips or swedes ; third year, barley or oats, with grass and clover seeds ; fourth year, seeds mown for hay ; fifth year, seeds fed, to be followed by wheat. A portion of the turnip break is often sown with mangold, rape, or thousand-head kale, and part of the wheat stubble with vetches, to be fed by sheep, and followed by late turnips. Peas are also occasionally taken after wheat, and the land may, in an early season, be afterwards sown with turnips, thus bringing it back again into course. On the better soils the ordinary Norfolk four-course rotation is occasionally adopted, when the crops are the same, the grass seeds being, however, only kept down for one year before being broken up for wheat ; but, where a large head of live stock is maintained, second year's seeds are found very useful for summer grazing, both for sheep and cattle. Some farmers again, adopt a six-course rotation, taking barley after wheat, followed by roots fed off as a preparation for oats, thus getting three corn crops in six years, as against two in the five-course system, but this, generally speaking, is not so suitable for the district, tending to the impoverishment of the soil, which is also more difficult to keep clean, owing to two corn crops following each other on the same land.

At the commencement of the nineteenth century we find that wheat was generally sown in July. Cobbett, in his *Rural Rides*, writing from

AGRICULTURE

Fairford on 30 September, 1826, says, 'Wheat sowing is yet going on, on the Wold ; but, the greater part of it is sown, and not only sown, but up, and in some places high enough to hide a hare.' Although very little is now sown before the end of September, and more frequently October and November are the busiest months for drilling, a stale furrow is the best, and the ploughing is done as far as possible in August. After the land has been rolled and a seed bed prepared with the harrows and drags, about nine pecks of seed are drilled to the acre and harrowed in. Now that wheat has so greatly depreciated in price it is seldom hoed, and remains until the spring, when it is rolled to consolidate the earth, and lightly harrowed. When ripe it is cut and tied by the self-binder.

As soon as the corn is safe in stack a start is made on the wheat stubbles, and as large an area as is possible is stirred by the cultivator. On light soils the cultivator is followed by the roll, and the couch dragged out on the surface and burnt. The first root crop to be drilled in the following spring is mangold, and for this a clean piece of wheat stubble is selected, given a good dressing of farmyard manure, and ploughed at once to ensure its working well in spring. The land intended for swedes and turnips is also ploughed, and the whole of the root land should have been ploughed once by the end of the year. In spring it is ploughed across, rolled, dragged, rolled again, and drilled. The water drill is largely used on the Cotswolds, and roots are drilled on the flat and not on the ridge. For mangolds 3 to 4 cwt. of salt is broadcasted previous to drilling, and about 1 to 2 cwt. of nitrate of soda or guano drilled in April with the seed. After the seed is up it is top-dressed with about 1 cwt. of either nitrate of soda or guano, if the smaller amount has been used with the drill.

The soil being generally speaking deficient in phosphates, about 3 cwt. of superphosphate of lime or sometimes 2 cwt. added to 1 cwt. of dissolved bones is drilled with a swede crop. Rather less is usually applied for turnips. Rape is often sown in March or April to provide early keep for lambs in July and August, and thousand-head kale may be drilled at almost any time to provide a succession of sheep-feed throughout the winter and spring. The greater part of the root land is sown with swedes to come in for food after the turnips are finished, towards the end of the year, and maintain the sheep until spring. It is of great importance that the root crop should be singled early, as soon as the rough leaf is developed, and as this coincides with the haymaking season there is a difficulty where labour is not over-plentiful in getting all the crop hoed over in proper time to secure the development of the plant.

Mangold and swedes are singled out and seconded, but as a rule turnips are only singled. As soon as they show well above ground, and afterwards throughout the summer at intervals, three or four horse-hoeings are given whenever the weather is favourable and the horses can be spared. The rainfall on the Cotswolds is considerable, and generally sufficient to produce a fair crop of roots even upon this light dry soil, but the plant is often irregular. Owing, however, to the available amount of lime, the disease called 'Finger and Toe' is almost unknown, and the roots are generally of good quality and free from mildew. The mangold should be pulled and secured in the clamp by the first week in November, and later in the month a proportion of the swede crop is pitted or trenched in the field as a precaution against frost.

Winter feeding of cattle for the production of beef is not customary on the Cotswolds, nearly all the roots being consumed on the land by sheep receiving hay and cake. To attempt to fatten cattle in yards or boxes to any considerable extent would necessitate increased expense in lifting and carting home the roots and drawing out the manure, with little or no profit now that beef is imported in such enormous quantities and values are so greatly diminished.

As the roots are being consumed the ploughs are kept going close behind the sheep-fold. The land that was ploughed in autumn is cross-ploughed in February or March, dragged, rolled, and harrowed. About three bushels of barley is drilled per acre, harrowed, and lightly rolled in. The mixture of seeds for the next year's hay crop and sown in the barley, varies with the nature of the soil and the taste of individuals, about twenty-eight pounds being sown for a two-years' lay, or if intended to be laid down with sainfoin four bushels per acre is a usual seeding. It may be noted that this limestone soil is not so liable to clover sickness as is the case where lime is deficient. The grass and clover seeds are sown with the seed barrow, or drilled across the barley in April or May, after which they are lightly harrowed and rolled in. When the land is dry enough a second rolling is given when the barley is about three inches high. The cultivations for oats are similar to those for barley, except that so fine a seed-bed is not absolutely necessary, and they can be sown when it would be too late to plant barley. From three to four bushels of oats are drilled to the acre.

The value of barley for malting purposes is now very much lower than that which prevailed up to the last quarter of the nineteenth century, when great care was taken to ensure an even-coloured sample. It was generally mown with the scythe so as to lie thinly and evenly on the ground, after which it was twice turned before being carted to the stack in order that it should all be exposed as far as possible to the same amount of sun and dew. It is now often cut and tied with the self-binding reaper, and although, in this case, the corn in the centre of the sheaves does not exactly match in colour that on the outside, the very small increased value that is now given for an even sample does not pay for the considerable addition to the cost of harvesting involved by the extra manual labour.

When the corn is off the land should be found covered with a close plant of seeds for the next year's hay crop, and the moist climate of Gloucestershire provides this with greater certainty than is the case in counties with a lower rainfall. The young seeds are often lightly grazed with sheep in autumn, but must not be stocked so heavily as to have an adverse effect on the succeeding hay crop. In winter it is good practice to give a dressing of farmyard manure as, irrespective of its fertilizing properties, the shelter and covering afforded are a great protection to the plant from frost, and not only result in an increased weight of hay, but also improve the succeeding wheat crop, for, as a general rule, a good crop of clover is followed by a good yield of wheat, caused by the accumulation of many necessary ingredients, nitrogen and potash in particular, in the clover root. Very little of the clover and seed hay is now mown with the scythe, the horse machine doing the work cheaply and well. The Cotswold farmer is an economical manager, and is careful to place a large proportion of his hay-ricks in convenient positions in his root fields, so as to save labour in carrying dry food to his sheep in the following autumn and winter. As a rule hay is well made in Gloucestershire, although agriculturists from other districts observe that owing to the practice of building such low ricks an unnecessarily large portion of the contents must consist of outsides, top and bottom. The lattermath is fed with sheep or young cattle, the latter doing better upon seeds than on old pasture. It is grazed until ploughed for wheat, which in the four-course system would be in the same year as it has borne the hay crop, or in the more customary five-course system a twelvemonth later. Winter vetches are drilled on a wheat stubble that has been manured, ploughed, rolled, and harrowed down to a seed-bed immediately after harvest, at the rate of 4 bushels to the acre. They should be ready to feed in the following May, but in recent years the large flocks of wood-pigeons so prevalent in the country have done great damage to vetches as well as clover in the winter. Spring vetches sown in March should be ready to feed in July. Peas are usually drilled in early spring on a stubble that has been broken up in autumn. The seed-bed must be got into a good tilth, and drilling should take place when the land is friable. The harrows follow the drill and cover the seed, and as soon as the plant is visible a second harrowing is given. When about three inches high the crop should be again harrowed and rolled.

On hill farms the proportion of meadow is usually small and is very frequently mown every year, being grazed after the crop has been carried and until May in the succeeding year, when it is again laid up for hay.

From this brief account of husbandry operations on the Cotswold Hills it will be seen that the object in view is to consolidate the arable land by treading, and to manure and stimulate it to bear corn crops by the consumption of the root crop by sheep having rations of hay and corn or cake. The soil is healthy for sheep, and they are generally well managed. Formerly the Cotswold breed predominated, but at the present time there are few working flocks that have not been crossed to some extent with the Down, and most now approximate to the Oxford Down type. The lambing pen is generally placed in a turnip field, and constructed of thatched hurdles divided into convenient pens well littered with straw, which is considered more healthy for both ewes and lambs than a permanent lambing pen at the homestead. After lambing and when the young lambs are well on their legs, the ewes run out daily on the turnips, or have a fold of kale and return to the shelter of the pen at night. If the land is very wet they are shifted to a dry pasture or seed field, and provided with some rough temporary shelter. In due course a water meadow, Italian ryegrass, or an early field of seeds provides food for both lambs and ewes, some roots being thrown to them daily. During summer they are run thinly on seeds until the lambs are weaned in July, when they are put on lattermath sainfoin or clover, the ewes being given a bare bite on pasture or seeds in order to dry up their milk. In September rape or early turnips provide food for the lambs, the wethers being pushed with cake for the butcher, and the ewe lambs kept in thriving condition in order to take their place in the breeding flock the succeeding year.

Although there are several excellent herds of Shorthorns kept on such farms as are suitable, cattle breeding is not largely practised on the hills on account of the small proportion of grass land, except from the few cows kept to supply milk to the farmer's house and to his neighbours. Calves are, however, on most farms bought from dairymen in the vale or from the neighbouring county of Wilts, and after being weaned are reared and generally sold as stores at about two years old. Not many pigs are kept, the breed of such as there are being usually a Berkshire cross.

2.—The portion of the Thames Valley that is situated within the county of Gloucester contains about 60,000 acres, much of the soil being agriculturally more important than that of the Cotswold Hills. It is, however, very variable, the greater part being upon the Forest Marble and Bradford Clay, partly overlaid by the Cornbrash. When the Forest Marble is fully exposed the soil is of a particularly obstinate nature, cold and retentive of moisture, at the same time difficult to drain on account of the layers of hard thin rock lying near the surface. The Thames meadows and adjoining arable land, extending from South Cerney to Lechlade, through Down Ampney and Kempsford, are on the Oxford Clay, for the most part covered with oolitic or calcareous gravel.

The farms in this division are of less area than upon the Cotswolds, and, as is naturally the case where the soil is of a more fertile nature, small holdings of 50 to 150 acres are found. Where, however, the Cornbrash, Forest Marble, and the moory gravels predominate, the holdings are larger. The course of husbandry is, generally speaking, very similar to that which is customary on the Cotswolds, with certain modifications necessitated by the variations of the soil. Some of the heavier tenacious arable land will not carry sheep in winter, and, instead of turnips or swedes to be fed off on the land, vetches are grown as fallow crops to be fed in summer; or swedes and mangold, to be drawn off and consumed in the cattle yards, are substituted, and beans occasionally precede wheat. It may, however, be said that for the most part agricultural operations on the arable land are very much the same as those that have already been described, and it is unnecessary to enumerate them in detail. Probably one-third to one-half of this district is now in permanent pasture, much of the more intractable arable land having been laid down to grass since 1880. On the border of the county of Wilts and in the immediate neighbourhood of the Thames dairy farms predominate. These were formerly devoted to the production of cheese, and although this industry still exists to a small extent, the greater number of farmers have now become milk-sellers, and the produce of their cows is sent away twice a day by rail to London and other large centres of population. Although the wholesale price is low, and the cost of carriage is high in proportion to the value of the commodity, this method of dealing with their milk finds great favour with those whose occupations lie within reasonable distance of the railway, but it is very doubtful if as much money is realized by this practice as if it were converted into cheese, as was at one time customary. Made into cheese, milk has been worth recently nearly 7d. a gallon, and, although the labour of the dairy is a considerable tax at certain times of the year on the female members of his family, the cheese-maker has in the whey a useful food for pigs, which should be a source of profit to the farmer, and a benefit to the farm on which they are reared and fed. It is probable that on the average not more than 6*d.* a gallon all the year round is realized from the sale of milk. This is, however, more profitable than butter-making, since it takes from 2½ to 3 gallons of milk to make a pound of butter, which will not sell throughout the year at an average of over 1*s.*

The irrigated meadows that have been formed in the Valley of the Churn and other rivers are a feature of this district. Since the decline of the flour-milling industry, that coincided with the huge imports of flour from the North American continent, the river banks have in many instances been allowed to fall into disrepair, and from this cause, as well as from the increased abstraction of water for other purposes, the supply has diminished, and the thorough irrigation of the meadows has not been so complete as was formerly the case. The importance, however, of meadows that come into profit in early spring before any other grass is available, and that will afterwards bear a heavy hay crop, can hardly be over-estimated. As soon as the autumn rains fill the rivers advantage is taken to flood the meadows, which are kept alternately covered with running water and dried, care being taken to prevent the tender grass being injured by severe frost. They are finally dried off, and in April a good bite of young grass is available for the lambs, or for the dairy cows. When this has been eaten off, the meadow is again flooded, and a heavy crop of grass will be ready to cut as soon as the hay has been got together on the upland pastures. Sometimes, though not always, a third flooding is possible, when the grass will again grow rapidly and provide a good lattermath to be grazed, or occasionally a second hay crop. Water meadows are somewhat costly to manage, owing to the numerous hatches that are required to regulate the flow of the water, and the necessity of keeping them, as well as the ditches or water carriers, in good repair; and it must be admitted that although the hay crop produced on these meadows is heavy, it is not of first-rate quality. To a hill farmer, however, an irrigated meadow is a very valuable adjunct, affording an early bite for the lambs at a season when sheep-feed is very scarce.

The Thames Valley has long been noted for its excellent Shorthorn dairy cattle and for the Oxford Down sheep that are here found in great perfection.

3.—The great vale of the Severn contains about 370,000 acres. It includes the fertile valleys of Evesham, Gloucester, and Berkeley, and contains the most valuable agricultural land in the county. The greater part is situated upon the Lias Clay, but in many places this is overlaid by a red marl or sandy loam of a very fertile nature. In the immediate neighbourhood of the Severn, the productive character of the soil is due to alluvial deposits. Near to the Bristol Coalfield, and in the vale of Berkeley, the New and Old Red Sandstone are met with.

By far the greater part of the surface of this district is now permanent pasture, for although described by Bravender in 1850 as being arable and pasture in about equal proportions, a great deal of the more tenacious soil was laid down to grass when wheat cultivation on such land became unremunerative, and only that which is more productive and less expensive to cultivate now remains in arable husbandry. Viewed from the escarpment of the Cotswolds the preponderance of pasture, the smaller inclosures, the luxuriant hedges, and the large quantity of hedgerow timber, chiefly elm, present a striking contrast to the bare landscape of the hills. The farmer of the vale chiefly relies on his cattle and his dairy, and although much milk is sent away to the towns a considerable quantity of cheese is made in the neighbourhood of Berkeley and Gloucester

The cheese known as Double Gloucester is a thick cheese weighing about 33 lb. and is made from March to October, the procedure at the County Council Dairy School being as follows :—The night's milk is sieved into a large vat in the dairy and left until morning. The cream is then skimmed, warmed up, and mixed with the morning's milk, which is added to that of the previous night. The whole is then heated by means of hot water to 82°–86° F. according to the time of the year. Rennet is now added at the rate of 1 drachm to 3–4 gallons (1 fl. oz. to 25–30 gallons) to form the curd, and the vat is covered and left for about an hour, when the contents should be sufficiently firmly coagulated to break clear over the thermometer. It is then cut with both vertical and horizontal American cutters, short intervals being left between the operations. Afterwards the curd is gently stirred and gradually heated to a temperature of 90°–94° F. It is then allowed to settle for fifteen to thirty minutes, piled to the centre of the vat and the whey let off, after which it is removed to a cloth on the rack and cut and turned at intervals of twenty to thirty minutes according to condition. When the curd is fairly dry it is ready to vat, and should have a decidedly acid taste and smell. It is weighed, ground, and salted at the rate of 1 oz. of salt to 4 lb. of curd before placing in the smaller vats, the full process of manufacture occupying from six to seven hours. On the first day the cheese is put into the press with only a slight pressure, and on the second day it is turned, a dry cloth put on and full pressure applied. The same treatment continues for five days, when it is removed to the cheese room, where it remains until ready for market, which will be in about eight weeks.

Single Gloucester is a thin cheese weighing about 14 lb., frequently made partly of skim milk, the cream taken from the night's milk not being returned to the vat when the morning's milk is added, as is the case with Double Gloucester. The principal difference lies in the fact that the curd obtained is not so firm and dry, and the same degree of acidity is not developed before vatting as in the case of Double Gloucester. The time occupied in making Single Gloucester is from five to six hours, and it should be ready for market in about six weeks.

The records relating to the milk used for cheese-making at the County Council Dairy School in 1904, the cheese being afterwards sold, show that when made into Stilton the milk realized 11d. a gallon, Double Gloucester 6d., and Cheddar returned over 7½d. a gallon, while milk made into Single Gloucester realized over 5d.

The arable land of the vale is now for the most part cultivated with the object of assisting the dairy as well as the production of corn, and the fallow crops are principally mangold or cabbage, followed by beans, which are succeeded by wheat. The whole of the manure made on the farm is usually applied to the arable land, which is managed so as to produce as heavy crops as it will grow. A regular rotation of cropping is seldom practised, the aim of the farmer being to get a corn crop as often as the season and the condition of the soil will allow. Although bare fallows are still found necessary if the seasons are unfavourable, they are much less frequent than formerly, owing to the fact that the greater part of the more intractable arable land has now been laid down to permanent grass. Root crops are almost invariably drawn off to be consumed by cattle in yards and sheds, and it is quite exceptional to see sheep feeding off roots on arable land in autumn or winter. When the land is foul a bastard fallow is given by sowing vetches on a wheat stubble directly after harvest. The vetches must be early sown so that they may be fed off on the land in time for it to be ploughed for the succeeding wheat or bean crop before the busy days of harvest. For a bare summer fallow the land is first ploughed in early spring and left until the spring planting is finished. Then, when it has lain long enough to get fairly dry, it is ploughed back again, and afterwards scarified as often as necessary and the season permits. The clods receive a thorough baking from the sun, and the greater part of the couch grass is thus killed.

Where milk-selling is practised it is the aim of the farmer to keep up the supply by having his cows downcalving all the year round, but more particularly in the winter months when milk is dear, and when, from the effect of climate and the necessity of foddering the cows on dry food, the quantity produced is less than when they are grazing the pastures in spring and summer. The heifer calves are usually retained in order to maintain the dairy stock, and the bull calves are sold to the hill farmers to be weaned and reared as steers. As in the Thames Valley, there are many famous herds of Shorthorn dairy cattle in this district, this breed largely predominating over others. The Longhorns and Old Gloucesters mentioned by Rudge are practically extinct. The grass land of the vale is not generally speaking healthy for sheep, as it induces fluke or liver rot, and trouble is experienced with foot rot. Many farmers, however, in the neighbourhood of Gloucester buy a few ewes of the Radnor breed in autumn, run them on the sounder grass fields with a Hampshire or Shropshire Down ram, and sell them out the following summer with their lambs as soon as they can be got fit for the butcher.

Although there is seldom any farmyard manure available for the grassland, the application of 5 to 7 cwt. of basic slag to the acre on fields upon the Lias has produced a most beneficial effect, increasing the growth of white clover and the finer grasses to an extent that, in the absence of proof, would not readily be believed.

The production of cider and perry is a considerable industry in the vale of Gloucester; the better qualities being obtained from orchards on the Red Marls and Sandstone soils. Speaking generally, orchards have not been as well managed as might have been the case, and have not been regularly replenished with young trees to take the place of those that have become unserviceable. Practical instruction in fruit culture, including the management of young and old orchards, and lectures on cider-making, followed by practical demonstrations and advice during the season at the various mills in the district, are now given by experts under the supervision of the County Council, and have led to increased attention being attracted to the industry with good results, the orchards being better tended, and a more methodical system of manufacture being adopted. The National Fruit and Cider Institute at Long Ashton near Bristol is also carrying out important investigations into the most suitable varieties and the most profitable methods of production, besides being engaged in chemical research in relation to the subject.

In the neighbourhood of Winchcombe and the Vale of Evesham the cultivation of fruit and manufacture of jam have undergone considerable extension, and a large and important industry has been established.

In the vicinity of the larger towns such as Cheltenham, Gloucester, Bristol, and Bath, market-gardening is largely practised. The soil of the district immediately adjoining Cheltenham is particularly suitable to this description of husbandry, the Lias Clay being here overlaid by a bed of warm sandy loam of a very fertile nature. This business has become much less profitable than formerly now that communication with the Channel Islands and the Continent is frequent and rapid. The earliest vegetables and fruit, which command the highest prices, are produced in their more genial climate, and the English grower is consequently under a great disadvantage in the lower prices that prevail when his crops are ready for market.

4.—That part of the county lying beyond the Severn contains about 73,000 acres. The Forest of Dean itself, which covers about 24,000 acres, presents few features of agricultural interest. Adjoining it on the north the soil is a light loam, for the greater part on the Old Red Sandstone, easy of cultivation, but deficient in lime, and of no great fertility. It is well adapted for barley and turnip husbandry, and the rearing of cattle and sheep. This district is called The Ryelands, and gave its name to a breed of fine-woolled sheep that is now very seldom met with as a pure breed, the sheep now found in the locality being almost entirely derived from the Clun Forest or Radnor breed either pure or crossed with the Shropshire Down.

On the arable land the four or five course system of cropping, as practised on the Cotswold Hills, is followed, and where the land is well farmed good crops are produced. The Old Red Sandstone and Carboniferous Limestone are also met with south of the forest, and a considerable area near the Severn is upon the New Red Sandstone, Red Marl, and the Lias. Here the land is very similar to that of the other part of the vale of Gloucester from which it is separated by the river. The farms are largely composed of pasture, and dairying and cattle-grazing prevail. The fine breed of Hereford cattle is met with in this district, and probably in its native home and the immediate neighbourhood is surpassed by no other variety for summer grazing.

Land is for the far greater part held upon yearly tenancies throughout the county. Upon the Cotswolds and arable farms of the Thames Valley they generally commence and terminate at Michaelmas, and where permanent pasture predominates at Lady Day.

Except in the neighbourhood of the towns, where manure may be easily brought on to the farm in return for produce sold, it is not customary for a tenant to sell hay and straw, but to consume them on the holding. An outgoing tenant is paid for the whole of the expense of his last year's root crop, for all work done for the benefit of his successor, and for the hay and straw left on the premises at consuming price. He is also entitled to be paid for the labour he has expended on the manure left, and a practice is growing up of allowing compensation for what is considered to be the unexhausted manurial value of corn and cake consumed during the last two years of the tenancy.

The farmhouses and buildings of Gloucestershire are as a rule sufficient, and on the Cotswolds the cost of keeping them in repair, which throughout the county almost invariably falls upon the landlord, makes a very serious inroad upon the rent. In this poor district the gross rental of agricultural holdings seldom amounts to more than the interest on the capital expended by the owner in providing this necessary equipment. The increased quantity of labour-saving implements now used upon a farm necessitates increased accommodation to protect them from the weather, and corrugated iron and timber have been largely substituted for stone and tile in meeting the demand. Such buildings are undoubtedly necessary, but do not add to the beauty of the landscape.

Although many new labourers' cottages have been provided, there still are a great many that do not satisfy the requirements of the present day. This is largely attributable to the pernicious system of life leases that formerly prevailed. It was in many districts the custom for a labourer to take a lease of his cottage at 1s. a year or thereabouts, for the longest of three lives, generally those of himself, his wife, and a child. When one of the parties died a younger life was often substituted on payment of a small fine. The lessees were under strict covenants to repair, but as the structure became old, and the roof-timbers and walls began to decay, there was no incentive to get an extension of the lease, or to carry out the necessary repairs. It consequently followed that, at the death of the last surviving lessee, the tenement reverted to the landlord worn out and valueless. Some have been newly roofed and repaired at great cost, and others have been permitted to go into ruin, being completely worn out. Since the agricultural labourer can only pay from 1s. to 2s. a week for his cottage, in return for which his landlord pays the rates and undertakes all repairs, it is evident that the building of labourers' cottages in country villages is a philanthropic work which landowners, with their incomes in many cases reduced by one-half, are not competent to undertake.

It is not the custom in Gloucestershire for labourers to be boarded and live in the farmhouse or with a foreman. Carters, undercarters, shepherds, and cattlemen are usually engaged by the year, and receive higher wages than daymen, and cottages rent-free, besides other privileges. There appears to be a sufficiency of agricultural labour in the county, although complaints are sometimes made of the quality, and there is an undoubted deficiency of boys for agricultural employment, especially for those required to attend live stock on Sundays, and it is difficult to get milkers. A satisfactory mechanical milker has not yet been discovered.

LIVE STOCK

No county of its acres is more distinguished for the excellence of its flocks and herds than is the county of Gloucester.

Reference has already been made to the breed of Cotswold sheep that was renowned in the middle ages, and stood its ground until the last quarter of the nineteenth century.

The Cotswold sheep of the fifteenth century inhabited broad, unenclosed, and bleak tracts of country with little natural shelter covered with short sweet herbage, and judging from the description of the country they occupied were probably very different from the Cotswold sheep of the present day. It is therefore not unreasonable to conclude that their altered and improved character is largely the result of the improved state of cultivation of their native hills, and is not altogether due to admixture with other breeds, as is sometimes asserted. There is, however, no doubt that early in the nineteenth century a cross with the new Leicester was introduced with benefit to the breed.

It is described by Rudge as being

> large and coarse in the wool, at three years old generally weighing from twenty-two to thirty pounds per quarter, and capable by forced feeding of being made even forty-five pounds. At the same age it produces nine or ten, and sometimes more weight of wool per fleece.

In his *Rural Rides* Cobbett, describing his journey over the Cotswolds in 1826, notes that ' there has come down to us from a distance of many centuries a particular race of sheep called the Cotswold Breed, which are, of course, the best suited to the County.'

When Bravender wrote his essay the Cotswold sheep were probably the same in all essential characteristics as at present. He notes that at that time many fat tegs were ' brought to the fairs in April and May, being from thirteen to fifteen months old, that have had neither cake nor corn, the clip of the tegs averaging about 7 lb. and that of the ewes 6 lb. each.' The Cotswold sheep of the present day are big and handsome animals, carrying a great weight of carcass upon clean wide-standing legs. Their white faces are set off by a long curly topknot, and the heavy white fleece is of long curled wool. That the wool-producing qualities of the Cotswold sheep are maintained is shown by the result of the clip of the celebrated Aldsworth flock in 1905, when 1,100 fleeces produced 417 tods of washed wool or an average of 10½ lb. per fleece. These sheep are very hardy in constitution, and quiet by disposition, seldom attempting to break bounds. There are now comparatively few pure-bred flocks on their native hills, their place having been largely taken by the various Down breeds and their crosses. The greatest demand for Cotswold rams at the present day comes from East Anglia, where they are much in request for crossing with black-faced ewes, giving size, constitution, and early maturity to the lambs.

Throughout the Thames Valley and upon the Cotswold Hills the greater proportion of the flocks now consist of the Oxford Down, or of cross-bred sheep in which the Oxford breed predominates. The Oxford Down originated in a cross between the Cotswold ram and Hampshire Down ewe, and having been bred since about the year 1835, has long been recognized as a distinct breed. In the Oxford the poll is well covered with wool, and has a topknot inherited from the Cotswold. The face is a uniform dark brown, fleece thick and heavy, the body being wide, level on the back, and supported by short legs. They are said to bear harder folding and to fatten with less food than the Cotswold.

These beautiful sheep have been brought to great perfection in the Thames Valley, and the old-established flock at Maiseyhampton has been the means of extending the popularity of the breed over the continent of Europe, in the United States, and our Colonies. That they also thrive in more exposed situations may be seen at Cowley Manor near Birdlip, much of the land being 800 ft. above sea level. Of other breeds the Hampshire and Southdown appear to make little headway, and the Shropshire breed is in this county for the most part used for crossing with the Radnor—a small breed carrying a short fine fleece, which is a favourite with the grassland farmers of the vale. The mutton is of excellent quality, and, being hardy in constitution, the sheep require and receive very little attention. This breed has been a good deal crossed, and the sheep that are sent to the fairs at Gloucester do not exhibit much uniformity.

While the conversion from arable husbandry of much land that does not at present prices produce wheat at a profit has naturally had the effect of reducing the number of sheep in the county, increased pasturage has been provided for cattle that are in appreciably larger numbers than before the change took place.

Excepting in the Tewkesbury district, where the Herefords are often met with, the prevailing breed is the Shorthorn, and Gloucestershire probably contains as fine herds of the latter as any county in England. The exhibition of Shorthorn cattle at the annual show of the Gloucestershire Agricultural Society has long been celebrated for its outstanding excellence. A noteworthy incident in connexion with the Shorthorn history of the county was the dispersion of Lord Sherborne's pedigree herd in 1848. Although the sale catalogue included the celebrated cows Jenny Denison and Ruth (by Harold), and other animals whose descendants have since become distinguished, the prices realized were moderate, and Gloucestershire breeders availed themselves of the opportunity to buy. In the list of purchasers are the names, well-known in Shorthorn history, of Colonel (now Sir Nigel) Kingscote and Messrs. Bowly, Garne, Lane, Mace, and Kendall, and there can be no doubt that the diffusion of so many highly descended animals was of great advantage to Lord Sherborne's neighbours.

At Tortworth in 1853 the great sale of Lord Ducie's herd took place, when sixty-two head totalled £9,361 16s., an average of £150 19s. 11d. This occasion is memorable for the contest between the American breeders and the late Colonel Sir Robert Gunter for the ownership of the animals of Mr. Bates's Duchess tribe. Colonel Gunter succeeded in buying a yearling heifer and two heifer calves, for which he paid 1,060 guineas.

In 1868 and 1869 the herd of Mr. Stiles Rich at Didmarton was dispersed, when 114 animals averaged £70 12s. 10d., and in 1873 at Broadmoor Mr. Thomas Garne's herd of 101 head averaged £58 17s. At this sale thirty-two animals of the old Pye tribe averaged over £82.

Prices continued to rise, and Mr. Edward Bowly had several successful sales at Siddington, the best being in 1875, when thirty animals averaged £217 18s. 8d. In the same year Sir Nigel Kingscote obtained an average of £179 4s. 8d. for forty head. At the Berkeley sale in 1879 Lord Fitzhardinge's thirty-two head averaged £147 9s. 10d. This sale was the last in the county where these inflated prices were obtained. The falling values of cereals, the disastrous seasons, which were followed by the loss of thousands of sheep from liver rot, and the general reduction in rents and consequent diminution of the means of landowners, induced something like a panic among all classes connected with agriculture, and prices came down with a run. This has probably not been an unmitigated misfortune to breeders, as the return to commercial values put trade on a business basis and enabled them to secure the best strains of blood for replenishing their herds at moderate prices. There are now in the county many grand herds in the hands of tenant farmers as well as landowners who, if the country continues to be kept free from disease, seem to be about to reap the result of their enterprise in the higher prices that have been realized at the sales of 1905 and 1906.

The great annual show and sale of Shorthorns at Birmingham, to which many Gloucestershire breeders send their young bulls and surplus heifers for disposal, has this year shown that there is a brisk demand for good stock, and values are again considerably higher than in 1905.

At Badminton and a few other places the old breed of Gloucester cattle is preserved, and at Maisemore and Poulton there are noted herds of the Aberdeen Angus breed. Jersey cattle are met with for the supply of gentlemen's houses with cream and butter, but are not kept commercially.

Horses are not largely bred in the hill district, the nature of the fences and size of the inclosures not being very well suited for this description of stock. Most of the larger farmers, however, try to maintain their teams by annually breeding a few colts that are brought in to work at two years, which enables them to sell a matured gelding or so every year for town work. In the vale, and where shelter is afforded by high hedges, more foals are bred. Although not attaining the standard of several of the midland counties in the general excellence of the horses used in agriculture, weight, quality, and soundness have greatly improved, largely due to the high-class studs of Shire horses at Batsford and Blaisdon, while those at The Hendre, Buscot, and Wantage in adjoining counties have contributed to this result. There are also several societies that hire a stallion for the benefit of their members, and individual landowners have done much to assist in this important matter. Although Shire horses are generally speaking not so saleable as before the days of motor lorries, the best animals have maintained their value, and there is no difficulty in obtaining a remunerative price for a heavy Shire gelding six years old and suitable for town work. Hunters are bred to a moderate extent chiefly in the vale, but the majority of horses of this description in the county are bred in Ireland, a large number being brought over by dealers and sold at Barton Fair, held at Gloucester at Michaelmas.

Pigs bred in the county are mostly Berkshires or crosses with that breed. Now that fat bacon is not so much appreciated the cross with the Tamworth is a favourite and produces a very saleable carcass. Large and Middle White pigs, and the breed of Large Blacks, are more generally seen than a few years back. There is a bacon factory at Cirencester dealing with a great quantity of pigs that is advantageous to feeders in that neighbourhood, which, however, does not nearly supply its requirements, and similar factories are at Ebley and Newmarket.

Of late years a great increase in the quantity of poultry has been evident. The large number of portable poultry houses seen in the fields enable fowls to be kept in a more healthy condition than when aggregated in large flocks about the homestead. As an adjunct to an agricultural holding poultry may doubtless be kept at a profit, but the soil and climate of the county is not as a rule suitable for poultry farms pure and simple.

The Cirencester Agricultural Society was founded by the third Earl Bathurst in 1828. Subsequently its scope of operations was enlarged, and it became the parent of the Gloucestershire Agricultural Society. An annual show of live-stock and implements is now held at the principal centres of population in rotation. There are also agricultural associations at Badminton and Lydney, while the Berkeley Hunt Society has instituted examinations in the various technical subjects connected with the business of agriculture that have been taken up by the young farmers of the district with commendable enthusiasm. The Cotswold Society holds an annual show at Northleach, Stow, or Chipping Norton, and the Moreton-in-Marsh and Lechlade Societies have for their object the promotion of the breeding of Shire horses. At Winchcombe and elsewhere one-day shows have been successful and popular, and excellent exhibitions of roots, grain, and produce are annually held at Gloucester and Cheltenham.

The Kingscote Farmers' Club was for many years a centre where addresses were given on agricultural topics followed by discussion throughout the winter months, and the Gloucestershire and Cirencester Chambers of Agriculture, and the North Cotswold Farmers' Club are affiliated to the Central Chamber, and debate matters relating to the practice of the farm and measures before Parliament affecting agriculture at their meetings throughout the year.

Several associations have recently been started in the county for the purpose of co-operation among farmers to enable them to buy seeds, artificial manures, and implements in larger quantities and on more advantageous terms, and are making satisfactory progress.

The markets making returns of sales of corn to the Board of Trade are Gloucester, Cirencester, Cheltenham, and Tewkesbury. For live stock there are markets at Gloucester, Tewkesbury, Berkeley Road, Cirencester, Andoversford, Fairford, Lechlade, Nailsworth, Tetbury, Chipping Norton, Bourton-on-the-Water, and Winchcombe. These have largely taken the place of the fairs that were formerly the only centres for the disposal of stock, but Barton Fair at Gloucester in September, Stow Fair in May, and at Cirencester the fairs for fat and store sheep in May and September, and the ram fair in August, attract large numbers of animals for disposal, and are attended by buyers from all parts of England.

No review of Gloucestershire Agriculture would be complete without a reference to the Royal Agricultural College at Cirencester, which was established in 1845, and was the first institution where opportunity was given to learn the science and practice of agriculture. It originated in an address to the Cirencester and Fairford Farmers' Clubs in 1842 on 'the advantages of a specific education for agricultural pursuits,' by the late Mr. Robert Jeffreys Brown, of Cirencester, who devoted an immense amount of time and energy to explaining his objects to landowners and agriculturists throughout the kingdom and interesting them in the subject. By Mr. Brown's efforts a large sum of money was raised by subscription, a charter obtained, and the erection of the college and farm buildings commenced on a farm offered by Earl Bathurst. Owing to the cost of the college and buildings having been greatly under-estimated there was some unforeseen delay, but the necessary funds were raised and the college was opened for the reception of students in 1845. At the present time from fifty to sixty in-students are received in the college, and there are about twenty to twenty-five out-students who reside in the town of Cirencester. The curriculum is divided into three courses. The full-diploma course has two branches, namely, what is called the estate branch for landowners, estate agents, and surveyors, and the farming and colonial branch for intending farmers and colonists. The full course occupies a period of two years, but there is also a special one-year course for out-students only. The subjects are Practical Agriculture and Dairy Farming, Agricultural Chemistry (theoretical and practical), Bacteriology, Physics and Mechanics, Geology, Botany, Entomology, Book-keeping, and Mensuration, Land Surveying and Levelling, and Veterinary Surgery. The special subjects for the Estate Branch Diploma are Estate Management, Forestry, Agricultural Law, Building Construction and Materials, and Architectural Drawing.

Besides the daily lectures and practical classes on the farm, instruction is given in butter and cheese making at a model dairy where Cheddar, Cheshire, Stilton, Wensleydale and cream cheeses are made.

At the present time the Earl of Ducie is the president of the council, which includes several other landowners, and the principal is the Rev. J. B. McClellan, M.A., who is assisted by a staff of resident professors. There are also several honorary professors of eminence, who act as external examiners. The value of the instruction given at the Royal Agricultural College is recognized by the Indian Government, which sends several native students over for the Diploma Course, granting them a financial allowance for the purpose, in order that they may qualify for appointments in the Indian Agricultural Service, in which there are now many who have received their agricultural education at Cirencester.

About 30 acres of land immediately adjoining the college buildings are reserved for the dairy and for experimental purposes, but the farm itself is not now managed by the college, but is in the occupation of Mr. Russell Swanwick, an old diploma student, who is well known, not only in Great Britain and the Colonies, but on the Continent and in the United States, as an eminent breeder of Cotswold sheep, Berkshire pigs, and thoroughbred horses. The farm consists of 465 acres, of which 204 are at present in permanent pasture, including some laid down in recent years. By arrangement with Mr. Swanwick the students have full access to the farm, the various operations being daily explained by the professor of agriculture.

The museum contains samples of seeds, models of cultivated roots, collections of wool, cereals, and grasses, and a dentition collection, &c. The laboratory is well equipped aud there is a large botanical garden. At a short distance is the veterinary hospital, fitted up for the reception of diseased or injured animals, with farrier's shed, and the necesssary accommodation and appliances for performing operations and conducting post-mortem examinations. The examinations for the diploma and other honours are largely conducted by the external examiners, who are recognized authorities in their respective subjects.

Since the opening of the college many practical experiments have been carried out on the various soils of the district in order to ascertain the quantities and descriptions of the manures best suited to the crops grown upon them, and feeding experiments on sheep and cattle. Many of these have been fully described in the journals of the Royal Agricultural Society of England, and have proved of great service to agriculturists.

Agricultural instruction is also given through the County Council by means of classes held throughout the county by experts for the benefit of young farmers, and others when such subjects as the Principles of Manuring Soils, Injurious Insects, Diseases of Crops, Farm Weeds, Feeding Stuffs, Management of Live Stock, Grasses and Clovers, &c., are explained by lectures followed by discussion. Dairy classes are also held at the Central School, Gloucester, as well as at other centres, and visits of advice are paid to cheese and butter making dairies where difficulties have been experienced. Popular lectures on Farriery, Horticulture, Poultry-keeping, and Bee-keeping, and instruction in Thatching and Hedging have also been given, with satisfactory results. The work of the County Council as regards cider-making has already been mentioned and has proved useful. The amount of money annually placed at the disposal of the agricultural sub-committee by the Education Committee of the County Council is only £1,500, although agricultural land pays a very large proportion of the county rate. Of this sum £100 is allocated to scholarships at agricultural schools or colleges, £100 is contributed to the National Cider Institute, and the remainder is absorbed in lectures, classes, examinations, research and establishment charges. At the present time several series of experiments in manuring are being carried out on different farms by Mr. Drysdale Turner, the Agricultural Director.

The present condition of agriculture in the county may be said to be satisfactory. Rentals on the hills have probably fallen since 1875 on the average at least fifty per cent., and in individual cases the reductions are still greater. In the vale the reduction may be averaged at twenty per cent. Landowners are, however, still required to pay the tithe rent-charge and keep their buildings in repair, which costs at least as much as when rents were at the higher standard. Meanwhile the tenant farmers have, with the help of their reduced rents and improved implements, together with increased attention to business, succeeded in adjusting their practice to the altered circumstances, and although fortunes cannot now be easily made in agriculture, there is no occupation presenting such attractive features to the man with moderate capital as that of a tenant farmer upon a large estate under a landlord who may be relied on to deal fairly with his tenants, as is happily the general rule in the county of Gloucester.

FORESTRY

ALTHOUGH the woods of Gloucestershire, covering some 61,184 acres, are surpassed in extent by those of at least five other counties, Yorkshire, Hampshire, Sussex, Kent, and Devon, yet in respect to forestry they yield in interest and importance to none. Not only does Gloucestershire possess a climate admirably suited for the growth of timber, but it contains in the Forest of Dean the largest block of crown woodlands which has been consistently utilized during a long period for the production of timber on more or less business-like principles. From the sixteenth century till the modern development of communication by land and water, the Forest of Dean formed the largest and most valuable oak-growing tract[1] within the kingdom. To-day it is the centre of the scientific forest management lately introduced by the State.

The county of Gloucester naturally falls into three great divisions, which run in nearly parallel lines from north-east to south-west, the rolling hills of the Cotswolds, the fertile valley between them and the Severn, and on that river's western bank a district 'all shaded with woods' which finds its most complete expression in the Forest of Dean.

As to the Cotswolds it is possible that at a remote period the range was clothed with beech woods. Aboriginal tribes at first clung to the hills, but when in the process of time these primaeval woods were cleared, the chalky soil would soon pass into a barren and treeless condition, incapable of becoming re-wooded in the ordinary course of nature. The complete denudation of lime and chalk hills can be performed in a very short space, while an attempt to reclothe them with timber forms one of the most difficult tasks in forestry and requires a long period for accomplishment. It is only here and there, as for instance on Earl Bathurst's estate near Cirencester, that remains of these primaeval beech-woods would seem to be in existence.

For the extent of woodland in the county in the pre-Conquest period we must largely depend on inferences from the casual entries of Domesday, and the evidence of place-names. But on a general view[2] it may be stated, with the proviso, however, that the central division was then far more heavily wooded than at present, that in the eleventh century the woodland was generally densest in the same parts of the shire as to-day. It may be convenient to collect here a few historical notes as to the forests east of the Severn before dealing with what must form the centre-piece of even the slightest discussion of the Gloucestershire woodlands—that

Queen of forests all that west of Severn lie[3]—

the Forest of Dean.

The Forest of Corse,[4] which lay within the Gloucestershire border, is generally considered in connexion with Malvern Chase and need not detain us here, but it is necessary to mention the woods in Kiftsgate hundred, at Sudeley,[5] Toddington, and Twyning,[6] which were of considerable extent. Indeed it is worth notice that in the north, as in the south and west, great masses of forest lay along the county boundary.

A reference to the Pipe Roll[7] of 1130 brings to our notice a royal forest of slight extent which brought in profits (*census*) amounting to 40s. There styled the Forest of Cirencester, it possibly included one if not both of the two woods entered in the great survey

---

[1] As Mr. Philip Baylis, His Majesty's Deputy Surveyor in the Forest of Dean, kindly points out, both the diarists Evelyn and Pepys, who may be regarded as expert witnesses where timber is concerned, pay a high tribute to that produced in the Forest ; Evelyn, *Diary* (ed. Wheatley, 1879), ii, 154 ; Pepys, *Diary* (ed. Wheatley, 1903), iii, 20.

[2] For a particular discussion of the Domesday woodland and the inferences derivable from the pannage entries see the Domesday article in *V. C. H. Glouc.* i.

[3] Drayton, *Polyolbion*, Song 7.

[4] The Forest of Corse or Cors, was apparently in the hands of the Clares at least as early as 1247, as appears from the inquisition held on the lands of Richard de Clare ; *Cal. Inq. p. m. Hen. III*, 156. Trespassers against the venison seem to have been imprisoned in Worcestershire, and Gloucestershire men much resented being thus haled across the border ; *Hund. R.* i, 179.

[5] Domesday mentions here a wood three leagues long by two broad.

[6] Twyning at least was said to have been at one time a parcel of the great Worcestershire Forest.

[7] (Ed. Hunter, 77.) Even in the Confessor's time, according to Domesday, part of the render at Cirencester was food for the king's hounds.

as belonging to the king's land in Cirencester hundred,[1] and was really an overlapping portion of the Wiltshire forest of Braden detached as an adjunct to the royal demesne of Cirencester. Its early status as a royal forest may also be gathered from a charter[2] of Henry I to the abbey of Cirencester in which is mentioned 'a water-course and the wood called Acley (Oakley), with the foresters and their land, and I retain nothing to myself out of the wood beside my hunting only, and the abbot may not assart it ;' while a further grant[3] or regrant of Richard I to the same house excepts only 'the pleas of our Crown and our forest of Mynthy, which we have reserved to ourselves.' This small forest is now represented by the fine woods on Earl Bathurst's estate already referred to.

No certain evidence has been adduced that Woodchester Park[4] was ever forest in a technical sense, even under the Angevins ; but the country between Huntingford and the Wood of Furches,[5] or Furcis, near Bristol, was for the most part afforested after the coronation of Henry II[6] either by that king or his sons and doubtless for reasons of revenue. A nucleus for this afforestation was however found in the ancient royal park of Alveston, which is specifically mentioned[7] in the Pipe Roll of 1130, and which was excepted from the disafforestation of 1228.[8] Alveston Park was, how-ever, in 1230 granted to Fulk FitzWarin, and a few years later stocked for his use with deer from the royal forests of Braden and Chippenham.[9] Within the area above-mentioned, which was often styled the Forest of Horwood, lay the manor of Pucklechurch, for which the bishop of Bath and Wells took out a special certificate of disafforestment, while the inhabitants in and about the forest paid a fine of 200 marks for the relinquishing of the royal rights.[10] In the Forest of Horwood the clearance of the woodlands since the Domesday time is specially noticeable, and was no doubt quickened in no ordinary degree by the forges of Iron Acton and its neighbourhood.

On the southern fringe of Horwood Forest proper, along the border of the shire, and over-lapping into Somerset, lay a wooded and furze-clothed tract appendant to the castle of Bristol, a portion of it being known at an early time as the wood of Furches. For example, in 1224 the king committed[11] the castle of Bristol 'cum bertona et foresta et chascia brullii de Kainesham et bosco de Furches et omnibus aliis ad castrum illud pertinentibus' to the custody during pleasure of Ralf of Wilinton. This tract at least as early as the reign of Edward I became known as the Forest or Chase of Kingswood, and frequent references to its keeper and other officers, or to trespasses against the king's vert or venison therein, are found on record.[12]

For instance, in 1275[13] Bartholomew Le Jevene, constable of Bristol Castle, was ordered to pay Hugh of Malvern, keeper, $7\frac{1}{2}d$. daily for the maintenance of himself and of three foot

---

[1] C. S. Taylor, *Dom. Surv. of Glouc.* 164.   [2] Dugdale, *Mon.* vi, 177.

[3] *Cal. Chart. R.* i, 145 ; Dugdale, *Mon.* vi, 178.

[4] It is not unlikely however that Woodchester Park may have been afforested in the reigns of the Conqueror's sons.

[5] In the account of the honour of Gloucester rendered by William de Faleisa and Master Swein we find an entry on the Pipe R. 2 John, of £17 1s. 1½d. for sales in the Wood of Furches.

[6] Close, 12 Hen. III, m. 10 d. ; and *Cal. Chart. R.* i, 75. The northern part of this region near Kingswood Abbey was probably royal forest as early as the reign of Hen. II (Dugdale, *Mon.* v, 427), while the Pipe R. 1 John shows that in the south the abbot of Glastonbury was fined 10 marks for old and new waste at Pucklechurch. It is possible that the afforestation of Pucklechurch was first made before the reign of Hen. II, since in his grandfather's time Theodric the miller of 'Popelicercha' owed 15 marks of silver to the king *pro placito cervi* ; Pipe R. for 1130.

[7] 'In terra lucrabili que capta est infra Parcum de Aluestan lxxij*s* numero.'

[8] *Cal. Chart. R.* i, 75.   [9] Close, 18 Hen. III, m. 6.

[10] *Cal. Chart. R.* i, 75, 104 ; Fine R. 12 Hen. III, m. 5 ; Pipe R. 12 and 13 Hen. III.

[11] Pat. 8 Hen. III, m. 2. In regard to the question of the early afforestation of this land near Bristol it is significant that in the reign of the Confessor 'Bertone' made a render of food (*panes*) for the king's hounds.

[12] Although the name Kingswood has occasionally been applied by modern writers to the whole area at one time afforested between Huntingford and the Avon, yet in the Patent Rolls of Hen. III (e.g. a°. 8 m. 10), the Forest of Harewood (Horwood) and Alveston is apparently distinguished from the tract afterwards known as Kingswood. It has also been most commonly assumed that Kingswood was disafforested by the charter procured by the men of Horwood in 1228. If so it could only have been in part, as a large parcel of Kingswood lay in Somersetshire. In this connexion it may further be suggested that the wording of this instrument does not forbid the interpretation that the 'Wood of Furches' is mentioned therein as a limit and need no more be regarded as necessarily situate within the metes of Horwood than 'the water of Severn' similarly named as a boundary. However this may be, as late as the reign of Edw. I, the royal writs assumed that there were verderers and regarders as well as foresters and agisters in Kingswood (Pat. 6 Edw. I, m. 19), and in 1285 the commission to R. de Hengham and W. de Wymburn to take all pleas touching the king's chase of Kingswood was coupled with a mandate to the sheriffs of Gloucestershire and Somersetshire apparently couched in terms usual when the forest law was in force (Pat. 13 Edw. I, m. 28). Mr. A. Braine, who in his interesting *Hist. of Kingswood Forest*, accepted the Horwood charter as referring to the Gloucester portion of Kingswood, found it necessary to add (p. 30) : 'But it is certain that the mandate was ignored, if not altogether set aside, by subsequent authorities.'   [13] *Cal. Close* (1272-9), p. 202 (m. 8).

serjeants as long as he shall have the custody.   On 22 September of the following year[1] we catch a glimpse of the early stage of industrial development which in modern times has made Kingswood one of the colliery districts of Western England, for then the same constable is ordered to permit Petronilla de Vivonia, wife of David Le Blund, to dig sea-coal in her wood within the king's chase of Kingswood, as the king learns by inquisition taken before him at Bristol that Petronilla and her ancestors from time out of mind were wont to dig sea-coal in the said wood until Robert Waleraund, then constable, wilfully hindered her.   The king, however, still cared for his deer, and although Thomas de Berkeleye was granted a licence[2] in 1283 to hunt the fox, hare, badger, and cat in the Forest of Mendip and in the Chase of Kingswood on both sides of the River Avon by Bristol except in the fence-month, it was with the proviso that he should take no deer nor course in the king's warrens.   Early in the reign of Edward III inquisition[3] was made into the condition of the Forest of Kingswood and the Somerset Chase of Filwood, which were still grouped together, and the keeper Michael de Aune was found to have felled a hundred oaks in the forest and taken 80 acres of 'gorst' and converted the profits to his own use, and also taken six bucks and six does of the king's venison without warrant.

A few years later, in 1336, a commission[4] was appointed to survey the wastes of the free chase of Kingswood, which was held for life by Queen Philippa, and to approve and lease these to tenants for life or for a term of years in order that they might assart them and bring them into cultivation.   But we are debarred from following in detail the history of this forest or chase.   During the reign of Henry VIII the rangership or custody of Kingswood was with the Berkeley family.   For a short time in the reign of Philip and Mary it was held by Sir Nicholas Poyntz, and a Star Chamber case[5] at that time throws considerable light on the condition of the forest.   Edward Reve, who acted as the deputy of Poyntz, complained that Richard Barkley of Stoke, 'a young gentilman of verey light disposition and havour,' with over twenty others, 'riotously arraid in harnes,' about midnight on Epiphany eve hunted in the forest and set on fire a great part of the furze and covert.   Challenged by Reve, Barkley called him 'villayne, with diverse other words of reproche,' and some of the attendant malefactors waylaid the ranger and beat him.   In the May following while Reve was away in the service of the crown on the high seas, Barkley broke into his house and carried away 'one hound called a brache.'   Again on 20 September 1 & 2 Philip and Mary the same offender sent a number of riotous persons, mainly his household servants, eight on horseback with 'long chasing staves,' and the rest on foot and assaulted two of the keepers Edward Bassett and George Reve, tearing them from their horses which they hamstrung.   So mangled with sword-cuts were the keepers that their lives were despaired of, the unfortunate Reve losing one hand clean cut off, while, in the language of the bill, the other arm 'unnethily hangith by the skynne.'

The Council immediately called on Barkley and his friends to answer these grave matters. The principal offender had evidently a weak case.   He first alleged spite on the part of Poyntz, and declared with respect to the first allegation that he had been peaceably 'byrdebeyting' with Hugh Partridge and other of his servants, but on his return within a quarter of a mile of his house of Stoke Park and a mile beyond the forest he was met by Reve and 'ij other wilfull and yvell disposed persons' who dogged his footsteps, and if they were assaulted by his servants they deserved everything they got.   As for the 'brache,' it of its own free will joined his hounds in a certain village, stayed two or three days and went home again.   The other allegations he absolutely denied, and disclaimed responsibility for the murderous attack on the keepers.

If this case fairly illustrates the lawlessness which prevailed at Kingswood, and if the constant encroachments of the coal-workings be considered, we are prepared for the picture drawn of the forest some sixty years after in Norden's Survey.[6]   Norden having taken 'the depositions of divers ancient borderers,' points out that the herbage for the deer was practically the only thing reserved to the Crown, for various claimants 'doe swallowe up the whole forest not allowinge his Majestie the bredth of a foote' while 'the timber, wood, bushes, soyle, coale mines and all other profittes altogether are carried from his Majestie by unknowne righte' whereas in other forests 'truely knowne owners cutt not downe their trees or woods of covert without the specyall lysence of the Justice of Oire.'

Kingswood Forest[7] was then divided into four 'walks' and as many keepers were allowed, 'all havinge under their charge by theire owne depositions not above 100 or 120 deere at the most.' As to the lodges, not one was in use for its original purpose; the oldest was utterly decayed, while a second dating from the reign of Henry VIII, which stood within the claim of Mr. Richard

---

[1] *Cal. Close* (1272–9), p. 310 (m. 4).   [2] Pat. 11 Edw. I, m. 23.   [3] Close, 2 Edw. III, m. 4.
[4] Pat. 10 Edw. III, pt. ii, m. 35 d.   [5] Phil. and Mary, $\frac{2}{23}$.
[6] S.P. Dom. Jas. I (1615), lxxxiv, 46.
[7] The name was now restricted to the Gloucestershire portion of the ancient Forest of Kingswood, the Somerset portion being known as Filwood Chase.   This distinction had been made at least as early as the reign of Edw. III, see text and *n.* 3 *supra*.

Barkley, had been 'converted to an alehouse' and was 'now fitt to harbor theves and enemes to the game.' Each of the four keepers received 40s. a year and certain known casual profits, while the ranger took an annual fee of £3 8s. 1½d. These payments were made by the sheriffs of Bristol, who were allowed an equivalent reduction in their 'accompt in the Chequer.'

Furthermore 'sheepe and goates[1] most pernitious cattle, intollerable in a forest make a farr greater shewe then his Majesties game; as for the goats they have confounded by their barkeing and pelling of the barke infinite manie faire hollyes the chefest browse now in use,' while the 'coale mines also devoure the principall hollies in all partes of the forest for the supportation of their pitts' and generally impair the herbage.

Formerly the keepers used to cut down oak boughs 'as bigge as a soare or soarell could turned over with his head' and sell the wood to their own profit. This however had been lately discontinued, but only apparently because 'euerie pretended owner presumes at his owne will to cutt downe his woodes.' The keepers were thus forced to take 'bush browse' or else famish the deer in winter, and even then were deprived by the woodwards of every division of the 'offal' of the 'small browse,' so that they became 'the more remisse in gaurdinge and releveinge his Majesties game.'

Other complaints were made as to the superfluity of cottages 'raysed upon the forest' and maintained under the toleration of the Statute for the erecting of houses in mining districts. The annual value of the coals taken was by deposition £200, but Norden understood 'by relation' that it should be £500.

The largest claim was one of 1,380 acres by Mr. Thomas Chester, but the surveyor had heard that 'there was a judgement for the king' as to this property. Many timber trees had here been felled and sold, and the waste was still going on, while Player the 'generall fermer of the coales' dug daily in the same division. 'Considering the judgement it were fit he were inhibited *quousque*.' Chester's bailiff had also received 32s. as 'wood-lease silver' from Filwood Chase payable at Martinmas. The Lord Barkley and Lady Newton claimed 1,350 acres; Sir Henry Billingsley 810 and Richard Barkley 540, while smaller holders with 218 brought up the whole area of the chase to some 4,298 acres.[2]

It is quite clear from this survey that Kingswood had, even in the early seventeenth century, ceased to be of much importance as a covert for deer, while waste of the vert and the extension of coal-mining were rapidly destroying its early character. The later history of the forest, largely made up of efforts on the part of the Crown to reassert its rights, and the resistance, active and passive, of grantees and squatters accompanied by the further deterioration of the remaining woodland, cannot be told here. When in the eighteenth century Whitefield[3] preached to the miners of Kingswood, and noted the tears that furrowed white runnels on their grimy cheeks, the king's deer had long vanished and little timber still remained.

The history of the Forest of Dean[4] can be carried back beyond the Conquest, for under the Confessor three thanes had held land in Dene free from geld by the service of guarding the forest.[5] The tract between the Severn and the Wye has always been the most heavily wooded in the shire, though even at this early period assarts had been made and the iron forges had begun to thin the brushwood if not the timber, for doubtless the render of iron[6] from Gloucester in King Edward's days came from Dean. The precise extent of this royal forest at the Conquest is unknown, but its boundaries at least on the south and east may not have differed widely from its present limits.[7] Quite early in his reign King William had made acquaintance with the Forest of Dean, for he was hunting here in 1069 when news was brought of the northern rising.[8] At his command[9] two manors, Hiwoldestone and Wigheiete, had been added to the forest before the date of Domesday, and after his death the further expansion of the area subject to forest law was determined as much by the necessities of revenue as by considerations of sport. According to the finding as to the ancient metes and bounds recorded on the Close Roll[10] of 12 Henry III, this extension of the forest to Gloucester and Newent on the north and Chepstow on the south had taken place

---

[1] This, as Mr. Philip Baylis kindly points out, illustrates Manwood's dictum that neither goats nor sheep were commonable in a forest. As to the case of sheep, compare the almost contemporaneous disputes in the forest of Essex or Waltham; *V.C.H. Essex*, ii, 'Forestry.'

[2] For a later survey of 1652 see Rudder, *Gloucestershire*, 458, n.w. The acreage within the metes and bounds there given was 3,432 acres and 2 roods.

[3] Gillies, *Life of Whitefield* (1772), 38.

[4] We are indebted in this section to the valuable assistance and suggestions of Mr. L. F. Salzmann, B.A.

[5] Dom. Bk. 167b.   [6] Dom. Bk. 162a.

[7] C. S. Taylor, *Dom. Surv. of Glouc.* 25. The present area of the Forest of Dean proper as defined by the Act of 1831 is about 24,000 acres. Outside this area to the west are the High Meadow Woods purchased by the Crown in the early part of the last century, and comprising within the Gloucestershire boundary nearly 3,000 acres.

[8] Ordericus, *Hist. Eccl.* (Migne), 317.   [9] Dom. Bk. 166b, 167a.   [10] m. 10d.

before the time of Henry II. And that the jurors referred to the reign of his grandfather can hardly be in doubt, if we consider the character and fiscal policy of Henry I and the parallel case of the forest of Essex.[1] Fosbrooke, however, in his *History of Gloucestershire*[2] quotes the finding of a jury about 1300 that the extension of the Forest of Dean was due to King John. But this statement was erroneous, or at best only partially correct, as we gather from other records[3] that in the anarchy of Stephen's reign his predecessor's additions to the forests were allowed to lapse, and only under the stronger Angevins was the enforcement of the forest law revived within the extended limits. An entry in the Pipe Roll[4] of 1130 records that Hugh, the son of William FitzNorman the Domesday holder of Dene, rendered account of the profits of the Forest of Dean and the enclosures (*haiis*) of Hereford[5] to the amount of £13. In the next reign the defection of Miles of Gloucester from Stephen to the empress won from Maud a grant in fee of the castle of St. Briavel and the whole of the Forest of Dean.[6] On Miles' death,[7] the castle and the forest were no doubt claimed by his son Roger, who had little to fear from the weakness of Stephen. But it is significant that on Roger of Hereford's submission to Henry Plantagenet the castle of St. Briavel and the Forest of Dean were excepted by name from the lands which Miles had held and which were now granted afresh to his son.

The constable of St. Briavel's Castle appointed by the Crown was usually warden also of the Forest of Dean, and the Pipe Rolls of Henry II and his sons abound in references not only to the regular profits of the Forest of Dean, but also to the large amercements derived from the rigorous enforcement of the forest laws within its extended boundaries.[8]

The period from 1217, the year when the Charter of the Forests was granted, till 1301, when the bounds of Dean and other forests were reduced to nearly the ancient limits of the Conqueror's days, furnishes abundant matter for the historian and a very small selection of illustrative details from inquisitions and plea-rolls can alone be given here.

Among the King's Remembrancer's records in the Exchequer has been preserved a very early estimate of the profits[9] of the forest of 'St. Breavell' or Dean which is attributed to the reign of Henry III, and some of the items mentioned throw a welcome light on the economy of the forest. The annual rent with the weirs was £44 11s. 10d. The customs duty for every load or seam of sea-coal crossing the Severn was fixed at one halfpenny, and this was farmed[10] to Payn of Lydney for £24. The toll on the forest road to Gloucester only brought in 20s. Considerable income was derived not only from the fees paid by owners of 'forgee forincece'[11] within the forest, but from the leasing of mines of coal and iron. Besides these there were apparently mines in the king's hands and a royal forge returned as worth £50 a year, but as to this last item a finding on inquisition which was attached to the estimate is instructive. The jurors were asked to determine how much wood had to be furnished to keep the forge at work, and what relation the value of the timber granted bore to the issues of the forge. The verdict returned was that each week two and sometimes three oaks were required, and that the value of the timber granted much exceeded the profits and issues of the forge.

The windfallen timber and branches (*cablicium et coporones vento prostrata*) were estimated to bring in about £10 per annum, but much depended on the season. The pannage fees produced about twice as much, and the perquisites of the forest and hallmote of St. Briavel 100s. An entry of

---

[1] For this see J. H. Round, *Geoffrey de Mandeville*, 'Appendix on Forest of Essex,' and *V.C.H. Essex*, ii, 'Forestry.'

[2] Page 98. Cf. Forest Proc. Exch. Tr. of Rec. 255.

[3] Cf. Verdict of the 'leet before the foresters of fee' in 1300, and note the very specific statement as to the similar history of the Staffordshire forests, Forest Proc. Anc. Chanc. 45.

[4] Ed. Hunter, 77.

[5] It may be noted that according to Close 12 Hen. III, m. 10 d. the Bishop of Hereford had a 'chacia' in Laxpeniard Wood parcel of the forest. In the reign of Edw. I, about 1300, the regarders found that part of Dean overlapped into Herefordshire ; Forest Proc. Exch. Tr. of Rec. 255.

[6] Round, *Geoffrey de Mandeville*, 56.

[7] He had been slain by a chance arrow shot at a deer, while under excommunication by the Bishop of Hereford. The foundation of the Cistercian abbey of St. Mary de Dene (Flaxley) by Roger was doubtless part of the post-mortem rehabilitation of his father ; see Introduction to *Cartul. of Flaxley, passim*.

[8] The Pipe RR. 1 and 2 John are particularly interesting in this respect. Among many entries may be noted the case of William de Huntele who was fined 2 marks for the loss of the first regard of the Forest of Dean which was burnt in his house, and that of the Lady of Blakeney who paid 2 marks 'ut carbonarii Regis amoveantur de baillia sua.' Some at least of the bailiwicks mentioned in the regard of 1282 were already in existence.

[9] Forest Proc. Exch. K.R. $\frac{1}{26}$.

[10] As the customs duty paid on every seam of iron-ore was also one halfpenny it is probable, although not directly stated here, that this farm included both coal and iron ; cf. article on 'Mining' in the present volume.

[11] Of these there were at the time twenty-six for the whole forest, a number trebled by the early years of Edw. I.

I mark for nuts and chestnuts reminds us of the famous wood of sweet chestnuts[1] within the forest.

But it is to the rolls of the forest eyres[2] that we must turn for the most intimate picture of the condition of the forest during the reign of Henry III and his successor. The terms of the writs, sent to the sheriff of Gloucester and other officers, in respect to the highest forest court, show how far-reaching were its powers. For instance, in 1232 the sheriff was ordered[3] to summon to Gloucester, on the Monday before St. John Baptist's Day, to the presence of John of Monmouth and other justices of the forest, all prelates, barons, knights, and free tenants within the bounds of the forest, also from each forest vill four men with the reeve and the foresters of the vills, and also all men dwelling outside the forest who owed suit to the forest pleas or have been attached in respect to the forest. All the king's foresters and verderers were also to be present ready to produce all indictments of vert or venison which had arisen since the last eyre, as well as the regarders with their regards duly signed with their seals, and the agisters with their rolls of agistment.

The interest of the earliest roll of a Gloucester forest eyre now extant, that for 1258, lies principally in the mention of wild boar venison, such entries being by no means common[4] in the rolls of most forests and in some occurring not at all. In one of these cases the slayer, John le Vilayn of Blakeney was dead; in the other, two offenders who had killed 'unum porcum in foresta de Dene' had been lodged in Gloucester gaol, but did not put in an appearance before the justices.[5] There is ample evidence that in the denser parts of the forest wild boars were found in plenty, and King John had some forty years before[6] shown his solicitude for their preservation by ordering John of Monmouth, constable and warden in 1216, to see that agistments were only allowed in the skirts of the forest and not in places where the wild boars (*porci silvestres*) congregate and haunt. The tithes of wild boar venison, as well as venison of deer in the Forest of Dean, were assigned to the abbey of Gloucester.[7]

The depredations of the forest wolves are once noticed on the rolls of this eyre. Geoffrey son of Bernard[8] had found a deer (*bestiam*) strangled by wolves and carried off two of its shoulders (*scapulas*). Like John le Vilayn, however, he was beyond the jurisdiction of any earthly court. The fines for trespasses on the vert were sometimes as low as 12*d.*, often 2*s.* and occasionally half a mark or higher; those for purprestures, assarts, and waste ranged from 1*s.* to over 20*s.* Other amercements were for keeping hounds or neglecting to law those dogs permitted.

The rolls of the next forest eyre held in Gloucestershire, before Roger de Clifford the younger and his fellows in 1270, introduce us to that commonplace of forest proceedings, the malpractices of the royal officers. Robert le Waleys[9] constable of St. Briavel's and warden of the forest under Robert Walerand took fines from all the foresters to appoint them, and they recouped themselves by profitable connivance at offences, and by encouraging iron forges and charcoal-burning. During the time of this warden the forest was damaged to the extent of £307 13*s.* 4*d.*, in the time of John Gifford the loss was £1,320, and under Thomas de Clare £1,048 12*s.* Even the very timber destined for the repairs of the castle of St. Briavel had been stolen by Adam the reeve and his accomplices.[10] So serious[11] was the damage done by the excessive number of charcoal burners, who bought wood from the foresters and stole still more, that an order was issued that in future no one should hold any pit for making coals (*foveam ad carbonandum*) within the forest. The itinerant forges were also a serious nuisance from their enormous consumption of fuel. No less than forty-three of their proprietors are named, and amongst them Payn of Lydney, already mentioned. A notion of the very serious waste of timber produced by even one forge may be gathered from the history of that owned by the privileged abbey of Flaxley. Henry II had granted the monks the right of receiving two oaks a week for their forge. Constant friction with the forest officers followed, with resultant appeals to the Crown, until finally the early privilege of the two oaks a week was surrendered to King Henry III in exchange for a parcel of the forest given in almoin to the monks[12] and afterwards

---

[1] The tithe of these chestnuts had been granted by Henry Plantagenet to Flaxley; Dugdale, *Mon.* v, 590. The original site of Flaxley was known as Castiard, probably from the abundance of chestnut trees.

[2] For an exact account of the various forest courts and their officers the reader must be referred to Mr. Turner's Introduction to *Select Pleas of the Forest* (Selden Soc.).

[3] Close, 16 Hen. III, mm. 9 *d.* 10 *d.*

[4] Attention was first drawn to this in Mr. Turner's *Select Pleas of the Forest* (Selden Soc.), xii.

[5] Forest Proc. Tr. of Rec. No. 28, m. 4 *d.*   [6] Close, 18 John, m. 1.   [7] Cf. Close, 11 Hen. III, m. 26.

[8] Forest Proc. Tr. of Rec. No. 28, m. 4 *d.*   [9] Ibid. No. 29, m. 1 *d.*

[10] Nicholls, *Personalities of the Forest of Dean*, 18.   [11] Forest Proc. Tr. of Rec. No. 29. m. 2.

[12] For this charter see the Appendix to the *Flaxley Cartul.* 110. Reservations of interest were the eyries of hawks and any minerals that might be found. In 1899 the Crown repurchased from Messrs. Crawshay & Co. 666 acres of the 800 odd granted to the abbey at this time (*ex informatione* Mr. Philip Baylis,).

known as Abbots Wood. In connexion with the iron-working in the forest it is worth notice that certain burgesses of Bristol,[1] when they came into the forest to buy iron, commonly arranged with the poachers to supply them with venison.

Some of the clergy, secular and regular, lent their countenance to evildoers of the laity and shared an amiable weakness for unlawful venison. One notorious poacher,[2] Jordan Hok, who was dead in 1270, had supplied the prior of Lanthony and his subjects, and been harboured by them. In consequence the prior was imprisoned till he paid a fine of 20 marks. Jordan had also found shelter with Brother Gervase, 'preceptor' at the Templars' house at Garway, who was his accomplice in these deeds. Furthermore the abbot of Tintern[3] kept a band of poachers, whom Nicholas, prior of Striguil, occasionally harboured. The abbot of Tintern,[4] moreover, had dug a pond and erected a mill between the forest bounds and the Earl Marshal's lands of Striguil, so that deer no longer came out of the earl's domains into the king's forest as they were wont, and the mill was harbour for ill-doers. At Lydney[5] the canons of Hereford habitually sheltered poachers at their house there, and when it was raided by the officers they found half a deer (*bestia*) hidden in the straw which had been brought thither from a well-known poacher, Walter Kappe, by William, reputed a chaplain of the Bishop of Llandaff; the other half had been sent to the Dean of Hereford, who, with the precentor and chancellor, shared in these exploits; while one of the canons,[6] Thomas de Ingoldes-thorp, when granted five deer by the king allowed his men to take at least two more.

The pleas of the forest of the next eyre of 1282 are recorded very fully, and throw considerable light on the customs of Dean. The signature of trees for sale is referred to in several entries. Hugh le Bowewrite[7] of Bicknor sealed three oaks in the bailiwick of Staunton 'with a certain false seal at the time of the sale in the forest, which, however, he did not fell.' William Wytebred of Alyaston was found in the forest carrying a 'certain seal cut off from an oak previously sealed for sale (*prius signata sigillo vendicionis*) which he wished to place on another oak,' but he was forgiven; while Adam,[8] the reeve of St. Briavel, who as one of the sellers was carrying a seal[9] when his fellows were in the forest, went on his own account and made John the Clerk, of Dean, sound a horn and meanwhile sealed a certain oak fraudulently in the king's wood. John his accomplice was then clerk to the sellers.

In one[10] case of trespass against the vert certain offenders were attached while carrying away four oaks on four waggons drawn by thirty-two oxen. This timber was claimed as housbote and heybote for the parsonage of Awre by its rector Henry de Mauley, who had died before the time of the eyre. The justices, however, refused to admit the claim and fined his agents.

The famous chestnut wood is mentioned in several cases. Ralf of Abbenhale,[11] and his forester John of Penyard, swore that one Roger de Bosco had been caught during the night of Christmas eve trespassing therein with a hauling-team of six oxen. Roger stoutly denied that his visit was after nightfall, alleging a previous quarrel with Ralf to account for the charge, and this version was borne out by the verderers, foresters, and serjeants. So Ralf was convicted of a false indictment, though Roger did not escape punishment for his trespass on the demesne, being sentenced to prison and only enlarged on paying 4s. fine. In another case Ralf Cole actually was caught by night 'cum quadam coxa castanearum' and a team of six oxen, and it is ominously recorded that the verderers had valued the oxen, and Walter de Snapes the constable will account for their price. Furthermore, the famous 'chestnut grove'[12] had been much deteriorated, by bad management, and thirty-four 'cippi' had been felled worth 2s. or 3s. each. There had also been great waste and many malpractices as to the vert in other parts of the forest, Ralf de Abbenhale, forester in fee, being a conspicuous offender. Charcoal-burning and itinerant forges, of which last at least sixty proprietors are named, were still grievously complained of. In many places the undergrowth was greatly destroyed so that it would scarcely grow again. As to the timber, the bailiff declared he cut trees in the winter for the support of the deer; but the regarders pointed out that it was needless to cut so many or so valuable trees, as the undergrowth would have been sufficient. The truth was that there existed an extensive illicit trade in timber and underwood stolen from the forest, and lists[13] are given of boat owners plying to Bristol and elsewhere and ready to ferry purchasers to or from the western bank of the Severn.

---

[1] Forest Proc. Tr. of Rec. No. 29, m. 5 *d*.
[2] Ibid. m. 4.
[3] Ibid. m. 5.
[4] Ibid. m. 7 *d*.
[5] Ibid. m. 5.
[6] Ibid. m. 6.
[7] Ibid. No. 30, m. 3 *d*.
[8] Ibid. m. 4.
[9] In a mutilated account of Ralf de Sandwich as constable of the castle of St. Briavel, 4 Edw. I, under the heading of 'Expenses' we read : 'In uno sigillo faciendo ad vendicionem bosce 18 [*d*?]'; Mins. Accts. $\frac{850}{18}$ (P.R.O.).
[10] Forest Proc. Tr. of Rec. No. 30, m. 2.
[11] Ibid. m. 4. Compare for cases of trespass in respect to 'special vert' *V.C.H. Essex* ii, 'Forestry.'
[12] Ibid. m. 17.
[13] Ibid. m. 19.

Wolves still proved troublesome in the winter months, and deer were found torn by these unauthorized hunters, while poor men who took the venison to their use were summoned before the justices.[1]

The forest law showed itself no respecter of persons, and a few cases in which men of rank were concerned may suitably conclude our quotations from the forest pleas of 1282. The Bishop of Hereford's woodward,[2] who had been convicted of poaching, was presented by his master as a fit person to have care of the king's venison. In requital the Crown seized the bishop's wood. A riding forester (*forestarius chiminarius*) of the Earl of Warwick killed a roe (*capriolum*) in Cinderford Moor in the third year of Edward I, and hid the venison under the bed of Stephen the miller of Cinderford 'et loquendum de dicto comite qui talem forestarium posuit in foresta in officio forestarii.' The Bigods[3] were already showing their characteristic qualities and defying the king's officers. Presentment was made that Roger earl of Norfolk when with his household he came to Striguil (Chepstow) was wont to spread his nets outside his own chase and set his dogs within the forest to drive the game. His predecessor Roger Bigod also sent in his dogs in the same way, and the foresters thrice removed them, but were unable to make an attachment owing to the power of the earl. Moreover all the poachers of the king's venison were made welcome within the earl's liberty when the county had become too hot for them, and made their head quarters there. One final case[4] may be mentioned as of some legal interest. John Tregoz when hunting in 1260[5] in the wood of Penyard, which was disafforested by the king ' as it is said,' started a stag which he pursued into the forest and there took. He did not appear at the following eyre, but it was supposed that as he held by barony he would be amerced *Coram Rege*. It now appeared that he was not, and he declared with truth that on the former occasion he was not a baron, his father being alive, but only ' bachelarius.' The matter was adjourned for the king's consideration at the next Parliament.

The perambulation[6] made on Ash Wednesday, 1282, in connexion with this eyre shows that the forest was divided into ten bailiwicks, Abbenhale (Abenhall) and Little Dean under Ralf de Abbenhale, Blakeney under Walter de Austune, Bleyth (Bley) under Ralf Hatheway, Berse under William Wodeward, Staunton under Richard de la More, Bicknor under Cecily de Michegros, Lea under Nicholas de Lea, with Ruardean and Great Dean in the special custody of the constable of St. Briavel's. The crown still claimed as forest the area between the extended boundaries recited in the Close Roll of 12 Henry III already referred to, but in the dawn of the fourteenth century, during the last years of the first Edward and the reign of his successor,[7] the outlying portions of the Forest of Dean were disafforested, and the area again approximated to the earlier conditions before even Hewelsfield had been added to it.

Our limits of space do not allow more than an allusion to the constant grants to privileged persons either of timber or venison, from the Forest of Dean. Occasionally at an early period even as many as 100 oaks[8] were given at a time, as to the abbot of Pershore in 1233; while in the years following the Earl Marshal[9] was enjoined to take fifty good oaks as near as may be to the river Wye for the repair of his keep of Chepstow (*ad turrim suam de Striguil gistandam*). As to venison deer were occasionally taken for the king's use in quite a wholesale fashion. On 20 August,[10] 1278, for instance, the constable of St. Briavel's was ordered to allow the king's huntsman to take a hundred bucks in Dean Forest, which were to be salted and delivered in barrels at Westminster by the quindene of the Michaelmas following. Constant reference may also be found on the rolls to the levy of miners and archers for the king's wars and the provision of material for ammunition.[11] On 15 February, 1336,[12] the king sent Richard Garne the king's fletcher whose wage was 6*d.* a day

---

[1] Forest Proc. Tr. of Rec. No. 30, mm. 6 and 8 *d.* The underwood in the wood of Hope Maloysel (Mansel) was a special covert for wolves; Pat. 9 Edw. I, m. 19, and cf. licences issued to wolf-hunters in the Forest of Dean about this time; ibid. mm. 20, 23.

[2] Ibid. m. 7. *d.*

[3] Ibid. m. 11 *d.* It was found in 1228 that the Earl Marshal had the warren of Tudeham 'et ibi potest capere coopertum quicquid de venatione invenit'; Close, 12 Hen. III, m. 10 *d.* Early in the reign of Edw. I a jury declared that the Earl Marshal's free chase extended of old time ' a ponte de Strugull usque ad campum de Alumpton,' but in the time of Hen. III he (the earl) had gone beyond these ' metes ' as far as the 'campum de Hualdesfeld'; *Hund. R.* i, 176.

[4] Forest Proc. Tr. of Rec. No. 30, m. 12 *d.*   [5] 44 Hen. III.

[6] Printed in part in *Trans. Brist. and Glouc. Arch. Soc.* xiv, 356 et seq. from Forest Proc. Exch. Tr. of Rec. No. 31.

[7] Cf. Perambulation cited by Fosbrooke, *Glouc.* 98 et seq., also a further one recited (Forest Proc. Anc. Chanc. 45, P.R.O.), and for the reign of Edw. II note the evidence of Pat. 15 Edw. III, pt. i, m. 9, that by writ of his predecessor a perambulation was made by which the forest was diminished by one-fourth. This, however, may only have been in confirmation of the disafforestation of the latter years of Edw. I. But note as to one parcel a specific assertion of disafforestation under Edw. II; Pat. 3 Edw. III, pt. ii, m. 19.

[8] Close, 17 Hen. III, m. 9.   [9] Close, 18 Hen. III, m. 9.   [10] Close, 6 Edw. I, m. 5.

[11] For early references to the provision of war material from the forest, see ' Mining ' in this volume.

[12] See writ to the Exch. enrolled; Close, 11 Edw. III, pt. i, m. 33.

and ten working fletchers earning 3*d.* a day to the Forest of Dean to stay there till they had made a great number of darts (*pilorum*) which when manufactured were to be sent to the king at Berwick-on-Tweed.

One episode in the history of the forest during the reign of Edward III must be briefly noticed before we pass on to the later history. In 1340 Guy Brian,[1] constable of St. Briavel's and keeper of the Forest of Dean, complained that whereas the king had lately appointed him to his office at the rent of £160 at the Exchequer, the entire issues thereof were not estimated at more than £84 13*s.* ¼*d.*, and that as he could not meet the exorbitant rent without unduly wasting the forest he prayed for inquiry and relief. On the receipt of this petition Gilbert Talbot[2] and John Gogh were appointed to make an inquisition into the circumstances, and in their report state that the value of all manner of profits pertaining to the castle and forest reached £117 4*s.* 5¾*d.* They point out that in the time of Robert Walram (? Walerand) farmer of the forest who first fixed the assessment at £160 and some of his successors, some great forges with other smaller forges of the king in the forest were put down to avoid destruction of the vert. These had rendered £26 19*s.* 3*d.* to the farmer. Other causes contributory to the reduction of income were to be found in the late disafforestation of large tracts, amounting under Edward II to one fourth of the forest, and to the alienation by various kings of fisheries, weirs and lands granted by charter. In consequence the render at the Exchequer was graciously reduced to £120,[3] and as this was still ridiculously high a further allowance of £30 out of the farm of £120 was permitted in 1349 'on account of the present pestilence and divers other causes.'[4]

In 1390 the Parliament of the realm[5] ratified a grant by the king to his 'very dear uncle,' Thomas duke of Gloucester, of the castle of St. Briavel, and the Forest of Dean, 'as a forest' in tail male. On his death the forest seems to have been held for a few years by John of Gloucester,[6] a natural son of the king, but late in 1399[7] it was granted to John the second son of Henry IV, then a lad ten years old, later to be better known as the great Duke of Bedford. In 1429, when the Duke of Bedford still held the forest, the bailiffs and burgesses of Tewkesbury petitioned Parliament and complained bitterly of the lawless interference of men of the forest with the vessels and trows which trafficked between Tewkesbury and Bristol, and moreover that they could obtain no redress for the despoiling of their goods 'in as muche as the saide Forest and Hundredes been large cuntrees, and wylde of peple and negh adjoynaunt to Wales and alle the Commones of oon affinite in malice and riot.'[8] For the next hundred years the history of the forest is mainly composed of details as to the appointments of various officers and the accounts of their administration, and these must be omitted here. At the Reformation the large interests of Flaxley and other religious houses within the Forest of Dean passed to lay hands, Flaxley itself being granted to the Kingstons, whose descendants in the seventeenth century sold it to the Boeves.[9]

Although no eyre had been held for more than two centuries previous to the reign of Elizabeth, the lesser courts of attachment or wood-motes still existed, and some attention was paid to the condition of the vert in the interests of local officials and farmers of forest rights. At a court[10] at Kennysley (Kensley) in 1568 we find presentations not only for hunting, with long bows and 'arrows with forked heads,' but also for a series of offences against the vert, to wit—bill-hewing, the collection of 'okecornes,' 'beatyng chestnutts,' cutting great branches called 'le Great Lymes,' for cutting 'Tower bowys,' rooting up hollies, hawthorns and hazels, stubbing 'crabbe stockes,' cutting 'Tynnett,'[11] for 'yardyng,' 'bestyng,' 'barkyng,' 'rodyng,' 'browsyng,' for an axe (frequently), and other forms of waste.

In the sixteenth century general concern was aroused by the rapid destruction of the woods in many parts of the kingdom, this waste having been encouraged in no slight degree by the transfer of the woods of the religious houses to private hands, when in too many cases they were promptly cleared of timber. An attempt was made to check this devastation and promote recovery by judicious restrictions and enclosures under the Statute of Woods[12] of 1543, which was reaffirmed and strengthened by an Act of 1570.[13] Other Acts as well of the reign of Elizabeth show that the preservation of the woodlands was being generally recognized as a matter of national and not merely local interest.

There was a tradition[14] current in the early seventeenth century that the admiral of the Armada had special instructions should he effect a landing to destroy the Forest of Dean and thus

[1] See writ to the Exch. enrolled ; Close, 11 Edw. III, pt. i, m. 33.
[2] Pat. 14 Edw. III, pt. i, m. 14 *d.*   [3] Pat. 15 Edw. III, pt. i, m. 9.
[4] *Cal. Pat. Edw. III*, 1348–50, p. 428.   [5] Parl. R. iii, 278*b*; cf. Stat. 8 Hen. VI, cap. 27.
[6] Nicholls, *Personalities of the Forest of Dean*, 23.   [7] *Cal. Pat. Hen. IV*, 1399–1401, p. 159.
[8] Parl. R. iv, 345.   [9] Later spelt Bovey and Boevey.   [10] Forest Proc. Exch. K. R. $\frac{1}{30}$ (P.R.O).
[11] 'Tynnett' is brushwood of thorn used for repairing fences.
[12] 35 Hen. VIII, cap. 17.   [13] 13 Eliz. cap. 25.
[14] Evelyn, *Silva* (1776), 564, and compare another version in S. Hartlib, *His Legacie* (2 ed. 1652), 84, 'The Spaniard sent an ambassador purposely to get this wood destroyed.'

cripple the navy of England, and it has been stated[1] that Burleigh was so moved by this discovery as to institute in Windsor Forest a systematic scheme for rearing oak woodlands from acorns. Experiments in the Elizabethan Age with acorns, beech-mast, and chestnuts, too often however proved abortive, owing perhaps to the depredations of field mice,[2] and the efforts made to re-afforest in Gloucestershire in the seventeenth century were generally by planting.

In the reign of James I various proposals were suggested to the king and his advisers for increasing the profits to be derived from the Forest of Dean. In one survey[3] and estimate the forest was said to contain of 'greate standing woodes 15,000 acres, parte beinge tymber and parte other, the most parte well sett, the lawndes not accompted.' It was, however, reported to be so wasted and of so ill condition that the preservation of the woods would neither yield pleasure to the hunter nor profit to the owner. On the skirts the waste had been especially serious, and the timber generally converted to 'dotards.' Numbers of 'poore creatures' lived on the spoil of the forest wood, while by negligence of former officers the inhabitants have 'much insulted by cuttinge of trees.' As to the ten 'woodwards or baylyfes of fee,' 'experience proueth that they, theire tenauntes and servantes are as great spoilers as any others.' In conclusion, it was pointed out that the conversion of the wood to 'coles for makinge iron' or the selling of the timber by the ton was almost equally profitable, but perhaps rather more could be got from the ironworks. In 1611 a grant[4] was made to William, earl of Pembroke, of the castle of St. Briavel and of the Forest of Dean, and all lands, mines, and quarries belonging thereto, the timber and underwood being excepted, on a forty years' lease, at the yearly rent of £83 13s. 4d., and an increase rent of £3 8s., and he also obtained for a further payment an annual grant of wood for his ironworks. Some care, however, seems to have been taken to ensure a recovery in the wasted portions of the forest, as on 20 June, 1611,[5] we hear of money being paid for enclosing and fencing coppices in the Forest of Dean, and a little later a warrant was issued to the Earl of Pembroke and his deputy-constable, Sir Walter Mountague, charging them to preserve the woods there and signify His Majesty's displeasure against recent spoilers.[6] As a result of the Earl of Pembroke's lease, riots took place, the cutting down of wood for his works being resented[7] by the men of the forest, who were probably stirred up by iron-masters already settled there, while the free miners asserted their claims to continue their industry. An information against certain of the miners was filed in the Exchequer, and this resulted in an order[8] of the court, which was practically a compromise, though regarded by the miners as to some extent a record in their favour, and a confirmation of their customary right, since no new diggers were to be allowed, 'but only such poor men as were inhabitants of the said forest.'

Other leases beside that to the Earl of Pembroke were granted in the reigns both of James I and his successor, and some of them led to serious disturbances. On 21 March, 1631, 500 persons,[9] with two drums, two colours, and a fife, assembled with guns and pikes before the house of Robert Bridges of Bicknor, a servant of Lady Villiers, a lessee, under letters patent, and threw down 100 perches of newly-made ditching, and ended by proclaiming with an 'O yes' that if Bridges re-erected it against May Day next they would be ready to do him the like service again. There exists incontrovertible evidence[10] that the rioters had considerable sympathy and even assistance from the gentry of the forest. One ringleader,[11] William Vertue, attached by John Wragg, a messenger of the Star Chamber, turned the tables on his captor by having him arrested on a trumped-up suit for £500 in a local piepowder court, and Wragg, carried protesting to gaol, was hardly used, though he showed the Council's warrant for Vertue's removal. But Vertue was ultimately fined £100, and suffered a year's imprisonment. Even Peter Simon[12] the curate of Newland was suspected of complicity in the riot, and haled before the bishop of Winchester on a charge of upholding the doctrine of the equality of all mankind, only to explain painfully that, on the contrary, he had always maintained 'that there is upon kings and princes, God's character, which makes their persons sacred as God's anointed.'

---

[1] Menzies, *Forest Trees and Woodland Scenery*, 132. With regard to this story, however, it is worth notice that Dr. Cox in his *Royal Forests*, p. 299, attributes Burleigh's order to 1580.

[2] Standish, *New Directions of Experience for the Increasing of Timber and Firewood* (1615), 14. Cf. the plague of mice or voles which visited both the Forest of Dean and the New Forest in the years 1813–15 ; Nicholls, *Hist. of Forest of Dean*, 95.

[3] Caesar Papers (B.M.), Lansdowne MS. 166, fol. 354.

[4] *Third Rep. of Com. of Woods and Forests* (1788), 11.

[5] *Cal. S.P. Dom. Jas. I*, 1611, p. 46.   [6] *Cal. S.P. Dom. Jas. I*, 1615, p. 296.

[7] S.P. Dom. Jas. I, lxx, 49 ; cf. similar friction in the case of Sir Wm. Throckmorton in 1618 ; Nicholls, *Personalities of the Forest of Dean*, 104 et seq.

[8] On information filed by the Attorney General, Hilary, 10 Jas. I.   [9] S.P. Dom. Chas. I, clxxxviii, 20.

[10] *Cal. S.P. Dom. Chas. I*, 1633, p. 151, and cf. the case of the escape of a ringleader, John Williams, 'alias Skimmington,' and the sheriff's reply, S.P. Dom. Chas. I, cciii, 36.

[11] S.P. Dom. Chas. I, cciii, 104.   [12] *Cal. S.P. Dom. Chas. I*, 1631, p. 36.

FORESTRY

A survey[1] of the trees in the Forest of Dean, taken in 1633 by John Broughton, showed that there were then 166,848, worth on an average a pound apiece, and if very small trees and brush-wood were included the whole of the wood might be valued at £177,681 6s. 8d. George Dunning, an experienced 'ship-timber man,' assured the surveyor that there was timber enough there to furnish the kingdom with shipping, but Broughton evidently thought that the wood was most profitably employed for the king's iron-works. Unauthorized private persons, however, were fully aware of the excellence of Dean timber, and John Purnell,[2] in the autumn of the same year, was building a ship[3] of wood cut in the forest without leave or order, and had actually taken for her keel a beech 60 ft. long which was sealed with His Majesty's mark.

The king's financial necessities had now become insistent, and there is evidence,[4] as in the parallel case of the Forest of Essex, that the disafforestation of Dean was being considered, and propositions were eagerly made by interested parties. However, in Gloucester as well as Essex, it was determined instead to hold an eyre or justice-seat and claim boldly the ancient limits of 1228 and 1282, which would prepare the way for a harvest of heavy fines. Care was taken that the jury of regarders[5] should be packed with persons well-affected to the prerogative. When the justice-seat was held in 1634 at Gloucester Castle before the Earl of Holland, the Lord Chief Justice in eyre south of Trent and his fellows, not only were the extended bounds of 1228 and 1282 re-established and fines imposed to the amount of some £100,000,[6] but apparently even the claims of the free miners to their customary rights were rejected.[7] The old limits were, however, soon to be restored by the Act 16 Chas. I, cap. 16, one of the measures of the Long Parliament.

In the autumn[8] of the same year, on 11 October, a fierce gale wrought havoc in the forest. In hardly more than two hours at least one thousand trees were blown down, and the 'rude country people' claimed the windfallen trees as their due, so that the king's surveyor had some difficulty in preserving them. A few months after this certain contractors,[9] in forwarding proposals to the government with regard to the timber in Dean Forest suitable for the Navy, offered to plant new trees in the room of those they shall be licensed to fell, while almost contemporaneously the Lords of the Treasury resolved[10] to preserve the forest for a perpetual revenue by enclosing, to put down all iron-works[11] within the precincts of the forest, to preserve the timber trees for the Navy, and to allow no oaks to be felled, and further 'to acquaint the king with the improvement of the lease, which will hinder all propounders.' They saw that the shifts of the king to raise money, and the rapacity of commercial speculators, were ruining the forest.

In 1638, however, an elaborate survey[12] was made of the greater part of the forest, and the total number of trees in Dean, the Lea Bailey[13] excepted, was returned at 70,971 oaks, of which 24,549 were timber trees, 20,823 beeches, and 13,763 'stogalls,'[14] containing 61,928 tons of timber and 150,808 cords[15] of wood, besides the underwood furnishing some 2,401 cords. The total value of this timber and underwood was estimated at £120,261 2s. 2d. Upon this survey an entire sale was made by the Crown to Sir John Winter of all woods and waste ground belonging to the Forest of Dean except the Lea Bailey, with the wood, timber, mines, and quarries, in consideration of £106,000 to be paid by instalments, and a fee-farm rent of £1,950 12s. 8d. for ever.[16] Winter aroused intense opposition by his enclosures and by grubbing up trees and underwood, and during the Civil War the people of the forest took the law into their own hands, threw down his fences, and for a time local anarchy prevailed, order being ultimately restored by the strong action of the Parliamentary Government. Four years[17] before the Restoration an Act was passed annulling Winter's grant, and the Forest of Dean was vested in the Protector for the use of the Common-

---

[1] *Cal. S.P. Dom. Chas. I,* 1633, p. 191. [2] S.P. Dom. Chas. I, ccl, 80.

[3] At a later time ships were built at Bullo for the Crown from the forest wood and iron (*ex informatione* Sir Charles Dilke, bart.) Many details as to shipbuilding at Lydney and elsewhere will be found in *Cal. S.P. Dom. Interregnum and Chas. II.*

[4] Cf. S.P. Dom. Chas. I, cclvii, 93. [5] *Cal. S.P. Dom. Chas. I,* 1634, p. 576.

[6] S.P. Dom. Chas. I, cclxxiii, 13.

[7] *Third Rep. of Com. of Woods and Forests* (1788), p. 12.

[8] *Cal. S.P. Dom. Chas. I,* 1634, p. 237. [9] S.P. Dom. Chas. I, 1634–5, cclxxxiv, 22.

[10] *Cal. S.P. Dom. Chas. I,* 1635, p. 607.

[11] Sir Sackville Crow, in the January of this year, had declared most of these to be unauthorized; *Cal. S.P. Dom. Chas. I,* 1634–5, p. 487.

[12] Forest Proc. K.R. $\frac{1}{5 0}$ (P.R.O.).

[13] A recent estimate cited by the surveyor allowed 23,220 oaks and beeches for the Lea Bailey, and not above 120 had been cut or blown down since it was taken. About a quarter were beeches.

[14] A 'stogall' was a tree cut short or broken down with the wind.

[15] A 'cord' of wood as reckoned by this surveyor was in height 4 ft. 3 in., in length 8 ft. 3 in., in breadth 4 ft. 4 in. The statute cord now contains 128 cubic ft. viz. 4 ft. by 8 ft. by 4 ft. Mr. Philip Baylis kindly points out that in the Forest of Dean wood is cut by a cord of 128·5 ft., viz. 4 ft. 6·75 in. by 13 ft. by 2 ft. 2 in.

[16] *Third Rep. of Com. of Woods and Forests* (1788), 13. [17] Ibid. 14.

wealth.[1] At the home-coming of the king this resumption was declared void, Winter entered again and proceeded to repair his enclosures. But so strong was the opposition of the freeholders and commoners, that a commission was appointed to inquire into the matter (28 December, 1661); another careful survey was made, and the trees remaining in the forest were returned as 25,929 oaks and 4,204 beeches; in all 30,233 trees containing 121,572 cords of wood and 11,335 tons of timber fit for the navy. Sir Charles Harbord stated in an official minute at the time of the appointment of this commission that the old trees standing in the Forest of Dean were of above three hundred years' growth, and yet as good timber as any in the world.[2] No doubt he referred to 'many trees there left at a great fall in Edward the Third's time by the name of forbid-trees, which at this day are called vorbid trees,' concerning which Winter discoursed to Pepys over a venison pasty at the 'Mitre' one August day in the following year.[3] In consequence of the report rendered by the commission, Sir John Winter surrendered his patent and received a fresh grant of the trees of the forest except 11,335 tons of timber reserved for the navy, together with the king's iron-works, and liberty to dig for and take iron-ore and cinders.[4] The fortunate grantee used his opportunities to the full. In April, 1663, he had 500 cutters of wood employed in Dean Forest, with the result that the timber was rapidly disappearing. And in spite of orders and recommendations of the House of Commons, the waste went on for three or four years longer, a new survey in 1667 actually revealing that of the 30,233 trees sold to Winter only 200 remained[5] in the forest, while only 1,100 tons of the timber reserved for the navy had been delivered, a shortage of 7,000 or 8,000 tons.[6] The consequence of these proceedings and of the report of the committee appointed to inquire into the complaints of the freeholders and commoners was the passing in 1668 of an Act for the Increase and Preservation of Timber within the Forest of Dean (20 Chas. II, C. 3). It provided, amongst other things, that 11,000 acres[7] out of a total estimated area of 23,000 acres might be enclosed within two years, and made and reputed a nursery for wood and timber only, while all lands of late disafforested were to be re-afforested, as they were in the tenth year of King Charles I, and governed by forest law. The deer at any one time were never to exceed 800 in number, and miners' lawful rights and privileges were to extend over all the forest except the parts enclosed.

Under the direction of the Marquis of Worcester and other commissioners appointed under the above Act of 1668, 8,487 acres of the forest were speedily enclosed and planted, while the remaining 2,513 acres were enclosed some time afterwards in order to complete the 11,000 acres sanctioned. Great attention was paid to the protection of the young woods and enclosures by Sir Charles Harbord, Surveyor-General of the crown lands, and his successors, and it was chiefly from these parts of the forest that supplies of dockyard timber became available from about 1740 onwards. On Sir Charles Harbord's advice the forest was divided into six 'walks' or districts, a keeper was appointed to each 'walk,' and six lodges were built and enclosures made for the accommodation of these keepers; and these lodges appear to have been the only houses then to be found within the forest bounds.[8]

For about twenty years after the passing of the Act of 1668 the woodmote and swainmote appear to have been regularly kept, and the miners were thus prevented from wasting the woodlands; but at the time of the Revolution (1688) and before the new government was fully settled encroachments were renewed, while during the reigns of William and Anne the miners seem to have made use of fuel (but not timber) from the forest. In 1705 a careful survey was made and a simple working plan drawn up for the management of the forest by Edward Wilcox, esq.,

---

[1] 'Cromwell in his Military Parliament resumed this forest and re-afforested the said 18,000 acres (granted to Sir John Winter), and so preserved the same by the forest law, with all the wood and trees; and expelled near 400 cabins of beggarly people living upon the waste and destruction of the wood and timber, and great numbers of goats, sheep, and swine that destroyed the young wood and soil thereof; all which (said he) now began to invade the same as formerly' (Memorial by Sir Charles Harbord, 28 Dec. 1661); *Third Report, ut supra*, 14.

[2] Ibid. 14.

[3] Pepys, *Diary* (ed. Wheatley, 1903), ii, 306. It is worth notice that on 5 Nov. 1662 Evelyn in his *Diary* (ed. Wheatley), ii, 154, reports a meeting of the Royal Society at Gresham College, 'where was a discourse suggested by me concerning planting His Majesty's Forest of Dean with oak, now so much exhausted of the choicest ship timber in the world.'

[4] 'Vast heaps of cinders which they find, and are now of great value,' as Winter told Pepys.

[5] Winter's spoliation had been seconded by the ravage wrought by the great storm of 18 Feb. 1662.

[6] *Third Report ut supra*, 15.

[7] 10,000 being part of the waste lands.

[8] Sir Robert Atkyns, in his *Ancient and Present State of Glouc.* (1712), p. 348, says that 'there are only six houses in this great Tract of Ground, which are the Lodges for so many Keepers, each of which have a salary of £15 yearly paid out of the Exchequer, and an Inclosure of Ground for their Encouragement. There had been many Cottages erected, but they have been lately pulled down as the best means to preserve the Wood.'

Surveyor-General of Woods, which was sanctioned by Lord Godolphin. In his memorial to the Treasury the Surveyor-General stated—

> that he had carefully surveyed the Woods in the Forest of Dean, and found them very full of young Trees, Two-third Parts whereof were Beech which overtopped the Oaks and would prevent them from ever growing up to be Ship timber, so as to answer the Purposes intended by the Act of Parliament ; and setting forth that 11,000 acres had formerly been inclosed ; and that if the same should be divided into Sixteen Parts and One Sixteenth Part, being near 700 acres, should be cut down each year and inclosed, leaving Standards of Oak or Beech, each Cutting would yield £3,500, and Room would be given for the Standards to grow and come to perfection.

The inhabitants of the forest strongly objected to this as interfering with their right to common of herbage and pannage, but the right of the Crown to enclose 11,000 acres was fully maintained as indisputable. About this time (1705–12) the forest was probably in its best state, but soon after 1712 all care of the forest seems to have ceased, the forest courts no longer being so regularly kept as formerly, and abuses and neglect on the part of officials increased to such a degree that the yield of timber for the navy was unsatisfactory, and great waste was made in the forest. For example, in a list of officials made up at a swainmote, or swanimote, court on 25 September, 1787, no regarder is named, though there ought to have been twelve regarders ; and encroachments had taken place to such an extent since 1712 that there were in 1788 'no less than 589 Cottages, and 1,798 Patches or small Inclosures of Land containing 1,385 Acres, encroached from the Forest.' The regular holding of the woodmote had long been discontinued and the swainmote was held only once a year, on 25 September, at the Speech House in the forest, when it seemed to be held merely for the sake of form.[1]

About the year 1758 John Pitt, then Surveyor-General of the Woods, proposed that 2,000 acres should be enclosed in the Forest of Dean, and order was given accordingly. In 1764 a survey had been made of the timber in the forest, when it was estimated that there were 27,302 loads fit for the Navy, 16,851 loads of about sixty years' growth, and 20,066 loads dotard and decaying. But six years later Pitt, who had been removed from office in 1763 and reinstated in 1767, reported to the Treasury that great quantities of wood and timber, amounting in value to £3,235, had been cut by order of his predecessor, Sir Edmund Thomas, without warrant. He accordingly recommended further enclosures which were authorized, and a survey in 1783 showed that there then existed in the forest 90,382 oak trees estimated to contain 95,043 loads and 17,982 beech trees reckoned at 16,492 loads.

Several Acts had been passed during the eighteenth century for the protection of woods in general and the promotion of a secure supply of timber for shipbuilding, but the outlook in these respects was not very hopeful, when an Act was passed in 1786 for appointing Commissioners to inquire into the state and condition of the Woods, Forests, and Land Revenues of the Crown. Of the seventeen reports issued by these Commissioners between 1787 and 1793 the third, issued in 1788, deals in an exhaustive manner with the later history of the Forest of Dean, and has been largely drawn upon for the purposes of this account. The officers of the forest existing at this time were the Lord Warden and six deputy wardens, four verderers, a steward of the Swanimote Court. nine foresters in fee, of whom one was chief forester and bow-bearer, nine woodwards, but not one regarder, and six keepers ; but most of these forest offices had become merely nominal, and the real government of the forest 'in every particular except the mines and coal' had been for many years in the hands of the Surveyor-General,[2] the Deputy Surveyor, and the six keepers. As to the abuses prevailing from the system of perquisites and other causes the Commissioners were very plain-spoken, and distinctly stated that 'it was not to be expected that the resident officers of the forest would point out the true causes of the devastation from which their advantages arose.' There were at this time believed to be about five hundred deer 'of all sorts' in the forest.

The main subsequent result of the inquiry into the state and condition of the Crown Woods and Forests was the passing in 1808 of *An Act for the Increase and Preservation of Timber in Dean and New Forests* (48 Geo. III, cap. 72). As its preamble states, it was designed to overcome the 'great and increasing difficulty' of procuring heavy timber by giving more thorough effect to the Acts of 1668 (Dean Forest) and 1698 (New Forest) 'which said Acts have not been duly put in

---

[1] The woodmote, or Court of Attachments, is now regularly held at the Speech House every forty days before the verderers (*ex informatione* Mr. Philip Baylis).

[2] By the Stat. 33 Hen. VIII, cap. 39, the Court of General Surveyors of the King's Lands was established, which was to consist of the king's general surveyors and other officials. This court was dissolved by letters patent of the same reign (38 Hen. VIII), and a new court, called the Court of Augmentations, was created with all the powers of the former court. One master, one surveyor of the woods for the south, and one of each for the north of Trent, were members of it. The duties of the office of Surveyor-General are now discharged by the Commissioners for the time being of His Majesty's Woods, Forests, and Land Revenues ; and the office of 'Deputy Surveyor' is the only survival of the Court of Augmentations connected with the management of the forests.

execution.' It reaffirmed the previously enacted orders, and formally laid down the procedure for future systematic enclosures to be made under royal commissions. About this time and previous thereto the Statute Book is full, more especially between the years 1796 to 1800, of private Acts of Parliament for enclosing open fields, commons, and waste grounds; and common lands were then often planted with the oak trees now in their full maturity.

What the hedges and the private woodlands were like, and what the general method of arboriculture was throughout the county about the end of the eighteenth and the beginning of the nineteenth centuries, we have a fairly good idea of from Marshall's *Rural Economy of Gloucestershire* (1789) and Rudge's *General View of the Agriculture of the County of Gloucester* (1807). According to the former [1] the chief hedgerow trees in the Vale of Gloucester were then elm and willow, there being few of oak or ash. 'Hedgerow timber is universally *lopped*; few, however, are *headed*, low, in the pollard manner, except willows, which . . . are here considered in a degree necessary to every farm.' The elm being of superior growth 'the color of iron; and in some instances almost as hard . . . the Bristol shipbuilders have a supply of keel-pieces from this quarter; and I know no country which is so likely to furnish good ones.' He speaks of coppices in the Vale (on poor clay 'not worth as arable land more than 8*s*. an acre; not estimated in this country at more than 5*s*. an acre') as often of high value. 'The species of wood is principally *oak*, *ash*, and *maple*; with some *sallow*, *hawthorne*, and *hazel*. The uses to which it is applied are principally rails, hurdle stuff, hedging materials, and fuel. *The age of felling* twenty years. And its estimated *value* at that age, twelve to fifteen pounds an acre. It growth is uncommonly luxuriant; the stools are thick upon the ground. . . In the latter stages of its growth it is the most impenetrable thicket I have seen'; while he recommends 'that many of the cold swells which occur in different parts of the Vale might be planted with great profit.' Of the remnants of the old woods and of the newer plantations on the Cotswold he, however, gives a poor account,[2] and points out that 'a spirit of planting has never been generally diffused' in that region.

The somewhat later details supplied by the Rev. Thomas Rudge, B.D.,[3] in 1807, are even more interesting. They form a chapter of one of the volumes then 'drawn up for the consideration of the Board of Agriculture,' which practically constituted an official survey of rural economy throughout the various counties in England, carried out by many local experts. He states that—

> on the Cotswolds beech and ash are the principal trees of the woods: beech, indeed, seems the natural growth of the soil, and probably at a remote period covered the greater part of this portion of the county. The principal woods now remaining in the interior of this district are those of the late Lord Chedworth, at Compton and Stowel; of Lord Bathurst, at Cirencester; and of the bishop of Durham at Rendcomb; but the declivities of the hills which border the Cotswolds towards the Vale, almost along the whole extent, and particularly from Birdlip to Wotton-under-Edge, are covered with the most luxuriant beeches, which present to the Vale a continued verdant screen. The most extensive are those of Sir William Hicks, at Witcomb; Mr. Sheppard, at Hampton and Avening; Mr. Kingscote, at Kingscote; but above all, in extent as in beauty, the magnificent woods at Spring Park, and on the Frocaster and Stanley hills, belonging to Lord Ducie. As these beech-woods reproduce themselves from seeds self-sown, they generally come up so thick as to require to be constantly drawn from the first twenty or thirty years. The remaining trees then stand for timber, and are supposed to come to their perfection in seventy or eighty years. Woods of the best timber will then be worth from £80 to £100 per acre.
>
> In the Vale there are but few tracts of woodland left: the principal belong to Lord Berkeley, near Berkeley; Lord Liverpool, at Hawkesbury; and Lord Ducie, at Tortworth. In the park of the latter, as in the adjoining chace of Micklewood, there are remains of the Spanish chestnut, so considerable as to authorize a conjecture that, in times not very remote, this formed a considerable portion of the timber of this part of the county; but above all, as a testimony of this fact, must not be unnoticed, the venerable chestnut tree growing in the garden at Tortworth-house, mentioned by Evelyn, in his *Sylva*, as being known to be 500 years old in the reign of King John. The tree, even now, makes a good appearance in branches and foliage, is in high proof, and in 1804 bore a considerable quantity of fruit. It was measured in 1791, and found to be 44 ft. and 4 ins. in circumference.[4]

He points out also that the elm-tree throve in almost every district, while the oak grew with much vigour in several parts of the Vale, particularly within the hundred of Berkeley. The great oak of Boddington,[5] burnt down in 1790, was a fine example, its girth at the ground more than 54 ft., and at its least dimensions 36 ft. The greatest extent of arm was 24 ft. from the stem. The principal oak-growing district, however, as we have already noticed, was the Forest of Dean.

Mr. Rudge draws particular attention also to the birch-trees of the forest, 'as in no place are they found more remarkable for size or beauty,' while the holly also grew in the forest

---

[1] Op. cit. i, 42–7.   [2] Op. cit. ii, 25–7.   [3] Op. cit. pp. 239–49.
[4] Marshall disputes the accuracy of these figures, see *Planting and Rural Ornament* (1796), ii, 127.
[5] Marshall, op. cit. ii, 299.

'to a large size and clean in its wood. It is much valued for inlaying cabinet work and turners' uses.'

In regard to plantations in general he points out that—

> if under this, we include grounds immediately attached to the seats of noblemen and gentlemen resident in the county, numerous are the planters who have screened the bleak spots of the Cotswolds, and have improved and adorned the general face of the county. But considering this part of the inquiry in an agricultural view there are no instances in the county of considerable tracts of waste (the forest excepted) being planted with the prospect of a future return in timber, whilst in every year many acres of beech-woods are destroyed and given up to the plough.

Mr. Rudge also gives an interesting description of the systems of planting and of the management of coppice-woods[1] then employed, especially noticing that used by J. Raymond Barker, esq., at Fairford. He further draws the attention of the planter to the walnut (*Juglans regia*) both for its timber and fruit. It was particularly abundant in Arlingham parish, but as the county had been ransacked for this wood by the Birmingham gun-makers, the stock of walnut-timber was much diminished and ' only here and there a solitary walnut tree seen growing.'

To resume the History of the Forest of Dean after 1808, provision was in 1819 made *for the better Collection and Recovery of the Gale Rents in the Forest of Dean* (59 Geo. III, c. 86) payable by the miners, and in 1831 was passed *An Act for ascertaining the Boundaries of the Forest of Dean and for inquiring into the Rights and Privileges claimed by the Free Miners of the Hundred of St. Briavel's and for other Purposes* (1 & 2 Will. IV, c. 12), the terms of which were extended in 1833 (3 & 4 Will. IV, c. 38) and 1834 (4 & 5 Will. IV, c. 59). In 1836 the office of Constable of the Castle of St. Briavel's was vested in the First Commissioner of Woods and Forests, and that of Keeper of the Deer in the Forest was vested in the Commissioners (6 & 7 Will. IV, c. 3), who were also in 1838 empowered *to confirm the Tithes to and to grant Leases of Encroachments in the Forest* (1 & 2 Vic. c. 42), their procedure being in accordance with *An Act for regulating the opening and working of Mines and Quarries in the Forest of Dean and Hundred of St. Briavel's* (1 & 2 Vic. c. 43), sanctioned on the same day, 27 July, 1838. Two Acts were passed relative to the Forest of Dean in 1842, *for the relief of the Poor in the Forest* (5 & 6 Vic. c. 48), and *to divide the Forest . . . into Ecclesiastical Districts* (c. 65), but neither of these affected the wood and timber. In 1845, Dean Forest and the New Forest were (14 & 15 Vic. c. 42) especially exempted from the provisions of the *Act to facilitate the Inclosure and Improvement of Commons* (8 & 9 Vic. c. 118, sect. 13). The Forest of Dean was not specifically affected by the Act of 1851 *to make better Provision for the Management of the Woods, Forests, etc.*, nor was it affected at all by *The Deer Removal Act*, 1851, which only applied to the New Forest ; but in 1852 the status of the Commissioners of Woods and Forests, in respect of Dean Forest and other royal properties, was determined by *An Act to alter and amend certain Acts relating to the Woods, Forests, and Land Revenues of the Crown* (15 & 16 Vic. c. 62), while their powers were extended by *An Act to authorise the letting Parts of the Royal Forests of Dean and Woolmer, etc.* (18 & 19 Vic. c. 16). In 1861, cap. 43 of 1838 was altered and amended by *An Act to make further Provision for the Management of Her Majesty's Forest of Dean, and of the Mines and Quarries therein and in the Hundred of St. Briavel's* (24 & 25 Vic. c. 40), and in that same year were passed the two statutes now having general application to the protection of woods, trees, &c., namely *An Act to consolidate and amend the Statute Laws of England and Ireland relating to Larceny and other similar Offences* (c. 96 sect. 16 as to ' any Forest, Chase, or Purlieu ' ; sects. 31, 32, 33, and 35 as to trees and woods) and the similar Act relating to *Malicious Injuries to Property* with regard to ornamental trees and shrubs (c. 97, sects. 20, 21, 22 and 53). In 1866, power was given to the Commissioners of Woods to grant licences for hunting, hawking, fishing, and fowling in any part of the New Forest and the Forest of Dean (29 & 30 Vic. c. 62, sect. 5), while in the same year a statute was passed *to extend the Provisions of the Acts for the Inclosure, Exchange, and Improvement of Land to certain Portions of the Forest of Dean called Walmore Common and The Bearce Common, and for authorising Allotments in lieu of the Forestal Rights of Her Majesty in and over such Commons* (c. 70). In 1871, further provision was made for the opening and working of mines in the forest and the hundred of St. Briavel's in *The Dean Forest (Mines) Act* (34 & 35 Vic. c. 85) ; but the friction was, and continued to be, so great that in 1874 a Select Committee of the House of Commons was appointed to inquire into and report on Dean Forest.

In May, 1889, another Select Committee of the House of Commons was appointed to inquire into the Woods and Forests and Land Revenues of the Crown, whose reports were

---

[1] It may be mentioned that at the present time (1906) the value of coppice-wood has fallen from various circumstances to a very low level, £2 to £7 per acre, according to locality and quality, being the ruling prices, while in some parts it is absolutely unsaleable (*ex informatione* Mr. Philip Baylis).

published on 26 July 1889, and 30 July 1890. With regard to the Forest of Dean (18,710 acres)[1]—

> The Committee are of opinion that having proper regard to the rights of commoners and the convenience of those engaged in mining industries, the best available income is obtained from the surface whilst, as in the New Forest, regard is paid to the preservation of the natural beauty of the woods.
>
> Possibly a large income might be obtained by the sale of the surface and the re-investment of the proceeds ; but a difficult question would have to be dealt with in the purchase of the right of commonage enjoyed by tenants and freeholders of certain parishes. This would be detrimental to the welfare of, and repugnant to the feelings of, the inhabitants of the district ; whilst the destruction of the forest would be most regrettable.

The first forty-one pages of the report of 1889 deal entirely with Dean Forest, and in that much interesting evidence is given by the Commissioner of Woods and Gaveller (Mr. Culley), the Deputy Surveyor (Sir James Campbell, bart.), and the Deputy Gaveller (Mr. Brown). Some of the chief points of interest regarding the timber were that the previous planting had chiefly been of oak, there being very little larch ; that most of the mature timber had been cut for the navy between 1854 and 1864, and that consequently the growing stock was still immature, fellings being limited to the cutting of decayed trees ; that the soil of Dean was superior to that of New Forest for growing oak, while two-thirds of it would also grow good larch ; that very great care was taken in the management in order to preserve the beauty of the district ; and that game was scarce in the forest, as it was considered better to give up the deer[2] than to risk the lives of the keepers against poachers.

From the remarks made by this Select Committee about a possible sale of the Forest of Dean, it may be presumed that some such idea had perhaps then been entertained. But at any rate, ever since then the endeavour has been made to manage the forest upon business principles as a timber-producing property. With this object in view, the late Mr. H. C. Hill was employed in 1897 to draw up a ‘working plan’ based more or less on the lines of the modern continental system, for the 20 years 1897–1917, which now forms the scheme of management adopted.[3] A few short extracts from Mr. Hill’s report can alone be given here. After a description of the forest and of the rights of the crown and a review of its past history he points out that—

> to maintain the Forest of Dean permanently under timber, the 11,000 acres which the Crown has the right to enclose ought to be placed under favourable conditions of growth with the view of establishing a complete crop of mixed beech and oak in ‘high forest,’ with scattered larch, chestnut, sycamore, and other trees. If this is done, its natural character will be restored and handed down to posterity, and the fine oak timber for which the forest is renowned may again be grown, and eventually harvested with other woods in the shape of a regular annual yield. The lower value of beech as compared with oak should in no way prevent its being grown in proper proportion, because it is only by the aid of the beech that fine oak can be grown, and the increased price which should be commanded by the latter over that of oak grown in pure open woods will more than compensate for the low price of the beech. The treatment now proposed has already been introduced by Mr. Philip Baylis, the present Deputy Surveyor, who at once realized that the whole of the forest was immature, and that consequently nothing of good size and quality was ripe for the axe. He further observed that the open woods were not growing satisfactorily, and entered on a scheme for re-enclosing as fast as possible up to the limit of 11,000 acres. He has opened out new nurseries, has extended planting operations, has stopped heavy thinnings in the young woods, and has projected new roads. These are all steps in the right direction, and the suggestions now made are more with a view of systematizing work than of introducing any new general scheme of management.
>
> *The chief work of the next twenty years.*—With the exception of the Lining Wood (80 acres, see also below) and some parts where oak is making no growth, the whole of the woods will have to be allowed to stand till they attain maturity—some 45 or 55 years. In the oldest woods a natural undergrowth exists (as in Russels, Chestnuts, and Lea Bailey enclosures) which should be allowed to grow up and complete the woods. The oaks are already too far apart, and for the next 15 years these

---

[1] Since 1896 the Crown lands (though not the ‘Forest’ area) have been increased by the purchase of the Abbot Wood estate (666½ acres) in the East Dean township and forming part of the Forest of Dean district of Gloucestershire, for £8,800 in December, 1899, but the wooded area thereon is not stated in the *Report of the Commissioners of Woods and Forests* (29 June, 1900, p. 74).

[2] It is said that 150 bucks and 300 does were either killed or removed from the forest in 1850 ; Cox, *Royal Forests of England*, 282. Dr. Cox is of opinion that in the first half of the thirteenth century red deer predominated in the forest, though there was a small admixture of fallow deer ; but the proportions were reversed before Edw. I came to the throne ; op. cit. 276. For details as to the deer in the forest during the nineteenth century the reader must be referred to Nicholls, *Forest of Dean*, 202. In 1855 Mr. Machen records ‘there is not now a deer left in the Forest, and only a few stragglers in the High Meadow Woods.’

[3] H. C. Hill, *Report on the Forest of Dean, with Suggestions for its Management.* 19 July, 1897. London : H. M. Stationery Office.

may be allowed to grow in girth. In part of Acorn Patch (812 acres), in Yew Tree Brake (183 acres), and in parts of Park Hill (141 acres), the underplanting of beech is recommended, but to be successful strong three-year-old plants must be put out. In the 56–62 years-old plantations there is some underwood coming naturally, but it is desirable to introduce beech generally by planting or sowing. In the 31–46 years-old plantations the sowing of beech-mast will, as a rule, succeed ; and an underwood once established, the overwood may be gradually thinned, so as to give to the oaks and larches that light needed to develop good crowns, but which must not be given by uncovering the soil. In the re-enclosed areas (which may aggregate 6,335 acres before the limit is reached, and of which 660 acres have already been fenced in) it has been decided to cut out the worst of the oaks, reserving or storing the more promising as standard trees. Under this shelter some self-sown growth of oak and ash may be expected to appear, which will survive if not allowed to be smothered by fern. Larch, and oak, and chestnut, as well as sycamore and willow, have been freely planted. Larch is so much exposed to attacks by insects and fungi that it is risky to plant it over any considerable area to the exclusion of other trees ; and further, the planting of all light-demanding trees should be limited to groups in the open places made by fellings and so located as to be free from the influence of the crowns of the stored oaks. Under the oaks, and generally where they are not natural seedlings or planted groups as above, beech should be thickly sown or planted. This work of fencing 6,335 acres, cutting out the bad oaks, and planting as now projected, will be heavy and costly, and it is thought that 20 years may well be given to its accomplishment. A difficulty in proceeding with it lies in the fact that beech-mast is only procurable at intervals probably of three or four years ; and the beech is the most important element in these plantations, where the oaks exist already in sufficient numbers, the chief object being to restore the natural condition of the wood as a mixed crop of oak and beech, and thus secure a better development of the oaks.

Arrangements are made to re-enclose areas averaging 300 acres a year, and to clear of inferior trees and replant as above, the following being the order kept in view :—Kensley Ridge and part of Beechenhurst and Serridge (662 acres enclosed in 1896) ; Staple Edge, N. Blakeney Hill and Lining Wood (1,500 acres enclosed in 1898) ; Lea Bailey, Buckholt, Sallow Vallets, Perch and part of Serridge (1,200 acres for enclosure in 1903) ; Nags Head, Barn Hill, Astonbridge (1,500 acres to be enclosed in 1907) ; Cockshoots and South Blakeney Hill (900 acres to be enclosed in 1912) ; Edge Hills, Bromley, Shutcastle, and part of Oaken Hill (900 acres to be enclosed in 1914).[1]

The area to be annually planted with larch, oak, &c., or sown with beech, would be 300 acres on an average, but as beech-mast can only be expected irregularly at intervals of several years, advantage must be taken of every year of mast to sow up the entire area enclosed, and also to establish nurseries to provide plants for years in advance.

These nurseries for beech need only be of a temporary nature, and they will probably succeed best if established within the enclosures, under the shelter of oak, in places near water and yet safe from frost. The question of fencing must be considered for each new enclosure as it is taken up.

The work second in importance during the next twenty-two years should be the introduction of underwood of beech in the enclosures, exceptionally of hornbeam, and possibly of spruce, in places where the soil is stiff or damage is likely to occur from frost.

Beech may be undersown with prospect of success in the 884 acres of wood not exceeding 46 years of age, exclusive of the Lea Bailey enclosure. Sowings may also succeed over portions of the older woods (such as part of Middle Ridge, Bourts, Crump Meadow, Deans Meend, Delves, East Bach Meend, Hangerbury, Light Moor), but elsewhere planting will have to be undertaken in the enclosures aged from 56 to 62 (except in Coverham, which is complete over the greater part, and in part of the Acorn Patch). Similarly, Yew Tree Brake, parts of Park Hill, and the 14 acres of old wood in Acorn Patch may be underplanted as plants become available.

In this way it is estimated that some 1,700 acres may be undersown as soon as beech-mast is obtainable, while 1,400 acres need underplanting within the next 20 years, or on an average of 70 acres a year. In order to effect this underplanting nurseries of beech should be formed within the different enclosures under the shelter of standard oaks as recommended for the newly enclosed areas.

He further pointed out that—

Lining Wood (80 acres), containing mature oak, should be enclosed and its natural regeneration undertaken. Certain areas also, such as, for example, Great Kensley with its 194 acres, where the oaks are not thriving, should be cleared and replanted with conifers, while small blank areas mostly caused by falls should be restocked.

As to the financial side of the scheme Mr. Hill stated that—

with only 80 acres of mature wood and almost the entire area very much over-thinned, there is little prospect of revenue for years to come. Receipts during the 19 years 1897–1916 will be restricted to the value of the inferior trees cut on areas averaging 300 acres annually, and that of the mature wood in the Lining Wood (80 acres). The clearance of the greater part of 300 acres where oak is not thriving will also give some return ; while later on the thinnings of young woods in which beech

---

[1] The following enclosures suggested by Mr. H. C. Hill have already been made :—New Beechenhurst, including Kensley Ridge and part of Serridge, enclosed 1897—666 A. 3 R. 38 P.; part of Serridge, enclosed 1900—133 A. 3 R. 9 P.; Staple Edge and part of Blakeney Hill, enclosed 1900—1,583 A. 1 R. 27 P. ; Sallow Vallets (part of), Buckholt, and part of The Perch, enclosed 1906—1,060 A. (*estimated*) ; *ex informatione* Mr. Philip Baylis.

underwood shall have been established will also yield some return. When once the oaks in the woods now 87–94 years old have reached a marketable size of about 6 feet in girth, and the woods become completely stocked, there will be no difficulty in raising the receipts to £12,000 or £14,000 a year, and in arranging for a sustained and steadily increasing yield from that time on until probably an income of £30,000 or £37,000 may be reached. But for the present the best plan is to allow the woods to mature under the best conditions. This involves considerable outlay in fencing and planting in order to make up deficiencies in the growing stock (or capital in wood) caused by ill-advised savings in abandoning fences which ought to have been maintained for the past 50 years and by too heavy thinnings ; and it therefore now becomes necessary to re-invest capital (in money) to make good the sums injudiciously saved over the past half-century. No accurate estimate can be made of the actual expenditure thus required, because it will vary with the amount of fencing needed for each enclosure, and will have to include extraordinary sowing of beech over considerable areas in addition to the regular planting or sowing of 370 acres a year.

As a rough forecast, however, an expenditure of £7,000 a year should suffice, while the average revenue from all sources (made up chiefly from inferior oaks, cut on 300 acres at £10 per acre, £3,000, trees in Lining Wood £500, and rents £2,500), will amount to a total of £6,000.

The surplus of late years amounting to £2,082 a year must for the time being be foregone and a certain deficit not exceeding £1,000 annually may have to be met.

A similar scheme of management for the period of thirty-five years (1897–1932), also drawn up by the late Mr. H. C. Hill, is being carried out in the Highmeadow Woods estate adjacent to the Forest of Dean and under the charge of the Deputy Surveyor of the latter.[1] This estate is the absolute property of the Crown free from any rights of common, and was acquired by purchase from Viscount Gage in 1817. It extends over about 3,285 acres of enclosed woods, of which 2,949 acres lie in Gloucestershire. The Tintern Woods, in the same district, have also been now (1906) brought under the provisions of a working plan drawn up by Mr. E. P. Popert, Superintendent Forester in the Forest of Dean.

This improved system of management of the woods of the Crown has further led to the establishment in January, 1904, of 'an experimental course of instruction for student woodmen who will be employed in these Crown woods during the time of their training.' The course was arranged with the sanction of the Treasury, and is held in the Crown Office, Whitemead Park. The course extends over two years, and includes instruction in forest botany, sylviculture, mensuration, and protection of woods. For the first course eight young men from the Forest of Dean and two from Windsor Forest applied to become students, this being as many as employment could be found for at that time ; but twice that number can now be instructed.

In order to try and give a fairly comprehensive summary of the general state of arboriculture throughout the private woodlands in Gloucestershire endeavours were made (1901) to collect direct information concerning the various large estates on such points as (1) the acreage of the woodlands and the ages of different portions, (2) the nature of the crops and the kinds of trees grown, (3) the past method of treating the woods, (4) the extent and nature of recent plantations, and (5) the method of planting usually adopted on each estate. All details below refer to conditions in 1901.

The information kindly furnished in response to this endeavour by many of the chief land-owners and their agents, and which is summarized below, shows that the conditions obtaining on private estates are similar to those throughout most of the other English counties. Except on the chalk hills, where there are large compact tracts of beech forming more or less pure highwoods, the woods are for the most part copses wherein the oak is the chief standard tree, along with which are also found ash, elm, beech, sycamore, chestnut, and conifers of various kinds (though mainly larch and Scots pine), while the underwoods are a mixture of hazel, ash, elm, sycamore, &c. The vast majority of the copses are irregular, showing that much of the art of forestry practised formerly for the sake of oak timber for shipbuilding has become lost, while the underwoods no longer receive the attention bestowed on them in former times, before the development of better communication by land and water, and before the economic and other changes took place which now cause coppice woods to have shrunk enormously in their profit-yielding capacity. Simultaneously with the great fall in the value of underwoods, however, their virtual enhancement as game coverts has been an additional cause of the coppices becoming less productive than formerly, because immense destruction is often caused by rabbits during hard winter weather, wherever these are preserved or at any rate permitted to breed in large number. So destructive are these little animals that large coverts of oak standards over hazel and ash coppice are at times denuded of all underwood just as if the young shoots of one year's growth had been cut down with a scythe.

The woodlands on the Badminton estate, the property of His Grace the Duke of Beaufort, aggregate 524 acres. Concerning the age, composition, and treatment of these, no details are obtain-

---

[1] *Working Plan Report for the High Meadow Woods*, by H. C. Hill, Conservator of Forests in India (on furlough), London, 19 July, 1897. Mr. H. C. Hill was afterwards, from October, 1900, until his death in November, 1902, Inspector General of Forests to the Government of India.

able except that the timber trees consist of oak, ash, and beech, with an underwood of hazel and ash, which is cropped at from 12 to 20 years of age. Recent plantations amount to about 30 acres of larch. The underwoods and the young plantations suffer from rabbits. There has been very little done in connexion with the woods for some years past, but they are now receiving attention.

On the Right Hon. the Earl of Ducie's estate (Tortworth, Falfield) in addition to a celebrated pinetum, the woodlands aggregate about 547 acres, and consist mainly of copse-woods of oak, ash, beech, wych elm, larch, Scots pine, and sycamore, while elms form the main hedgerow trees. The more recent plantations consist to a great extent of larch, with some oak and also a little Scots pine.

The woodlands on the Right Hon. the Earl Bathurst's Cirencester estate comprise about 2,500 acres, of which three large woods (Oakley 962 acres, Hailey 496 acres, and Overley 388 acres) form the group known as 'Cirencester Woods.'[1] The remaining 654 acres include Siccaridge, Francombe, Dorvel, Henwood, Sapperton, and other detached and smaller woods and plantations. Besides this there is a considerable quantity of park and hedgerow timber.

Cirencester Woods have been in existence for some centuries, and the greater part of the area is composed of old woods, the recent plantations being unimportant.

Allen, first Earl Bathurst (d. 1775), was a notable planter, whose skill was recorded by his friend and frequent guest, Pope, in the following couplet :—

> Who then shall grace, or who improve the soil ?
> Who plants like Bathurst, and who builds like Boyle ?

His successors have also taken continuous interest in the welfare of their woods. These large woods, composed of beech, with a moderate sprinkling of larch and of oak copse-woods, are systematically treated, about 90 acres of coppice being annually felled with a rotation of twenty years, and advantage being then taken to clear also a portion of the timber trees. The detached woods not being in regular crop are treated as circumstances demand, a portion being cut over annually. After the coppice and some of the timber overwood are cleared, bare spaces are planted with beech and larch, or else with ash for coppice. These spaces arise from the removal of branching trees and also from the depredations of ground game when the coppice-stools and seedlings are shooting after the previous cutting.

Ground game is now treated as vermin, and it is anticipated that gradually the coppice may be brought into a 16-year rotation, producing as much as twenty years' growth has hitherto done, and that natural regeneration may to a large extent take the place of artificial re-stocking, which has cost nearly £2 an acre with the necessary protection.

In forming new plantations it is necessary to use plants of 2 to 3 ft. high, and to set them 3 to 4 ft. apart, according to soil and elevation. Owing to the rapid growth of thistles, foulgrass, &c., on this class of land, notching of small plants is impracticable without a great expenditure in hoeing and cleaning, hence pit-planting is usual. The plantations that have succeeded best are those formed on old arable land. Those upon old rough turf, in spite of pains being taken to plant the trees carefully and well, are long in establishing themselves and have required much beating up of blanks.

The beech and larch timber produced in Earl Bathurst's woods is of exceedingly good quality and is much sought after. Owing to the matrix of beech, the protection afforded to the soil by the coppice, and the resulting deposit of leaf-mould, both beech and larch timber grow rapidly and are of higher value than timber grown under other circumstances in plantations of more recent origin.

At present these woods are somewhat thin ; owing to the discouragement of ground game, however, there is no doubt they will shortly be again more fully stocked and will carry more profitable crops.

On the Stanway estate, near Winchcombe, the property of the Right Hon. the Earl of Wemyss and March, the woodlands consist of about 1,000 acres, of various ages (of which 120 acres are young plantations formed within the last five years)[2] extending over both undulating hilly land and portions of the Vale. On the hilly ground the crops are principally larch, mixed with spruce, Scots pine, silver fir, beech, ash, wych elm, sycamore, oak, &c. A few Corsican pine have also been planted in recent years, and are doing remarkably well. In the Vale the covers consist principally of old oak trees, beech, a few chestnut, and large spruce, elm, Italian poplar, ash, lime, &c., with underwood of hazel and ash principally. The hedgerow and field timber consist of oak, elm, sycamore, silver fir, Spanish chestnut, ash, and beech.

---

[1] A well-known Gloucestershire landowner says that 'the large Woodlands on Lord Bathurst's estate are the best managed woods in the county, and the only ones that I know of which for two centuries have been regularly and carefully managed under competent supervision.' Earl Bathurst kindly permits these fine woodlands to be used for instructional purposes in connexion with the theoretical course in Forestry at the Royal Agricultural College, Cirencester.

[2] All details about area, age, &c., given here and in the following pages, refer to conditions in 1901.

The hill plantations are principally of larch 4 ft. apart, mixed with hardwoods (sycamore and ash being preferred) on fresh land. When the plants have fully established themselves, underlings, &c., and deformed trees are taken out. On the larch reaching its maturity the covers are cleared of them, while the best of the hardwoods are left standing in the best parts, and the worst parts are replanted with spruce for game cover, or with beech for the next crop. In many cases, where the plantations have been cleared, a crop of ash has come up of itself and has been left for poles, and will eventually be cut for underwood, leaving the best ash for timber.

In the Vale a portion of the underwood is cut each year, and the oaks and other trees (except ornamental specimens) that have attained maturity are felled and sold, unless required for estate repairs, a water-power saw-mill being used for the purpose of conversion in the latter case.

The underwood scarcely now pays for cutting, but it supplies the neighbourhood with fire-lighting wood, and with useful poles and stakes for many purposes.

Of the 120 acres planted in the last five years about 100 acres are chiefly of larch formed on old arable land, and 20 acres are mainly of sycamore, because experience here has shown that when land under larch is replanted with larch the young crop seems very liable to the attacks of the canker fungus.

Pit-planting in circular holes, about 18 in. in diameter and 8 in. deep, or 16 in. in diameter and 9 in. deep, according to the nature of the soil, is the usual method adopted on the hilly ground. The holing is done by piece-work, and the planting by day-work, the total cost being about 2s. 6d. per 100 trees to get the work done well.

For planting oak, ash, alder, Italian poplar, elm, &c. in open places in the woods in the Vale, plants about 6 ft. high are used, and each individual tree has to be protected from rabbits. They seem to do best when planted in groups, each kind by itself.

The woodlands on the Right Hon. Lord Sherborne's Sherborne (Northleach) and Standish estates are of large extent, as the enclosed plantations alone have an area of about 1,000 acres, while the many trees planted throughout the park and the grass-lands in the valleys give the whole a very well wooded appearance. The older plantations, formed about 80 to 100 years ago, are chiefly belts of trees with occasional clumps on the higher parts to shelter homesteads and stock. Here, about 440 ft. above the sea-level, the timber is mostly beech, which grows into fine trees, interspersed with a few oak, ash, elm, hornbeam, maple, and poplar in a fairly thriving condition. Larch, spruce, and Scots pine, originally planted along with the hardwoods as 'nurses' but left to grow into timber, have now in many cases become over-mature and unsound owing to their not having been removed in due time. At Lodge Park, about two miles distant at an altitude of about 540 ft., larch flourishes on thinner brashy soil, the beech thrives and ash grows well, while sycamore has been planted with much success on some of the thinnest soils, often thriving when other and less hardy trees set out along with it find difficulty in maintaining their existence.

There are some 80 acres or more of ash coppice, cut with a rotation of from twelve to twenty years (but most frequently seventeen to twenty), and these form the most profitable portions of the woodlands, generally giving a return of over 20s. per acre per annum. The ash are now planted very thick, so as to run up into clean poles, but assistance in this matter is also given for a few years by nipping off superfluous side-branches and removing double leaders formed as the result of frost.

On some parts of the estate, especially with a northern or western exposure, the larch thrives luxuriously, and is free from the canker disease; but many of the young plantations formed during the last thirty years have been attacked by this fungus and rendered unfit for timber, so that they will have to be cleared and used for fencing purposes. In consequence of this disease larch is no longer the chief tree numerically in the plantations formed during the last six years (about 40 acres) a preference having been given to mixtures of hardwoods (oak, ash, maple, and elm) with Scots pine, larch, spruce, and a few Douglas fir. The hardwoods are, without exception, planted in pits, as also the larger of the coniferous plants, while the smaller ones are notched into the soil with an L-shaped notch. Thinnings in the various woods are said to have been neglected up to about ten years ago, but since then work has been more regularly taken in hand to prevent the plantations becoming overcrowded and unhealthy.

The Sedbury Park Estate, near Chepstow, the property of Sir William H. Marling, bart., and Colonel P. S. Marling, V.C., extends altogether to 1,250 acres (of which 1,083 acres are old woods, and 167 acres are plantations) in the parishes of Tidenham, Woolaston, and Hewelsfield. They are situated on an exposed position between the Rivers Severn and Wye, on land varying from 50 to 750 ft. above sea-level.

In the 1,083 acres of old copsewoods the age of the standard timber trees cannot be ascertained, and the underwoods vary greatly in quality; they comprise a mixture of oak, hazel, birch, alder, blackwithy, lime, maple, whitebeam and chestnut, growing at random. These woods do not appear to have been planted, but seem to be remnants of the ancient woodlands formerly existing in this part of the county. The timber in the copsewoods comprises oak, ash, birch, elm and beech; but

FORESTRY

oak predominates, though ash is of first-class quality. The woods also contain a very large number of ancient yew trees.

The underwoods are cut at intervals of fourteen to eighteen years, when they are stored with young saplings as thickly as circumstances permit. The underwood is partially sacrificed to allow of a larger growth of stores, the best of which will be allowed to grow into timber, while the others will be cut down when from twenty to forty years of age along with the underwood at the current felling. At each cutting stores are left and the fall comprises timber, double stores (twenty to forty years), single stores (fifteen to twenty years), and the undergrowth.

There is a demand for pit-wood for the Forest of Dean coal mines near, but the sale of underwood is difficult to arrange unless included with timber and pitwood.

The 167 acres of plantations consist of 11 acres over fifty years, 21 acres of twenty to fifty years, 11 acres of ten to twenty years, and 124 acres under ten years; those over ten years of age are in all cases formed only of larch and Scots pine, while those below that are composed of mixed hard and soft woods (oak, ash, Spanish chestnut, lime, elm, beech, larch, Scots pine, Douglas fir, Austrian and Corsican pines, and spruce). Larch and spruce trees have been cut 90 feet in length, and containing upwards of 50 cubic feet of timber. The park and private grounds contain a large and fine variety of English and evergreen oak, ash, *Pinus ponderosa*, English and wych elm, cedar, and other trees.[1] Extensive planting of park trees has been done with selected standards of fifty varieties of oak, also elms, poplars, and other park trees.

The method of planting usually adopted is to select from 10 to 20 acres yearly, which are cleared ready for holing. The holes are all dug by piece-work, 4 ft. apart, and left ready for the forester and his men to fill. The plants are grown in the estate nursery, adjoining the forester's house, 600 ft. above sea level. Seedlings are purchased from nurseries in Scotland, and are transplanted twice in the estate nursery before being lifted for final planting. Hardwoods are raised from seed collected on the estate.

When the nursery supply is not sufficient for the year's planting the deficiency is made up by purchasing transplants from the north; but plants from the estate nursery appear to establish themselves more easily, and to stand the exposed positions open to all winds better than the plants purchased. The estate nursery has been established upwards of eight years, and is about 3 acres in extent. One section is reserved for the growth of standards of hardwoods suitable for park planting, the practice being to replace by new trees all windfalls and mature trees felled in the park.

Generally the estate is heavily timbered, especially in the south-west section; and as it contains a large proportion of poor hilly land, the revenue will ultimately be increased by the planting now taking place.

On the Lypiatt Park estate (Stroud) the property of the Right Hon. Sir John E. Dorington, bart., the woodlands amount to about 330 acres of all ages up to about 200 years. About 111 acres consist of beech (of 60, 80 and nearly 200 years of age) which attains maturity here at about 120 to 140 years, about 60 acres of larch, about 80 acres of mixed larch and beech, the latter forming an underwood that will be allowed to grow up into timber on the clearance of the larch standards, about 25 acres of mixed hardwoods, about 20 acres of copsewoods, now an unprofitable crop in this district, and some 36 acres of small miscellaneous woods and plantations.

On the Hatherop Castle estate (Fairford), the property of G. S. Bazley, esq., the woodlands extend to about 380 acres, out of a total area of about 5,800 acres. Of these, 80 acres are old copsewoods of from 120 to 150 years of age, and consist principally of oak, of indifferent quality, having a thin underwood of ash coppice cut with a rotation of about fifteen years; while the remaining 300 acres are plantations formed between 1867 and 1900, which vary from two to thirty-three years in age, and from a few perches to 60 acres in area, about 100 acres consisting of small clumps planted either for shelter or to improve the landscape, or else to join together or extend older plantations. These plantations are mixed, having been formed of beech, larch, Austrian pine, and spruce, with a fair proportion of sycamore ash, Norway maple and birch, and a sprinkling of alder hornbeam, Corsican pine, and other trees. On the whole, beech, larch, and spruce have done fairly well, but larch planted within the last twelve years is very subject to disease (*canker fungus*). Sycamore, ash and Norway maple have done well in most of the plantations, while birch and elder thrive in the most exposed situations, with shallow and stony soil.

The small clumps have been thinned regularly and rather heavily for effect. The larger plantations have been left alone; and where circumstances are sufficiently favourable, they are thick enough to furnish well-grown timber.

Until recently, the ground was trenched ('double dug') before planting, this has given noticeably better results. Also in some cases, a crop of potatoes has been grown first, and the young trees

[1] We understand from the courteous information of Sir Charles Dilke, bart., that the ilex at Sedbury is finer than at any other place in this county. He also reminds us that Sedbury is now famous as the birthplace of the late Miss Ormerod, the first authority on destructive insects.

kept clean by hoeing for some years. Trees so planted and cared for are very distinctly better than where a hole was dug, and a tree put in, but the expense of course has been great. Unfortunately the exposed situation and the shallow soil are rather unfavourable to the growth of good timber, and replanting has also often been necessary for this reason.

On the Failand estate (near Bristol) the property of the Right Hon. Sir Edward Fry, the wooded area consists only of about 30 acres, scattered in six patches; most of these are old mixed woods, of the usual character of English copses.

In the Lydney Park estate (Lydney: Charles Bathurst, esq.) the woodlands extend to 1,645 acres. With the exception of some 24 acres planted with larch about thirty years ago, the whole area has probably grown oak timber with underwood of mixed coppice for some hundreds of years. The custom was to cut the coppice every 17 years and fell a portion of the largest oak timber at the same time, and as evidently no planting was done for a long period of years, the woods have become thin from decay of stools, damage by rabbits,[1] and the gradual diminishing of the large timber.

About seven years ago a change was made in this system. As a preliminary measure, the difficult task of exterminating the rabbits was taken in hand, and it is only by persistent trapping, snaring and ferreting, that these pests can be kept down. The bulk of the oak timber (now mostly mature) is being felled on the various sections in their rotation as the coppice falls to be cut; and after being cleared, the whole area either is planted with hardwoods (oak, ash, sycamore, Spanish chestnut and beech) where the soil is suitable, or else larch has been extensively planted on the lighter lands where the soil is dry and gritty. On the boundaries of the woods, on exposed heights, shelter belts of non-deciduous trees, such as Scots, Austrian and Corsican pines and Douglas fir, have been planted, the latter in the most favourable situations.

About 781 acres of the woodlands have now been replanted in this way, and the larch is naturally showing most progress, the main difficulty being to keep the young plants from becoming overgrown by the coppice and fern, though the cost of clearing and the scarcity of labour are serious drawbacks to this necessary measure. The same difficulty arises with the hardwoods planted among the coppice, with the further disadvantage that considerable damage is caused to the young plants, (especially the ash), by caterpillars eating the leaders of the plants during dry seasons, when the young trees become more or less subject to serious blight.

On the Dyrham Park estate (Chippenham: the Rev. W. T. Blathwayt) there are about 100 acres of woodland. These are mostly old copsewoods with standards of oak principally, with elm, ash, and a few cherries, growing above an underwood consisting mainly of hazel, elm and ash. The young plantations of spruce, Scots pine and larch are small in extent.

On the Miserden Park estate (Cirencester: A. W. Leatham, esq., D.L.) the woods extend to about 518 acres, scattered in blocks varying from 20 to 70 acres in area. About 200 acres consist of copses with standards of ash and oak principally, 25 acres are young plantations of larch, and the rest is mostly beech of 100 to 130 years of age. Hitherto the system followed has been to clear the hardwoods when mature and plant larch; but it is now considered that selection felling among the standards and replantation of blank spaces in the coppice is a sounder method of treatment.

The Blaisdon estate (Newnham: Peter Stubs, esq.) contains 438 acres of woodlands. They consist of coppices, mostly of oak, interspersed with a few timber trees as standards, and are cut over with a rotation of eighteen to twenty years. No plantations have been formed recently.

On the Bowden Hall estate (J. Dearman Birchall, esq.) there are 250 acres of old beech woods, standing on 'common,' which entail endless disputes between the lord of the manor and the commoners. Selection fellings are made in these woods each year. No recent plantations have been made, owing to the enclosing of common now being illegal.

On the Haie estate (Newnham: Russell James Kerr, esq.) the woodlands aggregate about 250 acres. With the exception of a few acres of recent plantations, the woods are old copses of ash, birch, hazel, chestnut, holly, &c., with standards of oak, ash, beech, birch, elm, larch, fir, &c., cut over at twelve to fifteen years of age according to the condition of the underwood and the market rate for coppice at the time. The fall on such occasions includes mature standards and inferior trees interfering with the development of others. The small plantations formed during the last few years have been at 3ft. by 3ft. (4,840 per acre), with hardwoods for timber every 12 yards (33 per acre); but this is found unduly expensive, as early thinnings in this locality have no other market than as firewood.

On the estates of G. E. Lloyd Baker, esq., J.P., there are about 60 acres of wood at Hardwicke Court (Gloucester), and 112 acres at Uley (near Dursley), on the top of the Cotswold

---

[1] "Rabbits seem to have been well kept down by other animals which preyed on them about a hundred years ago; otherwise it would have been impossible to have raised the extensive larch, oak, and other plantations then so successfully and cheaply established all over Britain. This is confirmed by the examinations I have made of old manuscript game-books recording the game shot day by day'; Dr. J. Nisbet, 'Hist. of the Forest of Dean,' *Engl. Hist. Rev.* (July, 1906), 445 *n.*

FORESTRY

Hills. The former were mostly planted for sport or ornament, and consist chiefly of ash, cut every fifteen or twenty years for hurdle wood, with oaks amongst them. Part are about seventy years old, while the rest are very much older (up to 200 years). The estate has elms thickly grown in the hedgerows, and the value of the timber cut and sold comes to about £100 a year, besides a small quantity used for estate purposes.

The Uley woods are beech above a hundred years old. They were originally planted, but are now naturally renewed in most parts by seed. Ash occurs self-sown amongst the beech, and runs up into lanky trees which take up very little room, and sell for three to eight shillings each, when cut to make way for the beech. Sycamore also sows itself and grows into a fine tree. The beech is thinned heavily at about thirty years old, and then regularly thinned until a strong crop of seedlings is seen to be coming on, when the remaining large trees are cut, except where required for ornament. It is sold to neighbouring timber mills. The return is about £100 per annum for the 100 acres. Some portions are planted with larch, which makes a good and profitable change of crop.

On the Thornbury Castle estate (Thornbury: E. Stafford Howard, esq., C.B.) the woodlands consist of a few small coverts, the largest in the vale being about 8 acres. They were planted about seventy to eighty years ago and are mostly oak, which having been sufficiently thinned is now going on to maturity. There is one wood of coppice (principally alder, birch, and ash) which is cut in rotation every seven years; the ash and birch are now being stored. There is also a wood of 16 acres on the hill (about 770 ft. above sea-level) at Milbury Heath, which was planted about sixty years ago, when the common was enclosed. It is principally oak with a small admixture of larch, all growing very well in a dry sandy soil.

On the Boddington Manor estate (Cheltenham: J. S. Gibbons, esq.), where the celebrated 'Boddington Oak' stood, there are two or three old spinneys of oak, ash, and blackthorn, while within the last twenty years several small coverts, amounting to about 50 acres, have been planted, mainly for purposes of game preservation, with Scots pine, larch, birch, and black poplar.

The woods on the Over, Compton, and Elberton estates (Almondsbury: R. C. Cann-Lippincott, esq.) aggregate 255 acres and are distributed in strips, patches, and coverts varying from less than an acre up to compact blocks of over 40 acres. These woods have originally been copses, but many of them are now imperfectly stocked highwoods that were worked on an irregular system of selection, felling and replanting of blanks thus created. In some of the woods intended to be copses there are as many as seventy to eighty large oaks per acre, under which it is impossible for underwood to thrive. In other places the coppice of hazel, ash, &c., has been almost absolutely destroyed by rabbits, while in other parts the soil is covered with privet and rhododendrons (planted for game cover) or with weeds (blackberry, bracken, ivy, coarse grasses and moss).

On the Knole estate (Almondsbury: Colonel Chester Masters) there are about 184 acres of woods. Those on the plateau above the deer park range from 80 to over 150 years in age, and are mostly ornamental, while the coverts are intended for coppice and hardwood timber, of about forty years of age, with a few pine and larch of about twenty-five years. But in all the coverts in the Severn Marsh, the underwood of ash, wych elm, hazel, and poplar, has either been entirely destroyed by rabbits or to a great extent choked by blackthorn. The only recent planting at Knole consists of about 3 acres of ash.

On the Dodington estate (Sodbury, Dodington, and other parishes: Sir Gerald Codrington, bart.) there are about 300 acres of woods. The coverts contain timber of about forty years old, but except in the plantations running along the Bath and Gloucester road there is nothing but beech, Scots pine, a few larch, and a few spruce. In the pleasure-grounds round the gardens, there is a quantity of Turkey oak, which grows in the district very luxuriantly. On the Winterbourne or Bristol side of the estate, in the lower ground there are two coverts ranging about 20 acres and 10 acres respectively, in which the underwood is very thick and of fairly good quality (hazel, ash, and elm); box grows very plentifully in some of the coverts also. The recent plantations on the Dodington estate comprise some 40 to 50 acres, about 30 of which are larch and spruce, now from thirteen to fifteen years old, while 10 acres were formed about seven years ago, and the remainder are ash poles about ten years of age.

The method of treating the woods is to clear patches of the coverts where the ground is only imperfectly covered, and to replant (wherever suitable) with ash at 3½ ft. apart, the poles being looked over at the end of eight years, and the crooked ones coppiced, leaving the others to grow into timber trees. Places unsuited for ash are planted with larch and Scots pine. On the Knole estate marsh, it is intended to clear a covert of the worthless blackthorn, burn the roots with quicklime during the summer, and replant with oak, which does excellently in that district; in the case of the underwood, the practice is to cut it every ten to twelve years, and where possible then put in young trees after the crop of underwood is cleared.

Reference has already been made to the Tortworth chestnut and the Boddington oak; but the county abounds in large and celebrated trees of different kinds, and in particular it contains some of the finest elms in the whole of England. Within the Dean Forest one of the largest and oldest oaks is 'Jack of the Yat,' standing by the roadside near the sixteenth milestone on the Long Hill. In 1830, it girthed 17 ft. 8¾ in. at 6 ft. up, and in 1881, 18 ft. 0¼ in.[1] Back in the woods behind that stands the 'Crad Oak,' a fine specimen of the sessile oak. Though it seldom is to be found of extraordinarily large dimensions *Quercus sessiliflora* here forms closer, harder, and firmer timber than *Q. pedunculata*, and thrives better than this species in warm, dry, and elevated positions in the forest. Outside the forest bounds, on purlieu land, stands the 'Newland Oak' now girthing 43½ ft.[2] Loudon mentions[3] a group of three oaks, probably one of the most remarkable in England on account of the size of the trees :—

> At Razies Bottom, near Ashwick [says Professor Burnet], were growing, a few years ago, three fine oaks, called the King, the Queen, and the Duke of Gloucester. The King Oak was 28 ft. 8 in. in circumference at the collar; and about 18 ft. as the average girt to the height of 30 ft., where the trunk began to throw out branches. The Queen Oak, which girted 34 ft. at the base, had a clear cylindrical stem of 30 ft. high, and 16 ft. in circumference all the way; bearing two tree-like branches, each extending 40 ft. beyond the bole, and girting at the base 8 ft.; containing in all 680 ft. of measurable timber. The Duke of Gloucester had a clear trunk 25 ft. high, averaging 14 ft. in girt.

The elm here attains its finest development, and with respect to the height, girth, and beauty of the hedgerow and park timber, the elms of Gloucestershire are probably unequalled, and certainly not surpassed, by those of any other county. This fact was long ago noted by Marshall,[4] and it holds good to-day as well as it did about a hundred and twenty years ago :—

> The largest Elms we have seen, of the Fine-leaved sort, grow in the Vale of Gloucester. There are several in the parish church of Church-down which girt, at five feet high, from 10 to 12 feet. But the finest Elm in the Vale stands in the road between Cheltenham and Tewkesbury—within a few hundred yards of the Boddington Oak. It is known by the name of Piffe's Elm; and the turnpike gate, the fence belonging to which is fastened at one end to this tree, takes its name from it; being called 'Piffe's Elm 'Pike.' The smallest girt of this tree, which falls about five feet high, is at present (1783) exactly sixteen feet. At ten feet high it throws out large arms; which have formerly been lopped, but which now are furnished with tree-like shoots, rising, by estimation, to 70 or 80 feet high, with an extent proportionable, exhibiting all together the grandest tree we have seen; not so much from its present size, as from that fullness of growth and vigour which it now wears.

The whole of the district to the west and south of Almondsbury abounds in elms of magnificent dimensions and majestic appearance. Many of those on the Over Court, Compton, Ellerton, and Knole estates are remarkably fine. In 1902 trees were measured there girthing up to 19 ft. for elm (on Court Farm, Over), 13 ft. 5 in. for oak (sound trees), and 11 ft. for ash, while there were also much larger oaks of a purely ornamental character.

The most interesting tree in that particular district is, perhaps, however, the 'St. Swithin's Oak' at the top of the hill overlooking the deer-park at Over Court, and near the ancient chapel now forming the gardener's tool-shed at the back of the farmhouse of St. Swithin. It has a girth of 17 ft. 10 in. measured (1901) at 6 ft. above ground. It is an old pollard, and has large limbs spreading horizontally from about 10 ft. up the bole. At the base of the hill stands another very large oak of somewhat smaller girth.

Many of the old trees planted from two to three hundred years ago in Sherborne Park are now fine specimens of arboriculture. They include elms up to 19 ft. (at 3 ft. up), beech up to 14½ ft. in girth, and up to over 100 ft. high without a branch for 70 to 80 ft., cedar of 15½ ft., walnut of 13 ft., great maple of 12 ft. 4 in., yew of 12 ft., and Scots pine of 11½ ft. But perhaps the finest yew in the county is one growing in the old woods on the Sedbury Park estate (near Chepstow), which has a girth of 21 ft. 4 in. at 5 ft. above the ground; its bole is 8 ft. long and its height is 40 ft.

---

[1] John Smith, *On British Oaks*, Trans. of Royal Scottish Arboricultural Soc. xiii (1893), 43–4.
[2] Mr. Philip Baylis informs us that it is at this date (1906) a fine healthy pollard with a clean bole of some 12 ft. in height, at its base it measures 45 ft. 6 in. in circumference, and at 5 ft. from the ground 43 ft. 6 in. It is described in the *Trans. of the Woolhope Naturalists' Field Club for* 1889, p. 339.
[3] *Arboretum et Fruticetum Britannicum* (2nd edit. 1844), iii, 1760.
[4] *Planting and Rural Ornament* (1796), ii, 429. It is also mentioned by Loudon, op. cit. iii, 1393.

SPORT ANCIENT AND MODERN

STAG-HUNTING

IN the fifteenth and sixteenth centuries the wild stag was hunted on the hills of the Forest of Dean.[1] In 1688 the deer were limited to 800. In 1787 Mr. Charles Edwin, chief forester, told the Commissioners that he had as his perquisite the right shoulder of every deer killed in the forest, and also ten bucks and ten does. He also claimed liberty to hunt, fowl, and fish as he chose. His duty was to attend the king with six men, when he hunted in the forest.[2] In 1840 there were 1,000 deer which appear on occasion to have been hunted with staghounds, as we find record of a run from Trippen-Kennet, Herefordshire, to the Nag's Head enclosure in the forest. In the course of this run the stag swam the Wye three times.[3] In 1848, after a run of three hours, hounds killed in the forest a stag which weighed twenty-two stone. In 1850 government had all the deer killed to remove temptation from the path of the miners, and the forest ceased to be a forest save in name.

Turning now to the chase of the carted deer, we find that the Cheltenham Staghounds were established in 1837 by the Hon. C. F. Berkeley to provide sport when the foxhounds were meeting in the Berkeley country. The Cotteswolds form an ideal country for stag-hunting; there is little water, and as the stag can see a long way he is thus encouraged to make long points. At the election in July, 1847, Sir Willoughby Jones, a Conservative, beat Colonel Berkeley, the Liberal candidate, who held the seat for Cheltenham, by 105 votes; and Lord Fitzhardinge stopped his usual present of red deer for the staghounds and removed the hounds to Berkeley. Mr. Theobald then offered to get together a pack of staghounds, and the Cheltenham sportsmen accepting him as master, the opening meet of the new pack took place on

15 October, 1847, at the Plough Hotel, High Street. The stag was uncarted at Shurdington, and ran up by the Seven Springs, where it was taken after a short but hard run of about five miles.

Sir W. Jones, however, only sat for Cheltenham for a few months, and the feeling to which his election had given rise subsided. Lord Fitzhardinge began to hunt the district again, and in March, 1848, an immense crowd met his foxhounds on the Dowdeswell road, four miles from Cheltenham, where an address from the sportsmen of Cheltenham was presented to him in recognition of the fortieth anniversary of his annual visit to the town. There were 3,000 people on foot and 400 on horseback.

Mr. Theobald's whip was 'Old Sam,' a cripple, who only weighed seven stone. His position on horseback was not a graceful one, and he could not reach the saddle without help. Mr. Theobald was succeeded by Captain West, who resigned in 1857. Mr. W. White then took them, but the town and county could not support both the fox and staghound packs, and Mr. White gave up the latter after one season. In 1874 Mr. Richardson Gardiner of Cowley Manor, M.P. for Windsor, started a pack of staghounds at his own expense. He showed much sport for a few years, but gave up in 1878. Mr. W. B. Bingham of Cowley Manor had a pack of staghounds in 1885–6. These staghounds have had some famous runs. In 1878 Mr. Gardiner's met at Woodmancote, above Rendcombe, and ran by Combe End, through Williamstrip and Barnsley Park to the Leach, nearly thirteen miles beyond Bibury—a grand gallop over a grand country, 25 miles as the crow flies. A horse for which Mr. Croome gave £150 was so much exhausted by this run that he was of little use afterwards. Another stag from Edgeworth stood up for three hours and a half, and left the hounds hopelessly beaten, having passed Gloucester, and crossed the Severn near Minsterworth Mr. Croome only got to Matson, and he was the last of the field to give up. This was a fifteen-mile point, and the stag must have gone

[1] Gibbs, *A Cotswold Village.*
[2] H. G. Nicholls, *Forest of Dean.*
[3] *The Tewkesbury Reg.*

at least twenty-five miles. Mr. Croome also recalls a run with Mr. Gardiner's staghounds from Cowley right away past Colesborne and Northleach into the Heythrop country, on past Chipping Norton Junction and round to the left to Chipping Norton town, where the stag was taken. Hounds must have covered nearly forty miles.

FOX-HUNTING

THE BERKELEY HUNT

There is no doubt that up to the year 1796 hounds were kept at Berkeley and paid long visits to other districts, where they would stay for a time regulated by the supply of foxes. In the year named it is clearly recorded that the huntsman, Oldaker, took them to Gerrard's Cross, in Buckinghamshire, after which no one seems to know what became of them. At any rate there is no record of hounds being kept at Berkeley from that date till 1807, when Lord Dursley, who had just come of age, collected a pack from which that now existing is descended. Richard Cooper was then the huntsman. Soon after this, the pack hunted three countries, viz., ; the Berkeley in October, December, and February ; the Cheltenham in November, January, and March ; and while at Cheltenham horses and hounds would travel by road to Broadway (now the kennels of the North Cotteswold) and hunt the Broadway country on the Saturday, returning to Cheltenham on the Sunday. Part of the Broadway country, extending to the Ilmington Hills, was hunted in alternate months with the Warwickshire pack ; Bourton Wood, which is now hunted by the Heythrop, was also in the Broadway country. From 1808 to 1827 James Lepper was huntsman and was followed by Poole ; but in 1833, with the appointment of Harry Ayris as huntsman, the most flourishing days of the Berkeley seem to have begun. Ayris had come to Berkeley as whipper-in in 1826 ; he eventually retired in 1866 and lived on one of Lord Fitzhardinge's farms near Sharpness Point. Lord Dursley, who had become Lord Segrave, would hunt the hounds himself when with them, and especially when drawing coverts ; but he was not a bold rider, and when hounds really ran Harry Ayris was left to handle them. The country hunted from Berkeley Castle only extended as far as Almondsbury at the Bristol end, and Frampton at the Gloucester end. The best coverts in those days[1] were Bushey Grove, Red Wood, Hills Wood, Nuster Cliff Gorse (since called Nutstock), Parham brake, Fishing House Withy Bed, Newman's Withy Bed, Hay Wood, Tockington Park, Elmore, Clifford's Gorse, Tortworth Coppice, Tintock, Friar's Wood, Michael's Wood and Butler's Gorse. The mention of Elmore shows that occasional visits were paid to districts outside the regular hunting country. In 1858 Harry Ayris told the writer that some twenty years before that date hounds used to have an occasional day both at Elmore and at Corse Grove, now part of the Ledbury country. Lord Segrave planted on his own estate many capital gorse and blackthorn coverts, several of which can still be traced ; but they are now groves of oak and elm, which when cut down are replaced by larch and fir. 'Clifford's Gorse' is a puzzle, as there is no old gorse covert on the Frampton estate ; but it was perhaps the covert now known as the Blackthorn. It has always been a very favourite covert and would certainly have been mentioned. In the Cheltenham and Broadway countries the favourite coverts were Starwood, Chedworth and Withington Woods, Rendcombe Wood, Combend, Moor Wood, West Wood, Guiting Grange Gorse, Dowdeswell Wood, Chatcombe Wood, Stanton Wood, Dumbleton Wood, Haleswood, and Queen Wood, Foxcote Gorses (Mr. Canning's), Weston Park, Bourton Wood, Buckland Wood, Spring Hill, Meon Hill and several good gorses, the five last mentioned being hunted from Broadway. Harry Ayris states that the usual point of an Elmore fox was for Robin's Wood Hill. That was before the Gloucester and Berkeley Canal was made. Between Gloucester and Cheltenham were two favourite woods, Badgeworth and Hatherley. Lord Segrave, afterwards Earl Fitzhardinge, continued to hunt the three countries at his own expense[2] till his death in 1857. The earl was succeeded in 1857 by his brother, Admiral Sir Maurice Berkeley, afterwards first Baron Fitzhardinge. Sir Maurice gave up the Cheltenham and Broadway countries, but reserved the vale between Gloucester, Cheltenham, and Tewkesbury, and set to work to make the most of the real Berkeley country. The late Mr. Barwick Baker of Hardwicke Court, Gloucester, gave him invaluable help by planting in 1858 the two coverts known as Monk's Hill Gorse and Hardwicke Gorse. Though these consist more of blackthorn than gorse nowadays, trees have not been allowed to grow up and kill the undergrowth. Colonel Master planted the gorse below Knowle Park and a withy bed called 'Gus's'; and subsequently in 1877 the late Mr. Curtis Hayward of Quedgeley House, Gloucester, commenced the planting of Quedgeley Gorse,

---

[1] *New Sporting Mag.*

[2] The cost was about £4,000 a year, *Ann. of Sporting*, 1822.

which was completed by the present Lieutenant-Colonel Curtis Hayward. Mr. William Phelps of Dursley planted Rangeworthy Gorse. Thus the fox coverts in the Berkeley country were increased, and it became possible to hunt four days a week in the Vale, besides a day on the hills.

The Berkeley enjoyed its finest sport during the mastership (1857–67) of the first baron, who retained Harry Ayris as huntsman. On 14 January, 1860, there was a great run from Fishing House Withy Bed. Hounds got away close to their fox on the Severn bank, and ran very fast across the Marsh to Hay Wood ; forty minutes so far ; then slower to the New Passage at Aust and back along the river bank to the Old Passage, to ground. Dug him out and killed. One hour and forty minutes. On 1 March, 1860, they found at Tortworth and lost at Hardwicke. This is fifteen miles, the longest point recorded with this pack, but there is no doubt the hounds changed foxes. They ran through Michael's Wood, Berkeley Heath, Bushy Grove, Cats' Castle, Frampton and Moor Farm, and lost in the park in front of Hardwicke Court. The late Duke of Beaufort, Mr. John Bayley, Jim Mason, the steeplechase rider, Bob Chapman, and Mr. W. Kington, were among the strangers out.

On 13 January, 1862, late in the afternoon, a good fox from Hill's Wood chose an extraordinary line of country—hounds pressed him through the Deer Park and across the Pill, into the New Grounds at Purton, and parallel to the Severn almost to Frampton and recrossing the canal, killed at Cambridge. One hour and ten minutes. Colonel Berkeley (' the giant'), Harry Ayris, Mr. G. E. Lloyd-Baker, and Mr. W. Kington, were among the very few who saw it. The best day's sport on record with this pack is that of 25 January, 1864. In the morning they ran hard from Thornbury Park to Fishing House Withy Bed and lost. They then found in Hill's Wood, when the pack divided ; five couple broke for the Severn and were stopped and taken home, so hopeless was it to pursue the remainder. The body of the pack, twelve couple, ran by Daniel's Wood, Tortworth Copse, Charfield, leaving the Lower Woods just on the right, up Wortley Hill, past Newark and Ozleworth, to Tresham : hence back to the left by Ashcroft and Tyley to ground at Wotton Combe, where they bolted their fox and killed him. This was at best pace the whole way. The time is said to have been an hour and fifty minutes.

The 30 January, 1866, saw the last of about five that were always spoken of as ' Scrubby-tail's Runs.' This fox was known by his peculiar brush, the middle of which was bare to the bone. He was always to be found at Frampton and would run to Hardwicke. On his last day, hounds were taken to a halloa, while drawing the Blackthorn, and settled down to run hard at once. They were neither helped nor spoken to for one hour and twenty-five minutes, when they killed him almost by themselves at Elmore. The line was by Frampton Park, leaving Netherhills on the right, Moor Farm and Hardwicke Gorse on the left, nearly to Quedgeley and across the Gloucester and Berkeley Canal to Hawklow Hill, on the side of which they killed in the open. This was Harry Ayris's last season.

The first baron died in 1867 and was succeeded by his son, Francis W. Fitzhardinge, popularly known as ' the giant,' who held office for 29 years till 1896. In 1869 he lent the country between Gloucester and Tewkesbury to the Cotteswold Hunt for about four years and then resumed the loan. There was scarcely a fox in it when he lent this country, and it was well stocked when he took it back. He would give the Cotteswold Hunt a day or two during the season, but kept the country in his own hands that he might hunt there when he liked. In 1889 he lent it to the Cotteswold again, and they have hunted it ever since. Lord Fitzhardinge nearly always showed sport when he went there, but made very short days. He was a great man for going home early, but atoned for this to some extent by trotting very fast from covert to covert. He had a word for every one, and was exceedingly popular with the whole hunting fraternity.

Previous to 1807 the hunt servants undoubtedly wore yellow ; in Lord Segrave's time both they and the gentlemen of the hunt wore scarlet with a black velvet collar, on which was embroidered a silver fox with a gold brush. This continued until 1858 when Sir Maurice and his son ' the giant,' and the hunt servants, came out in yellow plush ; but the members of the hunt remained in scarlet without the gaudy collar. In 1867 the staff resumed the scarlet and the silver fox for the term of the second baron's mastership (1867–96), but in 1897 the present peer returned to the yellow, adopting cloth instead of plush. The dress uniform has for the greater part of the last century been an invisible-blue coat, with black velvet collar and crimson facings, and plain white waistcoat. The ladies of the Berkeley hunt wear a uniform, much the same as the gentlemen's dress coat ; viz. very dark blue, with crimson facings and black velvet collar. This was first worn in Sir Maurice's time, about 1860 ; Lady Gifford, Mrs. Barwick Baker, and Mrs. Berkeley, the wife of ' the giant,' being the first three who were asked to wear it. They were almost the only ladies hunting with this pack in those days ; now as many as forty are occasionally to be seen at a popular meet.

The Vale, as now hunted, from Gloucester to Bristol consists almost entirely of old grass ; it is peculiar in the rarity of ridge and furrow ; moreover, the little that exists is not nearly so deep as that found in most grass countries. About ten years ago a blackthorn, privet, and gorse covert was added to a wood known as Hunt Grove by Mr. Tidswell of Haresfield Court ; and in 1897 a new fox covert called ' Pancake ' was planted on Mr. Clifford's property at Frampton; in 1899 another was planted on the Frocester estate, named 'Adjutant' after the owner's son, Major Graham Clarke, who acted as Adjutant to the Imperial Yeomanry in the Boer War. At the present time there are about 70 couple of hounds in the kennels; they hunt four days a week in the Vale, and one day in the hills. The Berkeley is one of the few packs that have not followed the fashion of breeding for black and tan colour; the old white and badger-pies being greatly treasured; they have plenty of cry. In old days both packs were mixed, but now there are three, viz. dogs, bitches, and mixed. When founding his pack in 1808 Lord Dursley's own expression was, that he had to take what he could get from other kennels, namely those hounds 'whose capital sentence had been commuted to transportation.' Probably the most successful sire used was Lord Henry Bentinck's Contest in 1854. This hound was the father of Cromwell, perhaps one of the best hounds ever known. He was white marked with grey badger-pie. The late Rev. John Russell of Devonshire asked Harry Ayris how he came to send such a hound for Lord Portman to breed from. 'Because,' said the old huntsman 'I will back him to find a fox, hunt a fox, and kill a fox against any hound in England.' The Warwickshire Saffron and the Grove Barrister also did their share in improving the pack; latterly the Warwickshire Artifice and the Tickham Guider have been in high favour. Of late the Pytchley, Cottesmore, South Shropshire and Crawley and Horsham and the Blankney have patronized Berkeley blood.

Wire is far less common in the Berkeley than in any other country known to the writer. This is mainly a consequence of the natural sporting instinct of the farmers, many of whom are very fine riders; also the popularity of each successive master. The farmers passed a rule for their own Agricultural Society that no one should be allowed to take a prize who had had wire in or alongside his hedges during the previous hunting season. Danger signals are strongly objected to as being an excuse for keeping up wire. Perhaps the chief drawback to the country is its narrowness, the average distance from the Severn to the hills being only five miles. The bulk of the coverts are not three miles from the hills, and a good fox will make his point there in twenty minutes. The Midland Railway also cuts up the country badly, running its whole length from Tewkesbury to Bristol. In spite of this, very good sport is shown, and in two or three seasons as many as a hundred brace of foxes have been killed.

THE COTTESWOLD

The country now known as the Cotteswold was the scene of some famous runs in earlier

days. One of the finest took place in the days before the Berkeley Hounds visited the district with regularity. It occurred on 8 December, 1795; when the Warwickshire, then under the mastership of Mr. Corbet, sometimes drew as far west as the Cotteswold country. Finding at Welford, they ran by Leamington Heath, Norton Common, Evenlode Heath, Loughborough Lees, Donnington, Eyford, Cold Aston, Farmington Grove, Salperton, to Sandywell Park, 5 miles from Cheltenham, 25 miles straight and 35 miles as hounds ran, in 3 hours 50 minutes. The first hour and a half they ran without check; the second hour and a half they hunted slowly, and the last 50 minutes they ran without a check. There were fewer fences everywhere in those days, and the Cotteswolds were almost unenclosed. On 1 January, 1822, the Berkeley Hounds had the longest run, in point of time, ever known in the Cotteswold country. It was such a twisting journey that the distance cannot be calculated with any accuracy, but the time was five hours and a half! They met at Queenwood, Southam, 3 miles from Cheltenham, and ran up over Cleeve and Nottingham Hills, and down to the left to Gotherington, on to Winchcombe. Thence they ran back to Gotherington, Cleeve Hill, and down the western side of the hill to Agg's Hill. Turning up left, they ran east and were stopped at Guiting.

The history of the Cotteswold Hunt dates from 1857. On 22 December of that year a circular issued by Mr. W. N. Skillicorne, J.P., father of the present mayor of Cheltenham, announced that Mr. Cregoe Colmore of Charlton Kings was willing to hunt the Cheltenham and Broadway country, which had been given up by Sir Maurice Berkeley, three days a week for a minimum subscription of £1,500, guaranteed for three years. Mr. Colmore also undertook to hunt the Broadway country one day a fortnight, and to have a meet on that—the east —side of the Cheltenham country once a fortnight. The Broadway committee undertook to find him £400 a year for doing this, and for some years fulfilled the engagement. In 1865 there was a difficulty in getting the Broadway money, and the Cheltenham committee and the master proposed to hunt the Broadway country 'when convenient.' Lord Redesdale, then Chairman of Committee of the House of Lords, ex-M.F.H. of the Heythrop, and a large landowner, objected to this proposal, and was strongly supported by all the chief owners in a 'declaration' of 22 September, 1865, signed by Lords Harrowby, Wemyss and March, Beauchamp, Northwick, Sudeley, Sommerville, and others. The Cheltenham committee offered to refer the matter to arbitration, but the Broadway people refused. Their refusal was due to their apprehension lest their country should be partitioned between the Warwickshire, Cotteswold, and Heythrop. Thanks to Lord Redesdale and the other guarantors this step was avoided ; and the separation definitely took place at the end of the season 1866–7, the Broadway area adopting the name of the North Cotteswold, by which it has since been known. In 1858 Mr. Colmore bought the pack with which Lord Gifford had for three seasons hunted the old V.W.H. country, and took as his huntsman Charles Turner, who had turned hounds to Harry Ayris of the Berkeley for seven years. He did well as master, and made Cheltenham a fashionable provincial hunting centre. From 1858 to 1866 the Cotteswold subscription amounted to £1,800 a year. On two occasions when domestic bereavement caused Mr. Colmore to refrain from sport for a time his place was taken by his brother-in-law, Mr. Owen, and also by Mr. Watson and Mr. Barton. On Mr. Colmore's death in 1871 Sir Reginald Graham of Norton Conyers, Ripon, succeeded ; and a committee bought the hounds from the late master's executors by auction for 650 guineas. The new master carried the horn himself. His engagement of Charles Travess as a whipper-in, in 1872, was the most noteworthy incident of the short reign of Sir R. Graham. In 1873 he resigned, chiefly on account of the scarcity of foxes. This was due to neglect of earth-stopping, a very important duty in this country. His successor, Captain A. Sumner (1873–85), was one of the best masters the Cotteswold ever had. He could hold his own with the best over wold or vale, could keep his field in hand, and established and maintained the best relations with the farmers. On Captain Sumner's accession he promoted Charles Travess to carry the horn, and as huntsman Travess has remained with the Cotteswold ever since. A run, historical in the annals of the hunt, took place during this mastership. This occurred on 14 April, 1875. They met at Salperton, and finding at the New Gorse, ran through Hazleton Copse across the Northleach road to Compton Grove, and on over the brook to Withington village and up to the wood. The fox then ran right through Withington and Chedworth Woods, a distance of three miles—a very unusual thing—on by Chedworth village, leaving Foss Cross on the left, then while bearing right-handed for Barnsley, was pulled down just before reaching the park—eleven miles straight, about fifteen as hounds ran : the time is not recorded. Mr. W. O. Brigstocke, who had become honorary secretary on Captain Sumner's accession in 1873, resigned in 1876. Colonel Thoyts took up the duties in 1878 and officiated for a season, being followed by Mr. Le Blanc. Captain Sumner resigned in 1885, after a most successful reign of twelve years, and his place was taken by Mr. W. F. Hicks-Beach, whose accession to office saw a change in the constitution of the hunt. The hounds were permanently secured to it through the efforts of Mr. A. Le Blanc, and ownership was vested in the master,

Lord Fitzhardinge, and Mr. H. J. Elwes, as trustees. Mr. Le Blanc, who had been honorary secretary since the year 1879, resigned in the year which saw the success of his endeavours to secure the hounds to the hunt. His place was taken by Mr. G. B. Witts, who still holds office. Major de Freville followed Mr. Hicks-Beach as master in 1893, and retained office for six years. One of the best runs of the last ten seasons was enjoyed during his mastership. It took place about Christmas, 1898 ; hounds found in Chedworth Wood, and got away with their fox from the bottom part ; leaving Compton Cassey on the left, they crossed the stream near Starwood and ran on by Compton Abdale to Roel Gate. The point was nearly nine miles, but the distance was far more as hounds ran. Major de Freville resigned in 1899, and was succeeded by Mr. Algernon Rushout, who three years previously had resigned the mastership of the North Cotteswold (q.v.). Mr. Rushout's reign, if short, was very successful. Two fine runs occur to mind in connexion with his term of office. In January, 1900, hounds ran hard without a check all the way from Hazleton Brake, and killed their fox in Sherborne Park, having covered about ten miles under the hour. In January, 1902, they found just outside Andoversford, and ran, with only one check at Hazleton Brake, very fast to Farmington Grove, a nine-mile point and about twelve as hounds ran in a little over the hour. Mr. Rushout resigned in 1905, and was succeeded by Mr. E. B. Podmore, who had had a season's experience as master of the Vine Hunt. Mr. Podmore remained only one season, and gave place in 1904 to Mr. H. O. Lord, who continues in office. The Cotteswold country extends some seventeen miles from north to south, and fifteen miles from east to west. The North Cotteswold and Croome territories adjoin it on the north ; on the west lies the Ledbury country, on the south the Berkeley, and on the east the Heythrop and V.W.H. (Cirencester). Monday, Wednesday, and Saturday are the regular hunting days, with one by-day a week in addition, generally Tuesday or Friday. The subscription now exceeds the £2,000 which is guaranteed to the master. The Lords Fitzhardinge have for many years subscribed £100. Sir F. Goldsmid of Rendcombe gave £500 a year on condition that the hounds did not come near Rendcombe Park on Saturday, his Sabbath.

The meets considered best in the vale country are Combe Hill, Norton, Stoke Brake, Stoke Orchard, Boddington, and Odessa Inn. The vale is good riding country, with fair fences of every kind, and the water requires a big jumper. Except for small rails in the hedges there is little timber. East and south of the Cheltenham and Tewkesbury road there is little wire. On the hills the character of the country is quite different. The horseman can see a long way ahead; the uncoped walls are much alike; ditches on either side of the fences are rare, and wire is rarely seen. There is much grass, and the plough is very light. The winding 'deans' with steep sides are trying to horses. On the hills the best meets are at Hawling Downs, Andoversford, Puesdown, Foss Cross, Fivemile House, Rendcombe, Salperton, and North Cerney.

The Cotteswold Hounds have had only three huntsmen in forty-nine years, Charles Turner, T. Hill, and C. Travess, the last of whom has served during thirty-four seasons. Among famous followers of the Cotteswold may be mentioned the late 'Bob' Chapman, one of the largest hunter dealers in England; Chapman 'horsed' the Badminton hunt for many years; Mr. A. Le Blanc, formerly hon. secretary, who was seen at some meets in 1905–06 despite his ninety-two years, and Mr. Brigstocke. Other notable followers have been Mr. Hugh Owen and his brother 'Roddy,' who won the Grand National on Father O'Flynn, and died of cholera in the Soudan; Jacob, a dealer and a great performer in spite of his 16 stone, who afterwards became a picture dealer in London; Mr. Phillips, who died of heart disease in the hunting-field, aged seventy-four, and was the best man of his age in the hunt; and old Joe Titcomb who has been second horseman to the huntsman for over forty years. The most famous runner was Jack Cavanagh, who died in 1897. For over thirty years he was at every meet, and followed the hounds till they turned for home.

THE NORTH COTTESWOLD

The 'Broadway' country, which forms a large portion of the territory now known as the North Cotteswold, was hunted as far back as 1788 by a Mr. Dalton, whose name was originally Naper.[1] Mr. Dalton kennelled his hounds at Slaughter, and had as huntsman a man named Sebright. Sebright's name is memorable by reason of the fame of his son Tom, who, following his father's profession, became huntsman to Lord Fitzwilliam, and remained in the earl's service for nearly forty years. Tom Sebright was born at Stow-on-the-Wold. When the North Cotteswold became an independent country on 1 May, 1867,[2] the supporters of hunting in the district rose to their new responsibilities with energy. Between May and November a site was secured at Broadway, and kennels were built at a cost of £2,750. The Earl of Coventry accepted the mastership, and for six seasons hunted it at his own cost, showing excellent sport.

Among the runs of which Lord Coventry has preserved record, one on 26 November, 1868, deserves mention, though hounds failed to account for their fox. They ran in dense fog from Buckland by Snows-hill Bottom, Farncombe, Saintly Weston, Middle Hill, Letscombe and Slate-pits, where they lost after three hours and a half. Another noteworthy run occurred on 9 January, 1869, when Lord Coventry gave a breakfast at the 'Lygon Arms,' Broadway. After a run and kill they found at Buckland Wood, and ran up-hill three miles to Broadway Tower (where the master got his second horse), and then by Sharwell and through Northwick Park and Snowshill Farm to Cutsdean, where they checked. Thence they ran by Ford Hill Farm and Rock's Pool to Mr. Sarton's house at Swell, near Stow, where they killed in the garden, with only thirteen up. Distance, as hounds ran, fifteen miles; time, 70 minutes. Lord Coventry refers to 31 December, 1869, as 'the best day's sport I have seen in a long career.' After a brilliant twenty-five minutes ending in a kill, they ran a fox from Buckland Wood to Stow-on-the-Wold, a thirteen-mile point and fifteen as hounds ran, killing in the open near the quarry. Few got to the end of the run.

Lord Coventry resided at Croome, his seat near Upton, eighteen miles from the kennels at Broadway. In 1873 he felt that the distance was too great to enable him to do justice to the work of master, and to the regret of all, decided to resign office. He was succeeded in 1873 by Mr. Algernon Rushout, who had his own pack of hounds and hunted them himself. During his mastership good sport was the rule, and before Mr. Rushout resigned he could point in his kennels to twenty-five masks of foxes which his hounds had killed after runs of twenty miles or more. A twenty-five mile run from Porter's Plantation by Stump Cross and Stanway to Pexford, in 2 hrs. 10 min. deserves special mention. When Mr. Rushout took the country, he received a subscription, and the North Cotteswold has been maintained as a subscription pack ever since. The country, partly vale and partly hill, presents peculiar difficulties in the matter of stopping by reason of the rocks on the hills. In 1874 Mr. Rushout employed fifty earth-stoppers, and sometimes thirty of these were at work before a hunting day. The vale country, which is very strongly fenced, extends north from the hills and north-east of Winchcombe as far as Long Marston. Walls are the only fences in the hill districts. Lord Coventry considered the country a famous one in which to 'make' a pack of hounds, as the hill-sides carry a good scent and the rough nature of the ground precludes the possibility of interfering with them. On Mr. Rushout's retirement in 1876, Captain Cyril Stacey became master, purchasing the hounds from his predecessor. Captain Stacey carried the horn himself, hunting the country two days

---

[1] *Bell's Life*, 10 Feb. 1866.
[2] See *Cotteswold Hunt*, 291.

a week. He resigned in 1901, giving place to Mr. Charles McNeill, who in his turn purchased the hounds. Sport under McNeill, who, like his predecessors, was his own huntsman, was remarkably good. This was due in no small measure to Mr. McNeill's ability as a breeder of hounds. He sold the dog-hounds he had purchased from Captain Stacey, and purchased twenty-five couples of bitches from the Quorn, Mr. Fernie's, Pytchley, Badminton, and Atherstone kennels ; and during his six years of office he brought the pack to such a pitch of perfection that, on his retirement in 1906 he sold it with the entry for upwards of £3,600. The country acquired an enhanced reputation, and during the latter years of Mr. McNeill's mastership, Broadway, the most convenient hunting centre, became the resort of numerous visitors in the season. The pack hunts two days a week regularly, and on an occasional by-day. Sport in this country is carried on under very favourable conditions. The farmers are warm supporters of hunting, foxes are well preserved and plentiful, and what wire exists is always removed before the opening of the hunting season. Among the more noteworthy followers of the hunt in modern days, Mr. E. Hawkes of Talton may be mentioned. This gentleman, when on his death-bed, sent for Mr. Rushout, and wrote a cheque for his annual subscription, saying that he could die happily when he had discharged this obligation. He died two hours afterwards. Other well-known characters with the hounds were a yeoman of Broadway named Careless, who used to hunt six days a week on foot, with Mr. Rushout and the Heythrop ; and the Evesham sweep, who on occasion, would use his brush to bolt a fox if required.

THE VALE OF WHITE HORSE (CIRENCESTER)

The Vale of White Horse country owes its name to the 'White Horse' which adorns a locality long since separated from V. W. H. territory. The V. W. H. country, or a very large proportion of it, was originally hunted by Mr. Naper, who gave up his pack somewhere about the end of the eighteenth century and placed his country at the disposal of the landowners, who asked Mr. John Loder, then master of the Old Berkshire, to hunt it.[1] From this time forward until 1832 it formed part of the Old Berkshire territory, and as such was hunted by the masters of the latter from about the end of the eighteenth century. The first master concerning whom records have anything definite to tell was Mr.

Codrington of Codrington, member of a very old Gloucestershire family. Mr. Codrington took office in 1813 and remained until 1824 ; he does not appear to have been a very active man in the field, no doubt owing to his weight, and preferred gaps to fences. He lived at New House in Berkshire with Mr. Wyndham, a bachelor like himself, each having a distinct establishment. Mr. Codrington was succeeded by Mr. Harvey Combe, a member of the well-known firm of brewers. The country hunted by Mr. Combe from 1824 to 1826 extended from Cirencester to Scratch Wood, then 7 miles from London. To hunt this great area, 80 miles long, Mr. Combe purchased Sir J. Astley's pack from Norfolk. 'Nimrod' records a very fast run which took place in February, 1825, on the Gloucestershire side of the country. Hounds found at Williamstrip, and got their fox away toward Bradwell Grove ; then turning to the left and leaving the Grove on the right, they ran across the Bibury race-course near the grand stand, as it was in 1825, and past Aldsworth on the left. Then they crossed the Cheltenham-Oxford road, near Sherborne Park gates, and heading east, killed their fox about a mile from Farmington Grove, which was evidently his point. Ten miles in forty-seven minutes, of which seven were lost at a check. It was said of Mr. Combe that he covered a greater mileage of road going to meets and returning home than any man in England ; but before long he found it too much even for his energies, and in 1826 returned to the Old Berkeley.

Lord Kintore, who succeeded Mr. Combe in 1826, brought his own pack of hounds from Keith Hall, Aberdeenshire, to Wadley House. His establishment of second kennels at Cricklade for convenience of hunting the western side of the country may be regarded as the first step towards the creation of the V. W. H. as a distinct hunt. The necessity for such division was obvious : a letter[2] written by the master in the season of 1829 shows that different parts of the country were hunted at different times ; Lord Kintore in the letter referred to informs his correspondent that 'the hounds will hunt the east country in the autumn.' Lord Kintore was famed for the boldness of his horsemanship : in a ten-mile run from Crab Tree near Higleworth to Uffington he jumped the River Cole, a thing which has never been done since. He paid large sums for his horses : for one, named White-stocking, a wonderful jumper, he is said to have given £800. It may be noted that he always referred to the country as 'The Vale.'[3] The Hon. H. Moreton (afterwards earl of Ducie) followed Lord Kintore in the mastership in

---

[1] F. C. Loder Symons and E. Percy Crowdy, *A History of the Old Berks Hunt*, 1760–1904.

[2] F. C. Loder Symonds and E. Percy Crowdy, *A History of the Old Berks Hunt*, 1760–1904.
[3] Ibid.

1830. Mr. Moreton's term of office marks an epoch in the history of the hunt, as it was at his instance in 1832 that the original Old Berkshire was divided and the V. W. H. became a separate hunt. Mr. Moreton, who till this time had hunted from The Elms near Faringdon, moved to Cricklade, and in 1833 to Cirencester, where Lord Bathurst built kennels for the new V. W. H. in 1835. In this second move we find the first step towards the ultimate subdivision of the V. W. H. country into two parts. Mr. Moreton had as his huntsman Jem Hills, a famous servant in his day; he was somewhat excitable, and used frequently to quarrel with Hills in the field. Mr. Moreton, who became Lord Ducie in 1835, continued to hunt the country until 1842; his resignation, according to the *Sporting Magazine* of 1843, was due to 'the lukewarmness of the resident gentlemen and the scarcity of foxes.' He was succeeded by Lord Gifford, whose mastership was rendered memorable by the prolonged dispute with Mr. Morland, master of the Old Berkshire, concerning the boundary between the two countries. The right to draw certain coverts was hotly contested on either side, and feeling ran high; eventually in September, 1845, after more than two years of friction, it was agreed that the Rivers Thames and Cole should form the boundary, and that certain specified coverts should be neutral to both hunts. Lord Gifford resigned in 1847, and no master coming forward, the hunt was carried on until 1850 by a committee consisting of Lords Andover and Bathurst and Mr. Cripps (known as the 'A.B.C.' committee) with first Mr. Cripps and afterwards Mr. Barker as field master. In 1850 Mr. Villebois took office and ruled successfully until 1854 when Lord Gifford accepted the mastership for the second time and continued till 1857, when Mr. W. Fielder Croome succeeded him. This gentleman was a celebrated horseman, and kept his place in the wake of hounds on horses which no other man could ride; he met his death in the hunting-field, his horse falling over a little stone wall.

Mr. Henley Greaves, who succeeded Mr. Fielder Croome in 1861, only remained until 1863, when he gave place to Mr., afterwards Sir, M. Wharton Wilson. Mr. M. Wharton Wilson bought Mr. Duffield's pack of hounds for 800 guineas, and also engaged the Old Berkshire huntsman, Dale. Sir Wm. Throckmorton, who followed Mr. Wharton Wilson in 1869, first hunted the V. W. H. country from Buckland, Faringdon, but finding this inconvenient he moved to Cecily Hill, Cirencester. Sir William was well known as an owner of race horses, at one time was a member of the Jockey Club and the National Hunt Committee. His term of mastership, which closed in 1875, was particularly successful from every point of view. During the mastership of his successor,

the Earl of Shannon (1875-9), our present king paid two visits to him at Cecily Hill.

Mr. C. A. R. Hoare (1879-86) carried on the hunt in great style, hunting four or five days a week. Difficulties, however, arose between the master and his supporters. As the matter was in no way connected with hunting, but related to a scandal affecting Mr. Hoare's private life, we need only say that it served to alienate all the influential members of the hunt, and as he refused to resign the mastership, the trouble culminated in the division of the country. During Mr. Hoare's last season he hunted the Cricklade division of the country with the original pack of hounds, which afterwards passed to Mr. Butt Miller. Lord Bathurst, who took the Cirencester division, then formed a new pack, and from that date the old V. W. H. ceased to exist in its entirety.

With the accession to office of the late Earl Bathurst in 1886 begins the roll of masters of the V. W. H. (Cirencester) Hunt as it now exists. Lord Bathurst held the mastership until his death in 1897, when he was succeeded by his son the present master. Excellent sport has been the rule since the creation of the V. W. H. (Cirencester) as a separate country. Mr. Erle Drax of Cheltenham, who has hunted with the pack since Sir William Throckmorton's time, can recall several runs of nearly thirty miles. On a Saturday in March, 1885, the hounds had a wonderful run of three hours including checks, the distance being about 25 miles. Finding at Alvescot they ran towards Bampton, and leaving it on the right passed Witney on the left, and then Tar Wood, ending at Yarnton Junction, four miles from Oxford. Mr. H. Owen, Mr. C. Hoare, the master, and Mr. J. Adamthwaite of Siddington Lodge, Cirencester, were up at the end, and took the hounds back to Cirencester, arriving there at 12.15 on Sunday morning.

In March, 1886, they had a great run from Water Eaton by Red Lodge and Somerford Common to Cleverton near Charlton Park, where the fox was dug out from a drain under the road at 8.30 p.m. Distance over 15 miles, time about 80 minutes. Gibbs (*Cotswold Village*) describes a run on 1 January, 1897, from Stonehill Wood by Charlton Park and Gorston to Rodbourne in the Duke of Beaufort's country, in which hounds covered ten miles within the hour.

Among well-known covert owners and followers within the last thirty years, mention may be made of Mr. T. Chester Masters and Col. Chester Masters, Messrs. W. Musgrave of Barnsley, P. Barker of Fairford Park, Sir M. Hicks-Beach, Sir T. Bazeley, Mr. and Mrs. Van Notten Pole of Watermoor, the Hon. Mr. and Mrs. Agar Ellis of Highworth, Col. Arthur Archer of Lush Hill, Mr. T. and the Hon. Mrs. Kingscote, Mr. 'Eddie' Williams, then of Bibury Court, B. B. Cooper, now of Bibury

Court, Col. Buckle, Mr. Butler of Down Ampney, who was killed jumping a wall, Mr. Fox of Braddyl (Bradwell) Grove, Col. Dallas Yorke and his daughter (now Duchess of Portland), Mr. J. Adamthwaite, the Bowleys of Siddington, and Mr. and Mrs. Egginton, afterwards known as Erle Drax. Mrs. Egginton, for sixteen years, was one of the boldest riders with the V. W. H.

A sad event in the history of the hunt was the death of Major Whyte-Melville on 5 December, 1878, when hunting with the V.W.H. not far from Tetbury, where he had lived many years. He was galloping across a ploughed field, and his horse caught his fore-legs in a shallow drain, like a ' grip,' that had been just cut. The Major was thrown on his head and broke his neck.

HARRIERS

The earliest pack of which record remains was one kept by Mr. W. L. Barnard at Whitfield, near Apperley. Mr. Barnard achieved great popularity in the country, as would appear from the fact that in 1842 he was presented at Gloucester Shire Hall with a portrait of himself on a favourite hunter. The hide of this horse was eventually cut up into whip-thongs, some of which still exist. In 1849 the country round Cheltenham was hunted by the ' Cottiswold or Brockworth' Harriers,[1] Mr. S. Harman, a Cubberley farmer, being the first master. A pack called the Norton Harriers also existed about the same time, in the Cheltenham district. Mr. William Hawkins of the Hawthorns, Corse Lawn, maintained a pack of harriers for many years during the earlier half of the nineteenth century. He sold his pack to Mr. Parkes, who afterwards fought a duel on Kempsey Common with Mr. Russell of Powick, in consequence of a dispute in the hunting-field. Mr. Hawkins, who employed a woman as his kennel huntsman, was a most hospitable man ; he kept open house during the hunting season, with a table always standing in the hall. He died in 1860. Mr. Foley Onslow kept a pack at Newent for some years, in the fifties and early sixties; and about the same time, Mr. Crump of Walton Hill, near Coombe Hill, had a pack of harriers. The Cotteswold Harriers were owned by Mr. Hudson of Tocknalls, Painswick, in the early seventies. Mr. Hudson was subsequently joined by Sir Francis Ford and Mr. E. Potter, and the Cotteswold for several years hunted part of what is now the Boddington Harriers' country. They came to an end in 1882, and in the following

year Mr. T. S. Gibbons, who had purchased Boddington Manor, near Cheltenham, began to hunt the old Cotteswold country and some new territory with the pack he had bought from Mr. C. Morrell (the Berkshire Vale Harriers). For a time Mr. Gibbons hunted two days a week ; subsequently increasing the size of the pack, he hunted three days a week, and so continued for nine seasons, after which he dropped the extra day. The country hunted lies in the Vale of Severn. The Longford Harriers were established about the year 1840, by the Rev. W. Taylor, curate of Maisemore. During the sixty-four years of its existence the affairs of the hunt were managed by a committee of farmers. The kennels were at Longford, some two miles and a half from Gloucester, and the pack hunted twice a week the country in the neighbourhood of the county town ; also meeting by invitation in various parts of Gloucestershire, Worcestershire, and Herefordshire. The following gentlemen held office after Mr. Taylor's resignation :—Mr. F. Sevier of Maisemore assisted by Mr. Morris of Maisemore Court ; Mr. J. H. Priday of Brockworth (Mr. John Sivell, deputy master) ; Messrs. Harvey Melville, the Hon. T. L. Bampfylde, L. Fane Gladwin ; J. Gratwicke Blagrave and Oswald E. Part, as joint masters, and finally, Mr. Frank Green, whose resignation in 1904, after two seasons in office, was followed by the abandonment of the hunt. Mr. Gratwicke Blagrave, who held the mastership alone from 1899 to 1901, and with Mr. Part for another year, is remembered as an exceptionally successful and popular master.

COURSING

The principal public meetings held in the county before the passing of the Ground Game Act were those of Cirencester, Berkeley and Kingscote, the ground of each being well adapted for the sport. Cirencester was held over the stonewall district of the Cotteswold Hills where much of the land is arable, and the hares were always

remarkable for their strong running, affording excellent tests of the staying qualities of the greyhounds. A Cirencester club existed for some years in the 'sixties, and a two days' meeting was held each season under the patronage, and over the estates, of Mr. T. W. C. Master, about a mile from the town of Cirencester. Mr. E. Trinder was secretary to the club, and amongst the owners of greyhounds was the late Lord

[1] Gelert, *Guide to the Foxhounds of England.*

Gifford, well known as a master of foxhounds before he took an interest in coursing. After lying dormant for some years the meeting was revived in 1906, a new club having been formed, of whom Mr. F. T. Rawlins is the secretary. A meeting took place during the autumn of 1906, but does not call for any special remark. The Berkeley meetings held in the eighties, and known as the 'Berkeley (Open) and Yeomanry' meetings, took place by permission of Earl Fitzhardinge on the large meadows adjoining the River Severn, near the villages of Cambridge and Stonehouse, not far from the town of Berkeley. The meeting generally extended to two days, and being within easy reach of Gloucester was usually well patronized. The Kingscote meetings, abandoned in the early 'nineties, were for some years held over the estate of Sir Nigel Kingscote, K.C.B.; these were never of the same importance as the two mentioned.

Many good coursers at one time lived in the county. Among these, who lived in Cheltenham or its neighbourhood, were Dr. T. J. Cottle, Messrs. Jas. Leighton, Wm. Theyer, and C. J. Chesshyre.

Other noted members and good supporters of the Club were Lord Uffington, Messrs. J. H. Elwes, F. Cripps, E. Bowley, E. Reece, Chas. Randell, and H. Haywood, the two last-named, with Lord Uffington, being three most successful coursers in those days.

RACING

Gloucestershire held an important place in the early days of both Flat Racing and Steeplechasing. From time immemorial there has been racing on the great down lands in the neighbourhood of Burford. In the reign of Charles II Bibury, head quarters of the oldest Racing Club in England, was another Newmarket, and the meetings held there were visited by the king on at least three occasions. In 1681 the Newmarket Spring Meeting was transferred to Bibury; at that time Parliament met at Oxford, only thirty miles away, and Bibury was a convenient resort for racing legislators. The spread of railways eventually deprived the place of its prominence as a racing centre, and the club was removed to Stockbridge and later to Salisbury, after it had held its meetings at Bibury and Burford for 150 years. Nimrod, in his *Life of a Sportsman*, gives the following account of the Bibury Meeting in the reign of George III :—

Those were Bibury's very best days. In addition to the presence of George IV, then Prince of Wales, who was received by Lord Sherborne for the race week at his seat in the neighbourhood, and who every day appeared on the course as a private gentleman, there was a galaxy of gentlemen jockeys who alone rode at this Meeting, which has never been equalled. Among them were the Duke of Dorset, who always rode for the Prince ; the late Mr. Delné Radcliffe ; the late Lords Charles Somerset and Milsington ; Lord Delamere, Sir Tatton Sykes, and many other 'first raters.' I well remember the scenes at Burford and all the neighbouring towns after the races were over. That at Burford 'beggars description' ; for independently of the bustle occasioned by the accommodation that was necessary for the Club who were domiciled in the town, the concourse of people of all sorts and degrees was immense.

The old Sweating House still stands on the Downs near Aldsworth.

A successful meeting was held for years on the top of Cleeve Hill, where the Gloucestershire Stakes were run annually.

In more recent times Cheltenham, at that day one of the fashionable watering-places of England, was a resort for some of the keenest patrons of steeplechasing. Colonel Charretie, a very well-known figure in the sporting world, who made the Plough Hotel his head quarters, won the Cotteswold Handicap at Northleach in 1841 with Black Prince. Races were held here annually from 1840. The Colonel was a great match-maker, and always ready for a bet of any kind. In 1842 he made a bet that he would win a shooting match, the Imperial Steeplechase at Cheltenham, and play the Duke of York at the Assembly Rooms the same evening. He did not win, as his horse Napoleon, which he rode himself, was beaten by Mr. Robinson's Imperial Tom, at 10 st. 7 lb. and 13 st. respectively.

It was with Napoleon in 1833 that the Colonel made his celebrated match with Squire Osbaldeston's Grimaldi, over a six-mile course near Dunchurch. Captain Becher rode Napoleon, and the squire his own horse. During the race both horses fell into a river which had to be crossed, and Mr. Osbaldeston, first ashore, eventually won by a length and a half ; but was disqualified for going the wrong side of some flags. Colonel Charretie, however, anxious to avoid unpleasantness with his friends decided that the stakes should be drawn. The Colonel ran second in the Derby of 1843 with Gorhambury.

Mr. Fothergill ('Fog') Rowlands was another well-known Gloucestershire supporter of steeplechasing. He lived at Prestbury near Cheltenham, and was one of the best gentlemen riders of his day. To the efforts of Mr. Rowlands we owe the National Hunt Steeplechase, which he and his friends started as an experiment in 1859. The same complaints were being made in the fifties about the decadence of steeplechasing that we hear at this day. The regular steeplechaser was beginning to oust the old 'Cocktail' who had held his own in the thirties, described as the golden age of the sport, and many people being anxious to shut out the 'chaser in favour of the genuine hunter, Mr. Rowlands proposed a race in which bona-fide hunters alone should compete. He suggested that the various hunts should subscribe a liberal stake, as an inducement to farmers to breed high-class hunters. His proposal met with scant response, Mr. Rowlands declaring that not a single hunt, with the exception of the V.W.H., made any contribution. However, he and his friends themselves found the money, and a race took place as an experiment in 1859 at Market Harborough. The following year several hunts came to his help, and a very successful race was the result.

In 1861 the Grand National Hunt Steeplechase, through the kindness of a most popular nobleman residing in the neighbourhood, and also a contribution of £50 subscribed by the Cotteswold Hunt, was held at Cheltenham on a course at Southam under Cleeve Hill. It was not held in the county again until the present century, when it took place at Cheltenham two years running, in 1904 and 1905.

Cheltenham has for many years been a well-known training centre, and such famous men as William Holman, George Stevens, Tom Olliver and William Archer have been connected with the town as trainers or jockeys.

William Holman was settled in Cheltenham and was training and riding many winners about 1839. In 1841 he won two steeplechases at Andoversford, and on Xeno rode a dead-heat with Tom Olliver on Greyling at Cheltenham. In 1842, on Dragsman, he won the big race at Andoversford run over walls; and in 1843 the same race over a 6-mile course, on The Page, both his own horses. In the same year he rode in his first Grand National; he never succeeded in riding the winner, though in 1852 he was third, and in 1853 fourth on Sir Peter Laurie. He trained Freetrader, the winner of 1856, in which year he also had engaged Sir Peter Laurie, whose chance he fancied the better of the two. He asked William Archer to ride Freetrader, but the latter refused to waste to ride a 'second string,' and George Stevens had the mount and his first winning ride. Sir Peter Laurie spoiled whatever chance he might have had by refusing at 'Proceed's Lane,' in those days an in-and-out. In 1870 he trained The Doctor, when, with his second son George in the saddle, that horse was beaten a head by The Colonel. He also trained Globule, a little 15-hand horse who won the first big steeplechase at Croydon, when the course was so big as to be described as 'sensational'; Stanmore and Daddy Longlegs, winners of the Cheltenham and Leamington Grand Annuals of 1847; Penarth, on which George Holman won the Birmingham and Cheltenham Grand Annuals of 1862; Brick, who won the Prince of Wales' Steeplechase the first day and

Grand Annual the second in 1869; Master Mowbray, three times winner of this race, in 1874, 1875, and 1876; Chamade, Bantam, and Not Out, the last of which was just beaten for the Cesarewitch of Cardinal York's year (1870), and in 1871 won the Ebor Handicap. John, William Holman's third son, was also riding with great success on the flat and over a country at this time.

George Stevens was born in Cheltenham in 1833. His riding career extended from 1856 to 1870, during which he rode five Grand National winners: Freetrader in 1856, Emblem in 1863, Emblematic in 1864 and The Colonel in 1869 and 1870. In 1871 while riding home from Cheltenham to Emblem Cottage, a house he had built for himself on Cleeve Hill, he was thrown and killed. A stone inscribed 'G. S., 1871' now marks the spot at the foot of the hill.

William Archer was born at Cheltenham in 1826, and had his first mount when he was nine years old, riding a pony in a hurdle race at Elmstone Hardwick. He rode on the flat in his young days and for two years rode in Russia for the Czar. About 1844 he began riding between the flags and settled in Cheltenham, where he rode a great deal for William Holman. Of his two sons, William and Fred, the elder was killed while riding at Cheltenham in 1878. When Fred Archer was at the height of his fame he used to stay with his father, who then had the hotel at Andoversford, and hunt with the Cotteswold hounds.

Steeplechasing was first started in Cheltenham in the thirties. In 1834 Mr. William Vevers won the Rose Steeplechase on his horse Sailor Boy. In the same year a match of £200 a side was run between Mr. Lucas's Harlequin and Mr. Thompson's Primrose. In April of that year, and for several succeeding, a sweepstakes of £10 over a 4-mile course was run for. This was won in 1837 by Captain Becher on Vivian from thirteen opponents; the value of the race had by then increased to a sweep of £20 with £50 added, half by Lord Segrave and half by the town. Another race the same day was won by Tom Olliver on Railroad; in 1839 it was won by that great 'chaser Lottery. In the fifties a two-days' steeplechase meeting was held in the spring, and a flat-race meeting in the autumn. At the spring meeting was held the Cheltenham Grand Annual, which ranked with the other grand annuals of Aylesbury, Leamington, &c. In 1854 on the first day the Grand Annual, and on the second a Grand Military Steeplechase, were run under the following conditions: a sweepstake of £10 each with £100 added, the winner to give £20 towards expenses and six dozen of champagne. The meeting was held on various different courses round Cheltenham, but generally in Prestbury Park until about 1864, when it was moved to a course on Kayte Farm. It was there in 1866 that the meeting received a serious check by the collapse of the stand, a mishap which resulted in injury to a great many people. The committee was sued by some of the victims, and as the contractors who supplied the stand became bankrupt at the time, the committee lost a considerable sum of money. At this meeting Mr. Reginald Herbert, of Clytha, lately master of the Monmouthshire Hounds, won the Grand Annual of £500 with Columbia, beating among others Cortolvin, L'African, and Emblematic. The following year, 1867, the meeting was removed to a course at Prestbury, part of which is now covered by the Cheltenham cemetery; William Holman's eldest son, William R. Holman, managed these races for some years, holding a steeplechase meeting in the spring and a flat-race meeting in the autumn. He also managed a small flat-race meeting held at this time at Gloucester. In 1875 George Holman won the Grand Annual for his father's stable on Master Mowbray, giving Congress 1 lb. In this race R. Marsh, who had been living with Tom Golby at Northleach, and had just removed to Lordship Farm, Newmarket, was riding Furley, who swerved and fell at the first hurdles, bringing down Harbinger and Mistletoe; Alfred Holman, who rode the latter, was badly injured and was carried into the paddock for dead, at the moment his brother was led in as winner after a popular victory. In the eighties the races began to fall into disrepute in Cheltenham; they were finally abandoned in 1892.

It was not until 1898 that Mr. Jack Hargreaves and some friends got up a meeting at Prestbury Park, and revived the old Grand Annual. Alfred Holman maintained the family traditions by supplying the winner in Mr. R. C. B. Cave's Xebec, the writer having the mount. The horse had been done up and watered just before the race, as his owner had not intended to run him, but Holman was so anxious to be represented that Mr. Cave allowed him to be brought across from the Prestbury Park stables and started. After this the meeting again fell into abeyance; it was again revived in 1902, and very successful races are held in spring and autumn. The National Hunt Steeplechase, as already mentioned, was held there in 1904 and 1905.

Other meetings now held in Gloucestershire are Colwall and the annual hunt meetings of the V.W.H. at Oaksey and the Duke of Beaufort's hounds at Sherston; there are also point-to-point meetings held by other hunts, the best of which is that of the Ledbury over a fine natural course at Redmarley.

Gloucestershire has some excellent natural training-grounds on the Downs of the Cotteswold Hills. At present the principal training centres are Cheltenham and Cleeve Hill, but there are fine gallops on Bourton Hill, where Russell has a good string. In the old days of steeplechasing Tom Golby had training stables at Northleach, and used to gallop his horses at Stowell and Puesdown. Phryne was trained here by him for the Bristol Steeplechase. In the sixties Weaver had a very successful stable at Bourton Hill, where he trained Emblem and Emblematic for their successes in the Grand Nationals of 1863 and 1864 for Lord Coventry. Best known among later racing men in the county was Mr. H. S. Sidney, who settled in Cheltenham in 1896. He was then only twenty-five years old, but had already made a name for himself by his success in training and riding his own horses. He was very hardworking, a rare judge of a horse, a first-rate stableman, and an adept at 'placing' his horses. He turned out an extraordinary number of winners. In 1901 he headed the list of gentlemen riders. On three of his best horses—Gangbridge, Shortbread, and Cavill II—he won no less than forty-six races. In 1902 he moved to Weaver's old training ground at Bourton Hill; but on 26 December of the same year this popular all-round sportsman was killed in a race at Wolverhampton. Steeplechasing received a severe blow by his untimely death. Among present well-known trainers in the county are Alfred Holman, J. T. Rogers, and Mr. E. M. Munby at Cheltenham, and Russell at Bourton Hill. Messrs. Rogers, Munby, and Cuthbertson are also well-known gentlemen riders. Soldier riders have been represented by Mr. Hugh and the late Captain 'Roddy' Owen, who at one time lived in Cheltenham; Captain (now Colonel) J. W. Yardley, and Captain Elwes.

The Hon. Aubrey Hastings began his racing career with a little private establishment at Woodmancote near Cirencester, on the same ground on which Craddock trained a few horses for Mr. Charles Hoare, when master of the V.W.H. Other well-known gentlemen riders have at various times lived and trained on Cleeve Hill, notably Mr. G. Saunders Davies and Mr. A. W. Wood.

Flat-racing is, it is to be feared, a thing of the past in Gloucestershire, owing to the distance of our natural down courses from the railways; it is a county, however, in which steeplechasing in its best form has always been popular; and it has produced some of the finest horsemen in the world, both on the flat and across country.

SPORT ANCIENT AND MODERN

FALCONRY

In ancient times falconry was no doubt practised in many parts of Gloucestershire, as elsewhere in Britain; but after the great Civil War the sport was neglected. King John sent his falconer Hawkin de Hautville to Gloucester with a writ to the sheriff to provide proper food, lodging, and maintenance for him, his men, and his hawks—for the 'mewing,' or moulting of the birds.[1] Queen Elizabeth, when visiting the county, no doubt enjoyed many a flight; for her chief falconer, Sir Ralph Sadler, trained his hawks on the downs in the adjoining county of Wilts.[2] So recently as 1787 Mr. Charles Edwin, chief forester in fee and bow-bearer, informed the Commissioners of the Forest of Dean that he claimed by virtue of his office to be entitled to a licence to hawk, &c., within the forest.[3] For successful falconry an open country is necessary; hence the wooded hills and valleys along the range of the Cotteswolds are particularly unsuited to the sport. During a period of forty years, however, the late Major C. Hawkins Fisher kept peregrine falcons at his residence, The Castle, Stroud; and in that district, which he described as probably the worst country in all England for such flights, he took, in one season, thirty-two partridges, eight rooks, a crow, a wood pigeon and a magpie.[4] In the neighbourhood of Stroud, Major Fisher's falconer with his 'cadge' or portable frame, bearing three or four hooded hawks, was a familiar sight; and the far-sounding ringing of a hawk's bell, high in air, from a bird flown to the lure, or chasing a pigeon, was frequently heard. On the open land on the east side of the county much partridge hawking was enjoyed; and at a greater distance from home the hawks were flown at more difficult game, great numbers of grouse being killed in some seasons. At one time, Major Fisher let his young hawks out 'at hack' (at liberty) near Stroud; but many having been shot, he gave up rearing and obtained most of his birds full-grown from abroad. Shortly before his death, which occurred on 26 October, 1901, he published his *Reminiscences*, in which are recorded many and varied experiences of interest to the naturalist as well as to the sportsman.

SHOOTING

The county is well adapted to the rearing of most kinds of game. The wide range of dry light land, mostly arable, known as the Cotteswolds, the great Crown Forest of Dean, the woods of the large estates, the meadows of long rich grass, and the small enclosures of rough herbage with thick untrimmed hedges; and a plentiful supply of water are all favourable to the rearing of birds. During the last fifty years or thereabout, as the number of hares and rabbits killed has decreased, so the number of pheasants has increased. The reason being that, when from various causes, especially the working of the Ground Game Act, the supply of hares and rabbits diminished, game preservers reared more pheasants to replace the ground game. Previous to the passing of the Act, hares were very numerous in the county, but they gradually became rarer, except on some few estates. During the last two or three years in the neighbourhood of Lassington and elsewhere, for instance Hartpury, Tibberton, and Sherborne, they have been spared and are on the increase. In 1886, when the writer rented the shooting of the Grove Farm, Taynton, he killed a hare of a slate colour, evidently a cross with the blue hare, some of which had been turned out a few years before by a neighbouring squire.

Pheasants are now extensively reared on the large estates, and also on some game farms, such as that at Huntley. The old English pheasant is preferred by some to the Chinese bird as showing more sport. Reeve's pheasants have been naturalized at Tortworth, and these magnificent birds are on the increase as the owner allows only a few to be shot each season. In some of the wooded valleys of the Cotteswolds, and also at Flaxley and other places, the birds fly very high, taxing the skill of the best shot.

The partridge shooting in Gloucestershire is not as a rule first-class, but it is good on some of the Cotteswold estates, such as Sherborne; Corse Lawn is good partridge ground; and good sport may be had with partridges in the Newent district, at Taynton and at Hartpury. Red-legged partridges are numerous near Newent, so much so that in one day three brace out of the four bagged by the writer were 'Frenchmen.' Partridge shooting in some parts of the county

---

[1] C. Hawkins Fisher, *Reminiscences of a Falconer.* Nimmo, London, 1900.
[2] Badminton Library, *Coursing and Falconry*, 218.
[3] H. G. Nicholls, *The Forest of Dean*, 1851, p. 201.
[4] C. Hawkins Fisher, *Reminiscences*, 82.

has been steadily deteriorating, owing to the laying down of ploughland to grass; this is the case on Hartpury estate, and also on Highnam estate, on which one farm of 236 acres has all been laid down to grass. Very few people in this county now use setters or pointers for partridge shooting; retrievers or retrieving spaniels are employed. In the earlier part of the season the birds are walked up, and later on they are driven. Personal experience goes to show that for a quiet day with two guns nothing is better than a steady old setter who will stand birds and retrieve and, when told, break his point and hunt a hedgerow. The season of 1897 was the best for partridges within the writer's memory in the neighbourhood of Lassington; 145 birds were killed off about 500 acres at Malswick, and 314 were killed on the Newent Court estate.

The bags of partridges on Hartpury estate that season on six days in September were respectively 68, 56, 61, 42, 30 and 32 birds. Owing to the dearth of partridges from the wet weather in 1903, a good many Hungarian birds were turned out in Gloucestershire. The writer procured some eggs from Hungary and hatched, reared, and turned out two hampers of strong young birds in August, 1904, but he does not know that they have done him much good. In November, 1903, 50 brace of Hungarians were turned out on Hartpury estate, but a good many were killed by the wet, and on the whole the shooting has not been much improved by them. On the Sherborne estate, however, the introduction of fresh blood in the shape of Hungarians has had excellent results, over 100 brace of partridges having been killed in one day in 1905, and 126½ brace on another, the latter the record bag for Gloucester. On the Hartpury estate in 1905, on 1 and 2 September, 51 and 90 partridges were bagged. A few landrails are occasionally shot in September when beating clover or standing corn for partridges, but they are rarer than they were formerly. About 1893 two bevies of quails were seen on the Onslow estate near Newent, and about a dozen birds were shot. There were some quails at Quedgeley about twenty years ago.

Rabbits are very numerous in parts of Gloucestershire. This is in some measure the result of the Ground Game Act. The farmers preserve in order to enjoy ferreting at Christmas, and shooting young rabbits in the summer. The best way for the game preserver to have good rabbit shoots is to keep the fields round the coverts in his own hands. This is done at Tibberton and at Fretherne, at which latter the bag of rabbits on four days was: 1,214, 946, 388, 979; total, 3,527. In many cases it is not scarcity of rabbits which causes them to form so small an item in gentlemen's game books, but wiring by professional rabbit-catchers employed by the farmers. On one farm of 300 acres

near Gloucester 3,000 rabbits were destroyed in twelve months two years ago; whereas when the squire had his shoots only about 20 rabbits were shot in four days. There is one shoot of 1,200 acres in the Cotteswold where the shooting tenant undertakes to kill 4,000 rabbits in the year; of course, some of these would be wired. On certain estates such as Huntley and the Haie some white rabbits are kept, and if a keeper going his rounds sees these conspicuous animals out feeding he knows that trespassers have not been near lately. One way of ensuring good sport with rabbits is to ferret them out for several days, stop the burrows, and put bits of paper dipped in paraffin on the mouth of the holes. There are some fine shoots on the Cotteswolds where this method is practised; particularly that large tract which is rented by residents of Cheltenham and Gloucester.

Woodcocks do not frequent Gloucestershire in any considerable numbers. As a rule, at most shoots not more than two or three would be killed. There are woodcocks in the Forest of Dean; but the best place in the county known to the writer is May Hill, where on 28 December, 1898, 14 'cock were killed. Woodcock shooting on May Hill is not without its dangers, as a man walking at a higher elevation than another runs the risk of being hit by the latter. At one shoot the writer's servant, who was standing by him, got a shot through his hat. The rarity of the bird in some places causes every one to 'loose off' at it. A certain sportsman is reported to have said that when he heard the beaters call 'Woodcock forward,' he lay down flat till the danger was over.

In the winter a good many snipe visit the Severn meadows near Gloucester; there are also some in the Leadon meadows. About 1881 or 1882 quantities appeared at Hartpury, feeding in the mud beside heaps of rotten hay left by the flood. The snipe rose in wisps of five to eight, and seventy or eighty must have been put up out of one meadow.

The following records serve to show the nature of sport enjoyed on certain estates in the days of the muzzle-loader and in modern times:—

At Lassington (one day), 1845, 2 guns bag 112 head; 1848, 4 guns, 130 head; 1852, 4 guns, 150 head.

At Lassington (one day), 1896, 6 guns bag 108 head; 1897, 6 guns, 57 head; 1898, 6 guns, 45 head.

At Hartpury (one day), 1847, 4 guns bag 119 head; 1850, 7 guns, 173 head; 1857, 4 guns, 232 head.

At Hartpury (one day), 1903, 4 guns bag 742 head; 1904, 3 guns, 741 head and 721 head.

At Highnam (one day), 1848, 4 guns bag 90 head; 1850, 5 guns, 100 head.

At Highnam (one day), 1898, 8 guns bag 187 head (171 pheasants); 1899, 7 guns, 170 head (146 pheasants).

SPORT ANCIENT AND MODERN

The following records enable comparison to be made between the bags made in the whole season with the muzzle-loader and those made in recent times :—

At Highnam, seasons 1858-9, were killed 192 pheasants, 323 hares, and 1,767 rabbits ; season 1863-4, 307 pheasants, 672 hares, and 3,814 rabbits.

At Highnam, in 1881, 1,588 head were killed.

At Sherborne Park, in 1873, the bag for tbe season was : 577 pheasants, 302 partridges, and 587 hares ; in 1883, 351 pheasants, 421 partridges, 386 hares,

and 1,126 rabbits ; in 1904, 1,756 pheasants, 1,116 partridges, 961 hares, and 3,008 rabbits.

At Cowley Manor, in 1904, the season's bag of pheasants was 1,700, 1,138 being the largest day's bag.

At Hartpury, on 11 December, 1903, 3 guns killed 214 pheasants, 1 hare, 703 rabbits, and 4 various ; total, 922.

On 16 November, 1904, 3 guns killed 327 pheasants, 36 hares, 15 rabbits, 358 wild fowl, and 3 various ; total, 739 ; on 15 December, 1904, 3 guns killed 182 pheasants, 7 hares, 419 rabbits, 191 wild fowl, and 2 various ; total, 801.

WILD-FOWLING

In treating of the wild fowl of this county only those species are noticed which come in such numbers as individually to attract the attention of the sportsman, and to form an asset of a certain importance for the table. Such occasional visitors to Gloucestershire as the Brent Goose (*Bernicla brenta*), the Golden-eye (*Clangula glaucion*), the Grey Plover (*Squatarola helvetica*), and the Bar-tailed Godwit (*Limosa lapponica*) are of interest rather to ornithologists than to sportsmen.

The wild-fowling districts of the county fall under two categories, the permanent and the temporary. The former consist of the wider part of the Severn estuary for twenty-five miles from Avonmouth to Fretherne, and of a narrow transitional part running for another ten or twelve miles to Longney. Above Longney the ebb and flow of the tide are not such as to leave mud-banks or sands on which the wild fowl can feed and rest. Nor is any part of the water sufficiently far from land to offer the birds security from man. Off Avonmouth, on the other hand, the estuary is some $5\frac{1}{2}$ miles wide, and just below Fretherne over a mile wide.

The temporary districts for wild-fowling are certain low-lying meadow lands along the Severn which become flooded. To these are attracted many wild fowl, especially if such situations afford 'splashes'—'splash' being a local name for a shallow depression that retains the water after the main floods have subsided. These districts reach chiefly from Longney up to Tewkesbury, that is to say, along the narrower part of the river. The wild-fowling over them is necessarily carried on at uncertain times, and in a more or less casual and unscientific manner, chiefly by flight-shooting with a 12-bore gun. The uncertainty affects the birds as well as the wild-fowler, since the former scarcely have time to settle down in any regular haunts. Moreover, amid large tracts of water, covering in all perhaps seventy square miles, spots frequented by wild fowl, except those of the 'splashes' that follow on, are difficult to find. The big thorn hedges likewise check boating except in some ten or twelve situations where there is a tract of commonable land, or a grazing common termed

a 'ham,' or where dykes or 'reens' take the place of hedges. Wild geese and ducks, however, do frequent the flooded grounds in considerable numbers, and as the water subsides quantities of dunlins, snipe, and peewits feed over the sodden turf. One sportsman, at any rate, has made a systematic attempt to grapple with the geese and ducks. A chain-secured hut stands in the middle of the flood, and thither the shooter betakes himself with a 4-bore at flight time. The situation is towards the north of the Vale of Gloucester, and from the evidence collected it appears as though the majority of the ducks come from the north-east, and not from the Severn in the south-west. Their numbers vary according to the exact time of year of the floods and the prevailing wind of the evening. A strong south-west wind, for instance, considerably reduces their numbers. As often as not a good bag, chiefly of mallards, is obtained. During the day a good bag is made at times by working the floods with a boat or two. In the latter case, one boat is used to disturb the ducks, whilst the wild-fowler shoots from the other. If only one boat is used, and the ducks are fairly restful, they can be approached sufficiently close, say within 200 to 150 yards or less, to enable good results to be obtained with a 4-bore. Geese are seldom killed by either of these methods, and a bag consists chiefly of mallards, wigeon and teal, and occasional specimens of other ducks.

Returning now to the permanent districts, it is in these that the wild-fowler is at home. There the birds acquire habits, habits that change with a frost, the wind, the degree of moonlight, fog, the time of year, the tides, and with the amount of disturbance to which they are subjected. Still they are habits, and the man who correctly gauges the changes is the successful wild-fowler. These permanent districts have all much the same physical features, which vary in degree rather than in kind. When the tide is in there are no marshy tracts nor oozy shores bearing mixed vegetation, but the water reaches up to a bank which may be divided from fields by a foreshore, or by dry and scanty turf. Owing to the vagaries of the river a broad grass-covered foreshore capable of feeding herds of cattle may in two or three years be a channel of the river; and a fresh foreshore will spring up in another parish. When the tide is out there are wide stretches of mud alternating with sand-banks and stretches of seaweed-covered rocks. As a result of this, birds requiring food from vegetation must either be content with the meagre fare off the foreshore, or fly inland to the large peaceful meadows. They usually prefer the latter, since they are denied an oozy foreshore covered with miscellaneous herbage and weeds. Whether it is entirely due to the difficulties of working a punt on Severn waters, or whether it is partly due to this cause and partly to the fact that the feeding habits already mentioned check the presence of large flocks of birds along the estuary itself, except when resting or watering, we cannot say, but the punt-gunner is absent from the Severn. The swift currents, the rushing tides and 'bore,' the ground-swells, and heavy seas render a punt unsuitable and aiming uncertain. A small boat and a shoulder-gun comprise the outfit of the most successful wild-fowler, who, to succeed, must possess a thorough knowledge of the river and its ways. Having regard to the tides and currents, and to the fact that in many places a deep channel may become a mudbank in the course of even two or three tides, such knowledge is indispensable. Punt-guns have very occasionally been tried, but set aside after a few attempts to use them. The most successful wild-fowler on the Severn known to the writer has tried the punt-gun and every kind of shoulder-gun from a 28-bore to a 2-bore. A punt-gun was soon dismissed, a single 4-bore was a favourite for some time, and one cartridge has brought down thirteen wigeon, and another five geese, but all have given way to a double 10-bore as the most generally useful weapon. A considerable number of geese visit the Severn. They begin to arrive about the middle or end of September. Small flocks come at first, then large flocks, and with an interval their numbers are more or less maintained until the first southwest gale after about 21 February. Generally speaking, they feed during the day on the big meadows away from the Severn in scattered 'skeins.' They unite on the edge of the estuary or river to rest or to bathe between ten and eleven in the morning, and again between two and three in the afternoon, and stay for half-an-hour or an hour or more, but for the shorter time in the afternoon. After sunset they return to the river for the night, unless there happens to be a bright moon, when they sometimes stay inland all night. The flocks are nominally larger in a hard winter than in a mild one.

The Pink-footed Goose (*Melanonyx brachyrhynchus*) is the first species to arrive in the autumn. This goose comes during the latter half of September, and it is believed, forms the bulk of the flocks, numbering in all perhaps 2,000 or 3,000 birds, which stay until about the end of October, when nearly all this first lot leaves. A very few remain on, and towards the end of November the White-fronted Goose (*Anser albifrons*), begins to arrive and coming in large numbers of from 4,000 to 10,000, stays until the end of the goose season. The question of the Bean Goose (presumably *Anser arvensis* not *segetum*)[1] has not been settled. It certainly is not a mere straggler, as the Grey-Lag (*Anser anser*) is believed to be, or as the Barnacle Goose (*Bernicla leucopsis*) certainly is; for small flocks occur at various times during the goose season. Whether the bulk come with the first or the second lot of geese that arrive, or some with both is not definitely ascertained. Probably the bulk come with the first lot. To the wild-fowler the white-fronted geese offer the best sport. Whether he can get shelter or not, if he is in their line of flight as they come from inland to the river, he can kill birds out of the leading 'skeins,' and the others still come on and offer good shots. The pink-footed geese, on the other hand, are shy of a boat in view as it is when the birds approach from the open side of a 'gutter' or one-banked channel: the first shot at them under such conditions is the last. It is probably due to this boldness on the part of the white-fronted geese that the method of shooting them on the Berkeley estate is so successful. The shooters are placed about 200 yds. from the river behind shelter, and beaters drive the geese from the meadows when they are feeding. The geese make for the water, and passing over or between the shelters afford good shooting. The double 10-bore gun seems to be the favourite on these occasions. At night the wild-fowler has excellent opportunities of getting a shot on the river at the resting geese, and at such ducks as happen to have remained about the water. The methods adopted are either to let the boat drift with the current or tide, or to keep it steady and to allow the birds to drift to it. Food being obtained chiefly away from the river, and birds at dusk and dawn continually changing positions inland and on the water, the opportunities along the Severn banks also are many. But the wild-fowler's best chance of all is in a fog on the open river; still shooting in the fog is open to a grave objection. The sportsman can get well among flocks of birds on the water and make good bags; but the result is that birds, especially geese, scatter all over the country, even retreating high up on the Cotteswold Hills for days.

The only species of the duck tribe worth taking into account are the Mallard (*Anas boscas*), the Teal (*Nettion crecca*), the Wigeon (*Mareca penelope*), and the Pochard (*Fuligula ferina*). The order in which they are placed indicates their numerical precedence on the estuary, but from the point of view of the wild-fowler the wigeon should take precedence of the teal. The former

[1] cf. Alphéraky, *The Geese of Europe and Asia*, 1905.

bird is less readily enticed into the two decoys on the Berkeley estate, and its numbers are therefore less rapidly reduced along the Severn. The fact that the wigeon is a day-feeder may partly account for its shunning the decoys. The decoys also affect the distribution of mallards for the wild-fowler at certain periods, especially when the foreign birds begin to arrive. A certain number of mallards and teal stay on the Severn waters all night, and may be attracted with the aid of wooden decoy ducks combined with the notes of call-ducks. Artificial calls have been tried for them but without success. The call-notes of wigeon imitated by the human mouth bring down these birds to the water.

Curlew also may be attracted by imitations of their call-notes. The only species of wading-birds that appear in numbers worth considering are the Curlew (*Numenius arquata*), the Dunlin (*Tringa alpina*), the Lapwing (*Vanellus vulgaris*), and the Golden Plover (*Charadrius pluvialis*), although at times or in limited localities there may be fair numbers of the Ringed Plover (*Aegialitis hiaticola*) ; of the Whimbrel (*Numenius phaeopus*) in spring-time ; of the Knot (*Tringa canutus*) near Avonmouth ; and of the Redshank (*Totanus calidris*) as wanderers from Monmouthshire. Curlews are easily shot at their flight-time, which is as each tide covers the mudbanks and forces the birds inland.

Golden plover are most numerous when hard weather drives them from the fields to feed on the sands or mud-shores, and they are best shot when their heads are up-wind and kept intent on some moving object.

ANGLING

With regard to angling Gloucestershire is a most disappointing county. It lies within the watershed of four of our rivers, the Severn, Wye, Bristol Avon, and Thames. It has small rivers and brooks without number, yet with one single exception the angling is of a very second-rate order. In the Severn itself there is practically none ; the tide runs up as far as Tewkesbury near the northern border, and with the exception of some fishing at the navigation weirs and a little bottom-fishing here and there, there is really no angling worth mention. A somewhat similar state of things exists on the Wye, which forms the western boundary of the county. Although a number of salmon are taken by net in that part of the river which divides Gloucestershire from Monmouthshire there is practically no salmon angling, such sport as exists being of much the same nature as that on the Severn. In the brooks that run down from the Forest of Dean to the Wye and Severn there used to be plenty of small trout, these waters being very similar in character to the Welsh streams ; but the trout have greatly decreased of late years. This is due to two causes : (1) the increase of coarse fish, and (2) the increase of pollution.

There are still some streams where a fine basket of small trout can be caught, but they are few and difficult to fish, the banks of most of them being overgrown with bushes.

Pollution arises from the mines and manufactures in the Forest of Dean. In some places the brooks are so befouled that no fish can pass up or down ; such, for instance, is the case in the Lydney Pile. Another tributary of the Severn on the west bank, the Leadon, runs from Dymock to Gloucester, and affords a certain quantity of coarse fish, but the river is small, runs low in summer, and is much choked up with weeds. Something might be made of the Leadon, but at present it is not worth mention as an angling stream.

On the east bank the Bristol Avon has nothing in its Gloucestershire part but coarse fish, and not too many of them. There is some bottom-fishing, but it is hardly worth considering. From the Cotteswold Hills to the Severn there are a number of small brooks which ought to hold some good trout, and no doubt some of them do so. But they are not long enough to carry anything like a good stock of fish, and many of them are horribly polluted by the cloth works, the water being dyed a deep bluish black. Here again there is no angling worth the name. There is some good coarse fish angling, chiefly roach, in the Gloucester and Berkeley Canal which runs from Gloucester to Sharpness, and a skilful roach fisher may at times make a good bag. Above Gloucester the brooks are few and do not contain many fish. At Tewkesbury the Warwickshire Avon falls into the Severn, and the stream is in several places the boundary between Gloucestershire and Worcestershire. In the Avon there is very good coarse fishing, mainly roach, chub, and bream. Some pike are also caught. Dace have died out, and the number of perch has largely decreased. But in spite of all drawbacks the angler who understands bottom-fishing will find fair sport in the Avon. The great drawback is the number of anglers from Birmingham. Some of the clubs have rented water from the farmers and others, and claim, rightly, their monopoly of it. The continued fishing by the Birmingham Club makes the fish far shyer than they used to be, with the result that the takes are smaller. There are various legends of monster fish in the Avon, chiefly of pike ; one of them is said to be so large that he can only turn at one place on the river, so he swims up and down to get to it ! As a rule the fish do not run very large, although some large bream and chub are occasionally caught. The fish are almost invariably caught bottom-fishing. Worm, wasp, grub, stewed wheat paste are the baits most used. Good fish are often taken dibbling with the natural fly. There is very little, if any, fly-fishing. Pike are mostly caught with a live bait on snap tackle ; sometimes a dead frog is used.

So far as the watershed of the Severn is concerned Gloucestershire angling is of very little account. In the Thames watershed the case is different. The Coln, a tributary of the Upper Thames, rising in the Cotteswold Hills, affords some trout fishing. It is a clear, bright stream with very low banks, and it holds some very large trout which give the dry-fly angler sport as good as can be found anywhere in England. It resembles in character a Berkshire or Hampshire stream. The trout are shy and require considerable skill to catch, but are very game and well worth taking. The fishing is very carefully preserved, no lure but the fly being allowed, and any but dry-fly fishing being useless.

The Fairford fishing is an object-lesson to the rest of Gloucestershire, and in fact to the rest of England. In its lower waters the Coln has but few trout, and swarms with coarse fish. In its upper and middle waters the coarse fish are rigorously kept down, with the result that there is really fine trout fishing. A mill with an impassable weir marks the boundary ; below it the fishing is practically worthless, above it excellent. The Coln remains one of the best of the trout streams in mid-England. All the other Gloucestershire streams are ruined by coarse fish. They work up from the main river, breed rapidly, and exterminate the trout. The Stour, which runs into the Avon near Shipston, might be a fine trout stream, but it swarms with coarse fish. The same is the case with almost all the brooks that run down from the Cotteswold Hills into the Avon and Severn. In them the trout is rapidly becoming extinct. The same is the case in many of the brooks on the west side of the county, and until landowners unite and get rid of coarse fish Gloucestershire will be of little account in the eyes of anglers.

GOLF

The first club established in the county was that of Minchinhampton, in April, 1889. That of Stinchcombe Hill followed in October, 1889. The institution of the Minchinhampton Club was mainly due to the efforts of Mr. Arthur Playne ; the inhabitants of the surrounding villages having enjoyed from time immemorial certain rights over the common, which covers about 1,000 acres, were strongly averse from the establishment of a golf course on it. Their objections were overcome by Mr. Playne, who was greatly helped by Messrs. Clement Ritchie, F. H. Playne, A. E. Smith, J. T. Woolbright, and the Rev. E. H. Hawkins. There are now 390 members (including 150 ladies). The ladies have a separate club and separate 9-hole course ; both that and the course of 18 holes for men are on Minchinhampton Common, a level tract situated on a spur of the Cotteswold Hills, 1½ miles from Nailsworth and 3 miles from Stroud. The hazards consist of quarries, ancient entrenchments, roads, and a pond. The course, one of the finest of the inland links in England, was originally laid out by N. B. Wilson, but it has been a good deal altered and improved since, especially by the present professional, G. Brews. The game can be played all the year round, but the links are perhaps at their best in May and June, and in October. The lies are excellent, especially in these months. Many county matches, as well as club matches, are played here, and there are two meetings annually, which invariably attract many first-class players. There is an excellent club-house adjoining Ye

Old Lodge Inn. The Stinchcombe Hill Club was organized in October, 1889, through the initiative of Colonel W. Lloyd Brown and Miss G. Osborne (now Mrs. Walker), and the 9-hole course was laid out the same year by the writer and Mr. H. Goldingham. It was lengthened into an 18-hole course in October 1906. A gully 300 ft. deep, stone quarries, and ancient earthworks constitute the principal hazards. The greens are particularly good, the turf being very fine. There are over 100 playing members, including ladies. The Cheltenham Golf Club, established in 1891, has on Cleeve Hill, from 700 to 1,000 ft. above the sea, a course which was laid out by Tom Morris. In point of membership this is the largest club in Gloucestershire ; there are 363 members, of whom 110 are ladies. There is a separate club for ladies, who, however, play over the same course. The eighteen holes vary from 141 to 486 yards. The turf is close, resembling that of sea-side links, and the greens are excellent ; the rapidity with which the ground dries up after rain is noteworthy. Cleeve Hill is nearly 4 miles from Cheltenham. The members, about 100 in number, of the Cotteswold Hills Club, established in 1902, play over the same course. This latter club must not be confounded with the Cotteswold, whose course is at Stow-on-the-Wold ; this club was organized in November, 1891, chiefly through the instrumentality of the Earl of Eldon, Messrs. C. A. Whitmore, T. W. Stubbs, H. E. Rose, and Colonel Wynter. It consists of about sixty members. The 9-hole course is one with natural hazards. Play is not feasible in the summer.

The Painswick Club was also inaugurated in 1891. It numbers only thirty-two members. The course in 1906 was enlarged from nine holes to eighteen; the hazards are for the most part stone quarries. Sapperton Park Club, instituted 1893, has a 13-hole course, 4½ miles from Cirencester; the first five holes are played over again to complete the eighteen. Play is feasible all the year round. There are about ninety members. Amongst other courses in the county may be mentioned that of the Clifton Down Club on the Durdham Downs, a 9-hole course with natural hazards. As the downs are public property, play is not permitted after two o'clock on ordinary days, nor on Bank or public holidays. The club was established in 1895; the members number 200. The Bristol and Clifton Club has an 18-hole course at Failand, about 2½ miles from Clifton Suspension Bridge. The Long Ashton Club has a 9-hole course at Ashton Hill, about 3 miles from Bristol Joint station. These clubs have been established some four or five years.

The Gloucester Golf Club, established in 1896, consists of about one hundred members. The links are at Barnwood, two miles from Gloucester Cross. It is a 9-hole course on meadow land; the hazards are brooks and hedges; play is possible all the year round. A very flourishing club is the Rodway Hill, consisting of over three hundred members. The links are close to Mangotsfield station, 4 miles from Bristol. It is an 18-hole course over pasture and common land, with both natural and artificial hazards. The Churchdown Club, numbering nearly three hundred members, has its links lying round a spur of Chosen Hill, Churchdown, about 3 miles from Gloucester and Cheltenham respectively. They are somewhat hilly and have a clay subsoil, but the turf is excellent. The 9 holes err on the short side, but there is an immense amount of play from February to June. Play is possible all the year round. The course was laid out by G. H. Causey of Malvern in 1900.

Situate 2 miles from Tetbury lies the course of the Lark Hill Club, over which there is a great deal of play during the winter and early spring months. This club was established in January 1901, Lord Estcourt, Major Holford, Captain Gilbert Henry, and the writer being the main promoters. It is a 9-hole course over pasture and down land, with natural and artificial hazards, and is of a very sporting character. The land is the property of Lord Estcourt. The club con-

sists of 113 members, including ladies, who play over the same course as the men. In 1905 a golf-club was established at Badminton with a 9-hole course in Badminton Park. The hazards are entirely natural. H. Dunn from Westward Ho! professional and green-keeper, laid out the course. The Duchess of Beaufort and Captain Julian Spicer took a prominent part in establishing this club. There are at present some sixty-three members. The Henbury Club, instituted in 1891, has about 120 members. The course of 9 holes, varying from 135 to 653 yards in length, lies on Combe Hill, near Bristol, about 2½ miles from Clifton Down station. There is a separate club and 9-hole course for ladies.

The Alveston Club with seventy members, has a 9-hole course (natural hazards), about eight miles from Bristol. It was instituted in 1903. Wotton-under-Edge Club, instituted the same year, is a small club of forty-five members; the course of 9 holes is most beautifully situated on the slope of the Cotteswold Hills. The turf is good and the greens are well kept. The hazards are old Saxon and Roman banks and earthworks, a dry moat, a deep delkin, a sand cliff and brook.

Chipping Sodbury Club, instituted December, 1905, has forty members and a course 1½ miles from Chipping Sodbury station. Birdlip, instituted in January, 1901, has a 9-hole course on Birdlip Common, 6 miles from Cheltenham. Near Cirencester is a small club belonging to the Royal Agricultural College; it has a 9-hole course with natural hazards of stone walls and hedges. At Tewkesbury a club was instituted in 1892 with a course of 9 holes on Shuthonger Common. On Felton Common near Flax Bourton, 4 miles from Felton station (G.W.R.) is a course of 9 holes which was laid out for a flourishing club established about 1891.

The Gloucestershire Golf Union was founded in 1906. Its objects are to affiliate all the principal clubs in the county, to act as a central authority to decide all questions which may arise, to fix the par score of all courses in the county with a view to equalizing handicaps, to revise, and so far as possible bring into line local rules, and generally to promote the interests of the game; to institute County Club Championships and individual competitions in connexion therewith, to arrange matches with other counties, to arrange with railway companies for increased travelling facilities for golfers, and to act in conjunction with other county unions in all matters affecting the game. The members of the Gloucester Golf Club were the chief promoters of this union.

A HISTORY OF GLOUCESTERSHIRE

ATHLETICS

Athletic sports in Gloucestershire undoubtedly owe their origin to the example set by Cheltenham College in the year 1853, when the Rev. T. A. Southward, then head master of the civil and military department, was mainly instrumental in organizing what was destined to become a popular annual function. Certain cricket clubs followed suit; and, in rapid succession, many of the larger towns promoted sports on a more or less extensive scale.

For many years now the Cheltenham Athletic Sports (which though not connected with the sports of Cheltenham College were no doubt inspired by them) have been held. There are important level races and limited handicaps, and the best-known amateurs compete. Bristol is another great athletic centre. The Ariel Rowing Club's meeting in its day was a very large one. It has been succeeded by the sports of the Bristol Bicycle and Tricycle Club, at which many runners of more than average ability have made their début. The Bristol and Cotswold Harriers were once so strong in cross-country athletics that members figured prominently in some of the championships. Famous runners from that district were H. Whittick, E. C. Carter (now in America, where he has won championships and established records), and C. H. L. Clarke, famed for the graceful style of his running, and successful at many meetings in the south of England. Cirencester, Stroud, Tewkesbury, and, of course, Gloucester, are the scenes of well-known annual athletic meetings; and at each an attendance of something like 10,000 spectators is not uncommon.

THE COTTESWOLD GAMES

The Cotteswold Games were instituted about the year 1604 by Captain Robert Dover as a protest against the growing puritanical prejudices. James I having granted Dover licence to select a suitable place for the games, he chose a spot between Evesham and Stow-on-the-Wold: Dover's Hill marks the situation. Here was erected a wooden castle which seems to have been used as a pavilion by those who directed the proceedings. The programme comprised such exercises as cudgel play, wrestling, pike drill, running at the quintain, pitching the bar, throwing the hammer, &c. There was also horse-racing, country-dancing for the girls, and some kind of hare-hunting. It was Dover's express stipulation that the hare was not to be killed, so it is difficult to conjecture what form the sport took unless the ancient system of netting (not easy on open downs) was adopted. These games took place annually until 1644, surviving Dover's death (1641) by three years only. The founder appears always to have taken a very active part in the direction of the games, attired in a suit of the king's and mounted on a white horse. The sports attained to no small measure of fame in the west country, persons of social standing journeying long distances to be present in Whitsun week, the season chosen for them. Valuable prizes were given to the successful cudgel players and athletes, and with so liberal a hand were awards distributed, it is said that 500 persons wore 'Dover's yellow favours' a year after. An endeavour was made to revive the games in the time of Charles II, but their vitality was gone, and the revival was brief.

CRICKET

The cricket of Gloucestershire is even more intimately connected with the family of the Graces than that of Worcestershire is with the Fosters, and though the county record of Gloucestershire is one of singular unevenness, it presents many fine and attractive features. That the cricket of the county existed at all was for years due entirely to the one historic brotherhood, and when their influence ceased the energy of Mr. G. L. Jessop alone supported the unequal but improving side.

The first match played by Gloucestershire was at Lord's on 25 June, 1868, when the M.C.C. and Ground was beaten by 134 runs. This was a preliminary fixture, not dealt with in averages, but as usual the three Graces had the lion's share of the game, Dr. E. M. Grace—then the best bat in England—scoring 60 and 65 and taking twelve wickets. Nor was it until 1870 that county matches were arranged. A rattling start against Glamorganshire resulted in a victory by an innings and 268 runs, Dr. W. G. Grace compiling 197 and Mr. F. Townsend 105 towards a total of 418, Mr. G. F. and Dr. E. M. Grace dividing the opposing wickets. Genuine first-class county matches were that year limited to out-and-home engagements with Surrey, both of which were easily won—at the Oval 'W. G.' making 143 and Mr. Townsend 89, the unfortunate home side being the recipient of its twelfth successive defeat.

M.C.C. and Ground were not more fortunate, for though Alfred Shaw and Wootton were bowling, Dr. W. G. Grace scored 172, which the combined efforts of the Club in both attempts could only exceed by 16 runs. As will have been gathered, the western county had the nucleus of their future side. Dr. E. M. Grace had already passed the first prime of his batting before the Australians ever visited this country, but in earlier times he was a wonderful run-getter, obtaining huge scores by clean hard hitting, though his style was unique. He never grounded his bat, but used to stand upright holding it across the face of the stumps. At point he was marvellous, and in the days of lob-bowling he enjoyed great success with the ball.

To dilate on the cricket of his yet more illustrious brother, the champion, is even to-day superfluous. What Dr. W. G. Grace has achieved in the cricket field can never be emulated, and he has done more than any other individual to create enormous interest in the game. Mr. G. F. Grace, cut off in his prime in 1880 through sleeping in a damp bed, though he never equalled his brothers, was none the less a sterling cricketer, being a formidable bat, a capital fast bowler, and the best out-field of his time, the catch with which he dismissed Mr. G. J. Bonnor at the Oval being still quoted as being perhaps the finest ever made in the deep field. Mr. Frank Townsend was a lively bat, possessing a very pretty cut. Mr. J. A. Bush proved a really fine wicket-keeper, but his left-handed batting often furnished good-humoured diversion to the crowd. Mr. George Strachan, a serviceable bat, smart field, and change bowler, divided his cricket between Gloucestershire and Surrey. Mr. R. F. Miles was a slow left-handed bowler who enjoyed great efficacy on occasions, especially on a soft wicket.

It was not until 21 August, 1871, at Trent Bridge, that Gloucestershire was for the first time defeated, having until then six victories and a draw to its credit, but in that match 'W. G.' made 79 and 116. Against Surrey Mr. T. G. Matthews was eight hours at the wicket whilst obtaining a score of 201, going in first and being last out in a total of 400. In this match 'W. G.' kept wicket, dismissing five opponents. At Lord's, against M.C.C. and Ground, four Graces played, Mr. Henry Grace, an elder brother, being included. A keen tussle in 1872 saw Surrey victorious by a single wicket, whilst 'W. G.'s' chief county score was 150 against Yorkshire. In 1874, at Cheltenham, 'W. G.' and 'G. F.' dismissed Surrey for 27, and at Brighton the elder scored 179. On both occasions Yorkshire was beaten with an innings to spare, 'W. G.' making 167 and 127, and taking twenty-two wickets. Already the eleven had assumed its characteristics, that of playing fine cricket so far as the Graces and two or three others were concerned, whilst three or four places seemed allotted to any amateur available. Gloucestershire has tried more cricketers since its foundation than any other county, also fewer professionals. Indeed, until Midwinter appeared, the side was exclusively amateur.

The year 1875 saw the three Graces heading the batting averages and scoring more runs than the other sixteen amateurs who appeared on the side. In previous summers the once-famed Oxonian, Mr. T. W. Lang, had several times lent assistance. Mr. G. Neville Wyatt was also seen, though he did better work later for Sussex; and Mr. A. H. Heath, whilst still a schoolboy, received a trial. 1876 was a year of greater triumph, for not a single defeat could be set against five victories and three draws. Besides 177 v. Nottinghamshire and 104 v. Sussex, Dr. W. G. Grace went in first and carried out his bat for 318 out of 528 v. Yorkshire. He was batting eight hours, and only gave one chance. This was the largest individual score made in an inter-county match until Mr. A. C. Maclaren scored 424 at Taunton for Lancashire v. Somersetshire in 1899. Five days earlier, on the concluding day of the Canterbury week, Dr. W. G. Grace, for Gentlemen of M.C.C. v. Kent, had made 344 without a chance. This is still (1906) the fourth best score in first-class matches. Truly the Dominie's epithet, 'Pro-dee-gious !' comes to our lips, especially as those were not the days of mammoth scoring. Mr. W. O. Moberley enjoyed a long partnership with 'W. G.' and obtained his first hundred in the Yorkshire match. Though he never found a place in the University Eleven, he was a far better bat than many who have represented Oxford, and for many years he materially assisted his county. Mr. J. Cranston was also tried, and proved himself an excellent bat and good field. He left the county in 1883, and his best performances were after his return in 1889. Few left-handed bats ever played with such a uniformly straight bat. Mr. W. R. Gilbert, a cousin of the Graces, for some seasons proved a serviceable player, being a steady bat and slow bowler, occasionally effective. Still dwelling on 1876, the analysis of Mr. R. F. Miles at Brighton must be quoted—seven for 30 and five for 25—and between his two great batting achievements just mentioned, Dr. W. G. Grace, against Nottinghamshire, after scoring 177, took eight wickets for 69 in the second innings. Altogether in that August, in first-class fixtures, he aggregated 1,261 runs with an average of 140·1, besides taking twenty-eight wickets for 22 runs apiece.

Gloucestershire played England at the Oval in 1877, the first time any county had done so since 1866, but the victory by five wickets was not of much account owing to the wretched national side collected. The match was repeated in 1878, when a dull game ended in the defeat of the county by six wickets. In 1877, however, Gloucestershire were again unbeaten, having eight victories and a draw. The figures were far less sensational than in the previous year, Dr. W. G. Grace being more to the fore with the ball than with the bat, his county analysis showing that he captured eighty-eight wickets for less than 10 runs each, his great feat being *v.* Nottinghamshire at Cheltenham, when he actually captured seventeen for 89. The giant Australian, Midwinter, appeared under the residential qualifications. He was a steady bat, good out-field, and effective medium-paced bowler. It had been anticipated that he would assist the Australians in 1878, but when he was preparing to play for them at Lord's the brothers Grace arrived and took him in a cab to assist Gloucestershire at the Oval. He returned to Victoria in 1882, and came with the 1884 side to England. Unfortunately, misfortune ultimately affected his brain, and he died insane. His first appearance at Lord's was for Gloucestershire and Yorkshire *v.* England in July, 1877. In this match 'W.G.' made 52 and 110, and Mr. A. N. Hornby 105 and 33 not out.

The first coming of the Australians being the date of modern cricket, it is suitable to mention here the connexion Gloucestershire amateurs have had with Colonial teams. But first it may be interesting to give the achievements of the Graces up to this period for their county, when thirty-three victories could be set against seven reverses :—

	Runs	Average	Runs	Wickets	Average
W. G. .	4,051	48·67	4,331	346	12·179
G. F. .	2,367	32·31	2,647	138	19·25
E. M. .	1,560	25·10	1,243	66	18·55

Dr. E. M. Grace went with George Parr's team to Australia in 1863; Mr. G. F. Grace in 1873; Dr. W. G. Grace in 1873 and with Lord Sheffield's side in 1892; Mr. J. A. Bush and Mr. W. R. Gilbert in 1873 ; Mr. O. G. Radcliffe in 1892 ; Board in 1897 ; and Mr. G. L. Jessop in 1901.

It was a well-deserved compliment to select all three Graces to play for England in the first test march at the Oval, and it will be remembered that Dr. W. G. Grace scored a superb 152. Altogether in these pre-eminent fixtures he has obtained 934 runs in twenty-nine completed innings, with an average of 32, his highest contribution being 170 at the Oval in 1886.

Mr. J. Cranston represented England on the same ground in 1890, scoring 16 and 15, innings far more valuable under the circumstances than many a century. Mr. G. L. Jessop has scored 245 in seven complete innings, the chief performance being, of course, his stupendous 104 at the Oval in 1902.

Dr. W. G. Grace has represented the Gentlemen on every occasion until 1905 that they have been pitted against the Australians, and he has played for M.C.C. on eleven out of fourteen occasions. He also captained the fine eleven that Lord Sheffield selected, as well as twelve out of the fifteen matches played by the South against them. Altogether in this country his average against the Australians is 35·94 for an aggregate of 4,329 in 121 completed innings, whilst his 158 wickets have cost 3,281 runs, yielding an average of 20·121. Mr. J. A. Bush kept wicket for the Gentlemen in 1878 and 1884 against the Australians, and Messrs. E. M. and G. F. Grace and W. R. Gilbert played in 1878, Messrs. A. H. Newnham and O. G. Radcliffe in 1888, and Mr. G. L. Jessop in 1905. For M.C.C. and Ground against the Colonials Woof played in 1884, Board in 1896 and 1899, Wrathall and Mr. C. L. Townsend in 1899. It may be added that Gloucestershire twice beat the Australians (on both occasions in 1888) and have been defeated twelve times.

Reverting to 1878 the best feature was a clever victory over Lancashire on a soaking pitch by five wickets, Dr. W. G. Grace and Mr. W. R. Gilbert bowling unchanged, and Mr. G. F. Grace contributing 73 not out. Next summer, Somersetshire was met as a minor county, and had to field to an innings of 411, the champion and Mr. F. Townsend both running into three figures, though Mr. A. H. Evans was bowling. Dr. W. G. Grace was far ahead of his comrades in that wet summer, most of the side playing with a conspicuous absence of their old dash, but he averaged 54 for 709 aggregate, and took 76 wickets for 12 runs each, whilst the rest did very little indeed. It was notable that the defeat sustained at the hands of Nottinghamshire on the Cheltenham College ground was the first ever sustained by Gloucestershire at home since the institution of the club.

The excellent slow bowling of Woof materially assisted the eleven in 1880, and though handicapped by the lack of a wicket-keeper of any pretensions whatever, Gloucestershire showed fine cricket in August, with 'W. G.' in marked superiority to the others. Decisive improvement on the whole season was however shown in 1881, when six victories were set against two defeats, but seven defeats against two victories in 1882 reversed this. Shaw and Morley sent back the Westerners for 49, and a rattling game with Lancashire ended in an adverse margin of 13 runs in an aggregate of 901. Indeed, it was marked weakness in the batting after the Graces and Midwinter had been disposed of which accounted for much of the balance on the wrong side. The Australians compiled 450 at Clifton, Mr. T. Horan making 141 not out. The only first-class county beaten in 1883 by Gloucestershire was Lancashire, and this had to be set against six disasters. The feature in the Middlesex engagement was the enormous partnership of 324 runs compiled by Hon. Alfred Lyttelton (181) and Mr. I. D. Walker (145), the total being 537. Dr. W. G. Grace was in great run-getting vein, and Messrs. Cranston and Moberley also made centuries. Mr. W. W. F. Pullen, a big hitter, by this time was in the side, and so was Mr. H. V. Page—a keen, useful cricketer in every department. Mr. J. H. Brain also received his first trial. He was an attractive bat and beautiful field, who attained some distinction, but will always be memorable for an appalling series of disasters, going in first for Oxford v. Cambridge and for the Gentlemen v. Players on both metropolitan grounds and in his six efforts getting only two runs. Nicholls, who appeared in a few fixtures as an amateur, was the bowler who subsequently rendered such yeoman service to Somersetshire.

A victory by 7 runs over Lancashire alone redeemed 1884, when Gloucestershire fielded out to totals of 464 (to which they responded with 484) 404, 388, 314, and 301. Painter, an aggressive bat, now thoroughly justified the persistent trial he had received, but the rank and file were very weak. Mr. F. M. Lucas in 1885 compiled the first individual score of 200 ever made against Gloucestershire, while Dr. W. G. Grace carried his bat through a total of 348 v. Middlesex, of which his share was 221. In 1886 county matches were played both at Gloucester and Moreton-in-the-Marsh. At Nottingham, after Gloucestershire had accumulated 321, Nottinghamshire retorted with 343 for only three wickets. Woof bowled finely against the Australians, claiming 7 for 32. Mr. O. G. Radcliffe first came into the side. At his best he was a careful capable bat and a fair change bowler. Mr. H. Hale, an Australian, of the Cambridge eleven, took part in most of the fixtures with only moderate success. Middlesex at Clifton won by the bare margin of a wicket in 1887 after a splendidly contested match, but there was no seriously successful feature for the Westerners in a disastrous year except the superb batting of Dr. W. G. Grace, who in county fixtures alone scored 1,405 runs with an average of 63; the finest of all his great efforts for Gloucestershire. Roberts, a willing fast bowler destined to perform an enormous amount of hard work, made his first appearance, so did Mr. A. H. Newnham, a soldier whose bowling was not of first-class order though given exceptional opportunities in a year when the amateur attack was at its worst. Another soldier, Mr. W. Troup, subsequently proved a valuable bat. Better results characterized 1888 and Dr. W. G. Grace, without repeating his phenomenal work of the previous summer was once more the batting mainstay of the side. The double victory over the Australians caused genuine elation, against which had to be set totals against Surrey and Lancashire of 48, 39, 48, and 56. The opening of the county ground at Bristol happily inaugurated 1889, the feature of which was the return of Mr. Cranston, who scored 643, with an average of 29. Again in 1900 he was second only to 'W. G.,' making a wonderful 152 at Dewsbury, where Gloucestershire won by 84 runs after being 137 behind on first hands. The veteran Dr. E. M. Grace made scores of 96, 77, 78, and 69, remarkable for a man who had reached the zenith of his fame seven-and-twenty years before. Disasters followed in 1891, when the only cheerful feature was the capital wicket-keeping of Board, who presently developed into a lively bat. His excitable disposition perhaps prevented him from becoming quite so famous as his rattling services merited.

In the middle of June, 1892, the renowned Australian Mr. J. J. Ferris became qualified, but proved a complete failure as a bowler, whilst his stolid uninteresting batting in no way compensated for his falling off with the ball. After a few seasons his connexion with the county lapsed almost without comment. Dr. W. G. Grace was still far ahead of those he led, but three new batsmen deserve mention. Mr. S. A. P. Kitcat, whose appearances have been intermittent and who, despite a cramped and inelegant position, watched the ball very closely; Mr. R. W. Rice with every advantage of style never became as good as his correct play warranted; Captain Luard, a capital bat, was also a smart field. 1893 was depressing, but at its close, a Clifton schoolboy, Mr. C. L. Townsend, (a son of Mr. Frank Townsend) with leg-break, took twenty-one wickets for 21 runs each. This materially lightened the burden of Roberts and Murch, but in 1894 he failed to come up to this standard, the one hopeful sign being the trial given to Mr. G. L. Jessop.

Of this phenomenal cricketer, it is perhaps the truth to say that no more terrific hitter has ever scored off the best bowling with such punishing power. Possessing every stroke, he literally can 'knock the stuffing' out of the finest attack, and a catalogue of his achievements would occupy pages. Magnificent in the field, he was at times a decidedly dangerous fast bowler. When he became captain he infused into what was often a nebulous and scratch team something of his own energy, and often bore the burden of the side on his own shoulders. Like so many of the greatest cricketers, he never knew when he was beaten, and so long as he was at the wicket he was capable of saving the most hopeless match.

1895 was a year of great achievements for Gloucestershire. It displayed the marvellous renaissance of 'W. G.' who actually scored 1,000 runs in May, and had an average of 50 for his county for an aggregate of 1,424. On 17 May v. Somersetshire he scored his hundredth hundred, making 288 out of 463 in well under six hours, this being his second century in a fortnight, and in one week he made 500 runs. At Manchester Mr. Jessop took five wickets for 13 runs; but the feature of English cricket that July and August was the wonderful bowling of Mr. C. L. Townsend, who took 129 wickets for 12 runs apiece on all sorts of wickets: sixteen for 122 v. Nottinghamshire, eleven for 36 v. Yorkshire, twelve for 87 v. Sussex and thirteen for 111 v. Nottinghamshire being prominent performances.

Disasters came again in 1896, and except for the superb batting of Dr. W. G. Grace, the cricket was weak, Mr. Townsend's 101 wickets costing 21 runs apiece. The Grand Old Man of the cricket field in his fifty-first year scored 1,565, with an average of 53. His great contributions were against Sussex, for off the southern bowling at Brighton he compiled 243, and at Bristol 301. Mr. Hemingway showed himself a lively bat, and the South African, Mr. C. O. H. Sewell, played most stylish cricket when available.

Matters improved in 1897, Mr. C. L. Townsend at times showing much command over the ball, and the hitting of Mr. G. L. Jessop being recognized as phenomenal—126 in an hour and a half v. Warwickshire, 49 out of 59 in twenty minutes v. Lancashire, 90 v. Somersetshire in less than an hour, and 101 in ninety minutes against the Philadelphians are samples of his rate of progression. Mr. R. W. Rice and Board each obtained his first three-figure scores, and there was no falling off in the abilities of the renowned veteran so far as batting was concerned.

Aged twenty-two in 1898, Mr. Townsend reached the highest point he has attained as a cricketer. Like Mr. F. S. Jackson and Cuttell he scored a thousand runs and took a hundred wickets, his record being 1,270 runs and 145 wickets. He five times exceeded a century : v. Essex he took fifteen wickets for 141 runs ; in the month of August fifty-eight batsmen were his victims. Dr. W. G. Grace thrice achieved three figures, and made 1,141 in aggregate. Mr. Troup batted with splendid precision, as did Mr. Sewell, so it was not surprising that Gloucestershire took third place, only having Yorkshire and Middlesex as superiors.

The secession of Dr. W. G. Grace from the county much affected the rest of the side in 1899, and only ninth place was attained. Mr. C. L. Townsend alone seemed to succeed, and no left-handed batsman had ever before scored 1,694 runs for a county in one season. His average was 56, and no less than seven hundreds stood to his credit, his best work being against Essex, 181 not out at Leyton, and 224 not out at Clifton. Mr. Troup took up the captaincy, but could not do so well as Mr. Jessop, whose great feat, one of amazing brilliance, was to score 100 within the hour at Trent Bridge. Paish showed remarkable figures as a slow left-handed bowler : seven for 47 v. Middlesex at Lords, and fourteen for 196 v. Surrey, were two performances in an aggregate of 125 wickets for 2,367 runs. Until August Gloucestershire could not get a representative side in 1900, but then they beat Somersetshire, Kent, Essex, Surrey, and Worcestershire. It was Mr. G. L. Jessop's year both as captain and cricketer. Against Yorkshire he scored double hundreds, 164 and 139, seven times driving Rhodes out of the Bradford

ground for 6. At Old Trafford he made 66 and 44, and took eight wickets ; v. Surrey at Clifton he contributed 54 and 54, claiming nine wickets, and v. Essex captured eight wickets for 29 runs. Only twice before had his feat of scoring 2,000 runs and taking a hundred wickets been achieved, each time by a Gloucestershire representative, Dr. W. G. Grace and Mr. C. L. Townsend. The latter again batted well, so did Wrathall and Mr. W. S. A. Brown. Mr. R. W. Rice was the hero of the one-wicket victory over Somersetshire, as he carried his bat for 82, and Mr. A. H. C. Fargus did a fine bowling performance—twelve for 87—on his first appearance at Lord's, but was otherwise disappointing, and Roberts had to pound away with very little assistance.

Proxime accessit to the wooden spoon in 1901, the one happy feature for the Westerners was the batting of Mr. G. L. Jessop, who hit 125 not out v. Surrey, 124 v. Middlesex, 106 v. Warwickshire, and often took the sting out of opposing bowling in a few overs. Hale, engaged on the railway and only able to play in May, made a capital impression as a bat on the Southern Tour. It was sad to see that each of Mr. C. L. Townsend's wickets cost 56 runs, and the attack was altogether the weakest in England. Nor could any improvement be perceived in 1902, when the bowling was lamentable, though Huggins presented two fine performances in seven for 17 at Brighton and seven for 37 at Worcester, but this standard he could not maintain. Mr. Jessop scored with unremitting energy, but the only valuable support he received was from the strong defence of Mr. W. Troup. Again in 1903 matters were no better ; it was *aut Jessopus aut nihil*. He scored 1,307 runs with an average of 39, and no one else accumulated 650. At Brighton he made the largest score of his life, 286 out of 355 in less than three hours, and against Lancashire knocked up 168 in the same time. Nothing else was of consequence except the bowling of Dennett, who took five wickets for 6 runs v. Worcestershire, and twenty-four wickets for 230 in the three successive victories which wound up the season.

1904 saw a bracing revival, although only one century was to be noted, namely, 206 by Mr. Jessop in two and a half hours at Trent Bridge. The real source of the improvement was the admirable steadiness of Dennett with the ball, his 123 wickets for 19 runs apiece being a highly meritorious performance, his best work being seven for 28 and eight for 68 in the return with Middlesex. This he improved upon in 1905, just beating any Gloucestershire aggregate by capturing 131 wickets. Huggins was at times of service. Except for 234 v. Somersetshire, Mr. G. L. Jessop did little, and yielded pride of place to Mr. Sewell in 1905.

In conclusion, the following averages, specially

compiled, indicate who have had the lion's share in assisting the fortunes of the 'county of the Graces.'

BATTING

(End of 1906)

	Completed innings	Runs	Average
Dr. W. G. Grace .	583	22,465	38·311
G. L. Jessop . . .	341	10,878	31·307
C. L. Townsend. .	224	6,839	30·119
G. F. Grace . . .	121	3,419	29·10
C. O. H. Sewell. .	146	3,938	26·142
O. G. Radcliffe . .	208	4,319	20·159
Wrathall . . .	522	10,758	20·318
W. R. Gilbert . .	204	3,932	19·156
F. Townsend . .	261	4,922	18·224
Dr. E. M. Grace .	435	7,978	18·168
Painter	318	5,586	17·180

BOWLING

	Runs	Wickets	Average
R. F. Miles . . .	4,408	171	15·111
Midwinter . . .	4,992	312	16
Dr. W. G. Grace .	24,495	1,333	18·501
Woof	12,864	648	19·552
G. F. Grace . . .	3,208	167	19·35
W. R. Gilbert . .	3,763	191	19·134
Dennett . . .	9,307	469	19·396
C. L. Townsend.	13,364	627	21·197
Roberts . . .	24,184	1,102	21·1042
G. L. Jessop . .	11,289	495	22·399
Paish	13,517	573	23·358
Dr. E. M. Grace.	4,408	171	23·115

It will be noticed that the three Graces, Messrs. G. L. Jessop, C. L. Townsend, and W. R. Gilbert figure in both tables. Altogether Gloucestershire has won 147 matches and lost 210, leaving 157 unfinished.

SCHOOLS

THERE is, perhaps, no county in England which in ancient or modern times can boast a better supply of institutions for the advancement of secondary education than Gloucestershire. The ancient prosperity of the county, derived at first largely from the two great ports of Gloucester and Bristol, reinforced by the widespread development of its cloth-trade in the later fourteenth and succeeding centuries, studded it with great churches and their inseparable companions, flourishing grammar schools. The grammar schools of Gloucester and Bristol are, as will be seen, of immemorial antiquity, specific mention of them, not as new creations, but as previously existing institutions, being made in the twelfth century, à propos, as we should say, of new schemes for their government ; in both cases involving a transfer of power from the secular to the regular clergy. In both cities the Reformation movement was marked by the introduction of new schools, rivals to the old schools, with possibly the difference that the new schools were endowed and were free schools, instead of being fee-paying schools. The new school at Gloucester was the Crypt Grammar School ; and at Bristol, the Cathedral Grammar School. In neither case, oddly enough, did the new school prove an effective rival to the old school, until in quite recent times at Gloucester, through the apathy or error of the dean and chapter, the Crypt School took the front rank.

Both cities now enjoy an ample—if not, indeed, an excessive—supply of institutions for higher education ; for it is difficult to see how, with a population of rather under than over 50,000, Gloucester can support in real efficiency the Crypt Grammar School, the Cathedral Grammar School, and Sir Thomas Rich's School ; or Bristol, with about 330,000, can maintain the University College, Clifton College, the Grammar School, the Cathedral Grammar School, Queen Elizabeth's Hospital, Colston's Hospital, the Merchant Venturers' Technical College, and three so-called Higher Grade Schools ; and for girls, the Clifton High School, the Redland High School, Colston's Girls' Day School, the Red Maids' School, and the three Higher Grade Schools ; to say nothing of innumerable private schools, good, bad, and indifferent.

Outside the cities we find Cirencester Grammar School mentioned in the middle of the thirteenth century as an existing institution ; Wotton under Edge Grammar School, founded in 1384 ; Newland, now Coleford, Grammar School in 1445 ; Stow on the Wold in 1476 ; Chipping Campden Grammar School in 1487 ; Winchcombe Grammar School in 1521 ; Cheltenham Grammar School, at some unknown date before 1548. Westbury Collegiate Church, of very high antiquity, certainly maintained a grammar school, as it sent scholars to Oriel College, Oxford, on John Carpenter's foundation, and boarded, lodged, and clothed 12 choristers, while John Golde,

'Podidasculum,'[1] somebody's mistake for *hipodidasculum*, or usher, received a salary of £10 a year.

We may be sure that these are not all the schools that existed before the Reformation; but that there are many more which have no memorial, and are perished as though they had never been. No doubt some of the schools founded after the Reformation, such as Northleach in 1559, Tewkesbury in 1609, Tetbury in 1610, Thornbury in 1642, and Wickwar in 1683, like that of Chipping Sodbury, confirmed by a decree of Commissioners of Charitable Uses 4 September, 1694,[2] but mixed up with the gild and church lands of the borough, and now in abeyance, were really resuscitations or fresh endowments of pre-existing schools.

Of elementary schools before the Reformation we have scant traces. We see the Song School at Winchcombe; and the curious provision at St. Nicholas, Bristol,[3] in 1481, that

> the clerke aught not to take no boke oute of the quere for chulderyn to lerne in withowte license of the procurators [i.e. the churchwardens] undyr payne that the curate and procurators assign he.

But these two incidental references show the two main sources of provision for elementary schools in ancient days—the chantry priest, who taught the Song School; and, when there was none, the parish clerk, who, it should be remembered, was a literate and cleric of very much higher status than the later bearers of the title, and taught reading and elementary grammar out of the choir books.

The earliest post-Reformation endowment now forthcoming actually for elementary education, 'writing and ciphering,' was at Wotton under Edge in 1630. But only four more are in evidence before the eighteenth century.

GLOUCESTER SCHOOLS

The College School, Gloucester

The College School, otherwise the King's School, otherwise the Cathedral Grammar School, Gloucester, may claim a high antiquity; a great deal higher than that attributed to it by Nicholas Carlisle[4] of 'being coeval with the abbey,' meaning St. Peter's Abbey, Gloucester, now the cathedral church. This abbey is said to have been originally founded about 681,[5] as a nunnery.[6] It was afterwards a college of secular canons till the time of Wulfstan, bishop of Worcester, who ousted the clerks for monks and introduced the Benedictine rule in 1022.[7] It is probably owing to the

---

[1] *Valor Eccl.* ii, 435.
[2] *Char. Com. Rep.* xvii, 372.
[3] *Clifton Antiquarian Club Proc.* (1886), i, 148.
[4] *Endowed Grammar Schools*, i, 449.
[5] *Hist. Mon. Glouc.* (Rolls Ser.), i, 14.
[6] A similar tale is told of Carlisle and other places. The main object of such stories was to try to give a title to possessions, or more often claims to possessions, which could not otherwise be substantiated.
[7] *Hist. Mon. Glouc.* (Rolls Ser.), i, 8. The monkish writer says : 'The beauty of religion (speciositas religionis) in the minster of Gloucester was miraculously continued, after the transfer of the sisters existing there flying hither and thither, under secular power till the time of Bishop Wolstan in 1002, who in 1022 placed the clerks who had hitherto governed and kept St. Peter's church under the protection of God and the Apostles Peter and Paul and the rule of Blessed Benedict, and consecrated one Edric abbot.'

dispossession of the secular canons by the monks that when we first meet with Gloucester School in historical documents we find it under the tutelage not of the monastery of St. Peter, but of the canons of Llanthony Abbey, just outside the ancient city. The order or rule of the regular or Augustinian or black canons, who inhabited Llanthony, was intermediate between that of the monks, who were, theoretically, wholly immured in their cloister, and that of the secular clergy, who were wholly immersed in the world; for though bound by the threefold rule of poverty, chastity, and obedience, and supposed to live the common life in a common cloister and a common dormitory, the Augustinian canons, unlike monks, were allowed to hold vicarages and to move about to some extent in the world. Hence they were in many places recognized as not improper persons to be entrusted with the governance of public schools.

The first extant mention of the school is in a charter[1] of the first year of King John, 30 July, 1199. It is addressed to the church of St. Mary and St. John the Baptist and the regular canons of Llanthony, and witnesses that the king had ' granted and confirmed to the said church the donations which have been reasonably (*rationabiliter*) made to them of the gift of Henry our father ; the chapel in the castle of Gloucester (*capellam intra*[2] *castellum Gloucestrie*) and a school in the same town (*et unam scolam in eadem villa*) and half the fishery in Hersepol, which is of our demesne.' The recital and confirmation of other lands and grants made by other people follow, while the canons were to be ' quit of shire, hundred, &c. as our brother Richard's charter testifies.' The chapel in the castle is said in a deed of Miles,[3] constable of Gloucester, to have been given by his father Roger to the church of St. Owen, which he (Miles) gave to Llanthony in 1137, when the abbey church was dedicated. The school, therefore, existed before the foundation of Llanthony Abbey, under the government of the canons or chaplains of the castle chapel, probably a collegiate foundation like the similar chapels in Windsor Castle, the Tower of London, Pontefract Castle, Oxford Castle, Warwick Castle (the last three of which are known to have included schools as part of their foundation), and elsewhere.

The school was not, therefore, a monastic school in the sense of a school founded by or kept in a monastery for monks or by monks, or ' regulars' of any kind. All that was granted to the priory was the advowson or right of presentation or collation, as it was called; for a schoolmastership was looked upon as a form of ecclesiastical benefice, and was under ecclesiastical law, and so, often spoken of in the terms appropriate to ecclesiastical appointments ; indeed, 'rector' was a common *alias* for ' master,' and is still in use in Scotland, while the Rectors of Exeter and Lincoln Colleges at Oxford still show that the title was used in England. There is no evidence that the priory had to find, or did find, any endowment for the master. All they had to do with the school was to appoint and license the master to teach, perhaps to remove him on occasion, though of that we have no instance, and perhaps, though of that there is no evidence, to find a schoolhouse. Even their right of patronage was continually being

[1] *Rot. Chart.* (Rec. Com.), John, 7.
[2] In Dugdale, *Mon.* vi, 137, this is given as *juxta*, i.e. by the castle.
[3] Ibid. 136.

contested. Thus on 31 January, 1286–7, Bishop Godfrey Giffard [1] issued a commission to his Official Principal, or chancellor,

> to inquire as to the right of collation to the school in the borough of Gloucester and the possession or quasi-possession of this right, also how the collation has been hitherto accustomed to be made and by whom, and to do further thereon and concerning the premisses as the course of law demands, giving notice to those who are interested to be present at the inquiry.

The register, as usual, does not give us the return to the commission, but by a fortunate accident we learn it from an entry in a later register, that of Bishop Silvester de Giglis, when nearly two and a half centuries later the same dispute had arisen. À propos of this later dispute, which took place in 1512–3, Thomas Hanibal or Hannibal, LL.D., vicar-general of the bishop, who was in remote parts (as indeed he always was, being one of the Italian absentees whom the popes were fond of fattening on English endowments), recites [2] a mandate of Bishop Henry Wakefield in 1380, which itself recited a mandate of Bishop Godfrey Giffard, clearly the result of the inquiry ordered by him in the commission quoted. Bishop Wakefield says he has searched the registry of the date of Bishop Godfrey and found the letter and process underwritten. He then sets out letters patent of Bishop Godfrey dated 21 November, eleventh year of his consecration, i.e. 1287, addressed ' to his beloved son in Christ the archdeacon of Gloucester or his Official or other deputy.'

> The collation [3] of the school in the borough of Gloucester to which scholars flock, for the sake of learning, some from our diocese and others from divers parts, clearly belongs, as we have been informed by the evidence of trustworthy witnesses, and as clearly appears by inspection of the muniments and charters which they have concerning the same school, to the religious men the Prior and Convent of Llanthony by Gloucester, and is recognized as belonging to them of old time ; and they from the time during which they have held the collation, as we are informed by trustworthy witnesses, have held possession of the right of collation to the same, though others indeed may, though not without incurring the guilt of usurpation, perhaps claim the right.

Who these others were who claimed the right does not appear, but we may perhaps suspect that it was the monks of St. Peter's Abbey. Bishop Giffard therefore,

> to put an end to all controversy and prevent fierce disputes arising hereafter, commands (mandamus) the Archdeacon to cause public notice to be given on three Sundays during high mass, in all the parish churches in the municipality and others in the neighbourhood, of an inhibition against anyone calling himself a scholar keeping any school for the sake of teaching in the said borough, except that one the teaching (regimen) of which has been granted to a fit master (doctori ydoneo) by the collation of the Prior and Convent of Llanthony who have been and are notoriously in possession or quasi-possession of the right of collation to such school from time whereof the memory of man runneth not to the contrary.

' Other schools, if there are any there, to which anyone has been collated to the prejudice of the said religious' the bishop directed ' to be wholly suspended (totaliter suspendi).' Sixty years later, 1340–1, [4] the priory of

---

[1] Worc. Epis. Reg. Giffard, fol. 265. *Commissio Scolarum Glouc.* Officiali suo. Ad inquirendum de jure conferendi scolas infra municipium Gloucestrie ac de possessione juris hujusmodi vel quasi, necnon de modo quo ipsa collacio hactenus fieri consuevit, et per quas personas.

[2] Worc. Epis. Reg. Silvester, &c. fol. 202.

[3] Ibid. Pretextu siquidem scolarum in municipio Gloucestrie existencium ad quas nonulli scolares de nostra diocesi et alii de diversis partibus confluunt intuitu discipline.

[4] Chart. R. 14 Edw. III, m. 13, No. 26.

Llanthony found it necessary to get a royal charter confirming their right to the school (*unam scolam in eadem villa*), in the same terms as the charter of King John.

On 10 April, 1380,[1] Bishop Henry Wakefield, in a mandate to the archdeacon of Gloucester, recited Giffard's decree, and 'seeing that all and singular things contained in the process and letters were consonant to reason and equity, ordered them to be solemnly published and piously observed, canonically restraining all opponents and rebels by all ecclesiastical censures.'

In 1410 this school became the subject of a 'leading case'[2] in which the whole law of schools, essentially a matter of ecclesiastical jurisdiction, was discussed in the common law courts. As the case is of great importance in the history of education and has been somewhat misunderstood[3] a full account of it is necessary.

> Two Grammar School masters (masters de Grammer Schole) brought a writ of trespass against another master, their count being that whereas the collation of Gloucester Grammar Schole from time whereof memory runs not, &c., belongs to the Prior of Llanthony (Lantone) by Gloucester, and the said Prior had made collation to the plaintiffs to have the governance of the said scholars[4] and to inform children (*les enfants*) and others, &c., the defendant had set up a scole in the same town, by which, whereas the plaintiffs used to make of a child 40*d*. or 2*s*. a quarter, now they could only take scarce 12*d*., to their damage, &c.

Hill,[5] counsel for the defendants, demurred, 'the writ is worthless,' and eventually the demurrer was allowed and the judgement of the court was 'that the writ did not lie.' The arguments are set out at considerable length. They show that the real reason why the demurrer was allowed was twofold: (1) because the plaintiff masters had no estate at common law in their office, but merely a ministry or office which depended on the grant of the prior; and (2) 'that teaching and information of children was a spiritual matter,' and therefore the action could not be tried by that court. The last was the main point. Education was a matter of ecclesiastical law, and therefore for cognizance of the ecclesiastical courts, not of the common law courts. Lord Stanley, afterwards earl of Derby, quite correctly quoted this case in a debate in the House of Lords on an Education Bill in 1839, as showing that education was a matter for ecclesiastical cognizance. Mr. de Montmorency in disputing this dogma and maintaining that the case showed that the law of England recognized no restraint on the right of anyone to teach school where he pleased seems to misapprehend the effect of the case. It is true that there are *obiter dicta* in and during the course of the argument which could be interpreted in the sense urged by him, but they are *dicta* merely, and did not affect the final judgement of the court. For Skrene having argued for the defendants that there was a good action 'on the case' and that sufficient damage was shown, William Hankford, afterwards Chief Justice, then a puisne judge, said 'there may be damage without legal wrong (*damnum absque injuria*). Thus, if I have a mill and my neighbour sets up

---

[1] Worc. Epis. Reg. Silvester, fol. 202.

[2] Year Book, 11 Hen. IV, 47, case 21. The original is of course in Norman-French.

[3] J. E. G. de Montmorency, *State Intervention in English Education* (Camb. Univ. Press, 1902), 50–60.

[4] *Escholers*, but it looks as if it was a mistake for *escholes*, schools. The two plaintiff masters were no doubt the master and usher.

[5] Printed Till, not for Tickill, as Mr. de Montmorency suggests, p. 241, but for Hill, who as subsequently appears was one of the defendants' counsel.

another mill by which the profit of my mill is diminished, I should have no action against him, although it is damage to me.' William Thirning, the Chief Justice, granted that, but immediately took the objection that 'the teaching of children is a spiritual matter (*informacion des enfantes est chose espirituel*); and if a man retains a master in his house to teach his children, that might be damage to the common master of the town, still I think he would have no action.' Skrene answered 'The masters of Paul's claim that there may be no other masters in all the city of London except themselves.'[1] He claimed judgement and damages. Hill said:

> There is nothing in this case on which to maintain the action (*Il fault foundement en cet case de maintainer l'action*), since the plaintiffs have no estate, but only a temporary service (*ministery pur le temps*); and if another, who is as well taught in the faculty of science of Grammar as the plaintiffs are, comes to teach children, it is a virtuous and charitable action and to the benefit of the people, and so it cannot be punished by our law.

Thirning answered:

> Whether the Prior has such collation of schools or not, this Court can take no cognizance, because the teaching and information of children is a spiritual thing (*le doctrine et information des enfants est chose espirituel*); and moreover, as the plaintiffs have claimed the schools by the collation of the Prior, and thereon have founded their action, which is accessory and depends on the title of the Prior, who is the principal, and it is a spiritual matter, it appears that this action cannot be tried in this court.

Skrene still went on : ' If a market is set up to the nuisance of my market, I shall have an action for nuisance, and in a common case, if those coming to my market are disturbed or assaulted so that I lose my toll I shall have a good action on the case ; so here.' But Hankford replied:

> The two cases have no resemblance, for in the case you state you have a freehold and inheritance in your market, but here the plaintiffs have no estate in the schoolmastership (*le schole mastership*), &c., except for an uncertain period, and it would be unreasonable that a master should be disturbed in keeping school where he pleases, except in the case where a University was incorporate and schools founded in ancient time.'[2]

He then repeated the illustration of the mill, adding 'but if a miller disturb the water running to my mill or make any manner of nuisance, I should have an action.' The argument is that, even if the masters had an estate in the school, the mere setting up of a rival school would give no right of action, though if any boys were prevented by violence from coming to the school a right of action might in that case lie. 'And the opinion of the court was that the writ did not lie (*le brief ne gist my*); So it was agreed that they took nothing, &c. and so &c. (' *Per que fuit agarde que ils ne pristeront riens etc. eins etc.*'). It is difficult to understand how anyone could draw the conclusion from this report that teaching was a free profession, and that anyone could teach where he liked. So far as the common law courts[3] were concerned this might have been so ; and it would appear that they would have been ready to free the schools from clerical control under

---

[1] This is a most interesting remark, as it shows that the claim (enforced by a writ still extant of Henry of Blois, bishop of Winchester, as acting bishop of London during a vacancy of the see in 1137) of the schoolmaster of St. Paul's School to a monopoly of grammar school teaching was still recognized as binding nearly three centuries afterwards.

[2] ' Et il sera encounter reason que un Master serra disturbe a tenir schole ou luy pleist, sinon que le fuit en case ou un University fuit corporate, et escholes foundus sur auncient temps.'

[3] It is curious that Hankford should have expressed such anti-clerical views, as his own son was a commoner, and at this very time a scholar of Winchester College, founded to provide learned priests. He is concealed in Mr. T. Kirby's *Winchester Scholars* under the misreading of Haukford.

the Reformation movement then prevailing, if the law and the Lord Chief Justice had not been too strong for them. But they were. Education was recognized as a matter not for the common law courts at all, but for the ecclesiastical courts, and in the ecclesiastical courts the control of the ordinary in restraint of free trade in school-keeping was well established. The ecclesiastical law was, however, just as much a part of the law of England as the common law.

Whether the Gloucester schoolmasters having failed at common law then resorted to the spiritual court to put down their rivalry, and why they ever came to the common law court when the spiritual courts were open to them and had shown their efficacy in the matter only thirty years before, we are, in the usual tantalizing way of these records, left guessing.

The school must have been of very considerable status and repute in 1424, when[1] Mr. Richard Davy, master of Gloucester Grammar School, was especially invited to Winchester College on a vacancy in the head-mastership, and received 6s. 8d. for himself for his trouble, with 1s. for his clerk. A large field was got together, masters being sought from Maidstone, Oxford, and St. Albans. Davy was the only one who actually came to Winchester, apparently as a selected candidate, except Thomas Walewayn or Alwin from Newport Pagnell, who was elected, and probably owed his victory over Davy chiefly to being an old Wykehamist. It is a strong tribute to Davy's merits that, with the possible exception of William Waynflete, the next head master, no one not a Wykehamist was ever again in the running for the head-mastership till Dr. Burge was elected in 1901.

Once more, on 26 January, 1512–13, Bishop Silvester's *locum tenens*, Dr. Hanibal, had, as we said above, to reassert the rights of Llanthony Abbey over the school against fresh assailants. After reciting Bishop Giffard's commission and its results on Bishop Wakefield's confirmation in 1380, he proceeds

> We, treading in the steps of such mighty fathers and putting before our eyes letters, privileges, charters and instruments, confirmed not only by the Apostolic see, but by the most serene kings of England, confirm them by our authority as ordinary, and because it has come to our ears that lately new kinds of contention have arisen concerning the school (*scolarum*) in the borough of Gloucester through certain persons claiming the right of collation under the vice of usurpation, against the aforesaid recognised right, and they endeavour to appoint schoolmasters and scholars in the same borough ; for the appeasement of which contentions and controversies we caused all pretending an interest in the matter to be summoned for a certain day and place before us ; at which no one appearing or alleging any interest except the said Prior and Convent by their proctors, brother Robert Conde, cellarer of the monastery, and Mr. Robert Stynchrobe' (? Stinkrobe),

therefore the Official directed the archdeacon to cause to be proclaimed on three Sundays in all the parish churches of Gloucester and the neighbourhood

> a public inhibition[2] against anyone calling himself a scholar keeping any school for learning or sending anyone not of mature age to such schools, except those schools or school the teaching of which has been freely (*gratuita*) granted by the Prior and convent of Llanthony to a fit master.

[1] Win. Coll. Bursars' Roll. 'In datis Magistro Ricardo Davy, magistro gramaticalium scolarum Gloucestrie, venienti ad Collegium ut idem Ricardus esset informator scolarium collegii 6s. 8d. et in datis clerico suo 1s.' By an unfortunate error, due apparently to some notion that the so-called schools of the Jews were really public schools, an extract from this entry appeared in Mr. T. Kirby's *Ann. of Win. Coll.* 188 as 'scolarum giudicalium.' Mr. Kirby, however, informs me, and I have confirmed it by inspection, that the original entry is as given above.

[2] Publice inhibere ne quis pro scolari se gerens scolas aliquas discendi gracia exerceat, aut juvenem qui ad maturam etatem non provenerit scolis aliquibus tradat, nisi illis aut illi dumtaxat, quarum regimen Magistro ydoneo ex dictorum Prioris et conventus de Lanthon collacione gratuita est concessum.

The bishop, however, especially reserved to himself in the person of his Official 'the examination and approval (*examinacionem et approbacionem*) of the said master appointed by the convent.' At the same time the archdeacon was to suspend any school collated to anyone in prejudice of the rights of the said religious, compelling obedience by excommunication which 'we order and command shall be published and declared by you the said archdeacon or your official.'

The exact place where the Gloucester Grammar School was held has been ascertained. In the rental of Gloucester,[1] now among the town muniments, made in 1455 by a canon of Llanthony, is the following entry under 'Old Smyth Strete.' 'The prior of Llanthony holds in fee there a curtilage with a tenement where the school[2] is held with its appurtenances and contains in front [   ].' But here follows a blank never filled in, for the length of the frontage ; the MS. in this, as in many other cases, never having been completed as regards the measurements of the tenement.

We can fix the spot more exactly in the 'Rentall' of 1535, also prepared by a canon of Llanthony, ' Sir ' David Mathew.

> Old Smithestrette or the Scholhowse lane Is on the west side of the strett called Sowzyate street extending from hence downe to the Barelande.
>
> Gorlone extendyth from Trinitie churche into olde Smith strete and lyeth in length North and sowzte.
>
> Old Smyth street or the schole howse lane
>
> Memorandum the old scole howse, because he lyeth vacante, sum tyme in holdinge of Sir William scolemaster, folio xxxij[3] et numero lxv^{to} ; and it is now of value by yere but xiii*s*. iiij*d*.
>
> John Dyme occupieth a small tenement on the same syde of the stret between a tenement of John Okolte and a tenement perteynynge to Seynt Thomas service in the churche of the Trinite, sumtyme Nicholas Hope folio xxxiij et numero lxvi^{to}; and shulde paye by yere vij*s*., now he payeth v*s*.

The school, therefore, was on the right-hand side of the Schoolhouse Lane, now called Long Smith Street, going down it from Southgate Street, just above Gore Lane, which, like Kensington Gore in London, took its name from its shape, being narrow at one end and widening out to the other, and is now called Bull Lane.

Where the school had been moved to in 1535 does not appear. It is just possible that it had ceased, owing to the competition of the new Crypt School. But in that case we must antedate that school and assume (which is rather improbable) that it had been going on before a licence in mortmain had been obtained and before its formal foundation in 1537, and from shortly after the will of its founder in 1529. At all events the old school is thus shown to be nowhere near Llanthony Abbey itself, nor in or near St. Peter's Abbey, in no way therefore monastic, but in a central position in the middle of the town for which it catered.

---

[1] Edited for the Corp. by W. H. Stevenson. (John Bellows, Glouc. 1890.) Corp. Rec. No. 1365.

[2] ' Prior Llanthon in feodo tenet ibidem unum curtilagium cum tenemento ubi scole tenentur cum pertinenciis. Et continet in fronte.' Mr. Stevenson wrongly translated ' where a school is held.' It should be as given in the text, ' the school.'

[3] This refers to some earlier rental not now forthcoming unhappily.

SCHOOLS

The Refoundation of the Grammar School, Gloucester

If the old school had ceased, in 1535, which is very doubtful, its cessation was of no long duration. For on 3 September, 1541, the abbey of St. Peter, surrendered on 2 January, 1540, was refounded as the 'cathedral church of the Holy and Undivided Trinity' of the see of Gloucester, with a school as part of it. The king,

affecting from the bottom of his soul nothing more than that true religion and the true worship of God should not only not be abolished there but rather be restored in its integrity and reformed to its former rule with double sincerity, correcting the enormities into which the life and professions of the monks had through lapse of time deplorably lapsed, laboured . . . that for the future the muniments of sacred eloquence may be purely administered, and good morals be sincerely observed, that the youth may be freely instituted in letters and old age when shorn of its strength be worthily nurtured with necessaries, and lastly that the largesses of alms to Christ's poor, repair of roads and bridges and all other duties of every kind of charity be there performed, and spread thence far and wide ; and considering that the site of the monastery, in which were many splendid monuments of his illustrious progenitors, kings of England, there buried was a place fit, proper, and necessary for a bishop's seat,

he founded the bishopric and gave the bishop the Leaden Hall and the abbot's lodgings, and established the chapter to consist of a dean, the archdeacon of Gloucester, and six canons, and gave them the church and precincts. By another deed of the following day the dean and chapter were granted for endowment the possessions of the dissolved monastery.

The bishop, dean, and first 'prebendal priests' were named in the foundation deed. There seems to be no trace left of the parcelling out of the monastic buildings among the prebendaries and other ministers of the church for their houses, usually done by a royal commission by a formal deed of assignment. There is, therefore, no direct evidence of any allotment of a schoolhouse and masters' houses, for the grammar school, which in all the newly established cathedrals, except Winchester, formed an integral and important part of the new foundation.

At Gloucester the newly reinstated school first appears in the statutes which were promulgated on 5 July, 1544, by a commission consisting of Nicholas Heath, bishop of Worcester, George Day, bishop of Chichester, and Richard Cox, archdeacon of Ely and former head master of Eton.

The statutes were in general word for word the same as the statutes for other cathedrals of the new foundation, varying only in respect of the number and remuneration of the staff provided. Chapter 25 provides for the school :—

Of the schoolmasters. That piety and good learning may always give out shoots, grow and flower in our church to the glory of God and the use and ornament of the commonwealth we decree and ordain that by the Dean, or in his absence the Subdean, one be chosen who is learned in Greek and Latin, of good character and of godly life, with a faculty for teaching, who may train up in piety and good learning those children who shall resort to our school to learn grammar. And let him have the first charge (*primas obtineat*) and be Headmaster or Principal Teacher (*Archididascalus sive praecipuus Informator*). Another —well skilled in the Latin tongue and who hath a good faculty in teaching . . . shall instruct the youths under the headmaster in the first rudiments of Grammar, and shall therefore be called the undermaster or Second Teacher (*Hipodidascalus sive secundarius Informator*).

The masters were to obey 'those rules and orders which the dean, or in his absence the subdean, and chapter shall think fit to prescribe unto them.' If found ' idle, negligent or unfit to teach,' they might be deprived after three warnings.

The grammar school, it will be observed, was entirely free and open to all. The masters were to instruct any who came to learn grammar. The choristers are not even mentioned in connexion with it. There is not a vestige of foundation for the notion, sedulously inculcated by some writers and carelessly accepted by the public, that the school was solely or primarily or in any substantial degree intended for the choristers. The choristers were separately provided for by chapter 24 :—

> Of the choristers and their master. We decree that there be . . . by the election of the dean 8 choristers, youths who have good voices and are inclined to singing, who may serve, minister and sing in our choir. For the instruction of these youths and training them up as well in modest behaviour as in skilfulness of singing we will that . . . there shall be chosen one who is of a good life and reputation, skilful both in singing and in playing upon the organ, who shall diligently spend his time in instructing the boys in playing upon the organs and at proper times in singing divine service.

He also was removable after three warnings. At Gloucester there was not even the clause inserted in other cathedral statutes that the choristers should be eligible or have a preference for admission as scholars of the grammar school when their voices broke. The reason was that there was at Gloucester no provision for grammar scholars to be lodged, boarded, and clothed and taught gratis, at the expense of the cathedral establishment, as there was in most of the other cathedrals of the new foundation, ranging from 50 at Canterbury and 40 at Westminster to 20 at Peterborough ; consequently there would have been no adequate benefit to ex-choir boys in providing for their admission to the grammar school, to which they could, like everybody else, be admitted without special provision.

In other particulars, the statutes relating to the school were in identical terms with those in the other cathedrals of the new foundation, reference being made in the foundation deed here, by way of model, to the statutes of Westminster Cathedral, afterwards unfortunately dissolved by Queen Mary to reinstate the monastery.

The relative place which the grammar school bore in regard to the rest of the establishment may be gauged by the amount of the masters' salaries and allowances for liveries, or clothing, and commons, or board, compared with those of the other members of the establishment.

The dean had a salary of £27 a year, with an allowance of 4s. a day for every day at which he was present in his habit at mattins, mass, and vespers, including days on which he was absent for certain specified reasons, being a maximum of £73 ; or £100 a year in all. Each canon had a salary of £7 17s. 8d. and a similar allowance of 8d. a day, making a maximum of £12 3s. 4d., or £20 1s. in all. At Gloucester, differing in this respect from some other cathedrals, the canons were allowed or directed to have separate houses for themselves and their families, which did not at first mean wives and children, as they were still celibate priests, but servants and dependants ; but for the other members of the establishment a common hall was provided, where they were to be boarded together, and to wear a livery of one or two suits, which would have been called the gentlemen's and the servants' liveries. The living of these other members of the cathedral establishment was accordingly measured not by a daily allowance besides their stipend, which was to cover everything, but by a yearly allowance of livery and a monthly allowance for commons. The stipends were set out in chapter 30, the liveries in chapter 29, and the commons in chapter 28. They were :—

Office	Stipend			Livery of Cloth				Commons per Month		Commons per Year			Total		
	£	s.	d.		£	s.	d.	s.	d.	£	s.	d.	£	s.	d.
Minor Canon . . .	5	2	0	4 yds. at 5s. a yd. .	1	0	0	6	0	3	12	0	9	14	0
Choristers' Master . .	5	7	0	3 yds. at 5s. a yd. .	0	15	0	6	0	3	12	0	9	14	0
Deacon	2	19	2	3 yds. at 4s. 6d. a yd.	0	13	6	5	8	3	8	0	7	0	8
Lay Clerk	2	19	2	3 yds. at 4s. 6d. a yd.	0	13	6	5	8	3	8	0	7	0	8
Chorister	0	15	0	2½ yds. at 3s. a yd. .	0	7	6	3	4	2	0	0	3	2	6
Head Master . . .	8	8	8	4 yds. at 5s. a yd. .	1	0	0	6	0	3	12	0	13	0	8
Usher	2	19	2	3 yds. at 4s. 6d. a yd.	0	13	6	5	8	3	8	0	7	0	8

The head master therefore ranked in pay and position next to the canons, above the minor canons, while the usher ranked below the minor canons, with the deacon and lay clerks. In hall, however, the head master did not preside, one of the minor canons, who was steward and received an additional stipend for his trouble, supervising the arrangements and being responsible for the meals. The low position of the usher may be explained by the fact that he was usually a very young man, in or hardly out of his teens, and not intended to stay long, being on his promotion to orders and a head-mastership or a living. The pay allotted for the two masters together came to £20 1s. 4d. or 4d. more than the maximum allowance of a canon : and if the canon was non-resident beyond his allowed holidays of 80 days, or neglected any of the services when resident, as he was pretty sure to do, the allowance to the school considerably exceeded that to a canon.

The dean and chapter of Gloucester effectively prevented any full history of the school being written by the careless custody or destruction of all their Chapter Act books before 1617, and all their accounts before 1635.

Nothing at all is discoverable of the school before 1558, and then all we know is the name of the master, Robert Amfield.[1] In 1563 John Lightfoot was usher. In 1576 a new master and usher came in the persons of Tobias Sandford and Francis Pearson. We may say here once for all that as far as is known every master and every usher was in holy orders, if not when he came at all events shortly afterwards, though there was in fact no statutory obligation on them to be so. So that in every case the prefix of Reverend, which was not in fact commonly used till the seventeenth century, must be understood as an *epitheton constans*. Both master and usher were also, with few if any exceptions, Oxford men. Tobias Sandford, for instance, took his B.A. degree at Oxford 12 April, 1570, M.A. 19 June, 1574. He afterwards was incorporated at Cambridge, if the identification is correct, as Bachelor of Medicine in 1578. He left the school in 1580, apparently to go off to practise medicine. This was no uncommon thing with Elizabethan schoolmasters. Medicine was still, as it had been wholly in the Middle

---

[1] Rev. T. D. Fosbrooke, *New Hist. of Glouc.* (1819).

Ages, almost a branch of the clerical profession, and at least one famous head master of Winchester, Christopher Johnson, was afterwards president of the College of Physicians, and we have noted in Essex and Suffolk actual combinations of teaching school and practising medicine in the same individuals.

Thomas Wastell, appointed master in 1580, had taken his B.A. degree at Queen's College, 5 April, 1566. He held office for eight years.

Elias Wrench, who came in 1588, held office for ten years, vacating it to become canon of the cathedral and rector of Lassington and Rudford, and was buried in the cathedral in 1633. He has not been traced at Oxford himself, but four of his sons were there, with one of whom—a scholar and fellow of Corpus Christi College, entered in 1621, who bore the same name as himself—he has been confused.[1]

His successor, William Loe, was a Merton man, B.A. of St. Alban's Hall, Oxford 1597, M.A. 1600, and B.D. from Merton 8 June, D.D. 8 July, 1618. He also became a canon, sub-dean in 1605, and chaplain to James I.

The next head master, 1605, Thomas Potter, a scholar from Westmorland at Queen's College, where he matriculated 2 July, 1592, seems to have combined the mastership with the rectories of Hatherop and Sudeley. The name of his usher, Thomas Wood, is famous in that he was the father of the great Oxford antiquarian, Anthony Wood. He himself matriculated at Broadgates Hall, now Pembroke College, 20 June, 1600, and became B.A. at Corpus Christi College 15 March, 1603–4. Like most of the ushers, and indeed most of the head masters till the eighteenth century, he was quite a young man, only twenty-three, when he came to teach school. He only stayed at Gloucester for two years. John Clarke, a native of the county, the next head master, also matriculated at Broadgates Hall.

On 25 January, 1616–17 the first extant Chapter Act Book begins with a characteristic entry signed by William Laud, who inaugurated his new dignity as dean by a 'papistical' innovation, directing the removal of the communion table from the body of the choir to be placed altar-wise at the east end. On 9 March, 1617–18 a solemn entry in Latin records the admission of John Langley, B.A., to the place of

> headmaster of the free school in the college or cathedral church of Gloucester, the three articles required in that behalf being first signed by him, and an oath being made by him to observe the statutes and ordinances of the said church, and the oath of allegiance to King James first being taken by him as is provided.

This long entry and its special signature by Laud probably points to the forcible expulsion of his predecessor and the interest which Laud took in the school.

Laud's influence can be traced also in the appointment of Daniel Williams as usher on 14 October, 1618, he being a Warwick boy, of Laud's College of St. John's, where he matriculated 30 June, 1615, and had not yet taken his B.A. degree (which he did 19 October, 1619) when he became usher. He shortly returned to Oxford, being succeeded 8 October, 1621, by another boy from St. John's College, Thomas Daniel, who had taken his

[1] Rev. T. D. Fosbrooke, *New Hist. of Glouc.* (1819), 116 ; see Wood's *Ath. Oxf.* i, 11.

B.A. degree at the age of eighteen on 8 June previously. Laud's last signature as dean was to his admission. The ushers—who were not appointed by the head master but by the dean—were John Angell, elected 4 February, 1623–4; on 23 June, 1628, Giles Workman, a Gloucestershire boy, B.A. of Magdalen Hall; on 4 June, 1632, Ezra Grayle, B.A.; and on 25 October, 1634, John Grayle, of Stow, Gloucestershire, B.A. of Magdalen Hall. He afterwards attained fame as head master of Guildford Grammar School, where he reigned for half a century.

Langley the head master was a very distinguished person in the scholastic profession. Born at Banbury and probably educated at the Grammar School there, he matriculated at Oxford 23 April, 1613, and took his B.A. degree at Magdalen Hall 5 July, 1616. He did not become an M.A. till more than a year after his appointment to the head-mastership. Langley's services were much appreciated at Gloucester. A chapter minute of 11 May, 1628, exceptionally written in English, recites that he on 24 December previous did

> by resignation in writinge surrender and resigne uppe into the hands of Mr. Wrenche, then Sub-dean, his place ot High Schoolmaster within this churche, which he had dyvers yeares before that inioyed with good approbation of the Dean and chapter; and sithence that the said Mr. Langley by persuasion and request of dyvers of his friends is willinge to accepte of the same place againe, and to that purpose Mr. Doctor Wynniffe, Deane of this church, hath exprest his desire to Mr. Subdeane that Mr. Langley should be readmitted

therefore the sub-dean readmitted him 'into the place of High or Cheefe Schole Master in as ample a manner' as he had formerly held it. It is perhaps connected with this transaction that the same day 'Mr. Hosier, master of the choristers, is required to teach the catechism and principles of the Christian religion' to them. Perhaps Langley had objected to the head master being obliged to take time which should have been devoted to the school at large to give instruction of an elementary character to the choristers, whose attendance at grammar schools from the fourteenth century downwards has always been a difficulty, to the detriment of other scholars.

The first extant account of the Chapter Treasurer, for the year 1635, shows us 'stipends paid the head master (*archididascali*) John Langley, and usher (*hypodidascali*), John Grayle, £24 13s. 4d.,' while among 'extraordinary payments' (*In extraordinariis*) is 'In primis, To Mr. Langley, for increment of his salary 13s. 4d.' The account does not show what the payments to the master separately were. It is a curious thing that here, as in other cathedrals of the new foundation, there seems to be no evidence as to when the common table contemplated by the statutes of Henry VIII ceased. It was doomed from the time when matrimony became lawful to priests, such as head masters and minor canons. It had clearly ceased at Gloucester before this first extant account; the difference between the statutory salaries of £8 8s. 8d. and £2 19s. 2d. being accounted for by the commutation of the allowances for livery and commons into money. It was, as time went on, a disastrous exchange for all but the canons, as while they more than made up for the change in the value of money by increased rents and the fines paid for the renewal of leases, those who were not members of the governing body of the foundation received no such compensation. At this time the dean received £100, each canon £20, and minor canon £10, and the master of the choristers

£10. But two centuries later, while everybody else's pay had increased, even the minor canons getting £150 a year, the two masters were left with only £20 and £10 respectively. At this time the chapter took a truer and higher view of their duty to the school. Langley retired probably at Michaelmas, 1635, his successor being admitted 3 November, 1635. There is no foundation for the statement in the *Dictionary of National Biography* that he became a canon of Gloucester. On the contrary, he was either expelled from his post of master or driven to resign in consequence of Laudian persecution, because at Laud's visitation of the cathedral he displayed Puritan leanings. Whether he betook himself to keeping a private school in Gloucester or busied himself in clerical work, he was at hand in the neighbourhood for the benefit of the town when they wanted the Crypt School reinforced. For, as will be seen, when we come to deal with that school, on the usher going out of his mind and the master proving a failure as a teacher, Langley was in September, 1637, appointed usher and assistant to teach the Greek tongue at a salary of 40 marks. Six months later the head master's salary was reduced to 20 marks, when he appealed to Archbishop Laud. A writ of privy seal was sent down 22 April, 1640, to prohibit the corporation from removing the master, or from employing Langley, who had at Laud's visitation 'shown himself sedulously set against the government of the church and publicly refused to conform himself and deserted the college school.' However, Langley did better for himself, being elected high master of St. Paul's School 7 January, 1640–1. Here he was in high repute. He gave evidence against Laud before the Lords Committee for his persecution of a Puritan preacher at Gloucester, which caused the poor man's death. Langley was appointed by Parliament 23 June, 1643, a licenser of the press for works of philosophy, history, poetry, morality and arts, but complained of for remissness in 1648. In 1644 he published a rhetoric entitled, *Totius Rhetoricae adumbratio in usum Paulinae Scholae*, and an *Introduction to Grammar*. He died ten days after Oliver Cromwell, 13 September, 1657.

Thomas Widdows succeeded Langley as head master 3 November, 1635, and ten days afterwards Christopher Prior, a Balliol B.A., was admitted as usher. Widdows was from Mickleton, and matriculated at Gloucester Hall 13 April, 1627, at the age of fourteen, probably with a view to attending the Grammar School. He became a demy at Magdalen College in 1630, and there took his B.A. degree in 1630–1, and M.A. 17 December, 1633. He was only twenty-two when he became head master. The ushers were as usual evanescent, Prior having given place to William Collins of Magdalen College in 1636, and he to Richard Lovell of the same college, on 7 March, 1637, to be succeeded by William Eldridge of Bentham, Gloucester and Balliol on 21 May, 1639. On 10 November, 1636, the chapter passed a resolution that

whereas Mr. Thomas Widdows, master in arte and schoolmaster of the grammer schoole within this churche, hath since his admission to that place bin very diligent in his instruccion of the youth under his charge, as well in their manners as learninge, to the great good likinge of us the Deane and Chapter and the creddit of the said schoole We do therefore order that the same wages formerly paid to Mr. Langley his immediate predecessor in that place shall be continued and paid to him.

Accordingly we find in the accounts 1636–7, 'Mr. Thomas Widdowes for increment of sallery £2 3s. 4d.'; 1637–8, 'To Mr. Widdows' preferment sallery 13s. 4d.' besides £8 13s. 4d. salary. This payment is also made in 1640–1. There are no more chapter books or accounts after that year till after the Restoration. It is said[1] that Widdows was ejected from the mastership in 1640. If he was ejected, which we may take leave to doubt, it was not until 1642. But the Parliamentarians did not war against schoolmasters, at all events not at that date. It seems probable that Widdows being a Royalist, while Gloucester was the chief and, after the capture of Bristol, almost the sole, upholder of the Parliamentary cause in the west, he betook himself to more congenial surroundings at Woodstock School in the centre of the Royalist power. He afterwards, it is said, became head master at Northleach in Gloucestershire, and died there in possession of the mastership in 1655, in the full height of Commonwealth power under the Protectorate— strong evidence that Parliament warred not against schoolmasters.

William Russell, who succeeded in 1642, was a Gloucestershire man from Wickwar. He was educated at Lady Berkeley's Grammar School at Wotton under Edge, and went thence to Lincoln College, 22 January, 1635–6, where he became B.A. 24 October, 1639. He was a master at Sudbury in Suffolk before coming to Gloucester. He held office through the whole period of ' the troubles.' He seems to have been Presbyterian true blue.

We do not, thanks to the ' fool-fury' of the zealots of the Restoration, anxious to obliterate the proceedings and especially the good done by the Parliamentary party, know exactly what transpired at Gloucester about the school. But we know in general that the same committees which dealt with ' Scandalous Ministers' and with ' Plundered Ministers' dealt also with schoolmasters. Those committees had power to remove scandalous schoolmasters, and to provide augmentations for the poorest ones out of the estates of delinquents, and of bishops and deans and chapters which were sequestered by ordinance of 31 March, 1643.[2] Gloucester however was at first in the middle of the enemy's country, and it was not till 7 November, 1645,[3] that the estates of the dean and chapter of Gloucester were actually ordered to be sequestered and applied.

We learn from an order made in 1655 by the trustees for the maintenance of ministers and schoolmasters that by an ordinance of 8 July, 1646,

> the Lords and Commons in Parliament did settle William Russel scholemaster of Grammar schole of the Cathedral Church of Gloucester and ordered him £30 a yeare out of the lands and revenues of the said Deane and chapter—

a very considerable increase on the £19 6s. 8d., which it appears from the same order was ' the ancient stipend payable to the said Schoolmaster by the Deane and Chapter.' He no doubt received this from the sequestrators.

Deans and chapters were abolished by Act of Parliament on 30 April, 1649, but the schools and charities which formed part of the cathedral foundations were expressly saved. On 18 December following, the City Council

> agreed that Mr. Russell, scholemaster of the Colledge Schole, shall have paid unto him by the stewards for translating the foundation of the late Deane and Chapter out of Latin into English for the use of the Maior and Burgesses

40s., and Thomas Coll 13s. 4d. ' for faire writing the same.' By an ordinance passed 8 June, 1649, all the property of bishops, deans, and chapters which

---

[1] Foster, *Alumni Oxon.* ; Wood, *Ath. Oxon.* iii, 398 ; Bloxam, *Magd. Coll. Reg.* v, 127.
[2] Scoble, *Acts and Ordinances*, i, 37.   [3] *Commons Journ.* iv, 334.

appeared in the Valor Ecclesiasticus as spiritual possessions, that is, rectories and tithes, as distinct from temporal possessions like manors and lands, were vested in 13 trustees upon trust for salaries and augmentations of salaries to preaching ministers and schoolmasters. £13,000 a year was assigned for ministers and schoolmasters and £2,000 a year for the augmentation of the universities. On 16 March, 1649–50, the council agreed to petition Parliament for confirmation of the charitable objects of the foundation including

> the constant reparacione of the goodly fabricke of the colledge [1] and for the maintenance of a schoolmaster and usher in the colledge school, and for the charging thereof upon some of the lands belonging to the late Dean and Chapter.

Parliament had no intention of letting the schools suffer by the abolition of the chapters out of whose revenues they were supported. By another ordinance on 5 April, 1650, the duty of directing the grants to be paid by the trustees was given to the Parliamentary Committee for Reformation of the Universities. We learn from the order of 1655 already quoted that the council's request had been complied with, 'the amount of £19 6s. 8d. being secured by lands of the Dean and Chapter for the purpose reserved and settled on the trustees for the sale of Deane and Chapter lands.' But the augmentation of £10 13s. 4d. was not included in this settlement. When, under an Act of the Protectorate Parliament, 2 September, 1654, the direction of grants as well as the management of the property was given to the trustees for maintenance of ministers, thus making them a complete Ecclesiastical Commission, by an order [2] of the trustees of 5 April, 1654, it was provided that

> liberty be given unto the Scholemaster and Usher of the schoole in Gloucester to prove the pensions by them claymed and demanded from the said Trustees on the 7th day of May next, when the Trustees appoint to hear the same.

This they apparently did and were paid up to December, 1654. But a year later, 20 December, 1655,[3] the augmentation still remained unprovided for, and it was therefore

> ordered that the said yearly summes be paid untill further order of the Trustees and that Mr. Henry Langley and Mr. Matthew Langley receivers, doe pay the same out of the rents and profitts of the impropriated rectory of Churchedowne.

Nor was this the only augmentation, for on 2 June, 1655, the town added to their stipends :

> This House doth agree to give Mr. Russell, Schoolmaster, £10 yearely out of the chamber of this city for his better encouragement, to be paid quarterly, the first payment to begin at Michaelmas next and to continue during the pleasure of this house.

There was, however, a difficulty in getting payment, as on 26 June, 1656, payments though ordered to be continued, were on 25 June, 1657,[4]

> in arreare for [   ] years, amounting unto the summe of £63 6s. 8d. So Mr. Langley the receiver was ordered to pay those arrears out of the arrears of the rents and profits of the lands seized, not particularly disposed of for the said yeares, paying each yeare's arreare out of the rents and profits of the said yeare.

---

[1] So untrue are the common allegations against the Commonwealth's men that they destroyed or desired to destroy all the ancient churches. At Winchester at this time large funds were raised by subscription for the restoration of the cathedral.
[2] Lambeth MSS. Aug. 1005, fol. 236.
[3] Ibid. 972, fol. 383.
[4] Ibid. 493, fol. 250.

SCHOOLS

It is difficult to know what the precise relation of these orders was to certain proceedings taken at the same time in Chancery under the Elizabethan statute of charitable uses. A commission was issued under the statute[1] on 16 February, 1654–5, and the inquisition taken 21 January, 1655–6, before the mayor, Dennys Wise, and two aldermen, whereby it was found that on the erection of the cathedral Henry VIII had given £100 9s. 11d. of its revenues

for the pious and charitable uses hereinafter mentioned, viz. the upper schoolmaster or teacher of grammar in the school there the sum of £8 8s. 8d. for his salary, and also his constant diet at the first table in the common hall of the said college, with 4 yards of cloth yearly for his gown or outward garment. Afterwards, at the breaking up of the said common hall of the said college, the late dean and chapter of the said church allowed the said upper schoolmaster instead for salary, diet, and gown the yearly sum of £19 6s. 8d. The under master or usher of the school was given his constant diet at the common hall and 3 yards of cloth yearly for his gown. At the breaking up of the hall he was given the yearly sum of £8.

The said king also ordered by his letters patent that the schoole and houses of the said upper schoolemaster and usher should be well and duly kept from time to time in all manner of needful and necessary reparation out of the manors, lands, and revenues of the said late dean and chapter, which amounted yearly by estimation to £6 9s. 11d.

The upper schoolmaster was to be paid in all £25 16s. 7d. out of the manor of Tuffleigh, then in the hands of Richard Atkins, esq. The under master's salary of £8 is paid out of the manor of Rudford, in the hands of Andrew Wandlea, gent.

A further inquisition[2] was taken at the Tolsey, 8 April, 1657, before Luke Nourse, mayor, and others, and an order made thereon, which, after finding as in the previous inquisition as to the salaries of the masters, found that 'the yearly sum of £6 9s. 4d. now given to the 4 almsmen of the cathedral were to keep the schole and the houses of the said cheife or head schoolemaster and usher from time to time in all manner of neadful and necessary reparations.' The sums due were now ordered to be paid, and in response to a request from the jury that 'the Commissioners should sett downe such orders whereby the said Upper Schoolemaster, usher, almsmen, and poor may be elected, nominated, and appointed to have and receive the said several allowances,' on 22 May, 1657, the commissioners made a kind of scheme. They decided that 'the mayor and 5 senior aldermen and the town clerk should be governors of the said Free Grammer or Colledge Schoole'; on the death of any of whom others were to be chosen in their place. William Russell, who, as we have seen, had already been in office some fifteen years, was to be elected 'chief master in the schoole so long as he behaves well,' and William Bennet 'to be inferior master or usher.' In case of death or misdemeanour on the part of either, the majority of the governors 'can elect and nominate fresh men in their place, and have the power to remove or displace one of them if they have lawful and just right for so doing.' Anthony Edwards, the receiver, was to pay them, and the governors were to meet 'in one of the rooms or places, commonly called the Vestry or the Library, or the Chapter house, or some other convenient place within the precincts of the colledge.'

Next year the city obtained from the second Protectorate Parliament an Act, which appears now to be recorded nowhere except in an Inspeximus of

---

[1] P.R.O. Chancery Petty Bag. Inq. bdle. 23, No. 6, 1656.
[2] Ibid. bdle. 24, No. 3, 1657.

it by Oliver, Lord Protector, dated 4 August, 1657, preserved among the city muniments. The Act was made in the Parliament begun 17 September, 1656 :—

> Be it enacted by his Highness the Lord Protector and the Parliament now assembled and by the authoritie thereof that the late Cathedralle or Colledge church in the city of Gloucester and all the utensills thereof, with the Cloysters, Library and Free Schoole howse, and also those two severall howses or tenements with their appurtenances wherein the Schoolemaster and usher of the said Free Schoole there doe now inhabite and dwell, together with so much of the church goods and waste grounds adjoynyng (not already sold) . . . . shall henceforth be and remayne and are hereby enacted to be vested, settled and remayne henceforth in the real and actual possession and seizure of the Mayor and Burgesses of the said city of Gloucester and their successors for ever To and for the publique worship of God, the educacion of children in learninge and for such other publique religious and charitable uses and noe other as to them . . . . shall from time to time seeme most necessary and convenient.

Well would it have been for the school if this Act had never been brought to naught after three years by the Restoration, for under it the city showed every disposition to behave generously by the school. On 11 June, 1657, they directed the stewards to 'take care for the removing of the seates in St. Michael's Church and placing them fitt for the scholars of the two schools in this city so as the charges do not exceed 40s.'

'Mr. William Russell, school master of the Colledge was buryed 9 July, 1659, aged 42 years' in St. Michael's. On 13 April, 1660,[1] it was ordered that the receiver of Gloucestershire 'doe informe himselfe how much of the arreares of the salary due unto Mr. Russell late schoolemaster of the free schoole in Gloucester were unpaid unto him at the time of his death as well as of what was in pay unto him by order of the Trustees.' It is to be hoped that his family got the money. At all events they were looked after by the city council, who on 21 July agreed 'that Mrs. Russell the widow and relict . . . . shall have 20 nobles by the year allowed unto her and her children out of the chamber during the pleasure of this house.' Thus the city did what the chapter had never thought of doing, and gave a pension to the master's widow and children.

The next master was Mr. Benjamin Master. He had been a boy at Westminster School, then in the very height of its fame, and a Westminster student at Christ Church, Oxford, where he matriculated 29 November, 1633, and became M.A. 21 June, 1640. He was thus about twenty-five years old. He had apparently been master at Newark upon Trent Grammar School, an ancient school mentioned in the thirteenth century, and with a good endowment given by a successful cleric-diplomatist Archdeacon Thomas Magnus, in 1545. In these days it is to be feared, it would not be regarded as promotion to go from Newark to Gloucester School. On 7 November, 1659, the Gloucester Corporation 'agrees that Mr. Benjamin Maister, schoolmaster of the colledge House shall have' £12 'towards the charges of removal of his household and household stuff from Newark upon Trent to this city.' As 'cheife master' he was to have £10 per annum and Mr. Bays, usher, £5 per annum 'out of the chamber . . . . for their encouragement in their employ,' in addition of course to their stipends from the chapter revenues. But poor Master had the trouble of his removal for nothing. With the

---

[1] Lambeth MSS. Aug. 989, fol. 190.

Restoration his mastership and the augmentation of the school came to an end. At Michaelmas, 1660, the Chapter Accounts were resumed, and include ' to Mr. John Gregory, *archididascalo*, £13 13*s*. 8*d*.' Next year he had as usher Abraham Gregory, and was paid £4 besides his stipend 'for certain reasons which must not be taken for a president in the future.' John Gregory was first of Pembroke Hall New College, but took his B.A. degree at Cambridge. The usher was probably his nephew, a son of Francis Gregory of Woodstock, and came from Oriel College, where he matriculated on 7 December, 1660, aged 17, so that he began his scholastic career at the age of 18, while still an undergraduate. While still usher he took his M.A. degree at Cambridge, was vicar of Sandhurst, Gloucestershire, in 1664, and in 1671 retired from the usher-ship to become a canon of Gloucester, and rector of Cowley. Next year he was canon of Lincoln, in 1675 rector of St. Mary le Crypt, in 1679 precentor of Llandaff. He died at Gloucester, 29 July, 1690, and is buried in the cloisters. John Gregory, the head master, was also rector of Hempsted and Dursley, and became archdeacon of Gloucester in 1672. He died in 1678.

The mastership was kept in the family by the succession of Oliver Gregory, who had been usher of the Crypt School from 1670. He seems to have been a Cambridge man, while Nathaniel Lye or Luys, his usher, was of Brasenose. Lye only stayed three years, becoming vicar of Cowley, Gloucestershire, in 1673, afterwards canon of Bristol, archdeacon, and in 1723 at the age of 83, canon of Gloucester, dying at the age of 90 in 1737. Oliver Gregory remained head master till 1684, with Thomas Trippett for usher.

On 11 September, 1684, Mr. Maurice Wheeler, M.A. 1670 of New Inn Hall, and then chaplain at Christ Church, became head master. In 1685, Wheeler began a register of the school, ' The Census or Matriculation book of the King's School, Gloucester '—one of the very few instances of the use of the term King's School. The register has been continuously kept up to the present day. It is headed 'Scholae Regiae Glocestriensis Liber Censualis sive Matricula Alumnorum qui ibidem admissi, ingenium bonis moribus literisque excolendum tradidere; a Mauritio Wheeler, ejusdem Scholae Praeside, instituta A.D. MDCLXXXV.'

The list begins with 52 boys, whom Mr. Wheeler calls ' the aborigines who possessed the school at the time of the interregnum,' i.e. the time between his predecessor's departure and his own appointment (' Scholares aborigines, qui pridem initiati Scolam interregni tempore possiderent '). Those who entered afterwards he speaks of as ' scolares ascripti, qui, superius admissis et nominatis, denuo cooptarentur.' There were 54 ' aborigines,' of whom 30 came from the city and 23 from the county. The ' ascripti ' numbered 25 in 1684–5, and 32 in 1685–6. So that the school was well over a hundred. The boys included scions of the county families, among them Lysons of Hempsted, Kingscote of Kingscote, Maskelynes of Penton, Fusts and Jenners now fused into Jenner-Fusts, Phelps of Dursley, Crawley-Boevey, and so forth. From the town of Gloucester comes the well-known name of Abraham, son of Abraham Rudhall, the great bell-founder.

On 28 September 1686, is one of the all too rare entries concerning the school in the Chapter Books on a dispute as to 'the removal of children out of the Lower to the Upper Schole.' It was ordered that the

> antient custom should be observed, that is, that noe child shall be removed out of the Lower Schoole, nor admitted de novo into the Upper Schoole, untill he be so well grounded by the Usher in the rudiments of the Latin tongue as that he shall be able to make for his exercise 5 or 6 lines of plaine true Latine and shall understand the scanning and parsing of verses, and the making of 2 verses from one night's exercises.

The standard in the Lower School, presumably the three lowest forms, was not therefore very exalted. Presumably this entry was connected with the retirement of Mr. Trippett and the appointment of John Hilton, M.A., as usher.

With the eighteenth century long masterships became the rule. Wheeler held for twenty-eight years; and then became a canon of Lincoln and vicar of Wappenham, Northamptonshire. Among Wheeler's early pupils was George Whitefield, the celebrated preacher and joint founder of Wesleyanism, entered in 1725.

In 1692, Mr. Benjamin Newton, minor canon, was elected head master and sworn, but 'surrendered up his place as minor canon.'

On 30 November, 1724, William Alexander of Campden, Gloucestershire, and Trinity College, Oxford, 8 July, 1697, M.A. 1704, and already rector of Colesborne in 1713, came from Cheltenham Grammar School. Joseph Gregg, appointed usher 30 May, 1727, got into trouble, and was finally expelled for reasons which sound strange to modern ears. On 30 November, 1736, he was admonished 'for not attending divine service on holydays and holyday eves, and lying out of the precincts of the colledge without asking leave of the Dean.' On 19 May, 1739, he was warned a second time. He had been absent

> many whole days and nights holding his place with two ecclesiastical benefices in the country and an ecclesiastical office over the prisoners in the castle in violation of statute 21. Likewise it appears that the school has for some time been declining cheifly through Mr. Gregg's negligence of the proper school hours in the morning, for many years together, whereby the lower boys have not been duly forwarded in their learning, so that those parents and others are become generally prejudiced against the said school.

Also he had not attended early prayers on pretence of health 'which if true only shows him unfit for the business and he ought in conscience to resign.' On 26 May he was expelled. But the chapter had only themselves to thank if the usher had to hold benefices in the country and the prison chaplaincy to eke out his living. They still continued to pay him only £11 odd. Yet the salary of the master of the choristers, who in 1663 received only £7 10*s*., had been raised to £22 10*s*., or more than the head master, in 1665, to £30 in 1666, with £5 more for teaching them (*pro choristis instituendis*) or £35 in all.

Gregg's successor as usher, Edward Sparkes, became head master on 5 June, 1742, and held office for thirty-five years. Robert Raikes, the reputed founder of Sunday Schools, whose statue adorns the Thames Embankment in front of the late London School Board offices, entered the school in 1750; but Thomas Stock, 'an old boy' who entered the school in 1727, and became head master 18 December, 1777, is described on his monument in St. John's Church, Gloucester, of which he was rector, as having 'first suggested the institution of Sunday Schools, and in conjunction with Mr. Raikes established and supported the four original Sunday Schools in this parish and St. Catherine's in 1780.' Stock had for second master Thomas Evans, who retired in 1784 to the living of Chipping Norton. Stock retired 15 April, 1788. He survived until 1803 and was buried in St. Aldate's Church, the monument in St. John's being a cenotaph.

Arthur Benoni Evans, a Welsh parson's son from Monmouthshire, of Merton College, became second master 1 November, 1784, before he had taken his degree. Some four years afterwards, 15 April, 1788, he was admitted head master, David Carter Lewis, a compatriot, being at the same time admitted as second master.

In a *History of Gloucester* in 1829 by G. W. Arundel it is said 'The present very learned master, the Reverend A. B. Evans, is justly esteemed for the extent of his classical attainments as well as for his intimate acquaintance with most of the modern languages.' Dr. Phillpotts, famous in his day as Henry of Exeter, of which see he was made bishop in 1840, was a pupil of Evans, admitted in October 1783. Mr. Ellis Viner,[1] vicar of Badgeworth, whose father was there *circa* 1791, records how Evans drummed Greek repetition into the boys' heads ; his father could repeat a page of Homer on end without a mistake. Canon Hawkins of Llandaff, born in 1800, says that he went in 1807 as a day boy under 'the second master, and in 1810 became a boarder in Evans' house and under him in school. . . The system he adopted was an easier and sterner one than would meet with approval now,' but he gives no details. There were 30 boarders in the old house, which was entered from the small cloisters and was 'very small and confined.' There were fives courts against the then cathedral library, the old and present chapter-house. The schoolroom, the old and present cathedral library, was up some thirty or forty steps, so that Evans, lame from rheumatism or gout, in his later years took his class in his house. In 1810 the choristers, who have since come to be regarded, quite wrongly, as the real objects of the school, were again a trouble, the head master being paid £5 a year and the usher £15 a year for extra instruction to them. On 23 June, 1826, Thomas Evans, the son of the former usher, became usher, and on 30 November, 1827, was allowed £1 extra for every chorister learning to write ; an entry which shows how unsuitable choristers were for admission to the grammar school, grammar schools having far back in the Middle Ages never admitted boys who could not read or write first. Thomas Evans, who had been a Bible clerk at Oriel College, where he graduated in 1825, became also a minor canon in 1832, and was celebrated for his tenor voice and clear intoning ; in 1834–8 he was vicar also of Brookthorpe, in 1838 of St. Mary de Lode, chaplain of the county asylum, and precentor.

The return of ecclesiastical revenues in 1835 by the Ecclesiastical Commissioners shows a curious conception on the part of the dean and chapter of their obligation to the school. While the dean cleared over £900 a year and each canon £630, besides holding two or three livings apiece, they still only

---

[1] Frederic Hannam Clark, *Memories of the College School, Gloucester* (1890), 19.

paid the master £20 a year and the usher £10. It is true they also gave the usher a minor canonry, but that was only £50 a year. The proper proportionate amount payable to the masters was £630 a year. In 1840 a notice in the school register shows, besides the head master and under master, five assistant masters, Robert Anwyl Prichard, Mr. K. Shepcott, Henry Browne, with Marshal D'Aveny, no doubt French master, and Henry Jones, presumably writing master. On 30 November, 1841, being then M.A., Thomas Evans became head master, with another Welshman, R. A. Prichard, as second master. In 1843 the head master's old house in the precinct was given up for a fine old red-brick house in College Gardens, now St. Lucy's Nursing Home. Dr. Evans added to it at the back a fine new school and class room in the Gothic style, of which an interesting picture is given in the *Illustrated London News* of 30 November, 1844. Evans was a man of great activity, among other things a student of Sanskrit, and would sit up till 3 or 4 a.m. over his books and yet be at early prayers at 7.15 a.m. His Sunday holiday was occupied with a full Sunday service. It is no wonder, therefore, that his temper was none too good. An old boy records how

> the cane was used fiercely, such punishment being in no way reserved for great offences. One mode of severer flogging was corporal chastisement at the 'block,' a low kind of desk in the middle of the school, across which a boy was held and flogged. In 1843 or 1844 three boys, I think, ran away. After their capture and return an exciting scene was enacted. All of us, boarders and day-boys, were duly assembled at the new house, and marched down the street to the school, the culprits, I believe, being handcuffed and their coats being turned inside out. After an oration suitable to the occasion the sentence was a 'blocking.' The school being massed at the western end of the room, one culprit, a very powerful Welsh youth, resisted violently, whereupon he was handled by a combination of masters. The contest was exciting and prolonged. When it waxed fierce, and the Welsh boy was struggling violently on the floor, Dr. Evans jumped in the most cowardly way on his stomach. We could not stand this; a shout of indignation was raised, and a rush was made down the room by the boys, with a cry 'Throw them (i.e. the masters) out of the window.' Doubtless serious consequences would have ensued had not Evans piteously besought us to stay our hands. My memory fails me as to whether the Welshman was flogged or got off.[1]

It was excesses like this which ruined the smaller grammar schools, and, as means of communication improved, drove the upper classes, which used to attend them, more and more to the great public schools, where milder methods prevailed, and floggings, if frequent, were at least administered in a judicial manner. On 28 November, 1846, the second master, Prichard, was solemnly admonished by the chapter on a dispute with the head master. In 1850 he resigned and Herbert Haines succeeded him. In that year the chapter contributed £50 a year for a cricket ground. This was in Dean's Walk near Dockham ditch. In 1849 the old school was burnt and the present school, a room in the perpendicular Gothic style of architecture, built south of the chapter-house. Dr. Evans, as he became, died an old man, worn out by his multifarious exertions, in January, 1854, at the early age of fifty-three.

On the coming of Hugh Fowler, 11 February, 1854, the dean and chapter drew up a sort of scheme or rules for the school, under which the second master came more under the control of the head master and the

---

[1] Frederic Hannam-Clark, op. cit. 22.

salary of the masters was increased to £150 a year, of which the head master took £112 10s., and the under master the rest, £37 10s. Next year £10 was allowed for prizes. Mr. Hannam-Clark, who was in the school from 1859 to 1867, has in his *Memories of the College School* given a vivid picture of the school under Mr. Fowler and Mr. Haines. The methods were somewhat mediaeval. The head master kept a cane in his desk, and every Saturday morning, after hearing catechism, held an inquest in which the assistant masters reported to him the delinquents of the week, who were then caned on the hand, the whole school looking on. The system of *memoria technica* was used, English history and other subjects of instruction being compressed into unmeaning tags arranged in hexameters. The desks were used for marble trains and ink-rivers. Fighting 'the cads,' especially on 5 November, was a favourite pastime. But withal the boys liked Mr. Fowler and appreciated his geniality and sympathy. On his birthday presents of plate were made to him and a half-holiday obtained. One good 'howler' in translation is recorded by him, 'Parce metu' being rendered 'Spare me and you.'

Haines, called Badger Haines, is well known, to the antiquarian at least, by his monumental book on Monumental Brasses, the leading authority on its subject, published in 1861, when he was only thirty-one years of age. 'His gentle good nature combined with perfect strictness and justice, made him pre-eminently the popular master.' Yet the cane plays a striking part in the tales told of him by Mr. Clark. He took boarders first at Paddock House, and then in Hampden House, Barton Street. Though he died at the age of only forty-six on 14 October, 1872, he had been twenty-three years second master. His old pupils appropriately set up a memorial brass to him in the north transept of the cathedral.

From 1862 the head master was allowed £80 and the under master £40 a year for house rent. The Schools Inquiry Commission, represented by Mr. A. H. Stanton, found in 1866 a school of 96 boys, under the Reverend Hugh Fowler. Of these 42 were boarders in the head master's house, while there were some ten boarded with Miss Mascall in the cathedral precinct. The school consisted of one large schoolroom and one small classroom only. The education was that usual in public schools, mainly classical and mathematical. The boys, chiefly drawn from the professional classes, were preparing for the universities or professional life and paid tuition fees of £8 8s. to £10 10s. a year. It is strange to read that caning on the hand was still the usual punishment ; 'blocking or caning at the block' on another portion of the human frame for severer punishment 'not having lately been resorted to.' The work both in classics and mathematics was favourably reported on.

As a result of the passing of the Endowed Schools Act, 1869, in May, 1870, a joint committee of the dean and chapter and the town council made proposals for uniting the College School and the Crypt School and the endowments of the Blue Coat School under a single governing body, for the support of a single grammar school with classical and modern sides, an English (or third grade) school, and a girls' school. Unfortunately the Endowed Schools Commissioners were too busy elsewhere at the moment to take up the case, and the denominational difficulty of uniting the Cathedral School with the Crypt School, a school by foundation undenominational under the Endowed

Schools Acts, was put forward by Canon Tinling and others, while the local devotees of the Blue Coat School raised the cry of vested interests. So, unfortunately, the opportunity for union was allowed to pass, and not only did the Cathedral School and the Crypt School remain separate, but a third school, evolved from the Blue Coat School, was instituted as a rival and under-bidder to both. Mr. Fowler retired in 1872 to the vicarage of Barnwood. He was found dead in his bath-room 7 August, 1877.

The school had been falling in Fowler's later years, while the Crypt School was growing. The dean and chapter, instigated chiefly by Canon Tinling, were opposed to any fusion or, apparently, reform, and seem to have been desirous to reduce the school simply to the position of a choristers' school. Instead of augmenting the endowment of the school, removing it to a more suitable site, or at least enlarging the buildings, they inflicted a crushing blow on it by making the mastership an appendage to a minor canonry. The fleeting succession of masters testifies to the fatal success of their plans. as the place was simply used as a path to a better clerical living : March 1872, William Bedell Stanford, M.A., of Balliol College, Oxford ; July, 1875, J. A. R. Washbourn, M.A., of Pembroke College ; 1877, Philip William Sparling, M.A., of Sidney-Sussex, Cambridge, perhaps the first Cambridge head master ; 1884, Washbourn again ; April, 1886 (temporary), Ronald Macdonald, M.A.

In January, 1887, came Bernard Knollys Foster of Keble College, Oxford. He removed the master's house to Pitt House, an old-fashioned, rather rambling structure in Pitt Street, which runs north and south, parallel with the west wall of the cathedral precinct. Behind it is a pleasant lawn, with a field of about 5 acres, excellent for cricket and football. The chapter acquired the freehold of it for the school in 1890. He managed to stay for eleven years. He had a small boarding connexion, and the numbers under him rose to 63, but an outbreak of small-pox ruined the boarding-house and brought the numbers down. A. E. Fleming of Queen's College, Oxford, came in 1898 and combined the precentorship with the mastership ; and retained the former on his resignation of the latter. On 25 December, 1903, Oswald E. Hayden, whose prowess as a cricketer is recorded in the *History of Warwick School*, afterwards an exhibitioner of Christ Church, was appointed minor canon and head master. In spite of the clerical duties which consume his Sundays, he has devoted himself heartily to the school. He found 29 boys, of whom 18 were choristers or probationary choristers, and has raised the number to 52, of whom 5 are boarders, with two resident masters. Such vigour has he succeeded in instilling into them that they were able to play a drawn game with the Crypt School with its 150 boys at Association football and to beat them at cricket.

It is a strange thing that this school alone of the grammar schools of the cathedrals of the new foundation has been left unschemed by the Endowed Schools Commissioners and their successors, first the Charity Commissioners and now the Board of Education ; that no effort has been made to obtain an adequate endowment for it under sec. 27 of the Endowed Schools Act, 1869, from the Ecclesiastical Commissioners as owners of the chapter estates, though the claim is irrefutable ; or to make the school more public and popular by establishing a governing body, which should admit other elements besides the dean and chapter, who are constituted for wholly different purposes and with quite other interests.

The sole endowment of the school is now £180 a year, and that not paid to Mr. Hayden as grammar schoolmaster, but as teacher of the choristers. We saw that already in 1835 the proper stipends payable to the grammar school from the cathedral endowment amounted to over £630 a year. With the growth of population and the fall in the value of money the fair proportionate payment out of the revenues of the cathedral estates in the hands of the Ecclesiastical Commissioners would be represented by a much higher figure now.

THE NOVICES' SCHOOL, ST. PETER'S ABBEY, GLOUCESTER

Though St. Peter's Abbey, the chief monastic institution of Gloucestershire, had nothing to do with the public school of Gloucester, it seems to have done some educational work for the benefit of its own inmates, the novices, and in later times for its almonry or charity boys, who were also choristers in the Lady chapel. The only reference which is known to the monkish school, the school of the novices, is in 1378,[1] when Richard II held his first Parliament at Gloucester from 20 November to 17 December, staying by turns at Gloucester and Tewkesbury abbeys. When he was at Gloucester he and his whole court (*familia*) were lodged in the abbey, which was so crowded by them and the Parliament, the monks' refectory being used ' for the laws of arms,' i.e. for the Marshal's courts, and the Guest Hall for the Common Parliament, that

> for some days the convent had its meals in the dormitory, though afterwards, being better advised, in the schoolhouse, during the whole Parliament, as well on flesh days as on fish days, while their dinner was cooked in the orchard.

The chronicler laments the destruction of the turf in the cloister, in which the school was, in accordance with custom, situate, 'which was so worn by the exercises of wrestlers and ball-players that no traces of green were left on it.'

But this novices' school was no public school nor a school at all in our sense of the word. The novices could never have been more than ten at any time, and by analogy from even larger monasteries like Winchester and Durham must have generally consisted of only three or four youths and sometimes none ; while outsiders were strictly excluded.

GLOUCESTER COLLEGE, OXFORD

St. Peter's Abbey, however, seems to have taken a leading part in promoting education, à propos of the movement at the end of the thirteenth century for giving a university education to the Benedictine monks. About ten years after the foundation of Merton College at Oxford, the regulars seem to have thought it time to follow the lead of the secular clergy, and set up a permanent home for the members of the Benedictine order in the place which

[1] *Hist. Mon.* i, 53.

had now superseded Paris as the university of the English nation. Though the 'English nation' remained an integral part of the university of Paris, it was no longer English, nor recruited from England, but a mixed tribe of Scots, Germans, and Irish. Oxford had become the recognized resort for instruction in the higher faculties.

It has been alleged by Anthony Wood[1] that there was a Benedictine house at Oxford in 1175, but Wood was under the obsession of the monkish theory, and thought the monks the pioneers of learning and promoters of the university—an entire delusion. No documentary authority is forthcoming in support of his statement, which is wholly improbable in itself, and opposed to all existing documents.

It was not till a century later, after the administrative staff of Merton College was moved from Merton to Oxford, where the students of Walter of Merton's House of Scholars had already resided for ten years, that the proposition of a Benedictine college was first broached. It is stated that at the general chapter of the Southern Benedictines held at Abingdon in 1275 it was decided[2] to erect a house in which 'the brethren of our order who are to be sent from the various monasteries may live properly.' It is to be noted that they were not there already, but to go there. Each Benedictine house in the province of Canterbury was to contribute 2d. in every mark of its income for the first year and 1d. in after years for the purpose. Till this was done a lecturer was to be established. The proposal was repeated again at the next chapter at Abingdon in 1279[3] in the same form. But both resolutions seem to have remained mere resolutions.[4] The first definite mention of monastic students at Oxford occurs in a letter from Godfrey Giffard, bishop of Worcester, to the Chancellor and University of Masters at Oxford, on 8 April, 1283.[5] The preface suggests that the initiative in the matter had come from the pope, and that the house was an offshoot of the abbey of Gloucester only. It is probable that the whole proceeding arose from some suggestion made at the Council of Lyons in 1274, attended by Abbot Reginald of Homme of Gloucester, apparently as representative of Worcester diocese in the illness of the bishop. For the bishop tells the university that

> the supreme vicar of Christ thought that the study of theology ought to be increased so that it may by enlargement of the place of its tent make its ropes longer ; and we are informed of the praiseworthy and God-inspired devotion of the brethren of the abbey of St. Peter, Gloucester in our diocese, who now desire to depose ignorance the mother of Error and to walk in the light of truth that they may become proficient in learning.

The bishop, 'being desirous to help such a wholesome design,' asks the university

> that in the house they hold for this purpose in Oxford they may have a doctor in the divine page (i.e. a D.D.) to attend them, that the way of learning may lie open to those thirsting for wisdom, and so at last they themselves becoming learned may be able to instruct the people to the honour of God and the church.

[1] Anthony Wood, *City Documents* (Oxf. Hist. Soc.).
[2] So stated in *Worcester College*, p. 3, by C. H. Daniel and W. R. Barker (Univ. of Oxf. Coll. Hist.), F. E. Robinson, 1900. It is perhaps doubtful whether the meeting was not at Reading.
[3] *Chron. Petroburgense* (Camd. Soc. 1849), 31; Reiner, *Apostolatus Benedictinorum in Anglia* (1626), fol. 58.
[4] It is possible that the passing of the Statute of Mortmain in this year put a stop for the moment to any acquisition of land for the purpose.
[5] Worc. Epis. Reg. Giffard, fol. 206.

SCHOOLS

This seems to be the earliest mention of what was known as Gloucester College till 1540, afterwards as Gloucester Hall, and is now Worcester College. The university no doubt granted the request.

The Gloucester historian chronicles that, in the year 1283,

> our house at Oxford was founded by the noble man Sir John Giffard, a convent of monks being solemnly inducted there on St. John the Evangelist's Day (27 December) by the venerable Father Reginald, then abbot of Gloucester, Sir John Giffard being present and agreeing to the same.

The Worcester chronicle[1] in fuller and more specific terms says :

> A certain nobleman named John Giffard founded a place at Oxford outside the walls and gave possessions to maintain 13 monks, whom he chose out of the convent at Gloucester, wishing that his soul and the soul of Maud Longsword (de Longespey), formerly his wife, should receive perpetual benediction from the professors of St. Benedict.

Though no foundation is forthcoming, it is certain that one was actually made, as 'Henry, Prior of Oxford' is recorded last of the priors of the dependent priories or cells of Gloucester Abbey voting at the election of a new abbot, John of Gamage, on Sunday after Michaelmas, 1284.[2] But it seems that the Gloucester monks were recalled, for 7 years later, at a Benedictine chapter-general on 11 July, 1290,[3] a committee (*diffinitores*) was appointed to provide

> as well for those things which concern the priory at Oxford newly created by the aforesaid religious men for their studies as for the continuation of the building there and the contributions to be made in common to the building.

At the next general chapter, held in 1291 in Salisbury Cathedral on the day after the burial of Queen Eleanor at Amesbury, the committee presented their report.[4] By 5 instruments then produced and approved by the chapter, and presumably set out in order of date, the house at Oxford was settled or re-settled as a house for the whole order, and not for Gloucester Abbey only.

The first was a deed of John abbot and the convent of Gloucester which recited that

> Sir John Giffard, lord of Brimsfield, intended to establish *de novo* a house at Oxford for monks of the order of St. Benedict, to be held to be of his foundation, and thought that a place in Stockwell Street, which not sparing money or trouble he had bought from the hospital of St. John of Jerusalem, was specially suited for the purpose, because being in the Hospitallers' name it was exempt from all episcopal and archidiaconal jurisdiction.

The deed then stated that at the request of Giffard and of the presidents of the general chapter, Gloucester

> had sent monks to occupy this house in the stead of the community of the order, but had afterwards at the chapter's request recalled them, and sent Henry of Helm, one of their monks, to take possession in the name of the order and establish a convent there, without thereby claiming any private or special rights for Gloucester other than is enjoyed by any other member of the order.

In order to give effect to this and enable Henry of Helm to devote himself to this and fulfil his duties better the abbot thereby released him from all subjection to Gloucester Abbey.

---

[1] *Ann. Mon.* (Rolls Ser.), iv, 488. [2] *Hist. Mon. Glouc.* iii. [3] Ibid i.
[4] Reiner, *Apost. Benedict.* pt. ii, 52. Said to be from Cott. MS. Tib. A xv. The true reference seems to be Tib. A xiii, a Sherborne Abbey book which contains a collection of Benedictine statutes. But the leaf which should contain the passage quoted is missing.

The next instrument was a licence in mortmain of 12 March, 1290–1[1] to Giffard to grant 4 messuages and a toft to the prior and convent of the order of St. Benedict of Oxford, as if it was already established.

The third was a conveyance by which John Giffard, for the health of his soul and that of Matilda Longespee formerly his wife (she was widow of the earl of Salisbury's son when he had, it was alleged, raped her some thirty years before, and paid a fine to the king of 300 marks for doing so), granted to the prior and convent of St. Benedict of Oxford and the community of monks of the province of Canterbury sent there to study (*causa studii*), as governed by statutes of the order, the lands and tenements he had bought of John Hanvill, the prior of St. John of Jerusalem, of John of Hangenport, burgess of Oxford, of his washerwoman,[2] of John Watson and his wife Jdonea, and of Stephen Cove and Alice his wife, for the foundation, constitution, and perpetual maintenance[3] of the priory aforesaid, to receive all monks from the monasteries of the province of Canterbury there sent or to be sent to study, in pure and perpetual alms. Warranty of title was given on condition that (*ita quod*) the prior elected by the convent should be presented to Giffard and his heirs as patrons of the same, and the sub-prior and convent were to be permitted to take all rents and profits during the vacancy of the priory.

Next came another deed of Gloucester Abbey, repelling the false accusation brought by rivals that they claimed any special right in the property conveyed, and declaring that if any sufficient letter or charter of Abbot Reginald should be found differing from the grant to the community of the order, it was void and of no effect. Lastly, by a fifth instrument Henry Helm, prior of the house of St. Benedict in the suburb of Oxford and the convent of the same, declared that the priory was subject immediately to the presidents of the general chapter of Benedictines in the province of Canterbury, and that the student monks there should have the sole election of the prior, though bound to present him to the presidents or their representatives for approval.

It is a curious testimony to the permanence of a name once acquired, that in spite of these elaborate renunciations of the Gloucester rights, instead of the house being called St. Benedict's Priory, as it was evidently intended to be, it continued to be called Gloucester College till the dissolution of monasteries ; and afterwards when it belonged to St. John's College, who tried to call it St. John the Baptist's Hall, was called Gloucester Hall till 1715, when it was refounded as Worcester College.

In 1298,[4] on the morrow of St. Barnabas (i.e. 12 June),

> brother William of Brok incepted in theology (i.e. took his D.D. degree) under[5] Mr. Richard of Clyve, chancellor of the university, and was the first of the Black Monks in England who arose in that science ;

[1] Reiner, op. cit. 55, printed in Dugdale, *Mon.* iv, 407 ; Pat. 19 Edw. I.
[2] Worc. Epis. Reg. Giffard, 429. This appears in Reiner, and thence in Dugdale and Worcester Coll. as Eve Lotteris. The words in the Worc. Reg. are *sue lotricis,* i.e. the washerwoman or laundress of John of Hangenport, who presumably had a small piece of ground on which to hang out her washing.
[3] Misprinted *intentionem* in Reiner.
[4] *Hist. Mon. Glouc.* i, 34.
[5] This can hardly mean, as interpreted in *Worcester College,* that Clyve was the doctor lent by the university. For Richard of Clyve was much too big a person for that purpose, being Warden of Merton. 'Under' means under him as chancellor, not as teacher.

a pretty clear proof that the Benedictines had not previously enjoyed a university education. 'At his vespers his companion Laurence Honson,[1] bachelor of the same science, a monk of this place, responded to the question.' It was made a great occasion.

> The Abbot and all his monks with the priors, obedientiaries, cloister monks, clerks, esquires and other gentlemen to the number of 100 horses were there ; while the abbots of Westminster, Reading, Abingdon, Evesham, Malmesbury and many priors and other monks all gave the inceptor large presents, while nearly all the prelates of the Benedictine order who were absent sent gifts by their representatives. . . . And so this inception was consummated to the honour of this house and the whole order.

Giffard's deed above quoted is entered in the register of his cousin, the bishop of Worcester, in the same year, 1298, under the heading of

> Instruments of the foundation of the priory of St. Benedict of Oxford according to the articles of foundation delivered to the abbots and priors of the province of Canterbury on such and such a year and day at Oxford for the security of either party, viz. the founder and the religious.

It seems probable that this entry was made in view of the remarkable conduct of the founder, who in 1298 gave the go-by to all the former deeds by granting the site and buildings of the college to Malmesbury Abbey. The Worcester priory chronicler records that on the morrow of Blessed Clement, i.e. 24 November, 1298, three monks came to Oxford from Malmesbury there to stay for ever, one of whom on St. Katherine's Day (25 November) was made by Sir John Giffard perpetual prior, while on 29 May following Giffard, ' who gave the students of the order of St. Benedict a spacious place,' died, and was buried at Malmesbury. Malmesbury Abbey afterwards claimed the whole site and the exclusive use of the fishponds and the gardens, which still form the great attraction of Worcester College ; and the other monasteries had to ask the leave of Malmesbury to erect chambers for their students.

It has been estimated[2] that this college had 100 to 200 students. But the estimate is certainly excessive. It is founded on the supposition that every Southern Benedictine house did what it ought, and sent there its proper proportion, or something like its proper proportion, of monks, which, according to the Benedictine statutes of 1337 was 1 in 20 or five per cent. of its total numbers. But it is quite certain they never did. Even in 1342,[3] fifteen houses were reported to the general chapter for not sending students ; in 1426 seven abbeys ; in 1440 ten abbeys were in default, including Malmesbury the owner of the site. The neighbouring abbey of Abingdon itself, the abbot of which was a sort of visitor perpetuus of the college, only kept three students there. Gloucester, which ought to have kept four students, did not do so. Apart from this there are two facts which seem to show that the number was much smaller. First, it was ordered that if the students were under 60 they were to give the prior 5s. each, which would give him £15 a year, if more than 60 they were to give him a maximum of £20 a year, which means at the most 80 students. Secondly, the chapel was only[4] 40 ft. by 20 ft. Winchester College chapel which was

---

[1] So printed. But it is more probably Houson for Howson.
[2] *Worcester Coll.* 26.   [3] Ibid. 61.   [4] Ibid. 92.

for 105 foundationers, including choristers and lay clerks, was 93 ft. long by 30 ft. broad ; and the new chapel of New College, Oxford, which was for the same number, but men instead of boys, was 150 ft. long and 35 ft. broad ; excluding the ante-chapel. But the secular clerks were much less rich and less richly catered for than the monks, and it is impossible to believe that a chapel of considerably less than half the size of Winchester College and a third the size of New College could have been intended for 100, still less for 200 monks. We may fairly assume, therefore, that 60 was about the highest number at Gloucester College. In 1537 there were only 32 students.[1]

Gloucester having the best chambers in the place probably kept up its number of three or four students. As they were there for seven years at least, this represents a very small proportion of the whole number of monks receiving a university education, and cannot entitle St. Peter's Abbey to be regarded as a place of great learning. The abbey had no further special connexion with the college, in which at least 14 other monasteries had chambers for their students, while ' 38 can be definitely connected with Gloucester College.' It would, therefore, be out of place to pursue further the history of an institution, which only in its beginning and its name had any definite connexion with Gloucester.

ALMONRY SCHOOL AT ST. PETER'S ABBEY, GLOUCESTER

Soon after the beginning of the sixteenth century there seems to have been an organized movement for the reform of the monasteries and an endeavour made to turn them into something like colleges, or at least to make them societies of more or less learned men. The bishops in their visitations were in the habit of ordering the monks to provide themselves with grammar masters. We find this going on in the dioceses of Norwich and of Canterbury, and at Winchester, while quite a band of fellows at New College seem to have gone out as such teachers to various religious orders. Something of the sort must have happened at Gloucester, for we find Abbot William[2] and the convent on 16 April, 1515, making a grant headed[3] ' Writing of John Tucke, bachelor of arts, of his offices of Master of the Grammar School and of the song school or of the children of the chapel ' (' de officiis suis magistri Scole Gramaticalis et Scole cantus sive puerorum capelle '). It is noticeable that the word school is at this time in the singular. The grant included an annuity of £6, £3 from the cellarer and £3 from the master of the chapel ; a robe or gown ' of the best cloth such as the gentlemen in our house receive ' (' de meliori panno prout generosi in domo nostra recipiunt '), and two cartloads of fuel to be delivered at his house. Besides this the chapel-master was to give him a mark of silver to find himself a gown. At his house, too, he was to have every day in the year a large helping (*ferculum*) both of the first course and the second, as shall be set before a monk, and daily a loaf

---

[1] *Worcester Coll.* 27.
[2] Oddly written as Willielmus in *Hist. Mon. Glouc.* (Rolls Ser.), iii, 290. It must have been Willelmus in the original.
[3] Miss Rose Graham supplied the heading from the contemporary Index in the MS. It is not given in the printed edition in the Notts Series.

called 'le myech' [1] and a gallon of convent ale, while he might have in the chapel-house, when the singers dine with the boys, a daily refection at his pleasure. The grant was for eighty years, if the said John should so long live, but if prevented by illness from performing his service he was to have only £6 and half the livery (*liberatione*) aforesaid. The grant was on the condition that the recipient should be faithful to the abbot and convent,

> and teach the art of Grammar to all the youthful brethren of the monastery sent to him by the abbot and the 13 boys of the clerks' chamber; and shall teach and inform 5 or 6 of the boys, apt and ready to learn, in plain song, divided or broken song and discant, sufficiently and diligently, and shall devotedly with the same boys keep mass of the Blessed Virgin Mary and the antiphon belonging to it daily, and on Saturday mass of the name of Jesus with the antiphon belonging to it, and on feast days shall be present at both vespers and high mass and other times assigned by the precentor, solemnly singing and playing the organ

unless prevented by illness or other reasonable cause, or during a month's holiday in the year.

This combination of a grammar and song schoolmaster's duties in one person is a sure note of a not very exalted kind of school. Practically the school was a choristers' school pure and simple, as the three or four novices sent to learn grammar would not take up very much of the master's time.

The document is interesting, however, as containing the earliest evidence that at Gloucester, as in the other greater monasteries, a small charity school was kept, probably in the almonry, and that it consisted of the usual number of 13 boys, who also acted as choristers for the Lady chapel. In the dearth of Gloucester muniments we know no more of the date of its foundation or the extent of its work. The other inhabitants of the clerks' chamber were no doubt the lay singing men, whose services here as elsewhere were much sought after and highly paid in the latter part of the fifteenth and the first half of the sixteenth century, when the English were *par excellence* a musical nation. In 1535 it would appear from the Valor Ecclesiasticus that there were only '3 men and 5 boys, singing daily in the Lady chapel, by ordinance of St. Wolstan, bishop of Worcester, and Sir Serlo, abbot, receiving £5 a year,' while 'a poor scholar' serving the chantry priest of Abbot William Ferleigh 'at mass' received 4*d.* a week for doing so. These boys and clerks were reproduced on a less extensive scale on the dissolution of the abbey in the six lay clerks and eight choristers of the cathedral. The only other educational payment recorded is 'a distribution of 13*s.* 4*d.* a year to 4 poor scholars at Oxford by ordinance of Abbot Walter Froucettour,' which out of a total revenue of £1,550 (a great deal more relatively than £31,000 a year to-day) is not an excessive contribution to education.

---

[1] This word has been misinterpreted, *Hist. Mon.* iii, 324, following Ducange's Dictionary, as a small loaf. But this is through a confusion of the word with the French miche = mica, a particle, a crumb of bread. Quotations given in the Promptorium Parvulorum of 1440, under 'mychekyne,' a small mich, show that it cannot mean a small loaf. For the Register of Oseney in 1267 speaks of magne michie. So in 1351 the abbot of Lilleshall granted '8 magnas michias majoris ponderis de pane conventus.' 'Big small-loaves of the greatest weight' would be absurd out of Ireland. The Oseney passage contains a grant to Andrew of Langport on every day of 2 corrodies or canons' portions a day, specifying 2 loaves which are called magne michie, one bisan michiam, one salam michiam, one coarse (grossum) loaf and 2 gallons of the best beer. Bisa seems to mean brown, and salam is probably not, as Hearne guessed, a hall or court loaf (quasi a loaf you would cut in the salle à manger), but sala probably = sale, and means black. A myech is probably therefore simply a loaf of fine white bread, which might be either a great mich or a little mich, a 'mychekyne.' It is clear that the schoolmaster was being treated as a gentleman and on the same footing as the monks, and not put off with a small loaf and insufficient diet.

A HISTORY OF GLOUCESTERSHIRE

The Crypt Grammar School, Gloucester

The Crypt Grammar School was founded under John Cooke's will of 18 May, 1528, declaring the uses of lands in Gloucester and 'Begworth,' which he had granted to trustees on 12 May previous, for his wife for life and afterwards ' to such uses as she should declare by her learned counsel to the performance of his will as she knew his mind.' This was

> to purchase lands in fee-simple worth £20 a year and to enfeoff certain persons to the uses he had declared before Andrew, bishop of Christopolis, commendatory of the hospital of St. Bartholomew, that is, to make and edify in the parish of Christ a schoolhouse, and in the same establish and ordain a perpetual free school for the erudition of children and scholars there and ordain and establish a schoolmaster of the same school for the time, a priest, daily to keep school and teach grammar freely, within the said school and also to say mass

at certain times mentioned

> and pray for the souls of himself, his father and mother and of all christians for evermore and perform divers other alms, obsequies and deeds of charity . . . all which he had intended to ordain and establish himself, if it had pleased God to give him convenient space and time in this transitory world.

Joan Cooke, the widow, duly carried out her husband's will, by a deed of 11 January, 1539–40, made between herself, the mayor and burgesses of Gloucester of the second part, and the mayor and burgesses of Worcester of the third part. Letters patent—which, she is careful to say, she had obtained from the king at her own cost—had given the mayor and burgesses of Gloucester licence in mortmain to receive lands up to the value of not more than £50 a year to build, maintain, and continue a free grammar school within the said town, and to help certain poor people and help the repair of the bridge and causeway between Gloucester and Over on the west of it. She gave, subject to her own life interest, lands in Poddesmead, Hempsted, Elmore, Badgeworth, and Bentham, and a cottage in Brockworth, a little tenement in Westgate Street, Gloucester, and lands in Stonehouse, Ebley Oxlinch, Standish, Westbury, and Chaxhill. In consideration of the grant the corporation covenanted after Joan Cooke's death to

> find and provide an honest and well-learned schoolmaster, being a priest, if such could conveniently be had, to teach grammar to such children as might resort to the said free school then already built within the said parish of Christ, in the said town of Gloucester; and that the same schoolmaster, being a priest, should say mass every week within the parish church of Christ near adjoining unto the said free school and have for his stipend yearly £10; and, if it should fortune the said schoolmaster to be a layman, then the said stipend should be £9; and the said schoolmaster, whether priest or layman, should have a chamber in the said schoolhouse, which was appointed for him and his scholars only and not for his wife or family or for strangers.

From which we may infer that the worthy aldermaness was not in favour of the 'new religion' and did not like married clerics. The schoolmaster was to be 'named, chosen, ordered, and amoved by the mayor, recorder and two senior aldermen.' 3s. 4d. a week was to be paid out of the lands in Gloucester, Badgeworth, Bentham, and Brockworth to the poor of St. Bartholomew's Hospital, and the surplus of the rents was to go for repairs of the schoolhouse; while out of the rents of Stonehouse &c. £5 a year was to be spent on the West Bridge and causeway between Gloucester and Over. A yearly meeting was to be held to survey the repairs of the school. If the corporation of Gloucester failed to carry out the trusts the property was to go over to the corporation of Worcester for the repair of the walls of that city. By a subsequent deed of 20 November, 32 Henry VIII, an annuity of 6s. 8d. a year was charged in favour of the corporation of Worcester on the lands of Brockworth 'to the intent and purpose that they should see to the performance of the trust and confidence imposed by this deed.'

The parish of Christ was otherwise and more commonly known as that of St. Mary-le-Crypt, because of the crypt underneath the church. There is no evidence that the school was ever carried on in the crypt, and it was in fact until the eighteenth century commonly called Christ School. But in modern times it is called the Crypt School from the church parallel with the west front of which still stands the handsome building in the Tudor style, which used to be the school. But except the gateway which gives access to a small quadrangle on the north side of the church the whole buildings have been completely 'restored in' modern times, and the school has been removed to another site. The school seems to have been built before the extant city account books begin, so no record of its building or the cost of it remains.

The first notice we have of the school as a going concern is in the first extant account book of the corporation, of the date apparently (for the first page and date are lost) of 3 & 4 Edward VI, 1549–50. Out of a total rental of £86 1s. 11¾d. of city property, the 'manors, lands, and tenements geven by Dame Jone Coke, widow, deceased,' amounted to £26 6s. 3d.

Poddesmead manor was let for £13 6s. 8d.; Bentham in Begworth, now Badgeworth, for £5 6s. 8d.; other lands in Begworth for £2 8s. 3d.; mill in Ebley £3; grounds in Chaxhill 13s. 10d., in Standish 13s. 4d., and a tenement in Westgate Street 8s.

No mention of payment to any master appears in this account. A master, however, existed, as in the city rent-roll[1] for 1544 under St. Mary Lane is the

> Item. The Scholemaister of the Highe Schole holdeth at will another parcell or parte of the same lane extendynge from the parcell which widow Asbyns holdeth unto the church-yarde of Criste, and yeldeth by yere, 2s. 8d.

But in the next, 1550–1, is the entry 'Also in money paid to Thomas Bowland, scolemaster of the Gramer Scole of the said citie, for his wages by the tyme of this present accompte as in yeres precedent, £10.' Thomas Bowland had supplicated for his M.A. degree at Oxford 7 December, 1525. According to Rudge's *History of Gloucester* he was not the first master, but had been preceded[2] by John Disteley, whose history has not been traced, but he is no doubt the father of John Dysley of Gloucester, who became a scholar of Winchester in 1560 and subsequently a fellow of New College, Oxford.

The school finances were heavily taxed in this and the succeeding years for a law suit, 'expenses of suit with Massenger at London 20s., for Mr. Recorder of counsel, £4,' while next year saw £3 5s. 6d. expended, with Mr. Anthony Ronehill £2 16s. 8d. and Mr. Rastell £5 4s. 7d. Even if we

---

[1] City Muniments, No. 1369.   [2] Rudge, *Hist. of Glouc.*

multiply by 20 for the corresponding lawyers' fees now, the costs were not outrageous. This suit was the usual attempt of an heir-at-law, William Massinger, to upset a charitable devise. But it failed. A decree was made in favour of the school on 12 February, 1552. The enrolment of the decree in favour of the corporation cost £2 6s. 8d., while the Master of the Rolls and the Master of Requests were paid for the same 19s. 5d. An interesting payment this year, perhaps for the benefit of the school, was for 'Mr. Kingston's Abbot of Misrule coming to Gloucester at Christmas time, 10s.', while 'the players of the same Mr. Kingston,' who was lieutenant of the Tower and a neighbouring landowner, were paid 5s.

Next year, 1551–2, finds 'Nicholas Oldysworth, scoolemaister of the Free Gramer Scoole of the said citie,' receiving £10. In the following year his name appears as Woldisworthy. The accounts of that year show the political attitude of Gloucester in the payment of '2s. to him that brought the proclamacion of Lady Jane' and the same for the proclamation of 'Dudley traitor,' while no less than 60s. was paid 'to him that brought the proclamation of the Queen's grace that now is,' Queen Mary.

One wonders whether '20s. to Mr. Arnold's servants on May Day at the brynggyng yn of May' was for the boys' benefit and a mark of the reaction to Romanism. The reaction seems to have been bad for getting or keeping schoolmasters. For in 1553–4 Oldsworthy had given place to Richard Hewis, a distinguished person, of Magdalen College, Oxford, who had been usher of Magdalen College School in 1540 and a fellow 1547–8, being proctor of the university 1549, rector of West Walton 1550, and at Brandiston, Norfolk, 1551–6. But he only stayed a year at Gloucester, becoming rector of Rhoscrowther, Pembrokeshire, in 1554. Under Elizabeth he became a pluralist canon of Wells, Bristol, and St. David's.

For the next three years no master could be got to stay. The accounts record in 1554–5 'money paid to dyverse persons techynge the Gramer scoole this year £8 15s.,' next year £5 12s. 6d., and in 1556–7 £7 10s. for the same purpose. Did the schoolmasters refuse to come because the city spent '40s. in reward to the King and Queen's servants at the bryngyng down of Mr. Hooper to be brant,' '43s. 8d. on a dyner made and geven to Lord Chandos and other gentilmen that day Mr. Hooper was brant,' and '5s. 8d. for wyne by Mr. Kyngeston and others expended in the mornyng that the said Hooper was brante'? A payment which does not show enthusiastic loyalty was one of 6s. 8d. on the 'news that the Queen's highness was delivered.' 'The glasyng of the scole howse wyndowes' cost half that amount, 3s. 4d. At last, at the end of the Marian persecution, came Hugh Walker, and was paid for 1557–8, as 'scholemaister or teacher of the Gramer Schole for the whole yere, £10.' He proved a permanence and stayed till 1575–6. His successor, Gregory Downes, as he is called in 1576–7, and Downhall in 1577–8, appears in *Alumni Oxonienses* as both Downhall and Downall. He was of Pembroke Hall, Cambridge, and a B.A. there, but on coming to Gloucester took an *ad eundem* degree at Oxford in February, 1577. He was regarded as a catch, as he received double the salary of his predecessor, £20 a year. He is called in the accounts 'Schoolemaster of Crysts.' After a short two years he went off to the then more lucrative profession of the law, and became a master in

Chancery—then a highly paid official, almost Vice-Chancellor, ranking next to the barons of the Exchequer. The salary of his successors, Mr. Edmonde Crugley, 1579–81, Alexander Belshire, scholar of Winchester and fellow of New College, Oxford, 1581–2, Henry Aisgill of Queen's College, 1582–8, was cut down to the old figure of £10. The latter seems to have been a successful master, as in 1605–6 an usher was started at £4 a year, but he only stayed for a year and three-quarters, so that the increase of numbers which demanded him must have been temporary only. Aisgill became a canon of Gloucester and chancellor of St. David's Cathedral.

William Groves or Grove, a Gloucestershire boy, of Magdalen Hall, held the mastership from 1589 to 1612. From 1599 he combined the head mastership with the incumbency of the church of St. Mary-le-Crypt. In 1613 ushers began again to be appointed, and thenceforth remained a regular institution. This was in consequence of a bequest in 1611 of Alderman Laurence Wilshere, who gave £100 for the establishment of an usher. The next master was Floyde, who was removed probably for religious reasons in 1629.

John Bird, who followed, was eleven years later the subject of reprobation. In September, 1639,[1] Robert Bird, usher, and probably John Bird's son, 'in regard he is in a kind of distraction of mind,' was removed and his stipend of 20 marks (£13 6s. 8d.) ordered to be bestowed 'upon some other able man to be chosen in his roome.' At the same meeting it was recited that

> whereas the school founded . . . to teach gramer . . . is at this present and for divers yeeres past hath been very negligently and carelessly supplied by Mr. John Bird, school maister there, in so much that very few able schollers have been sent thence to the University in comparison of other free schools, and whereas the Greek tongue and other learninge are at this day taught in many free schools for the better instructing and fitting youth for the Universitie, whereof Mr. John Langley hath given good testimony in teaching and instructing many of the burgesses sonnes of this citye and others, and enabling them for the Universitye, it was thereupon ordered that Mr. John Langley shalbe an assistant to the said Mr. Bird to teach the Greek tongue and also shalbe usher in the roome of Mr. Robert Bird.

It was also stated that by the foundation of 'Crist School' the schoolmaster was only to have a single chamber and not have his wife and family there; but Bird had in fact had all the chambers, but one and a cockloft, and kept his wife and family there. He was now ordered to remove them by Lady Day. On 20 September the order appointing Langley as usher was revoked and he was 'elected to teach Greek and other languages and to have for his stipend 40 marks.' Langley had been, as we have seen, head master of the College School. How he came to be available for the Crypt School is a little mysterious. But he was not long allowed to occupy his peculiar position. On the following 3 January (1639–40) the corporation again returned to the charge against Mr. Bird.

> Whereas divers persons of this city both aldermen and others have of late made complaint that there is and hath been so much neglect by Mr. Bird . . . in so much that they shalbe enforced to withdrawe their sonnes from thence and to place them elsewhere, which will turne to their great charge and the disgrace of this citye . . . and whereas the lands appointed for maintenance of the said schoolmaister exceed not 20 marks, and £10 thereof

[1] I am indebted to Mr. C. H. Dancey (who has done a great deal for the history of Gloucester, in connexion with the Bristol and Gloucestershire Archaeological Society) for the extracts from the city minute books in regard to the school during the Commonwealth period and onwards to 1860.

at the most only allotted to the schoolmaister, untill Mr. Bird came to teach schoole there, and upon hope that the said Mr. Bird would have proved a diligent and painefull schoole maister, the said stipend hath been since increased to 40 marks out of the lands of this citye; Now in regard the said Mr. Bird is found to be very negligent careless and remiss in performance of the duty of his place,

they reduced his stipend to 20 marks, and also 'ordered that care be taken for the speedy removinge of the said Mr. Bird.'

But England was then under the government of the ex-Dean of Gloucester. Soon there arrived the following letter under the Privy Seal :—

Charles R.—Trusty and well-beloved wee greet you well. Wee understand that John Bird hath been Schoolmaister of the Towne Schoole of Gloucester for this many yeares, and that he is a very sober man of conversation and learned in that way, and hath deserved vere well of you and that City in the instruction and education of the children there. Notwithstandinge this wee are informed that there are some amongst you which indeavour to remove him from that place and attempt to bringe in one Langley a man sectiously sett agaynst the goverment of the Church of England, insomuch that at the late Metropolitical Visitation of the Most Reverend father in God the Lord Archbishop of Canterbury, hee, publiquely inn courte before the Vicar Generall, obstinatly refused to conform himself to those thinges which were required of him accordinge to lawe and forthwith deserted the Schools in Gloucester belonginge to the Deane and Chapter; We doe therefore hereby will and command you and any of you, that you suffer the aforesaid John Bird to continue Maister in the school, which he hath, and fairly and reasonably to allow him all such fees and profitts whatsoever belonging to his place, as have heretofore beene enioyed by him, without any interuption or molestation; and whensoever that place shall become void by death or otherwise, Wee doe further hereby enioyne and require you & any of you whom it may concerne, that you choose not the said Langley to succeede there, without the expresse consent of the Lord Archbishop of Canterbury for the time beinge first hadd and obteyned, as you or any of you will answer it at your perills. And our further pleasure is that our letter bee registered by you that the succeedinge Mayor and Electors may take notice of it. Given under our Signet at Our Pallace of Westminster, the Two & Twentieth day of April, in the Sixteenth yeare of Our Reigne [i.e. 1641].

In humble obedience to this calm interference with the chartered right of the corporation to manage their own school, it was on 4 May 'ordered at this house that Mr. Bird shall have restowered him out of the chamber all such fees and profitts as have heretofore been received by him.'

It is highly probable that this high-handed action on the part of the king and Laud largely contributed to the stalwart resistance made by Gloucester to the royal forces, which had no small effect on the result of the Civil War. Laud was sent to the Tower 18 December, 1640. In January, 1640–1, John Corbett, B.A., was appointed usher at a salary of £14 16s. 8d. On 13 May following an Act was made for removing and putting out of Mr. John Bird from being schoolmaster. The Act was read to him by Alderman Toby Bullock in the presence of the mayor, town clerk, sheriffs and others, and he was requested to remove from the master's chambers. 'Nevertheless he refused saying that he had wronges and would continue there.' On 25 May, however, an 'act' was passed 'to elect Mr. John Biddle schoolemaister of Criste.' He was a Gloucestershire boy, born at Wotton under Edge and educated in the grammar school there. While a boy he had translated Virgil's Eclogues and the first two satires of Juvenal into English verse, and composed an oration in Latin on the funeral of a school-fellow. He went to Magdalen Hall 27 June, 1634, and took his M.A. degree on 20 May, five days before his election as master. The mayor and corporation went out in their robes to meet and greet him on his way to the school. On 30 December, 1643, the schoolhouse was ordered to be repaired and the seats and glass taken out of St. Owen's church used for the purpose. Only six months later, on 2 May, 1644, Biddle's troubles began, and lasted for the rest of his life, which ended some twenty years afterwards. He was accused before the magistrates of holding Socinian opinions, which seems to mean denying the divinity of the Holy Ghost, and admitted doing so. In December, 1645, he was imprisoned by the Parliament's Commissioners for a book in support of these views, which had not been published, but had been stolen from his study. He was then apparently turned out of the head mastership, as in 1645 James Allen, 'master of Criste school,' who had been usher since 13 July, 1643, had his wages increased to 40 marks, and in 1647 Mr. John Cooper was chosen schoolmaster in place of Allen. Poor Biddle after six months' imprisonment was summoned to Westminster and examined at the bar of the House, and one of his books ordered to be burnt by the common hangman. On 2 May, 1648, an ordinance was passed making disbelief in the Trinity a capital offence, but it was never put into force. Cromwell protected him, but banished him to the Scilly Isles for three years. He founded a conventicle which is reckoned the beginning of Unitarianism. After the Restoration he was again, in 1662, seized and imprisoned, and died of the effects.

Allen was a Gloucester boy and New Inn Hall man, and Cooper came from Worcester, and was of Balliol. None of the masters are now of long continuance. On 5 January, 1650–1, Mr. Thomas Beavens succeeded Cooper with a salary of 40 marks (£26 13s. 4d.) 18 May, 1652, Nicholas Tailer was paid £30, while William Rowlins, B.A., chosen 21 July, 1653, was given £36 and a mark (13s. 4d.), and the new usher, Mr. Abraham Heague was to have 20 marks (£13 6s. 8d.). On 21 August, 1654, another new master, Mr. Francis Stedman, had only £30, while Heague, the usher, had his stipend raised to £16. In 1656 Heague became master, and so continued for nearly forty years, to 1696. John Grubbe of Christ Church succeeded for a year, then William King, 1697, of Brasenose and Balliol, to 1711. Philip Collier of Queen's was after eight years removed, 12 May, 1719; the Corporation order recording that 'The school is at present reduced to such a condition that 'tis of little benefit to this city and tho' admonition has been freely given no amendment had been made or is likely to be made, but parents tho' burgesses are obliged to send their children to other schools at great charges.' A further complaint was that Mr. Collier was not a priest, and so should only receive £9 a year. So he was deprived. On 16 May Mr. Richard Furney was elected in his place. He was of Oriel College. He wrote a history of Gloucester in six volumes—still in MS., four at Gloucester and two at the Bodleian Library at Oxford—from which subsequent writers have taken without verification the lists of masters. He was also rector of Doynton. He retired in 1723, and held livings in Hampshire and became archdeacon of Surrey. Daniel Bond, the usher, then became master. Thomas Gardiner, who had been appointed usher in 1737, succeeded to Bond in 1750, and after that no usher was appointed. From 1788 to 1802 Thomas Rudge, a Gloucester boy and of Merton College, held office. He too wrote a history of Gloucester and of the county, of considerable merit. He combined the mastership with two livings, and became, in 1814, archdeacon of Gloucester. Richard Solloway Skillern, a Bible clerk of All Souls College, was master for twenty years, 1802–22, and vicar of Chipping Norton also for the best part of that time. But the school had sadly fallen.

Carlisle [1] says of it in 1811, 'As to the school itself, it is now in every sense a Private School—the exertions of the Instructor being rewarded by payments from the friends of the Pupils.' But this remark evinces a total misconception of what is meant by a public school, which does not mean a free school but a school under public control, and to which the public generally, and not any particular class, such as clergy or licensed victuallers, are admitted.

Lord Brougham's Commission of Inquiry into charities found in 1838 John Goutter Dowling head master. He had entered on office at Midsummer, 1827. The largest number of boys he ever had was thirty-three, and at the date of the inquiry there were only twelve. All boys paid tuition fees of eight guineas a year. To W. H. Haviland, who on 15 June, 1830, gave him notice that having a large family he intended to avail himself of the advantage of having two sons taught free by virtue of Dame Joan Cooke's deed, Mr. Dowling replied that he would sooner give up the situation of schoolmaster than receive boys to be educated on the foundation. As the master received only £30 and a house, though the endowment was then worth £600 a year, it is not perhaps [2] surprising that the school was not free or successful. Under the Municipal Corporations Act, 1835, the trusteeship of charities was taken from corporations and vested in trustees to be named by the Court of Chancery. A body of Municipal Charity Trustees for Bristol was duly appointed on 31 May, 1836. But it was not until 7 May, 1844, that, under the presidency of Mr. J. H. Whitcombe, the corporation were required to hand over the management of the Crypt School to the trustees. On 12 December, 1844, the corporation definitely refused. On 5 May, 1845, they were served with a subpoena to answer to an Information in Chancery by the Attorney-General at the relation of Thomas Stanley and others. The suit dragged on in the way then usual, till on 13 May, 1851, the corporation gave instructions for a compromise. An order was made by the court to carry out this compromise, under which the corporation were to pay up eight years' arrears of rents and hand over the estates to the Municipal Charity Trustees. But before it was carried out a private person claimed a lease of the principal part of the estate at a nominal rent. This was not disposed of till March, 1856, when Vice-Chancellor Stuart dismissed the case of Hope v. Corporation of Gloucester. An appeal to the Lords Justices was taken, but also dismissed.

Then, in settling the scheme, a struggle began as to the provision of a new site for the school to be bought with the accumulation of rents, some £4,100. Eventually the present site of 3 or 4 acres in Southgate Street, known as the Bowling Green, with a house on it in which Mr. James Wintle and the Rev. C. J. Crawley lived, was bought for £5,000, a far larger and better site known as the Barton Street site, which had been previously bought from Mr. Hearne, being rejected because it was not in the 'Crypt Parish.' The Bowling Green site consisted partly of what had been the garden of the Grey Friars (whose manor still stands on the west side of 'Mare Lane' and partly of what came to be known as the Long Butts.

[1] Carlisle, *Endowed Grammar Schools*, ii, 452.　　　　[2] *Char. Com. Rep.* xxxii, pt. ii, 643.

SCHOOLS

The Long Butts acquired the name of Bowling Green because in 1631–2, when it was described as 'waste ground, now full of gravel pitts,' it was let by the corporation to Allen Kilminster for forty-one years at a shilling a year, he undertaking to fence it and level it and make it 'good and fitt for a Bowling ground—and permitt the Mayer and Burgesses to bowl there at all convenient times.' From that time it was known as the Bowling Green.

In the result it was not till 2 August, 1860, that a scheme was approved by the Master of the Rolls for what the court, ignoring the real founder, was pleased to call Dame Joan Cooke's Charity. A schedule attached to the scheme showed in parallel columns the value of the property in 1550 and in 1859:—

	1550			1859					
	£	s.	d.	£	s.	d.	£	s.	d.
Poddesmead Manor and lands, and lands in Hempsted and Elmore	13	6	8	545	0	0	—		
Messuage Westgate Street, let in 1830 for 40 years	0	8	0	1	18	10	5	0	0[1]
Badgeworth	2	8	3	89	6	8	—		
Bentham in Badgeworth, let in 1838 for 31 years	5	6	8	61	16	0	140	0	0[1]
Little Witcombe	—			57	0	0	—		
				755	1	6			

It will be noticed how absurdly under the mark is the common estimate of twenty times the value for estimating the value of money in Henry VIII and Edward VI's reign and now. A rental, excluding the house, in Gloucester of rural land of £21 1s. 7d. had grown to £753 3s. 8d., and should have been, but for an improvident long lease, £831, or practically forty times the amount. The fact is, those figures of twelve and twenty times are taken from estimates now nearly 100 years old, and to bring them to anything like approximate values now must be doubled, even as regards agricultural land ; while, when it is a question of land in or near towns, or in mining or manufacturing districts, they must be multiplied ten-fold or twenty-fold.

In the scheme a body of 17 trustees was appointed, who were directed to apply the whole income to the support of the school, except £78 a year to St. Bartholomew's Hospital, and £80 a year to the corporation for repair of the bridge and causeway between Gloucester and Over. The Court was more enlightened than the citizens in its ideas as to what it cost to maintain an adequate teaching staff. The head master was to have not less than £100 nor more than £300 a year salary, and £2 a year capitation fees up to 100 boys, and £1 a year beyond. The second master was to have only ' not less than £50, nor more than £150 a year,' with capitation fees of £1 up to 100 boys, and 10s. over that number. In the summer of 1861 the school was reopened as a day-school only, residences for the head and second masters, private houses bought for the purpose, adjoining. There was one large schoolroom for about 120 boys, two classrooms, and a room for drawing. It was to give an education which, on paper, differed not at all from that given by the College School, the subjects of instruction including Greek, Latin, French, German, English, mathematics, and history. The tuition fees

[1] Estimated value on expiry of leases.

were to be £3 to £6 a year. Mr. Brown stayed two years, during which the number in the school rose to 103. The Rev. J. R. Major followed for four years. The Schools Inquiry Commission[1] reported in rather unfavourable terms of the school, and mentioned that in the last two years sixteen boys had left after only a year's stay in the school. The trustees expressed themselves dissatisfied with the result of the scheme: 'It has neither brought people to the town to reside, nor afforded a good and cheap education to the people of the town.' The numbers fell, and the master did not get on with the trustees and resigned. On 15 July, 1867, the Rev. Christopher Naylor of Corpus Christi College, Cambridge, was appointed head master, and on 14 October, the Rev. John Cuming of the same college was appointed second master. The new masters were allowed to take boarders, so that the school became even more than before a mere reduplication and rival of the College School. On the other hand the fees were reduced to £4 a year. They found only 46 boys in the school. By 1870 the number had risen to 136. In this year the trustees concurred with the dean and chapter and the town council in the abortive proposals for amalgamation with the College School already related. The numbers continued to rise till they reached 156, and remained about 150 till the end of 1875. The Townsend Scholarship at Pembroke College, Cambridge, which had not been filled since 1853, was twice gained. The boarders did not form a very serious item in the school, the head master having only nine, and the second master one, the boarding fees being £30 or £32 a year. The school did what was then rare in schools of this kind, sent its boys in for the examinations and obtained the grants of the Science and Art Department at South Kensington, but only to the extent of about thirty boys out of the whole school. In 1877 the trustees of the school again formulated proposals for a scheme, this time in concert with the trustees of the Blue Coat School, Sir Thomas Rich's Hospital.

SIR THOMAS RICH'S HOSPITAL, GLOUCESTER

This Almshouse Elementary school was founded by Sir Thomas Rich of Sonning, Berkshire, a native of Gloucester, and son of a Gloucester alderman, who had made a fortune in the Turkey trade. He gave by will made in 1666[2] his house in Eastgate Street 'to be an Hospital for ever for the entertaining and harbouring of 20 poor boys and their maintenance, with diet, lodging, washing, clothing, and other necessaries in blue coats and caps according to the laudable usage of Christ's Hospital in London. An honest, able schoolmaster' was to live in the house 'to teach the said poor boys to write and read,' who were to be not under ten and none to continue beyond sixteen years of age. Six of the boys were to be apprenticed yearly, 'wherein his desire was' 'that 3 or 4 of them should be apprenticed in London to some honest handicraft trades there and with honest masters, not adhering in their opinions to the novelties of the times.' There were other provisions for doles of money and clothing to the poor, loans to young tradesmen, marriage portions for poor maidservants and the like. For endowment the very large sum of £6,000 was left to the mayor and burgesses of Gloucester,

---

[1] *Sch. Inq. Rep.* xv, 72. [2] *Char. Com. Rep.* xiv, 21.

estimated by the founder to produce an income of £300 a year, of which £6 13s. 4d. was to provide a dinner to the town council, £23 6s. 8d. for doles, &c., and the rest, or £270 a year, for the school. Invested in land at Awre and Blakeney, amounting to 954 A. 1 R. 39 P., the income in 1852 had risen to some £1,700 a year. Under a scheme of the Court of Chancery, 5 March, 1852, the hospital was rebuilt and the number of 'blue boys' increased to 34. But the education given remained wholly elementary. The trustees of this charity were the Municipal Charity Trustees, and concurred with the trustees of the Crypt School on 14 April, 1877, in asking for a scheme to unite the two charities.

On 10 August, 1878, the Charity Commissioners published a scheme under the Endowed Schools Acts to give effect to the trustees' proposals. Hot opposition was offered to the scheme, mainly by the old boys of the Blue Coat School, on the ground chiefly of the proposed abolition of the apprenticeships and the alleged disregard of the poverty qualifications. A public inquiry held on 17–19 June, 1879, showed that the payment of apprenticeship premiums was practically obsolete, and the apprenticeship had become merely a dole, and that the class from which the boys had been drawn was precisely the class that would obtain scholarships under the new scheme.

THE GLOUCESTER UNITED ENDOWED SCHOOLS

In the result the scheme was approved by Queen Victoria in Council on 3 May, 1882, with a few unimportant alterations. The scheme consolidated the Crypt and Blue Coat Schools and two connected charities as the Gloucester United Endowed Schools, under a governing body of 18, of whom 6 were appointed by the Town Council and 6 by the Municipal Charity Trustees, and 6 were co-optatives. There were to be 4 schools; the Crypt Grammar School for 160 boys, 120 day boys and 40 boarders at tuition fees of £5 to £10 a year, giving an ordinary second-grade grammar-school education, with 15 scholarships for boys from Rich's School, and with 3 £50 exhibitions to the University. Sir Thomas Rich's School was to be a lower-grade school at tuition fees of £2 to £4 a year, with 30 scholarships for boys from public elementary schools. There were to be upper and lower girls' schools corresponding to the two boys' schools. At this time the income of the endowments was over £3,000 a year.

The Crypt School went on much as before the scheme, averaging about 120 boys.

Rich's School was established under Mr. James Crofts, at tuition fees of £3 a year and £3 15s. in the 3 upper forms, the leaving age being 15. It soon rose in numbers and averaged about 240 boys, getting a good general education, French being taught in all classes, Latin as an optional subject pretty generally taken in the upper forms. Some 90 boys were in the science classes earning grants from the Science and Art Department, South Kensington. After 1888, owing to a falling off in the income from the endowment to the extent of some £600 a year, due to the depression in agriculture, the bulk of the scholarships had to be suspended.

The lower girls' school was set up in Mynd House in Barton Street in 1890 under Miss Barwell, B.A. of London University. The numbers gradually advanced till in 1903 they reached 227, and completely outgrew their housing. So in that year the school was temporarily transferred to Bearland House, formerly the town house of the earls of Berkeley, in Berkeley Street.

Meanwhile science and art schools had been set up by a committee by deed of 1 November, 1871, and in 1896 these were transferred to the corporation of Gloucester and carried on as the Municipal Technical School. Originally only evening and then day classes, after 1896 they became also an organized day school, which competed seriously with Sir Thomas Rich's School.

After the corporation, under the Education Act, 1902, became the local education authority for secondary education, a movement began which resulted in a new scheme under the Charitable Trusts Acts, sealed by the Board of Education on 13 February, 1906. Under this scheme all these schools were consolidated under one body of 21 governors; 3 appointed by the Gloucestershire County Council, 15 by the Gloucester City Council, and 3 co-optatives. The head masters of the Crypt School and of Sir Thomas Rich's School were pensioned off. The College School having then sunk into little more than a choristers' school, was treated as a *quantité négligeable*. The Crypt School is now to charge tuition fees of £8 to £18 a year as the first-grade school of the city, preparing for the universities, professions, and trades. Sir Thomas Rich's School is to be a second-grade school at fees not exceeding £12 a year, for boys up to seventeen years of age. The Technical School is to serve for a lower-grade school, with some attempt at manual and handicraft instruction, besides maintaining evening classes for artisans and the like, and day classes in science and art for elder pupils of all classes.

The girls' school is now to be called the High School, and to charge tuition fees of not less than £6 nor more than £15, and is to be the Upper Girls' School for the city.

Mr. Joseph Edward Barton became head master of the Crypt School in September, 1906. He was an old Crypt School boy, who went to Pembroke College, Oxford, with a Townsend Exhibition in 1894, and won a first class in classics in moderations in 1896, the Newdigate Prize Poem in 1897, and a first class in classics in the Final School in 1898.

THE TOWNSEND SCHOLARSHIPS

George Townsend, of Lincoln's Inn, by will, 14 December, 1682, gave Little Aston farm and tithes in Gloucestershire to the master, fellows, and scholars of Pembroke College, Oxford, in trust for 8 scholars, one to be chosen by the mayor and six of the senior aldermen of the city of Gloucester, and the chief master of the chief school thereof out of the scholars of the same school; another out of the scholars of Cheltenham School, in which he was a scholar; another out of Campden School, and a fourth out of Northleach School—the 3 last-named to be chosen by the chief schoolmaster, ministers, and bailiffs, or other chief officers of the same three towns, and in equality of votes the schoolmaster to have the casting vote. Each of them for eight years to have an eighth part of the rents; none but suitable grammar scholars fit to go to the university to be elected. In case any unsuitable scholar should be elected, it was his will that the master of the said college should refuse to admit him, and that in his stead another scholar of Gloucester School should be elected in manner aforesaid. His desire was that the scholars should for the last four years of residence direct their studies to divinity. For their better encouragement, four livings were to be given by his representatives to those scholars. The will was proved 29 November, 1683.

The first recorded nomination of a scholar from Gloucester is not till 2 December, 1696, from which time the Crypt School nominated pretty regularly every fourth year, and occasionally when the other schools failed to nominate.

Under the Universities Act, 1854, the Oxford University Commissioners in 1857 made an ordinance that the Townsend scholarships should be tenable for not more than sixteen terms from matriculation; and in 1858 the master and fellows, in default of sufficient merit from the schools, threw the scholarships open for that time.

The Crypt School being closed for a time, in 1860 Gloucester nominated a scholar from the Cathedral School, but the master of Pembroke rejected the nomination as irregular. An appeal to the visitor of the college, the earl of Derby, proved abortive for lack of jurisdiction.

In 1876 Gloucester nominated a scholar on Northleach failing to do so, but the master and fellows of Pembroke refused to examine him on the ground that the former residuary rights of Gloucester had been taken away by the ordinances of 1857 and 1858. They were upheld in their contention by Henry Cotton and Charles Bowen (afterwards Lords Justices of Appeal), to whom the case was submitted.

In 1881 new statutes for Pembroke College gave the four schools the right of presenting candidates for examination, but if the college did not consider them of sufficient merit for election, the four scholarships of £80 a year were to be thrown open.

In 1887, the master and fellows made a statute limiting the scholarships to as many of £80 a year as the income of the endowment could maintain. The income, which had been £400, was at that time reduced to £200 at most. Between 1880 and 1893 no candidates were sent by Gloucester; but in 1899, 1903, and 1905, it succeeded in obtaining the scholarship.

THE SCHOOLS OF BRISTOL

Bristol Grammar School

Bristol Grammar School in all probability existed before the Conquest. At all events it existed before St. Augustine's Abbey, now the cathedral church, as a public school under the government of the laity and secular clergy.

An inquiry was held[1] on 15 May, 1318, as to the rights and privileges of the Gild of the Kalendars held in All Saints' Church. Their rights had

---

[1] Bristol Little Red Book, fol. 82-3. This book was in 1900 edited by Mr. W. B. Bickley for the Corporation of Bristol. The entry is headed 'Of the rule of the house of the Brotherhood of the Kalendars' (' De regula domus Fraternitatis Kalend ').

apparently been infringed by the canons of St. Augustine's Abbey, who were especially summoned with the whole clergy and laity of Bristol to be present at the inquiry. The inquisition found that the gild of

> the said Brotherhood was formerly called the Gild or Brotherhood (*Gilda seu Fraria*) of the community of the clergy and people of Bristol, and that the place of assembly (*congregacionis*) of the brethren and sisters of the same used to be at the church of the Holy Trinity, Bristol, in the time of Aylward Mean and Bristoic his son, lords of the said town before the last conquest of England; the beginning of which gild and brotherhood passes the memory of man.

It must be admitted that Bristoic looks remarkably like an eponymous hero evolved out of the name of the town. But there is every reason to believe that the gild existed before the Conquest. It is confirmatory of the extremely early origin of the gild, which took its name from meeting on the Kalends, or first day of the month, that this gild is not unique in England, but had at least one other congener of the same name in the extremely ancient Kalendars' Gild of Winchester. The Inquisition proceeds to say that

> in the time of the Lord Henry Fitz Empress king of England, one Robert Hardyng, burgess of Bristol, by the consent of King Henry and Earl Robert and others interested, translated (*transtulit*) the said gild or brotherhood from Holy Trinity church to the church of All Saints, and established[1] the school of Bristol for teaching Jews and other little ones under the government of the said gild and the protection of the mayor of Bristol for the time being; and founded the monastery of St. Augustine in the suburb of the said town, and appropriated the church of All Saints to it, with a vicar to be elected from the chaplains of the said gild and brotherhood, to be presented by the abbot and convent to the bishop of Worcester, and made the monastery pay the vicar a certain portion under the title of rectory. All this was solemnly confirmed by the cardinal legate Gualo in the general council held at Bristol after he had crowned Henry III at Gloucester, and he enjoined William of Blois (le Bleys) bishop of Worcester to protect and approve the said gild and brotherhood to the praise of God and All Saints and the devotion and union of the clergy and people of Bristol, and procured the confirmation by the apostolic see of all the rights and goods [a term which included immovable as well as movable property] and took them under the protection of the apostolic see, and the bishops of Worcester approved and confirmed the said gild and brotherhood.

There the report suddenly ends, the dean of Christianity of Bristol, who held the inquiry, saying 'of many more things we inquired, all of which, on account of length, we could not write.' So the lazy commissioner has cheated us of further interesting details about the school and gild.

Enough is said, however, to show that the school was in existence before the abbey, though whether we are to infer that it existed in the church of All Saints before the transfer of the Kalendars' gild there, or that it was transferred there as part of the gild, or where it was, is left uncertain.

It is amazing that Robert Fitzharding or the gild should have established or maintained a school for Jews. But there was a great outbreak of persecution of the Jews owing to the anti-oriental and fanatically Christian feelings evoked by the second crusade, in which St. Bernard of Clairvaux was the prime mover, just at the time when Robert Fitzharding was founding the Augustinian Abbey. In 1146 the crusade was determined upon[2] by Conrad III of Germany, and in 1148[3] the abbey church was consecrated. The persecution of the Jews went to such lengths in Germany and

---

[1] Ac scolas Bristolie pro Judeis et aliis parvulis informandis sub disposicione dicte frarie stabilivit et proteccione Maioris Bristolie qui pro tempore fuerit.

[2] T. A. Archer, *The Crusades*, 212.   [3] T. Smyth, *The Berkeleys*, ed. by Sir J. Maclean.

France as to provoke an appeal on their behalf even from Bernard himself:
'You should not persecute the Jews, you should not slay them, you should
not even put them to flight,' as it would prevent their conversion promised in
Romans xi, 26.

A Hebrew historian says[1] 'in England the King of Heaven saved the
Jews through the king of England. He turned his heart so that he protected
them and saved their lives and property. Praised be the help of Israel.' But
another Hebrew historian, Joseph ben Meir,[2] under date 1146, says:

> The Lord saved the Jews by the hand of King Henry, for a king's heart is in God's hand.
> He took nothing, not even a shoe-string from them. Even those who in this year were
> compelled to defile themselves [i.e. be christened] found mercy from a priest, who led them
> not for silver and not for presents, to France, where they remained till the cruelty of the
> unbelievers had ceased.

This passage is, however, inconsistent with itself and untrustworthy. In the
first place Stephen, and not Henry, was king in 1146, and the salvation by
the king was not much of a salvation if the Jews were compelled to be
baptized and had to fly to France. However, the fact of the persecution and
the compulsory baptism may perhaps be considered to afford a reason for
Fitzharding founding a school for the enforced converts, or the children of
those who were killed, if any were. At all events, as will be seen, there was a
house in Wine Street known even in the sixteenth century as the Jews'
School, to give colour to the tale.

There is no further evidence of any connexion of the Kalendars' Gild
with the Grammar School. It does not seem to have remained long under
their control. For Leland, the itinerant antiquary of Henry VIII, tells us
that ' William Erle of Gloucester, founder of the monasterye of Cainesham,
gave the prefecture and mastershippe of the Schole in Brightstow to Cainesham
and took it from the Calenderies.'[3] Keynsham Abbey, in Somerset, about
6 miles from Bristol, was founded, according to Ricart's Calendar—the foundation deed itself was undated—in 1171. That being so, it is strange that
insistence should have been laid on the foundation of the school under the
Kalendars in the inquisition of 1318. The school is not, however, mentioned
in the foundation charter of Keynsham Abbey, and no accounts are left to
show the precise relations of the abbey to the school, whether it provided
any endowments, or, as is more probable, merely acted as governing body,
appointing and dismissing the masters. The transfer of authority over the
school to a body of Augustinian canons outside the town is curiously parallel
to that which we saw took place at Gloucester; the school there being handed
over to the Augustinian canons of Llanthony Abbey, outside that city.

We are enabled to fix the site of the school in the thirteenth century
from a document preserved, almost by accident, in the ' Great Red Book of
Bristol,' an MS. still in the council house. The book itself is of the fourteenth century, but on the fly-leaves at the beginning of it is copied a most
interesting rent-roll of the king's and the town's property in the borough, the
names of the tenants of which, followed as it is by an inquisition held for the

---

[1] Joseph Jacobs, *The Jews of Angevin England*, 258, quoting *Hebr. Berichte der Kreuzzüge*, 64.
[2] Wilken, *Geschichte der Kreuzzüge*, iii, App. p. 16. 'Ueber die Juden Verfolgung im Jahre 1146.' I
am indebted to Professor Margoliouth for this reference.
[3] *Itin.* (ed. Hearn, 1744), vii, 88.

crown by Richard of Rothewell and Robert le Rous on 24 August, 1285, fixes it to about that time, but after the expulsion of the Jews from England in 1290.

First comes 'Rentale of the farm of the Lord King of his town of Bristol.' Five items relating to the Jews are apparently all in Wine Street. Robert the Wiredrawer pays '8s. for the tenement formerly of Benedict the Jew of Winchester'; 6s. is due for the tenement formerly of Giles the Mason; formerly of Mossi of Kent, in Wynchestret (now Wine Street), while Joceus de Reigny, who was bailiff of Bristol in 1318, pays 6s. 8d. 'for the Jews' cemetery near St. Brandan's Hill.' Then comes '24s. from Thomas de Pridie for the king's tenement by the Butchers' stalls,' which in all probability represents the Jewish synagogue itself, or, at all events, from the largeness of the rent, some large building of a public character. Next comes 'From Geoffrey Justice and Alan Lorymer for the Jews school (*pro scolis Judeorum*) in Wynche stret which—16s.' The 'which' is tantalizing. It occurs in most of the items, and represents the beginning of some explanation about the size or former ownership of the property which the copyist omitted, to save himself trouble, or as irrelevant. The 22nd item is still more interesting. 'Of Roger Pert for Walter, parson of the church of St. Philip, for the old school opposite Saint Peter's which—(*pro veteribus scolis ex opposito Sancti Petri, que*) 12d.'

Here, then, we have first a Jews' school in Wine Street, disused, and another old and disused school in a quite different place in St. Peter's Street, opposite St. Peter's Church. Next follows a list of 'Rents of assize belonging to the town of Bristol yearly to be leased at Michaelmas.' It includes among 19 items, 'From the parson of St. Peter's Church for a piece of land under the old school which (*pro placea terre sub veteribus scolis quod*) 12d.;' and the next item but one is 'From a tenement of Joceus de Reigny next the old school (*juxta veteres scolas*) which, 6d.'

The old school being opposite St. Peter's Church is evidence that Leland's statement as to the transfer of the school to the government of Keynsham Abbey is correct, and gives an explanation of it. For the inquisition of 1285, already mentioned, includes among the tenancies in chief of the king in the town 'the Abbot of Keynsham for his tenements of his barony in Bristol which are in St. Peter's churchyard in the quarter of St. Mary le Port (*Beate Marie in burgo*).' St. Peter's Church was appropriated to Keynsham Abbey, and if the old school was by that church on the barony of the abbot, this may account for the transfer of the school to the government of the abbey. It is odd, however, to find that Adam de Bucton included among 'his tenements in barony' 'the tenement of the old school, opposite the church of St. Peter,' the next item being two tenements 'opposite the Jewry (*ex opposito Judaismi*), doing suit to the hundred of Bristol and also to the Market Court.' St. Peter's Church was only a little way from the old market. The explanation that suggests itself is that the old school had been sold by Keynsham Abbey to Adam of Bucton.

While the 'old School' thus appears several times, the Rental contains no mention of the then school. As will be seen, the next town rental which appears to be extant, that for 1532, shows it as existing in one of the town gates, Frome Gate, and there is evidence of its presence there some half a century before. But whether already in the thirteenth century the school had been transferred to that place we can but surmise.

It is a curious thing, in view of the subsequent history of the school, that half a century earlier than the mention of the site which we have been discussing, there is a mention of the school in connexion with the buildings which it occupied some 500 years later, 'the Hospital of St. Mark of Billeswick, otherwise Gaunt's.'

This hospital was founded by Sir Robert of Gournay some time before 1233, probably at the wish of Maurice de Gaunt, whose property he had inherited. Henry of Gaunt, the master or warden, largely increased the endowment, and in 1259 enlarged the establishment to a master and 12 brethren clerks and 5 lay brothers and 27 poor, 'of which number 12 were to be scholars, ministering, in the choir only, in black copes and surplices, as is more fully contained in the ordinance of Walter of good memory bishop of Worcester.'

This ordinance said that the clerks were to dress like the brethren of Lechlade Hospital, except the badge on their gowns, which was to be a white cross on a red shield with three white geese. The 12 scholars were

> to be admitted and removed at will of the master and to sing at the disposition of the Precentor (*cantoris*), and to be more plentifully provided for than the other poor according to the arrangement of the master and the means of the house; and one of the twelve scholars was to be elected of ability to keep in order and teach the others, and he was to be provided for even more plenteously and competently than the others.

One cannot help thinking that this provision for 12 select scholars being admitted to dine with the poor of the hospital was taken from the similar provision at the famous hospital of St. Cross at Winchester, where it was said to date from the ordinance of the founder, Bishop Henry of Blois, brother of King Stephen, in 1130,[1] and was probably the earliest establishment on record of an exhibition foundation, in the modern sense of support without full maintenance by charity. At all events, it is an interesting piece of evidence of the carrying on of the school in Bristol, and the presence of poor scholars of it in need of assistance.

By a later but undated deed, to which both Robert of Gournay and Henry of Gaunt were parties, the almshouse was taken out of the hands of the secular clergy, and the brethren there had to become regulars; and by arrangement with the prior of Maiden Bradley three of his brethren were sent thence to teach 'the regular use,' which was to follow that of Bradley, except that no women were to be admitted. In 1268 these ordinances were confirmed by Bishop Godfrey Giffard,[2] he apparently adding that no scholars were to eat or drink in the refectory, except by special leave of the master. They were only to enjoy the 'sufficient beer and pottage' of the outer poor. This hospital was bought from Henry VIII for £1,000, and granted by him to the city by letters patent 6 May, 1541.[3] Its chapel became the existing mayor's chapel, and the hospital in 1584 became Queen Elizabeth's Hospital for poor boys on the model of Christ's Hospital in London.

---

[1] Similar cases of scholars being fed occur in hospitals for the poor at Durham, and at Pontefract; *V.C.H. Dur.* ii; *Yorks.* ii, 'Religious Houses.'

[2] Worc. Epis. Reg. Giffard, fol. 15 *d*.

[3] Great White Bk. fol. 253.

It is nearly a hundred years later than that mention of the scholars fed in Gaunt's Hospital that in the dearth of documents we come across another indication of the Grammar School.

On 30 March, 1353,[1] on the election of a new abbot of St. Augustine's, William Cok, the usual examination of witnesses as to age and character took place, when William Hull, of the age of forty years and more gave evidence that 'from childhood he had been a companion and friend of the said elect at school and elsewhere (" ab infancia socius et sodalis dicti electi in scolis et alibi ") and therefore well knew his age.'

In the one monastic account of St. Augustine's Abbey quoted by Britton, that for 1491–2, which has been reasonably conjectured[2] to have been made up for and produced to the bishop on his visitation in 1493, Henry Burgges, collector of rents in Bristol, accounts for 13s. 4d. 'to John Griffith, vicar of St. Augustine the Less, for teaching the junior canons and other boys in the grammar school in the abbey ; and 13s. 4d. to him for his diet.' But this appears to refer to an almonry school. A record of the end of the fifteenth or early part of the sixteenth century, however, introduces us to renewed evidence of the public grammar school. A dispute—one of many similar disputes about this time—between the abbey and the town had arisen about some abbey choristers[3] who refused to pay ' the king's silver,' their goods were distrained upon by the town officers; the abbot arrested the distraining officers for trespass on his jurisdiction, abbey retainers were in turn imprisoned in the town prison called Newgate, which the abbot and his men attempted to force, but were repulsed. In the end the town officers were declared to be in the right, and the abbot and his successors were ordered on every Easter Sunday in the afternoon, and every Easter Monday in the afternoon, to meet the mayor and corporation ' at the door of the grammar school at Frome Gate,' and accompany them to St. Augustine's, where, according to custom, they went to attend service in state.

This inference that the school was then held in Frome Gate is confirmed by the earliest of the corporation accounts now in existence, the mayor's audit book for the year 1532. It begins ' A Rentall of all landis and tenements belonging to the Chamber of the Towne of Bristoll renewyd by William Nashe, chamberlayn ; Mr. Thomas Pacy then beyng maire.' Under the heading of ' Chrystynmasse streatt alias Knyfsmythstreate,' are the entries, 'a tenement under the scole howse in the tenure of William Whiting the yonger, 4s. A tenement over Frome Yate, which the Scolemaster of the Gramer hath rente free for the techyng of chyldyrn 36s. 8d.' Next year this item appears as ' a tenement in the tenure of Thomas Moffatt scolemaster, 20s. A tenement over Frome Yate which the Scolemaster hathe rente free for the techyng of childern 26s. 8d.'

[1] Worc. Sede vacante Reg. fol. 108 d.

[2] *Bristol Past and Present* ii, 64, from Britton's *Cathedral Antiq.* (1833). I have been unable to ascertain whether this document perished in the fire during the riots of 1832, and cannot therefore verify the words above. I doubt the phrase ' junior canons and other boys ' being correct.

[3] Britton, *Cathedral Antiq.* v, 22. This incident is quoted from ' an MS. calendar *penes* William Tyson,' said to be related under the time of Abbot Somerset, 1526–33, but to have referred to the time of Abbot Newland, who died in 1497. In *Bristol Past and Present*, ii, 64, it is confused with what was apparently a totally different incident connected with the election of Abbot Eliot in 1515, which Richard Fox, then bishop of Winchester, referred to Wolsey.

SCHOOLS

It is curious to find in what at this date is called 'Wynne Street' 'a tenement in the tenure of Thomas Snygge, called the Jewys Scole house, which John Ilkyns holdeth, 13s. 4d.'

In 1535 we find 'a tenement under the skolehouse in the tenure of Howell, labourer, 4s. A tenement over Frome gate with the skolemaster 36s. 8d.,' and in 1536 this item again occurs more fully as one which 'the Scolemaster hath rent free for the techyng of chyldern.' But in the next extant account, that for 1540, under 'Krystmas street' it appears as 'a tenement over Frome Yate, sometyme the schole house, in the tenure of William Dewe, coriar 36s. 8d.'

Frome Gate was then deserted by the school which had now gone into its fourth habitation, though only a few yards off. The reason was that a new endowment had been given to the school by new benefactors, which is erroneously treated as a new foundation. There cannot be a doubt that it was the same foundation, and not a new one that migrated to the new site, for Thomas Moffatt, the master, appears in the audit books in and after 1542, but not before. In 1542, 'paid to Moffatt skolemaister 6s. 8d.'; and in 1543 'paid to Mr. Thomas Moffatt for his rewarde of the Chamber, 6s. 8d.,' and in 1546 and later 'paid Mr. Moffatt for his annuytie a quarter 6s. 8d.'; and this continues to midsummer 1552, when it ceases. There can be little doubt that Moffatt retired in 1542, and received a pension of £1 6s. 8d. a year from the corporation on so doing, but that this was two years after the move to St. Bartholomew's Hospital, which had been acquired by the corporation for a new site, as now to be related.

The local historians and the official reports[1] have hitherto credited the origin of Bristol Grammar School to 'the will of Robert Thorne, 17 May, 1532, in which no specific bequest of money for erecting a grammar school appears, but among other dispositions it has "Also I will that there be in the power of my executors £1,000 to be distributed and ordered as to my executors shall seem best for my soul."'

The origin of the school must, as we have seen, be attributed to a much more ancient family of Bristol merchants than the Thornes, and to a far higher antiquity. But the new endowment is also incorrectly attributed. The will of Robert Thorne the younger in 1532 did in fact contain a specific bequest for the school, but the chief endowment is due not to this will, but to the will of his father of the same name in 1518. The Thornes were well-to-do Bristol merchants, who showed every disposition to do well to the town in which they had thriven. Robert Thorne the father was mayor in 1515.[2] He made his will 20 January, 1517–8.[3] He concludes :

also I make myne Executours Sir John Goodrygge, parson of Christ church, and William Wossley and John Wyatt, and to every of them I gyve £10 in redy money, and every of them a black gowne And to se my will and my debts paid and my will fulfilled, and the rest of all my goodes to be sold and doone for my soule where that ye fynd most nede, and I require as ye will aunser to for God that this be doone as God knowythe my mynde as I put my full trust in you for, and God send me space and grace I wold doo it myself.

[1] *Char. Com. Rep.* (1822), vi, 481 ; *Sch. Inq. Rep.* (1868), xv, 19.
[2] Great Red Bk. 260b.
[3] P.C.C. 19, Ayloffe, 6.

The will with this secret trust in it was proved in the Prerogative Court of Canterbury at Lambeth on 8 July, 1519, by William Wyatt, the other executor, Wossley, being admitted to probate also on 12 August following. What the secret trust was transpires in Letters Patent of Henry VIII,[1] dated at Chelsea, 17 March, 1531-2, whereby the king

> considering the pious purpose of our beloved Thomas West, knight, Lord La Warr, George Croft, chaplain, Robert Thorne and Nicholas Thorne, of our city of Bristol, and John Godrick (*sic*) clerk, executor of the will of Robert Thorne deceased, in the foundation, maintenance and support of a certain Grammar School (*scole gramatice*) to be made in the said town of Bristol or in the suburbs of the same for boys in the same school to be instructed in good manners and literature (*erudiendis in bonis moribus et litteraturis*) for the better sustenance of a master and one usher (*hostiarii*), or two ushers, of the same, and of other things necessary,

granted to the mayor, burgesses, and commonalty of Bristol and their successors that they might

> acquire and take the house or hospital of St. Bartholomew in the said town with the profits and advantages which now are or in time past have been accepted or reputed as parcel of the same hospital or which the aforesaid George Croft, master of the hospital aforesaid, ever held and enjoyed in right of the same hospital in the said town of Bristol or the parishes of Clifton, Stapleton, Sodbury and Wickwar, in the county of Gloucester and elsewhere within the kingdom of England, to the yearly value of £40 beyond all charges and reprises, as well from the aforesaid Thomas West, knight, Lord La Warr, the true patron and founder of the hospital aforesaid, as from the said George Croft, master and keeper of the house or hospital aforesaid, and from the brethren and sisters of the same house or hospital,

or from any one else having or pretending title in the premises.

All this was to be done without fine or fee paid to the Crown.

This patent had been preceded by an indenture of covenant, preserved among the school muniments in the possession of the Bristol municipal charity trustees. By this deed, made 31 January, 1531-2, between Sir Thomas West, knight, Lord La Warr and Robert Thorne, citizen and merchant of London, the latter covenanted that if a sure, sufficient, and indefeasible estate in fee simple be made by Lord La Warr and George Croft, the master of the hospital, to Thorne and his co-executors, within a year, of the hospital and its property, that then Thorne, within six years, shall

> ordain, prepare and make a convenient scole house for a free grammer scole to be taught and kept upon the said house or hospital or upon some part of the said lands and tenements belonging to the said house or hospital, and also the said Robert within the same term shall provide, establish and order a schoolmaster and usher to teche and kepe the said free scole, with such convenient waige to them to be appointed as shall or may conveniently come of the rents, issues and profits of the said lands, and also the said Robert shall appoint, make and establish within the same term of six yeres the foundacion, patents and ordinances of the said scole, after the mind and advice of John Barlowe, Deane of Westbury upon Trym, and of George Croft, Robert Thorne, Nicholas Thorne and John Goodriche.

In the ordinances 'the said Lord La Warre shalbe namyde and takyn as one of the principal founders of the said scole, and the said George Croft to be namid and takyn a singuler benefactor thereof' and provision was to be made that

> there shalbe a solemn obit to be kept yerely for ever on the eleventh daye of October at the said Bartilmews to pray for the souls of the said Lord La Warre, George and Robert and of Sir Thomas, now Lord La Warre, and for the soule of Sir Thomas West, knight, late Lord La Warre, and for the souls of all their ancestors and progenitors, and this obit to be kept

[1] Pat. 23 Hen. VIII, pt. ii, m. 36.

with ten prestes and six clarkes, at wiche obbit there shall be delt and distributed in alms among poore people 100d. at least, also that the said scolemaister and usher shall appoint and assign the scolers of the said scole to say such certaine prayers at their departing in the evening as shall be devised and appointed by the said Lord La Warre.

The existing almsfolk were to stay there for the rest of their lives with 5d. a week pension, and a priest kept 'until such time as the said scole be ordered and made and also a scolemaister resident and in possession there.' In consideration of all this Lord La Warr 'doth renounce and relinquish all his interest, title, right and claim to dwell in the said house, hospital and other the premises as in the patronage or foundacion thereof, saving only to him such preheminence in his name of the said foundacion and in such prayers and suffrages as before is rehearsed.'

Why fourteen years had been allowed to elapse before any steps were taken to carry out the elder Thorne's will we do not know. It may have been because the widow Jane or Johan Thorne was still alive; a declaration of the jewels given by her will to the church of St. Nicholas, made on 15 October, 1524, was enrolled in the mayor's court 14 March, 1524-5.[1] Or it may have been owing to the absence in Spain of Robert Thorne the younger.

No time was now lost in carrying out the deed of covenant, for we learn from a subsequent deed of 1561 that in Easter term 1531-2 'the said Robert Thorne, of London, merchant, Nicholas Thorne, of Bristow, his brother, and John Goodriche, clerk, by two severall writtes of entre in the post by them brought,' did recover against 'Crofte and Delaware, the master and the patron

6 messuages, 300 acres of land, fower score acres of mede, 200 acres of pasture, 10 acres of woodd and 40s. rente' the outlying property, and '40 messuages, 30 gardens, 10 acres of lande, 6 acres of mede, 20 acres of pasture and 40s. rent with th'appurtenances in the towne of Bristowe and the suburbes To the uses and intents that they their heires or assignes shulde geve the same premisses, specified in the said recoverie, to the Mayer aldermen and comynaltie of Bristowe and to their successors for ever to and for the errecion establisshement and contynuaunce of a fre Gramer schole to be erected within the said howse of the Bartillmewes, and to establishe theire one Scholemaster and one or two usshers for the same.

In other words the grantors suffered a recovery to uses and the grantees entered. But Robert Thorne the younger had delayed too long in carrying out his father's will. Only two months after the Letters Patent, 'beyng sekely but in my perfight mynde and reason such as it hath pleased God to geve me' he made his testament and last will 17 May, 1532.[2] After other personal legacies: 'Also I bequethe towarde the making upp of the Free scole of Saincte Barthilmews in Brystow £300 sterling and more that my Lord de la Warr owyth as by his obligacion apperithe.'

Besides that he bequeathed 'to Thomas Moffett, maister of the Grammer scole in Bristowe £25 and to Robert Moffett his sonne £10'; the gift to the son showing that, like so many other schoolmasters at this date, Moffatt was not in holy orders. He also gave £500 to the corporation of Bristol as a loan charity, to be lent free of interest to young men setting up in business as cloth-workers. The whole residue was given to his brother Nicholas. A mercer and three cloth-workers witnessed the will, which was proved in the Prerogative Court of Canterbury, 10 October, 1532.

[1] Great Red Book.
[2] Great Red Book, fol. 267.

He was buried in St. Christopher in the Stocks, London,[1] where ' there was a monument of pure touch,' i.e. touch-stone, with the inscription

> Robertus cubat hic Thornus mercator honestus
> Qui sibi legitimas arte paravit opes.
> Huic vitam dederat puero Bristollia
> Londinum hoc tumulo clauserat ante diem.
> Ornavit studiis patriam virtutibus auxit
> Gymnasium erexit sumptibus ipse suis.

Then follows the usual request for the reader's prayer for rest for his ashes, and a statement that he died at the age of 40. The use of the word gymnasium for a school is noteworthy. It is one of several indications that we were near being saddled, as the Germans were, with that pedantic term for a school.

In thus converting St. Bartholomew's Almshouse to a school the two Robert Thornes were not, as one local historian[2] has it, ' setting a rare example of a monastic foundation being sold to lay impropriation, and transformed in character some years before the Parliamentary dissolution of religious houses.'

Nor was Henry VIII, as other local historians have it, ' robbing a hospital to give it to the Thornes.' The connexion of hospitals and schools was, as we have seen here at Bristol itself in the case of Gaunt's Hospital, very ancient. The Thornes and Henry VIII were but following the example of Catholic popes and prelates and kings in converting to more useful purposes charities which had outlived their usefulness, or the incomes of which had outgrown their original purposes. Not only Edward II and Edward III but Henry VI and Henry VII had set the example. The appropriation of St. Julian's Hospital at Southampton to the support of Queen's College, Oxford, and of St. Bartholomew's at Oxford to Oriel College, had been improved upon by the bodily conversion of St. John's Hospital, Oxford, into Magdalen College, and St. Mary Magdalen's Hospital, Reading, and St. John's Hospital, Banbury, into Grammar Schools. These precedents have been followed over and over again, and in our own day the surplus revenues of the Wyggeston Hospital, Leicester, have furnished the most conspicuously successful of first grade secondary schools in the Midlands, the Wyggeston Schools for boys and girls.

Of St. Bartholomew's Hospital very little seems to be known. It was an almshouse for the poor and not a hospital for the sick, already in 1390,[3] when by his will Elias Spelby gave 40s. to the poor in it. It is said that it was in ruins at this time, when Leland visited it. But the statement rests on a conjectural reading by Hearne of a transcript of Leland by Stow. The fact that Lord De La Warr himself had lodgings there, and that there were almspeople in it in 1532, whose interests were preserved, is sufficient testimony that it was not in ruins.

Of Nicholas Thorne, the brother and heir of Robert the younger, having ' overlived ' his fellow-trustee Goodriche, it is said in the deed of 1561 that he ' did make a gramer schole within the said howse of the Bartilmewes and did place and sett one John Haris, scholemaster, to teche gramer there.' The exact date does not appear. But, as we saw, in 1536 Frome Gate was

[1] Stow's *Surv. of London* (ed. Strype, 1720), ii, 123. [2] *Bristol, Past and Present*, ii, 120.
[3] *Wills in Great Orphan Book.*

still occupied by the grammar schoolmaster, Mr. Moffatt, whereas in 1540 the mayor's audit book shows 'a tenement over Frome Yate sometyme the Schole house in the tenure of William Dewe, coriar,' and in 1542 Mr. Moffatt was pensioned. It seems, probable, therefore, that it was in 1538 or 1539 that under its old master, Moffatt, the ancient grammar school removed a few doors down Christmas Street, technically outside the town, in the suburbs, and found its fourth home in St. Bartholomew's Hospital, where it remained for nearly 290 years. The new master, Harris, does not appear to have come till three or four years after the removal in 1541 or 1542.

Of St. Bartholomew's Hospital all that remains to view is the beautiful fourteenth[1]-century gateway, with a Virgin and Child on one side, and a much battered figure on the other, which still remain to adorn the entrance to what is now entitled 'Brewer's Hall,' a little way to the right of the Christmas Steps, close to the top of which stand the chapel and chambers of Foster's Almshouse, otherwise the Three Kings of Cologne, to which Robert Thorne made a bequest. Some inner arches are also visible, but the whole place, which used to have a large quadrangle, is now so filled up with mean dwellings and a brewery office that few traces of antiquity or beauty are visible.

Unfortunately for the school, Nicholas Thorne, like his brother, a busy merchant, and much employed abroad, died without conveying the Bartholomew lands to the Corporation.

He made his will[2] on 4 August, 1546, describing himself as 'citezen and marchante of the cytie or towne of Bristowe '—it had become a city when it acquired a bishop in 1542. He was an exceedingly rich man, and he gave many charitable gifts, and especially remembered the schoolmaster and usher, and provided for the establishment of a school library. He gave his brother-in-law, William Harper, probably the merchant tailor who, as Sir William Harpur, founded Bedford School, '£60 and a gown jackett of tawny damask and to my sister his wife a ring with a diamond, a ring with emerall, a ring with a ruby, £10 and two gowns for 53s. 4d.' To Vincent Thorne, his brother Robert's illegitimate son, he gave

> 200 dukatts, and if he die under 21 yeres of age . . . to the use and behoofe of the Bartholomews in Bristowe there to be employed to the moste advauntage that may growe, of and towardes the buyldyng and reparacion of the same howse, or in purchasyng of landes for the mayntenance of the Free scoole there, after the dirreccion of myne executors or their assigns, or of such parsonnes that shall hereafter have the charge of the same, thinketh moste necessary for the behooffe and maytenaunce of the said free scole.

Then after giving £100 to one illegitimate son, apprentice to a haber-dasher in London, and £96 13s. 4d. to another at Biscay, he proceeds :

> Item, I geve and bequeth to Mr. Harrys, scolemaister of the free scoole at the Bartilmews, 5 markes sterling (£3 6s. 8d.) and a black gowne price 30s., for his paynes taking hereafter to bring upp youthe there in vertue to the pleasure of God, and he to have the same some that he nowe hathe for terme of his liffe, sicke and hole ; and yf the lands of the Bartilmewes may be hereafter ymproved by any meanes, the rents to be annye more than it is at this present day, then I will that his waigges be enlarged to £20 by the yeare. Item, I bequeth to Thomas Clarke of Allar, to John Serieaunt (Sergeant) ussher of the grammer scole, to John Sare notary . . to every of them 3 tonne of saulte.'[3] Item, I bequeth to the howse

---

[1] Not 13th century as in *Bristol Past and Present*.   [2] P.C.C. 18 Alen.
[3] Elsewhere it appears that a ton of salt was worth 20s.

of the Bartholomewes in Bristow towardes the mayntenaunce of the Free Scoole and to make a Library in suche place as Sir John Barloo, late Deane of the dissolved howse and college of Westbury-upon-Trym, John Drewis and Fraunces Codrington of Bristow afore-said, merchauntes, shalle thincke most best or meatest, with the master of the said Bartholo-mews, £30 sterling.   And more I geve and bequeth all such bookes as I have meete for the said lybrary, more my ostrolobia whiche is in the keping of John Sprint, potticary, with cartes and mappis, with such instruments as in my howse belonging to the science of astronomy or cosmografia.

This establishment of a school library with scientific instruments marks Nicholas, like his brother Robert, as a man much in advance of his age in learning and science.   As late as 1687 a catalogue of the books shows that most of them were preserved, together with a pair of globes with covers.   It is to the disgrace of later masters and later members of the corporation, in times which pride themselves on being more advanced and greater lovers of learning and conservers of antiquity, than those who reformed the monasteries or made the Civil War, that not a single one of these books is now forthcoming. The founder's astrolabe and instruments, worth hundreds or thousands of pounds to anyone who knew anything about the value of such things, were dispersed at a sale and acquired by a porter for a few shillings.

These were not all the gifts Nicholas Thorne gave the school.   'More I geve to the garnisshing of altars, vestments, aulter clothes and for the glasyng and reformyng of the windowes of the said churche and scoole whereas it is neade full £36 13s. 4d.'

He also gave £20 to be paid by the advice of the ex-dean and others

and of John Harris, Scolemaister of the saide scoole, to reteigne lerned counsell to assign and convey the landes belongyng to the said Bartilmewes to the chamber of Bristow of and for the assurance and contynuance of the saide Free scoole and I will that the said chamber to be bounde for the parfourmaunce of suche covenauntes as shall be thought most convenient or necessary for the establishment and contynuance of the same.

Mr. Barlow the ex-dean of Westbury was specially given 40s. and £5 in money to apply his mind to this and

to see that the said ordynaunces and rulis for the saide Free Scole of the Bartholomews in the said citie of Bristow be made to bring upp youth in vertuous customes and manners as well as in theare learning according to the very intent and true meaning of my saide brother Robert Thorne.

More than this.   He gave his children the residue of his estate, which must have been enormous, since he gave specific legacies of 100 marks and 100 ounces of plate 'halfe gilt and halfe parcell gilte' to each of his seven legitimate children, four sons and three daughters, and 'if any of them died under age the share was to go to the howse of the Bartholomews towards the building and purchasing of landes for the mayntenaunce of the Free Scoole there.'

This will was proved at Lambeth 15 October, 1546.   It was very bad for the school that Nicholas Thorne had not carried out the conveyance himself.   Very odd were the means adopted to carry it out by his successors. The legal estate in the lands descended to Nicholas's eldest son Robert, who died without issue, when it passed to Nicholas the second son.   He claimed the property as his own, the recovery having been suffered to Nicholas the elder and his heirs.   A compromise was effected by a deed of 15 February, 1558, made between William Tindall and Robert Butler, merchants of Bristol 'and burgesses of the Parliament of the same citie' and Nicholas Thorne 'the sonne.' By this Nicholas 'condiscended and agreed' that 'a sufficient assurance should be made by auctorite of Parliament' to the corporation 'of the Bartilmewes' and its lands 'to the use and maintenaunce of a free schole perpetually to be kept in the said howse.' The two M.P.'s on behalf of the corporation agreed that, within a year after Nicholas, then apparently a minor, came of age, they would grant him an estate for life or for 21 years in the property 'reserving the old accustomed rents,' while the corporation were to be bound to perform Nicholas the elder's will 'concerning the establishment and ereccion of the said schole.'

When Nicholas Thorne the younger had come of age he, by a deed of 1 July, 1561, 'for the accomplyshment as well of the good purpose and will of the said Robert my unkle and the said Nicholas my father' granted the Hospital and lands to the

> Mayor burgisses and cominaltie . . and to their successors for ever to the uses and intents of the fynding of a Free Gramer Schole within the said howse called the Bartilmewes for ever, and to fynde one sufficient and able person being sufficiently lerned and virtuouse to be Schole master their, and one or two other sufficient person or persons being also sufficient-lie lerned and virtuous to be usher or ushers, and they the said master and usher or ushers and their successors contynuallie to teache grammer within the said schole to all childrene and others that will repayre to the said schole for lerning and knowledge of the laten tonge and other good lerning, for the better educacion and bringing uppe of youthe in lerning and virtue, and that frelie without any thing to be taken other than fower pence onlie for the first admission of every scholer into the same schole.

So at last after more than forty years the title to the Bartholomews found rest in the persons originally intended by Robert Thorne the first and the second. But the fatal agreement with Nicholas Thorne II by which this conveyance was obtained had yet to be carried out. It was carried out by a deed of 20 September 1561, which in 1839 was among the corporation records, by which the corporation instead of giving Nicholas Thorne an estate in the property only for life or for twenty-one years, as stipulated, conveyed the whole of the Bartholomew estates to him and his heirs in fee-farm, i.e. on a perpetual lease at a rent of £30 a year.

> The capital house of St. Bartholomew and the school house and all other houses and edifices within the utter gate of the said capital house as they were or should be diuided by a main wall from the chapel or church of the said late hospital and the two aisles and small chapels within the said church

were excepted and reserved to the mayor and commonalty 'for the use and benefit of the said free school established and erected within the said capital house and to the master and usher of the same for the time being,' and Thorne undertook to keep these as well as the other premises in repair. But the whole of the endowment other than the school site and buildings were parted with out-and-out. What influence produced this astounding breach of trust on the part of the corporation, of which Mr. Nicholas Thorne himself was afterwards chamberlain, that is, treasurer or financial officer, does not appear. The Audit Book of 1563 shows payment of £100 by Thorne to the corporation in discharge of a bond by him, and as this was about two years' purchase of the endowment it would seem that this very moderate fine, which went not to the school but to the corporation, was the only one of the 'divers good causes and considerations' which moved them to take this extraordinary departure from the agreement of 1558.

It was a fatal transaction, for Thorne immediately proceeded to sell the greater part of the property. Thus a farm and 82 acres of land at Wickwar were sold by him in 1563 for £48, reserving the ancient and accustomed rent of £4, which is all that is now received by the school for this valuable property. Several farms and 153 acres of land in Stapleton and Horfield, both now parts of the city, Kingswood and Almondsbury were sold by him and his daughter and heiress for £138 6s. 8d., the ancient and accustomed rent of £3 6s. 8d. only being reserved. This property alone would in the present day produce an income which would be riches even to Eton or Winchester. Twenty acres in Clifton, now valued by the foot and worth £2,000 an acre, were sold by Alice Pykes, Thorne's daughter, for £320 and the school only gets from it a rent of £4 a year.

The immediate result of the transaction was that we find for the first time a payment from the corporation to the school. In the Mayor's Audit Book for 1562-3 appears 'Mr. Dyconson, scolemaister for the free scole, £7.' This was a quarterly payment, making £28 in the whole. The accounts for 1565-6 show that of this £28, £18 3s. 4d. was paid to the master and £9 6s. 8d. to the usher. From 1566-7 to 1601-2, however, the whole rent of £30 a year was paid, £20 to the head master and £10 to the usher.

In 1569-70 we have evidence that at Bristol as elsewhere the school supplied the public entertainments formerly found by the Corpus Christi and other gilds. The Audit Book of 1569-70 records the payment of £2 to the schoolmaster 'towards the painting of his pageant and charges for his plays at Christmas,' while 10s. 10d. was paid 'for drawing the town arms in a table set in the Grammar School, wherein be written on parchment the Orders of the school, wherein be drawn the pictures of Mr. Robert Thorne and Mr. Nicholas Thorne the founders of the said school.' So careless has been the management of the school, that these Orders which would have revealed the internal economy and curriculum of the school have wholly disappeared. In 1576-7 other charges for 'playes' in the school appear. From 1581 to 1591 Nicholas Thorne was himself chamberlain; and it is significant that though he had undertaken to keep the school in repair, in 1590 repairs are entered as done by 'the Chamber,' i.e. the corporation.

In 1591 he died, leaving three daughters Alice, Katharine, and Mirabel, co-heiresses. On 13 October, 1597, these three and the husbands of the two elder ones, John Pykes or Picks and Samuel Neale of Berkeley, made a partition of his estates, under which the Bartholomew lands were assigned as Alice Pykes's portion, she granting annuities of £5 and £6 out of them for equality of value to her sisters.

It is remarkable that the earliest Council Minute Book now extant begins in 1593, the year after Nicholas Thorne's death. The explanation appears to be that given by a later inquisition of charitable uses, that Thorne had got the earlier documents into his hands as concerning his title to the Bartholomew lands. They have never been recovered.

SCHOOLS

On 5 February, 1600-1,[1] Mr. John Whitson, alderman, himself a great benefactor to Bristol, and three others, were appointed a committee

> to consider of the Master and Usher of the Free Grammer Schooles peticion touching the raising of their stipends, and the Orders which they would have established in the Free School, and to bring in their opinions in writing.

On 10 May, 1602,[2] it was agreed that for five years following the chamberlain should pay £5 a year and the executors of Robert Kitchen should pay another £5 a year which he had given by his will, making £10 in all, to increase the master's salary by £6 13s. 4d. and the usher's by £3 6s. 8d. This made the master's salary £20 and the usher's £10; the amount contemplated by Nicholas Thorne the elder 60 years before. Now it was quite inadequate. In 1604 the master's salary was raised to £23 6s. 8d. and the usher's to £11 13s. 4d. But two years later the audit book ceases to show any payments to masters. It has been stated that the school was closed preparatory to the attack on the grant to Nicholas Thorne II which now followed. But it is more probable that the masters subsisted on their own resources pending these proceedings.

Under the Statute of Charitable Uses of 44 Elizabeth, 1603, passed on purpose to redress such breaches of trust, a commission was obtained from Chancery, 18 July, 1608, and an inquisition[3] under it was held at the Guildhall, Bristol, before Sir George Snigge and two others on 25 April, 1609. By the jury, nearly all members of the council, it was found that the said Nicholas II, 'pretending to inherit the same lands, procured a conveyance in fee farm under the yearly rent of £30 only,' though then they were of 'the cleare yearly value of £52 and upwards, and now are of a farre greater value over and above all charges and reprises.' They had been held by John Pykes deceased since Thorne's death, and were then held by Alice Pykes 'to the defrauding of the true intention of employment of the said lands . . . . and to the decay of the said school, schoolmaster and other the said uses.' The decree thereon made next day, 26 April, echoed the findings of the jury, asserted that N. Thorne had made away with the records, and had made conveyances of the lands to persons who were cognizant of the trust. The commissioners 'long endeavoured to appease the said persons,' and heard them all, but they 'obstinately refuse to conform themselves to such reasonable courses as equity in our opinion requireth.' So the commissioners

> do think fit that the said lands be returned to the said true first use and intent of employment thereof, that such said schoolmaster, ushers, and instructors of the said children and youths may hereafter live of the profits and revenues of the said lands, which now they cannot do; and that children may be better instructed in the said school . . . . do order . . . . that the schoolmaster should have yearly the yearly wages of £40 and the usher or ushers £20, which wages will be raised out of the said lands, unjust incumbrances being discharged.

Alice Pykes, however, put in exceptions to this decree before the chancellor, and also filed a bill against the corporation. Commissioners were

---

[1] Council Bk. 1598–1608, p. 47.
[2] Ibid. 58.
[3] P.R.O. Chan. Petty Bag. Inq. 7 Jas. I.

appointed to examine witnesses, who opened negotiations with the corporation for a compromise, to which they assented,

> being moved with the remembrance of manifold good deeds and acts of charity done by the ancestors of the said Alice Pykes unto and within the said city . . . . and also weighing what valuable consideration in other lands she had departed with to her sisters, and viewing her great charge, having seven daughters to provide for.

She retained the property, paying £41 6s. 8d. a year rent instead of £30 a year, including the cost of repairs to the school, estimated at £1 6s. 8d. a year. Lord Chancellor Ellesmere accordingly made a decree sanctioning this arrangement on 10 May, 1610, and giving the schoolmaster £26 13s. 4d. a year and the usher £13 6s. 8d., a third more than they got before.

The decree also confirmed the rights of the mayors to act as 'special governors of the school as in times past,' and

> that they should yearly visit the said school and choose overseers thereof . . . . and should with the advice of the aldermen and common counsil as often as they should see occasion displace and place the schoolmaster and usher of the said school . . . . freely without any reward taken therefore and . . . . make such orders and rules for the bringing up and education of youth there in grammar and other good learning as they should see fit so as they were not repugnant to the laws ordinances rule and government set down by the founders.

No sooner had Mrs. Pykes got this extremely favourable compromise than she began selling more of the lands : and in 1613 this poor widow, in spite of her seven daughters, was able to buy up her sisters' charges of £11 a year on the lands. She also granted no less than 44 new leases, no doubt taking large fines, at small quit-rents. It was perhaps to stop further alienations that on 26 September, 1616, the corporation resolved to offer £500 to Mr. Nicholas Pykes, her son, for the Bartholomew lands ; and eventually bought them for £650. They were accordingly conveyed by Alice Pykes by deed of 7 June, 1617, to John Whitson and three other aldermen and their heirs, they paying £41 rent to the school. Finally they came home again to the corporation by a conveyance by the two surviving aldermen trustees, 12 April, 1621.

From September, 1617, the accounts of the Bartholomew lands were kept by a separate bailiff in a separate book. After 1630, up to which date fines and 'overplus' in respect of the lands were entered, no payments in respect of them appear in the mayor's audit books. In spite of the somewhat ambiguous terms of the conveyance by Mrs. Pykes, the whole income of the lands was applied to the school.

The master throughout these troublous times, from 1597 to 1622, appears to have been William Swift, a Gloucestershire boy, who matriculated at Christ Church, Oxford, 2 July, 1585, aged 18, and took his M.A. degree there 7 February, 1589-90. On his death in 1622 the chamberlain and Mr. Barker and his men went 'on a journey to Oxford, being out 5 days, to provide a schoolmaster for the Grammar Schoole, all charges amounteth as by the particulars appeareth to £4 5s. 5d.'

On 22 June, 1622, the Council Book records :

> This day Mr. Payne, master of arts, commended by the vice-chancellor of Oxford to Mr. Mayor, aldermen and common council of this city to succeed Mr. William Swift deceased, late schoolmaster of the Free Grammar School . . . . is elected and chosen chief schoolmaster . . . . with the yearly pension of 40 marks formerly given . . . . with such other

duties [i.e., 4*d.* a head] for the admission of scholars as formerly have been usually given. And it is declared that . . . . he shall not admit or receive into the same school above the number of 12 scholars that shall be strangers and not freemen's sons, to be either tabled or taught by him or the usher at any one time, to the end that freemen's sons of the same city may be prepared and be better instructed, according to the true intent and meaning of the founder of the said school.

This was a quite illegal restriction on strangers, far from the 'true intent and meaning of the founder,' who would have expressed it if he had meant it. The reference to tabling shows that there were then boarders in the school, whose payments no doubt had enabled the schoolmasters to live in spite of the small salary they received after the corporation's breaches of trust. The restrictions were bad policy, as experience has shown that the more widely a school throws open its doors to strangers and boarders as well as to residents on the spot, the better school it becomes and the more residents' children it is likely to have in it. But to restrict the school not merely to residents but to a limited class of residents, the sons of freemen, was a suicidal policy, which in later days was one of the main causes of the narrow dimensions to which the school was reduced.

Payne, who was probably the Richard Payne of Gloucestershire who matriculated at New College, Oxford, 11 November, 1608, M.A. 1616–17, only held office for a few weeks. Probably the new restrictions made him go, for on 6 August, 1622, on the election of Mr. Richard Cheyney, the restriction was relaxed : he was 'not to take above 20 forain scholers at any one time, whereof 10 he may table at once and no more.' Richard Cheyney had taken his M.A. degree at Magdalen Hall, Oxford, 10 July, 1618, and was already, when elected master, rector of Tarrant Rushton, in Dorset. He held office till his death in 1636. At his coming the school library was much augmented. 'Paid Mr. William Brown for 107 books bought for the use of the library in the Grammar School, £14 10*s.*' and five years later, 1628–9, 'Paid Richard Roydon for books he delivered Mr. Cheyney for the library at the Grammar School, £4.' In 1626 Richard Whickham by will gave £100 to be converted to the use of the Free Grammar School. Only £68 was received in respect of this legacy, and employed on new building the library and furnishing it with several books, 'which were some time the books of Mr. William Swift, late master.' William Burns, by will 13 November, 1634, gave £10 to buy books for the library.

On 23 June, 1629, George Harrison, the usher, was 'utterly discharged and dismissed.'

Complaint hath often been made against him, as well for misdemeanours as for his neglect and insufficient training up and instructing such boys and youths in the rudiments and grounds of learning as have been committed to his care and charge, to the great disgrace of the city and especially the governors of the same school, insomuch that divers inhabitants of the said city have of late years for the reasons aforesaid sent their children out of this city to be taught and instructed, to their great and extraordinary charge. But in regard of his poverty and charge of his wife and children and to the end that he may be the better enabled to settle himself elsewhere,

the Corporation gave him £50 out of a fine paid by Thomas Cecil for insulting the mayor, and £17 2*s.* 11*d.* 'for divers implements, reparations and other things . . . . yet in the school.'

Mr. James Walsh, of Mangotsfield, was elected usher in his place. The same day, 23 June, 1629, after a long recital of the decree of Lord Ellesmere fixing the salaries, which the corporation 'do think too mean and not sufficient for their annual maintenance in a competent and meet manner . . . . for the more credit and honour of the said school,' the salaries were raised to £40 and £30 respectively, 'out of the issues of the said lands and such other monies or benefit or gift as are or shall be bestowed upon the said school.' The 'other monies' refers to a gift by will[1] of George Nathway, 27 September, 1628, of £50 'to be employed in some land or otherwise for the augmentation of the stipends of the master or usher of the Free School.' An annuity of £3 was paid by the executors in respect of this, which was redeemed by payment of £50 in 1671 : £1 10s. was paid to the master, and £1 5s. to the usher, afterwards reduced to £1 6s. 8d. and 13s. 4d. respectively, and called, for some mysterious reason, 'hat-money.'

The first extant bailiff's account of the school lands is for 1633–4, and shows a rental of some £85 with £20 for a fine on renewing a lease. Among the expenses is, 'For the charge of visitations at the Grammar School the week before Christmas £1 5s.'

In 1636–7 the city paid Mrs. Cheyney, widow of Richard Cheyney, a gratuity of £10 by way of pension.

On Cheyney's death 'Mr. Henry James, late master of Queen Elizabeth's Hospital, was appointed in his place.' This is a singular instance of the promotion of a master from this much lower grade school to the mastership of the high school. It was probably due to personal influence, Mr. Henry James having been a Bristol boy, who matriculated at Trinity College, Oxford, aged 17, on 30 April, 1619; M.A. from Hart Hall, 7 May, 1625. He does not seem to have been a success, as on 27 September, 1638, Bartholomew Man, recommended by the earl of Pembroke, the high steward of the borough, was chosen in his place.

In February, 1638–9, Elisha, son of Mr. Farmer, later minister of St. Werburgh's, having been 8 or 9 years in St. John's College, Oxford, was chosen usher in place of Walsh, removed 'for abuses by him in the disparagement of the school and retarding the boys learning.'

In the Council Book on 7 September, 1640,

> the whole house doth enact that there shall be a visitation of the Free Grammar School for examination of the scholars how they profit in learning twice a year viz. before Michaelmas and before Easter, on pain of 40s. per time each mayor making default, and the common and usual premium given the boys best deserving to be continued, whether out of the chamber's money or the Free School rents, as heretofore hath been done.

On 23 January, 1642–3, Man was ordered 'to remove at Lady Day, and Walter, son of John Rainsthorp, a free burgess, succeeded. He held office all through the Civil War. In December, 1657, his salary was increased to £60 a year. He died shortly afterwards, and on 23 March, 1657–8, a handsome eulogy of him was entered in the Council Book. He was 'exceeding faithful, diligent, and able in his place, and one whom God made especially instrumental in the educating, teaching, and bringing up of youth within this city, sending many able and useful scholars to the university.' He left a widow and six children and a very small estate. So £10 a year was directed to be paid for their use.

---

[1] Will Bk. No. 3. Vellum Bk. of Charities.

His successor was John Stephens of Trinity College, Oxford, matriculated there 16 October, 1640, aged 16, and B.C.L. 3 December, 1646, and afterwards M.A. He was appointed 18 March, 1657–8. At his incoming an inventory was taken of the school library. It consisted of about 160 volumes, comprising geographical and astronomical works, such as Manilius' *Astronomy* and Ptolemy's *Geography*, and Cornelius Agrippa's *De occulta Philosophia*, gifts no doubt from the Thornes' library.

On 20 September, 1658, on the resignation of Mr. Jonathan Price, usher, we learn that it was one of the ordinances of the school that both masters should be university graduates, for a special dispensation was voted to enable Mr. Ball, who was not a graduate, to be elected in his place. Mr. Stephens was probably a Puritan or Independent, as in 1662 he disappeared, a victim apparently to the Restoration reaction, Ball the unqualified usher being put in his place.

In 1666 new ordinances which bear the Restoration stamp were made for the school. The master was to be 'an M.A. of two years' standing, well learned in Latin, Greek, and Hebrew.' This last qualification may or may not have been a new importation. It is found in some Elizabethan school statutes, but is more common in Jacobean and later days, especially those of the Commonwealth, and is a mark of the spirit of theological controversy, which in Erasmus' time had introduced into the schools the study of Greek, with a view to the new learning in the New Testament, and now had carried the learned into similar dissection of the Old Testament. The Presbyterians especially affected this new study, which made it unpopular with the royalist rulers of Restoration schools, and it soon dropped out. Another new requirement was that the master was 'to be well affected to kingly government.' The usher was to be a B.A. of two years' standing, 'learned in Latin and Greek' only, but equally 'well affected.' Further restrictions were now imposed on the freedom of the school. 'Every scholar being the son of a burgess dwelling within the city and lawfully baptized' was to be admitted free, paying an entrance fee of 5s. instead of the ancient 4d.—a fair equivalent to the altered value of money. Others who were 'not to enjoy the privileges of the school' were to be admitted on such terms as the master and parents should agree upon. Besides admission fees, every scholar was to pay 1s. in winter for fire and 2d. a quarter for sweeping the school. Every scholar was to resort to church on the Lord's Day morning and evening. Another sign of reaction was that the visitation, or examination, of the school was again reduced to once a year on the Thursday before Easter, when premiums not exceeding 10s. might be given to the 'best deserving.'

In 1670 Stephens died, and Rowland Tucker the usher performed his duties, receiving £12 10s. for doing so until on 6 December, 1670, John Rainsthorp was appointed master. He had matriculated at St. John's College, Oxford, 25 June, 1659, and was probably the son of Walter Rainsthorp, the master in 1642–57. At his incoming the garden of the usher, which had been annexed by the two previous masters, was restored to him. Eleven years later, 31 May, 1681,

Mr. Tucker, the usher . . . having been taken notice by this house of his inabilities and insufficiency, by reason of age and other infirmities, for some time past to officiate as usher there, which has driven most of the youth out of the city to seek learning elsewhere, to the preventing the pious intention of the donor, and the desertion of the city and school, it is ordered that he be dismissed from the school at Midsummer day next, and to receive £10 yearly out of the salary of his successor towards his support during the life of the said Tucker.

The pension was afterwards increased to £20, and was not deducted from the salary of Mr. Thomas Stump, his successor.

On 12 July, 1676,

it being mentioned in the house that the Grammar School is neglected both by the master and usher . . . . seeing it would be very unprecedented and unfit that any be dismissed unheard, no proceedings were to be taken until articles are exhibited against them or either of them.

Probably Rainsthorp's neglect arose from his attention to clerical work, as he was vicar of St. Michael's.[1] In 1686 he became vicar of All Saints and a canon of Bristol Cathedral.

On 11 May, 1687, Mr. William Stephens, B.D., was appointed in his room, but after only two years was followed by Mr. Wotton with Richard Wotton as usher. In 1697 Robert Welstead was elected with 'condition not to take any cure or appointment.' But as long as the corporation carried the fines received in respect of the Grammar School estate into their own coffers instead of increasing the masters' pay, the masters necessarily took every opportunity of eking it out by clerical service. In 1699 the city were better advised, and fines to the extent of £5 spent on repairs to the school. In 1700 they expended another £100 from a similar source in a real effort to improve the status of the school. On 23 August, 1700, the city resolved to pay Balliol College, Oxford, this sum 'towards the buildings of chambers for the exhibitioners to be sent from our Grammar School to that College on condition that within three months Dr. Maunder does by proper instrument signify the concurrence of the college.' An act of the college is accordingly entered in the city books 19 November, 1700, by which the college

promised for themselves and their successors that all the encouragement which the statutes of the college allowed should be given to and all due care taken of all such exhibitioners as should from time to time be sent in order to their improvement in virtue and learning.

Welstead resigned in 1702, and was succeeded by Edward Pearce, of University College, Oxford, who held office till he vacated it in 1709 'by accepting cure of souls' in the vicarage of Pilminster, Somerset.

The ushers were very fleeting birds at this time; Deane who had held from 1697 to 1704 being succeeded by Bradford, who in 1706 was dismissed for misconduct. Henry Margetts then came on probation for a year and left at the end of it, then Thomas Creswick died during his probationary year, and 3 November, 1708, Walter Rainsthorp, no doubt of the same family as previous masters, came.

In 1709 William Golding became master, and 12 December, 1711, asked and received an augmentation of salary 'of £20 a year, during the pleasure of the house,' making it £80 a year in all. After seven years Golding retired on being presented by the crown to a benefice. His letter on resignation affords the only glimpse of the numbers of the school, which, in the absence of any registers, is obtainable. He says in his seven years' mastership 155 boys had left the school, of whom went :—To Oxford 12, to

---

[1] J. Latimer, *Annals of Bristol*, 17th cent. 179.

law 7, to physic 1, to the army 1, to shop trades 56, to merchants and sea 53, to business unknown 11, to county affairs 2, went from the upper school to other schools 6, died 6. The numbers leaving, the average time of attendance at school being five years, represents a school of about 110 boys.

Golding's successor, James Taylor, of Oriel College, Oxford, 'B.L.' i.e. B.C.L., not M.A., did not receive the augmentation of his predecessor, nor apparently did he deserve it. He retired to the vicarage of St. Michael 18 April, 1722. Alexander Stafford Catcott, B.C.L., of Merchant Taylors School, a fellow of St. John's College, Oxford, came in. Next year, 16 November, 1723, he petitioned for the augmentation, showing that in a year and a half ' he had increased the number of boys from 20 to 70, which might be looked upon as an instance of his past duty and an earnest of his care to come.' The augmentation was granted ' during the pleasure and as the free gift of this house.' The account book of the treasurer of the school lands contains a catalogue taken 23 September, 1725, by Catcott of the school library, the last that is extant. Catcott had dabbled in poetry before becoming master with ' The Poem of Musaeus on the loves of Hero and Leander,' and ' The Court of Love, a Vision from Chaucer.' These and some volumes of sermons have procured him a place in the *Dictionary of National Biography*. He held office for 22 years. Thomas Fry, President of St. John's College, Oxford, and Richard Woodward, bishop of Cloyne, are recorded as having been amongst his pupils. In 1743 he retired to the vicarage of St. Stephen's, Bristol.

On 18 January, 1743-4, Samuel Seyer, of Pembroke College, Oxford, who became the father of the historian of the Bristol charters, was elected head master. Next year new orders were made for the school, 1 May, 1745. The chief changes were that for ' well affected to kingly government ' the words ' well affected to the constitution in church and state ' were substituted in the masters' qualifications ; and the requirement of the scholars that they should be ' lawfully baptized ' was dropped. The opening hours of school were altered from 6 a.m. to 7 a.m. in summer and spring, and the dinner hour from 11 a.m. to 12 noon, and return from dinner from 1 p.m. to 2 p.m. Tuesday, as well as Thursday and Saturday afternoons, were to be half holidays and consecrated to writing lessons, while play-days were allowed on days appointed not ' by the church rules ' but ' by public authority.' Instead of finding a fire for the boys in the ' back kitchen,' the master was now to provide this luxury in the school itself.

It was not till 1757 that Mr. Seyer asked for and obtained the augmentation of £20 a year granted to his predecessor. This may have been because a large outlay was necessary on the school buildings, on which, between 1757 and 1762, no less than £2,040 was expended. Seyer retired in 1764 to the living of St. Michael.

Charles Lee succeeded him with a new usher, Walter Trevenna. Lee seems to have been successful in filling the school, as two years later, 7 June, 1766, a committee was appointed to consider what alterations and additions to the buildings should be made for the better accommodation of the scholars. This committee in July reported that

it would be a public benefit if the master and scholars of the Grammar School were removed to the buildings of Queen Elizabeth's Hospital, and the master and boys of that Hospital removed to the Grammar School . . . . for the present apartments belonging to the Grammar

School (though fit for all the purposes of the Hospital) are not large enough to secure and entertain many of the citizens' children, whose parents would choose to have them brought up and educated under their own view and inspection rather than at distant schools, and the buildings near College Green now employed for the said Hospital will better accommodate more than twice the number of young gentlemen than the present Grammar School.

The buildings of Queen Elizabeth's Hospital were the old St. Mark's or Billeswick, otherwise Gaunt's Hospital. But as the gift of them to Queen Elizabeth's Hospital by the corporation had been confirmed by Act of Parliament, another Act was thought necessary to effect the exchange, and a Private Act of 9 George III was accordingly obtained for the purpose. A great deal of abuse has been hurled by some local historians[1] at the corporation for this act, and it has been imputed to merely personal motives, the head master Lee having married one Alderman Dampier's daughter. But it would be odd if an alderman was able to make a whole corporation carry out such a transaction merely for the private benefit of his son-in-law ; and the fact is that Lee did not become Dampier's son-in-law until nearly two years after the council had determined on the exchange. It was, in fact, merely a case of suiting the long coat to the tall boy and the short coat to the small boy : giving the larger building to the school of over 100 boys of 13 to 19 years old, and the smaller to a merely charity school of 36 boys under 14. It was, however, a misfortune for the Grammar School, as it postponed the time for the provision of proper buildings long after Queen Elizabeth's Hospital was given new and palatial accommodation.

It is represented that the exchange of buildings took place before the Act was passed. But it seems to be doubtful whether this is not founded only on the fact that money was entered in the chamberlain's account for 1767–8, rendered, as usual, some time after the event.

The school is said to have prospered exceedingly under Lee at first. But, as usual with all public schools in the eighteenth century, he was allowed to stay on long after he had passed his zenith. He held the head-mastership for no less than 48 years, till his death in 1811. The result was that for several years it is said that the school consisted of one boy. In 1803 a committee of Old Boys called the attention of the council to the condition of the school. But the council refused to grant a retiring pension, and so Lee was allowed to stay on till he dropped.

On the appointment of his successor, John Joseph Goodenough, in March, 1812, the school orders were revised, chiefly by raising the entrance fee from 5s. to £4, while he was allowed to charge £16 16s. a year for instruction in all subjects but Latin and Greek, which alone, according to the convenient doctrine of the Court of Chancery, were free. The Commissioners of Inquiry concerning charities in 1822[2] found a school of only 50 boys, 35 boarders and 15 day boys. Four or five boys were 'on the foundation, there not having been more than ten for many years. They rather absurdly represented the admission fee as illegal, and it was reduced again to 5s., though as far as the Foundation deed went that was equally illegal, the sum mentioned by Robert Thorne being 4d. Dr. Goodenough was allowed, in 1820, to take a living in Buckinghamshire. In his later years the school sank almost to nothing.

[1] J. Latimer, *Annals of Bristol*, 18th cent. 375. He falls into the error of supposing that the Grammar School was then a day school.　　　　[2] *Char. Com. Rep.* vi, 481.

SCHOOLS

In 1827 the corporation claimed the school lands as their own. In 1837 the Municipal Charity Trustees, who, under the Municipal Corporations Act, 1835, had been substituted as the Governing Body of the school for the corporation, filed a Bill in Chancery on behalf of the school, and in January, 1842, its title to such of the lands given by the Thornes as still remained was affirmed by the Court. The endowment left brought in about £1,000 a year. The trustees then tried to get rid of Dr. Goodenough, whose usefulness had long been over, and succeeded in September, 1844, after a litigation which cost £3,220.

A new scheme was made by the Court of Chancery in 1847 which enabled tuition fees of £6 a year to be charged. Under Dr. Robert Evans the school reopened 24 June, 1848, with 200 boys. He died in the cholera epidemic of October, 1854. He was succeeded by the second master, C. T. Hudson, who resigned on the refusal of the Master of the Rolls in 1860 to allow boarders. This, and the inertia of the trustees in not moving the school to a new site where proper playgrounds and school-buildings could be provided, resulted in the foundation of Clifton College, and the supersession by it of this ancient grammar school as the chief school of the town. Some improvement was effected by an Act of 1859, 21 & 22 Vic. cap. 30, confirming a scheme of the Charity Commissioners under the Charitable Trusts Acts, by which the old exhibition endowments were consolidated and augmented by the unused accumulations, about £2,000, of Dr. Thomas White's charity for roads.

In 1866 the Schools Inquiry Commission found a school of 235 boys under the Rev. J. W. Caldicott. The masters were ill-paid. Very few boys went from the school to the universities.

> The situation is gloomy. . . . . There is a long schoolroom . . . . 5 class-rooms, though one should more properly form the head-master's study. The other masters . . . . have no private room whatever in which they can stay between school hours. . . . . The school buildings generally are not worthy of the city. . . . . They compare very unfavourably with those of Queen Elizabeth's Hospital or Clifton College.

After the passing of the Endowed Schools Act, 1869, a new scheme or rather schemes were published by the Endowed Schools Commissioners. They met with much opposition, but finally in their main features became law on the approval of Queen Victoria in Council 13th May, 1875.

The main scheme added to the Municipal Charity Trustees six governors, two representatives of the Town Council, two of the School Board, one of the Grammar School Masters, and one of the masters and mistresses of the various schools placed under them. The tuition fees were raised from £8 to £12 a year, and four leaving exhibitions of £50 a year were provided. By three subsidiary schemes for the Loan Money, the Prisoners Redemption Charities, and Mary Ann Peloquin's doles, all of which, being out of date, were of little use, and had large accumulations of income, sums of £4,250, £355 10s., and £5,000 were applied to the school in order to provide the much-needed new buildings, which were to be for 400 boys. On 15 February, 1879, the school moved into these buildings, erected in Tyndall's Park, just off the top of Park Road, the main street leading from Bristol to Clifton. They are in the late Perpendicular and Tudor styles, and form an imposing pile, the more striking from the use of the reddish-purple stone of the district, set off by white stone quoins and mullions. The most conspicuous feature is the Large Hall, 140 ft. long by 50 ft. high and 50 ft. broad. But it was unfortunate that a very large part of the £20,000 of the original building was lavished on this hall, just at the time when the more advanced schools had already abandoned the massing of battalions of boys in big schools for the division of them into quieter and more easily taught squads in separate class-rooms. There were only three class-rooms to begin with. In 1892 the city gave £2,000 of the money coming to it for technical education under the Local Taxation Act, 1890, out of which three more class-rooms and two Science Lecture theatres and a Physical Laboratory were added. These are now adequate for the 200 boys in the school, but by no means adequate for the 400 boys contemplated, and who in due course of development may soon be expected to arrive.

The weight of debt for the buildings was lightened by a scheme of 17 November, 1888, which appropriated some £6,000 from various obsolete charities to the school; and the income was increased by a scheme of 16 May, 1893, which appropriated the unused payment every fourth year of £104 from Sir Thomas White's charity. The total income from the endowment at the present time is just under £2,000 a year.

In 1883 Dr. Caldicott retired to the vicarage of Shipston, Worcestershire. He was succeeded by Robert Leighton Leighton, probably the first lay head master since the days of Edward VI. From Manchester Grammar School he won an exhibition at Balliol College, and took first classes in classics, both in Moderations and Final Schools. He had been eight years head master of Wakefield Grammar School when appointed. The most permanent memorial he has left behind him is the enlargement and laying out of the school playing fields, which till his time were unused and uncared for, effected by means of a subscription of £2,408 which he raised in 1891–2. One of the governors, Mr. O. Hosegood, being skilled in the matter, took charge of the culture of the ground. Now the cricket pitch is said to be excellent, and the games and sports are effectively organized.

Mr. Leighton also greatly modified the curriculum. He specialized classics and mathematics, establishing parallel VI and V Forms in each subject; and attempted a commercial department, in which French and German were substituted for Latin and Greek. But this proved a failure. The grant of £200 a year by the city in 1892 under the Local Taxation Act, 1890, enabled the teaching of science to be properly organized for the first time under a special science master. The laboratories then built, considered excellent at the time, are now being 'modernized' and remodelled. A carpenter's shop is in process of erection. The list of University successes gained by the boys from Bristol Grammar School was well maintained under Mr. Leighton. He retired at the end of the summer term 1905, and is living at Cambridge.

The present head master is Mr. Cyril Norwood. He was at Merchant Taylors School, and scholar of St. John's College, Oxford, where he obtained a first class in both Moderations and Final Schools. Having headed the list of candidates for the civil service in 1899, he abandoned an Admiralty clerkship in 1901 for an assistant mastership at Leeds Grammar School, and was elected head master at Bristol in May, 1906.

SCHOOLS

BRISTOL COLLEGE OR CATHEDRAL GRAMMAR SCHOOL

After the dissolution by surrender of St. Augustine's Abbey in 1538, Henry VIII by letters patent, 4 June, 1542, established in it the cathedral church of the Holy and Undivided Trinity, with a bishop, dean, and chapter of 6 canons prebendaries, 6 minor canons, a schoolmaster, and usher : with other minor ministers and officers. As the establishment and the statutes were in identical terms with those of Gloucester, the pay of the master and usher being the same, £20 and £10, and there being here also no foundation scholars, it is unnecessary to repeat the provisions made with regard to the school at Bristol. And it is not a little discreditable to the deans and chapters of these two western sees that they alone of the chapters of the cathedrals of the new foundation, merely to save their own pockets, allowed their grammar schools to be degraded to the position of mere chorister schools and elementary schools. At Bristol, however, as will be seen, the modern chapter did at length, too late indeed to retrieve the situation wholly, endeavour to restore the school to some useful work, and if not to its ancient and intended status, at least to some position as a secondary school.

In spite of these express directions for the maintenance of a grammar school, it has been stated in an official report that no cathedral grammar school was ever established. 'I learn,' said Mr. A. H. Stanton in his report to the Schools Inquiry Commission in 1866,

> that there is no trace of any such school having in fact been brought into existence in Bristol. Two grammar schools were founded in the city at about the same period when the statutes were granted to the cathedral, and one of them is situated close by. It is perhaps to be presumed therefore that their presence was one of the deterrent causes why the statutes were not acted upon.

At this time the dean and chapter were so oblivious of their statutory duty that they had actually appointed a certificated elementary schoolmaster to teach the school. Mr. Stanton adds :—

> I find that some school has long existed in connexion with the cathedral, and in a history of Bristol in 1809 is spoken of as 'the Cathedral Grammar School.' It would seem therefore that we must accept the present school as the imperfect development of the higher type contemplated by Henry VIII.

But this is all guesswork, and though, through the destruction of documents which is thought to have taken place at the Reform Bill riots in 1835, it is impossible to demonstrate the actual existence of the Cathedral Grammar School in the sixteenth century; yet there can be no reasonable doubt of the fact that one was established. In the first place Henry VIII was not the kind of person to brook the dereliction of duty which would have been implied by a failure to establish the school for which part of the endowment was expressly assigned. Two commissions were appointed, one under Henry VIII, one under Edward VI, to see that the deans and chapters duly carried out the charitable objects, of repair of bridges and roads and relief of the poor, provided in their statutes. It is impossible to suppose that neglect to maintain the school can have been, as it is supposed to be, one of the reasons for the establishment of the new cathedrals, since then an important object in the statutes for them would have been overlooked. If Henry had not intended Bristol Cathedral to maintain a grammar school he would have omitted the provision for it, as he did in the case of the only cathedral of the new foundation which did not have a school as part of its foundation, Winchester, and that we learn from Archbishop Abbot was because of 'that noble school of Wykeham's foundation,' which then took day boys as well as boarders.

But at Archbishop Laud's visitation, which took place in 1634, less than a hundred years after the foundation of the cathedral, we not only have positive evidence of the existence of the grammar school, but the evidence shows that it was then by no means new, but already on the decline; and at the same time, that it was not then, and never had been, or was intended to be, exclusively or mainly, or indeed partially, a choristers' school. Among the papers preserved in the House of Lords MSS.[1] relating to this visitation, are the following returns as to Bristol Cathedral :—

> [About the Choristers.] The weakenes, through age of their master causeth that they bee not so well ordered or instructed as they otherwise should, but for helpe hereof are committed to the care of some others of the quier, and some of them alsoe goe to the gramar schoole. Two of them are sent to the grammar schoole.
>
> [About the Grammar School.] The yearly allowance of the schoolemaster is by statute only 20 marckes, and for an usher 20 nobles, both which stipendes have beene conferred upon the schoolemaster heretofore undertaking the whole charge of the schoole, and receiveth the whole £20; and they conceive hee is diligent in his place.
>
> The yearely allowance of the schoolemaster is £13 6s. 8d., and of the usher £6 13s. 4d. But the whole £20 hath beene enjoyed by two or three schoolemasters, his immediate predecessours, and likewise by himselfe for these fifteene yeares by the consent of the bishop, deane, and chapter. . . . There is great want of an usher, the master being an ordinary preacher and chaplyn to the Lord Bishop. The schollers who of ould were wont alwaies to repair to the morning service in the cathedrall church half an hower after 6 do wholly absent themselves therefrom, and are not culpable. . . .
>
> The prebend, whose house is utterly decayed, hath the house auntiently the schoolmaster's. The schoolemaster the house of a petty canon, without any care for restitution thereof to that poore place.
>
> The whole churchyard is made a receptacle for all ydle persons to spend their time in stopball. . . . The schoolhouse standing on this site is made at all times as a common tennis court, and ys in a manner fitted for that use.

When deans and chapters were abolished in 1649 Parliament took care that the schools and other charities dependent on them should not suffer. The Trustees for Plundered Ministers were charged with seeing to the payment of the masters, with power to augment their salaries. Their proceedings have been very ill preserved. But we find an order on 28 November, 1651[3] :—

> Whereas the yearely pension of £13 6s. 8d. heretofore payable by the Dean and Chapter of Bristoll to the schoolmaster of the Free Schoole of Bristoll and £6 13s. 4d. to the usher of the said schoole is now charged upon and payable by the said trustees, which said service is performed by [   ] Adams, schoolmaster of the said schoole, It is ordered that the said £13 6s. 8d. and £6 13s. 4d. to bee from tyme to tyme paid unto the said Mr. Adams to bee accompted from the 16th day of October, 1650.

Mr. Richard Phelps, the receiver, was accordingly told to pay the money 'for and during such tyme as he shall contynue to perform the said service.' A rather curious entry about it occurs on 20 November, 1654: 'Mr. Richard Phelps, upon his account hath delivered up the respective

[1] *Hist. MSS. Com. Rep.* iv, 142.
[2] Marginal note in the original : ' It were well that the boyes came to church.'
[3] Lamb. MSS. (Lamb. Lib.), Aug. 969, fol. 91.

orders by which he was appointed to pay augmentations and allowances, together with his acquittances indorsed upon the said order, soe that he hath not sufficient warrant to pay such augmentations and allowances.' So he received a new order to pay up to Michaelmas, 1654, the sums scheduled, including 'Bristoll Schoole schoolemaster, Mr. Adams, £13 6s. 8d., usher £6 13s. 4d.' By a further order of 24 July, 1655,[1] the payment was charged on the impropriate rectories of Banwell, Puxton, and Churchill in Somerset. Two years later, 17 November, 1657,[2] Adams having either retired or died, the trustees ordered 'that Mr. William Thomas bee and he is hereby settled schoolemaster of the Free Schoole att Bristoll in the county of Somerset and that hee doe from time to time diligently discharge the duty of schoolemaster there,' with £20 a year out of the tithes of the same parishes.

In the absence of documents the next we hear of the Cathedral School is a most astounding and inaccurate return by the dean and chapter to the Cathedral Commission[3] in 1852. 'In the Choristers' School, which is a grammar school,' the statutable allowance of the head master is £8 8s. 8d. and of the under master £2 19s. 2d. An increased allowance is made to the head master of £51 11s. 6d., in all £60. There is no statutable house, but one is provided by the dean and chapter in which scholars may be boarded. They then make this astounding statement, 'The schools are open to others not by statute but by permission of the dean and chapter.' This in face of the statutes which made the school open to all. There were then in the school 6 choristers, 2 probationers, and 25 others. The school struggled on as a grammar school under the Rev. Robert Hancock, a minor canon, and the Rev. F. E. Skey, now vicar of Weare. But in 1866 it was placed under the control of a Mr. Morgan, a certificated master, and was degraded into a merely elementary school.

The Endowed Schools Commissioners took it in hand at the same time as the other secondary schools of Bristol and endeavoured to make it again take its place as a secondary school. But the scheme actually made and approved by Queen Victoria in Council, 4 February, 1875, was a compromise. It declared the

> object of the trust shall be to maintain the efficiency of the cathedral school founded by Henry VIII in Bristol, and in connexion therewith to train teachers for supplying education higher than elementary education, in accordance with the doctrines of the Church of England

and it gave the institution the name of Bristol Cathedral College, calling the upper part the Training College, and the lower part the College School. Towards the endowment the commissioners extracted £120 a year from the dean and chapter and £12,000 from the Ecclesiastical Commissioners for buildings; which was approximately the equivalent of what a canon received in 1835, without any allowance for the 150 years during which the school had been starved. The governing body was a quaint one consisting of 11, the bishop, the dean, and 5 nominees of the dean and chapter, one appointed by the Lord President of the Council, and 3 by the rival schools of Bristol, 2 by the governing bodies of the Grammar School and of Colston's Hospital, and one by the head masters of the Grammar School, Colston's Hospital, and Queen Elizabeth's Hospital.

---

[1] Lamb. MSS. (Lamb. Lib.), Aug. 967, fol. 12.   [2] Ibid. 993, fol. 280.   [3] Cath. Com. Rep. 1854, p. 218.

The school was made a very subordinate part of the establishment. The master was to be appointed by the principal of the college, 18 choristers were to be free, and 3 boys might be admitted up to the age of 15 at such fees as the chapter might appoint.

The school was, however, a success. The Rev. Henry W. Potes, of St. John's College, Cambridge, a senior optime, who had been six years at Cranleigh School, Surrey, was appointed head master in January, 1876. He found 18 choristers and 1 paying boy. In less than three years the full complement of 100 allowed by the scheme was reached, and was then raised to 120.

The Training College was placed under the Rev. Alfred Rosser, B.A. London, and the scholars in it had the school as a training school. But the only people who came to the college were those who had been given scholarships. When their two years had elapsed no more came, and the training college collapsed. This necessitated a new scheme. It treated the school as an ordinary secondary school, with leaving age of 17, and substituted for the rival schoolmasters' nominee on the governing body a representative of the Bristol School Board; but it still retained the representatives of the governing bodies of the rival Bristol Grammar and Colston Hospital Schools. The head master's status was raised to that of other grammar schools, with sole power of appointing and dismissing assistant masters. The fees were raised to from £5 to £10 a year and foundation scholarships by competition were provided; the choristers being still admitted free. The endowment, however, was not increased.

In the school Latin and French have been compulsory, Greek is optional and an extra, and no one learns it. Games and sports are kept up under difficulties, by means of a field hired near the Downs. There are now 102 boys and 4 assistant masters. The boys mostly go into business in the town. The endowment is only £200 a year.

Queen Elizabeth's Hospital

John Carr founded this school by will 10 April, 1586. He was a soap-boiler, having works in Bristol and at Bow, and is said to have acquired great wealth by a secret process of manufacture. He gave the manor of Congresbury and all his estates in Somerset for the erection of a hospital in Bristol

> for bringing up of poor children and orphans, being men children born in the city of Bristowe, or in any part of testator's manor, lands or tenements in Congresbury, and whose parents are deceased or fallen into decay, and not able to relieve them; and for those chiefly to provide in such order, manner, and form, and with such foundation, ordinances, laws, and government, as the hospital of Christchurch, nigh St. Bartholomew's Hospital, in London, is founded, ordered, and governed.

The corporation were appointed governors of the charity, and on Carr's death they at once began to make arrangements for the establishment of the hospital, and in March, 1590, obtained a charter from the crown.[1]

> This year aboute iij weekes in Lent there was presented in the house a patente from her majestie as concerninge a hospitall to be erected by the name of Queene Eliz. Hospitall, yssueinge oute of John Carres landes. Which said Hospitall was the same yeere, by the

[1] Mayor's Calendar, 62.

greate diligence and charitable endevour of the said William Birde, founded at the Gauntz, and xij poore children placed therein for a beginninge of the sayd good worke, to which the sayd William Birde was a bountifull benefactor and gave thereunto 530 li in money for the advancement thereof.

The school was opened in September, 1590. In June, 1596, Carr's trustees transferred the estate to the Corporation, who in the following year obtained an Act of Parliament which settled the property on the charity for ever. Anthony Standbank had given land and houses in Bristol before this date ; Lady Mary Ramsey gave £1,000, which with £450 of corporation money was by deed 22 March, 1609, laid out in land in Winterbourne. Alderman Barker, in 1658, gave six houses in Bristol and £100. Edward Colston in 1698 gave lands in parishes of Yatton and Congresbury. James Gollop in 1710 gave lands, and Samuel Hartnell in 1716 gave £700.

In 1651 the number of boys was raised to 24, in 1695 to 36 by Edward Colston's gifts, and in December, 1700, to 40. The hospital was rebuilt in 1706. We have already seen how in 1769 these boys were moved into St. Bartholomew's Hospital.

The common council increased the amount paid to the master for feeding, clothing, and educating the boys from £10 to £12 per head in 1789, and prescribed the diet. They were to have meat five days a week and milk pottage on the other days ; breakfast was limited to bread and beer.

In 1781 the corporation claimed to treat £3,000, which they had advanced for the building of the hospital in Elizabeth's reign, as a debt, bearing interest at 5 to 10 per cent., and unblushingly claimed to the Charity Commissioners in 1821 that the hospital was, therefore, indebted to them in the sum of £46,499. After the Municipal Corporations Act had transferred the management of the charities to the Municipal Charity Trustees, a Bill was filed in Chancery, and the corporation eventually agreed to a decree against themselves in January, 1842. The number of boys was then 42, which the trustees at once increased to 120. In 1847 the school was moved to new buildings on the north-west side of Brandon Hill, and the numbers again increased.

The Assistant Commissioner for the Schools Inquiry Commission in 1866 found 195 boys. He reported favourably on the education, some of the boys learning Latin and the earlier books of Euclid. If they stayed beyond the age of 14, which they could only do by special permission of the trustees, they were expected to go in for the Cambridge Local examination. But he pointed out that the results were not adequate to the size of the endowment—some £7,400.

By a scheme made under the Endowed Schools Acts, 13 May, 1875, for this and the Red Maids' School, which placed them under the same governing body as the Grammar School, very ambitious developments were contemplated. The hospital was to be for 160 boarders, while two purely day schools for boys were to be provided. But those were the days when rents were advancing by leaps and bounds. Then came a fall, and the net income now is only £5,172. So not only have the day schools never been started, but the hospital itself has had to be reduced in numbers, and at present contains only 127 inmates. These are all admitted by competitive examination by boys from public elementary schools in Bristol and the other districts contemplated by the founder, 60 of whom must be orphans. As all have to leave at 15 years old, the standard of education aimed at is that of the Cambridge Junior Local examinations.

RED MAIDS' SCHOOL

John Whitson, alderman, by will 27 March, 1627, bequeathed nearly all his property to the mayor and burgesses, out of which they were to pay £90 a year for one grave, painful, and modest woman, and for 40 poor women children, whose parents were burgesses deceased or decayed, to be furnished with convenient lodging, bedding, linen, and other necessaries. The mayor and aldermen were to pay 40s. for each, and to cause them to be apparelled in red cloth. The Red Maids' Hospital was opened in 1634, and the corporation, in a declaration of trust 21 April, 1634, directed the surplus of the funds to be given in sums of £10 or £20 for marriage portions for the maids. The premises originally granted were found inconvenient, and in 1658 a new hospital was built, which was rebuilt in Denmark Street in 1842. The school is now managed under a scheme of the Endowed Schools Commissioners of 1875. There are 80 girls, under Miss Eliza Charlotte Bowen, head mistress, with 4 assistant mistresses. The pupils are prepared for Cambridge local examinations, with good results, and on leaving obtain posts as pupil teachers, clerks, typists, &c.

COLSTON'S HOSPITAL

The foundation of this school dates from a deed of Edward Colston, 25 November, 1708, by which he conveyed to the Company of Merchant Adventurers lands in trust for a school for 100 poor boys to be provided with board, lodging, and clothing. They were to be all sons of freemen, or born within the city, save 20 who may be of another place. The school was opened in July, 1710, in a house on St. Augustine's Back, which had been converted from a sugar refinery.[1] In 1842 the Master of the Rolls gave judgement against the Merchants' Society in an action as to the surplus funds, after the expenses of the school had been provided, which they claimed.

The school was removed to the vacated bishop's palace at Stapleton in October, 1861. By a scheme of the Endowed Schools Commissioners in 1875, the nomination of boys was stopped. They were to be selected by order of merit; 80 from elementary schools in Bristol, and 20 from those of Gloucestershire, Wiltshire, and Somerset, and the governors were to admit other boys, besides those on the foundation, on payment of £30 a year. There are now about 50 boys paying fees, besides the 100 foundationers. The governing body was altered, and consists now of 23 governors, of whom 2 are ex officio, 18 nominated by the Merchant Venturers, the magistrates of Gloucestershire and Somerset, and the Bristol Education Committee, and 3 are co-opted. The head master is Mr. Anthony Finn, M.A. and LL.D., Trinity College, Dublin, and he has a staff of 6 assistant teachers, who prepare boys for the Board of Education Science and Art examinations.

[1] *Annals*, ii, 84.

SCHOOLS

COLSTON'S GIRLS' DAY SCHOOL

This school was opened in January, 1891, in Cheltenham Road, under a scheme of the Charity Commissioners of 1875 by which the surplus income of Colston's Hospital was to be used for a girls' day school. The governing body consists of 8 members of the Colston's Hospital governing body and 5 ladies co-opted by them. The fees are £6 a year, and there are 350 girls. Under Miss Evangeline Margaret Hughes, B.A. London, and a staff of teachers, six of whom have university qualifications, this school has rapidly developed into a secondary school of the highest type, preparing pupils for the London Matriculation examinations and for various colleges for women.

MERCHANT VENTURERS' TECHNICAL COLLEGE

A diocesan school was established in Nelson Street in 1812, which, being unsuccessful, was converted in 1856 into a trade school, taken over by the Society of Merchant Venturers, and transferred to Unity Street in 1885. No. 8, Unity Street, was added in 1899, and the Rosemary Street and Kingsdown Parade premises were added in 1903. The college includes a preparatory school and secondary day school for boys, who number about 360. The fees are £2 3s. 4d. a term; and there are evening classes for adults, for which 2s. 6d. to 10s. 6d. a session is charged, as well as the regular adult day students, who pay £10 10s. a year; and the total number of students in 1903 was 2,426. They enter for London Matriculation and Board of Education examinations, and become engineers of all kinds, chemists, surveyors, architects, teachers, civil servants, &c., on leaving the college. The principal is Professor Julius Wertheimer, B.Sc., B.A., who has a staff of 21 teachers under him, exclusive of visiting teachers and a large staff engaged for evening classes only. The school was burnt to the ground in 1906, and the classes are now held in various elementary schools, pending reconsideration of the whole establishment.

CLIFTON COLLEGE

The Clifton College Company was incorporated under the Companies Acts, 13 September, 1860, with a nominal capital of £10,000, in 400 shares of £25 each. The Rev. Charles Evans, assistant master at Rugby, formerly fellow of Trinity College, Cambridge, and Senior Classic 1847, was elected head master, and in September, 1861, opened the school in Arlington Villas, but just a year afterwards resigned on being elected to the head mastership of King Edward's School, Birmingham. Then came the Rev. John Percival, assistant master at Rugby, formerly fellow of Queen's College, Oxford, where he obtained double firsts in both mathematical and classical Moderations and Final Schools. By this time the building was sufficiently advanced for the schoolhouse and big school to be used, and the formal opening took place on 30 September, 1862. There were then 60 boys. The school was divided into classical and modern sides, and their numbers seem to have been nearly in the same proportion from the first.

A junior school was opened in April, 1863, at 7 Rodney Place, by Mr. Hartnell. In 1864 a second boarding-house was opened by Mr. T. E. Brown. New houses were added : in 1867, C. H. Lay ; 1870, E. Harris ; 1874, T. W. Lunn, 25 boys ; 1878, Jews' house, 30 boys, B. Heymann. In 1879 the numbers were limited to 600—460 in the upper and 140 in the junior school. A preparatory school for boys under 10 was started in September, 1874, in charge of Mr. Escott, at 4 College Terrace. In April, 1875, the day-boys were organized as houses, North Town under Mr. Wiseman and South Town under Mr. Tait, and consisted of 90 boys each.

On 19 December, 1864, the first stone of the chapel was laid, and it was licensed by the Bishop of Gloucester and Bristol on 15 June, 1867.

Organized school games began in the winter term of 1862 with Rugby football, and 'runs' were started with great vigour in the Easter term by H. W. Wellesley, the first head of the school. The great runs of the year are the 'Short Penpole' and 'Long Penpole' for the lower and upper 'packs' respectively, into which the school is divided.

The cricket has been on a high level from the first, Clifton providing many university players. The great match of the year is naturally against Cheltenham College.

The first number of the school magazine, *The Cliftonian*, appeared in December, 1867, and about the same time the debating society, which was started by a few boys in the schoolhouse, was thrown open to the sixth and fifth forms.

The Percival Library was built in 1870. A 'military side' was established in 1873, and contributes large numbers to Sandhurst and Woolwich every year. An engineer cadet corps was started in 1875, beginning with 100, and in 1878 the school eleven first competed for the Ashburton Shield at Wimbledon. In March, 1877, the school became a public school by a royal charter of incorporation, but there is no endowment beyond the site and buildings.

Dr. Percival resigned the head-mastership in 1879, having been elected President of Trinity College, Oxford. Another Rugby master, the Rev. James Maurice Wilson, succeeded him. He had been senior wrangler in 1859, and a fellow of St. John's College, Cambridge.

The Great Quadrangle was completed in 1890 with the Wilson Tower. The impressiveness of the buildings is much increased by the reddish-purple colour of the local stone used. During Mr. Wilson's last days at Clifton the last remaining available open space near the college and outside its territories was bought.[1]

Mr. Wilson was succeeded in January, 1890, by the Rev. M. G. Glazebrook, high master of Manchester Grammar School. He was a scholar of Balliol, and had been for ten years an assistant master at Harrow.

Mr. Glazebrook made various changes in the modern side, emphasizing the importance of English and improving the teaching of modern languages. That the classical side was in no way neglected under his care is proved by

[1] *Great Public Schools*, 'Clifton,' 219.

the fact that 14 first classes at Oxford and Cambridge were gained in 1902, the same number as in 1882.

Mr. Glazebrook retired to a canonry at Ely in 1906, and the Rev. A. A. David, fellow and tutor of Queen's College, Oxford, succeeded him. French and German have now become 'form' subjects on the modern side; and the teaching of English and history is being organized throughout the school, while more translation and less grammar grinding is being insisted on in Classics. In Forms V and VI a choice of specialization is offered in classics, mathematics, modern languages, science or engineering.

University College

A public meeting was held in Clifton on the 11 June, 1874, with the object of establishing a college in Bristol, which should combine technical training with general culture. Dr. Percival, then head master of Clifton College, now bishop of Hereford, and Dr. Jowett, master of Balliol, were among the chief movers, and subscriptions were raised, and a company incorporated under the Companies Act of 1862. The first session of the college was opened 10 October, 1876, under the presidency of Dr. Elliott, dean of Bristol, with a staff of two professors and four lecturers in the faculty of arts and science, and it was housed in temporary premises in Park Row. The Bristol Medical School, which was started with a course of lectures in 1814, and incorporated in 1832, was in 1893 incorporated with the University College, of which it became the faculty of medicine. A department of engineering was started in 1878. A day training college for women was affiliated in 1892, and a similar college for men in 1905; a secondary training department was added in 1902; lectures on law and on social problems are given under boards of legal and social studies.

There are now 9 professors, one assistant professor, 24 lecturers and 3 readers in the faculty of arts and science; 8 professors and 21 lecturers in the faculty of medicine. The buildings have cost upwards of £45,000.

The first principal, Professor Marshall, was appointed in 1877 and left in 1881, when he was succeeded by Professor, now Sir William, Ramsay, who held office till 1887. The present principal is Professor Lloyd Morgan, LL.D., F.R.S. There is a special tutor for women students, Miss M. J. Tuke. In 1904 there were 1,121 students in all—483 men and 638 women.

Clifton High School for Girls

A body of shareholders started this school in September, 1877, desiring no pecuniary advantage, but having the right of nominating pupils at a slightly reduced rate. The fees are from £3 3s. to £8 a term, and there are about 220 pupils under Miss Catherine S. Burns with a staff of 12 teachers, mostly from the universities, besides visiting masters and mistresses. The girls are prepared for London Matriculation and examinations of the Oxford and Cambridge Board.

A HISTORY OF GLOUCESTERSHIRE

REDLAND HIGH SCHOOL FOR GIRLS

This school is of much the same type as the last mentioned school. It was established in May, 1882, and is governed by a council of men and women who are co-opted. There are about 260 girls with Miss Elizabeth Ann Cocks, head mistress, and a staff of 12 mistresses, mostly of university qualifications. The fees are from £2 2s. to £5 5s. a term.

1. ST. GEORGE HIGHER GRADE AND TECHNICAL SCHOOL
2. MERRYWOOD HIGHER GRADE
3. HIGHER GRADE SCIENCE AND ART COUNCIL SCHOOL

These three schools are under the direct control of the Bristol Education Committee. The first was opened in August, 1895, in Church Road, the second in January, 1896, in Southville, and the third in November, 1898, in Fairfield Road.

They are all day schools for boys and girls, St. George having 540, Merrywood 420, and Fairfield Road about 162 pupils; and charge fees of from 3d. to 6d. a week. Pupils are prepared for London Matriculation and Board of Education examinations.

CIRENCESTER GRAMMAR SCHOOL

The first mention of Cirencester Grammar School, or rather its master, which is as yet forthcoming is in July (no day is given), 1242, when the schoolmaster of Cyrencester (*magister scolarum Cyrencestrie*) gave judgement as one of three judges in a case between Gloucester Abbey and the abbey of Lyra or Lire in Normandy, the priory of Acley, and Robert Foliot, rector of Fownhope, in favour of the defendants and against the abbey of Gloucester.

The *casus belli* was the right to the tithes of the chapelries of Ash and Strongford. The original judges appointed by the pope to hear the appeal were the abbot of Eynsham near Oxford, the prior of St. Frideswide's (now Christ Church, Oxford), and the dean (of Christianity) of Oxford. But they were all too busy to act. So as the case was to be heard in Cirencester parish church the abbot of Eynsham appointed the parish chaplain, the schoolmaster (*magistro scolarum*), and the warden of the hospital at Cirencester his deputies; the prior of St. Frideswide's appointed the sacrist and succentor of Cirencester Abbey, and the dean of Oxford appointed the dean of Cirencester and Sir Richard Poltevin as their respective deputies. One of the deputies of each original delegate sat. The fact that the schoolmaster was coupled, not with any of the officials of Cirencester Abbey, who were named as deputies by the prior of Oxford, but with two of the secular clergy, the parish chaplain, and the warden of the hospital, shows that he was the master not of the monastic school, the novices' school in the cloister, but of the public grammar school, the school of and in the town.

Whether the school was at this time endowed and who appointed the master does not transpire. But in 1458 John Chadworth, bishop of Lincoln, who had been a fellow of Merton College, Oxford, and was already an M.A. when made one of the first fellows of Henry VI's new foundation of

<hr/>

[1] Pat. 35 Hen. VI, pt. i, m. 6.

SCHOOLS

King's College, Cambridge, in 1443, and was a Cirencester man, obtained licence[1] for the foundation of a chantry of St. Mary in Cirencester, which was no doubt his native place. The chantry or Lady chapel is said still to contain his arms, azure a chevron, between three foxes' or wolves' heads erased or, which also appear in the window of the tower of the church. Unfortunately, instead of endowing the chantry itself with lands, the founder gave the endowment, probably a sum of money down, though possibly lands, to the abbey of Winchcombe, who undertook to pay a rent-charge or annuity, pension as it was then called, of £10 a year to the chantry priest, who was also a schoolmaster. This appears from the Valor Ecclesiasticus of 1535 and the Chantry Certificates of 1548. This endowment was a good one at the time, £10 being the pay of the head masters of Winchester and Eton. In 1487, when a subsidy was levied on the clergy of Worcester diocese for the archbishop of Canterbury,[1] Master Simond Morland, schoolmaster of Cirencester (*Magister Scolarum Cirencestrie*), paid at the highest rate, 13s. 4d., while two chantry priests of the Trinity and St. Mary and three stipendiary priests there paid at the lowest rate, 6s. 8d., which, it may be remarked, was also the rate at which the schoolmaster of Worcester paid.

There being no registers of Winchcombe or Cirencester forthcoming we know no more of the school till the Valor Ecclesiasticus[2] of 1535 records

> Humfrey . . master of the grammar school there has an annuity of £10 to himself for his exercise aforesaid (*pro exercitio suo*) yearly paid out of the monastery of Winchcomb for ever by the ordinance and foundation of Sir John Chedworthe formerly bishop of Lincoln £10, the tenth [payable to the crown] thence (*decima inde*) 20s.

It speaks well for the status of the school that there was a separate and distinct song school also kept in Cirencester, one of the stipendiary priest-ships in the parish church having been founded, or at all events applied, for the maintenance of a song school, which would be in part a preparatory school for the grammar school. For the Chantry Certificate of 1545[3] shows us

In the Deanery of Cirencestre

64. The parishe of Cirencestre,

> where are of houseling people the nombre of 1,400.

> Robert Ricardes seruice, *alias* St. Anthonies seruice or chauntry.

> Founded by one Robert Richardes, and Elizabeth, his wyff, and the landes and tenementes thereunto belonging putt in feoffment, to the entent to manteigne a priste, being a singing man, to celebrate at the alter of St. Anthonye in the seid churche, and also to teache frely 2 children from tyme to tyme to singe, to helpe the dyvyne seruice there, and to praye for the Founders sowles and all christien sowles for ever.

> Sir William Wylson, Incumbent there, of the age of 46 yeres, having no other lyving then in the seid seruice, which ys yerely, £6 0s. 14¾d.

> The landes and tenementes belonging to the same are of the yerely value of £7 13s. 5½d. Whereof

> In reprises yerely, 19s. 4d.

> And so remayneth clere by yere, £6 14s. 1½d.

---

[1] Worc. Epis. Reg. Marston, fol. 13.   [2] *Valor Eccl.* (Rec. Com.), ii, 447.
[3] A. F. Leach, *Engl. Sch. at the Reformation*, 81, from Chant. Cert. 22, No. 64.

The later certificate[1] of 1545 shows us that the endowment of the school, through being part of the Winchcombe Abbey property, though in trust, had been confiscated to the crown.

> The chauntry or servyce of our Ladye.
> The clere yerely value, £11 8s. 4d.
> Thomas Taylour, Incumbent, hath for his yerely Stypend, £7.
> *A Schole taught by him at this presente.*
> *Continuatur the schole with the accustumed wages quousque.*

> Memorandum : that this said towne of Cyrencester is an Auncyent Boroughe Towne. The greate numbre of People and the contynuall Accesse of the greater nombre Repayringe to the same Towne consydered, The Inhabytantes there are moste humble sutours, that it maye please the Kynges Maiestie and His mooste Honorable Counsell to lett theim hau therin stablysshed some learned man to teache a Grammar Scole for the vertuouse bryngynge vp of the youth there aboutes, where are many chyldren which heretofore haue been very rudely, ignorantly, and for lacke of suche a teacher, symplye brought vp, and withoute knowlege, tyll within these three yeres Paste, sythens which tyme the aforesaide Parishoners, with their whole assentes, dryven therunto of grete necessytie, did appoynte one of the abouesaide servyces in their saide Churche, called our Ladye servyce, to be conuerted to the Kepinge of a Scole, And the Incumbent therof, named (as is aforesaide) Syr Thomas Taylour, hath very diligently applyed him self in teachinge of childrene, and hath hadd for his Salarye yerely £7 and his Mansion howse.
> In whiche saide Towne, till the Dissolucion of the Monasterye of Wynchecome, there was Graunted and payed oute of the same Monasterye one yerely Pencion of £10 to and for a Free Scole there, to be maynteyned and Kept ; sythens the Dissolucion of whyche Monasterye the same yerely pencion of £10 hath been withdrawen, and not payed, vnto the grete discommodytie of the same Towne of Cirencester.

At the end of this certificate, which is not one of the regular certificates made by the Chantry Commissioners, but a sort of abstract or report on further inquiry made by Thomas Sternehold, 'partycular Surveyour' for the county, is a recommendation. 'Places for Grammer Scoles to be newly erected. The townes of Newent, Cirencestour, Tewkesbury, Cheltenham in the aforesaid countie of Gloucter.'

Meanwhile the school was continued by warrant of the Chantry Commissioners for Continuance of Schools, signed by Sir Walter Mildmay, 20 July, 1548.[2]

Accordingly we find in the Ministers' Accounts[3] in 1547–8 the item of £7 paid to Thomas Taylor, schoolmaster (*ludi magistro*) of the grammar school founded by our Ladye Chantry in Cirencester, by virtue of a warrant signed by Walter Mildmay one of the commissioners and supervisors of the Court of Augmentations. The same payment is continued throughout the reign of Edward VI and down to Michaelmas, 2 Philip and Mary 1534.[4] The payment then ceases. The Roman reaction among other things put a stop to the Court of Augmentations, and apparently the Court of Exchequer refused to pay any of the schoolmasters continued by these warrants unless and until they sued for them in the Court of Exchequer, where they do not appear to have got them, except on proof of orthodoxy and by way of a new grant.

The school, however, seems to have been continued by means of another chantry endowment which escaped the Chantries Act. It was stated in some legal proceedings in 1587 that, after Thomas Taylor, one Baker was

---

[1] A. F. Leach, *Engl. Sch. at the Reformation*, 84, from Chant. Cert. 23, No. 40.
[2] Exch. L.T.R. 2 Eliz. Hil. pt. i, R. 6.   [3] P.R.O. Mins. Accts. 1–2 Edw. VI, 107.
[4] Land Rev. Rec. Accts. 1–2 Phil. and Mary, bdle. 28.

appointed master by the bailiff, treasurers, churchwardens, and other the masters of the town, and received £6 or £7 a year from them. On 22 January, 1559–60, after application to the Court of Exchequer by William Arderne or Alderney, who said that though he and his predecessors had always done their work well and faithfully, the stipend ordered by the Chantry Commissioners had been withheld, letters patent were issued for the restoration of the payment. It was accordingly made at the old rate of £7 a year to William Arderne till Michaelmas 1582.[1] Yet, though the Ministers' Accounts record this payment yearly to William Arderne, when on 12 June, 1570,[2] the Court of Exchequer issued a commission to Richard bishop of Gloucester, as to whether certain schoolmasters to whom stipends were paid out of the exchequer were suitable persons, and the schools in proper places, on 17 October certain parishioners came before the vicar-general in Gloucester Cathedral, and their testimony was as follows :—

> The presentment and declaration of John Apennyngton, John Keyle, Henry Hopkins and William Aprice, parishiners of Cyceter, to the contents of the Queen's Highnees Commission, First we find and testify that we receive the sum of seven pounds yearly (deducting the portage money) to the use of our grammar school of Cyetr. Item we find and testify that our school of Cycetre aforesaid is well tidily and decently kept, continued and maintained. Item we find and testify that our schoolmaster named Anthony Ellys, B.A. is a sufficient meet well approved and able man to teach grammar and teacheth his scholars diligently. Item we say and believe that the said grammar-school cannot be placed in any other place more conveniently than where it is placed for the increase of learning.

On 8 October, 1571, the return of the bishop[3] to a further commission dated 4 July, 1571, as to due payment of the stipend and wages of £7 a year to William Arderne, schoolmaster, of the grammar school in the town of Cirencester, so granted to him by decree of the Court of Exchequer dated 2 January in the second year of Queen Elizabeth, states on the evidence of John Keyle, Philip Maryner, William Aprice, and Thomas Feryby :

> Cirencester. The scholemaister receives the sum of 20 marks yearly, and has been well paid. The £7 which we have allowed yearly by the Queen's Majesty is truly paid. The scholemaister is learned. The schole is in a convenient place and well kept.

Whether we are to infer from these returns that William Arderne was the schoolmaster and that he received the crown stipend but paid it in full to Anthony Ellys, B.A., who was usher, or whether Arderne's name was merely continued to save trouble, is not clear.

In 1582–3 the Ministers' Accounts[4] show an increase of the crown payment from £7 to £20.

> £20 aid to William Arderne, £7 as before and £13 increase for one undermaster (*hipodidasculus*) called an usher, to assist the schoolmaster for the better education of the scholars, by a warrant signed by William, Lord Burghley, Lord Treasurer, and Walter Mildmay, Chancellor of the Court of Exchequer, dated 21 November, 1583.

This payment is continued next year to William Arderne, but in 1584–5 is made to Thomas Helme.

[1] Land Rev. Rec. Accts. bdles. 28, 29, 30.   [2] Exch. Spec. Com. 12 Eliz. No. 867.
[3] Ibid. 13 Eliz. No. 868. The Commission is in Latin, the return in English.
[4] Land Rev. Rec. Accts. bdle. 30.

The increase was it seems due to a petition from George Lloyd and others, in the course of which it is stated that the school flourished under Ellys with 100 to 120 scholars, sons of gentlemen and others.

Helme or Helmes proved unsatisfactory. The local magnates tried to turn him out, and in 1587 he complained to the Court of Exchequer. In the course of the proceedings it appeared that the crown stipend of £7 had not been the sole revenue of the school but that the property of a chantry called Jones's chantry had been applied to the school. This chantry had been founded in 1508 for 60 years only, with a gift over at the end of the term for repairing the church, making and repairing highways, and doles to the poor at the discretion of the feoffees; so that not being perpetually devoted to 'superstitious uses' it had escaped confiscation under the Chantry Act. Helmes now complained that the feoffees withheld the income of Jones's lands from him. He declared that in 1567 the feoffees had by deed indented assigned £8 to the schoolmaster's stipend, and alleged that about eight years ago, Henry Elrington, for seven years running churchwarden, envious perchance at this stipend of £8 disposed to so good a use, did along with the others begin to oppose the payment, and afterwards when the crown had increased its endowment to £20, they had retained the £8 unthankfully as towards the crown, contrary to all equity and good conscience, and dead to the hindrance of good learning. A commission of inquiry was upon this issued to Sir Henry Poole and others. Henry Elrington and the rest said there was no certainty about Thomas Taylor's appointment, but that after him one Baker, schoolmaster, and his successors had been nominated, chosen, and admitted by the bailiff, treasurers, churchwardens, and others the masters of the town, with a stipend of £7 from the exchequer, and £6 or £7 more added by them. The schoolmaster had always been removable upon a quarter's or half-year's notice by the churchwardens, with consent of the bailiff and others, if there were cause of dislike. But when the queen augmented her £7 to £20, the treasurers, &c., thinking that to be enough, had employed their £7 in repairing the church, at the present greatly in decay, and likely to be more ruinous if it be not foreseen, also in amending some of the decayed houses of Jones's trust, in repairing of highways, and the poor. Moreover Thomas Helmes is so unskilful and slack that his scholars do not profit, and the school has dwindled down to 40 scholars, all which being considered by the bishop of Gloucester and the defendants, they gave half a year's notice to Thomas Helmes before the augmentation up to £20 was settled, so that they might provide a better schoolmaster. Albeit he Thomas Helmes hath heretofore proudly said that he will be schoolmaster in spite of the most part of the parishioners; all which indiscreet speeches, and lewd bearing, and other causes considered, they prayed the court to let them as before have the nomination of the schoolmaster. As to the £7, when the half-year's notice was expired, as they much disliked the contempt and obstinacy of the man in not departing, they had detained it, as was lawful according to the terms on which it was granted, but it was detained for no other cause, and not at all for the hindrance of learning. Thereupon the court considering that it was needful to have an usher in the said school, ordered the disputed stipend, which they fixed at £8, to be employed ever in maintaining an usher in the said grammar school, and the schoolmaster for the time being to be content with the £20 given by Her Majesty. It was also ordered that Helmes should be examined by the bishop of Gloucester and Dr. Rudd, the dean, concerning his abilities to teach and aptness to train up scholars, with power to remove him if they thought good.[1]

In the result Helmes was continued as schoolmaster, for his name appears as such as late as 1614, at which date the regular entries in the vestry book commence. But the churchwardens as plainly resisted the order concerning the payment of the £8 ; for on complaint of Helmes to the Lord Chancellor, in 1603, a Commission of Charitable Uses was issued under the Act of 1601, to Sir Henry Poole, Sir John Hungerford, George Master, esq., and others ; when a jury found that the churchwardens and others, as feoffees of Jones's lands, had by deed indented in 1567 apportioned £8 yearly to the free grammar school, which £8 having been regularly paid to the schoolmaster from 1567 to 1583, had since that time been withheld and detained.[2] A decree now finally settled the payment of the £8 as obligatory. Under the order power was given to the master to receive the £8 from the tenants of Jones's land direct ; but afterwards, on petition to Lord Chancellor Bacon by the churchwardens, this order was varied and the payment was again entrusted to the feoffees.

The suitable place in which the school would appear to have been held— in 1570—was Dyer Street, for in a list of unsold fee-farm rents arising from ancient chantry lands, &c., in 1649 appears a tenement in Dyer Street called the Schoolhouse.[3] In 1534 Elizabeth Tolle, widow of Robert Richard, formerly bailiff of the town and founder of the chantry of St. Anthony, bequeathed £10 towards ' the repairing of a new schoolhouse.'[4] The word ' repair ' is similarly used in a will of 1492, concerning the new porch of the church, *ad reparationem novi porticus*.[5] Whatever was done then, the building was much out of repair at the beginning of the seventeenth century, but owing to the general dissatisfaction with Mr. Helmes nothing was done to remedy matters. Accordingly in May, 1609, he wrote as follows :—

> To the right honorable the Earle of Salisbury Lord high Treasurer of England. Maie it please your good Lordship to understand that after many petitions exhibited to the late Lord Treasurer for the repairinge of the Kinges Majestie's free grammer schoole within the Towne of Cirecester he graunted a survey to be made of the same schole, which survey was accomplished and delivered to his Lordships handes according to his commandment, and the content thereof was, that 200 poundes would not repair it, with a letter from my Lord Davers[6] to justifie the needfulnes thereof. Your poore supplicant Thomas Helmes, schoolemaister driven to povertie by reason of a suite dependinge betwixt him there being and some of the chiefest of that towne, for the recoverye of eight poundes by the yeare due unto the saide schoole, which suite did continue for the space of twentie and one yeares, being nevertheless contenanced by the right Hon. the old Lord Treasurer, your father, and Doctor Master,[7] as long as they did live, most humbly therefore pray your good Lordship to be a

---

[1] Exch. Dec. and Ord. Vol. 14, fol. 33a.
[2] Vestry Bk. 122a, b.
[3] Harleian MS. 5013, fol. 76.
[4] Will at Somerset House, Hogan, quat. 17.
[5] Ibid. Doggett, p. 118.

[6] Henry Lord Danvers, afterwards created earl of Danby, was at that time the owner of what is now Lord Bathurst's Home Park, and built the first house there. His father, Sir J. Danvers, had bought the estate from Sir T. Parry, steward of Queen Elizabeth's household, who was the original grantee from the crown of that part of the abbey property.

[7] Dr. Master, physician to Queen Elizabeth, bought the site of the abbey with certain lands, and built the original modern Abbey House. He died in 1588. George Master, mentioned on this page, was his son.

meane to our most gratious Kinge which favoureth all goodnes, to bestow in timber or ells what shall seem good unto his majestie for the repairinge thereof, and your said supplicant shall according to his bounded dutie daily praie to God for your honnors' health and prosperitie.[1]

He did not get much by this letter, for the endorsement on it is : 'I am not to sollicite his majesty in other men's suites, especially in matters of this nature.'—R. SALISBURY.

So the school buildings continued out of repair apparently during the remainder of the tenure of Mr. Helmes. Helmes regularly received the crown stipend up to Michaelmas, 1621.[2]

In 1622 Henry Topp, who matriculated at Oriel College, Oxford, 8 May, 1607, and took his M.A. degree 5 May, 1620, was appointed, presumably by the bishop on the authority of the foregoing order.[3] All seems to have gone well till April, 1639, when Mr. Topp was complained of, and the vestry ordered him to be more diligent and forthwith to provide an usher ; and in the next month as he had paid no attention to their order they gave him notice to leave. They would not do any repairs to the school and he had to do them at his own cost. The buildings were then repaired.[4] In 1641 he agreed to go for £80. But having got the £80 Topp still held on, and did not finally give up possession till early in 1646.[5] So says Mr. A. E. Fuller in *Bristol and Gloucester Arch. Soc. Trans.* ; but if he retained possession of the master's house, he did not receive the stipend or teach school. For we learn from a certificate made 30 Oct. 1651, to the parliamentary authorities for sale of fee-farm rents of the stipends payable to schoolmasters and vicars, that William Taylor,[6]

who succeeded in the room of Henry Topp, received the said stipend for the years 1644 and 1645, and likewise Hector Foorde (*sic*) the present schoolmaster hath received the same for the years 1649 and 1650 ; the other years that are behind being unpaid, besides the year ended at Michaelmas 1651, and being 4½ years some of the townsmen of Cyrencester have byn suing unto the Committee of Revenue for the obliging thereof.

There being no bishop of Gloucester, the treasurers, minister, church-wardens, constables, &c., as of old exercised the right of election,[7] when Hector Foard, M.A., was appointed in 1646. The same manner of election was followed in March, 1660, when John Hodges was appointed,[8] on terms of keeping the school in repair himself. But the vestry in fact paid for repairs in 1663 and 1665.

John Gwynne was master about 1666. About 1678 a patent under the great seal was obtained for John Parkinson, who had been of Brasenose College, Oxford, for the payment of £20 for his life.[9] He was succeeded about 1683[10] by John Turner, who was of Wadham College, Oxford, and LL.D. Then followed John Reeves, also of Wadham ; Richard Arthur, about 1725 ; George Whitwick, about 1750 ; —— James, about 1755. He was the last appointed in the old way. Party feeling ran very high at that

[1] S.P. Dom. Jas. I, xlv, No. 78.   [2] Land Rev. Rec. Accts. 18–19 Jas. I, bdle. 39.
[3] Vestry Bk. 57b.
[4] Ibid. 50a–61b.   [5] Ibid. 56b–65b.
[6] P.R.O. Aug. Off. Particulars for Sale, portf. 6, files 46, 47, Certificates of Stipends of Vicars and Schoolmasters.
[7] Vestry Bk. 65b.   [8] Ibid. 73b.
[9] Ibid. 85b.   [10] Ibid. 92b.

time, and an application was made to the crown;[1] the result being that James was ousted, and a patent was issued to William Matthews of Repton School and Magdalen Hall, Oxford, about 1756. He was succeeded by his stepson, John Washbourn, about 1774. In his time for many years there was not a single free scholar in the school; not as Rudder[2] explains, because Washbourn was incapable, or because the people did not care for education, but they sent their children elsewhere. Dr. Washbourn considered boarders from the country more profitable than town scholars, who were accordingly discouraged, and the few that did offer themselves, besides being made to pay quite otherwise than free scholars used to pay, were by him excluded from the free school seats at church, and put upon a very different footing from the boarding scholars, who numbered between 20 and 30. Umbrage was taken at this, and about 1780 the churchwardens began to charge him the same price for sittings as they charged other persons. In 1783 Dr. Washbourn dismissed all his boarders.[3] He seems to have returned to Oxford, as he was vice-president of Magdalen in 1786, dean of divinity next year, and in 1797 bursar. Presumably he served the free scholars through an usher, as he retained the mastership till his death on 23 Nov. 1805.

The Grammar School continued on its old footing with varying fortunes under Rev. J. Buckoll, 1805; Rev. — Grooby, 1807; Rev. H. Wood, 1823; Rev. E. Wood, 1835; Rev. W. Bartrum, 1851.

When Mr. Stanton visited the school for the Schools Inquiry Commission in 1866[4] he found it desirable to repeat the old statement of Anthony Wood, which seems to be due to some confusion with another school, that it was founded by Bishop Ruthall (of Durham) in the early part of the reign of Henry VIII. We have already seen that it was founded by another bishop half a century before. There is no evidence that Ruthall built a schoolhouse or had anything to do with it at all.

Mr. Stanton found the buildings old and rambling and much out of repair, the trustees of Jones's charity refusing, in spite of 300 years' custom, to do any. 'To put the premises in decent repair would absorb the whole income for some years to come.' It is not surprising therefore that under the Rev. W. Bartrum there were only 25 boys, of whom 7 were boarders. 'It was about three weeks after the time for school after the Christmas holidays and 3 had not yet returned.' 'The upper class of 5 boys failed altogether in Latin and French . . . None understood decimals . . . a few had some notion of fractions.' The payments were 30 to 40 guineas a year for boarders; 4 guineas a year for day-boys. For at least five years, and probably much longer, no boy had gone to the University.

So things went on till Mr. Bartrum died in 1881. Then at last a new scheme was made under the Endowed Schools Acts by which the endowment given in 1722 by Mrs. Rebecca Powell for a Blue and Yellow School was added to that of the grammar school. The old buildings in Lawditch Lane were sold and new and good buildings erected in the New Road.

---

[1] Lord Bathurst had at a previous election tried to secure both seats for the borough for his two eldest sons, he having always before been content with one seat. This had produced great irritation, and the town in general was in opposition to Lord Bathurst. The calling in of the crown was a bit of retaliation (Kilner MSS.).

[2] Rudder's *Hist. of Cirencester*, 309.

[3] Kilner MSS.

[4] *Sch. Inq. Rep.* xv, 60.

Mr. S. Elford, M.A., retired in 1903. Under Mr. Arthur Cecil Kelway, M.A., from Somerset County School and Queens' College, Cambridge, appointed April, 1903, and four resident assistant masters, there are now over 100 boys, of whom 12 are boarders. Such have been the good results of a scheme.

WOTTON under EDGE GRAMMAR SCHOOL

The foundation of Wotton under Edge Grammar School is an interesting one in that it is the first we know of as being founded not by a successful cleric or merchant, but by a lady, and that as early as 1384. The lady was of high rank, Katherine daughter of Sir John of Clivedon, knt., and Emma his wife, and was married first to Sir Peter of Vele, and afterwards, 30 May, 1347, as his second wife, to Thomas, third Lord Berkeley, 'and was fruitful,' says the family chronicler, 'to her husband both in lands and children.' Lord Berkeley died in 1361, but she survived him 24 years, and it was not till nearly the end of her life that she founded the school. The original foundation deed is no longer to be found in its proper home, the school. But the whole process of the foundation, and the statutes or regulations of the school, have fortunately been preserved in a transcript in the Worcester Episcopal Registers.

The date of the foundation of Wotton under Edge School has been variously given hitherto as 1382[1] and 1385,[2] but it belongs in fact to the year 1384. On 16 June, 1384, for £20 fine paid by Walter Burnell and William Pendok, chaplains, King Richard II,[3] reciting the statute of mortmain, granted them dispensation from it and licence 'to erect a schoolhouse (*domum scolarum*) in a certain place in Wotton underege for the habitation or foundation of a master and 2 poor scholars of the art of grammar, the master and his successors to teach and inform all scholars coming to the same house, taking nothing for his labour from them or any of them.' In other words it was to be a free grammar school. Licence was also given to grant certain property specified for their support. A licence in similar terms was granted by Thomas, then Lord Berkeley, as immediate lord of Wotton, on 1 July, 1384. Then on 20 October, 1384, Katerina, or Kitherina as the register calls her, 'who was wife of Sir Thomas of Berkeley, lord of Berkeley,' with the two chaplains, her agents and trustees, executed the foundation deed, which reads very much like an echo of the foundation deed of Winchester College executed by William of Wykeham two years before, though probably both are derived from earlier examples.

> We the said Katherine attentively considering that the purpose of many desiring to be informed in grammar, which is the foundation of all the liberal arts, is daily defeated and frustrated by poverty and want of means; therefore for the maintenance and exaltation of holy mother church, and the increase of divine worship and other liberal arts and sciences, out of the goods bestowed upon us by God have procured the said Walter and William to acquire certain lands and tenements in fee, that they may newly build a school house in

[1] *Sch. Inq. Rep.* xv, 125.
[2] *Char. Com. Rep.* xvii, 34. Carlisle, *End. Gram. Schools*, i, 408. The discrepancy is due to the usual error of identifying the almanack year with the regnal year. The whole process was done between 16 June, 7 Ric. II, and 20 October, 8 Ric. II, both of which fall in A.D. 1384, that king's accession having been on 22 June, 1384.
[3] Pat. 7 Ric. II, pt. ii, m. 3; and *Cal. Inq. p.m.* iii, 64, Nos. 123 and 124.

SCHOOLS

Wotton-under-Edge for the habitation or foundation, and likewise dispose of them for the maintenance, of a master and two poor scholars of the art of grammar; which master and his successors shall govern and inform all scholars coming to the same house or school [1] coming for instruction in this art without taking anything for his trouble from them or any of them.

Then the two chaplains convey the property and found 'a perpetual house of scholars [2] of one master and two poor scholars clerks living college-wise therein for ever' (*pauperum scolarium clericorum collegialiter vivencium.*) They then say they have appointed John Stone, priest and M.A., as master to teach and keep school in the same (*ad scolas in eadem regendas sive gubernandas*); and now admit the two poor scholars-clerks John Beenlye and Walter Morkyn, to live together according to statutes to be made by them and Lady Berkeley. They then set out the property conveyed 'to be held in common (*communiter et in communi*) by the master and scholars-clerks.' The school-house with 2 acres of land, and seventeen messuages with their appurtenances, in Wotton itself; a garden of 2 acres held by Richard Panyter, six messuages, three tofts, 66 acres of arable land, 15 acres of meadow, 20 acres of pasture, 10 acres of wood, 10s. 7½d. rent, and a rent of one bunch of cloves in Nubbeleye (Nibley), Stancombe, and Woodmancote held by John Oldelond, clerk; and other lands in Nibley belonging to various persons, viz. two messuages, 24 acres of land and half a virgate, and a mill; and lastly, 10 acres in Stancombe. The deed was witnessed by Thomas, fourth Lord Berkeley, the grandson of Thomas III, by his brother Sir John Berkeley, and by Sir Peter of Veel, Sir Thomas Fitznichol, Sir Thomas of Veel and Sir Edmund of Bradeston, knts., John Sergeaunt of Stone, whom we may perhaps take to be a relation of the first master, John Stone, priest, and others.

The statutes follow. The first of them required, unfortunately for the future of the school, that the master should always be a priest, and should celebrate in the Lady chapel of the manor of Wotton when Lady Berkeley or other lords or ladies of the manor were there, and otherwise in the parish church of Wotton, for the souls of the then Berkeleys, Katherine, Thomas and Margaret his wife, John and Elizabeth his wife; for Thomas Lord Berkeley her husband, Peter of Veel her former husband, Sir John of Clyvedon and Emma his wife, her father and mother, and all the ancestors and parents of the said Thomas and Katherine, 'without taking any stipend or salary except the rents and profits given at the first foundation or hereafter to be given.' The master was to be appointed by the Lady Katherine during her life, and afterwards by the heirs of Lord Berkeley or his brother, or in default by the lord of the manor of Wotton for the time being; except that if the manor through minority or otherwise came into the king's hands, the abbot of St. Augustine's, Bristol, was to appoint. The appointee was to be presented to and instituted by the bishop of Worcester. The property was to be managed by the master, who out of the income was to provide the two

---

[1] *Scolam*, the house being spoken of, not the institution, is singularly in the singular.

[2] The reading of the words varies between *domus scolarum*, or schoolhouse, and *domus scolarium*, or house of scholars. But there is no doubt that while the house is spoken of as schoolhouse, the name of the institution was 'House of Scholars,' in imitation of the title of the House of Scholars of Merton, otherwise Merton College, Oxford. In like manner Lady Berkeley calls the two boys scholars-clerks, which was the proper legal title of boys at school or youths at the University. The 'warden and scholars-clerks' was the corporate title of Winchester College. We may remember Chaucer's 'clergeon' or little clerk for the boy at school in the Prioress's tale, and 'the clerk of Oxenford' for the undergraduate in the prologue to the *Canterbury Tales*.

poor scholars-clerks with all necessaries, except clothing and shoes, and take the rest for himself.

On admission the masters were to take their corporal oath

to teach school (*scolas regant*) faithfully and govern usefully according to their power, and to receive kindly all scholars whatsoever howsoever and whencesoever coming for instruction in the said art of grammar, and to duly inform them in the same art, without exacting claiming or receiving any benefit or gain for his pains in the name of stipend or salary, by reason of which the master may be accused of canvassing for money (*de quo poterit argui ambicio magistrorum predictorum*).

The holidays allowed were at Christmas from St. Thomas's Day (21 December) to the morrow of the Epiphany (7 January); at Easter from Palm Sunday to the Sunday after Easter; at Whitsuntide from Saturday before Whit Sunday to the Monday after Trinity Sunday; and in the autumn from St. Peter ad Vincula (1 August) to the Exaltation of the Cross (14 September). This is an extremely important ordinance, as it is sometimes said[1] that there were no holidays at school in ancient times except saints' days.

The scholars-clerks were not to be over ten years of age when admitted, ' but assuming ability we do not mean to interdict their admission under that age.' They were to stay for six years attending school (*scolis intendentes*) and obeying their master, and were not to be put by the master to perform any services or do any tasks, but to be kept continuously at their learning and studies (*sed erudicioni et studio continue vacare compellantur.*) If they were idle or disobedient, or refused to submit to chastisement, they could be removed on proof of the matter before the patron or his steward.

The master also was removable by the patron for offences against the statutes after three warnings. If through age or other cause, not his own fault, he had to give up teaching, his successor was to pay him a pension of five marks a year.

Not another word is said throwing any light on the inner life of the school, its curriculum or hours. No doubt these were strictly regulated by custom.

Very shortly after the completion of the foundation, on 13 March, 1485–6,[2] the foundress died and was buried by the side of her second husband in Berkeley Church.

The episcopal registers enable us to obtain a tolerably complete list of masters up to the Reformation. John Stone, though already master before the execution of the foundation deed, was not formally presented to the bishop till 3 August, 1387[3] ' to the perpetual school house (*ad domum scolarum*) late founded by Lady Katharine of Berkeley deceased, in which no one had yet been instituted ', so the said bishop formally admitted him and instituted him perpetual chaplain in due form of law. Oddly enough, though this institution was thus solemnly entered in the register, it was not until 29 December, 1390,[4] that the bishop bethought him of the necessity of confirming the foundation and statutes, when the documents were all duly copied

---

[1] e.g. in Kirby's *Ann. of Winch. Coll.* whom I have followed in *The Schoolboy's Feast.* The fact is that Winchester being wholly, as far as the scholars were concerned, a boarding school, and the boys coming from places so far off as Devonshire, Lancashire, Cheshire, and Wales, they could not all in early times go home for the holidays. But the holidays seem to have existed all the same.

[2] *Lives of the Berkeleys*, i, 346.   [3] Worc. Epis. Reg. Wakefield, fol. 48.   [4] Ibid. fol. 71.

into his register and formally ratified and confirmed, and so he preserved them for our information. The next mention of the school is on 13 September, 1405,[1] when William Hesulton, 'Warden (*custos*) of the perpetual house of scholars of Wotton-under-Edge,' was ordained acolyte 'to the title of the same house.' He was made subdeacon the same day, and deacon on 18 December, 1406,[2] when he is called master (*magister*). The ordination was no doubt to qualify the new master according to the statutes. On 26 October, 1407,[3] John Semour was presented to the perpetual chantry of Wotton under Edge, vacant by the death of William 'Hasleton'. John James came next, Mr. William Clyfton being on 16 February, 1415-16[4] admitted 'to the perpetual chantry of the house of scholars of Wotton vacant by the resignation of Sir John James' on presentation of Thomas Lord Berkeley.

On 21 August, 1423,[5] Thomas Joye, rector of Bromham, was admitted 'chaplain of the chantry perpetual of the school house (*scolarum* is written in full) of Wotton by exchange with Sir William Hogyn, chaplain of it, on presentation of the honourable man Sir John of Berkeley, knight.' On 2 June, 1427,[6] Sir John Paradys was admitted to the 'perpetual chantry otherwise called school house' on the free resignation of Sir Thomas Joye. Paradise held for no less than thirty years, when he resigned, and on 18 December, 1456,[7] Mr. Walter Frouceter was admitted 'to the school house and also to the chantry of Wotton subtus egge,' on presentation of Sir Maurice Berkeley of Beverstone. It was arranged that Paradise (as he is now called) should have a pension to be settled by the bishop. On 30 September, 1460,[8] on death of Sir Walter Frouceter, Sir Robin Haynys, chaplain, was admitted; but only four months later he died and was succeeded by Sir John Dale, 16 January, 1460–1.[9] He resigned for Sir John Town,[10] 5 November, 1462, who in his turn resigned, to be succeeded 30 July, 1465,[11] by Sir Richard West. He enjoyed no less than twenty-two years' tenure. On 2 July, 1487,[12] Mr. John Parker was admitted 'to the chantry of Wotton-undyr-egge' on presentation of Edward Berkeley. On 23 July, 1493,[13] on resignation of Mr. John Packer (*sic*), LL.B. 'John Chylcote, M.A. in priest's orders' was admitted 'to the perpetual chantry or house of scholars in the parish church of Wutton-under-Dege' on presentation of Edward Barclaye (*sic*), knight of the king's body. Chilcote was a fellow of All Souls College, Oxford, so the school held a good position.

On 24 April, 1511,[14] on resignation of Chilcott (*sic*), Robert Coldwell, B.A. was appointed

> to the chantry, mastership and wardenship of the house of the school and scholars (ad cantariam magisterium atque custodiam domus scole et scolarium ') of Wotton-under-egge on the presentation of the abbot of St. Augustine's, Bristol, the lordship of Wotton being in the king's hands by reason of the minority of Maurice Berkeley.

In 1539[15] the *domus scolar' de Wotton* is entered in the list of ecclesiastical benefices on which the king was entitled to the tenths, as 'worth clearly in

[1] Worc. Epis. Reg. Clifford, fol. 42*b*.
[2] Ibid. fol. 46*b*.
[3] Ibid. Sede Vac.
[4] Ibid. Thos. Peverell, fol. 15.
[5] Ibid. Philip Morgan, fol. 23.
[6] Ibid. Thos. Polton, fol. 19*b*.
[7] Ibid. John Carpenter, fol. 140.
[8] Ibid. fol. 155*b*.
[9] Ibid. fol. 157.
[10] Ibid. fol. 175.
[11] Ibid. fol. 189*b*.　[12] Ibid. John Alcock, fol. 19.
[13] Ibid. Morton.
[14] Ibid. Sylvester de Giglis, fol. 68.
[15] *Valor Eccl.* ii, 494.

rents and farms per annum £11 12s. 6½d., besides chief rents of 18s. 1d. a year to the king, 12s. 4d. to William Berkeley, and 6½d. to James Berkeley.' The names of the incumbents of benefices in Gloucestershire are not given, but we know from the subsequent returns under the Chantries Acts of 1545 and 1547 that Robert Coldwell was still in office.

It is a strange thing that both these chantry certificates made under the Acts of Henry VIII and Edward VI called the foundress Katharine Vele, and the school the Vele School, as if the founder had married Vele after Lord Berkeley, whereas she was Lady Vele for only a few years, and Lady Berkeley for the last twenty-nine years of her life. Yet we can hardly suppose that the parishioners who furnished the information on which the certificate was based invented the name. The use of the name leads one to suppose that the property given to the school was property the lady had acquired from her first husband, and almost to suspect that in founding the school she was carrying out, not her own design, but the will of her first husband who had died forty-one years before.

Henry VIII's Chantry Commission reported[1] under 'Wotton-under-Hedge,' 'Katheryn Vele Fre Scole foundyd to fynd a Scole maister and 2 pore scolers for ever and to hav the value of the landes, which is worth by yere, £17 15s. 2d. Vele Scole is nere the church.' The income is set out ; and payments 'for the maister,' whose name is not given, of £10 1s. 7¼d. and 'for one scoler, £4 ' and after deduction of rents resolute, 22s. 3½d.,[2] fees 28s. and the ' kynges tenthes' (showing that it was valued as an ecclesiastical benefice), 23s. 3½d., ' so remayneth, nil.'

Edward VI's Chantry Commissioners, who said there were 800 houseling people, i.e. communicants, in the parish, representing a population of some 4,000, reported

> Wotton Fre Scoole founded by one Lady Katheryne Vele for the findinge of a mayster there freely to teache gramer and for two poore scolars also there to be founde with the pro-fittes commyng of the same landes. Sir Robert Coldwell, scolemaister there, of the age of 60 yeres, being unweldy, and for that purpose neither mete in desciplyne nor behaviour, and hath no other lyving then the seid scolemaistership which ys yerely ,

The figure was never filled in. The whole of this entry is, however, crossed out in the original certificate, and written instead is a

> Memorandum that there is within the said parishe a free scole of the foundacion of oone Ladie Katheryn Veele, whoe gave certeyn lands and tenements to the yerelie value of £16 14s. 8d.

(No two values in the two sets of certificates agree) 'for the findinge of a mayster there to teach gramer freelye and for 2 poor scolers there also to be mayntayned and founde with the issues and profittes thereof.'

The effect of the substitution of the memorandum for the certificate was a finding that the school was not a chantry within the meaning of the Act. So the school escaped at the time the confiscation of its property and went on. But it did not escape subsequent attacks from the hunters after what were called ' concealements,' attorneys mostly, who ferreted out lands, which the crown might claim as passing under the Acts for the dissolution of monasteries or of chantries, laid informations against the holders before the law

---

[1] A. F. Leach, *Engl. Sch. at the Reformation*, 79, from Chant. Cert. 21.
[2] Ibid. from Chant. Cert. 22.

officers of the crown, and obtained grants of the lands conditional on proving the crown title and paying the crown part of the plunder. To become informer of concealed lands became quite a profession.

The following is the account of these attacks given by James Smyth, steward of Lord Berkeley *temp*. Elizabeth and James I : [1]

> In the utmost skirt of this burrowe [2] or market towne, or rather in Synwell (as some will) one of the hambletts of the manor called Wotton Forren (which in this place doe adjoyne) standeth a free grammer schoole, founded in 8° Richard II by Katherine Lady Berkeley, and in the ordinances and statutes the said Lady and her feoffees ordained that the schoolmaster should daily pray in the church of Wotton for the soules of her self, her father, mother, husband, and of others ; whereby through the statute of 1 Edward VI for the dissolucion of chantries it is now supposed to come to the crown. Whereupon divers patents were in the raigne of Queene Elizabeth and of King James, passed of the schoolhouse and lands as concealed (i.e. concealed from the crown so as to prevent them passing to the crown under the Act). Whereby much trouble and expence were occationed ; which soc continued till by the sole presente of myself, tenant to such part of the schoolhouse lands as lye in Nibley with my expence of £700 at least, as is knowne to you, the same was quieted by a Decree in Chancery in the end of King James his raigne. And the schoole of now incorporated with ordinances and statutes for the regulatinge thereof fittinge the present time and the doctrine of the Church of England ; in which condition it flourisheth at this day 1639 ; whereof I doe write here the lesse referringe him that desireth more to the records themselves, and to a sentence in the Star Chamber in the time of King Charles, against one Benjamin Crokey, almost ever since a runnigate in Ireland, in avoidance of the shame and punishment which now by the sentence of that Court to have byn inflicted upon him for his wicked liblinge and falsehoods ; and lately taken at Bristol upon his returne from Ireland, at this time a prisoner in the Fleetes at my suite, as both of you doe knowe, October 1639.

A very different tale is, however, told by other people in which Smith himself stands out as principal villain and defacer of the school. An inquisition taken on 19 September, 1621, found that a bill had been filed in the Exchequer by one Edward Byshope against John Smith as defendant to prove that the lands belonging to the school had been given to the crown by the Chantries Act, and an answer was put in by Smith, and a commission issued to take evidence, Smith pretending to defend the action, whereas in point of fact he had 'had the carriage of the commission and entertained Byshope at his house and endeavoured to prove the plaintiff's bill.' In fact the whole proceeding was 'a mere practice of the said Smyth to draw the foundacion within the statute of chauntries.' Further, a certificate to that effect signed by the archbishop of Canterbury and the bishops of London and Winchester was put in.

The depositions taken in the exchequer suit contain a most interesting picture of the school in the days of Robert Coldwell, the last of the pre-Reformation masters, and his successors. They were taken [3] at Stone 14 July, 1616. The oldest inhabitants, headed by John Moore, 'parishe clarke there, aged 83 years and upwards,' gave evidence. He said that the 'scholehouse, which hathe bene soe comonlye called since in the later tyme of Henry VIII and after, was more usuallie called the Chaunterye house.' Robert Coldwell 'usuallie called Sir Robert, who taught schoole in the said howse was called also the Morrowe Masse Preiste, for difference sake from two other preistes

---

[1] John Smyth's *Lives of the Berkeleys*, ii, 401–2.
[2] The borough only consisted of 60 acres, and dated from a grant of a fair and market 36 Hen. III, to have the same liberties and customs as Tetbury ; ibid. 399.
[3] P.R.O. Exch. Dep. Mich. 14 Jas. I, No. 23.

that were in Wotton, because the said Sir Robert did always singe and saye his masses in the mornynge.'

Moore was at school there three or four years before the end of the reign of Henry VIII, and during the first year of the reign of Edward VI 'till the masse was put down.' He and other boys helped Sir Robert

in his masses especially in the parte of the *Confiteor* and in the *Oremus pro animabus* and some other partes, and when he came to the *Memento* then they that helped in the said masses did take to theire master a libell or a paper wherein was the names of suche dead persons sett downe, as their friendes or kyndred desired there shoulde be prayed and remembered in the said masses, for every of which named they gave a penney, the odd penney whereof this deponent or his fellows most commonly had. Theire said master standinge before the alter and the waxe tapers that were allwayes kept burnynge standinge thereupon, alsoe this deponent and his fellowe in their surplices kneelinge there one on the one side of their saide master and the other on his other side uppon 2 cusheynes which were theire kept.

Sir Robert held the school lands and 'the tennants thereof came to a courte holden at the said schoolehouse or chaunteray house once in 2 yeres or oftener.' Sir Robert, though he was, as we saw, over sixty in 1548, 'kept him only to the schoole all King Edward's dayes as muche as his troubles woulde give him leave, being muche questioned about keepinge a yonge woman secretly in the said schoolehouse.' We may remember that the chantry commissioners had noted him as 'not mete in disciplyne nor behaviour.'

Moore named eight people still alive who had been with him in the school and assisted in the masses, including Thomas Pardye *alias* Mopars, who was afterwards belonging to the church at Berkeley, and Robert Thompson, 'afterwards clarke to oulde Sir Thomas Throckmorton.'

Thomas Plomer, aged 85, also remembered being a scholar, and said it was

thought to bee a pece of good learninge and a kynde of freindshipp to the parents in that part to have their children admitted to helpe the preiste . . . especiallie upon All Souls day (2 Nov.) when was rememberance of . . . soules most cheifely and in the richest robes.

And Sir Robert when he came to name the founders and pray for them would doe it with a verie greate obeysaunce and bowinge of his heade and bodye.' He named other boys of Combe, of Wortley, of Hawkesbury, who had been at the school with him. Thomas Cole, another 'old' boy, said that there were 'comonly aboute 20 or 30 schoolers at most tymes and seldom did any schooler staye above 7 or 8 yeares, but were then placed abroad.' He used to help to sing mass in his surplice 'as well as he coulde, wiche was but meanely, and did answer to certaine prayers in Lattine words, which he then understode not and hathe long since forgotten, as theire master beforehand had taughte him and others, whiche,' as he naively remarks, 'made theire fathers and mothers a great deale the more to esteeme of him and his masses.' He also mentions other boys who had helped in the masses 'for that the best sorte of the schollers did soe by turnes.' Another witness, Edward Dawe, 'broad weaver' (i.e. weaver of broad cloth), said that the 'ile' in which the mass was said came to be 'called Sir Robert's Ile for that he was preiste and schoole master there above 40 yeres, and outlived one or twoe generations of the other two preistes that in King Henry's dayes was in Wotton churche,' and told how he 'hath often tymes since talked with them (his school fellows) of suche old matters, as they have bene togeather havinge never dwelled farre asunder.'

Old Sir Robert came to an end at last, but not before he had seen the mass restored 'againe in Queen Marye's tyme, not longe before he dyed,' as Thomas Hewes, yeoman, aged 87, said :

> At whose buryall he this deponent was amongst a great many other people and all or moste of his schoolers ; and afterwards he (this deponent) had some of his bookes and papers that contayned the pedigree and names of the ladye that founded the said chauntry and schoole and of all the oldest of her house who were Berkeleys which papers he had till within 20 yeres past.

The next master was 'Master Knight,' who was never called the Morrow Mass priest, but kept the school there 'till he fell into trouble aboute the lands belonging to it and in thende was put out,' says Agnes Adams, in whose house old Sir Robert died. She remembered Knight before he was 'shaven and made preiste and did weare a long yellow bearde, which when it was shaven and his crowne also he seemed to be not the same man.' He seems to have been the Robert Knight who became B.A. at Oxford 20 October, 1540, M.A. 1545. About 1559 the first attack on the school lands was made, according to 'ould Moore,' who knew that Sir John Berkeley came 'when question was made to the saide landes by some that were come thither at that tyme to enquire about them and that by his meanes the same was stopped, and no more adoe was thereof made for 20 yeeres after, that ever this deponent hearde of.'

Meanwhile Sir Robert Coldwell had himself inflicted almost as bad a wound on the interests of his successors by granting a lease on 18 May, 1535, of the school lands at Nibley, then called Warren's Court, to one William Thomas for eighty-eight years at 48s. a year. To this lease John Smith became entitled on his marriage with Grace Thomas, William Thomas's daughter, in 1578.

The witnesses at the inquisition in 1619 said that about forty years before the second attempt was made on the school lands to bring it under the Chantries Act

> Then Master Thomas Duport, by the helpe of the old Lord Berkeley pacified the same again and afterwards when Master Stanton was schoolmaister under Master James Duport he stopped the matter again with other persons a third tyme, which he, ould Moore, knoweth because he was Master Duport's baylie of the schoolhouse lands and that stopping cost money.

This last stoppage appears to refer to an inquisition, held in 1588, which resulted in a grant by Queen Elizabeth of 31 March, 1589, to Charles Badghot and Bartholomew Yardley and their heirs of the school lands. As this grant would have superseded Smith's lease (it is stated in subsequent proceedings) Smith bought up the patentee's rights for £200.

By some means the school came to be a family appanage of the Duport family. An indenture is extant of 1 September, 1592, by which John Duport 'doctor of divinitie, master of Jesus College in Cambridge, and master of the perpetuall Scholehouse or grammer schole and two poore schollers clerkes founded in the towne of Wotton under edge,' leased to James Duport of Medhurst, Leicestershire, the whole of the capital messuage in Wotton and 'the manor of the said schole and all its property in Nibley and elsewhere, except only one chamber within the said schole house . . . and the usual place for the scholemaster to teach schollers in' for 99 years at a rent of 40s., and the duty of keeping the schoolhouse in repair, and also granted the reversion on the same lease. This lease was confirmed by Henry Duport of Shersted, Leicestershire, esquire, as the 'lawfull and undoubted patrone of the perpetuall scholehouse.' A more discreditable transaction can hardly be conceived. Apparently Master Stanton was allowed the use of the single chamber reserved, and the schoolhouse to teach school, as the deputy of this absentee pluralist and fraudulent lessee, John Duport. Probably this lease was arranged with John Smith, who for £100 bought the lease from James Duport in 1604, and four years later, by deed 3 August, 1608, bought the reversion on the lease for £300. This grant purported to be made by James Duport with 'Thomas Duport and John Duport the two poore collegiate schollers of the said schoole,' so that not content with robbing the schoolmaster by these fraudulent long leases they had filled up the poor scholars' places with members of their own family.

On 6 April, 1609, is preserved the admission by Henry bishop of Gloucester, of the next master, Edward Cowper, B.D., on the presentation of John Smith of North Nibley, 'true and undoubted patron of the same.' Another document records that John Smith was personally present and 'exhibited the resignation of John Duport, professor of sacred theology, of the said free school.' Cowper or Cooper took his B.A. degree at Trinity College, Oxford, in 1581, M.A. 1584, and was apparently a fellow of Merton when he became B.D. in 1591, and tutor to the son of Henry Lord Berkeley in the same year.[1] But whether Cowper was, any more than John Duport, the real and acting master seems doubtful. John Moore when re-examined under the commission of 1619 on behalf of the defendant John Smith, said: 'One Mr. Robert Pricharde is nowe Schoolemaster at Wotton free schoole and soe was under Mr. Duport before he soulde the launds, and veryely thincketh that he hathe all his mayntenance from the said defendant . . . . as well or better than he had before from Mr. Duport.'

The result of Bishop v. Smith was naturally a finding that the lands were concealed, and a fresh grant was made by James I, 15 December, 1617, to John Smith and an Anthony Clifton in fee-farm, so that Smith acquired a fresh title by royal grant.

Fortunately somebody pursued the contention under the Statute of Charitable Uses of 1601. By decree 13 January, 1603, the Lord Keeper, assisted by two judges, declared that the lands did not come to the crown, as the principal institution was for teaching grammar and not for superstitious uses; and that all the long leases were void. The lands were decreed to the school, and ordered to be surrendered to the crown to the intent that the same should be regranted. But in consideration of the long possession of Smith and the money he had expended, he was to be allowed a new lease for three lives at an increased rent of the third part of the value as ascertained by a survey made under the direction of the court. The survey showed the property to consist of 31 houses and 162 acres of land at a rent of £21 4s. 6d., though the true value was £121 17s. 2d. They therefore put the third part

---

[1] Foster, *Alumni Oxon.*

of the value to be £47 a year, out of which £26 13s. 4d. was to be given to the master, and £4 each to 5 poor scholars.

The premises were surrendered and a new patent granted on 24 May, 1624. By this the school was reincorporated by the name of ' Master and Schollers of the Free Grammer Schoole of the Lord Berkeley in Wotton Underege in the countie of Gloucester.' The scholars were now to be 5 in number or more, according to the income of the property ; and ' our well-beloved Edward Cooper, Bachiler in Divinitye,' was named ' to be the first and present master.' The nomination of future masters was vested in George Lord Berkeley and his heirs, 'and for default of such issue in the lord of the manour of Wotton Underege for the tyme being,' and on his default for 60 days in the mayor of Wotton. Power to make new ordinances was given to the patron with the consent of the bishop of Gloucester or his chancellor.

The ' Ordynaunces for the said Schoole ' annexed to the patent were not very interesting. The qualification of the master was merely that he was to be a ' religious, discreet, and learned man,' who ' shall inhabite and dwell in the said schoolehouse and teache Grammer Schollers there,' and upon him was cast the burden of keeping the school and house in repair. Instead of the foundation being, as designed by Lady Berkeley, open to the world on equal terms, it was provided that

> the master shall not demaund receave or take any somme of money or reward of the said schollers [i.e. the foundation scholars] or any of them for teaching them, nor of any other scholler borne or inhabiting within the said burrowe or village of Wotton Underege or North Nibley above the summe of 6d. the quarter for teaching them.

To what was to be done and taught in the school only two items refer. The first required that

> eache morning and evening at 6 of the clock contynuallye in the school house, prayer shall be said and a psalme sung by the Master and schollers in such sorte as is used in the Free Schoole of St. Paule in our citye of London and as is expressed in a little book thereof late printed.

The other (No. 9)

> that the scollers shall everye daye in the weeke that is not Sundayes or hollidayes be dilligently ymployed by theire master in the said schoole from 6 of the clock in the morning until 11, and from 1 of the clock in the afternoon untill 6 at nighte. Neyther shall it be lawful for the said Schoolmaster to graunt any playdayes . . . . save only Thursdayes in the afternoone, nor that neither if there be a hollidaye in the same weeke. Item our will and pleasure is that the said schollers be taught to write a fayre hand, to cypher and cast an accompte, and to use noe other language in the said schoole but Lattin, or in tyme of disporting themselves together, which place we will have alwayes to be neere the schoolemaster's house.

The visitor was to

> visite the Schoole house for reparacions, the master for his good behaviour and diligence, and the said schollers for theire fashionable carriage and proceeding in learninge, and to see these our constitutions put in execution.

On 7 July, 1624, Edward Cooper, still the nominal master, executed a series of leases in accordance with the decree and the letters patent. The main one to Smith himself is not among the eight leases now in possession of the governors.

Cooper died on 11 June, 1632, and John Smith, who had obtained a transfer of the patronage from Lord Berkeley, appointed John Turner, M.A., ' of Wiltshire, plebeian,' who had matriculated at Magdalen Hall, Oxford,

23 June, 1621, and became M.A. 15 June, 1626. After his retirement to a living on 28 June, 1640, Smith appointed Joseph Woodward, who covenanted to keep an usher or under master, a B.A. at least, if the number in the school was over 50. His successor, Mr. Thomas Byrton, was appointed by Lord Berkeley and Mr. Smith. He was himself a Wotton boy who had matriculated at Lincoln College 5 April, 1639, became B.A. in 1642, and M.A. 3 December, 1646. On 10 July, 1647, Byrton granted a new lease of the lands in Nibley to Smith, who made him covenant to resign the school when called upon under penalty of £500, so that if he or any succeeding master refused to renew this lease he could be turned out at a moment's notice. Thomas Byrton had a very long tenure, as a lease by him is extant among the school papers dated 14 November, 1687. Two of his sons, no doubt educated in the school, went to St. Edmund's Hall, Oxford, in 1665 and 1669 respectively.

From a deposition in the suit of Bennett v. Smith taken in 1715, we learn that a schoolmaster who left the school about 1703 was named Peirce, and that during the vacancy in the mastership after his departure, George Smith, grandson of John Smith of Nibley, had the school study and trunk broken open and purloined some documents.

Samuel Bennett, the next master, by contesting the usurped rights of the great-grandson of John Smith to the school property, saved the school from being starved to death. He was himself a Wotton boy, and 'before he went to the University spent some time as apprentice to a clothier in Wotton.' On 21 May, 1702, at the age of 19, he matriculated at University College, Oxford, and took his B.A. degree there 14 February, 1705–6. In April, 1706, he was appointed master 'at the request of some of the cheiff inhabitants' by George Smith, who then claimed the patronage. He was made to give a bond to resign when called upon to do so. Shortly afterwards George Smith obtained from Bennett a renewal of the lease of the school land at the rent of £32 10s. only without paying any fine. But in Trinity term, 1710, the Attorney-General at the relation of Bennett, with Richard Osborne, esq., who had been one of the poor scholars of the school, and John Austin, on behalf of themselves and all other inhabitants of Wotton, filed an information and bill against George Smith to set aside the lease of Warren's Court at Nibley and the other school lands which Smith had got into his possession, which were said to be worth £350 a year or more, ten times the rent which Smith paid for them.

On 16 December, 1718, the Master of the Rolls ordered the lease from Bennett to George Smith, and the bond for resignation to be delivered up ; but decided that the Smiths were still entitled to a lease of the original lands of Warren's Court at only one-third of the real value, but were to pay full value for the other lands at Nibley. On appeal the decree of the Master of the Rolls was confirmed 26 July, 1723, with a trifling exception as to some of the lands, and the defendants were ordered to pay £4,225 to the school. A scheme was confirmed by the court 1 March, 1725, by which George Smith's rent was increased to £60 a year, and the master's salary to £40 a year; the number of poor scholars was raised from 7 to 10, and they were to be distinguished by caps and gowns, while exhibitions were to be provided for them to the University.

SCHOOLS

The most important results of the case were that for the first time a body of trustees was appointed to manage the property, to consist of the mayor, the minister (i.e. the vicar) ex officio, and five others, who were to invest any superfluous rents in land, while the school was ordered to be rebuilt. The Smith family, in spite of the opposition of Lord Berkeley and the inhabitants, were left in possession of the power of appointing the master, and were given alternately with the trustees the nomination of the poor scholars.

The school was accordingly rebuilt, the cost of doing so allowed by the master in Chancery, 27 May, 1726, being £450, and, wonderful to relate, it only exceeded that sum by 12s. 4d. The large building thus erected is that still used for the school. It is of the grey stone of the district, with a grey tiled roof in two stories, and was said in 1801 to be sufficient not only for the day scholars but for 'the lodging and accommodation of a large number of boarders,' and was used for a dozen boarders until 1893.

On 1 August, 1726, Samuel Craddock Bennett, son of the master, and Benjamin son of Richard Pearse, apparently the former master, were admitted on the foundation, both of whom in 1732 were given exhibitions of £5 a year to Oxford. In 1727 we find : ' gave the boys that answered well at the examination 6s.,' which they no doubt preferred to prizes of books. In that year the first exhibition was given : ' paid Robert Bennett's son's allowance at Oxon for year £5.' On 10 June, 1728, it was agreed that a gallery should be built in the church for the boys.

Bennett held office till Lady Day, 1743, when he died, and Samuel Craddock Bennett, the ex-scholar, served the office for half a year till a new master was appointed. This was the Rev. Samuel Hayward, a Gloucestershire boy, of Exeter College, where he matriculated 15 March, 1723, and became M.A. in 1730.

Mr. Hayward was not a success. At a meeting of trustees on 26 November, 1746, it was agreed to petition the bishop to ' inquire into the conduct of the master because of the great detriment to the school as well through incapacity as by reason of a state of lunacy.' The bishop recommended paying Hayward £20 a year to go, but this he declined. On 30 June, 1747, the trustees resolved to pay Hayward no more. They paid Richard Smith, one of their University exhibitioners, who received £10 for his exhibition, ' for teaching the boys from Michaelmas to St. Thomas £7 10s.' From Midsummer, 1748, the Rev. Thomas Clissold—he afterwards appears as Clisson—who matriculated at Wadham College, Oxford, February, 1735-6, took his B.A. degree 1739 and M.A. 1744, was paid as master, to hold during the life of Mr. Hayward, who was thenceforward paid an annuity of £20. Clissold had for a pupil in his early days Edward Jenner, the inventor of vaccination. If Lady Berkeley's foundation had done nothing more than educate this one boy, supposing that his school education had any share in the result, it would have amply justified her name being esteemed among the benefactors of the world. It is fair to say that he finished his education at Cirencester school. The incubus of Mr. Hayward's annuity burdened the school finances until his death in 1780. One result seems to have been the suspension for a long time of any University exhibitions. But in 1767 ' Mr. John Cooper for the better support of his nephew, James Cooper, at the

University' received £20, and in 1772 Daniel Kysic succeeded him. He became a fellow and tutor of Oriel College, Oxford. Clissold died in the summer of 1788. He was succeeded by the Rev. Peter Monamy Cornwall, a scholar of Westminster School and fellow of Trinity College, Cambridge ; also vicar of Westbourne in Sussex.

In 1799[1] Nicholas Owen Smyth Owen, the descendant of the original John Smith, gave a farm in North Nibley called Starwell in exchange for a release of all the stolen lands which had been so intermixed with the proper Smith lands as to be unrecognizable. The exchange proved beneficial, as the income of the property which the school acquired had risen by 1819 from £107 to £136. In the year before Mr. Smyth Owen had sold the North Nibley estate to John Justin, including the patronage of the school.

In 1801 the income of the school having increased to about £400 a year, the master's salary was raised to £80 a year, and the exhibitions to £30. In 1818[2] Cornwall had as usher his son Eusebius Cornwall, who had been a poor scholar and exhibitioner from the school, and was also curate of Uley. Cornwall had boarders, charging fifty guineas for 'parlour boarders,' and thirty guineas for others. In 1824 the master's salary was increased by a 'gratuity' of £20 a year.

Lord Brougham's Commission of Inquiry concerning Charities on visiting Wotton in 1826 found 10 foundation scholars, each receiving £6 a year, and 14 others, making 24 in all, all being educated free. No mention is made of boarders. So they had probably been given up, owing to the advanced age of Mr. Cornwall, then 81 years old. This school was actually conducted by his son George, also an ex-gown boy and exhibitioner 'who appears to give satisfaction both as to morals and competency of learning.' In 1828 Cornwall's long reign of 41 years came to an end. In 1833 his grandson Peter Monamy Cornwall received an exhibition of £50 from the school at Cambridge.

The Rev. Joseph Barkett of Trinity College, Oxford, who succeeded to the mastership, held office for just 10 years. In 1839 the Rev. Benjamin Robert Perkins, who was then vicar of Wotton, and as such ex officio trustee of the school, obtained from the then patron, Mr. Jorkin, the appointment of master. Mr. Perkins was an undergraduate at Lincoln College, Oxford, in 1820; chaplain at Christ Church 1824 to 1831 ; and vicar of Wotton in 1829.

One of the earliest acts of the new head master, 28 May, 1839, was to appoint his eldest son to a probationary scholarship. Four of these had been instituted three years before to give education gratis, but without stipend. A year later the boy was admitted to a foundation scholarship before he had attained the statutory age of 10 years; another son was admitted a probationary scholar at the age of 8, and there were 3 more sons, who all in time held foundation scholarships.

The inevitable result of the merger in the master of the chairman of the trustees, one of whose main duties was to supervise the master, was the neglect by the master of his duties. This provoked an application to the Board of Charity Commissioners, 7 April, 1855, who certified the case to the Attorney-General. All that resulted was a scheme of 5 December, 1860, which increased the number of trustees to 17, required them—an

[1] *Char. Com. Rep.* xvii, 344.   [2] Carlisle, *Endowed Grammar Schools,* i, 497.

entirely novel and unwarrantable requirement—to be members of the Church of England, resident within 17 miles of Wotton, and raised the foundation scholars to 16 or 20, and provided that in future no master should hold a cure of souls. Tuition fees were to be charged at the rate of not more than £4 a year for Wotton and Nibley boys, and not more than £8 a year from elsewhere. The inefficiency of Chancery as an Endowed Schools Commission was perhaps never more clearly exhibited. The Schools Inquiry Commission six years afterwards found the vicar and schoolmaster, Mr. Perkins, drawing £180 a year. The usher, the Rev. C. Cripps, vicar of a parish five or six miles away, 'slept during the greater part of the week at the schoolhouse,' which was otherwise unoccupied. There were only 13 boys in attendance, though 16 were paid to come. Three only were more than 14 years old. Seven of them wrote 'fairly.' 'The arithmetic was very indifferent, none understood decimals, and but few fractions. Only one boy professed to have done Euclid or algebra.' The head boy, however, son of a neighbouring parson, could translate the Odyssey fluently.

Such were the results of an endowment which had now risen in value to £331 a year net.

At length in 1882 the vicar-schoolmaster retired. The Rev. J. P. Cranston was then appointed. He reduced the school to even lower dimensions than his predecessor, and to prevent further scandals the trustees bought the right of appointing the master from Colonel Robert Hale, under an order of the Commissioners, 25 January, 1884. On 26 June, 1886, a scheme under the Endowed Schools Act made by the Charity Commissioners was approved by Queen Victoria in Council. This created a governing body of eleven, two appointed by the petty sessions justices, four by the vestry, now by the Parish Council of Wotton, and the rest co-optatives. The tuition fees were fixed at £4 to £10 a year ; and all pay the same fees. Foundation scholarships are now attained by exertion in competitive examination and not by patronage. All clerical and denominational restrictions on master and trustees were abolished.

The Rev. Frederick William Morris of Shrewsbury School, scholar of Jesus College, Oxford, then second master of the Goldophin School, Hammersmith, was appointed head master under the new scheme. He found 5 boys ; soon got 12 boarders, and raised the numbers of the school to 70. In 1892 the old school buildings were completely rearranged internally, the master's dwelling-house being now devoted to school purposes. In 1894 a very complete chemical and scientific laboratory was built on a lavish scale.

In 1900 girls were admitted to the school, and boys and girls are now taught together in all the forms. This co-education has proved a very great success, the girls working well and inciting the boys to work better. In 1906 rooms were acquired where girls from a distance can have their luncheon, and the whole is under the supervision of a matron.

NEWLAND GRAMMAR SCHOOL

The Grammar School at Newland is one of considerable interest from several points of view. In the first place it was one of the products of that great educational movement which took place in the last decade of the first half of the fifteenth century, and seemed likely to anticipate the Tudor development, when it was abruptly checked by the Wars of the Roses. The movement seems to have taken its initiative from the efforts of the first generation of scholars of Wykeham's College at Winchester, in 1382 to 1412, who took the chief posts in church and state by storm, and were earnest to reproduce in other places the institution from which they themselves had ' come to great things.' The most conspicuous result of their efforts was the foundation by Beckington and Chicheley in the name of the king of St. Mary's College, Eton, and St. Mary and St. Nicholas, otherwise King's College, Cambridge. But Eton, first founded in 1440, was rivalled, and, for perhaps a century, eclipsed by St. Anthony's School, London, founded in 1441 by another Wykehamist, William Say, dean of St. Paul's and master of St. Anthony's Hospital, which was connected, and was affiliated to Oriel College, Oxford, by exhibitions there on the model of Winchester and New College ; while King's was equalled by Chicheley's foundation, also in the name of the king, of All Souls College and surpassed by Waynflete's Magdalen College, at Oxford, though the latter had to wait for its legal completion till the rival Roses had been united in the persons of Henry VII and his queen, while Corpus and Christ's Colleges at Cambridge, though on a lesser scale, were on the same model as King's College. Eton was a college and an almshouse with a grammar school attached. Of similar foundation was Archbishop Chicheley's Higham Ferrers College, Northamptonshire, 1437, Draper's Newport College, Shropshire, 1442, Wye College, Kent, 1447, and Bishop Stillingfleet's College of Acaster in Yorkshire about 1460. The Hospital and Grammar School of Ewelme in Oxfordshire, the Grammar School and Song School of Alnwick in Northumberland ; Sevenoaks Grammar School, Kent ; Wokingham Grammar School, Berkshire ; Towcester Grammar School, Northamptonshire, are others of the numerous grammar schools founded in the same twenty years.

Newland Grammar School was founded in the height of the movement and is of especial interest, in that it was not founded like most of those named, by successful clerical statesmen, who, being enforced celibates, were by custom, which in another form under Henry VIII assumed the force of law, almost bound to commemorate their names by charitable benefactions in their native places, but by a country gentleman, a married man, though one without heirs male of his body to perpetuate his name and lineage.

Thanks to the researches[1] of Sir John Maclean we know a great deal about the founder and his wife. Robert Greyndour was a son of Sir John Greyndour, knight, sheriff of Gloucestershire in 1405 and 1411, who had inherited from his mother, Margaret of Abinghall, the manor of Abinghall and half of the manor of Mitcheldean.[1] Sir John died in October, 1416, Robert succeeded to his estates, he married Jane, daughter of Thomas Rigge of Charlcombe, Somerset, and died 19 November, 1443.[2] He was described

---

[1] *Trans. Bristol and Glos. Arch. Soc.* vi, 144–8 ; vii, 117–25. Sir John Maclean, however, attributes two chantries to Robert Greyndour, the chantry school at Newland, and another, also a chantry school, in Mitcheldean church ; ibid. vi, 166, 263. This last attribution is an entire mistake, owing, apparently, to an erroneous copy of the Chantry Certificate which placed under Mitcheldean the Newland foundation. Sir John Maclean himself says that he could find no institutions to the Mitcheldean chantry. Naturally, as there was no such chantry.

[2] Inq. p.m. 22 Hen. VI, No. 34.

as 'squyer' in a bequest to him by will of Richard Dixton, 'squyer,' 8 August, 1438, of ' my serp of silver and my cheyne of gold,' while ' Jone Greyndor, his wyf,' was given by the same will ' a covered cup of silver the wich I was wont to drink of and a bracelet of gold.'

Greyndour had probably while alive[1] provided the brass on the floor of the south of Greyndour chapel which still bears his effigy and that of his wife Jane, in the costumes of the period.

A subsequent owner of the manor and descendant, Sir Christopher Baynham, knight, who died in 1557, has had the audacity to inscribe his own name on the brass, in which he, or some other sixteenth-century person, inserted a representation of a miner of the Forest of Dean. The result is that the figures of Greyndour and his wife were called Sir Christopher Baynham and Lady.[2] To Sir John Maclean must be given the credit of having restored the attribution to the rightful owners.

Greyndour had no doubt made provision by his will for the foundation of the chantry school, as his wife obtained a licence, 6 November, 1445,[3] for the foundation of a perpetual chantry at the altar of St. John and St. Nicholas and a further licence in mortmain dated the same day[4] to endow it with lands to the value of £12 a year in Lydney, Alveston, and Newland. John Clifford was named in the patent as the first chaplain of the chantry. Sir John Maclean identifies[5] him with a rector of Staunton of the same name admitted 26 April, 1426, a successor being appointed, on his resignation on 18 June, 1449. As it will be seen that his successor in the schoolmastership was appointed the same year, the identification is probably correct.

The patents, as is usual, are limited to the chantry provisions, and the creation of the chantry priest as a perpetual corporation sole, which alone required the royal licence, and nothing is said about the scholastic duties of the chantry-priest, which were left for the Ordinance of foundation, for the making of which power was given by the patents. This, unfortunately, has wholly disappeared, and all we know about this ancient and interesting foundation is derived from the documents which recorded it for the purpose of confiscation.

' In the certificate[6] of John Currell, esquyer, Richard Pate (afterwards re-founder or re-endower of Cheltenham Grammar School) and Edwarde Gostewyke, gentilmen,' commissioners under the permissive Chantries Dissolution Act of Henry VIII in 1545, under the heading of ' The Parishe of Newland within the Deanry of the Forest,' there appears ' Gryndoures Chauntrye foundyd To fynde a preste and a gramer scole half free for ever, And to kepe a scoller sufficientt to teche under hym contynually. And he to have for his salary by yere £10 4s. 2d. Gryndoures Chauntery is within the said churche.' The total yearly value is given as £11 16s. 8d., ' whereof for the priestes stipende, £10 4s. 2d. ; for renttes resoluttes, 2s. 10d. ; for the

---

[1] Sir John Maclean (*Trans. Bristol and Glos. Arch. Soc.* vi, 36) says that his wife had it made. But in the first place the armour is of a somewhat early type for 1443, and the dress of the lady is also the same. Secondly, few if any who left the erection of their monuments to their successors, unless with very stringent directions in their wills, ever obtained them. The great bulk of mediaeval monuments were erected by those who commemorated themselves in their own lifetime.

[2] Haines, *Manual of Monumental Brasses*, i, cxii.

[3] Pat. 24 Hen. VI, pt. i, m. 29.

[4] Ibid. pt. ii, m. 17.

[5] *Trans. Bristol and Glos. Arch. Soc.* vii, 255.

[6] A. F. Leach, *Engl. Sch. at the Reformation*, 78 ; from Chant. Cert. 21, No. 24.

kinges tenthes, 23s. 8d. ; for 2 obbytes yerely, 4s. ; for 2 tapers yerely, 2s. ; And so remayneth, nil.' There must have been some handsome chalices and plate belonging to the chantry, as the plate, ornaments, and jewels were valued at £15 3s. 9d., equivalent to upwards of £303 of our money.

The Chantry Grammar School was not touched by Henry VIII, whose right of entry on the possessions of any college or chantry or gild he chose, including the colleges in the universities, was very sparingly exercised.

Under the Chantries Act of Edward VI, which definitely abolished all chantries as from Easter, 1548, several certificates appear to have been taken. First, one[1] by nine of the commissioners for the county, headed by Sir Anthony Hungerforde and three other knights and ending with 'Thomas Sterneholde and Richarde Pates, gentilmen' ; then, another[2] by the same Thomas Sterneholde, 'partycular surveyor unto the Kinges maiestie, appointed for the said countie and cities unto certeyne articles here under wrytten, as doth here after ensewe,' being a special inquiry with a view to ascertaining what chantries which were also grammar schools or endowments for the poor and other works of charity such as bridges and havens had a right to continuance under sect. 2 of the Act, or where vicars or curates of necessity or new schools were required ; and lastly, particulars[3] of the foundation of the chantry set out when its confiscated possessions were to be leased or sold by the Court of Augmentations for the crown under the Act. In this case the last account is perhaps the fullest and best. Putting these various accounts together we get exceptionally full and clear details of the foundation.

> The[4] Chauntry of Blakbroke, *alias* dicta Greyndours [also Grynedowres] chauntrye or schole, founded by one Robert Gryndour, esquier, by licence' 'by[5] hym opteynd of Kinge Henry the VIth for th'errection of the same, dated 28 Feb. in the 24th yere of his regne' 28 February 1445–6, 'to th'entent that there shuld be an honeste and discrete preste, being sufficientlie lerned in the arte of gramer to kepe and teache a grammer scoole ther half free for ever ; that is to saie, to take of scolers lernynge gramer, 8d. the quarter, and of other lernynge lettres and to rede 4d. the quarter, within a house there called the Chauntrie house or scoole house.

The alternative name of Blackbrook Chantry was derived, as appears incidentally, from this chantry or schoolhouse being called, presumably from its geographical position on a stream of this name—Blackbrook. The master was also 'bounde[6] by the graunte of him the said founder to fynde one scoller to teache under him there gyvinge him meate, dryncke, clothe, and all other necessaries.' This institution of an usher who was also a pupil is quite common in these foundations. The pupil teacher instead of being a modern invention, the creation of the elementary school of the nineteenth century, was a well-known institution in the fifteenth century. We shall find him at Bredgar, Kent, in 1334, as we found him at Wotton under Edge in 1384, a century before this Newland foundation. The provision for one shows the school was expected to number from 60 to 80 scholars. Had the foundation stopped there it would not have fallen under the Edward VI Chantries Act, which in its preamble set forth as one of its objects the

---

[1] A. F. Leach, *Engl. Sch. at the Reformation*, 82, from Chant. Cert. 22, No. 70.
[2] Ibid. 83, from Chant. Cert. 23, No. 34.   [3] Harl. MS. 605, fol. 12, 13b.
[4] Chant. Cert. 22.
[5] Harl. MS. 605. The same words in a slightly different order and with different spelling are given in Chant. Cert. 23.   [6] Chant. Cert. 23.

conversion of superstitious uses to the foundation of grammar schools; but unfortunately it went on: 'Allso the said chauntrye prieste' was 'to celebrate [1] and praye at thaulter called St. John Baptist and Saynt Nicholas altar within the parisshe church of Newlande for the soules of the said Roberte Gryndoure hys successors and benefactors and for all Christen soules' 'for ever.' Being a chantry, to hire a priest to pray the dead out of purgatory, as well as a school, the foundation was 'for superstitious uses' and swept into the meshes of the Chantries Act, and included in the certificates taken under it. However, we must be thankful to those who made the certificates for the extremely interesting information which gives this foundation its special interest and makes it a 'fingerpost' instance on the much-vexed question as to the meaning of the term 'free grammar school.' For the curious record of the school being half-free, that is to say that while boys learning grammar paid the full customary tuition fees of 8d. a quarter, boys learning merely their A B C and to read paid only half that, an arrangement which made the school half-free, is as absolutely unique in itself as it is absolutely convincing evidence that the freedom of schools meant freedom from fees. The use of the term 'a half-free grammar school' shows conclusively that the word 'free' did not refer to the liberal education which free grammar schools gave, nor to freedom from ecclesiastical control, which not one of them in fact ever enjoyed, nor to freedom from the law of mortmain, from which they were not free, nor to any one of the numerous fanciful explanations invented for the term, to escape from its obvious, primary, and true meaning, which was simply and solely freedom from tuition fees; nothing more and nothing less. The assumption that the ordinary grammar-school fee was 8d., the half-fee being 4d., is a rather remarkable instance of the customary and general character of the school arrangements of England and their persistence. At Merton College in 1277 the fee of the master of 'Glomary' or grammar was 4d. a term, and it remained the same in 1309 and 1339; but about half a century later, in 1382, the payment had gone up to 8d. a term, with three terms in the year. As we said in the Gloucester School case in 1410, 2s. a year was regarded as the nominal fee, the masters complaining that unlicensed competition had reduced it to half that. The Oxford University statutes in the late fourteenth and fifteenth centuries fixed the grammar school fee at 8d. a term. At Ipswich in 1477 the fee was fixed at 1½d. for grammarians, 8d. for psalterians, and 6d. for primarians, but the tariff was lowered again in 1482 to 8d. a quarter.

We are enabled to trace the continuance of Greyndour's Chantry Grammar School in accordance with the foundation by the institutions of the masters in the registers of the bishops of Hereford, the deanery of the Forest of Dean having belonged to that diocese, and not, as the rest of Gloucestershire did, to the diocese of Worcester, until the constitution of the bishopric of Gloucester in 1541.

Incidentally we learn from these that Jane Greyndour did not long remain a widow after the death of the founder, Robert Greyndour. For on 4 March, 1448,[2] 'Sir John Barre knight and Jane his wife, late wife of Robert Greyndour,' presented William Coburley, chaplain, to the perpetual

---

[1] Harl. MS. 605. In Chant. Cert. 23 it is called 'Saynt Nicholas aulter' simply.
[2] Heref. Epis. Reg. Beauchamp, fol. 2.

chantry of Robert Greyndour on the resignation of John Clifford. For forty years Jane and her second husband survived. Sir John Barre, in right of his wife, presented, on 30 October, 1457,[1] to the perpetual chantry in honour of St. John Baptist and St. Nicholas,' Richard Devyn on the death of William Coburley. Devyn resigned in less than two years, and was succeeded by Edward Janyns, chaplain, admitted[2] to the chantry of Robert Greyndour on 20 July, 1459. On 7 December, 1463, Sir William Phen was appointed on the resignation of Janyns. On 5 June, 1465,[3] Philip ap Eynon succeeded on the death of Phen. Ap Eynon was no doubt a scion of the Ap Eynons who became Baynhams, and were prospective inheritors of Newland and Mitcheldean, for on 2 December, 1485, Thomas Stokes, vicar of Lydney, exchanged that vicarage with Sir Philip Baynham, and was admitted to the chantry of St. John Baptist and St. Nicholas, called Greyndours, on the presentation of Thomas Baynham, esquire, and Alice his wife. Sir John Barre had died 14 January, 1482–3,[4] and Jane his wife on 17 June, 1485. By her will dated 3 February, 1484–5,[5] proved 23 July, 1485, she directed her body to be buried in the chapel of St. John the Baptist and St. Nicholas, by the side of the husband of her youth, Robert Greyndour, the vicar was 'tenderly to pray in his daily masse and in his pulpitt for my soule and for myn husbandes' soules,' while 'a devout secular prest' was to 'sing in my chapel at Newlond 3 yeres continually . . . to say every day 6 psalms and 15 psalms with the litany, placebo and dirige with 9 lessons and commendations, for 12 marks (£8), while another priest was 'to say for my soul especially, during a whole year, St. Gregory's trentall with all the observances and fastings that pertain thereto' for £10. The fact that these were to be additional priests shows that the testatrix was aware that her own perpetual chantry priest would not be able to spare the time from his scholastic duties for all those special observances. Gorgeous plate, however, vestments, yellow velvet, white damask, russet satin, purple and yellow, she gave to the altar of St. John the Baptist and St. Nicholas, 'the which is my own chapel,' and 'to Sir Philip Beynham, my chantry priest, my fair little portues[6] of the Salisbury use covered with green cloth, lying for the most part in my parlour window in a bag; a book which is called *Pupilla oculi*, the which the said Philip hath in his keeping, my calendar, a great flat rose-piece of silver with a cover to the same of silver, and £10 in money.' The *Pupilla oculi sacerdotis*, though credited to a chancellor of Cambridge University, was not a school-book, but a religious book. Robert and Jane Greyndour's only daughter Elizabeth had married John Tiptoft, earl of Worcester, but had predeceased her mother, dying on 1 September, 1452. The inheritance went to Alice, granddaughter of William Walwayn, who had married Jane Greyndour, Robert's only sister. Alice Walwayn married Thomas Baynham, and by this marriage reunited the severed moieties of the manor of Mitcheldean and brought Newland into the Baynham family. In 1502 we learn that John Alexander was the chaplain of the chantry from a lease by him still in possession of Mr. R.

---

[1] Heref. Epis. Reg. Stanbery, fol. 37.

[2] Ibid. fol. 57. The name of the chaplain appears from St. John Maclean's list to be omitted in the institution; but it is mentioned on the appointment of his successor.

[3] Ibid. fol. 81. [4] Inq. p.m. 22 Edw. IV, No. 39.

[5] P.C.C. 16 Logge. [6] 'Portiforium,' or portable prayer-book, breviary.

Fryer of Coleford, which has attached to it the seal of the chantry, the figures of St. John and St. Nicholas, and a shield of the Beauchamp[1] arms. The legend is :—

SIGILLUM CANTARIE ROBERTI [GREYNDOUR ARMIG]ERI APUD NUL[AND].

On 16 May, 1521,[2] John Bolthar, B.A., was presented by the Sir Christopher Baynam (*sic*) who, as we saw, wrote his name on his predecessor's brass, on the cession of Sir Thomas Poumfrey, whose appointment is not given and who cannot be traced. The Oxford University registers now begin to throw light, though fitful and scanty, on some of these masters. We can trace[3] John Bolthar, for instance, as the John Bolter who supplicated for his B.A. degree on 4 December, 1513, and 17 May, 1514, and was admitted to it on 3 July, 1514. His successor, David Smith, appointed[4] on Bolter's resignation by Sir Christopher Baynham on 12 January, 1530, appears, under the spelling 'Smygth,'[5] supplicating for his B.A. degree 11 March, 1507–8, and 'determining' in 1508–9 ; and supplicating for his M.A. degree 20 February and 'incepting' 28 February, 1518–19, and dispensed from disputations on 10 March, 1518–19, probably because he was already teaching school somewhere, and again on 25 June, 1522. He died after little more than a year, being succeeded by Roger Wynter, appointed by Sir Christopher Beynam (*sic*), 17 November, 1531.[6] Wynter's appointment testifies to the high status of the school, for he was a fellow of Oriel College,[7] who supplicated for his B.A. degree 11 November, 1522, determined in 1523, and became fellow of Oriel 2 November, 1525, when he is described as from Salop. He supplicated for his M.A. degree 28 January, 1528–9, and incepted 15 March, 1528–9.

At the date of the chantry certificate of Edward VI, 1548, 'Sir Roger Forde' was 'at this present incumbent and scolemaster.' He is to be identified with 'Roger Ford, secular chaplain,' who in 30 January, 1531–2, was admitted to the degree of Bachelor of Grammar at Oxford. His being described already as chaplain, and his seeking only the inferior degree in grammar instead of that in arts, may be taken to imply that he was already incumbent and schoolmaster at that time.

A flattering testimonial to him, and to his predecessors, is given by the Chantry Certificates.[8] Sterneholde says :—[9]

> A man of honest conversacion and good learninge, and wholye geven and applyinge himself in the vertuouse bryngynge up of the same scollars, whereof are at this present good store, and the Scole very well haunted, to the grete commodytie of the countrey thereabouts.

This is more largely expressed, apparently from the original return, in the Particulars for Sale :—

> A man of honest conversacion and good lernynge, applyenge him selfe daylie in theducacion and bringinge upp of Scolers in vertue and leninge, the scoole now beinge well haunted and furnished with scolers, and hathe ben allweyes ; which is very requisite and necessarie that it shulde continewe ; or else hit shal be a greate lose and discomoditie to all the countrie there abouts, for that ther is not any other Gramer Scole free, nether otherwise, not by a grete distaunce, to have their childerne brought upp vertuouslie in lerninge.

---

[1] This must be a mistake for the Berkeley arms.
[2] Heref. Epis. Reg. Booth, fol. 64.
[3] C. A. Boase, *Reg. of the Univ. of Oxf.* 89.
[4] Heref. Epis. Reg. Booth, fol. 170.
[5] C. A. Boase, *Reg. of the Univ. of Oxf.* 59.
[6] Heref. Epis. Reg. Booth, fol. 173.
[7] C. A. Boase, *Reg. of the Univ. of Oxf.*
[8] Harl. MS. 601. fol. 12.
[9] A. F. Leach, *Engl. Sch. at the Reformation*, 84.

This testimonial could not save the endowment of the school from confiscation. On 22 June, 1548, it is noted:—

> My lorde Protectors grace's pleasure is that Lewis Williams shall have in ferme the premises, and therefore commandeth that a lease be made to hym of the same for 20 yeres under the seale of the Courte of the Augmentation, yeldinge to the Kings Highness the saide yerely rente, according to such order as other leases use to passe in the same courte : Provided allweies that yf at any tyme after the sealinge of the said lease the said Lewis Williams, his executors and assignes or any other for hym or them or in his or ther ryght, shall, or doe expell or put out of any of the premises any of the tenaunts or farmers having estate by Indenture, untill suche tyme as theire estates therein shall be tried or adjudged to be voyde in any of the king's Highnes courts having authoritie to hold plea of the same ; that then and from thenceforth the said lease to be voyde.

The excessive tenderness thus shown to the tenants, who were not the objects of the founder's bounty, while the general public was deprived of the endowment given for its benefit, is a curious commentary on the policy of Protector Somerset.

The school, however, went on, as a note to Sterneholde's certificate says 'the school is continued until further order (*continuatur the schole quousque*).' The warrant of Sir Walter Mildmay and Robert Kelway directing the continuance of the school and the payment of a sum representing the net rental of the confiscated lands of the chantry from the crown revenues in Gloucestershire is not forthcoming. But the Ministers' Accounts for 1549–50[1] show £11 'paid in cash to Roger Forde, school master (*ludimagistro*) of the grammar school founded by Greyndour's chauntry in the parish church of Newland and for his wages or stipend so granted to him during the king's pleasure' by virtue (*vigore*) of the warrant signed by Walter Mildmay, knight, a general surveyor of the Court of Augmentations and revenues of the king's crown. The payment was continued[2] till 1553–4, when it ceases, the Court of Augmentations having been abolished. As we saw was the case also at Cirencester the payments were stopped unless and until sued out again by way of a fresh grant in the Court of Exchequer. In this case perhaps Ford died. The grant seems never to have been renewed.

Whether the school had actually ceased before it was revived or newly endowed half a century later is unknown.

Some time before 1598 Edward Bell the elder had granted property on trust for the payment of £10 yearly to a master teaching grammar in the schoolhouse which he had begun, and £2 for repairs. By deed, 21 March, 1626–7, his son Edward Bell confirmed the grant.

Alderman Whitson, of Bristol, by will dated 27 March, 1627, bequeathed an annuity of £10 for increase of the schoolmaster's stipend, and in 1724 John Symons, by will, left £100 to be invested in land for the benefit of the school, provided that the master should be a layman and following no other business, but when he should be in holy orders, the rents should be divided among the almspeople ; but this direction has been neglected, the master, who generally has been in orders, always receiving the money. In 1650 ordinances were made for the school under which the trustees were to be satisfied by the approval ' of learned men such as the

[1] P.R.O. Mins. Accts. 3–4 Edw. VI, No. 90.
[2] Ibid. 4–5 Edw. VI, No. 90 ; 5–6 Edw. VI, No. 76 ; 1–2 Phil. and Mary ; Land Rev. Rec. Accts. bdle. 28.

trustees shall desire to take account of his sufficiency and ability to keep a free grammar school.' He was to teach freely all children 'that may come to him to be taught, being of the parish of Newland'—an unwarranted narrowing of the original intention—charging an entrance fee of 1s. 6d. In 1711, and for many years afterwards, the school was sacrificed to the almsfolk, the whole surplus after paying £10 a year to the school being divided among them.

At the time of the Schools Inquiry Report[1] in 1866 the master just appointed was an Etonian, F. L. A. Görtz, who after a roving life had settled down to teach this school, the endowment of which should have been half of £176, or £88, but was, through the almshouse being more favoured, only £65. He found 5 boys in the school, his predecessor having been a non-resident clergyman, who lived at Tidenham, and discharged his duties by deputy. Under the new master these had risen to 14—12 foundationers and 2 private pupils. The population had ebbed from Newland to Coleford. In 1868 the Rev. C. M. Perkins was appointed master, but from 1872 did duty by deputy, the school being practically elementary. The school was moved to Coleford under an order of the Charity Commissioners in 1875, the old building being sold and a new site purchased, and a large schoolroom and a class-room erected at Coleford. The school was not much more flourishing in its new habitat. The Rev. G. Burrows, 19 September, 1876, and Alfred Dykes Sylvester, 12 June, 1878, each held office for two years. Then came Mr. John Bond, an elementary Irish schoolmaster, but LL.D. of Dublin, and kept to Christmas, 1896, a school of about 30 boys. He was followed for five years by Mr. J. Talbot Gardiner. On 6 December, 1901, the present head master, Mr. William Hodder, M.A. of Clare College, Cambridge, was appointed. A scheme is now being made by the Charity Commissioners under the Endowed Schools Acts, apportioning the endowments between school and almshouses and creating a representative governing body.

CHIPPING CAMPDEN GRAMMAR SCHOOL

Chipping Campden Grammar School was founded in or about 1487, by John Ferby, or Feriby, and Margaret his wife. The earliest evidence yet produced of its foundation is in the certificate of the commissioners of Henry VIII.[2]

> The parishe of Campden.
>
> Feraby servis, otherwise callyd the Scolemaisters servys, founded and lands put in feoffment to fynde a preste for ever to kepe a Free scole and to have for his salary by yere £8 to kepe an obyt and to geve in almes yerely 40s. [yearly value] £13 6s. 8d. whereof for the prestes stipend £8 for the poore folk £10 ; and so remayneth clere £3 6s. 8d.

The foundation was left undisturbed by Henry VIII. In the certificate of the commissioners of Edward VI it appears as :—

> The Scolemaister Servyce alias dictum Ferbye Service. This servyce is left out in thother certificat. Founded by one John Ferbye and Margaret.

The date of 1487 is derived from a statement in a Bill in Chancery of 1627 that the school was founded 'about 140 years before.' It is confirmed

---

[1] *Sch. Inq. Rep.* xv, 88.

[2] A. F. Leach, *Engl. Sch. at the Reformation*, 36; from Chant. Cert. 21, No. 31 ; 22, No. 57.

by an inquisition post mortem held 4 November, 4 Henry VII, by which it was found that John Fereby, who died 6 December, 3 Henry VII, had enfeoffed certain feoffees of Knyghtes Place, Kent, with 12 marks a year held of the abbey of Lesnes, and that Margaret Fereby, aged 6, was his heir. The Feribys, or Ferbys, were anciently of Speldhurst, and then of Paul's Cray in Kent.[1] They were also connected with Surrey.

It appears from the Bill referred to that the endowment of Chipping Campden School consisted of the moiety of the manor of Lyneham, Oxfordshire, called in another document Fynes Court, which rather looks as if Margaret Feriby was a coheiress of the manor. Though hitherto nothing has been produced to connect the John Feriby who died in 1487 with the founder of Campden School, it may fairly be assumed that as he had an heiress Margaret, he is the same person.

The certificate of the Chantry Commissioners which would have established it to be a 'service' in the church, a kind of chantry, having been crossed out and a memorandum substituted treating it solely as a school, it escaped being confiscated under the Act. We must assume, therefore, that it went on in the even tenor of its way as a grammar school, first under Glaseman and then under unknown successors till it made its appearance in the Court of Chancery. The tale told in the Decree[2] is that about fifty years before, i.e. 1576, the surviving feoffees of the school lands made a fraudulent lease of the half manor of Lyneham, and subsequently sold the reversion for £1,100, buying in exchange lands worth £700 in Barton on the Heath, Warwickshire; the difference they pocketed, and the lands themselves they let at low rents to their friends. When, about 1625, the town arranged to appoint fourteen new feoffees, the fraudulent trustees, who had been paying the schoolmaster only £13 6s. 8d., made feoffment to John Gilby and others 'living far away,' and 'divers persons of their affinity and kindred, some of them young children who were not fit and capable in managing the estate or to control the others in misemploying the property.'

Sir Baptist Hickes, who had bought the manor of Campden and afterwards became Viscount Campden, Robert Lilly the vicar, and others then filed a bill in Chancery. The defence was that the rents had been applied 'for the corporacion of Campden' and the bridge. But 'his lordship did utterly mislike the same,' and 7 June, 1627, ordered the accounts to be taken and nothing allowed the defendants.

By a deed of 24 September, 1627, the land at Barton was assigned to thirteen trustees, including Sir Baptist Hickes and the famous Endymion Porter, for the advancement and benefit of the school and poor of the town, which probably meant the township 'of Chipping Campden,' and that they should 'pay to . . . the schoolmaster for the teaching of a free grammar school . . . such yearly salary or stipend for his pains as should be thought meet by the feoffees or the greater part of them,' the overplus 'towards the maintenance relief and succour and for the good and benefit of the poor . . . and for necessary uses in and about the same schoolhouse and poor.' The schoolmaster was to be named by the feoffees and to be 'of good and civil

---

[1] Hasted, *Hist. of Kent*, i, 146 ; Phillipots, *Villare Cantianum* (1657), p. 109.
[2] B.M. Lansd. MSS. 227, fol. 280.

conversation and diligently and discreetly demean himself or else to be removed by the said office.'

A distinguished alumnus during this troubled period was the Puritan President of Trinity College, Oxford, Robert Harris. Little is known about the school except from the accounts, the Governors' Minute Book consisting of little else than appointments of governors and grants of leases. Ambrose Jenks, 1630, was the first master after the re-settlement, and Samuel Edwards followed in 1634, Kirkham filled the post during the Commonwealth, and Taylor was appointed in 1669.[1]

In 1683 this was one of the four schools selected by George Townsend, a barrister of Lincoln's Inn, to compete for the exhibitions at Pembroke College, Oxford, which he established by his will. In 1695 a farm at Gretton was bought; it let in 1829 at £70 a year, but in 1890 at only £40 a year, thereby reverting to the amount for which it was let in 1780.

In 1702 the custom of barring-out the masters at the beginning of holidays gave trouble here as elsewhere. It was ordered by the governors 'If any of the Scholars be instrumental in pushing the master out of the school, they shall from thenceforth be incapable of having any benefit by the said school.'

In 1818 Rev. Joseph Wergan was master, with a salary of £50 a year. He took a limited number of pupils at £30 a year. The usher taught the free boys the three R's.

In 1829 the income from endowment was £170 a year. The head master received £50 a year and the under master £37 10s. There were about 60 boys, of whom 30 to 40 were free boys, 6 or 7 of whom were taught classics by the head master, who was Richard Otways Wilson, while the rest received elementary instruction from the under master.

In 1858 a subscription was begun for rebuilding the school and enlarging the playground. The work was completed in 1864 at a cost of £1,800. Mr. Stanton, the assistant commissioner who visited the school for the Schools Inquiry Commission in 1866, reported[2] 'There are few Grammar Schools . . . which can compare with Chipping Campden School either in the appearance of the buildings or the excellence of the accommodation.' There were then 34 boys under the Rev. S. F. Hiron, D.C.L., himself an old Campden boy, 10 boarders and 16 'free' boys at £2 a year and 8 paying day boys at £8 a year. The classical work and French were well taught and a mathematical master from Cambridge had just been imported to carry the mathematical work to the same level. Dr. Hiron held for 9 years. The Rev. Joseph Forster followed from 1871 to 1889, when the present master, Mr. Francis Bayley Osborne, probably the first lay head master of the school, was appointed. He was at Bedford Modern School and had been a master at Preston Grammar School.

A scheme under the Endowed Schools Acts, approved by Queen Victoria in Council, 20 March, 1891, put the school under a governing body of 12; including one representative of Pembroke College, Oxford, 2 of the justices of the Campden division, 2 of the town trustees and one of the Rural District Council of Campden. The tuition fees were fixed at £6 to £10 and boarding fees at £35 a year. The income from endowment had

---

[1] *Endowed Grammar Schools*, i, 444. 　　　　[2] *Sch. Inq. Rep.* xv, 50.

then shrunk to £140 a year, of which £13, the customary amount, was assigned for a bread dole.

There are now 35 boys in the school, of whom 8 are boarders.

A new scheme is in preparation by the Board of Education by which this, like other small grammar schools in rural districts, will be enabled to call in the softer sex to increase the numbers and give a new sphere of usefulness to this old foundation.

STOW ON THE WOLD GRAMMAR SCHOOL

Thomas Billing,[1] Chief Justice, and others conveyed lands in St. Olave, Southwark, to William Chestre and others. William Chestre, by will in May, 1476, declared the uses of these lands, including the maintenance of a Trinity chantry in Stow church. These lands came to Richard Chestre by survivorship, he having only one daughter, Joan, married to Thomas Bittlesden, against whom William Martin recovered in 1487. He[2] conveyed the lands, described as 'Glean Alley in St. Oliff's parish in Southwark,' to trustees in Stow, and appointed that £6 a year were to be paid to the chantry priest, who was to keep a school and instruct the children of the town. The school must have been duly built, as in the reign of Queen Elizabeth it is spoken of as 'Tenementum vocatum le Schole House modo ruinatum, et in decasu, in Stowe in le Owlde juxta cimeterium ecclesie.' It was probably rebuilt in 1594, as an old house adjoining the churchyard bears the inscription : 'Schola institutionis puerorum Ricardi Shepham civis et mercatoris Londinensis impensis exstructa 1594.' Richard Shepham,[3] citizen and merchant tailor of London, by will dated 20 July, 1604, devised lands in Southwark for the perpetual maintenance of a school and almshouse in Stow. The school was established by a charter of James I in 1612, which ordained that there should be 'one Free Grammar School for the instruction of boys and children in the Latin tongue and other more polite literature and science,' and nominated the bailiffs and burgesses of Chipping Norton as governors, and the governors covenanted that they would appoint a discreet, pious, and learned schoolmaster.

The school was existing at the time of the Charity Commissioners' Report in 1829, but though subscriptions were raised 'to repair the Grammar School' in 1848,[4] it seems to have come to an end in that year, and the income, a rent-charge of £13 6s. 8d., was paid to the national school.

WINCHCOMBE GRAMMAR SCHOOL

In the Valor Ecclesiasticus[5] of 1535 we find the abbey of Winchcombe paying

> In alms and payments (*elemosinis et pencionibus*) by foundation and ordinance of Lady Jane Huddelston, relict of John Huddilston (*sic*) knight, yearly to the Master of the Grammar School of Winchcombe, to the Master of the boys singing in the monastery aforesaid, and for the maintenance of 6 boys in the said monastery being instructed and taught in the art of grammar and of song ; and also for keeping the anniversaries of the said Lady Jane and the said Sir John her late husband at the monasteries of Hayles and Winchcombe yearly with distributions in bread to the poor on the said anniversary days, £21 6s. 8d.

[1] Rudder, *Hist. of Glouc.* ; not Belleny, as he prints.
[2] Atkyn's *Ancient and Present State of Glouc.* 366.
[3] *Char. Com. Rep.* xxi, 176.
[4] *Sch. Inq. Rep.* xv, 101.
[5] *Valor Eccl.* (Rec. Com.), ii, 459.

SCHOOLS

A note says 'Note.—The alms distributed among the poor, as that is allowed and the rest disallowed,' i.e. the tenths were payable on the singing boys' income as part of the monastic staff, but not on the payment to the poor, which was a charity to outsiders.

John Austin, master of the Lady chapel, had a separate endowment of £19 14s. 7d. out of which he paid

> in alms to six boys or choristers of the Blessed Mary's chapel viz. in the price of 6 gowns (*tunicarum*) and making and doubling the same ; in the price of 24 pairs of shoes and 12 shirts, according to a composition and ordinance of Richard, late abbot of the monastery aforesaid, made and confirmed under the common seal of the monastery, 62s.

The Song School therefore and the maintenance of the 6 choristers for whom alone, or primarily, it was intended, was actually a monastic school in the sense that it was maintained by and in the monastery. Song Schools being mainly intended to teach choristers to sing mass were regarded as superstitious and not favoured by the reformers. This school and its master therefore ceased on the dissolution of the abbey, but the Grammar School was continued. We learn from the account of the Receiver General of the Crown Revenues in Gloucestershire for the year 1566-7 more precisely its origin. Dame Jane Huddleston had left money for founding an almshouse, but as it was insufficient for that purpose, £400 was paid by her executors to Winchcombe Abbey for the purpose of founding a Free Grammar School. By an indenture between the abbots of Winchcombe and Hailes, 13 September, 1521, it was agreed that Winchcombe should buy lands to the value of £21 5s. 8d., the sum specified in the Valor. Out of this 6 scholars were to be maintained, and a schoolmaster, to be elected and removed by the abbot, with a stipend of £6 13s. 2d. a year, ' or such as could be agreed upon,' and a gown, or 20s. in lieu of a gown. An honest tenement or chamber was to be provided, together with fuel and meat and drink in the monastery.

This school ought to be called the Huddleston School, and not attributed, as it is in the Report of the Commissioners of Inquiry concerning Charities[1] in 1829, to Henry VIII and called the King's school. For in point of fact that king merely confiscated its endowment, which though held in trust and no part of the monastic property, was as usual treated as such, and taken by the Crown. The school, however, was continued. A payment of £10 a year seems to have been continuously made to the grammar schoolmaster, though it has not been actually traced further back than 1558, when £5[2] was paid to Richard Hide, but he is not called schoolmaster (*ludimagister*) till 1562, when a 'pension' of £10 was paid him out of the Crown revenues for Gloucestershire. From 1563 to 1566 Humphrey Dicke[3] was paid at the same rate.

A return for Winchcombe made 1 February, 1570–1, by John Cocke and Thomas Bolar, ' bayleis,' together with four churchwardens says[4]:—

> We have of the Queen's Majestie, by her receiver Mr. Fludd, £10 yearly, to the maintaininge of good lerninge to the virtuous bringing upp of youth in our schole of Winchelcombe. Oure Schoolemaister is one Phillip Brode, a B.A., and not onely allowed

---

[1] *Char. Com. Rep.* xxi, 163. In the *Annals of Winchcombe,* by Emma Dent (1877) it is boldly asserted ' The Grammar School was founded in 1522 by Henry VIII, and his endowment of £9 4s. 6d. per annum was confirmed by Elizabeth.'   [2] P.R.O. Land Rev. Rec. Acct. bdle. 28.

[3] E. Dent, *Ann. of Winchcombe*, 144, calls him ' master of the game.'

[4] Exch. Spec. Com. No. 867, 12 Eliz.

and admitted by the Ordinary, but allso for his good behaviour, conversacion and diligency in teaching well liked of the town. But we have no decent and convenient house, wherein our Schole may be kept; for the Abbey being suppressed our Scholehouse was taken awaye, and sythence that tyme we have had none but upon sufferance.

Another commission was issued next year, 4 July, 1571. To this the bishop made return 6 October, 1571,[1] that Edward Stratford, John Turner and Richard Parsons, sworn, said that the stipend of £10 had been paid to the schoolmaster of Winchcombe, and the school kept from the beginning of the queen's reign, and the schoolmaster 'has been at all times a man well learned and of honest conversacion.'

> Item, the schole house is in a decent and convenient place but is not of dutie but of sufferance and frendschipp.
> Item, the eleccion and placeynge of the Scholemaister is at the discretion of the baylies of the towne and other of the honest and substantiall men ther and att the confirmacion of the bishopp.

The returns seem to have been regarded as satisfactory, as thenceforth the stipend of the master was regularly paid by the Crown Receiver down to the Civil War. A return[2] of the year 1651 to Parliament stated that

> the said stipend hath bin constantly paid to the schulemaster there for the time being from yeare to yeare out of the revenues of the said county of Gloucester by the receivers thereof untill the feast of St. Michael the Archangel 1650, except only for half a year ended at Michaelmas 1642 and one whole yeare ended at Michaelmas 1643 in which time it was not paid by reason of their troubles.

Unfortunately the master's name is not stated.

The King's School was apparently rebuilt after the Restoration, as there is preserved in the Parish Chest a copy of articles dated 5 June, 1671, made between the two bailiffs and 10 other persons, ' on the behalf of themselves and the rest of the township of Winchcomb aforesaid,' with ' Henry Thorne, late of Oxford, Batchelor of art and now elected School master of his majestie's free school in Winchcomb.'

As the schoolhouse was built at the cost of the town, ' the said Bayliffs and others having the disposal thereof' granted that Thorne should hold it as long as he continued schoolmaster . . . 'keeping the said schoolhouse and mounds about the garden and yard' in repair. Thorne on his part covenanted to 'teach and instruct 10 freeschollars as shall be presented unto him by the bayliffs for the time being and their successors together with the former bayliffs or any six of them.' Similar agreements were made with Edward Rainsford in 1715 and Thomas Skealer in 1726 and Benjamin Roberts on 4 January, 1732, all of whom were also vicars.

Meanwhile, in 1621 Francis Lady Chandos built in Nicholas Street a free grammar school with rooms for a school and schoolmaster, who should be ' appointed according to the tenor of a certain feoffment made by her for the education . . . . of 14 children of the town of Winchcombe, as schollers in the said schole, as well in the science of grammar as in other learning fitt for their years to be instructed in, and that under such order and form of government as in the said feoffment was expressed.' The deed in question

---

[1] Exch. Spec. Com. No. 868, 13 Eliz.
[2] P.R.O. Aug. Off. Particulars for Sale of Fee farm rents.

was dated 13 November, 1621, and gave certain buildings and lands and stock producing £13 13s. 10d. per annum.

What the relation of this school to the 'King's School' was intended to be does not appear. It was stated in 1818 that 'the King's School and Lady Chandos' School have usually been holden by the Vicar,' the vicar being appointed master of both foundations and conducting a grammar school in the Chandos School buildings, the old school which was opposite to the church having fallen into decay. But when this began cannot be ascertained. The inevitable result of the combination of offices followed in the decay of the school. From the time of John James Latas, vicar, 1793–1832, the school had degenerated into a merely elementary school, the vicar taking the income of both schools and paying a deputy to perform the duty of teaching. In 1816, 20 to 24, in 1829, 34 boys were taught the three R's. In 1832 Mr. Charles Lapworth was appointed and was still master in 1866.[1] It was then reported that penmanship of an elaborate character was his chief care. The reading was indifferent, and in arithmetic none had reached fractions.

On Lapworth's death, Mr. Thomas C. Webb, the present master, was appointed, September, 1871, by the trustees of the Chandos School. He had been head master of Raye's Endowed School, Cheveley, and second master of the Grammar School, Newport, Isle of Wight. He quickly revived and has sustained the character of the school as a grammar school.

The salary was £80 a year for 14 foundation scholars, with power to take 10 more boys at four guineas a year each. At Christmas, 1873, he removed from the old school, which was 14 ft. by 12 ft. only, to the 'Club Room' in Gloucester Street, when the numbers went up to 50. In 1874–5 the present school adjoining the old school, 40 ft. by 18 ft., was built by subscription at a cost of £477, the old school being used as a dining-room. Desks were found by a subscription inaugurated by the vicar, the Rev. R. Noble Jackson, in 1882.

On 28 November, 1876, a scheme under the Endowed Schools Acts was approved by Queen Victoria in Council. This established a governing body of 7 governors, the high bailiff ex officio, 2 representatives of the Vestry, now of the Parish Council, one of the justices of the Petty Sessional Division, and 3 co-optatives headed by Lord Sudeley. The tuition fees were to be £2 to £5 a year, and the boys were to leave at 16. Latin but not Greek was included in the curriculum. By a scheme of the same date the King's School was incorporated, with leave to apply its endowment, if and when redeemed by the Treasury, for a sum of Consols to bettering the buildings. The name of the Chandos School was adopted for the united foundation ; so that poor Lady Huddleston, to whom the school was primarily due, bids fair to be wholly forgotten. The boys aim at the Oxford Local Examinations. About 1890 the numbers fell, but they have since revived, and there are now 30 in the school, of whom 20 are boarders. The endowment, which in 1840 brought in £74 a year, now yields but £55 a year.

---

[1] *Sch. Inq. Rep.* xv, 122.

A HISTORY OF GLOUCESTERSHIRE

CHELTENHAM SCHOOLS

Cheltenham Grammar School

The earliest knowledge we have of the school at Cheltenham is in the document which recorded its disendowment, though not its disestablishment.

The certificate[1] made under the Chantries Act of 1547 records in 'The Deanery of Wynchecombe':

> 53. In the parysshe of Cheltenham, where are of howselinge people,[2] 600.
>
> Saynt Kateryne Service. The clere yerely value, 118s. 11d. Edward Grove, incumbent, hath for his yerelye stypend, 100s.
>
> Memorandum; that the sayde Syr Edward Grove, one of the incumbentes, was charged by speciall Covenaunt betwene the Parysshoners of the saide Towne of Cheltenham and him, always to teache their children; which Towne is a markett Towne and muche youthe within the same, nere wherunto is no scolle kept. Wherefore it is thought convenyent to signifye unto your Mastershipps the same to be a meate place to establyshe some Teacher and erect a Gramer Scole, So it might stande with the Kynges Majesties pleasure.
>
> Continuatur Schola quousque.
>
> Places for Grammerscoles to be newlye erected. The townes of Newent, Cirencestour, Tewkesburye, Cheltenham, in the aforesaide countie of Glouceter.

The direction for the continuance of the school was duly carried out. In the accounts[3] of the Crown received for Gloucestershire 3–4 Edward VI, we find ' and in like cash (*denariis*) paid to Edward Grove, schoolmaster of a certain grammar school of the foundation of the chantry of St. Katherine in the parish of Cheltenham, and for his wages or stipend so (i.e. by warrant of Sir Walter Mildmay knight) granted to him at 100s. a year, in such allowances due for a year £5.'

This item is continued yearly up to and including 1–2 Philip and Mary, when it stops and appears no more.[4]

It is probable that the school was kept going in some form. For on 7 January, 1574, Richard Pate of Minsterworth, Gloucestershire, who had been one of the Chantry Commissioners, obtained a grant of the property or part of the property of St. Katherine's Chantry and also of that of Our Lady's Chantry in the parish church with other property; the queen being ' well pleased to make the said Richard Pate more hable and sufficient to perfect and accomplish that good work which he then intended in the edifying, building and perpetual foundation and maintenance of a Free Grammar School and an Hospital in the town of Cheltenham.' Pate had also acquired some other chantry land in Gloucester; three houses in St. Aldate's parish, Gloucester; the house of the Trinity College belonging to Our Lady Chantry in Trinity Church, Gloucester, and Grace Lane College belonging to the Lady Chantry in Saint Mary Grace Lane, Gloucester.

All these by deed of 1 October, 1585, he gave to Corpus Christi College, Oxford, ' in token of his thankful remembrance that he had been brought up heretofore in good letters' there ' for the perpetual maintenance

---

[1] A. F. Leach, *Engl. Sch. at the Reformation*, 85.   [2] Communicants.
[3] Mins. Accts. 3–4 Edw. VI, Roll 90.
[4] Mins. Accts. 4–5 Edw. VI, R. 90; 5–6 Edw. VI, R. 76; Ld. Rev. Rec. Accts. bdle. 28, 1 and 2 Phil. and Mary.

and foundation of the aforementioned Free Grammar School and Hospital in Cheltenham by him erected for that purpose.' One-fourth of the income the college was to take ' to the free and only use of the college.' With the other three-fourths the college covenanted that they would ' maintain the Free Grammar School of Cheltenham aforesaid, and the exercise of grammar and the other liberal arts there, and also the said Hospital or Almshouse ' for five poor people.

An elaborate ' Schedule idented ' annexed to the deed set forth the ' Rules, Orders, Statutes, and Ordinances ' for the school and hospital.

The president and seven senior fellows of the college were to manage the property and have ' the placing, displacing, and removing ' of the schoolmaster and usher, subject to gifts over of the appointment first to Magdalen College, Oxford, and then to the bishop, if it was not made within three months of a vacancy. The master was to be an M.A. 30 years old at the least, and both master and usher were to be

> whole and sound in body and examined and allowed touching religion by the ordinary of the diocese of Gloucester for the time being and as well lively examples and patterns of virtue and true godliness to their scholars in life and conversation as sufficient persons to teach and instruct them in the Latin and Greek tongues.

They were to ' teach the Grammar allowed and approved by the common authority of the Queen's Majesty that now is, and of her . . . . heirs and successors for the time being,' to take the scholars every Sunday and holiday at public prayers, and divine services, and sermons, at the parish church, ' examining and trying what benefit the scholars shall reap by every such sermon.' They themselves were not to preach above six times a year. If either of the masters became impotent and ' will accept the room of a poor man in the Hospital . . . that then he be preferred to one of those rooms, and have 2d. weekly more than any other there placed . . . and the best chamber.' The other five poor were to have the extra 2d. ' defalked out of their portion rateably.' The schoolmaster was to have £16 and the usher £4 a year.

Each scholar was to pay an entrance fee of 4d. ' if his parents be inhabiting or himself lodging in the parish,' 8d. if not, ' with which money the schoolmasters shall . . . buy and provide such Latin and Greek books as shall be most necessary for the public use of the said Scholars, to be tied fast with little chains of iron. ' For the reformation of divers enormities and disorders used in the often absence of scholars from school, especially in the time of harvest,' it was ordered that any scholar absent four whole school days ' shall be adjudged a stranger and shall not be admitted thither again without payment of as much as any strange scholar is at his first admission to pay.'

If there were not 30 scholars,

> of which number 4 at the least shall have knowledge in the Greek and Latin tongues and be able to make exercises in prose and verse in those tongues and to speak the Latin tongue extempore, and 5 others of that number able to translate any piece of familiar English speech into Latin, and 4 other able to make a sentence of true Latin between the nominative case and the verb ; and 14 others able and ready to learn the rules or accidence to the rules of construction and the residue of that number children of good aptness to learn

then as long as they are wanting the master was only to be allowed his wages at the rate of 20 marks (£13 16s. 8d.) and the usher at the rate of £2, 'which sums are left arbitrable to be by the said Patrons and Governors for the time being increased or diminished as to their grace wisdom and discretion shall be thought best and most convenient.' By the deed, the president or vice-president or one of the seven seniors of the college was to visit the school once a year, ' at such time as the lands of the college lying in Gloucestershire are to be visited or surveyed by the statutes of the college.' By the ordinances four days' notice was to be given and the visitors were to

> spend the time from 8 or 9 of the clock until 11 in the forenoon and 3 to 6 p.m. in apposing trying and examining the scholars of the said school and after such apposition ended shall determine and judge which 4 scholars of the said school have showed themselves best scholars of the whole number in the said disputations ; and also which 3 of the 3 next forms to the highest forms have proved themselves the best scholars severally of the said 3 forms ; and . . . shall with some convenient oration in Latin give conclusion to that day's exercise and dispose to the scholars such gifts and rewards as the said Richard Pate the founder (knowing that honour and reward yielded to virtue and learning doth greatly augment the same especially in youth) hath appointed.

The prizes were,

> to the best . . . a pen of silver wholly gilt of the price of 2s. 6d. To the second best . . . a pen of silver parcel gilt of the price of 1s. 8d. To the third a pen of silver of the price of 1s. 4d. To the fourth a penner and inkhorn of the price of 6d. which four shall be termed the four victors of the said school for that year. . . . The three best scholars of the next 3 several forms to the highest, have every of them a quire of paper price 4d. the quire for their reward.

Then they were to go two-and-two to the parish church,

> the 4 victors coming last next before the said schoolmaster and usher, each of them having a laurel garland on his head provided for that purpose and the 3 other rewarded scholars shall go together in one rank next before the said victors, each of them holding his quire of paper rolled up in his right hand.

Annexed was a budget showing a rental of £73 19s. 4d. gross and £53 19s. 7½d. net. The master and usher were to take £14.

Such were the elaborate and on the whole wise provisions made by Richard Pate for the foundation and permanence of this already ancient school. How long the provisions were properly carried out by Corpus Christi College and how long the school effectively purveyed the highest grade of secondary education to Cheltenham cannot be ascertained.

When light does fall on the school it is not one which reflects credit on the college. Carlisle[1] in 1818 received no answer to his letter asking for information. But it was ' stated that the parishioners are much dissatisfied with the management of the school and there is a dispute between them and the present master.'

Apparently the college thought they had fulfilled their obligations to the school by continuing to pay the master and usher £20 a year, the sums specified in Pate's time, instead of giving three-fourths of the value of Pate's lands. In 1828, however, judgement in a suit in Chancery, *Attorney-General* at the relation of James Matthews and others *v. The President and Scholars of Corpus Christi College, Oxford*, dispossessed the college of this erroneous conception of their obligations, and in 1832 a scheme was settled by which the master was to receive £35 a year instead of £16 from the day of his appointment at Michaelmas 1816, to Michaelmas 1832 ; while in future he was to receive

---

[1] *Endowed Grammar Schools*, i, 446.

£116 a year and £2 capitation fee. The usher was to receive £60 a year. The vicar and churchwardens' consent was rendered necessary to the granting of leases, and the system of beneficial leases on fines was abolished.

The school might then have been put on a firm basis as what it was intended by its founder to be, the principal school of the place. But unfortunately the Rev. Clement Hawkins, the master, had a vested interest in a small school. It was not till his death, in 1845, that anything could be done.

The school was wholly closed from 1840 to 1852. It was then reopened under a scheme of the Court of Chancery of 11 November, 1851. This limited the number of boarders to 30, and the tuition fees to 6 guineas a year, and a preference was to be given to inhabitants of the parish up to 500. No provision was made for new buildings on a new site, which was essential if the school was to take the place it ought to have taken.

But in the interval the more intelligent inhabitants had acted for themselves, and established by private enterprise Cheltenham College, the immediate success of which was a measure alike of the demand for a good school and the weakness of parochial narrowness and jealousy in the sphere of school management. From that time the grammar school was doomed to a lower plane, and has been the sport of parochial politics and constant conflicts of programme and principle.

The first head master of the resuscitated school was Dr. Humphreys, who brought the number of scholars up to 106. He was succeeded by Dr. Henry Hayman. At the time of the Schools Inquiry Commission in 1866 he had 127 boys, of whom 46 were boarders, 24 in the head master's house and 22 in the commercial master's house. The school was divided into classical and commercial departments, the two being quite distinct, even in their games. They were, in fact, two schools: the classical of 58 boys and commercial of 69. It was an unsatisfactory and unworkable arrangement, and the usual result of commercial schools was obtained, that the boys in it were 'not so far advanced in arithmetic or mathematics as the boys in the classical department.' Dr. Hayman left in 1867 to go to Bradfield and thence to Rugby.

Under Henry Martyn Jeffery, F.R.S., who had been second master, the school was gradually reduced to 17 boys.

A scheme made under the Endowed Schools Acts, 15 July, 1881, put an end to the governorship of the distant college, and placed the management of the school, including the appointment of the head master, in a governing body of 12 persons, consisting of the Mayor of Cheltenham *ex officio*, 3 representatives of the town council, 4 of the college, 2 of the justices of the peace of the Cheltenham division, and 2 of the parents of scholars. Mr. James Winterbottom, first honorary secretary and then chairman of the governing body, and Mr. W. H. Gwinnett, an 'old boy' and chairman to 1901, have done signal service to the school.

In February, 1882, the governors elected as head master Mr. John Style, M.A., Cambridge, then second master of Manchester Grammar School.

The buildings contained three class-rooms, which may have been the original school of Richard Pate. On its outer wall was the legend, 'Scola Grammatica.' It stood on the High Street end of the 'one furrow of land running from High Street to Back Street,' given by Richard Pate. Adjoining this building was the head master's residence. Two small additional class-rooms were separated by the width of the playground from the rest of the school.

After due deliberation the governors passed resolutions :

First (unanimously) : That new buildings were required.

Second : That they should not be built on the old site.

On the second point the majority failed to carry with them Mr. W. H. Gwinnett, a former pupil of the school, who exercised much influence in Cheltenham. After discussing the suitability of available sites the governors purchased, subject to the consent of the Charity Commissioners, about 14 acres of land in a more open part of Cheltenham, near Christchurch (now the playing-fields of the Ladies' College), at a price of £120 an acre. Here the school would have been surrounded by its own playing-fields.

A public meeting was called to protest against the change of site. It was neither large nor influential, but no public expression of opinion in favour of the change was made in opposition to it. The Charity Commissioners, after inspecting the proposed site, refused their sanction, and the governors were condemned to build on the old site in the High Street. The decision, together with the fixing, by scheme, of the usual leaving age at 17 years, had a prejudicial influence upon the future of the school.

On 14 December, 1887, the foundation-stone of new buildings (by Messrs. Knight & Chatters, the local architects) was laid by the Right Hon. Sir Michael Hicks-Beach, bart., with Masonic ceremonies.

During the two years spent in pulling down and rebuilding the school, the boys were taught in buildings formerly used by the Presbyterian Church, in the two detached class-rooms on the old site, one of which had been fitted up as a chemical laboratory, and the preparatory form and first form at Wolseley House, which had been rented on lease as a residence for the head master.

The new buildings were opened in 1889. They cost £10,000, of which £8,000 was raised by loan, repayable in 30 years. They contained a large hall, ten classrooms, an art room, chemical laboratory, and a science lecture-room.

From 1882 to 1892 the school enjoyed ten years of growing prosperity. The curriculum had been broadened by the introduction of drawing (freehand, model, and geometrical) as an ordinary school subject, and by teaching chemistry and physics throughout the upper school and singing in the junior school. An English author was read in every form. Efforts were made to increase the existing school lending library and to improve its character. Drill was introduced, and regular games organized. A successful class in manual instruction was conducted out of school hours by a skilled joiner, and optional classes in shorthand and book-keeping were well attended, when no charge was made. French, which was begun in the preparatory form, and Latin, begun in the second form, were part of the ordinary curriculum of the school. German and Greek were extra subjects. The mathematics and science of the upper school were taught with a view to the examinations of the Science and Art Departments at South Kensington.

SCHOOLS

The distinctions gained in outside examinations, and at the universities and university colleges, were more than is usual in such schools.

The following scholarships and exhibitions were founded :—

In 1883 Mr. Henry Martyn Jeffery established, in memory of Miss Curgenwen, an exhibition of the value of the school fees, which has been generally offered for competition among boys entering the school from the elementary schools of Cheltenham.

In 1888 Mr. W. H. Gwinnett, then chairman of the governing body, gave £100 to the school, which sum was increased by subscription among friends of the school, so as to provide a scholarship of the value of the school fees, and in 1902, after Mr. Gwinnett's death, a similar scholarship was founded in his memory by subscription.

Mr. W. Dades-Overton, of Swindon, near Cheltenham, bequeathed £1,000 to found an exhibition, tenable at either Oxford or Cambridge, open to all boys who have been in the school for three years.

The school had no playing-field for its own use, but shared a field with a local cricket club until 1896, when it obtained the use of playing-fields of about 12 acres at Battledown. A house at Battledown, overlooking the playing-fields, was rented in 1896 for the head master, who removed from Wolseley House with a small number of boarders.

The Local Taxation Act of 1890 had placed at the disposal of the Cheltenham Corporation a sum of money to be spent upon technical and scientific instruction. A portion of this grant was allotted to the grammar school for the maintenance of its science classes, a portion to the school of art carried on in the Clarence Street Buildings, and the rest to extending a collection of evening classes and classes for adults, which had been held for some time in laboratories adjoining the school of art and public library, and to setting up in connection with it a 'day and boarding school for boys.' The day-school for boys was conducted in the Clarence Street Buildings ; scientific and commercial subjects were taught under the direction of the science master, now head master, of 'The Public School of Science and Technical School,' at the low fee of £6 a year, and boarders were invited.

The school was not successful, but it caused indirectly considerable injury to the grammar school.

In 1894 an agreement was entered upon by which the grammar school governors took over the buildings, assets, and liabilities of the school of science, and agreed to set up a distinct 'modern side' in the grammar school, and to admit to it any scholars of the school of science. Certain members of the executive committee of the school of science were admitted to the meetings of the governing body, where, however, they had no legal status and no right to vote, and a so-called 'hybrid committee' of certain governors of the grammar school and certain members of the executive committee of the school of science was formed to administer the work of the evening classes.

An amending scheme of 1898 regularized the transaction already accomplished, and permitted the school to carry on the work of evening classes which it had been conducting since 1894. At the same time it extended the leaving age of pupils to 18 or 19 years, and removed limitations of the curriculum. Three additional representatives of the

Town Council were added to the governing body, and the 'hybrid committee' ceased to exist.

In July, 1900, the head master made arrangements for the whole upper school to pass through the four years' course of the Board of Education as a Class A School.

The numbers in the school—in spite of increased competition due to the founding of the Dean Close School, which was opened during the rebuilding of the grammar school—had risen from 17 to between 140 and 150 boys.

After the incorporation of the school of science the numbers showed a tendency to fall, and by the end of 1900 they had fallen as low as 115. The numbers remained at this low ebb during the troubled period which followed the remodelling of the governing body in 1900, and it was not until public confidence had become reassured that the numbers again increased, and in 1905 and in the beginning of 1906 there were 165 boys in the school, the present number being 153.

In 1900 a further amendment of the scheme provided for the appointment of five representatives by the County Council, five by the Town Council, together with the Mayor *ex officio*, four by Corpus Christi College, and two by the parents.

The County Council undertook to give a grant to the school of not less than £1,000, and the governors became the authority for the supply of higher education over a wide area of nearly 100 small towns and villages in the neighbourhood of Cheltenham, in which lectures and classes were held by the staff of the grammar school, assisted by visiting instructors. The governors also became responsible for the school of art, which had been languishing for lack of support.

In July, 1906, the head master availed himself of the opportunity offered by the new scheme to retire.

Harold Sydney Jones, M.A., of Christ's College, Cambridge, where he was 9th wrangler in 1888, then head mathematical and science master of University College School, is the present head master.

CHELTENHAM GIRLS' GRAMMAR SCHOOL

In 1901 the governors added a Pupil Teachers' Centre to the work they had undertaken. It was opened in the Clarence Street Buildings, and was taught by the staff of the grammar school, a mistress being specially appointed for the care and oversight of the girls, who greatly outnumbered the boy pupil-teachers. Other girls, too, who were not pupil-teachers were admitted as bye-students on the payment of fees—the numbers soon outgrew the accommodation, and before the end of 1904 there were about 90 girls and some 10 or 12 boys receiving instruction in the classes.

In 1904 the governors purchased Livorno Lodge, in North Street, which by alterations and additions was adapted for the purpose of a day-school for girls.

It was opened in January, 1905, as the County High School for Girls, under the head-mistress-ship of Miss Heatley, M.A., London, assisted by a well-qualified staff of mistresses, and in 1906 its numbers had already reached 140.

SCHOOLS

In order to provide the accommodation required by H.M. Inspector for the evening classes, and to provide a home for the school of art, buildings have been erected adjoining the grammar school. To enable a loan to be raised for this purpose, the County Council grant has been increased to £2,200 yearly, by agreement between the County Council, the Town Council, and the governors of the grammar school.

These laboratories and art rooms are available at separate times for the use of the pupils of the two schools of the foundation.

The new scheme of the Board of Education, 5 December, 1905, definitely provides for the girls' school upon Pate's foundation.

The governing body is increased by two additional representatives of the County Council, who must be women. The school is now administered by 19 governors :—The mayor, *ex officio*, 7 representatives appointed by the County Council, 5 by the Town Council, 4 by Corpus Christi College, Oxford, and 2 by the parents of the day scholars attending the schools of the foundation.

CHELTENHAM COLLEGE

Cheltenham was the first of the many public schools founded in the reign of Queen Victoria, and claims to be the first 'great public school' founded since Charterhouse School in 1620. In 1840 some parents of boys who were at private schools in Cheltenham and dissatisfied with them decided to start a public school under their own direction.[1] Among these founders were Mr. G. S. Harcourt, Capt. J. S. Iredell, whose name is kept alive by a school prize, and the Rev. Francis Close, afterwards dean of Carlisle, then incumbent of Cheltenham. It is probably owing to his influence that the school governors, masters, and boys were absolutely required to be members of the Church of England. Houses were bought for the school in the centre of the town. The Rev. Alfred Phillips, from King William's College, Isle of Man, was appointed the first Principal. Success was immediate, and at the end of a year, more space being wanted, the present site then outside the town was bought. The college buildings began with a large schoolroom, since known as the 'big classical.' One of the first boys was the present Lord James of Hereford, who after a brilliant career at the bar became Attorney-General in Mr. Gladstone's Government in 1880, but seceded on the question of Home Rule in 1885, and was made a peer in 1895. The boys used to go to churches in the town till 1858, when a chapel was built, for which in 1896 the present one, in commemoration of the school's jubilee, was substituted.

From the first the school was divided into classical and modern sides, and usually the modern side has been the larger. It used to be called the military and civil department. It has been largely a preparatory school for a military career, and probably the number of Cheltonians in the army exceeds that from any other school. The Rev. W. Dobson became Principal in 1845. He was of Charterhouse School and a Fellow of Trinity, Cambridge, and came to Cheltenham from a Nottinghamshire rectory. Mr. John Morley, Mr. Lecky, the historian of Ireland and of Rationalism, and

---

[1] *Great Public Schools*, article on Cheltenham College by E. Scot Skirving, M.A., from which most of this information is taken.

Mr. F. W. H. Myers, the author of *St. Paul*, were among his pupils. Four Balliol scholarships were won by Cheltenham boys between 1850 and 1854. Dobson was a successful head master in spite of the curious system invented by the directors, under which they managed the discipline, the Principal the actual teaching, and another man the religious training. When he was succeeded in 1859 by the Rev. H. Highton, friction began, and ended in his retirement. But on the appointment in 1861 of Dr. Alfred Barry, who had been head master of Leeds Grammar School, this absurd system was abandoned, and the Principal became responsible for all the teaching and the discipline as well. A council of 24 members, 12 elected by themselves, 12 by the proprietors or shareholders, was substituted for the directors. In Dr. Barry's time a junior school was built, and most of the boarding houses. Amongst his illustrious pupils—1859–64—was the present Lord Chancellor, Robert Reid, Lord Loreburn. When he was succeeded in 1869 by Dr. Jex-Blake there were 240 day-boys and 440 boarders. Dr. Jex-Blake left in 1874 to become head master of Rugby, and was succeeded by Dr. Kynaston, an Eton boy and master. In his time the day-boys were marshalled into two houses for the purposes of games, and had two house-masters to look after them. Dr. Kynaston retired in 1888, and the Rev. H. A. James, who had been head master of Rossall, and was dean of St. Asaph, was appointed. Two events[1] particularly marked his period of office. The first was the celebration of the College Jubilee in 1891, at which divers athletic entertainments and admirable performances of 'The Birds' of Aristophanes were given. Twice before Greek plays had been acted, when in 1888 and 1889 the 'Electra' and 'Oedipus Coloneus' of Sophocles were given in full.

The other event was the Act of Incorporation passed in July, 1894, which made Cheltenham a public school in name, as it had long been in reality and reputation. In 1895 Dr. James succeeded Dr. Percival as head master of Rugby, and the Rev. R. S. de Courcy Laffan, an exhibitioner of Winchester and of Merton College, Oxford, head master of Stratford-on-Avon Grammar School, was appointed. Under his rule the school flourished in both numbers and honours, but he resigned in 1899 and was succeeded by the Rev. Reginald Waterfield, scholar of Winchester and New College, who had been assistant master at Rugby for six years. On his accession the numbers were about 640, of whom about a third were day-boys. In addition to cricket, Rugby football, and all the games and sports common to all public schools, Cheltenham has the advantage of a boat club, though at some distance, for the members have to go nine miles by train to Tewkesbury and the River Severn. A rifle corps was founded in 1862, which in 1889 was changed into an engineer corps in which something is learnt of sand modelling and fortification, and an annual bridging competition is held.

CHELTENHAM LADIES' COLLEGE

On 30 September, 1853, a prospectus was drawn up at the house of the Rev. H. Walford Bellairs, then H.M. Inspector of Schools for Gloucestershire, for 'a college in Cheltenham for the education of young ladies, and

---

[1] *Public School Magazine*, Dec. 1899, p. 396.

children under 8 years of age."[1] Instruction was to include the liturgy of the Church of England, grammar, geography, history, arithmetic, French, music, drawing, and needlework. The college was to be confined to day scholars, and the fees were to be from 6 to 20 guineas a year. Shares of £10 each to the amount of about £2,000 were taken up, and the entire management and control were vested in the hands of the founders, the Rev. H. W. Bellairs, Rev. W. Dobson, Principal of Cheltenham College, Rev. H. A. Holden, Vice Principal, Lieut.-Col. Fitzmaurice, Dr. S. E. Comyn, and Mr. Nathaniel Hartland. They appointed as Principal Mrs. Procter, and as Vice Principal her daughter, Miss Annie Procter, who was understood to be the actual head. A well-built stone house, with good gardens, Cambray House, was taken on lease at a rental of £200 a year, and a schoolroom was added before the opening of the college, on 13 February, 1854. It started with over 100 pupils, and the numbers steadily increased for the first two years, but by the end of 1857 there were only 89 pupils. There was some disagreement between the Principal and Vice Principal and the council, and eventually Mrs. and Miss Procter resigned. Miss Procter opened a private school in Cheltenham, which she carried on for 30 years.

Miss Dorothea Beale, mathematical tutor at Queen's College, London, was appointed Principal on 16 June, 1858, and Miss Brewer, who was already on the staff, Vice Principal. Of the subscribed capital of £2,000 only about £400 was left, and there were only 69 pupils. Rigid economy had to be practised, but in spite of all care, at the end of 1860 the college was still being carried on at a loss, and the lease of Cambray House having expired no member of the council was willing to take the responsibility of renewing it. Fortunately, Mr. J. Houghton Brancker was asked to be auditor, and he drew up a financial scheme, lowering the fees, but making music and drawing extras. The owner of Cambray House agreed to grant a yearly lease, and from that time things began to mend. In 1864 the first regularly constituted boarding house was opened under Miss Caines. In the same year a change was made in the school hours, which caused an outcry, and the numbers declined for the first time since Miss Beale's arrival. The hours had been 9.15 a.m. to 12.15 p.m. and from 2.45 p.m. to 4.15 p.m., but now the morning hours were lengthened and afternoon school abolished. This was found to work satisfactorily, and next year the numbers once more increased.

In 1871 a portion of the site of the present college was bought, and the college entered into possession at Lady Day, 1873. In 1876 Miss M. Newman offered to provide a house for not more than 10 girls preparing as governesses, who should attend the college, paying Miss Newman unremunerative fees. Her offer was cordially accepted, and the house started, but Miss Newman unhappily died after one year. In January, 1878, Miss Beale issued an appeal for subscriptions to carry on this work, and about £1,200 was immediately collected, one-half from the staff. This sum was vested in trustees, who kept on the students in a private house till 1885, when St. Hilda's College was opened. It was the first training college established for secondary teachers.

---

[1] *History of the Cheltenham Ladies' College*, 1853–1904 (*Cheltenham Looker-on* Printing Works), from which most of these facts are taken.

It was resolved at a meeting of proprietors in May, 1879, that the company should register itself with limited liability under the Companies Acts, and on 31 January, 1880, the college was duly incorporated. The new constitution provided for a governing body of 24 members, of whom 18, namely 12 men and 6 women, were to be elected by the shareholders, and the remaining 6, each holding office for six years, were to be appointed by (1) the Bishop of Gloucester and Bristol, (2) the Hebdomadal Council of the University of Oxford, (3) the Council of the Senate of the University of Cambridge, (4) the Senate of the University of London, (5) the Lady Principal, and (6) the teachers. At that time the numbers were 469, and with the kindergarten, 501. There were 10 boarding houses. In 1889 'Eversleigh' was opened as a boarding house, and Cambray House, the original College, was bought by Miss Beale for £2,000, and started as a boarding house and school for those waiting admission to the college. It was enlarged in 1895, and two years later Miss Beale made over the property to the Ladies' College by deed of gift, though it was arranged that she should still continue there the school and boarding house. More boarding houses were added in 1891. The limit of numbers was raised from 500 to 600, which necessitated an extension of the college buildings. A new house for the Principal was added, and the whole work was completed in 1894.

Meanwhile, in 1892, Miss Beale bought Cowley House, Oxford, for £5,000, and opened it as a hall for women students from Cheltenham, under the name of St. Hilda's Hall. Mrs. Burrows was appointed Principal, and the hall was opened with 7 students in October, 1893. It was enlarged in 1895, and again in 1897, and in 1901 was amalgamated with St. Hilda's College, Cheltenham, the name of the joint association being 'St. Hilda's Incorporated College,' and to this Miss Beale has presented the Oxford property. Mr. John Alexander Hay, of Cheltenham, in 1903 bequeathed £3,000 to the college for exhibitions to St. Hilda's Hall. From this bequest an exhibition varying from £25 to £45 a year, and tenable for three years, is awarded annually.

In 1902 the total number on the books reached 1,014, including ordinary pupils, kindergarten pupils, foundationers of St. Hilda's, students in the training department, and by-students, a euphonious term for girls staying at school beyond the ordinary school age.

Numberless honours have been gained by Cheltenham girls, and many of the High Schools all over the country have chosen their head mistresses and assistants from among them. In 1902 the University of Edinburgh conferred on Miss Beale the honorary degree of LL.D, only once before given to a woman, in recognition of her services to education and of the position attained by the ladies' college. She died in November, 1906, leaving all her money to the college, of which she had been Principal 48 years, having raised it from a small and tottering establishment of some 70 pupils to the vast and firm organization of over 1,000, which has been the model to so many other foundations for girls' education.

On 20 March, 1907, Miss Lilian Mary Faithfull, M.A. Dublin, Vice Principal of the Women's Department, King's College, London, was elected Principal. Miss Faithfull had been an exhibitioner at Somerville College, Oxford, where she obtained a First Class in the Honours School of English language and literature.

SCHOOLS

TEWKESBURY GRAMMAR SCHOOL

In 1535[1] there is evidence of the existence of the usual Almonry, or charity school, in the abbey, with incidentally mention of what must have been the usual public or grammar school outside. The almoner gave

in alms distributed to certain poor scholars to the number of 16, as in woollen cloth to clothe them, in ordinary years £7 13s. 4d.; and to certain poor boys in the same office [i.e. the Almonry] limited by the ordinance of foundation as well in eatables and drinkables and other necessaries as in maintenance (*exhibicione*) of the same boys at school (*ad studium*) in ordinary years £3 11s. 8d.

In Edward VI's Chantry Certificates[2] of 1548 there is a memorandum that Tewkesbury 'is a verye grete markett Towne . . . Having many children likely and apt throughe good instruccion to atteigne to learninge,' therefore the inhabitants are 'humble suters' to the king to give 'some convenyent stypend for the mayntenaunce of a Free Scole there for ever,' and Tewkesbury is one of four places in Gloucestershire where 'Grammerscoles are to be newlye erected.'

A school was apparently established, as in 1609 Sir Dudley Digges[3] gave £160 for the purchase of lands settled to the use of the free school. Yet William Ferrers, citizen and mercer of London, has been popularly considered the founder of the school. By his will, 17 September, 1625, he devised to the mayor and burgesses of Tewkesbury two annuities out of his manor of Skellingthorpe, Lincolnshire, towards 'the maintenance of a schoolmaster who should freely teach poor men's children within the free school of Tewkesbury, and four poor men's children from the parish of Ashchurch.'

Charters were granted to the town by both James I and James II, in which provision was made for a 'Free Grammar School, which should consist of one master and one usher and scholars'; and in 1698 William III granted a charter for 'the better instruction of youths and boys in the borough of Tewkesbury,' and incorporated certain officials of the borough by the name of 'the governors of the goods, possessions, and revenues of the Free Grammar School of William Ferrers in Tewkesbury for ever, who were to nominate one honest man 'learning and fearing God' to be master, and one discreet and fit person to be usher, both of whom were to hold their office during the good pleasure of the governors.[4] William Alye gave £70 by will made in 1625, with which chief-rents were bought, for the education of 6 poor children in the grammar school, and in 1722 Mrs. Elizabeth Dowdeswell gave £40 to the school.[5]

A new scheme was made for the school by the Court of Chancery in 1851, by which the property was vested in 8 trustees annually elected by the corporation out of their own body. They were invested with all the powers of the old governors. The boys on the foundation were limited to 12 from Tewkesbury, to be elected by the governors, and 4 from Ashchurch, to be elected by the vicar and churchwardens of the parish. They might stay from 8 to 15, and were to learn Latin, Greek, and English, with reading, writing, geography, and arithmetic. If there were more than the 16 free

---

[1] *Valor Eccl.* ii, 483.
[2] A. F. Leach, *Engl. Sch. at the Reformation*, 85.
[3] Rudder's *Gloucestershire*.
[4] *Sch. Inq. Rep.* xv, 107.
[5] Rudder's *Gloucestershire*.

boys the master was to provide an usher at his own expense.[1] The school was carried on in a room attached to the north transept of the abbey church, formerly used as the chapter-house,[2] but in 1862 it was moved to the private house of the master, John Morgan, who was a layman, appointed in 1858. In 1867 there were the 16 free boys, 9 day boys paying 4 guineas each, and 7 boarders. A few of the boys learnt Latin, but none Greek or French, and the standard was not high in any subject.[3]

NORTHLEACH GRAMMAR SCHOOL

Hugh Westwood, of Chedworth, left by will, 1 May, 1559, his parsonage of Chedworth, consisting of tithes and lands there, to feoffees to found

> one grammar school for ever in the town of Northleach ; provided always, that the school-master and scholars shall every day say or sing one Anthempe, and the Paternoster, and Ave, or some other godlie or wholesome prayer, having in remembrance him the founder, and his heirs, for ever ; and provided that the said town of Northleach shall prepare a house convenient for the scholehouse and schollmaster meet and necessarie for that purpose, or else the school not to be there.

The town prepared the house, as we learn from the preamble to an Act of Parliament procured in 1606. But after this, various abuses in the trust arose. The surviving trustee of the will made a lease of the parsonage to his son at a very small rent, and conveyed the reversion to another son. Hugh Westwood's heir, Robert, a cousin, tried to upset the will, claiming the estate as heir. So the schoolmaster and inhabitants filed a Bill in Chancery. The result was an Act of Parliament in 1606, whereby the school was incorporated by the name of the ' Schoolmaster and Usher of the Free Grammar School of Hugh Westwood,' who were to have perpetual succession and a common seal. The provost and scholars of Queen's College, Oxford, were to appoint the master and usher, who were to be graduates of Oxford, to make all the orders and statutes for the school, and to have full power in all the government of it, to suspend and deprive the schoolmaster and usher, and to appoint ' how the rents and profits . . . shall be proportioned, . . . so as the whole rent be disposed between them the said schoolmaster and usher.'

The first schoolmaster was William Lickebarrow, B.A., and the first usher John Stone, B.A. Lickebarrow was a Queen's College man from Westmorland, who had just taken his B.A. degree, 14 December, 1605, and was only 24 years old.

In 1769 Queen's College made ordinances which to a large extent were a repetition of earlier ones. The schoolmaster must be an M.A. of Oxford, able to instruct scholars in Latin and Greek prose and verse. The usher also, if it may be, was to be a graduate of Oxford, or at least a good and ripe scholar who has been trained up there, and able to teach Latin and Greek, and also to write, cipher, and cast accounts ; he is to teach beginners A B C, the ordinary primer, and the Psalms of David, and when they can read, the ordinary accidence and grammar of the upper school.

---

[1] *Sch. Inq. Rep.* xv, 107.   [2] *Char. Com. Rep.* xxi, 195.   [3] *Sch. Inq. Rep.* xv, 108.

SCHOOLS

A long list of books for the use of the school is prescribed, including Isocrates, Æschines, Demosthenes, and Homer; Herodian, Cicero, Cæsar, Terence, Justin, Ovid, Prudentius, Virgil, Horace's *Epistles* and *Ars Poetica*, and a little Greek Catechism, set forth by authority. The usher was to teach Lilley's *Grammar*, Nowell's *Catechism*, and *Disticha Catonis*. The grammar of King Henry VIII, continued and authorized in the reigns of Edward VI and Queen Elizabeth, is to be used, and no other; and such other books as 'are without taint of atheism, epicurism, popish superstitions, lasciviousness and other like infections.'

At the time of these ordinances the income seems to have been £20 a year, and it was provided that if ever the income reached £60, the master was to have £40, and the usher £20, and so in proportion if there was a further increase. In 1818[1] the income was stated to be £600. The head master was then the Rev. John Nelson, and the usher the Rev. Thomas Tordiffe, and they divided this income between them in the proportion of two-thirds to one-third for the instruction of 3 free boys, 4 or 5 being the average, the education being confined exclusively to the classics.

In 1829 Lord Brougham's commission[2] reported that

the head master's situation is considered in the light of a mere beneficial sinecure in the gift of Queen's College, Oxford. He resides, however, at Northleach, and the school therefore may be considered as having the benefit of his supervision. The usher is personally employed in the instruction of the few boys who are sent to the school from the town of Northleach.

In 1847 Mr. Askew, the master, refused to take any boys till they were able, in the words of the statutes, to 'take instruction.' There were 20 boys in the school taught by a deputy, a decrepit old man paid by the usher. The Rev. C. H. Lowry on being appointed usher in these circumstances soon left for the head mastership of Carlisle Grammar School. In 1855 he was himself made head master at Northleach, and some effort was made at improvement. But in 1866 the Endowed Schools Inquiry Commission[3] found that all that Mr. Lowry, the head master, did was to open the school with prayers, and occasionally gave scripture lessons. He also took in his own house a 'classical department,' consisting of his son and the usher's sons and one other boy, a boarder, who after nine years in the school had just joined the classical department. The usher, who was vicar of Barrington, six miles off, where he lived, attended twice a week and took the upper classes in English history and Latin. Otherwise the school was run by a 'commercial master,' John Worder, an elementary teacher, who issued his own prospectus of the school as a commercial school, making no reference to the fact of its being a grammar school or to its master and usher. He had 58 boys, 43 of them boarders paying about £26 a year, and 15 day-boys, 6 foundationers gratis and 9 paying £6 a year. Worder went off to Cheltenham with his boarders in 1867. Other 'commercial' masters followed.

This scandal was put a stop to by a scheme under the Endowed Schools Act of 11 July, 1877, which divested Queen's College of the patronage and put the school under a governing body of 12, on which the college was cut down to 2 representatives, the rest being appointed, 2 by the justices of the

[1] Carlisle, op. cit. i, 458.   [2] *Char. Com. Rep.* xxi, 115.   [3] *Sch. Inq. Rep.* xv, 96.

Petty Sessional Division in which Northleach lay, 2 by the trustees of the Northleach Town Charities, 1 by the Board of Guardians, 1 by the Vestry, now Parish Council, of Chedworth, and 4 co-optatives.

Mr. Lowry, the head master, received a pension of £220 a year for life ; the usher, the Rev. Richard Rice, received a pension of £60 a year for life, and the commercial deputy was given the option of becoming head master.

TETBURY GRAMMAR SCHOOL

By an inquisition [1] taken 19 September, 1622, it was found that Sir William Romney, knight, held from Lord Berkeley the tolls on wool and yarn and other profits. He devised all these by will made in 1610 to the town, and from them £13 was to be paid yearly to a schoolmaster to teach the children of the parish gratis and he 'earnestly recommended that the Schoolmaster shall be very skilful in arithmetic, which art teacheth much wit.' By decree made on the inquisition the schoolmaster was to be chosen by thirteen townsmen elected for the rule of the town, and paid £20 yearly.

The Ordinances [2] made by the thirteen, 8 April, 1623, required that the schoolmaster

> shall teach the Latin tongue by the use of Lillie's [3] grammar and such ordinary books as are most approved in schools, and in like manner for the Greek, by such grammars and authors as are most usual, and not by any quaint, strange, or new devices of his own.

The town bought the lease and all his rights from Lord Berkeley in 1632, and then declared that £20 should be for ever continued to a schoolmaster and usher to teach the children of inhabitants.

The first master's name recorded is Mr. Debb, who appears in the St. John's College, Cambridge, register as master at Tetbury when George Long was admitted to St. John's, 5 March, 1644–5, at the age of 22. Presumably he had left the school some years before, as in 1642 Thomas Tully of Queen's College, Oxford, became head master and remained till 1657, when he was made Principal of St. Edmund's Hall, Oxford, and became Dean of Ripon in 1673. John Oldham, the poet, author of *Satires upon the Jesuits* and *A Satire against Virtue*, was in the school 1668–70. The next master known was Henry Heaven, appointed 1678. He matriculated at Wadham 2 July, 1658, and took his B.A. from Trinity College, 22 March, 1661–2. During his reign William Talboys, by will in 1680, left a yearly sum of 20s. for buying books for the poorer scholars. Philip Bisse, afterwards bishop of Hereford, is mentioned by the Rev. A. T. Lee as having been educated at this school, but he can only have used the school for a short time as a preparatory school, as he was admitted to Winchester College as founder's kin in 1686 [4] at the age of 14. Joseph Trapp, professor of poetry at Oxford 1708–18, is also claimed by Lee, but the *Dictionary of National Biography* says he was trained at home by his father and at New College School before matriculating at Wadham in 1695. Mr. Lee says the grammar school was held in a room over the church porch till the

---

[1] *Char. Com. Rep.* xviii, 350.   [2] Rev. A. T. Lee, *Hist. of Tetbury*, 1857, p. 177.
[3] Not Leltie's as misread by the reverend historian.
[4] This is the date given by Lee, but it was in fact 1682; Kirby, *Winchester Scholars*, 204.

church was rebuilt in 1777–81, but in a Chancery suit[1] in 1759 it appears that the room for the Free Grammar School was in the roof of the north aisle of the church, 'near 80 ft. long, and wide in proportion.'

The Rev. Christopher Hanley, M.A., from Merton College, Oxford, became head master in 1698, and was succeeded in 1703 by Mr. Hall, who died the same year. Then came the Rev. John Lewis, who stayed till 1721. The Rev. Henry Wightwick followed and reached a record of 42 years, holding office till his death, 22 November, 1763. After him the school sank into little more than an elementary school under three Welshmen, John Richardes, Robert Williams and J. Evans. In 1791 the Rev. Lancaster Dodgson of Shatton, Cumberland, was appointed. He matriculated at Queen's College, Oxford, 1783, and took his B.A. in 1786 and M.A. four years later, and was a Fellow till 1817, but does not seem to have been successful with the school which was discontinued in 1800, the tolls of the market proving insufficient to provide a salary for a master.

In 1824 a petition was presented to Chancery with regard to the Tetbury Charity estates for the removal of the trustees and a new scheme. This was approved in 1830, and directed a payment of £70 to a schoolmaster and £35 to a mistress. But this was for an elementary school and bore no relation to the ancient grammar school, which has never been revived. The national school still receives the payments ordered by the Chancery scheme.

THORNBURY GRAMMAR SCHOOL

This school was first mentioned in a deed poll of Robert Stone of Merton, 15 October, 1606, who conveyed to new feoffees a burgage and a half formerly given by John Jones the elder.

William White in 1642 gave to John Stafford and others a messuage and a close of pasture upon trust to allow the profits yearly to a schoolmaster to teach in Thornbury, who should be chosen by the feoffees, an unmarried graduate of one of the universities of England. If he should marry, the feoffees should make a new choice.

William Edwards by will, 10 June, 1648, gave lands for a schoolhouse which he had begun to build in his lifetime and also gave a library to the school. By an indenture, 20 October, 1655, the surviving trustees conveyed to John Stafford and others the newly-erected house and the residue of the premises for the maintenance of a schoolmaster who should freely and without payment teach three poor children of the parish, nominated by the trustees and vicar.

New feoffees have been from time to time chosen and the trust-premises regularly transferred.

A book of the transactions has been regularly kept. By an entry, 11 October, 1797, it appears that the free-school being in a ruinous state, Mr. Kingsmill Grove, of Thornbury, volunteered to advance the money for rebuilding, to be repaid out of rents. The master, William Llewellyn, was then paid £15 a year, but after the re-building, as soon as Kingsmill Grove was repaid, he was to receive the net yearly income arising from the estates.

---

[1] *Glouc. Notes and Queries*, 1881, vol. i, 245.

In 1826 the estates were worth £57 3s. 6d., of which 40 guineas a year were paid to the schoolmaster, but in 1867 he was only receiving £30 a year. The master from 1864–9 was the Rev. H. S. Roberts, LL.D., of Queens' College, Cambridge, who had been for many years second master at Bristol Grammar School. There were then 13 boys, all day-boys, who all learnt Latin, and a few had begun Greek. Mr. Roberts left in 1869 to become head master of Wigton Grammar School.

The school was placed under a partly representative governing body by a scheme made under the Endowed Schools Acts, 17 May, 1879. In 1906 Mr. George Nixon, LL.B., was head master. A scheme for its improvement is now under consideration.

WICKWAR—ALEXANDER HOSEA'S FREE SCHOOL

Alexander Hosea was a native of Wickwar, who, according to the county historian,[1] ran away from home as a boy, and becoming rich by his own industry in London, bequeathed by will, 19 March, 1683, two houses in Holborn and £600 to the mayor, aldermen, and borough of 'Weekworth' for support of a school for such children whose parents were poor, to be taught to read and write, and he especially ordained that the minister should not be schoolmaster. A scheme of the Court of Chancery ordered that there should be a master to teach Latin as well as one to teach reading and writing. Before 1700 no less than ten orders had been made by the Court of Chancery for the school. In 1835 a scheme was made which ordered that the master should be able to teach Latin as well as give a general English education, that the school should consist of 40 free boys of the parish and 30 girls, also free, to be taught by a mistress. Very few boys ever learnt Latin, and according to the Assistant-Commissioner's report in 1866 no boy had gone to the university or other place of education for many years, and the teaching was merely that of a national school.

The school was reconstituted by scheme under the Endowed Schools Acts, 30 April, 1894, as a public elementary school: with provision for exhibitions to higher schools to the extent of £30 a year.

BERKELEY

By will (5 October, 1696) Samuel Thurner, M.B., of Magdalen Hall, Oxon, gave lands, the income of which was to be employed in keeping as many poor children at school as that the schoolmaster should have 10s. a year for each child. He desired that the master should be chosen from Magdalen Hall. In 1717, John Smith, A.M., of Magdalen College, Oxford, gave a sum of money which, with £40 given by the countess of Berkeley, was laid out in lands for teaching 12 boys. The rents of all these lands were paid to the master, and the school was limited to 38 boys. The Corporation has usually appointed a graduate of the University as nominal master, and he appoints a deputy. By scheme under the Endowed Schools

---

[1] Atkyns, *Gloucestershire*, 430. This tale must be received *cum grano*. It is one of the usual attempts to represent great men as rising from the gutter, like similar tales of Whittington, Archbishop Chicheley, Cardinal Wolsey, Gresham, &c.

SCHOOLS

Acts approved by Queen Victoria in Council, 8 August, 1899, the endowment, about £80 a year, is applied to evening classes and exhibitions.

MINCHINHAMPTON: THE FREE SCHOOL OF SAINTLOE.

Some time before 1697 Nathaniel Cambridge, formerly of Hamburg, merchant, deposited £1,000 in the hands of trustees to purchase lands for the establishment and support of a free school for boys born in Minchinhampton or Woodchester. In 1697 they bought lands, and a house which was altered to make it convenient for a school. By a scheme under the Endowed Schools Acts 29 June, 1888, the school was to be conducted as a secondary school at tuition fees of £6 to £8 a year.

MARLING'S SCHOOL, STROUD

This school is a modern foundation, quite on the ancient model. It was founded by a scheme under the Endowed Schools Acts of 28 November, 1887. A site and £10,000 was given by Sir W. H. Marling, bart., Captain W. B. Marling, and Mrs. George Robertson, children of Sir Samuel Stephens Marling, bart., who had intended to found it. To this was added £1,000 given by Mrs. Dickinson, widow of Sebastian Stewart Dickinson, of Painswick, for a scholarship in honour of her husband. Accumulations of income of the very ancient charity for the town and church of Stroud, known as the Feoffees' Charity, dating in part from a deed of 4 August, 1304, and half the income of that charity so far as applicable for the poor ; one half of Samuel Watts' Charity for a lecturer, founded about 1634 ; the charities under the wills of Thomas Webb, 4 November, 1642, for 'a good schoolmaster in Stroud,' and Henry Windowes, 13 December, 1734, for an augmentation to the schoolmaster ; the Rev. William Johns' Charity for apprenticeship, founded by deed 12 July, 1776 ; William Hawker's Charity for the like purpose, by deed 8 January, 1676; and Richard Aldridge's Charity, by will 7 December, 1815, for his family monument in the church and other purposes—were all consolidated and applied for the erection and maintenance of a grammar school.

Seldom has an application of more or less useless charities to education been better justified by results. A school was built and opened in 1891 under William John Greenstreet, of St. Saviour's Grammar School, Southwark, and St. John's College, Cambridge, where he became a junior optime in the mathematical tripos of 1882. He was afterwards Vice Principal of the Hull and East Riding College. He came to Stroud from the Cardiff Proprietary College. The school is now flourishing, with 88 boys—12 of whom are boarders—and 5 assistant masters and a music mistress.

LYDNEY SECONDARY SCHOOL

Thanks to the generosity of Mr. Charles Bathurst, of Lydney Park, sen. and jun., the Lydney Institute, which has had a school attached since 1902, is in process of conversion into an endowed secondary school, under a scheme of the Board of Education. Mr. Frank Dixon, B.Sc. London, F.Chem.S., is head master over 80 boys and 40 girls, with 4 assistant masters and 3 assistant mistresses.

ELEMENTARY SCHOOLS FOUNDED BEFORE 1800[1]

WOTTON UNDER EDGE BLUE COAT SCHOOL.—Hugh Perry, alderman and mercer of London, by will (20 April, 1630) gave £8 for an usher to teach writing and ciphering in the free school, but if leave could not be obtained for him to teach there, then the mayor and brethren were to appoint a place for him to teach in. To this the General Hospital Trustees used to add £60 a year from their funds. In 1900–1[1] it was described as a church school, with an average attendance of 111 children.

MARSTON SICCA.—This school was founded by John Cooper who, by will (27 February, 1643) gave his house and close and £300 to trustees to maintain a schoolmaster to teach 22 poor children. Described in 1901 as a national school with an attendance of 79 children.

MICKLETON.—The origin of the endowment of this school was a grant in February, 1512, by Richard Porter of land for the repair of the church and the overplus to go to charitable uses. The Court of Chancery in Easter term, 1663, made a decree, in which it was settled that £20 yearly should be paid to a schoolmaster to teach the sons of poor inhabitants. By scheme under the Charitable Trusts Acts 17 June, 1898, this endowment is applied for prizes in, and for exhibitions from, elementary schools.

DYRHAM : REV. WILLIAM LANGTON'S CHARITY.—By will, dated 20 July, 1668, the Rev. William Langton gave £600, two-thirds of the income of which were to be spent in schooling for poor children of the parish. £32 a year was paid to the schoolmaster, and £16 to a schoolmistress at Hinton, which is a hamlet of Dyrham. The Rev. Peter Grand, rector of Dyrham, by will 18 January, 1791, gave £3,000 stock for various uses, including £10 a year to the schoolmaster of Dyrham and a house, and £5 a year for keeping it in repair. In 1900–1 the school was described as a church school, with attendance of 61 children.

CHELTENHAM OLD CHARITY SCHOOL.—Under George Townsend's will dated 14 December, 1682, £4 yearly was left to four towns, of which Cheltenham was one, for teaching poor children to read. As the estate improved in value the trustees paid more to the schoolmaster, who taught in a school carried on over the church porch. This appears to be represented by the parish church boys' school, average attendances in 1900–1, 326.

MINCHINHAMPTON : TOOK'S CHARITY.—By deed dated 21 January, 1698, Ursula Took granted 20 acres of arable land and £80, of which £8 a year was to be spent in keeping at school 6 boys from Minchinhampton to be taught to read, write, and cast accounts, and to be brought up in the doctrine of the true Protestant religion. By will 9 March, 1698, Henry King left the residue of his personal estate to the use of the poor of Minchinhampton and Rodborough. Lands were bought and the whole profits spent on the salary of a schoolmaster, who taught 8 poor boys to read, write, and cast accounts, and he taught with them the 6 boys of Took's Charity. This is now represented by the parochial school with an average attendance, 1900, of 297.

[1] The facts as regards Elementary Schools are, unless otherwise stated, derived from the Reports of the Commissioners of Inquiry concerning Charities, 1820–37, and the Board of Education Report for 1900–1.

SCHOOLS

RODBOROUGH : HENRY KING'S CHARITY.—The half of Henry King's legacy belonging to Rodborough was applied in the same way as at Minchinhampton.

FAIRFORD FREE SCHOOL.—The Honourable Elizabeth Farmor by will (8 August, 1704) left £1,000 for the purchase of lands, £10 of the yearly income of which was to be applied to a free school. In 1737 a decree of the Master of the Rolls ordered a schoolhouse to be built out of the funds, and in 1739 it was vested in James Lambe, the lord of the manor. Till 1817 only boys were admitted to the number of 60, but on 21 June an order of the Court of Chancery admitted the same number of girls. It is returned as a 'church' school in 1900–1 with average attendance of 174. Part of the endowment is, by a scheme under the Endowed Schools Acts of 30 April, 1894, made applicable for exhibitions to secondary schools.

GREAT BADMINTON FREE SCHOOL.—By deed (22 June, 1705) Mary, duchess dowager of Beaufort, granted a yearly rent-charge of £94 to be taken out of several fee-farm rents for an almshouse and a school for the boys and girls of Great and Little Badminton and Littleton Drew, to be taught to read well and learn the Church Catechism, and the girls to knit and sew plain work. It appears as a national school in 1901, average attendance 90.

PAINSWICK CHARITY SCHOOL.—By settlement (3 April, 1707) Giles Smith, of Painswick, released to trustees certain lands which were to be used for setting up a free school to teach poor boys the three R's, not to exceed 10 at one time. The school was held for many years in part of the town hall, 26 boys being taught there. By scheme under the Charitable Trusts Acts, 20 December, 1892, the school building was still to be used for elementary education, but the endowment applied for support of an evening, school and technical instruction.

BUCKLAND OR LAVERTON FREE SCHOOL.—James Thynne, of Buckland, erected a school building at Laverton in his lifetime, and Thomas, Lord Viscount Weymouth, endowed it by deed 19 June, 1710, with land at Stanton to pay £20 yearly to a schoolmaster to teach the sons of Protestant parents in elementary subjects. In 1901 it was called a church school, average attendance 38.

BRISTOL : COLSTON'S SCHOOL IN TEMPLE STREET.—This school seems to have been supported by voluntary contributions till 1711, when Edward Colston built the present house and school and gave an annuity of £80 for its support. Forty boys were to be taught the three R's and the Catechism, and entirely clothed.

BRISTOL : UNITED SCHOOLS OF ST. MICHAEL AND ST. AUGUSTINE.—This school was established in 1713 for the education and clothing of a certain number of boys and girls by voluntary contributions.

BRISTOL : STOKES CROFT SCHOOL.—The members of the congregation of Protestant Dissenters erected a united building for school and almshouse in 1722 by voluntary subscription. Forty boys were taught elementary subjects. Originally it was intended to board and lodge them, but as the funds were not sufficient they were only given a Sunday suit of clothes and a dinner on Sundays.

BRISTOL : ELBRIDGE'S SCHOOL IN ST. MICHAEL'S PARISH.—John Elbridge, in his lifetime, built a school and by will 20 February, 1738, bequeathed

£3,000 to it. In 1816 there were only girls in the school, and it has since been maintained only for girls, 24 being entirely clothed and brought up for domestic purposes. Represented in 1900–1 by St. Michael's national school, average attendance, 397.

BRISTOL: TEMPLE CHARITY SCHOOL FOR GIRLS. — This school was started by voluntary contributions about 1725, and supported by them till May, 1798. About 1787 the guardians of the charity, out of savings, bought an old house in Temple Street for £200, which house they pulled down and built the present school on the site. In 1798 the permanent property, by different donations and legacies, having reached the sum of £1,200 5 per cent. stock, the guardians resolved that they would be in no further need of subscriptions, and sent a notice to this effect to the subscribers. There were 40 girls on the establishment, who were clothed entirely and taught the catechism, reading, and needlework. Apparently represented by an infants' school, average attendance, 173.

GLOUCESTER : THE POOR'S SCHOOL.—By will (11 June, 1711) Dorothy Cocks devised lands at Taynton to the Poor's School at Gloucester, and John Hyett, by will 5 September, 1711, gave to the Poor Working Charity School at the East Gate of the city £100, and in case his son should die without issue, £1,000 for building a school, and £400 for the salary of a schoolmaster. The son, by will 17 December, 1713, gave effect to his father's dispositions.

CIRENCESTER : THE BLUE SCHOOL.—This school was instituted in 1714 by donations and collections made in the town. The first amount raised was £228 10s., which was increased to £428 5s. 6d. by 1755, and was the capital of the school. Various other sums applied to its use brought up the income to over £113. Twenty boys and 20 girls, who are all entirely clothed, receive instruction. The school was under the same management as the Yellow School.

THE YELLOW SCHOOL.—Founded by will (17 September, 1722) of Mrs. Rebecca Powell. It was ordered by the Court of Chancery, 16 July, 1816, that a house should be bought, in which 20 boys could be brought up and taught reading and writing and the art of weaving worsted stockings, and 20 girls taught to read and spin. In a further order, 21 July, 1739, the master reported that the attempt to establish the manufacture of worsted stockings had failed, so that part of the scheme should be abandoned, and 40 boys and 20 girls should be taught the three R's, the Church Catechism, and clothed. The school was kept in the premises originally built for the purpose in Gloucester Street. The Blue School is kept under the same roof. The number of children in all was, in 1867, 286—131 boys, and 155 girls. By schemes under the Endowed Schools Acts, 28 November, 1876, both schools were made secondary schools. By further scheme, 29 November, 1881, the ancient grammar school was united with it.

BOURTON ON THE WATER.—Anthony Collett of Bourton on the Water, by will (16 January, 1716) gave a rent-charge of £10 on his lands for a schoolmaster to teach 12 poor boys to read, write, and cast accounts, and to instruct them in the Church Catechism.

PUCKLECHURCH : HENRY BERROW'S CHARITY.—The Rev. Henry Berrow, vicar of Pucklechurch, by indenture, made 6 November, 1718, granted £200, the income of which was to be applied to teaching 10 boys and 10 girls of the parish, from the age of 4 to 10. By will, dated 14 December, 1724, he gave £300 more.

DURSLEY : SCHOOL OF THE PROTESTANT DISSENTERS.—Joseph Twemlow, in 1718, erected a house at Dursley, used for religious worship, and at other times for a schoolhouse for teaching poor children of Protestant Dissenters. Josiah Sheppard, by will (25 August, 1726) gave £100 to be laid out in lands for the support of the school, and a sum of £260 from the bounty of Mary Twemlow and others has also been expended in lands.

KINGSWOOD.—This school was endowed with lands in Gloucestershire in 1720 by the heirs of Israel Mayo, whose father, John Mayo, had by will (15 March, 1674), charged him to erect a free school and endow it with £30 a year. Israel Mayo paid the £30 a year during his lifetime, but did not endow it.

MARSHFIELD : THE CHARITY SCHOOL.—A ledger-book of accounts of this school beginning 25 March, 1722, shows the school supported by annual subscriptions, the first name being John Harington, who is said to have given the schoolhouse and half a year's subscription of £3. By indenture 3 February, 1731, Dionysia Long, of Golden Square, Middlesex, granted property in Gloucestershire to trustees to appoint a schoolmaster to teach 20 poor boys of the parish the three R's. The boys were also entirely clothed. In 1900–1, national school with average attendance of 120.

AMPNEY CRUCIS : ROBERT PLEYDELL'S CHARITY.—The sisters and co-heirs of Robert Pleydell, by an indenture dated 2 May, 1722, granted Ranbury Farm in Ampney St. Peter, pursuant to the design of Robert Pleydell, that out of the rents £65 should be paid for instruction of poor boys and girls, £15 for apprenticing, and they also granted the same trustees premises for the schoolhouse. In 1901, national school with average attendance of 107.

WOODCHESTER : ROBERT BRIDGES' CHARITY.—Robert Bridges, by will (23 October, 1722) gave to trustees £500 to purchase lands and apply the proceeds in teaching 3 poor boys to read and write and apprenticing 1 yearly. Saint Loes School at Minchinhampton being found sufficient for teaching the boys of this parish, the funds were applied to clothing and apprenticing. In 1900–1 this school had an average attendance of 91.

THORNBURY : ATWELLS' FREE SCHOOL.—John Atwells, by will (16 May, 1722) gave £500 in trust for setting up a free school and directed that a good master and mistress should be placed therein to instruct the children of the parishioners, gratis, in reading, and the girls knitting and sewing as well. Though 24 boys could have had their education free there were only 14 in the school in 1867. This was merged in the Grammar School foundation by scheme under the Endowed Schools Acts, 17 May, 1879.

TETBURY : HODGES' CHARITY.—In 1723 Elizabeth Hodges by will left £30 a year for teaching poor children in Tetbury the three R's. On this foundation a school was kept for many years in which 15 boys were taught, but when a scheme was made in Chancery in 1830 for all the charity estates this was merged in the national school, the master of which received £30 a year for teaching the boys on Hodges' foundation.

STAPLETON FREE SCHOOL.—Mary Webb, by will (15 October, 1729) bequeathed £450 in trust, the interest to be applied for a school and almshouse,

£15 a year to a master for teaching 20 poor boys and 10 poor girls. Various other donations brought up the capital amount to £785 15s., of which the duke of Beaufort was treasurer. A schoolmaster and his wife taught the stated number of children, and had a salary of £25. Represented in 1900–1 by Stapleton church school; average attendance, 133; now in the borough of Bristol.

CAM : FRANCES HOPTON's CHARITY.—By will, dated 11 March, 1730, Mrs. Frances Hopton gave an estate called Draycott Farm to trustees, to build a schoolroom with apartments for a master and mistress to teach 10 poor boys and 10 poor girls, the boys to learn the three R's and the girls reading, knitting, and sewing. The total income in 1826 was £163 10s., which had increased to £237 by 1867, when there were 22 boys and 21 girls. In 1900–1, average attendance, 82.

BISLEY : BLUE COAT SCHOOL.—John Taylor, clothier, of Stroud, by will dated 19th January, 1732, devised lands in trust for teaching 10 poor boys in Bisley to read and write and to clothe them. The rents of this land in 1829 were £55 10s. The master had a salary of 12 guineas, and £18 6s. 6d. was spent on clothing. In 1867 there were 18 boys on this foundation in the parish school, part of the income of the church lands being employed in the maintenance of a free school, and £13 14s. out of the rent being paid yearly to the schoolmaster, who is also master of the Blue Coat School. In 1900–1, national school, average attendance, 111.

RANDWICK CHARITY SCHOOL.—On 20 February, 1734, lands were conveyed to trustees for this school, in accordance with the will of Thomas Vobes, of Standish, dated 8 February, 1706. Richard Cambridge, merchant, of London, gave £50 and Ann Hawker £20, with which lands were bought in 1730. In 1749 £40 was subscribed by the inhabitants to buy a dwelling-house for the master. Thomas Genner, by will 27 May, 1756, bequeathed his house and garden, the rent to be disposed of in clothing for the poor scholars. Other bequests of property have later been made to the school, which in 1826 brought in an income of £40 19s. in all. There were then 38 boys and girls. In 1900–1, average attendance, 143.

CHURCHDOWN : HENRY WINDOW's CHARITY.—Henry Window, esq., by will dated 13 December, 1734, devised lands to pay the yearly sum of £20 to a schoolmaster to teach poor boys and girls of Badgeworth and Churchdown the three R's, and he gave a house for the master to live in. Two schools were being regularly kept after the death of the testator, 1745—one under a schoolmaster for boys and girls, and another under a schoolmistress for infants. The school was given a new governing body by a scheme under the Endowed Schools Acts. In 1900–1, represented by a board school, average attendance, 116.

HORSLEY : THE FREE SCHOOL.—Edward Webb, of Nailsworth, by will (15 April, 1744) gave to trustees £200 to be by them disposed of for the poor in such manner as they should think fit, and by indenture dated 7 December, 1752, Elizabeth Castleman assigned £200 to her trustees to apply the profits for the education of the poor children of Horsley. Land was bought in 1755 and the school established. Other gifts have since been made, and in 1823 a new school building was begun, and opened in March, 1824. The old school only accommodated 24, but in 1867 there were 76 boys and 63 girls. In 1900–1, average attendance, 135.

SCHOOLS

KEMPSFORD : LORD VISCOUNT WEYMOUTH'S CHARITY.—An inscription, undated, on the church-table says that Thomas, Lord Weymouth, gave £10 per annum to teach the poor children to read and write. A schoolhouse was built in 1750 on ground given by Thomas, Lord Weymouth, a descendant of the donor. The expense of the building was defrayed by subscription. The annual sum of £10 is regularly paid by the marquis of Bath to the master and mistress, who live rent and tax free, and teach poor children to read and write: 1900–1, average attendance, 59.

HENBURY : ROBERT SANDFORD'S CHARITY.—Robert Sandford, by will (13 January, 1756), gave £1,500 to trustees to provide instruction in reading and writing for the poor children of Henbury. By decree of the Master of the Rolls, 27 June, 1781, it was ordered that there should be two schools, one at Henbury and the other at Northwick. A house was hired at Northwick and the school established, where 40 boys and girls were taught reading and writing, and an agreement was made with the feoffees of the grammar school at Henbury to send boys there. For many years 40 boys were sent, a rent of £15 was paid, and £24 to the master and usher. In 1900–1, a boys' school, average attendance, 97.

NORTH NIBLEY : REV. WILLIAM PURNELL'S CHARITIES.—By indenture, dated 5 April, 1758, the Rev. William Purnell conveyed lands on trust for apprenticing poor boys. By his will, dated 15 September, 1763, he gave £300 for the purchase of an annuity to be applied in keeping 5 boys of the parish at school, 1 of whom should each year be apprenticed. From 1822 the master of the school has had for his salary £30 in consideration of his teaching these 5 boys. In 1867 there were 24 free boys in the school. In 1900–1, called a church school, average attendance, 35 boys.

MINSTERWORTH.—Susannah Crump, by indenture dated 15 November, 1763, granted an annuity of £4 to be paid to a discreet schoolmistress to teach 10 poor children to read. Her son-in-law, Daniel Ellis, by will 26 January, 1784, gave £100 to be spent in erecting a house for this school. The sum was allowed to accumulate till 1808 when a schoolhouse was built. In 1900–1 called a national school, average attendance, 63.

EASTINGTON FREE SCHOOL.—This school was established in 1764 by subscription to teach poor children of the parish to read. The general income is about £50, and there were about 70 boys and girls under a school master and mistress respectively in 1832. The number had risen to about 90 in 1867. In 1900–1, called national, with average attendance of 170.

ARLINGHAM : YATE'S CHARITY.—John Yate by will devised all his property to his mother, subject to the payment of certain annuities, one of which was for the support of a school. She, wishing that his desires should be carried out, executed an indenture of bargain of sale, dated 1 February, 1765, by which an annuity of £40 was to be paid for a charity school, £20 for the salary of a schoolmaster, £10 for a mistress, and the other £10 for fire, books, repairs, &c. The affairs of the charity came before the Court of Exchequer in 1825, when the Accountant-General was ordered to report on them. He found that all the sums payable for school purposes had been duly paid up to December, 1826. In 1867 there were 23 boys and 25 girls. In 1900–1, called national, average attendance, 34.

PEBWORTH.—Thomas Eden, by deed (6 December, 1773) granted lands in Gloucestershire and tenements in Bristol to maintain charity schools in Pebworth, Weston Subedge, Weston upon Avon, Broad Marston, Old Stratford in Warwick, and Newbold in Worcester, for poor children to be taught to read and to learn the services of the Church of England. The six schools were established in his lifetime. Broad Marston, Weston Subedge, and Weston upon Avon schools were all upon the same foundation. In 1900–1 Pebworth had an average attendance of 109, Weston Subedge of 58.

STONEHOUSE CHARITY SCHOOLS.—John Elliot, esq., and others, in 1774 gave sums of money amounting to £612 10s. to trustees to establish two charity schools, one at Stonehouse, the other at Ebley, for teaching poor children to read and for instructing them in the principles of the Church of England. In 1826 the number at Stonehouse was 28 and at Ebley 16, but in 1867 there were about 150 in all. In 1900–1, represented by board school at Ebley, average attendance 128, and national school at Stonehouse, 305.

MITCHELDEAN : CHARITIES OF WILLIAM AND AMY LANE.—William Lane, of Gloucester, by will (30 March, 1789) gave to trustees £1,000 to apply the income for various sermons and for a charity school for not less than 20 poor children to be taught on Sundays as well as other days, and Mrs. Amy Lane, his wife, by will 18 August, 1806, gave £300 to the same object. The money was all laid out in three per cent. stock, producing an annual dividend of £62 4s. 4d. In 1826 about 30 boys were taught the three R's and the Catechism, and taken to church twice on Sunday ; but 40 years later there were 70 boys and 50 girls. In 1900–1; average attendance 148.